Childhood and Adolescence

Childhood and Adolescence

Philip R. Newman
Barbara M. Newman
The Ohio State University

Brooks/Cole Publishing Company
I(T)P® *An International Thomson Publishing Company*

*Pacific Grove • Albany • Belmont • Bonn • Boston • Cincinnati • Detroit
Johannesburg • London • Madrid • Melbourne • Mexico City
New York • Paris • Singapore • Tokyo • Toronto • Washington*

Sponsoring Editor: *Jim Brace-Thompson*
Project Development Editor: *Heather Dutton*
Marketing Team: *Lauren Harp and Margaret Parks*
Editorial Assistant: *Terry Thomas*
Production Coordinator: *Kirk Bomont*
Project Management, Composition, Interior Illustration,
and Prepress: *GTS Graphics, Inc.*
Manuscript Editor: *Sheila Pulver*

Permissions Editor: *Mary Kay Hancharick*
Interior Design: *Ann Beurskens*
Cover Design: *Roy R. Neuhaus*
Photo Researcher: *Sue C. Howard*
Indexer: *Steve Sorensen*
Cover Printing: *Phoenix Color Corporation, Inc.*
Printing and Binding: *Quebecor Printing Hawkins*

Cover: *Carnival Time at Willow Bend,* by Jane Wooster Scott/SuperStock, Inc.

For more information, contact:

BROOKS/COLE PUBLISHING COMPANY
511 Forest Lodge Road
Pacific Grove, CA 93950
USA

International Thomson Publishing Europe
Berkshire House 168-173
High Holborn
London WC1V 7AA
England

Thomas Nelson Australia
102 Dodds Street
South Melbourne, 3205
Victoria, Australia

Nelson Canada
1120 Birchmount Road
Scarborough, Ontario
Canada M1K 5G4

International Thomson Editores
Seneca 53
Col. Polanco
11560 México, D. F., México

International Thomson Publishing GmbH
Königswinterer Strasse 418
53227 Bonn
Germany

International Thomson Publishing Asia
221 Henderson Road
#05-10 Henderson Building
Singapore 0315

International Thomson Publishing Japan
Hirakawacho Kyowa Building, 3F
2-2-1 Hirakawacho
Chiyoda-ku, Tokyo 102
Japan

Printed in the United States of America

10   9   8   7   6   5   4   3   2   1

Library of Congress Cataloging-in-Publication Data
Newman, Philip R.
    Childhood and adolescence / Philip R. Newman, Barbara M. Newman.
      p.   cm.
    Includes bibliographical references and index.
    ISBN 0-534-13686-9
    1. Child development.   2. Adolescence.   I. Newman, Barbara M.
II. Title.
HQ767.9.N5   1997   96-33529
305.23′1—dc20   CIP

*To
Sam,
Abe,
and
Rachel*

Brief Contents

Chapter 1   *Introduction*   *2*

Chapter 2   *Research on Children and Adolescents*   *26*

Chapter 3   *Psychosocial Theory*   *54*

Chapter 4   *Major Theories for Understanding Change*   *90*

Chapter 5   *Sexual Reproduction and Heredity*   *140*

Chapter 6   *Prenatal Development and Birth*   *180*

Chapter 7   *Developmental Tasks of Infancy*   *234*

Chapter 8   *Expanding the Psychosocial Analysis of Infancy*   *288*

Chapter 9   *Developmental Tasks of Toddlerhood*   *342*

Chapter 10   *Expanding the Psychosocial Analysis of Toddlerhood*   *392*

Chapter 11   *Developmental Tasks of Early School Age (Ages 4 to 6)*   *451*

Chapter 12   *Expanding the Psychosocial Analysis of Early School Age*   *500*

Chapter 13   *Developmental Tasks of Middle Childhood (Ages 6 to 12)*   *546*

Chapter 14   *Expanding the Psychosocial Analysis of Middle Childhood*   *596*

Chapter 15   *Developmental Tasks of Early Adolescence (Ages 12 to 18)*   *630*

Chapter 16   *Expanding the Psychosocial Analysis of Early Adolescence*   *674*

Contents

Preface   xxii

1 Introduction 2

A Journey of Discovery   4

The Study of Development: The Approach of This Text   4

The Content of Development   5
Domains of Development   6
Stages of Development   6
Developmental Tasks   8
Continuity   9

The Contexts of Development   11
Families   11
Culture   11
Ethnic Groups   11
Social Conditions   13

The Relationship of Heredity and Environment   16

Universal Characteristics of Childhood   17
First Experiences   17
Children in Families   18
Skill Development and Learning   19

Conclusions and Preview of the Remainder of the Text   20

Chapter Summary   23

References   23

2 Research on Children and Adolescents   26

Scientific Observation   28

Research Design   31
Selecting a Sample   32
Research Methods   33
Designs for Studying Development   43
Evaluating Existing Research   47
Ethics   47

The Ongoing Study of Child Development   50
Limited Applicability of Historical Data to Current and Future Generations   50
Self-Directed Creation of Experiences   50

Chapter Summary   52

References   53

3 Psychosocial Theory   54

What Is a Theory?   56

Rationale for Selecting Psychosocial Theory   57

Basic Concepts of Psychosocial Theory   59
Stages of Development   60
Developmental Tasks   65
Psychosocial Crisis   70
The Central Process for Resolving the Psychosocial Crisis   75
Radius of Significant Relationships   77
Coping Behavior   78

Evaluation of Psychosocial Theory   82
Strengths   82
Weaknesses   84

Chapter Summary   88

References   88

4 Major Theories for Understanding Change   90

The Theory of Evolution   92
Implications for Child Development   93
Links to Psychosocial Theory   96

Psychosexual Theory   96
Implications for Child Development   97
Links to Psychosocial Theory   99

Cognitive Developmental Theory   101
Basic Concepts in Piaget's Theory   101
Vygotsky's Concepts of Cognitive Development   105
Links to Psychosocial Theory   107

Theories of Learning   108
Classical Conditioning   108
Operant Conditioning   111
Social Learning   114
Cognitive Behaviorism   120
Summary of Learning Theories   121
Links to Psychosocial Theory   122

Cultural Theory   122
Implications for Child Development   124
Links to Psychosocial Theory   126

Social Role Theory   127
Implications for Child Development   128
Links to Psychosocial Theory   128

Systems Theory   129
Implications for Child Development   132
Links to Psychosocial Theory   135

Chapter Summary   135

References   137

5 Sexual Reproduction and Heredity   140

The Reproductive Process   142
The Male Reproductive System   142
The Female Reproductive System   143
Hormones and the Reproductive System   143
Fertilization Through Sexual Intercourse   145
Fertilization Through Reproductive Technology   149

The Cellular Basis of Sexual Reproduction   151
Gametes   151
Cell Division   153
The Timing of Meiosis for Males and Females   156

The Transmission of Genetic Information   156
The Replication of DNA   159
Mutations   161
The Laws of Heredity   161

Genetic Sources of Individuality   166
Genetic Determinants of the Rate of Development   166
Genetic Determinants of Individual Traits   167
Genetic Determinants of Abnormal Development   168
Genetic Technology and Psychosocial Evolution   169

Evaluating the Impact of Heredity on Behavior   173
Reaction Range   173
An Example of Behavioral Genetics: Hereditary Influences on Intelligence   174

Chapter Summary   176

References   178

6 Prenatal Development and Birth   180

The Phases of Prenatal Development   182
Development in the First Trimester   183
Development in the Second Trimester   187
Development in the Third Trimester   192

The Psychosocial Context of Pregnancy   194
  Maternal Nutrition   194
  Maternal Drug Use   196
  Obstetric Anesthetics   200
  Environmental Toxins   200
  Mother's Age   201
  Mother's Emotional State   202

The Impact of the Fetus on the Pregnant Woman   203

The Birth Process   207
  Stages of Labor   208
  Cesarean Delivery   208
  Infant Mortality   211

The Impact of Culture   212
  The Medical Birth Culture of the United States   213
  The Birth Culture in Sweden and the Netherlands   215
  Examples of Birth Cultures in Traditional Societies   215
  Cultural Complexity   218

Abortion   218
  The Abortion Controversy and the Legal Context   220
  Difficulties in Evaluating Abortion Research   223
  What the Research Shows   224

Optimizing Development in Pregnancy   227

Chapter Summary   228

References   229

7 *Developmental Tasks of Infancy*   234

Newborns   236

The Development of Sensory/Perceptual and Motor Functions   238
  Sensory/Perceptual Development   240
  Motor Development   244
  Temperament   249

Attachment   251
The Development of Attachment   252
Formation of Attachments with Mother, Father, and Others   255
Patterns of Attachment   255
Parental Sensitivity and the Quality of Attachment   259

Sensorimotor Intelligence and Early Causal Schemes   262
How Do Infants Organize Their Experiences?   262
The Development of Causal Schemes   263

Understanding the Nature of Objects and Creating Categories   265
The Nature of Objects   265
The Categorization of Objects   269

Emotional Development   270
Emotional Differentiation   271
Emotions as a Key to Understanding Meaning   273
The Ability to Regulate Emotions   274
Emotions as a Channel for Adult–Infant Communication   276

Chapter Summary   279

References   281

8 Expanding the Psychosocial Analysis of Infancy   288

The Psychosocial Crisis: Trust Versus Mistrust   290
Trust   290
Mistrust   291
Resolving the Crisis of Trust Versus Mistrust   294

The Central Process for Resolving the Crisis   294
Mutuality with the Caregiver   294
Coordination, Mismatch, and Repair of Interactions   295
Establishing a Functional Rhythm in the Family   297
Parents with Psychological Problems   297

The Prime Adaptive Ego Quality and the Core Pathology 300
   Hope   300
   Withdrawal   300

Factors in the Transition to Parenthood and Grandparenthood 302
   The Transition to Parenthood   302
   The Transition to Grandparenthood   308

Cultural and Ethnic Patterns That Create Distinctive Child-Rearing Environments 311
   Feeding and Weaning   313
   Safety in the Physical Environment   316

Social Issues: Parental Employment and Infant Child Care 320
   The Effects of Maternal Employment on Interactions with Infants   322
   Parental Values about Maternal Employment   323
   The Nature and Quality of Alternative Care   324
   Social Policies and the Care of Infants   327

Optimizing Development in Infancy 330
   Promoting Emotional and Cognitive Development   330
   Parents as Advocates   331
   Contextual Factors That Support Parenting   331

Chapter Summary 333

References 335

9 Developmental Tasks of Toddlerhood 342

Language and Communication 345
   Milestones in Language and Communication   346
   The Language Environment   354

Elaboration of Locomotion 361

Fantasy Play   366
The Emergence of Symbolic Play   367
Changes in Fantasy Play During Toddlerhood   368
The Importance of Fantasy Play   372
The Role of Play Companions   373
Imaginary Companions   374

Self-Control   376
Precursors of Self-Control in Infancy   378
Control of Impulses   379
Self-Regulated Goal Attainment   383

Chapter Summary   386

References   387

10 Expanding the Psychosocial Analysis of Toddlerhood   392

The Psychosocial Crisis of Toddlerhood   394
Autonomy   395
Shame and Doubt   395

The Central Process: Imitation   397

The Prime Adaptive Ego Quality and the Core Pathology   399
Will   399
Compulsion   399

Family Development During Toddlerhood   402
Parents as Play Companions   402
Parents as Socialization Agents   404
Managing Work and Family Life   409
Becoming a Sibling   413

Cultural and Ethnic Patterns That Create Distinctive Child-Rearing   416
The Value of Fantasy   417
Variations in Promoting Autonomy   418
Culture and Discipline Practices   420

Societal Issues That Provide Resources or Barriers to Development   422
Poverty   422
Day Care   427
Child Abuse   433

Optimizing Development in Toddlerhood   438
The Adult's Role   438
The Physical Environment   439
The Community   440
Toddlers Contribute to Their Own Development   441

Chapter Summary   443

References   445

11 Developmental Tasks of Early School Age (Ages 4 to 6)   451

Gender-Role Identification   452
Individual Differences Versus Constructivism   453
Understanding Gender   456
Learning Sex-Role Standards   457
Identifying with Parents   459
Forming a Gender-Role Preference   462

Early Moral Development   465
Learning Theory   466
Cognitive-Developmental Theory   468
Psychoanalytic Theory   472
Research on Empathy and Perspective Taking   474
Research on Parental Discipline   477

Group Play   480
Group Games   480
Friendship Groups   481

Self-Theory   484
   Developmental Changes in the Self-Theory   486
   Self-Esteem   488
   Self-Esteem and the Early-School-Age Child   491

Chapter Summary   492

References   494

12 Expanding the Psychosocial Analysis of Early School Age   500

The Psychosocial Crisis of Early School Age   502
   Initiative   502
   Guilt   503

The Central Process for Resolving the Crisis:
Identification   506

The Prime Adaptive Ego Quality and the Core
Pathology   509
   Purpose   509
   Inhibition   513

The Role of Parents and Other Family Members in Fostering
Development   514
   Parents as Educators   514
   Parents as Advocates   518

Cultural and Ethnic Patterns That Create Distinctive Child-
Rearing Environments   519
   Religion and the Moral Atmosphere of the Home   519
   Culture and Gender   522

Societal Issues That Provide Resources or Barriers to
Development   527
   School Readiness   527
   The Impact of Television   531

Optimizing Development for Early-School-Age Children   538

Chapter Summary   541

References   542

13 Developmental Tasks of Middle Childhood (Ages 6 to 12)   546

Concrete Operations   550
Conservation   551
Classification Skills   554
Combinatorial Skills   555

Skilled Learning   558
Features of Skilled Learning   560
Reading   561
A Model of the Developing Mind   562
The Social and Cultural Contexts of Skill Development   566

Self-Evaluation   568
Self-Efficacy   570
Social Expectations   571

Friendship   576
Family Influences on Children's Readiness for Friendships   577
Three Contributions of Friendship to Social Development   578

Team Play   583
Interdependence   584
Division of Labor   584
Competition   585
In-Group and Out-Group Attitudes   586

Chapter Summary   589

References   590

14 Expanding the Psychosocial Analysis of Middle Childhood   596

The Psychosocial Crisis: Industry Versus Inferiority   598
Industry   598
Inferiority   599

The Central Process: Education   603

The Prime Adaptive Ego Quality and the Core Pathology   606
Competence   606
Inertia   607

The Interactive Relationship Between the Development of Children and Parents   607
Forming the Parent–School Partnership   608
The Child as a Stimulus to Adult Learning   609

Cultural and Ethnic Patterns That Create Distinctive Child-Rearing Environments   612
Achievement Strivings and Culture   612
Multicultural Education and School Adjustment   615

Social Issues That Create Barriers to Development   617
Parental Divorce and Its Impact on Children   617
Violence in the Schools   620
Homelessness and Its Impact on Children   622

Optimizing Development in Middle Childhood   624

Chapter Summary   626

References   627

15 D*evelopmental Tasks of Early Adolescence (Ages 12 to 18)*   630

Physical Maturation   632
Physical Changes in Girls   635
Physical Changes in Boys   638
The Secular Trend   639
Psychosocial Consequences of Differences in Maturation Rate   640
Review of Major Trends in Physical Development   641

Formal Operations   644
Piaget's Theory of Formal Operational Thought   644
Six Characteristics of Formal Operational Reasoning   645
Egocentrism   646
Factors That Promote Formal Operational Thought   648
Criticisms of the Concept of Formal Operations   652

Emotional Development   652

Developmental Trends over the Course of Early Adolescence   652
Eating Disorders   653
Delinquency   654
Depression   655

Membership in the Peer Group   658

Cliques and Crowds   658
New Learning Linked to Peer-Group Membership   661

Sexual Relationships   661

The Transition to Coitus   663
Orientation Toward Sexuality   664
Problems and Conflicts Associated with Sexuality   665

Chapter Summary   667

References   668

16 Expanding *the Psychosocial Analysis of Early Adolescence*   674

The Psychosocial Crisis of Early Adolescence   676

Group Identity   678
Alienation   678

The Central Process: Peer Pressure   679

The Role of School Adults in Peer-Group Structuring   680
Affiliating with a Peer Group   681
Peer Pressure in Specific Areas   681
Conformity and a Sense of Belonging   681
Conflict, Tension, and Alienation   682

The Prime Adaptive Ego Quality and the Core Pathology   684

Fidelity to Others   684
Isolation   685

Significant Factors in the Development of Parents and Other Family Members   685
Parents and Their Adolescent Children   685
Parents Caring for Their Aging Parents   689

Cultural and Ethnic Patterns That Create Distinctive Child-Rearing Environments   691
Cultural Patterns of Rites of Passage   693
Ethnic-Group Identity   695

Societal Issues That Provide Resources or Barriers to Development   698
Parenthood in Early Adolescence   698
Adolescent Alcohol and Drug Use and Abuse   703
Work Experiences in Early Adolescence   708

Personal Identity: The Psychosocial Transition to Adulthood   710
Two Components of Identity: Content and Evaluation   710
Identity Status   712
Gender Variation in the Process of Identity Formation   714

Optimizing Development in Adolescence   718

Chapter Summary   720

References   722

Glossary   *729*

Indexes   *751*

Preface

We have written *Childhood and Adolescence* with an eye toward integrating much of what we have studied and read about the nature of development with what we have experienced firsthand. For us, the scholarly study of development and the personal roles of father and mother, husband and wife, student, teacher, and scholar have provided a dynamic synergy. We hope that this book captures some of the puzzlement, energy, and excitement that comes from trying to bring the critical problem-solving perspective of the social sciences to your real-world experiences with infants, children, and adolescents. At the same time, we hope that it stimulates you to relate the confusions, pains, and delights of what you experience with children to the typically abstract constructs offered by theory and research.

We hope that this book helps you take hold of the study of child development, to make new meaning of the observations and experiences you encounter. We also hope that the book allows the issues facing children and families today to take hold of you by encouraging you to bring renewed commitment and purposefulness to your dedication to improving the quality of life for future generations.

Perspective

Childhood and Adolescence takes a psychosocial approach to the study of child development from conception through about age 18. This means that we present development as a product of the ongoing interaction between individuals and their social and cultural contexts. We assume that human growth has a strong biological base that comes into contact with a wide range of environmental factors to produce an individual's life story. Increasingly, research in child development points to the impact of broad sociological factors such as race/ethnicity, gender, parents' education and work status, poverty, religion, and urban or rural community as forces that influence the tempo of growth, the content of behavior, and the quality of life for children. In addition, differences in the family environment, such as family structure, parenting style, the role of siblings and extended family members, and the existence of supportive networks all have an impact on patterns of development. Research is discovering and documenting that families are different settings for different children, due in part to temperamental differences, physical vulnerabilities, and unique talents of the children; the age and psychosocial maturity of parents; and the changes in cultural, economic, and historic forces that impinge on families over time. Finally, children influence and modify their environments, evoking novel responses from parents and other caregivers, engaging in interactions with new technologies, and seeking new experiences that stimulate adults in new directions.

The focus of *Childhood and Adolescence* is an analysis of patterns of consistency, change, and growth over these 18 years of life. The book focuses on five domains of development—physical, intellectual, emotional, social, and self-development—as they merge and interact over six stages of life: the prenatal period, infancy, toddlerhood, early school age, middle childhood, and early adolescence. Special attention is given to the way these domains interact to produce patterned changes in self-understanding, social relationships, and world view. At the same time, the book introduces topics that relate to the psychosocial development of those who are significant in the lives of children, especially mothers, fathers, siblings, grandparents, and teachers. Children do not raise themselves. They depend on the psychosocial maturity of those in their immediate social network to provide the necessary resources, protect them from harm, nurture and love them, teach and show them the ways of their culture. The story of child development is embedded in the challenges facing adults who are parenting and caring for children, the values and goals of the culture as they are transmitted by significant caregivers, and the resources, institutions, and policies of the society during the historical period in which a child grows up.

Organization

The book begins with four chapters that provide the basic tools for a critical examination of the study of development. The first chapter outlines the orientation of the book, including the dynamic interaction between nature and nurture, the concept of life stages, the concepts of continuity and change, and the notion of the role of complex social environments in shaping the quality and direction of childhood experiences. The second chapter introduces the research process and the importance of taking a systematic, scientific approach to the study of development. Methods of research, approaches to studying change, and the topic of ethics in the study of children are covered. The third chapter is an in-depth discussion of psychosocial theory, which serves as the integrating organizational framework for the book. The use of a detailed theoretical orientation is unique to this book. It offers students a set of clear assumptions, constructs, and themes around which to make meaning of a wide array of scientific literature. The theory is presented as a heuristic for guiding one's inquiry, with a discussion of strengths and weaknesses of the theory included. Chapter 4 provides a summary of other dominant theories that have influenced and guided the study of child development. Basic concepts from each theory are introduced along with ideas about the contribution of each theory to the study of development and links to psychosocial theory.

Chapters 5 and 6 focus on reproduction, the mechanisms of heredity, and the prenatal period of development. The explosion of information on genetics and the mapping of the human genome have had a significant impact on the presentation of information about genetics in this book. Chapter 5 covers the biology of sexual reproduction, the biochemistry of genetics, information on genetic anomalies, and illustrations of the interaction between heredity and environment with emphasis on the themes of temperament and intelligence. The psychosocial context is highlighted by considering topics such as the factors that contribute to attraction and commitment between partners and the factors that lead to the transition to sexual activity during adolescence. Chapter 6 focuses on fetal growth during each of the three trimesters of the prenatal period within the complex psychosocial environment. Changes in the status of mothers and fathers as a result of pregnancy are considered, as is the impact of the mother on the uterine environment. Cultural patterns of the treatment of men and women during pregnancy as well as the nature of the birth culture are discussed. The abortion controversy highlights the societal investment in decisions made during this stage of life.

Chapters 7 through 16 include two chapters each on the life stages of infancy (birth to 2), toddlerhood (2 and 3), early school age (4 to 6), middle childhood (6 to 12), and early adolescence (12 to 18). The first chapter of each two-chapter section focuses on the major developmental tasks of the period, highlighting changes in the domains of physical, cognitive, social, emotional, and self-development. The second chapter in the section focuses on expanding the psychosocial analysis of the stage by looking at the psychosocial crisis of the stage, the central process for resolving the crisis, and the major ego strengths and core pathologies that are likely to emerge during the period. In addition, these chapters address significant factors in the lives of parents and other family members that have an impact on development. Cultural patterns that create distinctive child-rearing environments and societal issues that provide unique resources and challenges to development are described. These chapters end with an overview of ideas about promoting optimal development during this period of life.

Special Features and Learning Aids

The book is written in a way that attempts to provide a complex analysis in a clear, easily comprehensible style. Photos, cartoons, figures, and tables are used to augment the narrative. Each chapter begins with a detailed outline and ends with a numbered summary that reminds the reader of the main ideas. Boxes are used to extend information and elaborate on new directions in research and practice. An extensive glossary of most boldfaced words is another resource for mastering new terms and concepts.

An important, innovative feature of the book is the Notebook Page exercises. These pages are intended to stimulate critical thinking and give the reader specific opportunities to link personal experiences with basic concepts, to record observations, and to preserve an ongoing record of how beliefs, observations, and new ideas are being integrated.

A supplemental student study guide has been prepared to accompany *Childhood and Adolescence*. The student study guide offers a step-by-step strategy for identifying and mastering basic concepts and integrating new ideas that are presented in each chapter. Along with the goal of enhancing critical thinking, the study guide includes sections that focus on examining personal beliefs and reviewing those beliefs after reading the chapters.

Acknowledgments

We are deeply indebted to our children, Sam, Abe, and Rachel, for their love and trust in us. They have been sources of continuous wonder and inspiration. Because of them, we have taken up the challenge to write this book, hoping that it will help other adults experience the satisfaction of contributing to the optimal development of children.

Many students, friends, and colleagues have responded to this work, commented on sections, and given suggestions for examples, cartoons, and illustrations. In particular, we want to thank Kirk Bloir, Alison Marlowe, Dana McCormick, Leslie Sexton, and Christy Snyder, each of whom assisted with aspects of manuscript preparation and revision. In addition, they brought joy, laughter, and an occasional box of doughnuts to the task.

The book has been enhanced by a very extensive review process. We deeply appreciate the constructive criticism and encouragement of our reviewers, including David Balk, Kansas State University; Mark Barnett, Kansas State University; Michael Bergmire, Jefferson College; Gail Bollin, West Chester University; Kenneth Bordens, Indiana Purdue Fort Wayne; Nancy Budwig, Clark University; Mary Anne Christenberry, College of Charleston; Cynthia L. Crown, Xavier University; Michelle Dunlap, Connecticut College; Warren Fass, University of Pittsburgh; Rebecca Glover, University of North Texas; Gordon Greenwood, University of Florida; Russell Isabella, University of Utah; Allen Keniston, University of Wisconsin-Eau Claire; Joe Kishton, University of North Carolina at Wilmington; Frank Salamone, Iona College; Caroline Salvatore, Salve Regina University; Carol Seefeldt, University of Maryland; Thomas Sommerkamp, Central Missouri State University; Arlene Sprague, Lincoln Memorial University; and Christine Ziegler, Kennesaw State College.

The idea for this book emerged when we were working with Paul O'Connel, a developmental editor with the Dorsey Press. He and David Folmer were enthusiastic about the idea and encouraged us to move ahead with sample chapters. In the meanwhile, Dorsey Press was purchased by Brooks/Cole. The new staff at Brooks/Cole could have pulled back from this project, but they too saw something of promise. Craig Barth visited with us at our home and talked with us about our ideas. Vicki Knight and then Jim Brace-Thompson served as our editors, encouraging us to remain focused on our goals for the book. Two very talented developmental editors, Pat Gadban and Heather Dutton, worked with us to sharpen our focus and tighten the text. Heather also kept reminding us of page length, preventing us from writing ourselves out of an audience. Many other very capable and dedicated members of the Brooks/Cole family have contributed to this book: Ellen Brownstein, Kirk Bomont, Lauren Harp, Sue Howard, Roy Neuhaus, Margaret Parks, and Terry Thomas. In addition, the staff at GTS Graphics, especially Heather Stratton and Margaret Pinette, have managed the details to produce the beautiful book you hold in your hands.

Philip R. Newman
Barbara M. Newman

Childhood and Adolescence

Introduction

Chapter 1

A Journey of Discovery

The Study of Development: The Approach of This Text

The Content of Development
  Domains of Development
  Stages of Development
  Developmental Tasks
  Continuity

The Contexts of Development
  Families
  Culture
  Ethnic Groups
  Social Conditions

The Relationship of Heredity and Environment

Universal Characteristics of Childhood
  First Experiences
  Children in Families
  Skill Development and Learning

Conclusions and Preview of the Remainder of the Text

Chapter Summary

References

Why study child development? Childhood is our past and our future. It is the past of each individual, the foundation on which the present is built. And it is the future of every society, the hopes and dreams of lives that continue beyond our own. The story of childhood, including patterns of child-rearing, the organization of family life, the educational system, the resources available for children and the risks to which they are exposed, is also the story of a society and its future.

Understanding child development is important for all people who work as parents, doctors, nurses, therapists, teachers, psychologists, social workers, and professionals in other fields giving direct service to children. By understanding child development, you can help children develop to their fullest potential. You can learn what is best for children and what is likely to put them at risk. You can provide an optimal environment for children, even those with severe physical, cognitive, and emotional challenges, and you can reap the benefit of watching them flourish and grow.

A Journey of Discovery

We invite you to join us on a journey of discovery of the period from conception through early adolescence. As your guides, we hope to expand and deepen your understanding of the process of change and growth during the first 18 years of life. As you gain new insights about the challenges and achievements of development, you will also participate in a process of self-discovery so you can understand the contributions of these years to your own development.

Anyone setting off on a journey of discovery is well-advised to take notes. A fundamental aspect of scientific training is the development of skills of observation, analysis, and interpretation. As you travel through new territory, you will have ideas and observations that had not occurred to you before. To guide your observations and to help you keep track of your insights, we have included a series of Notebook Pages throughout the book. These pages are designed to provide a personal database to help you understand processes of development. You will learn how to make systematic observations and to use these observations in order to critically evaluate and integrate information from the course. Even though you have many demands on your time, we urge you to be conscientious about completing the Notebook Pages. We believe that by keeping notes about your observations, your ideas, and your questions, you can follow the maturation of your own understanding of the subject matter. You can begin to link the concepts that you are studying with your personal observations and recollections, evaluate and modify your personal theories, and introduce new theories when they make more sense. Your understanding of child development will become more meaningful because the scientific information that you discover will be more fully integrated into your ways of looking at the world and making sense of your own experiences.

The Study of Development: The Approach of This Text

The study of infancy, childhood, and adolescence addresses patterns of change and continuity from conception to about age 18. In this text, we will describe and explain the sequence of changes in various capabilities. We will also examine what is known about characteristics that show consistency from stage to stage and how these continuities influence development. The focus of the text is on patterned changes in physical and psychological development that have implications for how infants, children, and adolescents make meaning of their experience, modify their self-understanding, and expand the depth and complexity of social relationships.

We take a *psychosocial orientation* to the understanding of development. This means that we assume that development is a product of the continuous interplay between individuals and their social and cultural environments. Development can be characterized by distinct stages during which basic developmental tasks are dictated by the interaction of biology and culture. There is also a predictable conflict in each stage, referred to as a *psychosocial crisis*, which is produced by the discrepancy between an individual's skills and abilities at a certain stage and the expectations and demands to participate in social life at that stage. In addition, there is a central process—which differs from stage to stage—that helps to resolve the conflict by the end of the stage. Development occurs within an expanding network of significant relationships that conveys society's expectations and requires increasingly complex social skills. These ideas will be explored in greater detail in Chapter 3.

Dev't influenced by social & cultural environments

We suggest that development is a product of the interaction and integration of three major factors:

1. Biological evolution and the biochemical bases of behavior;
2. The interaction of individuals and their environments, especially their immediate social groups and social institutions; and
3. Contributions that individuals make to their own development.

We also argue that development can be enhanced. Development is optimized when a person creates new behaviors and relationships as a result of skill acquisition and successful conflict resolution over the course of each life stage. Children and adolescents reach their highest levels of competence in conflict-free spheres of behavior, finding pleasure and enjoyment in the exercise of mastery. Even in the face of stress and crisis, individuals can redefine their situation or acquire new skills and resources that help them cope with the challenge and attain a higher level of functioning. Meaningful relationships provide encouragement and other resources in these times of challenge. New, more adaptive behaviors continue to be possible throughout life for adults as well as for children.

The Content of Development

Development encompasses a number of components, including emerging capabilities, patterns of change that occur over time, emerging consistent behaviors, and the learning, internalization, and integration that result from one's experiences. The text examines the strategies and systems that children use to organize and make sense of their experiences. We believe that children actively contribute to their development; things do not just happen to them. They think up things to do, projects to explore, and skills to master. *They try to take care of themselves.*

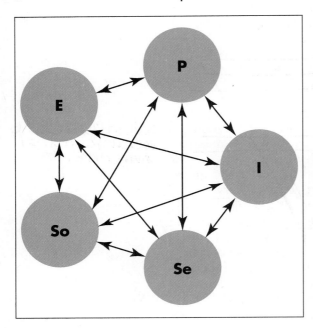

FIGURE 1.1

The content of five domains of development and their inter-connections. **P**hysical = Genetic bases of behavior; the brain and the nervous system; physiological systems; physical maturation and growth; motor activity and motor development; physical appearance; reproductive system and sexual activity; health and illness. **I**ntellectual = Consciousness; sensation and perception; memory; problem solving; language; planning; logical reasoning; hypothesis raising and testing; metacognition (thinking about one's thoughts). **E**motional = The emergence and differentiation of emotions; the expression of emotions; the control of emotions; the ability to recognize and respond to the emotions of others (empathy); defenses. **So**cial = Roles and role relationships; socialization; social identity; social skills; friendship formation; capacities for intimacy; family relationships; membership in various social groups; identification of reference groups; group identity. **Se**lf = Self-recognition; boundaries between self and other, self-awareness; self-control; self-esteem; self-efficacy; personal identity; self-understanding.

Domains of Development

The text focuses on changes in capabilities over time that occur for most children across five domains of development: *physical, intellectual, emotional, social, and self.* In real life, of course, these domains often overlap, as when emotions influence intellectual evaluation or when language becomes a vehicle for expression in the social, intellectual, or emotional domains. Changes in one area are influenced by changes in another. (See Figure 1.1.) For example, the physical changes associated with puberty affect an adolescent's thoughts, feelings, relationships, and views of the self. New skills in forming relationships in early childhood provide a child with new outlets for physical, intellectual, and emotional development. What one learns about oneself and how one feels about oneself set the tone for how events in other domains are processed. The changes that occur across the developmental domains from period to period in a person's life provide the framework for development. Typically, qualitative changes across several domains result in the movement from one stage of life to the next.

Stages of Development

We have identified six distinct stages of development in the period from conception until approximately 18 years of age. *Stages* refer to periods when there are qualitative differences in how life is experienced. Differences from one stage to the next are more than a matter of degree; they reflect fundamental distinctions in a person's ability to make meaning of experiences, conceptualize self and others, and interact as a member of the social group. The stages are typically experienced in a specific sequence; one cannot skip a stage, and each stage builds upon competencies achieved at an earlier stage. One can, however, anticipate issues that will occur in a future stage, recall experiences of a preceding stage, and, in some cases, reinterpret past events in a new light. By presenting development as a sequence of stages, we consider the interrelation

In these photos of Marta at infancy, early school age, and (on the following page) early adolescence, physical change is most readily observable. However, she has experienced equally remarkable growth in intellectual, emotional, and social competences as well as new levels of self-understanding.

among various domains which provides an integrated picture of the kinds of coping resources that a child is likely to have at a certain period of life.

We have done our best to calculate the age ranges when people tend to go through the stage changes, but we know that, at best, these ages are only approximate guidelines. The six stages of childhood and adolescence that are covered in this text are:

1. Prenatal (conception until birth)—Chapters 5 and 6
2. Infancy (birth to 2 years)—Chapters 7 and 8
3. Toddlerhood (2 and 3)—Chapters 9 and 10
4. Early school age (4 to 6)—Chapters 11 and 12
5. Middle childhood (6 to 12)—Chapters 13 and 14
6. Early adolescence (12 to 18)—Chapters 15 and 16 < Middle late

The text will examine the main accomplishments, conflicts, and challenges that confront individuals as a natural part of development. In order to illustrate the stage differences graphically, we present photographs of a child, pictured at three stages of development. We ask you to consider the multitude of changes across each of the five domains—physical, intellectual, emotional, social, and self—that are represented by these changing images of childhood and adolescence.

You might think of the stages by imagining the situation of a child becoming separated from his or her parent at a crowded and unfamiliar public setting like an amusement park or a fair. An infant can only cry to communicate distress. A toddler might be quite absorbed in watching some activities or playing with others and not notice that he or she had been separated for quite a while. Once the child realized the separation, she or he could probably tell an adult her or his name and maybe the parent's name. An early-school-age child would probably become very upset quickly, realizing more of the dangers of being separated. This child might try to find a police officer

or a guard and ask for help. The child could probably tell an adult his or her address, phone number, and something about the parents. By middle childhood, the parent and child may have already made a plan about what to do in case of separation, such as agreeing to meet at a certain landmark. When children reach this age, parents may even be willing to allow them to go off with a friend for an hour and meet back up at an agreed-upon spot. By adolescence, the child will probably want to be on his or her own and may only be willing to spend a few precious moments with the parents. Separation, by this point, is likely to be desired rather than feared.

For most people, children and adults, time is spent in the company of others. For children, these others are usually in stages of development that are different from their own. Much of the impact of the environment on children and adolescents can be conceptualized as the influence that people in significant social relationships have on one another. Our basic unit of analysis is each person functioning as an individual. However, throughout the text, you will find examples of the interdependence of people at various stages of development, and the transmission of values, goals, and beliefs from one generation to the next. How people were treated as children seems to influence how they treat their own children when they become parents themselves. Children watching their parents' interaction with their grandparents can anticipate how they might expect to interact with their parents when they become adults. Stages of life are linked because of the vital role of childhood in stimulating the behavior systems of adulthood and because of the vital importance of the behavior systems of adults in influencing the experiences of children.

Developmental Tasks

Each developmental domain is comprised of many specific capacities. The specific capacities undergoing transformation during a particular life stage are called *developmental tasks.* For example, within the domain of physical development, one task is the emerging capacity for voluntary, fine-muscle coordination. In infancy, fine-muscle coordination may involve finger–thumb opposition for grasping and manipulating objects. In early school age, it may involve using pens and pencils for writing. By early adolescence, fine-muscle coordination involves the coordinated use of both hands in performing complex tasks such as playing video games or the piano and manipulating materials to produce pottery, weaving, or sculpture.

Over the course of infancy, childhood, and adolescence, there are periods of heightened maturation in each of the developmental domains. Normally, progress in achieving new developmental tasks will depend on prior accomplishments so that advancement in each area builds on achievements from an earlier period. However, development does not occur evenly across all domains at every stage of life. Some periods are especially critical for the establishment of certain capacities, while a subsequent period might involve strengthening or consolidating that ability rather than expanding in new directions. The developmental tasks that become elaborated during a particular stage depend on the genetic plan for growth, the capacities of the individual child, and the requirements and demands of the culture.

Continuity

The study of child development emphasizes the nature and direction of growth and change. However, we could not be aware of differences if they did not occur against a backdrop of continuity. Think a moment about your own sense of self. You know, at a most basic level, that you are the same person you were yesterday or even last year. Despite the many new events and ideas that you experience, you maintain some sense of self-sameness.

Continuity in development can be thought of in several different ways (Kagan, 1980). Some qualities show very little change from stage to stage. Continuity is reflected when a quality becomes stable, rate of change slows down, or when it comes to a halt altogether. For example, after a period of growth, you achieve your adult height which does not change much over your life span.

Continuity can refer to a common response or behavior across settings. For example, some children are timid when they meet strangers; most of the time, they withdraw rather than initiate interactions with new people. Shyness shows continuity across settings when the conditions relate to meeting unfamiliar people.

Continuity can refer to the relationship between one person and others. For example, some children are intellectually gifted. The content and quality of their intellectual abilities change dramatically from one age to another. However, in relation to their age-mates, they always perform in a superior way. Their test scores consistently place them in the top group. Thus, even while they are changing in ability, they show continuity in their position relative to others.

Finally, continuity is a product of commitment to an ongoing set of roles and relationships. Parents, siblings, and other relatives establish a framework of continuity for children that contributes to self-definition. Continuity is sustained by the expectations that others have of you to be yourself, and your own expectations to present yourself with consistency (Caspi, 1993).

Notebook Page 1.1 gives you an opportunity to examine the ideas of continuity and change in reference to your own development.

Continuity and Change

In each developmental domain, individuals experience areas of change and growth as well as areas of continuity. For each domain listed below, try to identify two examples of change over the past 5 years and two examples of continuity in your own life. For example, in the physical domain, you may find that the pace of activity that seems best for you is about the same as it was 5 years ago. (Some people are basically active, whereas others are more contemplative.) However, the kinds of activities in which you participate may have changed. You may be involved in more or fewer team sports, more or less fitness activity, or more or less competitive activity today than 5 years ago.

Current age _____

Domain of Development	Change over 5 Years	Continuity over 5 Years
Physical	1.	
	2.	
Intellectual	1.	
	2.	
Emotional	1.	
	2.	
Social	1.	
	2.	
Self	1.	
	2.	

The Contexts of Development

Children are an integral part of a complex physical and social environment. One way of thinking about the contexts of development is to imagine the child as part of a kaleidoscope of changing, interconnected segments. Children are members of families. Parents and other relatives are members of other important work and community groups that can influence families. Children, as they grow, may become members of other institutions such as day-care programs, schools, religious groups, community clubs, or athletic teams. Communities are contained within cities, counties, states, and national governments. An assumption of this text is that an understanding of child development requires insight into each level of social organization as well as across the culture as a whole. These organizations influence what is expected of children, what resources children have to meet these expectations, and what risks children might encounter. They influence the options that children have for how to behave. In addition, the context of development embodies social, economic, and historic factors. Events such as war, political revolution, famine, or economic collapse may temporarily alter prevailing child-rearing values, opportunities for education, and availability of resources; in addition, these events may increase exposure to violence and separation of family members or other unpredictable stressors that may disrupt the course of development.

Families

All over the world, children are raised by small groups or families. *Family* seems to be the universal primary social context of childhood for most cultures. When we speak of family, we are speaking of a group of people, usually related by blood, marriage, or adoption, who share a common bond and who experience a sense of emotional intimacy. People in a family care about one another and take care of one another. We will be considering family and the specific relationship with mother, father, grandparents, and siblings as the major environmental system in the lives of most children. We will examine how this system places demands on children for organizing their thoughts and behaviors over the stages of development. Box 1.1 describes the characteristics of families that have been identified as significant for optimizing development.

Culture

Culture refers to the socially standardized ways of thinking, feeling, and acting that a person acquires as a member of a society. Culture includes the concepts, habits, skills, arts, technology, religion, and government of a people. Often, a culture exerts influence directly through families as well as through other social organizations such as churches and schools. The United States, like other societies, has a culture that has a strong, unifying impact on its citizens. We will note the vast differences in what life, including family life, is like in different cultures, and how the integration of various cultures and individuals produces distinctive personal experiences.

Ethnic Groups

Despite the common threads of culture that affect everyone who grows up or lives for a long time in the United States, there are also persistent subcultural forces that shape the daily lives of children and adults. The United States is

BOX 1.1

Optimizing Development: Vital Families

As we embark on the study of child development and consider those factors that provide optimal support for maturity, we appreciate once again how much a child's life exists within a parental and family context. The *relational system, that is, the quality of the* relationships between the adult(s) who are parenting the child, and the *family system,* the quality of the relationships among all those who comprise the child's significant and intimate family, are critical determinants of development. Research has shown, for example, that the quality of the parents' relationship with one another influences a young infant's adaptation (Belsky, 1984; Stoneman et al., 1989; Bornstein, 1995). Similarly, we understand that strong families have a number of important social characteristics that provide key resources for the developing child (Walker & Taylor, 1991; Belsky et al., 1991; Dubow et al., 1991; Garmezy, 1993).

What are the qualities of a vital marriage or partnership, and how are these qualities relevant for our understanding of a child's development? At least three features have been identified as central for establishing and maintaining a vital adult relationship. First, the partners must be committed to growth both as individuals and as a couple. They must accept the idea that each of them will change in important ways over the years and that the relationship will change. Obviously, this expectation of and openness to change between the partners is linked to a certain flexibility in regard to a child's inevitable change and growth. Mothers and fathers who can accept one another as individuals whose needs and concerns change over time are more likely to approach parenting with this same openness.

Second, vital relationships are characterized by effective communication. The partners make sure to have enough time to interact with one another. They listen to each other, encourage each other, convey love and caring, and interact honestly. They validate one another's concerns, try to express understanding, and provide support when necessary. Here, too, we see the benefit of effective communication for a child's development. Parents who are able to achieve open communication with one another are likely to approach their child with similar skills—listening, expressing encouragement and support, and permitting the child to be frank and direct.

Third, partners in a vital relationship make effective use of conflict. Rather than avoiding or denying conflict, they understand that it is inevitable for individuals with separate points of view to disagree. When these couples cannot resolve their conflicts, they are willing to leave the matter at stalemate rather than escalate their differences to increasing levels of hostility. Conflict sometimes even results in a new appreciation for one's partner's individuality. When conflict can be viewed positively, it provides a promising context for child development. Rather than shrinking from differences in point of view, couples who can accept conflict with each other are likely to view conflict with their child as a natural aspect of the individuation process. Children benefit by seeing their parents as individuals who have distinct outlooks and opinions on certain matters, as long as these differences do not result in intense or prolonged hostility. Acknowledging these differences gives children a certain space in which to establish their own individuality.

---

a complex society that is made up of people from a vast array of cultures throughout the world. We call these groups *ethnic subcultures* or *ethnic groups.* People who belong to ethnic subcultures share socially standardized ways of thinking, feeling, and acting with other members of their subgroup. The subculture may or may not be in conflict with the mainstream culture of the United States. Much of the literature on child development in this country is based on observations of white, middle-class children of European ancestry and their families. However, some attention has been given by researchers to the lifestyles, parenting practices, and family values of various other ethnic subcultures, and we will try to give special attention to studies that highlight ethnic group comparisons where possible.

The primary ethnic groups in the United States are of European origin, with the largest groups having ancestry traceable to the United Kingdom, Ger-

Family reunions build a sense of pride and tradition.

The family system has qualities that permit it to adapt in response to crisis and change, while preserving a sense of closeness and support (Hill, 1949, 1971; McCubbin et al., 1980; Boss, 1987; Wilson & Gottman, 1995). These qualities, often referred to as *family strengths*, are:

- Time to talk to one another

- Time to talk together as a family unit

- A respect for and acknowledgment of contributions from all family members

- Effective strategies for managing conflict and regulating negative emotions

- A spiritual or philosophical outlook on life

- A general sense of community; a willingness to help people who are not members of the family

- A sense of pride and pleasure in enacting certain family traditions and rituals

Children who grow up in strong families are fortified by these strengths. They have a clear sense of family identity and an important feeling of family support. As children, and later as adults, they understand how to extend the affection and support that they have experienced in their family to new relationships.

many, and Ireland. Major racial and national ethnic groups include African-Americans, Chinese, Filipinos, Japanese, Indians, Koreans, Vietnamese, Mexicans, Puerto Ricans, Cubans, and other Spanish-speaking peoples of the Americas. Table 1.1 shows the racial characteristics and Hispanic origin of the U. S. population projections for 1995.

Social Conditions

Throughout the text, we will be placing the study of development in a *sociohistorical context*, touching on the economic, political, and social conditions of a particular period. A parent's unemployment has an impact on his or her self-esteem and may influence interactions with his or her children (Elder, 1995). Low salaries and hazardous work conditions may influence the ways that teachers interact with students. Good and bad economic times, war, and

TABLE 1.1

U.S. Population by Race and Hispanic Origin, Percent Distribution, Projection for 1995

Hispanic origin	10.2
Non-Hispanic origin	
American Indian, Aleut, Eskimo	0.7
Asian, Pacific-Islander	3.5
African-American	12.0
White	73.6

Source: U.S. Bureau of the Census (1994). *Statistical abstract of the United States: 1994.* (114th ed.) Washington, D.C.: U.S. Government Printing Office. Adapted from Table 18.

demands in the work environment are examples of sociohistorical factors that seem to affect how people relate to each other and how they treat children. The social demands that are placed on the caregivers, role models, and teachers of children influence the environment that children encounter. Throughout the text, we will be paying attention to research on the effects of the environment on mother, father, siblings, other caregivers, and community because these factors have both direct and indirect influences on child development.

Any effort to consider the environmental contexts of development adds immeasurably to the complexity of the analysis. Consider the following matrix, which relates the five domains of development to the four critical environmental contexts that influence development. Variations in each of the contexts have the potential for modifying the directions of development in each domain at each stage of life. For example, try to fill in this matrix for the period of toddlerhood, ages 2 and 3. Consider how each environmental factor might contribute to or limit development in each of the domains of development during these years. Notebook Page 1.2 gives you an opportunity to develop these ideas further in relation to your ethnic group.

Matrix: Environmental Factors and Domains of Development

	Physical	Intellectual	Emotional	Social	Self
Families					
Culture					
Ethnic group					
Sociohistorical context					

Your Ethnic Group's Impact on Your Development

The matrix on environmental factors suggests that each factor can influence the direction of development in each domain. In this notebook page, explore this idea by focusing on your ethnic group's influence on the course of your development. Try to separate these influences from the overall impact of American culture.

First, identify your ethnic origins. Many students are of mixed ethnic background. Once you have identified your ethnicity, think about the importance of each ethnic strand on your identity. For some, ethnicity provides very obvious influences. Some students have grown up in ethnic neighborhoods where subcultural practices and attitudes were widely shared. For others, ethnic influences are less obvious and may be reflected in a family name, a sense of family history, or a curiosity about remote family ancestry.

Second, for each domain of development, consider the importance of ethnic influences and try to give one or two examples of these influences.

1. **Physical Development.** How important is your ethnic background in influencing your physical behavior or the pattern of your physical development? Give one or two examples of ethnic influences on some aspect of your physical development (e.g., diet, types of activities, genetically based diseases or vulnerabilities).

2. **Intellectual Development.** How important is your ethnic background in influencing your intellectual development or your intellectual interests? Give one or two examples of ethnic influences on some aspect of your intellectual development (e.g., information, problem-solving strategies, language, memories, myths, and stories).

3. **Emotional Development.** How important is your ethnic background in influencing your emotional development or the way you express your feelings? Give one or two examples of ethnic influences on some aspect of your emotional development (e.g., temperament, motives, topics about which you have strong feelings, your tendency to express or control the expression of emotions).

4. **Social Development.** How important is your ethnic background in influencing your social development or social relationships? Give one or two examples of ethnic influences on some aspect of your social development (e.g., roles, membership in groups, opportunities for leadership, family values, rites of passage).

5. **Self-Development.** How important is your ethnic background in influencing the development of your self-concept? Give one or two examples of ethnic influences on some aspect of your self-concept (e.g., models and heroes, personal history, self-esteem, goals for the future, values).

15

The Relationship of Heredity and Environment

NATURE
VS.
NURTURE

A recurring question in the field of child development is whether the forces of nature, that is, the influences of heredity and biological maturation, or the forces of nurture, that is, the influences of socialization and environment, are more central to directing the course of individual development.

Behavioral genetic research has demonstrated that the genetic influences on individual differences are substantial and pervasive. Genetic influences are found across the full range of human traits such as physical characteristics, intelligence, personality, and social styles. The same body of research also highlights the importance of the environment. These data indicate that nongenetic factors are responsible for more than half of the influence in most complex behaviors (Plomin et al., 1994; Plomin, 1995). This suggests that development is a product of both genetic and environmental influences. We will discuss this dynamic process in greater detail in Chapter 5.

Here, let us consider the contributions of heredity and environment in the hypothetical case of a temperamentally active child who is entering kindergarten. Considerable evidence supports the contribution of heredity to temperament (Thomas & Chess, 1977, 1986; Buss & Plomin, 1984, 1986; Sanson & Rothbart, 1995). *Temperament* refers to a person's usual way of handling physical and social stimulation. It includes such dimensions as activity level (whether a child is calm and generally slow moving or intense and active); sociability (whether a child is shy and reserved or outgoing); and sensitivity to stimulation (whether a child is easily upset by such stimuli as noise and touch or reacts minimally to most stimuli). These basic aspects of a child's orientation to the environment are a product of genetic information and can be observed in the first few months of life (Gunnar et al., 1995).

The temperamentally active child's experiences in coping with kindergarten will depend largely on the teacher's style and the classroom environment. If the teacher encourages active participation, group conversation, large-motor activities, and movement from one activity to another based on a child's interests, the active child will probably adjust to the class readily. If the teacher encourages quiet listening, requires following a group schedule, focuses on small-motor activities, and expects the children to sit in one place for long periods, the active child may experience the setting as frustrating and more stressful.

Development for this child may take very different paths depending on how the teacher arranges the situation and how the child is labeled as a consequence of his or her interactions in this environment. Factors such as the other children's attitudes—accepting or rejecting—or the child's own skills—verbal communication skills, motor coordination, or sociability—will also help determine what the kindergarten experience will be like and how it might guide subsequent development.

These early experiences in kindergarten provide the environmental influences that combine with genetic characteristics to guide development. They shape a child's self-esteem as a learner and his or her feelings of comfort with the learning process. If the child is treated as a cooperative, creative, and intelligent contributor to the classroom, that experience of success will be carried on to the next grade. If the child is always "getting into trouble" and being perceived as unruly, future learning will likely be tinged with that negative connotation.

The course of growth and change for an individual is guided by the continuous interplay between heredity and environment. No genetic plan can exist outside the context of a dynamic environment. The environment can provide both resources and barriers to the full expression of genetic potential. At the same time, the impact of the environment depends in part on the kinds of responses that are called forth by certain genetic characteristics. A single setting actually represents very different environments for the individuals who inhabit it (Caspi, 1993).

The exact contribution of the environment will be influenced by a child's own efforts to shape the nature of her or his personal experiences. Although many children suffer from destructive circumstances, certain resilient children are able to use inner resources and draw upon protective factors in the environment to thrive even in the most dire situations (Anthony & Cohler, 1988; Block & Block, 1980; Block, 1981; Clark, 1983; Cowan & Work, 1988; Garmezy, 1991, 1993; Rutter, 1985, 1987, 1993; Werner & Smith, 1982). The impact of the environment depends, in part, on the personal resources that children bring to it and on the nature of the psychological self. During childhood, a sense of self matures through acquisition of general skills in perception, information processing, memory, judgment, reality testing, problem solving, social competence, and emotional control. The self-concept is built upon experiences of mastering the challenges of daily life, identification with significant others, and the influence of those significant others on the way the self is reflected through acknowledging, approving, or disapproving one's actions and ideas. Understanding how the self develops, protects itself, and imposes itself on the environment is crucial to analyzing the interaction of heredity and environment.

[handwritten margin note: Dev't of self]

Universal Characteristics of Childhood

We have emphasized the many, many sources of genetic and environmental variation that can result in individual differences in life paths during childhood. At the same time, it is instructive to consider overarching themes that apply universally to the period of childhood. These themes bring into focus the experiences of childhood as compared with other periods of life, regardless of differences linked to culture, subculture, or historical period. In particular, we will consider the abundance of new experiences, the impact of the family, and the emphasis on skill development and learning new behaviors.

First Experiences

Many first experiences happen during childhood. Childhood may be defined, in part, by the fact that more new experiences occur per unit of time than at later periods. Examples of novel experiences in infancy are the tastes of each new food, each trip to an unfamiliar setting, and each song or story heard for the first time. As childhood continues, children expand their vocabulary, try out challenging motor activities, and experiment with new tools and materials. In adolescence, young people experience awakening sexual impulses, take on added social responsibilities, and have new thoughts about themselves and their relationships with others.

First experiences have a major impact on each of the domains of development, influencing both the content and the formation of various systems. Language acquisition provides a holistic example of how one set of early experiences influences both the structure of a system and its content. Infants

[handwritten margin note: First experiences influence content & formation of various systems.]

around the world can produce the basic sounds of all languages. However, as time passes, they acquire increased competence in recognizing and producing the sounds of the language spoken in their home environment, while losing that ability for other spoken languages. Thus, the spoken language system is shaped by the accumulation of early experiences.

Establish foundation of expectations

A child who is at basic levels of general concept formation, experiencing new situations, forms concepts that influence the way he or she interprets subsequent experiences (Rheingold, 1985). First experiences establish the foundation for what children and adolescents expect. These first experiences create the basis for what is judged to be familiar and what is judged to be novel. Subsequent experiences confirm or disconfirm the expectations established by first sets of events.

Influence self-concept formation. ↳ leads to organization & interpretation of other events through this lens of perception

First experiences help provide organizing ideas for self-concept formation. Suppose that a child, Maddy, is constantly being scolded and punished. She gradually develops the idea that she is not a good person. In comparison, Mark is usually praised and admired. He comes to believe that he is a valued and special person. If you were like the active child we referred to earlier, you may have developed a sense of yourself as unruly or incapable of self-control. Once you accept this self-concept, you are likely to organize and interpret other information that you receive about yourself in a similarly negative way.

Early experiences also establish the person's attitudes, standards, and values in such basic areas as family relations, sexuality, religious beliefs, and work ethics. In the early years, children do not have a basis for comparison. They are not able to think about their experiences in a relativistic or objective way. Thus, children incorporate the ideals, practices, and myths of those who rear them. Revisions and modifications of these childhood beliefs do take place, but slowly and with difficulty. These revisions occur as a result of new learning, new roles and relationships, and new insights that occur in adolescence and adulthood. For some, psychotherapy is the means through which childhood beliefs are reviewed and revised. For many people, however, certain childhood beliefs continue to guide behavior without much modification. Knowing this presents us with a great responsibility to understand development so that, as adults, we can better assure that a child's first experiences will foster a positive, hopeful outlook regarding self and others.

Children in Families

Most children experience childhood in the environment of their *family of origin, the family to which they are born*. Of course, this is not true for everyone. Some children grow up in foster families, adoptive families, or, in rare cases, in institutions. However, for those who grow up in families, some universal features of families are important to note. Families tend to promote the development of social attachments. In most families, these attachments are positive; they help children feel safe, loved, and confident that their important needs will be met. But even when the attachments are negative or conflictual, they establish the child's very early orientation about what children come to expect in an intimate relationship. (More will be said about attachments in Chapter 7.) Even though the content of the relationships may change from childhood to adulthood, attachments formed in childhood to parents or guardians, siblings, grandparents, and other close family members continue to be relevant throughout life (Ainsworth, 1985).

Children live in families as junior members. The implication is that family members in different power or status positions are exposed to different styles of interaction (Goffman, 1967; Homans, 1974; Berger et al., 1977). For example, people who are in higher or superior positions behave in different ways toward subordinates than they behave toward equals. Often, subordinates are regarded as somewhat ignorant or inept. In turn, people in subordinate positions behave differently toward superiors, equals, and subordinates. Subordinates may obey superiors unquestioningly and with humility, or they may respond with resentment and rebelliousness. In contrast, people in equal status positions tend to be more relaxed, informal, and on equal footing with each other. In adult life, most people find themselves in positions that provide a range of status and power positions. Generally, people prefer being in high-status positions, and they do not enjoy being in low-status positions.

Children are usually considered to be in subordinate positions to one or more adults in their families and other settings. Younger siblings may also be treated as subordinates by older siblings; and in some cultures, female children are subordinates to male children. Children are typically viewed as being less than fully capable. Their ideas and suggestions are typically less valued than are those of adults. And children are expected to submit to the advice and will of adults. Childhood is a time when we learn firsthand all the patterns and nuances of behavior associated with being in a subordinate position. It is also a time when we observe how people in positions of authority behave. These experiences of subordinate–superior relationships provide a model that many adults use as they embark on new roles as parents, teachers, supervisors, managers, and professionals. This phenomenon is central to the notion of *transference,* a process in psychotherapy where a client relates to a therapist in a manner based on the client's past experiences with authority figures, thereby revealing many emotional issues.

Skill Development and Learning

Human adaptation relies more on learning than on instinct. Humans are born in a relatively immature state, with only a few reflexes that are necessary for their immediate survival. Most of what it takes to become an accepted, self-sufficient member of a human group has to be learned. During infancy and childhood, a remarkably rapid period of neural maturation sustains complex cognitive functioning, including the accumulation of specific information, as well as more general concepts, strategies, and rules for solving problems. Young children evidence an intense curiosity that is expressed through sensory, motor, and intellectual exploration.

All cultures recognize that children need to be introduced to the essential knowledge, skills, attitudes, and values of the society. Adults and older children create systems to transfer information to younger children. Younger children are exposed to a cultural curriculum that includes those myths, facts, customs, and rituals that are seen as vital to adult functioning. Learning may take place in formal schools and apprenticeships or informally with the family, friends, or a community group. Often this learning focuses on work-related skills, but it also covers critical areas of social relationships and customs, religious observances, and survival skills.

Children learn new information, but, more importantly, they learn how to acquire knowledge. They discover which people to consider as wise or

[handwritten margin note: Adaptation relies on learning]

At age 7, a child in Ghana is encouraged to learn the basic skills of wood carving valued by his culture.

informed, and how much to trust their own senses and direct experiences in gaining new ideas and information. Thus, a fundamental perspective on the learning process is formulated during childhood.

The universal features of childhood, summarized in Table 1.2, provide a common set of psychological filters through which the world is viewed by children in all cultures. The first experiences provide a basic orientation toward self, family, work, and society. The child's role in the family provides lifelong loving relationships for most people and an understanding of differences between a child and an adult, including subordinate and superior relationships. The emphasis on learning skills helps children gain a sense of competence and membership in their society. In Notebook Page 1.3 we are asking you to recall some of your own early childhood memories in order to begin to identify the salient first experiences, family relationships, and skill development that were significant in your personal history.

Conclusions and Preview of the Remainder of the Text

Through the study of child development, you will have the opportunity to understand more about the principles and processes associated with growth and development during the first 18 years of life. We hope that you will find yourself in awe of children's many challenges and accomplishments, their creativity and resourcefulness, their energy and promise. This field combines a descriptive focus on basic patterns of continuity and change, with attention to individual differences, the impact of family dynamics, and cultural and historical variations. The text will focus on five domains of functioning across six stages of life. The story of development includes an appreciation of the interdependence of children and adults, and the integration of children and their families in broader community, cultural, and societal systems. The psychosocial approach emphasizes the ongoing interaction of children and their social worlds, viewing development as a product of biological processes, social interactions, and the self as an agent of purpose and will.

In the next three chapters, we introduce the scientific methods used in the study of child development, the basic concepts of psychosocial theory, and other theories and principles of change and growth. These chapters will serve as resources for your inquiry; they will help you bring a more critical, analytic approach to the material on development that is presented in this text or that you read in lay publications or professional journals. In Chapters 5 and 6, we begin the story of development with the discussion of sexual reproduction and the biological bases of heredity, fetal development, and birth. Chapters 7 through 16 provide two chapters on each of five additional stages of life. For each stage, the first chapter focuses on basic developmental tasks; the second chapter offers a psychosocial expansion. The developmental tasks highlight new competencies in the domains of physical, intellectual, social, emotional, and self-development. The psychosocial expansion introduces concepts related to the psychosocial crisis and its resolution, including an analysis of the resulting ego strengths and core pathologies. In addition, these chapters address issues pertaining to the development of significant family members and changes in the family system as the child matures. Cultural variations and societal issues that present challenges to development are also introduced.

Along this journey, we encourage you, through the Notebook Pages, to reflect on real children, both children you observe and memories of your own childhood, in order to connect the material you read here and elsewhere with

TABLE 1.2

Universal Characteristics of Childhood

The High Rate of First Experiences

Coding at basic levels of concept formation
Establishing a foundation for expectations
Organizing ideas for self-conceptualization
Establishing basic attitudes, standards, and values

The Family

Becoming socially attached
Forming lifelong attachments
Learning the interaction style of the subordinate–superior status relationship, with emphasis on the subordinate
Thinking of oneself as being in training to become fully capable

Emphasis on Skill Development and Learning

Introduction to essential knowledge and skills
Introduction to myths, facts, customs, and rituals
Absorption of fundamental aspects of the learning process
Development of a sense of competence
Development of a sense of societal membership

Childhood Memories

Early childhood memories provide a place to begin your own self-understanding and a basis for building empathy with children. In this notebook page, you will work on retrieving some early memories. First, relax as much as possible. Let go of the preoccupations of the moment. Now try to visualize your earliest recollection of your home setting.

1. Write down your earliest memories of home.

_____

_____

2. Visualize your mother. Write down the earliest memory associated with her.

_____

_____

3. Visualize your father. Write down the earliest memory associated with him.

_____

_____

4. Take a moment to return to your relaxed state. Let your mind wander. See if any earlier memory comes to mind—a sound, an emotion, a taste, or an image. Write it down.

_____

_____

5. Read over each of the memories, and write down an estimate of the age or stage in your life linked to each memory.

_____

_____

firsthand experiences. We want you to link the abstract concepts presented in the text with your own observations, both to clarify those concepts and to challenge them against the backdrop of your experiences. We know that all generalizations about children are open to exceptions. Your observations will help you keep the uniqueness of individual lives in focus as you become familiar with general patterns. Our goal is to provide you with a look into the study of child development that will engage new levels of critical thinking, provoke a higher degree of concern about the conditions surrounding childhood development, and deepen your insight into the many faces of childhood, including your own.

Chapter Summary

1. The study of development includes a description of emerging capabilities, patterns of change, patterns of consistency, and an analysis of the genetic, environmental, and personal factors that account for these patterns.
2. Development occurs in five major domains: physical, intellectual, emotional, social, and self. Changes in each area influence changes in the others.
3. The period from conception until approximately 18 years of age will be analyzed as six stages of development. The stages and approximate age ranges are: prenatal (conception until birth), infancy (birth to 2 years), toddlerhood (2 and 3), early school age (4 to 6), middle childhood (6 to 12), and early adolescence (12 to 18).
4. The social and physical environments are complex. Critical components of the environment, including parents, siblings, other caregivers, teachers, social organizations, physical and social settings, ethnic groups, and culture, all influence the nature of the resources and barriers that children encounter.
5. The course of growth and change for an individual is guided by the continuous interplay between heredity and environment.
6. Even though childhood is experienced differently in different cultures, there are some universal characteristics of childhood: the plethora of new experiences, the role of subordinate in the family group, and the emphasis on skill development and learning.

References

Ainsworth, M. D. S. (1985). Patterns of infant–mother attachments: Antecedents and effects on development. *Bulletin of the New York Academy of Medicine, 61,* 771–791.

Anthony, J. E. & Cohler, B. J. (1988). *The invulnerable child.* New York: Guilford.

Belsky, J. (1984). The determinants of parenting: A process model. *Child Development, 55,* 83–96.

Belsky, J., Youngblade, L., Rovine, M. & Volting, B. (1991). Patterns of marital change and parent–child interaction. *Journal of Marriage and the Family, 53,* 487–498.

Berger, J., Fisek, M. H., Norman, R. Z. & Zelditch, M., Jr. (1977). *Status characteristics and social interaction: An expectation states approach.* New York: Elsevier.

Block, J. (1981). Growing up vulnerable and growing up resistant: Preschool personality, preadolescent personality and intervening family stresses. In C. D. Moore (Ed.), *Adolescence and stress.* Washington, D.C.: U.S. Government Printing Office.

Block, J. H. & Block, J. (1980). The role of ego-control and ego-resiliency in the organization of behavior. In W. A. Collins (Ed.), *Development of cognition, affect, and social relations* (vol. 13). Hillsdale, N.J.: Erlbaum, 39–101.

Bornstein, M. H. (1995). Parenting infants. In M. H. Bornstein (Ed.), *Handbook of parenting, volume 1: Children and parenting.* Mahwah, N.J.: Erlbaum, 3–40.

Boss, P. (1987). Family stress. In M. B. Sussman & S. K. Steinmetz (Eds.), *Handbook of marriage and the family.* New York: Plenum Press, 675–724.

Buss, A. H. & Plomin, R. (1984). *Temperament: Early developing personality traits.* Hillsdale, N.J.: Erlbaum.

Buss, A. H. & Plomin, R. (1986). The EAS approach to temperament. In R. Plomin & J. Dunn (Eds.), *The study of temperament: Changes, continuities, and challenges.* Hillsdale, N.J.: Erlbaum.

Caspi, A. (1993). Why maladaptive behaviors persist: Sources of continuity and change across the life course. In D. C. Funder, R. D. Parke, C. Tomlinson-Keasey & K. Widaman (Eds.), *Studying lives through time: Personality and development.* Washington, D.C.: American Psychological Association, 343–376.

Clark, R. M. (1983). *Family life and school achievement: Why poor black children succeed or fail.* Chicago: University of Chicago Press.

Cowan, E. L. & Work, W. C. (1988). Resilient children, psychological wellness, and primary prevention. *American Journal of Community Psychology, 16,* 591–607.

Dubow, E. F., Tisak, J., Causey, D., Hryshko, A. & Reid, G. (1991). A two-year longitudinal study of stressful life events, social support, and social problem-solving skills: Contributions to children's behavioral and academic adjustment. *Child Development, 62,* 583–599.

Elder, G. H., Jr. (1995). The life course paradigm: Social changes and individual development. In P. Moen, G. H. Elder, Jr., & K. Luscher (Eds.), *Examining lives in context: Perspectives on the ecology of human development.* Washington, D.C.: American Psychological Association.

Garmezy, N. (1991). Resilience in children's adaptation to negative life events and stressed environments. *Pediatric Annals, 20,* 459–466.

Garmezy, N. (1993). Vulnerability and resistance. In D. C. Funder, R. D. Parke, C. Tomlinson-Keasey & K. Widaman (Eds.), *Studying lives through time: Personality and development.* Washington, D.C.: American Psychological Association, 377–398.

Goffman, E. (1967). *Interaction ritual.* New York: Anchor.

Gunnar, M. R., Porter, F. L., Wolf, C. M., Rigatuso, J. & Larson, M. C. (1995). Neonatal stress reactivity: Predictions to later emotional temperament. *Child Development, 66,* 1–13.

Hill, R. (1949, 1971). *Families under stress.* New York: Harper & Row (reprinted in 1971, Westport, Conn.: Greenwood Press).

Homans, G. C. (1974). *Social behavior: Its elementary forms* (revised ed.). New York: Harcourt, Brace, Jovanovich.

Kagan, J. (1980). Perspectives on continuity. In O. G. Brim, Jr., & J. Kagan (Eds.), *Constancy and change in human development.* Cambridge, Mass.: Harvard University Press.

McCubbin, H., Joy, C., Cauble, B., Comeau, J., Patterson, J. & Needle, R. (1980). Family stress and coping: A decade review. *Journal of Marriage & the Family, 42,* 855–871.

Plomin, R. (1995). Molecular genetics and psychology. *Current Directions in Psychological Science, 4,* 114–117.

Plomin, R., Owen, M. & McGuffin, P. (1994). The genetic basis of complex human behaviors. *Science, 264,* 1733–1739.

Rheingold, H. L. (1985). Development as the acquisition of familiarity. In M. R. Rosenzweig & L. W. Porter (Eds.), *Annual Review of Psychology, 36,* Palo Alto, Calif.: Annual Reviews Inc., 1–17.

Rutter, M. (1985). Resilience in the face of adversity: Protective factors and resistance to psychiatric disorder. *British Journal of Psychiatry, 147,* 598–611.

Rutter, M. (1987). Psychosocial resilience and protective mechanisms. *American Journal of Orthopsychiatry, 57,* 316–330.

Rutter, M. (1993). Resilience: Some conceptual considerations. *Journal of Adolescent Health, 14,* 626–631.

Sanson, A. & Rothbart, M. K. (1995). Child temperament and parenting. In M. H. Bornstein (Ed.), *Handbook of parenting, volume 1: Children and parenting.* Mahwah, N.J.: Erlbaum, 299–321.

Stoneman, Z., Brody, J. H. & Burke, M. (1989). Marital quality, depression, and inconsistent parenting: Relationship with observed mother–child conflict. *American Journal of Orthopsychiatry, 59,* 105–117.

Thomas, A. & Chess, S. (1977). *Temperament and development.* New York: Bruner/Mazel.

Thomas, A. & Chess, S. (1986). The New York longitudinal study: From infancy to early adult life. In R. Plomin & J. Dunn (Eds.), *The study of tempera-*

ment: *Changes, continuities, and challenges.* Hillsdale, N.J.: Erlbaum.

U.S. Bureau of the Census. (1994). *Statistical abstract of the United States: 1994.* (114th ed.). Washington, D.C.: U.S. Government Printing Office. Adapted from Table 18.

Walker, L. J. & Taylor, J. H. (1991). Family interactions and the development of moral reasoning. *Child Development, 62,* 264–283.

Werner, E. E. & Smith, R. S. (1982). *Vulnerable but not invincible: A study of resilient children.* New York: McGraw-Hill.

Wilson, B. J. & Gottman, J. M. (1995). Marital interaction and parenting. In M. H. Bornstein (Ed.), *Handbook of parenting, volume 4: Applied and practical parenting.* Mahwah, N.J.: Erlbaum, 33–35.

Research on Children and Adolescents

Chapter 2

Scientific Observation

Research Design

Selecting a Sample

Random Samples

Stratified Samples

Matched Groups

Volunteer Samples

Strengths and Weaknesses of Approaches to Sampling

Research Methods

Observation

Case Study

Interviews

Surveys and Tests

Experimentation

Designs for Studying Development

Retrospective Studies

Cross-Sectional Designs

Longitudinal Studies

Cohort Sequential Designs

Evaluating Existing Research

Ethics

The Ongoing Study of Child Development

Limited Applicability of Historical Data to Current and Future Generations

Self-Directed Creation of Experiences

Chapter Summary

References

P arents, teachers, and other professionals who care for and educate children generally have their own ideas about children's needs and how best to meet them. These ideas are usually shaped by personal experiences in families, schools, and communities, as well as by the mass media and other culture bearers. Social scientists, however, use research as a primary tool for generating accurate information and new knowledge on child development. The scientific approach challenges and complements our commonsense notions by providing information that has been gathered and evaluated through a rigorous and systematic process. In order to become more sophisticated consumers of research information, you must be able to recognize the qualities of good research, develop the capacity to criticize research, and apply research findings to the problems you need to solve. In this chapter, we consider basic elements of the research process, including the characteristics of scientific observation, research design, research methods, various approaches for studying changes in development over time, and the ethical considerations associated with research with children.

Scientific Observation

SCIENTIFIC OBSERVATION
1) Objective
2) Repeatable
3) Systematic

Scientific observation in child development, as in other areas of social science, is characterized by three essential qualities: It must be objective, repeatable, and systematic (Creswell, 1994). These qualities may or may not be characteristic of the way you make observations in your personal life. Notebook Pages 2.1 and 2.2 provide an opportunity to examine the challenges of making objective observations of behavior.

Objective observations accurately reflect the events that are taking place. They are not unduly influenced by what the observer expects or hopes to see.

This observer has been trained to record details of student–teacher interaction. She does not appear to be infering with the children's interest or focus of attention.

Objectivity I

Scientific inquiry typically begins with observation. As a student of child development, you need to learn to become a careful observer. For this Notebook Page, you will focus your observations on the issue of misbehavior. Develop a set of guidelines for categorizing what you consider to be misbehavior by children. Try to be as specific as possible about what types of behaviors qualify for which categories. Then go to a setting where children and adults are likely to be present together (e.g., a shopping mall, a park, a restaurant) and observe children for 30 minutes. Write down all the examples of misbehavior that you observe, and categorize each observation based on your definition.

1. Definition of misbehavior: _____

_____

2. Categories of misbehavior: _____

_____

Observations of Misbehavior	Category
1.	
2.	
3.	
4.	
5.	
6.	

29

Objectivity II

A scientific approach to child development strives for objectivity. It is important for scientists to recognize their personal beliefs and values and to understand how these beliefs may influence their observations and the meaning they attach to those observations.

Go back to the list of observations of misbehavior and the categories that you assigned to them in Notebook Page 2.1. Try to be conscious of threats to your objectivity in this exercise. Did you need to add to or modify your list of categories based on your observations? Did you have to "stretch" your categories to make them fit what you saw? How might your prior beliefs and values have influenced your definition of misbehavior? How might your experiences as a child have influenced your definitions? Did the gender or appearance of the child or the adult whom you observed influence how you categorized their behavior? For each observation in Notebook Page 2.1, suggest a possible source of observer bias that may have influenced your judgment.

Observations of Misbehavior	Possible Source of Observer Bias
1.	
2.	
3.	
4.	
5.	
6.	

Suppose, for example, that as a parent you want an objective assessment of your child's physical attractiveness. You cannot just go up to some friends or relatives and ask them to tell you whether they find your child attractive, because they presumably would not like to insult you and may be inclined to formulate their answers to please you. A more objective approach might be to include your child's photograph with photos of 100 other children chosen at random. You could then ask another person to give the photographs to 10 people who do not know you or your child and ask each of them to rate the photos for physical attractiveness. You may or may not like the outcome, but at least your method would be more objective. It would give you an unbiased assessment of your child's appearance.

Social science research is always vulnerable to the theoretical biases and value orientations of researchers. Certain practices of research design, sampling, and methodology are used to help overcome biases and build a higher level of objectivity into the process. However, many will argue that it is impossible to be entirely objective. One's orientation toward framing research questions and interpreting the results is always influenced to some degree by one's cultural and historical contexts which influence values, beliefs, and assumptions that guide the research process. That is why it is so important that the research carried out by any one investigator be repeatable.

If research is *repeatable,* then others can approach the research task and observe the same things as the original investigator. In order for this to occur, the original investigator must carefully describe all the procedures and equipment used in the study and define all the essential characteristics of the participants (such as age, sex, and social class background) and the setting or situation where the observations were made. Since there are so many ways that one group of participants might differ from another, and so many different ways that observations can be made, repeatability is a very important part of building a body of social science knowledge. Usually a problem or process is investigated by an individual or research team, taking great care to make sure that observations are unbiased, orderly, carefully collected and recorded, and comprehensive. In order to insure that the results of a study are accurate, the original researchers should encourage other investigators to repeat the study to see if the same results are observed.

A *systematic* approach ensures that research is done in a proper, orderly way. Scientists have a framework of essential questions that they strive to answer, based on what is already known and what certain theories predict. They approach research with clear objectives, carefully defining the purpose of the research and the specific methods they will use to reach those objectives. Although discoveries are sometimes made by accident, scientific research typically does not randomly investigate seemingly unrelated topics.

Research Design

Research investigations are designed, just as cars, bridges, and buildings are designed. In formal, scientific work, research design is often conducted by small groups of scholars who try to devise the most appropriate, objective, and systematic approach for answering their questions. Scientists know that the information they gain from conducting research will be heavily influenced by the characteristics of the participants who are involved in their study, the kinds of data that are gathered, and the conditions under which the data are gathered. In child development, the principles of research design focus on the sample population that is selected to participate in the study, the method that is used to gather information, the approach to studying change, and the statistical techniques that are used to analyze the data (Miller, 1991). In this chapter, we will focus on the first three factors: sampling, methods, and designs for studying change.

Selecting a Sample

Sampling is the approach to choosing participants who will be included in the study. The nature of the questions that are being addressed usually influences the method of identifying the appropriate sample. If the study involves some universal principle of development, children from a wide variety of family and social backgrounds should be chosen. For example, studies of normal language development should include children from various ethnic, racial, socioeconomic, and cultural backgrounds. One cannot establish universal principles if the research reveals the pattern to be true only for a certain homogeneous group of children.

Samples taken from a population

Every sample is taken from a population. The *population* is the large group to which the findings of the research are intended to apply. The relevant population depends on the purpose and scope of the research. The sample is a smaller subgroup of the larger population that will participate in the study. For example, the population of interest in a particular study might be children ages 3 and 4 who are enrolled in some form of preprimary school. In 1993, that population in the United States was about 3,275,000 (U.S. Bureau of the Census, 1995). No research study can include all of those children. So a sample is drawn that is expected to be representative of the population. Under ideal conditions, the children who actually participate in this study ought to have the same general characteristics with respect to gender, family structure, community setting, and socioeconomic levels as the population from which the sample was selected. In addition to the characteristics of the children, the variety of available preprimary schools ought to be reflected in the schools attended by the sample children.

The sample and the population from which the sample is taken determine what generalizations may be made from the research findings. If all the children in the study are from one urban, low-income community in the Midwest who attend Head Start, one would have to be cautious about generalizing the findings. Could the findings be generalized to children from rural settings, from other regions of the country, from church-based or other private preschool programs? We must be careful not to assume that research findings based on one sample are generalizable for children of both sexes, and all ages, social classes, religions, cultures, or areas.

The following four approaches to sampling are common in the research literature. Each one has somewhat different implications for the generalizability of the findings.

Random Samples

In a *random sample, each child in a given population has an equal chance of being included.* The researcher may ensure equal opportunity by putting each child's name on a slip of paper and then choosing some of the slips blindly, or by selecting names from a list at random by using numbers produced by a random number generator.

Stratified Samples

In a *stratified sample*, participants are deliberately selected from various types of children (strata) in the population. For example, the number of girls and boys in the sample might be selected to correspond to the proportion of girls and boys in the school district. Within each type, however, the participants are selected at random.

Matched Groups

In most studies using *matched groups*, the researcher selects two or more groups of subjects who are similar on many dimensions. Participants in one group typically receive some type of treatment or participate in some type of experimental intervention and the participants in the other group do not. In this way, the effects of the treatment can be observed, since the participants are thought to be very similar in all other respects.

Volunteer Samples

Most studies rely on *volunteer samples.* Participants are solicited by advertisements, or requests to teachers, professionals, parents, or groups of potential participants. Those who are included in the study are selected from among those who volunteer.

Strengths and Weaknesses of Approaches to Sampling

What are some of the strengths and weaknesses of these approaches to sampling? Random sampling and stratified sampling are most likely to ensure that a sample is representative of the population from which it is drawn. If each child in the population had an equal chance of being included in the study, then the outcome ought to be equally likely to apply to those who did not participate and those who did. The method that places the greatest limits on generalization is volunteer sampling. Can you think of how reliance on volunteers may produce special problems? For example, parents who volunteer to allow their children to participate in research may have different personality characteristics than those who do not. They may be experiencing problems with their child that they hope the study will help them solve. Or they may be unusually confident of their parenting skills and therefore more willing to allow their children to participate than the parents who refuse.

Regardless of these difficulties, volunteer samples are widely used because they are often the only possibility for studying a certain question. For instance, some of the research findings discussed in this text are based upon *clinical studies.* This usually means that the children, the parents, or the entire family have been involved in some type of treatment program or are on the waiting list to receive clinical treatment. Clinical studies seek to understand the causes of conditions, the developmental paths or patterns that these conditions exhibit, the impact of certain treatments, and the long-term impact of these conditions on adaptation in childhood, adolescence, and beyond. Without voluntary participation, there would be no way to begin to document the effectiveness of treatment for a condition. At the same time, one must be cautious not to generalize findings from clinical studies to the population as a whole.

Research Methods

A variety of methods has been used to study child development. Each one has its strengths and weaknesses, allowing the investigator to focus on some set of behaviors at the expense of others. The choice of method must fit the

5 CATEGORIES OF DEV'TAL RESEARCH ↓

observational studies yield correlations (relationship among variables)

problem under study. Five general categories of developmental research are described here: observation, case study, interviews, experimentation, and surveys and tests. These methods have all contributed to increased knowledge, and you will find examples of each method in this text. Some techniques, especially naturalistic observation, case study, and interview, are more commonly used in the exploratory phase of research when investigators are trying to formulate basic themes or define the dimensions of a problem. Other methods, especially observation using a predetermined coding scheme, experimentation, and surveys and tests, tend to be used in the hypothesis-testing phase of the research process.

Observation

Direct observation of children in their home and school environments is one of the oldest methods for studying child development (Kessen, 1965). Researchers have used parents' diaries and observation logs to gather information about behavior in intimate settings that could not be known in any other way. Jean Piaget (1929) was guided by the observations of his own children in the formulation of his theory of cognition. Today, some researchers conduct observations in homes, schools, and day-care centers, where children typically spend their time. Others bring children and their families or friends into "homelike" laboratory settings where they can watch children's behaviors under somewhat more constant and controlled physical conditions (Kochanska, Kuczynski & Radke-Yarrow, 1989).

Naturalistic observation, in which behavior in a nonlaboratory setting is carefully observed without any other kinds of manipulation, provides insight about how things occur in the real world. In some instances, researchers go into a particular setting to observe the full range of interactions and behavior patterns. Based on their field notes, they develop hypotheses or tentative explanations about the meaning of the behaviors. Then, they may test these hypotheses through more focused observation or through more controlled experimentation.

In other instances, researchers use observation to examine a specific behavior or relationship. They may be looking for different forms of peer aggression, patterns of social cooperation, or conditions that promote cross-gender interactions. In these cases, the observers have a predefined focus and limit the scope of their observations to behaviors relevant to their concerns.

The technology of videotaping has expanded the use of observational techniques for developmental research. A videotaped record can be reviewed over and over again. Several observers can watch a tape, pause it, and discuss what they saw. Videotapes can be slowed to frame-by-frame viewing, allowing for very detailed microanalysis of behavior. Facial expressions and motor sequences have been examined using this approach. The same events can be observed from several points of view. For example, researchers interested in children's play might videotape a child's free play in three or four different settings such as day care, a school playground, and at home with family or friends. Several observers might review the tapes, each one rating different aspects of the behavior.

Observational studies lend themselves to an examination of correlation (as opposed to causation, which we will explain shortly). *Correlation* refers to a statistical analysis of the strength and direction of relationship among vari-

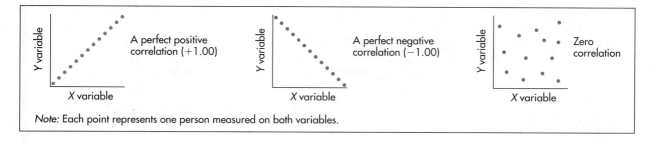

Note: Each point represents one person measured on both variables.

ables. It reflects the degree to which knowing the value of one variable, such as age, allows one to predict the level of another variable, such as helpfulness. In observational research, many correlational questions can be addressed. Do children who often play alone show more creativity in their play? Do younger children use fewer words to describe an object than do older children? Do children who are most aggressive with their peers at day care also act aggressively at home?

The *correlation coefficient* can range from values of +1.0 to −1.0. Let us take, as an example, the correlation between popularity with peers and aggressiveness. If increased aggressiveness is associated with higher levels of popularity, the correlation is positive (toward +1.0). If increased aggressiveness is associated with lower levels of popularity, the correlation is negative (toward −1.0). If there is no systematic relationship between aggressiveness and popularity, the correlation is close to 0. (See Figure 2.1.) (Research about the relationship between popularity with peers and aggressiveness is discussed in more detail in Chapters 11 and 13.)

A strong correlation between two variables only shows that there is an association between them. It does not provide information about *causation.* Knowing that aggression is negatively correlated with popularity does not necessarily mean that being aggressive causes children to be rejected by peers, nor that being unpopular causes children to be aggressive. It could be that some other factor, such as mistrust of others, accounts for both aggression and peer rejection.

Strong or weak correlations DO NOT yield causation

Strengths and Limitations of the Observational Method. One strength of naturalistic observation is the ability to capture natural responses as they occur. Another strength is the ability for children's behaviors to guide the researcher's conceptualization. Rather than setting up a specific task or group of questions and having children respond, the observer examines the full range of relevant behaviors and forms an interpretation of the events from the patterns that have been observed.

Observational research also has weaknesses, however. It is often difficult to establish agreement among observers about exactly what occurred. Think about the times that you and a friend have been in the same situation but have had entirely different reactions to or interpretations of the event. Typically, two or more observers' codings of the same situation are compared to determine whether different observers rated the same event in the same way. This is called *interobserver reliability.* When interobserver reliability is high, one can be confident that all the observers are describing or coding the events in the same way. When interobserver reliability is low, the researchers must determine why and correct the differences in observation criteria. This may result in changing the category scheme so that behaviors are more clearly associated with a category, or training observers more precisely on how to code each behavior.

Another difficulty with the observational method occurs when so much activity is taking place that it is difficult to select specific behaviors or to code events fast enough. Finally, some research focuses on a particular kind of behavior or behavioral sequence such as helping behavior, peer rejection, or conflict. In naturalistic observation, one cannot be assured that the behavior of interest will take place during the observational period.

Case Study

A *case study* is an in-depth description of a single person, family, or social group. The purpose of a case study is to describe the behavior of only that person or group. Case studies are often carried out to illustrate a general principle by providing specific details, to examine a phenomenon that does not conform to theoretical predictions, or to stimulate theory development in an area that has not been investigated. Case studies have been used to examine the sequence of life events that led up to a certain crisis or major turning point. They have also been used to document the course of mental disorder or to illustrate the treatment process (Runyan, 1982). Case studies can be based on various sources of information, including interviews, therapy sessions, prolonged observation, diaries or journals, letters, historical documents, and interviews with people who know the subject of study.

Some case studies document the lives of great individuals. In *Gandhi's Truth*, Erikson (1969) provided a psychosocial analysis of the life of the Indian pacifist, Mahatma Gandhi. Erikson considered Gandhi's childhood, adolescence, and young adulthood as they contributed to Gandhi's personality, moral philosophy, and the contradictions between his personal social relationships and his role as a powerful social leader.

Case studies may also focus on social groups, families, and organizations. One of Anna Freud's most famous psychiatric cases described the attachments that developed among a group of orphans who had lived together in a concentration camp during World War II (Freud & Dann, 1951). The study focused on the strong attachments that the children had to one another and their strategies for maintaining their connectedness once they were placed in a more normal social environment. The case illustrated a unique phenomenon, the intense emotional attachment of unrelated young children to each other, that had not been documented before.

Strengths and Limitations of the Case Study Method. Case studies have the advantage of illustrating the complexity and uniqueness of individual lives. Studies carried out with large samples often identify general principles, whereas case studies provide concrete examples of how these principles are realized in the lives of specific individuals. Some cases give the details of a rare experience that might not be captured in a large-scale study. A case study may bring a problem to the attention of researchers who then pursue it through other methods (Yin, 1994).

Case studies, however, have been criticized as being unscientific. In the first place, they are obviously not representative of large groups of individuals. One must be cautious about generalizing the conclusions drawn from a case study to other individuals or groups. Moreover, if the information that provides the basis of the case study is gathered in a biased or subjective way, then the results or conclusions of the study will be of little worth. Of course, this criticism applies to any type of research. Finally, critics argue that there is no reliably uniform, objective perspective in case studies. If different researchers wrote a case study on the same individual, they might come up with very different views of the events and their significance.

These limitations suggest that one needs a very clear idea of the purpose and a systematic, unbiased approach to gathering information in order to conduct case studies that meet the standards of scientific observation. At the same time, vividly written, compelling case material has had a consistent impact in stimulating theory and research in the field of child development.

Interviews

Many case studies are based largely on face-to-face *interviews*. This method can be used to gather data from large numbers of individuals and from groups in clinical settings.

Interviews can be highly structured, almost like a verbal survey, or very open-ended, allowing the participant to respond freely to a series of general questions. The success of the interview method depends heavily on the skill of the interviewer (Holstein & Gubrium, 1995). Interviewers are trained to be nonjudgmental as they listen to a child's responses. They try to create *rapport* with the child by conveying a feeling of trustworthiness and acceptance. In unstructured interviews, the interviewer must make use of this rapport to encourage the child to say more about a question and to share thoughts that may be private or personal. Matching the race and gender of the interviewer and the child being interviewed has been found to help foster rapport and improve the quality of the data that are produced.

The interview method has traditionally been associated with clinical research, and it is becoming a major method in the study of cognition and language as well. Piaget's structured interview technique (Piaget, 1929) provides a model for the investigation of conceptual development (see Box 2.1). The researcher who uses this technique asks a child a question (say, "Are clouds living or dead?") and then follows up on the answer with questions about how the child arrived at his or her conclusion. In other studies, Piaget asked children to solve a problem and then asked them to explain how they knew that their solution was correct. The child becomes an informant about his or her own conceptual capacities. This approach has been adapted in the study of moral development, interpersonal development, and positive, helping behavior.

Strengths and Limitations of the Interview Method.

The interview method has the advantage of allowing individuals to contribute their own views on the topic being studied. They can tell the interviewer what is important to them, why they might choose one alternative over another, or what they think is wrong with the investigator's view of the situation.

Children may also, however, present themselves in the way that they want the interviewer to see them rather than responding naturally; when they do so, they are said to be exhibiting a *self-presentation bias*. A child's responses are also vulnerable to influence by the interviewer. By smiling, nodding, frowning, or looking away, the interviewer can deliberately or inadvertently communicate approval or disapproval. There is a fine line between establishing rapport with an interview subject and influencing his or her responses.

BOX 2.1

Piaget's Interview Method

Piaget's use of the clinical interview method to pursue a young child's cognitive reasoning can be seen in two excerpts from his works. In the first, Piaget is exploring a 5-year-old child's understanding of dreams.

> *Where does the dream come from?*—I think you sleep so well that you dream.—*Does it come from us or from outside?*—From outside.—*What do we dream with?*—I don't know.—*With the hands? . . . With nothing?*—Yes, with nothing.—*When you are in bed and you dream, where is the dream?*—In my bed, under the blanket. I don't really know. If it was in my stomach(!) the bones would be in the way and I shouldn't see it.—*Is the dream in your head?*—It is I that am in the dream: it isn't in my head(!) When you dream, you don't know you are in the bed. You know you are walking. You are in the dream. You are in bed, but you don't know you are. (Piaget, 1929:97–98)

Here Piaget is describing a 7-year-old child's understanding of class inclusion:

> You present the child with an open box that contains wooden beads. The child knows they are all wooden because he handles them, touching each and finding that it is made of wood. Most of these beads are brown, but a few are white. The problem we pose is simply this: are there more brown beads or more wooden beads? Let us call A the brown beads, B the wooden beads: then the problem is simply that of the inclusion of A in B. (This is a very difficult problem before the age of 7 years.) The child states that all the beads are wooden, states that most of them are brown and a few are white, but if you ask him if there are more brown beads or more wooden beads he immediately answers: "There are more brown ones because there are only two or three white ones." So you say: "Listen, this is not what I am asking. I don't want to know whether there are more brown beads or more white beads, I want to know whether there are more brown beads or more wooden beads." And, in order to make it easier, I take an empty box and place it next to the one with the beads and I ask: "If I were to put the wooden beads into that box would any remain in this one?" The child answers: "No, none would be left because they are all wooden." Then I say: "If I were to take the brown beads and put them into that box, would any be left in this one?" The child replies: "Of course, two or three white ones would remain." Apparently he has now understood the situation, the fact that all the beads are wooden and that some are not brown. So I ask him once more: "Are there more brown beads or more wooden beads?" Now it is evident that the child begins to understand the problem, sees that there is indeed a problem, that matters are not as simple as they seemed at first. As we watch him we observe that he is thinking very hard. Finally he concludes, "But there are still more brown beads; if you take the brown ones away, only two or three white beads remain." (Piaget, 1963:283–299)

Source: Piaget, J. "The attainment of invariant and reversible operations in the development of thinking," *Social Research, 30,* 283–299.

Surveys and Tests

Survey research is a means of collecting specific information from a large number of participants. People responding to surveys must be able to read and write, unless the survey questions are read to them. Thus, the survey method is most commonly used with respondents in middle childhood, adolescents, and adults. Survey information about infants and toddlers is often collected from parents, child-care workers, physicians, nurses, and others who are responsible for meeting the needs of these young children. Thus surveys have contributed a great deal to our knowledge about the way that adults perceive the behaviors and needs of young children.

Survey methods can be used to collect information about attitudes ("Do you believe that teachers should be permitted to use corporal punishment with their students?"); current behaviors and practices ("How many hours per day do you watch television?"); aspirations ("What do you hope to do when you graduate from high school?"); and perceptions ("How well does your mother/father or son/daughter understand your views?").

Survey questions are prepared in a standard form, and the responses are usually coded according to a prearranged set of categories. In well-designed surveys, the questions are stated clearly and offer response choices that are not ambiguous or overlapping. In the most effective surveys, the sample of subjects is carefully selected to be representative of the population under study. Surveys may be conducted by telephone, through the mail, in class-rooms, at work, or in participants' homes (Fowler, 1993).

Tests are often similar in form to surveys. They consist of groups of questions or problems that the child is expected to answer. Usually tests are designed to measure a specific ability or characteristic. You are no doubt famil-iar with the kinds of tests that are typically given in school: You are presented with a group of items and asked to formulate the correct answer or to select the correct answer from among several choices. Intelligence tests and achieve-ment tests are of this nature. A researcher might give these tests along with some other measures in order to learn how intelligence relates to social life, emotions, or self-understanding.

Other tests are designed to measure a variety of psychological constructs, such as creativity, conformity, depression, and extroversion. Some tests are administered to assess whether a person has some form of mental illness, learning disorder, developmental disability, or handicap.

In order to be of use, psychological tests must be reliable and valid. Tests are *reliable* when they provide approximately the same score or the same diag-nosis each time a person takes the test. This does not mean that the test does not indicate when changes occur. But a child who takes a reliable test on two consecutive days should get approximately the same score on both days unless some deliberate training or intervention has been introduced in the interim. There ought to be a positive correlation (toward $+1.0$) between the two scores.

Tests are *valid* when they measure what they claim to measure. The peo-ple who design the tests have to define what it is they are trying to measure. They also have to provide evidence that their test really measures this con-struct (Messick, 1989). Consider the various tests that have been designed to measure intelligence in infants and very young children. The results of these tests are not very closely related to the results of intelligence tests given to the same subjects in adolescence and adulthood (Columbo, 1993; Neisser et al., 1996). Perhaps the underlying components of intelligence differ in babies and in adolescents and adults. Or perhaps intelligence evolves in so many ways that the intelligence of the adult bears little relation to that of the infant. Or perhaps these infant tests do not really test broad, adaptive intelligence, but instead measure sensory processing and central nervous system coordination.

Strengths and Limitations of Surveys and Tests.

Surveys and tests have certain advantages that make them applicable to developmental research. They allow us to compare the responses of large groups of respon-dents. Surveys and tests have been designed to address a wide variety of top-ics. With a prearranged coding or scoring system, many tests can be admin-istered and evaluated without difficulty.

This method also has limitations. Some surveys create attitudes in sub-jects where none existed before. For example, you might ask sixth-grade chil-dren questions about their satisfaction with their school curriculum, which they may not have given much thought to before. Another problem is the gap

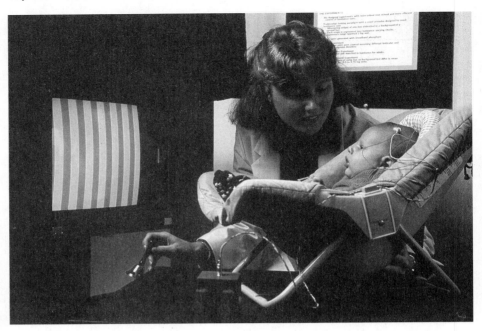

The experimental method has been used widely to determine infants' recognition of or interest in visual and auditory stimulation.

between answers to survey questions or test scores and actual behavior. Children may write on a survey that they would rather read than watch television, but in real life they may watch television during most of their spare time and rarely read. Similarly, parents may say that they allow their children to participate in family decisions, but when it comes to real family decisions, the parents may not actually give their children much voice.

The use of tests to determine school admissions and placement has come under serious attack (Weinberg, 1989). Some tests have been criticized for putting unfair emphasis on knowledge derived from a white, middle-class, Eurocentric cultural perspective. Some tests have also been criticized for the difficulty they pose for children whose first language is not English or who have different learning styles and modes of synthesizing information.

Intelligence tests in particular have been criticized for use in schools and treatment facilities because they are used to decide children's educational placement, but they do not encompass the full array of psychological factors associated with social competence and adaptive behavior (Neisser et al., 1996). Psychological tests continue to be used in research to explore the relationship among developmental domains.

Experimentation

Experimentation is best suited for examining causal relationships. In an experiment, some variable or group of variables is systematically manipulated while others are held constant. The variable that is manipulated by the experimenter is called the *independent variable*. The variable defined by the participant's responses or reactions is the *dependent variable* (Davis, 1995). The purpose of the research is to determine whether the independent variable or some combination of independent variables affects the dependent variable. (See Box 2.2.)

In some experiments, one group of participants is subjected to *treatment* that is not provided to another group. The group that experiences the treat-

BOX 2.2

Analysis of an Experiment

The following study was designed to investigate the relationship between the ability of infants to recognize and make reference to themselves and their ability to experience certain emotions (Lewis, Sullivan, Stanger & Weiss, 1989).

Hypothesis

Babies who can recognize and make reference to themselves will show the emotion of embarrassment. Babies who cannot recognize and make reference to themselves will not show embarrassment.

Participants

Twenty-seven babies in three age groups:

9–12 months (average 10.5 months)

15–18 months (average 17 months)

21–24 months (average 22.5 months)

Treatments

All babies were in a laboratory setting with their mothers. They all experienced three treatments:

1. The infant, seated in a high chair, was approached by a female stranger who walked slowly toward the baby, touched the baby's hand, turned, and left the room.
2. The child's mother placed the child in front of a one-way mirror.
3. The child's mother applied a dab of nonscented rouge on the baby's nose while pretending to wipe the child's face. The child was again placed in front of the mirror.

Variables

The children's facial expressions were videotaped through the one-way mirror and coded. Observers measured the following behaviors:

Self-recognition defined as nose touching; interobserver reliability was 100%

Fear/wariness/crying defined by certain predetermined facial expressions and vocalizations;

interobserver reliability was 90% for fear, 92% for wariness, and 98% for crying

Embarrassment defined as a smiling facial expression followed by a gaze aversion and movement of the hands to touch hair, clothing, face, or other body parts; interobserver reliability was 85%

Results

Twenty-three out of 27 infants showed a wary face when approached by the stranger. No babies showed a wary face when placed in front of the mirror. Ten babies touched their noses when they saw the dab of red rouge. Older babies were significantly more likely to touch their noses than younger babies. Eight of the 10 who showed self-recognition also showed signs of embarrassment. Babies who did not show self-recognition did not show embarrassment.

Conclusions

Wariness was the typical response to a stranger, not fear. However, wariness did not require self-recognition. On the other hand, embarrassment did require self-recognition.

Try to analyze this study:

What are the independent variables? (Age and treatments)

What are the dependent variables? (Self-recognition and emotional reactions such as wariness, fear, and embarrassment)

Try to critically evaluate this study:

What other factors would you want to know about this study in order to determine the generalizability of the findings? What are some possible limitations to this study based on the sample? The situation? The way that the variables were measured?

What type of experiment might you conduct next to confirm the results of this study?

---

ment is called the *experimental group.* The group that does not experience the treatment or manipulation is called the *control group.* Differences in behavior between the two groups are then attributed to the treatment. In other experiments, the behavior of a single group of participants is compared before and after treatment or across several treatments. Once again, systematic differences in behavior before and after the treatment are attributed to the experimental manipulation. In this case, each participant serves as his or her own control.

<u>Control is the key to successful experimentation</u>. The experimenter must exercise control in selecting the children or families who participate in a study so that they bring equivalent competencies to the situation. If this condition is not met, one cannot assume that differences in behavior between groups are due to the treatment.

The experimenters must control the way that a task is presented to the participants so that such factors as inability to understand the instructions, discomfort and unfamiliarity with the setting, and the order of events do not interfere with the participants' behavior. Control ensures that changes in behaviors do in fact result solely from the experimental manipulation.

Many studies in child development are *quasi-experimental.* This means that the treatment was not controlled by the experimenter but was a result of some pattern of life events (Wilson, 1995). Suppose that we are interested in the impact of parental unemployment on children at various ages. We cannot (nor do we want to) cause some parents to lose their jobs for an experiment, while others retain their jobs. We can, however, compare children of about the same age and social class whose parents have already experienced unemployment with children whose parents have not had this experience.

In a quasi-experimental study, assignment to a "treatment" occurs as a result of real-world events. The researcher tries to compare some of the consequences of this treatment—in this case, the experience of unemployment—and to deal with the limitations that are imposed on the results by factors outside her or his control. The researcher is thus able to compare children whose parents have experienced unemployment with those who have not, but is not able to claim that unemployment is the only factor that might account for the differences in outcome that are observed.

Strengths and Limitations of the Experimental Method.   The experimental method has the advantage of making conclusions about causal relationships possible. If we can show that the participants' behavior changes only when a certain variable in the experimental situation changes, we can conclude that the manipulation has caused the changes in behavior. This is a very powerful advantage, particularly for research on the effect of conditions that occur early in development on later outcomes.

Experiments also have limitations, however. We cannot be certain about how applicable a controlled laboratory situation is to the real world. Would the behaviors that are observed in the laboratory also be observed at home, at school, or at play with friends? For example, through studies of attachment (which is discussed in Chapter 7), we have learned that infants and young children do not behave the same way in the presence of their mothers as they do when their mothers are absent. This consideration makes it clear that experimental research with young children whose mothers are not allowed to be present may produce behavior that differs in quantity, quality, and sequence from behavior that would be observed under more normal conditions, when the mothers were present.

The conclusions of experimental studies tend to suggest that event *A* causes response *B*. In many domains of development, however, a multifaceted, reciprocal process promotes change. Just think a moment about the development of friendship among primary school children. A friendship depends on similarities in many domains for two children. Friendships may be influenced by the children's appearance, physical size, abilities, temperaments, intelligence, where they live, whether their parents encourage the friendships, whether other children in the school support their friendship or make fun of it, and so on. Friendships are sustained and promoted by continuous feedback and interaction rather than by one or two factors that could be said to promote or inhibit friendship. We should avoid imposing a unidirectional, causal explanation on behaviors that are more accurately described using an interactional model.

The advantages and disadvantages of the five research methods are summarized in Table 2.1.

Designs for Studying Development

The primary concern of developmental research is to describe and account for patterns of continuity and change. Four major research approaches have been established to examine development: retrospective studies, cross-sectional studies, longitudinal studies, and cohort sequential studies.

4 Research approaches:

TABLE 2.1

Advantages and Disadvantages of Five Methods of Developmental Research

Method	Definition	Advantages	Disadvantages
Observation	Systematic description of behavior	Documents the variety of ongoing behavior; captures what happens naturally, without experimental intervention	Time-consuming; requires careful training of observers; observer may interfere with what would normally occur
Case studies	In-depth description of a single person, family, or group	Focuses on complexity and unique experiences of individual; permits analysis of unusual cases	Lacks generalizability; conclusions may reflect bias of investigator; hard to replicate
Interviews	Face-to-face interaction in which each person can give a full account of his or her views	Provides complex first-person account	Vulnerable to investigator bias
Surveys and tests	Standard questions administered to large groups	Permits data collection from large samples; requires little training; very flexible	Wording and way of presenting questions may influence responses; response may not be closely related to behavior; tests may not be appropriate for use in schools or clinical settings
Experimentation	Analysis of cause–effect relations by manipulation of some conditions, while others are held constant	Permits testing of causal hypotheses; permits control and isolation of specific variables	Laboratory findings may not be applicable to other settings; focuses on a unidirectional model of causality

Retrospective Studies

A researcher engaged in a *retrospective study* asks the participants to report on experiences from an earlier time in their lives. Many early studies of child-rearing used parents' recollections of their parenting techniques to evaluate patterns of child care. Researchers who studied the effects of stress during pregnancy often asked women to recall their emotional states before, during, and after their children were born. Investigators of personality development use retrospective data by asking adolescent or adult subjects to recall important events of their childhood.

This approach produces a record of what memories a person has retained of past events. We cannot be certain if these events really occurred as they are remembered. For that matter, we cannot be certain that they occurred at all. Piaget described a vivid memory from his second year of life:

> I was sitting in my pram, which my nurse was pushing in the Champs Elysées, when a man tried to kidnap me. I was held in by the strap fastened around me while my nurse bravely tried to stand between me and the thief. She received various scratches, and I can still see vaguely those on her face. (Piaget, 1951:188)

Thirteen years later, when Piaget was 15, the nurse joined a religious order. She wrote to his parents and returned a watch that they had given her for protecting Jean from the kidnapper. She confessed that she had made up the story even to the point of scratching her own face. Piaget realized that he had probably created the visual memory from the story his parents had told him about the incident when he was a child.

The passage of time may change the significance of certain past events in a person's memory. As we gain new levels of cognitive complexity or change our attitudes, we reorganize our memories of the past in order to correlate them with our current level of understanding (Basic Behavioral Science Task Force, 1996). Sometimes, people claim to have recovered memories of past events that have been long forgotten or "repressed." It is extremely difficult to determine the accuracy of these memories (Loftus, 1993). They may be influenced by current experiences or ideas taken from books, movies, or conversations with others, or altered by suggestion. For these reasons, the usefulness of repressed memories as a tool for uncovering systematic data about the past is limited. However, retrospective data are of value for understanding how people make sense of their past and what role they perceive past experiences to have had in their present way of thinking. In Notebook Page 2.3 you are asked to evaluate the accuracy of your own memories.

Cross-Sectional Designs

Studies that compare people of different ages or social backgrounds or school or community settings on some variable at one point in time are called *cross-sectional designs*. Such designs are quite commonly used in research on child development. For instance, investigators may compare children of different levels of biological maturity or different chronological ages to learn how a particular developmental domain changes with age. One such study explored differences in the way that children ages 7, 9, and 12 were able to reason about problems in which more than one outcome was possible (Horobin & Acredolo, 1989). Even though the younger children were aware that there were multiple solutions, they were more likely than older children to settle on one solution and insist that it was correct.

Retrospective Studies

Retrospective information is often criticized because it may not be an accurate portrayal of what actually happened. Review your Notebook Page 1.3 of early memories. For each memory, think about what might be inaccurate about the memory. Write down your critique of the memory. Did events really happen as you recall them? Are you correct about your age when the event occurred? Have you experienced other events since the time of the memory that may influence how you recall the events in your memory? Is it possible that the event had a different impact or meaning when it occurred than it has now as you remember it? Is it possible that the event did not happen?

Memory from Notebook Page 1.3	Critique of the Memory

The limitation of the cross-sectional method is that it blurs the pattern of individual development. With respect to the study on reasoning, the cross-sectional approach tells us that most 12-year-olds are more flexible in their reasoning than most 7-year-olds. It does not tell us how the children who were the most flexible at age 7 perform at age 12 in comparison with those who were least flexible.

Longitudinal Studies

A *longitudinal study* involves repeated observations of the same subjects at different times. The time between observations may be brief, such as immediately after birth and again two or three days after birth. Or observations may be repeated over the entire life course, as in Leo Terman's longitudinal study of gifted children. Terman began collecting data from children in 1921, and the study of these individuals has continued for more than 65 years, even after Terman's death (Terman, 1925; Terman & Oden, 1947, 1959; Sears, 1977; Sears & Barbee, 1978).

Longitudinal studies have the advantage of allowing us to consider the course of development for a group of individuals. We can discover how certain characteristics of children in infancy or toddlerhood relate to those same characteristics when those individuals reach adolescence or adulthood. We can also learn whether certain qualities of childhood, such as intelligence or sociability, are relevant to overall social adjustment or life satisfaction in later years.

Longitudinal studies can be very difficult to complete, however, especially if they are intended to follow a group over a long period, such as the years from childhood into adulthood. Over this span of time, participants drop out of or lose contact with the study, investigators lose funding for or interest in the project, and methods or research issues become outdated. One of the greatest limitations of these studies is that they focus on only one generation of subjects, and historical and social factors that may be unique to that time inextricably influence the course of this group's development. Some examples of such factors are the Depression and the social unrest of the 1960s.

Cohort Sequential Designs

A *cohort sequential design* combines the cross-sectional and the longitudinal approaches into one method of study (Schaie, 1965). Groups of participants, called *cohorts*, are selected because they are a certain number of years apart in age. For example, we might begin with a group of adolescents who are ages 11, 14, and 17. Every 3 years, this group is interviewed until the 11-year-olds have turned 17. In addition, every 3 years, a new group of 11-year-olds is added to the study.

This combination of a longitudinal and a cross-sectional design is a very effective developmental research method. It produces immediate cross-sectional data, longitudinal data after 3 and 6 years, and a comparison of children who were the same age (11, 14, or 17) at three different times. This third comparison permits us to identify social and historical factors that may influence age-related differences. The elements of a cohort sequential design are illustrated in Figure 2.2.

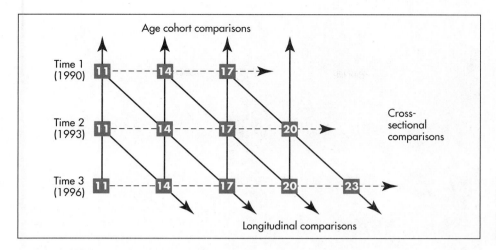

FIGURE 2.2
Elements of a cohort sequential design

Evaluating Existing Research

In addition to collecting new data, social scientists give considerable scholarly effort to reviewing and evaluating existing research. Statistical techniques allow us to compare the findings of a variety of studies in order to identify patterns of results. As a student, you may be asked to review research findings on some topic that is of interest to you. Such a review gives one a broad point of view on methods that have been used to explore the topic, patterns of research results, and aspects of the topic that remain unresolved. Most researchers use this method to keep well informed on the research being reported in their subject area. They analyze and synthesize the work of others to generate well-founded conclusions and to highlight directions for future research. The study, analysis, and evaluation of the current research literature constitute a special skill in its own right.

Ethics

In conducting research with people, especially children, social scientists continually confront ethical questions. *Ethics* refers to principles of conduct that are founded on a society's moral tenets. As part of their professional code, researchers are obligated to treat all research participants in a humane, morally acceptable manner (American Psychological Association, 1992).

Ethical guidelines for the treatment of human research participants encompass a variety of considerations (Barrett, 1995). Because researchers are concerned with a person's right to privacy, they must keep the identities of individual participants confidential. People must not be coerced into participating in a research project, and their refusal to participate should have no negative consequences. If children in a classroom, for example, decide that they do not want to participate in a research project, or if their parents do not give permission for them to participate, these children should not be criticized, given an undesirable alternative assignment, or given a lower grade.

Researchers must protect participants from unnecessary painful physical and emotional experiences, including shame, failure, and social rejection. Researchers must weigh the benefits of the new information that they may discover in a particular study against the potential risks or harm to the participants. Two questions must guide the researcher's decisions:

In order to meet ethical guidelines for research with children, the researcher must explain the purpose of the activity to the child as clearly as possible. The child must be free to withdraw from the study at any time.

1. How would you feel if you, or one of your family members, were a subject in this study?

2. Can the problem be studied in ways that do not involve pain, deception, or emotional or physical stress?

The American Psychological Association (1982) has published a guide for researchers titled *Ethical Principles in the Conduct of Research with Human Participants*. This guide stipulates that participants must be told about all aspects of the research that might influence their decision to participate. They must be free to withdraw from the study at any time. They are entitled to a full explanation of the study once it has been completed. When the participants are children, their parents must be given this information and must approve their children's participation. Researchers must also attempt to explain the nature of the research to the children who are involved in terms that they can understand and answer any questions that the children have about the study and their participation in it. Most schools, day-care centers, and hospitals also have their own review procedures for determining whether or not they will permit a research project to be carried out with the children in their programs. In Notebook Page 2.4 you are asked to assess the ethical implications of two published studies involving infants or children.

Since young children are inclined to try to please adults due to their subordinate position, and since they are likely to be gullible about any experimental deception, it is especially important for child development researchers to consider the possible impact of any research intervention on young children. Experimental treatments that make children feel embarrassed, guilty, frightened, or socially rejected must be carefully screened. In cases where the research does produce some type of stress, every effort must be made to forewarn children and discuss the research with them afterward to help them make sense of their experiences.

Ethics

Scholars and professionals working in the field of child development must establish a consistently high ethical standard. They must be careful not to exploit children or expose them to unnecessary risk or pain. They must not abuse the trust that parents and children place in the research process.

Review two studies published in one of the following journals: *Child Development, Developmental Psychology,* or the *Journal of Youth and Adolescence*. For each study, write down the ethical considerations that were involved in conducting the research. Then give your own assessment of what, if any, stresses the children or parents may have been exposed to as a result of participating in the research. In your opinion, were the risks or stresses outweighed by the potential contribution of the study to the body of knowledge?

1. Study 1: Reference: _____

_____

2. Ethical considerations: _____

_____

3. Stresses to children and/or parents: _____

_____

4. Assessment of relationship of risks to contributions: _____

_____

1. Study 2: Reference: _____

_____

2. Ethical considerations: _____

_____

3. Stresses to children/parents: _____

_____

4. Assessment of relationship of risks to contributions: _____

_____

49

The Ongoing Study of Child Development

Throughout history, people have written about children, given child-care advice to parents and teachers, and described the changes in behavior that occur over the childhood years. Why does that information not suffice? Why must we develop and sustain new research initiatives to understand development?

There are at least two reasons why the need for the systematic study of child development never ends. Perhaps you can think of others. (See Notebook Page 2.5.) First, historical data are of limited applicability to current and future generations due to changing social conditions. Second, because of the adaptive nature of humans, each person and each generation contributes something unique to the story of development.

Limited Applicability of Historical Data to Current and Future Generations

Stannard (1980) stated that the most important achievement of modern historians is their increasing recognition that life in the past was fundamentally different, both socially and technically, from our own. The implication is that at every historical period there is a unique historical context. For example, in American colonial times, white women and most African-Americans were considered to be the property of white men. Any scholarly work that addressed issues of child development, family life, or socialization during the colonial period would have been written within the context of a society that considered certain groups of people to be property. This view caused differences in socialization practices, educational practices, and beliefs about a person's fundamental abilities, rights, and resources for females and males, African-Americans and whites. What we can learn from the literature and wisdom of the past about child development and socialization practices is limited by the prevailing beliefs, social norms, and values of that era. As our knowledge increases and our cultural values change, wisdom of the past often becomes outmoded.

We can extend this line of reasoning by recognizing that the knowledge that guides our current thinking will probably be viewed as outmoded 20 or 30 years from now. We are meeting challenges today that stimulate new thinking and test the limits of our knowledge. We are studying the impact of new technologies that keep premature babies alive, that introduce information in massive quantities under high levels of personal control, and that allow very young children access to a vast array of electronic stimulation at the push of a button. In the future, we may come to regard current controversies about the impact of medical, television, or computer technology on young children as quaint preoccupations. What may have been novel conditions at one time may later become accepted, or they may alter or vanish in the light of new information, new technology, and changing values. As we study child development, conduct research, and socialize each new generation of children, we must be careful to take into account our tendencies to rely too heavily on our conceptions of the past and try to recognize when conditions have changed.

Self-Directed Creation of Experiences

The reality of self-directed development adds one more challenge to the study of development. Because people, including children, establish goals and make choices that will help them achieve their goals, the course of each person's

Your Own Research Questions

We have argued that the study of child development will never end. Use this Notebook Page to identify two areas where you believe that continuing research is needed.

1. *Research based on your own life:* Reflect on some aspect of your personal history or experience. Based on events in your life, what is one topic that you think deserves additional research? Write down some research questions related to this topic.

_____

_____

_____

_____

_____

_____

2. *Research based on a social or historical condition:* Think about conditions facing young children and adolescents in our society today. Identify an issue that you think deserves additional research. Write down some research questions related to this topic.

_____

_____

_____

_____

_____

_____

developmental history is unique. The human organism is genetically designed to produce a wide range of characteristics and behaviors. The combination of genetic variation, differences in experience, and individual choice make the specific life course of any single person extremely difficult to anticipate.

At every moment, we are building our lives. At different times, our capacities differ because of the potential competencies and resources linked to our level of development. An infant is not capable of having the same number of long-term, intimate relationships as an older person. An early-school-age child is not capable of resolving a quarrel with the same negotiation strategies as an adolescent. By understanding the capacities and potentials of development at different ages, we can better understand what accomplishments are desired by and possible for children. We use information based on research to improve our approach to the education, socialization, and nurturance of children. Each new generation of children can benefit from the advances of preceding generations. Adults can structure the environment so that children have the optimal freedom to build their lives by exercising their own decisions and choices, taking new paths and creating new stories that we have not experienced. Our study of children is then guided by the new paths that are forged by each succeeding generation.

Chapter Summary

1. Research helps us to develop accurate information through scientific observation and analysis of our observations. Objective, repeatable, and systematic scientific observation ensures that the research process will be successful in generating knowledge.

2. The research design and the approach to selecting a sample influence how possible it will be to generalize a study's findings.

3. Five of the most common research methods used in the study of development are observation, case study, interviews, experimentation, and surveys and tests. Each method has its advantages and limitations.

4. Four approaches have been used to study change over time: retrospective, cross-sectional, longitudinal, and cohort sequential designs. Cohort sequential studies are the most powerful of the four for distinguishing between developmental and historical contributions to patterns of change.

5. Research ethics are important for the protection of participants in all research and are particularly critical when dealing with infants, children, and adolescents. Child development researchers must maintain the highest ethical standards in protecting children from unnecessary pain, stress, or embarrassment associated with participation in research.

6. The study of child development is never complete. As historical and cultural factors change, so does the context for development. We use new understanding and technologies to change our approaches to the education, parenting, and socialization of children. This, in turn, leads to new behaviors that require new analyses.

References

American Psychological Association. (1982). *Ethical principles in the conduct of research with human participants.* Washington, D.C.

American Psychological Association. (1992). Ethical principles of psychologists and code of conduct. *American Psychologist, 47,* 1597–1611.

Barrett, M. (1995). Practical and ethical issues in planning research. In G. Breakwell, S. Hammond & C. Fyfe-Schaw (Eds.), *Research methods in psychology.* Thousand Oaks, Calif.: Sage.

Basic Behavioral Science Task Force of the National Advisory Mental Health Council (1996). Basic behavioral science research for mental health: Perception, attention, learning, and memory. *American Psychologist, 51,* 133–142.

Bayley, N. (1970). Development of mental abilities. In P. H. Mussen (Ed.), *Carmichael's manual of child psychology* (3rd ed.), volume 1. New York: Wiley.

Columbo, J. (1993). *Infant cognition: Predicting later intellectual functioning.* Newbury Park, Calif.: Sage.

Creswell, J. W. (1994). *Research design: Qualitative and quantitative approaches.* Thousand Oaks, Calif.: Sage.

Davis, A. (1995). The experimental method in psychology. In G. Breakwell, S. Hammond & C. Fyfe-Schaw (Eds.), *Research methods in psychology.* Thousand Oaks, Calif.: Sage.

Erikson, E. H. (1969). *Gandhi's truth: On the origins of militant nonviolence.* New York: Norton.

Fowler, F. L., Jr. (1993). *Survey research methods.* (2nd ed.) Thousand Oaks, Calif.: Sage.

Freud, A. & Dann, S. (1951). An experiment in group upbringing. In R. Eissler, A. Freud, H. Hartmann & E. Kris (Eds.), *The psychoanalytic study of the child* (volume 6). New York: International Universities Press.

Holstein, J. A. & Gubrium, J. F. (1995). *The active interview.* Thousand Oaks, Calif.: Sage.

Horobin, K. & Acredolo, C. (1989). The impact of probability judgments on reasoning about multiple possibilities. *Child Development, 60(1),* 183–200.

Kessen, W. (1965). *The child.* New York: Wiley.

Kochanska, G., Kuczynski, L. & Radke-Yarrow, M. (1989). Correspondence between mothers' self-reported and observed child-rearing practices. *Child Development, 60(1),* 56–63.

Lewis, M., Sullivan, M. W., Stanger, C. & Weiss, M. (1989). Self-development and self-conscious emotions. *Child Development, 60,* 146–156.

Loftus, E. F. (1993). The reality of repressed memories. *American Psychologist, 48,* 518–537.

Messick, S. (1989). Meaning and values in test validation: The science and ethics of assessment. *Educational Researcher, 18,* 5–11.

Miller, D. C. (1991). *Handbook of research design and social measurement.* (5th ed.) Newbury Park, Calif.: Sage.

Neisser, U., Boodoo, G., Bouchard, T. J., Jr., et al. (1996). Intelligence: Knowns and unknowns. *American Psychologist, 51,* 77–101.

Piaget, J. (1929). *The child's conception of physical causality.* New York: Harcourt, Brace. (Originally published in French in 1926.)

Piaget, J. (1951). *Play, dreams, and imitation in childhood.* New York: Norton.

Piaget, J. (1963). The attainment of invariants and reversible operations in the development of thinking. *Social Research, 30,* 283–299.

Runyan, W. M. (1982). *Life histories and psychobiography: Explorations in theory and method.* New York: Oxford University Press.

Schaie, K. W. (1965). A general model for the study of developmental problems. *Psychological Bulletin, 64,* 92–107.

Sears, P. S. & Barbee, A. H. (1978). Career and life satisfaction among Terman's gifted women. In J. Stanley, W. George & C. Solano (Eds.), *The gifted and the creative: Fifty year perspective.* Baltimore: Johns Hopkins University Press.

Sears, R. R. (1977). Sources of life satisfactions of the Terman gifted men. *American Psychologist, 32,* 119–128.

Stannard, D. E. (1980). *Shrinking history: On Freud and the failure of psychohistory.* New York: Oxford University Press.

Terman, L. M. (1925). *Genetic studies of genius.* Stanford, Calif.: Stanford University Press.

Terman, L. M. & Oden, M. H. (1947). *The gifted child grows up: Twenty-five years' follow-up of a superior group.* Stanford, Calif.: Stanford University Press.

Terman, L. M. & Oden, M. H. (1959). *The gifted group at mid-life: Thirty-five years' follow-up of the superior child.* Stanford, Calif.: Stanford University Press.

U.S. Bureau of the Census. (1995). *Statistical abstract of the United States: 1995* (115th ed.). Washington, D.C.: U.S. Government Printing Office.

Weinberg, R. A. (1989). Intelligence and IQ: Landmark issues and great debates. *American Psychologist* (special issue: Children and Their Development: Knowledge Base, Research Agenda, and Social Policy Application), *44(2),* 98–104.

Wilson, S. (1995). Quasi-experimental designs. In G. Breakwell, S. Hammond & C. Fyfe-Schaw (Eds.), *Research methods in psychology.* Thousand Oaks, Calif.: Sage.

Yin, R. K. (1994). *Case study research: Design and methods.* Thousand Oaks, Calif.: Sage.

Psychosocial Theory

Chapter 3

What Is a Theory?

Rationale for Selecting Psychosocial Theory

Basic Concepts of Psychosocial Theory

Stages of Development

Developmental Tasks

Psychosocial Crisis

A Typical Psychosocial Crisis

Psychosocial Crises of the Life Stages

The Interrelationship Between Developmental Tasks and
Psychosocial Crises

The Central Process for Resolving the Psychosocial Crisis

Radius of Significant Relationships

Coping Behavior

Prime Adaptive Ego Qualities

Core Pathologies

Evaluation of Psychosocial Theory

Strengths

Weaknesses

Chapter Summary

References

In the preceding chapter, we described a variety of strategies that researchers use to observe development. Often, the sheer number of observations can be overwhelming. Observations do not explain the process and direction of change and growth, nor do they reveal the underlying organizing structures. Theories provide frameworks that help make these many observations meaningful and allow us to study the underlying structures. Theories also help uncover new knowledge by suggesting where systematic observation might fruitfully reveal connections or structures that were previously unknown.

In this chapter, we will define the concept of theory and introduce the basic concepts of psychosocial theory, which provides the framework for our analysis of human development. In Chapter 4, we will discuss other theories that also account for growth and change. Some of those theories furnished the foundation upon which psychosocial theory was built. Others complement psychosocial theory by providing greater detail regarding specific aspects of development in the physical, intellectual, social, emotional, and self domains.

What Is a Theory?

A *theory* is a logical system of general concepts that provides a framework for organizing and understanding observations. The word *theory* can be used in an informal sense to refer to an intuitive hypothesis or best guess about why an event occurred ("My theory is that Collin was overtired, and that's why he cried at the party."). A formal scientific theory is a set of interconnected statements, which, taken as a whole, attempt to account for some broad-ranging phenomenon such as learning or mental illness. Scientific theories typically include precise definitions, axioms (basic assumptions accepted without proof), hypotheses (models or schemes for how and why something happens), intervening variables (factors that may modify the direction of influence), and laws (statements about the exact relationship among the axioms, hypotheses, and intervening variables).

A theory is like a flashlight that illuminates a path in a darkened woods. The light shines bright and wide enough to guide your exploration and investigation, but the beam does not light up the entire woods. If you shine the light on the path directly ahead, you will miss the activity taking place in the branches of the trees above. The function of a theory is to describe unobservable structures, mechanisms, or processes and relate them to each other and to observable events. For example, when we consider learning, the structures that store information are not observable. However, according to certain principles of learning theory, we can infer that new learning has occurred when we observe a relatively permanent change in behavior as a result of experience.

A formal theory should meet certain requirements. It should be logical and internally consistent with no contradictory statements. The theory should be testable. Hypothetical constructs should be translatable into testable hypotheses. The theory should be parsimonious, relying on as few assumptions, constructs, and propositions as possible. Finally, a theory should integrate previous research, and it should deal with a relatively large area of science (Miller, 1993). Most current developmental theories do not meet all the requirements of formal, scientific theories. However, they offer a language of shared constructs and hypotheses that allow scientists to compare observations and build new knowledge. To evaluate a theory, we must answer three questions.

1. *Which phenomenon is the theory trying to explain?* If a theory is being used to explain intellectual development, it may include hypotheses about the evolution of the brain, the growth of logical thinking, or the capacity for symbolism. We are less likely to expect such a theory to explain fears, motives, or friendship. Understanding the focus of the theory helps to identify its *range of applicability*. This is not to say that principles from one theory will have no relevance to another area of knowledge. Usually, however, we are not dealing with grand theories that explain behavior at the individual, family, and societal levels, but with theories that attempt to guide and clarify research related to a narrow range of observations.

[handwritten margin note: which phenomenon? —Is it applicable?]

2. *What assumptions does the theory make?* Assumptions are the guiding premises underlying the logic of a theory. In order to evaluate a theory, you must first understand what its assumptions are. Charles Darwin assumed that lower life forms "progressed" to higher forms in the process of evolution. Freud assumed that all behavior was driven by an unconscious "storehouse" of motives and wishes.

[handwritten margin note: what assumptions?]

   The assumptions of any theory may or may not be correct. They may be influenced by the cultural context, by the sample of observations from which the theorist has drawn inferences, by the current knowledge base of the field of study, and by the intellectual capacities of the theorist.

3. *What does the theory predict?* Theories add new levels of understanding by suggesting causal relationships, by unifying diverse observations, and by identifying the importance of events that may have gone unnoticed. Theories of human development offer explanations regarding the origins and functions of human behavior and the changes that can be expected from one period of life to the next.

[handwritten margin note: Predictions?]

We expect a theory of development to provide explanations about four issues:

1. The processes that account for growth from conception through old age, and how these processes vary across the stages of life.
2. The factors that account for stability and change across the life span.
3. How the domains of physical, cognitive, emotional, social, and self-development interact and how these interactions account for thoughts, feelings, behaviors, and social relationships.
4. How the social context affects individual development.

Rationale for Selecting Psychosocial Theory

We have selected psychosocial theory as an organizing framework for the text because it allows us to identify and integrate information from a wide range of disciplines covering a diversity of topics. Psychosocial theory is not the only or the most widely accepted framework for studying human development;

Psychosocial theory addresses continued development over the life course as well as the interdependence of people at different stages of life.

Psychosocial Theory
① growth across
*   lifespan*
*   -changes*
*   -relationships*
*   -environment*
② individuals
*   contribute to*
*   their psychological*
*   devt.*
③ Effect of culture
*   on individual*
*   growth.*

however, it combines three features that are not as clearly articulated or integrated in other theories of development.

First, psychosocial theory addresses growth across the life span. It identifies and differentiates among issues of central importance from infancy through old age. This perspective allows one to consider the changes that take place during childhood that affect functioning in later life. It also highlights the impact of relationships at various life stages, emphasizing that the quality of a child's environment depends on the developmental level and psychosocial competence of those who are responsible for the child's care.

Second, psychosocial theory assumes that individuals have the capacity to contribute to their own psychological development at every stage of life. The theory recognizes that people integrate, organize, and conceptualize their own experiences in order to protect themselves, to cope with the challenges they face, and to direct the course of their own lives. Therefore, the direction of development is not entirely dependent upon biological and environmental influences.

Third, the theory takes into consideration the active contribution of culture to individual growth. At each life stage, cultural goals, aspirations, opportunities, and social expectations make demands on individuals. These demands draw forth reactions. These reactions, in turn, influence the social systems within which the person's capabilities will be developed. This vital link between the individual and the wider world is a key mechanism of development.

One of the great theorists who identified and developed psychosocial theory is Erik H. Erikson. Erikson initially was trained as a psychoanalytic clinician (see the Biographical Sketch on page 60). An interest in the effects of sexuality on functioning and in the ideas of the biologist Julian Huxley led Erikson to focus on the influence of social instincts on development. His theory was influenced by the work of many others, including Sigmund and Anna Freud, Peter Blos, Robert White, Jean Piaget, and Robert Havighurst, whose ideas you will encounter in this text. His theory has provided a rich body of ideas which have been elaborated in our own writings, as well as in the work of many other students of human development.

Basic Concepts of Psychosocial Theory

Psychosocial theory presents human development as a product of the interaction between individual's mental representations, needs, and abilities (*psycho*) and societal resources, expectations, and demands (*social*). The theory accounts for the patterns of individual development that emerge out of the more global process of psychosocial evolution.

Psychosocial theory is linked to an earlier use of the construct offered by Julian Huxley (1941, 1942) who used the term *psychosocial evolution* to refer to those human abilities that have allowed us to gather knowledge from our ancestors and transmit it to our descendants. Cultures devise child-rearing practices, education, and modes of communication in order to transmit information and ways of thinking from one generation to the next. At the same time, people develop new information, new ways of thinking, and new ways of teaching their discoveries to others. Through this process, according to Huxley, psychosocial evolution has proceeded at a rapid pace, bringing with it changes in technology and ideology that have allowed us to create and modify the physical and social environments in which we live.

Psychosocial evolution has its basis in the biological system. Over millions of years, humans have evolved a complex neurological capacity that permits them to adapt to a wide range of physical and social conditions, as well as to create new environments and forms of social organization. Huxley's definition of psychosocial evolution can be interpreted to include all of the biologically driven processes that have allowed us to build civilizations, formulate systems of scientific inquiry, and create patterns of meaningful social relationships.

The theory of psychosocial development offers an organizational framework for considering individual development within the wider perspective of psychosocial evolution. In order to transmit values and knowledge across generations, individuals must develop capacities for internalizing knowledge, adapting it, and transferring it to others. People change and grow systematically, enhancing their potential for carrying their own and succeeding generations forward.

Psychosocial theory, as we view it, is based on six organizing concepts: (1) stages of development, (2) developmental tasks, (3) psychosocial crisis, (4) a central process for resolving the crisis of each stage, (5) a radiating network of significant relationships, and (6) coping—the behavior that people spontaneously generate to meet new challenges. Figure 3.1 on page 62 shows development as a building process that incorporates these six constructs. The figure

[handwritten margin notes:]
PSYCHOSOCIAL THEORY

Psychosocial evolution— generational transmission of knowledge.

Biological basis

PT based on 6 concepts

Biographical Sketch

Erik H. Erikson
1902–1994

PSYCHOSOCIAL
THEORY

Erik Erikson was born near Frankfurt, Germany, in 1902. His Danish mother was divorced before his birth, and she married Erikson's pediatrician, Dr. Homburger, before Erikson was 5. Erikson grew up in the home of this prosperous physician, not discovering until his adolescence that Dr. Homburger was not his biological father. During his childhood, he was exposed to some of the bigotry of growing up as the adopted son of a Jew (his mother was a Danish Lutheran). His friends at school teased him about being a Jew, yet friends of his father referred to him as "the goy" (a Yiddish term for gentile) (Hopkins, 1995).

At age 18, after completing gymnasium (a German secondary school that prepares students to study at a university), Erikson traveled around Europe for a year. He spent several months on the shores of Lake Constance, reading, writing, and enjoying the beauty of the setting. When he returned home, he enrolled in art school for the next few years. He next traveled to Florence, Italy, where he concluded that he was not going to succeed as an artist. He and some of his friends, including Peter Blos, wandered around for a time, searching for a sense of themselves and their personal resources (Coles, 1970).

Erikson and Blos accepted an invitation to teach at a private school that had been founded by Anna Freud for the children of students at her father's Vienna Psychoanalytic Society. In Vienna, Erikson studied the techniques of psychoanalysis and underwent a training analysis with Anna Freud. His decision to become an analyst was encouraged by the supportive, influential analysts of the Psychoanalytic Society, who were eager to help promising people enter their newly created field. Erikson's admission to training was unusual in that he had neither a university nor a medical degree.

During the period of his analytic training, Erikson met and married Joan Serson who was his lifelong intellectual partner as well as intimate companion. As a result of the political turmoil in Europe in the early 1930s, the Eriksons moved to America. He became a child analyst on the faculty of the Harvard Medical School. Three years later, he went to Yale, and two years after that, he went off to study the Sioux Indians in South Dakota. After completing his research observations on the Sioux, he opened a clinical practice in San Francisco. During this time, he also conducted a study of the Yurok Indians. In 1942, Erikson became a faculty member at the University of California at Berkeley.

expands at each stage as the radius of significant relationships widens and the achievements of earlier stages are integrated into the behaviors of the next stage of development.

Stages of Development

A *stage of development* is a period of life that is characterized by a specific underlying organization. A wide variety of behaviors can be viewed as an expression of the underlying structure of each stage. Every stage has some characteristics that differentiate it from preceding and succeeding stages. Stage theories propose a specific direction for development. Each new stage incorporates the gains made during earlier stages. At each stage, the accomplishments from the previous stages serve as resources for mastering the challenges presented by the developmental tasks, central process, psychosocial crisis, and

In 1950, he left Berkeley and became an analyst on the staff of the Austen Riggs Center in Stockbridge, Massachusetts. In the late 1950s, Erikson became a professor of human development at Harvard. He retained this position until his retirement in 1970. He and Joan continued to expand their analysis of human development with the notable publication of *Vital Involvement in Old Age* (1986) which probes the life histories of a number of octogenarians and examines issues associated with a fully developed self in old age.

Erikson's major theoretical work, *Childhood and Society*, was synthesized while he was at Berkeley and published in 1950, when he was 48 (a revised edition was published in 1963). In this book, Erikson presented a psychosocial theory of development, which he expanded and revised in many other books and papers. In two biographical case studies, he applied the principles of psychosocial analysis to the lives of Martin Luther and Mohandas Gandhi (Erikson, 1958, 1969).

When observations from his clinical practice raised questions that the research literature was unable to answer, he studied traditional cultures and historical figures. He followed his ideas, pursuing observations that would help him to clarify his analysis of human development.

Through his clinical and theoretical writings, he demonstrated that the evolved structure of each individual, although very complex, can be studied and understood. He identified a process, the psychosocial crisis, that links individuals and societies in a fundamental way and instigates development.

Erikson's life story reveals him to be a person who took a unique personal route to realize his potential. His writings blend compassion, keen observational skills, a poetic synthesis of ideas and experiences, and a persistent questioning about the interrelationships of individual lives and societies. In the course of his own intellectual development, he mastered several disciplines, including psychoanalysis, cultural anthropology, psychology, theology, and history. In his search for deeper understanding, he remained open to all human behavior that might inform his questioning mind, drawing on life histories, clinical cases, and fictional characters.

Erikson won the Pulitzer Prize and the National Book Award. In 1984, he received the G. Stanley Hall Award from the Division of Developmental Psychology of the American Psychological Association for distinguished contributions to developmental psychology.

Interrelationship between the individual and society.

significant relationships. The interplay of these factors provides the experiential base for new learning, and therefore for development. Each stage is unique and leads to the acquisition of new skills related to new capabilities (Davison et al., 1980; Flavell, 1982; Fischer & Silvern, 1985; Levin, 1986; Miller, 1993).

The stage concept suggests areas of emerging competence or conflict that may explain a range of behaviors. To some extent, you can verify the stage concept through analyzing your own past. You probably can recall earlier periods when you were preoccupied first by efforts to gain your parents' approval, then to win acceptance by your peers, and later to understand yourself. These concerns may have appeared all-consuming at the time, but eventually each gave way to a new preoccupation. At each stage, a person is confronted with a unique problem that requires the integration of personal needs and skills with the social demands of the culture. The end product is a new mode of orientation and a new set of capabilities for engaging in social interactions.

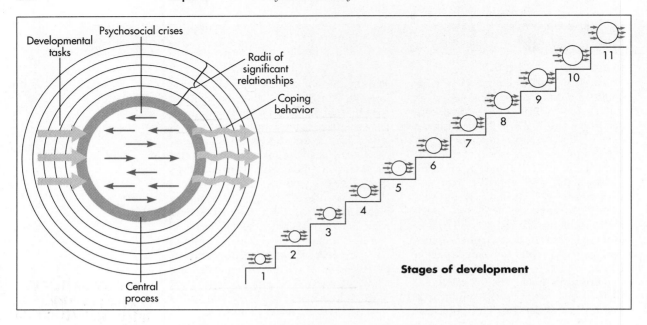

FIGURE 3.1

Six basic concepts of
psychosocial theory

Erikson (1950/1963) proposed eight stages of psychosocial development. The conception of these stages can be traced in part to the stages of psychosexual development proposed by Freud and in part to Erikson's own observations and rich mode of thinking.

Figure 3.2 is the chart that Erikson produced in *Childhood and Society* to describe the stages of psychosocial development. The shaded squares identify the main psychosocial conflicts of the various stages, with the resolution of each conflict producing new self-understanding and new social competence.

The concept of psychosocial stages of development is very good as far as it goes, but Erikson's road map seems incomplete. If the idea of psychosocial evolution has any validity—and we believe it does—new stages can be expected to develop as a culture evolves. We have identified 11 stages of psychosocial development, each associated with an approximate age range: (1) prenatal, from conception to birth; (2) infancy, from birth to 2 years; (3) toddlerhood, 2 and 3 years; (4) early school age, 4 to 6 years; (5) middle childhood, 6 to 12 years; (6) early adolescence, 12 to 18 years; (7) later adolescence, 18 to 22 years; (8) early adulthood, 22 to 34 years; (9) middle adulthood, 34 to 60 years; (10) later adulthood, 60 to 75; and (11) very old age, 75 until death. By discussing a prenatal stage, a second stage of adolescent development, and very old age, we are adding three stages to the ones that Erikson proposed. This revision is a product of our analysis of the research literature, our observations through research and practice, discussions with colleagues, and suggestions from other stage theorists.

The elaboration of psychosocial theory by adding three new stages provides a good demonstration of the process of theory construction. Theories of human development emerge and change within a cultural and historical context, as do patterns of biological and psychosocial evolution. The extension of the adolescent period, for example, is a product of changes in the timing of onset of puberty in modern society, the intensifying need for education and training before entering the world of work, related changes in the structure of

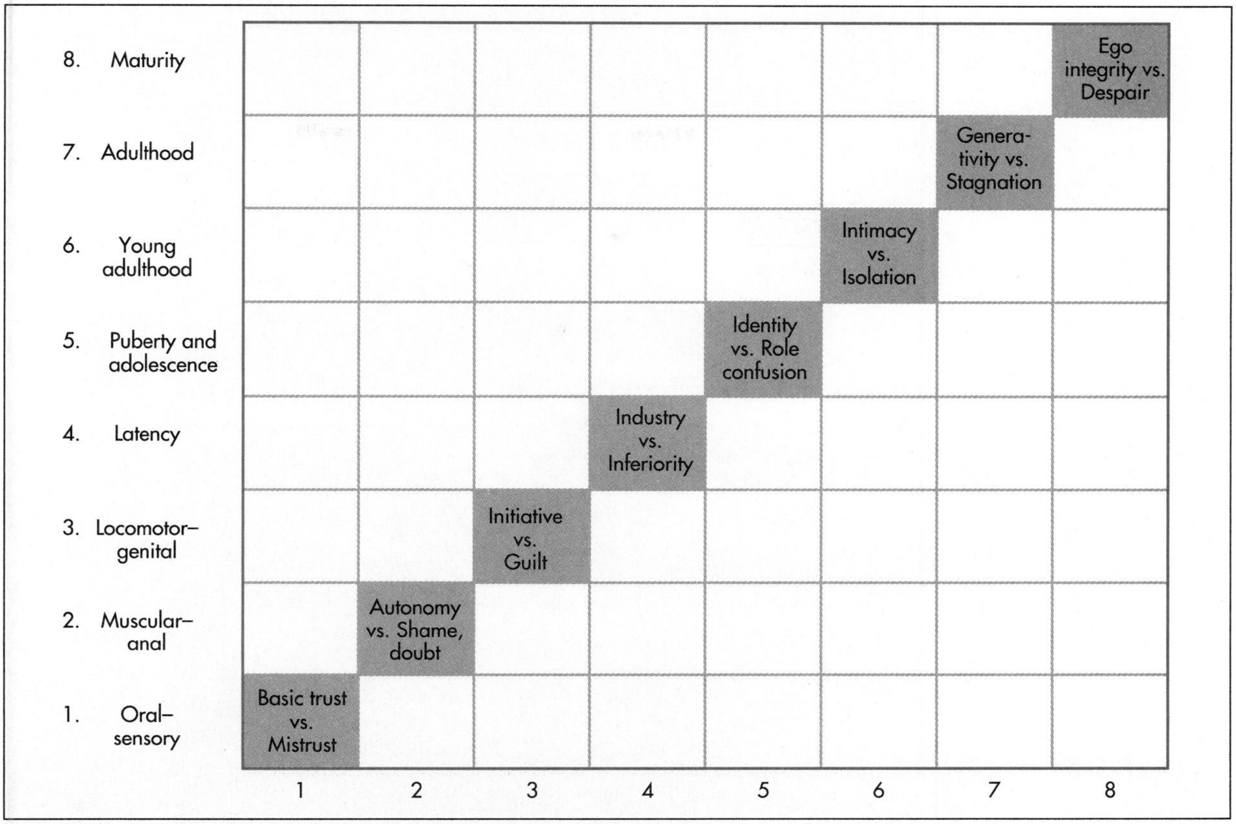

	1	2	3	4	5	6	7	8
8. Maturity								Ego integrity vs. Despair
7. Adulthood							Generativity vs. Stagnation	
6. Young adulthood						Intimacy vs. Isolation		
5. Puberty and adolescence					Identity vs. Role confusion			
4. Latency				Industry vs. Inferiority				
3. Locomotor–genital			Initiative vs. Guilt					
2. Muscular–anal		Autonomy vs. Shame, doubt						
1. Oral–sensory	Basic trust vs. Mistrust							

FIGURE 3.2

Erikson's psychosocial stages
Source: Erikson, E. H. (1950/1963). *Childhood and society.* New York: Norton.

the educational system, and the increasing variety of choices that are available in our society in regard to work, marriage, parenting, and beliefs. Our observations relating to the changing circumstances and preoccupations of certain age groups led to the clarification of new stages of development.

Figure 3.3 shows the 11 stages of psychosocial development that we have identified. The age range of each stage is only an approximation. Each person has his or her own timetable for growth depending on how long it takes to master the tasks of the stage and to resolve the challenges that are posed during that period.

An assumption of this and other stage theories is that the psychological development that takes place at each stage will have a significant effect on all subsequent stages. The stages are viewed as a sequence. Although one can anticipate issues that will occur at a later stage, one passes through the stages in an orderly pattern of growth.

Erikson (1963) proposed that the stages of development follow the *epigenetic principle;* that is, a biological plan for growth allows each function to emerge in a systematic way until the fully functioning organism has developed. In the logic of psychosocial theory, the entire life span is required for all the functions of psychosocial development to appear and become integrated. There is no going back to an earlier stage: Experience makes retreat impossible. However, one can reflect on conflicts and events of earlier stages and rework the meaning of those experiences based on new insights and a

Prenatal	Conception to birth
Infancy	Birth to 2 years
Toddlerhood	2 and 3 years
Early school age	4 to 6 years
Middle childhood	6 to 12 years
Early adolescence	12 to 18 years
Later adolescence	18 to 22 years
Early adulthood	22 to 34 years
Middle adulthood	34 to 60 years
Later adulthood	60 to 75 years
Very old age	75 until death

FIGURE 3.3
Eleven stages of the life span and approximate ages

new perspective. What is more, the issues of earlier life stages frequently reemerge in later periods of life.

The concept of life stages permits us to consider the various aspects of development at a given period of life and to speculate about their interrelatedness. It also encourages us to focus on the experiences that are unique to each life period, which deserve to be understood in their own right and in terms of their contribution to subsequent development. When programs and services are designed to address critical areas such as education, health care, housing, and social welfare, the developmental stage approach is very helpful in focusing attention on the specific needs and resources of the population to be served.

We caution you to avoid thinking of stages as pigeonholes. The mere fact that a person is described as being at a given stage does not mean that he or she cannot simultaneously function at other levels. It is not unusual to anticipate issues applicable to a later stage before they become dominant. Many children of toddler and preschool age, for example, play "house," envisioning the roles of husband or wife, parents and children. You might say that in this play they are anticipating the issues of intimacy and generativity that lie ahead. While some elements of the central psychosocial skills can be observed at all ages, it is the intensity with which they are expressed that marks their importance in defining a stage. Erikson puts it this way:

> The epigenetic chart also rightly suggests that the individual is never struggling only with the tension that is focal at the time. Rather, at every successive developmental stage, the individual is also increasingly engaged in the anticipation of

tensions that have yet to become focal and in reexperiencing those tensions that were inadequately integrated when they were focal; similarly engaged are those whose age-appropriate integration was then, but is no longer, adequate. (Erikson et al., 1986:39)

As one leaves a stage, the achievements of that stage are not lost or irrelevant to later stages. Erikson (1963) warned against becoming too structural in one's thinking about development because important ego strengths emerge out of the successful resolution of conflicts at every stage. However, one ought not to assume that these strengths, once established, are never challenged or shaken. Events can take place later in life that call into question the essential beliefs established in an earlier period.

For example, the positive outcome of the psychosocial conflict during early school age is initiative versus guilt. *Initiative* refers to a joy in innovation and experimentation and a willingness to take risks in order to learn more about the world. Once achieved, the sense of initiative provides a positive platform for the formation of social relationships, as well as for further creative intellectual inquiry and discovery. However, a child's experiences in a highly authoritarian school environment or in a very judgmental personal relationship could cause inhibition of this sense of initiative.

The concept of life stages should be used to highlight the changing orientations toward self and others that dominate periods of the life span. The essential idea is that the ways in which one perceives and experiences one's life vary qualitatively from stage to stage.

An alternative approach in the study of human development is to trace single processes or systems across the life span. One might, for instance, consider changes in emotional functioning from infancy through later life. This approach might provide greater detail regarding the emergence and modification of each system, but it would not contribute as much to an understanding of the interaction of systems within a person's life. If you wish to study the continuity and change within a particular system across the life span, you may wish to refer to the sections of each chapter that deal with the theme of interest to you.

To our minds, movement from one stage to the next is the result of changes in several major domains at approximately the same time. The new combination of needs, capabilities, and expectations is what produces a new orientation toward experience at each new stage.

Developmental Tasks

Developmental tasks, the second organizing concept of psychosocial theory, consist of a set of skills and competencies that contributes to increased mastery over the environment. These tasks define healthy, normal development at each age in a particular society. Generally, the developmental tasks reflect areas of accomplishment in physical, cognitive, social, emotional, and self-development during each stage. The tasks form a sequence: Success in learning the tasks of one stage leads to development and greater chances of success in learning the tasks of later stages. Failure at the tasks of one stage leads to greater difficulty with later tasks or may render them impossible to master.

Robert J. Havighurst (1972) believed that human development is a process in which people attempt to learn the tasks required of them by the society to which they are adapting (see the Biographical Sketch on next page).

*B*iographical *S*ketch

Robert J. Havighurst 1900–1991

HUMAN DEVELOPMENT

Robert J. Havighurst was born on June 5, 1900. He received his Ph.D. in chemistry in 1924 from Ohio State University, after which he did postdoctoral study in physics and chemistry at Harvard University. In 1930, he married Edythe McNeely and together they had five children. After teaching science at the high school and college levels for a few years, he made a major shift in career direction, focusing his interest on problems of adolescent development and the educational process. From 1934 to 1941, he worked for the General Education Board of the Rockefeller Foundation where he took a leadership role in sponsoring research programs in child development and innovative educational programs. Through his efforts, resources were directed to the relocation of European scholars during the war, especially psychodynamic scholars who were interested in child development, including Bruno Bettelheim, Peter Blos, Erik Erikson, and Fritz Redl. In 1941, he became a professor of education at the University of Chicago where he eventually formed the Committee on Human Development. At his retirement in 1974, he was named Professor Emeritus in Development and Education.

Havighurst is known for many contributions in the fields of psychology, sociology, and education. In the 1950s, he guided a major research project that demonstrated how children who are unsuccessful in school become socially alienated. At that time, he and his colleagues estimated that about 30% of adolescents were socially alienated young people of all social classes, although their backgrounds were predominantly lower middle class and working class (Havighurst et al., 1962). This is one of the few

estimates ever offered of the number of disaffected youth in American society.

Havighurst developed and expanded the concept of developmental tasks in his book, *Human Development and Education*, which was published in 1953, and applied this concept to a life-span analysis of development. Many theoretical systems have been built around this idea because of its relevance for understanding the basic process of human development. Havighurst also proposed the idea of the "teachable moment," a time when a person is most sensitive to learning a particular task. In collaboration with several anthropologists, Havighurst studied child-rearing practices across race and social class in the United States; emotional, social, and moral development of children in six Native American cultures; and retirement in six European countries. His research repeatedly clarified the significant contributions of social class and culture to development, as well as highlighting the concept of various paths for healthy development in adolescence and adult life. Havighurst was actually one of the very first to initiate course work and systematic research regarding the normal processes of adult development and aging, thus establishing the full life span as the appropriate domain for the study of human development. Over his life, he authored or coauthored more than 50 books and hundreds of articles, chapters, and monographs (Neugarten, 1993).

In 1969, Havighurst received the Thorndike Award in Educational Psychology from the American Psychological Association, and, in 1977, he received the award for Distinguished Scientific Contributions from the Society for Research in Child Development.

These tasks change with age because each society has *age-graded expectations* for behavior. "Living in a modern society is a long series of tasks to learn" (Havighurst, 1972:2). The person who learns well receives satisfaction and reward; the person who does not suffers unhappiness and social disapproval.

Although Havighurst's view of development emphasizes the guiding role of society in determining which skills need to be acquired at a certain

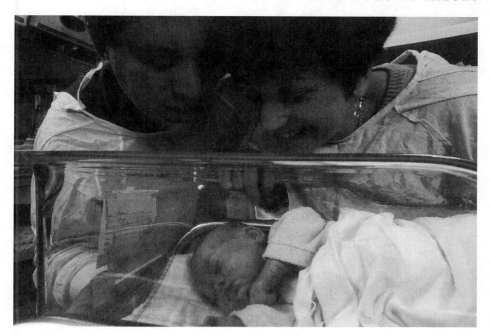

The birth of a child is often a teachable moment when parents are eager to acquire new information and skills related to parenting and child care.

age, it does not totally ignore the role of physical maturation. Havighurst believed that there are *sensitive periods* for learning developmental tasks, when a person is maturationally most ready to acquire a new ability. Havighurst called these periods *teachable moments*. Most people learn developmental tasks at a time and in the sequence appropriate for their society. If a particular task is not learned during the sensitive period, learning it may be much more difficult later on.

Learning during a sensitive period may enhance learning and performance in this task area later in life. Initially, skills are developed in a sensitive period when much is happening both internally and externally to stimulate that area of growth. Once the sensitive period has passed, however, learning may still continue. Language skills, for example, do not cease to develop after toddlerhood. New and complex ways of using language expand throughout the life span. Much elementary and high school curricula focus on developing language, including expanding one's vocabulary, developing skills in oral and written communication, and learning new languages.

The basic tasks that we identify differ from Havighurst's. Our choice of tasks focuses on general areas of accomplishment that have been identified by researchers as critical to psychological and social growth at each stage within a modern, technological culture. We recognize that the demands for growth may differ depending on the orientation and complexity of the particular society. The tasks that are presented as central for successful adaptation for children growing up in a postindustrial society such as the United States are not necessarily the appropriate standard for maturation and growth in a developing country or in a more traditional tribal culture.

We believe that a relatively small number of extremely important psychosocial tasks dominate a person's problem-solving efforts and learning during a given stage. As these tasks are mastered, new competencies enhance the

[handwritten margin note:] sensitive periods & teachable moments · time when person is sensitive to learning

Developmental Tasks

The developmental tasks of each life stage are associated with particular areas in which energy and attention are focused. With the mastery of each developmental task, children acquire new capacities and resources to meet challenges and expectations. At the same time, there is a persistent set of needs that must be met at all life stages. One must not assume that because children are focused on certain unique tasks at a particular life stage, there is no continuity of experience from one stage to another.

In some ways, all human beings are alike no matter what their age. Think of five examples of basic needs and abilities that are the same for any person from birth through age 18.

1. _____

2. _____

3. _____

4. _____

5. _____

Other needs and abilities change substantially from one life stage to the next. Describe one or two factors that are unique to each of the following stages.

1. Infancy (birth to 2 years):

_____

_____

2. Toddlerhood (2 and 3 years):

_____

_____

3. Early school age (4 to 6 years):

_____

_____

4. Middle childhood (6 to 12 years):

_____

_____

5. Early adolescence (12 to 18 years):

_____

_____

person's ability to engage in more complex social relationships. To our way of thinking, a successful culture stimulates behaviors that help its members learn the things that they need to know both for their own survival and for that of the group.

The tasks may reflect gains in physical, cognitive, social, and emotional skills, and the ability to conceptualize the self. One of the developmental tasks of infancy, for example, is forming a bond with the caregiver. Early in life, success in forming this crucial positive attachment determines the quality of subsequent social relationships. Notebook Page 3.1 asks you to identify areas of new development at each of five stages of childhood.

Keep in mind that the person is changing on several major levels during each period of life. Tasks involving physical, emotional, intellectual, social, and self-growth all contribute to the person's resources for coping with challenges. Table 3.1 shows the developmental tasks that we have identified as having major effects on the life experiences of most people in modern society and the stages during which each set of tasks is of primary learning value. There are 42 developmental tasks in the list. While the infant is learning orientations and skills related to the first five, the young adult has acquired skills related to 27 tasks from previous stages. New learning may continue in these areas, as well as in the four new developmental task areas. A very old person has the experience of all the areas of previous learning, while working on three tasks and the crisis of the final stage.

In this book, we focus intensively on the developmental tasks from infancy through early adolescence. Our understanding of development in later stages, however, will provide a strong basis for conceptualizing the dynamic interplay between people in different stages. For example, as an infant strives to develop a social attachment, he or she must depend on an adult who is capable of reciprocating and caring for the child. Looking at the developmental tasks of adulthood, one finds that childbearing and child-rearing are tasks for adults in the stages of early and middle adulthood. For adults who are involved in parenting or in some type of caregiving relationship with infants and young children, the task of achieving competence and satisfaction in the caregiving role corresponds to the infant's needs to attach to a caring adult. The infant and the adult are bound into complementary roles, and the developmental outcome for both the infant and the adult are interdependent.

Psychosocial Crisis

A *psychosocial crisis*, the third organizing concept of psychosocial theory (Erikson, 1950/1963), arises as a person makes psychological adjustments to social demands at each stage of development. The word *crisis* in this context refers to a normal set of stresses and strains rather than to an extraordinary set of events. At each stage of development, society and social groups make demands on the individual. The psychosocial crisis of a stage can be thought of as a state of tension that a person experiences when persistent guidelines and expectations from society exceed his or her skills. The expectations may involve demands for greater self-control, further development of skills, or stronger commitment to goals. During each stage of development, the individual tries to achieve a resolution by adjusting to society's demands while translating those demands into personal terms.

A Typical Psychosocial Crisis

The psychosocial crisis with which you are probably most familiar is that of identity versus identity confusion, which is associated with later adolescence. An *identity crisis* is a sudden disintegration of the framework of values and goals that a person relies on to give meaning and purpose to daily life (Erikson, 1968).

An identity crisis is usually associated with intense anxiety and depression. The anxiety stems from fears that, without the structure of a clear value system, unacceptable impulses will cause harmful or immoral behavior. The depression results from feelings of worthlessness. When previously established goals lose meaning, a person's actions seem to have no purpose or value.

TABLE 3.1

Developmental Tasks Associated with Life Stages

Life Stage*	Developmental Tasks
Infancy (birth to 2 years)	Social attachment
	Maturation of sensory, perceptual, and motor functions
	Sensorimotor intelligence and primitive causality
	Understanding the nature of objects and the creation of categories
	Emotional development
Toddlerhood (2 and 3)	Elaboration of locomotion
	Fantasy play
	Language development
	Self-control
Early school age (4 to 6)	Sex-role identification
	Early moral development
	Self-theory — *each have a theory of who we are (internal)*
	Group play
Middle childhood (6 to 12)	Friendship
	Concrete operations
	Skill learning
	Self-evaluation
	Team play
Early adolescence (12 to 18)	Physical maturation
	Formal operations
	Emotional development
	Membership in the peer group
	Sexual relationships
Later adolescence (18 to 22)	Autonomy from parents
	Gender identity
	Internalized morality
	Career choice
Early adulthood (22 to 34)	Exploring intimate relationships
	Childbearing
	Work
	Lifestyle
Middle adulthood (34 to 60)	Managing a career
	Nurturing the marital relationship
	Expanding caring relationships
	Managing the household
Later adulthood (60 to 75)	Promoting intellectual vigor
	Redirecting energy toward new roles and activities
	Accepting one's life
	Developing a point of view about death
Very old age (75 until death)	Coping with physical changes of aging
	Developing a psychohistorical perspective
	Travel through uncharted terrain

*We do not consider the concept of developmental tasks appropriate to the prenatal stage.

TABLE 3.2

Psychosocial Crises of the Life Stages

Life Stage*	Psychosocial Crisis
Infancy (birth to 2 years)	Trust versus mistrust
Toddlerhood (2 and 3)	Autonomy versus shame and doubt
Early school age (4 to 6)	Initiative versus guilt
Middle childhood (6 to 12)	Industry versus inferiority
Early adolescence (12 to 18)	Group identity versus alienation
Later adolescence (18 to 22)	Individual identity versus identity confusion
Early adulthood (22 to 34)	Intimacy versus isolation
Middle adulthood (34 to 60)	Generativity versus stagnation
Later adulthood (60 to 75)	Integrity versus despair
Very old age (75 until death)	Immortality versus extinction

*We do not consider the concept of psychosocial crisis appropriate to the prenatal stage.

A college student's identity crisis may be intensified under two conditions, both of which demand immediate, intense examination of value issues. First, the identity crisis may be heightened in students who attend a college with a significantly different value orientation and frequent interaction with faculty members. These students suddenly feel at a loss when significant adults they expect to admire and respect challenge their values. They may respond by desperately clinging to their old value system in order to maintain a sense of control.

The identity crisis may also be heightened in students who are exploring and experimenting if external demands force them to make a value commitment about which they are uncertain. The need to decide on a major, to make a commitment to a romantic relationship, or to take a stand on a campus controversy may cause some students to realize that they do indeed know what they want. Students who make this happy discovery will move in the direction of identity achievement. Other students, however, may experience even greater confusion by demands for commitment, throwing their existing tentative value structure into chaos.

Psychosocial Crises of the Life Stages

According to psychosocial theory, the nature of the psychosocial crisis is different in each stage of life. Table 3.2 lists the psychosocial crisis in each stage of development from infancy through very old age. The crises are expressed as polarities—trust versus mistrust, autonomy versus shame and doubt—indicating the most positive and negative possible outcomes of the crisis. According to psychosocial theory, most people's experiences are characterized by both the positive and the negative ends of the continuum. The inevitable discrepancy between one's level of development at the beginning of a stage and society's push for a new level of functioning by the end of it introduces at least some degree of stress. For example, even within a loving, caring social environment that promotes trust, an infant will experience some moments of frustration or disappointment that introduce sentiments of mistrust. Even the most industrious, skillful child of middle childhood will encounter some tasks that are too difficult or some sense of inferiority in comparison with a more talented peer. The outcome of the crisis at each stage is a balance or integration of the two opposing forces. For each person, the relative frequency and significance of positive and negative experiences will determine at what point along a continuum from extremely positive to extremely negative the resolution occurs.

The likelihood of a completely positive or completely negative resolution is small. Most people experience a generally positive resolution of the crisis, supported by natural maturational tendencies and favorable events. At each successive stage, the likelihood of negative experiences increases as the developmental tasks become more complex and the chances of encountering societal barriers to development increase. However, the achievement of a positive resolution to each crisis fosters new psychosocial strengths that help the person to meet the demands of the next stage.

If we are to understand the process of growth at each life stage, we must consider the negative pole of each crisis as well as the positive, because it offers insight into basic areas of human vulnerability. Experienced in moderation, negative experiences foster clarification of ego positions, individuation, and moral integrity. Although a constant attitude of suspicion is undesirable, for example, basically a trusting person must be able to evaluate situations and people for their trustworthiness. In every psychosocial crisis, both positive and negative experiences contribute to the total range of a person's adaptive capacities.

Why conceptualize life in terms of a series of crises? Does this idea adequately portray the individual's process of growth, or does it overemphasize conflict and abnormality? The concept of crisis implies that normal development does not proceed smoothly. Psychosocial theory hypothesizes that conflict and resolution are necessary elements in the developmental process that drive the ego system to develop new capacities. "Growing pains" occur at every stage of life. Those who expect their ego problems to be over after adolescence will be sorely disappointed.

The term *psychosocial* adds another dimension to the concept of developmental crises. These crises are the result of cultural pressures and expectations. The theory suggests that, in the process of normal development, individuals will experience tension regardless of their culture because of society's need to socialize and integrate its members. Although the tension itself is not solely a result of personal inadequacies, an individual's failure to resolve it can seriously limit future growth.

The exact nature of the conflict is not the same in all stages. Few cultural limits are placed on infants, for example; the outcome of the infancy stage depends greatly on the qualities of the caregiver. In early school age, the culture opposes the child's initiative in some matters and offers abundant encouragement to initiative in others. In middle childhood, the dominant cultural goal is the achievement of knowledge and skills that are valued by the society; mastery is highly valued, but not all skills are valued equally. In Notebook Page 3.2 you are asked to conceptualize the nature of the psychosocial crisis of middle childhood—Industry versus Inferiority.

In addition to these predictable crises, any number of unforeseen stressors can arise during a lifetime. Parents divorcing, the death of a sibling,

[margin notes, handwritten:]
Seek balance or integration of two opposing forces

Crises offer insight into vulnerability

conflict & resolution necessary to dev't

Culture and the Psychosocial Crisis

Each psychosocial crisis is the result of some tension between the developmental maturity of a person at the beginning of a stage and cultural expectations and demands for participation and contribution to society associated with that stage. These expectations and demands are usually communicated to children by family, friends, teachers, and the media. They may be embedded in the mythology and folk wisdom of the society as a whole.

The psychosocial crisis of the middle childhood years (approximately 6 to 12) is industry versus inferiority. This crisis focuses on the pressures that children feel to demonstrate competence in socially valued skills and to feel a sense of pride in achievement. The negative pole of this crisis is a sense of inferiority resulting from experiences of failure to achieve important skills.

The crisis of industry versus inferiority often assumes a cultural as well as a subcultural perspective. For example, almost all American children are expected to learn to play baseball during these years, and almost all Italian children are expected to learn to play soccer. By age 12, most farm children have already learned to drive a tractor; most urban children have figured out how to take the bus or subway. By age 12, many Jewish children have learned how to read some Hebrew and recite Hebrew prayers.

1. What kinds of pressures do children experience related to skill development and achievement during middle childhood?

_____

_____

2. How are these expectations communicated to children?

_____

_____

3. Which skills does American culture appear to value for children at this stage?

_____

_____

4. What are some consequences of success and failure in skill development at this stage?

_____

_____

5. What subcultural differences regarding expectations for achievement during middle childhood exist among various groups? What are one or two examples of subcultures that have unique expectations for children in middle childhood?

_____

_____

6. Based on your own experiences, memories, and observations of children, describe two or three of the most rewarding accomplishments that contribute to a sense of industry during the period of middle childhood.

_____

_____

exposure to violence, the loss of a job, and widowhood are crises that can come at many points in life. Coping with such unpredictable crises may be overwhelming, particularly if a person suffers several crises simultaneously. However, unanticipated crises can also lead to new growth and the emergence of new competencies at any stage. The concept of predictable developmental stress that is emphasized in psychosocial theory must be expanded to include the possibility of unanticipated crises. These chance events may foster growth, but they may also result in defensiveness, regression, or emotional paralysis. The impact of an unpredictable crisis will depend, in part, on whether or not the child is in a state of psychosocial crisis at the time (Cummings, Greene & Karraker, 1991; Larson & Ham, 1993).

Unanticipated crises can lead to growth and competencies during any stage they are experienced.

The Interrelationship Between Developmental Tasks and Psychosocial Crises

Success in mastering developmental tasks is influenced by the resolution of the psychosocial crisis from the previous stage, which fosters new social capabilities. Equipped with these capabilities, a person encounters the challenging experiences and relationships of the new stage with enhanced feelings of personal worth. The skills learned while meeting the developmental tasks of a particular stage then enable a person to resolve the psychosocial crisis of that stage. Task accomplishment and crisis resolution interact to produce human development.

The Central Process for Resolving the Psychosocial Crisis

Every psychosocial crisis involves some discrepancy between a person's developmental competencies at the beginning of the stage and societal pressures for more effective, integrated functioning. We have extended the concept

Central process

*Individual needs
w/ cultural
requirements*

of psychosocial theory by identifying a central process for resolving each psychosocial crisis. The *central process,* the fourth organizing concept of psychosocial theory, refers to a mechanism that links the individual's needs with cultural requirements at each life stage. Significant relationships and relevant competencies change at every life stage, so stage-specific modes of psychological work and social interaction must occur if a person is to continue on to the next stage.

For example, *imitation* is viewed as the central process for psychosocial growth during toddlerhood (2 to 4 years). Children expand their range of skills by imitating adults, siblings, playmates, television characters, and even animals. Imitation appears to give toddlers enormous satisfaction. Through imitation, they can increase the similarity between themselves and admired members of their social groups. They can also exercise some control over potentially frightening or confusing events by imitating elements of those occurrences in their play.

Moving toward a sense of autonomy in toddlerhood is facilitated by a child's imitative abilities and by the variety of models available for observation, which expand a child's mastery of a range of behaviors. Through persistent imitative activity, children increase their sense of self-initiated behavior and control over their actions.

Imitation is more dominant in the behavioral repertoire during toddlerhood than at any other time in life, although it is often used as a learning and social strategy at other stages. When a parent tells a child, "That's good, Cathy. Now watch Daddy, and do it just like him," the parent is also using the significant parent–child relationship to act as society's agent in encouraging imitation of culturally expected behaviors. The message conveyed repeatedly to the child is that imitation is a key tool for learning.

Table 3.3 shows the central processes that lead to the acquisition of new skills, the resolution of the psychosocial crisis, and successful coping at each life stage. Each of these processes appears to take on heightened significance

TABLE 3.3

The Central Process for Resolution of the Psychosocial Crisis

Life Stage*	Central Process
Infancy (birth to 2 years)	Mutuality with caregiver
Toddlerhood (2 and 3)	Imitation
Early school age (4 to 6)	Identification
Middle childhood (6 to 12)	Education
Early adolescence (12 to 18)	Peer pressure
Later adolescence (18 to 22)	Role experimentation
Early adulthood (22 to 34)	Mutuality among peers
Middle adulthood (34 to 60)	Person–environment fit and creativity
Later adulthood (60 to 75)	Introspection
Very old age (75 until death)	Social support

*We do not consider the concept of psychosocial crisis appropriate to the prenatal stage.

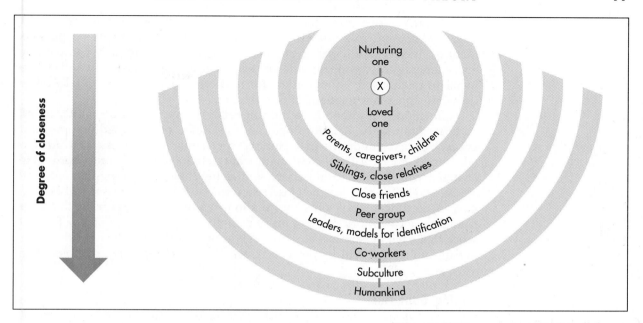

FIGURE 3.4
Radius of significant relationships

in the course of a particular stage. Each process can be encouraged through significant social relationships. <u>Personal and societal mechanisms for absorbing and reorganizing information lead to a revised self-awareness and consequent crisis resolution.</u>

Radius of Significant Relationships

Erikson (1982, p. 31) pointed to a *radius of significant relationships* at each stage of development (see Figure 3.4). Initially, a person focuses on a small number of relationships. During childhood, adolescence, and early adulthood, the number of relationships expands, and they take on greater variety in intensity. In middle and later adulthood, the person often returns to a small number of extremely important relationships that provide opportunities for great depth and intimacy. People in these significant relationships make most of the demands on a person, transmitting society's messages and producing tension.

In infancy, the significant social relationship is with a nurturing person. Most often, the mother is the significant other. However, father, siblings, a grandparent, or a substitute caregiver may also provide this significant relationship. One significant relationship is essential, but it is possible for an infant to have more than one.

Most toddlers establish relationships with a widening circle of caregivers. In early school age, relationships with family members, including siblings and grandparents as well as parents, become stronger and deeper. More relationships with friends and teachers become important.

At middle childhood, significant relationships extend to a widening circle of people, including acquaintances in the neighborhood and at school, friends made at camp, in clubs, and on sports teams. In early adolescence, the peer group, clubs and organizations, work, and religious groups provide new relationships that help young people define themselves and advance their complex social reasoning.

radius of significant relationships

In later adolescence, the radius of significant relations extends to mentors, leaders, and role models in the effort to create an integrated personal identity. In early adulthood, partners in friendship, sex, intimacy, competition, and cooperation provide significant relationships. There is a new and deeper focus on relationships. In addition, for most people, their children take precedence in significant relations at this time.

In middle adulthood, significant relations are based on family, work, and/or community. Relationships may be quite far-flung. Adults are influenced by their children's and parents' social relationships as well. In later adulthood and very old age, significant relationships become both more abstract, with a bond to humanity, and at the same time more focused, with a new level of caring for the close relatives and friends who are still living.

According to Erikson's formulation, readiness to engage in this ever-changing network of relationships is a result of the epigenetic plan. The network that each person has at each stage of life determines the care, demands, and meaning that will be derived (Duck, 1988; Grusec & Lytton, 1988; Higgins, et al., 1985).

Coping Behavior

Coping behavior, the sixth organizing concept of psychosocial theory, consists of active efforts to resolve stress and create new solutions to the challenges of each developmental stage. Robert White (1974) identified three components of the coping process: (1) the ability to gain and process new information, (2) the ability to maintain control over one's emotional state, and (3) the ability to move freely within one's environment.

Coping behavior is an important concept in psychosocial theory because it allows us to explain how new, original, creative, unique, and inventive behaviors occur. Coping behaviors allow for the development and growth of an individual, as opposed to the maintenance of a level of equilibrium in the face of threat. In Notebook Page 3.3 you are asked to recall examples of your own coping strategies in middle childhood and early adolescence.

White illustrated the coping process by describing high school seniors' strategies for coping with the imminent challenge of college. Those who visit the campus, talk to students there, start reading for courses they will take, or take summer jobs working with college students are devising coping strategies that will lead to increased information about the setting and increased competence in it.

Individuals create their own strategies for coping with life challenges. The variation in coping styles reflects people's talents and motives, as well as the responses of significant others to a particular strategy. Think of the first day of kindergarten for a group of 5-year-olds. Some children just sit, shyly watching the teacher and the other children. Others climb all over the equipment and eagerly explore new toys. Still others talk to the teacher or other children, asking names, telling about the bus ride to school, and making friends. Each of these strategies can be understood as a way of gathering information, while preserving a degree of autonomy and integrity in a new and potentially threatening environment. No one way is right or even best for everyone; each strategy serves some children by allowing access to information, exploration, and some control over emotions that are evoked by the new challenge.

An individual's characteristic style of coping appears to be influenced by a variety of factors, including gender, available resources, the nature of the

Coping Behavior

Normal lives are filled with problems. Psychosocial theory emphasizes that some of these problems are a result of a necessary tension between the level of maturity that a person has achieved at a particular age and society's expectations for new levels of functioning. The capacity for coping allows children to move ahead as they face critical developmental crises. Often, coping behavior involves using new resources, creating novel solutions, developing new skills, or reconceptualizing a problem as an opportunity rather than a threat. Rather than simply trying to maintain the status quo or defend themselves from external demands, children engage their energies in solving problems in ways that will preserve their feelings of self-worth and capability.

In the space below, describe two examples of your own coping behaviors during middle childhood (approximately 6 to 12 years old) and early adolescence (approximately 12 to 18 years old). Describe the problems that you faced and the strategies you used to handle these problems.

Problem   **Coping Strategies**

Middle childhood

1.

2.

Early adolescence

1.

2.

Fortified by a sense of hope, this family can still be playful even though their home was destroyed in a hurricane.

particular interpersonal relationships, and accumulation of life experiences. In addition, personality exerts a consistent influence over a person's coping style. Children who are temperamentally difficult, for example—that is, children who are irritable and fearful, who have difficulty establishing regular eating, sleeping, and toileting patterns, and who have high activity levels—have been found to adapt less readily to change. They are more likely to evidence behavioral and emotional problems when they encounter misfortunes such as divorce or economic hardship in their families (Hetherington, 1989; Rutter, 1987).

Everyone's coping style undergoes some developmental transformations. With increased maturity, people approach stressful events more philosophically. Adults are less likely than children or adolescents to use simplistic forms of coping, such as escape, denial, and blaming others for their misfortunes. Many adults are able to reconceptualize negative events, finding some positive consequences in them or redefining them in a more positive light. Adults who have reached a high level of maturity are better able to determine when it is best to try to change a situation and when it is best to adapt to it (Folkman et al., 1987; Labouvie-Vief et al., 1987). At each stage of development, those individuals who cope effectively with the challenges and resolve the crisis in a positive direction acquire new psychological strengths, referred to as prime adaptive ego qualities. Those whose reactions to the challenges of the stage are more defensive or whose coping styles result only in new levels of stress and disorganization are more likely to acquire core pathologies.

Prime Adaptive Ego Qualities

Erikson (1978) has postulated *prime adaptive ego qualities* that result from the positive resolution of a stage's psychosocial crisis and provide resources for coping in the next. He describes these qualities as mental states that form a basic orientation toward the interpretation of life experiences. A sense of competence, for example, permits a child to exercise his or her wits to solve problems without being hindered by a sense of inferiority.

The primary ego qualities and their definitions are listed in Table 3.4. The ego qualities contribute to the person's dominant worldview. Throughout life, an individual must reformulate this worldview to accommodate new ego qualities. Infants who develop a basic orientation of *hope* will believe that their needs have a good chance of being met. Toddlers who develop a sense of hope and a sense of will, will regard the world as a place where desires can be attained through a combination of caring from others and personal determination.

The importance of many of the prime adaptive ego qualities has been verified by research. For example, people with a hopeful attitude have a better chance of maintaining their spirits and strength in the face of crisis than people who are pessimistic (Mirowsky & Ross, 1986; Werner, 1989). Erikson and his co-workers' interviews with very old people found that those who maintained a sense of hope about their own future, as well as that of their children were more intellectually vigorous and psychologically resilient than those not characterized by this orientation (Erikson et al., 1986).

TABLE 3.4

The Prime Adaptive Ego Quality at Each Psychosocial Stage

[handwritten note: Mental states that provide framework for interpretation of experiences.]

Stage	Ego Quality	Definition
Infancy	Hope	An enduring belief that one can attain one's deep and essential wishes
Toddlerhood	Will	A determination to exercise free choice and self-control
Early school age	Purpose	The courage to imagine and pursue valued goals
Middle childhood	Competence	The free exercise of skill and intelligence in completing tasks
Early adolescence	Fidelity (I)	The ability freely to pledge and sustain loyalty to individuals and groups
Later adolescence	Fidelity (II)	The ability freely to pledge and sustain loyalty to values and ideologies
Early adulthood	Love	A capacity for mutuality that transcends childhood dependency
Middle adulthood	Care	A commitment to concern about what has been generated
Later adulthood	Wisdom	A detached yet active concern with life itself in the face of death
Very old age	Confidence	A conscious trust in oneself and assurance about the meaningfulness of life

Source: Based on Erikson, E. H. (1978). Reflections on Dr. Borg's life cycle. In E. H. Erikson (Ed.), *Adulthood.* New York: Norton, 1–32.

Core pathology develops when an individual is unable to effectively deal w/ a crisis.

Core Pathologies

Although most people develop prime adaptive ego strengths, there is also a potential *core pathology* or destructive force that may develop as a result of ineffective, negative crisis resolution at each stage (Erikson, 1982) (Table 3.5). Core pathologies also serve as guiding orientations for behavior. These pathologies serve as a barrier to relationships, exploration of the interpersonal domain, and resolution of subsequent psychosocial crises. The energy that would normally be directed toward mastering a stage's developmental tasks is directed instead toward resisting or avoiding change.

Evaluation of Psychosocial Theory

Although we believe that psychosocial theory provides a useful theoretical framework for organizing the vast array of observations in the field of human development, we recognize that it also has weaknesses. We want you to be aware of both its strengths and its weaknesses so that you can form your own independent assessment of the theory's usefulness in guiding your study of development. Table 3.6 contains a summary of the strengths and weaknesses of psychosocial theory that are discussed below.

Strengths

Psychosocial theory provides a very broad context for the study of development. The theory links the process of child development to later stages of adult life, to societal needs, and to the ability of societies to interact with one

TABLE 3.5

Core Pathology at Each Life Stage

Stage	Core Pathology	Definition
Infancy	Withdrawal	Social and emotional detachment
Toddlerhood	Compulsion	Repetitive behaviors motivated by impulse or by restrictions against the expression of impulse
Early school age	Inhibition	A psychological restraint that prevents freedom of thought, expression, and activity
Middle childhood	Inertia	A paralysis of action and thought that prevents productive work
Early adolescence	Isolation	Lack of companions
Later adolescence	Repudiation	Rejection of roles and values that are viewed as alien to oneself
Early adulthood	Exclusivity	An elitist shutting out of others
Middle adulthood	Rejectivity	Unwillingness to include certain others or groups of others in one's generative concern
Later adulthood	Disdain	A feeling of scorn for the weakness and frailty of oneself and others
Very old age	Diffidence	An inability to act because of overwhelming self-doubt

Source: Based on Erikson, E. H. (1982). *The life cycle completed: A review.* New York: Norton.

another. Although many scholars agree that such a broad perspective is necessary, few other theories attempt to address the dynamic interplay between individual development and society.

The emphasis of psychosocial theory on psychological development and processes provides insight into the directions of healthy development across the life span. Concepts central to psychosocial theory such as ego strengths, coping, well-being, social support, and interdependence have become thoroughly integrated into contemporary human development scholarship (e.g., Snyder, 1994; Ryff, 1995; Zimmerman et al., 1995). The theory identifies the tensions that may disrupt development at each life stage, providing a framework for psychotherapy and counseling. At the same time, it also recognizes the contributions that individuals make to their own well-being. Psychosocial theory stresses the interplay between a genetically guided plan for development and the powerful forces of culture and society at every life stage.

The concept of normative psychosocial crises is a creative contribution of the theory. It identifies predictable tensions between socialization and individual capability throughout life. Societies, with their structures, laws, roles, rituals, and sanctions, are organized to guide individual growth toward a particular ideal of mature adulthood. If individuals grew in that direction naturally according to a genetically guided plan, presumably there would be no need for these elaborate social structures. But every society faces dilemmas in attempting to balance the desires of the individual with the needs of the group. All individuals face some problems when they attempt to maintain individuality while still satisfying group requirements. Psychosocial theory gives us constructs to explore these natural tensions.

TABLE 3.6

Evaluation of Psychosocial Theory

Strengths	Weaknesses
The theory provides a broad context, linking development in various stages of life to the resources and demands of society.	The basic concepts of the theory are abstract and difficult to operationalize.
It emphasizes ego development and directions for healthy development across the life span.	Explanations of the mechanisms for resolving crisis and moving from one stage to the next are not well developed.
It provides a useful framework for psychotherapy.	The specific number of stages and their link to a genetic plan for development have not been adequately demonstrated, especially in adulthood.
It emphasizes the dynamic interplay between a genetic plan and the forces of culture and society in guiding individual development.	The theory is dominated by a male Eurocentric perspective that gives too much emphasis to the emergence of individuality and not enough emphasis to social competence and social needs.
The concept of normative psychosocial crises provides an effective set of constructs for examining the tension between the individual and society.	The specific way in which culture encourages or inhibits development at each life stage is not clearly elaborated.

Weaknesses

One weakness of psychosocial theory is that its basic concepts are presented in language that is abstract and difficult to examine empirically (Crain, 1985; Miller, 1993). Such terms as *initiative, personal identity,* and *generativity* are hard to define and even more difficult to measure objectively. Nonetheless, efforts have been made along this line. James Marcia, Alan Waterman, Anne Constantinople, and others have contributed to a rather extensive literature that examines the construct of personal identity. Other researchers have attempted to analyze the concept of intimacy, and still others have studied the concepts of generativity and integrity. A questionnaire measure based on Erikson's psychosocial theory, the Inventory of Psychosocial Development, has been used to trace the emergence of psychosocial crises and their resolution in samples varying in age from adolescence to later adulthood (Whitbourne et al., 1992; Walaskay et al., 1983–1984; Waterman & Whitbourne, 1981; Constantinople, 1969). In addition to studies that analyze psychosocial theory directly, other studies have a bearing on the clarification and extension of its constructs.

Another weakness of the theory is that the mechanisms for resolving crises and moving from one stage to the next are not well developed. Erikson did not offer a universal mechanism for crisis resolution, nor did he detail the kinds of experiences that are necessary for coping successfully with the crisis of each stage. We have addressed this weakness by introducing the concepts of developmental tasks and a central process for each stage. The developmental tasks suggest some of the major achievements that permit a person to meet the social expectations of each stage. The central process identifies the primary social context within which the crisis is resolved.

The specific number of stages and their link to a biologically based plan for development have been criticized, most notably in discussions of the stages of adulthood (Crain, 1985). Other human development theorists, such as Robert Peck, Robert Gould, Daniel Levinson, and Marjorie Lowenthal, take a more differentiated view of the stages of adulthood and later life. We have responded to these criticisms by treating adolescence as two distinct stages and by adding another stage of adulthood—very old age (Newman & Newman, 1995). You will also read about the important developmental issues of the prenatal period, a stage that Erikson's theory does not consider, but one that clearly plays a central role in setting the stage for a lifetime of vulnerabilities and resources. In our view, these revisions present no threat to the usefulness of the theory. Rather, they demonstrate the natural evolution of a theoretical framework that accounts for the observations of a new historical era.

Finally, the theory has been criticized as being dominated by a male, Eurocentric, individualistic perspective (Gilligan, 1982). The themes of autonomy, initiative, industry, and personal identity all emphasize the process of individuation. In this and other theories of development, ego development, separation from family, autonomy, and self-directed goal attainment have been equated with psychological maturity. Relatively little attention has been given to themes that have been identified as central to the developmental experiences of girls and young women, such as interpersonal competence, cooperation, and affiliation (Josselson, 1987). These themes also seem to be especially salient in more collectively oriented ethnic subcultures where maturity is equated more with one's ability to support and sustain the family or extended family group than with individual achievement of status or wealth.

Within the framework of psychosocial theory, the theme of connection is addressed directly through the crisis of trust versus mistrust in infancy, but then the thread is lost until early and middle adulthood when issues of intimacy and generativity refocus on relationships. The concept of the radius of significant relationships is present at every phase of life, however, suggesting that self-image is always intimately linked to meaningful social connections. We use this construct throughout the text to maintain the perspective of an individual's network of relationships, focusing especially on family and friends in childhood; on family, peer group, close friends, and love relationships in early and later adolescence; and on intimate partners, family, friends, and co-workers in various phases of adult life.

To further extend the theme of connection, the text elaborates on developing capabilities for social interaction and differences in male and female socialization at each life stage. A variety of social abilities, including empathy, prosocial behavior, interaction skills, and components of social cognition such as taking another's point of view, are traced as they emerge in the context of parent–child and sibling relations, friendships, and peer groups. Finally, the text considers subcultural as well as broader social influences on development and the importance of a collective orientation toward responsibility in caring for children and creating a sense of community.

Development will be optimal if a person retains the ability to create new behaviors and relationships as a result of skill acquisition, coping, and successful crisis resolution at each stage. Constriction of development is the result of core pathologies that inhibit behavior in general and new adaptive behaviors in particular (especially social behaviors). The mechanism for positive and negative development is diagrammed in Figure 3.5.

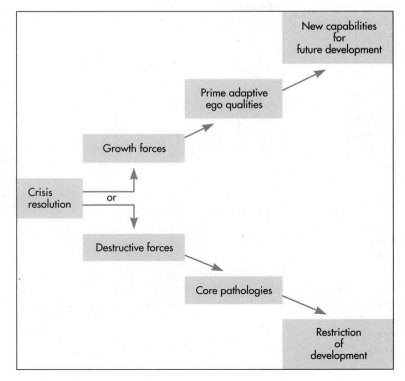

FIGURE 3.5

Mechanism for positive and negative psychosocial development

At the beginning of this chapter, we discussed the three questions that you must ask in order to evaluate a theory. Let us now answer these questions with respect to psychosocial theory.

1. *Which phenomenon is the theory trying to explain?* The theory attempts to explain human development across the life span, especially patterned changes in self-understanding, social relationships, and worldview.
2. *What assumptions does the theory make?* Human development is a product of three factors: biological evolution, the interaction between individuals and social groups, and contributions that individuals make to their own psychological growth.
3. *What does the theory predict?* There are 11 distinct stages of development. Developmental tasks are dictated by the interaction of the physical, intellectual, emotional, social, and self-domains with various societal systems during each stage. A crisis arises at each stage of

TABLE 3.7

Organization of the Stages

Life Stage	Developmental Tasks	Psychosocial Crisis	Central Process	Prime Adaptive Ego Quality	Core Pathology
Prenatal (conception to birth)					
Infancy (birth to 2 years)	Social attachment; Maturation of sensory, perceptual, and motor functions; Sensorimotor intelligence and primitive causality; Understanding the nature of objects and creation of categories; Emotional development	Basic trust versus basic mistrust	Mutuality with caregiver	Hope	Withdrawal
Toddlerhood (2 to 4)	Elaboration of locomotion; Fantasy play; Language development; Self-control	Autonomy versus shame and doubt	Imitation	Will	Compulsion
Early school age (4 to 6)	Sex-role identification; Early moral development; Self-theory; Group play	Initiative versus guilt	Identification	Purpose	Inhibition
Middle childhood (6 to 12)	Friendship; Concrete operations; Skill learning; Self-evaluation; Team play	Industry versus inferiority	Education	Competence	Inertia

Life Stage	Developmental Tasks	Psychosocial Crisis	Central Process	Prime Adaptive Ego Quality	Core Pathology
Early adolescence (12 to 18)	Physical maturation Formal operations Emotional development Membership in the peer group Sexual relationships	Group identity versus alienation	Peer pressure	Fidelity (I)	Isolation
Later adolescence (18 to 22)	Autonomy from parents Gender identity Internalized morality Career choice	Individual identity versus identity confusion	Role experimentation	Fidelity (II)	Repudiation
Early adulthood (22 to 34)	Exploring intimate relationships Childbearing Work Lifestyle	Intimacy versus isolation	Mutuality among peers	Love	Exclusivity
Middle adulthood (34 to 60)	Managing a career Nurturing the marital relationship Expanding caring relationships Managing the household	Generativity versus stagnation	Person–environment fit and creativity	Care	Rejectivity
Later adulthood (60 to 75)	Promoting intellectual vigor Redirecting energy toward new roles Accepting one's life Developing point of view about death	Integrity versus despair	Introspection	Wisdom	Disdain
Very old age (75 until death)	Coping with the physical changes of aging Developing psychohistorical perspective Travel through uncharted terrain	Immortality versus extinction	Social support	Confidence	Diffidence

development, and a central process operates to resolve it. Each person is part of an expanding network of significant relationships that convey society's expectations and demands. These relationships can also provide encouragement in the face of challenges. New behaviors continue to be possible throughout life.

Table 3.7 summarizes the major developmental tasks, the psychosocial crisis, the central process, and the possible prime adaptive ego strengths and core pathologies for each stage of development. You can use this table as a guide to the major themes of the text. It may help you to see the connections among topics within a chapter or to trace threads of continuity over several stages of development. You may also use this table to construct a life course for yourself, which will reveal tensions and major psychosocial factors that may affect your self-concept and your relationships with others.

Chapter Summary

1. A theory is a logical system of general concepts that provides a framework for organizing and understanding observations. To evaluate a theory, one must answer three questions: (1) What phenomenon is the theory trying to explain? (2) What assumptions does the theory make? and (3) What does the theory predict?

2. Psychosocial theory offers a life-span view of development as a product of interactions between individuals and their social environments. The needs and goals of both the individual and society must be considered in conceptualizing human development.

3. At each stage, a normative crisis is caused by tension between one's needs and personal resources and the new expectations and demands of one's society which are transmitted through a network of significant relationships. Resolving each stage's crisis provides new social abilities that enhance the resources available in the subsequent stage.

4. Predictability is found in the sequence of psychosocial stages, in the central process for resolving the crisis at each stage, and in the radius of significant relationships. Individuality is expressed in the achievement of the developmental tasks, the evolution of a worldview, and the style and resources for coping that a person brings to each new challenge.

5. As individuals progress through the stages of life, most develop an increasing capacity for innovative thought and action and initiating new relationships that help them to direct the course of their lives. These innovations contribute to the continuing evolution of social behavior, influencing other members of the social group and gradually modifying the social context. Thus, the theory offers a dynamic view of the integration of individual and societal development.

6. A critical analysis offers strengths and weaknesses of psychosocial theory, suggesting directions for modification and areas where additional theoretical perspectives are needed.

References

Coles, R. (1970). *Erik H. Erikson: The growth of his work.* Boston: Atlantic-Little, Brown.

Constantinople, A. (1969). An Eriksonian measure of personality development in college students. *Developmental Psychology, 1,* 357–372.

Crain, W. C. (1985). *Theories of development: Concepts*

and applications. (2nd ed.). Englewood Cliffs, N.J.: Prentice-Hall.

Cummings, E. M., Greene, A-L. & Karraker, K. H. (Eds). (1991). *Lifespan perspectives on stress and coping.* Hillsdale, N.J.: Erlbaum.

Davison, M. L., King, P. M., Kitchener, K. S. & Parker,

C. A. (1980). The stage sequence concept in cognitive and social development. *Developmental Psychology, 16,* 121–131.

Duck, S. (1988). *Handbook of personal relationships: Theory, research, and interventions.* New York: Wiley.

Erikson, E. H. (1950/1963). *Childhood and society.* New York: Norton.

Erikson, E. H. (1958). *Young man Luther.* New York: Norton.

Erikson, E. H. (1968). *Identity: Youth and crisis.* New York: Norton.

Erikson, E. H. (1969). *Gandhi's truth.* New York: Norton.

Erikson, E. H. (1978). Reflections on Dr. Borg's life cycle. In E. H. Erikson (Ed.), *Adulthood.* New York: Norton, 1–32.

Erikson, E. H. (1982). *The life cycle completed: A review.* New York: Norton.

Erikson, E. H., Erikson, J. M. & Kivnick, H. Q. (1986). *Vital involvement in old age.* New York: Norton.

Fischer, K. W. & Silvern, L. (1985). Stages and individual differences in cognitive development. *Annual Review of Psychology, 36,* 613–648.

Flavell, J. H. (1982). Structures, stages, and sequences in cognitive development. In W. A. Collins (Ed.), *The concept of development.* Hillsdale, N.J.: Erlbaum, 1–28.

Folkman, S., Lazarus, R. S., Pimley, S. & Novacek, J. (1987). Age differences in stress and coping process. *Psychology and Aging, 2,* 171–184.

Gilligan, C. (1982). *In a different voice.* Cambridge, Mass.: Harvard University Press.

Grusec, J. E. & Lytton, H. (1988). *Social development: History, theory, and research.* New York: Springer-Verlag.

Havighurst, R. J. (1953). *Human development and education.* New York: Longmans, Green.

Havighurst, R. J. (1972). *Developmental tasks and education.* (3rd ed.) New York: David McKay.

Havighurst, R. J. et al. (1962). *Growing up in River City.* New York: Wiley.

Hetherington, E. M. (1989). Coping with family transitions: Winners, losers, and survivors. *Child Development, 60,* 1–14.

Higgins, E. T., Ruble, D. N. & Hartup, W. W. (1985). *Social cognition and social development: A sociocultural perspective.* New York: Cambridge University Press.

Hopkins, J. R. (1995). Obituaries: Erik Homburger Erikson (1901–1994). *American Psychologist, 50,* 796–797.

Huxley, J. (1941). *The uniqueness of man.* London: Chatto & Windus.

Huxley, J. (1942). *Evolution: The magic synthesis.* New York: Harper.

Josselson, R. (1987). *Finding herself: Pathways to identity development in women.* San Francisco: Jossey-Bass.

Labouvie-Vief, G., Hakim-Larson, J. & Hobart, C. J. (1987). Age, ego level, and the life-span development of coping and defense processes. *Psychology and Aging, 2,* 286–293.

Larson, R. & Ham, M. (1993). Stress and 'Storm and Stress' in early adolescence: The relationship of negative events with dysphoric affect. *Developmental Psychology, 29,* 130–140.

Levin, I. (1986). *Stage and structure: Reopening the debate.* Norwood, N.J.: Ablex.

Miller, P. H. (1993). *Theories of developmental psychology.* (3rd ed.). New York: W. H. Freeman.

Mirowsky, J. & Ross, C. E. (1986). Social patterns of distress. In R. H. Turner (Ed.), *Annual Review of Sociology, 12,* 23–45.

Neugarten, B. L. (1993). Obituaries: Robert J. Havighurst (1900–1991). *American Psychologist, 48,* 1290–1291.

Newman, B. M. & Newman, P. R. (1995). *Development through life: A psychosocial approach.* (6th ed.). Pacific Grove, Calif.: Brooks/Cole.

Rutter, M. (1987). Psychosocial resilience and protective mechanisms. *American Journal of Orthopsychiatry, 57,* 316–331.

Ryff, C. D. (1995). Psychological well-being in adult life. *Current Directions in Psychological Science, 4,* 99–104.

Snyder, C. R. (1994). *The psychology of hope.* New York: Free Press.

Walaskay, M., Whitbourne, S. K. & Nehrke, M. F. (1983–1984). Construction and validation of an ego-integrity status interview. *International Journal of Aging and Human Development, 18,* 61–72.

Waterman, A. S. & Whitbourne, S. K. (1981). The inventory of psychosocial development. *JSAS: Catalog of selected documents in psychology, 11* (Ms. No. 2179).

Werner, E. E. (1989). Children of the Garden Island. *Scientific American,* April, 106–111.

Whitbourne, S. K., Zuschlag, M. K., Elliot, L. B. & Waterman, A. S. (1992). Psychosocial development in adulthood: A 22-year sequential study. *Journal of Personality and Social Psychology, 63,* 260–271.

White, R. W. (1974). Strategies of adaptation: An attempt at systematic description. In G. V. Coelho, D. A. Hamburg & J. E. Adams (Eds.), *Coping and adaptation.* New York: Basic Books, 47–68.

Zimmerman, M. A., Salem, D. A. & Maton, K. I. (1995). Family structure and psychosocial correlates among urban African-American adolescent males. *Child Development, 66,* 1598–1613.

Major Theories for Understanding Change

Chapter 4

The Theory of Evolution
 Implications for Child Development
 Links to Psychosocial Theory

Psychosexual Theory
 Implications for Child Development
 Links to Psychosocial Theory

Cognitive Developmental Theory
 Basic Concepts in Piaget's Theory
  Implications for Child Development
 Vygotsky's Concepts of Cognitive Development
  Implications for Child Development
 Links to Psychosocial Theory

Theories of Learning
 Classical Conditioning
  Implications for Child Development
 Operant Conditioning
  Implications for Child Development
 Social Learning
  Implications for Child Development
 Cognitive Behaviorism
  Implications for Child Development
 Summary of Learning Theories
 Links to Psychosocial Theory

Cultural Theory
 Implications for Child Development
 Links to Psychosocial Theory

Social Role Theory
 Implications for Child Development
 Links to Psychosocial Theory

Systems Theory
 Implications for Child Development
 Links to Psychosocial Theory

Chapter Summary

References

Psychosocial theory provides the conceptual umbrella for our approach to studying human development, but we need other theories to account for global evolutionary change, societal and cultural change, and individual change. We need concepts that will help explain the contributions of life experiences, maturational factors, and a person's own constructions of experience to patterns of physical, cognitive, social, emotional, and self-development.

In this chapter, we introduce the major theories guiding research and thinking in the field of child development. First, we will present evolutionary theory, which places the study of individual development in the broad context of the history of the species. Next, psychosexual theory will be discussed. This theory focuses on the relationship of mental activity to changing needs, wishes, and drives. Cognitive developmental theory offers a third view of stages of development that describes the maturation of capacities for logical thought. Four theories related to psychosocial theory—learning theory, cultural theory, social role theory, and systems theory—offer mechanisms that explain how the social environment uniquely influences the content as well as the direction of a child's growth. These theories attempt to account for individual differences by offering various processes of adaptation to the social environment.

Using a family of theoretical perspectives helps to maintain flexibility in interpreting behavior and facilitates our understanding of the integration of individuals and social systems. With each theory, a brief explanation of the focus of the theory and a few major constructs are presented, along with an analysis of the contributions of the theory to the study of child development and its links to psychosocial theory. In subsequent chapters, additional ideas from many of the theories will be presented as they relate to specific topics.

The Theory of Evolution

law of natural selection
- change in response to a change in environmental conditions

The theory of *evolution* explains how diverse and increasingly more complex life forms come to exist. Evolutionary theory, developed by Charles Darwin (see the Biographical Sketch on p. 93), assumes that the natural laws that apply to plant and animal life also apply to humans. The *law of natural selection* explains how, over generations, species gradually change in response to changing environmental conditions. The law of natural selection claims that behavior adapts to the environment in which it occurs. Natural selection operates at the level of genes that are passed, via an individual organism's reproductive success, from one generation to the next. Reproductive success, sometimes called *fitness*, varies among members of a species (Archer, 1991).

varying patterns of genetic makeup

Every species produces more offspring than can survive to reproduce because of limitations of the food supply and natural dangers. Darwin observed that there was quite a bit of *variability* among members of the same species in any given location due to genetic differences. As a result of varying patterns of genetic makeup, some individuals were better suited than others to their immediate environment and were more likely to survive, mate, and produce offspring. These offspring were also more likely to have characteristics that were appropriate for that location. Overall, the species would change to become more successful, or it would evolve into a new species. If

*B*iographical *S*ketch

Charles Darwin
1809–1882

*EVOLUTIONARY
THEORY*

Charles Darwin was born in 1809 into an educated English family with a long-standing tradition of belief in the concepts generated by the theory of evolution. Darwin's grandfather, Erasmus Darwin, was one of the pioneers in the development of evolutionary theory. As a schoolboy, Darwin rebelled against the classical pattern of learning by rote memorization. He preferred to spend long periods of time outdoors, exploring nature and puzzling over its mysteries.

As a young man, Darwin studied medicine but found the lectures boring and the work distasteful. He left medical school, gravely disappointing his father. Darwin was then sent to Cambridge University to study theology in preparation for entering the clergy, but he found this study even less interesting than medicine. He continued to spend much of his time outdoors, exploring nature.

In 1831, an opportunity arose that allowed Darwin to indulge his passion for the outdoors in a professionally ac-

ceptable way: He became the resident naturalist on *H.M.S. Beagle*. The crew's mission was to map the coast of South America and to sail to the Pacific islands to document the plant and animal life. The voyage lasted from 1831 to 1836. During those years, Darwin demonstrated unbounded enthusiasm for his exploration of the natural phenomena that he encountered.

Returning to England, Darwin settled down to reflect on his observations and the samples he had collected. With painstaking attention to detail, over a period of 20 years he developed his theory of how species can change and evolve into new plant or animal forms. However, he postponed writing about his views while he searched for examples that would support his argument. Not until 1859, when he learned that another naturalist, Alfred Russell Wallace, was about to introduce a very similar argument, was Darwin compelled to publish his groundbreaking *The Origin of Species*.

the environment changed (in climate, for example), only certain variations of organisms would survive, and again species would evolve. Forms of life that failed to adapt would become extinct. It is important to understand that it is the variability within a species that ensures the species' continuation or its development into new forms.

Ethology, the study of evolutionarily significant behaviors, is an extension of evolutionary theory into the realm of animal and human behavior. This field provides a systematic approach to analyzing reproductive practices, caregiving behaviors, strategies for obtaining resources, group behavior, and other behaviors that contribute to individual and species survival. In Notebook Page 4.1 you are asked to consider the relationship between an individual's reproductive decisions and species survival.

"Survival of the fittest"

Implications for Child Development

With its focus on reproductive success, evolutionary theory highlights three phases of life: healthy growth and development leading up to the reproductive period; success in mating and the conception of offspring; and the ability to parent offspring so they can reach reproductive age and bear offspring of their own (Charlesworth, 1992). An organism is most vulnerable during childhood; children require care if they are to survive to reproductive age. It is important to understand that biological capacities and the environments in which they can be expressed operate together to produce behavior. A genetic plan, shaped through hundreds of generations, guides infants' predispositions, capacities, and sensitivities. Evolutionary theory states that infants come into the world with a range of innate capacities and potentials. They have competencies that permit them to establish social contact, organize information, and recognize and communicate their needs. At the same time, these innate capacities are expressed within specific contexts. The quality of parenting, adequacy of resources, and competition for resources among siblings are examples of environmental factors to which infants must adapt. Childhood experiences shape the future by providing the context for the establishment of attachments, meaningful social competence, and problem-solving capacities, all of which have a bearing on an individual's behavior in adulthood, particularly the abilities to form intimate relationships and to parent offspring successfully.

The evolutionary perspective draws a connection between an individual's life history and the long-range history of the species. Principles of natural selection operate slowly over generations. However, the reproductive success of individuals over the course of their own life span will determine whether their genetic material continues to be represented in the larger population. Many general areas of human behavior are functionally relevant to the successful survival and fitness of individuals and groups (Charlesworth, 1992). They include:

Reproductive strategies, such as having few or many sex partners or early or later entry into sexual activity,

Infant immaturity requiring prolonged care,

Infant–caregiver attachment,

Parent–child conflicts and sibling rivalry,

Peer group formation and functions, especially cooperation, competition, dominance, and submission,

Pair-bonding and mate selection,

Helping behavior and altruism,

Learning as adaptive behavior,

Individual creation and modification of the environment, and

Social evolution and the elaboration of rites, rituals, and religions.

The evolutionary perspective focuses on the importance of variability for a species' survival. Although theories of development typically examine general patterns of continuity and change across individuals, evolutionary theory analyzes individual differences in the study of development in order to understand the capacity of the human species to adapt successfully to a wide variety of environmental conditions.

Evolutionary Theory and the Emphasis on Reproduction

Evolutionary theory focuses attention on those capacities and behavior patterns that contribute to the long-term survival and continued adaptation of the species. More specifically, the theory highlights those conditions that influence whether individual members of the species survive long enough to reproduce and protect their offspring until they are able to reproduce. It regards continuity and change in the gene pool over many generations as the central theme of development.

Take a moment to reflect on your own intentions regarding reproduction by answering the following questions.

1. Do you have or wish eventually to have children?

2. What factors in your own personal history or in your goals for the future influence these intentions?

3. What concerns or wishes have your own parents expressed to you related to your having children? If you decided not to have children, or were unable to have children, how do you think your parents would react?

4. What relationship do you think exists between an individual's reproductive decisions and species survival?

Links to Psychosocial Theory

Evolutionary theory is the larger framework within which broad issues of individual adaptation, species adaptation, and species survival are considered. Erik Erikson drew heavily on concepts first introduced in Julian Huxley's theory of *psychosocial evolution,* which examines the processes through which human beings influence their own adaptation. Huxley focused on the creation of new information and the invention of strategies for communicating that information from one generation to the next. Psychosocial theory translates the idea of species adaptation to the individual level through the concepts of the psychosocial crisis and coping. Each individual encounters a necessary, developmental struggle in which he or she repeatedly experiences tension between personal traits and capacities and the requirements and demands of the environment.

Each generation within a society faces similar challenges to deliver critical resources to the young, to nurture competence and a capacity for caring in a new generation of adults, and to inspire younger generations with hope and anticipation about the prospects of aging. Within cultural groups, the evolution of rites and rituals serves to preserve resources, direct the rearing of children, and assist individuals through key transitions. Groups that adapt successfully distribute resources effectively, help new members, and pass along information that will help individuals cope with future challenges.

One unique aspect of the human species is our ability to modify our environment in significant ways. We not only adapt to the environment but also alter it to suit our needs. Many of these modifications of the environment increase the chances that individuals within the group will survive; however, some modifications introduce grave risks. Psychosocial theory measures individual growth by the extent which the adults of a society use their competence and power to ensure the safety and well-being of future generations.

Psychosexual Theory

[margin note: dev't of emotional & social life]

Sigmund Freud's (1933/1964) psychosexual theory addresses the development of an individual's emotional and social life. Although much of this theory has been revised, refuted, or repressed, *psychosexual theory* continues to influence contemporary personality theories and the study of child development. Freud focused on the impact of sexual and aggressive drives on the individual's psychological functioning. He distinguished between the influence of sexual drives on mental activity and their effect on reproductive functions. Based largely on material from therapeutic sessions with his patients, Freud recognized the profound influence of sexuality on mental activity (see the Biographical Sketch on p. 98). In addition, he came to believe that very young children had strong sexual drives. He argued that although children are incapable of reproduction, their sexual drives direct aspects of their fantasies, problem solving, and social interactions.

[margin note: Influence of sexuality on mental activity]

[margin note: Domains of consciousness]

The most enduring contribution of psychosexual theory is the identification of domains of consciousness, referred to as the *conscious,* the *preconscious,* and the *unconscious.* Seemingly irrational behavior can often be explained by analyzing the conflicting needs, fears, and wishes that exist in the unconscious.

All humans have certain things in common but it is our variability that assures species survival.

Psychosexual theory describes three basic structures of the personality: the *id* (the sexual and aggressive impulses), the *ego* (the reality-oriented functions), and the *superego* (the moral, ethical principles). As ego develops, the child becomes increasingly adept at satisfying id impulses in ways that are socially acceptable and do not offend the moral and ethical content of the superego. Psychosexual theory outlines five stages of development: oral, anal, phallic, latent, and genital. At each stage, the focus of conflict around the expression of sexual and aggressive impulses changes. The stages reflect shifts in the body areas where pleasure is experienced and shifts in the orientation to self and social relationships.

In adolescence, a resurgence of sexual and aggressive energy challenges many of the ego's earlier coping strategies. The ego must find new ways to express and modify impulses. An essential aspect of this process is thought to be the separation of ego from earlier figures of attachment and investment of energy in the self as well as in new social relationships.

Implications for Child Development

Psychosexual theory emphasizes the importance of the tension between interpersonal demands and intrapsychic demands in shaping personality. The ego develops interpersonal skills for dealing with society. It also develops skills for satisfying personal needs, standards, and aspirations. The expectations of others, particularly parents, are internalized and given personal meaning in the formation of the superego. Freud was able to show how a child translates the demands of the interpersonal world into his or her own personal way of functioning, while new demands and experiences continue to play a role in the development of personality. Freud focused on the effects of sexual impulses on personal and interpersonal life.

ID, EGO, SUPEREGO

5 STAGES
1) oral
2) anal
3) phallic
4) latent
5) genital

*B*iographical *S*ketch

**Sigmund Freud
1856–1939**

*Psychosexual
Theory*

Sigmund Freud was born in Freiberg (now Pribor), Czechoslovakia, in 1856. His grandfather and great-grandfather had both been rabbis. One of Freud's early memories was of a strong resentment toward his baby brother, who had been born when Freud was 19 months old. Freud was filled with guilt over his angry feelings when the infant died at 8 months of age.

Freud was trained as a neurologist in Vienna during the 1870s. His early research focused on the functions of the medulla, the conduction of nerve impulses in the brain and spinal cord, and the anesthetic properties of cocaine (Freud, 1963). In 1882, Freud's interest turned from physiology to psychology because of his association with Josef Breuer. Breuer and Freud developed a theory of hysteria in which they attributed certain forms of paralysis to psychological conflict rather than to physiological damage (Breuer & Freud, 1895/1955).

As a physician, Freud continued to develop his scientific interests in psychology by keeping careful notes on his patients. In many of his writings, he presents cases from which he derived his theory of psychological functioning.

In 1905, Freud published his revolutionary theory of infantile sexuality and its relation to adult life, provoking furious criticism. His medical colleagues could not accept the idea of childhood sexuality. They considered his public lectures on the topic crude and distasteful. Freud was denied a professorial appointment at the University of Vienna primarily because of these lectures and writings. Even Breuer, his longtime colleague and collaborator, found Freud's preoccupation with sexual motives offensive and terminated their association.

In response to his exclusion from the medical community, Freud helped to form the International Congress on Psychoanalysis. Within the context of this professional organization, he developed his psychosexual theory and taught the principles of psychoanalysis to his followers.

Toward the end of his life, Freud, like Albert Einstein in Germany, was forced to leave Austria and move to England to protect himself and his family from the threat of extermination by the Nazis. In the 1930s, Freud and Einstein corresponded regarding their perceptions of anti-Semitism (Einstein & Freud, 1933/1964). They shared their experiences as men of science who had been subjected to the same form of bitter prejudice.

Freud died of cancer in England in 1939. He devoted the last years of his life to extensive writing which inspired other analysts and scholars to study his theory further.

Influence of childhood experience on adult behavior.

One of the major early contributions of psychosexual theory was identifying the influence of childhood experiences on adult behavior. Freud argued that the basic dynamics of personality are established by the age of 6 or 7. Psychoanalytic theory was unique in explaining ongoing adult behavior in terms of stages of development, family interactions, and unresolved family conflicts. The emphasis that Freud gave to parenting practices and their implications for psychosexual development provides one of the few theoretical frameworks for examining parent–child relationships. Many of the early empirical studies in developmental psychology focused on issues that derived from his theory, such as child-rearing and discipline practices, moral development, and childhood aggression.

Projection

The psychoanalytic approach recognizes the importance of motives, emotions, and fantasies in human behavior. Within this framework, human behavior springs at least as much from emotional needs as from reason. The theory suggests that underlying motives and wishes explain behaviors that otherwise might not seem logical. Many domains of mental activity, including fantasies, dreams, primary process thoughts and symbols, and defense mechanisms, influence how children and adolescents make meaning from their experiences. Through the construct of the unconscious, Freud provided a means for conceptualizing explanations for thoughts and behaviors that appear irrational, self-destructive, or contradictory. The idea that development involves efforts to find acceptable outlets for strong, often socially unacceptable impulses still guides therapeutic intervention with children, adolescents, and adults.

Another critical point is Freud's open recognition of the role of sexual impulses during childhood. Freud believed that a sexual relationship with a loving partner is important for healthy adult functioning. He concluded that sexual impulses have a direct outlet in adult behavior. Freud also recognized that children have sensual needs for stimulation and satisfaction, but they seemed to have no acceptable means to satisfy those needs. Today, we are more aware of a child's need for hugging, snuggling, and physical warmth with loving caregivers, but society still finds it difficult to acknowledge that young children have sexualized impulses. Childhood wishes and needs, repressed in the unconscious by defense mechanisms, guide behavior indirectly through symbolic expression and dreams or, in some cases, the symptoms of mental disorders. The acceptance and expression of sexual impulses continue to cause conflict in modern society. Controversies over sexual dysfunction, sexual abuse, rape by strangers and acquaintances, sexual harassment in the workplace, sexually transmitted diseases, contraception, abortion, infidelity, and homophobia reveal the difficulties Americans have in dealing with the expression of sexual impulses.

Links to Psychosocial Theory

Both psychosexual theory and psychosocial theory address basic, qualitative changes in self-understanding and social orientation over the period of infancy, childhood, and adolescence. Erikson, having been trained in psychoanalysis under Freud's daughter Anna, and mentored by Freud and other members of the Analytic Institute, readily acknowledged his intellectual ties to Freud's psychosexual theory. Freud and Erikson both posited five stages from infancy through adolescence. Psychosexual theory deals with conflicts that the child experiences in satisfying basic needs and impulses, especially

Human behavior influenced by emotional needs as much as reason.

sexual impulses during childhood.

Linda has an infant.

Linda is nervous.

Linda has loving feelings toward the infant.

Linda has angry feelings toward the infant.

Angry feelings are unacceptable to Linda.

She pushes angry feelings to the unconscious.

Linda becomes overly loving.

She feels better.

Reaction formation

sexual and aggressive impulses, within socially acceptable boundaries. Psychosocial theory expands this view by considering the broad range of social demands and expectations that confront children at each point in development, as well as the wide variety of competencies and social resources that children have for meeting those demands.

Of particular note is the difference between how Freud and Erikson conceptualized the period of middle childhood. Freud referred to this time as *latency,* and argued that it was a time of relative quiet with respect to sexual and aggressive drives when no new personality characteristics were emerging. Erikson emphasized these years as a time of critical mastery of ego skills, highlighting the social expectations for children during the period from ages 6 to 12 to begin developing competence in skills and knowledge that are valued by the culture.

Both psychosocial theory and psychosexual theory describe characteristics and functions of the ego system. However, psychosocial theory goes beyond childhood and adolescence, suggesting the direction for ego development in early, middle, and later adulthood. Psychosocial theory gives a greater role to the individual in guiding and shaping the direction of development through coping strategies that may redefine conflicts and identify new resources.

Sexual impulses and needs are central to psychosexual analysis. In the psychosocial framework, sexual behavior is considered within the complex network of social relations. Sex-role development, sexual relationships, sex-role identity, intimacy, marriage, and nurturing the marriage relationship are

all elements of psychosocial development that are addressed as the product of a complex synthesis of thoughts, wishes, behaviors, and social expectations at various stages of life.

Psychosexual theory suggests that basic issues of personal development are in place by adolescence. The results of this development influence the remainder of adult life in a person's defensive style, fixations, typical sexual behavior and sexual fantasies, and the strategies for sublimating sexual and aggressive impulses. Psychosocial theory suggests that development continues throughout life, as people learn skills from accomplishing new developmental tasks and achieve new social abilities. The radius of significant relationships expands, bringing new expectations and sources of social support. As new conflicts arise, they stimulate new growth, and new ego qualities emerge as a result of successfully coping with each new challenge.

Cognitive Developmental Theory — Piaget

Cognition is the process of organizing and making meaning of experience. Interpreting a statement, solving a problem, synthesizing information, and/or critically analyzing a complex task are all cognitive activities. Perhaps the most widely known and influential proponent of modern cognitive theory is Jean Piaget (see the Biographical Sketch on p. 103). His concepts provide the initial basis of this section. Recent interest in the social framework within which cognition develops has been stimulated by the work of L. S. Vygotsky. Several of his important contributions, introduced toward the end of this section, complement and expand the developmental perspective on how logical thought emerges and changes over the life course.

organizing & making meaning of experience

Basic Concepts in Piaget's Theory

According to Piaget, every organism strives to achieve equilibrium. *Equilibrium* is a balance of organized structures, whether motor, sensory, or cognitive. When structures are in equilibrium, they provide effective ways of interacting with the environment. Whenever changes in the organism or in the environment require a revision of the basic structures, they are thrown into disequilibrium (Piaget, 1978/1985). Piaget focused both on equilibrium with the environment, achieved through the formation of schemes (the structure or organization of action in thought) and operations (the mental manipulation of schemes and concepts) that form systematic, logical structures for comprehending and analyzing experience, and on equilibrium within the schemes and operations themselves.

strive to reach a state of equilibrium ⇒ effective interaction with the environment

Meet Bob.

He has strong unacceptable impulses.

He transforms the energy to accomplishment.

All in his head.

Sublimation

ADAPTATION
accomodation
assimilation

Equilibrium is achieved through *adaptation,* a process of gradually modifying existing schemes and operations in order to account for change or discrepancies between what is known and what is being experienced. Adaptation is a two-part process in which the continuity of existing schemes and the possibility of altering schemes interact. One part of adaptation is *assimilation*—the tendency to interpret new experiences in terms of an existing scheme. Assimilation contributes to the continuity of knowing. The second part of adaptation is *accommodation*—the tendency to modify familiar schemes in order to account for new dimensions of the object or event that are revealed through experience.

*B*iographical *S*ketch

Jean Piaget was born in Switzerland in 1896. Much like Darwin, he showed talent as a naturalist early in childhood. He observed and studied birds, fossils, and seashells, and at the age of 10 contributed a note on the albino sparrow to a scientific journal. While in high school, he began to publish papers describing the characteristics of mollusks. His work in this area was so impressive that he was invited to become the curator of the mollusk collection at the Geneva Museum. Piaget earned his doctorate from the University of Neuchatel in 1918; his dissertation was on the mollusks of Vallais. For cognitive psychology, the most direct consequence of Piaget's training as a naturalist was his sense that the principles of biology could be used to explain the evolution of knowledge. The observational skills that he had honed served him well as he developed his theory.

After several years of research, Piaget was able to define a set of problems and methods that guided his program of research and theory building. Between 1918 and 1921, he worked in the laboratory of Theodore Lipps, whose research focused on the study of empathy and aesthetics. He spent some time working at Eugene Bleuler's psychiatric clinic near Zurich, where he learned the techniques of psychiatric interviewing. He attended the Sorbonne in Paris, where he had the opportunity to work in the laboratory of Alfred Binet. Binet's laboratory was actually an elementary school in which studies on the nature of intelligence were being conducted. There, Piaget investigated children's responses to reasoning tests. He devised a clinical interview technique to determine how children arrive at their answers to reasoning problems. He became interested in the patterns of thought revealed by their incorrect answers. In essence, Piaget focused on how children think rather than on what they know.

Piaget's observations provided the basis for his first articles on the characteristics of children's thought processes. One of these articles brought him to the attention of the editor of *Psychological Archives,* who offered Piaget the job of director of studies at the Institute Jean-Jacques Rousseau in Geneva. There, he began to investigate the nature of children's moral judgments, theories about everyday events, and language. It was not until the period from 1923 to 1929, when Piaget conducted experiments and systematic observations with preverbal infants, that he began to unravel the basic mysteries of the development of logical thought. This work was significantly enriched by observations of his own children.

Piaget produced a massive quantity of research and theory about cognitive development, logic, the history of thought, education, and the theory of knowledge (epistemology). In 1969, the American Psychological Association gave Piaget the Distinguished Scientific Contribution Award for the work that had revolutionized our understanding of the nature of human knowledge and the development of intelligence. He continued his work on the nature of cognitive development until his death in 1980, at the age of 83.

*Jean Piaget
1896–1980*

*COGNITIVE
DEVELOPMENTAL
THEORY*

Piaget hypothesized that cognitive development occurs in four stages, each characterized by its own unique capacity for organizing and interpreting information. He attempted to explain the epigenesis of logical thought— the development of new structures for thought—not individual differences in knowledge and reasoning or differences resulting from cultural and subcultural experiences. At each new stage, the competence of earlier stages is not lost but instead is integrated into a qualitatively new approach to thinking and knowing.

The first stage, *sensorimotor intelligence,* begins at birth and lasts until approximately 18 months of age. This stage is characterized by the formation

Adaptation = assimilation
and accommodation

of increasingly complex sensory and motor schemes that allow infants to organize and exercise some control over their environment.

The second stage, *preoperational thought,* begins when the child learns a language, and ends about age 5 or 6. During this stage, children develop the tools for representing schemes symbolically through language, imitation, imagery, symbolic play, and symbolic drawing. Their knowledge is still very much tied to their own perceptions.

The third stage, *concrete operational thought,* begins about age 6 or 7 and ends in early adolescence, around age 11 or 12. During this stage, children begin to appreciate the logical necessity of certain causal relationships. They can manipulate categories, classification systems, and hierarchies in groups. They are more successful at solving problems that are clearly tied to physical reality than at generating hypotheses about purely philosophical or abstract concepts.

The final stage of cognitive development, *formal operational thought,* begins in adolescence and persists through adulthood. This level of thinking permits a person to conceptualize about many simultaneously interacting variables. It allows for the creation of a system of laws or rules that can be used for problem solving. Formal operational thought reflects the quality of intelligence on which science and philosophy are built.

At the start of each new stage, the child experiences a type of egocentrism or limitation in point of view. With experience, children gain new objectivity about their perspective and are able to step back from the situation and see it more flexibly. Each of the stages will be described in some detail in subsequent chapters.

Implications for Child Development

Piaget's theory has had an enormous influence on research on cognition. At the risk of oversimplifying, let us give a few of the implications of his theory for the study of child development. First, Piaget's theory suggests that cognition has its basis in the biological capacities of the human infant and that knowledge is derived from action. Second, discrepancies between existing schemes or concepts and contemporary experiences promote cognitive development. Encounters with all types of novelty, especially experiences that are moderately distinct rather than widely different from what is already known, are important for advancing new ideas and ways of organizing thought. Extending this concept, encounters with differences in opinions through discussion and reading are just as important in adolescence and adulthood as encounters with different types of sensory materials are in infancy and toddlerhood.

Third, Piaget believed that infants have the capacity for thinking and problem solving. Although infants do not make use of symbolic strategies, they are able to establish certain logical connections between means and ends that guide their problem-solving efforts. Fourth, infants, toddlers, and school-age children think in different ways, and the ways that they think are different from the ways adults think. This does not mean that their thinking is unorganized or illogical, but the same principles of logic that typically govern adult thought do not govern the thinking of young children. Fifth, beginning with the period of concrete operations, children can approach problems using many of the principles that are fundamental to scientific reasoning. They can also begin to reason about their reasoning, introducing the importance of *metacognition* or the many strategies that guide the way that people organize in order to think more clearly and effectively. Sixth, thinking about the social world is regulated by many of the same principles as thinking about objects in the physical world. As children learn about the principles that govern objects and physical relationships, they are also learning about themselves and others.

Vygotsky's Concepts of Cognitive Development

Piaget envisioned cognitive development as a process in which children investigate, explore, discover, and rediscover meaning in their world. Although Piaget acknowledged the significance of social factors, especially parents and peers, in the cognitive process, his theory focuses on individuals interacting with their environment. In contrast, Vygotsky, often referred to as a *contextualist,* argued that development can only be understood within a social framework. Vygotsky (1962, 1978) proposed analyzing *the child's activity in a setting* in order to study cognitive development, because the child and the culture are intricately interwoven through the process of social interaction. New levels of understanding emerge from interpersonal interactions between two individuals, initially the infant and a caregiving adult. Eventually, interpersonal collaboration becomes internalized to form the child's internal mental framework. Through continuous interaction with others, especially adults and older children, a child revises and advances his or her levels of understanding.

> New understanding, gained through collaboration, is a product of the child's original understanding, the partner's different understanding, the child's difficulties with the task and the ways they are expressed in the course of their interaction, the partner's response to those difficulties, and so on. Since this process evolves over time, and each person's responses depend on what the other has previously done or said, the outcome is one that cannot be attributed to either one or the other. The unit of analysis extends beyond the individual. (Tudge & Winterhoff, 1993, 76)

[handwritten margin note: individuals interacting with their environment]

Three of the central concepts in Vygotsky's theory are introduced here: culture as a mediator of cognitive structuring, movement from the intermental to the intramental, and the zone of proximal development.

Vygotsky argues that cognitive development can only be understood in the context of culture. Think for a moment about the many ways that culture shapes the content and processes of thought. A simple conversation between a mother or older sibling and a young child includes layers of cultural beliefs. Such daily interaction involves beliefs about children's thoughts; the skills they are encouraged to attain; the sources of information that are available to them; the ways that information is shared; the kinds of activities that children, adolescents, and adults are permitted to engage in; and the limits that are placed on participation in certain settings or forms of interaction (Miller, 1993).

Of the many elements of culture that shape cognition, one that was of special interest to Vygotsky was the invention of tools and signs. Technical *tools* like plows, cars, and weapons, and *signs,* sometimes referred to as psychological tools, like symbolic systems, counting systems, and strategies for remembering, modify the child's relationship to the environment. Through the use of tools, humans change the way that they organize and think about the world. Vygotsky viewed tools as a means through which the human mind is shaped and modified over the course of history.

Perhaps contrary to common sense, Vygotsky argued that high-level mental functions begin in external activity that is gradually reconstructed and internalized. He gave the example of pointing. Vygotsky claimed that initially an infant stretches a hand toward an object that is out of reach, making grasping motions with the fingers. This movement is directed to the object. But as soon as the mother recognizes that the child wants the object and satisfies the child's desire, the child begins to modify the reaching and grasping motion into a socially meaningful gesture—pointing. The mother's understanding of the child's gesture and the intermental coordination between mother and infant result in an intramental process for the infant, an understanding of the special relationship—in this case, between the desired goal, the mother as mediator, and pointing as a meaningful sign.

Taking the idea of internalization a step farther, Vygotsky offered the concept of the *zone of proximal development* as the immediate framework through which learning and development converge. The zone is "the distance between the actual developmental level as determined by independent problem solving and the level of potential development as determined through problem solving under adult guidance or in collaboration with more capable peers" (Vygotsky, 1978, 86).

We have all experienced a situation in which we were unable to solve a task by ourselves, but with the assistance and advice of someone else we were able to achieve success. The typical effort of a parent helping a child put together a jigsaw puzzle by suggesting strategies, like selecting all the straight-edged pieces first to make the border, or sorting pieces by color, is an example of how learning takes place within the zone. Vygotsky suggests that the level of functioning that a child can reach when taking advantage of the guidance of others reflects the functions that are in the process of maturation, as compared to those that have already matured. Learning within the zone of proximal development sets into motion the reorganization and internalization of existing developmental competence which then become synthesized at a new and higher intramental level.

With adult guidance, children can work on more complicated projects and solve more difficult problems than they might on their own.

Implications for Child Development

Vygotsky's theory suggests that the boundaries between the individual and the environment are much less clear than one might infer from most other theories of human development. In fact, he emphasizes the guiding role of social interaction and culture in shaping and orienting cognition, thus bringing the study of cognitive development into much greater harmony with many of the concepts of psychosocial theory than might be seen in Piaget's framework.

Several specific implications of Vygotsky's work can be inferred. First, the mental structures and functioning of people raised in a specific culture will be different from those raised in other cultures, just as the thinking of a toddler is different from the thinking of an adult. Second, because of the way that intermental experiences and networks structure intramental events, one's family and others who influence and control the structure of early learning and problem-solving experiences will also influence the structure of one's thinking. Third, individuals can promote their own cognitive development by seeking interaction with others who can help them develop higher levels of functioning within their zone of proximal development.

Links to Psychosocial Theory

Both cognitive developmental theory and psychosocial theory conceptualize development as a product of ongoing interactions between the individual and the environment. For both theories, psychological development is a result of some discrepancies, referred to as disequilibrium in cognitive developmental theory and as psychosocial crises in psychosocial theory. Piaget's theory, like psychosocial theory, proposes stages of development, with each stage growing from and integrating achievements of earlier stages. Piaget considered development in four stages that covered the period from infancy through adolescence. Erikson outlined these same years in five stages, drawing a greater

bluring of boundaries between individual and environment

culture specific

dev't a product of interaction between individual and environment.

distinction in functioning between early and middle childhood than did Piaget. Although contemporary scholars are addressing issues of changes in cognitive functioning during adulthood, Piaget's theory does not offer any hypotheses about the qualitative changes that might follow the period of formal operational reasoning, whereas psychosocial theory makes clear predictions about the direction of ego development in early, middle, and later life.

Perhaps the most significant distinction between the theories is their focus or range of applicability. Piaget's focus, as well as that of Vygotsky, is on the cognitive domain, especially the process of knowledge acquisition and logical reasoning. The meaning that a child makes of a situation depends largely on the stage of mental development that has been attained. Feelings, social relationship, and self-understanding are viewed as cognitive schemes that are constructed with the same logic that the child applies to understanding objects. Psychosocial theory considers the emotional domain as a pervasive filter through which a child organizes and interprets experience. The nature of the resolution of each psychosocial crisis guides a child's ability to adapt and mature within society. As a psychotherapist, Erikson was aware of the many instances in which one's reasoning abilities and problem-solving skills were disrupted by strong emotional conflicts, unconscious wishes and fears, and conflicting social demands. He described the broad array of outlooks and coping strategies, such as trust and mistrust, hope and withdrawal, that determine the direction of psychological development from one period of life to the next. For example, feelings of hope or hopelessness influence a child's level of enthusiasm or caution in new learning situations. The nature of one's cognition during any stage is influenced by one's psychosocial orientation.

Vygotsky's theory provides an important link between Piaget's emphasis on the maturation of logical reasoning and psychosocial theory's emphasis on the maturation of self in society by focusing on the interpersonal nature of cognition. The idea of a zone of proximal development relates closely to the construct of the radius of significant relationships, highlighting the unique interpersonal and cultural context of all aspects of knowing, whether it is knowing about the logic of the physical world or the logic of relationships.

Theories of Learning

Learning theorists have proposed mechanisms to account for the relatively permanent changes in behavior that occur as a result of experience. The reason that humans have such an extensive capacity to adapt to changes in the environment is that they are so well equipped to learn. Four theories of learning that have made significant contributions to the study of human development are reviewed below: (1) classical conditioning, (2) operant conditioning, (3) social learning, and (4) cognitive behaviorism.

Classical Conditioning – PAVLOV

The principles of *classical conditioning,* sometimes referred to as Pavlovian conditioning, were developed by Ivan Pavlov (1927/1960). Classical conditioning characterizes the types of learning that occur when events take place close together in time and thereby acquire similar meaning. In much of his work, Pavlov used the salivary reflex as a measure of response to various stimuli.

[handwritten margin note:] Cognitive developmental theory focuses on the acquisition of knowledge & logical reasoning

He carried out an extensive body of research in an effort to understand the conditions under which stimuli in the environment other than food would elicit or inhibit salivation.

The model for classical conditioning is illustrated in Figure 4.1. The basic elements in a classical conditioning experiment are the neutral stimulus (NS), the neutral response (NR), the unconditioned stimulus (US), the unconditioned response (UR), the conditioned stimulus (CS), and the conditioned response (CR). Before conditioning, the bell is a *neutral stimulus* (NS). It elicits a response of interest or attention, but nothing more (*neutral response*). The sight and smell of food are *unconditioned stimuli* (US) that elicit salivation, the *unconditioned response* (UR). During conditioning trials, the bell is rung shortly before the food appears. The dog is judged to have been conditioned when it salivates at the sound of the bell, even before the food is presented, because the bell is now associated with food. The bell, therefore, comes to control the salivation response and is known as the *conditioned stimulus* (CS). Salivation that occurs in response to the bell alone is called the *conditioned response* (CR). You may have experienced a conditioned response when you looked at your watch or the clock and realized that it was near dinner time. Often, just knowing that it is almost the time when you usually eat is a stimulus for feeling hunger pangs.

Conditioning does not take place randomly between any two events linked in time. A conditioned response is established only when there is a "meaningful" relationship between the CS and the US. They must occur together many times before conditioning is established. Furthermore, the CS itself is not totally neutral. A visual stimulus such as a colored light will prompt visual orienting, for instance, whereas an auditory stimulus may simply increase attention or arousal. In a conditioning experiment, the learner builds many associations simultaneously. Although a particular experiment may focus on establishing a link between one CS and one US, the learner will build links among many elements of the environment—its visual, auditory, and olfactory components, including the US. Pavlovian conditioning provides a model for understanding how multiple associations, sometimes stored at the unconscious level, can be established and triggered in the process of concept formation, memory, and problem solving (McClelland & Rumelhart, 1986; Rumelhart & McClelland, 1986).

Implications for Child Development

Classical conditioning can account for a great deal of the associational learning that occurs throughout life. When a specific symbol is paired with an image, emotional reaction, or object, that symbol takes on new meaning. The associations that are made through classical conditioning may involve labels and concepts, but they do not necessarily require language skills. During infancy and toddlerhood, a variety of positive and negative emotional reactions are associated with people, objects, and environments. An adult's reactions to the taste of a certain type of food or the feel of a particular material may be the result of conditioned learning that originated in childhood. Similarly, fears can be the results of classical conditioning. Many people recall at least one frightening experience from childhood, such as nearly drowning, being hit, or falling from the top of a slide. The association of fear or pain with a specific target may lead to systematic avoidance of that object, setting, or situation for the rest of one's life.

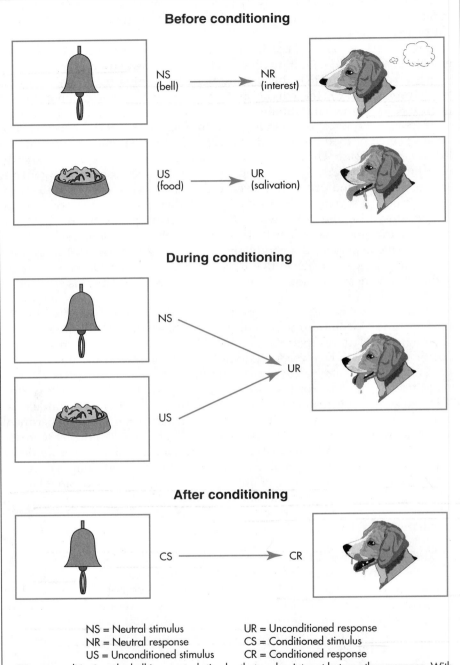

FIGURE 4.1
Classical conditioning

*B*iographical *S*ketch

Burrhus Frederic Skinner was born in 1904 in Susquehanna, Pennsylvania. As a child he liked to build such mechanical creations as roller-skate scooters, steerable wagons, and rafts. He was an eager explorer and enjoyed biking and canoeing with his friends along the Susquehanna River.

Skinner studied English literature at Hamilton College and graduated in 1926. After graduation, he tried to develop a writing career. Despite an encouraging letter from the poet Robert Frost, Skinner came to the conclusion that he had nothing important to say.

In 1928, Skinner enrolled in the graduate program in psychology at Harvard, where he studied animal behavior. He described his life as a graduate student as highly focused: "I would rise at six, study until breakfast, go to classes, laboratories, and libraries with no more than fifteen minutes unscheduled during the day, study until exactly nine o'clock at night and go to bed. I saw no movies or plays, seldom went to concerts, had scarcely any dates, and read nothing but psychology and physiology" (1967, 398).

Skinner received his Ph.D. in 1931 and continued at Harvard as a research fellow for five more years. He began his faculty career at the University of Minnesota, where he wrote *The Behavior of Organisms* (1938). During World War II, he worked on a research project to train pigeons to pilot torpedoes and bombs. Although this particular project was never implemented, Skinner continued to conduct much of his research with pigeons. He created unique experimental equipment that allowed pigeons to make complex responses. He even taught pigeons to play table tennis! After two years as a Guggenheim fellow, Skinner became chairman of the psychology department at Indiana University. In 1947, he returned to Harvard, where he remained until his retirement.

A major focus of Skinner's work was his empirical approach to understanding behavior. He searched for explanations that were tied to observed relationships between behaviors and their consequences. In the process, he devised a number of remarkable inventions, including the Skinner box, an apparatus in which animal behaviors could be modified, monitored, and recorded; a temperature-controlled mechanical crib that was intended to provide the ideal environment for an infant; and the teaching machine, which provided step-by-step instructions and immediate reinforcement. In addition to his experimental contributions to the field of learning, his utopian novel, *Walden Two* (1948), and his extension of behaviorist principles to social criticism in *Beyond Freedom and Dignity* (1971) provided strong arguments for the powerful role of the environment in determining and controlling behavior.

B. F. Skinner
1904–1990

OPERANT
CONDITIONING

Environment determines and controls behavior

Operant Conditioning ~SKINNER~

Operant conditioning emphasizes the role of repetition and the consequences of behavior in learning. In this type of learning process, behaviors are strengthened when they are followed by positive consequences and weakened when they are followed by negative consequences. One of the best-known American learning theorists, B. F. Skinner, developed many of the principles of operant conditioning (see the Biographical Sketch above).

Skinner's work focused on the modification of voluntary behaviors as a result of the consequences of those behaviors. In the traditional operant conditioning experiment, the researcher selects a response in advance and then waits until the subject makes the desired response (or at least a partial

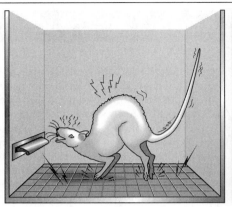

(a) Electric shock produces pain.

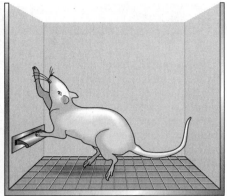

(b) Pressing the bar ends the shock and stops the pain.

Negative reinforcement

response). Then the experimenter presents a reinforcement. *Reinforcement* is operationally defined as any stimulus that makes a repetition of the response more likely.

There are two kinds of reinforcers. Some, such as food and smiles, increase the rate of response when they are present. These are called *positive reinforcers*. Others, such as electric shock, increase the rate of response when they are removed. These are called *negative reinforcers*. Suppose that a mother gets upset whenever she hears her baby cry. She may try a number of things to stop the crying—rocking, feeding, talking, changing the baby's diapers. If one of these behaviors causes the baby to stop crying, it is reinforced. The mother is more likely to try that behavior the next time. The baby's cry is a negative reinforcer because when it stops, the specific caregiving response is strengthened. In Box 4.1 we discuss the role of reinforcement in the establishment of superstitious behaviors.

Operant conditioning refers to the development of behavior patterns that are under the learner's voluntary control (Davey & Cullen, 1988). The person can choose to make a response or not, depending on the consequences associated with the behavior. In many instances, however, the behavior to be learned is one that has never been performed before. How can you be reinforced for making a complex response if you have never done it?

One means of developing a new complex response is *shaping*. Here, the response is broken down into its major components. At first, a response that is only an approximation of one element of the behavior is reinforced. Gradually, new elements of the behavior are added, and a reinforcement is given only when two or three components of the response are linked together. Once the person makes a complete response, earlier approximations are no longer reinforced. Parents often use the shaping process to teach their young children such complicated behaviors as using the toilet, practicing good table manners, and caring for their belongings.

[handwritten margin note:] positive and negative reinforcers

[handwritten margin note:] Operant conditioning effects learned behaviors or behavior under voluntary control.

BOX 4.1

Operant Conditioning and Superstitions

Do you have a "lucky" shirt? Do you avoid walking under ladders? Have you ever noticed that some baseball players talk to the ball before they pitch or swing the bat in a certain way? All these oddities are instances of superstitious behavior. We can usually see a logical connection between a behavior and its intended consequence: We wash our hands in order to remove dirt; we put on jackets in order to stay warm on a chilly day. Some behaviors, however, are repeated even though they are not clearly tied to some observable consequence.

According to the operant conditioning view, superstitious behavior is the result of the accidental pairing of a behavior and a reinforcement. Suppose that just before a batter gets up to bat, he knocks the mud from his cleats. On this turn at bat, he hits a

triple and scores the winning runs for his team. The next time he gets up to bat, he may knock the mud from his cleats on the chance that it might help him hit a triple again. If the behavior is followed by a positive consequence every once in a while, that will be enough to maintain it. Here, we see an intermittent reinforcement schedule in action.

Some people fear that something undesirable will happen if they do not perform some behavior—that they will have bad luck, say, if they fail to hold their breath as they pass a cemetery. They reduce the fear by performing the ritual. The fear reduction in itself is reinforcing, and the ritual continues to be performed. Behaviors that appear illogical to an observer may be tied to a reinforcement history that maintains them.

Much research has been devoted to determining which conditions of learning result in the strongest, longest-lasting habits. *Schedule of reinforcement* refers to the frequency and regularity with which reinforcements are given. A new response is conditioned rapidly if reinforcement is given on every learning trial. This schedule is called *continuous reinforcement*. Responses that are established under conditions of continuous reinforcement are very vulnerable to *extinction;* that is, if the reinforcement is removed for several trials, performance deteriorates rapidly (see Figure 4.2).

Some schedules vary the amount of time or the number of trials between reinforcements. This procedure is called *intermittent reinforcement*. The learner responds on many occasions when no reinforcement is provided, but does receive occasional reinforcement. Such schedules result in the most durable learning. Intermittent reinforcement lengthens the time that an operant behavior remains in the learner's repertoire after reinforcement has been permanently discontinued (Ferster & Culbertson, 1982).

A variable reinforcement schedule is probably truer to real life. It would be very difficult for anyone to learn a behavior if every instance of it had to be reinforced. Children often exhibit a new response when no caregivers are present or when they are attending to other matters, or children may exhibit the response in the context of other behaviors that are followed by a negative consequence. Research on operant conditioning demonstrates that conditions of intermittent reinforcement are precisely those under which the longest-lasting habits are formed.

Implications for Child Development

The principles of operant conditioning apply whenever the environment sets up priorities for behavior and conditional rewards or punishments for approximating a desired behavior. People change whenever their operant

Rewards or punishments based on behavior.

FIGURE 4.2

Continuous versus intermittent reinforcement. This figure shows runway speeds for two groups of rats once reinforcement has been discontinued. One group has previously been reinforced on every trial; the other has been reinforced on only 30% of the trials. Running speed declines rapidly for the group trained under continuous reinforcement. The group that has been trained under intermittent reinforcement continues to run quickly for the first 10 trials and remains above the 100% group for all 20 trials.

Source: Adapted from H. Gleitman (1986), *Psychology.* New York: Norton, p. 111. Copyright © 1991, 1986 by W. W. Norton & Company, Inc. Reprinted by permission of W. W. Norton & Company, Inc.

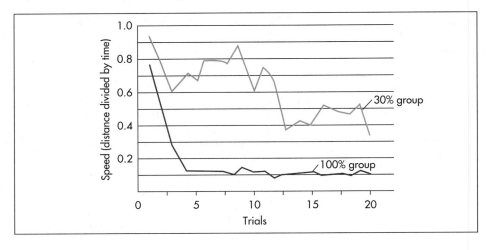

behaviors adapt to changes in environmental contingencies. The environment controls the process of adaptation by establishing and modifying contingencies (Skinner, 1987). Behavior can be modified in the desired direction as long as the person who is guiding the conditioning has control over the distribution of valued rewards. These principles are especially applicable to the learning that takes place during toddlerhood (2 and 3) and early school age (4 to 6). Children of these ages are unlikely to be able to analyze the existing framework of reinforcement. Once individuals can interpret a reinforcement schedule, they may choose to adapt to it, resist it, or redefine the environment in order to discover new sources of reinforcement. In Notebook Page 4.2 we ask you to take some time to consider your own reinforcement history.

There is no doubt that operant conditioning occurs often throughout life. Although one typically thinks of adults establishing the reinforcement schedules that shape children's behavior, it is also clear that a child's behavior is often a reinforcement for an adult. A child's smile, laughter, enthusiasm, or attention is often a reward that modifies a parent's or a teacher's behavior.

Social Learning

The concept of *social learning* evolved from an awareness that much learning takes place as a result of observing and imitating other people's behavior (Bandura & Walters, 1963). Changes in behavior can occur without being linked to a specific pattern of positive or negative reinforcement. They can also occur without numerous opportunities for trial-and-error practice. A child can watch someone perform a task or say a new expression and imitate that behavior accurately on the first try.

The role of *imitation* is the central process in resolving the crisis of autonomy versus shame and doubt in toddlerhood. At that age, imitation provides a mechanism for the rapid acquisition of new behaviors. Think about all the things a 3-year-old child can say or do. It would be impossible for parents deliberately to teach a child every single behavior; they would have no time left to eat, sleep, or work. Children must acquire much of their knowledge by observing and imitating others. Adults provide the *models* for many activities. They express feelings, voice attitudes, perform tasks, and espouse their moral values. By observing and imitating many of these behaviors, children become socialized into their family's and community's way of life.

learning takes place from watching others

Imitation

Models

Children imitate models
who have power and
control resources.

Vicarious reinforcement

Early research in social learning theory attempted to identify conditions that determine whether a child will imitate a model (Bandura, 1971, 1977, 1986). Children have been found to imitate aggressive, altruistic, helping, and stingy models. They are most likely to imitate models who are prestigious, who control resources, or who themselves are rewarded. Bandura and Walters (1963) suggested that children not only observe the behaviors carried out by a model but also watch what *happens* to the model. When the model's behavior is rewarded, the behavior is more likely to be imitated; when the model's behavior is punished, the behavior is more likely to be avoided. When bad behaviors go unpunished, they too are likely to be imitated. This process is called *vicarious reinforcement*. Through observational learning, a child can learn a behavior and also acquire the motivation to perform or resist performing that behavior, depending on what is learned about the associated consequences. Thus, observational learning can hold the key to self-regulation and the internalization of standards for resisting certain behaviors as well as for enacting behaviors (Grusec, 1992). In Notebook Page 4.3 we ask you to think about behaviors you may have imitated from significant models during three periods of your life.

Recent directions in social learning theory have added an increasingly cognitive orientation (Bandura, 1989). Through observational learning, the child becomes acquainted with the general concepts of the situation as well

Your Reinforcement History

A positive reinforcement is any stimulus that makes the repetition of a response more likely. A negative reinforcement is any stimulus that makes a repetition of a response more likely when the stimulus is removed.

Reflect on your childhood experiences. Think of three examples of deliberate efforts that someone made to alter your behavior through positive reinforcements. Perhaps your parents offered you a special treat if you cleaned up your room, or they let you stay up late to watch a TV program if you finished your homework. For each example, answer the following questions:

1. What response was being reinforced?

_____

_____

2. What was the reinforcement?

_____

_____

3. Who was controlling the reinforcement?

_____

_____

_____

4. Do you still perform this response?

_____

_____

_____

5. Are you still reinforced for this response? If so, what reinforcements continue to influence your behavior?

_____

_____

Now shift your focus to examples of negative reinforcements. Can you recall any deliberate efforts that someone made to alter your behavior through the use of negative reinforcements? Maybe your parents kept scolding you until you said that you were sorry. Or maybe you negatively reinforced your parents by whining and complaining until they bought you the toy you wanted.

1. What response was being negatively reinforced?

_____

_____

2. What was the negative reinforcement?

_____

_____

3. Who was controlling the reinforcement?

_____

_____

4. Do you still perform this response?

_____

_____

_____

5. Do you still experience negative reinforcement? If so, what kinds of negative reinforcements continue to influence your behavior?

_____

_____

_____

Can you recall some examples when a positive or negative reinforcement occurred accidentally? In other words, do you remember a time when a response was strengthened as a result of positive or negative reinforcement, but no one was deliberately trying to modify your behavior? This might have been the beginning of a superstitious ritual.

According to social learning theory, this girl's hesitance to dive into the pool is partly due to her observations of what happened to others in similar situations, as well as her own past experiences.

watch
learn
remember
recall
↓↓
requirements
expectations

as the specific behaviors. Direct reinforcement or nonreinforcement provides one type of information about how to behave in a certain situation. In addition, children watch others, learn about the consequences of their actions, remember what others have told or shown them, and recall what they have read or learned about the situation. Over time, a child begins to form a symbolic representation for the situation, the required behaviors, and the expected outcomes. A child may learn that in one teacher's classroom it is appropriate to ask lots of questions and offer suggestions for ways of solving problems, while in another teacher's classroom it is better to remain quiet, take notes, and not try to engage the teacher. The rules for behavior in each setting are abstracted from observations of others, consequences following one's own behavior in the past, and understanding the demands in the immediate situation.

Implications for Child Development

The principles of social learning theory are assumed to operate in the same way throughout life. The concept of social learning highlights the relevance of models' behavior in guiding the behavior of others. These models may be parents or grandparents, older siblings, peers, teachers, employers, entertainment stars, or sports heroes. Since new role models may be encountered at any life stage, new learning through the process of observational learning is always possible. Exposure to a certain array of models and a certain pattern of rewards or punishments results in some behaviors being imitated and others being inhibited. The similarity in behavior among people of the same ages reflects their exposure to a common history of models, rewards, and punishments. Recognition of the potential impact one has as a model for others, especially in the role of parent, teacher, clinician, counselor, or supervisor ought to impart a certain level of self-conscious monitoring about the behaviors that one exhibits and the strategies that one employs in the presence of children.

The Influence of Models on the Formation of New Behaviors

Social learning theory emphasizes that new behaviors can be acquired through the observation and imitation of models. This process can occur at any point in the life span. Focus on three periods in your life: later elementary school (grades 3 through 6), high school (grades 9 through 12), and the present. For each period, identify a person who was (is) important to you—someone you respected or idolized. Then try to recall two or three characteristics of that person that you may have imitated—it might be clothing, hairstyle, tone of voice, expressions, or any of a wide range of attitudes or behaviors.

Age Period	Person Who Served as Model	What Was Imitated
Elementary school		
High school		
Present		

Think back to the person and behaviors you mentioned in the two earlier periods. Do you still admire or idolize this person? Do you still exhibit the attitudes and behaviors you imitated at those times? At present, are you a model for any children, adolescents, or adults? What behaviors of yours have you seen them imitate?

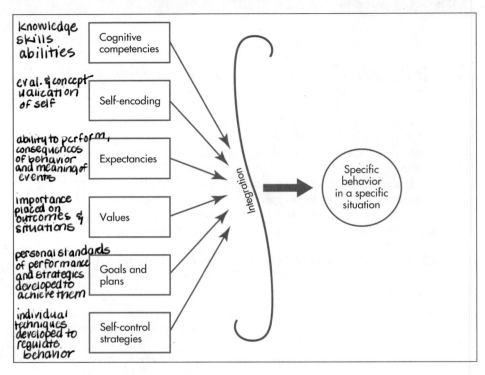

knowledge
skills
abilities

eval. & conceptualization of self

ability to perform, consequences of behavior and meaning of events

importance placed on outcomes & situations

personal standards of performance and strategies developed to achieve them

individual techniques developed to regulate behavior

FIGURE 4.3

Six cognitive dimensions that influence behavior

Internal mental activities that influence behavior

MISCHEL

SIX COGNITIVE FACTORS

Cognitive Behaviorism

One objection that has been raised frequently against classical and operant conditioning as theories of learning is that they have no language or concepts to describe events that occur in the learner's mind. *Cognitive behaviorism* studies the many internal mental activities that influence behavior. Edward Tolman (1932/1967, 1948) discussed the notion of an intervening set of responses that influence learning. He believed that a learner develops a *cognitive map,* which is an internal mental representation of the learning environment. Individuals who perform a specific task in a certain environment attend primarily to that task, but they also form a representation of the rest of the setting. The map includes expectations about the reward system in operation, the existing spatial relationships, and the behaviors accorded highest priority. An individual's performance in a situation represents only part of the learning that has occurred. The fact that people respond to changes in the environment indicates the existence of a complex mental map.

According to Walter Mischel (1973, 1979), at least six cognitive factors must be taken into account in understanding a person's behavior: cognitive competencies, self-encoding, expectancies, values, goals and plans, and self-control strategies (see Figure 4.3). *Cognitive competencies* consist of knowledge, skills, and abilities. *Self-encoding* is the evaluation and conceptualization of information about the self. An interesting finding in this area is that depressed people tend to evaluate themselves more realistically than those who are not depressed. Mischel (1979) argues that "to feel good about ourselves we may have to judge ourselves more kindly than we are judged" (p. 752). In other words, most people who are not chronically depressed may bias their evaluations of themselves in a self-enhancing way.

Expectancies refer to expectations about one's ability to perform, the consequences of one's behavior, and the meaning of events in one's environment.

Values consist of the relative importance that one places on the outcomes of situations. One person may value high levels of task performance, while another may value success in social situations. One's behavior in a situation is influenced by how one values its possible outcomes. *Goals and plans* are personal standards of performance and the strategies that one develops for achieving them. Obviously, individuals differ in their goals and plans; these differences lead to considerable variation in behavior. *Self-control strategies* are the techniques that an individual develops for regulating his or her own behavior. The more aware we are of the effects of stimuli on our behavior, the more effectively we may overcome, channel, or eliminate their influence. Of these six areas, expectancies has received considerable attention among those interested in learning and performance.

Implications for Child Development

Cognitive behaviorism suggests that the full range of learning processes, including classical conditioning, operant conditioning, and observational learning, enables a learner to acquire cognitive structures that influence subsequent learning and performance. We might say that the learner acquires an outlook on the learning situation that may influence the feeling of familiarity with the task, motivation to undertake it, optimism about performing successfully, and strategies for approaching the task. In addition to everything that a parent, a teacher, or a supervisor does to structure a learning environment, one must always take into account the outlook that the learner brings to the task. Differences in expectancies, self-control strategies, values, and goals all influence the way children approach a learning situation.

Summary of Learning Theories

All four of the learning theories contribute valuable insights into human behavior (see Table 4.1). Classical conditioning can account for the extensive network of associations that are formed between symbols and stimuli, enduring

---

TABLE 4.1

Four Learning Processes

Process	Description
Classical conditioning	When two events occur very close together in time, they acquire similar meanings and produce similar responses.
Operant conditioning	Responses that are under voluntary control can be strengthened or eliminated depending on the consequences associated with making the response.
Social learning	New responses can be acquired through observation and imitation of models.
Cognitive behaviorism	In addition to new responses, the learner acquires a mental representation of the situation, including expectations about rewards and punishments, which responses are appropriate, and the physical and social settings in which the behavior occurs.

emotional reactions to one's environment, and the organization of learning associated with reflexive patterns. Operant conditioning emphasizes the acquisition of behavioral patterns on the basis of their consequences. Social learning theory adds the important element of imitation. People learn new behaviors by watching others. Through social learning, individuals develop an understanding of the social consequences of behavior leading to new patterns of behavioral expression and self-regulation. Finally, cognitive behaviorism suggests that a complex set of expectations, goals, and values can be treated as behavior and can influence performance. Although information or skills can be learned, they will not be expressed in behavior unless expectations about the self and the environment justify their enactment. This perspective highlights the person's capacity to guide the performance of new learning.

Links to Psychosocial Theory

[handwritten margin note: learning theories provide insight into mechanisms of adaptation. -emphasize significance of immediate environment in directing growth]

The learning theories and psychosocial theory operate on different levels of abstraction. The learning theories provide insight into the laws that govern many of the basic mechanisms of adaptation. Psychosocial theory assumes that growth and change continue throughout the life span; however, the theory does not attempt to account for the exact processes by which new behaviors, new coping strategies, or new ego strengths are acquired. The learning theories provide a battery of explanations for the ways that the patterns of daily events might shape the direction of adaptation and growth. They offer insight into the processes through which the broad social environment becomes internalized and translated into habits, preferences, and expectations. The learning theories emphasize the significance of the immediate environment in directing the course of growth. They speak less to the epigenetic process to which Erikson referred when he described a predictable pattern in the nature and direction of development over the life span.

Cultural Theory

The concept of culture, although defined in a wide variety of ways by anthropologists, sociologists, psychologists, and political scientists, refers here to the learned systems of meanings and patterns of behaviors that are shared by a group of people and transmitted from one generation to the next. *Physical culture* encompasses the objects, technologies, structures, tools, and other artifacts of a culture. *Social culture* encompasses norms, roles, beliefs, values, rites, and customs (Herkovits, 1948; Triandis et al., 1980; Rohner, 1984; Betancourt & Lopez, 1993).

On a general level, culture has been described as a *worldview*, a way of making meaning of the relationships, situations, and objects encountered in daily life. Basic ideas such as whether people are considered to be in control of nature or a part of it; who is included in the definition of family; what characteristics are considered signs of mental health or mental illness; which acts are construed as hostile and which as nurturing; which aspects of the environment are considered dangerous and which are valued—all these and many other mental constructions are shaped by the culture into which one is born (Kagitcibasi, 1990). Culture guides development, not only through encounters with certain objects, roles, and settings, but through the meanings linked to actions.

*B*iographical *S*ketch

Ruth Benedict was born in New York City in 1887. Her father died very suddenly when Ruth was 21 months old. Her mother, now responsible for Ruth and a younger sister Margery, returned for a while to live with her parents on a farm in central New York state. The mother taught school and then, in 1899, settled as a staff member of the Buffalo Public Library on a salary of $60 per month.

Ruth suffered from two major childhood crises: hearing loss due to a severe attack of measles and emotional trauma associated with her father's death and her mother's extreme, prolonged grief. Ruth withdrew into an elaborate private world which was populated by beautiful dead people like her father and Christ, and an imaginary companion. In her real world, she was very uninvolved, even alienated from others.

Fortunately, her intellectual abilities earned her a scholarship to a preparatory school in Buffalo and then a place at Vassar where she studied English literature and graduated Phi Beta Kappa in 1909. Her early adult years were marked by confusion and depression. She worked as a social worker and a teacher, and then began an ambitious writing project that she never finished. In 1914, she married Stanley Benedict who became professor of biochemistry at Cornell University. After a brief period of happiness in this marriage, Benedict became frustrated by the lack of meaning and direction in her life. In 1919, she enrolled in the New School for Social Research and discovered the field of anthropology. She studied anthropology at Columbia University under Franz Boas and completed her Ph.D. in 1923. Her dissertation focused on the concept of the guardian spirit among North American Indians. Benedict maintained a strong interest in the contributions of a culture's literature, religions, language, and aesthetic dimensions to the overall impact of the culture on its members. She expressed her interest in the religious and aesthetic dimensions of life through her poetry, which she wrote under a pseudonym until the early 1930s.

Benedict served as an assistant to Boas on a year-to-year appointment from 1923 to 1931, when Boas finally arranged for her to be an assistant professor at Columbia University. At that point, her own theoretical analysis of patterns of culture and the ways different cultures have of defining and valuing certain personality types began to take shape. *Patterns of Culture* was published in 1934 and served as the primary introduction to the field of cultural anthropology for the next 25 years.

During the war, Benedict wrote a widely distributed pamphlet, *The Races of Mankind*. She conducted extensive research on contemporary cultures including Rumania, Thailand, and Japan while she worked for the Office of War Information. After the war, she used this research in a powerful book on Japanese culture, *The Chrysanthemum and the Sword* (1946). This achievement was followed by receipt of a large grant from the Office of Naval Research to study contemporary cultures. In the 1920s, Benedict could hardly get a salary or a faculty appointment, but in the 1940s she was the director of one of the largest projects that American anthropologists had ever undertaken. In 1947–1948, she was president of the American Anthropological Association, becoming the first woman to serve as the leading figure of an American learned society. In 1948, Columbia made her a full professor. She died that fall of heart disease.

Ruth Benedict
1887–1948

CROSS-CULTURAL THEORY

CULTURAL DETERMINISM
-psychological
experiences shaped
by cultural group.

The principle of *cultural determinism,* first described by Ruth Benedict (see the Biographical Sketch above), suggests that the individual's psychological experiences are shaped by the expectations, resources, and challenges posed by one's specific cultural group. The extent to which development is viewed as distinct stages of life depends on the degree to which socialization

Traditions, such as First Communion, are used to mark the transition to a new status within age-graded societies.

within a culture is characterized by continuity or discontinuity. You are asked to explore this idea further in Notebook Page 4.4.

Continuity is found when a child is given information and responsibilities that apply directly to his or her adult behavior. For example, Margaret Mead (1928/1950) observed that, in Samoan society, girls of 6 or 7 years of age commonly took care of their younger siblings. As they grew older, their involvement in the caregiving role increased; however, the behaviors that were expected of them were not substantially changed.

Discontinuity is found when a child is either barred from activities that are open only to adults or forced to "unlearn" information or behaviors that are accepted in children but considered inappropriate for adults. The change from expectations of virginity before marriage to expectations of sexual responsiveness after marriage in American society is an example of discontinuity. Sexuality and sex play are viewed as inappropriate behavior for young children but appropriate for adults.

Cultures that have discrete, age-graded expectations for individuals at different periods in the life span produce a pattern of development in which age groups have distinct characteristics and appear to function at different skill levels. These societies are marked by public ceremonies, graduations, and other rites of passage from one stage to the next. Cultures that are permissive and open and recognize few distinctions between the responsibilities of children and those of adults do not produce age-graded stages of development. In those societies, development is a much more gradual, fluid transformation in which adult competencies are built directly on childhood accomplishments.

Implications for Child Development

According to the concept of cultural determinism, the way that events of the various stages of development are experienced depends on how they are regarded by the culture. This diverse perspective is seen in the ways in which

A Cultural View of Life Stages

The theory of cultural determinism suggests that culture shapes the basic patterns of individual life experiences. More specifically, culture determines whether there are stages of development and how those stages are experienced. Based on your observations and experience in the United States, what are the culturally defined stages of life? For each stage, give a name (e.g., infancy), an approximate age range, and two or three critical cultural expectations for associated behaviors or accomplishments.

Life Stage	Approximate Age	Defining Cultural Expectations

Take note of ways in which your concept of the culturally defined stages of life coincide with or differ from the stages that are presented for psychosocial theory, Chapter 3, page 62.

different cultures mark an adolescent girl's first menstruation (Mead, 1949/ 1955). In some societies, people fear menstruation and treat the girl as if she were dangerous. In other societies, she is viewed as having powerful magic that will affect her own future and that of the tribe. In still others, the perceived shamefulness of sex requires that the menstruation be kept as secret as possible. The culture thus determines how a biological change is perceived and treated.

Societies vary in their expectations of people making significant life decisions during each period and in the range of available choices. American adolescents are expected to make decisions regarding sex, work, politics, religion, marriage, and education. In each of these areas, the alternatives are complex and varied. As a result, adolescence is prolonged, and there is a great risk of leaving this period without having found a solution to these problems. In cultures that provide fewer choices and a clearer path from childhood to adulthood, adolescence may be brief and relatively free of psychological stress.

The study of development must be approached with appreciation for the cultural context. Cultural expectations for the timing of certain life events, such as schooling, work, marriage, childbearing, and political and religious leadership, influence the tempo and tone of one's life history. Cultures also vary in the personal qualities that they admire and those they consider inappropriate or shameful. A society's standards of beauty, leadership, and talent and the importance placed on those traits determine its individual members' achievement of status.

One criticism of our scientific knowledge about child development is that it lacks the diversity of cultural contexts. If we accept the idea of cultural determinism, we must agree that development can only be fully understood by taking into consideration the particular ecological and cultural context in which it occurs. Much of what we know about development is based on a very small sample of the peoples of the world. In particular, advances in the social sciences in the United States, Canada, and Europe have not been matched by the studies in the developing nations of Africa, Latin America, and Asia. Thus, attempts to identify and establish universal principles of development must always be tempered by the realization that our scientific observations do not reflect the variations in cultural environments that guide the socialization process (Nsamenang, 1992).

A child's life course is influenced by his or her identification with subcultural norms and values, as well as by the overarching norms and values of the dominant culture. The relative contribution of subcultural influences to a child's development depends on the intensity of the family's loyalty to the subcultural group, the amount of time spent with members of the child's own and other subcultural groups, and the way the child's group is viewed or treated within the larger society. As we consider the dynamics of normative development, we must keep in mind that people of various ethnic subcultures may have unique views on such issues as appropriate child behavior and successful maturity, the nature of gender roles, and the proper balance between individual achievement and responsibility to family and community.

Links to Psychosocial Theory

Psychosocial theory is based on the assumption that culture makes a fundamental contribution in shaping an individual's development. In fact, Erikson argued that basic cultural values could be inferred from infant caregiving

culture is a fundamental part of individual dev't.

practices. By observing how adults respond to infants' needs, one can deduce key cultural values regarding generosity, self-control, independence, or cooperation. Just as evolutionary theory asserts that adaptation is a product of the interaction between the organism and the environment, psychosocial theory assumes that individual development is a product of continuous interaction between the developing child and the demands and resources of the culture.

In contrast to Ruth Benedict's view that the degree to which development appears stagelike depends on the continuity or discontinuity of the society, psychosocial theory supports the concept of an epigenetic plan for development. However, the stages themselves are derived from the view that all cultures must be able to adapt to changes in economic, environmental, and intercultural conditions. The stages of individual development are interwoven with the society's ability to adapt and remain viable. The psychosocial stages emerge as the mechanisms of socialization within each culture evoke them. Psychosocial theory suggests, for example, that the way that trust is established differs from one culture to the next, but that all societies have mechanisms for building levels of trust during the period of infancy.

Social Role Theory

Another approach to conceptualizing the effect of the environment on development is suggested by social psychologists such as Orville Brim (1966) and sociologists such as Talcott Parsons (Parsons & Bales, 1955). They trace the process of socialization and personality development through the person's participation in increasingly diverse and complex social roles. A *role* is any set of behaviors that has a socially agreed-upon function and an accepted code of norms (Brown, 1965; Biddle & Thomas, 1966; Biddle, 1979). The term *role* was taken from the context of the theater. In a play, actors' behaviors are distinct and predictable because each actor has a part to play and follows a script. You will recall this metaphor from Shakespeare's analysis in *As You Like It:* "All the world's a stage, and all the men and women merely players; They have their exits and their entrances; And one man in his time plays many parts" (Act II, Scene vii).

Role theory applies this same framework to social life (Biddle, 1986). The three elements of role theory are the patterned characteristics of social behavior *(role enactment),* the parts or identities that a person assumes *(social roles),* and the scripts or shared expectations for behavior that are linked to each part *(role expectations).*

Social roles serve as a bridge between the individual and the society. Every society has a range of roles, and individuals learn about the expectations associated with them. As people enter new roles, they modify their behavior to conform to those role expectations. Each role is usually linked to one or more related or *reciprocal roles.* The student and the teacher, the parent and the child, and the salesperson and the customer are in reciprocal roles. Each role is partly defined by the other roles that support it. The function of the role is determined by its relation to the surrounding role groups with which it is allied.

Four dimensions are useful in analyzing the impact of social roles on development: the number of roles that a person occupies; the intensity of role involvement or how deeply identified a person is with the role; the amount

Reciprocal roles

of time the role demands; and the degree of flexibility associated with each role.

Implications for Child Development

All cultures offer new roles as individuals move from one stage of life to another. These roles may be required at a certain age, such as the role of high school student. Other roles may be accessible only to those of a certain age who demonstrate other relevant skills, traits, or personal preferences. In many elementary schools, for example, the fifth-grade students become eligible to serve in the role of "crossing guard" to help younger children cross streets near the school, but that role is voluntary and subject to adult approval. Families, organizations, and the larger community have implicit theories of development that determine what role positions are available for children in each age group.

Some of the most important life roles persist across several stages. For example, we are someone's child from infancy until death; we are siblings over the entire life span. In each of these roles, there is both continuity and change (Feldman & Feldman, 1975). The expectations for role performance remain the same in some respects but change in others. We can begin to see how social roles provide consistency to life experiences and how they also prompt new learning.

[handwritten margin note:] provide consistency & prompt new learning

Links to Psychosocial Theory

Role relationships provide a central mechanism for the socialization process. In psychosocial theory, the radius of significant relationships serves as an interconnected web of reciprocal roles and role relationships through which society's expectations and demands are communicated. The idea of reciprocity in roles is closely linked to the concept of interdependence between people in different psychosocial stages. This text emphasizes the importance of considering the development of parents and other adults in understanding the development of the child. Social role theory helps clarify the many reciprocal roles that children and adults occupy.

In the following chapters, we describe a number of life roles specifically related to family, school, and friendship. As children assume an increasing number of roles, they must learn some of the skills of role playing, role differentiation, and role integration. The ability to integrate several diverse roles while maintaining a sense of personal continuity is crucial during the developmental crisis of later adolescence (individual identity versus identity confusion). With each new role, one's self-definition is modified, and the potential for influencing the world increases. At the same time, the addition of new roles places new demands on individuals to meet competing demands (see Box 4.2.).

diverse role integration is essential to the dev't of personal continuity.

Systems Theory

Systems theories attempt to describe and account for the characteristics of systems, viewing individuals as interconnected elements (Sameroff, 1982). To a large degree, these theories highlight *differences in perspective*. Any system, whether it is a cell, an organ, an individual, a family, or a corporation, is composed of *interdependent elements* that share some common goals, interrelated functions, boundaries, and an identity. The system cannot be wholly understood by identifying each of the component parts. The processes and relationships of those parts make for a larger coherent entity. Systems theories take the position that the whole is more than the sum of its parts. The language system, for example, is more than the capacity to make vocal utterances, use grammar, and acquire vocabulary. It is the coordination of these elements in a useful way within a context of shared meaning. Similarly, a family system is more than the sum of the characteristics and competence of the individual family members. Families are a composite with a sense of common destiny and the genetic heritage of the two parents and their developing children.

systems theories highlight differences in perspective

A system cannot violate laws that govern the functioning of the parts, but at the same time it cannot be explained solely by those laws. Biological functioning cannot violate the laws of physics and chemistry, but the laws of physics and chemistry cannot fully explain biological functioning. Similarly, the capacities of children for cognitive growth cannot violate the laws of biological functioning, but biological growth does not fully explain quality of thought.

Individuals, families, communities, schools, and societies are all examples of *open systems*. Ludwig von Bertalanffy (1950, 1968) defined open systems as structures that maintain their organization even though their parts constantly change. Just as the water in a river is constantly changing while the river itself generally retains its boundaries and course, so the molecules of human cells are constantly changing while the various biological systems retain their coordinated functions.

open systems – maintain organization even though parts change.

Open systems share certain properties. They take in energy from the environment, transform this energy into a product that is characteristic of the system, export the product into the environment, and draw on new sources of energy from the environment to continue to thrive (Katz & Kahn, 1966). As

BOX 4.2

Role Strain and Parenthood

A recurring theme in the literature on parenthood is the experience of role strain. *Role strain* can be defined as a sense of overload that results when too many expectations are associated with a role (Biddle, 1986). Each of the four dimensions of social roles may contribute to parental role strain. When parenting is added to other adult roles, especially those of worker and spouse, the demands of the new role may seem overwhelming. The intensity of the parent role carries over to the sense of involvement in all the behaviors associated with the role and provokes anxiety about failure to meet the expectations of the role. First-time parents especially may have little confidence in their ability to fulfill their roles.

The parent role does indeed take a lot of time. Most first-time parents underestimate how much time infants and toddlers require. When new parents, especially mothers, reflect on the time that they spend in a variety of social roles, they single out the parent role as being more time-consuming than any they have ever played.

Parental role strain is related to the structure of the role. Some adults have a very clear set of ideas about how they should enact their parent role, but many are unsure. Husbands and wives are likely to differ in their views on child-rearing techniques and issues. These differences require time to resolve. Because of the hardships or distress that many adults recall from their own childhoods, they do not want to raise their children the way they were raised; consequently, they have to learn a new script for this role.

There are at least four ways to minimize the strain associated with the parent role (Rollins & Galligan, 1978; Bahr, Chappell & Leigh, 1983; Cowan & Cowan, 1988):

1. When rewards for role enactment are frequent, the demands of the role seem less onerous. Adults who receive a lot of encouragement and support from family, friends, and community for their active involvement in parenting will probably feel less stressed by the amount of time and effort they invest in it.

2. The ability to delegate role responsibilities can reduce role strain. Adults who can afford to hire help with some parenting responsibilities or whose families can assist them experience less role strain than those who are solely responsible for the parenting role. Couples who can flexibly alter and share household responsibilities in response to the demands of parenting experience more satisfaction and less strain.

3. The ability to integrate several aspects of the parenting role or several different roles in one activity can reduce role strain. Some parents become quite inventive about ways to maintain contact with their children and still carry out their household and other work tasks and have time with each other.

4. Role strain is reduced when marriage partners reach consensus about their parent roles. New parents who have largely resolved their differences regarding child-rearing philosophy, child-care issues, and the division of household responsibilities experience less role strain and a higher level of marital satisfaction than do those who continue to have opposing views.

we have noted, this process requires an open boundary. The more open the boundary, the more vigorously the process operates. Each specific system has a unique set of processes that are appropriate to the particular forms of energy, product, and transformations relevant to that system. In analyzing systems, one focuses more on the processes and relationships among the parts that permit a system to survive and grow than on the characteristics of the parts themselves.

Systems adjust to or incorporate more of the environment in order to prevent disorganization resulting from environmental fluctuations (Sameroff, 1982). Adaptation seems to be a fundamental process, whether the concept is articulated by Darwin, Piaget, Skinner, or Bandura. Ervin Laszlo (1972) described this property of an open system as *adaptive self-regulation.* A system uses *feedback mechanisms* to identify and respond to environmental changes. The more information about the environment that the system is capable of detecting, the more complex these feedback mechanisms must be. When the oxygen level of the environment is reduced, for example, you tend to grow sleepy. While you sleep, your breathing slows and you use less oxygen. Some of these adjustments are managed unconsciously by the organization of biological systems. Others are managed by more deliberate efforts to minimize the effects of environmental changes. Most systems have a capacity for storing resources so that temporary shortages do not disrupt their operations.

When open systems are confronted by new and constant environmental conditions, they have the capacity for *adaptive self-organization.* The system retains its essential identity by creating new substructures, by revising the relationships among components, or by creating new, higher levels of organization that coordinate existing substructures.

From the systems perspective, the components and the whole are always in tension. One's observations and perceptions depend on one's perpective in this complex set of interrelationships. All living entities are both parts and wholes. A person is a whole—a coordinated complex system composed of physical, cognitive, emotional, social, and self-subsystems. A person is also a part of a family, a classroom or work group, a friendship group, a community group, an ethnic or religious group, and a society. Part of the concept of human development involves an analysis of the adaptive regulation and organization of those subsystems. Simultaneously, human development also must consider the ways that larger systems fluctuate and influence individuals, forcing adaptive regulation and reorganization as a means of achieving stability at higher levels of system organization.

In an effort to elaborate and clarify the interlocking system of systems in which human behavior takes place, Urie Bronfenbrenner (1979) offered the following topography of the environmental structure (see Figure 4.4):

> A *microsystem* is a pattern of activities, roles, and interpersonal relations experienced by the developing person in a given setting with particular physical and material characteristics.
>
> A *mesosystem* comprises the interrelations among two or more settings in which the developing person actively participates (such as, for a child, the relations among home, school, and neighborhood peer group; for an adult, among family, work, and social life).
>
> An *exosystem* refers to one or more settings that do not involve the developing person as an active participant, but in which events occur that affect, or are affected by, what happens in the setting containing the developing person.
>
> The *macrosystem* refers to consistencies in the form and content of lower-order systems (micro-, meso-, and exo-) that exist, or could exist, at the level of the subculture or the culture as a whole, along with any belief systems of ideology underlying such consistencies. (Bronfenbrenner, 1979, 22, 25, 26)

Thus, Bronfenbrenner argues that development is influenced directly by the interactions that take place within a single microsystem, such as the

FIGURE 4.4
A topography of the relationship among systems. Specific examples of microsystems and systems in the exosystem are given, but many other systems could be shown. Arrows in the mesosystem show a two-way, or bidirectional influence; arrows in the exosystem are undirectional, since the developing person does not participate in those settings.
Source: Adapted from: Bronfenbrenner, U. (1979). *The ecology of human development.* Cambridge, Mass.: Harvard University Press. Copyright © 1979 Harvard University Press.

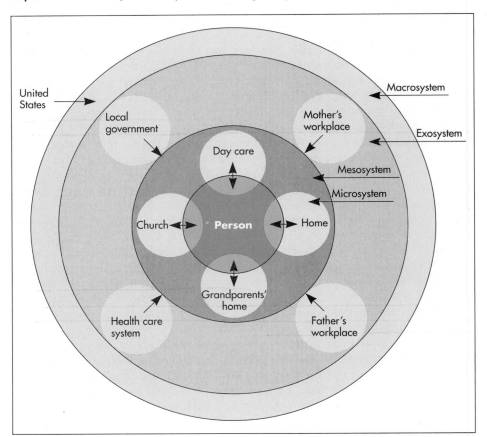

Family is viewed as a system

family, and by the similarities and differences in patterns of interaction that occur across the various systems in which the person functions (the mesosytem). In addition, events in other adjoining systems, such as decisions in the workplace that affect the parent's work schedule, or decisions in city government that affect resources for local schools, have an impact on a child's development even though the child does not participate directly in these settings. Further, the roles, norms, and resources within settings as well as the interrelationships among systems have a unique pattern of organization and reflect an underlying set of beliefs and values that differ from one culture or subculture to the next, and these distinctive cultural characteristics are transmitted to the developing person.

Implications for Child Development

The relevance of systems theory to child development can be most readily appreciated in its application to families. Family system theories focus on how families establish and maintain stable patterns of functioning. Families are viewed as emotional units that are identifiable by certain *boundaries* and *rules* (Kantor & Lehr, 1975; Giles-Sims, 1983). The boundaries of the family determine who is considered to be a family member and who is an outsider. They influence the way that information, support, and validation of the family unit are sought and how new members are admitted into the family. Some families have very strict rules that maintain a narrow boundary around the family. Few sources of information or contact are admitted. Other families extend the sense of belonging to a wide range of people who add ideas and resources.

Family systems are maintained by patterns of communication. *Positive* and *negative feedback loops* operate to stabilize, diminish, or increase certain types of interactions. A feedback loop is positive when a child offers a suggestion and a parent acknowledges and accepts the suggestion. In such a pattern, the child is encouraged to continue to offer suggestions, and the parent comes to view the child as someone who has valuable ideas. A feedback loop is negative if a parent ignores the child's suggestion or scolds the child for making it. The child is less likely to make further suggestions, and the parent is likely to view the child as someone who has no valuable ideas. Many positive and negative feedback loops operate in all families to sustain certain underlying qualities of the system, such as the power hierarchy, the level of conflict, and the balance between autonomy and dependency among the members.

One of the most commonly noted characteristics of family systems is the interdependence of its members. Changes in one family member are accompanied by changes in the others. Imagine for a moment that family members are standing in a circle and holding a rope. Each person tries to exert enough tension on the rope to keep it tight and preserve the circular shape. The amount of tension that each person must exert depends on what every other person is doing. Now imagine that one member of the family lets go of the rope and steps away. In order to retain the shape and tension of the rope, everyone else has to adjust his or her grip and position in the circle. Letting go of the rope is an analogy for many kinds of changes that can occur in a family—a parent's illness or death, a child's departure for college, or a parent's unemployment or taking a new and demanding job. The system adjusts by redefining relationships, modifying patterns of communication, and adjusting its boundaries. The members and their interdependencies change. Similar adjustments must be made if a member is added to the family system, or when the system undergoes some other major transition. In Notebook Page 4.5 we ask you to apply principles of family systems theory to a family you know well.

The system's perspective offers an especially productive approach to clinical problems. A person who has been identified as dysfunctional is treated as part of a family system rather than as a lone individual. From a system theory perspective, the person's problems occur as a result of the way the person is treated by other family members. The only way to bring about changes in the person's functioning is to alter the functioning of the other members of the system as well. If the person is "underfunctioning"—that is, acting irresponsibly, not communicating, not performing at his or her level of capability, or withdrawing—others in the family are assumed to be "overfunctioning"—that is, assuming many of the person's roles and responsibilities in order to "take up the slack." The dysfunctional behavior is maintained because it is a component of an emotional unit. In other words, the dysfunction belongs neither to the person nor to the other family members but to the particular interdependence among the family members that seems to preserve the viability of the family system as a whole (Bowen, 1978).

By definition, family systems are also interdependent with adjacent systems. Thus, understanding families requires analyzing not only the resources and demands of other social systems that impact families but also

[handwritten margin notes:] Family governed by boundaries and rules. Maintained by communication

Positive & negative feedback loops

Applying Concepts from Family Systems Theory

Families, as social systems, can be characterized by certain boundaries, rules, and patterns of interdependence among members, and with adjoining systems. Apply each of these system characteristics to a family that is very close to you—the family in which you grew up, the family you live in now, or the family of a very close friend. For example, what kind of boundaries exist that allow some people to feel close to or part of this family while others feel clearly outside of the family? How are these boundaries established and maintained? Are they rigid or permeable?

System Characteristic	Example from a Specific Family
Boundaries	
Rules	
Patterns of interdependence among members	
Patterns of interdependence with adjoining systems	

the opportunities that families have for influencing adjoining systems. A woman who is experiencing an extremely demanding, stressful, and sexist work environment, for example, may be constantly tired, tense, and irritable in her behavior toward her family members. Her resentments from work may affect the way she treats and expects to be treated by males in her family. If the job is important to her and to her family, no one may be willing to acknowledge the impact that her work is having on her family life. Family violence, the effects of parents' unemployment, participation of mothers in the labor force, day care, and the role of parents in their children's schooling are all being examined from a systems perspective.

Links to Psychosocial Theory

Psychosocial theory embraces the basic assumption of systems theory that understanding development requires an analysis of the child as a member of a number of interrelated systems. Systems theory, however, is not really a developmental theory. Systems are expected to change through adaptive self-regulation and adaptive self-organization. The direction of this change is not necessarily patterned except that it is expected to create new, higher levels of organization to coordinate newly developed substructures. According to psychosocial theory, however, change is developmental. With expanding cognitive capacities and the resolution of each new psychosocial crisis, a child is propelled into increasingly complex social systems and encounters new stimulation for growth through participation in a greater variety of social relationships. At each new stage, children develop new coping skills and devise strategies for new levels of participation in the social system. Eventually, they create innovative approaches for modifying the social system itself.

Chapter Summary

The seven theoretical perspectives that we have reviewed take distinct approaches to continuity and change across the life span.

1. Evolutionary theory provides an overall temporal framework within which to understand individual development. Although a life span of 85 or 90 years may seem long, it is but a flicker in the 1 to 2 million years of human biological adaptation. Evolutionary theory highlights the biologically and genetically governed aspects of growth and development. The environment provides the specific conditions that require adaptation. However, adaptive change can occur only if it is supported by the genetically based characteristics of the organism. The basic mechanism that accounts for species change over many generations is natural selection.

2. Ethology, the study of evolutionarily significant behaviors, provides a systematic approach to analyzing reproductive practices, caregiving behaviors, strategies for obtaining resources, group behavior, and other behaviors that contribute to individual and species survival.

3. According to psychosexual theory, development follows a biologically determined course along which changing patterns of social relationships are dictated by the unfolding of sexual impulses and the

sexualization of body zones. Culture plays a major role in establishing the taboos and acceptable patterns of sexual gratification that lead to conflicts, fixations, and strategies for sublimation. Sexual impulses, wishes, and fears, many of which are unconscious, guide behavior and give it meaning. Psychosexual theory asserts that basic personality patterns are established during infancy and childhood. It also identifies the family, especially the parent–child relationship, as the primary context within which conflicts related to the socialization of sexual impulses are resolved.

4. Psychosexual theory describes three basic structures of the personality: id, ego, and superego. As ego develops, the child becomes increasingly adept at satisfying id impulses in ways that are socially acceptable. In adolescence, a resurgence of id energy challenges many of the ego's earlier coping strategies. Ego must find new ways to express and modify impulses. An essential aspect of this process is thought to be the separation of ego from earlier objects of attachment and investment of energy in the self as well as in new social relationships.

5. Cognitive developmental theories focus on the etiology of rational thought and the capacity for scientific reasoning. Piaget's cognitive theory, like psychosexual theory, views development as a product of a biologically guided plan for growth and change. The elements that make cognitive growth possible are all present in the genetic information that governs the growth of the brain and nervous system. However, the process of intellectual growth requires interaction with a diverse and responsive environment. Cognitive development is fostered by recognizing discrepancies between existing schemes and new experiences. Through the reciprocal processes of assimilation and accommodation, schemes are modified and integrated to allow experiences to be organized and understood.

6. Vygotsky's contribution places the development of higher mental processes in a dynamic social context. Although thinking and reasoning are dependent on biologically based capacities, the organization of mental activity reflects unique characteristics of the culture, especially as culture is transmitted through language, tools, and social relationships.

7. Learning theories focus on the mechanisms that permit individuals to respond to their diverse environments and the permanent changes in thought and behavior that accompany changes in the environment. Behavior can be shaped and modified by systematic changes in environmental conditions. According to learning theorists, human beings have an especially flexible behavioral system. No assumptions are made about universal stages of growth. As conditions in the environment change, response patterns also change. Similarity among individuals at a particular period of life is explained by the fact that they are exposed to similar environmental conditions, patterns of reinforcement, and models.

8. Cultural theory, like learning theories, emphasizes the role of the environment in directing the course of development. Within this framework, the significance of biological maturation depends on the way that it is viewed by the culture. The possibilities for cultural variation are enormous. What we understand to be the normal or natural pat-

tern and tempo of change in competence, roles, and status depends heavily on the way that a society recognizes individuals of different ages, gender, and degrees of kinship.

9. Instead of examining the environment microscopically as do learning theories, considering every unique stimulus and its corresponding response, social role theory suggests that learning is organized around key social functions called roles. As people attempt to enact roles, they integrate their behavior into meaningful units. Meaning is provided by the definition of the role and the expectations of those in reciprocal roles. Development is a product of an increasing number of complex roles over the life span. As children acquire and lose roles, they modify their self-definitions and their relationships with social groups. Most societies define roles that are linked with gender, age, marital status, and kinship. These roles provide patterning for the life course. However, the patterns are understood to be products of the structures and functions of society rather than of genetic information.

10. Systems theory takes a unique scientific perspective. Rather than analyzing causal relationships, systems theory emphasizes the multidimensional sources of influence on individuals, and the simultaneous influence of individuals on the systems to which they belong. Each person is at once a complete individual system and a component of one or more larger systems. One must approach the study of child development from many angles, identifying the critical resources, their availability, and their transformation, which support an adaptive process of reorganization and growth.

References

Archer, J. (1991). Human sociobiology: Basic concepts and limitations. *Journal of Social Issues, 47*, 11–26.

Bahr, S. J., Chappell, C. K. & Leigh, G. K. (1983). Age at marriage, role enactment, role consensus, and marital satisfaction. *Journal of Marriage and the Family, 45,* 795–804.

Bandura, A. (Ed.). (1971). *Psychological modeling.* Chicago: Aldine-Atherton.

Bandura, A. (1977). *Social learning theory.* Englewood Cliffs, N.J.: Prentice-Hall.

Bandura, A. (1986). *Social foundations of thought and action: A social cognitive theory.* Englewood Cliffs, N.J.: Prentice-Hall.

Bandura, A. (1989). Social cognitive theory. *Annals of Child Development, 6,* 1–60.

Bandura, A. & Walters, R. H. (1963). *Social learning and personality development.* New York: Holt, Rinehart & Winston.

Benedict, R. (1934/1950). *Patterns of culture.* New York: New American Library.

Benedict, R. (1946). *The chrysanthemum and the sword.* Boston: Houghton Mifflin.

Bertalanffy, L. von (1950). The theory of open systems in physics and biology. *Science, 111,* 23–28.

Bertalanffy, L. von (1968). *General systems theory* (rev. ed.). New York: Braziller.

Betancourt, H. & Lopez, S. R. (1993). The study of culture, ethnicity, and race in American psychology. *American Psychologist, 48,* 629–637.

Biddle, B. J. (1979). *Role theory: Expectations, identities, and behaviors.* New York: Academic Press.

Biddle, B. J. (1986). Recent developments in role theory. In R. H. Turner & S. F. Short, Jr. (Eds.), *Annual Review of Sociology, 12,* 67–92.

Biddle, B. J. & Thomas, E. J. (1966). *Role theory: Concepts and research.* New York: Wiley.

Bowen, M. (1978). *Family therapy and clinical practice.* New York: Aronson.

Breuer, J. & Freud, S. (1895/1955). Studies on hysteria. In J. Strachey (Ed.), *The standard edition of the complete psychological works of Sigmund Freud* (vol. 2). London: Hogarth Press.

Brim, O. G., Jr. (1966). Socialization through the life cycle. In O. G. Brim, Jr., & S. Wheeler (Eds.), *Socialization after childhood.* New York: Wiley.

Bronfenbrenner, U. (1979). *The ecology of human development*. Cambridge, Mass.: Harvard University Press.

Brown, R. (1965). *Social psychology*. New York: Free Press.

Charlesworth, W. R. (1992). Darwin and developmental psychology: Past and present. *Developmental Psychology, 28,* 5–16.

Cowan, C. P. & Cowan, P. A. (1988). Who does what when partners become parents: Implications for men, women, and marriage. In R. Palkovitz & M. B. Sussman (Eds.), *Transitions to parenthood.* New York: Hawthorn Press, 105–132.

Darwin, C. (1859/1979). *The illustrated "Origin of species."* Abridged and introduced by R. E. Leakey. New York: Hill & Wang.

Davey, G. & Cullen, C. (1988). *Human operant conditioning and behavior modification*. New York: Wiley.

Einstein, A. & Freud, S. (1933/1964). Why war? In J. Strachey (Ed.), *The standard edition of the complete psychological works of Sigmund Freud* (vol. 22). London: Hogarth Press, 195–218.

Feldman, H. & Feldman, M. (1975). The family life cycle: Some suggestions for recycling. *Journal of Marriage and the Family, 37,* 277–284.

Ferster, C. B. & Culbertson, S. A. (1982). *Behavior principles* (3rd ed.). Englewood Cliffs, N.J.: Prentice-Hall.

Freud, S. (1933/1964). New introductory lectures on psychoanalysis. In J. Strachey (Ed.), *The standard edition of the complete psychological works of Sigmund Freud* (vol. 22). London: Hogarth Press.

Freud, S. (1963). *The cocaine papers*. Vienna and Zurich: Dunquin Press.

Giles-Sims, J. (1983). *Wife battering: A systems theory approach*. New York: Guilford Press.

Gleitman, H. (1986). *Psychology*. New York: Norton.

Grusec, J. E. (1992). Social learning theory and developmental psychology: The legacies of Robert Sears and Albert Bandura. *Developmental Psychology, 28,* 776–786.

Herkovits, M. (1948). *Man and his works*. New York: Knopf.

Kagitcibasi, C. (1990). Family and socialization in cross-cultural perspective: A model of change. In J. J. Berman (Ed.), *Nebraska symposium on motivation, 1989: Cross-cultural perspectives*. Lincoln, Nebr.: University of Nebraska Press.

Kantor, D. & Lehr, W. (1975). *Inside the family*. San Francisco: Jossey-Bass.

Katz, D. & Kahn, R. L. (1966). *The social psychology of organizations*. New York: Wiley.

Laszlo, E. (1972). *Introduction to systems philosophy: Toward a new paradigm of contemporary thought*. New York: Harper & Row.

McClelland, J. L. & Rumelhart, D. E. (1986). *Parallel distributed processing* (vol. 2). Cambridge, Mass.: MIT Press.

Mead, M. (1928/1950). *Coming of age in Samoa*. New York: New American Library.

Mead, M. (1949/1955). *Male and female: A study of the sexes in a changing world*. New York: Mentor.

Miller, P. H. (1993). *Theories of developmental psychology* (3rd ed.). New York: W. H. Freeman.

Mischel, W. (1973). Toward a cognitive social learning reconceptualization of personality. *Psychological Review, 80,* 252–283.

Mischel, W. (1979). On the interface of cognition and personality: Beyond the person–situation debate. *American Psychologist, 34,* 740–754.

Nsamenang, A. B. (1992). *Human development in cultural context: A Third World perspective*. Cross-cultural research and methodology series, vol. 16. Newbury Park, Calif.: Sage.

Parsons, T. & Bales, R. F. (Eds.). (1955). *Family socialization and interaction process*. New York: Free Press.

Pavlov, I. P. (1927/1960). *Conditioned reflexes*. New York: Dover Press.

Piaget, J. (1978/1985). *The equilibration of cognitive structures*. Chicago: University of Chicago Press.

Rohner, R. P. (1984). Toward a conception of culture for cross-cultural psychology. *Journal of Cross-cultural Psychology, 15,* 111–138.

Rollins, B. C. & Galligan, R. (1978). The developing child and marital satisfaction of parents. In R. M. Lerner & G. B. Spanier (Eds.), *Child influences on marital and family interaction: A life-span perspective*. New York: Academic Press.

Rumelhart, D. E. & McClelland, J. L. (1986). *Parallel distributed processing* (vol. 1). Cambridge, Mass.: MIT Press.

Sameroff, A. J. (1982). Development and the dialectic: The need for a systems approach. In W. A. Collins (Ed.), *The concept of development: The Minnesota symposia on child psychology* (vol. 15). Hillsdale, N.J.: Erlbaum.

Skinner, B. F. (1938). *The behavior of organisms*. New York: Appleton-Century-Crofts.

Skinner, B. F. (1948). *Walden two*. New York: Macmillan.

Skinner, B. F. (1967). Autobiography of B. F. Skinner. In E. Boring & G. Lindzey (Eds.), *History of psychology in autobiography* (vol. 5). New York: Appleton-Century-Crofts, 387–413.

Skinner, B. F. (1971). *Beyond freedom and dignity*. New York: Knopf.

Skinner, B. F. (1987). Whatever happened to psychology as the science of behavior? *American Psychologist, 42,* 780–786.

Tolman, E. C. (1932/1967). *Purposive behavior in rats and men.* New York: Appleton-Century-Crofts.

Tolman, E. C. (1948). Cognitive maps in rats and men. *Psychological Review, 55,* 189–208.

Triandis, H., Lambert, W., Berry, J., Lonner, W., Heron, A., Brislin, R. & Draguns, J. (Eds.). (1980). *Handbook of cross-cultural psychology* (vols. 1–6). Boston: Allyn & Bacon.

Tudge, J. R. H. & Winterhoff, P. A. (1993). Vygotsky, Piaget, and Bandura: Perspectives on the relations between the social world and cognitive development. *Human Development, 36,* 61–81.

Vygotsky, L. S. (1962). *Thought and language.* Cambridge, Mass.: MIT Press.

Vygotsky, L. S. (1978). *Mind in society.* Cambridge, Mass.: Harvard University Press.

Sexual Reproduction and Heredity

Chapter 5

The Reproductive Process
The Male Reproductive System
The Female Reproductive System
Hormones and the Reproductive System
Fertilization Through Sexual Intercourse
Twins
Fertilization Through Reproductive Technology

The Cellular Basis of Sexual Reproduction
Gametes
Cell Division
The Timing of Meiosis for Males and Females

The Transmission of Genetic Information
The Replication of DNA
Mutations
The Laws of Heredity
Alleles
Genotype and Phenotype
Sex-Linked Characteristics

Genetic Sources of Individuality
Genetic Determinants of the Rate of Development
Genetic Determinants of Individual Traits
Genetic Determinants of Abnormal Development
Genetic Technology and Psychosocial Evolution
Ethical Issues in Genetic Technology

Evaluating the Impact of Heredity on Behavior
Reaction Range
An Example of Behavioral Genetics: Hereditary Influences on Intelligence
Genetic Irregularities
Family Relationships

Chapter Summary
References

T his chapter begins by discussing the physiology of human sexual reproduction, giving special emphasis to fertilization and the technological alternatives to natural fertilization. Then, we examine the mechanisms of cell division that produce the special cells involved in the reproductive process. The third section of the chapter focuses on heredity, including the biochemistry of genetic material, the laws that govern inheritance, and the contributions of hereditary factors to individual traits.

In keeping with the psychosocial framework, we refer, when appropriate, to the behavioral context within which the biology of reproduction occurs. Human sexuality and reproductive activity involve coordinating motivation, attitudes and values, behaviors, and physiological processes. Many psychosocial factors determine which partners become sexually intimate, whether their intimacy results in sexual intercourse, and whether their sexual intercourse results in fertilization.

The Reproductive Process

Sexual reproduction is responsible for the perpetuation of life on earth through the generation of new organisms. For humans, a new organism begins in the union of nuclei from the cells of two different parental organisms. As noted in Chapter 4, genetic variation is key to the process of evolution by natural selection. Because sexual reproduction for humans involves combining genetic material from two different organisms, the process operates in such a way as to increase the amount of genetic variation in a population. It ensures that all humans, except identical twins, are genetically unique.

In sexual reproduction, special kinds of cells called *gametes* unite to form the first cell of the new organism. Gametes differ in appearance from other cells in the body, and they contain only half the genetic material present in other body cells. The two main types of gametes are *sperm cells*, produced in males, and *egg cells*, produced in females. We will describe the male and female reproductive systems as well as the hormones that regulate them. In reading about fertilization, you will start to appreciate the many factors that must "go just right" in order for a new life to begin.

The Male Reproductive System

In males, gamete and male sex hormone production occur in the testes which are located in a pouch called the *scrotum* just below the penis. The *penis* is used for reproduction and for the excretion of urine. From each testis the sperm flow into a long coiled tube called the *epididymis*, located behind the testes. If uncoiled, a typical epididymis would be about 20 in. or 50 cm long. The epididymis can hold billions of sperm.

Shortly before ejaculation, sperm are propelled from the epididymis into a long duct called the *vas deferens*, which carries the sperm to the seminal vesicles, a pair of sacs that produce seminal fluid, which is added to the sperm to produce semen. Secretions from the prostate increase the volume of the semen, which is ejaculated from the penis via the urethra during orgasm.

A male may release 200 million to 500 million sperm at one time. Sperm cells remain in the epididymis until they are released in sexual activity or reabsorbed by the body. The formation of sperm cells in mature human males takes about 72 days. The male reproductive system is presented in Figure 5.1.

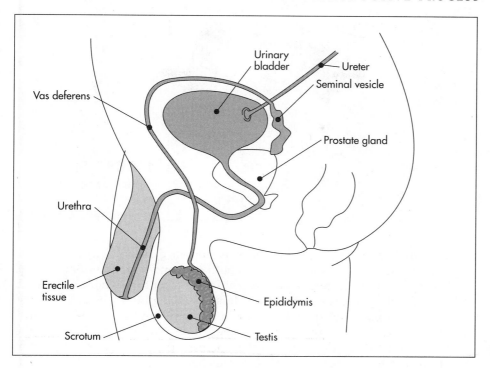

FIGURE 5.1
The male reproductive system

The Female Reproductive System

In females, gamete and female hormone production occur in the ovaries. There are two ovaries, each located low and on either side of the uterus within the abdominal cavity. Each ovary is situated close to a short tube called a *fallopian tube*. When an egg cell (or ovum) is expelled from an ovary, it is sucked into a fallopian tube. Millions of tiny hairlike cilia move the ovum along its course toward the *uterus*.

The uterus is a hollow, thick-walled muscular organ that becomes the environment for the developing child during the prenatal period. Each month, between puberty and menopause, an egg from one ovary is carried along the fallopian tube. If fertilized, it begins to divide and implants into the lining of the uterus to develop into an embryo. At birth, the baby is forced out via the cervix, a usually narrow passage that forms the neck of the uterus, which projects into the *vagina*. The vagina is a muscular passageway that connects the uterus to the outside of the body. The female reproductive system is depicted in Figure 5.2.

Hormones and the Reproductive System

A *hormone* is a substance, secreted by a cell or gland, that has a regulatory effect on cells and organs in other parts of the body. Hormones can be thought of as chemical messengers that travel in the blood to various organs. Hormones play a key role in regulating the reproductive process. The gonads (the ovaries and testes) that produce gametes also produce *sex hormones*. These sex hormones are produced as a result of stimulation by hormones in the brain. The three primary sex hormones are *estrogen*, named for the estrus or menstrual cycle; *testosterone*, named for the testis where it is produced; and *progesterone*, named for gestation. These names suggest that sex hormones are

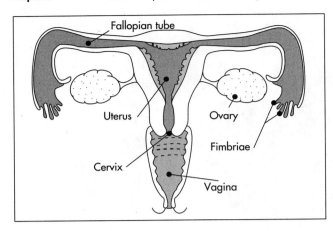

FIGURE 5.2
The female reproductive system

distinctly male and female. However, it is known that estrogen and testosterone are present to differing degrees in both men and women (Money, 1980).

Estrogen and testosterone are present in the body throughout childhood, but at relatively low levels. As John Money (1980) puts it, before puberty, the engine is in place but there is no gas in the car. With the onset of puberty, the car is fueled to go. At puberty, hormones produced in the brain signal the pituitary gland to secrete hormones that increase the production of estrogen in females and testosterone in males. These changes in hormone level stimulate the further development of primary sex characteristics, including the growth of the testes and penis in males and the onset of ovulation and menstruation in females. These changes in hormone levels also influence the emergence of secondary sex characteristics such as growth of facial and body hair, changes in body shape and proportion, deepening voice, and heightened sexual interest. Thus, changes in physical appearance signal a new level of sexual maturity, which is accompanied by new reproductive capacity.

Hormones guide the activation of the reproductive cycle by coordinating the functions involved in a woman's menstrual cycle. The menstrual cycle begins with each potential egg cell enclosed in a *follicle,* a small balloonlike sac on the surface of an ovary. A follicle reacts to hormones from the brain by producing estrogen during the 10 days before an egg cell is released. Estrogen stimulates the inner layer of the uterus, which fills with fluids and blood vessels and becomes much thicker in preparation for the possible arrival of a fertilized egg.

After a follicle releases its egg cell, its remaining cells fill the cavity that the released egg cell occupied. These cells appear yellow in color and are referred to as the *corpus luteum* (yellow body). The corpus luteum produces the hormone progesterone which helps maintain the thick layer of the uterus for about two more weeks. This is enough time for a fertilized egg to attach itself to the wall of the uterus. If the egg is not fertilized, the thick layer of the uterus disintegrates and the corpus luteum stops producing progesterone. The inner layer of the uterus breaks off and passes out of the body through the vagina. The loss of tissue and blood from the uterus is called *menstruation.* The menstrual flow usually lasts four or five days. This cycle of maturation and release of the egg cell, thickening of the uterine lining, and disintegration of the uterine lining when a fertilized egg fails to implant takes about 28 days.

Given this background on the male and female reproductive systems and the role that hormones play in reproduction, we can now turn to the process of fertilization. When the female and male systems are healthy and functioning well, fertilization of an egg cell by a sperm cell usually occurs through sexual intercourse. When problems arise in the reproductive systems, or when individuals do not want to have sexual relations with a person of the opposite sex, today's medical technology has made alternative methods of fertilization possible. In Notebook Page 5.1, we ask you to reconstruct your own knowledge about reproduction.

Fertilization Through Sexual Intercourse

During sexual intercourse, sperm cells enter the woman's body through the vagina. In a condition of sexual arousal, the male's penis fills with blood, enlarges, and becomes rigid. With stimulation to orgasm, the male reproductive system responds by ejaculating 3 to 4 mL (milliliters) of a whitish fluid called _semen_. The semen contains hundreds of millions of sperm as well as secretions of other glands. After they are expelled into the vagina, the sperm swim off in all directions, many moving up along the moist linings of the female reproductive tract into the uterus and the two fallopian tubes. Why are so many sperm needed to fertilize just one egg cell? Many sperm die as they come in contact with the vaginal environment. In addition, sperm secrete an _enzyme_ that helps break down the layer of cells enveloping an egg cell. The collective production of this enzyme by many sperm appears to be necessary to provide a sufficient quantity to penetrate the egg.

How do the sperm find the egg? Some research suggests that when eggs are ready to be fertilized, they produce a chemical substance that serves as a type of "homing device" for the sperm. Those sperm that are sensitive to this chemical attractant are guided to the egg in the fallopian tube (Roberts, 1991).

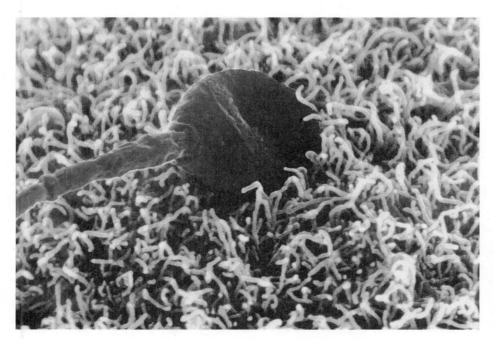

At the moment of fertilization, one sperm breaks through the outer layer of the egg and the genetic material from the two gametes combines.

BOX 5.1

The Social Context of First Intercourse

In order for a sperm cell to "find" an egg cell, a male and female must "find" one another. In each society and subculture, the norms governing the transition to sexual activity differ. Since reproductive activity can begin in early adolescence, researchers have tried to account for the factors that influence whether an adolescent will engage in sexual intercourse and, if so, when. The model illustrated in the figure at right was devised to explain this transition.

Three basic dimensions account for the adolescent's initiation into sexual activity: motivation, social controls, and attractiveness. *Motivation* can be accounted for by biological factors, especially new levels of hormone production; by a new level of desire for independence and adult behaviors; and by certain internalized norms and attitudes. *Social controls* provide the normative environment for sexual activity. According to the model, these controls are a product of parental socialization and practices, school achievement and educational aspirations, and the attitudes and sexual experiences of friends. One might add here the influence of religious beliefs and values. The third dimension, *attractiveness*, influences one's appeal to partners. Attractiveness is defined in part by one's level of physical maturation, social acceptance or popularity, and whether one is judged to be physically appealing.

In an effort to assess this model, researchers found that, for girls, various social controls, including parents, school achievement, and friends' attitudes and behaviors, all played an important part in predicting the timing of first sexual intercourse. For boys, the transition was most strongly predicted by hormonal levels and popularity with girls. Social controls, which are so meaningful in explaining the transition to first sexual experience for girls, did not have predictive power in determining the timing of this transition for boys.

This research supports the notion that hormone levels may be a strong predictor of the transition to sexual intercourse for boys, but that, for girls, hormone levels alone do not account for involvement in sexual activity. For girls, the transition to sexual intercourse is influenced largely by social context (Brooks-Gunn & Furstenberg, 1989; Hanson et. al, 1987; Newcomer & Udry, 1987; Udry & Billy, 1987).

Transition to first coitus in adolescence ▶

Source: Udry, J. R. & Billy, J. O. (1987). Initiation of coitus in early adolescence. *American Sociological Review, 52,* 842. Copyright © American Sociological Association. Reprinted by permission.

Swimming at a rate of an inch in 8 minutes, sperm may reach an egg in as little time as an hour. The journey usually takes about 6 hours, but sperm can stay alive in the uterus for up to 3 days during ovulation. The egg cell remains alive for about one to two days once it is released from the ovary, providing a window of about 24 to 36 hours for fertilization to occur (Turner & Rubinson, 1993).

The thousands of sperm that reach the egg emit an enzyme that softens the outer layer of the egg cell and makes it easier to penetrate. However, only one sperm cell can fertilize an egg cell. Just the head of the sperm, which carries the genetic material, actually enters the egg cell. Once a sperm penetrates the outer membranes of the egg cell, the membranes react immediately, forming a barrier to other sperm cells.

The child's development actually begins in the fallopian tube. In fertilization, the merging of the gametes produces the genetic information for a completely new and unique individual. The cell produced when the sperm fertilizes the egg is referred to as a *zygote.* This cell travels down the fallopian tubes, dividing as it travels toward the uterus without growing larger. After about one week, this mass of cells implants in the uterus. One cell produces two, two produce four, until, at the end of the period of prenatal devel-

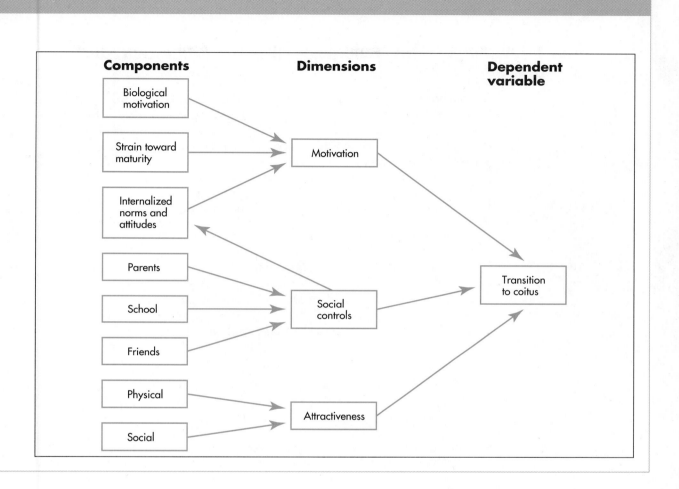

opment, a new individual composed of billions of cells is born. Scientific research has yet to fully unravel the mysteries of how this single cell with a complete set of genetic material is able to produce the wide range of different types of body organs, each with their own characteristics and functions, that make up a unique human being.

In most cases, the fertilization of the egg by the sperm leads to the development of only one zygote which matures into one fetus. In some cases, however, multiple births (most commonly twins) occur. These offspring, who share the same uterine environment, can be either identical or fraternal.

Twins

Occasionally, the zygote divides in two and separates into two individuals with exactly the same chromosomal composition. These individuals are referred to as *monozygotic twins* (MZ) because they come from a single zygote. These twins are always of the same sex, and they are strikingly similar in physical appearance, which accounts for the term *identical twins*.

Because identical twins are genetically the same, much research has been done with identical twins who have been raised together and identical twins who have been raised apart in order to understand the relative contributions of

Your Knowledge of the Biological Basis of Sexual Reproduction

The biological process of reproduction is a product of thousands of years of human evolution. The system and its mechanisms operate largely outside our conscious awareness. In fact, many adolescents and young adults of reproductive age do not understand the biology of reproduction or how sexual activity is related to fertilization.

Try to reconstruct your personal understanding of sexual reproduction.

1. a. What was your earliest idea of how babies were made or where babies

came from? _____

b. Where did you get this information? _____

2. a. At what age did you learn about sexual intercourse? _____

b. What did you think was the purpose of sexual intercourse?

_____

c. Where did you get this information?

_____

3. a. If you are a female, reread the section on the male reproductive system. What questions do you still have about how the male reproductive system functions?

_____

_____

b. At what age did you fully understand this process? _____

c. If you are a male, reread the section on the female reproductive system. What questions do you still have about how the female reproductive system functions?

_____

_____

d. At what age did you fully understand this process? _____

4. From an evolutionary perspective, what might be the reproductive advantage of having two and only two sexes?

_____

heredity and environment to intellectual, emotional, and social functioning. These findings will be discussed throughout the text.

Fraternal twins occur as a result of multiple ovulations during the same cycle. Each egg develops singly in a separate follicle, is shed and fertilized individually, and develops separately in the uterus. They are referred to as *dizygotic twins* (DZ), indicating that they are two-egg twins. Genetically, they bear no more resemblance to one another than other children of the same parents. They may be of different sexes and have quite distinct physical and personal characteristics. However, they do share the same uterine environment during the prenatal period. Approximately 1 in 90 pregnancies involves twins, most commonly dizygotic twins (Clayman, 1989).

Fertilization Through Reproductive Technology

Reproduction is a wonderfully intricate process through which a sperm, guided by a chemical signal, finds and penetrates an egg's outer membrane, followed by the zygote's journey through the fallopian tube to its proper location in the uterus, and the implantation in the uterine lining which is prepared to sustain a developing embryo for nine months. For approximately 1 couple out of 12 in the United States, however, this normal process does not work, and they have difficulty conceiving. In 1990, an estimated 1 million new patients sought treatment for infertility (Elmer-Dewitt, 1991).

Infertility can result from problems in the reproductive system of either the man or the woman. Conditions related to infertility among men include inadequate sperm production or production of sperm that do not contain the full complement of genetic information, cannot travel successfully to the egg, or lack the enzymes necessary to soften and penetrate the egg's outer membrane. Conditions that contribute to infertility for women can be related to a failure to ovulate, blocked fallopian tubes, a failure of the embryo to implant in the uterus, and miscarriage or extremely premature onset of labor. In some instances, a woman is allergic to her partner's sperm; the woman's body produces antibodies that destroy the sperm as they enter her body. For couples who are unable to conceive, some remarkable alternatives are currently being developed.

Artificial insemination is probably the most well-developed alternative to natural fertilization. A woman who wants to conceive goes to a clinic each month where sperm, which have been donated and frozen, are injected into her vagina. Some sperm banks keep the characteristics and medical history of the donors on file. A woman can select the sperm of a donor who closely resembles her partner. A single woman can select features that she desires in her offspring. Other banks blend the sperm of donors so that the donor's identity cannot be traced. The Office of Technology Assessment reported that approximately 172,000 women in the United States undergo artificial insemination each year and that about 65,000 babies are conceived annually from this procedure (Byrne, 1988). This method is effective only if a woman's reproductive system is functional.

Another alternative to natural fertilization is *fertilization in vitro*. In this process, an egg is removed from the ovary and placed in a petri dish inside an incubator. A few drops of sperm are added to the dish. If fertilization takes place and the cell begins to divide, the fertilized egg is returned to the uterus in order to develop. A survey of 146 clinics that perform in vitro fertilization found that the procedure is successful in about 9% of cases (Sperling, 1989).

This procedure is used when a woman has experienced difficulty in the fertilization process.

A third procedure, *gamete intrafallopian transfer* (GIFT), involves transferring eggs and sperm into a woman's fallopian tubes. Fertilization takes place, as it normally would, within the woman's reproductive system. However, the eggs and sperm could come from either the woman and her fertile male partner or from other donors. Thus, the fetus could be genetically related to both the male and female partners, to one, or to neither.

A fourth alternative is *in vivo fertilization*. In this procedure, a fertile male and an infertile female ask a second woman, who has demonstrated her fertility, to be artificially inseminated with the man's sperm. Once an embryo has formed, it is transferred to the first woman's uterus, which becomes the gestational environment. The child is therefore genetically related to the man but not to the woman who gives birth.

A fifth alternative involves a *surrogate mother*. Sperm from an infertile woman's fertile male partner are injected into a surrogate mother during the time of her regular monthly ovulation. Once the surrogate mother becomes pregnant, she bears the child and returns it to the parents at birth. About 100 babies per year are born to surrogate mothers (Byrne, 1988). In one remarkable case of this type, a woman agreed to be the surrogate mother for her own daughter who was born without a uterus. At age 42, she gave birth to her own twin grandchildren (Elmer-Dewitt, 1991).

One future plan involves flushing a fertilized egg from the uterus soon after conception, freezing the embryo, and implanting it in the uterus of a woman who has been unable to conceive naturally. This woman could then carry the baby through the regular gestation period and give birth.

All of these alternatives have raised many legal and ethical questions (Andrews, 1984; Elmer-Dewitt, 1991). For example, the husband of a woman who is artificially inseminated must consent to the procedure and agree to assume legal guardianship of the offspring. But who should be responsible if a child resulting from artificial insemination has a severe genetic defect? According to a report of physicians who perform artificial insemination, less than half of them screened potential donors for major genetic diseases or viruses that could be passed through the semen (Byrne, 1988). Sperm banks were found to be more thorough than individual physicians about taking these precautions. There are no official state or federal regulations for screening donors.

What rights does a sperm donor have to a relationship with his offspring? In 1983, a man from California was granted weekly visitation rights to a child who had been conceived with his sperm. Is he to be considered the "father" of the child?

What limits should be placed on the production of embryos in vitro? Should scientists be permitted to produce embryos from frozen sperm and egg cells for other purposes such as tissue use for medical treatments?

In the widely publicized case of Baby M., William and Elizabeth Stern paid Mary Beth Whitehead $10,000 to be a surrogate mother. After the baby was born, Ms. Whitehead decided that she wanted to keep her. In ensuing court battles, the New Jersey Supreme Court ruled that the contract between the couple and Ms. Whitehead was void and that it was illegal to pay women to bear children for others. Nonetheless, it granted custody of the child to the Sterns, arguing that they could provide the child with a more stable home environment. However, the court rejected the right of Elizabeth Stern to adopt the baby and supported Ms. Whitehead's rights for continued visitation. This complex pattern of decisions is likely to set a tone for other states, making surrogate parenting illegal or so tightly regulated that it will become an underground practice (Lacayo, 1988).

Another troubling ethical issue is the fate of frozen embryos. Some estimates suggest that more than 4,000 frozen embryos are being held in various medical and laboratory facilities in the United States (Elson, 1989). State laws governing their use as well as their rights are often conflicting and confusing. Questions are raised about the right of parents to determine the fate of these embryos, the embryos' rights to protection and inheritance, and the responsibility of institutes and laboratories to ensure the proper use of the embryos. A disturbing factor here is the obvious detachment of an embryo from his or her parental origins, which tends to encourage embryos being regarded as objects or products rather than as emerging beings. Notebook Page 5.2 asks you to state your own opinions regarding reproductive technology.

On a more encouraging note, one of the first studies on the quality of parenting and developmental outcome for children conceived through artificial insemination and in vitro fertilization was very positive (Golombok et al., 1995). In this study, conducted in the United Kingdom, 86 families with children conceived through alternative reproductive technologies were compared with families with naturally conceived or adopted children. In general, parents of children conceived through both types of assisted reproduction displayed more warmth and involvement with their children, higher levels of interaction, and lower levels of stress than the parents of children who were conceived naturally. Parents of adopted children typically scored in between the levels of the other two groups. There were no significant differences among the groups of children with respect to social and emotional development; all were well within the norms for their age groups.

The Cellular Basis of Sexual Reproduction

In this section, we move from the level of the female and male reproductive anatomy to the level of the critical cells involved in forming a new child. In sexual reproduction, only the special cells called gametes unite to form the first cell of the new organism. From an evolutionary perspective, you might say that all the other cells of the body are joined in the mission of making sure that healthy gametes are produced and have ample opportunity to achieve fertilization and reproduction.

Gametes

Sperm cells, produced by males, consist of a nucleus that carries genetic information, a tail that propels the cell, and a *mitochondrion* (plural: *mitochondria*) that generates energy. Sperm cells are quite small. Normal adult males produce approximately 200 to 300 million sperm cells every day.

Egg cells or ova (singular: ovum), produced by females, contain a nucleus and a reserve food supply in an area outside the nucleus called the *cytoplasm*. In humans, the egg cells are much larger than the sperm cells. They are also larger than other cells in the body, usually about 0.12 millimeters in diameter or the size of the head of a pin. Human females are born with an

Attitudes Toward Reproductive Technology

Roughly 6 million couples of childbearing age experience some form of infertility. Other groups such as single women, gay men, and lesbian couples see innovations in reproductive technology as an avenue for having their own, genetically linked, children.

What are your attitudes about alternatives to natural fertilization?

1. **a.** Under what conditions would you use an alternative reproductive technique in order to have children?

   _____

   b. Which techniques would you consider?

   _____

2. What research priorities do you think ought to be related to infertility and alternative modes of reproduction?

   _____

3. Suppose that a married couple who were very close friends of yours discovered that they were infertile.

   a. If you are a female, would you be willing to serve as a surrogate mother for this couple?

   _____

   b. If you are a male, would you be willing to donate sperm to be used in artificial insemination for this couple?

   _____

   c. What are your emotional responses to this question?

   _____

   d. What are your intellectual reactions to this question?

   _____

   e. Try to explain these reactions.

   _____

estimated 400,000 immature egg cells called *oocytes*. During a woman's fertile years, from puberty to menopause, one egg ripens and is released each month. Thus, only about 400 to 500 oocytes actually reach maturity, while the remainder degenerate and are absorbed by the body (Turner & Rubinson, 1993).

The nuclei of the gametes, like the nuclei of all cells, contain genetic information. But only the gametes can transmit parental genetic information to the offspring. The genetic information is carried on long, thin strands called *chromosomes*. After the discovery in the late nineteenth century that chromosomes in the cell nuclei could be stained, biologists were able to count and study them. They learned that the cells of each species contain a specific number of chromosomes. It was not until the 1950s that Joe Hih Tjio and Albert Levan of the Institute of Genetics in Lund, Sweden, determined that human cells contained 46 chromosomes. By comparison, the common fruit fly, which is used in a good deal of genetic research, has only eight chromosomes.

Chromosomes come in pairs. The number of chromosomes in a normal body cell is called the *diploid* number. The diploid number of human chromosomes is 46. Twenty-two pairs of human chromosomes are called *autosomal* since both members are similar in shape and size. They also contain the same kinds of *genes*. Genes are segments of a chromosome that code for specific hereditary characteristics. The twenty-third pair of human chromosomes is unique: Females possess two X chromosomes, whereas males possess one X and one Y chromosome. The X and Y notation is used because these chromosomes differ in shape and size; the X chromosome is longer than the Y chromosome. There are very few similarities in the genes present on the X and Y chromosomes.

Gametes are the only cells that contain half the number of chromosomes that are present in the body cells of the parent. This is called the *haploid* number. For humans, the gametes contain 23 chromosomes, half the diploid number of 46. This reduction of chromosomes by one-half in each gamete allows reproduction to occur. If the reduction process did not occur, the number of chromosomes in each body cell would double with each reproduction, and the cell nuclei would eventually fill with chromosomes.

During *fertilization*, a sperm and egg fuse together and merge their genetic information. This occurs when the first cell of the new organism is produced. Within this new cell, in each chromosome pair, one chromosome comes from the father through his sperm and one chromosome comes from the mother through her egg.

The 23 pairs of chromosomes in a fertilized egg contain the complete set of instructions for development, determining the structure and timing of the formation of the heart, the central nervous system, the immune system, and every other organ and tissue required for life. Messages are encoded in the chromosomes that determine when events such as the onset of puberty or menopause will occur. In order for one fertilized cell to transform to the billions of cells required for a healthy newborn, an amazing process of cell division takes place.

Cell Division

Cell division is occurring constantly in human body cells. The normal process of cell division occurs slightly differently in the formation of gametes than it does in most body cells. Gamete cell division is called meiosis; cell division in other body cells is called mitosis.

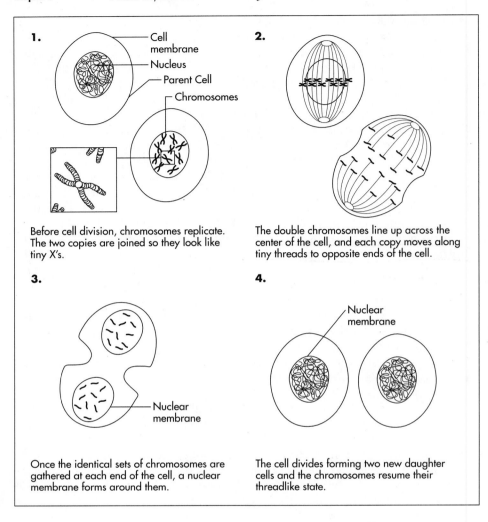

1.

— Cell membrane
— Nucleus
— Parent Cell
— Chromosomes

Before cell division, chromosomes replicate. The two copies are joined so they look like tiny X's.

2.

The double chromosomes line up across the center of the cell, and each copy moves along tiny threads to opposite ends of the cell.

3.

— Nuclear membrane

Once the identical sets of chromosomes are gathered at each end of the cell, a nuclear membrane forms around them.

4.

Nuclear membrane

The cell divides forming two new daughter cells and the chromosomes resume their threadlike state.

FIGURE 5.3

Phases of mitosis

Mitosis involves four steps which result in the formation of two new nuclei, each having the same number of chromosomes as the parent nucleus (see Figure 5.3). In this process, incredibly thin strands of genetic material are replicated, separated, moved to distinct areas of the cell, and gathered together again to form new cells. With each replication, two daughter cells are produced which have the exact same genetic material as the parent cell.

Meiosis occurs in the *gonads* (the ovaries in females; the testes in males) where the gametes are produced. Meiosis follows a different course and timetable in females and males. For females, cells begin meiosis during the prenatal stage but do not complete development into gametes until puberty when they are released one at a time as eggs or ova. In males, cells enter meiosis after puberty begins.

Meiosis consists of two cell divisions (see Figure 5.4). Meiosis begins as the DNA (molecules that carry genetic information) in each chromosome is copied. The 46 long, thin chromosomes thicken and shorten. While this is occurring, each chromosome strand finds the other member of its pair, and they set up next to each other along their lengths. At this point, 23 pairs of

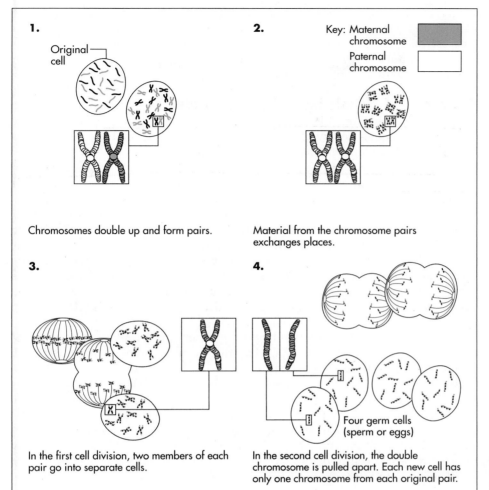

1.

Original cell

Chromosomes double up and form pairs.

2.

Key: Maternal chromosome
Paternal chromosome

Material from the chromosome pairs exchanges places.

3.

In the first cell division, two members of each pair go into separate cells.

4.

Four germ cells (sperm or eggs)

In the second cell division, the double chromosome is pulled apart. Each new cell has only one chromosome from each original pair.

FIGURE 5.4
Phases of meiosis

chromosomes are observed. The pairs lie very close to each other and are often twisted around one another. In many instances, chromatids (segments of a chromosome) break at various places and join with broken chromatids from the matching strand. This exchange process is called *crossing over*. As a result of crossing over, the genes in the chromatids are arranged in ways that differ from both the maternal and paternal genetic patterns, adding another source of genetic variation.

At the first cell division, the homologs (matching members) of each of the 23 pairs of chromosomes reach the two poles of the cell, and the cell divides, forming two new cells. Each of these new cells has 23 chromosomes, not 23 pairs as would be the case in a normal body cell.

During the second cell division, the two daughter cells separate, producing four new cells, each with 23 unpaired chromosomes.

There is a very important difference between meiosis in sperm cells and meiosis in egg cells. In egg cells, the division of the cytoplasm during meiosis is not equal. In both cell divisions, most of the cytoplasm goes to only one of the offspring cells. The other offspring cells, called polar bodies, are tiny cells that cannot produce a new individual. When meiosis is concluded in the female, the egg cell has one set of 23 chromosomes, just as a sperm cell has one set of 23 chromosomes. However, for females, each cell that completes meiosis produces only one egg cell with 23 chromosomes rather than the four sperm cells with 23 chromosomes that are produced through meiosis in males.

The Timing of Meiosis for Males and Females

In males, gametes are not generated until puberty is reached. Once gamete production begins, however, meiosis proceeds as described above. Gametes are produced throughout the remainder of the male's life.

In females, meiosis begins in the prenatal stage with the formation of potential egg cells. In female embryos, some normal cells from the ovary enter meiosis, producing roughly 400,000 potential egg cells that begin to be active. These active cells stop developing in prophase I and remain at this point for a number of years, allowing a great deal of time for crossing over to occur. Meiosis resumes when the female enters puberty. At monthly intervals, one egg cell resumes meiosis, and the course of gamete development proceeds into meiosis II; then the process stops again. (In most animals, many egg cells are produced at each ovulation, and a litter of offspring is produced. Humans sometimes produce two or more eggs, but usually one egg cell is released each month.)

Mature egg cell production begins at puberty and continues until menopause, during a woman's 50s. The fact that women have a finite number of fertile years has given rise to the notion of the biological clock which is discussed in Box 5.2. During *ovulation*, an egg cell is released from the ovary. Fertilization stimulates the egg cell to complete meiosis II. Just about all of the cytoplasm of the original cell remains with the egg cell. Some supplemental cytoplasm is produced in the periods between the cell divisions. The material in the cytoplasm is used for the building blocks and source of energy needed for early cell divisions in the developing organism. This supply lasts until the zygote implants itself into the inner layer of the uterus.

The Transmission of Genetic Information

Genetic factors guide the emergence of individual characteristics and the tempo of growth. In fact, many predispositions for behavior appear to be the result of genetic instructions. For some time, the impact of genetic factors could only be assessed indirectly by observing the common threads of specific characteristics among offspring or relatives. However, with current technology, it is possible to observe genetic commonalities directly, through analysis of DNA. The discovery of the *genetic code* and initial efforts to map the *human genome* (the complete genetic information for human beings) are scientific achievements of the latter half of the twentieth century.

Scientists predict that the full map of the human genome will be complete within the next 10 years (Jaroff, 1989; Olson, 1995). This will have enormous implications for our understanding of human development and aging, health and disease, and many aspects of personality and behavior. Therefore, it is more important today than it was in the past for students of child development to be knowledgeable about the biological bases of reproduction and heredity.

BOX 5.2

The Biological Clock

You have undoubtedly heard the expression "her biological clock is ticking" when speaking about a woman's fertile years. Actually, you might think of this clock as an hourglass filled at the top with oocytes. The roughly 400,000 oocytes that a woman is born with are her lifetime allotment. When puberty begins, only about 20,000 of these immature eggs are still viable. With each menstrual period, one egg reaches maturity and is released. As many as another thousand wither away and are absorbed into the body. Thus, eggs and oocytes are trickling to the bottom of the hourglass every month. The supply of eggs and the quality of the egg cells decline over time. Finally, during a woman's 50s, ovulation stops altogether.

Contemporary lifestyles place many women in a race with their biological clocks. The availability of effective contraceptives permits women to engage in sexual intercourse without the risk of conception. Economic factors and changes in social norms have contributed to greater involvement of women in the labor market. As a result, many women are able to postpone childbearing in order to advance in their careers. Norms toward later age at first marriage and smaller family size are other factors that result in decisions to postpone childbearing.

You might think that women age 35 or 40 who have postponed earlier childbearing are still young enough to begin a family. Today, as compared with the turn of the century, women can expect to live to 85 or 90, with an expanded healthy adulthood of 35 or 40 years beyond age 40, certainly long enough to rear a child to a stage of independence and social maturity. However, the reproductive system has not yet adapted biologically to accommodate this new era of increased longevity; menopause still begins sometime during the end of the fifth decade or the beginning of the sixth decade of life.

As with many other natural barriers and limitations, medical interventions are being devised to defy the biological clock. At age 52, Jonie Mosby Mitchell decided that she wanted to bear a child. Through hormone therapy, her physician was able to reverse the effects of menopause. Then, by fertilizing an egg from a younger woman with Mrs. Mitchell's husband's sperm, the physician was able to help Mrs. Mitchell give birth (Gorman, 1991). This is not a common practice, and certainly not very affordable. You can imagine just how committed Mrs. Mitchell must have been to bearing a child to go through the many procedures necessary to make this birth possible. This example illustrates one more way in which psychosocial factors influence the reproductive process.

This section of the chapter outlines the biochemistry of genetic information and the processes involved in copying genetic information from one cell to the next. This is the most microscopic level on which the reproductive processes will be described in this text. The purpose of providing this level of detail is to ensure that you appreciate the delicate complexity of the reproductive process and how miraculous it is that this process occurs so regularly with so few errors. We then introduce the laws of heredity, discovered by Gregor Mendel, which help explain how hereditary traits are transmitted from one generation to the next.

Genetic information provides a map and a set of instructions for development. The information that specifies the approximately 100,000 different proteins that carry out life's processes is encoded in a linear sequence of approximately 3 billion pairs of *bases*. The sequence is strung out over the 22 pairs of autosomal chromosomes (the two members of a pair of chromosomes have the same basic organization) and the two sex chromosomes (which may or may not be the same) that are present in each human cell (see Figure 5.5).

Chromosomes are made up of genes which are composed of *DNA* (deoxyribonucleic acid) molecules. A *gene* is a portion of DNA that codes for one hereditary characteristic, such as eye color, and occupies a specific place

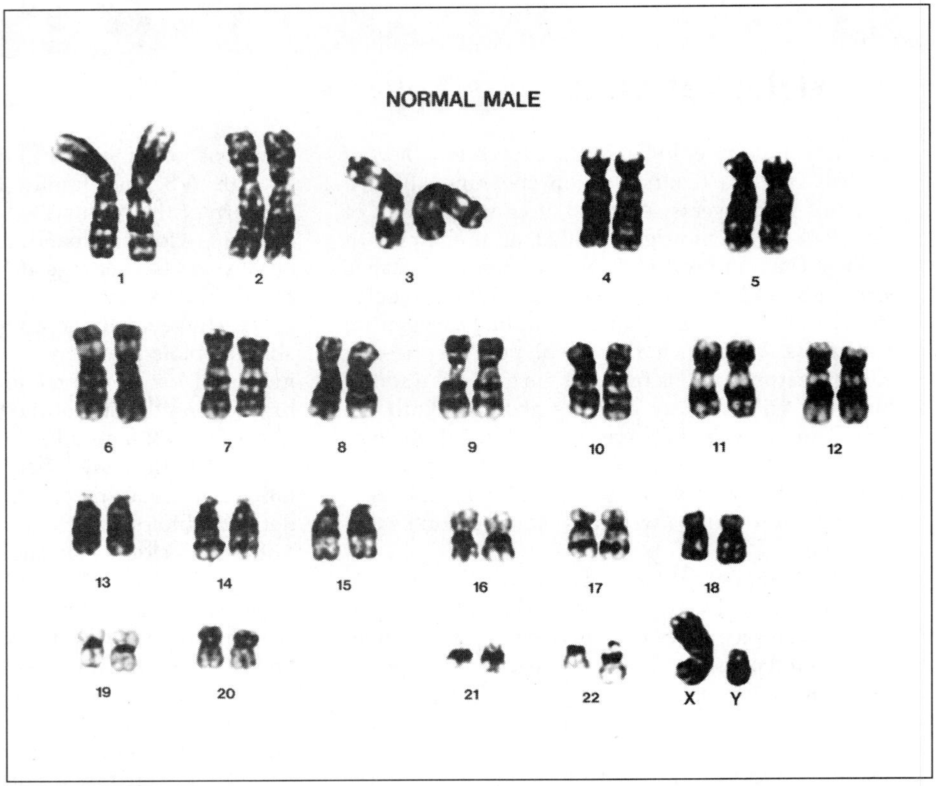

NORMAL MALE

FIGURE 5.5
Human male chromo-
somes. The chromosomes
are at the prometaphase
stage of mitosis and are
arranged in a standard
classification, numbered 1
to 22 in order of length
and with the X and Y
chromosomes shown
separately.
Photomicrograph courtesy of
Chin Ho, The Hospital for Sick
Children, Toronto.

on a chromosome. Human beings have about 100,000 functional genes distributed along the 23 pairs of chromosomes. Chromosome pairs differ in size, and it is estimated that some chromosomes contain over a thousand genes, while others contain over two thousand. The smallest human chromosome, chromosome 21, contains 50 million base pairs of DNA; the largest, chromosome 1, contains roughly 250 million base pairs (Thompson, McInnes & Willard, 1991).

This is ". . . one of the most remarkable facts in all of science: The development of a human being is guided by just 750 megabytes of digital information. In vivo, this information is stored as DNA molecules in an egg or sperm. In a biologist's personal computer, it could be stored on a single CD-ROM" (Olson, 1995, 396).

DNA is the basic ingredient of the genetic structure. The DNA molecule has the shape of a double helix, which is similar to a twisted rope ladder. The sides of this genetic ladder are composed of alternating units of sugar (deoxyribose) and phosphate. The rungs are made up of pairs of nitrogen bases. Four bases are involved. They are *adenine* (A), *guanine* (G), *cytosine* (C), and *thymine* (T). These bases are often referred to by their initial letter, and the letters A, G, C, and T are called the genetic alphabet.

A nitrogen base plus the sugar and phosphate molecules to which it is connected is called a *nucleotide.* The information code of DNA is distinguished by the four bases in the nucleotides. The order in which the nucleotides occur determines the meaning of the genetic message.

DNA replication includes its own amazingly sensitive mechanisms for identifying and repairing errors.
Source: From "The Molecular Genetics of Hemophilia," by R. M. Lawn and G. A. Vehar, p. 50. Copyright © 1986 by *Scientific American,* Inc. All rights reserved.

The Replication of DNA

Life depends on the accurate transmission of genetic information. Genetic messages are passed along through generations of dividing cells. In the context of species evolution, the organism must be able to achieve an optimal balance between avoiding errors in the replication of DNA and permitting some errors (mutations) that might contribute to a species' ability to adapt to new environmental conditions. ". . . The optimal efficiency of error avoidance and error correction depends on the organism and the conditions in which it finds itself. When life is good and easy, change is more a threat than a benefit; when life is hard, sometimes only change can help" (Radman & Wagner, 1988).

The genetic instructions for forming a human being from a single fertilized egg require about three billion units which must be replicated about a million billion times. Imagine tangling and untangling a microscopic thread of genetic material over and over again as chromosomes duplicate and divide. The actual rate of error in this amazingly accurate process involving copying, checking, and transmitting information from one cell to the next is approximately one in 10 billion (Radman & Wagner, 1988).

During DNA replication, the two strands of the DNA molecule separate at the connection of the two bases on the rung. This is often described as "unzipping." After the strands become unzipped, a new side is created on each of the single strands to complete the double helix structure. The nucleotides of the single strands create new nucleotides out of material that is available in the cell nucleus.

There is no choice about what to construct. For a nucleotide with a sugar and phosphate side and a thymine (T) half rung, adenine (A) is the only base that can be joined; when the nucleotide has guanine (G) as the half rung, only

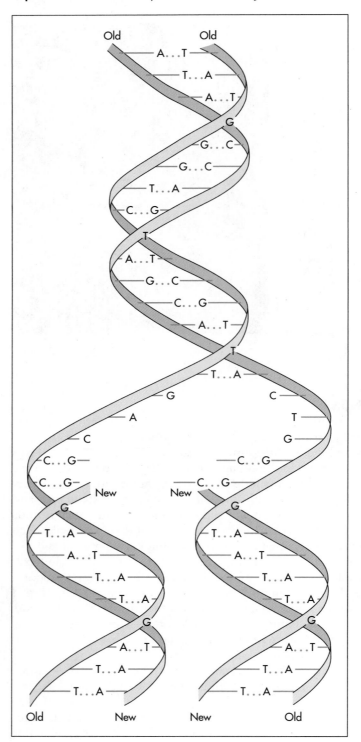

FIGURE 5.6
DNA replication

cytosine (C) will fit. From the two unzipped sides of the old double helix, two new double helixes are created. Figure 5.6 displays a schematic of DNA unzipping and beginning to synthesize new strands. Several enzyme-guided processes assure the accuracy of the replications so that errors can be expelled if the nucleotide matchup is incorrect (Radman & Wagner, 1988; Trefil, 1995).

Mutations

Any changes in the nucleotide sequence from the original DNA molecule is considered a *mutation.* Mutations can occur in the somatic cells during normal mitosis and in the gametes during meiosis. Mutations occur in two ways. Some errors arise in the normal process of DNA replication and transfer. Others are a result of exposure to certain toxins in the environment such as radiation. The errors that occur in normal DNA replication are rare, only one in every 10 million base pairs. And an estimated 99.9% of these errors are counteracted through self-correcting enzymes.

Mutations introduce new variability into the genome from parent to offspring only when they occur in the gametes. When groups of people are isolated from one another, mutations that arise in one population begin to establish characteristics that are unique to that group. Thus, mutations are what account for the genetically based differences among human races and among subpopulations described as ethnic groups that were established roughly 100,000 years ago (Thompson, McInnes & Willard, 1991).

The Laws of Heredity

Genetic information links each new person to the human species in general and to a specific genetic ancestry. Therefore, when we talk about inherited characteristics, we are actually referring to two different kinds of heredity. The first kind includes all the genetic information that we share as members of the human species. We inherit genetic information that is common to all human beings such as patterns of motor behavior (walking erect, for instance), brain size, and body structure, including the relative size of the head, torso, and limbs. Two of the most relevant of these species-related characteristics are the readiness to learn and the inclination to participate in social interaction. All humans share these attributes.

The second kind of heredity refers to characteristics that have been transmitted through a specific *gene pool.* Such traits as hair color, skin color, blood group, and height all result from the genetic information passed on from one generation to the next. Intellectual factors such as IQ, specific cognitive abilities, academic achievement, reading disability, and mental retardation also show significant genetic influence. Even personality factors such as extroversion and neuroticism, which are globally distributed, are genetically determined (Plomin, 1989). Some attitudes and beliefs, such as traditionalism, seem to be inherited (Martin et al., 1986; Tellegen et al., 1988), while various forms of psychopathology, including schizophrenia, affective disorders, and alcoholism, have been shown to have inheritable potential (Plomin, 1989). The principles of genetics that we will be discussing refer primarily to this second group of inherited characteristics, the products of specific gene pools.

There are 2^{23} possible combinations of chromosome separation for any individual's gametes. When one considers the chance meeting of one particular sperm and one particular egg cell, the possible number of different individuals that might be produced by two adults is $2^{23} \times 2^{23}$, or 64 trillion,

BOX 5.3

The Social Chemistry of Mate Selection

With all the possible pairings of human beings and the trillions of potentially distinct offspring that any two partners might produce, you might wonder why we see as much similarity between siblings as we do. Part of the answer comes from the process of mate selection. Even though we may believe that in the United States we are relatively unconstrained in the choice of a sexual partner, it turns out that mate selection is not random. Many filters are applied as couples progress from first meetings to a commitment to marry and reproduce. The figure to the right illustrates four phases of increasing involvement in the mate selection process (Adams, 1986). At each phase, a relationship can be terminated if the key issues of that stage produce undesirable information or evaluation on the part of either member of the couple. A relationship can also be disrupted if an alternative attraction reduces commitment to the original relationship. The alternative attraction could be another person, but it might also be a job, school, or pursuit of a personal goal.

Two of the major factors that reduce variability between mates are stratification and assortative mating. *Stratification* refers to the fact that the larger population is divided into subgroups that are unlikely to intermarry. In the United States, race and religion are two categories of stratification that reduce genetic variability between partners. *Assortative mating* refers to choosing a partner who has a particular trait. Usually, this means a person selecting someone who resembles him or her in certain highly valued areas. Consider the elements mentioned in each phase of the mate selection model. Many of them have a documented genetic base. Physical appearance, certain aspects of social behavior (like being outgoing or reserved), similarity of racial background, equality of intellectual potential, strength of sexual motivation, and the capacity for empathy are all examples of genetically inherited characteristics. Thus, to the extent that mate selection results in the pairing of partners who have many inherited characteristics in common, the vast range of potential individual differences among offspring is somewhat reduced.

The mate selection process in the United States ▶
Source: Adams, B. N. (1986). *The family: A sociological interpretation* (4th ed.). San Diego: Harcourt, Brace, Jovanovich. Reprinted by permission.

without taking crossing over into account! With crossing over introducing sequences of specific genetic information on a chromosome that are unlike either the original maternal or paternal code, the amount of expected variation among offspring is further increased. In Box 5.3, we explore some of the reasons that offspring are similar as a result of the similarities between their parents.

The laws that govern the process by which genetic information is transmitted from parent to offspring were discovered by Gregor Mendel, a monk who studied the inherited characteristics of plants, particularly garden peas (Mendel, 1866). His laws were formulated long before the discovery of the biochemical materials composing genes and chromosomes. Mendelian principles of inheritance are described below.

Alleles

In the 22 pairs of identical chromosomes, each gene has at least two states or conditions, one on each chromosome strand in the pair. These alternative states are called *alleles*. Whatever the allelic state of the gene from one parent, the other parent's allele for the gene may be either the same or different. If both alleles are the same, the gene is said to be *homozygous*. If the alleles are different, the gene is *heterozygous*.

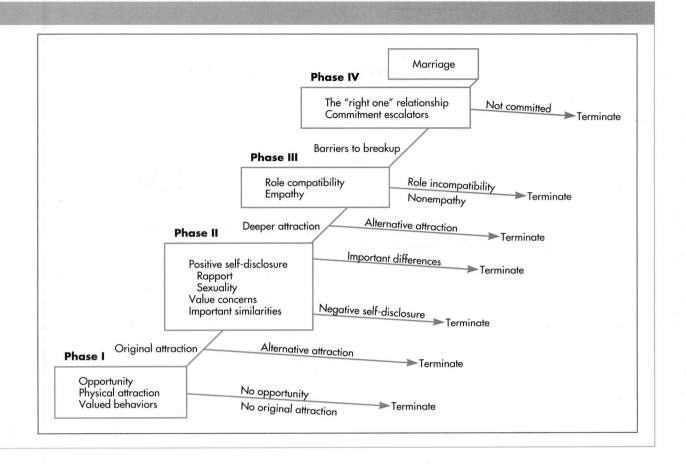

Genotype and Phenotype

The genetic information about a trait is called the *genotype*. The observed characteristic, i.e., the appearance of a living thing, is called the *phenotype*. There are three ways in which genotype influences phenotype: cumulative relations, codominance, and dominance relations.

Cumulative Relations. Sometimes, the differences in the allelic states of a gene result in a *cumulative relation,* in which more than one pair of genes influence the trait. An example of this kind of relation is the genetic contribution to height. If a person receives mostly "tall" genes, the person will be tall. If the person receives mostly "short" genes, then the person will be short. Most people receive a mix of "tall" and "short" genes and are of average height. The kinds of genes that a person has for height are the genotype; the person's actual measured height is the phenotype.

Codominance. In some instances, the differences between alleles can result in *codominance,* a state in which both genes are expressed in the new cell. An example of codominance is the AB blood type that results from the joining of an A allele and a B allele. This blood type is not a mixture of A and B, nor is A subordinated to B or B to A. Instead, a new blood type, AB, is formed.

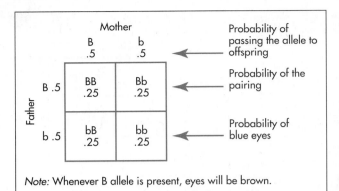

FIGURE 5.7

The probability of producing a blue-eyed offspring from two heterozygous brown-eyed parents

Dominance Relations.   The differences in the allelic states of a gene can also result in a *dominance* relation. Dominance means that if one allele is present, it is always observed, whether or not the other allele is the same. The allele that dominates is called the *dominant gene.* The allele that is present but is masked in the presence of the dominant gene is called the *recessive gene.* The recessive characteristic will appear or be observed only if the person's genes contain two identical alleles for the characteristic; in other words, the gene must be homozygous.

Eye color is the result of a dominance relation. The gene for brown eyes (B) is dominant over the gene for blue eyes (b). There are four possible gene combinations related to brown or blue eye color: BB, Bb, bB, and bb. Only if both parents carry the b allele and if that allele is present in both of the gametes that form the offspring will the child have blue eyes. The probability of the recessive trait of blue eyes emerging in the offspring of two heterozygous (brown-eyed) parents is illustrated in Figure 5.7. As the figure shows, on the average only 25 percent of the offspring of heterozygous (brown-eyed) parents would have blue eyes.

In the case of a dominance relation, genetic information (genotype) is not always observed in some outward characteristic (phenotype). For example, people with alleles BB or Bb have brown eyes, but their genetic information is different. Therefore, for brown or blue eye color, there are *two* phenotypes, brown and blue, but there are *three* genotypes, BB, Bb, and bb (BB and bb both represent homozygous genes; Bb and bB are heterozygous genes).

Sex-Linked Characteristics

Certain genetic information is said to be *sex-linked* because the allele for the specific characteristic is found on the sex chromosomes. The female ova bear only X chromosomes. Half of the male sperm bear Y chromosomes, and half bear X chromosomes. Male children can only be produced when a Y-bearing sperm fertilizes the egg, resulting in an XY combination in the 23rd chromosome pair. All unions between an X-bearing sperm and an egg result in female children. Since males are the only source of Y chromosomes, only males can provide the genetic information that results in male offspring.

Sex-linked traits are more likely to be observed in males even though they are present in the genotype of females. You will understand this more readily if you visualize the XY chromosome pair (refer to Figure 5.5). If a recessive trait is carried on the X chromosome, there will be no second X to pro-

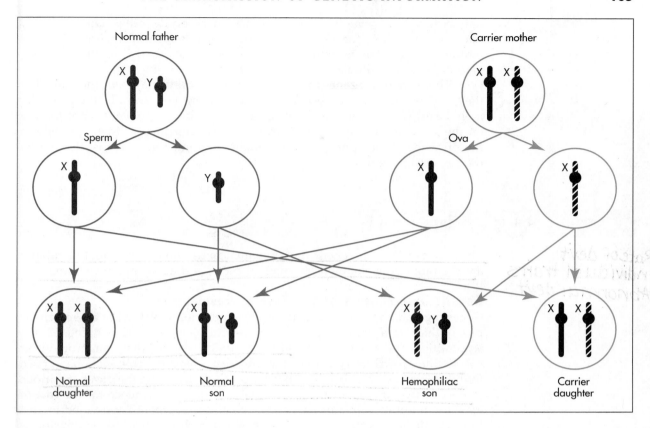

Normal father

Carrier mother

Sperm

Ova

Normal
daughter

Normal
son

Hemophiliac
son

Carrier
daughter

vide a dominant allele, so the recessive trait will always appear in the phenotype. *Fragile X syndrome* is an example of a sex-linked, chromosomal genetic disease. A small part of the tip of the X chromosome breaks off. The damage is linked to various levels of neurological deficit, including mental retardation and learning disabilities, as well as abnormal growth regulation. Boys are more likely to be severely affected by the condition than girls since they do not have a normal X to balance the deficits of the fragile X.

The Y chromosome is quite small, and very few Y-linked traits have been identified. However, when a trait is carried on the Y chromosome, it will be inherited and transmitted only by males, since only males have a Y chromosome. One of the key genes that does reside on the Y chromosome is referred to as TDF, testis-determining factor. This gene (or genes) is responsible for setting into motion the differentiation of the testes during embryonic development. Once the testes are formed, they produce hormones that account for further differentiation of the male reproductive system.

Hemophilia is an example of a sex-linked trait. (See Figure 5.8). The allele for hemophilia is carried on the X chromosome. Hemophiliacs do not have a specific blood protein that causes blood to clot after a wound is inflicted (Lawn & Vehar, 1986). Therefore, even a small cut or bruise is potentially life-threatening for a hemophiliac because any internal or external bleeding cannot be stopped. If the allele is either heterozygous or homozygous for the dominant characteristic (normal clotting), a female child will have normal blood-clotting capacity. Only if the female child is homozygous for the recessive characteristic will she be a hemophiliac. This is very rare, and there are

FIGURE 5.8

Sex-linked inheritance of hemophilia results from the location of the factor VIII gene on the X chromosome. A male carrying a mutant factor VIII gene lacks normal factor VIII and is a hemophiliac. A female carrier is protected by the normal gene on her second X chromosome, but half her daughters will be carriers and half her sons will be hemophiliacs. The sons of a hemophiliac father will not be hemophiliacs but his daughters will be carriers.
Source: Lawn, R. M. & Vehar, G. A. (1986). The molecular genetics of hemophilia. *Scientific American, 254,* 50.

only a very few female hemophiliacs. The male, on the other hand, has only one potential allele for the blood-clotting gene, which he inherits from his mother. If that allele is dominant, his blood clots normally. If it is recessive, he will be a hemophiliac.

There are other genes that are expressed in only one sex or the other, but they are not found on the sex chromosome per se. For example, the genes for male beard development and for female breast development are not located on the sex chromosomes. However, these characteristics will emerge only in the presence of the appropriate hormonal environment, which is directed by the sex chromosomes.

Genetic Sources of Individuality

— Rate of dev't
—Individual traits
— Abnormal dev't

Three areas in which genetic determinants contribute to individual variability are the rate of development, individual traits, and abnormal development.

Genetic Determinants of the Rate of Development

Genes regulate the rate and sequence of maturation. The idea of an epigenetic plan, which is a core proposition of psychosocial theory, is based on the assumption that there is a genetically guided system that can promote or restrict the growth of cells over the life span. Genetic factors also have been found to play a role in behavioral development, including the onset of various levels of reasoning, language, and social orientation. Evidence for the role of genetics in guiding the rate and sequence of development is provided in part from studies of identical twins. The rate at which identical twins develop is highly correlated, even when those twins are reared apart. A variety of characteristics, including the acquisition of motor skills, personality development, changes in intellectual capacity among adult twins, and the timing of physical maturation, all show a strong genetic influence (Holden, 1987).

genes as internal regulators

Genes can be viewed as internal regulators. They set the pace for maturation. They signal the onset of significant developmental changes across the life span, such as growth spurts, the eruption of teeth, puberty, and menopause. They also appear to set the limits of the life span, guiding the timing for physical decline and death. A small number of genes influence the number of times that cells from a specific organism can divide and replicate (Marx, 1988). Research with three different animal species including fruit flies, worms, and mice, show that by breeding the most long-lived of a species, the offspring have a longer life span than average (Barinaga, 1991).

Differences in the rate of development contribute to our understanding of psychosocial growth. The study of behavioral genetics has shown that the accomplishment of certain skills by a specific age is not wholly under a child's control. Maturation is partially dependent on the genetically determined rate of development. Children are not trying to be "slow" or "accelerated." They are responding to an inner plan for their own developmental growth. These differences bring children into contact with new aspects of their environments and provide them with changing capacities at different chronological ages. Adult expectations for the accomplishment of specific tasks such as toilet training, getting dressed without help, or being able to write should take into account the child's developmental level. Adults may convey unreasonable dis-

Many of the differences in physical appearance between these two children, including height, hair color, eye color, skin color, and facial features, are governed by genetic factors.

appointment to developmentally "late" children, as well as pride and approval to developmentally "accelerated" children. Well-documented consequences of the rate of development are discussed in Chapter 15 where we focus on early and late entry into puberty. Especially for boys, early maturing appears to be accompanied by distinct social advantages, while there are some social disadvantages for girls.

Genetic Determinants of Individual Traits

Genes contain specific information about a wide range of human characteristics, from eye color and height to the ability to taste a particular substance called phenylthiocarbamide (to tasters, it is bitter; to nontasters, it has no taste at all). Some of these characteristics are controlled by a single gene. In humans, however, most significant characteristics, such as height, weight, blood group, skin color, and intelligence, are controlled by the combined action of several genes. When multiple genes are involved in the regulation of a trait, the variability in that trait increases.

Recent work suggests that genetic factors play a substantial role in accounting for individual differences in personality (Holden, 1987; Plomin, 1990). Two basic characteristics, extroversion (a tendency to be sociable and outgoing) and neuroticism (a tendency to be anxious and emotionally sensitive), are pervasive dimensions of personality that appear to be determined largely by genetics. Even in rather specific areas of personality such as political attitudes, aesthetic preferences, and sense of humor, identical twins show greater similarity than fraternal twins.

Genetic factors do not tell the entire story of the direction of growth and adaptation. However, they are important in setting the stage or establishing significant parameters for development. The area of temperament provides a good example of how genetic determinants of individuality can influence the

temperament – response to environment

temperament influences how others respond and react to a person.

process of adaptation to the family group. *Temperament* refers to relatively stable characteristics of response to the environment that can be observed during the first months of life (Hubert et al., 1982; Lerner, 1983; Thomas & Chess, 1980). There is considerable evidence supporting the conclusion that aspects of temperament such as activity level, sociability, and emotionality have a strong genetic component (Buss & Plomin, 1984; Plomin, 1990).

A child's temperament influences the tone of his or her interactions, the frequency of interactions, the way others respond to the child, and the way the child responds to those reactions. A highly active, social child is likely to initiate a number of interactions and to respond positively to the attention of others. A more passive, introverted child will seek out interactions less frequently and may recoil from the advances of adults or children in the environment. From this example, you can see that the same home environment may not actually be experienced in the same way for two temperamentally distinct children. These two children have the potential to call forth different patterns of response from their parents, their siblings, and other caregivers.

To add to the picture, genetics contribute to the fit between the parents' temperaments and the child's temperament (Bates & Pettit, 1981; Buss & Plomin, 1975; Plomin, 1990). Chess and Thomas (1984) suggested that a *goodness of fit* model between parent and child determines whether the child experiences support for his or her temperamental style and develops optimally or encounters inappropriate and disruptive parental responses. For example, an active, socially outgoing parent might feel some disappointment with a baby who is withdrawn and does not respond eagerly to social interaction. The parent may become discouraged and stop initiating interactions, or the parent may become intrusive and demand behaviors that the child finds difficult or stressful. Of course, it is possible that the parent will become more accepting of the child's reserved nature or that the child will become more skilled at mutually satisfying interactions. In this sense, genetic individuality does not provide the final script, only the initial directions of the relationship. In Notebook Page 5.3, we ask you to consider the genetic ancestry that may account for some of your own individual characteristics.

Genetic Determinants of Abnormal Development

In addition to characteristics such as physical appearance, temperament, personality, talent, and intellectual capacity that are influenced by genetic information, a wide variety of abnormalities or *anomalies* have a genetic cause. The most dramatic anomalies result in spontaneous abortion, or miscarriage, of the fetus early in pregnancy. It is estimated that a majority of the spontaneous abortions occurring early in pregnancy are the result of chromosomal abnormalities in the fertilized zygotes that would cause major developmental defects or that interfere with basic mechanisms of mitosis and the formation of organ structures (Clayman, 1989).

In the United States, anomalies occur in about 6 to 7% of the population (Cunningham et al., 1989). Anomalies that are present at birth are referred to as *congenital disorders*. However, not all congenital disorders have a genetic cause (see Figure 5.9).

Some genetic and chromosomal disorders are listed in Table 5.1. About 300 genetic disorders that result from a dominant gene have been identified;

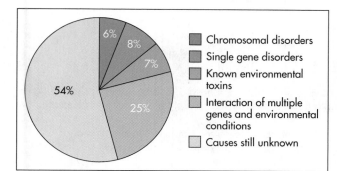

FIGURE 5.9
Causes of congenital disorders
Source: Adapted from Moore, K. L. (1988). *The developing human: Clinically oriented embryology* (4th ed.). Philadelphia: W. B. Saunders.

about 250 disorders that result from a recessive gene have been identified. Molecular biologists have been able to identify the chromosomal site of a number of genetic disorders. This work is leading to a clearer understanding of the molecular mechanisms that account for these disorders and, in some instances, to the development of gene therapies for some genetic and other metabolic diseases (Crystal, 1995).

The variety of genetic abnormalities serves to broaden the range of individual variability. Many of the irregularities pose a challenge to the person's adaptive capacities and to the caregiving capacities of adults in the culture. Even relatively mild irregularities may be significant factors in a person's psychological functioning. The presence of a white shock of hair, a birthmark, an elongated middle toe, or a long nose reminds each of us of our uniqueness. Because these characteristics may be present in our parents, grandparents, or great-grandparents, certain inherited features link us quite obviously with our ancestry. Although many of these irregularities may not be of medical concern or require treatment, they are relevant to an evolving sense of self. Sometimes, however, the irregularities pose a real threat to health or impede a person's level of functioning. Certain genetic diseases are linked directly to one's ancestry; the incidence of some genetic diseases is higher in certain populations than in others (see Box 5.4).

Genetic Technology and Psychosocial Evolution

The products of psychosocial evolution, including behavioral adaptations, the transfer of knowledge, new inventions, and new forms of social organization, were once considered to be carried by social mechanisms rather than incorporated into the genetic structure. However, current and future levels of technology and knowledge about human biology will allow us to intervene in order to modify the genotype. As a result of the human genome-mapping project, the locations of specific disease sites are becoming known. This information could lead to the correction of genetic errors, new treatments for genetic diseases, and, theoretically, the creation of new characteristics. Thus, our society is entering a potentially revolutionary new era of psychosocial evolution in which knowledge can be used to alter genetic material.

In 1988, the U.S. government approved the first transfer of a foreign gene into humans (Roberts, 1989). In this first test, the transplanted gene served as a *marker* to help track the progress of an experimental cancer treatment. This experiment was not considered *gene therapy* because the transplanted gene was not expected to produce a therapeutic benefit. As of 1995, there were 38

TABLE 5.1

Examples of Genetic and Chromosomal Disorders

I. Genetic disorders

A. Autosomal dominant gene

1. *Achondroplasia (dwarfism):* Abnormal bone growth, especially in the arms and legs, results in short stature, short limbs, a well-developed trunk, and a head of normal size except for somewhat protruding forehead.
2. *Huntington's chorea:* Rapid, jerky, involuntary movements. Deterioration of muscle coordination and mental functioning. Symptoms usually do not appear until age 35 to 50. Results from a genetic defect on chromosome 4.
3. *Marfan's syndrome:* Elongated fingers; deformed chest and spine; abnormal heart. Tendons, ligaments, and joint capsules are weak.

B. Autosomal recessive gene

1. *Albinism:* Hair, skin, and eyes lack the pigment melanin. Often accompanied by visual problems and a tendency to skin cancer.
2. *Cystic fibrosis:* Certain glands do not function properly. The glands in the lining of the bronchial tubes produce excessive amounts of thick mucus, which leads to chronic lung infections. Failure of the pancreas to produce enzymes necessary for the breakdown of fats and their absorption from the intestines leads to malnutrition. Sweat glands are also affected. Often fatal by age 30. Missing base pairs on chromosome 7.
3. *Sickle-cell anemia:* Malformation of red blood cells reduces the amount of oxygen they can carry. Results in fatigue, headaches, shortness of breath on exertion, pallor, jaundice, pain, damage to kidneys, lungs, intestine, and brain.
4. *Tay-Sachs disease:* Absence of a certain enzyme results in the buildup of harmful chemicals in the brain. Results in death before age 3.

C. X-linked recessive

1. *Color blindness:* Defect of light-sensitive pigment in one or more classes of cone cells in the retina of the eye and/or an abnormality or reduced discrimination of light wavelengths within the middle (green) and long (red) parts of the visible spectrum.
2. *Hemophilia:* Absence of blood protein, factor VIII, reduces effectiveness of blood clotting. Severity of disorder varies. Bleeding episodes likely to begin in toddlerhood.
3. *Duchenne muscular dystrophy:* Progressive degeneration of muscle fibers. Most common form of childhood dystrophies. Muscle weakness early in life. Few survive teen years. Thirty percent of affected males are also mentally retarded.

II. Chromosomal disorders

A. Autosomal abnormalities

1. *Down syndrome:* Usually three rather than two chromosomes 21. The excess chromosome results in physical and intellectual abnormalities, including IQ in the range of 30–80; distinctive facial features, heart defects, intestinal problems, hearing defects; susceptibility to repeated ear infections. Tendency to develop narrowing of the arteries in adulthood, with an attendant increase in risk of heart disease. Such people tend to be affectionate and friendly and get along well with other family members. Most are capable of some learning.

B. Sex chromosome abnormalities

1. *Turner's syndrome:* Usually caused by a lack of one X chromosome in a girl; sometimes, one of two X chromosomes is defective; occasionally, some cells are missing on an X chromosome. These abnormalities result in defective sexual development, absence of menstruation, infertility, short stature, narrowing of the aorta, and a degree of mental retardation.
2. *Klinefelter's syndrome:* One or more extra X chromosomes in a boy. This abnormality results in defective sexual development, including enlarged breasts and small testes, infertility, and often mental retardation.
3. *Fragile X syndrome:* A small portion of the tip of the X chromosome is susceptible to breakage under certain conditions. The damage results in mental retardation, learning disabilities, and abnormalities in growth regulation, such as a big head, higher-than-normal birth weight, large or protruding ears, and a long face. Behavior problems include hand flapping, hand biting, hyperactivity, poor eye contact, autism, social withdrawal, and shyness. More boys are affected than girls, and boys' problems tend to be more severe.

BOX 5.4

Race, Ethnicity, and Genetic Disease

Racial and ethnic identity have implications for carrying certain genetic diseases. The comparatively high rate of expression of certain genetic diseases in particular ethnic groups results from early isolation of certain ethnic populations from one another in the history of human evolution. Social norms that guide members of particular groups to marry within their group increase the expression of such diseases and add to the probability that the genes responsible for the disease will be passed along from one generation to the next.

In addition, some particular genetic features are valued by a culture, thereby giving individuals with that feature a reproductive advantage. As an example, among the Hopi Indians of Arizona, albinism is considered to be a highly esteemed feature. Albino males are consequently preferred as partners over their normally pigmented peers, thereby increasing the rate of albinism in this particular group. The following examples illustrate the prevalence of genetic diseases among various racial and ethnic populations.

Cystic fibrosis. In the United States, this disease is present in 1 out of 2,000 live births among white babies but is very rare among nonwhite babies. Only 1 in 90,000 African-Americans has the disease.

Familial mediterranean fever. This disease is found among Sephardic Jews (Jews who settled in Spain after the Diaspora, the dispersion of Jews out-side Palestine in 586 B.C.), Armenians, and Arab families. The symptoms begin between the ages of 5 and 15 and are expressed as episodes of fever, abdominal pain, arthritis, and chest pain. Episodes last from 24 to 48 hours.

G6PD deficiency. The disease, which affects the chemistry of red blood cells, is present in about 15% of U.S. African-American males. A related disease, *favism,* affects people of Mediterranean origin.

Sickle-cell anemia. In the United States, about 150 per 100,000 African-American children suffer from this disease. A high incidence is also found among persons of Mediterranean origin.

Spherocytosis. This is the most common form of inherited anemia in people of Northern European descent. In the United States, 1 out of 4,500 people has the condition.

Tay-Sachs disease. Among Ashkenazi Jews (Jews who settled in eastern Europe after the Diaspora), the incidence is 1 in 3,900, as compared with 1 in 112,000 among U. S. non-Ashkenazi Caucasians.

Thalassemia. The disease involves faulty production of hemoglobin, the material that carries oxygen in the blood. It is found most often in people from Mediterranean, Middle Eastern, and Southeast Asian origins.

Sources: Emery and Mueller, 1992; Thompson et al., 1991; & Clayman, 1989.

---

human studies in which evidence of gene transfer had been observed from one day to 36 months, depending on the disease target and the method of transfer. However, no human disease has yet been cured using this method. These techniques are highly specific, very expensive, and involve sophisticated medical and scientific expertise. We are nowhere near any kind of medical intervention that would have widespread impact via pills or injection of a protective gene to prevent or counteract a genetic disease (Anderson, 1992; Crystal, 1995).

Currently, widespread intervention consists of *genetic counseling,* which involves efforts to predict recurrences of a family's genetic disease. Individuals or couples whose families have a history of a genetic disease or who are otherwise concerned about the possibility of transmitting a genetic disease to their children can undergo blood tests that will identify genes that might result in the inherited disorder. Genetic counselors also help draw a family tree, tracing any history of certain diseases among a comprehensive group of blood relatives. Couples are advised about the likelihood of having children who would be afflicted with the disease and counseled about the consequences and demands for caring for a child with a particular disease.

Family Resemblance

Two adults have the potential for producing at least 64 trillion genetically distinct offspring. Despite this possibility for vast individual differences, we still observe and can measure areas of family resemblance.

What aspects of your own physical and behavioral characteristics do you attribute to heredity?

1. Which of your own physical and behavioral characteristics do you believe were inherited from your biological mother or her ancestors?

_____

_____

_____

2. Which of your own physical and behavioral characteristics do you believe were inherited from your biological father or his ancestors?

_____

_____

_____

3. Do you and your siblings share any characteristics that you consider to be genetically based family traits? What are they?

_____

_____

_____

4. If you were adopted, what information do you have about your genetic ancestry? What questions do you have about this?

_____

_____

_____

The decision about whether or not to have children is left entirely to the couple. However, genetic counseling leads some couples to a decision not to reproduce and thus has the potential for modifying the gene pool.

Ethical Issues in Genetic Technology

Gene transfer, genetic engineering, and genetic fingerprinting, used to help identify criminal suspects, are just some of the issues that are raising new ethical concerns. Although there is consensus that gene therapy for serious diseases such as hemophilia, cancer, or AIDS is ethical, there is much less agreement about the use of genetic intervention on zygotes to enhance aspects of normal development. Through discussion, research, observation, and court cases, we are hammering out a set of ethics that not only deal with specific issues but also set the tone for how we conceptualize life itself.

Evaluating the Impact of Heredity on Behavior

How can we determine the contribution of hereditary factors to behavior? It is almost impossible to distinguish between the influences of genetics and the environment. However, it is clear that the genetic code relies on certain minimum environmental supports such as air, food, and protection from predators and other dangers in order to be expressed.

Reaction Range

One way to summarize the influences of genetics on behavior is to consider the genotype as establishing a *reaction range*. This means that a particular genotype influences the range of possible responses to environmental conditions. Given similar environmental conditions, the impact of genetic differences is most likely to be expressed. However, when environmental conditions vary, the advantages of one genotype over another may be masked by the adversities or opportunities of the situation. This concept is illustrated in Figure 5.10, which shows the hypothetical reaction range for three children with respect to intelligence. Child A has greater genetic potential for intelligence than child B who has greater potential than child C. When all three children are in unstimulating environments, their IQs develop at the lower end of their potential ranges. When all three children are in stimulating environments, their IQs develop toward the upper end of their potential ranges. However, if child A were placed in an unstimulating environment and child C in a stimulating one, differences might not be so clearly observed. Each child's intellectual ability can be expressed as a range that is a product of the interaction of genetic potential and the environment.

A very clear example of the concept of reaction range can be seen in the outlook for children with Down syndrome (Patterson, 1987). This disease, which occurs once in every 700 live births, is the most common genetic cause of mental retardation in the United States. In the early part of this century, children born with Down syndrome had a life expectancy of 9 years. Today, the life expectancy of a Down syndrome child is 30 years, and 25% of these children live to age 50. Good medical care, early and constant educational intervention, physical therapy, and a nurturing home environment can have significant, positive results for a child with Down syndrome. Under optimal

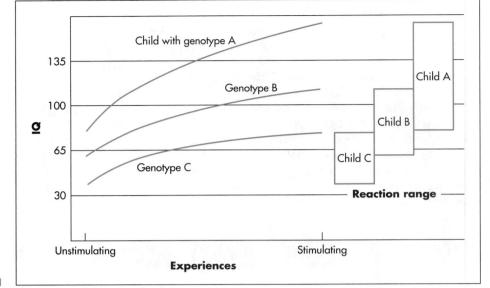

FIGURE 5.10

Hypothetical reaction ranges for intelligence *Source:* Adapted from Gottesman, I. (1963). Genetic aspects of intelligent behavior. In N. Ellis (Ed.), *Handbook of mental deficiency.* New York: McGraw-Hill, 255. Reprinted by permission of the author.

conditions, these children, whose IQs range from 30 to 80, are able to achieve a moderate degree of independence and participate actively in family life.

An Example of Behavioral Genetics: Hereditary Influences on Intelligence

An issue of interest to developmental psychologists, educators, and parents is the relative contribution of genetic and environmental factors to intelligence. This issue has enormous implications for parenting, early intervention, and education. How much can educational intervention make a difference in a child's intellectual development and cognitive attainments?

In fact, intelligent behavior requires the successful integration of both genetic and environmental factors. Genetically, intelligence relies on the structure of the central nervous system and the sense receptors which are a product of genetically guided information. However, the optimal functioning of these systems requires adequate nutrition, rest, and good health—conditions that vary among environments. Intelligence also relies on experience with diverse stimuli, appropriate social interactions, schooling, and the cultivation of problem-solving strategies, which are also elements of the physical and social environment.

The influence of genetic factors on intelligence can be studied in two ways: by observing the impact of genetic diseases on mental capacity and by comparing intellectual attainment among genetically related individuals.

Genetic Irregularities

First, we know that specific genetic irregularities can cause degrees of mental retardation. Two examples are Down syndrome and phenylketonuria (PKU). The Down syndrome child has three chromosomes or a partial triplicate of chromosomes at chromosome 21 rather than the normal two. The additional chromosome leads to an overproduction of enzymes, resulting in both intellectual and physical abnormalities. As we discussed earlier, the severity of developmental delay associated with Down syndrome depends in part on the quality of the child-rearing environment.

With optimal home and school support, a child with Down syndrome can enjoy interacting with peers and learn many skills required for self-sufficiency.

PKU is a condition that results from a recessive gene (p). When a child is homozygous for p, a specific enzyme is not produced. The outcome is that an amino acid, phenylalanine, accumulates in the body and leads to brain damage. If PKU is diagnosed within the first week of life, the negative effects of the condition can be minimized through systematic controlling of diet by reducing the intake of milk and other foods containing phenylalanine. Many other genetic diseases have some negative effect on intellectual growth. Thus, genetic diseases play an indisputable role in restricting intellectual potential, but the severity of their impact can often be modified by appropriate environmental intervention.

Family Relationships

A second approach to understanding the influence of genetics on intelligence is through studying family relationships. The more closely related family members are, the more similar their genetic makeups. If intelligence is influenced by genetics, close relatives should be more similar in intelligence than distant relatives.

Figure 5.11 shows the degree of similarity found in over 100 studies of intelligence for four types of relationships among siblings (Bouchard & McGue, 1981). As the figure illustrates, similarity in intelligence increases with the degree of genetic relatedness. Similarity in intelligence between identical (MZ) twins is striking evidence for the contribution of genetics to intelligence. Findings from the same study show that the correlation between identical twins reared apart is higher than that for fraternal twins reared together (0.72 compared to 0.60). Fraternal (DZ) twins who share the same prenatal experience, home environment, and child-rearing history show much less similarity than identical twins and are not much more alike than ordinary siblings. This comparison offers clear evidence regarding genetic influence on intelligence.

Many of the same studies that provide evidence for genetic contributions to intelligence also highlight the role of the environment. The correlation

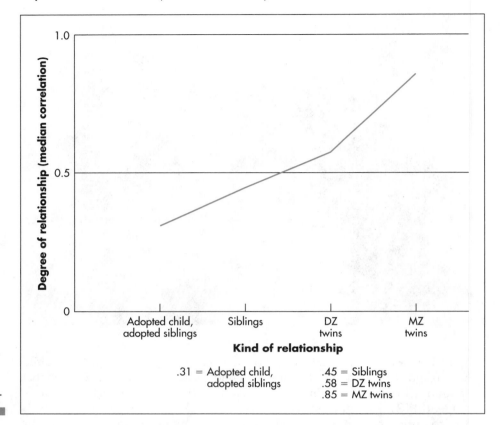

FIGURE 5.11

Similarity in intelligence
for four levels of sibling
relationship
Source: Bouchard, T. J.
and McGue, M. (1981).
Familial studies of intelligence: A review. *Science,*
212, 1055–1059. Copy-
right 1981 AAAS.
Reprinted with permission.

.31 = Adopted child,   .45 = Siblings
         adopted siblings   .58 = DZ twins
                                              .85 = MZ twins

between identical twins is not perfect, suggesting an environmental role even
among children who share identical genetic material. The correlation between identical twins reared apart is smaller than that for identical twins
reared together, once again demonstrating the contribution of environmental
factors in the expression of genetic potential. Plomin (1990) summarized a
large body of research on genetics and intelligence by concluding that roughly
50% of the difference in the way individuals score on IQ tests is due to genetic
differences in the test takers. This means that the remaining 50% is due to
environmental factors and measurement error. The challenge for social scientists, including students of child development, is to try to understand just how
these environmental factors make their contributions and at what point in
development they play their most significant part.

Chapter Summary

1. In sexual reproduction, special cells called gametes unite to form the
    first cell of a new individual. The new cell produced from the gametes
    combines genetic information from the male and female parent cells
    (sperm and egg cells), yielding a genetically unique new organism.

2. Normally, the gametes combine through sexual intercourse. At orgasm, the
    male releases 200 to 500 million sperm which swim into the female repro-

ductive tract to the uterus and the fallopian tubes. If sexual intercourse occurs at a time when an egg has been released, fertilization can occur.

3. Only one sperm can fertilize an egg. After the egg has been penetrated by the sperm, the cell membrane forms a barrier to other sperm cells.

4. In humans, twins are the result of two different processes. Identical twins result when the zygote divides and separates into two separate individual cells, each with identical chromosomes. Fraternal twins result when two eggs are fertilized by two sperm during the same ovulation.

5. Infertility can result from problems in the reproductive system of the male or the female. Artificial insemination, in vitro fertilization, gamete intrafallopian transfer (GIFT), and surrogate mothers are all types of reproductive alternatives or technologies used to overcome barriers to reproduction.

6. Gametes are formed in a process of cell division called meiosis, in which cells are produced that have 23 chromosomes rather than the 46 present in most human cells.

7. For males, gametes are not produced until puberty, and then they are produced for the remainder of the male's lifetime. For females, meiosis begins in the prenatal stage with egg development, continues at puberty with the release of one mature egg per month, and ends at menopause, in the age period 45 to 55.

8. Genetic information is encoded in chains of DNA molecules. DNA is shaped like a twisted rope ladder. The sides of the ladder are composed of sugar and phosphate. The rungs are made up of pairs of four nitrogen bases: adenine, guanine, cytosine, and thymine. These bases, known by their letters, A, G, C, and T, are only found in four combinations: C-G, G-C or A-T, T-A. This is the key of the genetic code.

9. Genes are segments of DNA that account for the production of amino acids and proteins that provide the basic building blocks of human life. There are an estimated 100,000 genes, each one involving 10,000 to 150,000 base pairs.

10. Each gene has at least two states or conditions called alleles. The alleles can be the same (homozygous) or different (heterozygous). Differences in alleles can be reflected in a cumulative, codominance, or dominance relation.

11. Some genetic characteristics are described as sex-linked because the allele is found on the 23rd pair of chromosomes which determines the biological sex of the individual. Females have two X chromosomes in the 23rd pair; males have one X and one Y chromosome. X and Y chromosomes do not contain the same genes.

12. Genes contribute to individual differences in three ways: they direct the rate and sequence of development; they account for individual traits; and they account for abnormalities that affect the pattern of growth and development.

13. Considerable research has been devoted to analyzing the contribution of hereditary factors to intelligence. Genetic diseases clearly impose limits to intellectual capacity. In addition, a range of intellectual ability is established genetically. The extent to which an individual functions at the low, middle, or high end of that range depends largely on the nature of the environment in which development occurs. The impact of heredity on intelligence is most clearly observed among individuals who have been exposed to similar environments.

References

Adams, B. N. (1986). *The family: A sociological interpretation* (4th ed.). San Diego: Harcourt, Brace, Jovanovich.

Anderson, W. F. (1992). Human gene therapy. *Science, 256*, 808–813.

Andrews, L. B. (1984). Yours, mine and theirs. *Psychology Today, 18*, 20–29.

Barinaga, M. (1991). How long is the human life-span? *Science, 254*, 936–938.

Bates, J. E. & Pettit, G. (1981). Adult individual differences as moderators of child effects. *Journal of Abnormal Child Psychology, 9*, 329–340.

Bouchard, T. J. & McGue, M. (1981). Familial studies of intelligence: A review. *Science, 212*, 1055–1059.

Brooks-Gunn, J. & Furstenberg, F. F., Jr. (1989). Adolescent sexual behavior. *American Psychologist, 44*, 249–257.

Buss, A. H. & Plomin, R. (1975). *A temperament theory of personality development*. New York: Wiley.

Buss, A. H. & Plomin, R. (1984). *Temperament: Early developing personality traits*. Hillsdale, N.J.: Erlbaum.

Byrne, G. (1988). Artificial insemination report prompts call for regulation. *Science, 241*, 895.

Chess, S. & Thomas, A. (1984). *Origins and evolution of behavior disorders*. New York: Brunner/Mazel.

Clayman, C. B. (1989). *The American Medical Association encyclopedia of medicine*. New York: Random House.

Crystal, R. G. (1995). Transfer of genes to humans: Early lessons and obstacles to success. *Science, 270*, 404–410.

Cunningham, F. G., MacDonald, P. C. & Gant, N. F. (1989). *William's obstetrics* (18th ed.). Norwalk, Conn.: Appleton & Lange.

Elmer-Dewitt, P. (1991). Making babies. *Time, 138*, 56–63.

Elson, J. (1989). The rights of frozen embryos. *Time*, July 24, 63.

Emery, A. E. H. & Mueller, R. F. (1992). *Elements of medical genetics* (8th ed.). Edinburgh: Churchill Livingstone.

Golombok, S., Cook, R., Bish, A. & Murray, C. (1995). Families created by the new reproductive technologies: Quality of parenting and social and emotional development of the children. *Child Development, 66*, 285–298.

Gorman, C. (1991). How old is too old? *Time, 138*, 62.

Gottesman, I. (1963). Genetic aspects of intelligent behavior. In N. Ellis (Ed.), *Handbook of mental deficiency*. New York: McGraw-Hill, 255.

Hanson, S. L., Myers, D. R. & Ginsburg, A. L. (1987). The role of responsibility and knowledge in reducing teenage out-of-wedlock childbearing. *Journal of Marriage and the Family, 49*, 241–256.

Holden, C. (1987). The genetics of personality. *Science, 237*, 598–601.

Hubert, N. C., Wachs, T. D., Peters-Martin, P. & Gandour, M. J. (1982). The study of early temperament: Measurement and conceptual issues. *Child Development, 53*, 571–600.

Jaroff, L. (1989). The gene hunt. *Time Magazine, 133*, (12), 62–67.

Lacayo, R. (1988). Baby M. meets Solomon's sword. *Time Magazine*, February 15, 97.

Lawn, R. M. & Vehar, G. A. (1986). The molecular genetics of hemophilia. *Scientific American, 254*, 50.

Lerner, R. M. (1983). A "goodness of fit" model of person-context interaction. In D. Magnusson & V. L. Allen (Eds.), *Human development: An interactional perspective*. New York: Academic Press, 280–294.

Martin, N. G., Eaves, L. J., Heath, A. C., Jardine, R., Feingold, L. M. & Eysenck, J. J. (1986). Transmission of social attitudes. *Proceedings of the National Academy of Sciences, USA, 83*, 4364–4368.

Marx, J. (1988). Are aging and death programmed in our genes? *Science, 242*, 33.

Mendel, G. (1866). Experiments with plant hybrids. *Proceedings of the Brunn natural history society*.

Money, J. (1980). *Love and love sickness: The science of sex, gender difference, and pair-bonding*. Baltimore: The Johns Hopkins University Press.

Moore, K. L. (1988). *The developing human: Clinically oriented embryology* (4th ed.). Philadelphia: W. B. Saunders.

Newcomer, S. & Udry, J. R. (1987). Parental marital status effects on adolescent sexual behavior. *Journal of Marriage and the Family, 49*, 235–240.

Olson, M. V. (1995). A time to sequence. *Science, 270*, 394–396.

Patterson, D. (1987). The causes of Down syndrome. *Scientific American, 257*,(2), 52–61.

Plomin, R. (1989). Environment and genes: Determinants of behavior. *American Psychologist, 44*, 105–111.

Plomin, R. (1990). *Nature and nurture: An introduction to human behavioral genetics*. Pacific Grove, Calif.: Brooks/Cole.

Radman, M. & Wagner, R. (1988). The high fidelity of DNA duplication. *Scientific American*, August, 40–46.

Roberts, L. (1989). Human gene transfer approved. *Science, 243,* 473.

Roberts, L. (1991). Does egg beckon sperm when the time is right? *Science, 252,* 214.

Sperling, D. (1989). Success rate for in vitro is only 9%. March 9. *USA Today,* 1D.

Tellegen, A., Lykken, D. T., Bouchard, T. J., Wilcox, K., Segal, N. & Rich, S. (1988). Personality similarity in twins reared apart and together. *Journal of Personality and Social Psychology, 54,* 1031–1039.

Thomas, A. & Chess, S. (1980). *The dynamics of psychological development.* New York: Brunner/Mazel.

Thompson, M. W., McInnes, R. R. & Willard, H. F. (1991). *Genetics in medicine* (5th ed.). Philadelphia: W. B. Saunders.

Trefil, J. (1995). How the body defends itself from the risky business of living. *Smithsonian, 26,* 43–49.

Turner, J. S. & Rubinson, L. (1993). *Contemporary human sexuality.* Englewood Cliffs, N.J.: Prentice-Hall.

Udry, J. R. & Billy, J. O. G. (1987). Initiation of coitus in early adolescence. *American Sociological Review, 52,* 841–855.

Prenatal Development and Birth

The Phases of Prenatal Development
  Development in the First Trimester
    The Germinal Period
    The Embryonic Period
    The Fetal Period
  Development in the Second Trimester
  Development in the Third Trimester

The Psychosocial Context of Pregnancy
  Maternal Nutrition
  Maternal Drug Use
    Alcohol
    Nicotine
    Caffeine
    Addictive Drugs
    Prescription Drugs
  Obstetric Anesthetics
  Environmental Toxins
  Mother's Age
  Mother's Emotional State
  The Impact of the Fetus on the Pregnant Woman
    Changes in Roles and Status
    Changes in the Mother's Emotional State

The Birth Process
  Stages of Labor
  Cesarean Delivery
  Infant Mortality

The Impact of Culture
  The Medical Birth Culture of the United States
  The Birth Culture in Sweden and the Netherlands
  Examples of Birth Cultures in Traditional Societies
    Reactions to Pregnancy and Childbirth
  Cultural Complexity

Abortion
  The Abortion Controversy and the Legal Context
  Difficulties in Evaluating Abortion Research
  What the Research Shows

Optimizing Development in Pregnancy

Chapter Summary

References

Chapter **6**

Guided by a miraculous genetic plan, fetal development takes place within the uterine environment which must provide the essential resources for sustaining full gestational growth. The fetus and mother form an interdependent relationship, an excellent example of the psychosocial framework. In addition, the mother, and through her, the fetus, are typically part of an intimate family relationship. This reproductive family system is an integral element in a social context that determines certain features of pregnancy and childbirth, such as how the pregnant woman is treated, what behaviors she is expected to perform or refrain from during pregnancy, how her behavior is expected to influence her unborn child, and how she will feel about herself. The social context also has implications for the expectant father, his behavior, and self-image.

Pregnancy is a time of heightened emotionality, with opportunities for both increased intimacy and stress. It is a time of arousal, during which both mother and father are motivated to protect the emerging life. In most cases, the intensity of this period evokes new levels of caring and concern between the expectant parents as they anticipate the extension of their relationship in the birth of their child. Sometimes, however, stress destroys the relationship. Men may abandon their pregnant partners; women may be resentful of the baby's father; the couple may be disappointed to find that pregnancy increases the distance between them rather than bringing them closer together. In Notebook Page 6.1 we ask you to consider how pregnancy might influence experiences of intimacy and isolation for a person and for the expectant couple.

The biological father is not always actively involved in the social aspects of a pregnancy. The presence or absence of close, supportive relationships available to a pregnant woman significantly influences her emotional and physical well-being. Social isolation clearly places a pregnant woman and her fetus at risk, not only during pregnancy but in the weeks and months following birth.

This chapter picks up where we left off in Chapter 5 at the moment of fertilization and traces the story of development through the three trimesters of prenatal growth and the birth process. The interdependent relationships among mother, father, and fetus are analyzed. At relevant points, we discuss the father's role as well as how the couple's relationship influences the pregnancy. We then examine the cultural framework surrounding the prenatal and childbirth experiences of the family system. The chapter closes with a psychosocial analysis of the issue of abortion.

The Phases of Prenatal Development

The period of pregnancy, typically 40 weeks after the last menstrual period or 38 weeks from ovulation, is often conceptualized as three 3-month periods called *trimesters*. Each of these trimesters brings changes in the status of the developing fetus and its supporting systems. Major developments for each trimester are summarized in Table 6.1.

Development in the First Trimester

The Germinal Period

After fertilization, the egg begins to divide. In the first series of divisions, the cells do not increase in mass or take on specialized functions. Rather, the cell material is redistributed among several parts of the cell body. In successful implantation, by the sixth day after fertilization the egg makes contact with the lining of the uterus and begins to attach itself. Sometimes, the egg does not reach the uterus but attaches to the fallopian tube or implants on some area of the intestine. The *embryo* may grow in these locations until the organ ruptures. This can pose serious risks to the pregnant woman, involving extensive internal bleeding.

The Embryonic Period

The three weeks following implantation are devoted largely to an elaboration of the support systems that contain the embryo. An *amniotic sac* filled with a clear, watery fluid surrounds the embryo. This fluid acts as a cushion that buffers the embryo, while permitting it to move and change position.

At this point, about three weeks after implantation, when the woman's menstrual period is about two weeks overdue, the first reliable tests can determine if she is pregnant. Once the embryo is firmly implanted in the uterus, special cells in the placenta produce a hormone that maintains the uterine lining. This hormone is excreted through the kidneys, so its presence can be detected in a urine sample.

The *placenta* is an organ that is newly formed for each pregnancy and discarded at birth. It is an exchange station for nutrients and waste, as well as a screen against some materials that could harm the growing embryo (see

TABLE 6.1

Major Developments During Three Trimesters of Fetal Growth

First Trimester	Second Trimester	Third Trimester
Fertilization	Suckling and swallowing	Nervous system matures
Growth of the amniotic sac	Preference for sweet taste	Coordination of sucking and swallowing
Growth of the placenta	Skin ridges on fingers and toes	
Emergence of body parts	Hair on scalp, eyebrows, back, arms, legs	Mechanisms for regulating body temperature
Differentiation of sex organs		More efficient digestion and excretion
Initial formation of central nervous system	Sensitivity to touch, taste, light	
	Sucks thumb	Degeneration of the placenta toward the end of the ninth month
Movement	6-month average size: 10 inches, 2 pounds	
Grasp reflex		9-month average size: 20 inches, 7 to 7½ pounds
Babinski reflex		
Heartbeat		
3-month average size: 3 inches, about 2/5 ounce		

Pregnancy's Relationship to Intimacy and Isolation

Most couples who decide to have children are usually in early adulthood, when the psychosocial crisis involves developing a sense of intimacy as opposed to a sense of isolation.

Intimacy can be defined as the ability to experience an open, supportive, loving relationship with another person without losing one's own identity in the process. Describe specific ways that the challenges of pregnancy might lead to the development of intimacy.

1. For a person:

_____

_____

_____

_____

2. For a relationship:

_____

_____

_____

_____

Isolation can be defined as a heightened sense of separateness from others, which may be experienced as loneliness, depression, or fear of close relationships. Describe specific ways that the challenges of pregnancy might lead to the development of a sense of isolation.

1. For a person:

_____

_____

_____

2. Signs of isolation in a relationship:

_____

_____

_____

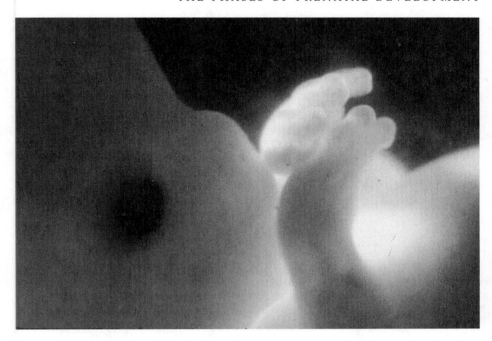

By 8 weeks, the fingers are clearly differentiated. Features of a human face are recognizable.

Figure 6.1). The mother's blood and the embryo's blood, which circulate independently, both pass through the placenta. However, the placenta is an imperfect screen. It permits the mother's blood to deliver oxygen and nutrients to the fetal system and remove waste products from it. In the process, some substances in the mother's system may affect the fetal system.

Agents that can produce malformations in the developing embryonic and fetal tissues and organs are referred to as *teratogens*. Teratogens take a wide variety of forms, such as viruses, medicines that a pregnant woman might ingest, alcohol and other drugs, and environmental toxins. During the first trimester, especially weeks 3 through 9, the embryo is especially sensitive to the disruptive influences of teratogens (Moore, 1993) (see Figure 6.2). Since many women are not aware that they are pregnant in these early weeks, they may inadvertently expose the fetus to drugs or environmental hazards during this critical period.

In the third and fourth weeks of pregnancy, a rapid process of cell differentiation takes place. Cells specialize into structures that will permit them to carry out unique functions in the body. Similar cells are grouped into tissues that gradually emerge as body organs.

The first essential changes in the embryo include the establishment of the body form as an elongated cylinder and the formation of precursors of the brain and heart. By the end of the fourth week, a head, upper trunk, lower trunk, and tail are visible. Limb buds and forerunners of the forebrain, midbrain, hindbrain, eyes, and ears can be observed. The embryo has increased 50 times in size and 40,000 times in weight since the moment of fertilization.

By the end of the second month, the embryo looks quite human. It weighs about 2.25 grams and is about 28 millimeters (an inch) long. Almost all the internal organs are formed, and the external features of the face, limbs,

(handwritten margin note:) teratogens – substances in mothers blood that can harm fetus

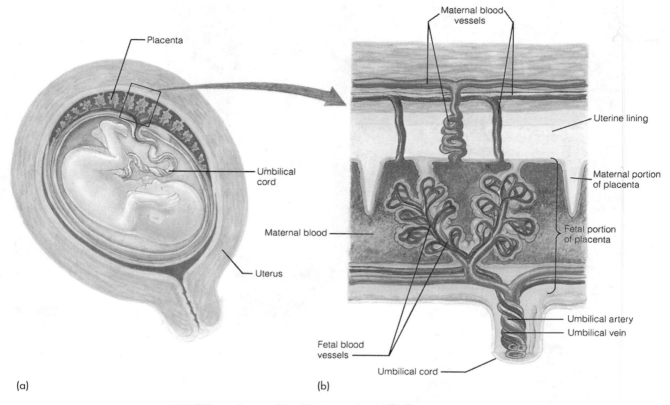

(a)   (b)

FIGURE 6.1

The placenta exchanges nutrients, oxygen, and waste products between the maternal and fetal circulatory systems. (a) The placenta attached to the uterine wall. (b) Close-up detail of placenta.
Source: From Robert Crooks and Karla Baur, *Our Sexuality,* 6th ed. Pacific Grove, Calif.: Brooks/Cole, 1996.

fingers, and toes are established. At eight weeks, the embryo will respond to mild stimulation. The embryonic period ends at about 10 weeks after the last menstrual period. Most of the essential structures are formed by this time.

The Fetal Period

The term *fetus* is used to describe the organism from this point, about ten weeks from conception, until birth. The fetal period consists largely of maturation and growth of structures. In the third month, the fetus grows to 3 inches and its weight increases to 14 grams. The head is about one-third of the total body length. During this month, the fetus assumes the "fetal position"—arms curled up toward the face and knees bent in toward the stomach. The eyelids are fused shut.

Also during this third month, a dramatic change takes place in the sexual organs. All embryos go through a stage in which no sex-linked differentiation can be made. Both females and males have a genital gland or gonad. If the embryo is a genetic male, then the Y chromosome will lead to the production of the H-Y antigen. Under this condition, at about six weeks of life, the gonadal tissues differentiate into testes. Under the XX condition, the gonadal tissues form the ovaries. If the testes are established, testosterone is produced, leading to the formation of the penis and scrotum. The "fallback" position in fetal development is the female pattern of genital structure. In other words, if, for some reason, testosterone is not produced, the baby will develop the reproductive structures of a female even if the chromosomal sex is male (Kimura, 1992; Stechler & Halton, 1982).

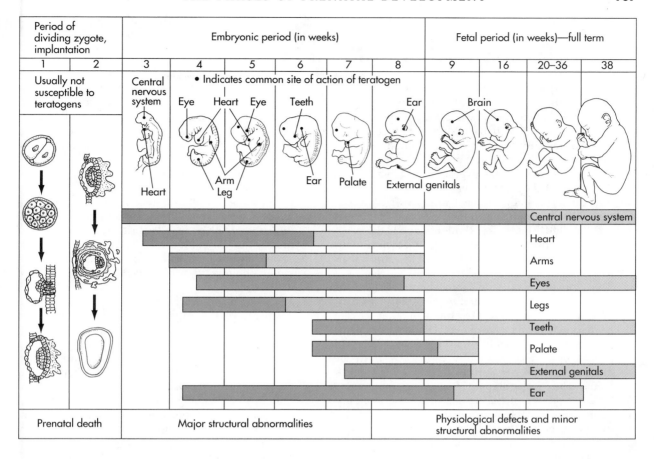

Period of dividing zygote, implantation		Embryonic period (in weeks)						Fetal period (in weeks)—full term			
1	2	3	4	5	6	7	8	9	16	20–36	38

Usually not susceptible to teratogens

• Indicates common site of action of teratogen

Central nervous system · Eye · Heart · Eye · Teeth · Ear · Brain
Heart · Arm · Leg · Ear · Palate · External genitals

	Central nervous system
	Heart
	Arms
	Eyes
	Legs
	Teeth
	Palate
	External genitals
	Ear

Prenatal death	Major structural abnormalities	Physiological defects and minor structural abnormalities

The genetic factors that differentiate the fetus as male or female appear to influence more than the formation of the reproductive organs. Research on the organization and structure of the brain suggests that, during fetal and early postnatal development, sex hormones direct male and female brains along slightly different paths, possibly relating to some gender differences in problem-solving orientation and cognitive skills (Kimura, 1992).

The three-month-old fetus moves spontaneously and has a grasp reflex and a *Babinski reflex* (the toes extend and fan out in response to mildly stroking the sole of the foot). With the use of an amplified stethoscope, the fetal heartbeat can be heard through the uterine wall. These strangely remote sounds, like a drum beating under water, provide very concrete evidence of the emergence of a new, independent life.

Development in the Second Trimester

During the second trimester, the average fetus grows from 3 inches to 10 inches and increases in weight from 1 ounce to almost 2 pounds. Beginning with the fifth month, the fetus will grow at the rate of about 1 inch every 10 days until the end of pregnancy. During the second trimester, the uterus itself begins to stretch and grow. It rises into the mother's abdominal cavity and expands until, by the end of the ninth month, it pushes against the mother's ribs and diaphragm. The reality of a growing life becomes increasingly

FIGURE 6.2

Critical periods in prenatal development. During the first two weeks of development, the embryo is usually not susceptible to teratogens; a substance either damages all or most of the cells of the embryo, resulting in its death, or damages only a few cells, allowing the embryo to recover without defects. Dark area denotes highly sensitive periods.
Source: Moore, K. L. (1993). *The developing human: Clinically oriented embryology* (4th ed.). Philadelphia: W. B. Saunders.

BOX 6.1

Father, Mother, and Fetus: After the Quickening

During the second trimester, a father is able to make contact with his unborn child as he places his hand on his wife's abdomen and feels the movements of the life within. For many fathers, this is a time of great joy as the prospect of parenthood becomes more than abstract empathy with his wife's pregnancy. Investment in the expected child increases as the reality of the fetus becomes more concrete. This time can foster a new intimacy for the expectant couple as they begin to talk about their plans and hopes for the child, share their thoughts about the pregnancy and upcoming birth, and explore their feelings related to assuming responsibility for the care of their new child.

Sometimes, the first movements of the fetus stimulate a negative reaction in the father. This may, in turn, have a negative effect on the mother, leaving her depressed and aware of her lack of support. Some men are not comfortable with the physical aspects of pregnancy and consequently turn away from the mother. They do not want to feel the fetus's movements. They feel extremely uneasy or embarrassed by explanations of the details of female anatomy. Some men feel that the fetus, and then the baby, threatens their own position with the mother, and they feel resentful and competitive toward the woman and the unborn infant. Some men worry about the increased economic responsibility toward the unborn child. If they are unemployed or underemployed, prospective fathers may long for more income, have low confidence and self-worth, or worry about losing the mother's income if she does not return to work after childbirth. Some men may become increasingly distant from the mother. In one study of low-income urban women, 38% had experienced violence from their male partner during the childbearing period (O'Campo et al., 1995). In these cases, both mother and father experience feelings of isolation rather than intimacy.

Emotions associated with isolation, including anxiety and depression, can have a negative impact on the fetus as well as the mother. As we will see in the next few sections, these emotions can increase the difficulties of pregnancy, the birth itself, and the early months of parenting—difficulties that can have strong negative effects on establishing a successful parent–child relationship (Field et al., 1985; Field et al., 1990).

The relationship between the mother and her partner have implications not only for the emotional state of the mother during pregnancy, but for the psychosocial development of the offspring. The figure provides an analysis of the possible attitudes of two partners under each of three conditions: happy about the pregnancy; ambivalent about the pregnancy; and unhappy or even angry about the pregnancy. Given the fact that about one-third of pregnancies are unplanned and may be undesired, it is likely that each of these possible pairings of attitudes could represent a significant percentage of expectant couples.

Research supports the idea of significant association between the quality of the parents' relationship during the prenatal period and the quality of their child-rearing in the early years. This in turn has implications for the child's growth and development. Partners who show high levels of detachment or neg-

evident to the pregnant woman during this trimester, as she observes changes in her profile and experiences the early fetal movements called "quickening." These movements are first experienced as light bubbles or twitches. Later, the fetal movement can be identified as the foot, elbow, or fist of a restless resident. Box 6.1 considers the involvement of expectant fathers after quickening.

During the fourth month, the fetus begins to suck and swallow. Whenever the fetal mouth opens, amniotic fluid enters and cycles through the system. The amniotic fluid provides some nutrients in addition to those absorbed through the placenta. The four-month-old fetus shows some preference for a sweet taste, as evidenced by the fact that the fetus swallows faster if sugar is introduced in the amniotic fluid (Gilbert, 1963).

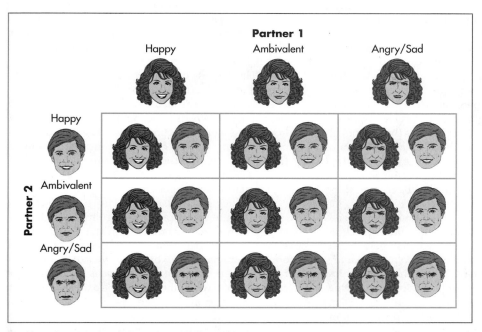

Possible combinations of partners' emotions regarding pregnancy

ative interaction during the prenatal period have difficulty providing an emotionally secure environment for their newborn. "Couples characterized by positive mutuality, partner autonomy, and the ability to confront problems and regulate negative affect are responsive to the needs of their infants, promote their autonomy, and have more secure and autonomous children, as seen throughout the first four years of life" (Heinicke, 1995).

In the fifth month, the skin begins to thicken, and a cheesy coating of dead cells and oil, the *vernix caseosa*, covers the skin. The fetus's individuality is marked by the pattern of skin ridges on the fingers and toes. Hair covers the scalp, eyebrows, back, arms, and legs.

The fetus's sensory receptors are well established by the end of the sixth month. The fetus is sensitive to touch and may react to touch with a muscle movement. At six months, the fetus will stick out his or her tongue at a bitter taste. Through the sixth month, the nostrils are plugged by skin cells. When these cells dissolve, the nose is filled with amniotic fluid, so smell is probably not possible until birth.

The external ear canal is filled with fluid, and the fetus does not tend to respond to sound until the eighth or ninth month. By the sixth month,

BOX 6.2

Development of the Human Brain

The brain begins to develop very early and continues to develop throughout the nine months of the prenatal period and well into childhood and adolescence. The figure provides a very general idea of the path of brain development over the prenatal period. What begins as a hollow tube becomes a mass of over 100 billion interconnecting neurons, each with an estimated 15,000 connecting branches. A *neuron* is a specialized impulse-conducting cell that is the functional unit of the nervous system. The neurons of the brain form a complex interconnected electrical circuitry. Most of the neurons are formed before birth, requiring an estimated 250,000 neurons to be formed during each minute of prenatal growth.

The formation of the brain into specialized areas with complex interconnections takes place in phases. The prenatal period is devoted largely to cell production and the migration of cells to particular areas of the brain. Once established in their correct location, neurons take on the properties of the cell type they are expected to become and begin to establish links to other related cells through the formation of networks of axons and dendrites. Axons transmit impulses away from the cell body; dendrites transmit impulses to the cell body. Bundles of axons from many neurons act as cables (information from many sources is combined in overlapping and interconnected neurons) sending information away from the billions of neural cell bodies. These grouped units are

called *nerve pathways*. After birth, the brain changes in weight and size as neurons grow and the number of axons and dendrites increase. Few neurons are added, but many die away.

The process of cortical development has been likened to carving a sculpture. The brain, which produces about twice as many neurons as will be needed to sustain effective functioning (Kolb, 1989), forms an exact pattern of connections and linkages, and the remaining bits seem to fade away, just as a sculptor carves away excess stone to reveal the desired form. The detailed features in the sculpture are a function of stimulation and experience.

Studies of the *visual cortex* clearly illustrate this process. In newborn cats, axons from the right and left eyes overlap considerably in the visual cortex. However, with experience, each eye establishes an area of dominance in which the eye axons are separated in the visual cortex. If one eye is kept closed for as long as one week, the open eye's axons spread out across a larger area of the visual cortex, and the closed eye's axons occupy a very restricted space (Shatz, 1992). Similarly, scientists suggest that, for humans, stimulation during infancy is critical in the completion of the neural networks that lead to the specialization and integration of brain functions.

Source: Kolb, B. (1989). Brain development, plasticity, and behavior. *American Psychologist, 44,* 1205.

Development of the human brain ▶
Source: Kolb, B. (1989). Brain development, plasticity, and behavior. *American Psychologist, 44,* 1205.

however, the semicircular canals of the inner ear are sensitive to stimulation. There is considerable evidence that fetuses respond to auditory stimulation, and that they may habituate to specific sounds such as the mother's voice, demonstrating the effects of this learning by behavior after birth. The nerve fibers that connect the retina of the eye to the brain are developed by six months. Infants born prematurely at six months respond to light.

The fetus at 25 weeks functions well within the uterine environment. It swallows, digests, excretes, moves about, sucks its thumb, rests, and grows.

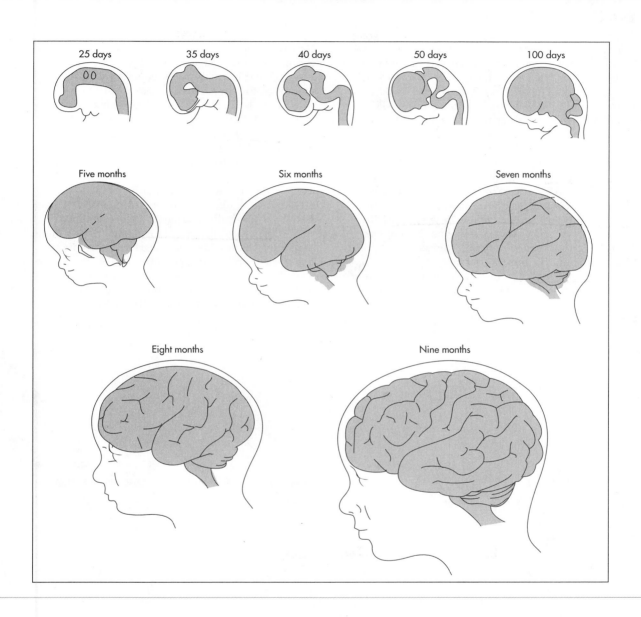

However, the nervous system, which began to develop at three weeks, is still not well enough formed to assure survival. Box 6.2 describes the development of the brain during the prenatal and neonatal periods. With advances in medical technology, the 25-week-old fetus, weighing about 1000 grams, has about a 70% chance of survival if it is placed in one of the nation's intensive care neonatal nurseries. Here, a complex network of medical professionals, using advanced devices to supplement the infant's respiratory, digestive, and regulatory functions, can preserve the lives of these very tiny babies.

BOX 6.3

Looking in on the Fetus

In recent years, great progress has been made in saving lives in utero. In the United States, the infant mortality rate has been reduced from 99.9 deaths per 1,000 live births in 1915 to 8.9 deaths per 1,000 live births in 1991 (U.S. Bureau of the Census, 1994). Much of this progress has been due to the development of new technology for monitoring the development of the fetus. Four such strategies are described here (Cunningham, MacDonald & Gant, 1989):

Ultrasound. Based on sonar technology that was developed for submarine warfare during World War II, ultrasound technique uses reflected sound waves to produce a visual image of the fetus. Ultrasound can be used to date the pregnancy more precisely, diagnose certain structural defects in a fetus, and detect multiple pregnancies.

Amniocentesis. About 20 cc of amniotic fluid are withdrawn from a woman's uterus, as shown in the figure at right. This procedure is carried out in the 16th week of pregnancy, to evaluate fetal cells for chromosomal or enzyme disorders. Later in a pregnancy, fetal cells can be assessed to evaluate the maturation of the lungs, and serious respiratory disorders can be prevented by delaying cesarean deliveries until the lungs are adequately developed.

Fetoscopy. A fetus can be examined directly and blood samples taken by inserting a fiber optic lens into a pregnant woman's uterus. This technique allows for the diagnosis of genetic disorders, particularly blood diseases that cannot be evaluated using amniotic fluid. Once diagnosed, some disorders can be treated surgically and medically before birth.

Electronic fetal heart rate monitoring. Birth attendants can monitor the fetal heart rate continuously, using electronic equipment that is painlessly attached to the pregnant woman's abdomen. This method is especially useful in detecting any disruption in the fetal oxygen supply during labor.

Amniocentesis ▶

Development in the Third Trimester

In the last trimester, the average fetus grows from 10 to 20 inches and increases in weight from 2 pounds to 7 or 7½ pounds. Weight appears to be more dependent upon environmental factors than length, so length is probably the better index of fetal maturity.

Increases in body size and weight are paralleled by a maturation of the central nervous system. The advantages of a full-term fetus over a premature, 28-week fetus include: (1) the ability to begin and maintain regular breathing; (2) a stronger sucking response; (3) well-coordinated swallowing movements; (4) stronger *peristalsis* (the alternating waves of contraction and relaxation of the alimentary canal) and, therefore, more efficient digestion and excretion of waste; and (5) a more fully balanced control of body temperature. Also, as the placenta begins to degenerate in the last month of pregnancy, antibodies

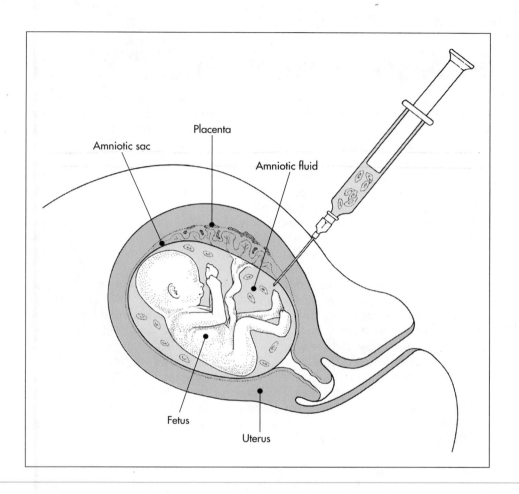

Placenta

Amniotic sac

Amniotic fluid

Fetus

Uterus

in the mother's blood that have been formed against various diseases pass into the fetal bloodstream. They provide the fetus with immunity to many diseases during the first few months of life. Box 6.3 describes some of the current technology that allows physicians to assess the maturity and health of the fetus.

The uterus cannot serve as the home of the fetus indefinitely. Several factors appear to coincide to bring the period of pregnancy to a close. First, as the placenta degenerates, antibodies form in both the mother's blood and the fetal blood that would destroy each other. Second, the placenta does not grow much larger than 2 pounds. As the fetus reaches its maximum size, it cannot obtain enough nutrients through the placenta to sustain life. Third, the fetal head cannot grow much larger than the mother's pelvic opening without endangering the infant's brain during the birth process.

We do not know the exact set of factors that signals the onset of uterine contractions and the birth process. The wide variation in the duration of pregnancies and in the size of "full-term" infants suggests that labor is signaled by a number of interacting factors that differ from one woman to another, and even from one woman's pregnancy to her next.

The Psychosocial Context of Pregnancy

Pregnancy affects a woman's social roles and social status. It influences the way people treat her and the resources that are available to her. Pregnancy also influences a woman's physical well-being and her emotional state. A mother's attitude toward her pregnancy and her developing attachment to her unborn child set the stage for the quality of her parenting after childbirth.

This section of the chapter focuses on characteristics of the mother, her lifestyle, and the physical and cultural environment that impact fetal development. The unborn child is influenced not only by the genetic information that guides biological development but by very specific aspects of the intrauterine environment, many of which are related to the mother's resources and her attitude toward her pregnancy. The impact of poverty on fetal development is discussed in some detail in Box 6.4.

One of the indicators of a newborn's developmental status is its weight for its gestational age. Many of the topics discussed in the following pages, including maternal nutrition, drug use, exposure to environmental toxins, and maternal age, are associated with low birth weight and other signs of developmental vulnerability. Babies who are small for their gestational age (*SGA*) are at considerable risk. They have a higher mortality rate, more complications during postdelivery care, and a higher incidence of mental and motor impairment than do babies who are average for their gestational age (Cassady & Strange, 1987). The evidence for the impact of a mother's lifestyle on her fetus is often derived from the association of certain maternal characteristics and the incidence of SGA babies.

[handwritten marginal note: SGA— gestational age]

Maternal Nutrition

The perception that a fetus will get what it needs for growth no matter what the mother eats is simply not true. Adequate nutrition for fetal development requires that the mother have access to a balanced diet and be able to transform nutrients into a form that the fetus can ingest. The placenta takes care of the latter process, but the mother must take care of the former (Lindblad, 1987). Children can suffer malnutrition at any time during the prenatal period or after birth. The most severe impact on growth occurs when resources are inadequate both during and after pregnancy (Brasel, 1974), as is the case in poverty-stricken areas of the world.

Much of the data on the effects of malnutrition on human fetal growth comes from studying the impact of disasters and crises, such as extreme poverty, wars, and famine, that restrict access to adequate nutrition. Malnutrition can be inferred from a baby's low birth weight in comparison with his or her gestational age. The relative contribution of malnutrition to SGA is difficult to estimate. Pregnant women who experience these disaster conditions are likely to encounter other stresses, including increased exposure to envi-

BOX 6.4

The Impact of Poverty

Probably the single most powerful psychosocial factor that influences the course of a fetus's development and the chances of survival is poverty. Poor women are likely to experience the cumulative effects of multiple factors associated with infant developmental vulnerabilities and infant mortality (Swyer, 1987). Poverty is associated with malnutrition, higher incidence of diabetes and cardiovascular disease, and higher rates of infection, which are all linked to low birth weight and physical vulnerability. Poor women are less likely to have been vaccinated against infectious diseases, such as rubella, that can harm the developing fetus. They are likely to get pregnant at an earlier age and to have repeated pregnancies into their later adult years—both are practices associated with low-birth-weight. Women who have had little education are less likely to be aware of risks to the fetus associated with alcohol, drug use, caffeine, and smoking, and they are more likely to abuse these substances.

Poverty is associated with poor prenatal care. Women with few financial resources and little education may not understand the importance of early prenatal care, and they cannot afford it (Cassady & Strange, 1987). Further, they may find that the quality of the medical care they receive is poor and that the costs of making prenatal visits are not worth the benefits. For example, Hansell (1991) found that the quality of prenatal care in a national sample varied systematically with the woman's sociodemographic background. Women who were less well-educated and who were living in metropolitan areas received less adequate care.

Many of the risks that increase the vulnerability of poor women's babies are preventable. A well-organized, accessible system of regional medical-care facilities, combined with effective educational programs about pregnancy, prenatal care, and nutrition, could significantly improve the health of babies born to poor women (Swyer, 1987). In a systematic evaluation of a coordinated maternity care program for women on Medicaid in North Carolina, it was clearly demonstrated that a comprehensive prenatal care program can improve birth outcomes, even for a high-risk population (Buescher et al., 1991). This kind of program involves more than prenatal visits; it includes nonmedical support services such as ensuring access to food stamps; the Women, Infants, and Children (WIC) food program; transportation to prenatal and postnatal health appointments; and housing assistance or job training, as necessary.

The survival opportunities of infants born to poor women provide a measure of the social justice of an entire society. In a just and humane society, improving the life chances and eliminating health risks for the children of poverty must concern all citizens.

ronmental toxins, diseases, and extreme anxiety, that could also affect fetal development.

Some studies have been designed to intervene by providing dietary supplements in situations where pregnant women are malnourished. There are mixed results concerning whether a pregnant woman's diet can be modified in order to increase a newborn's birth weight. When a sample of Guatemalan mothers' diets were augmented by 20,000 additional calories during the nine months of pregnancy, their newborn babies were 0.2 kilograms (7 ounces) heavier than the newborn babies of mothers whose diets had not been supplemented (Habicht et al., 1974). However, controlled studies in the United States have not found meaningful increases in the birth weights of newborn infants whose mothers were receiving dietary supplements (Cassady & Strange, 1987).

Some effects of prenatal malnutrition can be counteracted after birth. Infants' growth potential permits those who have access to adequate nourishment after birth to make up for a slowed prenatal growth pattern (Tanner, 1990). Infants who are born malnourished demonstrate increased activity levels, make greater demands on the environment, and give cues for more active caregiving responses (Brazelton, 1987). If caregivers respond appropriately to these demands, a positive pattern of interaction can offset deficits observed shortly after birth that have been caused by inadequate prenatal nutrition.

You may associate malnutrition and hunger with pictures of children in developing countries such as Bangladesh or Ethiopia. You may be surprised to learn, however, that according to a recent congressional report, roughly 30 million Americans suffered from hunger in the United States in 1991. Hunger was defined as "a condition where health is threatened because a person repeatedly does not eat enough nutrients" (*Columbus Dispatch,* 1992). Despite conclusive evidence for the importance of prenatal diet for fetal development, we are unable to prevent this easily treatable threat in our own country.

Maternal Drug Use

Pregnant women as a group use a wide range of drugs that are either prescribed or taken voluntarily. Iron, diuretics, appetite suppressants, tranquilizers, hormones, and antibiotics are commonly ingested. In addition, some women use drugs such as alcohol, caffeine, nicotine, marijuana, cocaine, crack, heroin, and other narcotics (Chasnoff, 1988). Although the mother and the fetus have independent circulatory systems, research shows that many drugs that are ingested by pregnant women are metabolized in the placenta and delivered to the fetus. What is more, the impact of a specific dosage of a drug may be minimal for the pregnant woman and yet be quite dramatic for the fetus.

As you review the following sections on the impact of drugs on fetal development, two principles must be considered. First, genetic predisposition may make some developing fetuses particularly vulnerable to the negative impact of certain drugs or toxins. Data on this point are very clear in animal studies since animals are more likely to have litters of offspring, some of which show greater resilience in the presence of prenatal teratogens than others (Vorhees & Mollnow, 1987). Second, the consequences to the central nervous system of exposure to a certain drug or toxin vary depending on the dosage, the duration, and the timing of exposure. In some instances, mild exposure may not have noticeable effects early in infancy, but may become evident as a child is challenged to perform more complex cognitive tasks (Vorhees & Mollnow, 1987).

Alcohol

There is conclusive evidence that alcohol is a teratogen. Prenatal exposure to alcohol can disrupt development of the brain, interfere with cell development and organization, and modify the production of neurotransmitters, which are fundamental to the maturation of the central nervous system (West, 1986). Alcohol has complex negative consequences for fetal development that have been grouped together and given the name *fetal alcohol syndrome* (Abel, 1984; Clarren & Smith, 1978; Jones et al., 1973). Fetal alcohol syndrome is related to disorders of the central nervous system associated with reduced intellectual functioning; malformations of the face, eyes, ears, and mouth; and low birth weight. The incidence of fetal alcohol syndrome among babies of women who drink heavily—about 1.5 ounces or more of alcohol a day—is 30 to 50%. At a rate of 1 to 3 infants affected per 1,000 live births, fetal alcohol syndrome is the greatest current source of environmental disruption to the prenatal central nervous system (Vorhees & Mollnow, 1987). Even moderate daily alcohol intake may produce some of the symptoms of fetal alcohol syndrome, especially if drinking occurs in conjunction with malnutrition during pregnancy.

The risks associated with prenatal exposure to alcohol cannot be overemphasized. In a longitudinal study of the effects of prenatal exposure to alcohol, children of mothers who drank 1.5 ounces of alcohol (one average-strength drink) a day during pregnancy had lower IQ scores at age 4 than did the children of mothers who used little or no alcohol (Streissguth et al., 1989). The use of alcohol significantly predicted reduced IQ scores even when many other factors, such as mother's educational level, family socioeconomic level, child's birth order, the quality of mother–child interaction, and child's involvement in preschool, were taken into account. Thus, many of the environmental variables that are known to have an enhancing effect on a young child's intellectual functioning did not overcome the damage to the central nervous system produced by exposure to alcohol during the prenatal period.

Cultural factors increase the likelihood of prenatal alcohol exposure. Alcohol is widely used in the United States, and the quantity of alcohol that can produce permanent negative consequences for fetal development may actually be considered socially acceptable or "safe" by many American adults. What is more, women who are experiencing some of the early discomforts of pregnancy, such as fatigue, irritability, or nausea, are often advised by family and friends to use alcohol to try to relieve these symptoms.

Nicotine

Pregnant women who are heavy smokers (20 or more cigarettes a day) are more likely to give birth to babies who are small for their gestational age (McDonald, Armstrong & Sloan, 1992). According to a review of 45 studies that examined this relationship, infants born to smokers weighed an average of 200 grams less than infants born to nonsmokers (U.S. Department of Health, Education, and Welfare, 1979). There is evidence that if a woman stops smoking by the fourth month of her pregnancy, she is no more likely than a nonsmoker to give birth to a low-birth-weight infant (Sexton & Hebel, 1984).

Women who smoke have a greater risk for miscarriages and stillbirths than women who do not smoke (Armstrong, McDonald & Sloan, 1992; Streissguth et al., 1989). Neurological examinations of newborn infants who are exposed to nicotine during the prenatal period reveal decreased levels of responsiveness and arousal at 9 days and 30 days after birth (Fried, et al., 1987). One hypothesis is that smoking exposes the developing fetus to carbon monoxide which accounts for central nervous system damage and related neurological symptoms (Mactutus & Fechter, 1984). Even if a pregnant woman does not smoke, she and her fetus may be exposed to the effects of nicotine by being around people who smoke. If the partner of a pregnant woman smokes, he may inadvertently be exposing his unborn child to related risks.

Caffeine

Caffeine, which is commonly consumed in coffee, tea, and certain sodas, freely crosses the placenta. Heavy caffeine consumption, defined in one study as more than 300 mg or roughly three cups of coffee per day or more, is associated with increased risk of low birth weight and has some modest relationship with preterm deliveries. Infants born to women who reduced the amount of caffeine that they drank after the sixth week of pregnancy showed no ill effects associated with early caffeine consumption (Fenster et al., 1991; McDonald, Armstrong & Sloan, 1992).

Addictive Drugs

The use of addictive drugs, especially heroin and cocaine, as well as methadone (a drug used to treat heroin addiction), is associated with higher risks for low birth weight, birth defects, and increased rates of infant mortality (Dinges, Davis & Glass, 1980; Zuckerman et al., 1989). Infants who have been exposed to cocaine, opiates, and methadone during the prenatal period demonstrate a pattern of high-pitched crying (evidence of neurological disorganization), extreme irritability, fever, sleep disturbances, feeding problems, muscle spasms, and tremors during the first week of life (Hans, 1987). Cocaine, crossing the placenta, impairs the fetal sympathetic nervous system which helps control many of the involuntary activities of the glands, organs, and other parts of the body. It also increases the constriction of blood vessels in the uterus and therefore reduces the blood supply to the fetus (Lester et al., 1991). Cocaine-exposed infants have a high risk for *sudden infant death syndrome*, the sudden, unexpected death of an apparently healthy baby who seems well when put to sleep but is later found dead. Often, these deaths cannot be explained, even after autopsy.

In the 1980s, the availability of "crack," an inexpensive, smokable form of cocaine, dramatically increased the number of cases of cocaine-exposed babies, especially in major cities such as New York, Los Angeles, Detroit, and Washington, D.C. One estimate suggests that there are about 1 million U.S. women who use cocaine. Babies born to these mothers are likely to require prolonged hospital stays, as well as foster care if their mothers continue to use drugs and are unable to care for them. Crack babies show evidence of problems with fine motor coordination, focusing and sustaining attention, and, perhaps as a result, school adjustment. As cocaine-exposed babies enter the school system, more teachers are recognizing their special patterns of learning difficulties. Some argue that these difficulties are not associated with cocaine exposure directly but with the combination of early neurological vulnerability and ineffective caregiving. Others suggest that early cocaine exposure produces significant disruption in the formation and functioning of the brain (Toufexis, 1991).

Law-enforcement officials are arresting and charging women who have exposed their unborn infants to these harmful and illegal substances (Sachs, 1989), which presents a moral dilemma. Prosecutors are attempting to hold pregnant women responsible for behaviors that jeopardize their infants' health by charging them with child abuse and placing the children in foster care. Nineteen states have laws that allow criminal charges to be filed against women who give birth to babies who have illegal substances in their blood. Those who oppose such actions argue that many legal substances such as alcohol, cigarettes, and coffee also have known negative effects on fetal develop-

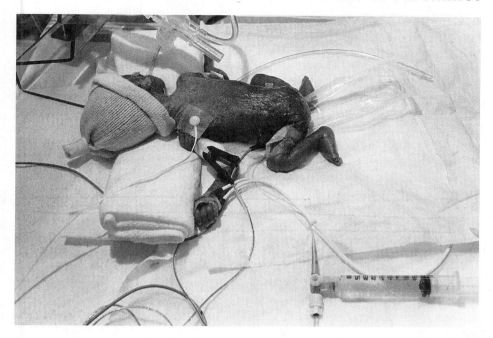

This cocaine-addicted premature infant will struggle to survive the effects of the prenatal environment.

ment, but women who use these substances are not charged with child abuse. Furthermore, it is difficult to ensure that babies who are taken from their birth mother and placed in foster care will actually thrive (Feinman, 1992; Willwerth, 1991).

Over the past ten years, a new complication associated with intravenous drug use is the spread of the human immunodeficiency virus (HIV) and the acquired immunodeficiency syndrome (AIDS) through the use of infected syringes. About 70% of women with HIV have been infected through their own drug use or that of a sex partner. These viruses can be passed from a pregnant woman to her fetus. Children born to mothers with HIV have about a 50% chance of developing the disease, and 95% of those infected die by age 3 (Darney et al., 1989; Judson, 1989). At present, there is no way to treat babies infected with AIDS. Because their immune system is deficient or inoperative, they cannot fight off the many infections that babies typically encounter during the early years (Seabrook, 1987).

Prescription Drugs

Other drugs have been prescribed to women during pregnancy to treat medical conditions. The tragic outcome of the use of thalidomide to treat morning sickness in the 1960s alerted us to the potential danger of certain chemicals for the fetus, particularly during the period of differentiation and growth in the first trimester. Taken during the 21st to 36th day after conception, thalidomide can cause gross deformities of a baby's limbs.

Some hormones are administered to help sustain pregnancy; however, in several instances, these therapies have been linked to physical or behavioral consequences in the offspring. In one study, prednisone was prescribed to a sample of 119 women to alleviate infertility and then to maintain their pregnancies. The birth weight of their babies was significantly lower than that of the babies of a control group (Reinisch & Karow, 1977). In another study, both male and female children who were exposed to testosterone-type hormones prenatally showed more masculine-style behaviors and responded in a more masculine way in tests of personality, gender role, and work and family values (Reinisch & Sanders, 1984). The effects of exposure to certain prenatal hormones may be direct, by altering the central nervous system, or indirect, by influencing the pattern of caregiver–infant interactions.

Obstetric Anesthetics

For the most part, pain-relieving drugs have been used during labor for the benefit and convenience of mother and physician. At first, their effect on the newborn went unnoticed. However, evidence suggests that the kind, amount, and timing of anesthetic used in delivery can all induce neonatal depression and affect the coping capacities of newborns (Naulty, 1987; Stechler & Halton, 1982). When babies whose mothers had received medication during labor were compared with babies whose mothers had not, the first group was observed to perform less well on measures of perception, motor skills, and attentiveness (Brackbill et al., 1974; Brackbill et al., 1985).

There is some controversy about the seriousness of this problem. Research has shown that a range of drugs, including general anesthetics, local anesthetics, and tranquilizers administered by inhalation, can interfere with the infant's behavior (Aleksandrowicz & Aleksandrowicz, 1974; Brackbill, 1977; Murray et al., 1981). Babies whose mothers received comparatively large doses of medication during delivery were difficult to arouse, difficult to feed, and difficult to soothe.

Other studies suggest that it may not be the drugs themselves that have a lasting impact on the infant. First, the mothers who request large doses of obstetrical anesthetics may be more anxious or distressed during pregnancy (Yang et al., 1976). Second, the behavioral effects of the drugs on newborns may influence their parents' perceptions of them. These perceptions may alter the quality of the early infant–care giver relationship, thus affecting infant performance (Lester, Als & Brazelton, 1982).

Environmental Toxins

Environmental toxins encompass a wide range of substances that can be encountered in the work setting, through foods, or in the home. As more and more women enter the work force and assume nontraditional work roles, concerns about the hazards of work settings for fetal development continue to grow. Exposure to radiation presents a clear risk to fetal growth. Other hazardous chemicals are also suspected of producing fetal abnormalities. In an Allied Chemical plant, fear that the fluorocarbon 22 might cause fetal damage led to the layoffs of five women workers. Two of those women chose to be sterilized in order to hold their jobs (Bronson, 1979). Wives of men who are employed in hazardous environments may also experience higher rates of miscarriages, sterility, and birth defects in their babies. In one study, paternal exposure to specific solvents and chemicals at work was linked to higher rates of spontaneous abortions among their wives (Lindbohm et al., 1991).

The workplace is not the only setting in which pregnant women can come in contact with environmental toxins. Methyl mercury was one of the first substances established as a human teratogen in the late 1950s. An industrial plant in Japan released a mercury-containing substance into the Mina-mata Bay. Through the food chain, mercury was consumed by fish that pro-vided a staple in the diet of people living in the area. The mercury was linked to over 40 cases of mental retardation and neurological impairment among children born in the area. Most of the women whose offspring suffered seri-ous symptoms did not themselves experience severe symptoms (Vorhees & Mollnow, 1987).

Research must continue on the effects of substances that are potentially toxic to fetuses. The danger of exposure to lead for young children is well doc-umented. However, the effects of various levels of exposure on infants and young children are still ill defined (Schroeder, 1987). The potential of herbi-cides and pesticides used in forests and farmlands to harm developing fetuses is also arousing concern (Morris, 1987). Many products have been discovered to be teratogens only after abnormal reproductive outcomes have been sys-tematically documented.

Research on drugs and environmental toxins alerts us to their potential impact on an immature and rapidly changing infant. Evidence about the effects of food additives on newborns and chemical pollutants on both fetuses and newborns warns us that infants may have some unique sensitivities to the environment that may not be observed in older children or adults (Gia-cola & Yaffe, 1987). Each unborn generation depends on its predecessors to protect them from these environmental hazards.

Mother's Age

The capacity for childbearing begins about a year to one-and-a-half years after the beginning of menarche and ends at the end of the climacteric, sometime during a woman's late forties or early fifties. Thus, a woman is potentially fer-tile for about 35 years during her lifetime. Pregnancy and childbirth may occur at any point during this period. The effects of pregnancy and childbirth on the physical and psychological well-being of a mother vary with her age and her emotional commitment to the maternal role. Similarly, these factors can have a significant impact on the health and well-being of her infant.

Women between the ages of 16 and 35 tend to provide a better uterine environment and to give birth with fewer complications than do women under age 16 or over 35. Particularly when it is their first pregnancy, women over 35 are likely to have longer labors than younger women, and labor is more likely to result in the death of either the infant or the mother. The two groups with the highest probability of giving birth prematurely are women over 35 and those under 16 (Schuster, 1986).

Adolescent mothers are more likely to experience complications during pregnancy that may endanger their infants and themselves. Premature chil-dren of teenage mothers are more likely than those of older mothers to have neurological defects. This may be a consequence of the fact that the repro-ductive organs of very young mothers, especially those under age 16, are not fully mature. In addition, adolescent mothers may not suspect that they are pregnant and may engage in a variety of behaviors such as smoking, drink-ing, and drug use that are harmful to the fetus during the first trimester. Very young mothers typically do not receive early and consistent prenatal care (Quilligan, 1983; Roosa, 1984).

A primary risk for infants of mothers who are over 40 is *Down syndrome* (Moore, 1993). A woman's ova are present in a premature form from birth; the longer she lives, the older those cells become. It has been hypothesized that some part of the high incidence of Down syndrome among older women is the result of deteriorating ova. However, older women typically are also likely to have male partners who are their same age or older. Although the male's sperm are produced anew daily, some evidence suggests that the rate of genetically defective sperm increases among older men. Thus, aging in one or both partners may contribute to the increased incidence of birth defects among babies born to older women. The association between parental age and Down syndrome is not entirely satisfactory as an explanation, since older women who have had multiple births are not as likely to have a Down syndrome child as are women who are having their first child at an older age. What is more, many Down syndrome babies are born to women who are under 35. It is likely that in some cases the syndrome is a result of errors that occur during cell division, and in others it is a result of a genetically transmitted condition.

Table 6.2 shows the live birthrates for women across the age range 10 to 44 from 1960 through 1990. The pattern shows that women in the United States are having fewer babies at every age period except the very youngest (10 to 14) than they were in the 1960s. Two other observations about the data presented in Table 6.2 are relevant to our understanding of pregnancy and childbirth in the United States. In contrast to 1960, the age periods from 20 to 24 and 25 to 29 have become equally likely times for childbearing. This suggests greater diversity in the timing of entry into motherhood now than there was 30 years ago. Second, the decline in the birthrate is also expressed in a shrinking of the childbearing period: Far fewer children are being born today to women 30 years and older than was the case in 1960. Even though we hear quite a lot in the media about delayed entry into childbearing and births to "older" mothers, the birthrate to women over age 30 does not come close to returning to the levels of childbearing in the older age ranges that was characteristic of the early 1960s.

Mother's Emotional State

Certain psychosocial factors are associated with increased anxiety and depression during pregnancy. Women who are having marital difficulties, who do not have adequate social support during pregnancy, and who have conflict

TABLE 6.2

Live Birthrates by Age of Mother, 1960–1990 (Births per 1,000 women)

Year	10–14	15–19	20–24	25–29	30–34	35–39	40–44
1960	0.8	89.1	258.1	197.4	112.7	56.2	15.5
1970	1.2	68.3	167.8	145.1	73.3	31.7	8.1
1980	1.1	53.0	115.1	112.9	61.9	19.8	3.9
1990	1.4	59.9	116.5	120.2	80.8	31.7	5.5

Source: U.S. Bureau of the Census, 1986, 1989, 1994.

about their own personal identity are likely to experience greater emotional stress (Fleming et al., 1988). It is possible that these strong emotional reactions, such as chronic anxiety or depression, may influence the fetal environment directly through the secretion of maternal hormones that may cross the placental barrier. However, evidence in this regard is mixed (Sameroff & Chandler, 1975; Vaughn et al., 1987).

Evidence suggests that a woman's feelings about her femininity, her unborn child, and her psychological stability are associated with the extent of difficulties experienced during pregnancy and labor. Women who have more stable personalities and a positive orientation toward pregnancy react more favorably to the stresses of labor than do anxious, irritable women. The latter are more likely to have longer labors and experience more complications. They tend to request and receive more medication during delivery, which may influence the responsiveness of their newborn infants (Standley, Soule & Copans, 1979; Yang et al., 1976).

The contribution of maternal anxiety to complications during labor and delivery was studied with a group of Guatemalan women (Sosa et al., 1980). The hospital normally did not permit any visitors to remain with an expectant woman on the maternity ward. Each woman in this study, however, was assigned a companion who stayed with her until delivery. This person talked, held the woman's hand, rubbed her back, and provided emotional support during labor. Women who had a companion had fewer complications during labor than a group who did not have the companion, and their babies showed fewer signs of fetal distress. The mean length of labor was over ten hours shorter for those women who had a companion than for those who were alone during labor. Recent studies support the idea that women who are accompanied by supportive companions during labor experience shorter labors and fewer difficulties during delivery (Kennell & McGrath, 1993).

Recent trends in the United States have shown a dramatic increase in fathers' involvement during labor and delivery. A Gallup poll conducted in the early 1980s found that approximately 80% of fathers attend the birth of their children, as compared with 27% in the early 1970s (Kliman & Kohl, 1984). The father's presence is clearly a great comfort to a pregnant woman during labor and delivery. When fathers are present, women tend to have shorter labors, report experiencing less pain, use less medication, and feel more positive about themselves and their childbirth experience. Fathers also describe their participation in the birth as a significant personal experience (Grossman et al., 1980). However, we cannot conclude that fathers who participate in the birth experience have a more intimate relationship with their children than do fathers who are not present at the birth (Palkovitz, 1985; Palm & Palkovitz, 1988). In Notebook Page 6.2 we ask you to consider the implications of what you have read about the psychosocial context of pregnancy for promoting a healthy pregnancy for the expectant mother and father as well as for the fetus.

The Impact of the Fetus on the Pregnant Woman

Now we consider some of the ways in which a fetus influences a pregnant woman. Being pregnant alters a woman's body image and her sense of well-being. A wide range of physical changes accompanies the various stages of pregnancy. Some women feel especially vigorous and energetic during much of their pregnancy; they are described as "glowing" or "radiant." Other women experience distressing symptoms such as nausea, backaches, swelling, headaches, and irritability. As the pregnancy advances, most women

Promoting Health for Mother, Father, and Fetus During Pregnancy

You have read quite a bit about the context of pregnancy, including the many ways that the mother's behavior influences fetal development, the impact of the pregnancy on the mother and father, and the possible impact of the couple's relationship on the mother's emotional state which indirectly or directly influences the fetus. Given all these many factors in an interdependent system, try to answer the following questions.

1. What considerations are necessary for the health of the baby during the prenatal period?

_____

_____

2. What considerations are necessary for the health of the mother?

_____

_____

3. What considerations are necessary for the health of the father?

_____

_____

4. What characteristics of the relationships among the father, mother, and fetus would be most likely to enhance each person's health?

_____

_____

_____

5. What characteristics of the relationships among the father, mother, and fetus might produce negative health outcomes?

_____

_____

_____

Pregnancy is a matter of both pride and modesty for this native Choco woman of Panama.

experience weight gain, some difficulty in movement, sleep disturbances, changes in basic digestive and urinary functions as the expanding uterus presses on other internal organs, and decreasing interest in sexual activity. In some cases, pregnancy actually poses a risk to the pregnant woman's health. In the condition known as *toxemia of pregnancy*, some unknown toxin gradually poisons the woman's system. During the second half of pregnancy, as the fetus grows, the afflicted mother may experience extreme high blood pressure, kidney failure, and, in some cases, convulsions.

Changes in Roles and Status

Pregnancy, especially first-time pregnancy, is associated with a variety of changes in social roles and social status. As we noted in Box 6.1, women who become pregnant may be treated in new ways by the baby's father. Many fathers become more solicitous of their pregnant partners. Others grow more distant and spend less time at home. With pregnancy, women are also viewed in a new light by their peers. To some extent, the impact of pregnancy on peer relations depends on the norms of the community. If the pregnancy is seen as desirable, expectant mothers are treated with a certain admiration and increased consideration. If the pregnancy is seen as undesirable and inappropriate, peers may make the expectant woman feel guilty or ashamed. As an example, in some communities, adolescent girls who become pregnant may feel guilty or try to hide their pregnancy. In other communities, becoming pregnant during adolescence is viewed by the peer group as an accomplishment—a sign of maturity.

In contemporary U.S. culture, pregnancy may be greeted with some ambivalence, especially as it relates to a woman's role in the labor force. For working couples, the decision to have children is made in the context of very real economic costs, both in the potential loss of the woman's income and in the potential risk to her career advancement. Women who become pregnant may be given fewer responsibilities or be passed over for promotions. In business settings, pregnancy may be viewed as a distraction, a life event that is likely to interfere with work productivity. Women who choose to have children may be perceived by their employers as not being really serious about their careers.

Within the family, a pregnant woman is likely to be treated with new levels of concern and care. Her pregnancy affects her spouse, parents, siblings, and in-laws. By giving birth to her first child, a woman transforms her husband into a father, her mother and father into grandparents, and her brothers and sisters into uncles and aunts. Being pregnant may affect the gender identity of the mother and/or father: Becoming pregnant may confirm a woman's sense of femininity; getting a woman pregnant may represent confirmation of a man's virility (Heitlinger, 1989).

In some societies, pregnancy and childbirth confer special status on a woman. In Japan, for example, traditional values place motherhood above all other roles that a woman can play. "Only after giving birth to a child did a woman become a fully tenured person in the family" (Bankart, 1989). When Japanese women become mothers, they can begin to have an impact on government, community, and public life as people who are uniquely responsible for molding the next generation. Among Mexican-American women, childbearing is viewed within a broad religious context. "It is considered the privilege and essential obligation of a married woman to bear children. But children come 'when God is willing' " (Hahn & Muecke, 1987).

Changes in the Mother's Emotional State

Women have emotional as well as physical and social reactions to pregnancy. Pregnancy is listed as the twelfth most stressful life change in a list of 43 life events in the Social Readjustment Rating Scale (Holmes & Rahe, 1967). There appears to be a relationship between the intensity of stress experienced by a pregnant woman and the stress level of her husband. The higher the wife's stress, the higher her husband's stress (Jarboe, 1986) (see Box 6.5). A woman's attitude toward her unborn child may be one of pride and acceptance, frustration and rejection, or—as is the case with most American women—ambivalence. Expecting a child is linked with both positive and negative emotions.

American women endorsed the following three reasons as the most important advantages to having a first child (Fawcett, 1988):

1. Children bring stimulation, fun, and activity to life.
2. Children bring love and affection.
3. Children strengthen the bond between a husband and wife.

Each of these reasons suggests powerful, positive emotional consequences associated with childbearing. At the same time, there are stresses associated with pregnancy and the anticipation of children. American women cite the following three disadvantages of having children:

BOX 6.5

Couvade

Although most of the literature on the prenatal period focuses on the relationship between the fetus and the pregnant woman, some evidence suggests that expectant fathers have their own emotional reactions to pregnancy. In some cultures, there is a formal practice of *couvade* in which the expectant father takes to his bed and observes very specific taboos during the period shortly before birth. Among the Arapesh of New Guinea, childbearing is believed to place as heavy a burden on the father as on the mother. Some cultures believe that by following the ritual couvade, fathers distract the attention of evil spirits so that the mother and baby can pass through the childbirth transition more safely (Helman, 1990).

Among groups that do not practice the ritual couvade, it is nonetheless common to find men experiencing some couvade symptoms such as general fatigue, stomach cramps, nausea, dizziness, or backache. Trethowan (1972) was one of the first to document the nature and extent of couvade symptoms among various populations. He suggested that these physical symptoms are a product of a man's emotional ambivalence toward his wife. The expectant father may experience empathy and identify with his wife's pregnant state. At the same time, he may experience some jealousy of his wife, resentment for the loss or potential loss of intimacy in their relationship, repulsion at his wife's physical appearance, or some envy for his wife's ability to bear a child. These psychological conflicts, many of which are probably unconscious or unexpressed, are amplified by an expectant father's conscious worries about the health and well-being of his baby. The combination of these stresses may produce the couvade syndrome.

In a study carried out in Rochester, New York, Lipkin and Lamb (1982) found that about 22% of a sample of men whose partners had recently had a child sought medical treatment for what the authors described as couvade syndrome symptoms. These complaints included feeling rundown and bloated and having stomach cramps and pain in the groin. The symptoms these men described could not be accounted for by other medical conditions. The implication is that expectant fathers can become emotionally and physically stressed by the events surrounding pregnancy and impending childbirth.

1. Children require significant financial resources.
2. Children bring a loss of freedom.
3. Parents worry about their child's health and safety.

In addition to these worries, most pregnant women experience some anxiety and depression. During the first trimester, symptoms of nausea and fatigue can result in depression. During the last trimester, sleeplessness, moodiness, and worrying about childbirth are associated with anxiety (Kaplan, 1986). Throughout pregnancy, there are constant worries and preoccupation about whether the baby will be healthy. One study reported that at the seventh month of pregnancy and again during the fourth month after birth, most women organized their thoughts about themselves as mothers around the theme of fear, including fears for their babies' well-being or for their own ability to provide for their infants' needs (Vizziello et al., 1993).

The Birth Process

Birth is initiated by involuntary contractions of the uterine muscles. The process that expels the infant from the uterus is called *labor.* The length of time from the beginning of labor to the birth of the infant is highly variable. The average time is 14 hours for women undergoing their first labors (primiparas) and 8 hours for women having subsequent labors (multiparas).

3 STAGES OF LABOR

I. Contractions. Diation of cervix

II. Expulsion of fetus.

III. Expulsion of placenta

Stages of Labor

The medical profession describes three stages of labor, two of which are illustrated in Figure 6.3. The first stage begins with the onset of uterine contractions and ends with full dilation of the cervix (the gradual enlargement of the cervical opening from only millimeters to about 10 centimeters in diameter); this is the longest stage. The second stage involves the expulsion of the fetus. This is the time when the mother pushes or "bears down." The baby also helps in the birth process by squirming, turning the head, and pushing against the birth canal. The second stage begins at full dilation and ends with delivery of the baby. The third stage, which lasts about five to ten minutes, begins with delivery and ends with the expulsion of the placenta.

These three stages of labor do not precisely parallel the personal experiences of childbirth. For example, although the expulsion of the placenta is considered a unique stage of labor in the medical model, it is rarely mentioned in women's accounts of their birth experiences. On the other hand, many of the signs of impending labor that occur in the last weeks of pregnancy are perceived by a pregnant woman as the beginnings of labor.

The psychological experiences of the birth process can be viewed as having five phases: (1) early signs that labor is approaching; (2) strong, regular uterine contractions signaling that labor has begun, generally accompanied by leaving home for a hospital or birthing environment; (3) the transition phase, during which contractions are strong, rest times between contractions are short, and women experience the greatest difficulty or discomfort; (4) the birth process, which allows for the mother's active participation in the delivery; and (5) the postpartum period which involves the initial interactions with the newborn, physiological changes that mark a return to a prepregnant state, and, if birth has taken place away from home, a return to home. The significant events of these phases are summarized in Table 6.3.

Cesarean Delivery

Sometimes a normal, spontaneous vaginal delivery is dangerous to the mother or the newborn (Cunningham, MacDonald & Gant, 1989). One alternative is to remove the baby surgically through an incision in the uterine wall. The procedure is named after the Roman emperor Julius Caesar, who, legend has it, was delivered this way. The likelihood that he actually was delivered surgically is questionable, since until as late as the seventeenth century, the operation was usually fatal to mothers. Most early cesarean deliveries were performed on dead or dying women in the hope of baptizing the unborn child (Cunningham, MacDonald & Gant, 1989).

The *cesarean delivery* makes childbirth a surgical procedure, requiring anesthetics, postnatal intravenous feeding of the mother, and a prolonged recovery period (Zahniser et al., 1992). The procedure undoubtedly saves many infants and mothers who would not survive vaginal childbirth. However, there is concern as to whether the procedure is being misused for the convenience of health professionals or busy mothers who want to schedule deliveries and thereby avoid the uncertainty of waiting for the onset of labor. The incidence of cesarean deliveries in the United States has increased from 5.5 percent of births in 1970 to 23.6 percent in 1992 (U.S. Bureau of the Cen-

Stage 1

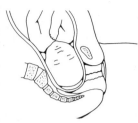 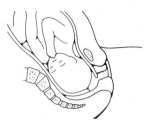 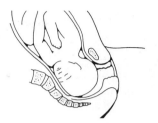

Early labor, where effacement, or thinning, has occurred and the cervix is starting to dilate.

The continuation of dilation of the cervix.

Approaching full dilation of the cervix.

Stage 2

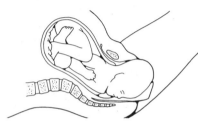 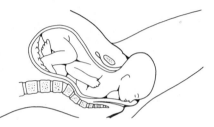

Face down, the baby's head is pressed against the perineum, which gradually stretches, widening the vaginal opening.

The baby's skull extends as it sweeps up over the perineum. First the top of the skull and then the brow emerge.

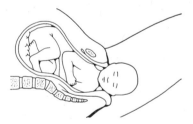 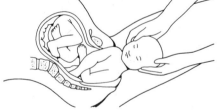

Once the head is born, the shoulders rotate in the pelvis, turning the head to left or right.

The top shoulder is born first; the rest of the body then slides out easily.

FIGURE 6.3
The first two stages of labor
Source: Clarke-Stewart, A. & Koch, J. B. (1983). *Children: Development through adolescence.* New York: John Wiley & Sons. p. 65.

sus, 1994). The U.S. Public Health Service goal statement, *Healthy People 2000*, calls for a reduction of the national cesarean rate from 24% to 15%, a goal that implies recognition that a substantial number of the current cesarean procedures are not required by the risk status of the mother or the infant (*Healthy People 2000*, 1990).

Some scholars have begun to examine the impact of the cesarean delivery on both the newborn and the parents. At this point, it appears that, in the short term, that is, within five minutes after birth babies delivered by cesarean are more likely to show signs of risk than babies delivered vaginally. This difference holds for babies who are delivered by cesarean section due to

TABLE 6.3

Significant Events of Five Psychological Stages of Labor

Phase I: Early signs that labor is approaching
   1. Lightening (about 10 to 14 days before delivery). The baby's head drops into the pelvic area.
   2. Release of the plug that has kept the cervix closed.
   3. Discharge of amniotic fluid.
   4. False labor   irregular uterine contractions.

Phase II: Onset of labor
   1. Strong, regular contractions 3 to 5 minutes apart.
   2. Transition from home to hospital or birthing center.

Phase III: Transition
   1. Accelerated labor, with contractions lasting up to 90 seconds and coming 2 or 3 minutes apart.
   2. Some sense of disorientation, heightened arousal, or loss of control.

Phase IV: Birth
   1. The baby's head presses down on the bottom of the birth canal.
   2. The mother experiences a strong, reflexive urge to push to expel the baby.
   3. The mother typically is moved from a labor area to a more sterile delivery room where the baby is born.

Phase V: Postpartum period
   1. Mother and infant have initial contact.
   2. Placenta is expelled.
   3. Rapid alteration of the hormone system to stimulate lactation and shrink the uterus.
   4. Mother and infant engage in early exploration; initial attempts at nursing.
   5. Return to the home and introduction of the newborn into the family setting.

the mother's previous cesarean section and who therefore are not at risk in other ways (Burt, Vaughan & Daling, 1988). However, long-term follow-ups of babies delivered by cesarean section find no effects on the child's IQ or standardized math and verbal test scores (Entwisle & Alexander, 1987). The short-term effects may be a product of the infant's exposure to an amount and type of anesthetic used during the surgical procedure that would not be used during a vaginal delivery.

How are parents affected by a cesarean delivery? One study found that mothers whose children were delivered by cesarean section expressed greater dissatisfaction with the childbirth experience itself than mothers whose children were delivered vaginally. However, they did not show more problems in postpartum adjustment. In this study, both mothers and fathers of babies delivered by cesarean section were more involved in their parental roles. They viewed their children in a more positive light and had higher expectations for their children's school success than other parents did (Padawer et al., 1988). One explanation for these findings is that special difficulties associated with childbirth increase the commitment that parents make to their child. We must be careful not to overgeneralize the results of limited research, but these findings suggest that events surrounding conception and birth that increase commitment to a newborn ought to be studied further for their long-term implications for family development.

Infant Mortality

The *infant mortality rate* refers to the number of babies who die during the first year of life per 1,000 live births. In 1991, this rate was estimated at 8.9 deaths per 1,000 in the United States, a mortality rate that is equaled only for groups 55 to 64 years old and older (U.S. Bureau of the Census, 1994). For African-American infants, the mortality rate was 17.6 deaths per 1,000 live births compared with 7.3 deaths per 1,000 live births for white infants (U.S. Bureau of the Census, 1994). About two-thirds of infant deaths occur during the first month after birth. Most of those babies who die have severe birth defects, are very premature (born before the 30th week of pregnancy), or experience sudden infant death syndrome (Clayman, 1989).

Infant mortality rates are influenced by many factors, including (1) the frequency of birth complications; (2) the robustness of the infants (which is influenced by prenatal nutrition and degree of exposure to viruses or bacteria, damaging X-rays, drugs and other teratogens in utero); (3) the mother's age; and (4) the facilities that are available for prenatal and newborn care. One-fourth of infant deaths occur as a result of complications associated with low birth weight. Interventions that help prolong gestation and improve interuterine growth would reduce infant mortality rates (Wilcox & Skjoerven, 1992).

Infant mortality rates vary a great deal from one country or region of the world to another. In Sweden, in 1990, the infant mortality rate was 6 deaths per 1,000 live births, whereas, in that same year, the mortality rate in thirteen countries of the world was over 120 deaths per 1,000 live births (U.S. Bureau of the Census, 1991). Although the U.S. rate of approximately 9 deaths per 1,000 live births appears quite low in comparison with worldwide estimates, the United States ranks sixteenth among industrialized nations, behind countries such as Australia, Canada, Denmark, France, Japan, Sweden, and the United Kingdom.

Within the United States, regional infant mortality rates range from a low of 5.8 deaths per 1,000 live births in Vermont to a high of 21 deaths per 1,000 live births in the District of Columbia (U.S. Bureau of the Census, 1994). Despite the overall decline in infant mortality rates over the past 40 years, the disparity between rates for African-American and white infants has persisted, and the ratio has increased so that the risk of infant death is now 2.2 times greater for African-American than for white infants (Singh & Yu, 1995). Differences in the infant mortality rates between races differ from region to region and city to city. In a comparison of 38 large metropolitan areas, the greatest difference between racial mortality rates was found in Pittsburgh, Pennsylvania (African-American rate = 24.07, white rate = 9.43). The smallest difference was in Anaheim, California (African-American rate = 10.59, white rate = 8.45) (Polednak, 1991). Even in the same city, factors contributing to segregation of neighborhoods and the related differences in quality of health care and educational resources can influence life chances for each new generation. Density of low-income population, availability of information on the impact of diet and drugs on the developing fetus, and adequacy of medical facilities for high-risk newborns all contribute to the regional and ethnic group variations in infant death rates among populations of different incomes.

In comparison with many countries that have national health-care benefits for expectant mothers and universal health insurance for infants, the United States does not guarantee maternity care benefits for all women of childbearing age. The extent of medical coverage available during pregnancy and during the early childhood years depends on the specific nature of a woman's health insurance. In 1987, five million women of childbearing age had private health insurance that did not cover maternity care. Medicaid, the public program that is intended to provide health care for individuals living below the poverty level, actually assists less than 40% of America's poor, including many women of childbearing age. Thus, many American women have inadequate maternity insurance or none at all (National Commission to Prevent Infant Mortality, 1988).

In addition to the availability of affordable insurance to cover the costs of maternity care and infant health care, the quality of care must be taken into account. In one analysis of pregnancy-related mortality, researchers found that roughly 44% of these deaths could be attributed to preventable causes. What is more, the rate of deaths from preventable causes was greater for African-American than for white women, and greater for women on Medicaid or with no insurance than for women who had private insurance (Mertz, Parker & Halpin, 1992). One must assume that one of the reasons that some women do not take advantage of prenatal health programs is that they are not at all confident of receiving quality care.

Each infant's chances for surviving the prenatal period and birth depend on the convergence of biological, environmental, cultural, and economic factors. As can be seen from the examples given above, despite a well-designed biological arrangement to sustain prenatal growth, many American infants start out their journeys on very different footing, depending on the social and economic circumstances in which they are conceived. Children of poverty are at greatest risk and receive the least and poorest-quality care.

The Impact of Culture

The events of pregnancy, childbirth, and the initial period following childbirth receive attention in every culture. The beliefs, values, and guidelines for behavior regarding pregnancy and childbirth have been referred to as the "birth culture" of a group (Hahn & Muecke, 1987; Jordan, 1983; Mead & Newton, 1967). One cannot assume that everyone in a particular cultural group adheres to all the guidelines of the birth culture, but, at the very least, they are part of the mythology or lore that a woman and her partner experience during her pregnancy.

The birth culture usually addresses several of the following aspects of pregnancy and childbirth:

- The decision to have a child, the best age for childbearing, and the value of childbearing.

- Interpretation of the experiences of pregnancy, including prohibitions or prescriptions regarding exercise during pregnancy, the way members of the community treat a pregnant woman, and the attitude of the father toward the pregnant woman.

- Changes in social status that accompany pregnancy and childbirth, including the relevance of having a male or a female child.

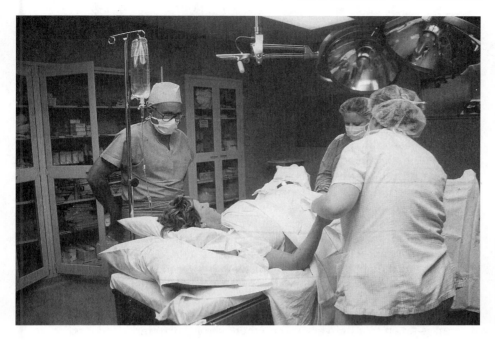

In the United States, the birth culture emphasizes dependence on technology and medical professionals in a hospital setting.

- Experiences and expressions of pain and the use of substances to alleviate pain.

- The particular style of help and social support that are available during childbirth, including the involvement of technical and/or spiritual aides to assist in childbirth.

- The setting where childbirth takes place.

- Expectations for the father's role during childbirth.

- Expectations for the mother, father, and newborn during the first few weeks following childbirth.

Although the biological processes of fertilization and fetal development are universal, the social, psychological, and technical contexts of pregnancy and childbirth vary widely from one cultural group to another.

The Medical Birth Culture of the United States

Contemporary obstetric practice in the United States has created a birth culture that has similarities with other technological societies, and also has some unique qualities that set it apart from other Western countries (Helman, 1990). The U.S. medical model is committed to saving as many babies and mothers as possible by altering, as necessary, the techniques of prenatal care and delivery in order to counteract naturally occurring difficulties. Access to the best care possible, however, depends on one's ability to pay. According to this birth culture, the ideal age for fertility is considered to be between the ages of 20 and 35. Women who are pregnant before age 20 or after age 35 are considered "high-risk" pregnancies.

Pregnant women are urged to have professional prenatal care throughout the pregnancy so that they and their fetuses can be monitored through urine and blood samples, weight gain, heartbeat, fetal heart monitoring, and, in some cases, ultrasound and amniocentesis. Pregnant women are advised of certain dietary restrictions, especially alcohol, salt, and caffeine consumption, and are often urged to take vitamin supplements. They may be counseled to restrict their physical activities, especially strenuous lifting, in the last trimester. Pregnant women and their partners may be encouraged to attend childbirth classes where they learn about the physical events of childbirth and about strategies for breathing and relaxation that can help relieve some of the discomfort associated with childbirth.

For the vast majority of pregnant U.S. women, labor and delivery take place in a hospital setting. Increasingly, women are accompanied during labor by the baby's father or a supportive partner. However, the obstetrician, who is usually a man, is considered "responsible" for the delivery. Less than 5% of births involve assistance by a midwife, although the practice is quite a bit more common among Native American and Hispanic families than among African-American, whites, and Asians (Parker, 1994).

Once in the hospital, a pregnant woman becomes a patient. An IV drips glucose into the woman's bloodstream, and in many instances a fetal monitor is inserted. The birth itself is usually attended by medical specialists including an obstetrician, a nurse, and an anesthesiologist. For the birth, the woman is taken to a delivery room where she is surrounded by medical technology. According to one description, the woman's "entire visual field is conveying one overwhelming perceptual message about our culture's deepest values and beliefs: technology is supreme, and you are utterly dependent on it and on the institutions and individuals who control and dispense it" (Davis-Floyd, 1987). The delivery room is usually chilly. The woman typically lies on her back with her feet propped up in stirrups. A surgical episiotomy, an incision that expands the vaginal opening, is performed. After a few moments of direct contact between mother and newborn, they are separated for roughly four hours while the baby's vital signs are observed. Mother and baby are considered distinct "patients," each now requiring separate kinds of medical expertise, the mother continuing to be observed by her obstetrician and the nursing staff; the infant now in the care of the neonatologists and the pediatrician (Lozoff, Jordan & Malone, 1988).

Many American adults accept this medical birth culture as the "right way" to approach childbirth, and they prepare themselves to adapt to its demands. However, over the past 20 years, this birth culture has been changing as a result of the dissatisfactions expressed by many couples and new beliefs about what is best for mothers and infants. Some hospitals provide a more "homelike" atmosphere on the maternity ward. Fathers are encouraged to participate in the labor and delivery, even to attend a cesarean delivery. Arrangements are made for sibling visitation in the hospital. Some hospitals are experimenting with a birthing chair that places the woman in a more upright position for delivery, using gravity to assist her as many nontechnological cultures do. And immediate and frequent contact between mother and newborn is encouraged, especially through rooming-in arrangements where the mother and baby share the same hospital room.

Comparisons between the U.S. birth culture and that of two other industrialized nations, Sweden and the Netherlands, illustrate some of the ways that cultural values and beliefs guide the events surrounding pregnancy and birth. Observations from nontechnological, traditional cultures provide another perspective on how birth-related events are treated.

The Birth Culture in Sweden and the Netherlands

Sweden and the Netherlands are two industrialized nations that have access to the full range of birth technology but provide birth cultures that differ in notable ways from that of the United States (Lozoff, Jordan & Malone, 1988). In 1990, the infant mortality rate in the United States was 10.4; in Holland, 7.0, and in Sweden, 5.9 (U.S. Bureau of the Census, 1991). In both Sweden and Holland, prenatal care is available to all citizens without charge. In both countries, trained midwives manage the prenatal care and attend the births. Most births take place in hospitals in Sweden; about 40% of births in Holland take place at home. In both societies, pregnant woman play a major role in determining the course of their treatment and care.

In Holland, childbirth is considered a natural event. Women do not expect to receive pain-relieving medication. Discomfort is managed through controlled breathing, relaxation techniques, and support from the birth team. In Sweden, a woman is advised about the medications that are available for pain, the appropriate use of these medications, and the known possible side effects. The decision about whether to take any medications is left to the pregnant woman.

In both Sweden and Holland, the birth team includes the pregnant woman, a midwife, a midwife's assistant, and a supportive attendant such as a husband, friend, or close relative. Dutch women prefer to deliver at home and are moved to the hospital only if complications are anticipated. Swedish women deliver at the hospital, but the environment of the hospital is made as "homey" as possible, and the woman is free to move about, watch television, play cards, and visit with friends during the early hours of labor. In both countries, a physician is on call to handle complications or emergencies, but the pregnant woman's preferences on seeking medical assistance are taken into account.

What can we learn by comparing the birth culture of the United States to those of Sweden and Holland? First, in Sweden and Holland, all prenatal care is free of charge, and women in those countries almost universally take advantage of these services. Second, those countries both foster the creation of a supportive birth team comprised of professionals and paraprofessionals who help manage prenatal care, provide information and support, and are present during the delivery. Third, in these countries, women have more control over decisions related to the pregnancy and delivery, including the use of pain-relieving medication. In Holland, in particular, birth is defined as a natural event requiring minimal medical intervention beyond that offered by a midwife. Finally, the birth setting is as homelike as possible. This birth culture is obviously effective, given the low mortality rate.

Examples of Birth Cultures in Traditional Societies

Data on methods of approaching pregnancy and childbirth in traditional cultures are drawn primarily from the Human Relations Areas Files (Murdock & White, 1969) and from Ford's (1945, 1964) comparison of reproductive behavior in 64 cultures. In most traditional societies, women are usually accompanied by other women during childbirth. Men and nontribal women are often excluded from the childbirth setting. Further, many of the events related to conception and delivery are considered too personal or sacred to discuss with outsiders. Thus, the data on childbearing practices are not systematic. Nonetheless, they serve to place the American birth culture in a comparative context.

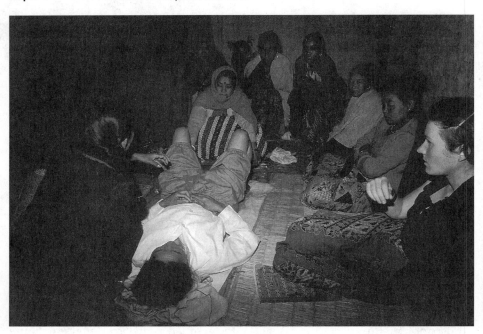

A French physician teaches midwifery to rural women in Nepal.

Reactions to Pregnancy and Childbirth

People of many cultures hold the assumption that the behavior of expectant parents influences the developing fetus and the ease or difficulty of childbirth. Of the 64 cultures studied by Ford (1945), 42 prescribed certain behaviors for expectant parents and prohibited others.

Many of the restrictions were dietary. "Among the Pomeroon Arawaks, though the killing and eating of a snake during the woman's pregnancy is forbidden to both father and mother, the husband is allowed to kill and eat any other animal. The cause assigned for the taboo of the snake is that the little infant might be similar, that is, able neither to talk nor to walk" (Roth, 1953, 122). In many Asian, Mediterranean, and Central and South American cultures, pregnancy is believed to be affected by the balance of what are considered "hot" and "cold" foods in the woman's diet. Pregnant women are advised to avoid very hot foods such as chili peppers, salty or fatty foods, and very cold foods such as acidic, sour, or cold fresh foods (Hahn & Muecke, 1987).

Attitudes toward pregnancy and childbirth can be characterized along two dimensions: (1) solicitude versus shame and (2) adequacy versus vulnerability (Mead & Newton, 1967).

Solicitude Versus Shame. *Solicitude* toward the pregnant woman is shown in the care, interest, and help of others. For example, "it is said among Jordon villagers that 'as people are careful of a chicken in the egg, all the more so should they be of a child in its mother's womb'" (Grandquist, 1950).

At the other end of this continuum, evidence of *shame* is seen in cultures that keep pregnancy a secret as long as possible. This custom may stem from a fear that supernatural demons will damage the fetus, or it may be a result of shyness about the sexual implications of pregnancy.

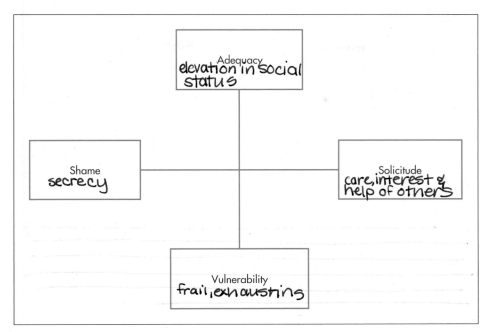

FIGURE 6.4
Two dimensions of attitudes toward pregnancy and childbirth

Societies that demonstrate solicitude increase the resources and care given to the pregnant woman and fetus. These attitudes emphasize the importance of birth as a mechanism for perpetuating the continuity of the group. By keeping pregnancy a secret, societies that instill a sense of shame about pregnancy may not promote the health of the mother or fetus during the prenatal period and do not appear to encourage propagation of the group.

Adequacy Versus Vulnerability. Evidence of _adequacy_ is seen when pregnancy is viewed as a sign of sexual prowess or a means of entrance into social status for a woman. Some cultures do not arrange a wedding until after a woman has become pregnant. In a *polygamous family*, one in which a man has more than one wife, the pregnant wife receives the bulk of her husband's attention and may prevent her husband from taking an additional wife (Grandquist, 1950). In some cultures, women are considered more attractive and sexually desirable after they have borne children (Gorer, 1938; Tichauer, 1963).

At the other end of this spectrum is *vulnerability*—the view that childbearing is exhausting, pregnant women are vulnerable, and women grow more frail with each pregnancy. In some cultures, a pregnant woman and her fetus are thought to be more readily exposed to evil spirits. Birth is considered an especially critical life transition during which the forces of life and death are engaged in particularly intense competition for the mother and the fetus.

One can think of solicitude and shame, and adequacy and vulnerability as two dimensions that create a matrix within which the birth culture of any society or subculture can be located (see Figure 6.4). The U.S. medical birth culture, for example, is characterized by solicitude and vulnerability. In comparison, Sweden and Holland might be characterized more by solicitude and adequacy. These broad dimensions help summarize the orientation of the pregnant woman, her family, her partner, and her community toward the events of pregnancy and childbirth. In Notebook Page 6.3 we ask you to draw upon your own observations and experiences to characterize our cultural orientation toward pregnant women and expectant fathers.

Cultural Complexity

The United States today is more culturally diverse than ever before. In 1992, the United States saw an influx of about 975,000 immigrants from over 60 countries. The religious, racial, and ethnic diversity of our population brings with it an array of subcultural beliefs, attitudes, and norms regarding reproduction, pregnancy, and childbirth. Even within cultural subgroups, some individuals are more acculturated and willing to embrace the medical birth culture, while others still endorse certain traditional beliefs.

Events at the time of birth influence a mother's feelings about herself and her ability to enact her parenting role. Efforts on the part of the community, especially family members, close friends, and health-care professionals, to acknowledge a woman's competence and control of the situation, as well as to express caring and support for her, seem to promote a woman's positive orientation toward herself and her mothering role. Messages of social rejection, doubts about a woman's competence, and attempts to take away her control or to isolate her from her infant or her social support system may undermine her self-esteem and interfere with her effectiveness as she approaches the demanding and exhausting task of labor.

Conflicts arise as pregnant women of other birth cultures encounter the birth culture of the U.S. medical model. Separated from their traditional birth attendants, exposed to men at a time when their birth culture dictates a need for modesty, placed in a highly technological and impersonal hospital setting, or encouraged to take medications or permit procedures that are unfamiliar or rejected in their own culture, these women are likely to feel isolated, alienated, and highly suspicious of the people who are in charge of the birth experience. They may experience depression and feelings of helplessness caused by the unfamiliarity of the U.S. birth culture. Obstetrical medicine needs a new level of sensitivity and flexibility toward the birth culture of a pregnant woman and her family (Hahn & Muecke, 1987). New efforts need to be made to interpret the key elements of the U.S. medical birth culture to those patients who are not familiar with it so that those aspects that cannot be modified can at least be understood and perhaps be viewed as less intimidating or disrespectful to the beliefs of the mother and her kin.

Abortion

Abortion is the termination of pregnancy before the fetus is able to live outside the uterus. Pregnancies may be terminated through spontaneous abortion, usually referred to as a miscarriage, or through physical intervention. Although the technology for inducing abortions has evolved, the practice of abortion, along with infanticide, as a means for controlling population growth is ancient (Krannich, 1980). Both the Aranda of central Australia and the Hopi of Arizona are examples of traditional societies that have induced abortions by tying a belt very tightly around a mother's abdomen (Murdock, 1934). In modern China, in an effort to control population, official policy permits each

The Birth Culture of the United States

We have discussed the idea that each society has a unique birth culture that can be located along the continuum between solicitude and shame and between adequacy and vulnerability. Think about your own observations of how pregnant women and expectant fathers are treated.

1. What evidence have you observed of solicitude toward pregnant women?

2. What evidence have you observed of shame regarding pregnant women?

3. What evidence have you observed of adequacy toward pregnant women?

4. What evidence have you observed of vulnerability toward pregnant women?

5. What would you say is the cultural attitude toward expectant fathers? What observations support this view?

married couple to have only one child, so many pregnant women who already have one child are forced to have an abortion.

In obstetrical practice, abortions are induced differently before and after 12 weeks of gestation. Before 12 weeks, the pregnancy is aborted by instrumental evacuation, usually by dilating the cervix and then either suctioning out the contents of the uterus with a vacuum aspirator (vacuum curettage) or scraping out the uterus (surgical curettage). After 12 weeks, abortion can be induced by an injection of a saline solution or prostaglandin, which stimulates labor. The fetus can also be removed surgically by means of a procedure similar to that used in the cesarean section (Cunningham, MacDonald & Gant, 1989).

Research in France has led to the development of a drug, RU 486, that interrupts pregnancy by interfering with the synthesis and circulation of progesterone (Baulieu, 1989). The drug is most effective if it is taken within the first seven to nine weeks after the last menstrual period. It results in a shedding of the uterine lining, thereby replacing vacuum aspiration or other surgical intervention. From January through September, 1989, it was used by more than 2,000 French women *per month* with a success rate of over 95% when taken within the seventh week of pregnancy. At present, the drug is being evaluated in the United States. Many physicians who would not perform abortions on moral grounds say they would be willing to prescribe RU 486 to women who requested it (Rosenblatt et al., 1995).

The Abortion Controversy and the Legal Context

The United States is currently engaged in an intense and sometimes violent controversy over the issue of abortion. The conflict arises because of the strong, and seemingly irreconcilable, differences in beliefs about society's responsibility to protect a woman's rights and the rights of an unborn child. On one side are those who insist that a woman has a right to privacy and an absolute right to choose or reject motherhood. On the other side are those who seek to protect the rights of the unborn fetus, which is incapable of protecting its own interests.

The former position, often referred to as "pro-choice," draws on constitutional protection from governmental intervention into matters that are fundamentally private and affect personal freedom. This view endorses the elimination of all legal restrictions on a woman's decision to have an abortion. Those who uphold this view may differ about whether they approve of the use of abortion for purposes of regulating family size or because of economic hardship. However, they support the view that any decision about an abortion is a private matter that ought to be reached between a woman and her physician.

The latter position, often referred to as "pro-life," argues that the unborn child has an inalienable right to life and society is responsible for protecting this right. This view endorses the position that abortion ought to be illegal. Those who uphold this view may differ about whether abortions may be performed under special circumstances, for example, when pregnancy threatens a woman's life. But, generally, they believe that from the moment of conception a new life is formed that deserves society's complete protection. Notebook Page 6.4 gives you an opportunity to consider factors that may influence your own view about abortion.

The abortion controversy reflects passionately held values about the relationship between the individual and the society.

In the case of <u>Roe</u> v. <u>Wade</u>, the U.S. Supreme Court proposed a developmental model supporting the idea that pregnancy could be divided into three trimesters. The justices considered abortion to be a woman's right in the first trimester, guarded by the Constitution's protection of privacy. They said that some restrictions could be placed on access to abortion in the second trimester, on the basis of the risk posed by abortion to the mother. The fetus's rights were still not an issue during this period. In the final trimester, however, when the fetus was considered to have a good chance of surviving outside the uterus, states could choose not to permit abortion. This ruling endorsed a <u>woman's right to full control over the abortion decision until the fetus reaches a point of *developmental viability*.</u> At that point, the court ruled, the society's responsibility to the unborn child outweighs the woman's right to freedom and privacy. Within the context of *Roe* v. *Wade*, any efforts to restrict a woman's access to an abortion until the last trimester were considered unconstitutional.

In recent years, states have challenged the ruling in *Roe* v. *Wade* by proposing various limitations or restrictions on access to abortion. In 1989, the Supreme Court upheld a Missouri law that made it illegal for any public institutions or any public employee of the state to perform an abortion. The law requires that a physician who is going to perform an abortion after 20 weeks of pregnancy must first conduct tests to determine viability. If the fetus is capable of independent survival, abortion is illegal. Finally, the Missouri law defines life as beginning at conception, implying the state's responsibility to protect the fetus much earlier than was established by *Roe* v. *Wade* (*Economist*, 1989). By upholding the Missouri law, the Supreme Court opened the door for each state to decide whether or not to impose similar restrictions.

In 1992, the Supreme Court reviewed a set of laws passed by the Pennsylvania legislature. In their decision, they confirmed that *Roe* v. *Wade*

Your Views on Abortion

Take some time to consider your own personal views about abortion. Do you place yourself in the pro-choice or pro-life camp or some other position?

1. What factors in your own upbringing or personal experiences influence your views?

_____

_____

_____

_____

_____

2. Imagine that you were pregnant or that you were the father of an unborn child. What conditions might lead you to consider an abortion of this pregnancy?

_____

_____

_____

_____

_____

3. In your opinion, why is abortion such an intense controversy in the United States? What other cultural, historical, and psychosocial factors might be fueling this issue?

_____

_____

_____

_____

_____

"established a rule of law and component of liberty we cannot renounce" (Greenhouse, 1992). The court argued that state laws ought not impose an *undue burden* on a woman by placing major obstacles in her way if she seeks an abortion before the fetus has reached viability. However, of five sections of the Pennsylvania law, the court considered four acceptable and agreed that they did not place an undue burden. These restrictions were as follows:

1. Requiring a woman to wait 24 hours for an abortion after hearing a presentation at a physician's office intended to persuade her to change her mind.
2. Requiring teenagers to have the consent of one parent or a judge before having an abortion.
3. Requiring the physician to specify a medical emergency that would justify waiving requirements 1 or 2.
4. Requiring the physician or clinic to make regular reports to the state.

The fifth provision, requiring a married woman to tell her husband of her intention to have an abortion, was rejected. Thus, states are defining, in their own ways, the degree to which they will make resources available for abortions and the extent to which they will try to direct the abortion decision through the presentation of certain types of information and the exclusion of others.

In an attempt to establish a more scientifically based framework for limiting the right to abortion, in 1987 President Reagan asked Surgeon General C. Everett Koop to evaluate the impact of abortion on women's physical and mental health. If abortion were found to be associated with increased risk for certain types of physical or mental illnesses, this could provide a basis for framing abortion-related policies to promote the public welfare.

Dr. Koop and his staff reviewed more than 250 studies that dealt with the psychological impacts of abortion. In 1989, he wrote to President Reagan stating that he would not issue a report because he found no basis for limiting the right to abortion based on public health risks. In subsequent testimony, he concluded that gynecologists and obstetricians had already determined that the physical consequences of abortion were no different than those for women who carried their pregnancy to term. In addition, he concluded that the psychological risks of abortion were very minimal from a public health perspective. What is more, Dr. Koop found that the research on the psychological impact of abortion was so methodologically flawed that the results could not be used to support either side of the abortion debate (Koop, 1989a, 1989b; Wilmoth, 1992).

Difficulties in Evaluating Abortion Research

What accounts for the difficulties in evaluating the results of abortion research? The following problems have been identified, each of which illustrates the psychosocial framework within which the abortion decision is made (Adler et al., 1992; Wilmoth, de Alteriis & Bussell, 1992).

1. Abortion is a sensitive and controversial subject. Many women who have had abortions do not wish to disclose this information. Therefore, many women who are asked to participate in research on abortion refuse to do so or give false information. Given the published data provided by hospitals, physicians, and abortion clinics, national studies

of fertility estimate that only about one-half of women who have an abortion report it. Thus, the sample of participants in most abortion research is not necessarily representative of the population of women who have had abortions. One might hypothesize that those who admit to having had an abortion differ psychologically from those who do not admit it.

2. The estimation of psychological risk associated with abortion needs to be made in relation to some comparison group, but the nature of the comparison group is often difficult to establish. Women who have unwanted pregnancies and who choose abortion to end the pregnancy are probably not comparable with women who want to be pregnant and who choose to carry their pregnancies to term. Women who have unwanted pregnancies that they carry to term are difficult to identify. Multiple comparisons are probably needed, which makes the research much more difficult and expensive.

3. The context of abortions differ: Some are performed for therapeutic reasons, others are elective; most current abortions are legal, but some are illegal; most are related to an unwanted pregnancy, but not all; some result from the diagnosis of a fetal abnormality; some have been preceded by counseling; most are carried out in the first trimester, but others have been delayed to the second trimester and require a more difficult procedure; some are carried out in clinics that have been targets of demonstrations.

4. Different studies use a variety of outcome measures which are not always comparable in order to assess impact. The reliability and validity of the measures have not always been established, and they are not all equally relevant to various populations.

5. The prevalence of various consequences of abortion has not always been established. For example, suppose one wanted to determine the extent to which abortion was followed by a high risk for intense emotional reactions such as depression or guilt. One would need to determine the extent to which the population being assessed was at risk for these kinds of emotional reactions under other types of stressful life events. In addition, one would need to determine the extent to which the population being assessed differed from some comparison group, such as women who gave birth to unwanted children, in being at risk for these types of reactions.

6. Finally, the abortion decision occurs in the context of a wide variety of lifestyle frameworks, making generalizations very questionable (Russo, Horn & Schwartz, 1992). In addition to differences in race, religion, and socioeconomic status, women seeking abortions differ in age, marital status, and whether they already have other children.

What the Research Shows

The number of reported abortions has increased dramatically since the *Roe* v. *Wade* decision, involving a great diversity of women of different backgrounds with a variety of family and cultural contexts and with different reasons for wanting abortions. Some of the characteristics of U.S. women who had legal abortions in 1990 are summarized in Table 6.4. There has been a good deal of research since 1973, but it does not present any single conclusion about abortion. The effects of abortion are complex and depend on many circumstances.

The most common emotion among women who have an abortion is relief (Lemkau, 1988). Especially when the pregnancy was unwanted and the abortion is performed within the first 12 weeks, women generally resolve any negative feelings and thoughts they may have had soon after the abortion is completed (Adler et al., 1990). Although abortion is a stressful life event, most women are able to recover quickly from whatever distress they might experience. Several psychosocial factors appear to be linked with avoiding long-term feelings of regret or emotional distress. Among women undergoing abortion, those who have an *androgynous* gender identity, that is having flexible access

TABLE 6.4

Legal Abortions: Selected Characteristics, 1990

Total legal abortions	1,609,000
Abortion ratio	280
(Number of abortions per 1,000 abortions and live births)	
Age of women, %	
Less than 15	1
15–19	22
20–24	33
25–29	22
30–34	13
35–39	7
40 and over	2
Race, %	
White	65
African-American and other	35
Marital status, %	
Married	18
Unmarried	82
Number of prior live births, %	
None	49
1	25
2	17
3	6
4 or more	3
Number of prior induced abortions, %	
None	55
1	28
2 or more	17
Weeks of gestation, %	
Less than 9 weeks	53
9–10 weeks	26
11–12 weeks	12
13 weeks or more	10

Source: U.S. Bureau of the Census. (1994). *Statistical abstract of the United States: 1994* (114th ed.). Washington, D.C.: U.S. Government Printing Office, 85, table 112.

to both masculine (e.g., competitive, assertive, independent) and feminine (e.g. emotionally expressive, sociable, nurturant) characteristics, report less sense of loss, less anxiety, fewer physical symptoms, and fewer thoughts about death than do other women. These women tend to have a less traditional gender-role orientation and expect to find a variety of sources of satisfaction in their lives in addition to or instead of child-rearing (Alter, 1984; Miller, 1992).

Another factor is a woman's views about the acceptability of abortion. Not surprisingly, those women who believe that abortion is an acceptable solution to an unwanted pregnancy and who feel that abortion is also acceptable to their friends, family, and partner are less likely to experience strong feelings of regret or emotional upset following an abortion (Miller, 1992).

Elective abortion is sometimes followed by lingering negative feelings. For example, in a study of 292 patients interviewed two weeks after their abortions, 76% said their strongest emotion regarding the abortion was happiness, but 17% said their strongest emotion was guilt (Lazarus, 1985). Although the short-term response to an abortion may be relief and a sense of having taken responsibility for an important decision, in the longer term, feelings of shame, guilt, regret, grief, anger, and depression may surface (Speckhard & Rue, 1992). In a review of clinical cases in which abortion produced strong, unresolved negative emotions, a number of factors were identified (Lemkau, 1988). Sometimes, when an abortion is performed late in the pregnancy due to the discovery of a genetic anomaly in the fetus, a woman grieves for the loss of a child to whom she has already become attached. In other second-trimester abortions, the ambivalence that caused the delay in the decision to have an abortion is exacerbated by the physical discomfort associated with a late abortion. Some women discover that they are unable to conceive after an abortion, which evokes feelings of guilt, shame, anger, and regret. Women who are divorced, separated, or widowed at the time of an abortion also appear to be more vulnerable to strong, negative emotional reactions.

A significant number of women decide to have an abortion because their boyfriends or husbands are not ready for a baby or because problems in their relationships make it a bad time to have a baby. Women who say that these reasons are very important in their decision to have an abortion are likely to experience greater emotional upset and regret than women who do not appear to be pressured toward abortion by their partners (Miller, 1992). Once the abortion is over, these women are likely to find that they have compounded their losses, having given up the child they conceived in hopes of saving a relationship that does not work out.

This brings to our attention the issue of the role and reactions of fathers in the reproductive process. In 1976, the Supreme Court ruled that a woman did not need the consent of her husband or the child's father in order to have an abortion. This position was upheld again in 1992, overturning the part of the Pennsylvania law described earlier requiring that a woman inform her husband about her intent to have an abortion. From the concern over requiring a father's consent, one might infer that many men do not approve of their wives' or partners' decisions to have an abortion. However, the survey cited above suggests that it is often a father's reluctance to be responsible for parenting a child that motivates a woman's decision to have an abortion.

What are men's reactions and views about abortion? There is not much literature addressing this point. Shostak and McLouth (1985) interviewed 1,000 men who had accompanied women to abortion clinics across the United States. Of these men, 93% said they would alter their birth-control methods as a result of the experience; 83% believed that abortion was a desirable way of resolving an unwanted pregnancy. Many of these men expressed anxiety, frustration, and guilt in relation to the unwanted pregnancy and the abortion. Clearly, more research is needed to understand how the psychosocial maturity of the father and the mother as well as the nature of their relationship contribute to the abortion decision-making process.

Optimizing Development in Pregnancy

Regardless of who you are and the circumstances surrounding your pregancy, you want it to be physically and psychosocially healthy. If you are a seventeen-year-old whose boyfriend isn't sure he wants to have a baby, your concerns may be different in some ways from a 28-year-old, married woman and her husband who are looking forward to the baby. Both of you may be different, in turn, from a 38-year-old single executive whose biological clock is telling her that she must have a child soon if she ever hopes to have one. In many ways, however, all pregnant women have a lot in common. Pregnancy is a critical period for development. Even though it occurs for a relatively brief time, it sets the tone for much of the parent—child relationship. Table 6.5 summarizes ideas from the chapter that are relevant to optimizing development during the prenatal period.

TABLE 6.5

Optimizing Development During the Prenatal Period

1. To prevent health risks for the developing fetus, women who are sexually active and who might become pregnant ought to take certain precautions, such as cutting down on the use of alcohol, cigarettes, and caffeine; avoiding exposure to known environmental toxins; and restricting use of most drugs, including certain over-the-counter drugs.

2. Caring, supportive relationships are vital for physical as well as psychological health. Loneliness and alienation lead to different physical conditions for a pregnant woman than does a support system of a loving partner, good friends, and family members.

3. Pregnancy is often accompanied by heightened levels of stress and anxiety, for both mothers and fathers. This stress can be reduced through appropriate coping behavior, including regular visits to a reliable prenatal clinic to monitor the pregnancy and detect and treat any abnormalities and seeking expert information by reading books and pamphlets about pregnancy or attending childbirth classes.

4. Most women feel some frustration and loss of control during their pregnancy. One way to deal with these negative feelings is to take as much responsibility for the direction and management of the pregnancy and birth as possible. This may mean attending childbirth classes, reading about pregnancy and childbirth, staying active, and keeping a sense of humor about the routine difficulties of pregnancy. However, there are factors, such as the onset of labor, over which one has no influence, so one must learn to be flexible. Moreover, pregnancy is a preamble to child-rearing, and any parent will tell you that you simply do not have as much control over your child's behavior as you might expect. In order to retain a healthy frame of mind, a pregnant woman must find ways to accept some of her experiences without feeling demeaned or diminished.

Chapter Summary

1. Fetal development occurs within the context of a complex psychosocial framework, including the lifestyle and psychosocial maturity of the mother and the father, the relationship between the mother and the father, and the orientation of the larger family and culture toward the pregnant woman.

2. The period of gestation, typically lasting 38 weeks, is divided into three trimesters. In the first trimester, the organism's supportive structures are established and a critical process of differentiation of cells and organs takes place. In the second trimester, the fetus grows rapidly, sensory systems are established, and fetal movement can be detected. The third trimester is devoted largely to increases in body size, improved coordination of muscle movement, and more fully developed regulatory functions. The nervous system, which is established very early, continues to develop throughout the gestational period.

3. Many aspects of the pregnant woman's lifestyle, health, and emotional well-being can influence the health and development of the fetus. Of specific concern are maternal nutrition and drug use, the administration of anesthetics during childbirth, exposure to environmental toxins, and the mother's age at pregnancy. Women living in poverty are exposed to many of the conditions that place fetal growth at risk.

4. The developing fetus also has an impact on the mother, the father, and the couple. Pregnancy produces a wide range of direct physical changes for the woman. In addition, it evokes changes in roles and status for mother, father, and extended kin, as well as in the emotional states of both parents.

5. The birth process itself has five phases. The early signs that birth is approaching orient the parents and ready the birth canal for the baby's passage. Labor and delivery involve involuntary uterine contractions. The length of labor is quite variable, although it is usually shorter for women who have already had a child. The most difficult phase of delivery is the transition to full labor, when the contractions are strongest and last the longest time. In the postpartum period, mother and infant make their initial contact, and the mother—infant dyad make a transition back into the daily life of family and community.

6. The infant mortality rate refers to the number of babies who die during the first year of life per 1,000 live births. The rate in the United States ranks this country sixteenth among industrialized nations. There are notable differences in infant mortality by race, region, and urban setting within the United States.

7. The events of pregnancy and childbirth take place in the framework of a "birth culture" that shapes beliefs, values, and guidelines for behavior. The U.S. birth culture is guided largely by medical obstetrical practices. This birth culture differs from other industrialized countries, as well as patterns in more traditional societies. The birth culture can be described quite broadly within a matrix of adequacy and vulnerability on one dimension, and shame versus solicitude on the other.

8. The societal conflict over abortion provides a powerful example of the convergence of many psychosocial factors. The legal and cultural contexts, the health and well-being of the mother, the rights of the unborn child, the new technologies that permit extrauterine conceptions and extend viability to smaller and more vulnerable babies, and the life circumstances that might lead to an unwanted pregnancy are all elements in this debate. The vast majority of abortions occur as a result of unwanted pregnancies and take place within 10 weeks of gestational age. In a society such as ours, where abortions are legal, the abortion decision rests largely on a woman's evaluation of the costs and benefits of a new child in her life, her perceptions about the impact of the pregnancy on her relationship with the father, her moral and religious beliefs, her support from family and partner on the decision, and her access to safe, affordable medical intervention.

References

Abel, E. L. (1984). *Fetal alcohol syndrome and fetal alcohol effects*. New York: Plenum.

Adler, N.E., David, H. P., Major, B. N., Roth, S. H., Russo, N. F. & Wyatt, G. (1990). Psychological responses after abortion. *Science, 248*, 41–44.

Adler, N. E., David, H. P., Major, B. N., Roth, S. H., Russo, N. F. & Wyatt, G. E. (1992). Psychological factors in abortion. *American Psychologist, 47*, 1194–1204.

Aleksandrowicz, M. K. & Aleksandrowicz, D. R. (1974). Obstetrical pain-relieving drugs as predictors of infant behavior variability. *Child Development, 45*, 935–945.

Alter, R. C. (1984). Abortion outcome as a function of sex-role identification. *Psychology of Women Quarterly, 8*, 211–233.

Armstrong, B. G., McDonald, A. D. & Sloan, M. (1992). Cigarette, alcohol, and coffee consumption and spontaneous abortion. *American Journal of Public Health, 82*, 85–87.

Bankart, B. (1989). Japanese perceptions of motherhood. *Psychology of Women Quarterly, 13*, 59–76.

Baulieu, E. (1989). Contragestion and other clinical applications of RU 486, an antiprogesterone at the receptor. *Science, 245*, 1351–1357.

Brackbill, Y. (1977). Long-term effects of obstetrical anesthesia on infant autonomic function. *Developmental Psychology, 10*, 529–535.

Brackbill, Y., Kane, J., Manniello, R. L. & Abramson, D. (1974). Obstetric premedication and infant outcome. *American Journal of Obstetrics and Gynecology, 118*, 377–384.

Brackbill, Y., McManus, K. & Woodward, L. (1985). *Medication in maternity: Infant exposure and maternal information*. Ann Arbor: University of Michigan Press.

Brasel, J. (1974). Cellular changes in intrauterine malnutrition. In M. Winick (Ed.), *Nutrition and fetal development*. New York: Wiley.

Brazelton, T. B. (1987). Behavioral competence of the newborn infant. In G. B. Avery (Ed.), *Neonatology: Pathophysiology and management of the newborn*. Philadelphia: Lippincott, 379–399.

Bronson, G. (1979). Issue of fetal damage stirs women workers at chemical plants. *Wall Street Journal*, February 9.

Buescher, P. A., Roth, M. S., Williams, D. & Goforth, C. M. (1991). An evaluation of the impact of maternity care coordination on Medicaid birth outcomes in North Carolina. *American Journal of Public Health, 81*, 1625–1629.

Burt, R. D., Vaughan, T. L. & Daling, J. R. (1988). Evaluating the risks of cesarean section: Low Apgar score in repeat C-section and vaginal deliveries. *American Journal of Public Health, 78*, 1312–1314.

Cassady, G. & Strange, M. (1987). The small-for-gestational-age (SGA) infant. In G. B. Avery (Ed.), *Neonatology: Pathophysiology and management of the newborn*. Philadelphia: Lippincott, 299–331.

Chasnoff, I. J. (1988). *Drugs, alcohol, pregnancy, and parenting*. Hingham, Mass.: Kluwer.

Clarke-Stewart, A. & Koch, J. B. (1983). *Children: Development through adolescence*. New York: John Wiley & Sons.

Clarren, S. K. & Smith, D. W. (1978). The fetal alcohol syndrome. *New England Journal of Medicine, 298,* 1063–1067.

Clayman, C. B. (1989). *The American Medical Association encyclopedia of medicine.* New York: Random House.

Columbus Dispatch (1992). "30 million Americans hungry, House committee report says." Thursday, September 10, 1992.

Cunningham, F. G., MacDonald, P. C. & Gant, N. F. (1989). *Williams' obstetrics* (18th ed.). Norwalk, Conn.: Appleton & Lange.

Darney, P. D., Myhra, W., Atkinson, E. S. & Meier, J. (1989). Sero survey of human immunodeficiency virus infection in women at a family planning clinic: Absence of infection in an indigent population in San Francisco. *American Journal of Public Health, 79,* 883–885.

Davis-Floyd, R. E. (1987). The technological model of birth. *Journal of American Folklore, 100,* 479–495.

Dinges, D. F., Davis, M. M. & Glass, P. (1980). Fetal exposure to narcotics: Neonatal sleep as a measure of nervous system disturbance. *Science, 209,* 619–621.

Economist (1989). The fearful politics of abortion. July 8, 21–23.

Elson, J. (1989). The rights of frozen embryos. *Time,* July 24, 63.

Entwisle, D. R. & Alexander, K. L. (1987). Long-term effects of cesarean delivery on parents' beliefs and children's schooling. *Developmental Psychology, 23,* 676–682.

Fawcett, J. T. (1988). The value of children and the transition to parenthood. In R. Palkovitz & M. B. Sussman (Eds.), Transitions to parenthood. *Marriage and Family Review, 12,* 11–34.

Feinman, C. F. (1992). *The criminalization of a woman's body.* Binghampton, N.Y.: Haworth Press.

Fenster, L., Eskenazi, B., Windham, G. C. & Swan, S. H. (1991). Caffeine consumption during pregnancy and fetal growth. *American Journal of Public Health, 81,* 458–461.

Field, T. M., Healy, B., Goldstein, S. & Guthertz, M. (1990). Behavior-state matching and synchrony in mother–infant interaction of non-depressed versus depressed dyads. *Developmental Psychology, 26,* 7–14.

Field, T. M., Sandberg, D., Garcia, R., Vega-Lahr, N., Goldstein, S. & Guy, L. (1985). Pregnancy problems, postpartum depression, and early mother–infant interactions. *Developmental Psychology, 21,* 1152–1156.

Fleming, A. S., Ruble, D. N., Flett, G. L. & Shaul, D. L. (1988). Postpartum adjustment in first-time mothers: Relations between mood, maternal attitudes, and mother–infant interactions. *Developmental Psychology, 24,* 71–81.

Ford, C. S. (1945). *A comparative study of human reproduction.* New Haven, Conn.: Yale University Publications in Anthropology, no. 32.

Ford, C. S. (1964). *A comparative study of human reproduction.* (Reprinted from the 1945 edition). New Haven, Conn.: Human Relations Area Files Press.

Fried, P. A., Watkinson, B., Dillon, R. F. & Dulberg, C. S. (1987). Neonatal neurological status in a low-risk population after prenatal exposure to cigarettes,{normal} marijuana, and alcohol. *Journal of Developmental and Behavioral Pediatrics, 8,* 318–326.

Giacoia, G. P. & Yaffe, S. J. (1987). Drugs and the perinatal patient. In G. B. Avery (Ed.), *Neonatology: Pathophysiology and management of the newborn.* Philadelphia: Lippincott, 1317–1348.

Gilbert, M. S. (1963). *Biography of the unborn.* New York: Hafner.

Gorer, G. (1938). *Himalayan village: An account of the Lepchas of Sikkim.* London: Michael Joseph.

Grandquist, H. (1950). *Child problems among the Arabs.* Helsinki: Soderstrom.

Greenhouse, L. (1992). Surprising decision: Majority issues warning on White House effort to overturn Roe. *The New York Times,* Tuesday, June 30, 1992, A1, A7.

Grossman, F. K., Eichler, L. S., Winickoff, S. A. (1980). *Pregnancy, birth, and parenthood.* San Francisco: Jossey-Bass.

Habicht, J. P., Yarbrough, C., Lechtig, A. & Klein, R. E. (1974). Relation of maternal supplementary feeding during pregnancy to birth weight and other sociological factors. In M. Winick (Ed.), *Nutrition and fetal development.* New York: Wiley.

Hahn, R. A. & Muecke, M. A. (1987). The anthropology of birth in five U.S. ethnic populations: Implications for obstetrical practice. *Current Problems in Obstetrics, Gynecology, and Fertility, 10,* 133–171.

Hans, S. L. (1987). Maternal drug addiction and young children. *Division of Child, Youth, and Family Services Newsletter, 10,* 5, 15.

Hansell, M. J. (1991). Sociodemographic factors and the quality of prenatal care. *American Journal of Public Health, 81,* 1023–1028.

Healthy People 2000: National Health Promotion and Disease Prevention Objectives. (1990). Washington, D.C.: U.S. Department of Health and Human Services, Public Health Service, DHHS publication PHS 91-50212.

Heinicke, C. M. (1995). Determinants of the transition to parenting. In M. H. Bornstein (Ed.), *Handbook of parenting, Vol. 3: Status and social conditions of parenting.* Mahwah, N.J.: Erlbaum, 277–303.

Heitlinger, A. (1989). Current medical, legal, and demographic perspectives on artificial reproduction in Czechoslovakia. *American Journal of Public Health, 79,* 57–61.

Helman, C. G. (1990). *Culture, health and illness* (2nd ed.). London: Wright.

Holmes, T. H. & Rahe, R. H. (1967). The social readjustment rating scale. *Journal of Psychosomatic Research, 11,* 213–218.

Jarboe, P. J. D. (1986). A comparison study of distress and marital adjustment in infertile and expectant couples. Unpublished doctoral dissertation, The Ohio State University.

Jones, K. L., Smith, D. W., Ulleland, C. N. & Streissguth, A. P. (1973). Patterns of malformation in offspring of chronic alcoholic mothers. *Lancet 1,* 1267–1271.

Jordan, B. (1983). *Birth in four cultures: A cross cultural investigation of childbirth in Yucatan, Holland, Sweden and the United States* (3rd ed.). Montreal: Eden Press.

Judson, F. N. (1989). What do we really know about AIDS control? *American Journal of Public Health, 79,* 878–882.

Kaplan, B. J. (1986). A psychobiological review of depression during pregnancy. *Psychology of Women Quarterly, 10,* 35–48.

Kennell, J. H. & McGrath, S. (1993). Effects of environment on perinatal behavior: Perinatal effects of labor support. Paper presented at the meetings of the Society for Research in Child Development, New Orleans.

Kimura, D. (1992). Sex differences in the brain. *Scientific American, 267,* 119–125.

Kliman, D. G. & Kohl, R. (1984). *Fatherhood USA.* New York: Garland Press.

Kolb, B. (1989). Brain development, plasticity, and behavior. *American Psychologist, 44,* 1203–1212.

Koop, C. E. (1989a, January 9). Letter to President Reagan. In *Medical and psychological impact of abortion.* Washington D.C.: U.S. Government Printing Office, 68–71.

Koop, C. E. (1989b, March 16). Testimony before the Human Resources and Intergovernmental Relations Subcommittee of the Committee on Government Operations, House of Representatives. In *Medical and psychological impact of abortion.* Washington, D.C.: U.S. Government Printing Office, 193–203, 218, 223–250.

Krannich, R. S. (1980). Abortion in the United States: Past, present, and future trends. *Family Relations, 29,* 365–374.

Lazarus, A. (1985). Psychiatric sequelae of legalized first trimester abortion. *Journal of Psychosomatic Obstetrics and Gynecology, 4,* 141–150.

Lemkau, J. R. (1988). Emotional sequelae of abortion: Implications for clinical practice. *Psychology of Women Quarterly, 12,* 461–472.

Lester, B. M., Als, H. & Brazelton, T. B. (1982). Regional obstetric anesthesia and newborn behavior: A reanalysis toward synergistic effects. *Child Development, 53,* 687–692.

Lester, B. M., Corwin, M. J., Sepkoski, C., Seifer, R., Peucker, M., McLaughlin, S. & Golub, H. L. (1991). Neurobehavioral syndromes in cocaine-exposed newborn infants. *Child Development, 62,* 694–705.

Lindblad, B. S. (1987). *Perinatal nutrition.* San Diego: Academic Press.

Lindbohm, M., Hemminki, K., Bonhomme, M. G., Anttila, A., Rantala, K., Heikkila, P. & Rosenberg, M. J. (1991). *American Journal of Public Health, 81,* 1029–1033.

Lipkin, M. & Lamb, G. S. (1982). The couvade syndrome: An epidemiological study. *Annals of Internal Medicine, 96,* 509–511.

Lozoff, B., Jordan, B. & Malone, S. (1988). Childbirth in cross-cultural perspective. In R. Paldovitz & M. B. Sussman (Eds.), Transitions to parenthood. *Marriage & Family Review, 12,* 35–60.

Mactutus, C. F. & Fechter, L. D. (1984). Prenatal exposure to carbon monoxide: Learning and memory deficits. *Science, 223,* 409–411.

McDonald, A. D., Armstrong, B. G. & Sloan, M. (1992). Cigarette, alcohol, and coffee consumption and prematurity. *American Journal of Public Health, 82,* 87–90.

Mead, M. & Newton, N. (1967). Cultural patterning of perinatal behavior. In S. A. Richardson & A. F. Guttmacher (Eds.), *Childbearing—Its social and psychological aspects.* Baltimore: Williams & Wilkins.

Mertz, K. J., Parker, A. L. & Halpin, G. J. (1992). Pregnancy-related mortality in New Jersey, 1975 to 1989. *American Journal of Public Health, 82,* 1085–1088.

Miller, W. B. (1992). An empirical study of the psychological antecedents and consequences of induced abortion. *Journal of Social Issues, 48,* 67–93.

Moore, K. L. (1993). *The developing human: Clinically oriented embryology* (4th ed.). Philadelphia: W. B. Saunders.

Morris, R. A. (1987). The use of legislatively mandated birth registries in conducting research on behavioral teratology/toxicology. *Division of Child, Youth, and Family Services Newsletter, 10*(4), 12.

Murdock, G. P. (1934). *Our primitive contemporaries.* New York: Macmillan.

Murdock, G. P. & White, D. R. (1969). Standard cross-cultural sample. *Ethnology, 8,* 329–369.

Murray, A. D., Dolby, R. M., Nation, R. L. & Thomas, D. B. (1981). Effects of epidural anesthesia on newborns and their mothers. *Child Development, 52,* 71–82.

National Commission to Prevent Infant Mortality. (1988). *Death before life: The tragedy of infant mortality.* Washington, D.C.

Naulty, J. S. (1987). Obstetric anesthesia. In G. B. Avery (Ed.), *Neonatology: Pathophysiology and management of the newborn.* Philadelphia: Lippincott.

O'Campo, P., Gielen, A. C., Faden, R. R., Xue, X., Kass, N. & Wang, M. (1995). Violence by male partners against women during the childbearing year: A contextual analysis. *American Journal of Public Health, 85,* 1092–1097.

Padawer, J. A., Fagan, C., Janoff-Bulman, R., Strickland, B. R. & Chorowski, M. (1988). Women's psychological adjustment following emergency cesarean versus vaginal delivery. *Psychology of Women Quarterly, 12,* 25–34.

Palkovitz, R. (1985). Fathers' attendance, early contact, and extended care with their newborns: A critical review. *Child Development, 56,* 392–406.

Palm, G. F. & Palkovitz, R. (1988). The challenge of working with new fathers: Implications for support providers. In R. Palkovitz & M. B. Sussman (Eds.), *Transitions to Parenthood.* New York: Haworth, 357–376.

Parker, J. D. (1994). Ethnic differences in midwife-attended U.S. births. *American Journal of Public Health, 84,* 1139–1141.

Polednak, A. P. (1991). Black–white differences in infant mortality in 38 standard metropolitan statistical areas. *American Journal of Public Health, 81,* 1480–1482.

Quilligan, E. J. (1983). *Pregnancy, birth, and the infant.* U.S. Department of Health and Human Services. Washington, D.C.: U.S. Government Printing Office. NIH publication no. 82-2304.

Reinisch, J. M. & Karow, W. G. (1977). Prenatal exposure to synthetic progestins and estrogens: Effects on human development. *Archives of Sexual Behavior, 6,* 257–288.

Reinisch, J. M. & Sanders, S. A. (1984). Prenatal gonadal steroidal influences on gender-related behavior. In G. D. DeVries, J. P. C. DeBruin, H. B. M. Uylings & M. A. Corher (Eds.), *Sex differences in the brain: The relation between structure and function. Progress in Brain Research* (vol. 61). Amsterdam: Elsevier.

Roosa, M. W. (1984). Maternal age, social class, and the obstetric performance of teenagers. *Journal of Youth and Adolescence, 13,* 365–374.

Rosenblatt, R. A., Mattis, R. & Hart, L. G. (1995). Abortions in rural Idaho: Physicians' attitudes and practices. *American Journal of Public Health, 85,* 1423–1425.

Roth, W. E. (1953). Precautions during pregnancy in New Guinea. In M. Mead & N. Calas (Eds.), *Primitive heritage.* New York: Random House.

Russo, N. R., Horn, J. D. & Schwartz, R. (1992). U. S. abortion in context: Selected characteristics and motivations of women seeking abortions. *Journal of Social Issues, 48,* 183–202.

Sachs, A. (1989). Here come the pregnancy police. *Time,* May 22, 104–105.

Sameroff, A. J. & Chandler, M. J. (1975). Reproductive risk and the continuum of caretaking casualty. In F. D. Horowitz, M. Hetherington & S. Scarr (Eds.), (1992). Developmental theories for the 1990s: Development and individual differences. *Child Development, 63,* 1–19.

Schroeder, S. R. (1987). Behavioral toxicology: Assessment technology for neurotoxic effects of lead exposure in humans. *Division of Child, Youth, and Family Services Newsletter, 10*(1), 14–15.

Schuster, C. S. (1986). Intrauterine development. In C. S. Schuster & S. S. Ashburn (Eds.), *The process of human development.* Boston: Little, Brown, 67–94.

Seabrook, C. (1987). Children—"third wave" of AIDS victims. *Atlanta Journal,* February 19, 1A, 12A.

Sexton, M. & Hebel, J. R. (1984). A clinical trial of change in maternal smoking and its effect on birth weight. *Journal of the American Medical Association, 251,* 911–915.

Shatz, C. J. (1992). The developing brain. *Scientific American, 267,* 60–67.

Shostak, A. & McLouth, G. (1985). *Men and abortion.* New York: Praeger.

Singh, G. K. & Yu, S. M. (1995). Infant mortality in the United States: Trends, differentials, and projections, 1950 through 2010. *American Journal of Public Health, 85,* 957–964.

Speckhard, A. C. & Rue, V. M. (1992). Postabortion syndrome: An emerging public health concern. *Journal of Social Issues, 48,* 95–119.

Sosa, R., Kennell, J., Klaus, M., Robertson, S. & Urrutia, J. (1980). The effect of a supportive companion on perinatal problems, length of labor, and mother–infant interaction. *New England Journal of Medicine, 303,* 597–600.

Standley, K., Soule, B. & Copans, S. A. (1979). Dimensions of prenatal anxiety and their influence on pregnancy outcome. *American Journal of Obstetrics and Gynecology, 135,* 22–26.

Stechler, G. & Halton, A. (1982). Prenatal influences on human development. In B. B. Wolman (Ed.), *Handbook of developmental psychology.* Englewood Cliffs, N.J.: Prentice-Hall, 175–189.

Streissguth, A. P., Barr, H. M., Sampson, P. D., Darby, B. L. & Martin, D. C. (1989). IQ at age 4 in relation to maternal alcohol use and smoking during pregnancy. *Developmental Psychology, 25,* 3–11.

Swyer, P. R. (1987). The organization of perinatal care with particular reference to the newborn. In G. B. Avery (Ed.), *Neonatology: Pathophysiology and management of the newborn.* Philadelphia: Lippincott, 13–44.

Tanner, J. M. (1990). *Foetus into man: Physical growth from conception to maturity* (rev. ed.). Cambridge, Mass.: Harvard University Press.

Tichauer, R. (1963). The Aymara children of Bolivia. *Journal of Pediatrics, 62,* 399–412.

Toufexis, A. (1991). Innocent victims. *Time,* May 13, 56–60.

Trethowan, W. (1972). The Couvade syndrome. In J. Howells (Ed.), *Modern perspectives in psycho-obstetrics.* New York: Brunner-Mazel.

U.S. Bureau of the Census. (1991). *Statistical abstract of the United States: 1991* (111th ed.). Washington, D.C.: U.S. Government Printing Office.

U.S. Bureau of the Census. (1994). *Statistical abstract of the United States: 1994* (114th ed.). Washington, D.C.: U.S. Government Printing Office.

U.S. Department of Health, Education, and Welfare. (1979). *Smoking and health: A report of the surgeon general.* Washington, D.C.: U.S. Government Printing Office.

Vaughn, B. E., Bradley, C. F., Joffe, L. S., Seifer, R. & Barglow, P. (1987). Maternal characteristics measured prenatally are predictive of ratings of temperamental "difficulty" on the Carey Infant Temperament Questionnaire. *Developmental Psychology, 23,* 152–161.

Vizziello, G. F., Antonioli, M. E., Cocci, V. & Invernizzi, R. (1993). From pregnancy to motherhood: The structure of representative and narrative change. *Infant Mental Health Journal, 14,* 4–16.

Vorhees, C. V. & Mollnow, E. (1987). Behavioral teratogenesis: Long-term influences on behavior from early exposure to environmental agents. In J. D. Osofsky (Ed.), *Handbook of infant development.* New York: John Wiley & Sons, 913–971.

West, J. R. (1986). *Alcohol and brain development.* London: Oxford University Press.

Wilcox, A. J. & Skjoerven, R. (1992). Birth weight and perinatal mortality: The effect of gestational age. *American Journal of Public Health, 82,* 378–382.

Willwerth, J. (1991). Should we take away their kids? *Time,* May 13, 62–63.

Wilmoth, G. H. (1992). Abortion, public health policy, and informed consent legislation. *Journal of Social Issues, 48,* 1–17.

Wilmoth, G. H., de Alteriis, M. & Bussell, D. (1992). Prevalence of psychological risks following legal abortion. *Journal of Social Issues, 48,* 37–66.

Yang, R. K., Zweig, A. R., Douthitt, T. C. & Federman, E. J. (1976). Successive relationships between maternal attitudes during pregnancy, analgesic medication during labor and delivery, and newborn behavior. *Developmental Psychology, 12,* 6–14.

Zahniser, S. C., Kendrick, J. S., Franks, A. L. & Saftlas, A. F. (1992). Trends in obstetric operative procedures, 1980 to 1987. *American Journal of Public Health, 82,* 1340–1344.

Zuckerman, B., Frank, D. A. & Hingson, R. (1989). Effects of maternal marijuana and cocaine use on fetal growth. *New England Journal of Medicine, 320,* 762–768.

Developmental Tasks of Infancy

Newborns

The Development of Sensory/
Perceptual and Motor Functions

Sensory/Perceptual Development

Hearing

Vision

Taste and Smell

Touch

The Interconnected Nature of Sensory/Perceptual Capacities

Motor Development

Organization and Progression of Motor and Movement Skills

The Contributions of Nature and Nurture in Motor Development

Temperament

Attachment

The Development of Attachment

Five Sequential Stages

Stranger Anxiety

Separation Anxiety

Formation of Attachments with Mother, Father, and Others

Patterns of Attachment

The Strange Situation

Four Patterns of Quality of Attachment

Is the Strange Situation Procedure Valid in Different Cultures?

Parental Sensitivity and the Quality of Attachment

Sensorimotor Intelligence and Early Causal Schemes

How Do Infants Organize Their Experiences?

The Development of Causal Schemes

Understanding the Nature of Objects and Creating Categories

The Nature of Objects

Object Permanence

Precursors of Object Permanence

Object Permanence and Attachment

The Categorization of Objects

Emotional Development

Emotional Differentiation

Emotions as a Key to Understanding Meaning

The Ability to Regulate Emotions

Emotions as a Channel for Adult–Infant Communication

Social Referencing

Chapter Summary

References

Chapter 7

Infancy is a stage of strikingly rapid development. During the first year of life, the infant's birth weight almost triples. Imagine if your weight tripled within one year at any other time in life! Along with this extraordinary rate of physical growth comes a remarkable process of increased control and purposefulness leading to the integration of simple responses into coordinated, meaningful configurations of behavior. The baby seems to be growing before your very eyes. Parents remark that they go to work in the morning, and their baby seems to have changed by the time they return in the evening. Most infants are marvelous, flexible, complex organisms capable of adapting to any of the enormously varied social environments into which they may be born. By the age of 2, the fundamentals of movement, language, and concept formation can be observed. The global behaviors of early infancy become well-differentiated requests for the satisfaction of specific needs.

In recent years, as American families have become smaller, we have seen a change in the emphasis that society places on infancy. Children are taken much more seriously, and each child is considered special. Complex medical technologies save the lives of babies born at 1,200 grams (39 ounces) and even 1,000 grams (32 ounces). Psychologists study infant temperament and the early origins of personality, focusing on individual differences among infants from the very first weeks of life. A growing "baby industry" produces special equipment, foods, toys, books, and other paraphernalia intended to enrich the infant's sensory and motor development and to support the parent–infant bond. Parents take child-care classes, read books and magazines, and join support groups so that they can "get it right the first time."

From the perspective of psychosocial development, five major developmental tasks are especially critical during infancy. These are:

1. Formation of an attachment to at least one person;
2. Establishment of the perceptual, motor, and sensory systems for sensing and processing stimuli;
3. Elaboration of the sensorimotor intellectual system;
4. Initial understanding of the nature of objects and creation of categories for organizing the physical and social world; and
5. Differentiation of the emotional system.

For each of these tasks, one finds evidence of the complex interaction of genetics and environment in directing growth. This chapter begins with a description of the physical status of the newborn and then takes up each of the developmental tasks listed above.

Newborns

In the United States, the average full-term baby weighs 3,300 grams (7 to 7.5 pounds) and is 51 centimeters (20 inches) long. Boys are slightly heavier and longer than girls. At birth, girls' nervous systems and bones are about two weeks more mature than boys'.

In the first minute after birth, and then again at five minutes, the newborn's life signs are evaluated using the *Apgar scoring method*, named for its originator, Virginia Apgar (see Table 7.1). Five life signs are scored on a scale

TABLE 7.1

The Apgar Scoring Chart

Sign	Score		
	0	1	2
Heart rate	Absent	Slow (less than 100 beats/minute)	Over 100 beats/minute
Respiratory effort	Absent	Slow or irregular breathing	Good crying, strong breathing
Muscle tone	Flaccid or limp	Weak; some flexion of extremities	Active motion; strong flexion of extremities
Reflex irritability	No response	Weak cry, grimace, cough, or sneeze	Vigorous cry, grimace, cough, or sneeze
Color	Blue, pale	Body pink, extremities blue	Completely pink

Source: Apgar, V. (1953). Proposal for a new method of evaluating the newborn infant. *Anesthesia and Analgesia, 32,* 260–267.

from 0 to 2: heart rate, respiratory effort, muscle tone, reflex irritability, and body color. A score of 7 to 10 means that the infant is in good condition. Scores of 4 to 6 mean fair condition and indicate the need for the administration of supplemental oxygen. Scores of 0 to 3 suggest extremely poor condition and the need for resuscitation. Even among the highest-scoring group, those with scores of 7 or 8 show less efficient attention and less habituation to stimuli than the highest-scoring infants. The most important use of the Apgar is for determining the need for immediate intervention rather than for assessing subsequent development (Francis et al., 1987).

Babies differ in their physical maturity and appearance at birth. Differences in physical maturity have distinct consequences for their capacity to regulate survival functions such as breathing, digesting, waking, and sleeping. Infants who weigh less than 2,500 grams (about 5 pounds, 8 ounces) are called *low-birth-weight babies.* Low birth weight may be a result of being born before the full period of gestation, that is, prematurely. It may also result from the mother's inadequate diet, smoking, or use of drugs, as discussed in Chapter 6. These factors tend to lower the fetus's weight for a given gestational age. Babies who are small for their gestational age (SGA) are at greater risk than those who are born prematurely but are of average weight for their gestational age (Cassady & Strange, 1987). Box 7.1 discusses some of what is known about the development of very small babies.

Differences in appearance may influence the reaction and responsiveness of caregivers, including the infant's mother and nurses or other staff in the newborn nursery. In an observational study of mothers and their newborns while they were in the hospital, mothers of more attractive babies spent more time in affectionate and playful interactions with them. Mothers of less attractive babies spent more time interacting with others; the time they spent with

BOX 7.1

Very Small Babies

Today, many babies are born before they are fully developed. Modern technology has pushed back the boundary of fetal viability to about 24 weeks of gestational age, or a weight of about 500 grams (slightly over one pound). These tiny babies, not much bigger than the palm of your hand, receive weeks of round-the-clock care in their struggle to survive. About 17,000 infants who weigh less than two pounds are cared for in the nation's intensive-care nurseries. These babies have about a 70% chance of survival; the smallest babies have only a 20% chance (Kantrowitz, 1988).

What do we know about the developmental progress of these very small babies? How is the quality of the relationship with their parents altered by the prolonged hospitalization and their obvious vulnerability? How do parents cope with the anxieties and frustrations of caring for a very tiny baby? What are the outcomes with respect to a child's cognitive capacities and later intellectual development? Because this is really a very new population that has survived in appreciable numbers only in recent decades, many of these questions are still being addressed. But we are beginning to get a picture of the psychosocial development of very small babies.

When we think about the formation of an attachment between a parent and an infant, we have to realize that very-low-birth-weight preterm babies are clearly different from full-term babies. They are less physically attractive; they have higher-pitched, unpleasant cries; they are more easily overstimulated and more difficult to soothe; and they are less able to establish rhythmic patterns of social interaction. What

is more, the early weeks and months of parental contact with these babies take place in the intimidating environment of the hospital, where babies are usually hooked up to monitors, have tubes in their bodies, and are going through periodic physical crises in the struggle for survival. In this situation, it's a wonder that any kind of attachment can develop at all.

But with opportunities to interact and give care during the hospital stay, parents have an almost irresistible tendency to become absorbed in their very small babies, just as parents of full-term babies do. The process of attachment, however, appears to face greater challenges. Parents find that it is harder to synchronize their parenting activities with the activities of their babies. They perceive their babies as difficult, and find that they receive few cues of satisfaction or responsiveness from them. In other words, the establishment of a sense of reciprocity between parent and infant is more difficult to establish in the early months of life (Levy-Shiff et al., 1989). Nonetheless, in assessments of attachment at age two, very-low-birth-weight babies and full-term babies did not differ in the quality of their attachments with their mothers or their fathers (Easterbrooks, 1989). Preterm infants were just as likely to form secure attachments with both their mothers and their fathers as were full-term babies. Depending on the health and robustness of the infants, and with the appropriate parental responsiveness, approximately 65% of parents and low-birth-weight babies are able to establish a framework of secure, trusting interactions by the end of the child's infancy just as parents and full-term infants do (Goldberg & DiVitto, 1995).

their infants was more likely to be focused on caregiving functions rather than affection and play (Langlois et al., 1995).

The Development of Sensory/Perceptual and Motor Functions

During the first months of life, the sensory/perceptual system—vision, hearing, taste, smell, touch, motion sensitivity, and responsiveness to internal cues (proprioception)—is developing rapidly and appears to function at a more advanced level than the motor system. Since most muscle movements are not yet under the infant's voluntary control in the early months of life, researchers have had to apply considerable ingenuity to study infants' sensory/perceptual competencies. They cannot simply ask an infant to point to a circle or

When Ceci Burke was born, three months prematurely, she weighed 12.9 ounces. After she spent four months in the hospital, her mother and father finally got to take her home.

Extreme-low-birth-weight infants appear to be at risk for problems in subsequent cognitive development. Infants who are born weighing less than 1500 grams are likely to suffer serious brain hemorrhages. In addition, their undeveloped lungs cannot deliver an adequate supply of oxygen to the brain. These insults to the nervous system have an impact on a variety of information-processing skills that can be measured in newborns. High-risk preterm infants show deficits in regulating arousal and attention, visual recognition of familiar stimuli, and reactivity to novel stimuli (DiPietro et al., 1992; Millar et al., 1992; Rose et al., 1992). Severe respiratory distress experienced during the early months of life is associated with cognitive deficits that can be observed in the first year of life, and with learning and language deficits during the preschool years and on into the early school years (Brooks-Gunn et al., 1993; Rose et al., 1992). Babies born before 30 weeks to parents who have very limited educational and financial resources are at greatest risk for cognitive delays.

press a button to respond to a certain change in color or taste. Behaviors such as gazing time, changes in heart rate, the strength and/or frequency of sucking, facial action, and head turning are used as indicators of infants' interest or change in response to stimuli (see Box 7.2).

Using these strategies, researchers have begun to document infants' sensory capacities. Infants respond to and process much of the sensory stimulation that confronts them. They are certainly not adrift in sensory confusion. What is more, sensory capacities undergo rapid development during the first months of life. The genetic plan that has been carried out during the gestation period provides most newborn infants with intact sensory organs and a well-formed brain at birth. The infant's brain contains about 100 billion neurons, or nerve cells, which are already connected in pathways that are designed to execute definite functions. The fundamental organization of the brain does not change after birth, but details of its structure demonstrate

BOX 7.2

Looking in on the Newborn

One of the adaptive mechanisms that applies to all sense modalities is the infant's capacity to habituate to any particular repetitive stimulation. *Habituation means that the infant's response decreases after each presentation of an identical stimulus* (Rovee-Collier, 1987). These responses might be in the form of head or eye movements or changes in heart rate, respiration, or gazing time. As an adaptational mechanism, habituation allows the infant to shift attention to new aspects of the environment as certain elements become familiar. However, if a new stimulus is presented, such as a new level of loudness or the same tone presented to a different ear, the infant shows an increase in alert responsiveness. Habituation is one of the most primitive forms of learning, and it is observed in many other mammalian species.

Habituation is often used as a means of determining whether an infant can discriminate between two different stimuli. The researcher first habituates the infant to one stimulus; then, a second stimulus is presented. If the infant shows signs of renewed interest or alertness, this is taken as evidence that the infant has detected a difference between the two stimuli. If the infant shows no new signs of interest or responsiveness, this is taken as evidence that the differences between the two stimuli were too slight to be perceived.

Habituation depends in part on the nature of the stimulus. For example, newborns did not habituate to the sound of a door buzzer after 15 presentations. However, they did habituate to a blue light that stayed lit for 20 seconds after six presentations. Some babies are fast habituators; others are slow. Some infants quickly decrease their attentiveness to repeated stimuli, while others continue to respond to each presentation. Differences in speed of habituation may be related to the maturity of the infant at birth, the amount of anesthetic used during delivery, or innate differences in intellectual competence.

Researchers have used the phenomenon of habituation to assess infants' cognitive capacities. An infant's ability to differentiate among complex stimuli can be evaluated by observing the patterns of habituation and dishabituation. For example, four-month-old infants were habituated to a three-element mobile. Then the babies were allowed to gaze at an identical mobile or some variation of the mobile for one-half hour each day at home for three weeks. At the end of the three weeks, the babies were observed in response to the original mobile. Looking time was longest when there was a moderate difference between the original and the home mobiles. Identical stimuli or extremely discrepant stimuli did not appear to be as interesting as stimuli that were somewhat different from the original (Super et al., 1972). Similar findings have been observed in infants' responses to patterns of musical notes, phonetic sounds, and complex shapes. These studies support the notion that young infants are capable of forming and retaining a scheme for sensory experiences against which they can compare new events (Bornstein, 1992).

---

plasticity for some time (Singer, 1995). This means that sights, smells, sounds, tastes, touches, and posture activate and, over time, strengthen specific neural pathways, while others fall into disuse (Aoki & Siekevitz, 1988). Thus, the infant's interaction with the immediate environment begins to stimulate the organization of neural connections, creating very early patterns of familiarity and meaning.

Sensory/Perceptual Development

It would be difficult to review the full range and detail of sensory capacities that emerge and develop during infancy. Maturation in these domains is breathtaking. Our discussion focuses largely on those abilities that appear to permit infants, even from birth, to participate in and adapt to their social environment. From birth, sensory/perceptual capacities are vital resources that help infants establish emotional links with their caregivers, gather information about their environment, and cope with sources of stress.

PLASTICITY

Hearing

You may be surprised to learn that hearing, rather than vision, is the sense that provides the very earliest link between the newborn and the mother. Research has confirmed that the fetus is sensitive to auditory stimulation in utero (Aslin, 1987; DeCasper & Spence, 1986). Before birth, infants hear their mother's heartbeat. This sound continues to soothe the infant in the days and weeks after birth. Newborns show a preference for the sound of their mother's voice in comparison with an unfamiliar female voice (DeCasper & Fifer, 1980). They show a preference for the sound of melodies that their mother sang during pregnancy and even for the sound of prose passages read by their mother during the prenatal period. One must assume that an infant's indication of preference for these auditory stimuli is based on familiarity with the sounds from exposure in utero.

Young infants can distinguish changes in loudness, pitch, duration, and location of sounds (Kuhl, 1987). Many of these capacities are present among newborns but become increasingly sensitive by six months. Infants can use sounds to locate objects in space. In one study, babies between 6 and 8 months of age were placed in a darkened room. Objects that made sounds were located within reach and out of reach, and off to the right or left of midline. The babies made reaching motions in the correct direction of the sounds and made more efforts to reach objects that sounded as if they were within reach than objects that sounded out of reach (Clifton et al., 1991).

The human voice is one of the earliest stimuli to evoke an infant's smile. Infants appear to be particularly sensitive to language sounds. Very young babies are able to differentiate basic sound distinctions used in human speech throughout the world. Infants from all language environments are able to perceive and distinguish among speech sounds that could be used in one or more of the world's languages. During the second six months of life, after exposure to a native language, the infant's ability to make some of these sound distinctions drops out. Speech perception becomes more tied to the native language as infants begin to attach meaning to certain sound combinations, indicating a reorganization of sensory capabilities as the child listens to people speaking a particular language (Bornstein 1995; Werker, 1989). Here is an example of the plasticity referred to earlier—a fine-tuning of the neural network as a result of experience.

Vision

Infants respond to a variety of visual dimensions, including movement, color, brightness, complexity, light/dark contrast, contours, depth, and distance (Banks & Dannemiller, 1987; Hickey & Peduzzi, 1987). The vast majority of research on sensory development in infancy has concentrated on assessing the acuity or sensitivity of vision and analyzing the ways that infants use vision to understand their environment as well as to coordinate exploratory behaviors. Visual behaviors have also served as one of the primary windows for research into the infant's sensory and cognitive capacities. For instance, the time that an infant takes to scan an object and the length of time spent fixating on a novel object appear to be indications of infant intelligence. Shorter fixation time is apparently a result of greater speed and efficiency in visual processing (Colombo et al., 1991; Jacobson et al., 1992).

Visual acuity improves rapidly during the first four months. Pattern perception and movement perception mature as well. By two months, infants appear to form an expectation of a visual sequence. As they watch a pattern of events, they show evidence of anticipating the next event in the sequence (Aslin, 1987; Canfield & Haith, 1991). Three-month-old infants respond to wavelengths of light as though they perceive distinct hues of blue, green, yellow, and red (Aslin, 1987; Bornstein, Kessen, & Weiskopf, 1976; Teller & Bornstein, 1987). Four-month-old babies perceive objects as adults would, although they do not have the same set of cognitive associations with objects that imply specific functions or categories. They recognize shapes and detect complex patterns of motion like human walking. A great deal of infant learning occurs through listening and watching (Bornstein, 1995).

Faceness. The human face and *"faceness"* in general appear to have special appeal for newborns. Infants show preference for facelike stimuli. In the early weeks following birth, infants have optimal focus on objects that are about 20 cm away, about the distance of a mother's face if she were cradling her baby in her arms. Newborns can shift focus to scan and keep track of a moving target but not as easily and smoothly as older babies. Young infants appear to focus their attention on the contours or external borders of objects rather than on the internal details. Thus, if you were holding a young baby, the child might appear to be staring at your hairline or your chin rather than at your mouth. Faces have many of the properties that infants seem to prefer: Hairline is a type of contour; eyes provide a dark/light contrast; facial expressions provide a changing, moving stimulus.

In addition to the form, shape, and movement of the human face, certain facial expressions appear to have meaning to very young babies. One- and two-day-old babies are able to discriminate between and imitate the happy, sad, and surprised expressions of a live model (Field et al., 1982). This very early capacity for imitation wanes and is replaced between the ages of one and two with a voluntary capacity for imitation of facial expressions when the model is not present. Sometime between four and seven months, infants are able to recognize and classify some expressions such as happiness and anger (Caron et al., 1982; Ludemann, 1991; Nelson, 1987; Nelson & Dolgin, 1985).

Lack of motion in an adult face appears to have a disturbing effect on infants. When adults pose with a still face, babies stop looking at the adult and, in some cases, begin grimacing or showing other signs of distress. This reaction suggests that infants anticipate a certain normal sequence of facial movements in a human interaction. The absence of facial movements is interpreted as distressing (Segal et al., 1995; Stack & Muir, 1992).

Some two-day-old infants discriminate between a mother's face and the face of a stranger (Field et al., 1984). By three months, almost all infants distinguish a parent's face from that of a stranger (Zucker, 1985). These visual perceptual skills illustrate the highly developed capacities for orienting toward social stimuli that permit infants to participate so readily in the social context upon which their survival depends.

Taste and Smell

The sense of taste is at least partially functioning in utero (Mistretta & Bradley, 1977). Newborns can differentiate sweet, sour, bitter, and salty tastes. Facial responses to salty, sour, and bitter solutions share the same negative upper- and midface response but differ in the accompanying lower-face

Babies use the sense of touch to gather information about new and unusual objects.

actions: the lips purse in response to a sour taste, the mouth gapes in response to a bitter taste, and no distinctive lower facial reaction is seen in response to a salty taste. Two hours after birth, an infant's facial responses to a sweet taste (sucrose) are characterized primarily by relaxation and sucking. Sucrose has an especially calming effect on newborns and appears to reduce pain (Blass & Ciaramitaro, 1994). In one experiment, one- to three-day-old infants who were undergoing circumcision or heel prick to test for phenylketonuria cried much less when they were given a small sucrose solution to suck (Blass & Hoffmeyer, 1991).

Breast-fed babies are particularly sensitive to their mothers' body odors (Cernoch & Porter, 1985). One study found that seven-day-old babies could use the sense of smell to distinguish their own mothers' nursing pads from those of other mothers (MacFarlane, 1975). The mother's odor may play an important role in stimulating early mother–infant interactions (Porter, Balogh & Makin, 1988).

Touch

The skin is the largest sensory organ and the earliest to develop in utero. A variety of evidence from animal and human research suggests that touch plays a central role in development. Gentle handling, including rocking, stroking, and cuddling a baby all have soothing effects. *Swaddling*, the practice of wrapping a baby snugly in a soft blanket, is a common technique for soothing a newborn in many cultures. One of the effective techniques for caring for low-birth-weight babies is to introduce regular gentle stroking, rocking, and other forms of soothing touch.

Kinesthetic stimulation can have an arousing, as well as a soothing, effect. Some theorists view kinesthetic stimulation as a common method for maintaining an optimal level of arousal, using soothing techniques when the baby is upset or stressed and more vigorous arousing techniques such as jiggling or bouncing in order to engage the baby in social interaction or to get the baby's attention (Yarrow, Pedersen & Rubenstein, 1977). In many cultures, babies are carried on the mother's back, in a side sling, or front pouch where they have continuous physical contact with the caregiver as well as opportunities to encounter a wide range of visual, auditory, and olfactory stimulation as they are carried about the house or through their community.

Touch is an active, as well as a passive, sense; babies use touch to explore objects and people, including their own bodies. Sucking is one of the earliest coping strategies that infants use to calm themselves (Blass & Ciaramitaro, 1994). Sucking and mouthing also comprise an early form of exploratory touch. Babies can recognize qualities of objects from the way the objects feel in their mouths—nubby or smooth, chewy and flexible or rigid (Rose & Ruff, 1987). Of course, for older infants, most tactile information comes through touching with the hands and bringing objects to the face in order to take a closer look or to explore with the mouth. By five or six months of age, infants can use their hands for controlled examination of objects, fingering the surface to explore small details and transferring the object from hand to hand to detect corners, shapes, texture, and flexibility, as well as the overall size of the object (Gibson, 1962; Ruff, 1984).

The Interconnected Nature of Sensory/Perceptual Capacities

The sensory/perceptual capacities function as an interconnected system to provide a variety of sources of information about the environment simultaneously. Consider the situation when an infant is being nursed. At first, the mother guides the baby toward her breast, but the baby makes use of visual, tactile, olfactory, and kinesthetic cues to find and make contact with the nipple. If the baby is very hungry, she may close her eyes in order to concentrate exclusively on bursts of sucking behavior, coordinating sucking and swallowing as efficiently as possible. But as the initial swallows of milk satisfy the strong hunger pangs, the baby pauses to take in other aspects of the situation. She may gaze at the contours of her mother's face; playfully lick the milk dripping from her mother's breast; smell its fragrance and taste its distinctive sweet taste; listen to the sounds of her mother's voice offering comfort or inviting conversation; reach up to explore her mother's skin or relax in the comfort of her mother's gentle embrace. All the sensory information is integrated to create familiarity with this scenario, including a growing recognition of the mother and a rich mixture of sensory impressions associated with this delightfully intimate situation in which hunger is satisfied. In Notebook Page 7.1, we ask you to imagine yourself as an infant taking in sensory and perceptual experiences.

Motor Development

Organization and Progression of Motor and Movement Skills

At birth, an infant's voluntary muscle responses are poorly coordinated. Most early motor responses appear to be *reflexive,* meaning that a specific stimulus will evoke a particular motor response without any voluntary control or direction. Many of these built-in responses help infants survive and lead them on the road to developing more complicated sequences of voluntary behavior. The sucking reflex is a good example of this. At birth, inserting something in an infant's mouth produces a sucking reflex. This helps infants gain nourishment relatively easily before sucking behavior is under their control. Before

The Infant's Sensory World

As adults, we attach so many meanings to the objects in our world that we often fail to attend to the pure sensory information itself. Try to imagine that you are a four-month-old infant inspecting your world as you lie in your crib. You are in a familiar room, sunlight is coming in through a window, and you are lying on your back in a calm, alert state, gazing around. Describe your sensory experiences:

1. What do you see?

2. What kinds of sounds do you notice?

3. What types of textures do you feel?

4. What smells can you detect?

5. What kinds of movements/motor feedback do you experience?

long, infants become skillful at controlling the strength and sensitivity of sucking behavior. They use sucking and mouthing as strategies for tactile exploration. In some research, infants have been shown to use their mouths to explore objects that they can then identify visually, thus transferring information from the tactile sense to the visual sense (Gibson & Walker, 1984; Meltzoff & Borton, 1979).

In Table 4.1 in Chapter 4, you learned of a number of common infant reflexes, the evoking stimulus, and the response. Infant reflexes include sucking, grasping, rooting (turning the head in the direction of the cheek that is stroked), coughing, and stepping. With time, many of these behaviors make a transition from an involuntary to a voluntary behavior. In the process, infants may appear to lose a response before they regain control over simple movements. Then they blend several of these new voluntary movements into increasingly coordinated and complex patterns of behavior (Fentress & McLeod, 1986). For example, very young infants can support their full weight through the strength of their grasping reflex. When propped in an infant seat, they will reach and grasp reflexively at an object—and reach their target about 40% of the time. At four weeks of age, this reflexive reaching behavior seems to disappear, but by five months it is replaced by voluntary reaching, accurate grasping, clutching, and letting go (Bower, 1987). The transition from involuntary to voluntary reaching and grasping appears to result from a process of repeated discovery, exploration, and practice of controlled, coordinated muscle movements guided by visual and auditory cues, particularly cues about size, distance, and direction (Bower, 1989).

Motor skills also develop as a result of physical growth, and maturation of bones, muscles, and the nervous system. Figure 7.1 shows the normal sequence of development for motor and movement skills during the first year of life. Babies vary in the sequence and rate at which they acquire these skills. Individual children grow in spurts, interspersed with times of slow growth and some periods of regression (Fischer & Rose, 1994). Usually, however, during the first 12 months, babies begin to hold their heads up and to roll over by themselves; they learn to reach for things and grasp them; they sit, crawl, stand, and walk. Parental expectations seem to influence the timing of the onset for some of the milestones (Hopkins & Westra, 1990). During the second year, walking becomes increasingly steady; crawling may be used for play but is no longer the preferred method for locomotion. Babies explore stairs, climbing up and down using a variety of strategies. They start to slide or jump down from modest heights. Each of these accomplishments requires practice, refinement, struggle, and, finally, mastery.

Although the normative pattern of motor development suggests a preprogrammed sequence of stages that is heavily guided by genetics and neural structures, recent views of the process of motor development challenge this view. Rather, researchers now view the regularities in motor behavior as the result of a dynamic process of exploration in which infants coordinate their physical actions with the demands and opportunities of the situation. Perception and action work hand in hand, giving the infant information about the physical properties of the situation and feedback about the consequences of a specific motor strategy. This information guides the next motor action. Over time and with practice in similar situations, the infant discovers the combination of action, intensity, direction, and speed that will create the desired

INFANT REFLEXES

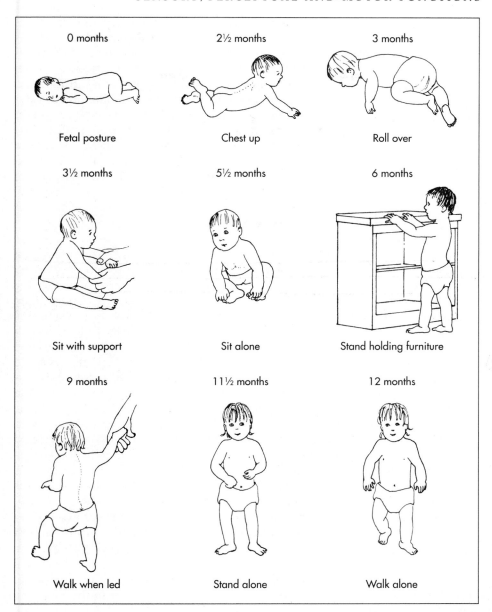

| 0 months | 2½ months | 3 months |

Fetal posture   Chest up   Roll over

| 3½ months | 5½ months | 6 months |

Sit with support   Sit alone   Stand holding furniture

| 9 months | 11½ months | 12 months |

Walk when led   Stand alone   Walk alone

FIGURE 7.1
The pattern of development of motor and movement skills. *Note:* The age at which 50% of babies mastered each skill is indicated. These norms were established in the 1960s by means of the Denver Developmental Screening Test.
Source: Based on Frankenberg, W. K. & Dodds, J. B. (1967). The Denver Developmental Screening Test. *Journal of Pediatrics, 71,* 181–191.

outcome. With additional practice, this pattern then becomes most likely and increasingly efficient (Thelen, 1995).

Consider a baby boy's efforts to crawl. He is placed face down in the middle of a gaily colored blanket. His mother kneels at the edge of the blanket and dangles a favorite stuffed bear. She smiles and says encouragingly, "Come on, come get Teddy." The baby looks intently, reaches toward the bear, and, by kicking and squirming, manages to move forward. This snakelike movement is his first accomplishment en route to well-organized crawling. Before he masters crawling, however, he must learn to raise himself on his knees, coordinate hand and leg movements, and propel himself forward rather than backward. Most babies reach a point when they rock in a stationary position on all fours before they can crawl. In repeated observations of 15 infants as they made the transition to crawling, a key precursor of crawling was found to be the establishment of a strong hand preference. When infants fell from a seated position onto their hands, they tended to fall onto their nonpreferred hand so that the preferred hand was available to reach out and begin to crawl. Confidence in being able to maintain one's body weight on one arm and two legs while reaching out with the preferred hand is part of the motor sequence necessary for forward crawling (Goldfield, 1989). The crawling behavior that tends to be regarded as natural and easily performed in infancy is in fact achieved by long and patient effort in the coordination of head and shoulder movement, reaching, and kicking.

The Contributions of Nature and Nurture in Motor Development

Motor development provides an excellent illustration of the interaction between the genetically guided plan for growth and the contributions of experience. The development of motor capacities is guided by genetics, beginning as it does with the presence of a wide range of reflexive responses that are "hard wired" into the infant's neurological system (McClearn, 1970; Plomin, 1987). At the same time, within this plan, one can observe both individual differences and group differences. Differences in motor behavior have been assessed along dimensions such as activity level, soothability, reactivity to stimuli, calm and fluid movement or spastic and jerky movement, and cuddliness (Brazelton et al., 1987). Not only are babies different from one another at birth, but they show different rates of motor advancement.

Layered atop these individual differences are cultural differences in child-rearing practices that encourage certain types of motor behavior and restrict others. Two cross-cultural examples illustrate the range in these practices. Among the Zinacantecos of southeastern Mexico, the newborn infant is draped in a long skirt held in place by a belt or wrap. "Then the newborn is wrapped in additional layers of blankets to protect him from 'losing parts of his soul.' This swaddling acts as a constant suppressant to motor activity. . . . Infants' faces are covered except during feedings, especially during the first three months, to ward off illness and the effects of the 'evil eye'" (Brazelton, 1977, 155).

Mothers rarely speak to their babies or try to evoke any type of social response. Babies are rarely on the floor. Rather they are held in the mother's lap, in her arms, or carried on her back. Mothers use breast feeding as a frequent quieting strategy. They respond to any signs of restlessness or crying by offering the breast. In comparison to many U.S. parents, the Zinacanteco mothers rarely urge their babies to perform new motor behaviors and show no special recognition or excitement when a new behavior is accomplished.

The Zinacanteco babies are quieter and less demanding than typical U.S. babies. Most of the babies evaluated in this study lagged behind U.S. babies by one month in motor development. However, despite what might be considered a very restrictive environment for motor development, all the babies showed about the same pattern of motor skill acquisition over the first year.

In contrast, Brazelton, Koslowski, and Tronick (1977) described the reaction of Zambian mothers to their newborns. Zambia is a country of south-central Africa with a population of about 8.5 million. Babies in the study were

by culture Motor dev't influenced

observed at less than 24 hours of age and again at five and ten days. At 24 hours, the babies were limp, unresponsive, and thin. Because of inadequate diets of mothers who had had repeated pregnancies and minimal access to protein, the newborns showed all the signs of intrauterine malnutrition. Nevertheless, after 24 hours, the Zambian mothers tucked their babies on their hips, bound them to their waists, and left the hospital for the village. At five days, the babies had begun nursing. They were alert and responsive. By ten days, the Zambian babies scored above American norms in social interest, alertness, consolability, and cuddliness on the Brazelton Infant Assessment scale. The African mothers expected their babies to respond in a vigorous, energetic way. Through active handling, including holding, rubbing, and caressing their babies, accompanied by frequent nursing and constant physical contact, the mothers evoked the lively responsiveness that they believed their babies ought to demonstrate.

The two examples suggest that motor behavior, like language, is shaped by the socialization context. Nurture plays a role in offering various opportunities for exploration and movement and in modulating the pace and perhaps the style of expressing motor behaviors. The social context can subdue and temper or evoke and encourage the way that babies maneuver through their environment.

Motor behavior shaped by socialization

The achievement of competence in each of the motor skill areas depends on a child's maturational level and environmental conditions and on the strength of the child's desire for mastery. Each advance in motor coordination brings an infant into a new type of contact with the environment. Increases in motor control permit children to experience more varied simulation, explore objects more deliberately, and voluntarily pursue their goals.

Temperament

Temperament is a theoretical construct that refers to relatively stable characteristics of response to the environment that can be observed during the first months of life (Hubert et al., 1982; Lerner & Lerner, 1983; Thomas & Chess, 1980). In early work on this construct, Escalona (1968) focused on individual differences among infants in the permeability of the boundary between the self and the stimulus environment, and the differential sensitivity of the infant to various sense modalities. Thomas, Chess, and Birch (1970) rated newborn infants on nine temperamental qualities, including activity level, rhythmicity, approach/withdrawal, adaptability, intensity of reaction, threshold of responsiveness, quality of mood, distractibility, and attention span and persistence. You can see that these dimensions of temperament are closely linked to the sensory/motor system and to the adaptive mechanisms that infants have for orienting to and withdrawing from stimulation. Based on their research, Thomas, Chess, and Birch were able to classify infants into three temperamental groupings: easy, slow to warm up, and difficult. Table 7.2 summarizes the characteristics of each of these temperamental types and the percent of the sample that could be clearly identified as belonging to one of the three categories. Roughly 35% of the sample could not be classified.

largely influenced by genetics

There is considerable evidence that some aspects of temperament, including activity level, sociability, and emotionality, are largely influenced by a person's genetic makeup (Braungart et al., 1992; Buss & Plomin, 1984, 1986; Goldsmith & Campos, 1986; Goldsmith et al., 1987; Thomas & Chess, 1977, 1986; Wilson & Matheny, 1986). In addition, dimensions of temperament,

TABLE 7.2

Three Types of Infant Temperament

Type	Description	% of Total Sample
Easy	Positive mood, regular body functions, low or moderate intensity of reaction, adaptability, positive approach rather than withdrawal from new situations	40
Slow to warm up	Low activity level, tendency to withdraw on first exposure to new stimuli, slow to adapt, somewhat negative in mood, low intensity of reaction to situations	15
Difficult	Irregular body functions, unusually intense reactions, tendency to withdraw from new situations, slow to adapt to change, generally negative mood, *hypersensitive*	10

especially emotionality and activity level, show modest stability over adjacent periods of infancy and toddlerhood (Bates, 1987; Calkins & Fox, 1992).

One ought not to overestimate the stability of infant temperament, however. Measures of temperament in infancy do not correlate all that highly with measures in the early and middle school years. In all likelihood, temperamental characteristics can be modified as children come into contact with socialization pressures at home and at school as well as with new internal capacities to regulate behavior. Thomas and Chess (1977, 1986) found that when parents were calm and allowed their children to adapt to novelty at a leisurely pace, their difficult children grew more comfortable and had an easier time adapting to new routines. However, if parents were impatient and demanding, their difficult children remained difficult and had a hard time adjusting to new situations as they grew older.

A child's temperament has consequences for the tone of interactions, the frequency with which interactions take place, the way others react to the child, and the way the child reacts to the reactions of others. Highly active, social children are likely to initiate interactions and to respond positively to the attentions of others. More passive, inhibited children will be less likely to initiate interactions and may withdraw when other children or adults direct attention to them. Many studies emphasize the relevance of the fit or match between the parents' temperament and that of the child (Plomin, 1990).

temperament effects interaction

As an example, Aletha is an active, socially outgoing woman who has looked forward eagerly to motherhood. She has prepared her baby's room with brightly colored wallpaper. She likes to sing and listen to music, and she has even bought a cassette player so she and her baby can listen to music together. Her infant, Patrice, is very sensitive to stimulation and does not react well to novelty. Aletha is disappointed and frustrated that Patrice is so irritable. Patrice seems to cry every time Aletha turns on the tape player. The baby does not like to be bounced or jiggled, and she seems to withdraw whenever her mother tries to show her a new toy or tickle her or try to evoke a response. As time goes along, Aletha simply lets Patrice lie in the bassinet for longer periods of the day. Aletha wonders if she does not know how to be a good mother or if maybe Patrice is abnormal.

Research findings are mixed about the extent to which parents actually alter their responses based on a child's temperament. Many studies find that mothers are equally warm and responsive to their babies regardless of infant temperament. Other studies find differences in maternal responsiveness related to how easy or difficult the child is. In some instances, mothers are more responsive to more difficult children; in other studies, mothers are less responsive to difficult children. More research in this area is needed, especially an assessment of parental values and beliefs, socioeconomic conditions, and subcultural context, as these factors may influence a parent's perceptions of his or her child as easy or difficult (Bates, 1987).

Attachment

Have you ever wondered how feelings of love and connectedness form between babies and their caregivers? At birth, an infant would be content to be taken home from the hospital by any adult. The newborn baby has not yet clearly differentiated his or her parents from others. Yet, by the end of the first year of life, babies not only know their caregivers but have very strong, emotional preferences for these adults over all others. _Attachment is the process through which people develop specific, positive emotional bonds with others._ As discussed in Chapter 4, John Bowlby proposed the notion of the attachment behavior system as an organized pattern of infant signals and adult responses leading to a relationship founded on infant trust and adult protection during the very earliest stage of development. The nurturing responses of the caregiver comprise a corresponding behavioral system that we often refer to as _parenting_ or _caregiving_ (Ainsworth, 1985; Bowlby, 1988).

The construct of attachment offers a perspective for understanding infant–caregiver interactions that is quite different from Freud's description of the oral stage. Freud emphasized a view of infants as more dependent, using the image of nursing to highlight the infant's role as a passive recipient of nurturance and care. The oral stage is characterized by an initial fusion between the infant and the caregiver which is gradually differentiated through experiences of delayed gratification. Attachment focuses on the active, social orientation of the infant in a behavioral system that is designed to protect the infant. Many of the sensory and motor competencies that are discussed in subsequent sections of this chapter contribute to an infant's ability to form a vivid mental concept of the caregiver and to evoke caregiving behaviors.

Certain patterns of caregiver–infant interaction in the first months of life contribute to the formation of attachment. One of the most significant of these is _synchrony of interaction_ (Isabella & Belsky, 1991). Parent–infant pairs that show positive attachment relations at one year are characterized in the early months by interactions that are rhythmic, well-timed, and mutually rewarding. When the caregiver is unresponsive to the infant's signals of distress or overly intrusive when the infant is calm, a less positive attachment is formed. Quantity, as well as quality, of interaction plays a key role in establishing the infant's confidence about the caregiver's capacity to protect and comfort (Cox et al., 1992).

Evidence that an attachment has been formed is seen in at least three behaviors. First, infants try to maintain contact with the object of attachment

Positive attachment

① *maintain contact*
② *show distress at absence*
③ *more relaxed w/ object*

(Ainsworth, 1973). Second, infants show distress when the object of attachment is absent (Schaffer & Emerson, 1964). Third, infants are more relaxed and comfortable with the object of attachment and more fretful with other people (Bronson, 1973).

The Development of Attachment

Five Sequential Stages

Ainsworth (1973, 1985) described a series of five stages in the development of attachment (see Table 7.3). In the first stage, during the first three months of life, infants engage in a variety of behaviors, including sucking, rooting, grasping, smiling, gazing, cuddling, and visual tracking, that serve to attract and maintain closeness with a caregiver. However, these behaviors do not appear to be aimed at a specific person. Through these contacts, babies learn about the unique features of their particular caregivers.

In the second stage, from about three months until about six months of age, an infant's attachment is expressed through preferential responsiveness to a few familiar figures. Infants smile more at a familiar caregiver than at a stranger, show more excitement at the caregiver's arrival, and appear to be upset when he or she leaves.

In the third stage, from about six to nine months, babies seek physical proximity with the object(s) of attachment. The ability to crawl and to coordinate reaching and grasping enable greater control over the outcomes of their actions.

In the fourth stage, from about nine to twelve months, babies form the first internal representation of their caregivers, which provides the first robust working model of an attachment relationship. Specific characteristics of a caregiver and patterns of expectations about his or her responses to the infant's actions are organized into a complex attachment scheme comprised of internal, mental representations.

TABLE 7.3 — AINSWORTH

Five Sequential Stages in the Development of Attachment

Stage	Age	Characteristics
1	Birth to 3 months	Infants use sucking, rooting, grasping, smiling, gazing, cuddling, and visual tracking to maintain closeness with caregivers.
2	3 to 6 months	Infant is more responsive to familiar figures than to strangers.
3	6 to 9 months	Infant seeks physical proximity and contact with object(s) of attachment.
4	9 to 12 months	Infant forms internal mental representation of object of attachment, including expectations about the caregiver's typical responses to signals of distress.
5	12 months and older	Child uses a variety of behaviors to influence the behavior of objects of attachment to satisfy needs for safety and closeness.

Not person specific →

preferential →

seek physical proximity →

internal representation of caregiver →

In the fifth stage, in toddlerhood and later, young children use a variety of behaviors to influence the behavior of their parents and other objects of attachment in order to satisfy their own needs for closeness. Children may ask to be read to, cuddled at bedtime, and taken along on errands.

As children mature from toddlerhood to the early and middle school years, they begin to conceptualize new risks and threats to their security. They may initiate new strategies for maintaining closeness to the objects of their attachment. Especially when they are undergoing unusual stress, as in times of illness, rejection, or parents' divorce, children of any age who have a secure attachment may try to activate the attachment system by sending signals that will result in adult responses of comforting and closeness.

Stranger Anxiety

During the second half of the first year, two signs of the child's growing attachment to a specific other person are observed: stranger anxiety and separation anxiety. *Stranger anxiety* refers to a baby's discomfort or tension in the presence of unfamiliar adults. Babies vary in how they express their objection to strangers and in how intensely they react. They may cling to their parents, refuse to be held, stiffen at the stranger's touch, or merely avert their eyes from the stranger's face.

A baby's response to a stranger depends on some very specific factors in the situation, including how close the mother is, how the stranger approaches the baby, and how the mother responds to the stranger (Keltenbach, et al., 1980). For example, if a mother speaks in a positive tone of voice to her baby about a stranger, the baby's response to the stranger is likely to be positive (Feinman & Lewis, 1983). A baby's response is also influenced by the amount of prior experience with unfamiliar adults. Normally, we take wariness of strangers as a positive sign—that is, babies are able to detect the differences between their parents and adults whom they do not know. Of course, wariness of strangers continues to be expressed throughout life; in fact, we often see more distinct expressions of suspiciousness or fear among adults encountering strangers than we do among babies.

Separation Anxiety

At about nine months, infants give another indication of the intensity of their attachment to their parents by expressing rage and despair when parents leave. This reaction is called *separation anxiety*. Separation can evoke two different kinds of behavior. Under some conditions, separation from the caregiver will stimulate attachment behaviors, especially efforts to find the caregiver and regain physical contact (Ainsworth et al., 1971). Separation can also evoke protest, despair, or detachment, depending on the length of the separation (Bowlby, 1960; Robertson & Robertson, 1989).

Separation from the mother for periods of 30 minutes has been identified as a distinct source of stress for babies nine months of age and older. Neurological and biochemical evidence of stress, including increases in adrenocortical activity and concentrations of cortisol in the saliva, have been associated with 30 minutes of separation from the mother in a laboratory situation (Gunnar et al., 1992; Larson et al., 1991). The impact of stressful separations can be seen in the disruption of basic physical patterns, especially sleep disturbances. The effects of prolonged periods of maternal separation, as when a mother goes away to attend a conference or for a brief vacation, can also be

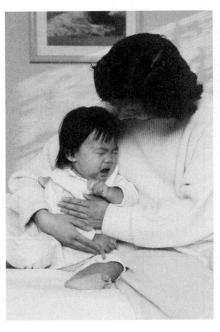

Protest against separation is a clear sign that an attachment has been formed.

observed in the child-care setting by regression to more immature forms of play behavior, aimless wandering, and altered interactions with peers and teachers (Field, 1991).

A baby's response to separation depends on the conditions of separation. Infants are less distressed when mothers leave them alone in a room at home than when they leave them in a laboratory (Ross et al., 1975). They are less likely to protest if the mother leaves the door to the room open than if she closes the door as she leaves. The protest response to separation seems to be tied to the baby's strong desire to maintain contact with the object of attachment. The importance of contact may be to (1) meet physical needs, (2) help the child overcome physical barriers, (3) provide protection or comfort, or (4) offer novel and stimulating interactions (Hay, 1980). When there are high levels of responsiveness and warmth in the parent–infant relationship, the infant has many reasons to want to maintain access to the caregiver.

Babies' responses to separation may also be related to their temperament (Gunnar et al., 1989; Gunnar et al., 1992; Izard et al., 1991). Babies who have a strong negative reaction to uncertainty, those who are especially distressed when they are confined or prevented from attaining a goal, and those who tend to withdraw from or become upset by novelty may find the experience of separation more stressful than others. Unique strategies of caregiving may help buffer these babies from the stressful impact of separation.

We expect babies to become more flexible over time about a parent's temporary departures. Young children learn to tolerate brief separations. At two years of age, children are able to use a photograph of their mothers to help sustain their adaptation to a new setting in the mother's absence (Passman & Longeway, 1982). By the age of three, children may even look forward to a night with a baby-sitter or an afternoon at their grandfather's house. Once the attachment is fully established, children can comfort themselves by creating mental images of their parents and by remembering their parents' love for them. During infancy, however, the parents' physical presence remains a focal point of attention and concern. Parents who, for one reason or another, are forced to leave their infants for a prolonged period may return to discover that their children are temporarily withdrawn and cold to them. They may find that previously loving and affectionate infants express sudden outbursts of rage. Since infants' language skills are inadequate for expressing complex inner thoughts and feelings, these behaviors are a means of communicating anger and frustration at their experiences of abandonment. In Notebook Page 7.2, we ask you to think about your current strategies for coping with separation and how they may be linked to childhood experiences.

Formation of Attachments with Mother, Father, and Others

An infant may establish an attachment with any person who performs a large portion of his or her care. Most commonly, the first object of attachment is the mother, but fathers, grandmothers, and child-care professionals can also become objects of attachment. Infants' attachments with their fathers and their mothers are established independently and depend on the amount and quality of time spent together (Fox et al., 1991). Early studies of infants' attachment to their mothers and fathers found that the babies tended to have playful interactions with their fathers—smiling, laughing, and looking—and comforting, stress-reducing interactions with their mothers. When only one parent was present, the babies showed evidence of attachment to that parent. When both parents were present, the babies demonstrated a different pattern of interaction with each (Lamb, 1976).

In Israel, kibbutz-reared infants showed great similarity between their attachment to their fathers and to their specially trained caregivers (called metapelets). However, there was no consistent pattern of similarity in the quality of their attachments to mother and father and to mother and metapelet (Sagi et al., 1985). In subsequent research, when these kibbutz children had reached the age of five, the quality of their infant attachment to the metapelet was a significant predictor of their socioemotional development as observed in school and at free play in their communal children's house (Oppenheim et al., 1988). This research suggests that infants are able to have a variety of attachment relationships. Exactly how the infant synthesizes the internal representations of various attachments is not well understood. Distinct relationships may have relevance for different interpersonal domains or become central as individuals assume a variety of social roles (Bretherton, 1985; Bridges et al., 1988).

Patterns of Attachment

The quality of attachment varies from family to family and from one parent–child dyad to another. The adults' acceptance of the infant and their ability to respond to the infants' varying communications are critical to a secure attachment. The parents' patterns of expressing affection and rejection influence how well babies' needs for reassurance and comfort are fulfilled (Tracy & Ainsworth, 1981).

The Strange Situation

Differences in the quality of attachment have been highlighted by observations of babies and their caregivers in a standard laboratory procedure called the *strange situation* (Ainsworth et al., 1978; Bretherton, 1990), in which, during a 20-minute period, the child is exposed to a sequence of events that are likely to stimulate the attachment system (see Table 7.4). The infant and caregiver enter an unfamiliar laboratory environment, a stranger enters, the

Coping with Separation

Although you might not describe your reactions to separation as "separation anxiety," most people continue to have emotional reactions to separation throughout life. You might not consider a brief separation very distressing the way an infant does when his or her mother walks into another room and closes the door behind her. Yet long separations, such as when you say good-bye to good friends for the summer or when you leave your family and friends to go off to college, may be a source of some distress.

1. Describe your typical reaction to meaningful separations, that is separations in which you and someone you care about are going to be apart for a while. What are your typical emotional reactions? What is your strategy for coping with separation?

2. Think back to your memories of separation in early childhood. What is your earliest memory of being separated from a loved one? What can you recall of this event—your emotions, how you expressed those emotions, how you behaved? Who helped you to handle those reactions?

3. What are the links between your memories of childhood separation and the way that you handle separations now?

TABLE 7.4

The Strange Situation Laboratory Procedure

Episode	Duration	Participants*	Events
1	30 sec	M, B, O	O shows M and B into the room, instructs M on where to put B down and where to sit; O leaves
2	3 min	M, B	M puts B down close to her chair, at a distance from the toys. She responds to B's social bids but does not initiate interaction. B is free to explore. If B does not move after 2 minutes, M may take B to the toy area.
3	3 min	M, B, S	This episode has three parts. S enters, greets M and B, and sits down opposite M without talking for 1 minute. During the second minute, S engages M in conversation. S then joins B on the floor, attempting to engage B in play for 1 minute. At the end of this episode, M leaves "unobtrusively" (B usually notices).
4	3 min	B, S	S sits on her chair. She responds to B's social bid but does not initiate social interaction. If B becomes distressed, S attempts to comfort B. If this is not effective, M returns before 3 minutes are up.
5	3 min	M, B	M calls B's name outside the door and enters (S leaves unobtrusively). If B is distressed, M comforts B and tries to reengage B in play. If B is not distressed, M goes to sit on her chair, taking a responsive, noninitiating role. At the end of the episode, M leaves, saying, "Bye-bye; I'll be back."
6	3 min	B	B remains alone. If B becomes distressed, the episode is curtailed and S enters.
7	3 min	B, S	S enters, comforting B if required. If she cannot comfort B, the episode is curtailed. If B calms down or is not distressed, S sits on her chair, taking a responsive role as before.
8	3 min	M, B	M returns (S leaves unobtrusively). M behaves as in episode 5.

*O = observer, M = mother, B = baby, S = stranger.
Source: Bretherton, I. (1990). Open communication and internal working models: Their roles in the development of attachment relationships. In R. Dienstbier & R. A. Thompson (Eds.), *Nebraska Symposium on Motivation, 1988: Socioemotional Development, 36*, 60–61. Copyright © 1990 by University of Nebraska Press. Reprinted by permission of University of Nebraska Press.

caregiver leaves briefly, and the caregiver and infant experience opportunities for reunion. During this situation, researchers make systematic observations of the child's behaviors, the caregiver's behaviors, and characteristics of their interactions to compare these behaviors across segments of the situation.

Four Patterns of Quality of Attachment

Four patterns of attachment behavior have been distinguished using the strange situation methodology: (1) secure attachment, (2) anxious-avoidant, (3) anxious-resistant, and (4) disorganized attachment. In American samples, about two-thirds of the children tested have been characterized as securely attached. Of the remainder, more children fall into the anxious-avoidant category than into the anxious-resistant category (Ainsworth et al., 1978). Only a small percentage of infants from functioning families show the disorganized pattern (Carlson et al., 1989; Radke-Yarrow et al., 1985; van Ijzendoorn et al., 1992). More research is needed in order to identify subsequent developmental outcomes linked to this attachment pattern, but it is likely that this highly disorganized attachment is associated with very serious mental health problems in later childhood and beyond.

Infants who have a *secure attachment* actively explore their environment and interact with strangers while their mothers are present. After a brief separation, the mothers' return reduces infants' distress and permits them to return to exploration of the environment. Infants who show an *anxious-avoidant attachment* avoid contact with their mothers after separation or ignore their efforts to interact. They show less distress at being alone than do other babies. Infants who show an *anxious-resistant attachment* are very cautious in the presence of a stranger. Their exploratory behavior is noticeably disrupted by the caregiver's departure. When the caregiver returns, the infants appear to want to be close to the caregiver, but they are also very hard to soothe or comfort. In the *disorganized attachment*, babies' responses are particularly notable in the reunion sequence. In the other three attachment patterns, infants appear to use a coherent strategy for managing the stress of the situation. The disorganized babies have no consistent strategy. They behave in contradictory, unpredictable ways that seem to convey feelings of extreme fear or utter confusion.

Within the home environment, babies who have a secure attachment are observed to cry less than other babies (Ainsworth, 1985; Tracy & Ainsworth, 1981). They greet their mothers more positively upon reunion after everyday separations and appear to respond more cooperatively to their mothers' requests. One senses that securely attached babies have a working model of attachment in which they expect their caregivers to be accessible and responsive. This confidence permits the securely attached infant to explore the environment and to accept brief separations with little protest.

Mothers of babies who were characterized as anxious-avoidant seem to reject their babies, almost as if they were angry at them. They spend less time holding and cuddling their babies than do other mothers, and more of their interactions appear to be unpleasant or even hurtful. At home, these babies cry a lot but are not readily soothed by contact with the caregiver, and yet they appear to be quite distressed by separations. These babies have strong needs for security, but it appears that their appeals for comfort will be rejected. Thus, they do not seek to make contact with the caregiver in the laboratory situation, defending themselves against rejection.

The third group, infants who are characterized as anxious-resistant, have mothers who are inconsistent in their responsiveness. Sometimes, these mothers ignore clear signals of distress. At other times, they interfere with their infants in order to make contact. Although these mothers appear to be able to enjoy close physical contact with their babies, they do not necessarily do so in ways that are appropriate to the babies' needs. The result is the formation of an internal representation of attachment that is highly unpredictable. These babies try to maintain proximity to their caregivers and to avoid any unfamiliar situation that will heighten the uncertainty of accessibility to them. Their responses reflect frustration at their inability to predict or control the responsiveness of their caregivers.

More research is needed to characterize the home-environment behaviors of children who have been identified as having a disorganized-insecure attachment. This categorization is overrepresented among mothers who appear to have serious deficits in maternal behaviors that may be linked to various psychological problems including being abusive, depressed, or suffering from other mental illnesses. These mothers are likely to be psychologically unavailable and unpredictable (van Ijzendoorn et al., 1992).

Is the Strange Situation Procedure Valid in Different Cultures?

Questions have been raised about whether the strange situation is a valid method for assessing attachment across cultures. The strange situation was designed to be novel enough to stimulate exploratory behavior but not so novel that babies would be terrified from the moment they entered the situation. Cross-cultural research suggests that this premise holds true. Children from different cultures behave very similarly as they attempt to cope with the stressors that are evoked by this situation.

Is it reasonable to expect that patterns of child-rearing in different societies will produce the same patterns of attachment that are found in the United States? In an analysis of 32 studies of attachment in eight countries—the United States, Germany, Great Britain, the Netherlands, Sweden, Israel, Japan, and China—secure attachment was found to be the modal pattern (van Ijzendoorn & Kroonenberg, 1988). What is more, the proportions of children categorized as anxious-resistant and anxious-avoidant varied more in studies carried out using different populations within countries than in those that compared children of different countries. One of two studies conducted in Japan, for example, found that 32% of the children were anxious-resistant; the other study found only 19% in this category. Similarly, studies carried out with different populations of children in the United States found very different patterns of attachment. Differences that are linked to subcultural or socioeconomic status within a country appear to be greater than differences among countries, especially when one compares the United States and the Western European countries.

Parental Sensitivity and the Quality of Attachment

How can we account for differences in the quality of the attachment? Early work on the formation of a secure attachment proposed that a cornerstone in this process was maternal sensitivity (Ainsworth et al., 1978). *Sensitivity* is generally defined as attentiveness to the infant's state, accurate interpretation of the infant's signals, and well-timed responses that promote mutually rewarding interactions (Isabella et al., 1989). Mothers who are psychologically available, responsive, consistent, and warm in their interactions with their babies, especially during the first six months of the baby's life, are found to be most successful in establishing a secure attachment relationship by the time the baby is 12 months old.

Three very general factors appear to produce the kind of sensitivity that underlies secure attachments (Figure 7.2). First, certain aspects of a caregiver's own personal experience contribute to his or her ability to serve as a secure base for a child. What does the caregiver bring to the relationship that supports sensitivity and responsiveness? What mental representations of a caring, parental role does the caregiver have? Adults who recall their own parents as accepting, responsive, and available are more likely to be able to transmit those qualities in the caregiver role. Adults who have experienced early loss or disruption of an attachment relationship themselves have more difficulty providing a secure base for their offspring (Ainsworth, 1989; Fonagy et al., 1991; Ricks, 1985).

Second, contemporary factors can influence an adult's ability to provide a secure base for attachment. Among them are the caregiver's self-esteem, the degree of control the caregiver believes that he or she should have over the infant's behavior, the quality of the relationship between the intimate partner

[Handwritten margin notes:]
FACTORS THAT PROMOTE SENSITIVITY
1. caregivers personal experience
2. self esteem, control, relationship, social network, etc...
3. infants characteristics

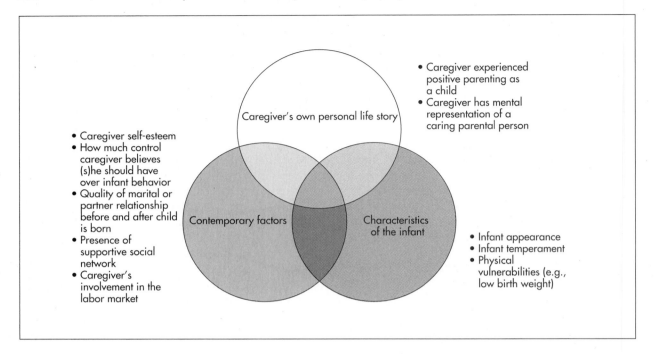

- Caregiver self-esteem
- How much control caregiver believes (s)he should have over infant behavior
- Quality of marital or partner relationship before and after child is born
- Presence of supportive social network
- Caregiver's involvement in the labor market

Caregiver's own personal life story

- Caregiver experienced positive parenting as a child
- Caregiver has mental representation of a caring parental person

Contemporary factors

Characteristics of the infant

- Infant appearance
- Infant temperament
- Physical vulnerabilities (e.g., low birth weight)

FIGURE 7.2

Factors affecting a caregiver's sensitivity to an infant's needs

or spouse both before and after the child is born, the presence of a supportive social network that validates the person's caregiving efforts, and the caregiver's involvement in the labor market (Chase-Lansdale & Owen, 1987; Donovan & Leavitt, 1989; Howes & Markman, 1989; Jacobson & Frye, 1991).

Third, the quality of the attachment can be influenced by the infant's characteristics. Certain aspects of the infant's temperament, especially fearfulness, sociability, and the intensity of negative emotions, may influence the way that the attachment relationship is established (Izard et al., 1991). Most studies have shown, however, that temperament per se does not determine whether or not a secure attachment can be established. Rather, it influences the kinds of caregiver responses that are most likely to create an internal sense of security for the infant (Thompson et al., 1988; Vaughn et al., 1989). In Notebook Page 7.3, we ask you to try to imagine specific parenting behaviors that would be most effective for establishing a secure attachment with babies of different temperament.

A sensitive caregiver adapts to the individual needs and demands of each infant, providing a sense of security despite marked differences in infant temperament, intelligence, and sensory/motor capacities (Sroufe, 1985). Individual differences among infants may elicit unique and creative approaches to parenting, but they do not prevent the establishment of a predictable, comforting attachment. Social support and family and community resources give caregivers the necessary skills and confidence to form relationships with challenging infants.

In usual circumstances if a caregiver has an infant that is easily overaroused, the caregiver will be prompted to provide modulated stimulation, smooth transitions, and so forth. In time the infant develops sufficient arousal tolerance and self-modulating capacity. A placid, hard to arouse infant elicits more vigorous

Temperament and Attachment

According to Sroufe, a sensitive parent modifies her or his caregiving strategies depending upon the temperament of the child so that a secure attachment can be formed, regardless of the child's initial physiological tendencies toward irritability, activity level, etc. Return to the discussion of temperament in the earlier section of this chapter and review the characteristics of the easy, difficult, and slow-to-warm-up babies. Imagine that you were the parent of each of these types of babies. What specific strategies might you use to establish a secure attachment with each type of child? Try to think of details of parenting behavior in areas such as soothing, playing, protecting, and stimulating the baby.

1. Parenting an easy baby:

2. Parenting a difficult baby:

3. Parenting a baby who is slow to warm up:

stimulation and articulated expressiveness. In time the infant becomes more actively engaged. Within this perspective, which truly respects infant plasticity, such change is viewed in terms of real transformation. . . . The "child effects" idea is turned around to imply prompting of required parental care, rather than as causing poor parenting. (Sroufe, 1985, 11)

Sensorimotor Intelligence and Early Causal Schemes

How Do Infants Organize Their Experiences?

According to Piaget's theory of cognitive development (1970), the chief mechanism governing the growth of intelligence during infancy is *sensorimotor adaptation*. From the very earliest days of life, infants use their reflexes to explore their world. At the same time, they gradually alter their reflexive responses to take into account the unique properties of objects around them. Infants do not make use of the conventional symbolic system of language to organize experience. Rather, they form concepts through perception and direct investigation of the environment. The notion of sensorimotor intelligence, then, encompasses the elaboration of patterns of movement and sensory experiences that the child comes to recognize in association with specific environmental events.

Think for a moment of a familiar experience such as tying a shoelace. The process of tying the shoelace requires little, if any, language. In fact, explaining how to tie a shoelace to a young child is particularly difficult because very few words or concepts are involved. This kind of motor routine is an instance of sensorimotor intelligence. When infants begin to adapt their sucking reflex to make it more effective, or when they use different techniques of sucking for the breast and the bottle, they are demonstrating sensorimotor intelligence. The familiar scheme for sucking is modified so that it takes into account the specific properties of the breast and the bottle.

One of the most important components of sensorimotor intelligence is the capacity to anticipate that certain actions will have specific effects on objects in the environment. In other words, infants develop an understanding of *causality* based solely on sensory and motor experience. Babies discover that if they cry, Mama will come to them; if they push a ball, it will move, and if they let go of a spoon, it will fall to the floor. These predictable sequences are learned through repetition and experimentation. The predictability of the events depends on the consistency with which objects in the world respond, as well as on the child's initiation of the action. Babies learn to associate specific actions with regularly occurring outcomes. They also experiment with their own actions to determine the variety of events that a single behavior may cause (Keil, 1975; Rovee & Rovee, 1969). Eventually, they are able to work backward: They can select a desirable outcome and then perform the behavior that will produce it.

In an intriguing analysis, researchers made videotapes to document the emergence of the use of a spoon as a tool for eating (Connolly & Dalgleish, 1989). The infants were observed once a month for six months in their home during a mealtime. At first, actions involving the spoon appeared to focus on exploration of the spoon itself. The infants banged the spoon, sucked it, or rubbed it in their hair. Then the babies showed an understanding of the purpose of the spoon as a tool by repeating the action sequence of dipping the

[handwritten margin notes:]
SENSORIMOTOR ADAPTATION

formation of concepts through perception and direct investigation.

causality based on sensory and motor experience.

Learning to manage a spoon is a good example of sensorimotor problem solving.

spoon in the dish and bringing it to the mouth. However, no food was on the spoon. In the third phase, babies began to integrate the function and the action by loading the spoon with food and then bringing it to the mouth. During this phase, they made so many errors that very little food actually got to the mouth via the spoon. Finally, babies were able to coordinate the action and the function by using the other hand to steady the bowl, altering the angle of the spoon, picking up food they had dropped, and devising other strategies to enhance the function, depending on the type of food involved. Here we see a demonstration of how one rather complex motor behavior becomes part of a problem-solving action sequence during the sensorimotor period of development.

The Development of Causal Schemes

The achievement of complex, purposeful causal behaviors develops gradually during the first two years of life. This achievement requires that infants have an understanding of the properties of objects in their environment and a variety of strategies for manipulating those objects. Finally, they must be able to select the most effective strategies for coordinating actions to achieve specific goals: One uses different behaviors to reach a ball that has rolled under the couch or to tape a new drawing on the wall.

Piaget and Inhelder (1966/1969) described six phases in the development of causal schemes (see Table 7.5). Subsequent research and related theoretical revisions confirm these levels of cognitive development (Fischer & Silvern, 1985). In phase 1, *reflexes,* cause and effect are linked through involuntary reflexive responses. The built-in stimulus–response systems of key reflexes are viewed as the genetic origin of intelligence. Babies suck, grasp, and root in response to specific types of stimulation. Piaget viewed the reflexes as adaptive learning systems. In detailed observations of his youngest child, Laurent,

TABLE 7.5 PIAGET

Six Phases in the Development of Sensorimotor Causality

Period	Approximate Age	Characteristic
1. Reflexes	From birth	Reflexive responses to specific stimuli
2. First habits	From 2nd week	Use of reflexive responses to explore new stimuli
3. Circular reactions	From 4th month	Use of familiar actions to achieve new goals
4. Coordination of means and ends	From 8th month	Deliberate use of actions to achieve new goals
5. Experimentation with new means	From 11th month	Modification of actions to reach goals
6. Insight	From 18 months	Mental recombination of means and ends

[handwritten: action connected w/outcome → (points to row 3)]
[handwritten: action to achieve outcome → (points to row 4)]

Source: Adapted from Piaget, J. & Inhelder, B. *The psychology of the child.* (1969). New York: Basic Books.

he noted daily changes in sucking behavior during the first month of life. Laurent became increasingly directed in groping for the breast and also appeared to form very early associations between those situations in which he was fed and those where he was not fed (Gratch & Schatz, 1987; Piaget, 1936/1952).

In the second phase, *first habits,* the reflexive responses are used to explore a wider range of stimuli. Babies explore toys, their fingers, parents' noses, and blankets by sucking on them. Gradually, they modify their responses according to their discoveries of the unique properties of those objects. The fact that a baby can satisfy his or her need to suck by bringing an object to the mouth is a very early form of purposive causal behavior.

The third and fourth phases involve coordination of means and ends, at first with familiar situations and then with new ones. In the third phase, *circular reactions,* babies connect an action with an expected outcome (Wentworth & Haith, 1992). They shake a rattle and expect to hear a noise; they drop a spoon and expect to hear a crash; they pull Daddy's beard and expect to hear an exclamation of "ouch." They do not yet understand why their specific action leads to the expected outcome, but they will signal surprise when it does not occur.

In the fourth phase, *coordination of means and ends,* infants use familiar actions or means to achieve new outcomes. They may shake a rattle to startle Mommy or pull Daddy's beard to force him to look away from the television set. The means and the outcomes have become quite distinct. There can be no question about the purposiveness of behavior at this point.

Coordination of means and ends are likely to be very closely tied to a specific context at this stage. For example, a baby may know how to make certain kicking motions to move a mobile in the crib. But in another room with the same mobile, the baby may not make the same connection. This may explain why babies sometimes perform less competently in the laboratory environment than they do at home. Many of the causal strategies that become part of a baby's daily repertoire are supported by a familiar context; these same connections are not necessarily evoked in a new environment (Rovee-Collier et al., 1992).

The fifth phase, *experimentation with new means*, begins with experimentation with familiar means to achieve new goals. When familiar strategies do not work, children modify them in light of the situation. One can think of this stage as sensorimotor problem solving. Children may try to reach a drawer by standing on a chair, to fix a broken toy with a string, or to make a gift by wrapping a toy in a piece of tissue. In Notebook Page 7.4, take some time to consider how toys promote means–end reasoning in infancy.

The last phase in the development of sensorimotor causality, *insight*, involves mental manipulation of means–end relationships. Children carry out trial-and-error problem-solving activities and planning in their minds. Instead of actually going through a variety of physical manipulations, they anticipate the outcomes of some actions in their minds. They can sort out possible solutions and reject some without having to try them out. The result is insight. Mental experimentation brings the child to the best solution, which is the only one necessary to enact.

The capacity to perceive oneself as a causal agent and to predict the outcome of one's actions is essential to all subsequent experiences of mastery. This capacity is the cornerstone of developing a sense of competence. It involves investigation of the environment, directed problem solving, and persistent efforts toward a goal (MacTurk et al., 1987; Yarrow et al., 1983). Adults' abilities to formulate a plan, execute it, and evaluate its outcome depend on this skill.

[handwritten margin note: capacity to see self as causal agent & to predict outcomes essential to all other experiences of mastery. => competence]

Understanding the Nature of Objects and Creating Categories

Rather than being passive spectators, babies are active explorers of their environment (Rochat, 1989). From birth, they try to make direct, sensory contact with objects. They reach for, grasp, and mouth objects. They track objects visually and alter their gaze to maintain visual contact with them. Not all manipulative behavior is exploratory, but certain combinations of mouthing, looking, and manipulating objects have been categorized as a type of examining behavior that provides infants as young as five months with a scheme for gathering information about novel objects (Ruff et al., 1992). From this active engagement with the object world, two related but independent aspects of infant intelligence develop: an understanding of the nature of objects and the ability to categorize similar objects.

[handwritten margin note: Babies actively explore their environments => understanding & categorization of objects]

The Nature of Objects

Through looking, manipulating, and examining, infants establish that objects have basic properties. In the discussion of vision (pp. 241–42), we reported that very young babies recognize the contours of objects and that by four months they seem to perceive objects just as adults would. That is, babies see objects as separate from each other, defined by boundaries, taking up space, having depth, and having certain attributes of weight, color, malleability, texture, and the capacity to contain something else or not. All of these

Toys and the Coordination of Means—End Relationships

Beginning at about 8 months of age, infants show the capacity to use familiar actions to achieve new outcomes. This phase of sensorimotor causality, phase 4, soon leads to phase 5, experimentation with new means, and then to phase 6, insight. Spend some time in a toy store looking at toys that have been designed for infants in the age range 8 to 18 months. Select two toys for your analysis. Explain how these toys might stimulate means—end coordination and promote new levels of experimentation in the use of familiar means to achieve novel goals.

1. Describe the toy. What age child is this toy designed for? What features of the toy might promote causal reasoning? What aspects of means—end coordination are most likely to be enhanced through the use of this toy?

2. Describe the toy. What age child is this toy designed for? What features of the toy might promote causal reasoning? What aspects of means—end coordination are most likely to be enhanced through the use of this toy?

properties influence the types of actions that infants use to explore the object and the ways that objects are eventually combined with other actions or causal schemes (MacLean & Schuler, 1989; Sera et al., 1988; Spelke et al., 1989; Palmer, 1989).

Object Permanence

One of the most carefully documented of these properties is *object permanence* (Wellman et al., 1986). Piaget (1954) argued that understanding the properties of objects was one of the foundations of logical thought. He discussed object permanence as a gradual process through which infants develop the concept that objects in the environment continue to exist even when they are out of reach or out of view. A permanent object retains its physical properties even when it cannot be seen.

Piaget suggested that initially the infant is aware only of those objects that are in the immediate perceptual field. If a six-month-old-girl is playing with a rattle, it exists for her. If the rattle drops out of her hand or is taken away, she may show some immediate distress, but she will not pursue the object. In a very real sense for a six-month-old, out of sight is out of mind. Attaining object permanence frees children from total reliance on what they can see. The ability to retain a mental image of an object is the first step toward complex representational thinking (Ramsay & Campos, 1978).

To understand object permanence, we might remove a rattle from a baby's grasp and hide it under a cushion. If the baby makes no effort to pursue the rattle, we can assume that he or she has no sense of its continued existence. If the baby pursues the rattle and looks for it under the cushion, we take our experiment one step farther. Again we take the rattle from the baby and place it under the cushion. Then we remove it from beneath that cushion and place it under a second one. This transition from cushion 1 to cushion 2 takes place in the child's full view. Adults would go directly to the second cushion to retrieve the rattle, as will a child who has developed a sense of object permanence. Some children, however, will look for the rattle beneath the first cushion and, not finding it, cease their search. Slightly older children will trace each location of the rattle by looking first under cushion 1 and then under cushion 2. The last two groups of children have learned some of the steps in pursuing an object but have not yet attained the concept of object permanence.

As a final test of a child's certainty about object permanence, we can once again transfer the rattle from cushion 1 to cushion 2 in the child's view and then stealthily hide it in a third place. The child who has attained the concept of object permanence will look beneath cushion 2 and, failing to find the beloved rattle, continue to search, fully convinced that it is somewhere. The child who earlier followed the path of the rattle from cushion 1 to cushion 2 will do the same thing this time. Not finding the rattle beneath cushion 2, this child will cease searching.

Progress in developing the concept of object permanence can be traced through the child's reactions when objects are removed from the perceptual field or displaced from one location to another (Bertenthal & Fischer, 1983; Harris, 1975; Sophian & Yengo, 1985). Babies as young as 9 months can understand that an object has been moved from one location to another. If babies of 8 or 9 months are permitted to search for an object immediately after it is hidden, they are very effective in finding it. However, if they have to wait for

Object permanence- ability to maintain mental image of object

5 or 10 seconds before they can search, or if the object has been moved from one container to a very similar container, they may become confused. By the age of about 17 months, infants can solve complex object permanence tasks in which objects are moved from one hiding place to the next in such a way that the infant cannot follow the path of the object (Gopnik & Meltzoff, 1987; Uzgiris & Hunt, 1975). However, even 2-year-olds can get confused if the object is displaced more than two or three times.

Certain experiences appear to help build the scheme for object permanence. Babies who are adept at crawling or who have mobility through the use of an infant walker seem to be more effective in their search strategies for objects that are hidden from view (Benson & Uzgiris, 1985; Kermoian & Campos, 1988). As babies gain greater control over their movement through the environment, they are better able to use landmarks other than their own body to locate objects. They can also experiment with the notion of leaving and retrieving objects, and discovering familiar objects in novel locations.

Precursors of Object Permanence

There is some controversy among scholars about the accuracy of Piaget's interpretation that infants do not understand that objects continue to exist when they are hidden from view. Piaget suggested that the capacity to understand that objects continue to exist requires a level of representational or symbolic thinking that would permit an infant to hold the idea of the object in mind while it was hidden. It also requires a combination of sensory motor capacities that permit the infant to become actively engaged in reaching, tracking, and uncovering hidden objects and learning about the spatial properties of objects in the environment. Thus, the first real evidence that infants have the ability to pursue a hidden object could not really be observed much before 8 or 9 months when babies begin to crawl. And full object permanence could probably not emerge much before 16 to 18 months, when babies have access to representational thinking. By this age, babies can imagine various movements and displacements of objects without actually viewing them.

In a series of experiments, Renee Baillargeon has tried to determine how infants evaluate objects that are hidden from view. One feature of her experiments is that she has deleted the motor search component. Most of her experiments use infant looking time as evidence of habituation in pretest conditions and reaction in test conditions. Even at very early ages, before infants can search for and retrieve objects, they appear to have a memory of the locations of objects and can anticipate that objects take up space (Baillargeon, 1987; Baillargeon & Graber, 1988). In the most recent experiments, infants as young as four months appeared to be able to retain the image of an object as it disappeared behind a screen and to emit surprise when the object emerged from the screen when it ought to have been blocked (Baillargeon & DeVos, 1992). In one of these experiments, the female infants were significantly more sensitive to the condition in which expectations were violated than were the male infants (see Figure 7.3 for a description of the experiment).

The question remains whether an infant's visual response to hidden objects is evidence that object permanence exists long before Piaget expected. Baillargeon argues that her evidence supports the view that infants as young as 3.5 to 4 months can represent the continued existence of objects when they are out of view. Others suggest that Baillargeon's visual task highlights an important perceptual precursor of the more complex scheme of object per-

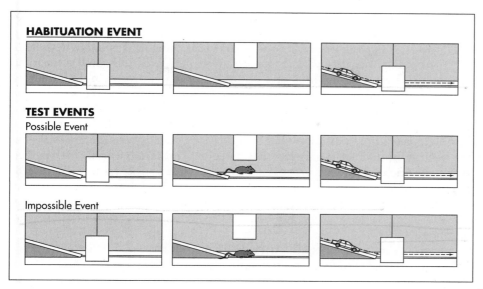

FIGURE 7.3
Habituation and test events in a study of object permanence. Prior to the experiment, the infant explores the toy car and the mouse. The infant sits on a parent's lap facing the apparatus. In the *familiarization* phase, the infant sees the mouse sitting on the track or behind the track with the screen raised. In the *habituation* phase, the screen is lifted and then lowered, then the car is pushed down the ramp at the left, rolling across the apparatus behind the screen, and continuing out the right side. These trials continued until habituation was achieved. In the *impossible* test, the mouse was placed on top of the track, the screen was raised so the baby could see the mouse, then the screen was lowered and the car was propelled down the track, emerging at the other side of the screen and rolling off to the right. The *possible* test was the same as the impossible test except that the mouse was placed about 10 cm behind the track so that it would not impede the rolling car.
Source: Baillargeon, R. & DeVos, J. (1992). Object permanence in young infants: Further evidence. *Child Development, 62,* 1237. Copyright © 1991 The Society for Research in Child Development, Inc. Reprinted with permission.

manence that is observed more fully developed toward the end of the first year. The infant's ability to anticipate an object's trajectory behind a screen is considered to be an early step in a sequence of abilities that eventually produce the complex search process that Piaget described (Fischer & Bidell, 1992).

Object Permanence and Attachment

The process through which infants establish a scheme for objects as permanent and subject to all the laws of nature is closely linked to their understanding of themselves and their relationships with others. Each step taken to analyze and organize the object world provides insight about self as well as about others.

The scheme for the permanent object applies to both humans and inanimate objects. One reason that babies experience separation anxiety is that they do not have the certainty that a person to whom they are attached will continue to exist when that person is out of sight or inaccessible. Once the infant has a clear understanding of object permanence, the fear that a loved caregiver has vanished forever when he or she leaves the house is reduced. Interestingly, some qualities of maternal care are associated with the emergence of object permanence during the first seven months of life. The babies of mothers who communicate with them frequently, who express positive feelings toward them, and who actively stimulate their achievements are more likely to apply the scheme of permanence to people as well as things (Chazen, 1981). The growth of attachment and the achievement of object permanence may thus be mutually enhancing.

The Categorization of Objects

Objects have properties and functions. As infants explore and experiment with objects, they begin to devise schemes for grouping objects together. They modify these schemes to add new items to the category and to differentiate one category from another. Categories can consist of the physical properties of

[margin note: physical properties and functions of objects]

objects, such as "smooth" and "rough," or they can consist of the functions of objects, as in "something to sit on" and "something to dig with."

The classification of objects and events into categories is one way infants have of coping with the vast array of new experiences that they encounter. *Categorization* is a fundamental element of information processing. By treating certain individual objects as similar because they belong to the same basic grouping, like two individual red blocks or two wiggly goldfish, the potential amount of information to process is reduced (Rosch, 1978; Younger, 1992). If an item is classified as a member of a category, then all the information that has been accumulated regarding that category can automatically be applied to the specific object. This process aids in the storage and recall processes of memory, in reasoning and problem solving, and in the acquisition of new information. Classification of objects, both animate and inanimate, into categories is a cognitive capacity that becomes increasingly sophisticated over the childhood years.

[margin note: Foundational category—distinction between social and nonsocial realms]

One of the most robust categories that appears early in infancy is the distinction between persons and inanimate objects (Ellsworth et al., 1993). Infants have been observed to smile, vocalize, and become more active in interaction with people as compared with things. By three months of age, infants already show their ability to categorize stimuli as people or things by smiling almost exclusively at people. Infants may look with equal interest at inanimate objects, especially novel objects, but their smiles are reserved for people. This distinction between the social and the nonsocial realm can be considered a *foundational category*. It provides a basis for our emphasis on the unique role of social relationships in the process of adaptation and growth. From this basic distinction between a person and a thing, many further subdivisions of categories emerge that begin to differentiate the infant's social world.

[margin note: Categorizing and naming are closely linked]

Research on infant categorization skills typically involves sorting objects into categories. By 15 months, babies touch all the objects that belong to one category and then touch all the objects in another category. By 18 months of age, children can perform multidimensional categorization tasks, for example, sorting eight objects, such as four brightly colored yellow rectangles and four human-shaped plastic figures, into two distinct groups (Gopnik & Meltzoff, 1987, 1992). This kind of sorting does not require the ability to give names to objects. However, shortly after children demonstrate the capacity to manage two-group sorting, they often show a rapid acceleration in the acquisition of names for objects (Gopnick & Meltzoff, 1992). Thus, categorizing and naming appear to be closely linked. By the close of the second year of life, babies know that objects have certain stable properties, that some objects "belong" with others, and that objects have names. With these achievements, infants impose a new degree of order and predictability on their daily experiences.

Emotional Development

Emotional development during infancy can be understood along three dimensions. First, new emotions emerge and are differentiated along dimensions of intensity. Second, with cognitive maturation, a child interprets events differently. New emotions may become attached to familiar situations. An experience that once caused wariness, such as a new toy or a loud noise, may become a source of excitement as the child gains mastery over exploring the situation. Third, children develop strategies for regulating their emotions so that they are not overwhelmed by their intensity.

Emotional Differentiation

Emotions gradually become differentiated during the first two years of life. Peter Wolff (1966) described seven states of arousal in newborn infants. Each is characterized by a distinctive pattern of respiration, muscle tone, motor activity, and alertness (see Table 7.6). In these states, one observes the earliest differentiation among distress (crying), interest (alert inactivity), and excitement (waking activity). A newborn's state of arousal influences his or her capacity to respond to the environment.

Changes in arousal state also serve to cue responses from caregivers. A baby's crying usually evokes a caregiver's effort to comfort or soothe. Visual alertness is likely to prompt social interactions. Parents try to interact with their infants, achieve eye contact, and initiate nonverbal exchanges during alert phases (Tronick et al., 1979).

Crying is an especially important emotional expression that contributes to the infant's survival. Until about six or seven months of age, the infant's mobility is quite limited. Crying is one of the primary signals available that will bring the caregiver to the infant. Infant cries vary in pitch, as well as in tempo and duration. Studies from laboratory and natural field settings, as well as across cultures, suggest that higher-pitched cries are considered more upsetting to the caregiver and are treated as a signal of a more urgent nature

TABLE 7.6 WOLFF

States of Arousal in Newborns

Regular sleep (RS)	Full rest; low muscle tonus, low motor activity; eyelids firmly closed and still; even, regular respiratory rhythm, about 36 breaths per minute.
Irregular sleep (IS)	Slightly greater muscle tonus; gentle motor activity; frequent facial grimaces and smiles; occasional rapid eye movement; irregular respiration, about 48 breaths per minute.
Periodic sleep (PS)	Intermediate between RS and IS; bursts of rapid, shallow breathing alternate with bursts of deep, slow breathing.
Drowsiness (D)	More active than RS but less active than IS or PS; eyes open and close; eyes, when open, are dull and glazed and may roll upward; respiration variable but of higher frequency than during RS.
Alert inactivity (AI)	Slight activity; face relaxed; eyes open and "bright"; respiration constant and more rapid than in RS.
Waking activity (WA)	Frequent, diffuse motor activity; vocalizations; skin flushed when active; irregular respiration.
Crying (C)	Vigorous, diffuse motor activity; facial grimaces; skin red; eyes open or partially closed; crying vocalization.

Source: Adapted from Wolff, P. H. (1966). Causes, controls, and organization of behavior in the neonate. *Psychological Issues, 5* (1, whole no. 17). Copyright © 1966 International Universities Press, Inc. Reprinted with permission.

than are low-pitched cries. In addition, information is contained in the pauses within and between cries. Crying that involves shorter pauses is perceived by adults as more arousing and unpleasant (Zeskind et al., 1992).

A broader palette of emotions gradually emerges from the basic states of arousal and distress. The differentiation of emotions follows a regular pattern, as Table 7.7 suggests. This table describes age-related changes on three dimensions of emotion: *pleasure–joy, wariness–fear,* and *rage–anger.* Emotional responses during the first month are closely tied to the infant's internal state. Physical discomfort, arousal, pain, and changing tension in the central nervous system are the major stimulants for emotions. During the period from one to six months, emotions begin to be associated with a separation of self and environment. Babies smile at familiar faces. They show interest in and curiosity about novel stimuli. They express rage when nursing is disrupted or when they are prevented from viewing an activity that they have been intently watching.

The period from 6 to 12 months reflects a greater awareness of the context of events. Emotions of joy, anger, and fear are tied to a baby's ability to recall previous experiences and to compare them with an ongoing event. These emotions also reflect a baby's ability to exercise some control over the environment and frustration when goals are blocked. At this age, the distinctions among some of the negative emotions such as anger, fear, and sadness

[Handwritten margin notes:]
EMOTIONAL RESPONSES

0–1 month
– tied to internal state

1–6 months
– separation of self & environment

6–12 months
– awareness of the context of events

1–2 yrs
– sense of self

TABLE 7.7

Age-Related Changes in Three Dimensions of Emotion

Month	Pleasure—Joy	Wariness—Fear	Rage—Anger
0–3	Endogenous smile; turning toward	Startle/pain; obligatory attention	Distress due to covering the face, physical restraint, extreme discomfort Rage (disappointment)
3	Pleasure		
4–5	Delight; active laughter	Wariness	
7	Joy		
9		Fear (stranger aversion)	Anger
12	Elation	Anxiety; immediate fear	Angry mood, petulance
18	Positive valuation of self	Shame	Defiance
24	Affection		Intentional hurting
36	Pride, love		Guilt

Note: The age specified is that of neither the first appearance of the affect in question nor its peak occurrence; it is the age at which the literature suggests the reaction is common.

Source: Sroufe, L. A. (1979). Socioemotional development. In J. D. Osofsky (Ed.), *Handbook of infant development.* New York: Wiley, 462–516. Copyright © 1979 John Wiley & Sons, Inc. Reprinted by permission of John Wiley & Sons, Inc.

In the second year of life, emotions of elation and delight are often linked to mastery.

may be blurred and difficult to detect by someone who is not familiar with the child (Camras et al., 1991).

Emotions that are observed during the second year of life—especially anxiety, pride, defiance, and shame—suggest an emerging sense of self. Infants recognize that they can operate as causal agents. They also begin to respond to the emotions of others. They can express love through hugs, kisses, and tender pats. They can share toys, comfort another distressed child, and imitate another person's excitement. In becoming a more distinct being, a toddler achieves a new level of awareness of the capacity to give and receive pleasure as well as the vulnerability of self and others.

The dimension of wariness–fear becomes more differentiated during the second year. The theme of anxiety was introduced in the discussion of attachment and the emergence of stranger anxiety at about six months and separation anxiety at about nine months. Anxiety of a more nonspecific form is observed during the second year. Babies begin to anticipate negative experiences and express fear of objects or events that have been associated with negative experiences in the past. Anxiety is a major dynamic in describing patterns of attachment, especially in relationships characterized by potentially rejecting or unpredictable caregivers.

[handwritten margin note: 1-2 yrs Emergence of non-specific anxiety.]

Emotions as a Key to Understanding Meaning

An infant's emotional reactions provide clues to the meaning he or she makes of a specific situation. Often, these reactions are studied by systematic coding of babies' facial expressions. In one study, when babies were videotaped after an inoculation at 2 and 4 months of age, their emotional reactions included closed-eye expressions of physical distress and anger. However, when they were filmed at 19 months, their expressions involved more open-eyed anger, suggesting greater awareness of the source of their discomfort (Izard et al., 1983).

Another example of how emotions provide a window on meaning comes from a study of infants in an operant conditioning experiment. Infants ages two, four, and six months were observed while they learned an operant arm-pulling task. A string was attached to the infant's wrist. When the string was pulled, it activated a switch that turned on a color slide of an infant smiling accompanied by the sound of children singing the *Sesame Street* theme. During the learning phase, pulling the string produced the visual and auditory stimulus. During the extinction phase, nothing happened when the string was pulled. In Box 7.3 we consider the variety of meanings of infants' smiles.

Even as young as two months old, the babies' expressions changed from interest and enjoyment during the learning phase to anger and sadness during the extinction phase. The findings were interpreted as demonstrating that infants' anger is associated with violation of expectations, and that expressions of interest and enjoyment are associated with learning and increased control. What is more, individual differences in emotional response to the task showed stability over the two-month period, particularly the expressions of interest during learning and anger during extinction (Sullivan et al., 1992).

The Ability to Regulate Emotions

Infants develop strategies for coping with intense emotions, both positive and negative. Most research in this area has focused on the ways infants deal with distress (Dodge, 1989). Even newborns have some strategies for reducing the intensity of distress such as turning their heads away, sucking on their hands or lips, or closing their eyes. As infants gain new motor coordination and control, they can move away, distract themselves with other objects, or soothe themselves by rocking, stroking themselves, or sucking their thumbs (Kopp, 1989). However, you surely have observed many instances when infants are not able to regulate the intensity of their emotions. Any researcher who works with infant subjects will tell you of babies who had to be eliminated from a study because they simply could not be calmed enough during the experimental procedure to attend to the task.

One of the most important elements in the development of emotional regulation is the way caregivers assist infants to manage their strong feelings (Kopp, 1989; Tronick, 1989). Caregivers can provide direct support when they observe a child's distress, such as cuddling, hugging, rocking, or swaddling. They may offer food or a pacifier or nurse the baby as a means of comfort. Through words and actions, they may help a child interpret the source of the stress or suggest ways to reduce the stress.

Some mothers have a hard time comforting their babies. In fact, they may even interact in ways that provoke anger rather than satisfaction. For example, when depressed and nondepressed mothers and their three-month-old infants were filmed in face-to-face interactions, depressed mothers and their infants were found to spend less time in matched behavior states than the nondepressed mothers and their infants (Field et al., 1990). What is more, the quality of those interactions was different. Depressed mothers and their infants spent more of their matched time in states of anger/protest or disengagement/looking away. Nondepressed mothers and their infants spent more of their time in play.

BOX 7.3

The Meaning of an Infant's Smile

The infant's smile is a social treasure. Parents and grandparents may go to great lengths to elicit this sweet expression. Yet researchers have discovered that an infant's smile can have a wide variety of meanings and be the response to many stimuli.

The very earliest smiles, observed during the first month of life, may occur spontaneously during sleep or in response to a high-pitched human voice. Gentle tactile stimulation—touching, tickling, and rocking—can produce these early smiles. A baby's first smiles are not a true form of social communication, although they are likely to produce positive feelings in the adult caregiver (Wolff, 1963, 1987).

Social smiles begin to be observed at about five weeks of age. These smiles are first produced in response to a wide range of stimuli—familiar faces and voices (especially the mother's), strangers, and nonhuman objects. After about 20 weeks, the smiling response becomes differentiated. Infants continue to smile broadly and frequently at people, especially familiar people, but they no longer smile readily at strangers or objects. The social smile conveys both a recognition of familiarity and an invitation to further communication or interaction (Ambrose, 1963; Sroufe et al., 1984).

The *cognitive smile* seems to develop with the social smile. Infants smile in response to their own behaviors, as if they were expressing satisfaction with their accomplishments (Papousek & Bernstein, 1969; Watson, 1970). At three months, babies smile in response to events that are moderately familiar, as if expressing pleasure in understanding the situation (Kagan, 1984). Infants smile elaborately when they are able to make something happen, as when they wiggle a mobile or make a bell jangle by kicking their feet (Cicchetti & Schneider-Rosen, 1984). These "mastery" smiles do not appear to have a social intention. By eight months, infants smile when they are able to grasp a new concept (Kagan, 1984). In the second year of life, smiling is associated with a primitive form of humor. Babies smile when they recognize an incongruity, such as a picture of their mother drinking from a baby bottle or crawling on her hands and knees. These smiles suggest that the baby appreciates something about the discrepancy between what is being presented and what is normally observed (Cicchetti & Schneider-Rosen, 1984).

Babies smile in a variety of contexts. The conditions that evoke smiles change as the baby matures. Thus, smiles, like other emotional expressions, should be interpreted in relation to the infants' existing schemes and goals.

Concern has focused on babies who are characterized as showing negative emotionality early in infancy. These babies tend to be at risk for subsequent behavior problems. Therefore, studies have been directed toward analyzing continuity and discontinuity in negative emotionality and the family characteristics that might be associated with reduced negativity over the first year of life. In one such study involving 148 babies and their parents, characteristics of the mothers and the fathers were examined separately to learn what might lead to increased negativity in infants from three to nine months of age. In addition to the direct quality of interactions between the mother–infant and father–infant pairs, researchers found that high levels of marital dissatisfaction on the part of the mother or father and the father's emotional insensitivity were associated with increases in an infant's negativity during this period. This is quite significant since it suggests that the emotional climate of the parental system is communicated in ways that the infant can perceive as early as three to nine months of age (Belsky et al., 1991).

Caregivers' approaches to the issue of emotional regulation vary with the culture. In some cultures, caregivers regulate emotions by protecting a child from certain arousing situations. Japanese mothers, for example, try to prevent their children from being exposed to anger. Young Japanese children are shielded from frustration so that they will not experience anger, and their parents rarely express anger to them, especially in public. Thus, Japanese parents try to regulate their children's anger by minimizing their experiences with it (Miyake et al., 1986).

In another example, Anglo and Puerto Rican mothers were compared with respect to what they considered ideal and negative behavior in the strange situation (Harwood, 1992). Anglo mothers thought that it would be undesirable if the baby clung to the mother during the initial phase and cried the whole time when the mother left the room. They also thought it would be undesirable if the baby was unhappy when the mother returned and came to her for comfort or expressed anger toward her. Puerto Rican mothers thought it would be undesirable if the baby was extremely active and ignored the mother during the initial phase or when she left the room, and if the baby continued to play actively when the mother returned without acknowledging her. Cultural values about the expression and control of distress influence how mothers respond to distress signals and what they teach their babies about how to regulate feelings of wariness, fear, and anxiety.

Emotional regulation can also be achieved by observing emotional reactions of others (Campos et al., 1989). Children observe anger, pride, shame, or sadness in others, often in response to their own emotional expressions. For example, when Connie stumbles and falls in trying to take a step on her own, she looks up at her mother. If her mother looks upset and frightened, Connie may begin to cry. If her mother laughs or speaks to her in a comforting tone, Connie may just get up and try again. Children can be distracted from their sadness by seeing laughter and joy in someone else. Through empathy, children can reduce their angry feelings toward someone else by seeing how sad or frightened the other person is.

As children understand the consequences or implications of a situation, they have new motives for regulating or failing to regulate their emotions. Children may extend or expand their signals of distress if they think it will help them achieve their goals, such as special attention or nurturing. Children may try to disguise their distress if they think that it will provoke additional pain. Emotional regulation, just like emotional signaling, takes place within an interpersonal context.

Emotions as a Channel for Adult–Infant Communication

Emotions are a major component of the communication system during infancy (Campos & Barrett, 1984). An infant has the capacity to produce a range of emotional expressions, including fear, distress, disgust, surprise, excitement, interest, joy, anger, and sadness. Parents and other caregivers rely on facial, vocal, and behavioral cues in order to determine and respond to an infant's emotions (Malatesta & Izard, 1984). In cycles of interaction, responsive caregivers monitor changes in a baby's affect as a way of ascertaining whether their interventions are effective. When interactions go astray and an adult cannot understand what a baby needs, the adult tries to repair or revise the communication (Tronick, 1989).

Think of a six-month-old baby who wants a toy that is out of reach. The baby waves her arms in the direction of the toy, makes fussy noises, and looks distressed. As her father tries to figure out what the baby wants, he watches her expressions in order to discover whether he is on the right track. Parents who are attuned to this form of communication are more likely to help babies achieve their goals, and babies are more likely to persist in attempts to communicate because they have experienced success in such interactions.

Babies can detect and differentiate the affective expressions of others. Very young infants can differentiate facial expressions of fear, anger, happiness, sadness, and surprise (Caron et al., 1988; Hornik et al., 1987; Ludemann & Nelson, 1988; Walker-Andrews, 1986). Similarly, adults can detect and differentiate the affective expressions of infants. The most readily recognized facial expressions are those of joy, interest, surprise, and distress (Oster et al., 1992). Take a look at the child's facial expression in Notebook Page 7.5. What does it mean to you? How would you respond?

The domain of emotions is a two-way channel through which infants and their caregivers can establish *intersubjectivity*. In our previous discussion of categorization, we pointed out that, from their earliest months, infants interact differently with people than they do with objects. Babies and caregivers are able to engage in reciprocal, rhythmic interactions; they appreciate state changes in one another and modify their actions in order to take into account information being sent by the other. Through a shared repertoire of emotions, babies and their caregivers are able to understand one another and to create shared meanings. Thus, emotional expression becomes a building block of trust.

emotional expression building block of trust.

Social Referencing

One of the most notable ways that infants and adults have of co-constructing their reality is the mechanism of *social referencing*. Under certain circumstances, infants make use of the emotional responses of another person to guide their own behavior. Infants often use their mothers as a social reference, but other adults can serve this function as well (Hornik & Gunnar, 1988; Klinnert et al., 1986; Walden & Ogan, 1988). As infants approach an unfamiliar adult, an ambiguous situation, or a novel object, they look to their mothers and use their facial or verbal expressions as a source of information about the situation. If a mother expresses wariness or a negative emotion, her infant is more likely to withdraw or to explore with caution. If the mother expresses a positive emotion, her infant is more likely to approach the situation or the unfamiliar person with confidence. By 12 months of age, infants consistently use this mechanism to try to appraise an ambiguous situation (Rosen et al., 1992).

Social referencing is an interactive process that illustrates how members of a cultural group begin to build a shared view of reality during infancy. Infants actively request information by looking to their mothers or other adults present in the situation. The adult's expression, either positive or negative, cues the infant about whether to approach or withdraw. Infants reduce their uncertainty and begin to appraise their world in the context of their caregivers' emotional responses. You can probably imagine the wide range of objects and situations that can be evaluated through this mechanism. Foods, toys, people, animals, sounds, plants, and objects of all sorts can be discerned as positive and approachable or negative and a cause for wariness. Depending on the cultural perspective, infants in different societies begin to categorize their experiences differently based in part on these early appraisals derived from social referencing.

Responding to an Infant's Emotions

Facial expressions play a vital role in parent–child communication, especially during infancy when other verbal and representational means for communication are not well developed. Infants can "read" some adult expressions and adults can "read" some infant expressions with little prior experience. Consider the photo of Cindy shown here.

1. What emotion is Cindy expressing?

_____

_____

_____

_____

_____

2. How does her expression make you feel?

_____

_____

_____

_____

_____

3. Suppose that you are taking care of Cindy. What might you do in response to Cindy's emotional expression?

_____

_____

_____

_____

Chapter Summary

1. Newborns vary in physical maturity. Those who weigh less than 2,500 grams are called low-birth-weight infants. Those who are small for their gestational age are at special risk for later problems in health and cognitive functioning.

2. Although the genetic plan plays a major role in guiding physical and sensory/perceptual maturation during infancy, there is considerable evidence for plasticity in neurological development as an infant's sensory/motor system interacts with the social and physical environment.

3. Hearing is the earliest link between the infant and the mother. The fetus is sensitive to auditory stimulation in utero. Babies can use sound to localize objects in space. They show special responsiveness to language sounds.

4. Visual acuity improves rapidly during the first four months. Infants respond to movement, color, brightness, complexity, light/dark contrast, contours, depth, and distance. Visual attention shifts from the contours of an object in the early months to the internal details by four months. The human face is a highly preferred stimulus. Infants not only recognize familiar faces but are able to imitate certain facial expressions.

5. Newborns can differentiate sweet, sour, bitter, and salty tastes. Sweet tastes have an especially calming effect.

6. The skin is the largest sensory organ and the earliest to develop in utero. Gentle stroking and handling have a soothing effect. Infants use the sense of touch to explore objects.

7. The sensory systems function in various degrees of interconnection. Sounds guide visual tracking; touch and taste can have a soothing effect; smell, touch, sound, and sight can all contribute to object recognition.

8. The motor system is less well developed at birth than the sensory system. Many early motor behaviors are reflexive. During the first year, some reflexive, involuntary responses gradually come under voluntary control; others simply fade away.

9. Motor development illustrates the interaction between the genetically guided plan for growth and the contributions of experience. Culture plays an important role in establishing expectations for infants' motor behavior and translating these expectations into specific child-rearing strategies.

10. Temperament refers to relatively stable characteristics of response to the environment that can be observed during the first months of life. These characteristics are closely linked to the sensory/motor system and to the adaptive mechanisms that infants use to orient to and withdraw from the environment.

11. Attachment is the process through which people develop specific positive emotional bonds with others. The attachment behavior system is linked to survival needs for safety and protection.

12. Synchrony in parent–infant interaction is fundamental to the formation of attachment.

13. By 9 to 12 months of age, infants form an internal mental representation of the object of attachment. Prior to that time, stranger anxiety and separation anxiety are two types of evidence that the baby is working on a stable representation of the attachment figure.

14. The strange situation is a major laboratory technique for assessing the quality of attachment. Using this paradigm, four patterns of attachment have been identified: secure, anxious-avoidant, anxious-resistant, and disorganized.

15. Parental sensitivity is an underlying factor in determining the quality of attachment. The three factors that appear to influence sensitivity are the adult's past experiences, including the way that he or she was cared for as a young child; contemporary factors that influence the caregiver's well-being, self-esteem, and emotional availability; and characteristics of the infant.

16. One of the most important components of sensorimotor intelligence is the formation of causal schemes. Causal schemes develop through six phases from an initial dependence upon reflexes as adaptive learning systems to the final stage of internal representation of means–end relationships.

17. Another essential aspect of sensorimotor intelligence is understanding the nature of objects. Object permanence refers to the concept that objects in the environment are permanent and do not cease to exist when they are out of view. The same physical laws govern the behavior of objects whether they are in view or not.

18. Piaget traced the development of object permanence through a task involving searching for a hidden object. He concluded that 18-month-olds could solve complex object permanence tasks. Other scholars have argued that much younger infants understand that objects continue to exist when they are out of view and that complex, representational skills are not required.

19. Categorization is another aspect of sensorimotor intelligence. One of the earliest categories is the distinction between persons and objects. By 12 months of age, infants can select objects that form a single category, and by 18 months they can solve multidimensional sorting tasks.

20. The earliest differentiation of emotions is seen in the distinctions among seven states of arousal. Over the first two years, three domains of pleasure–joy, wariness–fear, and rage–anger show clear evidence of elaboration.

21. Emotional regulation is possible even for very young infants. Caregiving strategies are often aimed at helping infants manage strong feelings through soothing and cuddling. Sometimes, caregivers try to provoke emotions, especially through playful tickling, vocal games, and other strategies aimed at increasing the baby's level of arousal.

22. Emotions are a major channel for communication. They provide an avenue for achieving intersubjectivity between infants and adults.

23. Through social referencing, infants make use of the emotional reactions of others to guide their own reactions, especially in ambiguous situations.

References

Ainsworth, M. D. S. (1973). The development of infant–mother attachment. In B. M. Caldwell & H. N. Ricciuti (Eds.), *Review of child development research* (vol. 3). Chicago: University of Chicago Press.

Ainsworth, M. D. S. (1985). Patterns of infant–mother attachments: Antecedents and effects on development. *Bulletin of the New York Academy of Medicine, 61,* 771–791.

Ainsworth, M. D. S. (1989). Attachments beyond infancy. *American Psychologist, 44,* 709–716.

Ainsworth, M. D. S., Bell, S. M. V. & Stayton, D. J. (1971). Individual differences in strange-situational behavior of one-year-olds. In H. A. Schaffer (Ed.), *The origins of human social relations.* London: Academic Press.

Ainsworth, M. D. S., Blehar, M. C., Waters, E. & Wall, S. (1978). *Patterns of attachment: A psychological study of the strange situation.* Hillsdale, N.J.: Erlbaum.

Ambrose, J. A. (1963). The concept of a critical period in the development of social responsiveness. In B. M. Foss (Ed.), *Determinants of infant behavior* (vol. 2). New York: Wiley.

Aoki, C. & Siekevitz, P. (1988). Plasticity in brain development. *Scientific American, 259,* 56–64.

Apgar, V. (1953). Proposal for a new method of evaluating the newborn infant. *Anesthesia and Analgesia, 32,* 260–267.

Aslin, R. N. (1987). Visual and auditory development in infancy. In J. D. Osofsky (Ed.), *Handbook of infant development* (2nd ed.). New York: John Wiley & Sons, 5–97.

Baillargeon, R. (1987). Object permanence in 3½- and 4½-month-old infants. *Developmental Psychology, 23,* 655–664.

Baillargeon, R. & DeVos, J. (1992). Object permanence in young infants: Further evidence. *Child Development, 62,* 1227–1246.

Baillargeon, R. & Graber, M. (1988). Evidence of location memory in 8-month-old infants in a non-search AB task. *Developmental Psychology, 24,* 502–511.

Banks, M. S. & Dannemiller, J. L. (1987). Infant visual psychophysics. In P. Salapatek & L. Cohen (Eds.), *Handbook of infant perception* (vol. 1). Orlando, Fla.: Academic Press.

Bates, J. E. (1987). Temperament in infancy. In J. D. Osofsky (Ed.), *Handbook of infant development* (2nd ed.). New York: John Wiley & Sons, 1101–1149.

Belsky, J., Fish, M. & Isabella, R. (1991). Continuity and discontinuity in infant negative and positive emotionality: Family antecedents and attachment consequences. *Developmental Psychology, 27,* 421–431.

Benson, J. B. & Uzgiris, I. C. (1985). Effect of self-initiated locomotion on infant search activity. *Developmental Psychology, 21,* 923–931.

Bertenthal, B. I. & Fischer, K. W. (1983). The development of representation in search: A social-cognitive analysis. *Child Development, 54,* 846–857.

Blass, E. M. & Ciaramitaro, V. (1994). A new look at some old mechanisms in human newborns: Taste and tactile determinants of state, affect, and action. *Monographs of the Society for Research in Child Development, 59* (1).

Blass, E. M. & Hoffmeyer, L. B. (1991). Sucrose as an analgesic for newborn infants. *Pediatrics, 87,* 215–218.

Bornstein, M. H. (1992). Perception across the life cycle. In M. H. Bornstein & M. E. Lamb (Eds.), *Developmental psychology; An advanced textbook* (3rd ed.). Hillsdale, N.J.: Erlbaum, 155–209.

Bornstein, M. H. (1995). Parenting infants. In M. H. Bornstein (Ed.), *Handbook of parenting, Volume 1: Children and Parenting.* Mahwah, N.J.: Erlbaum, 3–41.

Bornstein, M. H., Kessen, W. & Weiskopf, S. (1976). The categories of hue in infancy. *Science, 191,* 201–202.

Bower, T. G. R. (1987). *Development in infancy* (2nd ed.). New York: W. H. Freeman.

Bower, T. G. R. (1989). *The rational infant: Learning in infancy.* New York: W. H. Freeman.

Bowlby, J. (1960). Separation anxiety. *International Journal of Psychoanalysis, 41,* 69–113.

Bowlby, J. (1988). *A secure base: Parent–child attachment and healthy human development.* New York: Basic Books.

Braungart, J. M., Plomin, R., Defries, J. C. & Fulker, D. W. (1992). Genetic influence on tester-rated infant temperament as assessed by Bayley's Infant Behavior Record: Nonadoptive and adoptive siblings and twins. *Developmental Psychology, 28,* 1, 40–47.

Brazelton, T. B. (1977). Implications of infant development among the Mayan Indians of Mexico. In P. H. Leiderman, S. T. Tulkin & A. Rosenfeld (Eds.), *Culture and infancy: Variations in the human experience.* New York: Academic Press, 151–187.

Brazelton, T. B., Koslowski, B. & Tronick, E. (1977). Neonatal behavior among urban Zambians and Americans. *Annual Progress in Child Psychiatry, 15,* 97–107.

Brazelton, T. B., Nugent, J. K. & Lester, B. M. (1987). Neonatal behavioral assessment scale. In J. D. Osofsky (Ed.), *Handbook of infant development* (2nd ed.). New York: John Wiley & Sons, 780–817.

Bretherton, I. (1985). Attachment theory: Retrospect and prospect. In I. Bretherton & E. Everett (Eds.), *Growing points of attachment theory and research. Monographs of the Society for Research in Child Development, 50* (1–2 serial no. 209), 3–35.

Bretherton, I. (1990). Open communication and internal working models: Their role in the development of attachment relationships. In R. Dienstbier & R. A. Thompson (Eds.), *Nebraska Symposium on Motivation 1988: Socioemotional Development, 36,* Lincoln: University of Nebraska Press, 57–113.

Bridges, L. J., Connell, J. P. & Belsky, J. (1988). Similarities and differences in infant–mother and infant–father interaction in the strange situation: A component process analysis. *Developmental Psychology, 24,* 92–100.

Bronson, G. W. (1973). Infants' reactions to an unfamiliar person. In L. J. Stone, H. T. Smith & L. B. Murphy (Eds.), *The competent infant.* New York: Basic Books.

Brooks-Gunn, J., Klebanov, P. K., Liaw, F. & Spiker, D. (1993). Enhancing the development of low-birth-weight, premature infants: Changes in cognition and behavior over the first three years. *Child Development, 64,* 736–753.

Buss, A. H. & Plomin, R. (1984). *Temperament: Early developing personality traits.* Hillsdale, N.J.: Erlbaum.

Buss, A. H. & Plomin, R. (1986). The EAS approach to temperament. In R. Plomin & J. Dunn (Eds.), *The study of temperament: Changes, continuities, and challenges.* Hillsdale, N.J.: Erlbaum.

Calkins, S. D. & Fox, N. A. (1992). The relations among infant temperament, security of attachment, and behavioral inhibition at twenty-four months. *Child Development, 63,* 1456–1472.

Campos, J. J. & Barrett, K. C. (1984). Toward a new understanding of emotions and their development. In C. E. Izard, J. Kagan & R. B. Zajonc (Eds.), *Emotions, cognition, and behavior.* Cambridge: Cambridge University Press, 229–263.

Campos, J. J., Campos, R. G. & Barrett, K. C. (1989). Emergent themes in the study of emotional development and emotion regulation. *Developmental Psychology, 25,* 394–402.

Camras, L. A., Malatesta, C. & Izard, C. E. (1991). The development of facial expression in infancy. In R. Feldman & B. Rime (Eds.), *Fundamentals of nonverbal behavior.* New York: Cambridge University Press, 73–105.

Canfield, R. L. & Haith, M. M. (1991). Young infants' visual expectations for symmetric and asymmetric stimulus sequences. *Developmental Psychology, 27,* 198–208.

Carlson, V., Cicchetti, D., Barnett, D. & Braunwold, K. (1989). Finding order in disorganization: Lessons from research on maltreated infants' attachment to their caregivers. In D. Cicchetti & V. Carlson (Eds.), *Child maltreatment: Theory and research on the causes and consequences of maltreatment.* New York: Cambridge University Press, 494–528.

Caron, A. J., Caron, R. F. & MacLean, D. J. (1988). Infant discrimination of naturalistic emotional expressions: The role of face and voice. *Child Development, 59,* 604–616.

Caron, R. F., Caron, A. J. & Myers, R. S. (1982). Abstraction of invariant face expressions in infancy. *Child Development, 53,* 1008–1015.

Cassady, G. & Strange, M. (1987). The small-for-gestational-age (SGA) infant. In G. B. Avery (Ed.), *Neonatology: Pathophysiology and management of the newborn.* Philadelphia: Lippincott, 299–331.

Cernoch, J. M. & Porter, R. H. (1985). Recognition of maternal axillary odors by infants. *Child Development, 56,* 1593–1598.

Chase-Lansdale, P. L. & Owen, M. T. (1987). Maternal employment in a family context: Effects on infant–mother and infant–father attachments. *Child Development, 58,* 1505–1512.

Chazan, S. E. (1981). Development of object permanence as a correlate of dimensions of maternal care. *Developmental Psychology, 17,* 79–81.

Cicchetti, D. & Schneider-Rosen, K. (1984). Theoretical and empirical considerations in the investigation of the relationship between affect and cognition in atypical populations of infants. In C. E. Izard, J. Kagan & R. B. Zajonc (Eds.), *Emotions, cognition, and behavior.* Cambridge: Cambridge University Press, 366–408.

Clifton, R., Perris, E. & Bullinger, A. (1991). Infants' perception of auditory space. *Developmental Psychology, 27,* 187–197.

Colombo, J., Mitchell, D. W., Coldren, J. T. & Freeseman, L. J. (1991). Individual differences in infant visual attention: Are short lookers faster processors or feature processors? *Child Development, 62,* 1247–1257.

Connolly, K. & Dalgleish, M. (1989). The emergence of a tool-using skill in infancy. *Developmental Psychology, 25,* 894–912.

Cox, M. J., Owen, M. T., Henderson, V. K. & Margand, N. A. (1992). Prediction of infant–father and infant—mother attachment. *Developmental Psychology, 28,* 474–483.

Crittenden, P. M. (1985). Maltreated infants: Vulnerability and resilience. *Journal of Child Psychology and Psychiatry, 26,* 85–96.

De Casper, A. & Fifer, W. (1980). Of human bonding: Newborns prefer their mothers' voices. *Science, 208,* 1174–1176.

De Casper, A. J. & Spence, M. J. (1986). Prenatal maternal speech influences newborns' perception of speech sounds. *Infant Behavior and Development, 9,* 133–150.

DiPietro, J. A., Porges, S. W. & Uhly, B. (1992). Reactivity and developmental competence in preterm and full-term infants. *Developmental Psychology, 28,* 831–841.

Dodge, K. A. (1989). Coordinating responses to aversive stimuli: Introduction to a special section on the development of emotion regulation. *Developmental Psychology, 25,* 339–342.

Donovan, W. L. & Leavitt, L. A. (1989). Maternal self-efficacy and infant attachment: Integrating physiology, perceptions, and behavior. *Child Development, 60,* 460–472.

Easterbrooks, M. A. (1989). Quality of attachment to mother and to father: Effects of perinatal risk status. *Child Development, 60,* 825–830.

Ellsworth, C. P., Muir, C. P. & Hains, S. M. J. (1993). Social competence and person-object differentiation: An analysis of the still-face effect. *Developmental Psychology, 29,* 63–73.

Escalona, S. K. (1968). *The roots of individuality.* Chicago: Aldine.

Feinman, S. & Lewis, M. (1983). Social referencing at ten months: A second-order effect on infants' responses to strangers. *Child Development, 54,* 878–887.

Fentress, J. C. & McLeod, P. J. (1986). Motor patterns in development. In E. M. Blass (Ed.), *Handbook of behavioral neurobiology, vol. 8, Developmental psychobiology and developmental neurobiology.* New York: Plenum.

Field, T. M. (1991). Young children's adaptations to repeated separations from their mothers. *Child Development, 62,* 539–547.

Field, T. M., Cohen, D., Garcia, R. & Greenberg, R. (1984). Mother—stranger face discrimination by the newborn. *Infant Behavior and Development, 7,* 19–25.

Field, T. M., Healy, B., Goldstein, S. & Guthertz, M. (1990). Behavior-state matching and synchrony in mother—infant interactions of nondepressed versus depressed dyads. *Developmental Psychology, 26,* 7–14.

Field, T. M., Woodson, R. W., Greenberg, R. & Cohen,

C. (1982). Discrimination and imitation of facial expressions by neonates. *Science, 218,* 179–181.

Fischer, K. W. & Bidell, T. R. (1992). Ever younger ages: Constructive use of nativist findings about early development. *Newsletter of the Society for Research in Child Development,* Winter, 1, 10, 11, 14.

Fischer, K. W. & Rose, S. P. (1994). Dynamic development of coordination of components of brain and behavior: A framework for theory and research. In G. Dawson & K. W. Fischer (Eds.), *Human behavior and the developing brain.* New York: Guilford, 3–66.

Fischer, K. W. & Silvern, L. (1985). Stages and individual differences in cognitive development. *Annual Review of Psychology, 36,* 613–648.

Fonagy, P., Steele, H. & Steele, M. (1991). Maternal representations of attachment during pregnancy predict the organization of infant—mother attachment at one year of age. *Child Development, 62,* 891–905.

Fox, N. A., Kimmerly, N. L. & Schafer, W. D. (1991). Attachment to mother/attachment to father. *Child Development, 62,* 210–225.

Francis, P. L., Self, P. A. & Horowitz, F. D. (1987). The behavioral assessment of the neonate: An overview. In J. D. Osofsky (Ed.), *Handbook of infant development* (2nd ed.). New York: John Wiley & Sons, 723–779.

Frankenberg, W. K. & Dodds, J. B. (1967). The Denver Developmental Screening Test. *Journal of Pediatrics, 71,* 181–191.

Gibson, E. J. & Walker, A. S. (1984). Development of knowledge of visual-tactual affordances of substance. *Child Development, 55,* 453–460.

Gibson, J. J. (1962). Observations on active touch. *Psychological Review, 69,* 477–491.

Goldberg, S. & DiVitto, B. (1995). Parenting children born preterm. In M. H. Bornstein (Ed.), *Handbook of parenting, Volume 1: Children and parenting.* Mahwah, N.J.: Erlbaum, 209–232.

Goldfield, E. C. (1989). Transition from rocking to crawling: Postural constraints on infant movement. *Developmental Psychology, 25,* 913–919.

Goldsmith, H. H., Buss, A. H., Plomin, R., Rothbart, M. K., Thomas, A., Chess, S., Hinde, R..A. & McCall, R. B. (1987). Roundtable: What is temperament? Four approaches. *Child Development, 58,* 505–529.

Goldsmith, H. H. & Campos, J. J. (1986). Fundamental issues in the study of early development: The Denver twin temperament study. In M. E. Lamb & A. Brown (Eds.), *Advances in developmental psychology.* Hillsdale, N.J.: Erlbaum, 231–283.

Gopnik, A. & Meltzoff, A. (1987). The development of categorization in the second year and its relation to other cognitive and linguistic developments. *Child Development, 58,* 1523–1531.

Gopnik, A. & Meltzoff, A. N. (1992). Categorization and naming: Basic-level sorting in eighteen-month-olds and its relation to language. *Child Development, 63,* 1091–1103.

Gratch, G. & Schatz, J. A. (1987). Cognitive development: The relevance of Piaget's infancy books. In J. D. Osofsky (Ed.), *Handbook of infant development* (2nd ed.). New York: John Wiley & Sons, 204–237.

Gunnar, M. R., Larson, M. C., Hertsgaard, L., Harris, M. L. & Brodersen, L. (1992). The stressfulness of separation among nine-month-old infants: Effects of social context variables and infant temperament. *Child Development, 63,* 290–303.

Gunnar, M. R., Mangelsdorf, S., Larson, M. & Hertsgaard, L. (1989). Attachment, temperament, and adrenocortical activity in infancy: A study of psychoendocrine regulation. *Developmental Psychology, 25,* 355–363.

Harris, P. (1975). Development of search and object permanence during infancy. *Psychological Bulletin, 82,* 332–334.

Harwood, R. L. (1992). The influence of culturally derived values on Anglo and Puerto Rican mothers' perceptions of attachment behavior. *Child Development, 63,* 822–839.

Hay, D. F. (1980). Multiple functions of proximity seeking in infancy. *Child Development, 52,* 636–645.

Hickey, T. L. & Peduzzi, J. D. (1987). Structure and development of the visual system. In P. Salapatek & L. Cohen (Eds.), *Handbook of infant perception* (vol. 1). Orlando, Fla.: Academic Press.

Hopkins, B. & Westra, T. (1990). Motor development, maternal expectation, and the role of handling. *Infant Behavior and Development, 13,* 117–122.

Hornik, R. & Gunnar, M. R. (1988). A descriptive analysis of infant social referencing. *Child Development, 59,* 626–634.

Hornik, R., Risenhoover, N. & Gunnar, M. (1987). The effects of maternal positive, neutral, and negative affective communications on infant responses to new toys. *Child Development, 58,* 937–944.

Howes, P. & Markman, H. J. (1989). Marital quality and child functioning: A longitudinal investigation. *Child Development, 60,* 1044–1051.

Hubert, N. C., Wachs, T. D., Peters-Martin, P. & Gandour, M. J. (1982). The study of early temperament: Measurement and conceptual issues. *Child Development, 53,* 571–600.

Isabella, R. A. & Belsky, J. (1991). Interactional synchrony and the origins of infant–mother attachment: A replication study. *Child Development, 62,* 373–384.

Isabella, R. A., Belsky, J. & von Eye, A. (1989). Origins of infant–mother attachment: An examination of interactional synchrony during the infant's first year. *Developmental Psychology, 19,* 418–426.

Izard, C. E., Haynes, O. M., Chisholm, G. & Baak, K. (1991). Emotional determinants of infant–mother attachment. *Child Development, 62,* 906–917.

Izard, C. E., Hembree, E., Dougherty, L. & Spizziri, C. (1983). Changes in two-to-nineteen-month-old infants' facial expression following acute pain. *Developmental Psychology, 19,* 418–426.

Jacobson, S. W. & Frye, K. F. (1991). Effect of maternal social support on attachment: Experimental evidence. *Child Development, 62,* 572–582.

Jacobson, S. W., Jacobson, J. L., O'Neill, J. M., Padgett, R. J., Frankowski, J. J. & Bihun, J. T. (1992). Visual expectation and dimensions of infant information processing. *Child Development, 63,* 711–724.

Kagan, J. (1984). The idea of emotion in human development. In C. E. Izard, J. Kagan & R. B. Zajonc (Eds.), *Emotions, cognition, and behavior.* Cambridge: Cambridge University Press, 38–72.

Kantrowitz, B. (1988). Preemies. *Newsweek,* May 16, 62–70.

Keil, P. F. (1975). The development of the young child's ability to anticipate the outcome of simple causal events. Denver: Paper presented at the meeting of the Society for Research in Child Development.

Keltenbach, K., Weinraub, M. & Fullard, W. (1980). Infant wariness toward strangers reconsidered: Infants' and mothers' reactions to unfamiliar persons. *Child Development, 51,* 1197–1202.

Kermoian, R. & Campos, J. J. (1988). Locomotor experience: A facilitator of spatial cognitive development. *Child Development, 59,* 908–917.

Klinnert, M. D., Emde, R. N., Butterfield, P. & Campos, J. J. (1986). Social referencing: The infant's use of emotional signals from a friendly adult with mother present. *Developmental Psychology, 22,* 427–432.

Kopp, C. B. (1989). Regulation of distress and negative emotions: A developmental view. *Developmental Psychology, 25,* 343–354.

Kuhl, P. K. (1987). Perception of speech and sound in early infancy. In P. Salapatek & L. Cohen (Eds.), *Handbook of infant perception* (vol. 1). Orlando, Fla.: Academic Press.

Lamb, M. E. (1976). Twelve-month-olds and their parents: Interaction in a laboratory playroom. *Developmental Psychology, 12,* 237–244.

Langlois, J. H., Ritter, J. M., Casey, R. J. & Sawin, D. B. (1995). Infant attractiveness predicts maternal behaviors and attitudes. *Developmental Psychology, 31,* 464–472.

Larson, M. C., Gunnar, M. R. & Hertsgaard, L. (1991). The effects of morning naps, car trips, and maternal separation on adrenocortical activity in human infants. *Child Development, 62,* 362–372.

Lerner, J. V. & Lerner, R. M. (1983). Temperament and adaptation across life: Theoretical and empirical issues. In P. B. Baltes & O. G. Brini (Eds.), *Life span development and behavior, 5.* New York: Academic Press, 197–231.

Levy-Shiff, R., Sharur, H. & Mogilner, M. B. (1989). Mother-and father-preterm infant relationship in the hospital preterm nursery. *Child Development, 60,* 93–102.

Ludemann, P. M. (1991). Generalized discrimination of positive facial expressions by seven- and ten-month-old infants. *Child Development, 62,* 55–67.

Ludemann, P. M. & Nelson, C. A. (1988). Categorical representation of facial expressions by 7-month-old infants. *Developmental Psychology, 24,* 492–501.

MacFarlane, J. A. (1975). Olfaction in the development of social preferences in the human neonate. In *Parent–infant interaction.* Ciba Foundation Symposium 33, 103–113.

MacLean, D. J. & Schuler, M. (1989). Conceptual development in infancy: The understanding of containment. *Child Development, 60,* 1126–1137.

MacTurk, R. H., McCarthy, M. E., Vietze, P. M. & Yarrow, L. J. (1987). Sequential analysis of mastery behavior in 6- and 12-month-old infants. *Developmental Psychology, 23,* 199–203.

Malatesta, C. A. & Izard, C. E. (1984). The ontogenesis of human social signals: From biological imperative to symbol utilization. In N. A. Fox & R. J. Davidson (Eds.), *The psychobiology of affective development.* Hillsdale, N.J.: Erlbaum, 161–206.

McClearn, G. E. (1970). Genetic influences on behavior and development. In P. H. Mussen (Ed.), *Carmichael's manual of child psychology* (vol. 1). New York: Wiley, 39–76.

Meltzoff, A. N. & Borton, R. W. (1979). Intermodal matching by human neonates. *Nature, 282,* 403–404.

Millar, W. S., Weis, C. G. & Supramaniam, G. (1992). The influence of perinatal risk status on contingency learning in six-to-thirteen-month-old infants. *Child Development, 63,* 304–313.

Mistretta, C. M. & Bradley, R. M. (1977). Taste in utero: Theoretical considerations. In J. M. Weiffenbach (Ed.), *Taste and development.* DHEW Publication no. NIH 77-1068. Bethesda, Md.: U.S. Department of Health, Education, and Welfare, 279–291.

Miyake, K., Campos, J., Kagan, J. & Bradshaw, D. (1986). Issues in socioemotional development in Japan. In H. Azuma, I. Hakuta & H. Stevenson (Eds.), *Kodomo: Child development and education in Japan.* New York: W. H. Freeman, 239–261.

Nelson, C. A. (1987). The recognition of facial expressions in the first two years of life: Mechanisms of development. *Child Development, 58,* 889–909.

Nelson, C. A. & Dolgin, K. (1985). The generalized discrimination of facial expression by 7-month-old infants. *Child Development, 56,* 58–61.

Oppenheim, D., Sagi, A. & Lamb, M. E. (1988). Infant–adult attachments on the kibbutz and their relation to socioemotional development four years later. *Development Psychology, 24,* 427–433.

Oster, H., Hegley, D. & Nagel, L. (1992). Adult judgments and fine-grained analysis of infant facial expressions: Testing the validity of a priori coding formulas. *Developmental Psychology, 28,* 1115–1131.

Palmer, C. F. (1989). The discriminating nature of infants' exploratory actions. *Developmental Psychology, 25,* 885–893.

Papousek, H. & Bernstein, P. (1969). The functioning of conditioning stimulation in human neonates and infants. In A. Ambrose (Ed.), *Stimulation in early infancy.* London: Academic Press.

Passman, R. H. & Longeway, K. P. (1982). The role of vision in maternal attachment: Giving 2-year-olds a photograph of their mother during separation. *Developmental Psychology, 18,* 530–533.

Piaget, J. (1936/1952). *The origins of intelligence in children.* New York: International Universities Press.

Piaget, J. (1954). *The construction of reality in the child.* New York: Basic Books.

Piaget, J. (1970). Piaget's theory. In P. H. Mussen (Ed.), *Carmichael's manual of child psychology* (3rd ed.). New York: Wiley.

Piaget, J. & Inhelder, B. (1966/1969). *The psychology of the child.* New York: Basic Books.

Plomin, R. (1987). Developmental behavioral genetics and infancy. In J. D. Osofsky (Ed.), *Handbook of infant development* (2nd ed.). New York: John Wiley & Sons, 363–414.

Plomin, R. (1990). *Nature and nurture: An introduction to human behavioral genetics.* Pacific Grove, Calif.: Brooks/Cole.

Porter, R. H., Balogh, R. D. & Makin, J. W. (1988). Olfactory influences on mother–infant interactions. In C. Rovee-Collier & L. Lipsitt (Eds.), *Advances in infancy research* (vol. 5). Norwood, N.J.: Albex, 39–68.

Radke-Yarrow, M., Cummings, E. M., Kuczynski, L. & Chipman, M. (1985). Patterns of attachment in two- and three-year-olds in normal families and families with parental depression. *Child Development, 56,* 591–615.

Ramsay, D. S. & Campos, J. J. (1978). The onset of representation and entry into stage six of object permanence development. *Developmental Psychology, 14,* 79–86.

Ricks, M. H. (1985). The social transmission of parental behavior: Attachment across generations. In I. Bretherton & E. Waters (Eds.), *Growing points of attachment: Theory and research. Monographs of the Society for Research in Child Development, 50* (1–2, serial no. 209), 211–227.

Robertson, J. & Robertson, J. (1989). *Separation and the very young.* New York: Free Association Books.

Rochat, P. (1989). Object manipulation and exploration in 2- to 5-month-old infants. *Developmental Psychology, 25,* 871–884.

Rosch, E. (1978). Principles of categorization. In E. Rosch & B. Lloyd (Eds.), *Cognition and categorization.* Hillsdale, N.J.: Erlbaum, 27–48.

Rose, S. A., Feldman, J. F. & Wallace, I. F. (1992). Infant information processing in relation to six-year cognitive outcomes. *Child Development, 63,* 1126–1141.

Rose, S. A. & Ruff, H. A. (1987). Cross-modal abilities in human infants. In J. D. Osofsky (Ed.), *Handbook of infant development* (2nd ed.). New York: John Wiley & Sons, 318–362.

Rosen, W. D., Adamson, L. B. & Bakeman, R. (1992). An experimental investigation of infant social referencing: Mothers' messages and gender differences. *Developmental Psychology, 28,* 1172–1178.

Ross, G., Kagan, J., Zelazo, P. & Kotelchuck, M. (1975). Separation protest in infants in home and laboratory. *Developmental Psychology, 11,* 256–257.

Rovee, C. K. & Rovee, D. T. (1969). Conjugate reinforcement of infant exploratory behavior. *Journal of Experimental Child Psychology, 8,* 33–39.

Rovee-Collier, C. (1987). Learning and memory in infancy. In J. D. Osofsky (Ed.), *Handbook of infant development* (2nd ed.). New York: John Wiley & Sons, 98–148.

Rovee-Collier, C., Schechter, A., Shyi, G. C. W. & Shields, P. (1992). Perceptual identification of contextual attributes and infant memory retrieval. *Developmental Psychology, 28,* 307–318.

Ruff, H. A. (1984). Infants' manipulative exploration of objects: The effects of age and object characteristics. *Developmental Psychology, 20,* 9–20.

Ruff, H. A., Saltarelli, L. M., Capozzoli, M. & Dubiner, K. (1992). The differentiation of activity in infants' exploration of objects. *Developmental Psychology, 28,* 851–861.

Sagi, A., Lamb, M. E., Lewkowicz, K. S., Shoham, R., Dvir, R. & Estes, D. (1985). Security of infant–mother, –father, and –metapelet attachments among kibbutz-reared Israeli children. In I. Bretherton & E. Everett (Eds.), *Growing points of attachment theory and research. Monographs of the Society for Research in Child Development, 50* (1–2, serial no. 209), 257–275.

Schaffer, H. R. & Emerson, P. E. (1964). *The development of social attachments in infancy. Monographs of the Society for Research in Child Development, 29* (whole no. 94).

Segal, L. B., Oster, H., Cohen, M., Caspi, B., Myers, M. & Brown, D. (1995). Smiling and fussing in seven-month-old preterm and full-term Black infants in the still-face situation. *Child Development, 66,* 1829–1843.

Sera, M. D., Troyer, D. & Smith, L. B. (1988). What do two-year-olds know about the sizes of things? *Child Development, 59,* 1489–1496.

Singer, W. (1995). Development and plasticity of cortical processing architectures. *Science, 270,* 758–764.

Sophian, C. & Yengo, L. (1985). Infants' understanding of visible displacements. *Developmental Psychology, 21,* 932–941.

Spelke, E. S., von Hofsten, C. & Kestenbaum, R. (1989). Object perception in infancy: Interaction of spatial and kinetic information for object boundaries. *Developmental Psychology, 25,* 185–186.

Sroufe, L. A. (1979). Socioemotional development. In J. D. Osofsky (Ed.), *Handbook of infant development,* New York: John Wiley & Sons, 462–516.

Sroufe, L. A. (1985). Attachment classification from the perspective of infant–caregiver relationships and infant temperament. *Child Development, 56,* 1–14.

Sroufe, L. A., Schork, E., Motti, F., Lawroski, N. & La Freniere, P. (1984). The role of affect in social competence. In C. E. Izard, J. Kagan & R. B. Zajonc (Eds.), *Emotions, cognition, and behavior.* Cambridge: Cambridge University Press, 38–72.

Stack, D. M. & Muir, D. W. (1992). Adult tactile stimulation during face-to face interactions modulates five-month-olds' affect and attention. *Child Development, 63,* 1509–1525.

Sullivan, M. W., Lewis, M. & Allesandri, S. M. (1992). Cross-age stability in emotional expressions during learning and extinction. *Developmental Psychology, 28,* 58–63.

Super, C. M., Kagan, J., Morrison, F. J., Haith, M. M. & Weiffenbach, J. (1972). Discrepancy and attention in the five-month infant. *Genetic Psychology Monographs, 85,* 305–331.

Teller, D. Y. & Bornstein, J. H. (1987). Infant color vision and color perception. In P. Salapatek & L.

Cohen (Eds.), *Handbook of infant perception* (vol. 1). Orlando, Fla.: Academic Press.

Thelen, E. (1995). Motor development: A new synthesis. *American Psychologist, 50,* 79–95.

Thomas, A. & Chess, S. (1977). *Temperament and development.* New York: Bruner/Mazel.

Thomas, A. & Chess, S. (1980). *The dynamics of psychological development.* New York: Bruner/Mazel.

Thomas, A. & Chess, S. (1986). The New York longitudinal study: From infancy to early adult life. In R. Plomin & J. Dunn (Eds.), *The study of temperament: Changes, continuities, and challenges.* Hillsdale, N.J.: Erlbaum.

Thomas, A., Chess, S. & Birch, H. (1970). The origin of personality. *Scientific American, 223,* 102–109.

Thompson, R. A., Connell, J. P. & Bridges, L. J. (1988). Temperament, emotion, and social interactive behavior in the strange situation: A component process analysis of attachment system functioning. *Child Development, 59,* 1102–1110.

Tracy, R. L. & Ainsworth, M. D. S. (1981). Maternal affectionate behavior and infant–mother attachment patterns. *Child Development, 52,* 1341–1343.

Tronick, E. Z. (1989). Emotions and emotional communication in infants. *American Psychologist, 44,* 112–119.

Tronick, E. Z., Als, H. & Brazelton, R. B. (1979). Early development of neonatal and infant behavior. In F. Falkner & J. M. Tanner (Eds.), *Human growth* (vol. 3). *Neurobiology and nutrition.* New York: Plenum, 305–328.

Uzgiris, I. C. & Hunt, J. M. V. (1975). *Assessment in infancy: Ordinal scales of psychological development.* Urbana: University of Illinois Press.

van Ijzendoorn, M. H., Goldberg, S., Kroonenberg, P. M. & Frenkel, O. J. (1992). The relative effects of maternal and child problems on the quality of attachment: A meta-analysis of attachment in clinical samples. *Child Development, 63,* 840–858.

van Ijzendoorn, M. H. & Kroonenberg, P. M. (1988). Cross-cultural patterns of attachment: A meta-analysis of the strange situation. *Child Development, 59,* 147–156.

Vaughn, B. E., Lefever, G. B., Seifer, R. & Barglow, P. (1989). Attachment behavior, attachment security, and temperament during infancy. *Child Development, 60,* 728–737.

Walden, T. A. & Ogan, T. A. (1988). The development of social referencing. *Child Development, 59,* 1230–1240.

Walker-Andrews, A. S. (1986). Intermodal perception of expressive behaviors: Relation of eye and voice? *Developmental Psychology, 22,* 373–377.

Watson, J. S. (1970). Smiling, cooing, and "the game." Miami Beach: Paper presented at the annual meeting of the American Psychological Association.

Wellman, H. M., Cross, D. & Bartsch, K. (1986). *Infant search and object permanence: A meta-analysis of the A-not-B error. Monographs of the Society for Research in Child Development, 51* (3, serial no. 214 whole).

Wentworth, N. & Haith, M. M. (1992). Event-specific expectations of 2- and 3-month-old infants. *Developmental Psychology, 28,* 842–850.

Werker, J. F. (1989). Becoming a native listener. *American Scientist, 77,* 54–59.

Wilson, R. S. & Matheny, A. P., Jr. (1986). Behavior genetics research in infant temperament: The Louisville twin study. In R. Plomin & J. Dunn (Eds.), *The study of temperament: Changes, continuities, and challenges.* Hillsdale, N.J.: Erlbaum.

Wolff, P. H. (1963). Observations on the early development of smiling. In B. M. Foss (Ed.), *Determinants of infant behavior* (vol. 2). New York: Wiley.

Wolff, P. H. (1966). Causes, controls, and organization of behavior in the neonate. *Psychological Issues, 5* (1, whole no. 17).

Wolff, P. H. (1987). *The development of behavioral states and the expression of emotions in early infancy.* Chicago: University of Chicago Press.

Yarrow, L. J., McQuiston, S., MacTurk, R. H., McCarthy, M. E., Klein, R. P. & Vietze, P. M. (1983). The assessment of mastery motivation during the first year of life. *Developmental Psychology, 19,* 159–171.

Yarrow, L. J., Pedersen, F. A. & Rubenstein, J. (1977). Mother–infant interaction and development in infancy. In P. H. Leiderman, S. R. Tulkin & A. Rosenfeld (Eds.), *Culture and infancy: Variations in the human experience.* New York: Academic Press, 539–564.

Younger, B. (1992). Developmental change in infant categorization: The perception of correlations among facial features. *Child Development, 63,* 1526–1535.

Zeskind, P. S., Klein, L. & Marshall, T. R. (1992). Adult's perceptions of experimental modifications of durations of pauses and expiratory sounds in infant crying. *Developmental Psychology, 28,* 1153–1162.

Zucker, K. J. (1985). The infant's construction of his parents in the first six months of life. In T. M. Field & N. A. Fox (Eds.), *Social perception in infants.* Norwood, N.J.: Ablex.

Expanding the Psychosocial Analysis of Infancy

The Psychosocial Crisis: Trust
Versus Mistrust

Trust

Mistrust

Resolving the Crisis of Trust Versus Mistrust

The Central Process for Resolving the Crisis

Mutuality with the Caregiver

Coordination, Mismatch, and Repair of Interactions

Establishing a Functional Rhythm in the Family

Parents with Psychological Problems

The Prime Adaptive Ego Quality and the Core Pathology

Hope

Withdrawal

Factors in the Transition to Parenthood and Grandparenthood

The Transition to Parenthood

Parenting as a Stimulus for Adult Development

The Transition to Grandparenthood

Defining the Grandparent Role

The Impact of Grandparents on Grandchildren

Cultural and Ethnic Patterns That Create Distinctive Child-Rearing Environments

Feeding and Weaning

Breast and Bottle Feeding

Weaning

Safety in the Physical Environment

Disease

Environmental Toxins

Dangers in the Home

Social Issues: Parental Employment and Infant Child Care

The Effects of Maternal Employment on Interactions with Infants

Maternal Employment and Infant Attachment

Parental Values about Maternal Employment

The Nature and Quality of Alternative Care

Availability

Quality

The Costs of Infant Care

Social Policies and the Care of Infants

Chapter Summary

References

Chapter 8

I n this chapter, we extend the psychosocial analysis of infancy by examining the dynamics of the psychosocial crisis of trust versus mistrust and the central process that contributes to its resolution—establishing mutuality with the caregiver. This chapter also examines the social context within which infancy takes place, focusing on the psychosocial adjustments of the infant's first-time parents and grandparents. This exploration of changing roles directs attention once again to the dynamic interdependence between children and their significant adults. The cultural context of infancy is explored in two examples of diversity in the child-rearing environment: feeding and weaning patterns and concerns about safety in the environment. The societal context is highlighted by exploring the current crisis in infant care in the United States. The chapter ends with suggestions on optimizing development for people who are or will be caregivers for infants.

The Psychosocial Crisis: Trust Versus Mistrust

The term *psychosocial crisis* refers to a state of tension between the individual's developmental needs and the culture's social expectations. At each stage of life, the crisis is expressed as a struggle between the positive and the negative poles of a critical dimension. In infancy, the specific nature of the crisis, trust versus mistrust, focuses on an infant's fundamental sense of connection to the social world.

Trust

In adult relationships, *trust* refers to confidence in the predictability, dependability, and genuineness of another person (Rempel, Holmes & Zanna, 1985). Trust emerges in the course of a relationship as one person discovers that the other is honest, understanding, and dependable. As the level of trust grows, the partners may take some risks by disclosing information or feelings that could lead to rejection. Relationships that endure through periods of risk deepen in feelings of trust. However, trust is more than a summary of the past: It is a faith that the relationship will survive the uncertainties of an unpredictable future. This faith begins in infancy. A trusting relationship links confidence about the past with faith about the future.

For infants, trust is an emotion—a sense of confidence that their needs will be met and that they are valued. Trust is inferred from the infant's increasing capacity to delay gratification and from the warmth and delight that are evident in interactions with family members. The sense of trust expands from confidence in immediate figures in the social environment to an expectation about the supportiveness and responsiveness of the broader social and physical world. Infants also learn to trust their sensory systems in processing stimulation from the environment—in other words, trusting themselves.

The sense of basic trust is related to, but not identical to, Bowlby's concept of attachment (Bowlby, 1980). Attachment is a more limited construct that refers to the behavioral system ensuring safety and security for the infant. Gradually, the internal representation of the attachment relationship general-

Infants can draw on their sense of trust to overcome wariness in a new situation.

izes to other dyadic relationships, especially where issues of intimacy and protection are relevant.

Trust is a broader construct. Within the framework of trust, infants not only assess the trustworthiness of central social figures in their world but also achieve a sense of their own value and trustworthiness. Over time, a basic sense of trust expands to a global optimism about how one expects to be treated by others and about one's ability to cope with life's challenges. Trust is an integrating force that helps synthesize emotions, cognitions, and actions under uncertain conditions, allowing the pursuit of goals with a basic orientation that things will work out well.

Mistrust

During infancy, experiences of *mistrust* can arise from at least three sources: infant wariness, lack of confidence in the caregiver, and insecurity about one's own lovability. Wariness, one of the earliest infant emotions, is linked initially to at least two infant reflexes, the startle response in reaction to loud noises and the Moro reflex in response to sudden loss of support. One might say that all infants are instinctively prewired to be alert to certain environmental dangers. One of the caregiver's functions is to minimize the infant's exposure to stimuli that evoke these reflexes and to comfort and reassure babies when they encounter stimuli that are interpreted as threatening.

Second, babies can lack confidence in the good intentions of others. If the caregiver is unable to understand and respond appropriately to the infant's needs or is unusually harsh, seeds of doubt about the trustworthiness of the environment may be planted in the infant. Third, as babies experience the powerful violence of their own rage, they may doubt their own lovability.

MISTRUST IN INFANCY:
- wariness
- lack of confidence in intentions
- doubt own loveability

BOX 8.1

Is There a Critical Period for Attachment?

A *critical period* is a time of maximal sensitivity or readiness for developing certain skills or behavior patterns. The particular skill or behavior pattern is not likely to emerge before the onset of the critical period, and it is extremely difficult, if not impossible, to establish once the critical period has passed. The successful emergence of any behavior that has a critical period for development depends on the coordination of biological readiness and environmental supports (Scott, 1987).

Examples of critical periods for physical development were discussed in Chapter 6 when we considered the vulnerability of the fetus to certain viruses, drugs, and environmental toxins. Exposure of a human embryo to the rubella virus during the first trimester of gestation can cause massive disruption in the formation of body organs. The third month of gestation is a critical period for sexual development. In the presence of the hormone testosterone, the bisexual fetus becomes an anatomical male. In the absence of that hormone, the fetus becomes an anatomical female.

Konrad Lorenz (1935, 1937/1961) was one of the first ethologists to compare the critical periods in physical development and those in behavioral development. Lorenz described a process of social attachment among birds that he called *imprinting*. In this process, the young bird establishes a comparatively permanent bond with its mother. In her absence, the young bird will imprint on other available targets, including a model of its mother or a human being. For birds, the onset of the critical period coincides with the timing of their ability to walk. The critical period

ends when they begin to fear strangers. After this point, no new model or species can serve as a substitute for imprinting. The long-lasting results of imprinting include not only the early maintenance of contact with the mother bird, but also influence courting and mating behaviors during a bird's reproductive period.

In human development, the concept of a critical period for attachment, that is, a specific time during infancy when the child develops a strong, well-differentiated preference for one person, is controversial. It is fairly obvious that, soon after a child's birth, a parent's attachment to his or her child becomes quite specific—that is, a parent would not be willing to replace that child with any other child of similar age. The question is whether there is a distinct time when children are most likely to form such an attachment to their primary caregiver and whether such attachments can be formed after this period.

The most direct way to answer this question is to separate an infant from his or her mother and observe the consequences in the infant's ability to establish a bond with a new caregiver. Since such experimentation would be highly unethical, relevant evidence has been systematically gathered from situations in which the mother–infant relationship has been disrupted naturally.

Leon Yarrow (1963, 1964, 1970) observed 100 infants who were adopted after living in foster homes. The infants who were separated from their foster mothers at six months or earlier showed minimal distress. They did not tend to express prolonged anger or depression over separation if their physical

Most parents also contribute to experiences of mistrust by their inevitable mistakes in responding to their infant's signs of distress, particularly when babies are very small. They may try giving the baby a bottle and, if crying continues, changing diapers, rocking and singing, or putting the child to bed until something "works." Over time, however, they learn to interpret their child's signals correctly and to respond appropriately, thereby fostering the infant's sense of trust in the environment (Kropp & Haynes, 1987).

It appears that feelings of doubt or anxiety about the bond of trust are more common than may have been expected. About one-third of American infant–mother pairs who have been systematically observed show evidence of an insecure attachment. Cross-cultural research provides further evidence

and emotional needs continued to be met. As separation anxiety is not usually observed before about nine months, it is not surprising that these infants adapted so well to longer separations before this age.

All the infants who were transferred from foster mothers to adoptive mothers at eight months or older showed strong negative reactions, including angry protest and withdrawal. These infants found the disruption of their earlier relationships very stressful. One cannot, however, infer from these observations that these infants did not eventually form new attachments to their adoptive parents.

Later research by John Bowlby (1980) focused on adolescents who had moved repeatedly from one foster home or institution to another. These children never had any opportunity to form an enduring, stable loving relationship with a caring adult. As adolescents, they were described as *affectionless,* unable to form mutually trusting or close relationships with others. Other more recent studies confirm that children who spend their infancy in institutions where the turnover in caregivers is high show disruptions in social functioning, including indiscriminate friendship formation and difficulty in forming close relationships and finding emotional support from peers (Rutter, 1995).

From these real-world examples of disruption in the mother–infant relationship, we can say that the onset of a critical period for attachment must begin some time after six months of age. This does not mean that the first six months are unimportant for forming a strong bond between the child and the caregiver. On the contrary, these early months provide the foundation of consistency, warmth, and familiarity upon which the specific attachment is built.

If the critical period for attachment begins at about six months of age, when might this period be over? This question is more difficult to answer. The quality of the attachment relationship is established well before 24 months. Longitudinal studies have reported consistency in the quality of attachment from 12 to 18 months, from 12 to 20 months, and from 12 months to 6 years. Barring prolonged separation, it appears that the mental representation of the attachment is shaped by the end of the first year of life (Main, Kaplan & Cassidy, 1985). The question that remains to be answered is whether there really is a time after which a secure attachment can no longer be established. If there is no opportunity to form a consistent, long-term relationship with a loving adult, as in the case of the young people whom Bowlby studied, no attachment will be formed. In a study of children who spent their first years of life in an institution where the quality of care was good but staff turnover was high, children who were adopted at age 2 were able to form secure attachments to their adoptive parents. However, at ages 8 and 16, they showed evidence of difficulty in peer relations that were similar to the children who remained in the institution (Hodges & Tizard, 1989). Although this question continues to be explored, we can surmise that lack of continuity in caregiving during infancy, such as might occur in institutions or in shifts from one foster home to the next, is likely to produce long-lasting disruptions in relationship formation, even if a secure attachment with a caregiver is formed at a later time.

that a significant proportion of infants have difficulty deriving emotional comfort or security from their attachment relationships (Posada et al., 1995, van Ijzendoorn & Kroonenberg, 1988;).

In addition to the mistrust that emerges from inconsistent or unresponsive caregiving, there are many situations that disrupt the mother–infant relationship (see Box 8.1). In extreme cases, parents grossly neglect their infants. They may leave a baby alone without anyone to care for his or her needs. They may neglect to change or bathe the baby. They do not treat the baby's illnesses or protect the child from danger. They may consistently express hostility to the infant or provide almost no communication at all (Lyons-Ruth et al., 1987). Under these circumstances, infants discover that their parents are physically and psychologically unavailable (Egeland & Sroufe, 1981). The infant's growing mistrust stems from an inability to gain physical or psychological comfort.

Mistrust may manifest itself in an infant's withdrawal from interaction and in symptoms of depression and grief, which include sobbing, apathy, lethargy, and loss of appetite (Field et al., 1988). Mistrust may also be observed in the interpersonal distress expressed by angry, anxious, and resistant children with insecure attachments or in their inability to form close, satisfying relationships with others as they grow older. Finally, mistrust may provide a foundation for the emergence of a negative scheme about the self that is elaborated over time by attributes such as cautiousness, nervousness, or introversion (Malle & Horowitz, 1995).

Resolving the Crisis of Trust Versus Mistrust

In infancy, as in each of the other life stages, resolving the psychosocial conflict is integrated with mastering the relevant developmental tasks. All infants experience some aspects of the negative pole, mistrust, either as a result of mismatches between their needs and the caregiving they receive or their own difficulties in modulating strong feelings of fear or anger. Thus, resolving the crisis of trust successfully represents a real psychological achievement in minimizing wariness of the environment and regulating inner passions.

A positive resolution of the crisis of trust versus mistrust will facilitate psychological growth. Children who experience a basic sense of security are able to engage fully in relationships. They are in a strong position to explore their environment and to encounter novelty with curiosity and self-confidence (Aber & Allen, 1987).

Over the life course, the sense of trust is transformed and matures into an inner paradigm for understanding life. Among older adults who have a strong sense of trust, many of life's disappointments and complexities are minimized by a growing faith in God. A basic sense of trust evolves into a powerful belief in a universal source of goodness and love that can transcend daily tragedies and give integrity and meaning to death as well as to life (Erikson, Erikson & Kivnick, 1986).

The Central Process for Resolving the Crisis

Mutuality with the Caregiver

To resolve the crisis of trust versus mistrust an infant must establish a feeling of *mutuality* with a caregiver. Initially, this mutuality depends on the consistency with which the caregiver responds appropriately to the infant's needs. When a baby cries because of thirst, the caregiver should be able to interpret that cry and give the child water rather than changing the child's diaper. The caregiver learns to appreciate the variety of an infant's needs, and the infant learns to expect that personal needs will be met.

An infant influences a caregiver's responses in many ways. The degree of an infant's irritability contributes to the kinds of responses that adults make to them. Infants can reject or end an interaction by fussing, becoming tense, crying, or falling asleep. They can maintain an interaction by smiling, cooing, snuggling, or maintaining eye contact. Comforting techniques do not call forth the same responses from all babies (Campos, 1989). A pacifier helps comfort some babies, while others respond to being wrapped snugly in a blanket.

An infant and a caregiver learn to regulate the speed required in satisfying a need. In a study of mother–infant interactions, Bell and Ainsworth (1972) observed mothers' responses to infant crying during the first year of life. Over the course of the year, the infants' crying decreased and mothers tended to respond more quickly to their cries. This finding suggests a process of mutual adaptation by mothers and infants. Some mothers came quickly and ignored few cries. Other mothers waited a long time and ignored much of the crying. A striking finding was that the longer mothers delayed in responding to their infants' cries, the more crying the infants did in later months. Babies whose mothers responded promptly in the first six months of life cried less often in the second six months.

Coordination, Mismatch, and Repair of Interactions

The study of mutuality with the caregiver focused in some detail on patterns and rhythms of social interaction, especially coordination, matching, and synchrony (Brazelton, Koslowski & Main, 1974; Tronik & Cohn, 1989). _Coordination_ refers to two related characteristics of interaction: matching and synchrony. _Matching_ means that the infant and the caregiver are involved in similar behaviors or states at the same time. They may be playing together with an object, cooing and smiling at each other, or feeling angry at each other. _Synchrony_ means that the infant and the caregiver move from one state to the next in a fluid pattern. When infants are paying attention to their caregivers, the caregivers attempt to stimulate them. As infants withdraw attention, caregivers learn to reduce stimulation and wait until the infants are ready to engage again (see Notebook Page 8.1).

In the normal pattern of development, mother–infant interactions become increasingly coordinated (Isabella & Belsky, 1991; Tronick & Cohn, 1989); however, this does not mean that most of the interactions are coordinated. In fact, especially when babies are very young, matched interactions appear to become mismatched rather quickly. A mother and infant may be engaged in a period of cooing and laughing. The mother makes a funny noise, the baby reacts by cooing and laughing, the mother makes the noise again, and the baby laughs. On the third try, the mother cannot get the baby to make eye contact. She may try shifting the baby to another position or making the noise at a different pitch, but the baby looks away and squirms. The game is over and the connection temporarily broken. The explanation for these frequent failures in coordination may lie partly in the infant's rapid shift of need states and inability to sustain coordinated communication and partly in the adult's inability to sustain lengthy nonverbal communication. In normal mother–infant pairs, however, periods of mismatch are usually followed by _communication repairs,_ so that infants and mothers cycle again through periods of coordinated interactions.

At a theoretical level, this process of coordination, mismatch, and repair can be viewed as a fundamental building block for mutuality. Infants and caregivers gain confidence in their ability to communicate. Infants have many opportunities to experience the satisfaction of shared communication and the sense of being integrated in a responsive social environment. They also experience frequent recovery from a mismatched state to a state of effective communication, so that they learn to be hopeful about the ability to make these repairs in the future.

Coordination, Mismatch, and Repair

The coordination of social interaction is a fundamental element in creating a sense of mutuality in the mother–infant relationship. This process continues to underlie the quality of communication in adult relationships as well. Think for a moment of a situation in which you were having a conversation with someone and you either thought to yourself or said to the other person, "You don't understand what I mean" or "You just don't get it." Your conversation had shifted from a state of coordination to one of mismatch. At that point, you have the choice of either trying to repair the conversation or giving up.

Think of two examples in your own experience when you tried to repair a mismatch in a conversation. For each example, describe the nature of the conversation, what were you talking about, what may have caused the mismatch (for example, you made a joke, but the other person took you seriously), and what you did to try to repair the conversation in order to return to a state of coordination. If possible, choose one example when you were talking with a peer and one example when you were talking with someone older or younger than you.

1. Example 1.

    a. The conversation was about: _____

    _____

    b. The mismatch was a result of: _____

    _____

    c. To repair the mismatch, I: _____

    _____

2. Example 2.

    a. The conversation was about: _____

    _____

    b. The mismatch was a result of: _____

    _____

    c. To repair the mismatch, I: _____

    _____

Establishing a Functional Rhythm in the Family

The match or mismatch between an infant's rhythms and the family's rhythms is an important factor in a family's overall adjustment to a new baby (Sprunger, Boyce & Gaines, 1985). Some babies are quite predictable; their sleeping, eating, playtime, and even fussy periods follow a clear pattern. Other babies are much less regular. All babies are changing rapidly during the first 24 months of life, so daily patterns are bound to change, and families must make frequent adjustments in order to continue to meet the infant's needs. The essential spirit of mutuality depends on confidence that basic needs will be met. Because of this confidence, both the child and the parents are willing to modify their behavior. The product is a rhythmic, interdependent system (Osofsky & Connors, 1979).

Initially, most parents act on the infant's needs and schedule, which establishes the foundation of trust and mutuality. In American culture, by the end of the first year of life, babies are typically expected to modify their schedule of needs so that they sleep when the rest of the family sleeps, play when the rest of the family is awake, and eat three or at most four times a day, generally when the other family members eat.

During the second year of life, the demands of parenting change. Infants become more mobile and have new capacities to initiate activities. Their attention span increases, and they require more stimulation. They also have new areas of wariness and resistance—things they don't want to do (like take a nap) or people they don't like (such as a certain baby-sitter). These and other changes require adaptation on the parents' part in order to sustain the mutuality that had been achieved or to rectify problems in attachment and trust that may now be evident. The rhythmic pattern in the family is not permanent. Infants' new developmental competencies, changes in the demands on caregivers, shifts in the relationship between the child's parents, and new expectations for socially appropriate behavior from slightly older children can all disrupt the equilibrium of mutuality during the second year of life and stimulate revisions in the pattern, tempo, and quality of family interactions (Heinicke & Guthrie, 1992).

Parents with Psychological Problems

The importance of reciprocal interactions in building trust and hope during infancy is evident from studies of parents with psychological problems. Sensitivity to an infant's emotional states, the ability to respond appropriately to an infant's needs, and the quality of common, daily interactions can all be impaired by *family risk factors*. Studies of parents who are experiencing marital discord, who have been victims of child abuse or neglect, who are depressed, or who are mentally ill suggest that the interactional cycles of these parents and their children lack synchrony (Rutter, 1990). For example, in a comparison of mothers who had been maltreated as children and those who had not, the maltreated mothers were less involved with their children during play, used fewer strategies to direct their children's activities, and spoke more negatively to their children (Alessandri, 1992).

When depressed and nondepressed mothers and their three-month-old infants were filmed in face-to-face interactions, depressed mothers and their infants were found to spend less time in matched behavior states than nondepressed mothers and their infants (Field et al., 1990). We cannot be certain of the influence of this pattern of interactions on the long-term psychosocial

Civil war has destroyed this Peruvian woman's village. Hunger, homelessness, and fear make it hard for many women to bring joy, trust, and hope into their infants' lives.

development of the infants, but some seem to experience depression and a sense of mistrust. If the mothers recover from their depression, or if the infants have opportunities to interact with other, nondepressed adults, the dyad may establish more positive social interaction patterns (see Box 8.2).

An early intervention study with mother–infant pairs assessed as having anxious attachments helps clarify those aspects of mutuality that may be most amenable to repair. The study involved 100 Spanish-speaking mothers who had recently immigrated from Mexico or Central America and their 12-month-old babies (Lieberman, Weston & Pawl, 1991). These families were considered to be at risk for attachment disturbances because the combination of poverty, unemployment, and sudden cultural transition increased both anxiety and depression among the mothers. The mother–infant dyads were assessed using a home visit and observation in the strange situation. Of those who could be clearly classified, 34 anxious dyads were placed in the experimental intervention program, 25 anxious dyads were placed in the anxious control group, and 34 secure dyads were placed in a second, secure control group. The intervention involved weekly home visits with a trained intervenor over the second year of life.

The intervenors' efforts focused on two themes. First, they tried to encourage the mother to express her own feelings, including her longings for security, her concerns for protection and safety during her childhood and in the present, and her negative feelings of self-doubt and anger toward others, including the child and the intervenor. Second, intervenors provided developmentally relevant information about the child, including observations about the child's temperament, suggestions about age-appropriate opportunities for exploration, and strategies for negotiating mother–infant conflicts that would help restore synchrony.

BOX 8.2

Looking in on the Brain

Even at very early ages, infants are sensitive and responsive to the content and mood of their mother's interactive style. This sensitivity is evidenced not only in the manner of the infants' emotional expression and patterns of interaction but also by their pattern of frontal brain activity associated with emotion-evoking situations (Dawson et al., 1992). Infant brain activity can be monitored using the EEG (electroencephalogram, a painless technique in which electrodes are temporarily placed at specific locations on the infant's head). In normal adults and very young infants, the left frontal brain is activated under conditions of joy and interest; the right frontal brain is associated with distress and disgust. Unlike babies of nondepressed mothers, the infants of depressed mothers did not show the level of left frontal brain activity typically associated with joy and other positive emotions during playful interactions with their mothers. In a situation designed to produce negative emotions, the babies of depressed mothers showed increased left frontal brain activity when their mothers left them, a pattern opposite to expectations and totally unlike the responses of the babies of nondepressed mothers.

One interpretation of this observation is that depressed mothers fail to evoke positive emotional responses from their infants or to respond positively to their infants' positive emotions. Thus, the threshold for experiencing joy and happiness is increased in positive situations, and the babies' reactions tend to be neutral. In negative situations, the depressed mothers are also poorly coordinated with their babies, so that the babies are left to regulate negative affect on their own. A breakdown in mutual regulation of affect results in identical patterns of brain activity in depressed mothers and their babies.

The impact of the intervention was assessed at 24 months using videotapes of a 1½ hour laboratory session. The session included free play between mother and baby, play with a female stranger while the mother was present, child-directed play while the adults were unavailable, separation from the mother while the stranger remained in the room, reunion with the mother when the stranger left the room, and snack with mother, child, and observer.

Mothers in the experimental anxious attachment group showed significantly greater levels of empathy toward their children during this laboratory session than did the anxious controls. These mothers also initiated more interactions with their babies. The children showed fewer angry, avoidant, and resistant behaviors than did the anxious controls. Upon reunion after the brief separation, the mothers and children in the experimental group showed more evidence of eagerness to resume interaction than did the anxious controls. There were no significant differences between the intervention group and the securely attached controls on any of the behavioral measures at 24 months, which suggests that the intervention was effective in repairing the attachment system.

The results of this study suggest that interventions that engage the mother and support her emotional involvement in the parenting process can have a beneficial impact on the child's emotional development. We assume that this is due to the mother's greater self-acceptance and reduced frustration and her increased empathy for the child's needs and developmental level, as well as the child's improved capacity to coordinate his or her behavior with a more predictable, responsive partner.

The Prime Adaptive Ego Quality and the Core Pathology

Hope

Erikson (1982) has argued that positive resolution of the psychosocial crisis of trust versus mistrust leads to the adaptive ego quality of hope. As you will recall from Chapter 3, prime adaptive ego qualities promote openness to experience and information, the capacity to identify strategies to achieve goals, a willingness to be assertive, and a positive approach to forming close relationships. Even in the face of difficulties and stressful life events, these qualities contribute to higher levels of functioning and the preservation of a sense of well-being.

As the first of the prime adaptive ego qualities, hope pervades the entire life story. *Hope* is a global cognitive orientation that one's goals and dreams can be attained and that events will turn out for the best. As Erikson describes it, "hope bestows on the anticipated future a sense of leeway inviting expectant leaps, either in preparatory imagination or in small initiating actions. And such daring must count on basic trust in the sense of a trustfulness that must be, literally and figuratively, nourished by maternal care and—when endangered by all-too-desperate discomfort—must be restored by competent consolation" (1982, 60).

The hope that is born during infancy provides lifelong optimism in the face of risk. Throughout life, the capacity for hope stimulates us to seek new solutions to difficult challenges.

The construct of hope has received very little attention in the developmental research literature. Research has shown that adults who have a hopeful, optimistic outlook about the future have different beliefs about and emotional reactions to achievement than do people with a pessimistic outlook (Dweck, 1992; Norem & Kantor, 1988). People who have higher levels of hopefulness have more and varied goals and select more difficult tasks. Hopefulness is generally associated with higher goals, more confidence that goals will be reached, and greater persistence in the face of barriers to goal attainment, thus leading to higher overall levels of performance (Snyder et al., 1991).

Within the psychosocial framework, hope can be seen as the platform from which very young children take certain "leaps of faith." Hope provides the positive orientation for active exploration of the environment, a process upon which much of subsequent cognitive growth depends. When you see an infant overcome doubts and hesitancy in taking that first independent step, you see the dividend of hope. When you watch a toddler clamber over the bars of her crib and lower herself to the floor, you see the dividend of hope. And as a parent, when you give your adolescent the keys to the car and watch as he or she drives off alone, you see the dividend of hope. There are so many instances in life when we are faced with the choice of growing by taking a leap into an unknown future or stagnating by withdrawing from those risks. Without hope, neither the individual nor society could bear the weight of uncertainty in our changing world.

Withdrawal

As a core pathology, *withdrawal* refers to a general orientation of wariness toward people and objects. Withdrawal is especially disturbing during infancy since healthy development depends on a pattern of outward motion, extension, and increasing engagement with the social and physical worlds. Infants typically achieve mobility by learning to reach and grasp, crawl, stand, and walk. They explore through gazing, mouthing, and manipulating objects. Their behavior is typically characterized by interest in novelty, joy in learning, and frustration at encountering barriers to achievement of goals. Over the first year, babies become increasingly connected to significant figures in their social world, following them about, devising strategies to engage them in interaction, and depending on them for consolation when they are distressed. Infants who withdraw may show evidence of passivity, lethargy, and neutral or negative affect. They are not readily engaged in social interaction and do not show the self-directed exploration typical of most healthy infants.

One of the earliest descriptions of withdrawal in infancy was provided by Rene Spitz's (1945, 1946) analysis of children who had been institutionalized before one year of age. The babies who suffered the most had been placed in a foundling home in which eight babies were cared for by one nurse. These babies went through a phase of initial rage, followed by a period of physical and emotional withdrawal. They lay passively in their cribs, showing limited motor exploration and little emotionality. They rarely smiled or showed excitement. Their babbling and language were extremely delayed. They deteriorated physically. Their measured developmental level dropped substantially over a year's time. These babies suffered from a combination of a loss of their attachment figure, a lack of meaningful social interaction, and an absence of appropriate sensory stimulation, all of which produced what Spitz called *anaclitic depression.* The diagnostic manual of the American Psychiatric Association (1993) refers to this disorder as *reactive attachment disorder of infancy.* Subsequent research on the effects of prolonged, early institutionalization confirms that the most detrimental elements of this type of care are the high turnover in caregivers and the lack of opportunity to form a close attachment to any single person (Rutter, 1995). Other conditions that can produce this type of withdrawal are associated with maternal neglect caused by severe maternal depression, maternal isolation, extreme deprivation and neglect in the mother's own childhood, and prolonged disruption of contact between the mother and her baby.

Withdrawal may stem partly from genetically determined temperamental characteristics. As we discussed in Chapter 7, some babies have a very low threshold for pain. They are highly sensitive to sensory stimulation and recoil from contact that other babies find comforting or pleasurable. Some babies are more passive than others, requiring little stimulation and demonstrating less exploratory behavior than active babies.

At the extreme, some babies suffer from *infantile autism.* This condition is characterized by impaired social interaction, such as an inability to use direct gazing, facial expressions, or body postures to regulate social interactions, a delay in or total absence of verbal communication, and "restricted, repetitive, and stereotyped patterns of behavior, interests, and activities" such as "repetitive motor mannerism" or "compulsive adherence to motor routines" (American Psychiatric Association, 1993). Infantile autism is very rare, affecting about two to four cases in 10,000 babies, and is more prevalent in boys than girls. It is associated with incomplete brain development and impedes learning, especially in social competence and language skills. Autistic babies may perform certain tasks well, including motor skills and memory problems, but they seem almost oblivious to social interaction.

Is this just due to variations in personality type?

Within the more normal range of infant behavior, an orientation of withdrawal can be seen in the babies who have an anxious-avoidant or anxious-resistant attachment. For these babies, the kind of confidence and predictability that characterizes the secure attachment is missing. They show evidence of wariness and doubt in interactions with their primary caregivers, with strangers and in their investigation of the physical world. They rely on constancy and ritual to maintain a sense of control.

Babies who are excessively wary of social interaction and who recoil from novelty in the environment cannot experience the diversity of stimulation that is so crucial for new levels of cognitive complexity. They rely on the repetition of certain ritual behaviors to protect themselves from novelty and change. As they get older, children who suffer from withdrawal are likely to become preoccupied by inner fantasies and compulsive behaviors in order to achieve a sense of order and safety.

Although withdrawal and signs of depression are the primary core pathology associated with a failure to resolve the psychosocial crisis of trust, there are other maladjustments. Children of clinically depressed mothers or those who have been abused during infancy often display *aggressiveness*, particularly toward siblings and peers (Crittenden, 1992; DeMulder & Radke-Yarrow, 1991). Heightened anger and aggression during infancy and toddlerhood may disrupt the formation of social relationships and lead to peer rejection and social isolation. The increased violence among contemporary youth, the widespread use of guns and other weapons to resolve peer conflicts, and the open hostility of adolescents toward adults and peers alike suggest the need to examine conditions that may foster unresolved infantile rage.

Factors in the Transition to Parenthood and Grandparenthood

The birth of a child brings about major transitions in the lives of parents and others in the kinship network. A first child turns partners into parents, sons and daughters into fathers and mothers; fathers and mothers into grandfathers and grandmothers; and brothers and sisters into uncles and aunts. The infant's life story is embedded in the story of the generations of kinship relations. These kin will worry about the health and future of the child. Their social status will form the basis of the child's social status, and their values and beliefs will shape the child's socialization. The immediate child-rearing environment will be influenced by the psychosocial maturity of the parents, grandparents, aunts and uncles, and others who contribute to a child's care. These family members, especially the mother and father, but often extended kin, typically comprise the immediate radius of significant others through whom the infant first encounters the social world. Therefore, it is important to understand the psychosocial issues that accompany the transition to parenthood and grandparenthood.

The Transition to Parenthood

In contrast to the elated anticipation of and preparation for a first child, the actual arrival of the newborn often brings a period of stress to the new parents (Cowan & Cowan, 1988). The birth of a child introduces disequilibrium into the family system, requiring role adjustments, reorganization and redistribution of resources, and the formation of new relationships within the family. Disequilibrium introduces new opportunities for learning, coping, and adapting. It may also bring about maladaptation if the partners lack the ego strengths to adapt to these new demands or if the marital relationship is already distressed. On the average, the presence of children in the family is associated with lower marital satisfaction and less marital happiness, although ratings of marital satisfaction do not usually drop dramatically (Belsky & Pensky, 1988; Glenn & McLanahan, 1982).

Belsky and Rovine (1990) found clear evidence of individual differences among couples regarding this pattern. In their longitudinal study of 128 families, they observed four patterns of change in the assessment of marital quality. Some couples showed rapid decline in marital quality after the baby was born. Some showed a slow, steady decline. A third group showed no significant change, and a fourth group showed slight increases in marital quality. These findings caution us against overgeneralizing about individual cases from group trends.

Generally, the quality of marital adjustment over the transition to parenthood is closely related to marital quality before the child was born (Heinicke, 1995). Couples who are in close, confiding, satisfying marriages before their children are born tend to show higher levels of marital adjustment three months after childbirth (Cox et al., 1989; Wallace & Gotleib, 1990). The idea that having a baby will bring a couple closer together does not seem to be supported by the research literature. If the husband and wife have high levels of conflict and are disappointed in the quality of their marriage before a baby is born, these difficulties are likely to increase after childbirth.

The decline in marital satisfaction that often accompanies the transition to parenthood can be accounted for in several ways (see Box 8.3). For the first months after a child is born, both parents are exhausted from lack of sleep. They have new responsibilities and a new schedule. Many parents feel inadequate to care for their babies, and they turn to their parents, friends, pediatricians, and books for parenting advice. This lack of self-confidence may create tension between the marriage partners.

Potential conflicts may arise about child-rearing philosophies or childcare practices. Feelings of jealousy, competition, and abandonment may arise between partners in the first months after their child is born. The exclusiveness of the couple's relationship is interrupted by the baby's constant demands. In comparison with childless couples, new parents find themselves making more traditional, gender-specific assignments of family and household roles, which cause increased dissatisfaction (Cowan & Cowan, 1988). Feelings of resentment may be stronger when a couple's sex-role attitudes conflict with their assignments (Belsky, Lang & Huston, 1986).

It is not surprising that one's own childhood experiences influence one's reactions to the parent role. It might be a bit more surprising to realize that the level of marital satisfaction experienced after the birth of one's first child is related to one's childhood environment. One study reported a more pronounced decline in marital quality after the birth of the first child when either the husband or wife recalled their own parents as cold, rejecting, and involved in a conflictual marriage. In addition, negative childhood experiences were related to greater discrepancies between husbands' and wives' assessments of their marital quality after their children were born (Belsky & Isabella, 1985).

BOX 8.3

A Comparison of Parents and Nonparents

In an attempt to clarify the relationship of changes in marital satisfaction to the transition to parenthood, researchers compared marital activities and evaluations of the marriage by parents and nonparents who had been married the same number of years (MacDermid, Huston & McHale, 1990). Over the first three years of marriage, couples' ratings of *love* and *satisfaction* in their marriage declined somewhat. There were no differences in the magnitude of the decline for parents and nonparents. Having children did not account for a greater drop in love or satisfaction than appears to occur simply as a result of adjusting to marriage in general. This observation provides new insight into much of the earlier research on marital satisfaction and the transition to parenthood.

However, having children did have a clear impact on marital *companionship*. The percentage of leisure activities shared by the husband and the wife dropped sharply after their baby was born, but declined only slightly for couples without children. During the third year of marriage, parents had a greater number of shared activities per day than nonparents, but very few of those activities occurred when the child was not present. The figure at right shows the number of minutes of joint leisure per day without the child for two groups of parents in comparison with joint leisure for nonparents in the first, second, and third years of marriage. After the birth of their children, couples have only about one-third as many minutes together alone as they had when they were childless. The nature of companionship in mar-

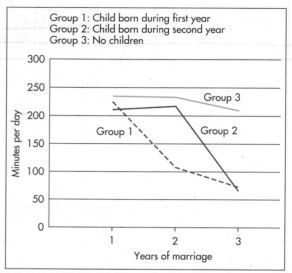

Minutes of joint leisure for parents and nonparents

Source: Based on MacDermid, S. M., Huston, T. L. & McHale, S. M. (1990). Changes in marriage associated with transition to parenthood. *Journal of Marriage and the Family, 52,* 475–486. Copyright © 1990 by the National Council on Family Relations, 3989 Central Ave. NE, Suite 550, Minneapolis, MN 55421. Reprinted by permission.

riage clearly changes to incorporate a baby and therefore may become less intimate.

One interpretation of these observations is that memories of negative childhood experiences are reawakened by the child's birth and stimulate increased defensiveness. Another interpretation may be that adults whose parents were cold and rejecting may not have developed adequate parenting skills. They encounter increased conflict with their spouses when they become parents because they are less competent in this new role.

It is ironic that many couples decide to have a child as an expression of their desire to become even closer, but most of them discover that pregnancy and the early years of child-rearing actually introduce a new degree of separateness in their relationship. The majority of household tasks and child-care responsibilities often fall to the mother. If she withdraws from the labor force, her partner may need to spend more time at work in order to compensate for the loss of income. In some instances, women try to compensate for their loss of involvement in areas outside the home, such as work, community service, and friendships, by investing more energy in their mothering role.

Consequently, fathers may actually be discouraged from spending as much time with their babies as they may wish (Cowan & Cowan, 1988). In some instances, the father simply does not have the personality characteristics that orient him toward an active role in his infant's care, so more child-care responsibilities are left by default to the mother (Volling & Belsky, 1991). When one partner is disappointed in the amount of time and involvement that the other is giving to household tasks and child care, the outcome is often an increase in marital dissatisfaction, as well as perceived stress surrounding the parental role (see Notebook Page 8.2).

Parents who experience higher levels of partner support and closeness also provide a more optimal environment for child development. Especially for men, the quality of the relationship they have with their partner is a strong predictor of the quality of their relationship with their infant. The more engaged and satisfied a man is with his partner, the more likely he is to be actively involved in the care of his child and to express satisfaction with the father role (Parke, 1995).

A number of studies have found a close relationship between marital support and parental competence. Other studies link parents' marital conflict to their children's cognitive delays, difficulties in school adjustment, and antisocial behavior with peers (Miller et al., 1993). Husbands and wives look to each other for reassurance that they are capable and valued. The encouragement that partners give to one another permits them to function in a warm, responsive, and positive manner with their children. Looking back to the psychosocial framework for adult development, the capacity to achieve intimacy in an adult relationship has important implications for individual adjustment and the ability to care for the next generation.

Parenting as a Stimulus for Adult Development

Parenting is a unique stimulus for psychosocial development (Newman & Newman, 1988). There may be some developmental antecedents to parenting, such as baby-sitting, caring for younger siblings, or working with children as a camp counselor or teacher. However, none of these roles involves the emotional investment and total responsibility of parenthood. In parenting, adults have opportunities to discover new aspects of their personalities.

[handwritten margin note: Parenting leads to the discovery of new aspects of personality.]

Infants actively engage parents, evoke unique responses, and, through their behaviors, begin to shape adults' parenting behaviors. As infants achieve new competence, such as motor skills or comprehension of language, adults modify the quality of their interactions with them (Bornstein, 1995). Mutuality is important in increasing the parents' capacity to experience intimacy. Successful child care is defined by the ability to anticipate children's needs, stimulate their interests, and delight their senses. Infants respond with unrestrained laughter, smiles, squeals, and coos. Through their open demonstrations of affection, they teach adults about the expression of love.

The parent role brings demands that are quite distinct from the role of the spouse. A parent must respond to an infant who cannot truly reciprocate one's generosity or caring. Parents discover qualities of nurturance, playfulness, and authoritativeness by interacting with their children. Memories of their own childhoods are revived and reviewed. Conflicts with their own parents, sibling jealousy, school experiences, peer relations, fears, and secret dreams are all reviewed. A new opportunity arises to put old ghosts to rest, reinterpret past events, and achieve an expanded sense of adult maturity.

Reducing Stress in the Transition to Parenthood

The transition to parenthood has been identified as a life event that can have negative consequences for the marital relationship. Review the preceding section and identify the various sources of stress in this transition, including those related to parents' views about their adult roles, their backgrounds and their own childhood experiences, the demands of infant care, characteristics of the infant, and changes that a baby brings to the marital relationship. Give four sources of possible stress that can occur in the transition to parenthood, and, for each, think of one or two strategies for preventing or reducing this stress.

Four Sources of Stress	How to Reduce or Prevent This Stress
1.	
2.	
3.	
4.	

Little has been written about the psychological growth stimulated by the decision to bear children. This is a unique and significant life decision. Even unplanned babies are products of some kind of decision, whether it was to have sexual relations knowing that pregnancy was possible, to avoid using effective means of birth control, or to go through with an unplanned pregnancy. During early adulthood, the issue of reproduction is confronted not just once, but many times. Adults make choices to delay parenting, to have another child, to wait awhile longer before having another child, or to stop having children altogether. These decisions reflect powerful psychosocial themes linked to one's sense of fulfilling a masculine or feminine role by having children, one's childhood socialization and identification with parental figures, and one's religious beliefs about sexuality, contraception, or abortion. Reproduction is the means by which the species perpetuates itself. Regardless of the decisions one reaches on this issue, it cannot help but heighten one's sense of being and one's belief that the decisions of adulthood make a difference.

The psychosocial development of parents and their children are intertwined. For parents in early adulthood, the development of a sense of intimacy is the positive resolution of the psychosocial crisis of that stage. Parents who have a close, confiding relationship—a cornerstone of intimacy—have better marital adjustment before the birth of a child than couples who do not. What is more, these couples are able to sustain higher levels of marital adjustment after the birth of their child. Better levels of marital adjustment ensure higher levels of marital satisfaction and warmer, more sensitive, and more affectionate parenting which is better for the child.

psychosocial dev't of parents and children are intertwined

This relationship is further documented in a 36-year prospective study of children who were initially studied at age 5 by Sears, Maccoby, and Levin (1957). Having a warm and affectionate father or mother was significantly associated with adult social accomplishments such as having a long, happy marriage, children, and relationships with close friends at midlife (Vaillant, 1977). People who were rated as more socially accomplished at age 41 were significantly more likely to engage in affiliative behaviors and to report warm relationships with significant others. They also reported higher levels of psychological well-being, work accomplishment, generativity, lower levels of strain, and less use of immature coping styles (Franz, McClelland & Weinberger, 1991). This analysis suggests the possible conclusion that warm parenting, which is likely to be a result of skills acquired in developing a sense of intimacy, leads to children's enhanced social functioning when they are adults.

Successful parenting is one factor that seems to lead to the development of feelings of generativity rather than stagnation in middle adulthood (McAdams & de St. Aubin, 1992). High generativity scores were associated with having children, though the generativity score was unrelated to marital status per se. The effect for parental status was particularly strong for men, who tended to show lower generativity scores if they had never been fathers. While these results are associational and cannot determine cause and effect, they lend support to studying psychosocial relationships and outcomes suggested by our guiding theory (see Figure 8.1). Positive parenting seems to be related to developing a sense of trust in infancy, a sense of intimacy in early adulthood, and a later sense of generativity. Intimacy is related to marital effectiveness and positive parenting. Parenting seems to be related to the development of feelings of generativity. It is possible that positive parenting

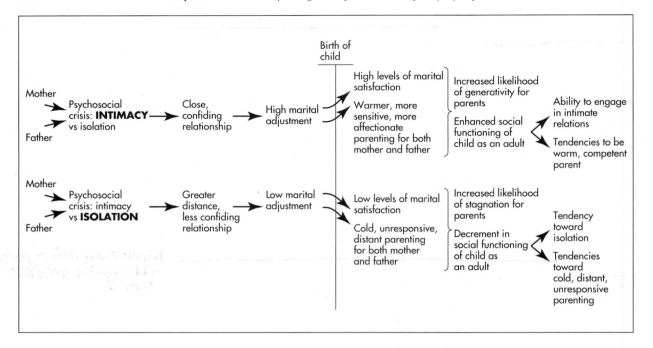

FIGURE 8.1

The relationship between intimacy in the adult generation, marital satisfaction, parental effectiveness, and enhancing psychosocial development in children

leads to enhanced psychosocial development for both child and adult, making child-rearing a vital factor in human psychosocial growth.

The Transition to Grandparenthood

Infants typically have living grandparents who influence them directly, through various forms of support and resources, as well as indirectly by providing support and resources to their parents. Research on the grandparent role has increased in the past 20 years as more families count on grandparents to provide direct assistance to children as a result of teen parenthood, single parenthood following divorce, and two-income families (Smith, 1995). Whereas this section focuses on the nature of the grandparent role and the impact of grandparents on their grandchildren, it is important to note that grandparenthood also provides a stimulus for development for the grandparent as well. The grandparent role has the potential for promoting a new perspective on time, purpose, and the meaning of life that can serve as a source of reassurance during later adulthood (Erikson, Erikson & Kivnick, 1986).

Defining the Grandparent Role

Adults differ in how they define the role of grandparent. Grandparents may see themselves as carriers of family traditions and wisdom, as experts in child care, as convenient and trusted baby-sitters, or as admirers from afar. Grandparents are asked to reinvest energy in small children. The quality of the relationship that develops between grandparents and grandchildren depends not so much on the fact that they are relatives as on the kinds of experiences that the two generations share. Adults must learn to define and enact a new role.

In one of the first empirical studies of grandparenthood, Neugarten and Weinstein (1964) interviewed grandparents in 70 middle-class families. Five grandparenting styles were identified, each expressing a rather distinct interpretation of the role.

1. *Formal.* These grandparents were interested in their grandchildren but careful not to become too involved in parenting them other than by occasional baby-sitting.
2. *Fun-seeker.* These grandparents had informal, playful interactions with their grandchildren. They enjoyed mutually self-indulgent fun with them.
3. *Surrogate parent.* This style was especially likely for grandmothers who assumed major child-care responsibilities when both parents worked outside the home.
4. *Reservoir of family wisdom.* This was an authoritarian relationship in which a grandparent, usually the grandfather, dispensed skills and resources. Parents as well as grandchildren were subordinate to this older authority figure.
5. *Distant figure.* This was a grandparent who appeared on birthdays and holidays but generally had little contact with the grandchildren.

It is clear from this description of grandparenting styles that the role prescriptions for the grandparent are ambiguous enough to permit wide differences in their enactment.

In a more recent analysis of grandparent styles, Cherlin and Furstenberg (1986/1992) conducted telephone interviews with a national sample of 510 grandparents. They classified their sample into three groups: remote, companionate, and involved. The *remote grandparents* (29% of the sample) had seen their grandchildren less than once every two or three months in the past year. Most of these grandparents lived far away from their grandchildren, but in some cases the lack of contact was a result of emotional rather than physical distance.

The *companionate grandparents* (55% of the sample) had seen their grandchildren at least once every two or three months in the past year, but there was little exchange of services or resources with the child's family and very little parentlike behavior toward the child. These grandparents were likely to characterize their relationship as one in which they could have fun with their grandchildren and then send them home. They observed a "norm of noninterference" in conflicts that a child was having with parents or any concerns about the child's behavior or the parents' child-rearing strategies.

The *involved grandparents* (16% of the sample) saw their grandchildren at least once every two to three months and showed both high levels of exchanges in services and resources and high levels of parentlike behavior. In fact, most of these involved grandparents had very frequent interactions with their grandchildren. This involvement is likely to be especially concentrated when the children are young. Almost all grandparents noted that they had less time together with their grandchildren during the teen years because the children had become involved in many activities on their own. But involved grandparents were more likely to take direct action by contacting their adolescent grandchildren and making plans to spend time together. Factors such as physical proximity, the grandparent's age and health, the quality of the relationship with the child's parents, and the grandparent's views about the grandparent role all influence the grandparent style (Smith, 1995).

The Impact of Grandparents on Grandchildren

Grandparents can influence the development of grandchildren directly and indirectly. Their *direct impact* occurs as a result of the quality of their interactions. The more frequently that grandparents interact with their grandchildren and the more these grandparents perform certain parentlike functions, such as baby-sitting, giving advice, or correcting or disciplining the child, the more likely the grandchild is to perceive the grandparent as a significant family member (Cherlin & Furstenberg, 1986/1992). Grandparents' *indirect impact* occurs through providing emotional support, child-rearing advice, and various resources, including money and skills, to their own child, thereby fostering this child's parenting ability.

There are relatively few studies of the quality of interaction between grandparents and their young grandchildren. Two studies that made use of the strange situation found that the more contact that grandmothers had with their grandchildren, the more likely that infants were to treat their grandmothers as a secure base (Myers et al., 1987; Tomlin & Passman, 1989). In one observational study of grandparents and their grandchildren at play, the grandparents were viewed as highly effective play partners. They tended to be more gentle with grandchildren than were the child's parents, but also somewhat less flexible, less calm, and less confident (Tinsley & Parke, 1987). Another study focused specifically on teenage mothers and their infants who were living at home with their own fathers and mothers (Radin, Oyserman & Benn, 1991). The study involved 66 working class families, 76% white and 24% minority families. The quantity and quality of the grandfather's participation in the child-rearing of his grandchild were significantly related to the grandchild's social, emotional, and mental development. Grandfathers who were highly involved and nurturant in their interactions had a strong positive impact on their grandchildren, especially their grandsons.

Grandparents play an especially important role in supporting the development of their grandchildren under conditions of family stress (Werner, 1991). In contemporary American society, grandparents frequently serve as a resource when difficulties arise for parents. In the case of parental divorce, grandparents often assume a more central role in the lives of young children. Some custodial mothers move back home with their parents. Grandmothers often assume more child-care responsibilities during this time. Following the parents' divorce, the grandchild's relationships with his or her maternal grandparents are more likely to be enhanced, whereas the relationships with the paternal grandparents are likely to decline. Conflicts between grandparents and parents about visitation with the grandchildren have led to the passage of statutes in all 50 states permitting grandparents the legal right to petition for visitation rights even over parental objections (Thompson et al., 1989). Several longitudinal studies have shown that a child's having good, ongoing relationships with his or her grandparents during the years following divorce is associated with the ability to cope with school demands, positive relationships with peers and teachers, and fewer behavior problems. Grandfathers can play an especially important role for their grandsons who are in the custody of their mothers (Hetherington et al., 1985, 1989).

Grandparents can also play a key role when their young, unmarried daughters become pregnant, especially when the teen mothers continue to live with their parents. This pattern has been studied extensively among African-American families in which roughly 30% of the children live in an extended family (Tolson & Wilson, 1990). African-American grandmothers are likely to perceive themselves and to be perceived by their daughters as actively involved in child-rearing (Werner, 1991). In one study of 64 African-American families, a grandmother's presence was associated with a high level of moral–religious orientation in the family climate (Tolson & Wilson, 1990). Families that included two caregivers, whether they were mother and grandmother or mother and father, had somewhat lower emphasis on organization and greater opportunity for independence. Having a grandmother in the home may allow the mother to be more flexible because she doesn't have to singlehandedly enforce compliance and arrange for the accomplishment of daily tasks. This pattern of active involvement of grandparents is also seen among Native Americans where grandparents are expected to serve as mentors and disciplinarians for grandchildren. If a biological grandparent is not available to perform these functions, the child's parent may adopt an elder in the community to play this role (Miller, 1979; Werner, 1991).

Maternal employment is a third condition in which grandparents are likely to give direct support. In a national sample of 796 mothers who had children under age 5 and who were employed, 24% said that one of the child's grandmothers was the principal child-care provider (Presser, 1989). These grandmothers provided an average of 27 hours per week of child care, and almost 40 hours per week when the mothers were employed full time. Clearly, these grandmothers were intimately involved with the daily lives of their grandchildren and played a key role in the grandchildren's adjustment and well-being.

The role of grandparent is interpreted very differently by different adults. The literature suggests that, in contemporary American families, there is a range of involvement from quite distant to intimate contact in the daily rearing of grandchildren. Expectations for grandparents' direct involvement in the care and education of grandchildren differs across ethnic groups and cultures. Although the grandparent role has the potential to serve as a significant outlet for expressions of generativity, some older adults are not able to connect to their grandchildren in this way. For grandparents with either the companionate or involved styles, the role has behavioral, emotional, and symbolic significance for them and their grandchildren. Erikson (1950, 1963) links the essential continuity of the psychosocial process from one generation to the next to the ways that young children view the role of elders in their lives. When older adults are treated with dignity and serve meaningful roles in the lives of children, their integrity and sense of purpose reinforce a sense of hope in the very young (see Notebook Page 8.3).

Cultural and Ethnic Patterns That Create Distinctive Child-Rearing Environments

From an evolutionary perspective, the next critical determinant of species survival following reproduction is the parents' ability to help the newborn thrive. The two sections that follow on feeding and weaning, and safety in the physical environment, illustrate the many ways that cultures create distinctive child-rearing environments during infancy in order to increase the chances for infant survival.

Remembering Your Grandparents

Take some time to recall your grandparents and your relationships with them. For each grandparent whom you remember, try to answer the following questions.

1. What are your earliest memories of interacting with your grandparent? If your grandparent was not alive during your lifetime, what is the earliest story you can recall having heard about that person?

_____

_____

_____

_____

2. Review the material on grandparenting styles. Assign each of your grandparents to one of those styles. Give an example that illustrates why that grandparent fits the style you selected.

   a. Maternal grandmother: _____

   _____

   _____

   b. Maternal grandfather: _____

   _____

   _____

   c. Paternal grandmother: _____

   _____

   _____

   d. Paternal grandfather: _____

   _____

   _____

3. Give two examples of ways that one of your grandparents has influenced you.

a. _____

_____

_____

b. _____

_____

_____

4. Give two examples of ways that you have influenced one of your grandparents.

a. _____

_____

_____

b. _____

_____

_____

~~~~~~

From the perspective of psychosocial theory, the process of individual growth is intimately linked to cultural values and cultural adaptation. An infant's needs are comparatively simple, and survival can be assured through a few basic parenting behaviors. However, each society, with its unique environmental conditions, economy, social structure, religious beliefs, and moral values, creates and refines its own child-rearing environment.

[handwritten margin note: individual growth linked to cultural values & adaptation]

Feeding and Weaning

Survival requires access to an appropriate diet. For human newborns, this diet begins with milk. One of the distinguishing characteristics of mammals is that they feed their young with milk produced by the mother's mammary glands. Mammals can be further categorized as _continual feeders_ or _spaced feeders_. Continual feeders include those species where the baby clings to the mother or follows the mother. Spaced feeders are animals whose young spend their

313

first weeks in a nest. The milk composition of the continual and spaced feeders differs, the former having lower fat and protein content, the latter having a more concentrated composition. Continual feeders suck more slowly; spaced feeders suck more rapidly. The milk composition and sucking patterns of humans suggest that they were originally continual feeders (Konner, 1977a).

Today, most people in Western societies are spaced feeders. Even mothers who say they feed their babies on demand generally limit nursing to once every two hours or so. However, evidence of the early pattern can still be observed in some traditional cultures. The !Kung San is a hunting and gathering society living in the Kalahari Desert of southwest Africa. Konner described their nursing patterns as follows:

> Infants are fed whenever they cry and frequently when they do not cry. . . . When the infant is able to reach for the breast, he feeds himself at his leisure. This results in short (a few seconds to fifteen minutes), frequent (several times an hour during the day) feeds. At night, infants sleep immediately beside their mothers, face to face, and are fed several times, at least whenever they cry. Such feeds may occur without the mother awaking. (Konner, 1997b, 292)

The consequences of the marked shift from continuous to spaced feeding in modern, technological societies have not really been evaluated (Konner, 1977a).

Breast and Bottle Feeding

Today, one of the major decisions facing new mothers is whether to breast-feed or bottle-feed their infants. Cultures vary in their enthusiasm about breast feeding, and certain cultural subgroups are more likely to breast-feed than others. The mother's decision is heavily influenced by cultural values about infant care and beliefs about being a good mother. Among the U.S. middle class, breast feeding is coming back into fashion. It is still less popular among poor, young, and minority-group mothers. Among the traditional Sioux Indians, a woman expected to nurse her infant and did so with extreme dedication (Erikson, 1950, 1963). During the 1960s in England, working-class women regarded breast feeding as grotesque (Hubert, 1974). In a study of over 3,000 infants in Shanghai, roughly 35% of the babies were bottle-fed. Bottle feeding was more likely among more highly educated families and with male children (Chen, 1992). An historical analysis of feeding practices in Australia found that the proportion of babies who had ever been breast-fed fell from 90% before 1960 to 70% in the 1970s. The most highly educated Australian mothers were the trendsetters. They were more likely to breast-feed their babies before 1950, the first to abandon breast feeding in the late 1950s, and the first to increase the rate of breast feeding in the early 1970s (Siskind et al., 1993).

American child-care literature suggests that the method of feeding does not determine the nature of the mother–infant bond (Eiger & Olds, 1987). Nevertheless, breast feeding and bottle feeding are distinct. Mothers who are nursing can respond more immediately to an infant's signal of hunger, whereas mothers who are bottle feeding must first prepare a formula. The amount and kind of sucking on the breast and the plastic nipple differ. The quality of interactions between mother and infant are different during breast feeding and bottle feeding. Breast feeding sessions usually last longer and involve more intimate contact between mother and child (Corter & Fleming, 1995). The amount consumed and the frequency of feeding are different for the two methods. Breast feeding is more closely linked to an infant's needs: When infants need more milk, they nurse more often, thereby stimulating more milk production. In bottle feeding, there is a tendency to assume that the child is satisfied when the bottle is empty.

Breast milk has many advantages for the developing infant. The composition of proteins, sugars, and fat in breast milk is perfectly matched to an infant's nutritional needs. Through breast feeding, mothers pass immunities to their babies that protect them from certain diseases, including respiratory infections and diarrhea (Jeliffe & Jeliffe, 1983). Low-birth-weight babies and premature babies benefit from breast milk because it is easy to digest and the fat is easily absorbed (Bitman et al., 1983). Even malnourished mothers are able to provide adequate nutrition to their babies by breast feeding, although the quantity may be low. Poor women are also able to nourish their babies economically by breast feeding. The American Academy of Pediatrics (1982) advises that breast milk is the best food for newborn infants unless the mother or baby have some condition that makes nursing inadvisable. Mothers who have a serious illness or are taking medication that could be transmitted through their milk should not breast-feed. Likewise, mothers taking drugs can pass them to the baby through their milk. Nursing mothers are advised to use all the same precautions related to drugs and medications as pregnant women.

Despite the ease and availability of breast feeding and its many advantages, certain cultural factors intervene to make many mothers reject this mode of feeding. In some developing countries, bottle feeding replaced traditional breast feeding in an effort to achieve modernization (Popkin et al., 1990). However, because of the poor water quality in many of these countries, infants who are bottle-fed suffer from intestinal infections and malnutrition. Among American women, the technology of formula feeding has great appeal. Mothers feel confident that the product is "scientifically designed" to meet their babies' needs. They may view formula feeding as more sanitary than breast feeding. In addition, concerns about modesty, the need to return to work, and the fear of being tied down to the baby are all reasons that women choose the bottle over the breast (Eiger & Olds, 1987).

A recent action by the Florida legislature indicates the cultural context of breast feeding. The Florida Senate amended their statutes on indecent exposure to exempt nursing mothers. The bill was passed in response to complaints from women who had been harassed by police, security guards, and other employees when they nursed their babies in movie theaters, bus stations, parks, restaurants, hotel lobbies, and department stores. The bill protects a woman's right to breast-feed in any public or private location (*Columbus Dispatch,* 1993). The need for such a bill illustrates the social norms that forbid the exposure of the female body under certain natural circumstances, while sanctioning it for other purposes such as advertising.

Weaning

There has been little research on patterns of *weaning* and their impact on infant development. Konner (1977a) suggested that there has been a dramatic drop in the age at weaning among humans, from about four years of age among early hunters and gatherers, to just a few months in many modern societies. The earlier pattern was typically tied to the birth of the next offspring. However, weaning today is linked to cultural values regarding nutrition, indulgence, independence, and accessibility of mothers to their babies.

In cultures where infants are fed on demand, nursing is intimately linked to the attachment process. In her description of Ganda babies, Mary Ainsworth noted the active role that infants played in engaging the mother for feeding:

> A conspicuous feature of the feeding of the majority of Ganda babies from about the middle of the first year onward was the degree of initiative they took in seeking the breast when they wished it. They would approach the mother, fumbling in the folds of her dress, and sometimes find and manage the breast without assistance. This active initiative was most characteristic of demand-fed babies especially those who had been given the breast for comfort. (Ainsworth, 1977, 125)

Given the central role that nursing plays in the Ganda babies' relationships with their mothers, weaning is a delicate and sometimes stressful procedure. Ganda mothers wean their babies gradually, first decreasing the daytime feedings and then, about two weeks later, the nighttime feedings. Ainsworth observed that demand-fed babies had the most difficult time with weaning. Four of these babies were weaned at 32, 49, 50, and 57 weeks. They showed many signs of an insecure attachment following weaning, "crying easily, constantly hanging onto mother's skirts, trying to get at her breast, and becoming very distressed if she left for even a minute" (Ainsworth, 1977, 127). The one baby who was weaned at 22 months responded well, showing new signs of self-reliance.

Freud's psychosexual theory was an important stimulus for the early anthropological exploration of nursing and weaning (Whiting, 1977). Freud argued that both overindulgence and inadequacy in oral gratification could result in forms of fixation on the oral mode of sexual gratification and, beyond that, in the formation of passive, dependent personality characteristics. From the attachment perspective, Ainsworth (1977) took a slightly different view. She suggested that feeding is only one of many behaviors involved in the attachment process. When infants are fed on demand, and especially when nursing is used as a means of comforting as well as feeding, weaning is associated with disruption in the attachment relationship. However, when feeding occurs on more of a schedule and is less central to the opportunities for interaction between mother and infant, weaning is accomplished more readily and with less impact on the attachment system. In most American families, women who nurse do so for only the first six months or less, until the baby's diet is supplemented with solid foods and the baby's digestive system is able to tolerate cow's milk. Therefore, the relationship between weaning and disruption of the attachment relationship has not been a topic of great interest to researchers.

Safety in the Physical Environment

environmental dangers

A second component of ensuring infant survival is the ability to protect infants from environmental dangers. These dangers vary by culture and the degree of a society's modernization. In addition to physical risks, some cultural perceptions of danger are linked to superstitions and religious beliefs. This section addresses only dangers associated with disease, environmental toxins, and dangers in the home.

To protect the child from dangers or risks in the environment, caregivers usually make some effort to restrict a child's movement through swaddling, carrying the baby in a sling, or placing the baby in a playpen. Caregivers also invoke certain prohibitions, such as warning the child "No, don't touch that" or pulling a child away from something dangerous. As children become more mobile, in the second half of the first year, the need for prohibitions and monitoring the child's exploratory activities increases. Depending on the cultural values for independent exploration, caregivers may heighten their restrictions and prohibitions or try to modify the environment in order to permit safe, unrestricted exploration.

Disease

Parents try to create an environment that will protect their child from known diseases. Parental understanding of diseases and their preventions and cures is shaped by culture. As we discussed in Chapter 6 in the analysis of pregnancy and childbirth, cultures differ in how they define disease and health and in the steps they take to ensure health or cure diseases. In two rural villages in what was then Yugoslavia, researchers found that mothers of infants spent a large part of their time doing laundry. Few homes had hot running water, and some had no indoor water at all. Mothers' fear of exposing babies to bacteria resulted in long hours boiling water on the stove and hand laundering diapers (Lewis & Ban, 1977).

exposure to different diseases varies by culture

In Guinea, children are at high risk for malaria. Young children may experience three to five serious bouts of fever in a year. Although there is a drug that can treat malaria if administered in the first day of the fever, it is not widely used due to lack of access to a reliable source of the drug and information about its use (Glick et al., 1989). Many suggest that access to sensitive health-care workers who can establish rapport with mothers plays a large part in both prevention and treatment of childhood illnesses in rural settings (Sandiford et al., 1991).

In a comparative study of Native Americans, Hispanic whites, and other whites in New Mexico, the Native American children consistently showed higher death rates from infectious diseases than did the other ethnic groups (Becker et al., 1990). This heightened vulnerability is related to many factors, including poor living conditions, crowding, difficulty in reaching health-care services, and preferences for care from traditional medicine men which often delay attempts to seek modern treatment.

AIDS. Cultural changes have been linked to the recent spread of AIDS (Cowley, 1993). Congenital AIDS (acquired immunodeficiency syndrome) and associated deaths among infants and children are increasing in the United States (Kilbourne, Buehler & Rogers, 1990; Wittenberg & Lazenby, 1989). An estimated 1,500 HIV-infected infants are born each year in the United States (Goedert & Cote, 1994). African-American and Hispanic babies are at relatively greater risk for AIDS than are white babies (Selik, Castro & Pappaioanou, 1988). The increase in the number of babies who are HIV positive or already have AIDS presents new challenges for health-care and child-care professionals to devise new strategies of care for babies who are highly vulnerable to all forms of infection, particularly to the wide range of infectious diseases that are likely to occur in any group-care setting. Not only are these babies vulnerable to illness as a result of their health status, but many experience the death of their mothers during their infancy, leading to severe grief reactions and associated physical and emotional withdrawal.

Efforts to prevent babies being born with HIV span the full range of cultural domains, including educating young people about the risks of unprotected sexual activity and the link between substance abuse and high-risk sexual behavior, disseminating information about abortion, treating pregnant HIV-positive women for drug use, and using new birthing procedures that help limit the transmission of the virus from mother to newborn. However, medical technology has limits in addressing the prevention of this disease, which will largely be controlled through altering social behavior (Shelov, 1994).

Environmental Toxins

Many agents are toxic to infants and young children. Lead poisoning is one of the major environmental health problems in the United States (Sargent et al., 1995; Sciarillo et al., 1992). Although the dangers of lead poisoning have been known for a long time, babies continue to be exposed in older homes where the walls have been covered with lead-based paint or by old furniture such as cribs painted with lead-based paint. Exposure usually comes through touching lead-painted surfaces that have become powdery. The powder sticks to the child's fingers, and when children suck their fingers or bite their nails, the lead enters the mouth. Knowing this, it is not surprising that some parents adopt a very restrictive policy toward infant exploration   prohibiting certain touching, chewing, and mouthing behaviors in very small infants that other parents might consider to be normal and appropriate forms of investigation.

Exposure to tobacco smoke is associated with a higher risk of respiratory illnesses among infants (Chilmonczyk et al., 1990). The presence of insecticides and other chemical pollutants in the water supply is also known to affect children's health. Knowledge of these dangers may cause parents to alter their behavior or modify the environment. Concerns about pollutants as well as bacteria in the water supply are closely tied to sterilization practices in infant feeding.

Dangers in the Home

Certain child-rearing practices arise as a means of protecting young children from known dangers. For example, Robert LeVine (1977) described a practice among many African cultures of adults carrying infants 18 months of age and older on their backs even though the infants were able to walk. He learned that this practice was an effort to prevent toddlers from getting burned by the open cooking fires at an age when they were mobile enough to walk or stumble into the fire but not old enough to understand the need to stay away from fires. Other local hazards such as falling off steep cliffs or into lakes, rivers, or wells prompt this same carrying behavior.

In societies with high infant mortality rates, infants are more likely to be carried for long periods of the day and for a longer part of their infancy (Goldberg, 1977). This practice enables continuous monitoring of the infant's needs and protection from harmful agents. Practices such as swaddling and carry-

lead
smoke
chemicals

This Native American infant is tucked into a cradle board. The beads rustle when he wakes, letting his parents know he is stirring.

ing may severely limit exploratory behavior, discouraging or preventing activities in which infants act as causal agents, discovering the consequences of their actions. Very close, prolonged swaddling actually places infants at high risk for developing serious respiratory infections (Yurdakok, Yavuz & Taylor, 1990). However, a caregiver's primary concern for the baby's survival dominates his or her approach to child care, diminishing other considerations.

In industrialized countries, different types of dangers present hazards to young babies. Electrical outlets, steep stairs, open containers of insecticides, cleaning agents, and other poisons are all examples of possible threats to infant safety. In many American families, babies are protected from these dangers by putting up gates in doorways or at the tops of staircases, or by placing an infant in a crib or playpen to restrict exploration. In other homes, parents "baby-proof" the home by removing as many known dangers as possible so that the baby can have maximum freedom for exploration. These two different strategies reflect different values about child-rearing. In the former case, parents try to preserve their adult environment and modify children's behavior in order to keep them safe. In the latter case, parents modify the environment to accommodate the baby's developmental needs, while protecting them from danger.

A strong cultural value in the United States for encouraging independence during infancy has led to the adoption of devices such as jumpers, climbers, and walkers that promote early motor competence. Just as swaddling is associated with some risks, walkers, in particular, have been involved in many accidents. With a walker, infants can move about before they actually are able to walk independently or to make accurate judgments about distance and depth. Infants become so confident about their ability to move

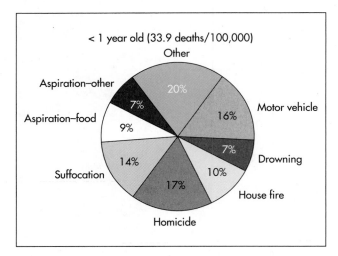

FIGURE 8.2
Percentage of deaths associated with major causes of injury for children less than 1 year old
Source: Waller, A. E., Baker, S. P. & Szocka, A. (1989). Childhood injury deaths: National analysis and geographic variation. *American Journal of Public Health, 79,* 311. Copyright © 1989 American Public Health Association. Reprinted by permission.

around in the home that they can tumble down stairs or crash into sharp edges of furniture.

An alarming irony regarding safety in the home comes from statistics on childhood deaths from injury in the United States for the years 1980 through 1985 (Waller, Baker & Szocka, 1989). Figure 8.2 shows that homicide was the most common cause of injury-related death for babies under one year of age, accounting for 17% of such cases. These data remind us that some American children are at risk from abusive treatment by the very adults who are expected to protect them (see Notebook Page 8.4).

The issues related to nurturing infants and protecting them from diseases and dangers illustrate the dynamic interaction between the universal needs of infants for food and safety and the varied cultural contexts in which these needs are met. Beliefs about infant-care practices may be supported in part by scientific research in some societies, but they are formed mostly through the transmission of family and community wisdom handed down from one generation to the next. Contemporary practices arise in response to newly emergent dangers.

Social Issues: Parental Employment and Infant Child Care

↑ # of ♀ (young mothers) in labor force

Each historical era poses new challenges and offers new resources for children and families. One of the most profound changes that has impacted American infants in the last 25 years is the rapidly increasing number of young mothers participating in the labor force. In 1960, the labor force participation rate of married women with children under the age of 6 was 19%; by 1993, the rate was 60%. Focusing on married women with children one year old and under, in 1975, the labor force participation rate was 31%; in 1993, the rate was 57.5%. Another change is the growing number of children who live with only one parent, usually the mother. In 1970, 11% of children under age 18 lived with their mother only; in 1993, that group had increased to 23% (U.S. Bureau of the Census, 1994).

Combining labor force participation outside the home with parenthood and marriage is not a new phenomenon. Among married African-American

Safety in Your Home Environment

One of the factors that guides a parent's approach to child care is his or her perception of dangers and risks to infant safety and health. These beliefs may be informed in part by scientific knowledge, but to a large extent they are built on past parenting practices, personal observations, and stories passed from one generation to the next, as well as access to resources that might help reduce risk or prevent dangers.

Think back to your own family environment during childhood.

1. What *dangers* do you recall being aware of in your home or neighborhood (for example, electric outlets, opening the door to strangers, or running out into the street)?

_____

_____

_____

2. What aspects of your parent's child-rearing behavior were intended to protect you from these dangers? For example, did they restrict your behavior, warn you, punish you, explain dangers to you, threaten you?

_____

_____

_____

3. What *diseases* did your parents worry about you and other children in the family contracting?

_____

_____

_____

4. What strategies did they use to protect you from diseases?

_____

_____

_____

321

women, 50% of the mothers of infants under one year of age were in the labor force in 1975. However, the pattern of combining work with mothering an infant has now become normative for all groups in the United States (U.S. Bureau of the Census, 1992). A combination of increased opportunities for women in many fields, changing social norms about women's participation in the work force, a high divorce rate, and increased economic pressures on families have accounted for this change.

The social implications of this rapid change in family lifestyle are far-reaching. In order to assess the impact of parental work outside the home on infant development, we must consider at least four factors. First, the effort required to combine work and parenting an infant affects the quantity and quality of time that mothers have to spend with their babies. Second, the increase in mothers' involvement in the labor force should change the role expectations for both parents in the division of family responsibilities, especially child care. Third, parents are likely to turn to other sources of child care, including other family members, family day care, and child-care centers, which raises questions about the availability, quality, and affordability of alternative child-care arrangements for infants. Fourth, the ease with which parents can coordinate child care and work depends on policies in the workplace, especially those regarding parental leave, the use of sick time to care for ill children, and permitting fathers as well as mothers to take time off to meet the needs of their small children.

The Effects of Maternal Employment on Interactions with Infants

The earliest studies of the relationship between maternal employment and infant development focused on whether maternal employment might damage the mother–child relationship. In general, studies comparing mothers who are employed 20 hours per week or more with nonemployed mothers find that the employed mothers have less time with their infants. However, the employed mothers tend to spend more time directly interacting with their infants than the nonemployed mothers, and they spend more time with their children during nonwork and weekend hours than do nonemployed mothers (Hoffman, 1989). This pattern has come to be referred to as "quality time," using the time available in a way that is child-oriented and meaningful. When the quality of interactions between children and their mothers has been compared, a consistent difference is that employed mothers appear to emphasize independence more than nonemployed mothers do (Weinraub, Jaeger & Hoffman, 1988).

When married women work full-time, fathers typically take on a more active role in child care and perform a wider range of child-care functions (Parke, 1995). Participation by fathers in child-rearing and more frequent father–child interactions have been linked to higher scores on measures of intelligence, academic achievement, and social competence in both single-earner and dual-earner families (Gottfried, Gottfried & Bathurst, 1988). Thus, to the extent that mothers' employment draws fathers into a more active partnership in parenting, children appear to benefit.

Maternal Employment and Infant Attachment

The impact of employment on infants' overall emotional development has also been studied within the framework of attachment theory. When results were combined for a large number of studies that compared attach-

IMPACT OF PARENTS WORKING OUTSIDE HOME
1) effort to balance work & parenting
2) expectations
3) alternate child care choices
4) policies of the workplace

ment relationships for infants of mothers who were employed full-time with infants of mothers who were employed part-time or who were not employed, 36% of the infants of full-time working mothers were classified as having an insecure attachment compared with 29% of the part-time or nonemployed mothers (Belsky, 1988, 1990; Clarke-Stewart, 1989). The differences were not found in each study but were observed when the results of many studies were considered together. This observation has led to an active debate about the risks associated with infant care. Jay Belsky (1988, 1990) has argued that, based on the research findings, infants who experience 20 hours per week or more of some type of alternative child care during the first year of life are at greater risk for insecurity in maternal attachment and for later disruption in social adjustment.

Other scholars have countered that the studies do not provide a sound basis for this conclusion (Clarke-Stewart, 1989; Fox & Fein, 1990; Zigler & Lang, 1991). Across many studies of attachment, it is not uncommon for about one-third of the samples to be evaluated as insecurely attached. The percentage of insecure attachments in this composite analysis does not differ substantially from the patterns found in many studies of nonemployed mothers. Insecurity in attachment may result from exposure to poor-quality infant care, or it may be the result of stress on the mothers who are working full-time. These two factors may be compounded in that mothers who are highly stressed may make hasty decisions about infant care or fail to take the time to evaluate the quality of care that their babies are receiving. Some scholars suggest that the strange situation itself is not an appropriate context for evaluating attachment for babies who are accustomed to frequent separations from their mothers. These babies may be able to handle their mothers' departure more easily and may not show evidence of seeking proximity upon reunion, both of which are behaviors typically considered evidence of secure attachment. The scientific literature has not yet thoroughly resolved this controversy.

Parental Values about Maternal Employment

The problem with comparing attachment among infants of mothers who work full-time and infants of those who work part-time or are not employed is that these employment categories subsume a great many other differences that might affect mother–infant attachment. Research has considered at least two of these factors: (1) the values and beliefs that mothers and fathers have about combining work and parenting, and (2) the quality and stability of the alternative child-care arrangements that the family can obtain. These issues lead to a more differentiated perspective on the impact of maternal employment.

Women and men are struggling over the new definitions of motherhood and fatherhood. As they become parents, adults are under pressure to revise the scripts that they may have learned during their own upbringing. It may take some time and effort for adults to integrate new expectations and behaviors with socialization values that were learned during a different historical context. For women, the conflict may focus on difficulties in giving up some responsibility for child care to their partners or other child-care providers, feeling guilty or sad about relinquishing a traditional part of their maternal role. Mothers may feel that it is demeaning or inappropriate for their male partners to function as an infant's direct caregiver. Some women believe that they are the only ones who can provide optimal care for their children, yet they

[handwritten margin note: discrepancies between values and behaviors can lead to anxiety, anger & depression]

[handwritten margin note: ♂ playing more active role in parenting]

are compelled by economic factors to return to work. Others remain home with their infants because they feel a moral responsibility to their children, but they would really prefer to be working. This group appears to show the greatest evidence of stress and depression as a result of role conflict (Hock & DeMeis, 1990). Discrepancies between one's values and one's behaviors are likely to be associated with feelings of anger, anxiety, and depression which are, in turn, disruptive to the mother–infant relationship (De Meis, Hock & McBride, 1986; Rooparine, 1990; Shuster, 1993).

With more women working outside the home, men are expected to participate more directly in fathering their very young babies. This means going beyond the few minutes of playful tickling and bouncing that were once typical for young American fathers. Fathers are expected to perform direct care-giving functions such as bathing, changing, feeding, and comforting the baby. They are also expected to become more involved in basic support functions such as taking time off from work to care for a sick baby, helping to select appropriate child-care arrangements, or providing child care during times when mothers are at work. Some fathers feel incompetent and awkward assuming primary infant-care responsibilities. They have no role models for active, engaged fathering during infancy. Many find that they have no support from work in assuming these tasks and no male peers with whom to discuss their concerns.

Perhaps as a result of many of these conflicts and doubts, increased father participation in child care has been linked to higher levels of marital dissatisfaction in dual-earner couples. Fathers in these marriages are somewhat more likely to worry that their wives are not available to meet more of their children's needs and that their own careers may suffer due to the amount of time they spend on child care (Hoffman, 1989). These unhappy fathers may add tension to mother–infant interactions. The risks to children associated with a mother's full-time employment are partly a result of mismatches between her work situation and her beliefs about mothering as well as her partner's views about responsibility for child care (see Notebook Page 8.5).

The Nature and Quality of Alternative Care

Another domain that may affect infants' emotional development is the quality of the substitute care that they receive. In the United States, infant child care falls short in availability, quality, and affordability.

Availability

Family day care or day-care centers for infants are in short supply. In one survey of 129 hospitals that had their own infant-care settings, there was one opening for every three babies whose parents applied (Children's Defense Fund, 1988). As another example, in 1991 a child-care needs assessment was conducted for Franklin County, Ohio, an urban county of about 379,000 households. Considering only households at or below 185% of the federally defined poverty level, only three spaces were available in licensed centers and registered day-care homes for every ten infants and toddlers who could have been placed (Action for Children, 1993; Metropolitan Human Services Commission, 1991). The inability of the community to establish infant-care centers that meet minimum standards for quality is striking. This same problem is found in most urban areas of the United States. Many parents have to combine several

Your Views on Combining Work and Infant Care

You have read about the conflicts that many adults experience in trying to balance their roles as worker, parent, and spouse. What are your own views about this issue?

1. In your opinion, what is the ideal infant-care arrangement, assuming that both parents were employed before the birth of their child?

_____

_____

2. Do you expect that you would want to take six weeks or more off from work if you had a new baby?

_____

_____

3. How should fathers and mothers share the responsibilities of infant care? Who should do what? Should one parent assume the primary child-care role? Which one?

_____

_____

4. How might your work influence how you enact the parent role? Try to be specific.

_____

_____

5. How might your role as parent influence how you enact your role as worker? Give examples.

_____

_____

types of child-care arrangements, including parental care, care by other relatives, and family day care in order to cover the working day. Short supply often leads to instability in the caregiving arrangements for many babies.

Quality

The availability and quality of infant child care are affected by the low salaries that are usually offered for child-care professionals. "Child care providers today are paid less per hour than animal caretakers, bartenders, or parking lot attendants. Only one-half of all child care workers receive health benefits; not even one in five has a retirement plan" (Children's Defense Fund, 1988). Low wages lead to high staff turnover, one dimension of child-care quality that has been shown to have negative effects on young children. High turnover is disruptive to children's efforts to form an attachment to a day-care teacher and subsequently impedes their ability to experience positive social interactions with peers (Howes & Hamilton, 1990).

Many infant-care arrangements are admittedly poor quality. Many states do not have any provisions for regulating quality in family day-care homes or centers operated by churches. More than half the teachers in child-care centers and over 85% of the people providing care for children in their homes do not have a college degree. There are no preservice training requirements for establishing child-care services in the home (National Commission on Children, 1993). Even though they might not prefer to do so, many parents leave infants in the care of elderly relatives who are unable to supervise their play adequately or in the care of older siblings who might themselves benefit from some type of supervised child care.

Components of Quality Infant Care. The evidence is clear that high-quality infant care contributes positively to infant development. Characteristics of high-quality infant care include small adult:child ratios and group size and well-trained child-care teachers. For infants, the optimal adult:child ratio is one adult for every three infants and a maximum group size of six in any one area. In addition, quality infant care addresses health-care and safety practices, the teacher behavior toward young children, and a program of activities that promote physical, cognitive, and social development in a group setting (Godwin & Schrag, 1988; Young & Zigler, 1986). Figure 8.3 illustrates how different structural aspects of child care can lead to positive developmental outcomes (Howes, Phillips & Whitebook, 1992). Two structural aspects of infant-care programs that can be regulated (the adult:child ratio and group size) predict appropriate caregiving by the staff and developmentally appropriate activities. These in turn are associated with secure relationships between infants and teachers and a positive social orientation. Both secure relationships and positive social orientations with teachers are associated with social competence with peers.

Early participation in high-quality infant-care centers has been associated with higher levels of sociable behavior with adults and peers and advanced cognitive functioning (Clarke-Stewart, 1989). Long-term effects of participation in high-quality infant care have been associated with teachers' ratings of emotional well-being, attractiveness, and assertiveness among sixth-graders. In this same study, children who spent more time in high-quality infant care were more affectionate toward their peers, received higher math grades, and were more likely to be assigned to a program for gifted students

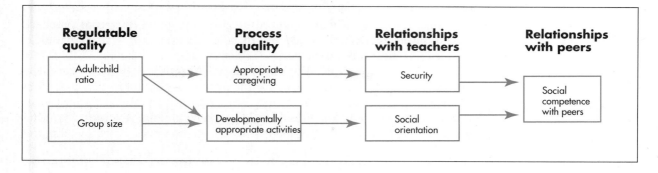

(Field, 1991). In a study conducted in Sweden, children who entered day care before age one performed better in school at ages 8 and 13 and were rated more positively on social and emotional dimensions than were babies who entered day care at older ages (Andersoon, 1992).

The Costs of Infant Care

Even when high-quality infant care is available, it is unlikely to be affordable for most families. Most quality infant-care programs cost between $125 and $150 a week. Even though staff salaries are low, the optimal infant:adult ratio makes infant care extremely expensive. Using a 1990 estimate of $21,600 as the mean income of a household in which the householder is aged 18 to 24, the family would have to spend 28% of their earnings for 50 weeks of infant care if they could find an infant-care center space available at $125 per week. For many single parents who earn roughly half that amount or less, quality infant care would consume almost half their annual income (Children's Defense Fund, 1988).

Another cost associated with group care of infants is the increased exposure to infectious diseases. For children under three years of age, the frequency of infections and hospitalization and the cost of medical care were far greater for children in day-care centers of varying quality than for children who were cared for in their own homes (Bell et al., 1989). The costs of medical care were higher for the child-care group, as were the percentage of children needing hospitalization and the number of days parents took off from work to care for sick children.

Social Policies and the Care of Infants

The availability, quality, and affordability of infant-care settings all depend on a broader social context. Public policies that permit and regulate full parental employment, flexible work hours and job sharing, parental leave, health-care resources, parent-education resources, and the funding and operation of child-care alternatives (Melhuish & Moss, 1991) support parents in their efforts to combine work and family life. Such policies can only be formed through collaboration among many sectors of society, including families, businesses, government, schools, health-care institutions, and social service agencies. In the case of single parents, policies that support advanced education and job training are crucial. Support for families with children who have special challenges and chronic illnesses must also be provided. In the United States, these

FIGURE 8.3

The relationship between structural aspects of infant-care settings and infant social development
Source: Howes, C., Phillips, D. A. & Whitebook, M. (1992). Thresholds of quality: Implications for the social development of children in center-based child care. *Child Development, 63,* 458. Copyright © 1992 The Society for Research in Child Development, Inc. Reprinted with permission.

integrated policies need to be flexible, permitting families with varying configurations and diverse values regarding parental roles, child-care practices, and combining work and family life to take advantage of a combination of resources that best meet their needs (Zigler & Lang, 1991).

In 1993, the Medical and Family Leave Act, part of which guarantees workers six weeks of unpaid leave for the birth of a new baby, was passed by the U.S. Congress. Thus, workers do not have to risk job loss in order to care for their newborns, and they do not have to seek child-care alternatives during this critical first period of life. This policy does not cover workplaces where there are 50 employees or less (see Notebook Page 8.6).

At present, in the United States, we are a long way from having an integrated policy that meets infants' needs, is truly supportive of diverse American families, and advances satisfaction and productivity in the workplace (Zigler & Stevenson, 1993). For a comparison with policies in Sweden, France, and Germany, see Table 8.1 (Allen, 1985). The lack of a comprehensive

TABLE 8.1

Parental Leave Policies in Four Countries

Sweden

Birth–9 Months	10–12 Months	13–18 Months
90% reimbursed	$150 per month	Unpaid, with job guarantee
Leaves financed through employer and employee contributions to general social insurance system		

France

Birth–4 Months	5–28 Months
90% reimbursed	Unpaid, with job guarantee
Paid from the social security system	Applicable only to companies with more than 100 employees (about one-third of the work force)

Federal Republic of Germany

Birth–3 Months	4–7 Months
100% reimbursed	$285 per month
Supplemented by employer payments to employees	
Funded primarily through disability coverage in social insurance fund	

United States

Birth–6 Weeks
Unpaid leave with guarantee of rehire (not applicable to companies with less than 50 employees)

Source: Adapted from Allen, J. P. (1985). Durations of funding sources of parental leaves in Sweden, France, and the Federal Republic of Germany. *The Networker, 6,* 5–6.

Policies Regarding Parental Leave and Infant Care

Work settings and communities differ in policies and resources for combining work and family responsibilities. Explore policies at your college or university and in another corporation in your community. Answer the following questions.

1. What are the policies on maternity leave? How much leave is provided? Is it paid or unpaid? Are there similar policies related to the adoption of a child? Are pregnancy and delivery covered under health-care benefits?

_____

_____

2. Is a parental leave available for fathers? For how long? Paid or unpaid?

_____

_____

3. Is there a guarantee of returning to the job or an equivalent after parental leave?

_____

_____

4. What support does the workplace provide for infant care? Does it sponsor a child-care center? Does it include spaces for infants? Is there a sick-baby setting? Is there a flexible benefits program permitting parents to set aside funds to pay for infant care?

_____

_____

5. Can a parent use her or his own sick leave to care for a sick child?

_____

_____

6. In your own words, summarize the policies of the two settings you investigated. To what extent do you consider each setting to be supportive of the goals of balancing work and family life?

_____

_____

329

program of policies and services for families with infants and young children is especially problematic since the United States has the highest divorce rate in the world and an increasing birth rate to unmarried women, resulting in one child out of four living in a single-parent (usually a single mother) household (National Commission on Children, 1993). The less a parent earns, the less likely she or he is to be able to afford quality infant care. For low-income parents, infant care is likely to be an unstable combination of arrangements, some of which are admittedly undesirable or even dangerous (Wolf & Sonenstein, 1991). The lack of child-care resources deters many single parents from working or seeking further education that would increase their chances of becoming economically independent. This pattern, combined with the rapid increase in labor force participation by mothers of infants, contributes to the current crisis of child care in America.

Optimizing Development in Infancy

Having read Chapters 7 and 8, you can appreciate the demanding nature of a parent's role in promoting optimal development during infancy. We have portrayed infants as active, adaptive, and eager to master the environment. At the same time, we have discussed the need for environmental support to facilitate growth.

Promoting Emotional and Cognitive Development

Many of the behaviors that appear to be important for the development of strong emotional bonds between infants and parents are also central to fostering intellectual growth. Let us look at some examples. Social attachment and object permanence were discussed earlier as two developmental tasks of infancy. What should parents do to encourage attachment? They must respond consistently and appropriately to their infant's needs. They should maintain contact with their infants by holding, cuddling, looking and smiling at, and speaking to them. These behaviors help infants achieve a well-differentiated image of their parents, including positive feelings of warmth and a wish to stay close to them.

Once specific attachments have been formed, children will pursue their parents all around the house. When parents leave the room, infants will cry out to them, crawl after them, or gaze intently in the direction they went. All of these behaviors are evidence of attachment, but they are also signs of an emerging concept of object permanence. The fact that children will pursue parents when the parents are out of sight means that they have an image of them in their minds that is more permanent than their mere visual perception of them. Parents perform a dual function: In maintaining a close bond with their children, parents nurture emotional attachment and provide a basis for conceptual growth (Pipp, Easterbrooks & Harmon, 1992).

If you have ever observed a child and parent in a novel environment, such as a doctor's office, you may have seen another example of this dual function. The parent serves as a home base of safety and reassurance from which the child can explore (Ainsworth, 1979; Bowlby, 1988). Each time the child leaves, he or she may wander a bit farther, investigating toys, magazines, furniture, or other children before returning to the parent. Parents can use the trust and confidence they have built with their infants to encourage their children's exploration, introduce them to new and unfamiliar objects, and support their efforts to master difficult motor tasks (Heckhausen, 1987; Zahn-Waxler, Radke-Yarrow & King, 1977).

Another way that parents foster both emotional and intellectual growth is by structuring the environment to suit an infant's developmental level (Bornstein, 1985; Bradley, Caldwell & Rock, 1988; Stevens & Bakeman, 1985). Parents should take the infant's perspective into account in providing toys and other sources of stimulation. They need to initiate interactions with their infants, as well as responding to infants' demands for attention. An infant's environment should allow a variety of experiences, a reasonable amount of frustration, and adequate opportunities to experience success. As infants' skills develop, parents should alter the environment appropriately, adding more complex stimuli, providing more opportunities for autonomy, and helping the child learn to tolerate some frustration.

Parents as Advocates

In addition to providing direct care, parents must serve as advocates for their infants. This role may involve selecting a competent health-care professional, identifying appropriate treatment for any disability, and arranging alternative care arrangements for their infants that meet their infants' needs within the parameters of work demands and economic resources.

In order to function as advocates for their children, parents may have to engage in an unfamiliar kind of thinking, for which they may feel unqualified. For example, parents must evaluate the competence of caregivers in meeting their child's needs for security and stimulation. They must assess the caregiver's motivation. They must consider the degree to which alternative caregivers reflect their own child-rearing philosophy.

Parents must assess whether their children's child-care setting is continuing to provide the kind of responsive, stimulating environment that will enhance development. In the best situations, alternative care settings can complement and enrich the parent–infant relationship. In the worst settings, infants can be neglected and abused. Parents must be willing to intervene as necessary to ensure their infants' well-being, despite pressures to continue with an established caregiving arrangement.

Contextual Factors That Support Parenting

A variety of contextual factors play a part in parents' ability to promote their children's optimal development. Parents must rely heavily on their own psychological well-being and on the loving support of caring friends and family to sustain the ego strengths, creative energy, and emotional resources necessary for the task. The ways that parents conceive their roles have major implications for infant development. Adults who themselves have had difficult experiences with a caregiver come to the parent role with special challenges. They may not have experienced the comfort, responsiveness, or

Japanese families take their infants to the beach, a place where parents and infants can relax and play together. Infants enjoy sensorimotor exploration under a parent's watchful eye with few restrictions and plenty to investigate.

appropriate stimulation that are essential for effective parenting. Some factors, however, offset these deficits. The quality of the parents' relationship and the emotional support they give each other are crucial in sustaining positive parent–child relationships (Cox et al., 1989, Dickstein & Parke, 1988; Egeland, Jacobvitz & Sroufe, 1988). Additional support from the child's grandparents and other family members, health and mental health professionals, and friends is helpful (Levitt, Weber & Clark, 1986; Stevens, 1988). The effective use of a social support network ensures that other adults are available to help the parent identify and solve child-rearing problems. Often the help is very direct, such as providing child care, clothes, playthings, furniture, or household help. Support may also come through providing companionship and validating the importance of the parenting role.

A third contextual factor is a parent's prior experience with child-rearing and child-care responsibilities. Adults who have had previous child-rearing experiences are likely to be more effective and accurate in solving child-rearing problems (Holden, 1988). They are also more likely to recognize meaningful infant signals and to consider the infant's developmental level in interpreting the child's behavior (Adamson et al., 1987). The role of parent makes considerable cognitive and emotional demands, but attachment to a child also provides opportunities for a parent's own psychological development. The elements of parenting that we have identified or implied as contributing to optimal development are listed in Table 8.2.

TABLE 8.2

Optimizing an Infant's Development

Provide appropriate and timely stimulation.

Provide warmth and affection; express positive feelings toward the baby verbally, by touching and hugging, and through playful interactions.

Encourage the infant's active exploration of the environment; encourage mobility.

Try not to control the infant's behavior too much.

Help the infant understand that he or she caused things to happen.

Help the infant engage in directed problem solving.

Encourage the infant to persist in efforts to reach a goal.

Keep a predictable schedule, especially when the infant is very young.

Spend time with the baby; be available when the baby needs you.

Communicate directly with the infant; engage the baby in verbal interaction, even if it is at the level of imitative gurgling and cooing.

Guide language development by using words to name and categorize objects and events.

Accept the baby's efforts to achieve closeness.

Be responsive; be sensitive to the child's state; learn to interpret the child's signals accurately.

Find effective ways to soothe and comfort the child in times of distress.

Help the infant interpret and find ways to regulate sources of distress.

To the extent possible, prevent the baby from being exposed to intensely negative, hostile, and frightening situations.

Be aware of the visual and auditory cues you send when you interact with the child.

Pay attention to ways that the baby is changing over time.

Monitor the infant's emotional expressions to evaluate the success of specific actions and interventions.

Create a safe environment in which the baby can explore.

Identify and use the resources needed to promote the child's physical health, including inoculations, medical checkups, and treatment for any chronic illnesses or disabilities.

Provide an appropriate diet.

Consider the infant's physical health, safety, and cognitive, emotional, and social needs in selecting any alternative child-care arrangements.

Monitor any alternative child-care arrangements to ensure that they continue to meet the baby's needs at new developmental levels.

Chapter Summary

1. In infancy, the psychosocial crisis is trust versus mistrust. For infants, trust is an emotional confidence that their needs will be met and that they are valued. Over time, trust expands to an orientation of optimism. Mistrust is an emotional wariness, a lack of confidence in the good intentions of others, and doubt about one's own lovableness.

2. The crisis of trust versus mistrust is resolved in an overall balance toward trust when the infant and caregiver achieve a sense of mutuality in their relationship. Through a process of mutual regulation and coordination, caregivers and infants build a pattern of meaningful, rhythmic interactions. Infants come to expect that they will be understood.

3. Parents who are experiencing marital discord, who have been victims of child abuse or neglect, who are depressed, or who are mentally ill are more likely to be psychologically unavailable and insensitive to their infants' needs, thus placing the process for achieving mutuality at risk.

4. A positive resolution of the psychosocial crisis of trust versus mistrust leads to the adaptive ego quality of hope. Hope is a cognitive orientation that one's goals and dreams can be attained and that events will turn out for the best.

5. The core pathology associated with a negative resolution of the psychosocial crisis of trust versus mistrust is withdrawal. High turnover in caregivers, lack of opportunity to form close attachments to any single person, and prolonged maternal neglect can result in forms of withdrawal.

6. The birth of a child transforms many members of the kinship network. The transition to parenthood is often associated with reduced levels of marital satisfaction for parents, especially when marital satisfaction was low prior to the child's birth.

7. Harmony in the marital relationship is associated with advanced development for infants and toddlers.

8. Establishing mutuality and a warm, sensitive, and affectionate relationship between parents and child appears to promote adult development by fostering new levels of intimacy and establishing the basis for generativity.

9. In the United States, there is great flexibility in how grandparents enact their role.

10. The more frequently that grandparents interact with their grandchildren and take on parentlike behaviors, the more significant they become in their grandchildren's lives.

11. Grandparents are especially likely to be directly involved with their grandchildren's care when parents divorce, when their teenage daughters have babies, or when mothers work full-time.

12. Cultures differ in the strategies that they adopt to ensure infant survival. Feeding, weaning, and strategies for ensuring safety in the physical environment are aspects of infant care that are enacted quite differently across cultural groups.

13. Although the scientific literature suggests that breast feeding has multiple physical, emotional, and social advantages for newborns, many cultural factors intervene to encourage bottle feeding instead. The use of formula is associated with modernization, concerns about cleanliness, and modesty.

14. Weaning can be a difficult time for babies when nursing is part of the attachment relationship. In some traditional societies, weaning is delayed until the birth of the next sibling.

15. Dangers in the environment can arise from many sources, including diseases, environmental toxins, and dangers in the home and local

environment. In each of these areas, knowledge of known risks, family traditions and wisdom, and beliefs and values about infant behavior converge to shape parenting practices.

16. One of the major social issues facing American families is the rapidly increasing employment of mothers of young infants. This change, including increased employment of single mothers and married women with infants, has produced a crisis in the availability and affordability of good alternative infant care.

17. Maternal employment is associated with less time spent in overall mother–child interaction, but more time in direct child-oriented interaction. When mothers are employed outside the home full-time, fathers interact more with babies, which has positive consequences for infant development.

18. There is debate regarding the impact of mothers' employment on the quality of attachment. Higher risks for insecure attachment are associated with poor-quality infant care, frequent changes in caregivers and caregiving arrangements, and high maternal stress associated with role conflict.

19. Infant child care falls short in the availability and affordability of quality settings. Many infant-care providers are unlicensed and unregulated. Salaries for child-care professionals are very low, leading to high staff turnover, which disrupts attachments.

20. Quality infant care can enhance both cognitive and social development.

21. The United States has yet to devise a broad public policy that supports parents in establishing a supportive family environment while, at the same time, permitting full employment.

22. Parents can play a central role in promoting optimal development during infancy. Through sensitive, consistent caregiving, they can foster both cognitive and emotional development. A successful attachment relationship serves as the basis for the formation of social competence and subsequent positive personal relationships. In addition to the importance of direct caregiving, parents should also create a safe, stimulating environment that permits exploration and mastery as well as serving as advocates for their children with other agencies and services.

References

Aber, J. L. & Allen, J. P. (1987). Effects of maltreatment on young children's socioemotional development: An attachment theory perspective. *Developmental Psychology, 23,* 406–414.

Action for Children. (1993). Personal communication, Dr. Susan Jakob.

Adamson, L. B., Bakeman, R., Smith, C. B. & Walters, A. S. (1987). Adults' interpretation of infants' acts. *Developmental Psychology, 23,* 383–387.

Ainsworth, M. D. S. (1977). Infant development and mother–infant interaction among Ganda and American families. In P. H. Leiderman, S. R. Tulkin & A. Rosenfeld (Eds.), *Culture and infancy: Variations in the human experi-ence.* New York: Academic Press, 119–150.

Ainsworth, M. D. S. (1979). Infant–mother attachment. *American Psychologist, 34,* 932–937.

Alessandri, S. M. (1992). Mother–child interactional correlates of maltreated and nonmaltreated children's play behavior. *Development and Psychopathology, 4,* 257–270.

Allen, J. P. (1985). Durations of funding sources of parental leaves in Sweden, France, and the Federal Republic of Germany. *The Networker, 6,* 5–6.

American Academy of Pediatrics. (1982). The promotion of breast feeding. *Pediatrics, 69,* 654–661.

American Psychiatric Association (1993). *Diagnostic and statistical manual of mental disorders* (3rd ed., rev.). Washington, D.C.: American Psychiatric Association.

Andersoon, B. (1992). Effects of day-care on cognitive and socioemotional competence of thirteen-year-old Swedish school children. *Child Development, 63,* 20–36.

Becker, T. M., Wiggins, C., Peck, C., Key, C. R. & Samet, J. M. (1990). Mortality from infectious diseases among New Mexico's American Indians, Hispanic whites, and other whites, 1958–87. *American Journal of Public Health, 80,* 320–322.

Bell, D. M., Gleiber, D. W., Mercer, A. A., Phifer, R., Guinter, R. H., Choen, J., Epstein, E. U. & Narayanan, M. (1989). Illness associated with child day care: A study of incidence and cost. *American Journal of Public Health, 79,* 479–484.

Bell, S. M. & Ainsworth, M. D. S. (1972). Infant crying and maternal responsiveness. *Child Development, 43,* 1171–1190.

Belsky, J. (1988). The "effects" of infant day care reconsidered. *Early Childhood Research Quarterly, 3,* 235–272.

Belsky, J. (1990). Parental and nonparental child care and children's socioemotional development: A decade in review. *Journal of Marriage and the Family, 52,* 885–903.

Belsky, J. & Isabella, R. A. (1985). Marital and parent–child relationships in family of origin and marital change following the birth of a baby: A retrospective analysis. *Child Development, 56,* 342–349.

Belsky, J., Lang, M. & Huston, T. L. (1986). Sex typing and division of labor as determinants of marital change across the transition to parenthood. *Journal of Personality and Social Psychology, 50,* 517–522.

Belsky, J. & Pensky, E. (1988). Marital change across the transition to parenthood. *Marriage and the Family Review, 12,* 133–156.

Belsky, J. & Rovine, M. (1990). Patterns of marital change across the transition to parenthood. *Journal of Marriage and the Family, 52,* 5–20.

Bitman, J., Wood, D. L., Hamosh, M. & Mehta, N. R. (1983). Comparison of the lipid composition of breast milk from mothers of term and preterm infants. *American Journal of Clinical Nutrition, 38,* 300–312.

Bornstein, M. H. (1985). How infant and mother jointly contribute to developing cognitive competence in the child. *Proceedings of the National Academy of Science,* USA, 82, 7470–7473.

Bornstein, M. H. (1995). Parenting infants. In M. H. Bornstein (Ed.), *Handbook of parenting. Vol. 1: Children and parenting.* Hillsdale, N.J.: Erlbaum, 3–39.

Bowlby, J. (1980). *Attachment and loss. Loss, sadness, and depression* (vol. 3). New York: Basic Books.

Bowlby, J. (1988). *A secure base: Parent–child attachment and healthy human development.* New York: Basic Books.

Bradley, R. H., Caldwell, B. M. & Rock, S. L. (1988). Home environment and school performance: A ten-year follow-up and examination of three models of environmental action. *Child Development, 59,* 852–867.

Brazelton, R. B., Koslowski, B. & Main, M. (1974). The origins of reciprocity: The early mother–infant interaction. In M. Lewis & L.A. Rosenblum (Eds.), *The effect of the infant on its caregiver.* New York: Wiley-Interscience, 49–76.

Campos, R. G. (1989). Soothing pain-elicited distress in infants with swaddling and pacifiers. *Child Development, 60,* 781–792.

Chen, Y. (1992). Factors associated with artificial feeding in Shanghai. *American Journal of Public Health, 82,* 264–267.

Cherlin, A. J. & Furstenberg, F. F. (1986/1992). *The new American grandparent: A place in the family, a life apart.* Cambridge, Mass.: Harvard University Press.

Children's Defense Fund. (1988). *A children's defense budget: FY 1989.* Washington, D.C.: Children's Defense Fund.

Chilmonczyk, B. A., Knight, G. J., Palomaki, G. E., Pulkkinen, A. J., Williams, J. & Haddow, J. E. (1990). Environmental tobacco smoke exposure during infancy. *American Journal of Public Health, 80,* 1205–1208.

Clarke-Stewart, K. A. (1989). Infant day care: maligned or malignant? *American Psychologist, 44,* 266–273.

Columbus Dispatch. (1993). Florida set to approve breast-feeding in public. 4A.

Corter, C. M. & Fleming, A. S. (1995). Psychobiology of maternal behavior in human beings. In M. H. Bornstein (Ed.), *Handbook of parenting. Biology and ecology of parenting.* (vol. 2) Hillsdale, N.J.: Erlbaum, 87–116.

Cowan, C. P. & Cowan, P. A. (1988). Who does what when partners become parents: Implications for men, women, and marriage. *Marriage and Family Review, 12,* 105–132.

Cowan, P. A. & Cowan, C. P. (1988). Changes in marriage during the transition to parenthood: Must we blame the baby? In G. Michaels & W. A. Goldberg (Eds.), *The transition to parenthood: Current theory and research.* Cambridge, England: Cambridge University Press, 114–154.

Cowley, G. (1993). The future of AIDS. *Newsweek,* March 22, 46–52.

Cox, M. J., Owen, M. T., Lewis, J. M. & Henderson, V. K. (1989). Marriage, adult adjustment, and early parenting. *Child Development, 60,* 1015–1024.

Crittenden, P. (1992). Children's strategies for coping with adverse home environments: An interpretation using attachment theory. *Child Abuse & Neglect, 16,* 329–343.

Dawson, G., Klinger, L. G., Panagiotides, H., Hill, D. & Spieker, S. (1992). Frontal lobe activity and affective behavior of infants of mothers with depressive symptoms. *Child Development, 63,* 725–737.

DeMeis, D. K., Hock, E. & McBride, S. L. (1986). The balance of employment and motherhood: Longitudinal study of mothers' feelings about separation from their first-born infants. *Developmental Psychology, 22,* 627–632.

DeMulder, E. K. & Radke-Yarrow, M. (1991). Attachment with affectively ill and well mothers: Concurrent and behavioral correlates. *Development and Psychopathology, 3,* 227–242.

Dickstein, S. & Parke, R. D. (1988). Social referencing in infancy: A glance at fathers and marriage. *Child Development, 59,* 506–511.

Dweck, C. S. (1992). The study of goals in psychology. *Psychological Science, 3* (3), 165–167.

Egeland, B., Jacobvitz, D. & Sroufe, L. A. (1988). Breaking the cycle of abuse. *Child Development, 59,* 1080–1088.

Egeland, B. & Sroufe, L. A. (1981). Attachment and early maltreatment. *Child Development, 52,* 44–52.

Eiger, M. S. & Olds, S. W. (1987). *The complete book of breastfeeding.* New York: Bantam.

Erikson, E. H. (1950). *Childhood and society.* New York: Norton.

Erikson, E. H. (1963). *Childhood and society* (rev. ed.). New York: Norton.

Erikson, E. H. (1982). *The life cycle completed: A review.* New York: Norton.

Erikson, E. H., Erikson, J. M. & Kivnik, H. Q. (1986). *Vital involvement in old age.* New York: Norton.

Field, T. (1991). Quality infant day-care and grade school behavior and performance. *Child Development, 62,* 863–870.

Field, T., Healy, B., Goldstein, S. & Guthertz, M. (1990). Behavior-state matching and synchrony in mother–infant interactions of nondepressed versus depressed dyads. *Developmental Psychology, 26,* 7–14.

Field, T., Healy, B., Goldstein, S., Perry, S., Bendell, D., Schanberg, S., Zimmerman, E. A. & Kuhn, C. (1988). Infants of depressed mothers show "depressed" behavior even with nondepressed adults. *Child Development, 59,* 1569–1579.

Fox, N. & Fein, G. G. (1990). *Infant day care: The current debate.* Norwood, N.J.: Ablex.

Franz, C. E., McClelland, D. C. & Weinberger, J. (1991). Childhood antecedents of conventional social accomplishment in midlife adults: A 36-year prospective study. *Journal of Personality and Social Psychology, 60,* 586–595.

Glenn, N. D. & McLanahan, S. (1982). Children and marital happiness: A further specification of the relationship. *Journal of Marriage and the Family, 44,* 63–72.

Glick, W., Ward, W. B., Gordon, A. & Haba, F. (1989). Malaria treatment practices among mothers in Guinea. *Journal of Health and Social Behavior, 30,* 421–435.

Godwin, A. & Schrag, L. (1988). *Setting up for infant care: Guidelines for centers and family day care homes.* Washington, D.C.: National Association for the Education of Young Children.

Goedert, J. J. & Cote, T. R. (1994). Public health interventions to reduce pediatric AIDS. *American Journal of Public Health, 84,* 1065–1066.

Goldberg, S. (1977). Infant development and mother–infant interaction in urban Zambia. In P. H. Leiderman, S. R. Tulkin & A. Rosenfeld (Eds.), *Culture and infancy: Variations in the human experience.* New York: Academic Press, 211–244.

Gottfried, A. E., Gottfried, A. W. & Bathurst, K. (1988). Maternal employment, family environment and children's development: Infancy through the school years. In A. E. Gottfried & A. W. Gottfried (Eds.), *Maternal employment and children's development: Longitudinal research.* New York: Plenum, 11–58.

Heckhausen, I. (1987). Balancing for weaknesses and challenging developmental potential: A longitudinal study of mother–infant dyads in apprenticeship interactions. *Developmental Psychology, 23,* 762–770.

Heinicke, C. M. (1995). Determinants of the transition to parenting. In M. H. Bornstein (Ed.), *Handbook of parenting: Status and social conditions of parenting* (vol. 3). Hillsdale, N.J.: Erlbaum, 277–303.

Heinicke, C. M. & Guthrie, D. (1992). Stability and change in husband–wife adaptation and the development of positive parent–child relationships. *Infant and Behavior Development, 15,* 109–127.

Hetherington, E. M., Cox, M. & Cox, R. (1985). Long-term effects of divorce and remarriage on the adjustment of children. *Journal of the American Academy of Psychiatry, 24*, 518–830.

Hetherington, E. M., Stanley-Hagan, M. & Anderson, E. R. (1989). Marital transitions: A child's perspective. *American Psychologist, 44*, 303–312.

Hock, E. & DeMeis, D. (1990). Depression in mothers of infants: The role of maternal employment. *Developmental Psychology, 26*, 285–291.

Hodges, J. & Tizard, B. (1989). Social and family relationships of ex-institutional adolescents. *Journal of Child Psychology and Psychiatry, 30*, 77–97.

Hoffman, L. W. (1989). Effects of maternal employment in the two-parent family. *American Psychologist, 44*, 283–292.

Holden, G. W. (1988). Adults' thinking about a child-rearing problem: Effects of experience, parental status, and gender. *Child Development, 59*, 1623–1632.

Howes, C. & Hamilton, C. E. (1990). *Children's relationships with child care teachers.* Los Angeles: University of California at Los Angeles.

Howes, C., Phillips, D. A. & Whitebook, M. (1992). Thresholds of quality: Implications for the social development of children in center-based child care. *Child Development, 63*, 449–460.

Hubert, J. (1974). Belief and reality: Social factors in pregnancy and childbirth. In M. P. M. Richards (Ed.), *The integration of a child into a social world.* London: Cambridge University Press, 37–52.

Isabella, R. & Belsky, J. (1991). Interactional synchrony and the origins of infant–mother attachment: A replication study. *Child Development, 62*, 373–384.

Jelliffe, D. & Jelliffe, E. F. P. (1983). Recent scientific knowledge concerning breastfeeding. *Review Epidemiology et Sante Publ., 31*, 367–373.

Kilbourne, B. W., Buehler & Rogers, M. F. (1990). AIDS as a cause of death in children, adolescents, and young adults. *American Journal of Public Health, 80*, 499–500.

Konner, M. (1977a). Evolution of human behavior development. In P. H. Leiderman, S. R. Tulkin & A. Rosenfeld (Eds.), *Culture and infancy: Variations in the human experience.* New York: Academic Press, 69–118.

Konner, M. (1977b). Infancy among the Kalahari San. In P. H. Leiderman, S. R. Tulkin & A. Rosenfeld (Eds.), *Culture and infancy: Variations in the human experience.* New York: Academic Press, 287–328.

Kropp, J. P. & Haynes, O. M. (1987). Abusive and nonabusive mothers' ability to identify general and specific emotion signals of infants. *Child Development, 58*, 187–190.

LeVine, R. A. (1977). Child rearing as cultural adaptation. In P. H. Leiderman, S. R. Tulkin & A. Rosenfeld (Eds.), *Culture and infancy: Variations in the human experience.* New York: Academic Press, 15–28.

Levitt, M. J., Weber, R. A. & Clark, M. C. (1986). Social network relationships as sources of maternal support and well-being. *Developmental Psychology, 22*, 310–316.

Lewis, M. & Ban, P. (1977). Variance and invariance in the mother–infant interaction: A cross-cultural study. In P. H. Leiderman, S. R. Tulkin & A. Rosenfeld (Eds.), *Culture and infancy: Variations in the human experience.* New York: Academic Press, 329–355.

Lieberman, A. F., Weston, D. R. & Pawl, J. H. (1991). Preventive intervention and outcome with anxiously attached dyads. *Child Development, 62*, 199–209.

Lorenz, K. F. (1935). Der Kumpan in der Urwelt des Vogels. *Journal Ornithologie, 83*, 137.

Lorenz, K. F. (1937/1961). Imprinting. In R. C. Birney & R. C. Teevan (Eds.), *Instinct.* Princeton, N.J.: Van Nostrand.

Lyons-Ruth, K., Connell, D. B., Zoll, D. & Stahl, J. (1987). Infants at social risk: Relations among infant maltreatment, maternal behavior, and infant attachment behavior. *Developmental Psychology, 23*, 223–232.

MacDermid, S. M., Huston, T. L. & McHale, S. M. (1990). Changes in marriage associated with transition to parenthood. *Journal of Marriage and the Family, 52*, 475–486.

Main, N., Kaplan, N. & Cassidy, J. (1985). Security in infancy, childhood, and adulthood: A move to the level of representation. In I. Bretherton & E. Everett (Eds.), *Growing points of attachment theory and research. Monographs of the Society for Research in Child Development, 50* (1–2, Serial No., 209), 60–104.

Malle, B. F. & Horowitz, L. M. (1995). The puzzle of negative self-views: An explanation using the schema concept. *Journal of Personality and Social Psychology, 68*, 470–484.

McAdams, D. P. & de St. Aubin, E. (1992). A theory of generativity and its assessment through self-report, behavioral acts, and narrative themes in autobiography. *Journal of Personality and Social Psychology, 62*, 1003–1015.

Melhuish, E. C. & Moss, P. (Eds.). (1991). *Day care for young children: International perspectives.* London: Routledge.

Metropolitan Human Services Commission. (1991). *Franklin County child care needs assessment.* Columbus, Ohio: MHSC.

Miller, D. (1979). The Native American family: The urban way. In E. Corfman (Ed.), *Families today* (vol. 1). Washington, D.C.: U.S. Government Printing Office.

Miller, N. B., Cowan, P. A., Cowan, C. P., Hetherington, E. M. & Clingempeel, W. G. (1993). Externalizing in preschoolers and early adolescents: A cross-study replication of a family model. *Developmental Psychology, 29,* 3–18.

Myers, B. J., Jarvis, P. A. & Creasey, G. L. (1987). Infants' behavior with their mothers and grandmothers. *Infant Behavior and Development, 10,* 245–259.

National Commission on Children. (1993). *Just the facts: A summary of recent information on America's children and their families.* Washington, D.C.: National Commission on Children.

Neugarten, B. & Weinstein, R. (1964). The changing American grandparent. *Journal of Marriage and the Family, 26,* 199–204.

Newman, P. R. & Newman, B. M. (1988). Parenthood and adult development. In R. Palkovitz & M. B. Sussman (Eds.), *Transitions to parenthood, marriage and family review, 12,* 313–337.

Norem, J. K. & Cantor, N. (1988). Capturing the "flavor" of behavior: Cognition, affect, and integration. In A. Isen & B. Moore (Eds.), *Affect and social behavior.* New York: Academic Press.

Osofsky, J. D. & Connors, K. (1979). Mother–infant interaction: An integrative view of a complex system. In J. D. Osofsky (Ed.), *Handbook of infant development.* New York: Wiley, 519–548.

Parke, R. D. (1995). Fathers and families. In M. H. Bornstein (Ed.), *Handbook of parenting. Status and social conditions of parenting* (vol. 3). Hillsdale, N.J.: Erlbaum, 27–63.

Popkin, B. N., Fernandez, M. E. & Avila, J. L. (1990). Infant formula promotion and the health sector in the Philippines. *American Journal of Public Health, 80,* 74–75.

Posada, G., Gao, Y., Wu, F., Posada, R., Tascon, M., Schoelmerich, A., Sagi, A., Kondo-Ikemura, K., Haaland, W. & Synnevaag, B. (1995). The secure-base phenomenon across cultures: Children's behavior, mothers' preferences, and experts' concepts. *Monographs of the Society for Research in Child Development, 60,* 27–48.

Presser, H. B. (1989). Some economic complexities of child care provided by grandmothers. *Journal of Marriage and the Family, 51,* 581–591.

Rabin, R. (1989). Warnings unheeded: A history of child lead poisoning. *American Journal of Public Health, 79,* 1668–1674.

Radin, N., Oyserman, D. & Benn, R. (1991). Grandfathers, teen mothers and children under two. In P. K. Smith (Ed.), *The psychology of grandparent-*

hood: An international perspective. London: Routledge, 85–99.

Rempel, J. K., Holmes, J. G. & Zanna, M. P. (1985). Trust in close relationships. *Journal of Personality and Social Psychology, 49,* 95–112.

Rooparine, J. (1990). Dual-earner wives' and husbands' perceptions of their children's day care experiences: Relationships to personal well-being, marital stress, and job satisfaction. *Early Education and Development, 1,* 205–216.

Rutter, M. (1990). Commentary: Some focus and process considerations regarding effects of parental depression on children. *Developmental Psychology, 26,* 60–67.

Rutter, M. (1995). Maternal deprivation. In M. H. Bornstein (Ed.), *Handbook of parenting: Applied and practical parenting* (vol. 4). Hillsdale, N.J.: Erlbaum, 3–31.

Sandiford, P., Morales, P., Gorter, A., Coyle, E. & Smith, G. D. (1991). Why do child mortality rates fall? An analysis of the Nicaraguan experience. *American Journal of Public Health, 81,* 30–37.

Sargent, J. D., Brown, M. J., Freeman, J. L., Bailey, A., Goodman, D. & Freeman, D. H., Jr. (1995). Childhood lead poisoning in Massachusetts communities: Its association with sociodemographic and housing characteristics. *American Journal of Public Health, 85,* 528–534.

Sciarillo, W. G., Alexander, G. & Farrell, K. P. (1992). *American Journal of Public Health, 82,* 1356–1360.

Scott, J. P. (1987). Critical periods in processes of social organization. In M. H. Bornstein (Ed.), *Sensitive periods in development: Interdisciplinary perspectives.* Hillsdale, N.J.: Erlbaum, 247–268.

Sears, R. R., Maccoby, E. E. & Levin, H. (1957). *Patterns of child-rearing.* Evanston, Ill.: Row, Peterson.

Selik, R. M., Castro, K. G. & Pappaioanou, M. (1988). Racial/ethnic differences in the risk of AIDS in the United States. *American Journal of Public Health, 78,* 1539–1545.

Shelov, S. P. (1994). The children's agenda for the 1990s and beyond. *American Journal of Public Health, 84,* 1066–1067.

Shuster, C. (1993). Employed first-time mothers: A typology of maternal responses to integrating parenting and employment. *Family Relations, 42,* 13–20.

Siskind, V., Del Mar, C. & Schofield, F. (1993). Infant feeding in Queensland, Australia: Long-term trends. *American Journal of Public Health, 83,* 103–106.

Smith, P. K. (Ed.). (1991). *The psychology of grandparenthood: An international perspective.* London: Routledge.

Smith, P. K. (1995). Grandparenthood. In M. H. Bornstein (Ed.), *Handbook of parenting. Status and social conditions of parenting* (vol. 3). Hillsdale, N.J.: Erlbaum, 89–112.

Snyder, C. R., Harris, C., Anderson, J. R., Holleran, S. A., Irving, L. M., Sigmon, S. T., Yoshinobu, L., Gibb, J., Langelle, C. & Harney, P. (1991). The will and the ways: Development and validation of an individual-differences measure of hope. *Journal of Personality and Social Psychology, 60*, 570–585.

Spitz, R. A. (1945). Hospitalism: An inquiry into the genesis of psychiatric conditions in early childhood. *Psychoanalytic Study of the Child, 1*, 113–117.

Spitz, R. A. (1946). Anaclitic depression. *Psychoanalytic Study of the Child, 2*, 313–342.

Sprunger, L. W., Boyce, W. T. & Gaines, J. A. (1985). Family–infant congruence: Routines and rhythmicity in family adaptations to a young infant. *Child Development, 56*, 564–572.

Stevens, J. H., Jr. (1988). Social support, locus of control, and parenting in three low-income groups of mothers: Black teenagers, black adults, and white adults. *Child Development, 59*, 635–642.

Stevens, J. H., Jr. & Bakeman, R. (1985). A factor analytic study of the HOME scale for infants. *Developmental Psychology, 21*, 1196–1203.

Thompson, R., Tinsley, B. R., Scalora, M. J. & Parke, R. D. (1989). Grandparents' visitation rights: Legalizing the ties that bind. *American Psychologist, 44*, 1217–1223.

Tinsley, B. J. & Parke, R. D. (1987). Grandparents as interactive and social support agents for families with young infants. *International Journal of Aging and Human Development, 25*, 259–278.

Tizard, B. & Rees, J. (1975). The effect of early institutional rearing on the behavior problems and affectional relationships of four-year-old children. *Journal of Child Psychology and Psychiatry, 16*, 61–73.

Tolson, T. F. J. & Wilson, M. N. (1990). The impact of two- and three-generational Black family structure on perceived family climate. *Child Development, 61*, 416–428.

Tomlin, A. M. & Passman, R. H. (1989). Grandmothers' responsibility in raising two-year-olds facilitates their grandchildren's adaptive behavior: A preliminary intrafamilial investigation of mothers' and maternal grandmothers' effects. *Psychology and Aging, 4*, 119–121.

Tronick, E. Z. & Cohn, J. F. (1989). Infants–mother face-to-face interaction: Age and gender differences in coordination and the occurrence of miscoordination. *Child Development, 60*, 85–92.

U.S. Bureau of the Census (1992). *Statistical abstract of the United States: 1992.* (112th ed.). Washington, D.C.: U.S Government Printing Office.

U.S. Bureau of the Census. (1994). *Statistical abstract of the United States: 1994.* (114th ed.). Washington, D.C.: U. S. Government Printing Office.

U.S. Department of Labor. (1987). Employment in perspective: Women in the labor force. Report 749.

Vaillant, G. E. (1977). *Adaptation to life.* Boston: Little, Brown.

van Ijzendoorn, M. & Kroonenberg, P. (1988). Cross cultural patterns of attachment: A meta-analysis of the strange situation. *Child Development, 59*, 147–156.

Volling, B. L. & Belsky, J. (1991). Multiple determinants of fathering during early infancy in dual-career and single-earner families. *Journal of Marriage and the Family, 53*, 461–474.

Wallace, P. M. & Gotleib, I. H. (1990). Marital adjustment during the transition to parenthood: Stability and predictors of change. *Journal of Marriage and the Family, 52*, 21–29.

Waller, A. E., Baker, S. P. & Szocka, A. (1989). Childhood injury deaths: National analysis and geographic variation. *American Journal of Public Health, 79*, 310–315.

Weinraub, M., Jaeger, E. & Hoffman, L. W. (1988). Predicting infant outcomes in families of employed and nonemployed mothers. *Early Childhood Research Quarterly, 3*, 361–378.

Werner, E. E. (1991). Grandparent–grandchild relationships amongst U.S. ethnic groups. In P. K. Smith (Ed.), *The psychology of grandparenthood: An international perspective.* London: Routledge, 68–82.

Whiting, J. W. M. (1977). A model for psychocultural research. In P. H. Leiderman, S. R. Tulkin & A. Rosenfeld (Eds.), *Culture and infancy: Variations in the human experience.* New York: Academic Press, 29–48.

Wittenberg, J. & Lazenby, A. (1989). AIDS in infancy: Diagnostic, therapeutic, and ethical problems. *Canadian Journal of Psychiatry, 34*, 576–580.

Wolf, D. A. & Sonenstein, F. L. (1991). Child-care use among welfare mothers. *Journal of Family Issues, 12*, 519–536.

Yarrow, L. J. (1963). Research in dimensions of early maternal care. *Merrill-Palmer Quarterly, 9*, 101–114.

Yarrow, L. J. (1964). Separation from parents in early childhood. In M. L. Hoffman & L. W. Hoffman (Eds.), *Review of child development research* (vol. 1). New York: Sage.

Yarrow, L. J. (1970). The development of focused relationships during infancy. In J. Hellmuth (Ed.),

Exceptional infant (vol. 1). New York: Brunner/Mazel.

Young, K. T. & Zigler, E. (1986). Infant and toddler day care regulations and policy implications. *American Journal of Orthopsychiatry, 56,* 43–55.

Yurdakok, K., Yavuz, T. & Taylor, C. E. (1990). Swaddling and acute respiratory infections. *American Journal of Public Health, 80,* 873–875.

Zahn-Waxler, C., Radke-Yarrow, M. & King, R. A. (1977). The impact of the affective environment on young children. Paper presented at the biennial meeting of the Society for Research in Child Development, New Orleans.

Zigler, E. F. & Lang, M. E. (1991). *Child care choices: Balancing the needs of children, families, and society.* New York: The Free Press.

Zigler, E. F. & Stevenson, M. F. (1993). *Children in a changing world: Development and social issues* (2nd ed.). Pacific Grove, Calif.: Brooks/Cole.

Developmental Tasks of Toddlerhood

Chapter 9

Language and Communication

  Milestones in Language and Communication

      Communication Accomplishments in Infancy

      Communicative Competence in Toddlerhood

      Language Development Beyond Toddlerhood

  The Language Environment

      Interaction and Language Development

      Scaffolding and Other Strategies for Enhancing Language Development

      Language at Home and at School

Elaboration of Locomotion

Fantasy Play

  The Emergence of Symbolic Play

      Distinguishing Pretense from Reality

  Changes in Fantasy Play During Toddlerhood

  The Importance of Fantasy Play

  The Role of Play Companions

  Imaginary Companions

Self-Control

  Precursors of Self-Control in Infancy

  Control of Impulses

      Increasing Sensitivity to the Distress of Others

      A New Sense of Future Time

      Strategies That Help Children Manage Their Impulses

      Individual Differences in the Ability to Control Impulses

  Self-Regulated Goal Attainment

      Speech and Goal Attainment

Chapter Summary

References

Toddlers seem to be bubbling over with unpredictable, startling thoughts and actions that amaze adults. Toddlers are extremely busy—talking, moving, fantasizing, and planning all the time. The vigor, constancy, and complexity of their physical activity are remarkable. Equally impressive is the toddler's flood of cognitive accomplishments, especially language production and unique forms of playful fantasy.

On the foundation of trust and optimism laid during infancy, toddlers construct a sense of personal autonomy, an enjoyment and confidence in doing things for themselves and expressing their will. The successful integration of these two capacities for trust and autonomy provides a strong, protective basis for the young child's ego system. From this basis, children are able to venture into satisfying and meaningful social relationships, engage in playful problem solving, and face their future with hopefulness and assertiveness.

A positive conclusion to the period of toddlerhood rests largely on the quality of the home environment. Toddlers, with their high energy level, their improbable ideas, their impish willfulness, and their needs for mastery, run headlong into the full range of limits in their physical and social environment. Parenting during toddlerhood is like paddling a canoe through rapids: It requires vigilance, good communication, flexibility, and a certain joie de vivre that keeps the whole journey fun. A child's cognitive and social development during this period can be facilitated by the parents' own ego development, by the way they approach the challenges of toddlerhood, and by the quality of the relationship between the child's parents (Miller et al., 1993). A high level of discord, conflict, and stress in the parents' lives brings special risk for some toddlers.

Aggression between parents increases the risks of violence toward toddlers. Although we discuss the positive experiences of most toddlers, for some the world is harsh, unpredictable, and dangerous. A toddler who pulls down blocks in a noisy clatter or spills juice on the breakfast table may be shaken to death by his or her mother's boyfriend. More common are children who are routinely hit by angry adults or exposed to repeated violence between the adults in the family. These children may experience fear, loathing, and frightening fantasies. Continuous exposure to rough treatment increases the likelihood that toddlers will act aggressively in their interactions with others, an orientation that begins to disrupt their social relations with siblings, peers, and child-care providers. This becomes a serious problem for some children during the early school age and middle childhood years when the peer rejection is so intense that access to learning social skills is severely disrupted. Many never recover. The tendency for aggression is also revealed when these children become parents themselves, with a tendency to physically abuse their own children (McCloskey et al., 1995).

Toddlerhood refers to two-and three-year-olds. The developmental tasks of toddlerhood—language and communication skills, expanded locomotion, fantasy play, and self-control—all contribute to the child's emerging independence within the boundaries of the social group. Some theorists refer to this as the first individuation process (Blos, 1979; Mahler et al., 1975). Obviously, three-year-olds are not ready to set out for life alone in the big city. But they are ready to express independent thoughts, exercise some control in making choices, and try doing things on their own in their own way. The psychosocial crisis during this period of life, autonomy versus shame and doubt, is a struggle to establish a sense of separateness without disrupting the bonds of affection and protection that are critical to a young child's physical survival and emotional connection to the family.

autonomy vs. self doubt.

Language and Communication

A major developmental transformation of toddlerhood is the emerging capacity for *semiotic thought*, the capacity to let one object, word, picture, or gesture stand for something else (DeLoache, 1991). Both the flood of accomplishments in the area of language and the astonishing talent for fantasy play depend on this new capacity for symbolization. Symbolization adds enormous flexibility to human thought. The symbol represents an idea of something separate from the thing itself. With the elaboration of various types of symbols, children can begin to recount events apart from the situation in which they occurred. They can invent worlds that never existed. The domains of make-believe, poetry, fairy tales, and folklore that we often associate with childhood open up to the toddler as the ability for symbolization expands.

capacity to recognize symbols

In the process of language development, children acquire *communicative competence:* They become adept at using all the aspects of language that permit effective participation in the language environment of their culture (Harris, 1992). This includes learning the sound system, the system of meanings, the rules of word and sentence formation, vocabulary, the necessary adjustments to the social setting to produce and interpret communication (pragmatics), and the ability to express thoughts in written as well as oral form. Through the achievement of communicative competence, children become increasingly integrated into their culture. They learn the expressions, tone of voice, and gestures that link them intimately to the language environment of their home and community. They learn when to speak and when to remain silent; how to approach communication with peers, parents, and authority figures. They learn the terms that are applied to kin, close friends, acquaintances and strangers; the words that are used to disparage or devalue and those used to recognize and praise. If nurturing is the primary vehicle for cultural socialization in infancy, communication is the primary vehicle in toddlerhood.

language dev't integrates the child into the culture

Communicative competence begins during infancy and develops throughout life. But toddlerhood encompasses the most dramatic expansion in verbal competence, when remarkable achievements are made in an exceptionally brief period. The discussion of language and communication is divided into two major segments: language milestones and the language environment. The first section outlines the communication accomplishments of infancy and toddlerhood, including the expanded use of words with meaning, the formation of two-word sentences, more complex sentence formation, grammar, and other milestones of language acquisition. The second section identifies factors in the social environment that help facilitate and optimize communicative competence.

FIGURE 9.1
Word production from 8 to 16 months
Source: Fenson et al. (1994). Variability in early communicative development. *Monographs of the Society for Research in Child Developments, 59* (5), 38. Copyright © 1994 The Society for Research in Child Development, Inc. Reprinted with permission.

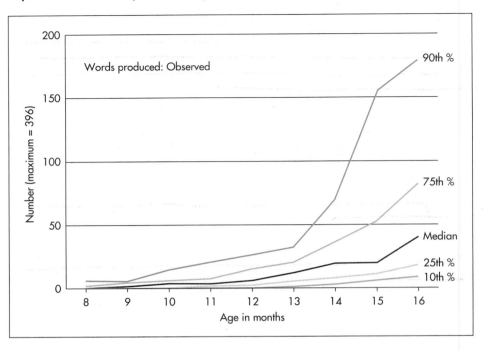

Milestones in Language and Communication

We will discuss patterns of accomplishment in language and communication from infancy through about age four. At the outset, however, it is important to recognize the wide variability in the development of communicative skills. Certain sequences of ability appear to be quite common across children in many language environments. For example, communicative gestures precede the production of spoken words, and the production of a substantial vocabulary of spoken words precedes the capacity for two-word sentences. But the timing of the onset of various abilities and the rate of growth in these abilities vary from child to child. For example, in a large national study of infant-toddler language, word production for 12-month-old infants ranged from the 90th percentile who used 26 words or more to the 10th percentile who produced no words. By 16 months of age, those in the 90th percentile were using 180 words, and those in the bottom 10th percentile produced 10 words or less (Fenson et al., 1994) (see Figure 9.1). All these children were healthy, normal children with no known history of developmental delay, prematurity, or genetic disease. As you read about modal or typical patterns, try to remember that these patterns disguise important variations.

Communication Accomplishments in Infancy

Thought and language seem to travel independent courses that intersect during the second year of life (Molfese et al., 1982). Before that time, one can observe vocalization without meaning; that is, cooing (mostly vowel sounds noticeable at one to two months) and babbling (consonant-vowel sounds repeated over and over, which begin at about four months). One also observes thoughtful action patterns without verbal labels—reaching and grasping, or learning to use a spoon. (We discussed this type of behavior as sensorimotor intelligence in Chapter 7.)

BOX 9.1

Looking in on the Brain: How the Brain Processes Language

Research evidence confirms that linguistic competence, especially verbal material, is based within the left hemisphere of the brain. Further, with the use of positron emission tomography (PET), one can observe different areas of activity in the brain related to varying language activities, including speaking, seeing, and hearing words. Verbal communication is distinct from other cognitive functions such as symbolization or associative memory. Studies involving deaf users of sign language as well as hearing subjects who use spoken language show that injury to the left hemisphere can result in a form of language aphasia. For the deaf, this injury does not interrupt the capacity to make other types of gestures, confirming that language functions are differentiated from other symbolic and motor functions that might be involved in the communicative process (Corina et al., 1992). Using pictorial information, studies have suggested that the right hemisphere applies conventional rules for determining meaning, whereas the left hemisphere is better suited for detecting deviations from standard meaning and for assigning meaning when the stimuli are unfamiliar (Cronin-Golomb, 1995). Researchers may eventually be able to observe substantial changes in organization and activity in this area of the left hemisphere during the period of toddlerhood when many new stimuli are encountered and few rules are already established.

Language Perception. Infants are able to recognize sounds and differentiate between sound combinations before they understand the meanings of the sounds (Bates et al., 1987). This capacity to recognize language sounds, including the phonetic combinations of letters and words, and the intonation of sentences, is called *language perception*. Very young infants appear to be able to hear and distinguish among all the major language sounds used in natural language. By the age of 4½ months, infants show recognition of the sound of their names (Mandel et al., 1995).

ability to differentiate between sounds

Babies also appear to be especially sensitive to a particular rhythmic manner of adult talking that is characteristic of the ways adults interact with preverbal babies. Anne Fernald calls this talk "parentese"; you might call it baby talk (Fernald & Kuhl, 1987). She found that, as an adult speaks to a baby, he or she "raises pitch, exaggerates intonation, shortens utterances, and greatly lengthens pauses between utterances" (Raymond, 1991, p. A7). This pattern was observed in seven different spoken languages. Babies seem to catch the emotional tone of these communications, perceiving the meaning as reassuring, approving, or disapproving (see Box 9.1).

Babbling. Babbling, initially characterized by sounds used in many languages, begins to reflect the sounds and intonation that infants are most likely to hear. Sounds that they do not hear drop out of their babbling, and, at about this same time, the capacity to differentiate among language sounds not found in their native language diminishes (Bates et al., 1987). This environmental shaping of language competence provides another example of plasticity of brain functions, discussed in Chapter 7, where some networks grow and become strengthened by experience while others wither and are absorbed into the neural mass.

Babbling begins to take on a special character of connecting consonants and vowels and repeating these combinations at around six to ten months. Although parents may eagerly receive this type of babbling as evidence of first words *(baba-mama-dada)*, research suggests that these repetitions of babbling sounds do not have a symbolic value.

Communication with Gestures.   By eight months, infants also use sounds, like grunting and whining, in combination with gestures to achieve a goal. Thus, sounds combined with gestures and looks in a certain direction become part of purposeful communication—such as trying to get mother to reach a cookie or to get a certain toy off the shelf. A common first gesture is to raise the arms up toward the caregiver in a desire to be picked up (Fenson et al., 1994). Sounds may also be used to express emotion or to get attention (Bates et al., 1987; Garton, 1992). Two other major communicative strategies emerge at about 9 to 11 months. Infants begin to seek adult interest and attention by *showing objects* and thereby initiating an interaction. Soon after showing, the infant begins *giving objects*. Adults who are willing to engage in this type of exchange will find the baby bringing them a whole variety of toys, utensils, and scraps of dust for inspection. Following giving, a common next step in communication is *pointing.* There is some debate about whether pointing is a form of reaching or a way of getting an adult's attention to notice an object. In either case, it is an example of an infant's initial ability to establish a shared reference point with respect to some object in the environment. Our first child, Sam, used pointing combined with a "whasziss?" sound to ask for the names of things at about ten months.

First Words.   Around the age of eight months, infants understand the meanings of some individual words and phrases (Fenson et al., 1994; Harris, 1992). This ability to understand words, called *receptive language*, precedes the ability to produce spoken words and phrases. You can direct a baby's glance by saying, "Look at the flowers," or "Do you want some crackers?" At this age, babies are accomplished at the ever-delightful game of "point to your nose, eyes, ears, etc." The number of words that infants understand increases rapidly after 12 months. According to one analysis, 16-month-old infants have a receptive vocabulary of between 92 and 321 words (Fenson et al., 1994).

One of the first significant events in the development of *language production* is the naming of objects. With repetition, a sound or word becomes associated with a specific object or a set of related objects. For example, a child may say *ba* whenever she sees her bottle. If she is thirsty and wants her bottle, she may try saying *ba* in order to influence her mother to produce the bottle. Gestures, actions, and facial expressions often accompany the approximate word and help establish its meaning in the caregiver's mind. If the baby's word has meaning to the mother and serves to satisfy the baby's needs, it will probably be retained as a meaningful sign. *Ba* may come to mean *bottle* and other liquids the child wishes to drink, such as juice, water, or soda.

The important characteristic of first words is their shared meaning. Even though *ba* is not a real word, it functions in the same way that any noun does: It names a person, place, or thing (Greenfield & Smith, 1976). These single-word utterances accompanied by gestures, actions, vocal intonation, and emotion are called *holophrases.* They convey the meaning of an entire sentence. For example, saying *ba, ba* in a pleading tone while pointing to the refrigerator and bouncing up and down conveys the meaning "I want a bottle." Gradually, the child discovers that every object, action, and relationship has a name.

[handwritten margin note:] receptive language - the ability to understand words.

[handwritten margin note:] Naming of objects

Holophrases convey the meaning of an entire sequence or thought.

Young children first talk about what they know and what they are interested in. Common first words include important people (*Mamma, Dadda,* names of siblings), foods, pets, toys, body parts (*eye, nose*), clothes (*shoe, sock*), vehicles (*car*), favorite objects (*bottle, blanket*), other objects in the environment (*keys, trees*), actions (*up, bye-bye*), pronouns (*you, me*), states (*hot, hungry*), *yes, no, please, down,* and *more.* Lois Bloom (1993) has suggested that a principle of relevance guides the early acquisition of new words. Babies are likely to attend to words and expressions that are most closely linked with what they are doing and thinking about at the time. For that reason, the actual vocabulary that is acquired during infancy is quite idiosyncratic, reflecting the themes and experiences of each child's everyday life.

Communicative Competence in Toddlerhood

Vocabulary. During the period from 12 to 16 months, infants make significant progress in learning the names of objects and applying those names to pictures or real examples. There is a rapid expansion of vocabulary during these four months. Sometime around 18 months, the child acquires a large number of new words, and vocabulary continues to expand at a rapid rate throughout the toddler and early school years (Rice, 1989). As reported above, the average toddler of 30 months has a spoken vocabulary of about 570 words. In order to accomplish this feat, children seem to *fast-map* new meanings as they experience words in conversation. Fast-mapping is forming an initial, partial understanding of a word's meaning quickly. It is an information-processing technique in which children relate the word to the known vocabulary and restructure the known-word storage space and its related conceptual categories (Carey, 1978). The child has to hear the new word only once or a very few times in a context that makes its meaning clear. Thus, without direct word-by-word tutoring, children accumulate numerous samples of their culture's language from the speech they hear and attach a minimally satisfactory definition to each word or phrase.

The early phase of vocabulary development seems to focus on broad semantic categories such as animals, cars, fruits, clothes. New words, particularly nouns, are treated like the name of a category of things rather than one specific object or part of an object. For example, when a child learns the word "cup," that word is used to refer to all objects that have the general shape and function of a cup (Golinkoff et al., Jones et al., 1991; Smith et al., 1992).

A much slower process of vocabulary development occurs as children and adults learn the distinctions among words within categories (Miller & Gildea, 1987). You may have a very good idea about the distinction between annual and perennial flowering plants, but you may not know the difference between the many, many types of each group and how to recognize them. In fact, building a vocabulary of subcategories may become an entire field of study, such as botany or zoology, in which the types and subtypes of a larger category are identified, classified, and named.

Two-Word Sentences. At 16 months of age, few children use two-word sentences, but by 30 months almost all children make these kinds of word combinations (Fenson et al., 1994). These two-word sentences are referred to as *telegraphic speech*. Children link two words that are essential to communicate what they intend to say. Just as in a telegram, however, other words—verbs, articles, prepositions, pronouns, and conjunctions—are left out. A child will say: "big ball," "more juice," "Daddy gone." Before this point, children tend to utter single words accompanied by gestures and actions. By stringing two words together, they convey more meaning through verbal communication and rely less heavily on gestures and actions to convey their intentions. The acquisition of telegraphic speech allows a child to make fuller use of the symbolism inherent in language to communicate meaning.

Children are quite innovative in using two-word sentences. They continue to understand more than they are able to say, but they appear to use their limited number of words and the newfound ability to combine them to get their point across. Children may convey different meanings with the same sentence. "Daddy go," for example, may be used to tell someone that Daddy has left, or it may be used to tell Daddy to leave. Children often indicate their meanings by tone of voice or by the words they stress. The use of two-word sentences is characteristic of toddler-age language learners in many cultures (Slobin, 1985).

Braine (1976) analyzed the first word combinations spoken by children in English, Samoan, Finnish, Hebrew, and Swedish. His goal was to identify the kinds of rules or patterns that governed these early combinations. Ten patterns of word combination were found in those early language samples:

1. Making reference to something: See + X (see mother).
2. Describing something: Hot + X (hot stove).
3. Possession: X has a Y (Billy has a bottle).
4. Plurality: Two + X (two dogs).
5. Repetition or other examples: More + X (more up).
6. Disappearance: All gone + X (all gone milk).
7. Negation: No + X (no sleep).
8. Actor–action relations: Person + X (Daddy sleep).
9. Location: X + here (Grandma here).
10. Requests: Have + X (Have it, ball).

Braine found that, although he could identify some common patterns of word combinations, they were not guided by the grammatical categories of

[handwritten margin note: telegraphic speech— two word sentences]

the spoken language but by the meanings that the child wished to express and by the variety of objects, people, and interactions in the immediate environment. The patterns of word combinations used by some children did not overlap at all with patterns used by other children within the same culture.

Early language appears to be closely tied to the representation of sensorimotor schemes—the kinds of activities that dominate the child's life such as eating, sleeping, playing games with mommy or daddy or the siblings, going places, coming back home, and so on. It expresses the properties and relationships of objects and people that are important in a child's life. Language use emerges within a larger communication system and reflects a child's cognitive capacities. At the same time, it reflects the perceptual and functional characteristics of the environment. The kinds of objects and relationships that are central to daily life influence the content and complexity of a child's early language (Nelson, 1981).

Grammatical Transformations. By combining words according to the set of rules of grammar for a given language, a person can produce a limitless number of messages that can be understood by another person. Remarkably, by the age of four, children appear to be able to structure their sentences using most of these rules without any direct instruction. The *grammar* of a particular language is a set of rules that permits the complexity and variety of one person's thinking to be readily understood by someone else. Consider the difference in meaning between "The boy hit the ball" and "The ball hit the boy." The simple matter of word order in a sentence is critical for preserving meaning. The basic format of an English sentence, noun phrase followed by verb phrase, is a central part of its grammar. In order to ask a question or to produce a negative sentence, the speaker transforms this word order according to a specific set of rules (e.g., You are going. Are you going?). The addition of certain inflections and modifiers conveys information about time, possession, number, and relation. As children learn the grammatical transformations of their language, they become much more effective in conveying exactly what they have in mind.

When Brown (1973) analyzed the development of grammar in three children, he found that, although the rate of acquiring inflections varied among the children, the order was surprisingly constant. The typical order in which children learn basic grammatical inflections is listed in Table 9.1.

A surprising observation is that children use correct transformations for the past tenses of irregular verbs (*went, gave, run*) before they use correct inflections of regular verbs (*talked, walked, jumped*). It appears that children first learn the past tenses of irregular verbs through rote memory. Once they learn the rule for expressing the past tense by adding -ed, they *overgeneralize* this rule and begin making errors in the past tense. So a two-year-old is likely to say "I ran fast," but a three-year-old may say "I runned fast."

The errors that young children make alert us to the fact that they are working to figure out a system of rules with which to communicate meaning. It is unlikely that these errors result from imitation of adult speech. Children say such things as "What dat feeled like?" or "Dose are mines." They have certainly not copied those expressions from adults; rather, these errors suggest the beginning of a grammar that becomes more specialized and accurate as children acquire the opportunity to match their speech to that of others (Schatz, 1983).

TABLE 9.1

Basic Sequence in Adding Grammatical Inflections

Inflection	Example
-ing	Puppy is runn*ing*.
in	*in* the pot
on	I am *on* the bed.
Plural: -s	Apple*s*
Past irregular	*Fell, hit, ran*
Possessive: -s	Baby's toy
Use of *to be* as main verb without contraction	The boys *are* home.
Articles	I want *a* bottle.
Past regular	You walk*ed* too fast.
Third-person regular	He walk*s*.
Third-person irregular	She *has*, he *does*.
Uncontractible progressive auxiliary	This *is* going fast.
Use of *to be* as a main verb with contraction	That'*s* Bill.
Contractible progressive auxiliary	I'*m* talk*ing*.

Source: Brown, R. (1973). *A first language: The early stages.* Cambridge, Mass.: Harvard University Press.

The milestones in language development during the first four years of life are summarized in Table 9.2. During the first year of life, babies are highly sensitive to spoken language. They use vocalization in a playful way as a source of sensory stimulation. Gradually, babies produce vocalizations that imitate spoken language. In the second year, babies understand words and phrases. They develop a vocabulary and begin to form two-word phrases. During the third year, language is definitely used to communicate ideas, observations, and needs. Comprehension of spoken language seems almost complete. Some of their speech may not be easily understood by people outside the family, partly because they are unable to produce clear phonetic sounds and partly because their knowledge of adult grammar is limited. During the fourth year, most children acquire an extensive vocabulary. They can create sentences that reflect most of the basic rules of grammar. Their language is a vehicle for communicating complex thoughts that are usually understood by children and adults outside the family.

Language Development Beyond Toddlerhood

Although the fundamentals of language are well established by age four, there are still some refinements of which toddlers are incapable. For example, Mary may raise a fuss about wanting the biggest piece of cake. If you allow her to choose, she selects a smaller piece with lots of frosting. Clearly, the word *biggest* is not being used correctly. Even though Mary is able to memorize and repeat the words *big, bigger,* and *biggest,* she does not yet fully understand the concept. Other observations suggest that two- and three-year-olds have difficulty using verbal instructions to control or guide their behavior (Tinsley & Waters, 1982). They may be able to tell themselves to "stop" or "go slow,"

TABLE 9.2

Milestones in Language Development

At the Completion of:	Vocalization and Language
12 weeks	Markedly less crying than at 8 weeks; when talked to and nodded at, smiles, followed by squealing-gurgling sounds usually called cooing, that is, vowellike in character and pitch-modulating; sustains cooing for 15–20 seconds.
16 weeks	Responds to human sounds more definitely; turns head; eyes seem to search for speaker; occasionally, some chuckling sounds. Recognizes the sound of his/her name.
20 weeks	The vowellike cooing sounds begin to be interspersed with consonantal sounds; acoustically, all vocalizations are very different from the sounds of the mature language of the environment.
6 months	Cooing changing into babbling resembling one-syllable utterances; neither vowels nor consonants have very fixed recurrences; most common utterances sound somewhat like *ma, mu, da,* or *di.*
8 months	Reduplication (or more continuous repetition) becomes frequent; intonation patterns become distinct; utterances can signal emphasis and emotions. Produces meaningful gestures like wanting to be picked up, showing or giving. Understands a small number of meaningful words and phrases.
10 months	Vocalizations are mixed with sound play such as gurgling or bubble blowing; appears to wish to imitate sounds, but the imitations are never quite successful; expanded comprehension of words.
12 months	Identical sound sequences are replicated with higher relative frequency of occurrence and early word production (*mamma* or *dadda*); understands about 50 words and simple commands ("Show me your eyes.").
16 months	Has a definite repertoire of about 40 words (the top 90th percentile has 180-word vocabulary); still much babbling, but now of several syllables with intricate intonation; words may include items such as *thank you* and *come here,* but there is little ability to join items into spontaneous two-item phrases; understanding is progressing rapidly.
24 months	Vocabulary of more than 300 items (some children seem to be able to name everything in environment); begin spontaneously to join vocabulary items into two-word phrases; all phrases appear to be own creations; definite increase in communicative behavior and interest in language.
30 months	Continuing increase in vocabulary with over 550 words; many new additions every day; no babbling at all; utterances have communicative intent; frustrated if not understood by others; utterances consist of at least two words, many have three or even five words; use of linguistic suffixes for possession, plural, and past tenses; frequent use of irregular plural noun (foot/feet) and irregular verbs; intelligibility is not very good yet by those unfamiliar with the child's speech.
3 years	Vocabulary of some 1,000 words; about 80% of utterances are intelligible even to strangers; grammatical complexity of utterances is roughly that of colloquial adult language, although mistakes still occur.
4 years	Language is well established; deviations from the adult norm tend to be more in style than in grammar.

Source: Adapted from Lenneberg, E. H. (1967). *Biological foundations of language.* New York: Wiley; and Fenson et al. (1994). Variability in early communicative development. *Monographs of the Society for Research in Child Development, 59* (5).

but these commands are not effective in slowing them down. Both of these examples demonstrate that toddler's language development can be somewhat misleading. One may assume that toddlers fully understand the more abstract meaning of the words they use, but in fact their language continues to be very idiosyncratic.

As the process of fast-mapping implies, children may add a word to their vocabulary without understanding the several meanings that this word has in different contexts. During the periods of early and middle childhood, considerable time and attention is devoted to exploring vocabulary, correcting some meanings that were incorrectly learned, and expanding the full range of meanings and underlying concepts that are linked to the many words that were acquired so rapidly during toddlerhood. One estimate is that the reading vocabulary or comprehension of dictionary entries of a ten-year-old child is close to 40,000 words, with perhaps another 40,000 proper names, places, and expressions unique to the child's own family, neighborhood, and cultural group (Anglin, 1993).

Important language functions develop more fully during early school age and middle childhood. Older children can use language to help them plan a problem-solving strategy, guide a complex series of motor activities, or identify the relationships among objects. Vocabulary expands, and words increasingly are used in the ways they are used by adults. Sentences become more complex, including conditional and descriptive clauses. Irregular verbs and nouns are learned and used correctly (Moskowitz, 1978). Children learn to conceptualize the grammatical structure of their language in school. Beyond the formal elements of vocabulary, grammar, reading, and writing, language becomes a vehicle for creative expression. Children write poems, essays, and stories. They begin to use sarcasm, puns, and metaphors to elaborate their speech. They create secret codes with their friends. They make up riddles and jokes, perform plays and puppet shows, publish school newspapers, and write enigmatic or corny messages in their friends' yearbooks. Language plays a critical role in subsequent psychosocial crises, especially the establishment of group identity, intimacy, and generativity. It is primarily through the quality of spoken language that one achieves the levels of emotional disclosure that sustain significant personal relationships. Language also serves as a mechanism for resolving conflicts and building cohesiveness within groups, whether of friends, co-workers, or family members.

The Language Environment

Language is a means for socializing and educating young children, creating a sense of group identity, and passing the mythology, wisdom, and values of the culture from one generation to the next. Language is integral to the psychosocial environment. Competence in the use of language solidifies the young child's membership in the immediate family and in the larger cultural group (Rogoff & Morelli, 1989). Although there is strong evidence for a genetic capacity for language learning, the specific content and tone of a child's communication are strongly influenced by the language environment. In this section, we focus primarily on the nature of the language interaction between toddlers and their caregivers, with some attention to the issue of bilingualism and the relationship of the language environment at home and school.

The time Vicky spends in playful interactions with her dad makes a major contribution to her cognitive development.

Interaction and Language Development

Probably the most important contribution that caregivers make to cognitive growth is the opportunity for interactions. An interactive adult can answer a child's questions, provide information, react unexpectedly and surprise the child, explain plans or strategies, and offer praise or criticism. With the achievement of language skills, children and their caregivers begin to explore a vast array of topics through spoken language. Together, they explore their needs—hunger, thirst, sleepiness, and companionship. They share emotions—anger, sadness, delight, pride, and shame. They talk playfully with one another, examining new objects, discussing kinship relations, and creating fantasy situations. Adults and children discuss philosophical and moral questions such as obeying rules, lying, helping others, empathizing with others, and various real and hypothetical dilemmas. As children verbally reveal their own point of view, parents begin to know and appreciate their child's concerns and needs in a new way. Similarly, children can ask questions and expand their understanding through family discussion.

Burton White compared the child-rearing practices of mothers whose children were judged to be socially and intellectually competent with those of mothers whose children were judged to be below average (White et al., 1979). The mothers of the competent children spent more time interacting with them than did the mothers of the below-average children. This was true at every age period from 12 to 33 months. "The amount of live language directed to a child was perhaps the strongest single indicator of later intellectual and linguistic and social achievement" (White et al., 1979). This does not mean that it is necessary to talk with a child continuously, but it is clear that children benefit from frequent opportunities for interaction.

The causal relationship between a child's language competence and the frequency of parent–child interaction is still a matter of some controversy.

Consider these three different explanations:

1. Parents and their offspring may share a genetic predisposition for verbal competence which is evident in the frequency of parent–child interaction and in the early acquisition of verbal skills.
2. Parents who interact frequently with their children provide a rich array of verbal stimuli and thereby promote high levels of verbal comprehension and production.
3. Children who are more verbally competent stimulate more interaction from their caregivers which then establishes a more active and diverse verbal environment.

Over time, research will no doubt clarify the nature of these relationships.

Certain characteristics of a caregiver have been shown to facilitate a child's language acquisition and communication skills (Snow, 1984). When talking to toddlers, adults tend to modify their speech so that they are more likely to be understood. They use simplified, redundant speech that corresponds to the child's level of comprehension and interest. It is noteworthy that caregivers speak to infants in long, complex sentences, but as soon as babies begin to speak, their caregivers' speech becomes exaggerated and simplified (Moskowitz, 1978). When speaking to toddlers, adults and older children adjust their spoken language in the following ways (Rice, 1989):

1. They simplify utterances to correspond with the toddler's interests and comprehension level.
2. They emphasize the here and the now.
3. They use a more restricted vocabulary.
4. They do a lot of paraphrasing.
5. They use simple, well-formed sentences.
6. They use frequent repetitions.
7. They use a slow rate of speech with pauses between utterances and after the major content words.

These characteristics of caregiver speech are not universal; they seem to reflect cultural norms for addressing toddlers (Pye, 1986). They are most typically observed in white, middle-class Western societies. In one cross-cultural analysis, for example, it was observed that African-American adults in the rural South do not simplify or censor their speech for young children (Heath, 1989). They frequently do not address children directly but expect the children to listen to adult conversation and to interrupt if they have something to add. African-American adults and children tend to direct one another's behavior with specific commands. It is just as acceptable for a toddler to command an adult as the other way around. Adults tease children, especially in the presence of others, in order to give the children a chance to show off their quick wit and to practice assertiveness. Within this particular language environment, children have the opportunity to hear a variety of opinions, gather information that extends their direct experience, and observe shifts in language tone and style that accompany changes in the topic or purpose of the conversation.

This example illustrates the wide variation in parenting styles that characterize American families, producing substantial differences in the language-learning environment of the home. In one longitudinal study, 40 families (15 African-American and 25 white families) with preverbal children were observed once per month over 2½ years (Hart & Risley, 1992). The observations covered the period shortly before, during, and after the child learned to talk. The number of words spoken to a child in an hour varied from 232 to 3,606; the percentage of time that parents were in the same room as the child during the observation ranged from 38% to 99%; and the average number of turns (parent speaks–child speaks) in an interaction ranged from 1.8 to 17.4.

One question raised in this observational study was whether parenting style during the period of toddlerhood was related to the child's measured IQ at 37 months. Three dimensions of parenting style were identified (see Table 9.3). The first and third factors, parental activity and quality of a parent's speech to the child, were positively related to the child's IQ. The second factor, performance as a social partner, was not correlated with the child's IQ. Both the first and third factors were correlated with the family's socioeconomic status, whereas the second factor was not. Children in lower socioeconomic-status families of both racial groups experienced less time with their parents, fewer moments of joint play, and exposure to fewer words. They were less likely to have their speech repeated or paraphrased by their parents or to

TABLE 9.3

Parenting Style During Language Learning

Factor	Criteria
1. Parental activity	The percentage of time that the parent was present in the same room with the child.
	The percentage of time that the parent joined the child in play.
	The number of words directed to the child.
	The number of *different* words directed to the child.
2. Performance as a social partner	The likelihood that a parent will respond to a child's initiation.
	The length of a social interaction as measured by the number of turns the parent takes.
	The relative length of a parent's phrases in comparison with the child's phrases.
3. Quality of a parent's speech toward the child	The likelihood that parents will ask their child questions.
	The likelihood that parents will repeat or paraphrase their child's speech.
	The frequency with which the parent imposes prohibitions on the child's behavior.

Source: Adapted from Hart, B. & Risley, T. R. (1992). American parenting of language-learning children: Persisting differences in family–child interactions observed in natural home environments. *Developmental Psychology, 28,* 1102–1103. Copyright © 1992 by the American Psychological Association. Reprinted with permission.

be asked questions and more likely to have prohibitions placed on their behavior. Those parents who were most likely to place prohibitions on their child's activities during this age period were less likely to listen intently to their child's speech, repeat what the child had said, or ask the child questions.

Scaffolding and Other Strategies for Enhancing Language Development

The process of language learning involves a pattern of mutual regulation and upward *scaffolding*. Children try to match the verbal expressions used by adults, both in pronunciation and in selection of words (Nelson, 1973). Sometimes a child may be misunderstood due to pronunciation that is discrepant from the real word (*ambiance* for *ambulance*, *snuffin'cake* for *stomach ache*). At the same time, adults may use simplification or some other strategy to make sure that children understand them. Through frequent interactions, adults encourage language development by establishing a good balance between modifying their speech somewhat and modeling more complex, accurate speech for children.

Adults make use of several strategies to clarify a child's meaning when the speech is unclear. One such strategy is *expansion*, or the elaboration of the child's expressions:

Child: Doggie wag.

Parent: Yes, the dog is wagging her tail.

Another strategy is *prompting*, which often takes the form of a question. Here, the parent urges the child to say more:

Child: More crackel.

Parent: You want more what?

In both of these interactions, the adult is helping the child to communicate more effectively by expanding or asking the child to elaborate on something of interest to the child. In addition, the kinds of sentences that parents use teach children to produce new sentences that are more grammatically correct and therefore more meaningful to others.

Reading and Language Games. Socially interactive rituals such as telling stories, playing word games, verbal joking and teasing, and reading books together also seem to enhance language development, especially by building vocabulary and preparing children to use language comfortably in social situations. Reading aloud has been identified as an especially important language activity, not only for literacy but also for expanding language skills (Crain-Thoreson & Dale, 1992; Valdez-Menchaca & Whitehurst, 1992). During toddlerhood, an adult may start out by reading picture books and asking the child questions about the pictures. The adult may try to relate the picture to some event in the child's life or ask children what they notice about the picture. Over time, the child becomes more and more of the storyteller, while the adult listens, encourages, and expands the tale. Some books are read aloud so often that the toddler begins to "read" them from memory or retell the story in their own words as they look at the pictures.

As children enter early school age, this type of ritualized reading activity provides a framework for the child's concept of reading, including the ideas that printed letters make up words; that stories usually have a beginning, middle, and end; and that printed words and spoken words are similar in some ways. Depending on the context in which children read, they may also discover that they can learn things from printed words that they can't always know from the pictures, and that reading enables them to learn about the world beyond their direct experiences (Schickedanz, 1986).

Parents often engage their children in language games to expand their use of words and phrases. These games are usually part of ongoing family life. They are introduced not as a separate activity, but as an extension of a related activity. Hoffman (1985, 90) described one of her 3½-year-old son David's spontaneous games that began to link speech to literacy. The object was for David to point to road signs as he rode with his mother to nursery school and for her to read as many of the signs as possible. David had created this game, and his mother played along willingly:

> On the way to nursery school, David said, "Let's talk about signs! What does that sign say?"
> I answered, "Right turn signal."
> David proceeded with, "And what does that yellow and red shell say?"
> I answered him, "It says 'Shell'—that's a gasoline station."
> He asked, "Does it have seashells in it?"
> I answered, "No."
> We proceeded to read signs. I read the majority as he requested. However, David read "Speed Limit 35," "Bike Route," "No Parking Any Time." When we came to "No Parking This Side of Street," he thought it was "No Parking Any Time."
> These were the signs that I was able to read as he requested while I was driving. They were not the only ones on the route.

Reading aloud as a family welcomes toddlers into the world of literacy.

SPEED LIMIT 40	WATCH CHILDREN
SPEED LIMIT 35 (12 times)	SIGNAL AHEAD (3 times)
NO PARKING ANY TIME (20 times)	NO LITTERING
SCHOOL SPEED LIMIT (2 times)	DRIVEWAY
NO PARKING ON THIS SIDE OF STREET (7 times)	BIKE ROUTE (2 times)
NO TURN ON RED (3 times)	

Source: From Hoffman, S. J. (1985). "Play and the Acquisition of Literacy" *Quarterly Newsletter of the Laboratory of Comparative Human Cognition, 7,* 89–95. Reprinted with permission.

Families and ethnic groups vary, not only in the language or dialect they speak but also in their reliance on verbal as opposed to nonverbal expression, their typical patterns of communication, and the importance they place on language as a means to help children achieve competence in various domains. One area that has received special attention in recent years is the role of family conversation about feelings and its relation to a child's ability to express feelings and to identify emotional states in others (see Box 9.2).

BOX 9.2

Family Talk about Feelings

Among the many areas of talk that are explored during toddlerhood, one that is especially important for the continuation of emotional and social development is talk about feelings. Children's use of words to refer to feelings and to describe emotions increases notably at three and four years of age. At this same time, children become more skilled at recognizing feeling states in others and in understanding how a person might feel in a certain situation (Brown & Dunn, 1992). Toddlers who have frequent experiences of talking with their parents when they are in distress or conflict appear to be more effective at the age of six in understanding others' points of view and in anticipating others' needs (Dunn et al., 1991). The implication is that the family's ability to identify a child's emotional states and talk about feelings influences a child's understanding of emotions and subsequent sensitivity to the emotions of others.

Brown and Dunn (1992) recorded mother–child and older sibling–child interactions at home visits when the study child was 33 and 47 months old. By the age of 47 months, child–sibling interactions had increased substantially. At that point, the quality of mother–child talk about emotions was distinct from the quality of sibling–child talk. Mothers talk more about the child's feelings. They acknowledge the child's feelings, talk about being hurt or hurting others, and help children interpret their feelings. Siblings, on the other hand, tend to draw attention to their own feelings. They are more likely to express feelings by laughing and joking or teasing the child. Perhaps partly as a result of their older siblings' tendency to draw attention to their own feelings, the younger children were more likely to talk about others' feelings at 47 months than they were at 33 months.

In contrast to environments in which talk about and expression of feelings are open and free, observations have revealed that maltreated children are more constrained in their speech (Coster et al., 1989). Maltreated toddlers speak in shorter phrases and are less likely to talk about their own activities or feelings. Their talk is often not relevant to the situation taking place. The more often that mothers of maltreated toddlers made reference to their own emotional states, the more likely toddlers were to talk about their own feelings and behaviors. This group's experience illustrates the extent to which an adult's inability to identify and express feelings in talk can restrict a child's early language development and establish powerful norms against certain types of communication.

tntontmontnt

the present time, the United States faces critical challenges in the education of young children. Many of these challenges are related to the quality of the young child's language environment, its correspondence with the language environment of the schools, and the relevance of the school's approach to the requirement of oral and written communication in the workplace. Language proficiency has at least two components (Snow, 1987). One is the use of language in face-to-face interactions in specific social situations. The other is language removed from any specific context, as it is usually measured by tests of vocabulary, verbal reasoning, and writing. Proficiency in one area may not predict proficiency in another (see Notebook Page 9.1).

Consider *bilingualism,* which is a social as well as a linguistic characteristic. Children who are proficient in two or more languages also exist in a complex sociocultural environment (Hakuta & Garcia, 1989). In some European countries, many sections of Canada, and certain areas of the United States, bilingualism is the norm. People who speak only one language are left out of important transactions in their community. Research has found that learning two languages generally does not hamper children's cognitive development, especially if being a native speaker of a particular language has no stigmatizing consequences (Diaz, 1983). It appears that young bilingual children are adept at switching from one language to another as the conversational situation demands. In one study of bilingual Hispanic children in Miami, Florida, the children had access to a nonoverlapping vocabulary in Spanish and English. In this instance, knowing the two languages actually expanded their access to concepts in comparison with children who spoke English or Spanish only (Umbel et al., 1992). In addition to the potential advantage in language performance, bilingual children may use their two languages to impose boundaries on social interactions and to add a degree of clarity to social relationships.

The concept of multicultural education underscores the need to recognize and value differences in the context and style of language use in various subcultures, and to introduce opportunities for children with different language competencies to build on their strengths in the educational environment. In the United States, however, schools assign high priority to proficiency in English. Even at a time when educators bemoan American schoolchildren's ignorance of foreign languages, the criterion for success in bilingual education is proficiency in abstract, academic English-language skills. Thus, schools may impose a conflict between proficiency in English and in the native language, which challenges children's language competence as well as their social identification (Olsen, 1988).

Elaboration of Locomotion

Use of the word *toddler* to describe the life stage for ages two and three is in itself a clue to the important part that locomotion plays. In fact, it is only during the first year of this stage that the child actually toddles. By age three, the child's walk has changed from the precarious, determined, humorous waddle known as the toddle to a more graceful, continuous, effective stride. Removal of diapers probably plays an important role in that progress;

What Was Learning to Speak Like for You?

The following questions are intended to help you recall or reconstruct your early language-learning experiences. Use any props you can find—early photos, toys, or childhood scrapbooks—to help you retrieve memories.

1. What do you remember about important features of your own language development, such as your first words; unique expressions; favorite stories, poems, songs, or word games; and cute verbal mistakes that became a family joke or expression? (You may include memories that occurred after toddlerhood.)

2. Ask your parents or any older person who interacted with you frequently when you were a toddler what they remember about your language learning. About how old were you when you began to say your first words? two-word phrases? three- and four-word sentences?

3. What were your first words?

4. Do your parents remember doing specific things to help you learn to talk or to help develop your vocabulary? What were they?

5. Do your parents or other relatives remember reading to you? What were some of your favorite books or stories?

_____

_____

_____

_____

6. Did you have any especially cute or unusual language behaviors that they remember? (Example: One child memorized the books that his parents read to him, giving them the impression that he could read when he was only about three.)

_____

_____

_____

_____

without thick padding between their legs, toddlers quickly make the transition from the gait of an ugly duckling to that of a swan. Of course, physical development, including changes in the shape and strength of leg muscles, contributes significantly to this transformation as well.

Locomotion plays a central role in the toddler's psychosocial development, facilitating the transformation of ideas into action and prompting new types of interactions with the social and physical environment. As locomotor skills develop, the child has more ways of remaining close to the object of attachment, new avenues for investigating the environment, and increased strategies for coping with stressful situations. Locomotor skills also figure prominently in the elaboration of play during this period. To the extent that coping, as we have defined it in Chapter 3, involves the ability to maintain freedom of movement under conditions of threat, the locomotor skills acquired during toddlerhood provide a fundamental arsenal of lifelong strategies for "fight" or "flight."

Advanced locomotor skills may also increase conflicts with caregivers, introducing new struggles of willfulness and new behavioral constraints (Biringen et al., 1995). When Ellen was about 2½ years old, she enjoyed watching her older brother climbing up a tree in a neighbor's yard. She begged her

Between the ages of 2 and 3, hurried walking becomes gleeful running.

brother to lift her up so she could get into the tree with him. One afternoon, her brother lifted her into the tree and then ran off to play with a friend. Ellen tried to get down from the tree, but she got her foot stuck in a crack between the branches. She cried and yelled until her mother came to get her. Her mother scolded Ellen for being in the tree and warned her never to go up there again. But, the next afternoon, Ellen was back trying to figure out how to climb into the tree on her own. Especially when locomotor skills occur early in a developmental period, before the maturation of verbal and cognitive competence, toddlers and caregivers may find themselves at odds in limiting locomotion to protect the child as well as other people and objects in the environment.

It is important to recognize the amazing complexity of the locomotor skills acquired by infants and toddlers in only two years. Difficulties encountered by engineers and inventors in trying to duplicate human locomotor skills with robots have demonstrated just how intricate and exquisite a toddler's accomplishments are (Pick, 1989). Research on motor development suggests that qualitative changes in locomotive behavior are not simply a result of maturation of the cerebral cortex (Kalverboer et al., 1993). Changes in body weight and muscle mass, combined with new capacities to coordinate neurological feedback from the limbs and to judge the effort needed to achieve a motoric goal, are all components in a regular progression in motor behavior (Getchell & Roberton, 1989). Some landmarks of motor development over the years from two to six in the skills of walking, running, jumping, hopping, throwing and catching, pedaling, and steering are described in Table 9.4. The achievement of these skills depends on opportunity and encouragement, as well as on the maturation of the cognitive and motor systems.

As walking becomes a more comfortable form of locomotion, new skills are added to the child's repertoire. Running and jumping are the first to emerge. By the age of four, children are likely to leap from stairways, porches, or ladders. They have begun to imagine what it might be like to fly, and jumping is their closest approximation to flying. Evidence suggests that the underlying structure of the jumping pattern remains stable throughout childhood and into adulthood (Clark et al., 1989). The child's delight in exploring jumping behavior may result from the acquisition of a fundamental movement pattern that gives the child a basic sense of mastery and lifelong possibilities.

TABLE 9.4

Changes in Gross Motor Skills During Toddlerhood and Early School Age

Age	Walking and Running	Jumping	Hopping	Throwing and Catching	Peddling and Steering
2–3 years	Walks more rhythmically; widely spaced feet narrow; opposite arm–leg swing appears. Hurried walk changes to true run.	Jumps down from step. Jumps several inches off floor with both feet, no arm action.	Hops 1 to 3 times on same foot with stiff upper body and non-hopping leg held still.	Throws balls with forearm extension only; feet remain stationary. Awaits thrown ball with rigid arms outstretched.	Pushes riding toy with feet; does little steering.
3–4 years	Walks up stairs, alternating feet. Walks downstairs, leading with one foot. Walks in a straight line.	Jumps off floor with coordinated arm action. Broad jumps about 1 foot.	Hops 4 to 6 times on same foot, flexing upper body and swinging nonhopping leg.	Throws ball with slight body rotation but little or no transfer of weight with feet. Flexes elbows in preparation for catching; traps ball against chest.	Pedals and steers tricycle.
4–5 years	Walks downstairs, alternating feet. Walks circular line. Walks awkwardly on balance beam. Runs more smoothly. Gallops and skips with one foot.	Improved upward and forward jumps. Travels greater distance.	Hops 7 to 9 times on same foot. Improved speed of hopping.	Throws ball with increased body rotation and some transfer of weight forward. Catches ball with hands; if unsuccessful, may still trap ball against chest.	Rides tricycle rapidly, steers smoothly.
5–6 years	Walks securely on balance beam. Increased speed of run. Gallops more smoothly. True skipping appears.	Jumps off floor about 1 foot. Broad jumps 3 feet.	Hops 50 feet on same foot in 10 seconds. Hops with rhythmical alternation (2 hops on one foot and 2 on the other).	Has mature throwing and catching pattern. Moves arm more and steps forward during throw. Awaits thrown ball with relaxed posture, adjusting body to path and size of ball.	Rides bicycle with training wheels.

Source: Berk, L. E. (1993). *Infants, children, and adolescents.* Boston: Allyn & Bacon, 299. Copyright © 1993 by Allyn & Bacon. Reprinted with permission.

Children's running abilities become more elaborated throughout toddlerhood. In films used to study the emergence of running, it appears that, for toddlers, running and walking are very much alike, with little increase in velocity and little or no "flight" (the time when both feet are off the ground) in running. At the beginning, toddlers appear to be running when they move a bit faster, but their action is not much like adult running. Over time, however, the movements become smoother, and flight time and velocity increase (Whitall & Getchell, 1995).

At first, youngsters may run for the sake of pleasure. Later in toddlerhood, running changes from a kind of game in itself to a valuable component of many other games. The absolute speed of toddlers is limited by their somewhat precarious balance and short legs. This does not discourage them, however, from devoting a great deal of time and energy to practicing running. The goals of mastery and exploration motivate their enthusiasm.

Toddlers are often exposed to a wide variety of other forms of locomotion, such as swimming, skiing, skating, sledding, and dancing. Children seem eager to use their bodies in a variety of ways, and they learn quickly (Ridenour, 1978). One of the vehicles of locomotion that has special meaning for the American toddler is the tricycle. The tricycle provides enormous pleasure because of its potential speed, reversibility, turning capacity, and horn. It is also an object through which the toddler can identify with older children and adults. The connections between tricycle, bicycle, and car are quickly and easily made by the toddler. The tricycle combines the joys of physical movement, the thrill of danger and independence, and the social significance of mechanized transportation. A tricycle (or comparable pedal toy) usually has great value for the child for the fun it provides and for the opportunities it offers to experience new levels of mastery. It also has symbolic significance for parents who recognize it as the first in a chain of objects that will foster the child's increased independence from the family and heightened identification with the peer group.

Fantasy Play

Dev't of representational skills

During toddlerhood, children acquire five representational skills that allow them to conceive of objects mentally rather than by actual physical manipulation. These representational skills are: imitation in the absence of the model, mental images, symbolic drawing, symbolic play, and language. Each of these skills allows children to communicate and process experiences independently of the immediate objects or events that the symbols represent. Children can explore relationships that they may have known in the past by imitating, drawing, or acting them out in fantasy. They can portray events and relationships that they wish would occur or that they wish to alter in some way from the original form. They can talk about these relationships in private or egocentric speech to plan and develop strategies.

Fantasy play and language are contrasting forms of representation. In acquiring language, children learn to translate their thoughts into a shared system of signs and rules. For language to be effective, children must use the same words and grammar as older members of the family to communicate their thoughts. Fantasy serves almost the opposite function. In fantasy, children create characters and situations that may have very private meanings.

There is no need to make the fantasy comprehensible to an audience. In fact, Vygotsky (1962) argued that fantasy play emerges as a result of prolonged unmet needs. Children often have strong feelings but lack words to express them. They may be frustrated by their helplessness or angry at being neglected. They can express and soothe these feelings through imagination, even though such feelings may never be communicated in a conversation.

The Emergence of Symbolic Play

During infancy, play consists primarily of repeated motor activity. Infants delight in sucking their toes or dropping a spoon from the high chair, which are typical *sensorimotor play* activities. As infancy progresses, there are increasing amounts of social play with the mother and other caregivers who form the content of the first complex mental representations. Toward the end of infancy, sensorimotor play includes deliberate imitation of parental acts. Children who see their caregivers washing the dishes may enjoy climbing up on a chair and getting their hands wet too. At first, these imitations occur only when they are stimulated by the sight of the caregiver's activity. As children enter toddlerhood, they begin to imitate caregiver activities when they are alone. A vivid mental image of a caregiver's action permits them to copy what they recall instead of what they see. This is the beginning of symbolic play.

A critical new capacity for thought is reflected in imaginary play. The meaning of objects and actions is derived from the ideas that children have about the pretend situation. Adults easily grasp the concept of using blocks to represent buildings, but for children that idea is a dramatic change in thinking that takes place during the preoperational years (Vygotsky, 1978). Two-year-olds (28 months) appear to be able to understand the context of a pretend situation quite clearly. They can pretend to feed a stuffed animal with pretend props. They can assign a pretend function to a substitute prop, treating a wooden block as a banana or a piece of cake. And they can follow through on a pretend situation, like spilling pretend tea or smearing pretend toothpaste, with a pretend remedy, like wiping up the pretend water with a towel (Harris & Kavanaugh, 1993). In trying to account for this flexible adaptation to pretend routines, Harris and Kavanaugh suggest that these very young children are able to construct a make-believe world in which objects can be stipulated to stand for other things (toy blocks for bananas) and in which words can be used in a nonliteral way ("feed the monkey a banana" is acted out by putting a toy block up to the mouth of a toy monkey).

Distinguishing Pretense from Reality

The capacity for pretense, whether through symbolic play, symbolic drawing, or telling make-believe stories, requires that children understand the difference between pretense and reality. Sometimes adults wonder whether children can in fact distinguish between what is real and what is pretend. The line between make-believe and reality can become blurred for all of us when we watch television, for instance. Which of the things we see on television are pretend and which are real? Are the situations depicted in commercials real or pretend? Are dramatic reenactments of historical events real or pretend?

In very simplified situations, children as young as three can tell the difference between what an object really is and what someone is pretending that it is (Flavell et al., 1987). Three-year-olds understand that a sponge is really a sponge, for example, but that you can pretend it is a boat floating in the water.

BOX 9.3

Deception in Toddlerhood

Do toddlers deceive people? Have you ever seen a child between the ages of two and four look at you with a mirthful expectation to see whether they have been successful in deceiving you? The biggest deceit we can remember occurred when our four-year-old told us that he had been invited to the birthday party of an older child who lived across the street, and he actually went to the party even though he had not been invited. He had really wanted to go so he made up a story that he was invited. He felt terrible when he got home because his plan didn't work. A good deal of such trickery occurs in toddlerhood, often in playful ways, as children try to get something they want.

Currently, researchers are studying what two- to four-year-old children understand about deception. It appears that an important change in the ability to conceptualize occurs between the ages of three and four. Most researchers agree that children in this age range begin to say things that aren't true (Dunn, 1988; Hala et al., 1991; Lewis et al., 1989; and Vasek, 1986). What is not fully understood is whether the child understands that, by telling something that is false, he or she changes the beliefs that another person has about the situation. In fact, many studies show that three-year-olds have difficulty giving misinformation about something they know to be true. For example, Joan Peskin (1992) set up a study in which children chose their favorite sticker from among three. They were told that a puppet would come in and try to take their favorite sticker. The experimenter encouraged the child to tell the puppet something or do something so the puppet wouldn't take their favorite sticker. Three-year-olds tried to pull the sticker away from the puppet, sit on the sticker, or push the puppet away, but they did not try to deceive the puppet by trying to act as if a different sticker was their favorite. The five-year-olds were quite successful in concealing information so that the puppet wouldn't guess which sticker was their favorite. They repeatedly defended their pretend choice to the puppet so the puppet could not logically deduce that another sticker really was the favorite.

On the basis of their observations, Ruffman et al. (1993) theorized that three-year-olds do not understand how deception creates a false belief. Further, if they know that something is true, they have a hard time fostering the misconception that it is false. That is why most three-year-olds get caught when they lie—they are not very good at it.

Once the capacity for symbolic thought emerges, children become increasingly flexible in allowing an object to take on a wide variety of *pretend identities* (see Box 9.3 and Notebook Page 9.2).

Changes in Fantasy Play During Toddlerhood

Toddlers are able to direct their play in response to mental images that they have generated by themselves. Initially, toddlers' symbolic play is characterized by the simple repetition of very familiar activities. Pretending to sweep the floor, to be asleep, to be a dog or cat, and to drive a car are some of the early play activities of toddlers. Over time, fantasy play changes along four dimensions (Lucariello, 1987; Rogers & Sawyers, 1988):

1. The action component becomes more complex as the child integrates a sequence of actions.
2. The child's focus shifts from the self to fantasies that involve others and the creation of multiple roles.
3. The play involves the use of substitute objects, including objects that the child only pretends to have, and the eventual invention of complex characters and situations.
4. The play becomes more organized and planned, and play leaders emerge.

In a complex solitary play episode, Chandler is explaining to Sugar Bear that he has to get his boots on before they can get into the spacecraft.

First, children incorporate a number of actions in a play sequence. From pretending to sweep the floor or take a nap, children devise a series of activities that are part of a complex play sequence. While playing fireman, the child may pretend to be the fire truck, the hose, the ladder, the engine, the siren, the people being rescued, and the firefighters. All the elements of the situation are brought under the child's control through this fantasy enactment.

Second, children become increasingly able to include others in their play and to shift the focus of the play from self to others (Howes, 1987; Howes et al., 1989). One can see a distinction here between solitary pretense, social play, and social pretend play. Children engaged in solitary pretense are involved in their own fantasy activities. They may be pretending that they are driving a car or giving a baby a bath. Children engaged in social play join with other children in some activity. They may dig together in the sand, build with blocks, or imitate each other's silly noises. Children engaged in social pretend play have to coordinate their pretense. They establish a fantasy structure, take roles, agree on the make-believe meaning of props, and solve pretend problems. The fact that two- and three-year-olds can participate in this type of coordinated fantasy play is quite remarkable, especially given their very limited use of language to establish and sustain coordination.

Fantasy play changes along a third dimension as children become more flexible in their ability to use substitute objects in their play. Fantasy play begins in areas closest to a child's daily experience. Children use real objects or play versions of those objects as props in their pretense. They pick up a toy telephone and pretend to call Grandma, or pretend to have a picnic with toy cups, plates, and plastic foods. But as they develop their fantasy skills, these props are no longer essential. Children can invent objects, create novel uses for common objects, and sometimes pretend to have an object when they have nothing.

Are You Still Pretending?

What has happened to your ability to pretend? Is it in active use and shiny bright like a new penny, or is it lying in your mental attic with the other dust-covered remnants of your childhood? Fantasy play involves the construction of a pretend world in which the constraints and demands of the real world are set aside. Pretending requires making a commitment to an "as-if" reality.

1. What were some of your favorite childhood pretend games or fantasies?

_____

_____

_____

2. What kinds of props did you use in your childhood fantasies?

_____

_____

3. With whom did you usually pretend (a special friend, parent, sibling, by yourself)?

_____

_____

4. What place does pretense have in your life now? Are you involved in passive pretense (going to movies, theater, watching TV drama) or active pretense (making up your own stories, games, characters)?

_____

_____

5. When was the most recent time that you pretended? Describe the situation. Who was with you? What did you do? How did you feel? What value does this kind of activity have for you?

_____

_____

_____

The play moves away from common, daily experiences to invented worlds based on stories, on television programs, or on purely imagined characters and situations. Children may take the roles of characters with extraordinary powers. They may pretend to fly, become invisible, or transform themselves into other shapes with the aid of a few secret words or gestures. Identification with a particular fantasy hero or heroine may last for days or even weeks as the child involves the characters of the story in a variety of fantasy situations.

Fourth, fantasy play becomes more planned and organized. The planning element is in part a product of the desire to coordinate play among several players. It also results from a new realization of and desire to include the elements that make pretend play most fun. In a preschool or day-care group, certain children are likely to take the lead in organizing fantasy play. They may initiate the play or give it direction by suggesting the use of certain props, assigning roles, or describing the context of the play. In the following example, we see a child demonstrating this kind of leadership:

Stuart: (climbing up on a tractor tire): This will be our shark ship, OK? Get on quick, Jeremy! The sharks will eat you!

Jeremy: No! This is my police helicopter!

Stuart: Well, OK. We're police. But we need to chase the sharks, OK? I see the sharks way down there! Come on!

Jeremy: OK. Let's get 'em! (They both make helicopter noises and swat at make-believe sharks with plastic garden tools.) (Trawick-Smith, 1988, 53)

Some people distinguish symbolic role playing from games with rules, implying that the latter is guided by a formal set of mental operations that constrain play, while the former is open and flexible. However, it is clear from observations that pretend play operates within a rule-bound structure as well (Harris & Kavanaugh, 1993; Vygotsky, 1978). In order to coordinate symbolic play with a partner, the children have to come to some mutual understandings about the situation, the props, the characters, and the plot. In order to sustain the pretense, the players have to limit their behaviors in ways that conform to the unspoken or latent rules of the play. If a brick is a substitute for a kind of food, it can't be used to build a house or to shoot an enemy. If one player is assigned to be Mommy, he or she cannot act like a baby. In games with rules, the rules are more clearly spelled out, but in both types of play, part of the fun is to function within certain boundaries.

Dramatic role playing, in which a child takes on the role of another person or creates a fantasy situation, increases steadily between the ages of three and five. By the age of six, however, children become increasingly involved in games with rules. They tend to use their fantasy skills during play by making up new games or new rules rather than by engaging in pretend play. They may fantasize about becoming a soccer or baseball star and they may then elaborate the fantasy into real-life skill development such as attending a special soccer camp or going to all the home games of their favorite baseball team. If you are looking for the experts in diversified, elaborated symbolic play, observe four- and five-year-olds (Cole & La Voie, 1985).

The Importance of Fantasy Play

Fantasy play is not simply a diversion. Children use fantasy to experiment with and understand their social and physical environments and to expand their thinking (Hutt et al., 1988; Piers & Landau, 1980). Views of the importance of fantasy play vary widely. Piaget (1962) emphasized the assimilative value of play. Through fantasy and symbolic play, he believed, children are able to make meaning of experiences and events that are beyond their rational comprehension. Fantasy play is a private world in which the rules of social convention and the logic of the physical world may not necessarily apply. From this perspective, fantasy play frees the child from the immediacy of reality, permitting mental manipulations and modifications of objects and events.

Vygotsky (1978) saw fantasy play quite differently. He argued that "play creates a zone of proximal development of the child. In play a child always behaves beyond his average age, above his daily behavior; in play it is as though he were a head taller than himself. As in the focus of a magnifying glass, play contains all developmental tendencies in a condensed form and is itself a major source of development" (p. 102).

When Vygotsky used the term *zone of proximal development*, he was referring to a range of potential performance. When trying to assess a child's developmental level, it is important to understand not only what the child already knows and can perform, but the domains that are "in progress" so to speak, the areas that are emerging as new fields of mastery. Normally, Vygotsky argued, adults, especially parents and teachers, and more advanced peers promote development by engaging children in activities and problem-solving tasks that draw children into their zone of proximal development, the new directions in which their capacities are moving. However, in play, Vygotsky saw a cognitive process that in and of itself foreshadows the child's next higher level of functioning. In pretend play, children try to act as if they are competent in areas where they do not yet feel competent in their real lives. They set and abide by certain rules for their performance. So if a child is pretending to be a good mother, she applies the ideas she has about how to be a good mother to the pretend situation. Similarly, if a child is pretending to be a superhero, she imposes all her knowledge of power, goodness, and helpfulness and tries to limit her actions accordingly. Vygotsky regarded fantasy play as a window into the areas of competence that the child is striving to master but which are still out of reach.

Erikson (1972) considered play as serving a vital function in promoting personality and social development. For example, he valued play as a mechanism for dramatizing the psychological conflicts that a child is struggling with, such as angry feelings toward siblings or parents or jealousy over a friend's new toys. Often, according to Erikson, play not only represents the problem but also offers a solution so that the child experiences some new sense of resolution and a reduction in tension. Symbolic play provides a certain flexibility or leeway in structuring the situation and, at the same time, imposes some limits so that the child can experience a new sense of mastery or control over issues that are perplexing or overwhelming in real life. This idea is similar to Vygotsky's notion of play as establishing zones of proximal development. The function of play is "the restoration and creation of a *leeway of mastery* in a set of developments or circumstances" (Erikson, 1972, 133).

Researchers who have studied children who do not engage in much pretend play and others who have tried to increase the level of pretend play among toddlers find that pretend play actually fosters cognitive and social development (Rubin, 1980; Saltz & Saltz, 1986). Children with well-developed pretending skills tend to be well liked by their peers and to be viewed as peer leaders (Ladd et al., 1988). Well-developed pretending skills are associated with advanced communication skills, greater ability to take the point of view of others, and greater ability to reason about social situations, all of which contribute to social competence. Children who have experiences that encourage a playful, imaginative approach to the manipulation and exploration of materials and objects through fantasy show evidence of more complex language use and more flexible approaches to problem solving (Burke, 1987). Clearly, the importance of fantasy play in the social, intellectual, and emotional development of young children cannot be underestimated. Some parents and teachers tend to measure a young child's cognitive growth in terms of the acquisition of words and concepts that seem relevant to the "real world." They emphasize the importance of learning numbers and letters, memorizing facts, and being able to read. However, research on cognitive development suggests that a well-developed capacity for symbolic thought provides the basis for subsequent intellectual abilities such as abstract reasoning and inventive problem solving.

The Role of Play Companions

Parents, siblings, and child-care professionals can enrich a child's fantasy play by serving as play companions who elaborate on a child's fantasy, legitimize fantasy play, and help the child to explore new domains of fantasy. Consider the following incident. In a university preschool, where college students were having their first supervised experiences teaching young children, a child of three attempted some pretend play with a student teacher. The child picked up a toy telephone and made ringing noises. The student teacher picked up another phone and said "Hello." The child asked, "Is Milly there?" The student teacher said "no" and hung up the phone. In this interaction, the student teacher had not yet learned how to help expand the child's play.

Research has shown that when mothers are available as play companions, the symbolic play of their two-year-old children is more complex and lasts for a longer time (Slade, 1987). When adults are trained to engage in and encourage pretend play with toddlers, the toddlers show an increasing capacity to coordinate their responses with those of an adult. Over the period from 16 to 32 months, toddlers become increasingly skillful at directing an adult's behavior and negotiating changes in kinds of play (Eckerman & Didow, 1989). In observations of mother–toddler play, the mother's language use within the play situation was important in promoting the child's language competence (Bornstein & O'Reilly, 1993). Other studies suggest that early and frequent opportunities to pretend with older siblings as well as with a parent contribute to the young child's ability to understand other people's feelings and beliefs. As toddlers experiment with various roles, co-construct fantasy situations, and manipulate objects with a play companion, they must establish many channels of shared meaning, thus fostering a new degree of awareness about another person (Youngblade & Dunn, 1995).

Within child-care settings, frequent interaction with the same stable group of age-mates results in more complex, coordinated play. Children who have had many changes in their child-care arrangements are less likely to engage in complex social pretend play with other children (Howes &

Stewart, 1987). Since toddlers rely so heavily on imitation and nonverbal signals to initiate and develop their social pretend play, the more time they have together, the more complex their fantasy play can be (Eckerman & Didow, 1996).

Imaginary Companions

Probably the most sophisticated form of symbolic play involves the creation of an imaginary friend (Singer, 1975). An imaginary friend is born, complete in concept, from the mind of a child. He/she may be an animal, child, or some other creature with a personality that is consistent from day to day. He/she has likes and dislikes that are not necessarily the same as those of his or her creator. He/she occupies space. Several functions are served by the imaginary friend:

1. He/she serves as a play companion for pretend play.
2. He/she takes the place of other children when there are none around.
3. He/she serves as a confidant for private expressions.
4. He/she is often involved in a child's efforts to differentiate between right and wrong. When a child has difficulty accepting responsibility for misdeeds, the imaginary companion may become a scapegoat.

Although it has been assumed that imaginary companions are quite rare, studies have found that as many as 65% of preschoolers have imaginary companions, and some children have more than one (Singer & Singer, 1990). In one study, researchers invited children who had imaginary companions to play with them in a laboratory setting and found that the children were quite willing to involve their imaginary companions in this type of setting. The children behaved as if the experimenter could also see and touch their imaginary friends. Thus, even though many parents do not appear to be all that well informed about the nature of their preschoolers' imaginary friends, the children themselves appear to be willing to share these imaginary companions with others (Taylor et al., 1993).

In Table 9.5, you will find the characteristics of 23 imaginary companions (Taylor et al., 1993). Study 1 and Study 2 were about six months apart, indicating that, for most children, the imaginary companion remained consistent over time and retained an active part in the child's fantasy life over this period. Fifteen children in this study were thought not to have an imaginary companion. They were asked about a real friend. However, it turned out that several of the children actually did have imaginary companions of whom their parents were unaware.

In general, imaginary friends can be seen as evidence of toddlers' ability to differentiate themselves from others and of their attempts to gain control over their impulses. An imaginary companion is a device that helps a toddler remain playful at even the most trying times. When studying toddlers, it may be very difficult to see the world through their eyes, especially since their views of mental functions and logical relationships are so different from those of adults. They also seem to be able to engage in imaginary activity for a very prolonged time, often outlasting the capacity of even the most well-meaning adult to function as a play companion. The imaginary companion provides a good vehicle for helping us think about the inner world of three- and four-year-old children (see Notebook Page 9.3).

TABLE 9.5

Toddlers' Descriptions of Their Imaginary Companions (IC)

Name	Sex	Age	Size[a]	Hair	Eyes	Clothes
		ICs of children in Study 1 and Study 2				
Bla-Bla						
Study 1	Male	3 yr, 6 mo	Same	Purple	Blue	"###"[rb]
Study 2	Male	5 yr	Bigger	White	Purple	"###"
Mr. Ghost						
Study 1	Male	9 yr	Same	White	White	None
Study 2	Male	15 yr	Bigger	White	White	All white
Ruthie						
Study 1	Female	3 yr	Smaller	Yellow	Green	Dress
Study 2	Female	4 yr	Smaller	Yellow	Blue	Dress
Tina						
Study 1	Female	6 yr	Bigger	Black	Shy	Dress
Study 2	Female	6 yr	Smaller	Red	—	Dress
Sara						
Study 1	Female	13 yr	Smaller	Blue	Gray	Pants
Study 2	Female	1 yr	Smaller	White	Blue	Dress
Little Chop						
Study 1	Male	1 yr	Smaller	Grayish-silver	Blue	T-shirt & shorts
Study 2	Male	1 yr	Smaller	Black	Green	T-shirt & shorts
Shedog						
Study 1	Female	4 yr	Same	Brown	Red	None
Study 2	Child does not remember Shedog					
Tompy						
Study 1	Male	5 yr	Same	Blond	Blue	Blue
Study 2	Child says Tompy was "defective" and is dead now					
Thunder						
Study 1	Male	17 yr, 6 mo	Bigger	Black	Green	Batman
Study 2	Child says he doesn't have Thunder anymore					
		ICs of children in Study 1 only				
Nutsy	Female	3 yr	Smaller	Black	White	Nutsy clothes
Baby	Female	3 yr	Smaller	No hair	Peach	Jammies
Boys	Male	26 yr	Bigger	Gray	White	Green
		ICs of children in real-friend pilot and Study 2				
Ariel						
Pilot	Female	6 yr	Smaller	Red	Green	No clothes
Study 2	Female	6 yr	Bigger	Red	Green	No clothes
Jacob						
Pilot	Male	Child did not know the answers to these questions[c]				
Study 2	Jacob was no longer an IC					

(continued)

TABLE 9.5 (continued)

Toddlers' Descriptions of Their Imaginary Companions (IC)

Name	Sex	Age	Size[a]	Hair	Eyes	Clothes
Acher						
Pilot	Male	5 yr	Same	Brown	Brown	T-shirt
Study 2	Male	5 yr	Same	Black	Orange	T-shirt
ICs of children in real-friend pilot only						
Chelsea	Female	5 yr	Bigger			
My Girls	Female	4 yr	Smaller	Yellow	Ugly	No clothes
New ICs of children in Study 2						
Steel-Dinosaur	Male	4 yr, 6 mo	Bigger	None	Blue	None
Lisa	Female	4 yr	Bigger	Red	Green	Dress
Bazooie	Male	5 yr	Allergic to kittens			
Nothing	Male	1,000 yrs ("older than my mom")	Bigger	Multicolored	Multicolored	Green
Baby	Female	?	Fatter	Black	?	Yellow dress with black
Gadget	Female	7 yr	Smaller	Blond and dark	Black and yellow	Smaller

[a]Child was asked if the IC was bigger, smaller, or the same size as the child. [b]Child used an incomprehensible word to describe the IC's clothes. [c]This description was the most incomplete in the sample, although the IC was the only one that was based on a real person (the child's cousin who lived in another state).
Source: Taylor, M., Cartwright, B. S. & Carlson, S. M. (1993). A developmental investigation of children's imaginary companions. *Developmental Psychology, 29,* 279. Copyright © 1993 by the American Psychological Association. Reprinted with permission.

Self-Control

Colin, aged 2 years, 9 months, is just starting nursery school:

> In his relations with children, Colin progressed quickly from a quiet, friendly, watching relationship on the first few days to actively hugging the other children. The hugging seemed to be in an excess of friendliness and was only mildly aggressive. Having started hugging he didn't know how to stop, and usually just held on until he pulled the child down to the floor. This was followed very closely by hair pulling. He didn't pull viciously, but still held on long enough to get a good resistance from the child. He grabbed toys from others. When stopped by an adult from any of these acts, he was very responsive to reason, would say, smiling, "I won't do it anymore," would tear around the room in disorganized activity, and then return to hugging or pulling hair. (Murphy, 1956, 11–12)

Self-control has been defined as the ability to comply with a request, modify behavior according to the situation, postpone action, and behave in a

Creating an Imaginary Companion

1. Did you have an imaginary companion(s) as a child that you can remember? Name and describe your companion.

_____

_____

2. What things do you remember about your activities with your companion? How was the companion useful to you?

_____

_____

_____

3. Ask your parents or other relatives if they remember you having an imaginary companion and, if so, what they remember about this companion.

_____

_____

4. Create an imaginary companion for yourself now. Think of a character that you would like to bring to life—a person, animal, or fictional character—who would be fun to play with, to talk to, or to keep you company. What are his or her physical features and unique personal qualities? Name and describe your companion.

_____

_____

_____

5. In going about your day, commune with your new imaginary companion from time to time, and then answer the following questions. Have you talked with your imaginary companion in the past day? If yes, what did you say? If no, try again!

_____

_____

377

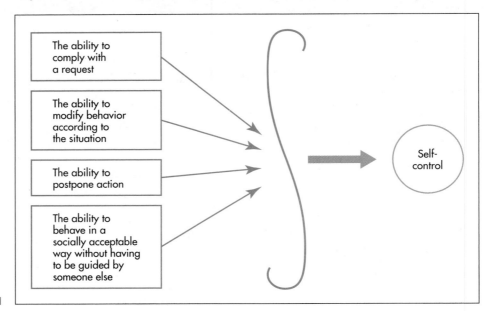

FIGURE 9.2

Components of self-control

socially acceptable way without having to be guided or directed by someone else (Kopp, 1982) (see Figure 9.2). These abilities reflect a growing sense of selfhood. In order to control one's behavior, a child needs to understand that he or she is a causal agent and that the behavior and its consequences are a product of action over which the child has some control. Self-control also reflects the cognitive ability to assess a situation and to compare it with previously learned guidelines on how to behave. Finally, the capacity for self-regulation reflects the ability to express or redirect impulses in order to reduce their intensity (Edwards, 1995).

Precursors of Self-Control in Infancy

Early in infancy, babies can increase or reduce their level of arousal (Kopp, 1982). By sucking or rocking, for example, babies can soothe themselves. Babies can resist overstimulation by turning away, crying, or going to sleep. From about 3 to 9 months, motor development permits increasing control over objects and behavior. Reaching and crawling give babies experiences in directing action and experimenting with the consequences of action. From 9 to 18 months, infants show the ability to comply with a request. They can give a hug, pass a toy to another child, or stop if a parent says "No." They also begin to inhibit their own behavior. A child may reach for a knife on the counter, shake her head, say "Don't touch," and pull back her hand. During toddlerhood, self-control develops in two directions: improved control of impulses and self-regulated goal attainment. Of course, we can all recall at least one instance when our self-control failed us. We shouted angrily at someone who cut ahead of us in traffic, ate hungrily before everyone at the table was seated, or partied too late even when we knew we had to get up early the next morning. Working on self-control is a lifelong challenge.

When Chris is overtired or afraid, he soothes himself by sucking his fingers and fingering his soft blanket. These are excellent strategies for achieving control over impulses.

Control of Impulses

During the years from two to four, children are increasingly able to modify and control their impulses. The ability to regulate or restrain behavior is a product of changing cognitive, social, and emotional competence. The case of Colin illustrates how toddlers can fall prey to their impulses. Sometimes they simply cannot interrupt an ongoing action, even one that they know is inappropriate. Over time, however, children become increasingly sensitive to the distress of others, better able to tolerate delays in the gratification of their impulses, and more skillful at managing the frustrations they experience (Vaughn et al., 1984; Zahn-Waxler, Radke-Yarrow, Wagner & Chapman, 1992).

Increasing Sensitivity to the Distress of Others

Toddlers are able to observe and empathize with expressions of distress from both children and adults. In addition, toddlers begin to understand when they have been the direct cause of someone else's distress (Zahn-Waxler, Radke-Yarrow, Wagner & Chapman, 1992; Zahn-Waxler, Robinson & Emde, 1992). Often, parents or teachers point out the child's action and its consequence, and this socialization focuses the toddler's attention on her/his role in causing someone else's distress. The following observation illustrates how this kind of conversation about negative consequences and a child's concern over his caregiver's distress can contribute to self-regulation of impulses (Brown & Dunn, 1992, 347–348).

Danny is 33 months old. He and his mother are at the sink washing dishes. Danny blows a handful of suds at his mother and some gets in her eyes. Danny is laughing at this new game.

Mother: No! Nuh uh, Danny. Danny, you got it in my eye. (Mother shows mild negative affect.)

(Danny stops laughing.)

Mother: Don't do that in my eye, ok? It hurts to get soap in your eye.

Danny: (very serious): I won't.

A New Sense of Future Time

In addition to becoming increasingly sensitive to expressions of distress in others, children gain in self-control as they begin to develop a rudimentary sense of time, including a new appreciation of the future. Toddlers repeatedly discover that, even though what they want is not available to them at the moment, it is often available after only a brief delay. Their sense of trust helps children to appreciate this. As they become aware that after a period of delay their needs will very likely be met, the delay itself generates less frustration. This sequence depends heavily on the caregivers' responsiveness and willingness to provide the gratifications that they have asked the children to delay. If children learn that they can trust their caregivers to keep promises, it is much easier for them to learn to wait.

Strategies That Help Children Manage Their Impulses

Language and fantasy are the most useful tools that toddlers have for managing their impulses. The more articulate children are in expressing their wishes, the better the chances that their needs will be met. When their needs cannot be met, children can use language to express how they feel. Feelings that are expressed are easier for children to control than those that are not. Children also learn to use language in order to interrupt an impulsive act or to resolve a conflict (Caplan et al., 1991).

One of the first tactics that toddlers use to inhibit an impulse is to divert their attention from a forbidden object. In a study of the ability to delay behavior, an adult showed two-year-olds an unusual telephone and asked them not to touch it, then stepped out of the room for a few moments. In the experimenter's absence, the children's behaviors were observed, and the time that elapsed before they touched the phone was measured. The experimenter returned as soon as a child touched the phone, or within 2½ minutes, whichever was first. Behaviors associated with an ability to delay touching the phone were looking away from the phone, playing with their hands or covering their faces with their hands, and talking about something other than the telephone. Delay strategies become more focused and effective by ages three and four (Vaughn et al., 1986).

When children are asked to resist temptation, they use a variety of verbal strategies, including talking quietly to themselves and singing songs to distract themselves (Mischel et al., 1989). Toddlers who can talk to themselves may be able to control their fears, modify their anger, and console themselves about disappointments. They may repeat comforting words that their parents have spoken to them, or they may develop their own verbal strategies for reducing their distress. When a little boy who feels bad about something says that "superheroes don't cry," he is making an effort to control his emotional state.

Through the use of fantasy, children create imaginary situations in which disturbing problems can be expressed and resolved. They can pretend to con-

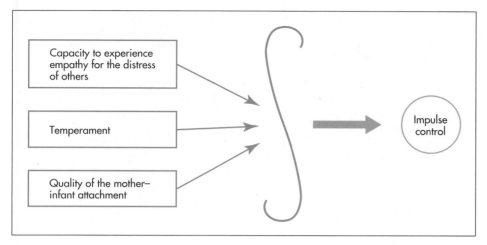

FIGURE 9.3

Factors associated with the ease or difficulty toddlers have in controlling their impulses

trol situations that are far beyond their real-world capacities (Singer & Singer, 1990). They can punish and forgive, harm and heal, fear and conquer fear, all within the boundaries of their own imaginations.

Individual Differences in the Ability to Control Impulses

The ability to delay gratification varies with the individual. At least three factors are associated with differences in the ease or difficulty that children have in controlling their impulses (see Figure 9.3). First, toddlers differ in their capacity to experience empathy for the distress of others. Empathy itself appears to have a genetic as well as an environmental basis. In a study of monozygotic and dizygotic twins who were two years old, the monozygotic twins showed greater similarity in their emotional concern and response to others' distress than did the dizygotic twins. In addition, mothers who had a stronger orientation toward concern for others in their child-rearing strategies had children whose empathy was more fully developed. Further, girls were observed to be more empathic than boys (Zahn-Waxler, Robinson & Emde, 1992). These differences in sensitivity to the distress of others lead to gradations in the distress that a child might feel in finding that his or her behavior has caused someone pain and in the child's willingness to curb that behavior in the future.

Second, individual differences in temperament have implications for self-control. Children who are more aggressive, active, or socially outgoing may experience more situations in which their actions are viewed as disruptive or in need of control. Children who are more socially inhibited, withdrawn, or passive may encounter fewer expectations to curb or restrict their behavior (Kochanska & Radke-Yarrow, 1992).

Third, some evidence supports the idea that the capacity for self-regulation may depend on the quality of the caregiver–infant attachment. Children who have an insecure attachment are more likely to exhibit irritability, avoidance, resistance, and aggressiveness as preschoolers (Teti et al., 1991). These toddlers have more difficulty calming themselves and reducing the intensity of their impulses (see Box 9.4). Put in a more positive perspective, one of the benefits of a secure attachment is the child's capacity over time to internalize

capacity to experience empathy

temperament

quality of attachment

BOX 9.4

The Control of Angry Feelings

The expression of anger, which is important to the child's developing sense of autonomy, constantly generates tension between parents and children (Wenar, 1982). A toddler gets angry for many reasons, including inability to perform a task, parental restrictions on behavior, conflicts over toys and other resources, and peer or sibling rivalry. As toddlers become increasingly involved in directing the outcomes of their activities, they get angry when someone interrupts them or offers unrequested assistance (Bullock & Lutkenhaus, 1988). In addition, some children are temperamentally more aggressive than others.

Although the expression of anger is inevitable and understandable, it is never pleasant. Even parents who have encouraged their children to be independent, to try new things, and to express their feelings find it difficult to accept the hostility that accompanies growing selfhood. Parents are faced with the tasks of providing acceptable mechanisms for the expression of anger and teaching children how to control angry feelings.

Children rely heavily on parents as models for learning how to control anger. Children learn as much or more about the expression of anger from watching their parents when they are angry as they do from verbal explanations or punishment (Bandura, 1977). Children are sensitive to anger when it is expressed between their parents, even when it is not directed to them. Parents' hostility to each other, expressed through quarrels, sarcasm, or physical abuse, increases a child's sensitivity to anger and is closely related to disturbances in development (Cummings, Pellegrini, Notarius & Cummings, 1989).

The child who can express anger and not lose control makes tremendous gains in the development of autonomy. Anger and conflict with parents give toddlers evidence that they are indeed separate from

their parents and that the separateness, although uncomfortable, is legitimate. Children who are severely punished or ridiculed for their anger are left in a state of doubt. They see models for the expression of anger in the way their parents respond to them and yet are told that their anger is not appropriate.

Adults can use several strategies to help young children manage or reduce the intensity of their anger (Berkowitz, 1973). These include:

- Ignoring the aggression.

- Providing brief "time-out" periods in a nearby quiet area until the anger has subsided.

- Arousing feelings that are incompatible with anger, especially empathy for the victim.

- Minimizing exposure to stimuli that arouse aggressive impulses.

- Explaining the consequences of aggressive actions for the other person.

- Explaining the circumstances that may have led to the initial feelings of anger or frustration.

For the sake of the child's emerging self-concept, angry feelings must be allowed some form of legitimate expression. In the process of expressing angry feelings, children learn to control themselves and to channel these emotions into constructive rather than destructive activity. Between the ages of two and five, the frequency of angry, aggressive behaviors declines as children develop effective strategies for self-control (Cummings, Iannotti & Zahn-Waxler, 1989).

---

many of the soothing, reassuring strategies that a caregiver has used to comfort and protect him or her and apply them to intense emotional states.

For 30 years, Walter Mischel and his colleagues have investigated the process by which children delay gratification. Mischel has found that, by age four, children who can delay gratification longer tend to be more intelligent and more likely to resist temptation, to demonstrate greater social responsibility, and to have higher achievement goals (Mischel et al., 1989). According to Mischel's research, a four-year-old's ability to use self-regulatory strategies to delay gratification seems to have enduring effects. More than ten years later, children who at age four had waited longer in an experimental situation that required self-imposed delay of gratification were described by their parents as socially and academically more competent than their peers. Parents rated these children as more verbally fluent and able to express ideas; they used and responded to reason, and they were more competent and skillful. They were more attentive and able to concentrate, plan, and think ahead. They were also seen as better able to cope with frustration and to resist temptation.

As Freud hypothesized, the ability to delay gratification seems to be an important component of ego development. The work of Mischel and his colleagues suggests that toddlers who are able to delay gratification made greater strides in ego development throughout childhood. Even though most children eventually acquire the skills needed for more successful delay, the ones who demonstrate these skills earliest seem to gain an advantage by using the growing network of ego skills more effectively.

Self-Regulated Goal Attainment

Beyond controlling impulses, self-control develops as toddlers learn that they can direct their behavior and the behavior of others to achieve intended outcomes (Messer et al., 1987). During infancy, children become increasingly aware of themselves as causal agents. In toddlerhood, children become much more assertive about their desire to initiate actions, to persist in activities, and to determine when these activities should stop. Their sense of *agency*—their view of themselves as the originators of action—expands to include a broad array of behaviors. Children make efforts to participate in decisions about bedtime, the clothes they wear, the kinds of foods they eat, and the family's activities. They want to do things that they see their parents and older siblings doing. Their confidence in their own ability to handle very difficult tasks is not modified by a realistic assessment of their skills. According to toddlers, "Anything you can do, I can do better." When they have opportunities to do some of these new and complex things and succeed, they gain confidence in themselves and their abilities.

A number of abilities must come together before the toddler can engage in these self-regulated, goal-directed behaviors (Bullock & Lutkenhaus, 1988):

- Thinking about a goal that has not yet been reached.

- Thinking about the kinds of activities that might lead to achieving the goal.

- Selecting the specific means that will be used to reach the goal.

- Keeping one's attention focused on reaching the goal.

This last point, keeping focused on the goal, is especially difficult for toddlers. They are inclined to become distracted, to be frustrated by obstacles to their efforts, or to have difficulty assessing how near or far they are from achieving their goal (see Notebook Page 9.4).

Speech and Goal Attainment

It may be obvious that many of the goals that toddlers try to attain involve fine and gross motor skills. They want things they cannot reach, try to keep up with older siblings who move more quickly, or want to play with toys or perform tasks that involve strength or coordination they have not yet

Self-Directed Goal Attainment

1. How do you think your current patterns of goal setting and goal attainment might be related to experiences of toddlerhood? Describe an example of something about which you have goals, aspirations, and conscious plans (for example, a career step, a purchase, or a competence).

_____

_____

2. How did you set your goal?

_____

_____

3. How do you keep focused on this goal?

_____

_____

4. How often do you revise this goal?

_____

_____

5. What are your strategies for attaining the goal? Do you use inner speech when you are planning and problem solving? Do you encourage yourself or scold yourself while you work toward a goal or solve a problem?

_____

_____

_____

6. Given your description of your own personal example, what happened during toddlerhood that influences how you address self-directed problem solving today?

_____

_____

Internalization of social speech

achieved. It is perhaps less obvious to appreciate the role of language in goal attainment. Vygotsky (1978) has argued for an especially central role for speech in self-directed goal attainment and practical problem solving. He theorized that _egocentric speech, or speech directed toward the self, and actions are part of the same problem-solving function_. The more difficult the problem is, the more necessary speech is in order for the child to find a solution. "Children solve practical tasks with the help of their speech, as well as their eyes and hands" (1978, 26).

Speech gives children a new degree of freedom, flexibility, and control in approaching tasks and working toward a goal. They can use words to call to mind concepts that are not visible. They can plan steps toward a goal and repeat them to guide their actions. They can use words like "slowly" or "be careful" or "hold tight" to control their behavior as they work on a task.

Speech that guides problem solving emerges from the social speech that characterizes children's interactions with adults. Often, when young children are trying to solve a problem, they turn to adults for help. Vygotsky suggested that the kinds of talk that adults use as they guide young children is then used by the children themselves to support and guide their own behavior. He refers to this process as the "internalization of social speech." Through this mechanism, the social environment shapes the child's thinking, planning, and problem solving. Thus, a child's capacity for self-directed goal attainment depends largely on the spoken practical advice and guidance from the adults and older peers who have helped the child solve problems in the past.

Sometimes toddlers' enthusiasm and self-confidence go beyond their potential for performance. They watch parents who are managing a task easily and think they can do it just as easily. If left to try the task on their own, they fail. They become discouraged and frustrated because they expected a

Internalization of social speech.

successful outcome. If parents tell them not to try, they are also frustrated, because they are certain that they would do a good job. Probably the best solution to this problem is to cooperate with toddlers, allowing them to do what they can but giving assistance when they need it. As Vygotsky might suggest, adults and older siblings can foster self-directed goal attainment by encouraging children to take on tasks that are just a step ahead of what they can manage easily, that is, in the zone of proximal development. As children engage in tasks that are somewhat beyond their capacity, they learn to evaluate their strength and skill more realistically without feeling humiliated by failure. By the end of toddlerhood, children are better able to evaluate the requirements of a wide variety of tasks. They can judge whether or not they can accomplish a task by themselves.

We have considered two rather different phenomena under the development task of self-control: control of impulses and self-directed goal attainment. Both abilities foster toddlers' growing sense of agency. To function effectively as family members, toddlers must feel successful in their ability to control the inner world of their feelings and to influence the outer world of decisions and tasks. As toddlers discover that they can tolerate stress, express or withhold their impulses as appropriate, and succeed at difficult tasks, they also gain a growing self-confidence.

Chapter Summary

1. The developmental tasks of toddlerhood, language and communication skills, expanded locomotion, fantasy play, and self-control all contribute to the child's emerging independence within the boundaries of the family group.

2. Semiotic thought transforms mental activity, allowing one object, word, picture, or gesture to stand for something else.

3. In infancy, milestones of language and communication include language perception, cooing and babbling, communication with gestures, and first words.

4. In toddlerhood, language comprehension expands markedly, vocabulary increases, and grammar emerges, first with two-word telegraphic speech and then with more complex sentences and grammatical transformations. In both infancy and toddlerhood, there is a wide range of normal variation in the rate of development and scope of language competence.

5. Language is a cultural tool that contributes to overall socialization. The child's language environment has substantial implications for intellectual development and social competence.

6. A parent's characteristics as an appropriate language partner and the use of specific scaffolding strategies enhance language competence.

7. Qualitative changes in locomotor skills bring toddlers into contact with new aspects of the environment and stimulate new caregiving responses. As with language, the pattern and rate of motor development is subject to wide individual differences.

8. Landmarks of motor development during toddlerhood include more stable and confident walking, running, jumping, hopping, throwing and catching, pedaling, and steering.

9. Fantasy play, like language, requires semiotic thinking. Early pretense usually involves the imitation of actions without the presence of a model. Over time, the pretense becomes more sophisticated. Action components become integrated into a sequence, the fantasy involves multiple characters and roles, a variety of props and objects may be invented, and the direction of the play becomes more organized. Play may go on for several days and weeks when play companions get together.

10. Fantasy play contributes to cognitive, social, and emotional development. It stimulates language skills, helps foster self-control, and provides insight into the minds and thoughts of others. Through play, children can attempt to experiment with problems and find solutions. Play stimulates children to function at a level beyond what they can achieve within the constraints of reality.

11. As with language, the nature of one's play companions is important in nurturing the capacity for play and for extending its complexity.

12. Imaginary companions are quite common during this period. They are a very sophisticated form of symbolic play in which the child produces and maintains a fully functional character without the use of props.

13. Self-control requires advances in cognitive, emotional, social, and self-development. It includes the ability to comply with a request, modify behavior according to the situation, and postpone actions that are socially unacceptable or inappropriate.

14. Self-control develops in two directions during toddlerhood: first, in the ability to identify and control unacceptable impulses; and second, in the ability to direct behavior to achieve specific goals. Both capacities contribute to a child's sense of urgency and personal confidence.

References

Anglin, J. M. (1993). Vocabulary development: A morphological analysis. *Monographs of the Society for Research in Child Development, 58.*

Bandura, A. (1977). *Social learning theory.* Englewood Cliffs, N.J.: Prentice-Hall.

Bates, E., O'Connell, B. & Shore, C. (1987). Language and communication in infancy. In J. D. Osofsky (Ed.), *Handbook of infant development* (2nd ed.). New York: John Wiley & Sons, Inc., 149–203.

Berk, L. E. (1993). *Infants, children, and adolescents.* Boston: Allyn & Bacon.

Berkowitz, L. (1973). Control of aggression. In B. M. Caldwell & H. N. Ricciuti (Eds.), *Review of child development research* (vol. 3). Chicago: University of Chicago Press.

Biringen, Z., Emde, R. N., Campos, J. J. & Appelbaum, M. I. (1995). Affective reorganization in the infant, the mother, and the dyad: The role of upright locomotion and its timing. *Child Development, 66,* 499–514.

Bloom, L. (1993). Word learning. *SRCD Newsletter,* Winter, 1, 9, 13.

Blos, P. (1979). *The adolescent passage.* New York: International Universities Press.

Bornstein, M. H. & O'Reilly, A. W. (1993). *The role of play in the development of thought.* San Francisco: Jossey-Bass.

Braine, M. D. S. (1976). *Children's first word combinations. Monographs of the Society for Research in Child Development, 41* (1).

Brown, J. R. & Dunn, J. (1992). Talk with your mother or your sibling? Developmental changes in early family conversations about feelings. *Child Development, 63,* 336–349.

Brown, R. (1973). *A first language: The early stages.* Cambridge, Mass.: Harvard University Press.

Bullock, M. & Lutkenhaus, P. (1988). The development of volitional behavior in the toddler years. *Child Development, 59,* 664–674.

Burke, B. (1987). The role of playfulness in developing thinking skills: A review with implementations strategies. In S. Moore & K. Kolb (Eds.), *Reviews of research for practitioners and parents.* Minneapolis: Center for Early Education and Development, (3), 3–8.

Caplan, M., Vespo, J., Pedersen, J. & Hay, D. F. (1991). Conflict and its resolution in small groups of one- and two-year-olds. *Child Development, 62,* 1513–1524.

Carey, S. (1978). The child as word learner. In M. Halle, G. Miller & J. Bresnan (Eds.), *Linguistic theory and psychological reality.* Cambridge, Mass.: MIT Press, 264–293.

Clark, J. E., Phillips, S. J. & Peterson, R. (1989). Developmental stability in jumping. *Developmental Psychology, 25,* 929–935.

Cole, D. & La Voie, J. C. (1985). Fantasy play and related cognitive development in 2 to 6 year olds. *Developmental Psychology, 21,* 233–240.

Corina, D. P., Vaid, J. & Bellugi, U. (1992). The linguistic basis of left hemisphere specialization. *Science, 255,* 1258–1260.

Coster, W. J., Gersten, M. S., Beeghly, M. & Cicchetti, D. (1989). Communicative functioning in maltreated toddlers. *Developmental Psychology, 25,* 1020–1029.

Crain-Thoreson, C. & Dale, P. S. (1992). Do early talkers become early readers? Linguistic precocity, preschool language, and emergent literacy. *Developmental Psychology, 28,* 421–429.

Cronin-Golomb, A. (1995). Semantic networks in the divided cerebral hemispheres. *Psychological Science, 6,* 212–218.

Cummings, E. M., Iannotti, R. J. & Zahn-Waxler, C. (1989). Aggression between peers in early childhood: Individual continuity and developmental change. *Child Development, 60,* 887–895.

Cummings, J. S., Pellegrini, D. S., Notarius, C. I. & Cummings, E. M. (1989). Children's responses to angry adult behavior as a function of marital distress and history of interparent hostility. *Child Development, 60,* 1035–1043.

DeLoache, J. S. (1991). Symbolic functioning in very young children: Understanding of pictures and models. *Child Development, 62,* 736–752.

Diaz, R. M. (1983). Thought and two languages: The impact of bilingualism on cognitive development. *Review of Research in Education, 10,* 23–54.

Dunn, J. (1988). *The beginnings of social understanding.* Oxford, England: Basil Blackwell.

Dunn, J., Brown, J. & Beardsall, L. (1991). Family talk about feeling states and children's later understanding of others' emotions. *Developmental Psychology, 27,* 448–455.

Eckerman, C. O. & Didow, S. M. (1989). Toddlers' social coordinations: Changing responses to another's invitation to play. *Developmental Psychology, 25,* 794–804.

Eckerman, C. O. & Didow, S. M. (1996). Nonverbal imitation and toddlers' mastery of verbal means of achieving coordinated action. *Developmental Psychology, 32,* 141–152.

Edwards, C. P. (1995). Parenting toddlers. In M. H. Bornstein (Ed.), *Handbook of parenting. Children and parenting* (vol. 1). Hillsdale, N.J.: Erlbaum.

Erikson, E. H. (1972). Play and actuality. In M. W. Piers (Ed.), *Play and development.* New York: W. W. Norton, 127–167.

Fenson, L., Dale, P. S., Reznick, J. S., Bates, E., Thal, D. J. & Pethick, S. J. (1994). Variability in early communicative development. *Monographs of the Society for Research in Child Development, 59* (5).

Fernald, A. & Kuhl, P. K. (1987). Acoustic determinants of infant preference for motherese speech. *Infant Behavior and Development, 10,* 279–293.

Flavell, J. H., Flavell, E. R. & Green, F. L. (1987). Young children's knowledge about the apparent-real and pretend-real distinctions. *Developmental Psychology, 23,* 816–822.

Garton, A. F. (1992). *Social interaction and the development of language and cognition.* Hillsdale, N.J.: Erlbaum.

Getchell, N. & Roberton, M. A. (1989). Whole body stiffness as a function of developmental level in children's hopping. *Developmental Psychology, 25,* 920–928.

Golinkoff, R. M., Hirsh-Pasek, K., Bailey, L. M. & Wenger, N. R. (1992). Young children and adults use lexical principles to learn new nouns. *Developmental Psychology, 28,* 99–108.

Greenfield, P. M. & Smith, J. H. (1976). *The structure of communication in early language development.* New York: Academic Press.

Hakuta, K. & Garcia, E. E. (1989). Bilingualism and education. *American Psychologist, 44,* 374–379.

Hala, S., Chandler, M. & Fritz, A. S. (1991). Fledgling theories of mind: Deception as a marker of

3-year-olds' understanding of false belief. *Child Development*, 62, 83–97.

Harris, M. (1992). *Language experience and early language development: From input to uptake.* Hillsdale, N.J.: Erlbaum.

Harris, P. L. & Kavanaugh, R. D. (1993). Young children's understanding of pretense. *Monographs of the Society for Research in Child Development, 58*, (1).

Hart, B. & Risley, T. R. (1992). American parenting of language-learning children: Persisting differences in family–child interactions observed in natural home environments. *Developmental Psychology, 28*, 1096–1105.

Heath, S. B. (1989). Oral and literate traditions among black Americans living in poverty. *American Psychologist, 44*, 367–372.

Hoffman, S. J. (1985). Play and the acquisition of literacy. *Quarterly Newsletter of the Laboratory of Comparative Human Cognition, 7*, 89–95.

Howes, C. (1987). *Peer interaction of young children. Monographs of the Society for Research in Child Development, 53* (1, Serial no. 217).

Howes, C. & Stewart, P. (1987). Child's play with adults, toys, and peers: An examination of family and child-care influences. *Developmental Psychology, 23*, 423–430.

Howes, C., Unger, O. & Seidner, L. B. (1989). Social pretend play in toddlers: Parallels with social play and with solitary pretend. *Child Development, 60*, 77–84.

Hutt, S. J., Tyler, S., Hutt, C. & Foy, H. (1988). *Play exploration and learning: A natural history of the preschool.* New York: Routledge.

Jones, S. S., Smith, L. B. & Landau, B. (1991). Object properties and knowledge in early lexical learning. *Child Development, 62*, 499–516.

Kalverboer, A. F., Hopkins, B. & Geuze, R. (1993). *Motor development in early and later childhood: Longitudinal approaches.* New York: Cambridge University Press.

Kochanska, G. & Radke-Yarrow, M. (1992). Inhibition in toddlerhood and the dynamics of the child's interaction with an unfamiliar peer at age five. *Child Development, 63*, 325–335.

Kopp, C. B. (1982). Antecedents of self-regulation: A developmental perspective. *Developmental Psychology, 18*, 199–214.

Ladd, G. W., Price, J. M. & Hart, C. H. (1988). Predicting preschoolers' peer status from their playground behaviors. *Child Development, 59*, 986–992.

Lenneberg, E. H. (1967). *Biological foundations of language.* New York: Wiley.

Lewis, M., Stanger, C. & Sullivan, M. W. (1989). De-

ception in 3-year-olds. *Developmental Psychology, 25*, 439–443.

Lucariello, J. (1987). Spinning fantasy: Themes, structure, and the knowledge base. *Child Development, 58*, 434–442.

Mahler, M., Pine, F. & Bergman, A. (1975). *The psychological birth of the human infant.* New York: Basic Books.

Mandel, D. R., Jusczyk, P. W. E. & Pisoni, D. B. (1995). Infants' recognition of the sound patterns of their own names. *Psychological Science, 6*, 314–317.

McCloskey, L. A., Figueredo, A. J. & Koss, M. P. (1995). The effects of systemic family violence on children's mental health. *Child Development, 66*, 1239–1261.

Messer, D. J., Rachford, D., McCarthy, M. E. & Yarrow, L. J. (1987). Assessment of mastery behavior at 30 months: Analysis of task-directed activities. *Developmental Psychology, 23*, 771–781.

Miller, G. A. & Gildea, P. M. (1987). How children learn words. *Scientific American*, September.

Miller, N. B., Cowan, P. A., Cowan, C. P., Hetherington, E. M. & Clingempeel, W. G. (1993). Externalizing in preschoolers and early adolescents: A cross-study replication of a family model. *Developmental Psychology, 29*, 3–18.

Mischel, W., Shoda, Y. & Rodriguez, M. L. (1989). Delay of gratification in children. *Science, 244*, 933–938.

Molfese, D. L., Molfese, V. J. & Carrell, P. L. (1982). Early language development. In B. B. Wolman (Ed.), *Handbook of developmental psychology.* Englewood Cliffs, N.J.: Prentice-Hall, 301–322.

Moskowitz, B. A. (1978). The acquisition of language. *Scientific American, 239*, 92–108.

Murphy, L. (1956). *Personality in young children. Colin, a normal child* (vol. 2). New York: Basic Books.

Nelson, K. (1973). *Structure and strategy in learning to talk. Monographs of the Society for Research in Child Development, 38* (1–2).

Nelson, K. (1981). Individual differences in language development: Implications for development and language. *Developmental Psychology, 17*, 170–187.

Olsen, L. (1988). *Crossing the schoolhouse border: Immigrant students and the California public schools.* San Francisco: California Tomorrow.

Peskin, J. (1992). Ruse and representations: On children's ability to conceal information. *Developmental Psychology, 28*, 84–89.

Piaget, J. (1962). *Play, dreams, and imitation in childhood.* New York: Norton.

Pick, H. L. (1989). Motor development: The control of action. *Developmental Psychology, 25*, 867–870.

Piers, M. W. & Landau, G. M. (1980). *The gift of play.* New York: Walker.

Pye, C. (1986). Quiché Mayan speech to children. *Journal of Child Language, 13,* 85–100.

Raymond, C. (1991). Cross-cultural study of sounds adults direct to infants shows that 'baby talk' can be serious communication. *The Chronicle of Higher Education,* January 23, A5, A7.

Rice, M. L. (1989). Children's language acquisition. *American Psychologist, 44,* 149–156.

Ridenour, M. V. (Ed.). (1978). *Motor development: Issues and application.* Princeton, N.J.: Princeton Books.

Rogers, C. S. & Sawyers, J. K. (1988). *Play in the lives of children.* Washington, D.C.: National Association for the Education of Young Children.

Rogoff, B. & Morelli, G. (1989). Perspectives on children's development from cultural psychology. *American Psychologist, 44,* 343–348.

Rubin, K. H. (1980). Fantasy play: Its role in the development of social skills and social cognition. *New Directions in Child Development, 9,* 69–84.

Ruffman, T., Olson, D. R., Ash, T. & Keenan, T. (1993). The ABCs of deception: Do young children understand deception in the same way as adults? *Developmental Psychology, 29,* 74–87.

Saltz, R. & Saltz, E. (1986). Pretend play training and its outcomes. In G. Fein & M. Rivkin (Eds.), *The young child at play: Reviews of research* (vol. 4). Washington, D.C.: National Association for the Education of Young Children, 155–173.

Schatz, M. (1983). Communication. In J. H. Flavell & E. M. Markman (Eds.), *Handbook of child psychology* (vol. 3). New York: Wiley, 841–889.

Schickedanz, J. A. (1986). *More than the ABCs: The early stages of reading and writing.* Washington, D.C.: NAEYC.

Singer, D. G. & Singer, J. L. (1990). *The house of make-believe: Children's play and developing imagination.* Cambridge, Mass.: Harvard University Press.

Singer, J. L. (1975). *The inner world of daydreaming.* New York: Colophon Books.

Slade, A. (1987). A longitudinal study of maternal involvement and symbolic play during the toddler period. *Child Development, 58,* 367–375.

Slobin, D. I. (1985). *The cross-linguistic study of language acquisition* (vols. 1 & 2). Hillsdale, N.J.: Erlbaum.

Smith, L. B., Jones, S. S. & Landau, B. (1992). Count nouns, adjectives, and perceptual properties in children's novel word interpretations. *Developmental Psychology, 28,* 273–286.

Snow, C. E. (1984). Parent–child interaction and the development of communicative ability. In R. L. Schiefelbusch & J. Pickar (Eds.), *Communicative competence: Acquisition and intervention.* Baltimore: University Park Press, 69–108.

Snow, C. E. (1987). Beyond conversation: Second language learners' acquisition of description and explanation. In J. P. Lantolf & A. Labarca (Eds.), *Research in second language learning: Focus on the classroom.* Norwood, N.J.: Ablex, 3–16.

Taylor, M., Cartwright, B. S. & Carlson, S. M. (1993). A developmental investigation of children's imaginary companions. *Developmental Psychology, 29,* 276–285.

Teti, D. M., Nakagawa, M., Das, R. & Wirth, O. (1991). Security of attachment between preschoolers and their mothers: Relations among social interaction, parenting stress, and mothers' sorts of the attachment Q-Set. *Developmental Psychology, 27,* 440–447.

Tinsley, V. S. & Waters, H. S. (1982). The development of verbal control over motor behavior: A replication and extension of Luria's findings. *Child Development, 53,* 746–753.

Trawick-Smith, J. (1988). "Let's say you're the baby. OK?": Play leadership and following behavior of young children. *Young Children, 43,* 51–59.

Umbel, V. M., Pearson, B. Z., Fernandez, M. C. & Oller, D. K. (1992). Measuring bilingual children's receptive vocabularies. *Child Development, 63,* 1012–1020.

Valdez-Menchaca, M. S. & Whitehurst, G. J. (1992). Accelerating language development through picture book reading: A systematic extension to Mexican day care. *Developmental Psychology, 28,* 1106–1114.

Vasek, M. E. (1986). Lying as a skill: The development of deception in children. In R. W. Mitchell & N. S. Thompson (Eds.), *Deception: Perspectives on human and nonhuman deceit.* New York: State University of New York Press, 271–293.

Vaughn, B. E., Kopp, C. B. & Krakow, J. B. (1984). The emergence and consolidation of self-control from 18 to 30 months of age: Normative trends and individual differences. *Child Development, 55,* 990–1004.

Vaughn, B. E., Kopp, C. B., Krakow, J. B., Johnson, K. & Schwartz, S. S. (1986). Process analyses of the behavior of very young children in delay tasks. *Developmental Psychology, 22,* 752–759.

Vygotsky, L. S. (1962). *Thought and language.* Cambridge, Mass.: MIT Press.

Vygotsky, L. S. (1978). *Mind in society.* Cambridge, Mass.: Harvard University Press.

Wenar, C. (1982). On negativism. *Human Development, 25,* 1–23.

Whitall, J. & Getchell, N. (1995). From walking to running: Applying a dynamical systems approach to the development of locomotor skills. *Child Development, 66,* 1541–1553.

White, B. L., Kaban, B. T. & Attanucci, J. S. (1979). *The origins of human competence.* Lexington, Mass.: D. C. Heath.

Youngblade, L. M. & Dunn, J. (1995). Individual differences in young children's pretend play with mother and sibling: Links to relationships and understanding of other people's feelings and beliefs. *Child Development, 66,* 1472–1492.

Zahn-Waxler, C., Radke-Yarrow, M., Wagner, E. & Chapman, M. (1992). Development of concern for others. *Developmental Psychology, 27,* 126–136.

Zahn-Waxler, C., Robinson, J. L. & Emde, R. N. (1992). The development of empathy in twins. *Developmental Psychology, 28,* 1038–1047.

Expanding the Psychosocial Analysis of Toddlerhood

The Psychosocial Crisis of Toddlerhood
    Autonomy
    Shame and Doubt
The Central Process: Imitation
The Prime Adaptive Ego Quality
and the Core Pathology
    Will
    Compulsion
Family Development During Toddlerhood
    Parents as Play Companions
    Parents as Socialization Agents
        Socialization Styles
        Discipline Practices
        Discipline Is Co-Constructed
    Managing Work and Family Life
        The Intermingling of Developmental Tasks: Work and Parenting
        Conflict Between Work and Family Life
        The Impact of Conflict on the Family Environment
    Becoming a Sibling
        Sibling Rivalry
Cultural and Ethnic Patterns That Create Distinctive Child-Rearing Environments
During Toddlerhood
    The Value of Fantasy
    Variations in Promoting Autonomy
    Culture and Discipline Practices
        Fables, Stories, and Myths
        Religions and Discipline
        Physical Punishment and Power Assertion
Societal Issues That Provide Resources or Barriers to Development
    Poverty
        Conditions Leading to Poverty
        The Influence of Poverty on Child Development
        Factors That Mediate the Impact of Poverty
        Poverty and Toddlerhood
    Day Care
        The Impact of Day Care
        Directions for the Future of Child Care
    Child Abuse
        The Effects of Abuse on Children
Optimizing Development in Toddlerhood
    The Adult's Role
    The Physical Environment
    The Community
    Toddlers Contribute to Their Own Development
Chapter Summary
References

Chapter **10**

393

The margin notes read:

CRISIS
autonomy vs. shame & doubt

test the limits

This chapter expands the psychosocial analysis of toddlerhood by examining the psychosocial crisis of the stage (autonomy versus shame and doubt), the central process through which the crisis is resolved (imitation), the related ego quality (will), and the core pathology (compulsion). The dynamics of this psychosocial crisis occur within the context of an increasingly complex social environment as toddlers move out of the home and into new domains, including day care, preschool, play groups, and community. They may accompany their parent(s) on errands to stores, go with family members to restaurants and sporting events, and make visits to relatives' homes. Thus, toddlers are exposed to more people, and parents begin to interpret community norms to their toddlers. Not only is the toddler changing, but the family group is changing as well. Parents must take on new roles in order to provide appropriate nurturing and socialization for their children; they become more active as play companions and socialization agents. At the same time, they may be encountering new conflicts in trying to balance work and family life as their children's needs change. In many families, a second child is born before the first child reaches the age of four, leading to new family dynamics and new roles for the toddler as "big brother or sister."

The psychosocial analysis also directs our attention to the unique cultural patterns that influence the child-rearing environment for toddlers. In this chapter, we take a closer look at three aspects of culture—attitudes and practices related to fantasy, cultural views of autonomy, and cultural variations in discipline and child-rearing practices. Each of these dimensions of culture influences the kinds of competence that are likely to be valued and the pattern of common socialization practices that toddlers are likely to encounter. Poverty, day care, and child abuse are three specific social issues that have a role in shaping the direction of a toddler's growth. We introduce these topics here because their clear and enduring impact on the course of development begins in toddlerhood. Within each topic, we attempt to clarify the ways that toddlers may be affected, as well as the coping skills that may emerge in the process of adaptation. The chapter ends with a consideration of the factors associated with promoting optimal development in toddlerhood.

The Psychosocial Crisis of Toddlerhood

During toddlerhood, children become more aware of their separateness. They experience a new level of self-consciousness which permits them to realize that they are the object of other people's affection, anger, encouragement, or scorn. They also become more aware of their own needs, wants, and goals. Using language and fantasy, toddlers begin to represent their inner world to others, and conscious activity expands greatly. With advances in locomotor skills and self-control, purposeful, energetic exploration expands as well. One consequence of this direction of growth is an increase in the conflicts that toddlers experience with adults and other children. Toddlers push the limits of safety and courtesy, violating or ignoring most social norms, not necessarily due to any deliberate desire to offend but out of ignorance of what is expected and an unbridled energy and enthusiasm for autonomous action. As a result, they encounter new levels of socialization pressures, efforts to guide, redirect, change, or suppress their words and actions. This is the basic context for the psychosocial crisis of autonomy versus shame and doubt.

Autonomy

The positive pole of the psychosocial crisis of toddlerhood is autonomy. At this period of life, *autonomy* refers to the ability to behave independently, to perform actions on one's own. The unique characteristics of growth toward autonomy are energy and persistence. At this age, children prefer to do most things on their own—in fact, they *insist* on doing so. Once children begin to work on a task such as putting on pajamas or tying shoes, they will struggle time after time until they have mastered it. They may reject help adamantly and insist they can manage on their own, allowing someone else to help them only when they are sure they can progress no further by themselves. Establishing a sense of autonomy requires tremendous effort by the child and extreme patience and support from parents.

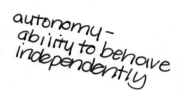
autonomy—
ability to behave
independently

Toddlers' demands for autonomy often are exasperating. They challenge parents' good sense, goodwill, and good intentions. Parents must learn to teach, encourage, absorb rejection, wait, and praise. By encouraging toddlers to engage in new tasks, parents promote a sense of competence. They hope and believe their children will succeed at much of what they try.

From two to four, toddlers shift from a somewhat rigid, naysaying, ritualized, unreasonable style, displayed around two, to an independent, energetic, persistent style by four (Erikson, 1963). In the early phases of toddlerhood, children use rather primitive devices to explore their independence. They may say "no" to everything offered to them whether they want it or not. Toddlers may be very demanding and insist on having things done their own way. They seem to refuse to listen to reason. This is the period that parents often refer to as the "terrible twos."

The behavior of older toddlers is characterized by the phrase "I can do it myself." Toddlers demonstrate an increasing variety of skills. Each new accomplishment gives them great pride and a growing sense of autonomy (see Box 10.1). Toddlers begin to create an image of themselves as being able to manage situations competently and satisfy many of their own needs. Children who have been allowed to experience autonomy should, by the end of toddlerhood, have a strong foundation of self-confidence and delight in behaving independently.

Shame and Doubt

Some children fail to emerge from toddlerhood with a sense of mastery. Because of a pattern of failure at attempted tasks or continual discouragement and criticism from parents or, most likely, both, some children develop an overwhelming sense of shame and self-doubt. This is the negative resolution of the psychosocial crisis of toddlerhood (Erikson, 1963). *Shame* is an intense emotion that can result from two different types of experiences: social ridicule or criticism and internal conflict (Morrison, 1989).

Shame produced by *social ridicule* or *criticism* generally has its origins in an interpersonal interaction in which you feel that you have violated a valued social standard or where you have been embarrassed or ridiculed for behaving in a stupid, thoughtless, or clumsy way. Most people recall the shame of social ridicule as an extremely painful emotion.

BOX 10.1

Toilet Training

Freud identified conflicts around toilet training as the central psychodynamic conflict of toddlerhood. In the Victorian era, biological functions were considered crude and offensive. Young children were toilet trained as quickly as possible, with great emphasis on cleanliness and privacy. The struggle, as Freud saw it, was between the natural impulses of the child and the society's insistence on bringing those impulses under control (Freud, 1920). He also thought that the child experienced physical pleasures through elimination, so that the adult's attempt to impose rules about elimination and to punish failure could intensify a child's conflicts about these behaviors.

As Robert White (1960) pointed out, in this particular conflict children are destined to lose. They must subordinate their autonomy to parental expectations for a specific routine for elimination. However, the way that toilet training is handled determines whether toddlers emerge from this experience feeling that they have mastered a challenging routine or that they have been exploited and dominated by a capricious force that is focused on crushing their will.

Toddlers must master a number of skills in order to succeed at toilet training. They must have some word or signal that they can use to communicate their need to go to the bathroom. They must be able to get to the bathroom either by finding their own way there or by finding someone to direct them. They must be able to delay elimination until they have arrived at the bathroom and removed their clothes.

For the child to experience a sense of competence during the toilet-training period, a number of things must occur: (1) The child's body must be ready; (2) the child must be able to give a signal when it is time to go; and (3) the child must be able to respond to an internal cue and anticipate necessary action. If parents wait to begin toilet training until children show signs of readiness in all areas, children are more likely to approach this task with feelings of pride and accomplishment in self-control rather than seeing it as a struggle of wills. Their success will increase their self-confidence.

In shame, the object of concern is the entire self. The "bad thing" is experienced as a reflection of a "bad self," and the entire self is painfully scrutinized and negatively evaluated. With this painful scrutiny of the self, there is a corresponding sense of shrinking, of being small, and of being worthless and powerless. (Tangney et al., 1992, 670)

Some cultures rely heavily on public humiliation as a means of social control. Children in those cultures grow up with strong concerns about "saving face," and may grow to adulthood with enhanced social skills for polite, thoughtful gestures in social interaction in order to keep the likelihood of public humiliation low.

Another source of shame is *internal conflict*. As children construct an understanding of what it means to be a good, capable person, they build a mental image of an ideal person, the *ego ideal*. Children feel shame when they recognize that even though they have not broken a rule or done something "naughty," they have failed to live up to their own private idea of how they think they should behave.

Researchers who study shame found that college students who have high levels of shame were also characterized by higher levels of resentment, irritability, anger, suspiciousness, and a tendency to blame others. The expression of strong feelings in response to repeated experiences of shame changes over time. First, the person directs hostility toward the self, feeling worthless

Using imitation, Ellie can become her mother's fitness partner.

and stupid. Later, the hostility is redirected in fantasies of retaliation toward the person who has rejected them (Kaufman, 1989; Lewis, 1987; Miller, 1985).

Under normal conditions, all children experience some failures amid their many successes. Even the most patient parent may occasionally shame a child for making a mess or disturbing others. Children who resolve the crisis in favor of autonomy will still sometimes doubt that they can succeed, and they may still experience shame when they fail. However, they will usually feel competent and be predisposed toward trying many activities. Children who resolve the crisis in favor of shame and doubt will avoid new activities and cling to what they already know, often creating ritualistic behavior patterns that they believe will protect them from being shamed.

The Central Process: Imitation

Ironically, the central process through which toddlers emerge as autonomous individuals is imitation. _Imitation_ is the primary vehicle through which toddlers learn new skills (Bandura, 1977). Success in these new skills leads to feelings of competence. In addition, through imitation, children develop a repertoire of language and actions that enables them to express their own needs and coordinate their behavior with that of others.

Imitation as a mode of learning emerges very early in infancy with the imitation of very simple facial expressions like smiling, sticking out the tongue, and frowning. By five months, babies can imitate new sounds that adults make in a back-and-forth kind of game, and at nine to ten months, babies engage in systematic imitation of sounds and gestures in games like "peek-a-boo" or "how big is the baby? Sooo big" (Bates et al., 1987). These forms of simple imitation through which babies incorporate sounds and actions become a basis for the more complex imitative sequences that are observed in toddlerhood.

The emphasis on imitation highlights the central role of culture at this period of life, giving the child a vocabulary not only of language but also of action. Daily events provide models for imitation which reflect the culture of family and community: the way visitors are greeted when they arrive at the home; the way adults prepare food, wash clothes, groom themselves, and speak to one another; the way household tasks and chores are performed; the way older children amuse themselves; the way younger people and older people treat each other.

Although imitation requires the presence of active models, once toddlers succeed in imitating a certain action, that action belongs to them and they can use it for any purpose. Toddlers seem driven to imitate almost everything they observe—the silly way a playmate goes down the slide, the peculiar voice on a television commercial, or their parent's expressions of exasperation. Toddlers' vocabularies expand markedly through the imitation of words heard in adults' conversations, on television, and in stories that are read to them. Their interest in dancing, music, and other motor activities stems from imitation. As soon as one child in a play group makes a funny noise or performs a daring act, other children appear to be compelled to re-create this novel behavior.

In studies of imitation in the home environment, toddlers show an impressive pattern of imitating parents' household, self-care, and caretaking activities. They show increasing interest in imitating behaviors that are socially meaningful, valued, and part of their everyday lives. These observations led researchers to suggest that imitation serves a critical function in satisfying the toddler's need for social competence (Kuczynski, Zahn-Waxler & Radke-Yarrow, 1987). Through imitation, children may also derive pleasure from the similarity they perceive between themselves and the model. Perceived similarity to an admired older sibling or adult is a secondary benefit of the imitative process.

Imitation is also a means of participating in and sustaining social interactions. Within a peer setting, imitation emerges as a dominant strategy whereby children coordinate their behaviors with those of other toddlers. Before verbal communication becomes much of a useful tool for establishing or maintaining social contact, toddlers imitate one another. Through imitation, toddlers can feel connected to one another and begin to invent coordinated games (Eckerman et al., 1989). Once toddlers can participate in coordinated, imitative play with a peer, they appear to begin to form a more detailed understanding of their play partner, and subsequently use additional verbal strategies to improve the coordination in their play (Eckerman & Didow, 1996). With increasing cognitive maturity, children draw from their repertoire of previously imitated behaviors to advance their own autonomy and improve the meaningfulness of social interactions.

As we discussed in Chapter 9 in the section on language and communication, imitation provides a means for accumulating words and expanding one's vocabulary. But in order to use language autonomously, children must figure out the rules through which their thoughts can be translated into words. The relationship between imitation of words and autonomy of language also holds for imitation of activities and autonomy of personality. The wide range

Imitation serves need to be socially competent

social interactions

of actions that children learn through imitation is gradually ordered to suit their preferences. Children rely on imitation to acquire many skills, but the unique use of those skills soon comes under the management of their own will.

The Prime Adaptive Ego Quality and the Core Pathology

Will

Erikson identified the prime adaptive ego quality that emerges through the successful resolution of the psychosocial crisis of toddlerhood as will (Erikson et al., 1986). Will is the capacity of the mind to direct and control action. It is directly linked to the idea of self-directed goal attainment. Will is the inner voice—focusing attention, encouraging, urging you on, especially in the face of obstacles. It provides the psychological energy that allows people to press harder in competition, to work to surpass previous achievements, and to reach for new goals. In the face of disability, it is the force that urges the person to make peace with the loss and to focus on alternate goals. In the face of crisis, people often refer to their will to survive or their will to live as the fundamental strength that kept them looking for new solutions or that prevented them from giving up hope. In older people who experience potentially spirit-crushing, painful losses or disabilities, it is the force that provides buoyancy as they learn to accept their decline, look for areas of continued mastery, and reflect nostalgically on past achievements.

Sometimes, we think of will in a negative way as associated with stubbornness or overbearing dominance, "bending to someone's will." But the meaning of will in the psychosocial context refers to the sense of inner determination and purpose that permits a person to set goals freely and make persistent efforts to achieve them. Will leads to a positive belief in oneself as someone who can make things happen. When you see a child struggling to carry a heavy box or drag a wagon filled with toys up a steep hill, you see will in action. When you watch an older child chew and twist a pencil trying to figure out a tough math problem, you see will in action. And when you go to the high school swimming pool at six o'clock in the morning and see students working out and swimming laps to get ready for the upcoming meet, you see will in action.

Compulsion

Will provides a voluntary energy and focus to action. In contrast, compulsions are repetitive behaviors that are motivated by impulse or restrictions on the expression of impulse. They are nonspontaneous and unchanging. Compulsions are a close relative to the ritualization that is developed in toddlerhood. Children in this stage typically devise some well-ordered rituals, especially around important transitions such as going to bed, getting dressed, and leaving the house (Albert et al., 1977). They insist that these rituals be followed precisely and become extremely angry if the rituals are violated. Rituals represent efforts to bring control and order to the environment. They also help provide feelings of sameness and continuity during changes in setting or state that may threaten toddlers' feelings of selfhood. Toddlers' rituals usually are not mere imitations of adult rituals. Toddlers' rituals, however, like those of

Ego quality: WILL minds capacity to direct and control action.

adults, serve an important psychological function of bringing order and a sense of mastery to the unknown or the unpredictable. This in turn provides a feeling of security as toddlers pursue well-learned behaviors that work and may also have symbolic value. In comparison with adaptive rituals, which actually provide a sense of comfort and relief from uncertainty, compulsions must be carried out again and again, never adequately resolving the anxiety that motivates them (see Notebook Page 10.1).

Obsessions are persistent, repetitive thoughts that serve as mechanisms for binding anxiety. Compulsions are repetitive, ritualized actions that serve the same function. The idea of binding anxiety means that the person feels that the thoughts or behaviors reduce some other source of distress. For instance, a person with a compulsive neurosis may feel driven to repeat a certain phrase over and over again in order to ward off a dangerous event even though the phrase has no realistic chance of altering the event. Or the person may become committed to repeated hand-washing to get rid of uncleanness. The compulsive handwasher "scrubs his hands in tortured solitude, until they become raw, and yet he never feels clean" (Erikson, 1977, 78). Over time, a neurosis may become very disruptive to daily life since it takes a lot of time, makes it hard to concentrate on tasks, and causes feelings of a loss of control.

The peculiar thing about compulsions is that they are typically experienced as irresistible impulses, often felt as pressing a person to do things against their will. In a sense, people who suffer from obsessions and compulsions have a damaged will. Their ability to willfully direct their thoughts and actions toward a goal is impaired. They feel that their thoughts and actions are being controlled by some powerful force outside their voluntary control. It is not the same as an hallucination. They do not think that a voice from outer space or the spirit world is telling them what to do. They recognize the directive as coming from their own mind, but not from their will.

Obsessive-compulsive behaviors are observable in the normal person's concern with order, cleanliness, and planning. Well thought out, impulse-free obsessions and compulsions can lead to careful planning and be helpful strategic devices for goal attainment. They are usually under the person's control and can be useful tools for personal organization. In the neurotic individual, however, such thoughts and behaviors are beyond personal control and often impede effectiveness. The obsessive-compulsive personality is overly preoccupied with details, rules, and schedules. A perfectionistic standard is applied to most every action so that, despite long hours of work, tasks often cannot be completed. Money is hoarded, objects that are generally worthless are saved, and relationships are strained because other people never seem to be able to match up to the person's exacting standards (American Psychiatric Association, 1993).

According to psychosocial theory, the sources that motivate lifelong obsessive and compulsive behavior are basic doubts about one's worth and continuing doubts about everything else, typically produced by strong feelings of shame. Compulsions represent the ego's attempts to provide some structure to reality, but they do not work to promote further development because they are not meaningful (Erikson et al., 1986). The experience of the doubt-filled, shame-ridden person tends to be continuously unpleasant, uncertain, and sometimes tortuous. Life is organized around carefully organized patterns of meaningless, compulsive behaviors.

Will and Compulsion

The prime adaptive ego quality of toddlerhood is will; the core pathology is *compulsion.* Both will and compulsion are elements of normal, adaptive functioning, but both can become maladaptive in the extreme.

1. Reflect on your behavior over the past week. Identify examples of your expression of will. In what ways did you consciously guide your behavior, impose control over your impulses, or choose a course of action?

   a. _____

   b. _____

   c. _____

   d. _____

   e. _____

2. Reflect again on your behavior over the past week. What are some examples of *compulsion* operating in your behavior? Did you go over something time and time again in your mind? Did you feel drawn to repeat an action unnecessarily? Did you perform some "ritual" or superstitious "habit"?

   a. _____

   b. _____

   c. _____

   d. _____

   e. _____

Family Development During Toddlerhood

As the child changes and grows, an adaptive family system changes as well. Toddlerhood brings with it new capacities for motor activity, fantasy, spoken communication, and willful, goal-directed behavior. Parents and children engage in many entirely new domains of activity—some prompted by the parents' desire to stimulate and foster new cognitive and motor skills, some prompted by the parents' roles as protectors and socialization agents, and some prompted by the child's expression of needs, talents, and interests. Simply from the perspective of time management, toddlers are much more challenging than infants. They do not nap twice a day, they cannot be carried easily from one spot to another, they require more playful activities and more careful supervision, and they are often oppositional. They will not go along anywhere a parent may want to go or stay as long as a parent may want to stay.

Much of what actively engaged caregivers do is to teach their toddlers. Caregivers dedicate countless hours to teaching across numerous domains—how to speak, how to play, how to treat other people, and how to perform hundreds of small tasks. Many caregivers have never taught before. The interaction of teaching and learning stimulates new growth for both the caregiver and the child, as well as reawakening many familiar areas of learning for the caregiver.

In this section, we consider four ways that family life changes in coordination with the period of toddlerhood. The first three focus especially on the development of adult caregivers as play companions, socialization agents, and managers of the role competition between work and family life. These examples illustrate the interdependence of development for people at various life stages. The developmental tasks of toddlerhood introduce new parental responsibilities and new demands for role enactment. The fourth topic, becoming a sibling, focuses on the development of the toddler as he or she enters the new role of sibling and examines the changes in family life that accompany the birth of a second child.

Parents as Play Companions

When our oldest child Sam was born, we realized that, after so many years of being serious, we had forgotten how to play. We talked it over and decided that it was probably OK, maybe even good, for adults to be playful. We began to explore play by remembering what we had enjoyed as children. We walked through toy stores and identified toys and games from our childhood that were still on the shelves. We remembered what it felt like to be playful. Once playfulness was reawakened, it became clear to us how important this orientation is. Even though we waver in our behavior from time to time, we continue to be reminded how important play abilities are even in the worst of circumstances. Playfulness is at the heart of successful learning and teaching in all areas. It allows a person to keep some emotional distance and to entertain a number of possible outcomes to a situation. Playfulness helps parents remain patient and supportive during even the toughest of toddler demands.

As we discussed in Chapter 9, parents are a child's first play companions. From early infancy, when parents and children engage in simple play like making funny noises or tickling, to more complicated ritual games like

Julie has to set aside her embarrassment at looking ridiculous in order to join in her children's fantasy play.

pat-a-cake or peekaboo, they weave playfulness into the fabric of their relationship. At toddlerhood, the play takes on a new complexion as children explore the world of fantasy and symbolic pretend play. It takes a special sensitivity and willingness for parents to be effective play companions at this stage. Three aspects of becoming a good play companion are emphasized, each of which challenges an adult's typical way of functioning and requires a special willingness to commit to fantasy as a valued activity (Rogers & Sawyers, 1988) (see Table 10.1).

First, parents have to value fantasy play in order to allow it to flourish. Adults who express impatience with pretend play or who constantly interrupt children who are in the midst of pretending will discourage the further elaboration of this form of play. Parents have to let go of their product or outcome orientation and be willing to give time and attention to activity that has no tangible outcome. Adults also have to be willing to support pretend play by providing some resources to foster the play. These resources include ideas, space for pretend, and access to "props" like dress-up clothes, old boxes, blocks, and other play materials.

Second, adults must be willing to join in the co-construction of the fantasy. A parent has to find the right level of involvement, permitting the child as much autonomy as possible in making decisions about the direction of the play but responding appropriately and with positive energy to the child's suggestions (Denham et al., 1991). A good play companion responds with enthusiasm to the child's ideas rather than insisting that the play "make sense" or follow the conventions of reality. A good play companion lets the child take the lead, resisting the temptation to organize the play into a more logical plot or insisting that the story end up with a certain conclusion. And a good play companion is not overly judgmental within the play scenario. If a toddler wants to act like a baby and makes the kinds of baby noises or clumsy baby

TABLE 10.1

The Dos and Don'ts of Being a Good Play Companion for a Toddler

Do	Don't
• Commit to fantasy as a valued activity in order to let it flourish	• Insist that play make sense or follow the conventions of reality
• Be willing to give time and attention to the activity	• Be impatient or interrupt children in the midst of pretending
• Be willing to provide resources to foster play	• Focus too much on teaching a particular concept or skill
• Be willing to join in the co-construction of fantasy	• Attempt to organize the play so that it is more logical
• Respond with enthusiasm to the child's ideas	• Be overly judgmental
• Let the child take the lead	• Insist that stories end with certain conclusions
• Extend the play by introducing slightly new and more advanced elements	• Shame the child

Source: Based on Rogers, C. S., & Sawyers, J. K. (1988). *Play in the lives of children.* Washington, D.C.: National Association for the Education of Young Children.

actions that he or she has seen in a younger sibling, a good play companion does not say, "Oh, you're too old to act like such a baby."

Third, parents find ways to extend the play, urging the toddler to the zone of proximal development, without dominating the play. This may mean using props in a novel way, suggesting an adventure to a new type of pretend place, or broadening the child's information about a pretend situation, for example, offering more information about how cars really work or about how to care for a sick baby, as the pretense unfolds.

Parents as Socialization Agents

Socialization is a process through which individuals are guided to function in ways that are acceptable to the group or groups of which they are members. Beliefs as well as behaviors are modified through socialization. Socialization is carried out through *open discourse* (talking about how to behave or what one expects, and stating the rules and explaining why they are important), through *modeling* (showing appropriate behavior in one's own actions and words), and through what is typically called *discipline* (calling attention to both the positive and negative aspects of behavior through various forms of rewards and punishments). In childhood, the first and primary socialization agent is the parent (two parents if they are present). But the socialization process is carried on by a variety of other agents throughout life, and new facets of one's socialization are added each time one enters a new social organization or becomes a member of a new social group. Thus, even as a parent is socializing her or his children, other authority figures, including people at work, friends who have already had children, religious leaders, or the parent's own parents, are socializing them.

Toddlers' naive egocentrism and physical exuberance frequently bring them into conflict with a parent, siblings, and peers. *Negativism,* or the clear refusal to comply with the requests of others, is a hallmark of toddlerhood (Haswell et al., 1981; Wenar, 1982). In addition, as we discussed in Chapter 9, toddlers have difficulty controlling their impulses. They may find it difficult to interrupt an action, even when they know it is wrong. Eventually, the child's refusal to comply will conflict with a parent's insistence on a particular behavior. Thus, we can expect occasions for discipline to be an inevitable element of parent–child interactions during toddlerhood. As we suggested in the discussion of the psychosocial crisis of toddlerhood, the ideal result of parental discipline is to foster a toddler's ability to impose limits on his or her own behavior without feeling unduly coerced or extremely inhibited by fears of the parent's reaction.

Socialization Styles

Different parents prefer different socialization styles in order to teach and enforce the rules of the household, the community, and the society. Some parents are *disciplinarians.* They have a certain set of expectations for their child, and they use a combination of firm talk and swift correction to enforce these expectations. When unsatisfactory behavior is observed, punishment or drill is used to correct it.

Others act more as *teachers* in their role as socialization agents. They attempt to teach their children how to behave by explaining how and why the child needs to modify behavior in a certain situation.

Still others think of themselves as *trainers.* They emphasize imitation as a way to guide children, and they use rewards and punishments to train the child in proper behavior. Trainers, teachers, and disciplinarians all make different assumptions about their children's capabilities and about their own adult role as socialization agents.

Discipline Practices

In toddlerhood, the immediate aim of discipline is to achieve compliance (Kochanska et al., 1995). A parent typically wants children to stop doing something ("Don't touch those figurines; they might break") or to do something ("Help me put the toys away now, it's time to go to bed"). If the child complies, a parent might respond positively by smiling, patting the child or giving a hug, or complimenting the child for being good, helpful, or obedient. If the child does not comply, a parent may try some form of distraction or offer some choice ("You can help clean up now or in five minutes"). But if compliance is not forthcoming, some type of discipline is likely to ensue.

Discipline practices have been described in three general categories (Hoffman, 1977):

1. *Power assertion.* Physical punishment, shouting, attempts to physically move a child or inhibit behavior, taking away privileges or resources, or threatening any of these things.
2. *Love withdrawal.* Expressing anger, disappointment, or disapproval; refusing to communicate; walking out or turning away.
3. *Inductions.* Explaining why the behavior was wrong; pointing out the consequences of behavior to others; redirecting behavior by appealing to the child's sense of mastery, fair play, or caring.

In addition to these three general categories of discipline techniques, parental modeling and reinforcement of acceptable behaviors are significant in the development of internal control (Maccoby, 1992). In order to correct their behavior, children must know what acts are considered appropriate as well as how to inhibit their inappropriate acts. Modeling and reinforcement aid children in directing their behavior; discipline serves to inhibit or redirect that behavior.

The manner in which the discipline is carried out over time is associated with child outcomes, especially increases in compliance, prosocial behavior, and the eventual internalization of moral standards or, alternatively, increases in noncompliance, aggressiveness, and low levels of moral reasoning. Three features of the approach to discipline appear to be important (O'Leary, 1995):

1. *The discipline should be immediate or as close in time to the situation as possible.* Laxness in discipline, such as laughing at an undesirable behavior, waiting too long to respond, inconsistently reprimanding the child for the same misconduct, or inadvertently rewarding a child for misconduct are all practices that are likely to increase rather than decrease the undesired behavior.

2. *The discipline should be appropriately firm, but not overreactive.* Practices that are intensely harsh, abusive, or cruel, whether they involve physical or emotional intensity, are associated with increases in problem behaviors. The infrequent use of power assertive punishment within an overall context of a warm, nurturing relationship may prove effective in fostering compliance. However, intense and frequent harsh punishment is associated with a variety of maladaptive consequences for children (Weiss et al., 1992).

3. *The discipline for a toddler should be brief.* It is important to make sure the toddler understands what the misbehavior was and why it was wrong, but the explanation should be concise and presented at the toddler's level of understanding. Punishment involving love withdrawal is especially likely to be carried on too long. The parent should make sure the toddler knows when she or he is back in the parent's "good graces," and not let the child spend hours thinking the parent is still angry.

Discipline Is Co-Constructed

Parents and children influence one another through a continuous stream of interactive behaviors. Rather than viewing socialization as unidirectional, with the parent's actions producing outcomes in the child's behaviors, scholars now view socialization as a *co-constructed* process. Parents and children "develop coherent expectations concerning each other's behavior, joint goals, shared scripts from which each acts, and shared meanings that make fuller coordination of their activity possible" (Maccoby, 1992, 1014). Three aspects of the socialization process support this interactive perspective: the parent's beliefs, the discipline situation, and the child's responses.

The Parent's Beliefs. An adult's personal theory about the appropriate role of a parent in guiding the behavior of children at various ages influences the way that person interprets and reacts to a child's actions. This theory is shaped by adults' recollections of how they were parented, their level of psychosocial maturity, cultural assumptions regarding children and how they should be treated, and the adults' earlier experiences in observing and interacting with young children.

Parental beliefs influence discipline in several ways. An adult's approach to discipline is guided by a subjective assessment of a child's actions. For example, adults are likely to be more lenient about punishing an action if they believe that the child did not understand that what he or she did was wrong. They feel angrier and tend to be more stern when they conclude that a child was in fact deliberately responsible for the misdeed (Dix et al., 1989).

A parent takes a child's age and relevant skills into account in assessing the seriousness of a misdeed. Gralinski and Kopp (1993) asked mothers of infants and toddlers what they insist that their children must *not do* and what things they insist or encourage their child *to do*. The responses to these two questions provided a framework for considering the kinds of rules that young children are exposed to and how those rules might change with the child's age. In Table 10.2, the categories of rules are listed along with the description of those rules and the frequency with which rules of each type were mentioned. The rules for the very youngest children were comparatively few in number and focused on trying to protect the baby's physical safety, trying to protect family possessions, and restricting certain hurtful behaviors (for example, no biting). Mothers of older children imposed rules across a broader

TABLE 10.2

Rules and Prohibitions for Infants and Toddlers

1. *Safety rules* ($N^* = 377$) refer to protecting children from their own acts.
2. *Personal property rules* ($N = 81$) involve safeguarding others' possessions from children's intrusiveness, exploration, or inadvertent destructiveness.
3. *Interpersonal rules* ($N = 180$) transmit information related to the expression of prosocial behavior and the control of aggressive behaviors directed toward parents, other children, or animals.
4. *Food-related rules* ($N = 75$) center around family eating habits and eating etiquette.
5. *Independence requests* ($N = 50$) are concerned with attempts to get children to try new activities, practice existing ones, or perform activities correctly.
6. *Self-care rules* ($N = 105$) center around activities related to children's personal care and hygiene.
7. *Family routines* ($N = 64$) focus on activities that contribute to a neat, orderly household.
8. *Delay* ($N = 10$) refers to requests that involve children's waiting for attention.
9. *Manners* ($N = 7$) focus on attempts to get children to behave politely.
10. *Obedience rules* ($N = 13$) refer to general comments about children's attitudes toward parental authority.

*N = The number of open-ended responses coded under each category.
Source: Gralinski, J. H. & Kopp, C. B. (1993). Everyday rules for behavior: Mother's requests to young children. *Developmental Psychology, 29,* 576. Copyright © 1993 by the American Psychological Association. Reprinted with permission.

domain, including safety and property, but went beyond these into family routines, self-care, and other rules or expectations for independence. For the oldest age group, the rules became more differentiated. Rules about social norms took on a new level of complexity reflecting concern about the child's expanding contact with the larger community. "Do not scream in a restaurant, appear naked in front of company, pretend to kill, hang up the phone when someone is using it, fight with children in school, play with guns, pick your nose, or go to a neighbor's house too early in the morning" (Gralinski & Kopp, 1993, 581).

Children show a gradual improvement from 13 months to 30 months in their ability to control their behavior. At the same time, mothers change their expectations of their children as a result of a combination of their children's ability to comply with some of the more basic rules and their children's exposure to a wider social environment.

A final element in a parent's assessment of misconduct is whether the parent believes a child's behavior is a product of a personal trait or a product of the situation (Mills & Rubin, 1990). A parent who concludes that a child is "naturally" aggressive and boisterous may react calmly to an aggressive outburst. A parent who believes the child is being purposefully defiant may react with greater force. This pattern depends heavily on the parent's cultural outlook and values (Kochanska et al., 1989).

The Discipline Situation. The situation may influence both whether and how a child is disciplined. Loud singing or asking Mom to play house may be acceptable when everyone is relaxed. The same behavior may not be acceptable, however, when Mom is on the phone or trying to pay the bills. In a laboratory simulation, mothers were in a room with their two children, one in the three-to-five-year age range and one under three (Zussman, 1980). Parental behavior toward the children was observed under two conditions: when the mothers could play with the children and when they were preoccupied with a task that competed with the children for attention. When the mothers were involved in the competing task, they had fewer positive interactions with their older child and more frequent critical or punishing interactions with their younger one.

The Child's Response. The child's response to a parent's initial request may influence subsequent actions. A discipline situation is interactive. With very young children, a parent's request or command is often followed by compliance. The father says: "No, don't touch!" and the baby withdraws her hand. In other instances, an adult can redirect a young child's misbehavior by distracting the child and offering some alternative activity or object. As children reach the age of three or four, however, they become more active advocates for their own wishes. They may resist a command by negotiating: "I do it later"; "I already tried some"; or "Just a little more." When parents point out a mistake or a misdeed, a three-year-old can offer a justification and try to avoid punishment: "Baby did it"; "I'm tired"; "I need it"; "It's mine." These justifications can lead to new negotiations. Sometimes, after hearing a child's reasoning, a parent may decide to allow the child to continue the behavior. In general, toddlers are more effective in offering reasonable justifications and negotiating alternative behaviors when their parents engage in these types of interactions than when parents issue stern commands and use physical punishment (Dunn & Munn, 1987; Kuczynski et al., 1987).

Generally, toddlers are very sensitive to expressions of parental disapproval. As they move through toddlerhood, they begin to appreciate the extent of their dependence on their parent(s). They want to please the parent, and they want to feel that their behavior is "in control." Most children's behavior can be regulated with minimal adult intensity. Often, children know immediately after a misdeed that they have done the wrong thing. Extensive punishment or shaming at that point serves only to generate a child's anxiety and further disorganize thinking rather than to reinforce the child's internal recognition of an inappropriate act.

In deciding on a discipline strategy, a caregiver must be sensitive to the child's changing motives, aspirations, competence, and fears. If a discipline technique does not succeed in inhibiting a specific behavior and if punishment has to be threatened repeatedly, it must be concluded that from the child's point of view the technique is not meaningful. Consider a boy who becomes very boisterous, overactive, and rude whenever company is present. His father consistently sends him out of the room as a punishment. If the pattern is repeated a number of times, one would assume that the boy knows the consequence of his behavior and does not see it as negative. Perhaps he becomes very anxious by the presence of so many strangers and is glad to be removed from them without having to ask. Perhaps the special attention that his father gives him as he removes him from the room is exactly what the child wants in the midst of all the adult-centered activity. A punishment is effective only if it succeeds in reducing the likelihood of a particular behavior.

The goal of effective discipline is to promote a child's autonomy while ensuring the child's safety, promoting conformity to social norms and expectations, and enhancing the child's ability to function effectively in the social group. Over time, and through a large number of interactions, the child's ability to comply with a caregiver's requests most of the time and to negotiate successfully for his or her own needs some of the time leads the way to the internalization of a positive moral orientation and a positive identification with the caregiver. Toddlers who have been exposed to effective discipline discover that they can experience mastery and self-directed goal attainment on many occasions and still feel pleasure at receiving approval and satisfaction at being able to control their behavior in accord with social expectations. The costs of ineffective discipline, especially the escalation of harsh discipline or the child's coercive and out-of-control behavior, can be great. The quality of the relationship deteriorates, parental affection for the child is likely to diminish, and the child feels increasingly alienated from satisfying social interactions (Chamberlain & Patterson, 1995) (see Notebook Page 10.2).

Managing Work and Family Life

We introduced the topic of managing work and family life in Chapter 8 in discussing the transition to parenthood. In toddlerhood, the matter becomes even more critical since the child's needs for supervised play and opportunities for focused, reciprocal interaction increase. A mom or dad who comes home after a full day at work cannot slip easily into the parent role by cradling the baby, looking at a few picture books, playing pat-a-cake, and then putting the baby to bed for the night. Toddlers want more. They want to run and chase, climb on your back for a horsey ride, roughhouse, build, bake, splash water with

Remembering a Discipline Situation

Parents differ in their approach to socialization, including the use of different discipline techniques such as power assertion, love withdrawal, and inductions, and different styles of discipline, such as disciplinarian, teacher, and trainer. These different strategies, when used consistently over many episodes, have a marked impact on the child's internalization of rules and prohibitions.

Try to recall a discipline situation from your childhood that occurred before the age of 5 or, if you cannot remember, think about the earliest discipline encounter you can recall.

1. Describe the situation. What was involved? What had you done? What type of discipline strategy was used?

2. Was this a typical discipline encounter for you or something unusual?

3. What impact did it have on you? Why do you think you still remember it?

4. If roles were reversed and you were the adult, how might you handle this kind of situation?

the hose, talk on the phone to grandma, go for ice cream, draw a picture, and tell stories. And all this before bath and bedtime! In this section, we consider two aspects of the relationship of work and family life: the intermingling of the developmental tasks of work and parenting, and the impact of conflicts between work and parenting on the family environment.

The Intermingling of Developmental Tasks: Work and Parenting

As you remember from reading Chapter 3 on psychosocial theory, marriage, nurturing of intimate relationships, childbearing and parenting, work and management of a career, and management of the household are major areas of new learning in early and middle adulthood. For most adults, these developmental tasks interact to structure thought and action in regular and systematic ways. Experiences related to learning these tasks command a good measure of attention. It is not surprising that the demands from these task areas overlap and sometimes come into conflict.

Family and work life are interconnected. No adult with young children manages his or her career independently of considerations of family roles. A decision to assume more authority at work, work longer hours, accept an offer with another company, quit one's job and look for another, or accept a transfer to another location will each touch the lives of other family members. One of the most consistently challenging aspects of adult development is the effort to coordinate continuously changing and often conflicting demands and expectations from one's marital, parental, and occupational roles.

A growing body of research focuses on the relationship of a person's work environment to her or his child-rearing values and parenting behaviors (Menaghan & Parcel, 1990). Parents in white-collar and entrepreneurial-type jobs are more likely to value independence and self-reliance in their children, whereas parents in blue-collar jobs are more likely to value obedience and respect for authority in their children. These differences are reflected in differences in disciplinary techniques: Parents in white-collar positions are more likely to try to encourage internalization and self-control by using inductions and love withdrawal, while parents in blue-collar positions are more likely to use power assertion to enforce compliance to authority (Kohn, 1983; Kohn et al., 1986). These differences in child-rearing values and parenting styles reflect the parent's understanding of requirements for success in the workplace.

A second line of inquiry has focused on the relationship of specific demands of the job and parenting behaviors. Adults whose jobs are *substantively complex*, requiring both cognitive and interpersonal problem solving and permitting a relatively high degree of independent decision making, tend to be more flexible and less harsh in their discipline, exhibit more warmth, and be more likely to offer explanations when disciplining their children. Another job characteristic described as *time urgency*, the sense of a heavy work load with severe time pressures, is associated with emotional withdrawal in interactions with children and a greater likelihood of harsh discipline practices (Greenberger et al., 1994; Repetti, 1992).

Thus, the nature of parents' work experiences is likely to shape their approach to parenting. The influence of work at home may contribute to the child's optimal development, especially when a parent is enthusiastic and stimulated by the challenges of work. The influence may be detrimental, especially if the parent is depressed, overwhelmed, or bored at work.

Conflict Between Work and Family Life

Conflict results when the demands of work and family roles make participation in one or both of these roles more difficult or inadequate (Tiedje et al., 1990; Voydanoff, 1988). This conflict is usually a result of competing demands on time or the psychological spillover of one role to the other. Some of the characteristics of the work setting that contribute to this conflict are:

- Long work hours,
- Shift work, especially evenings or weekends,
- Role ambiguity or role conflict at work, and
- Work overload.

Some of the characteristics of family life that contribute to this conflict are:

- Number of hours spent in child care and housework,
- Number and ages of children (especially toddlers and early-school-age children), and
- Husband's and wife's perceptions regarding appropriate role enactment.

The more that mothers and fathers identify with both the parent role and their work role and feel committed to spending time both with their children and fulfilling work demands, the more likely they are to experience psychological stresses associated with role strain (Simon, 1992).

Two factors that can minimize potential conflict include the perception that work hours and demands can be controlled and an outlook that enacting both work and family roles is enriching and worthwhile. Both of these factors are psychological—in other words, they refer to a way of seeing the world that gives a person a sense of greater control and meaning in the face of role conflict and role strain.

The Impact of Conflict on the Family Environment

The conflicts that couples have about balancing work and family have implications for both the quality of their marriage and for the child-rearing environment to which their young children are exposed. Even when both husband and wife are employed outside the home, couples tend to see child care and certain household maintenance tasks as primarily the wife's domain. This outlook is as common in Canada, Sweden, and Norway as it is in the United States (Kalleberg & Rosenfeld, 1990). When both husband and wife are in the labor force, the wife may experience considerable strain in trying to meet her work commitments while allowing adequate time for nurturance and recreational activities with her children.

An analysis of dual-career couples focused on how husbands and wives shared their household responsibilities. Half the sample were university faculty and half were business professionals (Biernat & Wortman, 1991). All the couples in this sample had at least one child under the age of five. Both husbands and wives in these families agreed that the wives carried out more of the child-care responsibilities than husbands, with the exception of play which was about equal. They also agreed that wives performed more of the household chores, with the exception of repairs and maintenance. Surprisingly, the wives said they were quite satisfied with this distribution of responsibilities.

Yet, when it came to evaluating their roles, wives felt guilty about not doing a better job as a parent or spouse, although they were doing more than their husbands. In comparison, husbands were quite satisfied with their own role performance as parents and as spouses. Husbands and wives who were doing the larger share of the child-rearing activities tended to be less positive about their roles as spouses. The greater the wife's income in comparison with her husband, the worse both the husband and the wife felt about their roles as a spouse. Career success for women was accompanied by increased conflict about marital as well as parental roles. Thus, even in professional couples where both husband and wife have demanding and equally high-status jobs, the partners continue to hold traditional expectations about their responsibilities in the areas of child care and household tasks, producing greater conflict and self-doubt among career women than among career men.

Ongoing conflicts between parents about child-rearing practices and responsibilities produce an undesirable environment for the developing child. In a study of 200 mothers of three-year-old boys, the greater the amount of parental disagreement about child-rearing, the greater the variety of behavior problems identified in the boys (Jouriles et al., 1991). Although it is possible that more difficult boys stimulate higher levels of child-rearing disagreements, it is also possible that exposure to parental conflict has a disruptive impact on toddlers. Exposure to parental quarrels causes toddlers to wonder if they are to blame for their parents' arguments. Further, parents who are involved in frequent disagreements over child-rearing are likely to be psychologically unavailable to respond to their child's needs. Finally, open exchange of angry talk between parents provides a model for aggressive behavior that may be transformed by the child into increased aggression with peers.

Becoming a Sibling

Important changes occur in the family when a second child is born. Parents have to attend to the needs of both children, thus reducing some of the intensity of their involvement with the firstborn. As parents observe familiar patterns of development in the second child, they begin to appreciate some of the regularities of development and can learn to anticipate future changes. Parents also begin to be sensitive to the temperamental differences between their children. The first child may have been more active or more sensitive to touch. The second child may be more calm or more frightened of novelty. With two or more children, parents may be able to identify these temperamental characteristics as belonging to the child's "nature." They may begin to be more accepting of both children as they are, rather than trying to change them according to some abstract idea of a child.

The experience for both children is also quite different. They each have a more diverse group of people with whom to interact. For the older child, there are opportunities to assume a dominant, teaching role with the younger child, a role rarely possible in a two-adult and one-child constellation. The older child may also see the younger as a welcome play companion, especially if parents are preoccupied or tired. Thus, the socialization environment changes with the birth of a sibling, creating intraenvironmental differences that contribute to each sibling's unique family experience (Plomin, 1990).

When there are two children in the family, each one is a potential *model for imitation* for the other. The younger child imitates behaviors that were not yet part of the older child's repertoire at the same age. When Joe was one and a half, he was actively pretending about superheroes in imitation of his older brother Rick's fantasy play. Rick, at one and a half, was far less sophisticated about the content of his play. He was more likely to pretend about cars, dogs, or family members. Conversely, Rick frequently imitates aspects of his younger brother's behavior. He blows bubbles in his soda, talks baby talk, or splashes wildly in the tub, repeating Joe's antics. Rick actually has an opportunity to participate in a variety of regressive behaviors that he missed out on as a single child in a three-person family group trying to imitate two adults.

Sibling Rivalry

The addition of a sibling brings new variety to the emotional side of the children's interactions (Brown & Dunn, 1992; Dunn et al., 1991). Siblings are more likely to fight with each other, to engage in fantasy with each other, or to tease each other, than either is to do these things with adults. One of the characteristics of sibling interaction that has received attention in child-care manuals and developmental textbooks is *sibling rivalry*, or jealousy. Rivalry among siblings has been theorized to result from three sources. First, older siblings are jealous of the love, attention, and time that new babies draw from parents; they feel dethroned by a new brother or sister. Second, younger brothers and sisters are jealous of the advantages in competence and authority that older siblings have (Adler, 1959; Freud, 1965). Third, the siblings are in competition for resources or may perceive themselves to be. An evolutionary perspective suggests that, while parents are invested in the survival of all offspring to give them the best chance of passing on their genetic material to the next generation, each sibling is most invested in his or her own survival, thereby motivating competition.

Judy Dunn (1985) described the reaction of firstborn children under the age of five to the birth of a sibling as *vigilant interest*. Toddlers are especially attentive during the times when the mother is focusing her attention on the new baby. The most common reaction to the newborn is an increase in "naughtiness" directed not so much at the baby as at the mother. "One child, whose mother and baby sister were gazing at each other in a long, absorbed exchange, picked up his cup, which had a lid with holes in it, and, looking across to the baby and his ecstatic, cooing mother, started to sprinkle his milk all over the sofa" (Dunn, 1985, 12).

Another consequence of the birth of a sibling is an increase in the older child's worries and ritualistic behaviors. Dunn described the results of studies showing that, while naughtiness declined after about 8 months, 38% of young children showed heightened anxiety during the year after a new sister or brother was born, and 35% showed new levels of ritualistic behavior. "Bedtime, bathtime, and mealtime rituals were particularly strong, as were rituals for saying goodbye to parents. One child would not go to sleep unless all his teddies had been kissed, his mother had kissed him between each bar on the cot, and the door was left open at a certain angle" (Dunn, 1985, 112–113).

It is so great to have a younger sibling whom you can bury and rescue—just like a real superhero!

The intensity of distress, expressed as naughtiness, increased anxiety, or sibling rivalry and conflict, that occurs after the birth of the second child is difficult to predict. It has been found to relate to a number of variables. Children under five are more likely to show signs of distress than are older children. Siblings show more signs of distress and ritualistic behavior when their mothers are especially tired or depressed following the birth of the second child. Sibling conflict and rivalry are determined in part by the temperaments of the children. Two active, impulsive children are more likely to experience conflict over space, possessions, noise level, and privacy than two children who are more reflective or passive (Stoneman et al., 1989). Children who are more withdrawn are more likely to show signs of increased anxiety rather than outbursts of hostility (Dunn, 1985).

Sibling conflict can be stimulated or reduced by parental behaviors. If parents spend considerably less time with an older child once a new baby is born or if a parent persistently praises one child and criticizes another, children are likely to identify these behaviors as evidence of parental preference. If parents are able to intervene in sibling conflicts in a way that is consistent and fair, pointing out what principles are involved and how a solution might be reached, children will recognize that the same guidelines for behavior apply equally to both of them (Brody et al., 1987; Stocker et al., 1989.) Fathers play a particularly important role in promoting sibling harmony. When fathers have a close, loving relationship with the first child, that child seems to have an easier time accepting the new sibling, and the sibling interactions tend to be more positive. Fathers can continue to provide parental closeness to the older child when the mother's attention is periodically distracted by caring for a newborn sibling. In addition, fathers who treat both children equally and emphasize family harmony when sibling conflicts arise appear to contribute in a positive way to the relationships that develop between brothers and sisters. In families where there are frequent disagreements between parents or where fathers are unavailable, sibling conflicts tend to be greater (Brody, Stoneman & McCoy, 1992; Brody, Stoneman, McCoy & Forehand, 1992; Volling & Belsky, 1992).

But it would be a mistake to focus only on the difficulties that firstborns have in adjusting to a new sibling. Many observations attest to the important contributions that siblings make to one another. Older siblings learn to consider the needs and wants of their younger brothers and sisters, which promotes a new understanding of the inner state of another person. Adapting to a new sibling facilitates perspective taking and a prosocial orientation (Garner et al., 1994, Howe, 1994). Siblings share private conversations, jokes, and teasing about things that are usually not part of adult talk. It is not uncommon for siblings to comfort one another, to seek each other out for help, and to teach each other new tricks, games, and skills. Older siblings take pride in helping younger brothers or sisters learn to use a spoon, tie their shoes, or button a button. The presence of a younger sibling can help stimulate a toddler's sense of mastery and self-control and a new perspective on his or her competence in comparison with a younger brother or sister. And it is not long before a younger sibling takes pleasure in drawing a picture for an older sibling or offering to share a bag of candy, building a bond of affection and admiration for the older sibling (see Box 10.2).

Cultural and Ethnic Patterns That Create Distinctive Child-Rearing Environments During Toddlerhood

The concept of socialization suggests that each culture has a set of values to which it ascribes. The customs, prohibitions, encouragements, courtesies, and restraints to which a child is exposed are intended to produce the parents' concept of the optimal features for someone of a certain age, gender, and social status, based on the parents' understanding of their culture. Socialization and development do not always complement one another. Depending on the values of the culture, some developmentally emerging capacities are fostered, and others are discouraged.

The important link between culture and child-rearing practices is the beliefs that adults have about the meaning and value of the child's behavior. Child-care practices are associated with certain ideologies or outlooks that may be implemented in a variety of ways. The more traditional and homogeneous the society, the more likely it is that child-rearing will be similar from one family to the next. The impact of child-rearing practices on children must be understood within its cultural context. Providing an abundance of toys and actively stimulating play may appear positive for a middle-class American mother, but it would not be viewed as an appropriate strategy by a Zambian mother. In traditional Sioux society, boys collected and played games with small animal bones gathered at the site where cattle were slaughtered, playthings that would probably be viewed with disgust among most American mothers today. We are only beginning to understand the influence of culture and subculture on development; much more research is needed.

In toddlerhood, we see clear evidence of the impact of culture on the development of young children, including their beliefs, conflicts, activities,

BOX 10.2

Siblings, Work, and Family Life

In our local newspaper, the daily weather is usually accompanied by a brief essay on a random topic. This particular essay seems to be a perfect link between our themes of work, family life, and sibling relations.

The Joys and Problems of Being No. 1

When I sat down to write this column, I intended some sort of paean [song of praise] to November.

However, my 4-year-old, Joey, who was sitting on my lap while I wrote, didn't like the direction the column was heading.

"What's a paean, Dad?" Joe asked.

"I'm not sure, son," I had to admit. "But it has a nice ring, doesn't it?"

Joe would have none of it.

"Write about me, Dad. Write about Mikey too."

Mikey is Joe's 1-year-old brother.

"You might not like what I have to say," I warned.

Joe is a first child and as such has a skewed view of the universe.

Like all first children, he experienced a time when he was Child the Omnipotent—the center of creation with no competition for affection or attention.

As a first child, Joe is still very—insistent.

"What's insistent?" Joe asked.

"It's like when the commercial for Magna Doodle comes on TV and you say, 'Buy me that toy, Dad. Buy me *every* toy.' "

"But you did not buy every toy for me."

"True," I said. "As a first child myself, I can be just as headstrong as you."

"What's headstrong?" Joe asked.

"It's like this morning, when you ordered Mike to go to his room and Mom told you, 'You're not Mike's boss.' Then you said, 'Oh yes I am.' "

"But I *am* his boss," Joe said.

"That's what I always said about my siblings," I told him. "When they would protest, I would pound them. But your grandma and grandpa were on to me. They were oldest children too."

"Were they the boss?" asked Joe.

"Not until they had me," I said. "Someday you will have kids and can be the boss."

"I don't want any kids," Joe said.

"Wise choice," I replied, trying to get around him to the keyboard.

"Go ahead and write about me some more," Joe said.

"Sorry, son. Now I have to tell all the people that today will be cloudy with a bit of sunshine, maybe a sprinkle or flurry, and a high of 43. Tonight will be cloudy with a low of 28."

"No, it won't," said Joe. "*I want it to be snowy.*"

Source: Stephens, S. (1992). The joys and problems of being No. 1. *Columbus Dispatch,* November 30, 6C. Reprinted with permission.

understanding of kinship relations, and orientation toward the acceptability of certain behaviors. In the sections that follow, we provide comparative examples of child-rearing environments for their impact on the child's involvement in fantasy and pretend play, autonomy, and discipline practices.

The Value of Fantasy

Cultural differences in the value placed on fantasy influence the extent to which parents encourage their children's fantasy play. By sharing folk tales, songs, and games, adults and older siblings pass down some of the cultural imagery around which children's play evolves. Melvin Konner (1977) suggested that play serves an adaptive function, providing opportunities for exploring the environment and sharpening survival and social skills. In play, children discover for themselves many things that it would take adults a very long time to teach them. When a society is not overly authoritarian, adults may even learn something from the novel and untutored ways in which young children playfully explore their environment.

The Hopi Indians of northern Arizona were observed extensively in the mid-twentieth century. They encouraged pretend play where children imitate the activities of adults (Queen & Habenstein, 1974).

> The girls play house. Their make-believe houses are peopled by dolls made of sticks or different parts of the forefeet of calves. Around the house are placed make-believe gardens, fields, and orchards. In these play houses the girls carry on, in miniature, the traditional activities of the Hopi women. They make small pots and grind corn. The boys build imitation corrals in which peach seeds play the part of sheep. They also construct little fields. They do not, however, play house, since traditionally the men have nothing to do with housework. (Queen & Habenstein, 1974, 64)

Among the Yanomamo of South America, little boys build small huts of old twigs and leaves and slip inside to play. But girls are encouraged to play only at being grown up and are soon required to assist their mothers in household chores. Whereas boys may continue to engage in pretend play well into their teens, girls by that age are actively involved in the daily work of the family (Chagnon, 1977). Among the Bali, play is permitted when it reflects efforts to solve real-world problems. Adults give little emphasis to fantasy (Mead, 1955).

In some cultures, such as the Sioux, dreams and visions are actively encouraged in order to help people formulate a life plan and to clarify their destiny. Erikson (1963) described the importance of the vision quest among the Sioux Indians. The vision quest, usually taken in early adolescence, involved going out to the prairie alone, unarmed, and dressed only in a loincloth. The young boy would wait for a vision which usually came on the fourth day, all the while risking the dangers of being alone without food, weapons, or shelter. After the vision, the boy would return home and describe it to a group of experts who would help the boy interpret its meaning. Although there is no way to really prepare for this experience through play, young Sioux boys were encouraged to value spiritual forces and to explore ways of overcoming the limits of their physical selves through fantasy.

Variations in Promoting Autonomy

According to psychosocial theory, the most intense emotional theme during toddlerhood is the desire to be autonomous, to do things for oneself. Toddlers experience a struggle between willfulness and self-regulation on the one hand, and the need to ensure continued parental approval and support on the other. Toddlers may reject an adult's offer to help tie their shoes or zip up their jackets and then in the next moment turn to an adult for help in something they have done independently many times before.

It appears that autonomy is a theme of greater significance and centrality for most families in the United States than it is in many other cultures. The Declaration of Independence is a key national document. American families are likely to foster and value independence in their children to an extent that is not seen in traditional cultures or even in many industrialized nations, especially during the toddler years. American babies are more likely than babies in other cultures to be placed in a separate sleeping area, away from their parents. American mothers wean their babies relatively early and encourage self-feeding. In contrast to many other cultures, American babies are not carried around on the mother's back for most of the day.

Cayapo Indian children in the Amazon River region of Brazil enjoy a childhood of affectionate playfulness with relatively few restrictions or rules.

Evidence of this emphasis on independence can be seen in a variety of child-rearing studies. In Robin Harwood's (1992) comparison of Anglo and Puerto Rican mothers' perceptions of attachment behaviors, she reported that Anglo mothers were more likely to be concerned when the babies would not play by themselves in the laboratory setting and when they fussed or clung too closely. In contrast, Puerto Rican mothers were concerned when the babies ignored their mothers or acted in a boisterous or rude manner in a public setting. They did not seem to mind at all if the babies clung to them or fretted. In their study of everyday rules for behavior, Gralinski and Kopp (1993) found that mothers of infants and toddlers (from 13 to 30 months) had a variety of rules and requests for compliance that focus on independence (walking instead of being carried, using words to make requests, and trying new toys or games), self-care (using the toilet, washing up or brushing one's teeth, and getting dressed without help), and family routines (clearing the table, putting toys away, and throwing away scraps of art materials). Thus, in addition to the rules that place restrictions or prohibitions on children's behavior (don't touch the knives or eat the cat litter), American mothers appear to expect a significant level of self-directed, autonomous behavior from toddlers.

Descriptions of traditional societies suggest that, in many cultures, not much is expected of children under the age of four. They are often nursed until about two, expected to learn culturally accepted patterns of elimination, and generally permitted to play without much structured guidance. As an example, consider child-rearing among the Baganda, a Bantu-speaking people of Uganda, a country in central Africa.

> In the home the child is usually allowed to play on the dirt floor, more or less unattended. Little attention is given to early cleanliness training or to the child's learning to walk. The mother may hug or caress the child and comfort it when hurt or in distress. . . . Baganda boyhood may not be idyllic, but in many ways

it is a rather carefree time of their lives. They wear little or no clothing until the age of six or seven years and are subject to very few duties or responsibilities. . . . Girls, perhaps sooner than boys, are taught a variety of household and agricultural duties. (Queen & Habenstein, 1974, 83–85)

Although we may believe that U.S. society is extremely strong in its value for autonomy, some societies have an even higher expectation for self-reliance among young children. In a study of child-rearing practices among Chinese, immigrant Chinese, and Caucasian-American parents, Chinese parents were found to be higher in their endorsement of parental control strategies, independence, and academic achievement than Caucasian-American parents. The groups were equally strong in their emphasis on expressing affection. The greater emphasis on independence among the Chinese parents was of some surprise to the investigators who had expected to find less value on individualism among the Chinese parents and more importance given to "knowing one's place" (Lin & Fu, 1990). However, they interpret the finding as related to the Chinese value for achievement. The Chinese believe that achievement is within one's own control, and that to achieve one must be self-reliant. The emphasis on individual achievement, however, is accompanied by a strong value on bringing honor to one's family through personal accomplishments.

From these examples, we see that autonomy has different cultural significances. From the U.S. perspective, autonomy is fostered through early separation from mother, demands for self-regulation, and encouragement of independent actions and self-care. In other societies, autonomy is encouraged by broad acceptance of the child's natural behaviors and will within an environment that fosters interdependence through sustained, gentle comforting. In still other societies, autonomy is encouraged through setting high standards and encouraging self-reliance, but the value of individual achievement is valued for the contribution it makes to the reputation and social status of the family.

Culture and Discipline Practices

Developmental research has highlighted four characteristics of optimal parenting strategies among families in the United States. These include:

- A high level of warmth and acceptance in which the child experiences an emotional climate characterized by caring, optimism, and humor.

- Firm control and willingness to impose clear expectations for responsible, self-regulated behaviors appropriate to the child's developmental abilities.

- A value for the child's psychological autonomy, expressed by the willingness to take the child's point of view into consideration and to involve the child in decision making.

- Full engagement or psychological commitment to the parenting process over a long period (Baumrind, 1973, 1991; Greenberger & Goldberg, 1989; Maccoby, 1992; Steinberg et al., 1989).

From a cross-cultural perspective, we might ask whether these same characteristics apply across cultures and how alternative approaches to discipline correspond to cultural values. Erikson (1963) emphasized this point as a primary rationale for studying child-rearing systems from a cross-cultural perspective. "Values do not persist unless they work, economically, psychologically, and spiritually; and I argue that to this end they must continue to be anchored, generation after generation, in early child training; while child training, to remain consistent, must be embedded in a system of continued economic and cultural synthesis" (Erikson, 1963, 138).

Discipline practices across cultures encompass a wide range of strategies. Parents have a big "bag of tricks" available for conveying ideals, rules, and prohibitions. Three of these are the culture's fables, stories, and myths; its religion; and its acceptance of physical punishment and power assertion.

Fables, Stories, and Myths

One of the strategies that adults in many societies use to guide their children and shape their behavior is to tell them stories that have "morals." In our culture, some of these common tales include "The Boy Who Cried Wolf" which encourages children not to make a big fuss over small things or whine and cry for an adult's attention unless it is really serious; or "Hansel and Gretel" which shows how children, through their own resourcefulness, can overcome adversity. Among the Yurok, a Native American tribe living along the Pacific coast, salmon fishing is the major focus of their economy. They value self-restraint as a means of achieving economic success and emphasize the evils of impatience or impulsiveness. "The buzzard's baldness is the result of his having impatiently put his whole head into a dish of hot soup. The greedy eel gambled his bones away" (Erikson, 1963, 177–178).

Stories, fables, and myths condense complicated issues and give young children a vivid solution to the conflicts that they face. They can call up these images to help reinforce their efforts to conform to social expectations or to resist antisocial impulses.

Religion and Discipline

Religious beliefs often influence the way that children are disciplined and the kinds of fears that children develop about the spirit world. For Catholic children, stories of saints and their sacrifices suggest models of ideal moral behavior. Threats of the possibility of hell and purgatory reinforce the serious consequences of certain sinful acts. Among the Hopi, the primary disciplinarian in the family is the mother's brother. When a child has been very naughty, the mother's brother will seek help from the Kachinas or ancestral spirits to help correct the child. The Kachinas, impersonated by masked men, come to the child's home and threaten to eat the naughty offender. The mother's brother and the child's parents plead with the Kachinas, trying to block the door and offering the Kachina food if it will spare the child. This technique demonstrates the parents' love and care to the child, as well as the fearful consequences of his or her actions from the spirit world (Queen & Habenstein, 1974).

Physical Punishment and Power Assertion

Most American child-rearing literature emphasizes the negative impact of physical punishment and power assertion for young children. Nevertheless, harsh, rigid punishment appears to play a consistent part in the child-rearing strategies of certain cultures and subcultures as well as among many U.S. families. The Yanomamo are a warfaring people who admire aggressiveness. Their lives are preoccupied with forming alliances among villages and raiding enemy villages. Male children are valued more highly than female children and are permitted a great range of freedom of behavior. Young boys are encouraged to be fierce by their parents.

> Although Ariwari is only about four years old, he has already learned that the appropriate response to a flash of anger is to strike someone with his hand or with an object, and it is not uncommon for him to give his father a healthy smack in the face whenever something displeases him. He is frequently goaded into hitting his father by teasing, being rewarded by gleeful cheers of assent from his mother and from the other adults in the household. (Chagnon, 1977, 84)

These examples of cultural variety in discipline practices illustrate that cultural transmission of values through socialization is multifaceted. Cultures may have many messages that they wish to impart to young children. The need to shape or mold behavior early in toddlerhood differs from one society to the next. In ascribing meaning to any particular child-rearing strategy, the context of preparation for challenges to survival must be considered.

Societal Issues That Provide Resources or Barriers to Development

In this section, we will examine the influence of three issues on the psychosocial development of children in toddlerhood: poverty, day care, and abuse. Although we introduce these topics in discussing toddlerhood, it is clear that the consequences of these early experiences are relevant to the child's entire developmental history. They are viewed in the context of the United States and its values, traditions, and policies that impact the current cohort of children.

Poverty

Poverty is both an economic and a psychological condition. Each year, the federal government establishes a poverty level for families of varying sizes. In 1992, the official poverty threshold for a family of four was $14,335. This way of defining poverty as an absolute dollar amount does not allow gradations of poverty, nor does it differentiate poverty based on location and cost of living. Poverty is also experienced psychologically when a family undergoes significant income loss or financial instability and is unable to live at the accustomed level in their community. Sudden loss of income from unemployment or divorce can result in a sense of poverty even if actual income is above the level designated by federal guidelines. Facts regarding children in poverty in the United States are summarized in Box 10.3 on page 424.

Conditions Leading to Poverty

In the first half of this century, most poverty was a result of nonemployment, unemployment, or work involving low wages or temporary wages (Hernandez, 1993). Since the 1960s, however, three major factors have contributed to the increase in the number of children living in poverty: the decline in well-paying, blue-collar jobs; large increases in single-mother house-

The stressors linked to poverty weigh on a parent's mind, creating emotional distress and often leading to harsh or critical responses to a child's behavior.

holds due to increases in births to adolescent mothers and increases in the divorce rate; and the decline in the value of federal benefits such as Aid to Families with Dependent Children (Huston et al., 1994).

Poverty is transitory for some families, when a wage earner loses one job and then finds new work, but persistent for others. For never-married women who become mothers in adolescence, poverty is often a result of interrupted education, the inability to work full time (usually because of caring for their children), and the low-paying jobs that are available to those who have limited educational attainment. In addition, many of these women have grown up in families that are already poor.

Divorce casts many women and their children into poverty. In many instances, the family was already encountering financial strain, which is known to be one of the primary factors associated with divorce. Following divorce, 27% of divorced women and their children fall below the poverty line (Chase-Lansdale, 1993). The level of poverty experienced by newly divorced women is aggravated by the failure of many fathers to pay child support. Poverty for these families is often temporary, since many divorced women remarry or are able to find adequate employment after a year or two. However, the negative impact of poverty on children, coupled with the stresses of experiencing parental divorce, is likely to affect a child's adjustment (Demo & Ganong, 1994).

Job loss within a two-parent family can also drag a family into poverty. Once again, this can be temporary or permanent. Job loss is known to introduce conflict and tension in the marital relationship, leading to withdrawal or to increases in open arguing and even physical violence between partners. The parental discord that may arise in the face of job loss and chronic unemployment has both direct and indirect effects on a child's emotional state (Grych & Fincham, 1990). Parents who are harsh, critical, and emotionally unavailable are likely to increase sentiments of shame and doubt in their toddlers

BOX 10.3

Facts Regarding Children in Poverty in the United States

Many of these facts were gathered by the National Commission on Children and reported in a summary of their research, *Just the Facts*, published in 1993. The term *poverty* as it is used here refers to federal guidelines for poverty level.

- In constant 1991 dollars, the median family income for families with children ($34,990) was *lower* than the median family income for families without children ($36,943).

- Children are the poorest age group today in America. Twenty percent of children under the age of 18 live in poverty; 25% of infants and toddlers under 3 live in poverty; 24% of children under age 6 live in poverty. In contrast, 12.4% of the elderly (those over 60) live in poverty.

- Roughly 14 million children live in poverty. Over half these children (about 7.5 million) are white. Minorities are disproportionately represented among the poor. Forty-six percent of all African-American children and 40% of all Hispanic children are poor, as compared with 17% of white children.

- Children living in poverty are about equally divided between those who live in urban areas and those who live in rural and suburban areas.

- Living in a single-parent home puts children at greater risk for poverty. For children under the age of 6, the poverty rate in a single-parent family is 57% (about 3 million children). However, a large number of children in two-parent families grow up in poverty. The poverty rate for children under 6 in married-couple families is 12% (about 2 million children).

who worry that these outbursts are directed toward them or that they have contributed in some way to their parents' misfortunes.

The Influence of Poverty on Child Development

Poverty in and of itself does not place inevitable limits on a child's development. There are many instances of children who grew up in poverty and achieved eminence. However, it is well documented that poverty increases the risks that children face, including risks associated with malnourishment, poor-quality health care, living in a hazardous physical environment or a dangerous neighborhood, receiving poor-quality or inadequate child care, and participating in an ineffective school system. Thus, poverty is linked with reduced access to the basic resources for survival (Duncan et al., 1994).

Futhermore, poverty is often associated with parental behaviors that are disruptive to optimal development. As a result of high levels of emotional distress among parents, economic hardship is likely to produce parent–child interactions that are not supportive of the child's intellectual or emotional development (McLoyd, 1990). Poor mothers are more likely than more affluent mothers to use power assertion and physical punishment as a form of discipline. One national study of poverty, parenting practices, and children's mental health found that the amount of spanking parents do was directly related to their current level of poverty. This pattern was the same for African-American, Hispanic, and non-Hispanic white families. In addition, the more likely that parents were to use spanking and harsh discipline, the more likely their children were to show signs of emotional distress (depression, fearfulness, and crying) as well as externally directed behaviors such as arguing, disobedience, destructiveness, and impulsiveness (McLeod & Shannon, 1993).

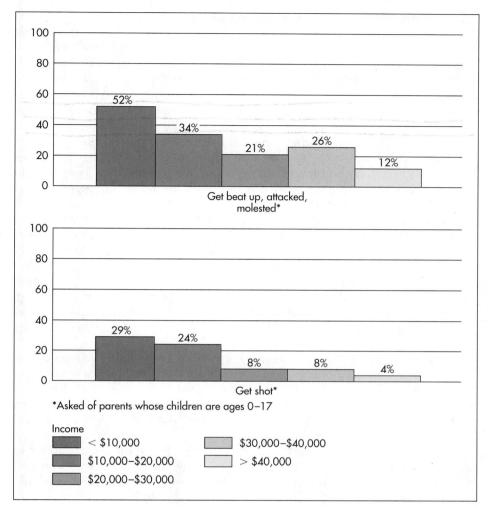

FIGURE 10.1
Percentage of parents, by family income, who worry "a lot" that their child will be beaten or shot
Source: National Commission on Children. (1991). *Speaking of kids: A national survey of children and parents.* Washington, D.C.: National Commission on Children, 31.

Parents living in poverty emphasize obedience and are less likely to use reasons and explanations in their discipline practices. They are less likely to reward their children through praise and encouragement or to ask their children for their ideas and opinions. In general, parents living in poverty have been characterized as less sensitive to their children's needs and less emotionally supportive. As we have discussed above, this approach to parenting may be due in large part to the emotional distress created by conditions of poverty. Frustration and anger at being poor may give way to feelings of weakness, victimization, and loss of control. These factors are often associated with both physical and mental health problems that may be expressed as pessimism, loss of hope, depression, drug and alcohol abuse, and psychosomatic ailments (McLoyd, 1990).

Another explanation for the association between poverty and harsh parenting that emphasizes obedience is that poor families tend to live in high-risk neighborhoods where children are likely to be exposed to violence. As a result, poor parents worry more about their children's safety and may be more emotionally reactive when children defy their authority on safety issues (see Figure 10.1).

Factors That Mediate the Impact of Poverty

Like every other environmental factor, poverty has a differential impact on children and families. Although we are still a very long way from fully understanding how some children escape its negative effects, we do know that many poor children continue to develop optimally. Some scholars have emphasized the notion of *resilience* as a characteristic of children who appear to have inner strengths that permit them to obtain necessary resources, define their situation in a positive way, and transcend the challenges of their lives (Garmezy, 1991). These children are characterized by an easy, sociable temperament. They are active, seeking out stimulation and evoking responses from others. They are bright and able to solve problems readily. They usually have at least one supportive, loving relationship with a family member, and they have access to supportive contacts outside the family.

In addition to children's resilience, some parents have resources that help them buffer the impact of poverty. Among low-income, single African-American mothers, for example, level of education, the presence of an emotionally supportive social network, and strong religious beliefs all help reduce the negative effects of poverty (Jayakody et al., 1993; Kelly et al., 1992; McLoyd, 1990;). Other studies of factors that mediate the negative effects of poverty on children have identified aspects of the mother's mental health, especially low levels of depression and active behavioral coping, as important (Duncan et al., 1994).

The impact of persistent poverty has more detrimental effects on development than transitory poverty. Persistent poverty in the life of a small child is a strong predictor of a wide variety of physical and mental health problems. Parents who are able to see their poverty as transitory and to take steps to overcome poverty may also differ with respect to their supportiveness and responsiveness to their children.

The persistence of poverty is a factor that clearly differs according to racial/ethnic group. Poverty is more long lasting for African-American and Hispanic families; families within these ethnic groups who are not currently poor are much more likely than similar white families to have lived in poverty at some time in their recent past. For African-American and Hispanic families, the stresses associated with racism and cultural alienation are likely to be combined with the emotional distress associated with persistent poverty, producing a greater challenge with regard to carrying out their parenting functions in a developmentally appropriate manner (Duncan et al., 1994; McLoyd, 1990).

Poverty and Toddlerhood

From a psychosocial perspective, how are toddlers likely to be affected by poverty? How might poverty systematically influence the developmental tasks of toddlerhood—the elaboration of locomotion, the experiences of fantasy and play, learning language, and the development of self-control? How do the conditions of poverty affect the expression of autonomy or the experiences of shame and doubt?

Current literature does not address these questions directly. Despite wide social interest and extensive policy debates regarding the needs of poor children, little research focuses on the consequences of poverty for specific developmental tasks. We hypothesize that toddlers are not directly aware of their poverty status. In comparison with older children who might understand from watching television, reading the newspaper, or interacting with other children in school that they are in a relatively impoverished situation, toddlers are not likely to have any comparative perspective. They assume that what they experience from day to day is what most everyone experiences. Toddlers probably do not feel bad about being poor or define themselves in this way. Poverty probably does not produce the same level of frustration and anger for toddlers that it does for adults.

However, toddlers suffer the effects of poverty directly. Two major consequences of poverty are poor health and inadequate nutrition. A national study found that children from families with incomes below $10,000 were three times more likely to be in poor health than were children from families with incomes above $35,000. Many children from low-income families have not been immunized for measles and other infectious diseases. Repeated bouts of illness combined with poor nutrition detract from a child's energy. The combination of malnutrition and illness are thought to have multiple consequences, including some structural brain damage, lethargy, delayed physical growth, and resultant minimal exploration of the environment. All these factors taken together produce delayed psychomotor and cognitive development in toddlerhood (Brown & Pollitt, 1996; Pollitt, 1994).

We can speculate that other aspects of poverty may interfere with the achievement of developmental tasks. Living in especially crowded conditions with many other children and adults in the same small living quarters may result in limited exploration; in addition, many poor neighborhoods lack safe play spaces in or near the home (Bradley et al., 1994). Lack of access to a variety of play materials may have a negative impact on language development as well as symbolic play. Crowding may also make it difficult for toddlers to have the private, uninterrupted opportunity for fantasy. On the other hand, some children may use fantasy to block out some of the more negative or troubling aspects of their environment or to create an inner space where their situation is less stark. Language development may be deterred if parents do not interact much with their toddlers, if they tell their children what to do rather than involve them in discussion, or if they consistently admonish their children to be quiet. Self-regulation may be achieved early, especially if parenting is harsh and the costs of impulsive action are high. However, if parenting is chaotic and unpredictable or if the levels of anger and aggression in the home are high, children may find it difficult to organize or direct their behavior in any systematic way.

This picture is disturbing. It suggests that toddlers are exceedingly susceptible to negative consequences of poverty in developing competencies for effective intellectual and interpersonal functioning (see Notebook Page 10.3).

Day Care

Toddlers seek out time during waking hours and transitions between waking and sleep to elaborate locomotion, engage in fantasy play, interact verbally in developing effective language abilities, and learn self-control. A child's psychosocial development depends on opportunities to engage in and continuously extend these abilities with supportive adults and other children, as well as during time alone. There must be numerous opportunities to explore issues related to individuality and self-directed action, as well as experiences of reassurance, connection, and support.

Some Possible Effects of Poverty on Toddlers

Poverty places toddlers at risk for optimal development but certainly does not seal a child's fate. List some circumstances that would generate positive and negative forces for the development of a toddler living in poverty. For example, living in a crowded apartment with siblings and other relatives might give many opportunities for conversations and the elaboration of language skills, but it might also mean that adults are too busy and too stressed to interact with toddlers in sustained conversation.

1. The elaboration of locomotion:

_____

_____

_____

2. Experiences of fantasy and play:

_____

_____

_____

3. Learning language:

_____

_____

_____

4. Development of self-control:

_____

_____

_____

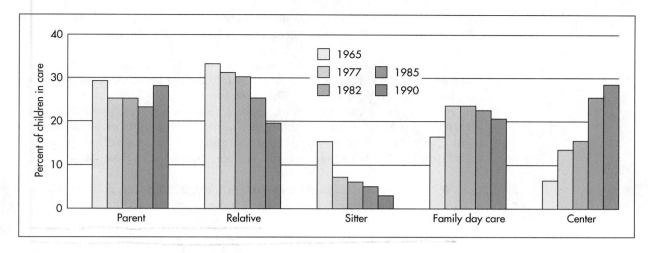

Many of the issues raised in Chapter 8 in the section on infant care are extended in this discussion of day care. Many more toddlers than infants are involved in some type of school or institutional setting. Figure 10.2 illustrates changes from 1965 to 1990 in patterns of child care for preschool-age children whose mothers are employed. Use of centers has steadily increased so that, in 1990, about the same percentage of toddlers were cared for in centers as were cared for by their parents. Child-care arrangements for toddlers vary with the presence of a father in the family, the child's age, and whether the mother is employed full- or part-time. About 13% of all toddlers have several child-care arrangements each day, but little is known about the developmental consequences of having this kind of variety in daily care (National Commission on Children, 1993; U.S. Bureau of the Census, 1991).

In the United States, there is a highly diverse "market" of child-care arrangements with minimal federal and state regulations (Holloway & Fuller, 1992). Caregivers have varying types of educational backgrounds, ranging from no specific training in child development to bachelor's and master's degrees in the field. Child-care arrangements reflect a wide variety of philosophies about the care of young children, wide differences in curriculum, and a great range in the physical settings where young children spend time.

Within a national context of growing needs for child care and a wide range of child-care arrangements, parents, educators, and policy makers are asking critical questions: What is the effect of day care on the development of young children? What is our obligation to ensure quality day care for children whose parents are in the labor force? What is our obligation as a society to ensure that the health, nutrition, and safety needs of children from low-income families are met?

The Impact of Day Care

Early-childhood programs have their roots in two rather distinct historical paths. One path emerged from university initiatives to promote optimal development in young children through nursery school programs that focused on health care, nutrition, and early peer socialization. These programs and similar activities in churches and community centers usually served children from middle- and upper-middle-class families. The other path had a child

FIGURE 10.2

Primary care arrangements for preschool children of employed mothers, 1965–1990
Source: Hofferth, S. L. et al. (1990). National child care survey. *Urban Institute Report,* 91–5. Copyright © 1990 Urban Institute Press. Reprinted with permission.

welfare orientation toward providing services for poor, abused, and immigrant children that their parents could not afford or did not know about (Holloway & Fuller, 1992).

The impact of day-care experiences on children has generally been assessed with regard to consequences for intellectual abilities, socioemotional development, and peer relations. Research tends to focus on the impact of day care on children of very poor families or children who are at special risk for school failure, illiteracy, and subsequent minimal employment or unemployment. Evaluations of day care often do not include data regarding the physical health, mental health, and family support provided by Headstart.

IQ and Academic Achievement. Although there are many questions still to be answered, researchers are reaching agreement on the positive impact of quality day care for toddlers. Data from model programs show that quality day care contributes to intellectual achievements, as reflected in higher IQ scores, during both preschool years and first grade (Burchinal et al., 1989). Achievement in specific areas such as mathematics is also higher in the early elementary grades for children from quality day care. However, both IQ and achievement test advantages dissipate so that, by the later elementary grades, children who experienced early day-care programs do not score significantly higher than control subjects (McKey et al., 1985).

In addition to test-score benefits, children who have participated in model day-care programs are less likely to be placed in special education classrooms or be held back a grade. Both of these advantages are significant in justifications for the costs of providing early educational experiences to children who are at special risk for school failure (Haskins, 1989).

The Perry Preschool Project has carried out extensive longitudinal research on a number of indicators of academic success. By age 19, those children who had experienced a quality child-care program had higher grades, fewer failing grades, a more positive attitude toward schooling, and a higher literacy rate than a comparable group of young adults who had not participated in a quality child-care program (Schweinhart & Weikart, 1988).

In studies of the impact of day care on intelligence and school achievement, researchers in the United States have focused on the ability of quality child care to modify the negative effects of poverty. This leaves open the question of whether early day-care experiences are enriching for middle-class children, whose resources are likely to be more supportive of intellectual achievement. In a national study, the effects of day-care participation during the first three years of life were related to reading and mathematics performance scores at age five or six (Caughy et al., 1994). The children were divided into three groups based on family income: below $15,000; $15,000 to $29,000; and $30,000 and above. Children in the lowest income group who attended day care in any one of the first three years of life had higher reading scores than children in the lowest income group who were not enrolled in day care. However, children in the highest income group who attended day care during the first year of life had lower reading scores than those who did not; and there were no differences in reading scores between those who attended day care in the second and third years and those who did not. For mathematics scores, day care again had a significant benefit for those in the impoverished home environments, but not for children from higher-income groups. Relatively few studies have compared both family income and the kinds of day-care experiences to cognitive competencies. We do not have enough systematic data to understand exactly which conditions would make formal day care the optimal environment for children of middle-income families.

Socioemotional Competencies. With respect to socioemotional competencies, quality day care is associated with higher levels of social competence, self-esteem, and empathy. Children who have positive interactions with adults in their day-care settings are more likely to continue to interact positively and comfortably with teachers and classmates in the elementary grades (Vandell, Henderson & Wilson, 1988). Some studies have found that children with day-care experience are less compliant with their parents and more aggressive with their peers than children who have not been in day care (Clarke-Stewart & Fein, 1983). This evidence of willfulness may be a result of a greater need to assert oneself in a group in order to have one's needs met. It may also reflect an advanced level of independence as a result of functioning in more than one socialization setting (Clarke-Stewart, 1989). Whether these qualities of non-compliance and aggressiveness lead to long-term problems in social adjustment has not yet been determined. Few evaluation studies have reported on long-term social consequences. However, results from the Perry Preschool Project found that, by age 19, fewer day-care children had committed delinquent acts or been processed by the courts, fewer had been on welfare, and more had been employed (Berrueta-Clement et al., 1984; Haskins, 1989).

Quality day care also has an impact on peer relations. Children benefit from opportunities to interact with a variety of peers in settings where adults are readily available to help them make choices and resolve differences. The quality and complexity of social play are especially enhanced when children remain in the same child-care setting rather than moving from one to another. Under conditions of stability, toddlers with limited verbal skills develop expanded strategies for coordinating their play with others and for exploring shared fantasies (Clarke-Stewart, 1989; Howes & Stewart, 1987). By the time they reached age eight, children who had experienced quality day care at age four were more likely to engage in friendly interactions with their age-mates, less likely to play alone, and less likely to be described as shy in comparison with children who had low-quality day-care experiences (Vandell et al., 1988).

Directions for the Future of Child Care

We face a critical gap between the demand for and availability of *afford-able, quality day care*. Although there appears to be an ample supply of child care, the settings that meet the standards for high quality are comparatively scarce (Phillips et al., 1994). In addition, services for certain groups, including children who are ill or have disabilities, children whose parents have evening work schedules, and children who need year-round programs, are in short supply (National Commission on Children, 1993).

Concern over the need for affordable, quality day care is expressed by parents who are currently in the labor market as well as by those who want to enter it. We now have a national parental leave policy so that parents can take time off from work to care for their newborns without risking the loss of their jobs. But parental concerns about child care continue throughout toddlerhood and well into the elementary school years when children need adult supervision before and after school hours. Policies and resources are needed to improve the training of child-care professionals, to upgrade their salaries, to provide subsidies to help cover the cost of child care, and to strengthen the licensing regulations for people who provide day care in their homes (Buie, 1988).

Corporations are beginning to address their employees' child-care needs. Workers who are worried about the difficulty of making adequate child-care arrangements experience anxiety, missed workdays, and lost productivity. Companies are addressing this issue in several ways (Quinn, 1988):

Emergency care. Temporary care is provided for those days when an employee's regular arrangement fails.

Discounts. The company arranges for a 10% discount with a national child-care chain or picks up 10% of the fee.

Vouchers. The company makes payments toward whatever child-care arrangement a parent selects. One company provides special assistance for all employees who earn less than $30,000. Another provides a subsidy during a child's first year of life.

Referral services. Companies recommend quality day-care centers to their employees.

On-site day care. Day-care centers are created at the workplace. Congress provides on-site day care for its members and employees.

Flexible benefits. Employees arrange to have child-care costs deducted from their salaries. This money does not count as taxable income.

Day care is clearly not the best choice for all families. Parents who are able to devote the time and attention to caring for their toddlers in the home environment with enthusiasm, patience, and an understanding of their role in promoting optimal development can do a wonderful job. They are rewarded by the intimate experience of watching their children grasp new ideas and achieve new levels of competence.

But for many families, some kind of child-care arrangement is not only necessary but also desirable. In order for day-care settings to have the desired beneficial impact, they must be adequately funded. Quality programs require a highly trained staff who can coordinate social service programs and resources, an effective family involvement component, and a developmentally appropriate curriculum that is adequately linked to the community's cultural strengths. Although innovation in early childhood education programs is important, all preschool and day-care centers should be held accountable to meeting basic standards of quality.

In considering education policies for children from low-income families, attention must be given to sustaining the gains made beyond the preschool years. Most poor children are not just poor when they are toddlers. They remain poor throughout their elementary and middle-school years. Research has shown that, beginning in the early elementary grades, poor children lose

Optimizing Development Through Child Care

Review the developmental tasks that were discussed in Chapter 9. Select one for the focus of this notebook page.

1. Give examples of strategies that could be used within a day-care or preschool curriculum that might promote development in this area.

2. What advantages might there be to having other children the same age or slightly older for promoting development in this area?

3. What special role should the child-care provider play?

4. What resources might be needed?

5. What specific criteria would you use to evaluate whether your plan works in practice?

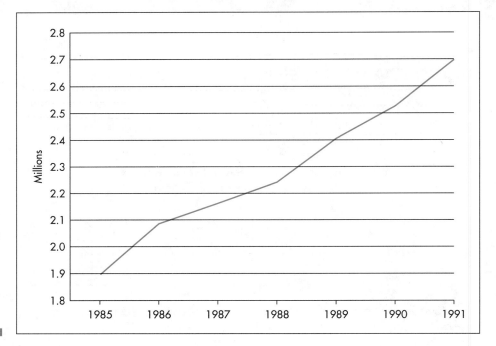

FIGURE 10.3

Cases of child abuse and neglect, 1985–1991
Source: National Commission on Children. (1993). *Just the facts: A summary of recent information on America's children and families.* Washington, D.C.: National Commission on Children, p. 151.

educational ground during the summers in comparison with their more afflu-ent peers who continue to be exposed to new experiences and resources when school is out (Entwisle & Alexander, 1995). Involvement in intellectually stim-ulating activities through summertime and after-school programs, weekend workshops, or clubs may sustain academic motivation and encourage a pos-itive orientation toward learning and problem solving for poor children in the middle-school and high-school years.

Child Abuse

The United States has a serious problem with child abuse. Ever since passage of the Child Abuse Prevention and Treatment Act of 1974, professionals of all sorts have been under legal obligation to report cases of suspected abuse to authorities. Nearly 3 million children were involved in cases reported in 1991. Figure 10.3 shows the reported victims of abuse and neglect from 1985 to 1991, with roughly 40% of cases being substantiated. The steady increase in reported cases may be due in part to greater pressures for reporting, in part to more openness about discussing abuse and recognition of its signs, and in part to greater stressors on families, including higher rates of parental alcohol and drug abuse, poverty, and economic hardship that result in abuse (Coulton et al., 1995, Garbarino & Kostelny, 1992). Instances of abuse may be inflated by false allegations due to community hysteria (for example, where many chil-dren in a preschool report being abused by a single teacher) or by fear of being sued for failure to report a suspected incident. Others contend that the num-ber of cases kept behind closed doors is still vastly underestimated. There are often no outward signs of maltreatment in child sexual abuse. There is no way of knowing how many children who have experienced sexual abuse keep it

BOX 10.4

Barriers to Efforts to Prevent and Treat Child Abuse

Current efforts to prevent and treat child abuse have been criticized on many fronts.

- There is a lack of consensus about definitions of child abuse, neglect, sexual abuse, and maltreatment. Some definitions use readily observable indicators like the extent of the injury, whereas others include the intent of the abuser and the psychological impact on the victim. In a summary of reported instances of abuse, the severity can vary from spanking and shoving to severe beatings and attempted homicide (Rogosch et al., 1995).

- Children in poor families are more likely to be victims of abuse. In many instances, abuse in poor families is confounded by substance abuse, job loss, and lack of knowledge about child development and parenting practices. Funds to provide counseling, treatment, or support to these families are inadequate (National Commission on Children, 1993).

- Since prevention programs are comparatively underfunded and programs for placement of children in substitute care are well funded, many abused children are separated from their families. Thus, abused children lose twice: They suffer from abuse, and then they are removed from their families and homes (National Commission on Children, 1993).

- Instances of child abuse are likely to go unreported when community members and professionals are reluctant to inform authorities about well-regarded families or abuse that occurred in a school or church setting. Children themselves are usually deeply intimidated by reporting their own abuse.

- Cases of abuse are difficult to assess because of the difficulties of evaluating young children's testimony. Recent research has found that children can be relatively easily swayed by an adult interviewer's suggestions; such suggestions may cause their memories of an incident to be revised to include elements that did not actually occur (McCarthy, 1993). Children may want to tell the truth, but their understanding of the truth can be altered by an interviewer's approach.

- Cultural values related to family privacy and corporal punishment of children inhibit broad educational initiatives for preventing violence toward children. Cultural myths of rugged frontier individualism support harsh treatment of children. The early Puritan value system endorses strong punishment to prevent and correct sin. In addition, many contemporary religious groups support inflicting pain on children to teach obedience and humility and to cleanse improper, sinful thoughts and behaviors (Hyman & Pokalo, 1992).

secret because they are afraid or embarrassed to discuss it or because they do not understand the implications of sexual contact between an adult and a child.

Child abuse has been defined in a variety of ways and can include a number of different kinds of experiences, such as physical, sexual, and emotional abuse. It can also include experiences in which children are repeatedly exposed to violence among adults, particularly their parents. Child abuse typically involves some form of intimidation, domination, manipulation, and exploitation by older adolescents or adults. It is differentiated from *neglect,* in which children are abandoned, confined, maintained in dirty conditions, or starved. According to a U.S. Census Department report, in 1987 an estimated 7,736 children ages 3 and 4 of working mothers cared for themselves while the parent(s) were at work (U.S. Bureau of the Census, 1991). This kind of arrangement could be considered a form of parental neglect (see Box 10.4).

The Effects of Abuse on Children

The effects of abuse on children are diverse. Maltreated children suffer a wide range of difficulties across many domains, including increased behavior problems, especially high levels of aggression, depression, impaired peer relations, lower performance on cognitive problem-solving tasks, insecure attachments and delays in social development that are normally associated with the formation of insecure or disorganized attachments (Emery et al., 1992). Abused children have been found to suffer from many psychological problems, but there is no clear causal link between one specific type of abuse and one specific pattern of symptoms. Furthermore, it is difficult to separate the negative effects of a child's observing violence between parents, family disorganization and the disruption of family ties, and stresses induced by economic hardship (each of which often accompanies abuse toward children) from the negative effects of abuse per se.

There is a common assumption in the literature that abuse is generationally transmitted—that children who experience abuse end up being abusive toward their own children. This assumption is currently being examined more fully to determine the mechanisms that might account for such a process. According to social learning theory, children who grow up being exposed to harsh parenting practices such as beating, whipping, or slapping tend to use those same practices when they have children of their own. However, some critics have claimed that the economic stresses of lower socioeconomic status (SES) produce these types of harsh parenting strategies and that the continuity of poverty from one generation to the next, rather than the modeling of specific parenting behaviors, contributes to intergenerational transmission of violence. In fact, abuse does occur more frequently in poor families, but the reason is not fully understood (National Research Council, 1993).

One study tried to sort out the role that socioeconomic status plays in the relationship between family environment and development outcomes for abused and nonabused children (Trickett et al., 1991). Higher-SES families were more likely to encourage autonomy and independence among their children in both abusive and nonabusive families. However, when SES was controlled, abusive families still had lower scores than nonabusive families on measures of closeness of family relationships, taking advantage of community resources, enjoyment in the parental role, and encouraging the child's autonomy. Abusers tend to be more authoritarian in their child-rearing practices. In one example, illustrated in Figure 10.4, as SES increased, scores on enjoyment of the child increased for nonabusive families and decreased for abusive families. As family resources increase, it is clear that children are more an annoyance than a source of enjoyment in abusive families, while they provide increasing pleasure in nonabusive families.

Researchers concluded that the family climate is distinctive in abusive homes. Although many abusive homes are also characterized by poverty, the effects of poverty do not fully account for the emotional tone and parental orientation associated with abuse. "For the abusive families, a picture emerges of worried parents with little enjoyment of parenting and little satisfaction with and expressed affection for the child, of isolation from the wider community, and of lack of encouragement for the development of autonomy and independence in the child while nonetheless holding high standards of achievement for the child" (Trickett et al., 1991, 155).

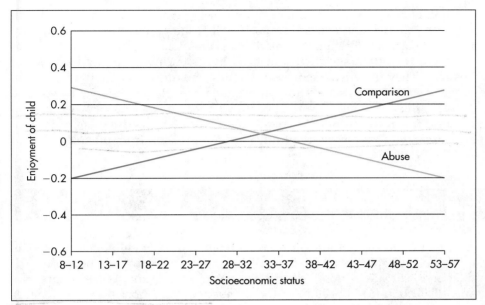

FIGURE 10.4
Enjoyment of the child among abusive and comparison families
Source: Trickett et al. (1991). Relationship of socioeconomic status to the etiology and developmental sequelae of physical child abuse. *Developmental Psychology, 27,* 154. Copyright © 1991 by the American Psychological Association. Reprinted with permission.

The dynamics of abuse are being pursued at another level among scholars with a more cognitive orientation. These researchers are examining the possibility that higher levels of aggressiveness and disruptions in social competence among children who have been abused are a result of modifications in cognitive functioning. Children who have been abused appear to process information in a different manner than children who have not been abused. They tend to be less attuned to social cues in an interpersonal situation and more likely to attribute aggressive intention in hypothetical situations. Further, they are more likely to anticipate an aggressive solution to a hypothetical problem (Weiss et al., 1992). When presented with a nonsocial, information-processing task, abused children tend to be more distracted by aggressive imagery, whereas comparison children are more successful at tuning out aggressive distractions. One interpretation of these observations is that abused children have become "hypervigilant" to any possibility of aggressive stimuli in the environment in order to be responsive to impending danger (Rieder & Cicchetti, 1989). Over the years, this adaptation to unpredictable threat leads to being overly preoccupied with the aggressive potential in an interaction, perceiving even neutral situations as aggressive and approaching most peer interactions with fear. These children are less able to filter out the social noise that is common in the flamboyant, awkward behavior of preschool and early-school-age children, interpreting gestures that might be intended as friendly as a signal to fight.

The picture that is taking shape of abused children, especially those suffering physical abuse, is that they not only have models of aggressive behavior to imitate in their dealings with others but also exposure to violence that predisposes them to make meaning of social interactions in a way that is disruptive to establishing trusting, positive relationships. These children have been restricted in the development of their own sense of autonomy and exposed to extreme feelings of shame and doubt as a result of unpredictable, harsh treatment. They have difficulty expressing their own thoughts and feelings for fear that self-expression itself will result in punishment. And they have difficulty interpreting the emotional expressions of others since they tend to ignore important social cues in their hypersensitivity to any evidence of hostility. They are distracted by constantly monitoring the environment in order to protect themselves from anticipated acts of aggression. And as time goes on, this fearfulness leads to confined behavior as well as a wariness in forming new relationships. Aggressiveness toward others can become a defensive strategy of preparation for anticipated aggression from others.

Optimizing Development in Toddlerhood

As a result of research in child development and early childhood education, quite a bit is known about optimizing development during the period of toddlerhood. The ideas presented in this section were introduced in Chapters 9 and 10. To optimize development, one must pay attention to toddlers' needs to expand their ability to move freely in the environment and to manipulate and investigate a great variety of sensory materials. Since knowledge grows through encounters with discrepancy, toddlers benefit from opportunities to explore as many types of objects and to experience as many different auditory, visual, and proprioceptive stimuli as possible.

Toddlers also need interactive language partners who can expand their vocabulary and conduct conversations about a wide array of topics that stimulate expression as well as comprehension. They need space, resources, and encouragement to engage in fantasy play, as well as play companions who can extend the content and direction of that play. Opportunities to exercise self-control come through trying new tasks and selecting activities. Toddlers also need help in gaining control over strong impulses.

The Adult's Role

To optimize development, adults must be aware of their role. Vygotsky's concept of the zone of proximal development is especially relevant for the relationship of adults and toddlers. The ideal adult companion for toddlers is patient, talkative, eager to stimulate language development, playful, and capable of teaching the day-to-day skills necessary for achieving new levels of self-reliance. As supportive, interactive partners, adults can lead toddlers toward new levels of cognitive, social, and emotional functioning. Through both playful and task-oriented interactions, adults' talk with toddlers expands a toddler's vocabulary. As play companions, adults prompt expanded fantasy play and, at the same time, often encourage new and more complex motor activity without dominating the direction of the play. Adults who understand the importance of the development of autonomy for toddlers can offer a child the chance to make meaningful, age-appropriate choices and decisions. A child who experiences the power of making decisions feels less subordinated to the will of others. Choosing books from the library, music to listen to, stories to read at bedtime, clothes to wear, or flavors of jello to eat are just a few examples of the many ways that adults can foster children's independent decision making.

In the High/Scope Preschool model, the formula that guides teachers is "plan, action, and review." This model suggests that adults share control of the learning process with children. Adults listen carefully and observe children so that they can help children express their intentions. As the children carry out their intentions, adults participate in appropriate ways, asking questions, assisting, or making suggestions without taking over leadership of the activity. As the activity comes to a close, the adult helps the child reflect on what has taken place, suggesting ways to share the activity with others and reviewing what was achieved. Over time, this approach helps children plan and direct their learning activities and gives them experiences in recognizing and accepting the outcomes of their actions (Hohmann & Weikart, 1995).

One implication of the High/Scope model is that, in order to promote optimal development for toddlers, adults need to be invested in the child's successful autonomy. They have to be willing to resist the urge to assert their will over the child's in a domineering, intimidating manner. They need to really listen and respect a toddler's ideas and wishes and be sensitive to the child's needs, while at the same time helping the child to meet those needs in ways that will increase a sense of self-confidence rather than dependence. Adults should be pleased about a child's increasing autonomous activity. A child's enjoyment of cooperative, collaborative activity can be fostered by the development of effective communication skills, a desire to help, and a caring, empathic view toward others.

The great capacity for imitation in toddlerhood is critical in conceptualizing the optimal environment. Children learn new skills, expressions, and behaviors by watching others. They expand their repertoire of motor activities, fantasy scenarios, songs, stories, and skills by observing those around them. Children benefit from imitating peers, older children, and adults.

In considering optimal development in toddlerhood, one must think of all those practices that promote positive socialization, and strategies that foster ability to engage in trusting, cooperative, and helpful interactions with others. Toddlers typically enjoy social interaction; they like to be with other children and to play either side by side or in coordination with their peers. However, toddlers often do not think about the impact of their actions on others. They may behave in ways that appear selfish, inconsiderate, and demanding. Sometimes they lack the ability to express their needs or control their impulses. They may be so focused on one element in a situation that they can't see other factors that may be contributing to the problem. Children eventually learn to regulate their behavior in order to engage in friendly, cooperative interactions and avoid harming others. This is accomplished through positive socialization practices, especially modeling cooperative and helpful communication and behaviors; by explaining rules and why they were made; by recognizing and praising helpfulness and cooperation; and by using discipline practices that emphasize the impact of a child's actions on others.

The Physical Environment

Development also depends on the nature of the physical environment. Most quality preschool and day-care facilities are designed to be used by "little" people who are just about three feet tall. The tables and chairs, the shelves and countertops, the light switches and doorknobs, the toilets and sinks, the art and carpentry materials are all within reach. In these settings, toddlers do not have to ask for help to do many of the things that they have in mind. They can see clearly what toys are available. They can reach the paint, the scissors, and the glue. The blocks and costumes are stacked and stored where they can be reached. And the floors are easily cleaned, the tables and counters are durable, and there is little worry about spills, stains, and other hazards of inexperienced hands. The more the environment is designed to be used by toddlers, the less often adults have to say "no" and the more initiative children can take in expressing their ideas without adult mediation. To the extent that the home environment resembles this user-friendly physical design, toddlers can function at a highly self-guided, autonomous level at home as well as at school.

The Community

In addition to family and school, optimal development is influenced in part by the nature of the community. What are a community's responsibilities to toddlers, and how do communities contribute to fostering optimal development? A community should provide settings where young children can explore the environment in safe, comparatively unrestricted ways. Many communities have public parks and play spaces that are suited to young children and activities designed for exploring the outdoors. Settings intended to enhance language skills and provide opportunities for social interaction between children and adults, as well as among children of varying age groups, are important community assets. Public television, public libraries and storytime programs, and traveling bookmobiles are examples of community resources directed toward this goal.

In addition to fostering toddlers' development directly through providing resources that enhance their abilities, communities need to support parents. Many communities sponsor parent-education programs, Baby and Me activities for mothers or fathers and their toddlers, Gymboree or other physical activity sessions for parents and their toddlers, support groups for parents who are at risk for abusing their children, and safe havens for mothers and children who are at risk of family violence. Parents also need information about the health and nutritional needs of toddlers, safety issues regarding toys and play materials, and community activities and resources for young children. The Cooperative Extension Service often provides this information to county residents. Other agencies such as the Chamber of Commerce, Headstart programs, pediatric clinics, and early-childhood centers may also have information of this type.

Some children are especially vulnerable and may rely more heavily than others on the community to promote their optimal development. These children may be growing up in families who are experiencing poverty, unemployment, parental drug or alcohol abuse, or homelessness. They may be growing up in neighborhoods characterized by high rates of violence and crime. They may have experienced abuse and/or neglect. They may have certain physical or psychological problems that are beyond the expertise or coping capacities of their parents. These children depend on the effective coordination of community services in order to sustain an optimal path of growth. Programs to promote health care, education, nutritional resources,

Toddlers like to make things happen!

mental health services, transportation, housing, and a variety of emergency services all need to be integrated into a coordinated network. Furthermore, successful communities provide prevention and early intervention programs that help parents cope with the challenges of child-rearing and improve their access to community services and knowledge about how to promote development.

The challenge for any community is to support parents in their roles and to hold them responsible for promoting their children's physical, emotional, social, and intellectual development. At the same time, communities need to provide high-quality services to facilitate parents' efforts to enact their roles successfully. These services must include preventive programs that will reduce conditions that cause parents stress in relating to their children. When parents are unable to enact their roles, communities must be resolved and prepared to intervene in ways that respect the intimate link between parents and children but that respect a child's independent needs and rights.

Toddlers Contribute to Their Own Development

Toddlers have some advantages over infants in being able to foster their own development. Through the use of language, they can express their needs and desires. They can begin to negotiate with adults to alter the pattern of caregiving—more time outside, more playtime with friends, more trips to the zoo or the library, more visits to daddy's house or to a favorite relative, and so on. And as the radius of significant others expands, toddlers can complement their experiences at home with parents, guardians, and siblings with experiences at day care or preschool with friends and teachers. Toddlers who are encouraged to express their natural curiosity and friendly, playful outlook toward others find that social contact is a major source of fun and stimulation for new ideas.

Toddlers like to make things happen, and in the course of their exploration and investigation they discover special activities that are of unique interest. Toddlers discover certain kinds of play that are especially satisfying—riding a tricycle, building with blocks, painting and drawing, looking at books, pretending to be superheroes or space travelers. These activities can provide hours of unconflicted activity; they serve to integrate language, motor skills, sensory exploration, planning, and problem solving and a personal sense of self-directed decision making. These interests often become the basis for new and expanded skills.

In Table 10.3, we list the factors that have been mentioned or implied as contributing to optimal development in toddlerhood.

TABLE 10.3

Optimizing Development in Toddlerhood

Make a psychological commitment to the parenting process.

Continue to think of ways of drawing children into their zone of proximal development.

Promote experimentation with various forms of locomotion.

Encourage fantasy by providing space, resources, and permission to pretend.

Join in as a play companion with children, but don't take over leadership of the play.

Extend play by suggesting new uses for objects, new situations, etc.

Be an active and frequent communication partner.

Talk about a wide range of subjects and use as wide a vocabulary as possible.

Ask questions.

Extend a child's speech through expansions, rephrasing, and prompting.

Talk about feelings and emotional reactions, not just about how to do things or about facts.

Foster empathy by pointing out the consequences of one's actions for others.

Continue to foster secure attachment by responding in a sensitive, timely way to a child's needs.

Do not introduce unnecessary prohibitions or constraints on a child's behavior.

Help children gain control of intense, angry feelings through calm talk, time-out, and encouraging empathic feelings for the victim.

Minimize exposure to violence and to stimuli that arouse aggressive feelings.

Permit some acceptable expression or outlet for strong feelings of frustration and anger.

Use language to help guide children in the process of stating goals and solving problems.

Encourage children to take on tasks that are a step beyond what they can manage comfortably.

Encourage and support self-directed goal attainment.

TABLE 10.3 (continued)

Optimizing Development in Toddlerhood

Show pride and enthusiasm in a child's ability to accomplish tasks or to complete a project.

Be patient as children try to do things on their own.

Don't ridicule or embarrass children.

Keep in mind that you are a significant model for imitation. Demonstrate behaviors that you want to promote in your child.

In child-rearing practices, show warmth and acceptance.

Create an affectionate climate in the home.

Establish clear, firm expectations for responsible, self-regulated behaviors that are appropriate to a child's developmental level.

Involve children in decision making.

Avoid escalating a discipline situation into a conflict of wills or a pure assertion of power.

Consider the reasons behind a child's misbehaviors and try to tie the discipline to the motives.

Remain playful in outlook as well as in behavior.

Try to achieve a positive outlook on the challenges posed by combining work and family life.

Try to achieve as much control as possible over the demands of your work schedule.

Communicate openly and often with your partner about expectations for enacting the parent role and for balancing work and family responsibilities.

Strive toward an equitable balance of responsibilities between partners for child care.

Be sure that the demands of work do not leave you psychologically unavailable to hear and respond to a toddler's needs.

Chapter Summary

1. The positive pole of resolving the psychosocial crisis of toddlerhood is autonomy, the ability to behave independently and perform actions on one's own. The negative pole is shame and doubt, a feeling of worthlessness that comes from being ridiculed and humiliated or feeling that one has failed to live up to the expectations of others.

2. The central process of this stage, imitation, provides a mechanism for incorporating the words, actions, skills, and customs that are enacted in the child's social environment. Once all these words and actions are taken in through imitation, the child brings a unique personal agenda to their further expression.

3. As a result of a positive resolution of the psychosocial crisis, the prime adaptive ego quality of will emerges. Will, the capacity to direct and control actions, tends to be associated with a positive belief in oneself and an accepting orientation toward others. The core pathology of this

stage is compulsion, irresistible impulses toward repetitive, ritualized thoughts or actions that seem to be beyond the control of will.

4. During toddlerhood, the family system undergoes important changes. Parents become important play companions. In order to foster and extend a child's fantasy, parents must value fantasy and allow a child time and space to be playful. Parents must join in the co-construction of the fantasy without taking it over. And parents must extend the play, broadening the domains within which pretense occurs.

5. As socialization agents, parents begin to regulate the child's behavior so that it conforms to the expectations and norms of a larger society. Of the many components of the socialization process, the one that has received the most attention is discipline.

6. Discipline practices have been categorized into three styles: power assertion, love withdrawal, and inductions. The kind of discipline that is used is influenced by parents' beliefs about what the child can or should be able to do, by the situation in which the behavior is taking place, and by the way the child responds to an initial effort to modify the behavior.

7. Work commonly affects family life. Parental role strain is increased during a child's toddlerhood, especially when husband and wife are in conflict about sharing household and child-care tasks.

8. Parental conflicts about role enactment, whether related to work or home, have a negative impact on toddlers.

9. The birth of a sibling dramatically changes the family configuration. Siblings often experience a sense of jealousy or rivalry which can be exaggerated when parents spend less time with the older child, intervene unfairly or inconsistently in the children's relationship, or become unavailable. Children who have a positive relationship with their father are likely to experience the addition of a new sibling more positively.

10. Each culture has a pattern of socialization that is intended to prepare the child to be a fully functioning member of the larger social group. Child-rearing practices are linked to cultural values and ideologies. The way that cultures convey the value of fantasy, autonomy, and various discipline practices shapes the direction of development.

11. Within the United States, certain social issues have a strong impact on a toddler's opportunities and future growth. Poverty places children at special risk for encountering barriers to development, including malnourishment, poor-quality health care, hazardous living arrangements, dangerous neighborhoods, poor-quality child care, ineffective school systems, and disruptive parental relationships characterized by high levels of emotional distress.

12. Children can be buffered from the effects of poverty through their own resilience and through their parents' effective coping strategies.

13. Day care in the United States is largely unregulated and varies tremendously in quality. Quality child care has been shown to have positive consequences for children, especially those from poor families who are at risk for subsequent school failure. Quality child care has been associated with immediate advantages in IQ and achievement and with longer-term advantages in positive attitudes toward

school, fewer school failures, and fewer placements in special education classrooms.

14. Social advantages of quality child care include higher levels of social competence, self-esteem, and empathy. Some studies show higher levels of willfulness and aggressiveness with peers among children in day care, but the long-term consequences of these trends have not been determined.

15. Cases of child abuse and neglect have been on the rise since 1985. Many factors combine to make intervention in and treatment of child abuse extremely difficult. At present, scholars are formulating a rather complex understanding of how abused children may become child abusers themselves as adults, but efforts to prevent abuse have been largely ineffective.

References

Adler, A. (1959). *Understanding human nature.* New York: Premier Books (Fawcett Publications).

Albert, S., Amgott, T., Krakow, M. & Marcus, H. (1977). Children's bedtime rituals as a prototype rite of safe passage. San Francisco: Paper presented at the annual convention of the American Psychological Association.

American Psychiatric Association (1993). *DSM-IV draft criteria.* Washington, D.C.: APA.

Bandura, A. (1977). *Social learning theory.* Englewood Cliffs, N.J.: Prentice-Hall.

Bates, E., O'Connell, B. & Shore, C. (1987). Language and communication in infancy. In J. D. Osofsky (Ed.), *Handbook of infant development,* 149–203.

Baumrind, D. (1973). The development of instrumental competence through socialization. In A. D. Pick (Ed.), *Minnesota symposium on child psychology* (vol. 7). Minneapolis: University of Minnesota Press, 3–46.

Baumrind, D. (1991). The influence of parenting style on adolescent competence and substance abuse. *Journal of Early Adolescence, 11,* 56–94.

Berrueta-Clement, J. R., Schweinhart, L. J., Barnett, W. S., Epstein, A. S. & Weikart, D. P. (1984). *Changed lives: The effects of the Perry Preschool Program on youths through age 19.* Ypsilanti, Mich.: High/Scope Press.

Biernat, M. & Wortman, C. B. (1991). Sharing of home responsibilities between professionally employed women and their husbands. *Journal of Personality and Social Psychology, 60,* 844–860.

Bradley, R. H., Whiteside, L., Mundfrom, D. J., Casey, P. H., Kelleher, K. J. & Pope, S. K. (1994). Early indications of resilience and their relation to experiences in the home environments of low birthweight, premature children living in poverty. *Child Development, 65,* 346–360.

Brody, G. H., Stoneman, Z. & Burke, M. (1987). Child temperaments, maternal differential behavior, and sibling relationships. *Developmental Psychology, 23,* 354–362.

Brody, G. H., Stoneman, Z. & McCoy, J. K. (1992). Associations of maternal and paternal direct and differential behavior with sibling relationships: Contemporaneous and longitudinal analyses. *Child Development, 63,* 82–92.

Brody, G. H., Stoneman, Z., McCoy, J. K. & Forehand, R. (1992). Contemporaneous and longitudinal associations of sibling conflict with family relationship assessments and family discussions about sibling problems. *Child Development, 63,* 391–400.

Brown, J. L. & Pollitt, E. (1996). Malnutrition, poverty, and intellectual development. *Scientific American, 274,* 38–43.

Brown, J. R. & Dunn, J. (1992). Talk with your mother or your sibling? Developmental changes in early family conversations about feelings. *Child Development, 63,* 336–349.

Buie, J. (1988). Efforts for better child care increase. *APA Monitor, 19,* 28.

Burchinal, M., Lee, M. & Ramey, C. (1989). Type of day-care and preschool intellectual development in disadvantaged children. *Child Development, 60,* 128–137.

Caughy, M. O., DiPietro, J. A. & Strobino, D. M. (1994). Day-care participation as a protective factor in the cognitive development of low-income children. *Child Development, 65*, 457–471.

Chagnon, N. A. (1977). *Yanomano: The fierce people* (2nd ed.). New York: Holt, Rinehart and Winston.

Chamberlain, P. & Patterson, G. R. (1995). Discipline and child compliance in parenting. In M. H. Bornstein (Ed.), *Handbook of parenting. Applied and practical parenting* (vol. 4). Hillsdale, N.J.: Erlbaum, 205–225.

Chase-Lansdale, P. L. (1993). The impact of poverty on family processes. *The Child, Youth, and Family Services Quarterly, 16*, 5–8.

Clarke-Stewart, K. A. (1989). Infant day care: Maligned or malignant? *American Psychologist, 44*, 266–273.

Clarke-Stewart, K. A. & Fein, G. G. (1983). Early childhood programs. In P. H. Mussen (Ed.), *Handbook of child psychology. Infancy and developmental psychobiology* (vol. 2). New York: Wiley, 917–1000.

Coulton, C. J., Korbin, J. E., Su, M. & Chow, J. (1995). Community level factors and child maltreatment rates. *Child Development, 66*, 1262–1276.

Demo, D. H. & Ganong, L. H. (1994). Divorce. In P. C. McKenry & S. J. Price (Eds.), *Families and change: Coping with stressful events*. Thousand Oaks, Calif.: Sage, 197–218.

Denham, S. A., Renwick, S. M. & Holt, R. W. (1991). Working and playing together: Prediction of preschool social-emotional competence from mother–child interaction. *Child Development, 62*, 242–249.

Dix, T., Ruble, D. N. & Zambarano, R. J. (1989). Mothers' implicit theories of discipline: Child effects, parent effects, and the attribution process. *Child Development, 60*, 1373–1391.

Duncan, G. J., Brooks-Gunn, J. & Klebanov, P. K. (1994). Economic deprivation and early childhood development. *Child Development, 65*, 296–318.

Dunn, J. (1985). *Sisters and brothers*. Cambridge, Mass.: Harvard University Press.

Dunn, J., Brown, J. & Beardsall, L. (1991). Family talk about feeling states and children's later understanding of others' emotions. *Developmental Psychology, 27*, 448–453.

Dunn, J. & Munn, P. (1987). Development of justification in disputes with mother and sibling. *Developmental Psychology, 23*, 791–798.

Eckerman, C. O., Davis, C. C. & Didow, S. M. (1989). Toddlers' emerging ways of achieving social coordinations with a peer. *Child Development, 60*, 440–453.

Eckerman, C. O. & Didow, S. M. (1996). Nonverbal imitation and toddlers' mastery of verbal means of achieving coordinated action. *Developmental Psychology, 32*, 141–152.

Emery, R. E., Fincham, F. D. & Cumming, M. D. (1992). Parenting in context: Systemic thinking about parental conflict and its influence on children. *Journal of Consulting and Clinical Psychology, 60*, 909–912.

Entwisle, D. R. & Alexander, K. L. (1995). A parent's economic shadow: Family structure versus family resources as influences on early school achievement. *Journal of Marriage and the Family, 57*, 399–409.

Erikson, E. H. (1963). *Childhood and society* (2nd ed.). New York: W. W. Norton & Company.

Erikson, E. H. (1977). *Toys and reasons*. New York: W. W. Norton & Company.

Erikson, E. H., Erikson, J. M. & Kivnick, H. Q. (1986). *Vital involvement in old age*. New York: W. W. Norton & Company.

Freud, A. (1965). *Normality and pathology in childhood*. New York: International Universities Press.

Freud, S. (1920). (J. Riviere, Trans.) *A general introduction to psychoanalysis*. New York: Washington Square Press.

Garbarino, J. & Kostelny, K. (1992). Child maltreatment as a community problem. *Child Abuse & Neglect, 16*, 455–464.

Garmezy, N. (1991). Resilience in children's adaptation to negative life events and stressed environments. *Pediatric Annals, 20*, 459–466.

Garner, P. W., Jones, D. C. & Palmer, D. J. (1994). Social cognitive correlates of preschool children's sibling caregiving behavior. *Developmental Psychology, 30*, 905–911.

Gralinski, J. H. & Kopp, C. B. (1993). Everyday rules for behavior: Mothers' requests to young children. *Developmental Psychology, 29*, 573–584.

Greenberger, E. & Goldberg, W. (1989). Work, parenting, and the socialization of children. *Developmental Psychology, 25*, 22–35.

Greenberger, E., O'Neil, R. & Nagel, S. K. (1994). Linking workplace and homeplace: Relations between the nature of adult's work and their parenting behaviors. *Developmental Psychology, 30*, 990–1002.

Grych, J. H. & Fincham, F. D. (1990). Marital conflict and children's adjustment: A cognitive-contextual framework. *Psychological Bulletin, 108*, 267–290.

Harwood, R. L. (1992). The influence of culturally derived values on Anglo and Puerto Rican mothers' perceptions of attachment behavior. *Child Development, 63*, 822–839.

Haskins, R. (1989). Beyond metaphor: The efficacy of early childhood education. *American Psychologist, 44*, 274–282.

Haswell, K., Hock, E. & Wenar, C. (1981). Oppositional behavior of preschool children: Theory and intervention. *Family Relations, 30*, 440–446.

Hernandez, D. J. (1993). Childhood poverty: Trends, causes, and policies. *The Child, Youth, and Family Services Quarterly, 16*, 3–4.

Hoffman, M. L. (1977). Moral internalization: Current theory and research. In L. Berkowitz (Ed.), *Advances in experimental social psychology*, (vol. 10). New York: Academic Press.

Hohmann, M. & Weikart, D. P. (1995). Active learning: The way children construct knowledge. *High/Scope Resource, 14*, 4–8.

Holloway, S. D. & Fuller, B. (1992). The great child-care experiment: What are the lessons for school improvement? *Educational Researcher, 21*, 12–19.

Howe, N. (1991). Sibling-directed internal state language, perspective taking, and affective behavior. *Child Development, 62*, 1503–1512.

Howes, C. & Stewart, P. (1987). Child's play with adults, toys, and peers: An examination of family and child-care influences. *Developmental Psychology, 23*, 423–430.

Huston, A. C., McLoyd, V. C. & Coll, C. G. (1994). Children and poverty: Issues in contemporary research. *Child Development, 65*, 275–282.

Jayakody, R., Chatters, L. M. & Taylor, R. J. (1993). Family support to single and married African-American mothers: The provision of financial, emotional, and child care assistance. *Journal of Marriage and the Family, 55*, 261–276.

Jouriles, E. N., Murphy, C. M., Farris, A. M., Smith, D. A., Richters, J. E. & Waters, E. (1991). Marital adjustment, parental disagreements about child rearing, and behavior problems in boys: Increasing the specificity of the marital assessment. *Child Development, 62*, 1424–1433.

Kalleberg, A. L. & Rosenfeld, R. A. (1990). Work in the family and in the labor market. *Journal of Marriage and the Family, 52*, 331–346.

Kaufman, G. (1989). *The psychology of shame.* New York: Springer.

Kelley, M. L., Power, T. G. & Wimbush, D. D. (1992). Determinants of disciplinary practices in low-income black mothers. *Child Development, 63*, 573–582.

Kochanska, G., Aksan, N. & Koenig, A. L. (1995). A longitudinal study of the roots of preschoolers' conscience: Committed compliance and emerging internalization. *Child Development, 66*, 1752–1769.

Kochanska, G., Kuczynski, L. & Radke-Yarrow, M. (1989). Correspondence between mothers' self-reported and observed child-rearing practices. *Child Development, 60*, 56–63.

Kohn, M. L. (1983). On the transmission of values in the family: A preliminary formulation. In A. Kerchoff (Ed.), *Research in sociology, education, and socialization.* Greenwich, Conn.: JAI Press, 3–112.

Kohn, M. L., Slomczynski, K. N. & Schoenbach, C. (1986). Social stratification and the transmission of values in the family: A cross-national assessment. *Sociological Forum, 1*, 73–102.

Konner, M. (1977). Evolution of human behavior development. In P. H. Leiderman, S. R. Tulkin & A. Rosenfeld (Eds.), *Culture and infancy: Variations in the human experience.* New York: Academic Press.

Kuczynski, L., Kochanska, G., Radke-Yarrow, M. & Girnius-Brown, O. (1987). A developmental interpretation of young children's noncompliance. *Developmental Psychology, 23*, 799–806.

Kuczynski, L., Zahn-Waxler, C. & Radke-Yarrow, M. (1987). Development and content of imitation in the second and third years of life: A socialization perspective. *Developmental Psychology, 23*, 276–282.

Lewis, H. B. (1987). Shame and the narcissistic personality. In D. L. Nathanson (Ed.), *The many faces of shame.* New York: Guilford Press, 93–132.

Lin, C. Y. C. & Fu, V. (1990). A comparison of child-rearing practices among Chinese, immigrant Chinese, and Caucasian-American parents. *Child Development, 61*, 429–433.

Maccoby, E. E. (1992). The role of parents in the socialization of children: An historical overview. *Developmental Psychology, 28*, 1006–1017.

McCarthy, K. (1993). Kids' eyewitness recall is focus for conference. *APA Monitor, 24*, 1, 28–29.

McKey, R. H., Condelli, L., Ganson, H., Barrett, B. J., McConkey, C. & Plantz, M. C. (1985). *The impact of Head Start on children, families, and communities.* (DHHS Publication No. OHDS 85-31193). Washington, D.C.: U.S. Government Printing Office.

McLeod, J. D. & Shannon, M. J. (1993). Poverty, parenting, and children's mental health. *American Sociological Review, 58*, 351–366.

McLoyd, V. C. (1990). The impact of economic hardship on black families and children: Psychological distress, parenting, and socioemotional development. *Child Development, 61,* 311–346.

Mead, M. (1955). Children and ritual in Bali. In M. Mead & M. Wolfenstein (Eds.), *Childhood in contemporary cultures.* Chicago: University of Chicago Press.

Menaghan, E. G. & Parcel, T. L. (1990). Parental employment and family life: Research in the 1980s. *Journal of Marriage and the Family, 52,* 1079–1098.

Miller, S. (1985). *The shame experience.* Hillsdale, N.J.: Erlbaum.

Mills, R. S. L. & Rubin, K. H. (1990). Parental beliefs about problematic social behaviors in early childhood. *Child Development, 61,* 138–151.

Morrison, A. P. (1989). *Shame: The underside of narcissism.* Hillsdale, N.J.: Analytic Press.

National Commission on Children. (1991). *Speaking of kids: A national survey of children and parents.* Washington, D.C.: National Commission on Children.

National Commission on Children. (1993). *Just the facts: A summary of recent information on America's children and their families.* Washington, D.C.: National Commission on Children.

National Research Council. (1993). *Understanding child abuse and neglect.* Washington, D.C.: National Academy Press.

O'Leary, S. (1995). Parental discipline mistakes. *Current Directions in Psychological Science, 4,* 11–13.

Phillips, D. A., Voran, M., Kisker, E., Howes, C. & Whitebook, M. (1994). Child care for children in poverty: Opportunity or inequity? *Child Development, 65,* 472–492.

Plomin, R. (1990). *Nature and nurture: An introduction to human behavioral genetics.* Pacific Grove, Calif.: Brooks/Cole.

Pollitt, E. (1994). Poverty and child development: Relevance of research in developing countries to the United States. *Child Development, 65,* 283–295.

Queen, S. A. & Habenstein, R. W. (1974). *The family in various cultures* (4th ed.). Philadelphia: J. B. Lippincott.

Quinn, J. B. (1988). A crisis in child care. *Newsweek,* February 15, 57.

Repetti, R. L. (1992). Social withdrawal as a short-term coping response to daily stress. In H. F. Friedman (Ed.), *Hostility, coping, and health.* Washington, D.C.: American Psychological Association, 151–165.

Rogers, C. S. & Sawyers, J. K. (1988). *Play in the lives of children.* Washington, D.C.: National Association for the Education of Young Children.

Rogosch, F. A., Cicchetti, D., Shields, A. & Toth, S. L. (1995). Parenting dysfunction in child maltreatment. In M. H. Bornstein (Ed.), *Handbook of parenting. Applied and practical parenting* (vol. 4). Hillsdale, N.J.: Erlbaum, 127–159.

Schweinhart, L. J. & Weikart, D. P. (1988). The High/Scope Perry preschool program. In R. H. Price, E. L. Cowen, R. P. Orion & J. Ramos-McKay (Eds.), *Fourteen ounces of prevention.* Washington, D.C.: American Psychological Association, 53–66.

Shore, M. F. (1993). Doing the right thing. *Readings, 8,* 4–7.

Simon, R. W. (1992). Parental role strains, salience of parental identity and gender differences in psychological distress. *Journal of Health and Social Behavior, 33,* 25–35.

Steinberg, L., Elmer, J. D. & Mounts, N. S. (1989). Authoritative parenting, psychosocial maturity, and academic success among adolescents. *Child Development, 60,* 1424–1436.

Stephens, S. (1992). The joys and problems of being No. 1. *Columbus Dispatch,* November 6, 6C.

Stocker, C., Dunn, J. & Plomin, R. (1989). Sibling relationships: Links with child temperament, maternal behavior, and family structure. *Child Development, 60,* 715–727.

Stoneman, Z., Brody, G. H. & Burke, M. (1989). Sibling temperaments and maternal and paternal perceptions of marital, family, and personal functioning. *Journal of Marriage and the Family, 51,* 99–113.

Tangney, J. P., Wagner, P., Fletcher, C. & Gramzow, R. (1992). Shamed into anger? The relation of shame and guilt to anger and self-reported aggression. *Journal of Personality and Social Psychology, 62,* 669–675.

Tiedje, L. B., Wortman, C. B., Downey, G., Emmons, C., Biernat, M. & Lang, E. (1990). Role compatibility in women with multiple roles. *Journal of Marriage and the Family, 52,* 63–72.

Trickett, P. K., Aber, J. L., Carlson, V. & Cicchetti, D. (1991). Relationship of socioeconomic status to the etiology and developmental sequelae of physical child abuse. *Developmental Psychology, 27,* 148–158.

U.S. Bureau of the Census. (1991). *Statistical abstract of the United States: 1991* (111th ed.). Washington, D.C.: U.S. Government Printing Office.

Vandell, D. L., Henderson, V. K. & Wilson, K. S. (1988). A longitudinal study of children with day-care experiences of varying quality. *Child Development, 59,* 1286–1292.

Volling, B. L. & Belsky, J. (1992). The contribution of mother–child and father–child relationships to the quality of sibling interaction: A longitudinal study. *Child Development, 63,* 1209–1222.

Voydanoff, P. (1988). Work roles, family structure, and work/family conflicts. *Journal of Marriage and the Family, 50,* 749–761.

Weiss, B., Dodge, K. A., Bates, J. E. & Petit. G. S. (1992). Some consequences of early harsh discipline: Child aggression and a maladaptive social information processing style. *Child Development, 63,* 1321–1335.

Wenar, C. (1982). On negativism. *Human Development, 25,* 1–23.

White, R. W. (1960). Competence and the psychosexual stages of development. In M. R. Jones (Ed.), *Nebraska symposium on motivation* (vol. 8). Lincoln: University of Nebraska Press.

Zigler, E. (1993). *Head Start and beyond: A national plan for extended childhood intervention.* New Haven, Conn.: Yale University Press.

Zigler, E. & Muenchow, S. (1992). *Head Start: The inside story of America's most successful educational experiment.* New York: Basic Books.

Zussman, J. V. (1980). Situational determinants of parental behavior: Effects of competing cognitive activity. *Child Development, 51,* 792–800.

Developmental Tasks of Early School Age (Ages 4 to 6)

Chapter 11

Gender-Role Identification
> **Individual Differences Versus Constructivism**
> **Understanding Gender**
> **Learning Sex-Role Standards**
> **Identifying with Parents**
> **Forming a Gender-Role Preference**

Early Moral Development
> **Learning Theory**
> **Cognitive-Developmental Theory**
>> Moral Transgressions Versus Social Convention
>>> Transgressions
> **Psychoanalytic Theory**
>> Research on the Development of Conscience
>> Neopsychoanalytic Theory
> **Research on Empathy and Perspective Taking**
>> Empathy
>> Perspective Taking
> **Research on Parental Discipline**

Group Play
> **Group Games**
> **Friendship Groups**
>> Conflicts among Friends
>> Sex-Segregated Friendship Groups
>> Groups and Dyads

Self-Theory
> **Developmental Changes in the Self-Theory**
> **Self-Esteem**
> **Self-Esteem and the Early-School-Age Child**

Chapter Summary

References

From a psychosocial perspective, the early-school-age period is a critical transition as children internalize more and more of their parents' values and ideals, thus laying the childhood foundation for their own ability to function as adults. Although children at this age continue to have many of the fanciful, energetic, and spontaneous qualities of toddlers, they also begin to take on more serious concerns, trying to make sense of the various complex social settings in which they participate and figure out what expectations others have for them. They begin to experience a new self-awareness, employing their own, albeit childlike, understanding of social and moral values to assess their sense of worth.

Family and school are the primary socialization contexts of this period. In addition, peer groups, neighborhood, and media exert social influences. These forces both provide models and apply pressure for developing scenarios about the self and others. To match this exposure to a diversity of social influences, most early-school-age children exhibit wide-ranging curiosity about all facets of life. Familiar patterns of behavior and family rules become legitimate material for questioning. Why do I have to go to bed? Why are you so angry at me? Why can't you buy me that toy? Why is it night? The independence of action that is seen in the toddler is extended through an independence of thought in the early-school-age child.

In this chapter, we will discuss four primary tasks of psychosocial development. The task of *gender-role identification* includes physical, cognitive, emotional, and social domains as they become integrated into an early scheme for thinking of oneself as male or female. Issues of right and wrong surface constantly as a result of the child's newly acquired abilities for independent thought and exposure to a much wider range of social influences. These experiences provide the basis for early *moral development*. A third area of new development involves increased levels of participation in *group play*. The skills for learning the rules and playing cooperatively with others require repeated experiences. As a result of participation with age-mates, children begin to form meaningful friendships and mental representations of participating in groups. Finally, understanding and experiencing the self expand markedly during early-school-age years. We conceptualize this developmental task as the acquisition of a personal *self-theory* that becomes increasingly complex as it is stimulated by newly expanded social influences. Accompanying the development of the self-theory is the development of a set of complex feelings about the self called self-esteem. In Chapter 12, we will expand the psychosocial analysis and give more attention to how these developmental tasks contribute to school readiness and adaptation to school.

Gender-Role Identification

Human societies are marked by patterns of organization based partially on gender. Males and females are typically assigned different roles, engage in different tasks, have access to different resources, and are viewed as having different powers and attributes. The specific content of these gender roles varies widely from one culture to another. For example, in contrast to many societies in which males appear to have a favored and dominant position, some cultures give special priority to girls and women. Among the Kanjar of Pakistan

young children continue to internalize parents values and ideals.

experience increasing self awareness

family & school provide socialization

independence of thought.

452

and northern India, **girls** and women provide more than half the family income through the sale of ceramic and papier-mâché toys, dancing, begging, giving carnival rides, and prostitution (Cronk, 1993). Kanjar men are described as "passive, cooperative and subordinate to females, whereas Kanjar women dominate public and private affairs and are socialized to be aggressive and independent" (Cronk, 1993, 279).

Our goal in the discussion that follows is to understand how children begin to conceptualize gender as a dimension of their self-concept, an organizing principle of social life, and a guide to their behavior. We focus on how children conceptualize their own gender, how they learn about the cultural expectations that are tied to gender, and how gender shapes aspects of their social experience. The discussion is presented in the context of the ongoing controversy over the origin of gender differences by introducing both the individual differences and the constructivist perspectives on this topic.

look at how children conceptualize gender as a dimension of their self-concept → effects on social life and behavior.

Individual Differences Versus Constructivism

The question is not whether gender differences exist, but how to explain their cause (Bohan, 1993; Thompson, 1993). The *individual differences* perspective suggests that gender differences are persistent, internal, individual attributes. Whether the differences are due to biology, socialization, or an interaction between the two, this perspective suggests that differences between males and females are stable characteristics that individuals bring to various situations.

INDIVIDUAL DIFFERENCES
internal, individual, persistent attributes

The *constructivist* perspective suggests that gender differences are a product of particular interactions that have a certain, socially agreed-upon, gender-related meaning. In this view, the specific behaviors that are described as masculine or feminine depend largely on the situation, including the expectations for people to behave in gender-appropriate ways. Gender differences, then, are not so much stable characteristics of individuals, but a product of how individuals have been socialized to behave, given the demands of the situation. As an example, consider the results of a study of social interaction between pairs of toddlers (Jacklin & Maccoby, 1978; Maccoby, 1990). The question being investigated was whether male and female children could be characterized as using different social styles during play. Investigators observed children during free play, noting the quality of their play when they were with a same-sex or an opposite-sex play companion.

CONSTRUCTIVIST
interactions, socially agreed upon, take on masculine or feminine qualities.
∴ gender differences are result of individual socialization.

One variable that was measured was the amount of time that one partner stood watching while the other child played with toys, a behavior called *passive.* No sex differences were observed overall in the frequency of passive behavior. However, the frequency of girls' passivity depended on the circumstances in which they were observed. In same-sex pairs, girls were rarely passive, but in mixed-sex pairs the girl frequently stood watching while the boy played with toys.

This kind of finding is replicated at older ages, showing that girls and boys, as well as men and women, interact in stereotypically gender-defined ways, particularly when they are observed in public settings and in mixed-sex groups. The constructivists offer the idea that gender differences are a product of social norms that define appropriate behaviors for males and females. This point of view places greater emphasis on the societal causes than on the biological causes as a source for gender differences in behavior (see Notebook Page 11.1).

Thinking about Gender Differences

Recent research on brain functioning has identified differences in how men and women process information and in how their brain structures are involved in various types of problem solving (Begley, 1995). Nonetheless, evidence that men and women use their brains differently to solve problems does not resolve the question of whether these differences are primarily a result of genetics or experience. What do you think?

1. When it comes to problem solving and cognitive functioning, do you think that men and women have different areas of strength and weakness? If so, what are these areas?

_____

_____

_____

_____

_____

2. What accounts for these differences? To what extent are these gender differences primarily a product of genetic information and hormonal differences? What might be the evolutionary basis for genetic gender differences in cognitive functioning?

_____

_____

_____

_____

_____

3. To what extent are these gender differences a result of socialization practices, such as differences in the kinds of toys that male and female children are encouraged to play with or the kinds of social expectations that are conveyed to male and female children? What might be the societal benefits for encouraging different patterns of cognitive functioning among boys and girls, men and women?

_____

_____

_____

_____

_____

4. To what extent might these gender differences be contextual? In other words, under what types of circumstances might you observe differences in the cognitive functioning of males and females? When might their performance be more similar?

_____

_____

_____

_____

_____

We do not expect gender identity to have been completed by the end of early school age. During this period, however, gender becomes a defining dimension of the way children understand themselves and others. This achievement is especially noteworthy in that it reflects the dynamic interaction of the physical, intellectual, emotional, and social domains as they are interpreted within a cultural context. Aside from their genital differences, male and female children may not appear very different based on their physical

gender is a defining dimension of the way children understand themselves and others.

It is not always easy to distinguish girls from boys by their outward appearances. What is your guess about these five children?

appearance. When boys and girls are dressed in shorts or jeans and a T-shirt, it is difficult to tell them apart. On average, five-year-old girls are only one or two centimeters shorter than five-year-old boys and weigh only a pound or two less. Yet, for both girls and boys, their sex and the sex-role expectations to which they are exposed become powerful organizing principles that guide their behavior, their social relationships, and the content of their self-concepts.

Four broad topics are explored in order to understand the process of gender-role identification in early school age: understanding gender, learning sex-role standards, identifying with parents, and establishing a gender-role preference. In this discussion, the term *gender* refers to an inner sense of being male or female, whereas *sex* refers to one's designation as a male or a female, a designation that is typically based on biological characteristics. *Gender role* means all the behaviors, attitudes, and personality traits that a society designates as appropriate or typical for male and female children (Bailey & Zucker, 1995).

Understanding Gender

Understanding gender involves four components that emerge in a developmental sequence from toddlerhood through early school age (Kohlberg, 1966) (see Figure 11.1). The first component is correct use of the gender label. The second component is understanding that gender is stable: If one is a boy, one will grow up to be a man. The third component is gender constancy: Even if a child plays with toys that are preferred by the opposite sex or wears clothes or a hairstyle like those of the opposite sex, he or she will still remain the same sex. The fourth component is the genital basis of gender.

The correct use of the appropriate gender label is the earliest component of gender-role identification to be achieved. The categorization of people as male and female is a natural category, much like the distinction between the

FIGURE 11.1
The development of the gender concept

familiar and the strange or between people and inanimate objects, which we discussed in Chapter 7. Even before the abstract categories *male* and *female* are understood, children learn through imitating parental expressions to refer to themselves as boys or girls. From infancy, parents make continual reference to a child's gender in such sentences as "That's a good boy" or "That's a good girl."

By the age of 2½, children can accurately label other children as boys or girls, and by the age of three they can sort photographs of boys and girls. They are also able to apply gender labels such as *Mommy* and *Daddy*, *brother* and *sister,* and *boy* and *girl* accurately (Leinbach & Fagot, 1986; Thompson, 1975). Children seek out cues that will help them apply these gender labels correctly. Their attention is thereby directed to the differences between males and females.

Understanding gender constancy appears to emerge somewhat later, usually between ages four and seven (Serbin, et al, 1993). A critical feature of understanding gender constancy is understanding the genital basis of gender. In research involving three-, four-, and five-year-olds, the majority of children who understood the genital differences between the sexes could also tell that a child's sex was not changed simply because the child was dressed like a member of the opposite sex. These young children understood that gender is a constant feature of a person, no matter how the person is dressed or whether their hair is long or short. The majority of the children who had no knowledge of genital differences were unable to respond correctly to questions about constancy (Bem, 1989).

Learning Sex-Role Standards

Sex-role standards are cultural and subcultural expectations about appropriate behavior for boys and girls, men and women. As you read this section, you may take issue with the content of the sex-role standards as they are reflected by current measures. There is no doubt that sex-role standards are currently in flux in U.S. society and probably differ from one ethnic subculture to the next. Future research involving children reared in the current and coming decades may find different patterns from those revealed in recently published research. However, you may also be surprised to find how pervasive some of the traditional sex-role standards are, especially as they are reflected in expectations of behavior that are conveyed to young children.

In research involving the construct of sex-role standards, children are usually asked to identify whether certain activities, occupations, or traits are more frequently associated with males, females, or both. As an example, in the Sex-Role Learning Index, U.S. children are shown 20 drawings of objects, 10 of which were traditionally associated with the male sex role (such as hammer, shovel, fire helmet) and 10 with the female sex role (such as iron, stove, dishes). By age seven, most children make a perfect score on this type of test, illustrating that they know fully how their society links gender and activities or occupations (Beere, 1990; Edelbrock & Sugawara, 1978; Serbin et al., 1993). Knowledge of culturally sex-typed personality traits such as gentle and affectionate or adventurous and self-confident emerges somewhat later. In one study of over 550 children, sixth-graders answered about 90% of these questions correctly (Serbin et al., 1993).

Once children recognize, and presumably accept, sex-role standards, these standards begin to shape their preferences and behaviors. For example, once children identify certain toys as more appropriate for girls and others as more appropriate for boys, then their own toy preferences are guided by these standards. Conversely, when they like a toy that is not obviously sex-stereotyped, they are inclined to think that other children of their same sex would like that toy as well (Martin et al., 1995). One consequence of this sex-typed thinking is that it limits a child's willingness to play with certain toys and games and therefore reduces the child's opportunities to learn from a variety of play experiences.

Accompanying sex-role standards are conditional rewards, incentives, and sanctions. Adults not only have expectations of a child in relation to the child's sex but also act to produce compliance with these expectations. The nature of parental influences on children's sex-role stereotyping is very complex (Turner & Gervai, 1995). Some parents believe that boys should be assertive and fight for their rights. Others believe that boys should think carefully about what is right and wrong and guide their actions by reason rather than impulsive aggression. Each of these sets of parents has a conception of male attributes that is communicated to their sons by a variety of means over a long period of time. The toys that parents give their children, the experiences to which they expose them, and the activities in which they encourage them to participate all reflect some dimensions of the parents' sex-role standards. By the time children reach school age, they have been encouraged to adopt those standards and punished for behavior that their parents viewed as gender-inappropriate. Young girls may be shamed for their assertiveness by being told that they are acting "bossy," and young boys may be warned to "stop acting like a sissy."

Current research on gender-role development suggests that, as the cognitive underpinnings related to the concept of gender mature, children form *gender schemes*, or personal theories about cultural expectations and stereotypes related to gender. Children tend to organize their perceptions, focus their attention, and interpret information in such a way as to be consistent with their gender schemes (Bem, 1981; Levy & Carter, 1989; Martin & Halverson, 1987). By kindergarten, both boys and girls recall information that is consistent with their gender stereotypes better than information that is counter to the stereotype or that is more relevant to the opposite sex (Bauer, 1993; Liben & Signorella, 1993). Among children ages 5 to 12, the greater the knowledge of sex-role standards, the greater the preference for same-sex peers and for sex-typed adult activities and occupations (Serbin et al., 1993).

Not all children are equally rigid in applying sex-role standards for themselves or others. Flexibility about the application of sex-role standards for oneself and for others is influenced by both cognitive factors and socialization. Children appear to learn the stereotypes and expectations related to their own gender before learning the expectations for the opposite gender (Martin et al., 1990). Girls are generally more flexible in their thinking about sex-role standards than boys. Early-school-age children are more likely than children aged six and seven to think that gender-role "transgressions," i.e., boys playing with dolls or girls pretending to be firemen, are permissible (Lobel & Menashri, 1993; Smetana, 1986). Children who have more advanced abilities to differentiate between moral norms (like telling the truth) and social norms (like saying "please" and "thank-you") are also less stereotyped in their play activities and toy choices (Lobel & Menashri, 1993). Among five- to ten-year-olds, training in multiple classification skills (sorting objects in more than one category) is associated with more flexible, less stereotyped responses to gender-related tasks (Bigler & Liben, 1992) (see Notebook Page 11.2).

Variations in family environment and the socialization context influence sex-role conceptualization. For example, young boys whose fathers live in the home typically have earlier knowledge of sex-typed roles. However, if these fathers participate in nontraditional activities in the home, sex-typed knowledge is delayed. Children whose mothers are involved in nontraditional tasks develop a more flexible attitude, seeing more activities and occupations as appropriate for both males and females, and they themselves are more flexible in their preferences for activities, occupations, and friends (Serbin, et al., 1993).

Identifying with Parents

In addition to understanding gender and learning the sex-role standards of one's culture, the third component of gender-role identification involves identifying with parents. _Identification_ is the process through which one person incorporates the values and beliefs of another. To identify with someone is not to become exactly identical to that person but to increase one's sense of allegiance and closeness to that person. Through the process of identification, ideals, values, and standards of the family and community become internalized so that they are embraced as part of the individual's own system of beliefs. During early school age, most children admire and emulate their parents. They begin to internalize their parents' values, attitudes, and worldviews. Identification is a major mechanism of socialization in childhood, but it can occur at any point in the life span.

Identification has received a great deal of attention in the psychological literature. The most persistent question raised is why children alter their

IDENTIFICATION-
incorporation of
another's values and
beliefs.
=> ↑ allegiance &
closeness

Learning about Sex-Role Standards

How are a culture's sex-role standards communicated to young children? Where do the images of an ideal boy or girl come from? Spend some time thinking about the sources and content of these images in your own childhood.

1. What do you recall from your childhood as images of an ideal boy and girl (e.g., girls are neat; boys are rough and tumble)? You will probably have sharper memories about the sex-role standards related to your own sex than to those of the opposite sex.

   _____

   _____

   _____

2. What were the sources of those images? What can you recall from your exposure to childhood stories and fairy tales? From pictures in books and magazines? From television? From your religious studies? From your parents' efforts to compare you to other male or female children?

   _____

   _____

   _____

3. As you think about these things now, which of these images do you still apply to your own behavior? Which of the childhood sex-role standards, if any, do you still consider appropriate when thinking about how you should behave as a male or a female?

   _____

   _____

   _____

4. Which of these early sex-role standards have you abandoned? Why?

   _____

   _____

   _____

behavior to become more like one parent or the other. What motives are satisfied in this process? There appear to be four substantially different theories about motives for identification: fear of loss of love, identification with the aggressor, identification to satisfy needs for power, and identification to increase perceived similarity (see Table 11.1).

The *fear of loss of love* is a very primitive motive. It is founded on a child's initial realization of dependence on the parents. A child behaves like a parent in order to ensure a continued positive relationship. Eventually, the child incorporates aspects of the loved one's personality into his or her own self-concept. The child can then feel close to the loved person even when the two are not physically together (Jacobson, 1964). If a child can be like a loved parent, the parent's continuous presence is not required to reassure the child about that love.

Identification with the aggressor was described in detail by Anna Freud (1936). This motive is aroused when children experience some degree of fear of their parents. In order to protect themselves from harm, they perform behaviors that are similar to those they fear. This kind of identification may give children a magical feeling of power as well as decrease the parents' tendency to aggress against them. Parents who see a great deal of similarity between themselves and their children are less likely to threaten or harm them.

Social learning theory focuses attention on a third motive for identification, the *need for status and power* (Bandura, 1977, 1986; Mischel, 1966). Studies of modeling show that children are more likely to imitate the behavior of a model who controls resources in a situation than they are the behavior of a model who is rewarded. The imitative behavior is motivated by a vicarious feeling of power.

Kagan (1958) contributed a fourth motive for identification by suggesting that children behave like their parents in order to increase the *perceived similarity* between them. Children attribute a number of valued characteristics

Note in right margin: MOTIVES FOR IDENTIFICATION

TABLE 11.1

Four Motives for Parental Identification

Motive	Definition
Fear of loss of love	A child behaves like a parent in order to ensure a continued positive love relationship.
Identification with the aggressor	A child behaves like a parent in order to protect himself or herself from the parent's anger.
Identification to satisfy needs for power	A child behaves like a parent in order to achieve a vicarious sense of the power associated with the parent.
Identification to increase perceived similarity	A child behaves like a parent to increase his or her perceived similarity to the parent and thereby to share in the parent's positive attributes.

to their parents, including physical size, good looks, special competencies, power, success, and respect. Children can more readily share these positive attributes when they perceive a degree of similarity between themselves and their parents. There are three principal ways in which children can experience this sense of similarity: (1) by perceiving actual physical and psychological similarities, (2) by adopting parental behaviors, and (3) by being told about similarities by others. Increasing perceptions of similarity promote stronger identifications.

These four motives for identification can operate singly or in combination to promote a child's identification with one or both parents. To the extent that children have opportunities to observe and interact with both parents, they are likely to take on characteristics of both. However, when the matter of gender-role identification is salient, that is, when children think about how they should behave as a male or female, they are likely to focus on the same-sex parent as a primary source of information. In some cases, the same-sex parent is not available for observation and identification. For example, when boys are raised by a single mother, they are likely to identify with other males who play a significant role in their lives, such as grandfathers, uncles, or older brothers. In addition, they are likely to rely heavily on information that they receive from their mothers about qualities that are desirable in boys and men.

Forming a Gender-Role Preference

The fourth component of gender-role identification is the development of a personal preference for the kinds of activities and attitudes that are associated with the masculine or feminine gender. Preferences for sex-typed play activities and same-sex play companions have been observed among preschoolers as well as older children (Caldera et al., 1989; Maccoby, 1988). The attainment of these preferences is a more complex accomplishment than might be imagined. In fact, one's gender-role preference may fluctuate throughout life.

Gender-role preference depends primarily on three factors. First, the more closely a child's own strengths and competencies approximate the sex-role standard, the more he or she will prefer being a member of that sex. Children vary in the expression of sex-typed behaviors and play preferences during early childhood. Some girls seem to enjoy masculine-typed play activities more than others, and some boys seem to enjoy feminine-typed play activities more than others. A few studies have investigated the subsequent sexual orientation of children who engage in more cross-sex play than is typical. These studies, all involving male children, evaluated play preferences in early childhood and sexual orientation in later adolescence or early adulthood. They have all found that, among boys who showed an unusual degree of cross-sex play preferences and activities, a greater than expected percentage were either bisexual or homosexual in their later adolescence and young adulthood (Green, 1987; Zucker, 1990). The most strongly held interpretation of these findings, although based on a small number of children, is that biological factors at work in the prenatal or early postnatal period guide both early childhood play preferences and later sexual orientation (Bailey & Zucker, 1995). Thus, to some degree, gender-role preference is guided by biological factors that influence the masculinization or feminization of the hormonal environment and the neural structures.

Second, the more that a child likes the same-sex parent, the more that child will prefer being a member of that sex. Retrospective studies, for example, find that there is some tendency for gay men to recall their relationships with their fathers as more distant and their relationships with their mothers as close. No parallel studies examine the relationship of lesbians with their mothers and fathers (Bailey & Zucker, 1995).

The two factors, enjoying sex-typed play activities and having a close relationship with your same-sex parent, begin to have a significant impact on a child's gender-role preference as the self-concept becomes more clearly differentiated. As children enter school and are exposed to the process of evaluation, they begin to have a more realistic sense of their unique qualities. As they acquire this self-reflective ability, they are able to appreciate the similarities and discrepancies between self and (1) the sex-role standard and (2) the same-sex parent (see Box 11.1).

The third determinant of gender-role preference consists of environmental cues as to the value of one sex or the other. The cues can emanate from the family, ethnic and religious groups, media, social institutions (such as the schools), and other culture carriers. Many cultures traditionally have valued males more than females and have given males higher status (Huber, 1990). To the extent that such culturally determined values are communicated to children, males are likely to establish a firmer preference for their gender group, and females are likely to experience some ambivalence toward, if not rejection of, their gender group. In other words, it is easier for children to be happy and content with themselves if they feel highly valued and more difficult if they feel less valued.

Some families develop a strong preference regarding the sex of an expected child. In a sample of over 6,000 married women in the United States, 63% of those who had never had children expressed a preference that their first child be a male and their second a female. Women who considered an even number of children to be ideal wanted to have an equal number of boys and girls. Women who preferred an uneven number of children wanted more sons than daughters (Westoff & Rindfuss, 1974). If the wish for a child of a particular sex is not fulfilled and the parents do not shed their commitment to the "missed" sex, the family may present obstacles to the formation of a positive sex-role preference for the child.

In a longitudinal study of Swedish children from birth to age 25, parents' prenatal preferences for a son or daughter were related to perceived problems in the mother–child and father–child relationships (Stattin & Klackenberg-Larsson, 1991). Mothers' perceptions of problems in the parent–child relationship, especially the relationship between fathers and their nonpreferred daughters, was significantly related to fathers' disappointed hopes for a son. Looking back on their relationships with their parents at age 25, nonpreferred daughters were especially likely to note problems in their relationships with their parents, saying that their mothers did not have time for them and their fathers were stricter with them, had less time for them, and that their relationships with their fathers were, in general, worse than the relationships described by preferred daughters.

Thus, it is possible for children to know what sex they are and what behaviors are expected of that sex and yet wish they were members of the opposite sex. In our own experience, when groups of male and female

BOX 11.1

Children Reared by Gay or Lesbian Parents

A growing number of gay and lesbian couples are rearing children. In most cases, the children were conceived in heterosexual marriages, but then one parent established a lesbian or gay relationship and continued to rear the child. In addition, some lesbian couples have conceived children through artificial insemination, and both lesbian and gay couples have adopted children (Bailey et al., 1995; Flaks et al., 1995). The emergence of this unique family structure provides an opportunity to better understand the process of sex-role socialization and the development of sexual orientation. Many questions about child-rearing environments and child outcomes can be posed. Do parents who have a homosexual orientation differ from heterosexual parents in their parenting strategies or parent-role behaviors? How relevant is a parent's sexual orientation in shaping a child's gender-role identification? One might predict that girls raised by lesbian couples would have a strong identification with female role models but would be less exposed to sex-role stereotypes than girls raised by heterosexual couples. One also might hypothesize that boys raised by gay couples would be more likely to adopt a homosexual orientation, given the opportunity for early identification with men who are supportive of nontraditional sexual preferences. One might wonder whether boys raised by lesbian couples or girls raised by gay couples would have more conflict over their sex-role preferences than children raised by heterosexual couples.

Research has just begun to address some of these issues. Several studies have reported that, when compared with heterosexual couples, lesbian couples exhibit more sensitive parenting and more egalitarian role relationships. Open disclosure of the lesbian relationship, the ability to maintain ties with the rest of the child's family, and a perception that the partners share equally in household and child-care tasks all contribute to the child's emotional well-being (Patterson, 1995). Studies of the well-being and cognitive and emotional adjustment of children growing up with lesbian mothers find no differences between these children and those growing up in heterosexual families. The two groups of children have similar sex-role preferences (Flaks et al., 1995; Patterson, 1992).

One study of the sexual orientation of young men who were raised by gay fathers found that about 90% of the sons whose sexual orientation could be determined were heterosexual (Bailey et al., 1995). This rate suggests that the process of identification with the father does not typically lead to an internalization of the father's sexual orientation. The authors argue that this finding, confirmed by data from other studies, is more supportive of a genetic than an environmental or socialization explanation for sexual orientation among males.

Research in this area is relatively new, and one must approach any conclusions with caution. The published studies are limited to small, volunteer samples who have usually been recruited through public advertisements. Participants are typically white, middle- or upper-middle class couples who are comfortable enough about their children's sexual orientation to be willing to discuss it with researchers. In addition, few studies include comparison groups which would permit a more systematic assessment of the rate of gay or lesbian sexual orientation among children raised by heterosexual parents (Bailey et al., 1995; Baumrind, 1995). Future research with larger, more diverse samples will undoubtedly help to clarify the genetic, environmental, and personal contributions to gender-role identification and sexual orientation.

students were asked whether they ever wished to be the opposite sex, many more females than males admitted to having wished to be of the opposite sex. This observation may reflect some perceived advantages of the male role in our culture or the more serious sanctions against men who value or exhibit behaviors defined as feminine. Or it may reflect the greater flexibility that girls and women exhibit in their gender schemes, permitting them to perceive a wider range of behaviors as desirable and possible.

The four components of acquiring gender-role identification—(1) developing an understanding of gender, (2) learning sex-role standards, (3) identi-

TABLE 11.2

Dimensions of Gender-Role Identification

Dimension	Gender-Role Outcome
Developing an understanding of gender	I am a boy; I will grow up to be a man.
	I am a girl; I will grow up to be woman.
Acquiring sex-role standards	Boys are independent; they play with trucks.
	Girls are interpersonal; they play with dolls.
Identifying with the same-sex parent	I am a lot like Daddy. I want to be like him when I grow up.
	I am a lot like Mommy. I want to be like her when I grow up.
Establishing a gender-role preference	I like being a boy. I'd rather be a boy than a girl.
	I like being a girl. I'd rather be a girl than a boy.

fying with parents, and (4) forming a gender-role preference—are summarized in Table 11.2. The outcome of the process for an individual child depends greatly on the characteristics of his or her parents and their approach to sex-role socialization, personal capacities and preferences, and the cultural and familial values placed on gender.

A child's gender-role identification becomes a basic cognitive scheme that influences the interpretation of experiences (Bem, 1981; Martin, 1989). Children learn that people are grouped into two sexes, males and females. In our society, this dichotomy tends to impose itself in a wide array of social situations, including home, work, and play. Once children have this powerful scheme, they go about the business of figuring out how to apply it. They recognize people as boys and girls, men and women, and they identify themselves as members of one of these groups. They form expectations based on this conceptualization that certain toys, interests, and behaviors are appropriate for boys and others are appropriate for girls; certain activities, dispositions, and occupations are appropriate for men and others for women. These expectations are generally reinforced by the beliefs of the older boys and girls, men and women with whom they interact. Thus, the gender schemes that are conceived during childhood shape the direction of a child's daily activities and contribute to a preliminary vision of the future.

[margin note: gender role identification influences interpretation of experience.]

Early Moral Development

Morality, the ability to judge right and wrong and to act accordingly is another major conceptual scheme that serves as an organizing principle during the early-school-age period. Early moral development involves a process called *internalization,* which means taking society's standards and values as one's own. Internalization takes place gradually over the early-school-age years. During toddlerhood, a child's attention is focused on the limits of and

INTERNALIZATION
taking standards
& values of society
& making them
your own.

standards for behavior. Children feel that demands for proper behavior do not come from within themselves but from elements of the external world. As we discussed in Chapter 9, the precursors of moral development in toddlerhood can be seen in the child's capacity to comply with parental requests and to control unacceptable or destructive impulses. During the early-school-age period, standards and limits become part of a child's self-concept. Specific values, acquired from parents, teachers, and other adults, become integrated elements of a child's worldview.

A three-year-old boy, for example, may take great delight in hitting his dog with a stick. In the midst of one of these attacks, his mother scolds him. She insists that he stop and explains that it is cruel to hurt the dog. If her punishment is not very harsh, she may have to remind the boy on several other occasions that hitting the dog is not permitted. As the boy internalizes this standard, he begins to experience internal control over his own behavior. He may see the dog lying calmly in the sun and, with a gleam in his eye, start to pick up a stick. At that moment, his behavior is interrupted by a feeling of tension, which is accompanied by the thought that it is wrong to hit the dog. If the standard has been successfully internalized, the emotional tension and the thought that hitting the dog is wrong will be sufficient to inhibit the boy from performing the act.

ACHIEVEMENTS IN MORAL
DEV'T:
① knowing "moral
code" of conduct
in community.
② experience of various
emotions
③ acting to inhibit
negative impulse

For early-school-age children, achievements in moral development include the following:

1. *Knowledge.* Learning the moral code of one's community and using it to make judgments about whether something is good or bad, right or wrong.
2. *Emotions.* Experiencing the array of emotions that foster caring about others and that produce anxiety, guilt, and remorse when a moral standard has been violated.
3. *Actions.* Taking appropriate actions to inhibit negative impulses or to give help and act in a prosocial manner when the situation calls for it.

There are a variety of theoretical explanations for how these domains of knowledge, emotion, and action evolve to produce the internalized moral behavior that we consider appropriate for the early-school-age child. In the following sections, we present the basic concepts from learning theory, cognitive developmental theory, and psychoanalytic theory that have been applied to the development of morality in childhood. These theoretical analyses are followed by a discussion of research on the contributions of empathy, perspective taking, and parental discipline to moral development.

Learning Theory

BEHAVIORAL
behavior influenced
by rewards and
punishments

Behavioral learning theory provides explanations for shaping moral behavior. Within this theoretical perspective, one can view moral behavior and the process of internalization as a response to environmental reinforcements and punishments (Aronfreed, 1969). Moral behaviors, like other operant responses, are shaped by the consequences that follow the behavior. A positive, prosocial behavior, like offering to help put toys away or comforting another child who is distressed, is likely to be repeated if it is rewarded. If a behavior is ignored or punished, it is less likely to occur. If a child performs a misdeed or defies authority and suffers negative consequences, the likelihood is that such behavior will not recur. If a child is in an unpleasant or painful environment and performs a behavior that reduces or eliminates the unpleasantness, he or she is more likely to perform this same behavior again in similar situations. For example, if a child says, "I'm sorry, I'll try to do better next time," and this apology reduces the parent's anger, this behavior is likely to be repeated at other times when the parent is angry at the child. Internalization may result, therefore, as behaviors that lead to a more comfortable and pleasant or less threatening environment become more common and the behaviors that produce parental anger or conflict disappear.

Avoidance conditioning is often viewed as a paradigm for understanding the concept of internalization in behavioral terms. A child who has been punished in the past for wrongdoings is likely to experience tension when he or she thinks about performing a misdeed. Avoiding or inhibiting the impulse to misbehave reduces the tension and is therefore reinforcing. This process can take place even when the caregiver who administered the punishments is absent. In other words, the scenario of thinking about a wrong or naughty action, feeling the anxiety that is associated with past punishments, and reducing that anxiety by exercising restraint can take place mentally without any observable behavior. Over time, the reinforcement of tension reduction that is linked to controlling an unacceptable impulse strengthens the tendency to inhibit the impulse, and the child's behavior becomes less and less impulsive.

avoidance conditioning

Social learning theory offers another source of moral learning: the observation of models. By observing and imitating helpful models, children can learn prosocial behavior. By observing the negative consequences that follow the misdeeds of models, children can learn to inhibit misbehavior. Their moral behavior is not limited to the actions they have performed. It can be based on expectations formulated from observations of the rewarded or punished conduct of relevant models (Bandura, 1977). If a respected older brother is punished for lying, the younger brother may develop the expectation that lying leads to negative consequences. Children may formulate abstract rules, concepts, and sets of propositions about moral behavior by extracting meaningful elements from several incidents of observational learning. In the process, a child forms a mental representation by selecting and organizing observed responses and uses this mental model to guide, compare, and modify moral behavior (Bandura, 1991).

SOCIAL observation

Finally, cognitive learning theory describes how moral behavior is influenced by the interaction of situational factors and expectancies, values, and goals that have been derived from earlier learning (Mischel, 1973). For example, some people place great value on success in athletics and so may be more tempted to violate rules in order to succeed in an athletic competition than in an academic setting. The expectation that a misdeed will be observed and punished leads to greater resistance to temptation than does the expectation that a misdeed will go unnoticed. Similarly, the expectation that positive, prosocial behaviors are valued and will be noticed influences a child's generosity and helpfulness (Froming, Allen & Jensen, 1985). These factors suggest that, although a general moral code may be internalized through consistent reinforcement of empathetic, sensitive, and just responses, a child's assessment of the specific situation also influences the extent to which moral behavior is displayed (Carroll & Rest, 1982).

COGNITIVE interaction of situation & expectation

Cognitive-Developmental Theory

Cognitive-developmental theorists have focused on the orderly development of a child's thoughts and reasoning about moral issues. Piaget (1932/1948) described the major transition in moral judgment as a shift from heteronomous to autonomous morality. With *heteronomous morality*, rules are understood as fixed, unchangeable aspects of social reality. During early school age, children's moral judgments reflect their subordination to authority figures. Young children are being told what is right or wrong by powerful adults. They do not have much of an opportunity to argue about this or to view these decisions from any perspective other than that of their family. As a result, an act is judged as right or wrong depending on the letter of the law, the amount of damage done, and whether or not the act was punished. With the shift to *autonomous morality*, children begin to understand that rules are products of cooperative agreements. An autonomous view of moral judgments occurs as a result of a child's participation in a variety of social roles and an egalitarian relationship among friends.

Expanding upon this view, cognitive-developmental theorists have described a sequence of stages of moral thought (Damon, 1980; Gibbs, 1979; Kohlberg, 1976). Moral judgments change as children become increasingly skillful at evaluating the abstract and logical components of a moral dilemma. At the core of these changes is the mechanism of *equilibration*. Children base their moral reasoning on certain principles and logical assumptions. From time to time, they encounter situations in which these principles do not seem appropriate or another person reaches a different conclusion about what would be fair or just. This places the child in disequilibrium. At this point, children are open to considering new justifications and a new logic in order to reach a judgment about which is the moral course of action.

Consider the following example. Linda is five. Her mom has told her many times that telling the truth is very important and that it is not right to tell lies. This is the rule, and Linda knows that her mother will punish her if she lies. So Linda tells the truth in order to avoid getting punished. Then one afternoon, Linda and her mom are visiting Linda's cousins. One of the cousins just bought a new outfit, and she is showing off for everyone, saying "Isn't this beautiful? Don't you love my new outfit?" Linda thinks the clothes look silly and says so. Her mother gets very angry and tells Linda that it was wrong to hurt her cousin's feelings. "But Mom, you told me to tell the truth, so I did," says Linda. Now Linda has two rules—don't lie and don't hurt people's feelings—which can sometimes be in conflict. She is in disequilibrium: The single scheme regarding moral behavior, don't lie, is no longer adequate to guide her moral behavior. Since Linda's mother is still in charge of her and is likely to know best, Linda decides that she will try to pay closer attention to what her mother thinks is right and wrong, believing that, if she can act as much like her mother as possible, she will be acting properly.

Stage changes in moral reasoning are associated with efforts to reconcile new perspectives and ideas about basic moral concepts such as justice, intentionality, and social responsibility with existing views about what is right and wrong. Children's reasoning can be thrown into disequilibrium through external sources, such as parental use of explanations and inductions regarding a moral dilemma, or encounters with friends who reason differently about a moral conflict. In addition, a child's own cognitive maturation, especially the

[handwritten margin notes:]
heteronomous morality- belief that rules are fixed & unchangeable
↓
autonomous morality- rules part of cooperative agreements

Equilibriation- reasoning based on principles and assumptions

ability to think abstractly and hypothetically about interrelated variables, determines how reasoning about moral dilemmas will be structured (Piaget, 1975/1985; Walker, 1988).

Kohlberg (1969, 1976) described three levels of moral thought, each characterized by two stages of moral judgment (see Table 11.3). At level I, *preconventional morality*, stage 1 judgments of justice are based on whether a behavior is rewarded or punished. Stage 2 judgments are based on an instrumental view of whether or not the consequences will be good for "me and my family." The first, and, to some degree, the second stages of level I characterize children of early school age. Level II, *conventional morality*, is concerned with maintaining the approval of authorities at stage 3 and upholding the social order at stage 4. Level III, *postconventional morality*, brings an acceptance of moral principles that are viewed as part of a person's own ideology rather than simply imposed by the social order. At stage 5, justice and morality are determined by a democratically derived social contract. At stage 6, a person develops a sense of universal ethical principles that apply across history and cultural context.

Research indicates that stage 6 reasoning is rarely achieved, and very few people function at this level consistently. One can think of a few individuals, such as Mahatma Gandhi, Mother Theresa, and Martin Luther King, Jr., whose moral judgments were based on ethical principles that apply across time and culture, transcending the laws and conventions of a specific society. Kohlberg (1978) admitted the rarity of this type of thinking and argued that

TABLE 11.3

Stages of Moral Judgment

Level I: Preconventional

Stage 1	Judgments are based on whether behavior is rewarded or punished.
Stage 2	Judgments are based on whether the consequences result in benefits for self or loved ones.

Level II: Conventional

Stage 3	Judgments are based on whether authorities approve or disapprove.
Stage 4	Judgments are based on whether the behavior upholds or violates the laws of society.

Level III: Postconventional

Stage 5	Judgments are based on preserving social contracts based on cooperative collaboration.
Stage 6	Judgments are based on ethical principles that apply across time and cultures.

Source: Based on Kohlberg, (1969, 1979).

stage 6 reasoning was more of a hypothetical construct to which moral reasoning might progress. Most of the research in this area has included children, adolescents, and young adults as subjects. From a psychosocial perspective, it is reasonable to conclude that stage 6 reasoning may only begin in middle adulthood, when people become preoccupied with issues of generativity and concerns that transcend their own lifetime.

Research on movement through the stages suggests that they reflect a developmental sequence. People do not necessarily use only one level of moral reasoning at a time. Over time, however, there is a gradual shift toward the maximum use of one perspective and the decreasing use of less mature views (Carroll & Rest, 1982; Kohlberg, 1979; Rest, 1983). The process of movement from one stage to the next appears to involve a period of consolidation, followed by a period of transition (Snyder & Feldman, 1984; Walker & Taylor, 1991a). During consolidation, most people use one modal stage of reasoning, with some reasoning at one stage below and very little at one stage above the mode. In a period of transition, reasoning changes in the direction of the next more advanced stage and becomes more evenly divided between two adjacent stages, with more reasoning occurring at the more advanced stage over time.

This theory of moral development gives rise to the expectation that early-school-age children will function at a preconventional stage and that their reasoning about moral situations will be dominated by concerns regarding the consequences of their behavior. At stage 1, judgments of good and bad, right and wrong, are based on whether a behavior has been rewarded or punished. At stage 2, moral judgments are based on whether the behavior brings about benefits for the child or for other people the child cares about. Thus, the young child's moral outlook has a utilitarian orientation (Kohlberg, 1976). Research with first-graders confirms that this outlook is quite common, whether children are discussing hypothetical moral dilemmas or real-life moral situations (Walker, 1989).

Behavior linked to moral principles

The preoccupation with consequences highlights the significance of the home and school environments for establishing and supporting a young child's moral code. In order to build a basis for making moral judgments, children need to understand the consequences of their behaviors for others. One can appreciate why inductions—explanations that emphasize the effects of a child's actions on others—are such a key disciplinary method for young children. In addition, the moral climate of the home and school provides the early content of the moral code. Behaviors that are linked to moral principles, such as telling the truth, respecting the feelings of others, and being respectful of authority figures, are woven into a child's concepts of right and wrong. The clarity of this moral code depends on the consistency with which positive examples lead to positive outcomes and negative examples lead to negative outcomes (Garrod, 1993) (see Notebook Page 11.3).

Moral Transgressions Versus Social Convention Transgressions

Not all rules or prohibitions have to do with moral concerns. There is a difference between the moral domain, which usually involves the rights, dignity, and welfare of others, and the domain of *social convention*, which involves socially accepted norms and regulations (Turiel, 1983). For example, in the preschool context, a moral transgression would involve stealing another child's toy; a transgression of social convention would be getting up and wan-

Imparting a Moral Code

Imagine that you are responsible for guiding the moral development of a young child. Think about what moral principles you believe are essential for a child aged four to six to learn.

1. What are three or four basic moral principles that you believe a child of four to six ought to begin to internalize? Examine your own reasons for placing such a high value on each of these principles.

Moral Principle	Reason That It Is Important
a.	
b.	
c.	
d.	

2. Now go back to each principle that you listed above and think about how you would help a young child to internalize it. For example, what might you say or do; what discipline strategies might you use; what stories, fantasy games, or problem-solving situations might you pose in order to help a child understand why these principles are important and to which situations or conditions they apply?

Moral Principle	Ideas for Helping a Child Internalize This Principle
a.	
b.	
c.	
d.	

471

moral transgressions hurt others while social-convention transgressions create disruption.

dering away during large-group time. Preschool-age children are consistently able to differentiate between moral and social-convention transgressions. They understand that moral transgressions negatively affect the welfare of others, but social-convention transgressions are disruptive or create disorder (Smetana, 1985).

Social-convention transgressions depend on the situation. At home, it might be permissible to get up from the table during dinnertime before everyone has finished eating and go off to play, whereas it is not permissible to get up from the snack table at preschool until the teacher says that everyone may leave. Moral transgressions apply more consistently across settings: It is morally wrong to steal at home, at preschool, or at a friend's house. It is significant that children as young as three and four make this distinction when they evaluate transgressions. In addition, in contrast to social-convention transgressions, young children tend to judge moral transgressions as being more serious, deserving greater punishment, and transcending the rules or authority in a particular situation (Smetana et al., 1993).

Psychoanalytic Theory

internalization of factors that contribute to control of temptation.

The focus of the psychoanalytic theory of moral development is on the internalization of values and the factors that sustain impulse control under conditions of temptation. You will recall from Chapter 4 that, according to psychoanalytic theory, personality is comprised of three distinct structures: id, ego, and superego. The *superego* includes moral precepts, often referred to as the conscience, and ideals about how a moral person ought to behave, referred to as the ego ideal. Both of these aspects of the superego are formed as a result of parental identification. Motivated by love, fear, and admiration, children actively imitate and incorporate their parents' characteristics and internalize their parents' values.

superego formed by parental identification

Classical psychoanalytic theory holds that the superego is formed during the phallic stage, between the ages of about four and seven, as a result of the conflict between internal sexual and aggressive impulses and parental treatment of the behavioral manifestations of those impulses. Once the superego is formed, it becomes the guardian of those internalized values. It monitors id impulses and ego's efforts to satisfy those impulses, sounding the alarm, usually in the form of anxiety or guilt, if the acceptable code of conduct is likely to be violated, and motivating sentiments of pride when ego performs in morally admirable ways. Freud suggested that the normal superego is harsh and inflexible, developed as it is within the context of an early-school-age child's cognitive structures. Thus, children at this age focus on bold distinctions between right and wrong, giving little consideration to intentions or circumstances that might alter one's interpretation of an act.

superego forms basis of personality and mental life

Once the superego is in place, an ongoing dynamic is set into action which forms the basis of personality and mental life. Id impulses strive for expression, ego tries to identify effective means of satisfying those impulses, and superego determines whether or not ego's solutions are acceptable. Ego must have the energy and resources to find flexible, satisfying, and socially acceptable outlets. An overly powerful id results in behaviors that are viewed as impulsive, self-centered, or antisocial. An overly powerful superego results in severe restrictions in thought and behavior.

According to psychoanalytic theory, the more severely a parent forces a child to inhibit impulses, the stronger the child's superego will be. Freud

(1925/1961) assumed that males would develop more highly differentiated and punitive superegos than females because he believed that males' impulses are more intense. He also believed that, because of the greater impulsive energy demonstrated by males, boys would be treated more harshly by their parents than would girls. Finally, Freud suggested that males identify with the father for two reasons: fear of losing the father's love and fear of the father as an aggressor. The identification with the father is an intense one and should lead to a fully incorporated set of moral standards. According to Freud, a female identifies with her mother for a single reason: fear of loss of love. Since Freud considered this motivation for identification to be less intense than that of the male, he believed that the female's superego would be correspondingly weaker.

Research on the Development of Conscience

Research on the development of conscience has failed to support many of Freud's hypotheses about the nature of the superego. Studies that have investigated the ability to resist temptation or to confess after wrongdoing have found that young girls, who are better able to resist temptation than boys, show a pattern of decreasing moral transgressions over the toddlerhood and early school years (Mischel et al., 1989). Studies that have attempted to assess the relative contributions of mothers and fathers to children's moral behavior have found that mothers' values and attitudes are strongly related to the moral behavior of their male and female children, whereas the values and attitudes of fathers show little relationship to their children's moral behavior (Hoffman, 1970). Finally, studies that have explored the relationship between parental discipline techniques and moral behavior have found that the children of parents who employ harsh physical punishment do not have higher levels of internalized moral standards. They are likely to inhibit impulsive behaviors in the presence of their parents, but when they are observed with peers away from home they tend to be physically aggressive and do not control their behavior well (Hart et al., 1990; Pettit et al., 1988). In contrast to Freud's emphasis on the strictness of parental discipline, research suggests that parental warmth, deemphasis on power assertion, democratic decision making, and the modeling of resistance to temptation all contribute to high levels of prosocial behavior and social responsibility (Kochanska, 1991; Maccoby, 1992).

Neopsychoanalytic Theory

These findings raise doubts about Freud's views on the formation of conscience and the relative strength of the superego in males and females. In fact, psychoanalytic theory now sets the critical time for the beginnings of moral development in infancy rather than in early school age (Kohut, 1971; Mahler, 1963). Infants develop an awareness of three domains: the body and its physical experiences and needs, the existence of others, and the relations between the self and others (Beit-Hallahmi, 1987). All subsequent psychological growth must be assimilated into these three domains. Thus, according to this view, the origins of moral reasoning and behavior have links to very early feelings about the self and its needs, especially feelings of pleasure and pain. Morality has a basis in awareness of others who are valued in a young child's life and of behaviors that strengthen or threaten the bonds between the self and others. This view suggests that some basis of early morality lies in the child's own sense of self-love, a wish to enhance and not harm or violate the self. Another basis is the extension of this self-love to the other and the wish to preserve the feelings of connection, trust, and security that have been established in the early parent–infant relationship. The moral aspect of the self is built on the close, affectional bond with the caregiver, including the positive feelings of empathy and connectedness that emerge in this early relationship and the internalization of early prohibitions that are accompanied by emotional signals such as anger and disapproval (Emde et al., 1987; Emde et al., 1991).

Freud's work remains a significant contribution to the area of moral development because he drew attention to the powerful role of the superego and the ego ideal in motivating and inhibiting behavior. He also pointed to the key role that parents play in establishing moral beliefs in early childhood. However, his description of the process whereby parental values are incorporated into a child's moral code appears to be faulty. Most likely, Freud underestimated the power of the need to reassure oneself about parental love. The strong affectional bonds between a parent and a child are the most effective forces in promoting positive moral behavior. Freud's analysis of gender differences in morality reflected a cultural stereotype that characterized men as more rational, logical, and in control of their emotions and impulses than women. Women were portrayed as temptresses, distracting men from their responsibilities and luring them into immoral behaviors. In contrast to this characterization, it appears that, in general, boys have more difficulty controlling their impulses than girls. Girls are more attuned to the implications of their actions for others than are boys, thus leading to a greater ability on the part of girls to resist temptation.

Research on Empathy and Perspective Taking

None of the theories discussed above focused specifically on children's capacity to recognize and care about the emotional distress that their actions might cause another person. The achievement of empathy and perspective taking add another dimension to understanding moral development in childhood.

Empathy

Empathy has been defined as sharing the perceived emotion of another, as "feeling with another" (Eisenberg & Strayer, 1987, p. 5). This definition emphasizes one's emotional reaction to the observation of another person's emotional condition. Children can identify another person's emotion and feel it personally by observing facial expressions, body posture, and vocalizations. The range of emotions with which one can empathize depends on the clarity of the other person's cues and on one's own prior experiences.

The capacity for empathy changes with development. Hoffman described four levels of empathy, especially in reference to the perception of another person's distress:

Global empathy. You experience and express distress as a result of witnessing someone else in distress. *Example:* A baby cries upon hearing the cries of other infants.

Egocentric empathy. You recognize distress in another person and respond to it in the same way you would respond if the distress were

[handwritten margin note: ability to share anothers emotions]

Marcus demonstrates his capacity for perspective taking. He doesn't have any trouble zipping up his coat, but he knows that his younger sister does, so he is glad to help her.

your own. *Example:* A toddler offers his own cuddle blanket to another child who is crying.

Empathy for another's feelings. You show empathy for a wide range of feelings and anticipate the kinds of reactions that might really comfort someone else. *Example:* A child sees another child crying because his favorite toy is broken. She offers to help fix the toy.

Empathy for another's life conditions. You experience empathy when you understand the life conditions or personal circumstances of a person or group. *Example:* A child learns of children in another town who have become homeless after a flood. The child asks his mother if he can send some of his clothes to the children in that town (Hoffman, 1987).

The capacity for empathy thus begins in infancy and evolves as a child achieves new levels of understanding about the self and others and a greater capacity to use language to describe emotions. Very young children appear to be able to recognize and interpret others' auditory and facial cues to emotions. In the newborn nursery, when one infant starts to wail, the other infants begin to cry (Martin & Clark, 1982; Sagi & Hoffman, 1976). Three- and four-year-olds can recognize the emotional reactions that children might have to specific problem situations. Both American and Chinese children were able to recognize "happy" and "unhappy" reactions by age three. The differentiation among "afraid," "sad," and "angry" developed slightly later. The specific cues for these feelings were linked to cultural patterns of expressing emotions. Nevertheless, it was clear that the youngest children in both cultural groups had the capacity to recognize emotional states in another person (Borke, 1973).

In addition to being able to recognize another's emotions, early-school-age children can usually identify the circumstances that may have produced a child's emotional response, especially anger and distress. Children are most likely to think that external events produce emotional reactions: "The teacher made her put her toys away" or "He tripped over the blocks." But they can also think about internal states that may produce strong emotions: "He's mad because he didn't get a turn" or "She's sad because her stomach hurts" (Fabes et al., 1988; Fabes et al., 1991; Hoffner & Badzinski, 1989).

The ability to identify pleasurable and unpleasurable emotions in others and to empathize with those emotions makes the child receptive to moral teachings. Empathy can serve a proactive function by enlisting a child's efforts to help another person. It can also serve a reactive function by generating remorse for having caused a negative emotional state in another person. In either case, empathy allows the child to experience how the other person feels, and therefore to be willing to modify his or her own behavior in order to reduce or remediate the sad or angry feelings of others (Hoffman, 1987).

Perspective Taking

Another element that expands the capacity for moral development is *perspective taking,* the ability to consider a situation from another person's point of view (Chandler & Boyes, 1982). This faculty requires a recognition that someone else's point of view may differ from one's own. It usually includes the ability to analyze the factors that may account for these differences. When children are able to assess these factors, they can begin to transcend their personal perspective and attempt to look at a situation from another's point of view.

Imagine that a child wants to play with another child's toy. If the child thinks, "If I had that toy, I would be happy, and if I am happy, everyone is happy," then the child may take the toy without anticipating that the other child will be upset. Although empathy provides an emotional bridge that enables a child to discover the similarities between self and other, it does not teach a child about differences. This requires perspective taking. Several psychologists have argued that, whereas empathy begins in infancy, the capacity to take the perspective of another person is achieved only gradually through peer interaction and peer conflict (Flavell, 1974; Piaget, 1932/1948; Selman, 1971).

Children of four and five frequently exhibit prosocial behavior that shows their understanding of the needs of others. The most common of these behaviors are sharing, cooperating, and helping. Two examples illustrate the nature of this kind of social perspective taking:

> The path of a child with an armload of Playdough was blocked by two chairs. Another child stopped her ongoing activity and moved the chair before the approaching child reached it.
> A boy saw another child spill a puzzle on the floor and assisted him in picking it up. (Iannotti, 1985, 53)

Robert Selman (1980) studied the process of social perspective taking by analyzing children's responses to a structured interview. Children viewed audiovisual filmstrips that portrayed interpersonal conflicts. Then they were asked to describe the motivation of each actor and the relationship among the various performers. Four levels of social perspective taking were described.

At level 1, the youngest children (four to six years old) recognized different emotions in the various actors, but they assumed that all the actors viewed the situation much as they did. The children at level 4 (about 10 to 12 years old) realized that two people can take each other's perspective into account before deciding how to act. Furthermore, they realized that each of those people may view the situation differently from the way they did.

Many moral dilemmas require a child to subordinate personal needs for someone else's sake. To resolve such situations, children must be able to separate their personal wants from the other person's wants. Selman's research suggests that children under the age of ten are rarely able to approach interpersonal conflicts with this kind of objectivity (see Box 11.2).

Research on Parental Discipline

The last contribution to understanding moral development that we will consider comes from the research on parental discipline that was discussed in detail in Chapter 10. In the process of disciplining a child, a parent emphasizes that certain behaviors are wrong and should be inhibited, while other behaviors are positive or desirable and should be repeated. This distinction between good and bad behaviors and the accompanying parental approval or disapproval begin to form the content of the child's moral code.

parental approval/ disapproval sets foundation for the dev't of a childs moral code.

In addition, parents use specific techniques of discipline. Four elements seem to be important in determining the impact of these techniques on the child's future behavior.

1. The discipline should help the child interrupt or inhibit forbidden actions.

   interpret or inhibit

2. The discipline should point out a more acceptable form of behavior so that the child will know what is right in a future instance.

   positive alternatives

3. The discipline should provide some reason, understandable to the child, that explains why one action is inappropriate and the other more desirable.

   reasoning

4. The discipline should stimulate the child's ability to empathize with the victim of misdeeds. In other words, children are asked to put themselves in their victim's place and see how much they dislike the feelings they caused in the other person.

   illustrate empathy

In considering discipline as a mechanism for teaching morality, one becomes aware of the many interacting and interrelated components of a moral act. The discipline techniques that are most effective in teaching morality to children are those that help them control their own behavior, understand the meaning of their behavior for others, and expand their feelings of empathy. Discipline techniques that do not include these characteristics may succeed in inhibiting undesired behavior but fail to achieve the long-term goal of integrating moral values into future behavior.

Kochanska (1991, 1993) has argued that the child's temperament is an often-overlooked factor in determining how effective certain discipline techniques are likely to be. In particular, children who are temperamentally fearful, whose response to novel stimuli is inhibition, and who choose to retain close proximity to their mothers as young children are especially sensitive to

BOX 11.2

Reasoning about Beliefs and Desires

Think about a situation in which a girl brings some candy to school and another child steals the candy. How do children understand this situation? What feelings do they attribute to the victim whose candy was stolen? In order to feel empathy for the victim, children must understand that the victim is going to be unhappy to discover that the candies that she thought were in her pocket are missing. Research with children in the United States has shown that by the age of four or five, children understand that people pursue goals because of their beliefs and that sometimes these beliefs can be mistaken. Children begin to have a sense of another's mind, and they can predict how another person might feel or act by knowing what the other person believes to be true in the situation (Wellman, 1990; Wellman & Bartsch, 1988).

Just how universal is this reasoning, and at what age is it likely to emerge? To what extent is reasoning about another person's beliefs, desires, and emotional reactions related to schooling or specific kinds of cultural socialization? To begin to address this question, Avis and Harris (1991) studied the reasoning of children of the Baka, a hunting and gathering culture of southeast Cameroon. These children do not attend school, and neither the children nor the parents read.

"Baka children spend much of their time at play, often in the miniature play village (Ndabala) behind the main camp; there they practice the arts of hut building, spear shaping, and fire making. They also participate in the practical tasks of camp life" (Avis & Harris, 1991, 461).

The testing situation was conducted by two Baka visitors, Mopfana and Mobissa, who were familiar with many of the children. Each child was brought into the cooking area with his or her mother. The child watched Mopfana cook mango kernels, a special treat for the Baka. Mopfana noted how delicious and tasty these kernels would be. He put the kernels in a bowl, covered them with a lid, and said he would be right back to eat his treat after he went to the men's meeting place to have a smoke. Once he was gone, Mobissa urged the child to play a game by taking the kernels out of the bowl and hiding them. Once the kernels were hidden, Mobissa asked the children three questions:

1. When Mopfana comes back, where will he look for the kernels—in the covered bowl or wherever the child had hidden them?
2. Before Mopfana lifts the lid of the bowl, will his heart feel good or bad?
3. After he lifts the lid, will his heart feel good or bad?

Children in this study ranged in age from almost 3 to 6 years; 17 were in the age range 2.11 to 4.3, and 17 were in the age range 4.4 to 6.1. In each group, 15 of the 17 children hid the kernels appropriately when Mobissa asked them. Only 6 of the younger children but 12 of the older children answered all three of the questions in a way which suggested that they understood how Mopfana's beliefs would guide his actions and how his mistaken beliefs would produce unhappiness.

The increase in competence from the toddler to the preschool period about predicting a person's reactions based on that person's beliefs and desires has been noted in similar studies in China, Japan, the United States, and the United Kingdom. Cultures may differ in how they perceive mental events; nonetheless, it appears that, during early school age, children become increasingly capable of analyzing the link between another person's beliefs and desires and their actions and emotions. This ability is clearly linked to a child's readiness to engage in moral reasoning and to consider the implications of his or her actions for others.

messages of disapproval. For these children, a small dose of parental criticism is adequate to promote moral internalization, and too much power assertion appears to be counterproductive. In contrast, children who are highly active and insensitive to messages of disapproval appear to require much more focused and directive discipline, especially a consistent program of recognizing and rewarding good behaviors while minimizing the situations and stimuli that might provoke impulsive or aggressive actions.

In addition to parental approval or disapproval, parents guide moral development by modeling positive, prosocial behaviors and talking with their children about moral issues. Parents can use scaffolding techniques to expand their child's moral reasoning just as they use scaffolding to advance communicative competence. When raising questions about moral decisions their children are facing, they can introduce new arguments or alternative points of view (Walker & Taylor, 1991b).

The child of early school age is in the process of developing an initial moral code. Five contributions to understanding the development of morality during the early-school-age period are summarized in Table 11.4. Each highlights an essential element of the larger, more complex phenomenon. Learning theory points out that an external reward structure inhibits or reinforces behavior. Cognitive theory suggests that an element of conceptual immaturity characterizes this early phase of moral development. Psychoanalytic theory is especially concerned with the relationship between parental identification and

TABLE 11.4

Contributions to the Study of Moral Development

Conceptual Source	Significant Contributions	Consequences for a Particular Aspect of Moral Development
Learning theory	Relevance of an external system of rewards and punishments	Moral behavior
	Imitation of models	Internalization of a moral code
	Formation of expectations about the reward structure	
Cognitive theory	Conceptual development of notions of intentionality, rules, justice, and authority	Moral judgments
	Stages of moral judgment	Distinction between moral transgressions and social-convention transgressions
Psychoanalytic theory	Parental identification	Internalization of parental values
	Formation of the superego	Experience of guilt
Research on empathy and perspective taking	Ability to experience another's feelings begins very early and changes with age	Empathy heightens concern for others and helps inhibit actions that might cause distress
	Ability to recognize differences in point of view emerges slowly during early school age and middle childhood years	Perspective taking can foster helping and altruism
	Peer conflict, peer interactions, and specific role-taking training all increase perspective-taking skills	
Research on parental discipline	Parents define moral content	Moral behavior
	Parents point out the implications of a child's behavior for others	Moral reasoning
	Creation of a reward structure	Internalization of moral values
	Differential impact of power, love withdrawal, warmth, and inductions	Empathy and guilt

[handwritten margin note: Moral behavior shaped by judgement, cognition, ability to empathize & identification.]

the development of conscience. The work on empathy and perspective taking shows that moral behavior requires emotional and intellectual understanding of the needs of others. These skills help children to appreciate how other children or adults may be experiencing a situation. With this insight, children can modify their own actions so that they can benefit others. Theory and research on parental discipline suggest that moral development is promoted when parents try to increase children's understanding of the implications of their behavior for others. It seems reasonable to conclude that moral behavior involves an integration of moral judgments, cognitions about the reward structure, parental identifications, empathy for others, and cognitions about the needs of others.

Group Play

Although family experiences continue to play the primary role in guiding a young child's construction of the social world, interactions with peers offer important opportunities for physical, cognitive, social, and emotional development. The quality of play expands during the early-school-age period, introducing more complex kinds of games with larger numbers of participants. In addition, children form friendship groups which allow them to sustain more elaborate fantasy play, to experience group conflict and group problem solving, and to encounter varying ideas about the two topics we discussed earlier—gender and morality.

Group Games

[handwritten margin note: fantasies w/ rules and boundaries ↓ shifting roles ↓ reciprocal nature of relationships]

Early-school-age children combine a continuing use of vivid fantasies in play with their newfound need to impose rules and boundaries on their play. Children show interest in group games that are more structured and somewhat more reality-based than the fantasy-based play of toddlerhood. Games like ring-around-a-rosy, London Bridge, and farmer-in-the-dell are examples of early group play. Hide-and-seek and Statue Maker are more complex games of this type. They involve more cognitive complexity, physical skill, and ritual. These group games combine the element of fantasy with an emphasis on peer cooperation. Group play can be seen as a form of play that is transitional between the fantasy play of the toddler and the team sports and other games with rules of middle childhood (Erikson, 1977).

Group games involve a few rules that are simple enough so that a child can effectively complete a game and determine a winner without the help of an adult. Usually, no team concept is involved in these games. A game is played repeatedly so that many children have an opportunity to win. The particular pleasure that children derive from these games seems to result more from peer cooperation and interaction than from the need to be a winner (Garvey, 1977).

Many of these games permit children to shift roles. A child is the hider and then the seeker, the catcher and then the thrower, the statue maker and then the statue. Through group play, children have a chance to experience the reciprocal nature of role relationships. Whereas many of their social roles are fixed—son or daughter, sibling, student—in play with peers, children have opportunities to experience a variety of perspectives (Lee, 1975; Sutton-Smith, 1972).

Tag, in its many forms, is a favorite group game among early school-aged children.

Watching early-school-age children at play, one senses their lively, fun-filled attitude. They use their emerging motor skills, especially running and chasing, dodging and jumping, to tease and trick one another. The minimal structure of the game allows them to experience feelings of mastery. Many of their play actions fill them with a sense of pride that can be observed in their laughter, smiles, and comic expressions.

game structure can lead to feelings of mastery

Friendship Groups

Friendships during early school age are typically based on proximity and the mutual enjoyment of activities. Friendships are maintained through acts of affection, sharing, or collaboration in fantasy or constructive play. By the age of four or five, children who have stable friendships become skilled at coordinating their interactions with their friends, creating elaborate pretend games, and being willing to modify their play preferences so that each member in the friendship group has a chance to enjoy the kinds of play he or she likes best (Park et al., 1993). Children may build a snow fort together, play space adventure with one another, or sleep over at one another's houses. Friendships can be broken by the taking of a toy, hitting, or name calling (Damon, 1977) (see Notebook Page 11.4).

Conflicts among Friends

As we discussed in the section on moral development, young children tend to evaluate situations on the basis of outcomes rather than intentions. Therefore, they are often harsh in assigning blame in the case of negative outcomes. For example, in one study, children were asked how much they should be blamed for a child's getting hurt. The "injury" took place in six different hypothetical situations. In the case of the lowest level of responsibility, a child was accidentally hurt by someone else's toy, but the toy owner did not

Early Friendships

Try to remember one of your earliest friendships—if possible, from the time you were four to six years old. Think about how you came to know this person and what you did together.

1. Describe this friend. What do you remember about her or his physical appearance, temperament, and special abilities?

_____

_____

_____

_____

2. What kinds of things did you do together?

_____

_____

_____

_____

3. What can you remember about how long the friendship lasted? Why did it end?

_____

_____

_____

4. Looking back on all the friendships you have had since early childhood, what was the significance of this particular early childhood friendship for you? In what ways did that friendship influence your approach to new friendships or expectations of a friend?

_____

_____

_____

actually cause the injury. At this low level of responsibility, six-year-olds were more likely than older children or adults to blame themselves for the outcome (Fincham & Jaspars, 1979). Because of the rigid approach to social responsibility at this age, peer play is frequently disrupted by quarrels, "tattling" on others, and hard feelings about injustices.

Even though children appear to be drawn into the active world of peer friendships, this is an uneven, difficult, and often extremely frustrating terrain for many to master. For example, many five- and six-year-olds participate in play fighting. In a study of children's perceptions of play fighting, Italian and British children ages 5, 8, and 11 were surveyed about the differences between real fighting and play fighting (Smith et al., 1992). About half the children liked play fighting, including more boys than girls. But about 80% thought that there was a risk that play fighting could lead to a serious, "real" fight. This might happen if there was an accidental injury, retaliation for an accidental injury, or mean name calling. Five-year-olds said that if play fighting turned into real fighting they would tell an adult. No matter if the other child was a friend or not, they believed that such a transgression had to be handled with a serious intervention by a grown-up. The older children were more likely to forget about it, especially if the other person was a friend.

Sex-Segregated Friendship Groups

One of the most noticeable characteristics of young children's friendship groups is that they are likely to be segregated by sex. When boys and girls are free to choose play companions, they tend to choose others of their own sex. This pattern of same-sex social groupings among children is found not only in the United States but in most other cultures (Edwards & Whiting, 1988). In one longitudinal study, children age 4½ were found playing with same-sex friends about three times more often than with opposite-sex friends. By age 6½, they were 11 times more likely to be playing with same-sex friends (Maccoby & Jacklin, 1987).

The important implication of the formation of same-sex social groups is that boys and girls grow up in quite distinct peer environments (Maccoby, 1988, 1990). Boys and girls tend to use different strategies to achieve dominance or leadership in their groups. Boys are more likely to use physical assertiveness and direct demands; girls are more likely to use verbal persuasiveness and polite suggestions. The verbal exchanges in all-boy groups tend to include frequent boasts, commands, interruptions, heckling, and generally playful teasing. Boys try to top one another's stories and establish dominance through verbal threats. The interactions in all-girl groups tend to include agreement with and acknowledgment of the other person's comments, listening carefully to one another's statements, and talking about things that bind the group together in a shared sentiment or experience. In mixed-sex groups, girls discover that the leadership and interpersonal skills that they have developed in their all-girl groups are not very effective in controlling the behaviors of boys. As a result, their negative views of boys are reinforced, and their tendency to seek all-girl peer interactions increases.

Of course, many young children do form friendships with children of the opposite sex. These friendships can begin as early as infancy or toddlerhood between children who live in the same neighborhood or attend the same day-care center. These friendships seem to be sustained as a result of compatible interests and play preferences and can survive the trend toward seeking same-sex friendships, even during middle childhood (Howes & Phillipsen, 1992).

However, the general tendency to form same-sex friendship groups is an important aspect of social development that is established during the early childhood years and continues into adolescence (Bukowski et al., 1993). Even though a boy and a girl grow up in the same culture, in the same neighborhood, and even in the same family, the social milieus in which the two are embedded have some very distinctive features. Through the development of same-sex friendships, girls and boys learn gender-linked communication strategies. These same-sex friendships also strengthen a child's positive feelings toward and identification with his or her own gender.

Groups and Dyads

In addition to the preference for same-sex friends, boys and girls tend to prefer to interact in different size groups. Early-school-age girls seem to enjoy dyadic interactions over larger group situations, whereas boys seem to enjoy the larger group settings (Benenson, 1993). This is not to say that boys and girls cannot function effectively in both dyadic and larger peer-group situations, but when given their choice, boys tend to prefer the group and girls the dyad. These two configurations, the group and the dyad, provide formats for different opportunities for intimacy, different needs to exercise dominance and control, and different problems in the coordination of action. They provide templates for somewhat different forms of adult social relationships: the dyad associated with intimacy between partners or in parent–child relationships, and the peer group associated with sports teams, work groups, and families.

Self-Theory

The idea of *self* was introduced in the discussion of infancy as we considered the emergence of the self in relation to others through the attachment process and in the infant's ability to categorize objects, including the self. Development of self was further explored in the treatment of the interrelated processes of self-regulated goal attainment and self-control in toddlerhood. In early school age, we consider new facets of the sense of self: the self-theory and self-esteem.

The early-school-age child's self-concept becomes a theory that links a child's ideas about the nature of the world, the nature of the self, and interactions between the two (Epstein, 1973, 1991; Epstein et al., 1993). One's theory about oneself draws on inner phenomena such as dreams, emotions, thoughts, fantasies, and feelings of pleasure or pain. The theory also develops as a result of transactions with and feedback from the environment. As with any set of concepts, a child's maturing cognitive abilities add to the complexity and logic of the self-theory. Further, since the self-theory is based on personal experiences and observations, it is modified throughout life by a person's changing physical and socioemotional competencies, as well as by participation in new roles.

One of the earliest psychological analyses of self-theory was provided by William James (1892/1961). He described the self as comprised of two elements, the "me" and the "I." The "me" is the self as object, including physi-

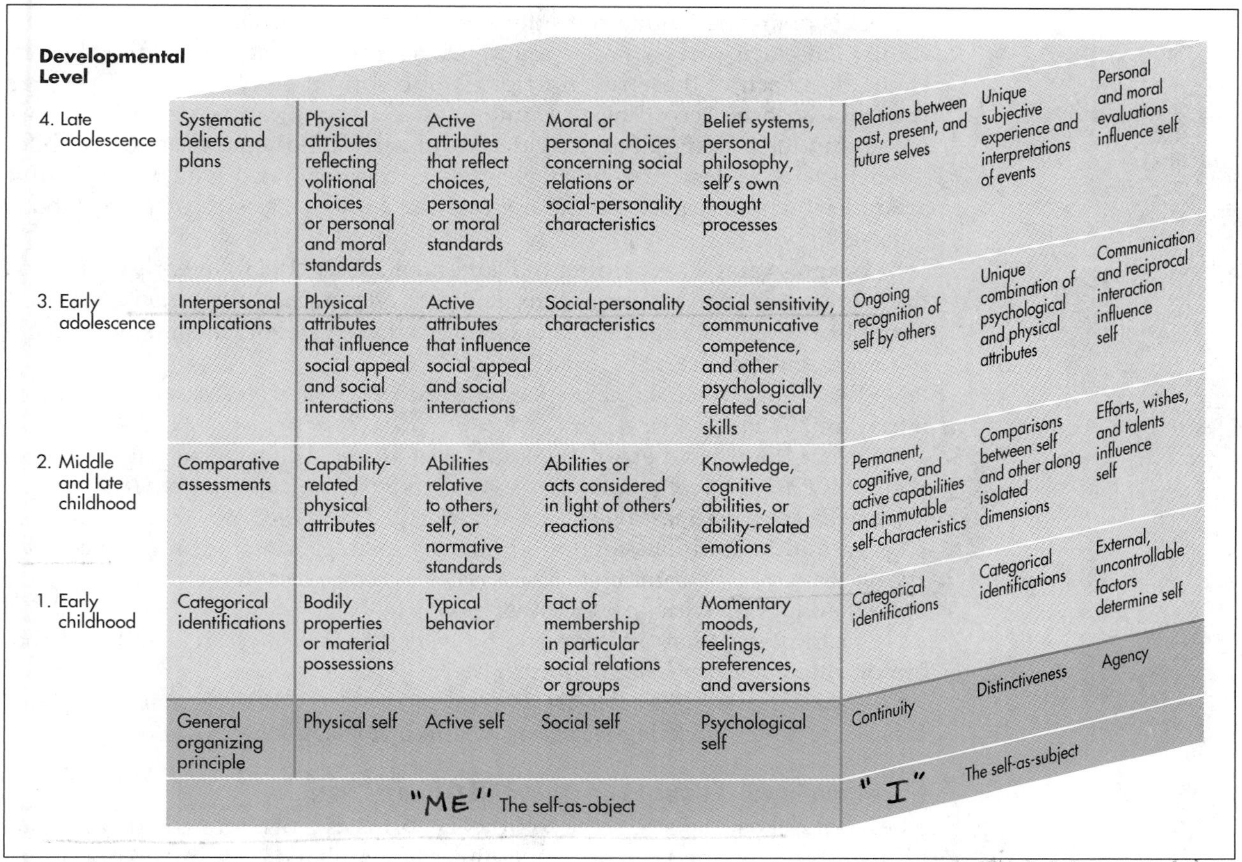

Developmental Level	General organizing principle →	Physical self	Active self	Social self	Psychological self	Continuity	Distinctiveness	Agency
4. Late adolescence	Systematic beliefs and plans	Physical attributes reflecting volitional choices or personal and moral standards	Active attributes that reflect choices, personal or moral standards	Moral or personal choices concerning social relations or social-personality characteristics	Belief systems, personal philosophy, self's own thought processes	Relations between past, present, and future selves	Unique subjective experience and interpretations of events	Personal and moral evaluations influence self
3. Early adolescence	Interpersonal implications	Physical attributes that influence social appeal and social interactions	Active attributes that influence social appeal and social interactions	Social-personality characteristics	Social sensitivity, communicative competence, and other psychologically related social skills	Ongoing recognition of self by others	Unique combination of psychological and physical attributes	Communication and reciprocal interaction influence self
2. Middle and late childhood	Comparative assessments	Capability-related physical attributes	Abilities relative to others, self, or normative standards	Abilities or acts considered in light of others' reactions	Knowledge, cognitive abilities, or ability-related emotions	Permanent, cognitive, and active capabilities and immutable self-characteristics	Comparisons between self and other along isolated dimensions	Efforts, wishes, and talents influence self
1. Early childhood	Categorical identifications	Bodily properties or material possessions	Typical behavior	Fact of membership in particular social relations or groups	Momentary moods, feelings, preferences, and aversions	Categorical identifications	Categorical identifications	External, uncontrollable factors determine self

"ME" The self-as-object   "I" The self-as-subject

cal characteristics, personality traits, social roles and relationships, and thoughts and feelings. The "me" can be described and, to a certain extent, measured; therefore, the "me" is the element that we are most familiar with in developmental research. The "I" is the self as subject, as one who is aware of one's actions, thoughts, and feelings. It can be characterized by four fundamental features (Damon & Hart, 1988):

1. A sense of agency or initiation of behaviors,
2. A sense of uniqueness,
3. A sense of continuity from moment to moment and day to day, and
4. An awareness of one's own awareness—metacognition.

James thought of the "I" as the essential domain through which one experiences a vivid, compelling sense of self-sameness and meaning from day to day. Yet he thought of it as largely unmeasurable. However, building on these ideas and more contemporary research and theory, Damon and Hart (1988) devised a model of self-understanding that is comprised of both the me (self-as-object) and the I (self-as-subject) (see Figure 11.2). The self-as-object, the me, represented along the front face of the cube, is broken down into four fields: physical self, active self, social self, and psychological self. The self-as-

FIGURE 11.2

A developmental model of self-understanding
Source: Damon, W. & Hart, D. (1988). *Self-understanding in childhood and adolescence.* Cambridge: Cambridge University Press, 56. Copyright © 1988 by Cambridge University Press. Reprinted with the permission of Cambridge University Press.

subject is delineated along the side face of the cube, through three fields: continuity, distinctiveness, and agency. Development, shown by the vertical changes in each of these seven fields, is traced from early childhood through late adolescence. According to Damon and Hart, one can recognize evidence for self-understanding in each field even in early childhood. From early childhood to late adolescence, what changes is the general organizing principle around which all aspects of the me and the I are synthesized (see Notebook Page 11.5).

As an example, according to Damon and Hart (1988), in early childhood the self is understood as an accumulation of *categorical identifications*. No additional linkage or significance is taken from these categorical statements, simply a recognition that they exist.

Examples: What kind of person are you? *I have blue eyes.* Why is that important? *It just is.*

What kind of a person are you? *I'm Catholic.* What does that say about you? *I'm Catholic, and my mother is, and my father is, and my grandmother, and my grandfather, and I'm Catholic too* (Damon & Hart, 1988, 59–60).

In middle and late childhood, the organizing principle shifts to *comparative assessments*. Self-understanding relies on comparisons with social norms and standards or with specific other people.

Examples: What are you like? *I'm bigger than most kids.* Why is that important? *I can run faster than everybody.*

What are you like? *I'm not as smart as most kids.* Why is that important? *It takes me longer to do my homework* (Damon & Hart, 1988, 62–63).

Developmental Changes in the Self-Theory

At each psychosocial stage, the self-theory forms as a person's cognitive capacities and dominant motives encounter stage-related cultural expectations (Stipek et al., 1992). In the first year of life, the self primarily consists of an awareness of one's independent existence. The baby discovers body boundaries, learns to identify recurring need states, and feels the comfort of loving contact with caregivers. During the second year, self-recognition and the evolving sense of being as a causal agent add new dimensions to the child's self-theory. Gradually, these experiences are integrated into a sense of the self as a permanent being who has an impact on the environment, existing in the context of a group of other permanent beings who either do or do not respond adequately to the infant's internal states.

In toddlerhood, the self-theory expands through an active process of self-differentiation. Children explore the limits of their physical, cognitive, social, and emotional capacities and the nature of their impact on others. Because of toddlers' inability to entertain abstract concepts and their tendency toward egocentrism (the perception of oneself as the center of the world) their self-theories are likely to depend on being competent and being loved. There is little recognition of social comparisons, being better or worse than someone else, but increasing sensitivity to the positive and negative reactions of others. By the age of 3½ or 4, children seem to understand the idea of competition in a game, and they seem to take pleasure in winning as well as to experience some disappointment in losing. However, the extent to which they actually reflect on the self, make judgments of their strengths and weaknesses, or distinguish among various arenas of competence is unclear (Emde & Buchsbaum, 1990).

[handwritten marginal note: cognitive capacity & motives encounter expectations & lead to dev't of self-theory.]

A Model of Self-Understanding

Refer to the developmental model of self-understanding created by Damon and Hart (1988) in Figure 11.2. Create an imaginary child who is in the early-school-age years. Fill in each of the cells in the model, the four dimensions of the self-as-object and the three dimensions of the self-as-subject, for this child. Try to build a consistent picture of a unique child, emphasizing categorical answers to the question: What kind of person are you?

1. Physical self: _____

_____

2. Active self: _____

_____

3. Social self: _____

_____

4. Psychological self: _____

_____

5. Sense of continuity: _____

_____

6. Sense of distinctiveness: _____

_____

7. Sense of agency: _____

_____

How easy or difficult was it for you to complete this task? Did you find yourself wanting to use more mature levels of understanding, such as comparative assessments (e.g., I am smarter than my friends) or interpersonal implications (e.g., People like me because I am a good listener)? Once you have become accustomed to defining yourself in more abstract, interpersonal, and ideological dimensions, it can be very difficult to think of the self in such concrete, categorical terms.

E.S. Age

realself vs.
   idealself

During early school age, the self-theory is modified further through processes of categorization and evaluative judgments. Children can distinguish between the real self (how one actually is) and the ideal self (how one would like to be). They can recognize some discrepancies between how they describe themselves and how their parents or friends might describe them (Oosterwegel & Oppenheimer, 1993).

During the period from four to six, children become more aware of the differences in perspective among people. An understanding of logical relations contributes to an appreciation of the concept of cultural norms: If one is in a certain role, one is expected to act in a certain way. Sex-role standards are especially important in this regard. Children are very sensitive to any implication that they are not living up to others' expectations for how a boy or girl ought to act. Children are also aware of moral imperatives that define good and evil. All these cognitive gains make a child more responsive to social pressure, more likely to experience feelings of guilt or failure, and more preoccupied with issues of social comparison, self-criticism, and self-evaluation. At the same time, the child remains largely dependent on adults for material and emotional resources, and therefore highly attuned to positive and negative parental feedback messages. For these reasons, the issue of self-esteem becomes especially salient during the early-school-age years.

Self-Esteem

For every component of the self—the physical self, the social self, or the self as represented by personal aspirations and goals—a person makes an evaluation of worthiness. This self-evaluation, or *self-esteem*, is based on three essential sources:

Basis of
  self-esteem

1. Messages of love, support, and approval from others,
2. Specific attributes and competencies, and
3. The way one regards these specific aspects of the self, both in comparison with others and in relation to one's ideal self (Pelham & Swann, 1989).

Feelings of being loved, valued, admired, and successful contribute to a sense of worth. Feelings of being ignored, rejected, scorned, and inadequate contribute to a sense of worthlessness. These very early affective experiences contribute to a general sense of pride or shame, worthiness or worthlessness, which are captured in global statements that children make about themselves even as young as three or four years of age (Eder, 1989; Eder et al., 1987): "I'm stupid," "I'm a fast swimmer," "I'm a big girl now."

Information about specific aspects of the self comes from experiences of success and failure with daily tasks and when particular aspects of one's competence are challenged. A young child may develop a positive sense of self in one or more domains such as athletics, problem solving, or social skills through the encouraging reactions of others as well as through the pleasure associated with succeeding in each of these areas (Harter, 1985).

Not all abilities are equally valued at home, at school, or by friends. People can believe that they have abilities in some areas but not in those they consider highly important. Others can believe that they have only one or two areas of strength, but they may highly value those areas and believe them to be critically important to overall success. Self-esteem is influenced by the

Doing something well, receiving a trophy for his performance, and being admired by his peers and a younger sibling all contribute to Adam's feelings of positive self-worth.

value that one assigns to specific competencies in relation to one's overall life goals and personal ideals. Thus, it is possible to be a success in the eyes of others and still to feel a nagging sense of worthlessness. Similarly, it is possible to feel proud and confident even though others may not value the activities and traits in which one takes great satisfaction (see Box 11.3).

Feelings of positive self-worth provide a protective shield around the self. A person with a positive, optimistic self-evaluation will likely deflect messages that are negative and incongruent. A person with high self-esteem will explain a failure by faulting the task, the amount of time needed for completion, the other people involved, or the criteria for evaluating success and failure, rather than placing all the blame for failure on his or her own incompetence. People with high self-esteem use a variety of strategies to minimize the importance of negative feedback. They might try to learn from a failure experience, but they do not permit failure to increase doubt about their basic worth. By contrast, people with low self-esteem will see failure as new evidence of their lack of worth (Brown & Gallagher, 1992; Brown & Mankowski, 1993).

Low self-esteem appears to be associated with a lack of clarity about one's essential defining features. For example, a person with low self-esteem may describe herself or himself using contradictory pairs of descriptive terms, seeing the self as both timid and bold or flexible and rigid. This confusion is linked to inconsistency, instability, and lack of confidence about one's essential nature. As a result of this confusion, people with low self-esteem are likely to have difficulty deciding about what social situations to participate in. They are likely to place themselves in situations where they receive contradictory or negative social messages about their worth and thereby expose themselves to even greater confusion (Brockner, 1984; Swann, 1990). For example, Kyle, who has low self-esteem, decided to join in a sports contest because a lot of

Contextual Dissonance and Self-Esteem

Children are influenced by the social groups that immediately surround them. During early school age, children emerge from the continuity of their families and neighborhoods into the more diverse context of school. This new context can complement or contrast with the major social characteristics of the family—specifically, religion, race, and social class. Rosenberg (1979) defined contextual dissonance as the difference between characteristics of one's own primary rearing environment and other environments in which one participates. He studied the impact of contextual dissonance on self-esteem, citing evidence of the negative effects of a dissonant environment. Catholics who had been raised in a non-Catholic neighborhood were likely to have lower self-esteem than those raised in a Catholic one. Similar findings were observed among Protestants and Jews raised in dissonant neighborhoods. Racial dissonance and economic dissonance have also been found to be related to low self-esteem. For example, African-American preschool-age children in an all-African-American Mississippi rural town reportedly had higher self-esteem than did those in a racially mixed Michigan urban area (McAdoo, 1985). The implication of these studies is that self-esteem is bolstered by a feeling of continuity and belongingness. Conversely, experiences of dissonance and lack of fit between personal values or qualities and the qualities valued by the community can result in lowered self-esteem.

Many people are thrust into dissonant situations that undermine a basically positive self-esteem (Setterlund & Niedenthal, 1993). Some examples of circumstances that might lead to disruption in the basic sense of self-worth for specific groups of people include adolescents who move to a new high school where the peer values are discrepant from their home and personal values, immigrants who are viewed as outsiders by the members of their new community, or individuals hired to perform an important leadership role in an organization where other employees have a very different background and training. One might imagine that finding oneself as the only minority child in a classroom of white students or the only female on a soccer team might have similar undermining effects on self-esteem.

the popular children in the class were participating. But Kyle really does not like sports very much. So he has to spend time doing something he does not like and is not very good at, which leads to being further rejected by the other children who make fun of him when he fails. Over time, lack of certainty about one's self is likely to be related to problems with identity achievement and greater vulnerability to negative feedback that increases confusion and produces negative emotions (Baumgardner, 1990; Campbell, 1990; Setterlund & Niedenthal, 1993).

Some scholars have speculated about the possible negative consequences of an unrealistically positive self-esteem. For example, people with high self-esteem seem to deflect failure messages in one area by exaggerating their abilities in another area (Brown & Smart, 1991). This strategy could be viewed as producing an inappropriately grandiose assessment of the self that is not validated by the views of others. Others suggest that parents and teachers can be so intent on providing self-enhancing strategies for children, focusing on building up the "me," that children become indifferent to the plight of others and lose sight of the kinds of positive feelings that are associated with helping others (Burr & Christensen, 1992).

It seems to be very important for children who have low self-esteem or whose self-esteem has declined as a result of recent experiences of failure or loss to develop strategies to enhance self-esteem. This type of intervention might help prevent the occurrence of more serious episodes of depression (Pelham, 1991). However, it is not clear whether it is advisable to take active steps for self-esteem enhancement among children who already possess a healthy, positive sense of self-worth.

Self-Esteem and the Early-School-Age Child

At each life stage, as individuals set new goals for themselves or as discrepancies in competencies become apparent, temporary periods of lowered self-esteem may be anticipated. However, research on self-esteem suggests that early-school-age children may be especially vulnerable to fluctuations in feelings of self-worth (Cicirelli, 1976; Kegan, 1982; Long et al., 1967). Here, we explore some explanations for this particular vulnerability.

Toddlers have been described as highly egocentric. In general, they feel good about themselves and do not differentiate between competence and social approval. Rather, they respond to all positive experiences as evidence of their ultimate importance and value. They are much more likely to react to positive feedback after a success than to negative feedback after a failure (Stipek et al., 1992). They use imitation to increase their own sense of mastery (Butler, 1989).

Toddlers don't differentiate between competence & social approval.

Early-school-age children, by comparison, are increasingly aware of the discrepancy between their own competencies and what they recognize as the skills expected of them by teachers and parents, or those exhibited by older children. They are aware of being evaluated by others. They are also aware of the importance of acceptance by adults and peers outside the family, especially teachers and classmates (Weinstein et al., 1987). These newly valued others may not be as proud of children's skills or as understanding about their limitations as family members are. Girls in the early school years are more critical of their abilities than boys and have lower expectations for success (Butler, 1990; Frey & Ruble, 1987).

Under conditions of peer competition, children begin to experience anxiety about their performance and about the way their abilities will be evaluated in comparison with others (Butler, 1989). At school, for example, young children often make critical comments about one another's work. Criticisms tend to outnumber compliments, and boys more than girls tend to be critical of their peers' work (Frey & Ruble, 1987). The combination of open peer criticism and a heightened emphasis on peer competition can make school an environment in which one's self-esteem is frequently challenged.

Finally, early-school-age children are beginning to achieve a degree of internalization of social norms, including ideals and prohibitions. They apply these norms in a rather strict, rule-bound way, often becoming highly critical of rule violations, whether committed by themselves or by others. Intentions, motives, and special circumstances are less significant to early-school-age children than the overt consequences of behavior. Thus, their newly formed capacity for guilt may lead to heightened anxiety over failure to live up to their moral code.

For all these reasons, the early-school-age child is likely to experience some feelings of depression and worthlessness. This decrease in self-esteem can be seen as a temporary fluctuation. Young children need frequent reassurance from adults that they are competent and loved. They need numerous opportunities to discover that their unique talents and abilities are useful and important and that they can have a positive impact on others. As children's competencies increase, as thought becomes more flexible, and as meaningful friendships are formed, their self-esteem rises.

Chapter Summary

Think about some of Disney's early animated fairy tales—*Cinderella, Snow White and the Seven Dwarfs*, and *Pinocchio*. Each in its own way captures the major developmental tasks of the early-school-age period. Each is a morality play, a struggle between good and evil, in which a child faces society's expectations for what a male or female child should be like. These serious themes, however, unfold within a context of playfulness, humor, and friendship. Cinderella has the companionship of the mice, Snow White frolics with the dwarfs, and Pinocchio seeks out the friendship of the "bad boys" who lure him to a land where children play all day and never work. The tale of Pinocchio is perhaps the most obvious portrayal of the tasks of this period, wherein the struggle to become a "human child" requires that Pinocchio embrace and internalize his "father's" goodness and his society's definition of what a human boy ought to be like. Eventually, through bravery and self-sacrifice, by returning the love that has been shown to him, Pinocchio claims his selfhood as a living human child, not merely a puppet carved of wood.

The tasks of the early-school-age period are closely interrelated. Clarification of the self-concept and the accompanying feelings of self-worth or self-esteem are established within the framework of sex-role expectations, moral standards, identification with parents and other meaningful adults, and playful interactions with peers. Because of the strict rule orientation and categorical thinking that characterize this period, children are likely to assume some basic equivalence between sex-role standards and moral standards. They may feel a moral obligation to uphold sex-role standards, and they may feel guilt if they violate these standards. The development of conscience, with its capacity to reward and punish, is accompanied by a constant inner voice, fueling the sense of self-worth for some children and leaving others with a pervasive sense of guilt.

The years from four to six bring children into contact with a wider social network beyond family, day care, and neighbors. As children interact with peers, they become aware of the variety of perspectives that other children bring to their play. They learn to be more sensitive to the fact that others do not always perceive events as they do. The resulting reduction in egocentrism and the increased feelings of caring about other children as close friends have implications for children's moral reasoning and for their emerging self-concepts. Children begin to think of themselves as liked or disliked by teachers, friends, and classmates. They become more concerned about how their actions affect others and whether other adults and children value them. As a result, they formulate a set of powerful early scripts about fundamental rules that govern their definition of self and their transactions with others. By the age of six, children demonstrate clear evidence of internalizing a broad range of cultural beliefs and values that have been transmitted through identification with family members, teachers, classmates, and friends. They have become the "human children" of their society.

1. Two contrasting explanations for gender differences focus on (a) individual differences, suggesting that gender differences are stable across situations, and (b) constructivism, suggesting that gender differences reflect situational adaptations.

2. Four components of understanding gender in childhood include appropriate use of gender labels, understanding that gender is stable over one's life, understanding that gender is constant despite external changes in activities or clothing, and comprehending the genital basis of gender.

3. During early childhood, children learn culturally endorsed sex-role standards that guide their play preferences as well as their choice of play companions.

4. Identification with parents contributes content to gender-role identification. Four motives for parental identification are fear of loss of love, identification with the aggressor, need for status and power, and a desire to increase perceived similarity.

5. Gender-role preference contributes to gender-role identification. This component is based on the match between one's own personal preferences and the sex-role standards of the culture, as well as on evidence of certain status benefits for one gender over the other.

6. Early moral development involves a process of internalizing society's standards and values as one's own. Morality involves three dimensions: knowledge of the moral code of one's culture, emotions that foster caring about others and remorse over wrongdoings, and moral actions.

7. Learning theory, cognitive developmental theory, and psychoanalytic theory each contribute to our understanding of the processes underlying moral reasoning, caring, and action.

8. Learning theory provides concepts, including avoidance conditioning, observational learning, and the role of expectations, values, and goals in guiding moral behaviors.

9. Cognitive developmental theory suggests a structural maturation in the capacity for making moral judgments. During the early-school-age period, children's moral judgments are likely to be guided by the rewards or punishments for a behavior or an instrumental assessment of the behavior's benefits for the child or the child's loved ones.

10. According to psychoanalytic theory, the superego emerges during the early-school-age period, resulting in the internalization of parental moral standards. The superego creates feelings of guilt when children threaten to violate moral standards, or, conversely, feelings of pride when they act in accord with prosocial, moral standards.

11. The neopsychoanalytic perspective suggests that morality emerges in infancy as a result of the close, affectional bond that forms between the child and the caregiver.

12. Empathy, which provides a vehicle for experiencing the emotions of others, and perspective taking, which allows one to consider a moral dilemma from another person's point of view, both contribute to moral judgments, emotions, and actions.

13. Parental discipline makes its own contribution to the development of morality, providing guidance about the content of the moral code, as well as strategies for redirecting behavior and increasing a child's awareness of the consequences of one's actions for others.

14. Group games give children practice in role playing and role exchange.

15. Early-school-age friendships may be difficult to sustain because children are very rule oriented and intent on making judgments based on consequences rather than intent.

16. Early friendships are largely sex-segregated. The quality of interaction in these same-sex groups differs for boys and girls, with boys favoring rough-and-tumble play and more acts of dominance and girls favoring verbal persuasion and more talk that increases mutual empathy.

18. The self-theory links ideas about the self, the world, and interactions between the two. It includes ideas about the self-as-I (the knower), and the self-as-me (the one who is known). According to Damon and Hart, the self-as-I can be described in terms of continuity, distinctiveness, and agency. The self-as-me can be described in terms of the physical, active, social, and psychological self.

19. The self-theory changes with development. In early school age, the self-theory is predominantly categorical. Children also begin to make evaluative judgments about the self, reflecting messages they receive about how well they are living up to the standards others have for their behavior. Many of these evaluative judgments relate to issues of gender and morality.

20. For every component of the self, there is an evaluation of worthiness. Taken as a whole, these evaluations form a sense of global self-esteem. Positive self-esteem is associated with optimism; low self-esteem is associated with a tendency to expect failure or to avoid difficult challenges.

References

Aronfreed, J. (1969). The concept of internalization. In D. A. Goslin (Ed.), *Handbook of socialization theory and research*. Chicago: Rand McNally.

Avis, J. & Harris, P. L. (1991). Belief-desire reasoning among Baka children: Evidence for a universal conception of mind. *Child Development, 62,* 460–467.

Bailey, J. M., Bobrow, D., Wolfe, M. & Mikach, S. (1995). Sexual orientation of adult sons of gay fathers. *Developmental Psychology, 31,* 124–129.

Bailey, J. M. & Zucker, K. J. (1995). Childhood sex-typed behavior and sexual orientation: A conceptual analysis and quantitative review. *Developmental Psychology, 31,* 43–55.

Bandura, A. (1977). *Social learning theory.* Englewood Cliffs, N.J.: Prentice-Hall.

Bandura, A. (1986). *Social foundations of thought and action.* Englewood Cliffs, N.J.: Prentice-Hall.

Bandura, A. (1991). Social cognitive theory of moral thought and action. In W. M. Kurtines & J. L. Gewirtz (Eds.), *Handbook of moral behavior and development: Theory* (vol. 1). Hillsdale, N.J.: Erlbaum, 45–103.

Bauer, P. J. (1993). Memory for gender-consistent and gender-inconsistent event sequences by twenty-five-month-old children. *Child Development, 64,* 285–297.

Baumgardner, A. H. (1990). To know oneself is to like oneself: Self-certainty and self-affect. *Journal of Personality and Social Psychology, 58,* 1062–1072.

Baumrind, D. (1995). Commentary on sexual orientation: Research and social policy implications. *Developmental Psychology, 31,* 130–136.

Beere, C. A. (1990). *Gender roles: A handbook of tests and measures.* New York: Greenwood.

Begley, S. (1995). Gray matters. *Newsweek,* March 27, 48–54.

Beit-Hallahmi, B. (1987). Critical periods in psycho-analytic theories of personality development. In M. H. Bornstein (Ed.), *Sensitive periods in development: Interdisciplinary perspectives.* Hillsdale, N.J.: Erlbaum, 211–221.

Bem, S. L. (1981). Gender schema theory: A cognitive account of sex-typing. *Psychological Review, 88,* 354–364.

Bem, S. L. (1989). Genital knowledge and gender constancy in preschool children. *Child Development, 60,* 649–662.

Benenson, J. F. (1993). Greater preference among females than males for dyadic interaction in early childhood. *Child Development, 64,* 544–555.

Bigler, R. S. & Liben, L. S. (1992). Cognitive mechanisms in children's gender stereotyping: Theoretical and educational implications of a cognitive based intervention. *Child Development, 63,* 1351–1363.

Bohan, J. S. (1993). Regarding gender. *Psychology of Women Quarterly, 17,* 5–21.

Borke, H. (1973). The development of empathy in Chinese and American children between 3 and 6 years of age: A cross-cultural study. *Developmental Psychology, 9,* 102–108.

Brockner, J. (1984). Low self-esteem and behavioral plasticity. In L. Wheeler (Ed.), *Review of personality and social psychology, 4,* Beverly Hills, Calif.: Sage, 237–271.

Brown, J. D. & Gallagher, F. M. (1992). Coming to terms with failure: Private self-enhancement and public self-effacement. *Journal of Experimental Social Psychology, 28,* 3–22.

Brown, J. D. & Mankowski, T. A. (1993). Self-esteem, mood, and self-evaluation: Changes in mood and the way you see you. *Journal of Personality and Social Psychology, 64,* 421–430.

Brown, J. D. & Smart, S. A. (1991). The self and social conduct: Linking self-representation to prosocial behavior. *Journal of Personality and Social Psychology, 60,* 368–375.

Bukowski, W. M., Gauze, C., Hoza, B. & Newcomb, A. F. (1993). Differences and consistency between same-sex and other-sex peer relationships during early adolescence. *Developmental Psychology, 29,* 255–263.

Burr, W. R. & Christensen, C. (1992). Undesirable side effects of enhancing self-esteem. *Family Relations, 41,* 480–484.

Butler, R. (1989). Mastery versus ability appraisal: A developmental study of children's observations of peers' work. *Child Development, 60,* 1350–1361.

Butler, R. (1990). The effects of mastery and competitive conditions on self-assessment at different ages. *Child Development, 61,* 201–210.

Caldera, Y. M., Huston, A. C. & O'Brien, M. (1989). Social interactions and play patterns of parents and toddlers with feminine, masculine, and neutral toys. *Child Development, 60,* 70–76.

Campbell, J. (1990). Self-esteem and clarity of the self-concept. *Journal of Personality and Social Psychology, 59,* 538–549.

Carroll, J. L. & Rest, J. R. (1982). Moral development. In B. B. Wolman (Ed.), *Handbook of developmental psychology.* Englewood Cliffs, N.J.: Prentice-Hall, 434–451.

Chandler, M. & Boyes, M. (1982). Social-cognitive development. In B. B. Wolman (Ed.), *Handbook of developmental psychology.* Englewood Cliffs, N.J.: Prentice-Hall, 387–402.

Cicirelli, V. G. (1976). Effects of evaluating task competence on the self-concept of children from different socioeconomic status levels. *Journal of Psychology, 94,* 217–223.

Cronk, L. (1993). Parental favoritism toward daughters. *American Scientist, 81,* 272–279.

Damon, W. (1977). *The social world of the child.* San Francisco: Jossey-Bass.

Damon, W. (1980). Patterns of change in children's social reasoning. A two-year longitudinal study. *Child Development, 51,* 1010–1017.

Damon, W. & Hart, D. (1988). *Self-understanding in childhood and adolescence.* Cambridge: Cambridge University Press.

Edelbrock, C. & Sugawara, A. I. (1978). Acquisition of sex-typed preferences in pre-school-aged children. *Developmental Psychology, 14,* 614–623.

Eder, R. A. (1989). The emergent personologist: The structure and- content of 3½-, 5½-, and 7½-year-olds' concepts of themselves and other persons. *Child Development, 60,* 1218–1228.

Eder, R. A., Gerlach, S. G. & Perlmutter, M. (1987). In search of children's selves: Development of the specific and general components of the self-concept. *Child Development, 58,* 1044–1050.

Edwards, C. P. & Whiting, B. B. (1988). *Children of different worlds.* Cambridge, Mass.: Harvard University Press.

Eisenberg, N. & Strayer, J. (1987). Critical issues in the study of empathy. In N. Eisenberg & J. Strayer (Eds.), *Empathy and its development.* Cambridge: Cambridge University Press, 3–13.

Emde, R. N., Biringen, Z., Clyman, R. B. & Oppenheim, D. (1991). The moral self of infancy: Affective core and procedural knowledge. *Developmental Review, 11,* 51–270.

Emde, R. N. & Buchsbaum, H. K. (1990). "Didn't you hear my mommy?" Autonomy *with* connectedness in moral self-emergence. In D. Cicchetti & M. Beeghly (Eds.), *The self in transition: Infancy to childhood.* Chicago: University of Chicago Press, 35–60.

Emde, R. N., Johnson, W. F. & Easterbrooks, A. (1987). The do's and don'ts of early moral development: Psychoanalytic tradition and current research. In J. Kagan & S. Lamb (Eds.), *The emergence of morality in young children.* Chicago: University of Chicago Press, 245–276.

Epstein, S. (1973). The self-concept revisited; or, a theory of a theory. *American Psychologist, 28,* 404–416.

Epstein, S. (1991). Cognitive-experiential self-theory: An integrative theory of personality. In R. Cutis (Ed.), *The self with others: Convergences in psychoanalytic, social, and personality psychology.* New York: Guilford, 111–137.

Epstein, S., Lipson, A., Holstein, C. & Huh, E. (1993). Irrational reactions to negative outcomes: Evidence for two conceptual systems. *Journal of Personality and Social Psychology, 62,* 328–339.

Erikson, E. H. (1977). *Toys and reasons.* New York: W. W. Norton.

Fabes, R. A., Eisenberg, N., McCormick, S. E. & Wilson, M. S. (1988). Preschoolers' attributions of the situational determinants of others' naturally occurring emotions. *Developmental Psychology, 24,* 376–385.

Fabes, R. A., Eisenberg, N., Nyman, M. & Michealieu, Q. (1991). Young children's appraisals of others' spontaneous emotional reactions. *Developmental Psychology, 27,* 858–866.

Fincham, F. & Jaspars, J. (1979). Attribution of responsibility to the self and other in children and adults. *Journal of Personality and Social Psychology, 37,* 1589–1602.

Flaks, D. K., Ficher, I., Masterpasqua, F. & Joseph, G. (1995). Lesbians choosing motherhood: A comparative study of lesbian and heterosexual parents and their children. *Developmental Psychology, 31,* 105–114.

Flavell, J. H. (1974). The development of inferences about others. In W. Mischel (Ed.), *Understanding other persons.* Oxford: Blackwell, Basil & Mott.

Freud, A. (1936). *The ego and mechanisms of defense.* New York: International University Press.

Freud, S. (1925/1961). Some psychical consequences of the anatomical distinction between the sexes. In J. Strachey (Ed.), *The standard edition of the complete psychological works of Sigmund Freud* (vol. 19). London: Hogarth Press.

Frey, K. S. & Ruble, D. N. (1987). What children say about classroom performance: Sex and grade differences in perceived competence. *Child Development, 58,* 1066–1078.

Froming, W. J., Allen, L. & Jensen, R. (1985). Altruism, role-taking, and self-awareness: The acquisition of norms governing altruistic behavior. *Child Development, 56,* 1123–1228.

Garrod, A. (1993). *Approaches to moral development: New research and emerging themes.* New York: Teachers College Press.

Garvey, C. (1977). *Play.* Cambridge, Mass.: Harvard University Press.

Gibbs, J. C. (1979). Kohlberg's moral stage theory: A Piagetian revision. *Human Development, 22,* 89–112.

Green, R. (1987). *The "sissy boy syndrome" and the development of homosexuality.* New Haven, Conn.: Yale University Press.

Hart, C. H., Ladd, G. W. & Burleson, B. R. (1990). Children's expectations of the outcomes of social strategies: Relations with sociometric status and maternal disciplinary styles. *Child Development, 61,* 127–137.

Harter, S. (1985). Competence as a dimension of self-evaluation: Towards a comprehensive model of self-worth. In R. Leahy (Ed.), *The development of the self.* New York: Academic Press, 55–121.

Hoffman, M. L. (1970). Moral development. In P. H. Mussen (Ed.), *Carmichael's manual of child psychology* (3rd ed., vol. 2). New York: Wiley.

Hoffman, M. L. (1987). The contribution of empathy to justice and moral judgment. In N. Eisenberg & J. Strayer (Eds.), *Empathy and its development.* Cambridge: Cambridge University Press, 47–80.

Hoffner, C. & Badzinski, D. M. (1989). Children's integration of facial and situational cues to emotion. *Child Development, 60,* 411–422.

Howes, C. & Phillipsen, L. (1992). Gender and friendship: Relationships within peer groups of young children. *Social Development, 1,* 230–242.

Huber, J. (1990). Macro-micro links in gender stratification. *American Sociological Review, 55,* 1–10.

Iannotti, R. J. (1985). Naturalistic and structured assessments of prosocial behavior in preschool children: The influence of empathy and perspective taking. *Developmental Psychology, 21,* 46–55.

Jacklin, C. N. & Maccoby, E. E. (1978). Social behavior at 33 months in same-sex and mixed-sex dyads. *Child Development, 49,* 557–569.

Jacobson, E. (1964). *The self and the object world.* New York: International Universities Press.

James, W. (1892/1961). *Psychology: The briefer course.* New York: Harper & Row.

Kagan, J. (1958). The concept of identification. *Psychological Review, 65,* 296–305.

Kegan, R. (1982). *The evolving self: Problems and process in human development.* Cambridge, Mass.: Harvard University Press.

Kochanska, G. (1991). Socialization and temperament in the development of guilt and conscience. *Child Development, 62,* 1379–1392.

Kochanska, G. (1993). Toward a synthesis of parental socialization and child temperament in early development of conscience. *Child Development, 64,* 325–347.

Kohlberg, L. (1966). A cognitive-developmental analysis of children's sex-role concepts and attitudes. In E. E. Maccoby (Ed.), *The development of sex differences.* Stanford, Calif.: Stanford University Press, 82–172.

Kohlberg, L. (1969). Stage and sequence: The cognitive-developmental approach to socialization. In D. A. Goslin (Ed.), *Handbook of socialization theory and research.* Chicago: Rand McNally.

Kohlberg, L. (1976). Moral stages and moralization: The cognitive-developmental approach. In T. Lickona (Ed.), *Moral development and behavior.* New York: Holt, Rinehart & Winston.

Kohlberg, L. (1978). Revisions in the theory and practice of moral development. In W. Damon (Ed.), *Moral development: New directions for child development* (vol. 2). San Francisco: Jossey-Bass, 83–88.

Kohlberg, L. (1979). *The meaning and measurement of moral development.* Worcester, Mass.: Clark University, Clark Lectures.

Kohut, H. (1971). *The analysis of the self.* New York: International Universities Press.

Lee, L. C. (1975). Toward a cognitive theory of interpersonal development: Importance of peers. In M. Lewis & L. A. Rosenblum (Eds.), *Friendship and peer relations.* New York: Wiley.

Leinbach, M. D. & Fagot, B. I. (1986). Acquisition of gender labels: A test for toddlers. *Sex Roles, 15,* 655–667.

Levy, G. D. & Carter, D. B. (1989). Gender schema, gender constancy, and gender-role knowledge: The roles of cognitive factors in preschoolers' gender-role stereotype attributions. *Developmental Psychology, 25,* 444–449.

Liben, L. S. & Signorella, M. L. (1993). Gender-schematic processing in children: The role of initial interpretations of stimuli. *Developmental Psychology, 29,* 141–149.

Lobel, T. E. & Menashri, J. (1993). Relations of conceptions of gender-role transgressions and gender

constancy to gender-typed toy preferences. *Developmental Psychology, 29,* 150–155.

Long, B. H., Henderson, E. H. & Ziller, R. C. (1967). Developmental changes in the self-concept during middle childhood. *Merrill-Palmer Quarterly, 13,* 201–215.

Maccoby, E. E. (1988). Gender as a social category. *Developmental Psychology, 24,* 755–765.

Maccoby, E. E. (1990). Gender and relationships: A developmental account. *American Psychologist, 45,* 513–520.

Maccoby, E. E. (1992). The role of parents in the socialization of children: An historical overview. *Developmental Psychology, 28,* 1006–1017.

Maccoby, E. E. & Jacklin, C. N. (1987). Gender segregation in childhood. In E. H. Reese (Ed.), *Advances in child development and behavior* (vol. 20). New York: Academic Press, 239–287.

Mahler, M. S. (1963). Thoughts about development and individuation. *Psychoanalytic Study of the Child, 18,* 307–324.

Martin, C. L. (1989). Children's use of gender-related information in making social judgments. *Developmental Psychology, 25,* 80–88.

Martin, C. L., Eisenbud, L. & Rose, H. (1995). Children's gender-based reasoning about toys. *Child Development, 66,* 1453–1471.

Martin, C. L. & Halverson, C. F. (1987). The roles of cognition in sex roles acquisition. In D. B. Carter (Ed.), *Current conceptions of sex roles and sex typing: Theory and research.* New York: Praeger, 123–137.

Martin, C. L., Wood, C. H. & Little, J. K. (1990). The development of gender stereotype components. *Child Development, 61,* 1891–1904.

Martin, G. B. & Clark, R. D., III (1982). Distress crying in neonates: Species and peer specificity. *Developmental Psychology, 18,* 3–9.

McAdoo, H. P. (1985). Racial attitude and self-concept of young black children over time. In H. P. McAdoo & J. L. McAdoo (Eds.), *Black children: Social, educational, and parental environments.* Newbury Park, Calif.: Sage, 213–242.

Mischel, W. (1966). Theory and research on the antecedents of self-imposed delay of reward. In B. A. Maher (Ed.), *Progress in experimental personality research* (vol. 3). New York: Academic Press, 81–132.

Mischel, W. (1973). Toward a cognitive social learning reconceptualization of personality. *Psychological Review, 80,* 252–283.

Mischel, W., Shoda, Y. & Rodriguez, M. L. (1989). Delay of gratification in children. *Science, 244,* 933–938.

Oosterwegel, A. & Oppenheimer, L. (1993). *The self-system: Developmental changes between and within self-concepts.* Hillsdale, N.J.: Erlbaum.

Park, K. A., Lay, K. & Ramsey, L. (1993). Individual differences and developmental changes in preschoolers' friendships. *Developmental Psychology, 29,* 264–270.

Patterson, C. J. (1992). Children of lesbian and gay parents. *Child Development, 63,* 1025–1042.

Patterson, C. J. (1995). Families of the lesbian baby boom: Parents' division of labor and children's adjustment. *Developmental Psychology, 31,* 115–123.

Pelham, B. W. (1991). On the benefits of misery: Self-serving biases in the depressive self-concept. *Journal of Personality and Social Psychology, 61,* 670–681.

Pelham, B. W. & Swann, W. B., Jr. (1989). From self-conceptions to self-worth: On the sources and structure of global self-esteem. *Journal of Personality and Social Psychology, 57,* 672–680.

Pettit, G. S., Dodge, K. A. & Brown, M. M. (1988). Early family experience, social problem-solving patterns, and children's social competence. *Child Development, 59,* 107–120.

Piaget, J. (1932/1948). *The moral judgment of the child.* Glencoe, Ill.: Free Press.

Piaget, J. (1975/1985). *The equilibration of cognitive structures: The central problem of intellectual development* (T. Brown & K. Thampy, trans.). Chicago: University of Chicago Press.

Rest, J. R. (1983). Morality. In J. H. Flavell & E. M. Markman (Eds.), *Handbook of child psychology: Cognitive development* (vol. 3). New York: Wiley.

Rosenberg, M. (1979). *Conceiving the self.* New York: Basic Books.

Sagi, A. & Hoffman, M. L. (1976). Empathic distress in the newborn. *Developmental Psychology, 12,* 175–176.

Selman, R. L. (1971). Taking another's perspective: Role-taking development in early childhood. *Child Development, 42,* 1721–1734.

Selman, R. L. (1980). *The growth of interpersonal understanding: Developmental and clinical analysis.* New York: Academic Press.

Serbin, L. A., Powlishta, K. K. & Gulko, J. (1993). The development of sex typing in middle childhood. *Monographs of the Society for Research in Child Development, Serial No. 232, Vol. 58.*

Setterlund, M. B. & Niedenthal, P. M. (1993). "Who am I? Why am I here?": Self-esteem, self-clarity, and prototype matching. *Journal of Personality and Social Psychology, 65,* 769–780.

Smetana, J. G. (1985). Preschool children's conceptions of transgressions: Effects of varying moral and conventional domain-related attributes. *Developmental Psychology, 21,* 18–29.

Smetana, J. G. (1986). Preschool children's conceptions of sex-role transgressions. *Child Development, 57,* 862–871.

Smetana, J. G., Schlagman, N. & Adams, P. W. (1993). Preschool children's judgments about hypothetical and actual transgressions. *Child Development, 64,* 202–214.

Smith, P. K., Hunter, T., Carvalho, A. M. A. & Costabile, A. (1992). Children's perceptions of play fighting, play chasing and real fighting: A cross-national interview study. *Social Development, 1,* 211–221.

Snyder, S. S. & Feldman, D. H. (1984). Phases of transition in moral development: Evidence from the domain of spatial representation. *Child Development, 55,* 981–989.

Stattin, H. & Klackenberg-Larsson, I. (1991). The short- and long-term implications for parent–child relations of parents' prenatal preferences for their child's gender. *Developmental Psychology, 27,* 141–147.

Stipek, D., Recchia, S. & McClintic, S. (1992). Self-evaluation in young children. *Monographs of the Society for Research in Child Development, 57* (1, Serial No. 226).

Sutton-Smith, B. A. (1972). Syntax for play and games. In R. E. Herron & B. Sutton-Smith (Eds.), *Child's play.* New York: Wiley.

Swann, W. B., Jr. (1990). To be known or be adored? The interplay of self-enhancement and self-verification. In E. T. Higgins & R. M. Sorrentino (Eds.), *Handbook of motivation and cognition: Foundations of social behavior.* New York: Guilford Press, 404–448.

Thompson, L. (1993). Conceptualizing gender in marriage: The case of marital care. *Journal of Marriage and the Family, 55,* 557–569.

Thompson, S. K. (1975). Gender labels and early sex role development. *Child Development, 46,* 339–347.

Turiel, E. (1983). *The development of social knowledge: Morality and convention.* Cambridge, England: Cambridge University Press.

Turner, P. J. & Gervai, J. (1995). A multidimensional study of gender typing in preschool children and their parents: Personality, attitudes, preferences, behavior, and cultural differences. *Developmental Psychology, 31,* 759–772.

Walker, L. J. (1988). The development of moral reasoning. *Annals of Child Development, 5,* 33–78.

Walker, L. J. (1989). A longitudinal study of moral reasoning. *Child Development, 60,* 157–166.

Walker, L. J. & Taylor, J. H. (1991a). Stage transitions in moral reasoning: A longitudinal study of developmental processes. *Developmental Psychology, 27,* 330–337.

Walker, L. J. & Taylor, J. H. (1991b). Family interactions and the development of moral reasoning. *Child Development, 62,* 262–283.

Weinstein, R. S., Marshall, H. H., Sharp, L. & Botkin, M. (1987). Pygmalion and the student: Age and classroom differences in children's awareness of teacher expectations. *Child Development, 58,* 1079–1093.

Wellman, H. M. (1990). *Children's theories of mind.* Cambridge, Mass.: Bradford, MIT.

Wellman, H. M. & Bartsch, K. (1988). Young children's reasoning about beliefs. *Cognition, 30,* 239–277.

Westoff, C. F. & Rindfuss, R. R. (1974). Sex preselection in the United States: Some implications. *Science, 184,* 633–636.

Zucker, K. J. (1990). Gender identity disorders in children: Clinical descriptions and natural history. In R. Blanchard & B. W. Steiner (Eds.), *Clinical management of gender identity disorders in children and adults.* Washington, D.C.: American Psychiatric Press, 1–23.

Expanding the Psychosocial Analysis of Early School Age

The Psychosocial Crisis of Early
School Age
   Initiative
   Guilt

The Central Process for
Resolving the Crisis: Identification

The Prime Adaptive Ego Quality and the Core Pathology
   Purpose
      Play and Purpose
   Inhibition

The Role of Parents and Other Family Members in
Fostering Development
   Parents as Educators
   Parents as Advocates

Cultural and Ethnic Patterns That Create Distinctive Child-Rearing
Environments
   Religion and the Moral Atmosphere of the Home
   Culture and Gender
      Individualism and Collectivism
      Masculinity and Femininity
      The Yanomamö: The Fierce People
      The Maasai

Societal Issues That Provide Resources or Barriers to Development
   School Readiness
      Readiness
      How to Measure Kindergarten Readiness?
      What Obstacles Stand in the Way of School Readiness?
      Who Is Responsible for Meeting the Goal of School
         Readiness?
   The Impact of Television
      Cognitive Consequences
      Socioemotional Consequences
      Television as a Stimulus for Optimal Development
      Advice to Parents, Teachers, and Caregivers about Guiding
         Children's Television Viewing

Optimizing Development for Early-School-Age Children

Chapter Summary

References

Chapter 12

I n this chapter, we expand the psychosocial analysis of the early-school-age period by defining the psychosocial crisis, <u>initiative versus guilt</u>, and the central process, <u>identification</u>. We discuss the prime adaptive ego quality, purpose, and the core pathology, <u>inhibition</u>. These concepts provide a sense of the ongoing psychosocial tension between the curious, investigative child and societal constraints that attempt to curb or prohibit certain types of inquiry.

We also discuss parents and caregivers as educators and advocates, illustrating the responsibilities that fall on adults as they try to pave the way for their children's entry into the more complex and bureaucratic environment of the school. Cultural and ethnic patterns are emphasized around two of the major developmental tasks of the early-school-age period: religion and the moral atmosphere of the home, and cultural variations in the definition of gender roles. Two societal issues are introduced: the concept of school readiness and the impact of television on young children. The chapter closes with a summary of ideas drawn from this and the preceding chapter about strategies for promoting optimal development during the early-school-age period.

The Psychosocial Crisis of Early School Age

As children resolve the toddlerhood crisis of autonomy versus shame and doubt in a positive way, they emerge with a strong sense of themselves as unique individuals. During the early-school-age period, children shift their <u>attention toward investigating the external environment.</u> They attempt to discover the same <u>kind of stability, strength, and regularity</u> in the external world that they have discovered within themselves.

Initiative

Initiative is an expression of the I, the executive branch of the self, as compared with the me, the observed characteristics of the self (Damon & Hart, 1988). *Initiative* is an outgrowth of early experiences of the self as a causal agent which continues to find expression as children impose themselves on their social world. Initiative is the active, conceptual investigation of the world in much the same sense that autonomy is the active, physical manipulation of it (Erikson, 1963). The child's motivation for and skill at investigation depend on the successful development of a strong sense of autonomy. When children <u>acquire self-control and confidence in themselves,</u> they are able to perform a <u>variety of actions and observe the consequences.</u> They discover, for example, the kinds of things that make parents or teachers angry and the kinds of things that please them. They may deliberately perform a hostile act in order to evoke a hostile response. Children's curiosity about the order of the universe ranges from the physical to the metaphysical. They may ask questions about the color of the sky, the purpose of hair, the nature of God, the origin of babies, or how fast fingernails grow. They take things apart, invent toys and games out of odds and ends, and explore the alleys and dark corners of their neighborhood.

One expression of initiative is children's playful exploration of their bodies. It is not uncommon to find five- and six-year-old children intently playing "doctor," oftentimes with both "doctor" and "patient" undergoing curious examination. Boys of this age can occasionally be observed in a contest to achieve the longest urine trajectory. Girls report attempting to urinate from a standing position "in the same way a boy does." Both boys and girls engage in some form of masturbation. These behaviors are evidence of children's growing interest and pleasure in their bodies and their physical functioning.

Initiative can be expressed when children are alone, as they try to discover how things work and build or invent novel devices. It can also be expressed in social situations as children ask questions, assert their presence, and take leadership. In one study of social competence, children described the strategies they used to enter a peer-group play situation (Dodge et al., 1986). Two children were playing a game (they were referred to as the hosts) and a third child was told to enter the room and try to initiate play with the others. The entry episode was videotaped and coded. In addition, both the child who tried to initiate play and the two hosts were interviewed about the episode and asked to evaluate how successful the entry child was. Three strategies for initiating interaction were judged to be effective and were associated with other evidence of social competence:

1. The entering child established common ground by giving meaningful information in response to questions.
2. The entering child engaged in a positive, friendly interchange with the others.
3. The entering child did not show evidence of negative, irritable behaviors.

The children who were least successful in initiating entry into the play "were disruptive, . . . made nagging, weak demands, . . . engaged in incoherent behaviors, or . . . disagreed with hosts without citing a rule or reason" (Dodge et al., 1986, p. 25).

Children who experience a positive sense of initiative can apply this orientation to investigation of the physical as well as the social world. They create "magic potions" by mixing together soap, perfume, pine cones, leaves, and other powerful ingredients. They make up plays, stories, puppet shows, dances, and ceremonies. They dress up in costumes, entertain company by standing on their heads, engage in daring acts by hanging from tree limbs or walking on high ledges, and impose themselves in any and all curious and private discussions. They spend time trying to figure out ways to catch a glimpse of Santa Claus on Christmas Eve or the tooth fairy when she comes at night to collect her treasures. These are the "Little Rascal" years when a sense of initiative is associated with a naive, exuberant, entrepreneurial spirit and a desire to discover, direct, and dominate. All manner of investigation and inquiry is fair game.

Guilt

Guilt is an emotion associated with the sense that one has been responsible for an unacceptable thought, fantasy, or action (Izard, 1977). Guilt is a negative emotion, usually accompanied by a sense of self-blame, remorse, and a desire to make amends for real or imagined wrongdoing. It has an adaptive function by promoting social harmony because it inhibits aggressive actions and leads people to seek forgiveness or make compensation for wrongs that they may have done. Three slightly distinct explanations for the dynamics of guilt are considered: psychoanalytic theory's concept of superego, the

[handwritten margin note: guilt inhibits aggressive action & leads people to seek forgiveness]

☆ GUILT ☆

PSYCHOANALYTIC
emotional reaction
to unacceptable
impulses

EMPATHIC
emotional arousal
& sensitivity to
anothers
distress

COGNITIVE
DEV'TAL

results when a
person doesn't
follow personal
standards &
beliefs.

empathic view of guilt, and the cognitive developmental view of self-evaluation (Zahn-Waxler & Kochanska, 1990).

The psychoanalytic perspective views guilt as an emotional reaction to unacceptable sexual and aggressive impulses. These impulses are especially threatening during the phallic period when a child's wishes focus on hostility and sexuality toward parents, which must be repressed. The superego, which is formed through the internalization of parental values and standards, monitors the ego's efforts to gratify id impulses. It punishes the ego through experiences of anxiety and guilt when it identifies behaviors that are socially unacceptable.

Research on empathy by Martin Hoffman (1982) suggests that guilt can be awakened at a very early age through emotional arousal and sensitivity to another person's emotional distress. This view of guilt, unlike the psychoanalytic perspective, is based on empathy and is not defensive. Instead, it is closely linked to prosocial feelings and the basic emotional bonds between infants and their caregivers.

The third perspective looks at guilt from a cognitive viewpoint. This approach suggests that guilt occurs when one fails to act in accord with personal standards and beliefs. The cognitive view assumes that, as a child's cognitive capacities mature, guilt is associated with increasingly complex situations. Hoffman (1990) suggested that the earliest forms of guilt take place over transgressions. With transgressions, a child can readily observe the harm or damage he or she has caused. At a more advanced level, guilt over inaction (not helping or failing to warn someone of a danger) occurs. Guilt over thinking about causing someone distress or letting someone down would require an even more complex level of reasoning. Finally, abstract guilt over the life conditions that others must endure (guilt about the fact that many children in the United States suffer from malnutrition) or the inequities that allow one to benefit while another person or group suffers requires cognitive reasoning plus a more complete internalization of ideals, values, and standards that typically do not develop until adolescence or adulthood.

Every culture imposes some limits on legitimate experimentation and investigation: Some questions may not be asked; some acts may not be performed. Adults' reactions determine whether the child learns to view specific behaviors such as aggressiveness, sexual play, or masturbation as wrong or acceptable. Children gradually internalize cultural prohibitions and learn to inhibit their curiosity in taboo areas. One taboo shared by most cultures is the prohibition against incest (Turner & Rubinson, 1993). Most children learn that any behavior that suggests sexual intimacy between family members is absolutely forbidden. Even the thought of such a relationship generates feelings of anxiety and guilt. The child's exploration of other domains depends on the extent to which the family and the school impose restrictions on legitimate inquiry or action.

The psychosocial crisis of initiative versus guilt is resolved positively when a child finds pleasure and growing knowledge through an active, questioning investigation of the environment. In the positive development of initiative, inquiry is tempered by a respect for personal privacy and cultural values. Even so, the preponderant psychological state is curiosity and experimentation. The child learns that, even though certain areas are off limits, efforts to understand most aspects of the world are appropriate (see Box 12.1).

BOX 12.1

Childhood Phobias

Occasionally, a child will experience an increasingly burdensome amount of guilt rather than the usual sense of initiative. One expression of overwhelming guilt is the development of a strong, irrational fear of some object or situation, a *phobia*. Some common phobias that develop during early childhood are fear of going to school, of the dark, or of an animal such as dogs. A phobic child tends to think a lot about the feared object and to experience a great deal of anxiety in connection with these thoughts. This limits his or her ability to explore the environment.

The case of school phobia is an interesting example. An estimated 17 children per 1,000 experience school phobia each year (Davison & Neale, 1990). The phobia consists of a dread of some aspect of the school situation, such as a teacher, another child, a janitor, or even eating school food. As the time to go to school arrives each morning, the child's anxiety increases. The child may complain of nausea or stomach pain and may even vomit. Once parents agree to let the child stay home, the anxiety and symptoms fade quickly—until the next morning (Coolidge, 1979).

From a psychoanalytic perspective, school phobia is seen as a conflict related more closely to separation from parents—usually the mother—than fear of school itself (Phelps et al., 1992). At a symbolic level, the child fears that his or her mother is in danger of serious illness or death, which is a projection of the child's unacceptable hostile feelings toward the mother. This threat to the mother can be averted only if the child stays home to protect her. Going to school thus is equated with losing mother, childhood, and safety. Since the actual fears of school are not confronted and the unconscious hostility toward the mother is not expressed or addressed, the idea of going to school continues to be frightening.

A phobia can be understood as a means of directing anxiety and guilt over unacceptable thoughts, behaviors, or fantasies to a specific target. Rather than accept personal responsibility for inappropriate behavior, the child projects the unacceptable impulses to an element of the environment, such as a teacher or the school building. The child is not doing fearful and harmful things; they are being done by something out there that evokes the child's fear.

The phobia provides a way for the child to express guilty feelings without having to take personal blame. Therefore, the phobia serves as a temporary protective device until the child can identify and control those impulses that are specifically linked to social disapproval. For the child who cannot take responsibility for socially devalued impulses or who experiences a great deal of anxiety in many areas, the range of feared objects and settings may grow rather than diminish. The extremely phobic child fears danger in most of the environment and cannot distinguish between fears that emanate from personal impulses and those that are realistic appraisals of external danger.

Guilt, like the negative poles of other psychosocial crises, can have an adaptive function. As children's sense of empathy grows and they take more responsibility for their actions, they are increasingly able to acknowledge the harm that their actions or words may have caused to someone else. Moderate levels of guilt have been associated with positive levels of prosocial behavior and high levels of empathy (Tangney, 1991). Research has shown that children who have a strong sense of guilt demonstrate lower levels of acting out and delinquent behavior, better academic performance, and more frequent helping behavior (Williams & Bybee, 1994). With development, experiences of guilt become more intense and are linked to more complex situations. For example, a young child may feel guilty about accidentally breaking something that was valuable or that had personal meaning to her father or mother. An older child might feel guilt about not living up to a parent's expectations of what she could accomplish or about realizing that he had been inconsiderate in taking the car so that his parent missed an important appointment (Williams & Bybee, 1994).

Girls and boys may show different patterns in the experience of guilt, based on different patterns of socialization and relationships (Maccoby, 1990). Girls tend to have higher levels of empathy and boys higher levels of aggression. Girls are socialized to be concerned about and preserve connections with others. Thus, they are more likely to experience guilt when they have lied or been inconsiderate to others. They are also more likely to experience guilt when they blame themselves for causing unhappiness or conflict among others. Boys are socialized to be assertive and to control the expression of their emotions. Therefore, they are more likely to experience guilt over overt actions like fighting, victimizing other children or animals, or damaging property (Williams & Bybee, 1994).

At the extreme, however, some children suffer from an overwhelming sense of guilt. These children feel that each of their questions or interventions is inappropriate. They frequently experience guilt about their own impulses and fantasies, even when they have taken no actions and no negative consequences have resulted. They begin to believe that their thoughts and actions are responsible for much of the misfortune or unhappiness of others. For example, young children of depressed mothers express unusually high levels of distress, concern, and feelings of responsibility for someone else's unhappiness. Mothers who are consistently sad are a model for blaming oneself when bad things happen. In addition, depressed mothers are likely to withdraw love when the child has misbehaved, a discipline technique associated with high levels of guilt and anxiety (Zahn-Waxler et al., 1990). In this kind of environment, a child learns to restrict new behaviors out of fear that they may cause harm or unhappiness to someone else. In effect, the child comes to feel that curiosity itself is taboo and so feels guilty whenever it is aroused. The child who resolves this crisis in the direction of guilt is left to rely almost totally on parents or other authorities for guidance on how to operate in the world (see Notebook Page 12.1).

The psychosocial crisis of initiative versus guilt highlights the intimate relationship between intellectual curiosity and emotional development. During this stage, family and school transmit cultural attitudes toward experimentation, curiosity, and investigation. They also direct the child's curiosity away from familial, subgroup, and cultural taboo areas. Children are expected to develop the ability to control their own questions and behavior. Whereas violations may bring disapproval and punishment, successful self-control may attract no notice whatsoever. Children must develop a strong internal moral code that will help them avoid punishment. They must also develop the ability to reward themselves for correct behavior. The more areas of restriction that are imposed, the more difficult it is for children to distinguish between legitimate and inappropriate areas of investigation. The only way that children have of coping with this problem is to develop a rigid moral code that restricts many aspects of thought and action.

The Central Process for Resolving the Crisis: Identification

The discussion of gender-role identification and moral development as major developmental tasks during early school age points directly to *identification* as the central process for resolving the conflict between initiative and guilt. Children at this age actively strive to enhance their self-concepts by incorporating

Understanding the Origins of Guilt

Guilt is a powerful human emotion that underlies our capacity to function in a morally responsible way within our social group. Consider the role of the following four sources of guilt in the socialization of young children. Write down one or two examples of your own experiences of guilt during childhood that are linked to each source.

1. Guilt that is a result of witnessing someone else's distress or pain:

2. Guilt experienced as a result of violating or thinking about violating personal standards or beliefs:

3. Guilt over unacceptable sexual or aggressive impulses:

4. Guilt over violating or thinking about violating cultural taboos:

Parental identification increases a child's sense of closeness to a parent and, at the same time, fosters independence.

Identification gives child a sense of security

into their own behavior some of the valued characteristics that their parents exhibit. Parental identification allows children to feel that their parents are with them even when the parents are not physically present. This feeling of connection with parents provides an underlying sense of security for children in a wide variety of situations.

Parental identification figures in the child's development in two rather different ways. First, closeness with parents provides the basis for the incorporation of parental sanctions and prohibitions. Once children have integrated these guidelines for behavior, they are bound to feel guilty any time they anticipate abandoning them. Second, identification allows the child to feel a growing sense of independence from parents (Jacobson, 1964). Children who know how their parents would respond in a given situation no longer need their parents' physical presence to direct their behavior. Children who can praise or punish themselves for their actions are less dependent on their parents to perform these functions. The security that results from strong parental identification allows children increased freedom from their parents. The child whose parental identifications are strong is more likely to challenge the environment, take risks, and initiate action.

Formation of an ideal self-image

Identification with parents results in a strengthening of the child's personality. An important outcome of early-school-age identifications is the formation of an ideal self-image, which psychoanalytic theorists sometimes refer to as the *ego ideal* (Freud, 1929/1955; Sandler et al., 1963). The ego ideal is a complex view of the future self, including skills, profession, values, and personal relationships. This ideal self is a fantasy, a goal that is unlikely to be completely attained even in adulthood. Nonetheless, the discrepancy between the real self and the ideal self is a strong motivating factor. As children strive to achieve their ideal, they attempt new activities, make plans that strain the limits of their abilities, take risks, and resist temptations that might interfere with attaining their desired goals.

EGO IDEAL

The ego ideal is more unrealistic during early school age than it is at later stages. Children can fantasize anything about themselves in the future. They use their parents' values very literally to project an ideal person of mythical proportions. The ideal self might include the strength of Hercules, the wealth of Queen Elizabeth, the wisdom of Confucius, and the compassion of Jesus. The lack of realistic constraints on the ego ideal allows the child to investigate and vicariously experience certain qualities that may always be beyond reach. As people grow older, it is important that the fantasy of the ideal self-image become increasingly attainable, albeit still beyond what has been attained. People who find it difficult to modify their ideal self-images are vulnerable to personal frustration and psychological despair because they fail to reach or even come close to their goals.

Identification with parents is the process by which the ideal self-image and moral prescriptions are integrated into the child's personality. Children who are unable to control their behavior so that it corresponds to the sanctions and ideals that they have internalized will experience guilt. Children whose behavior approaches their ideals and conforms to internalized sanctions will experience feelings of self-confidence that will allow them to take initiative. The balance between guilt and self-confidence determines the eventual resolution of the psychosocial crisis of initiative versus guilt.

The crisis of initiative versus guilt encompasses the child's need to question existing norms and the accompanying feelings of moral concern when norms are violated. This crisis does not focus specifically on intellectual development; rather, one must assume that the level of questioning that takes place during this stage is possible only because of an increase in cognitive complexity. The process of positive parental identification promotes the incorporation of cultural norms and strengthens the child's sense of competence. Socialization during this stage can foster a creative openness or an anxious dread of novelty (see Notebook Page 12.2).

The Prime Adaptive Ego Quality and the Core Pathology

As a result of efforts to resolve the crisis of initiative versus guilt, children emerge from the early-school-age period with the prime adaptive ego quality of purpose or the core pathology of inhibition. These predispositions suggest an orientation toward agency that leaves a child with coping resources to support directed, action-oriented problem solving or a more passive, self-protective approach to stress in which the child is more likely to allow others to guide his or her behavior.

Purpose

Purpose is thought or behavior with direction and, therefore, with meaning. "Purposefulness is the courage playfully to imagine and energetically to pursue valued goals" (Erikson, 1978, 29). Purpose is a cognitively more complex extension of the will gained in toddlerhood in that it combines a sense of agency with a plan. In contrast to the toddler who exercises his or her will through mere delight in action, the early-school-age child imposes intention and goals on action. This difference is illustrated by a toddler's typical running around the yard, laughing and shouting, as opposed to playing tag, which is more likely for early-school-age children. Toddlers may enjoy stacking

Identification and Social Interactions

According to psychosocial theory, the central process for resolving the conflict of initiative versus guilt is parental identification. Children are eager to discover as much as possible about the adult world, especially in the areas of sex-role expectations and morality. Their families teach them about how to behave in ways that are acceptable to the larger social group. The process of identification requires opportunities for children and parents to interact. In this exercise, try to estimate how many interactions are involved in socialization activities and see if you can create a model for understanding how socialization occurs as a result of interactions with others.

1. How many interactions do you have in the course of a day? (By interactions, we mean conversations, however brief, and nonverbal communications in which meaning is shared between two or more people.) Take some time to think about this. Spend a day trying to count the number of interactions that you have.

2. Try to remember your own interactions at ages four, five, and six. Observe some children of that age to improve your impression of typical interactions. What kinds of interactions are likely to take place, and about how many interactions might occur?

Wake-up:

Morning:

Afternoon:

Evening:

Bedtime: _____

During the night: _____

Now make a guess about how many interactions a child has in a day:

_____

_____

Multiply this number by 365 (days per year) × 3 (three years of the early-school-age period) = 1,095 days to estimate the number of interactions that a child has during early school age:

_____

_____

3. How many of these daily interactions do you think are initiated by parents to influence the child's behavior in valued ways? Multiply this number by 1,095 (days in three years):

_____

_____

Divide the number of interactions intended to influence the child by the total number of interactions to give the percentage of socialization interactions:

_____

_____

4. What do you think is the relationship between the percentage of socialization interactions and the level of the child's internalization of social standards and values? One possibility is that the higher the percentage of socialization interactions, the more fully socialized the child will be. Another possibility is that socialization interactions decline from age four to six, suggesting that the child has internalized parental teachings. How do *you* explain the relationship between the percentage of socialization interactions and socialization outcomes?

_____

_____

During the early-school-age period, play is typically accompanied by a plan. It looks like the plan here is to build a snake and reptile pit.

actions have a direction→
play has a plan

blocks on one another or splashing in water; early-school-age children want to transform materials and toys into a story or a project. Their actions follow some direction; their play has a plan.

A sense of purpose suggests that not only does the action have meaning, but the person initiating the action has meaning. Ricky enters a play situation and says, "I have an idea. Let's play trains." This suggestion reflects Ricky's sense of a goal-directed plan and his sense of confidence about introducing his idea into the ongoing activities of the group.

Play and Purpose

Toys

Erikson pointed out how important play and playfulness are in the process of resolving the crisis of initiative versus guilt. In *Toys and Reasons* (1977) he referred to this period of life as the Toy Stage, pointing out that children of four, five, and six almost always use toys to engage in intense play. Out of initiated actions that occur in a playful way emerges a basic ego strength—purposefulness. Children who can direct their behavior have acquired an essential tool—a basic sense that behavior that is directed and has a purpose allows them to reach their goals.

We discussed play as a major developmental task of toddlerhood in Chapter 9. We explored the development of the capacity for symbolic play, the role of the environment in fostering playfulness, and the significance of play for social and cognitive development. Here, we want to acknowledge the importance of play activities for resolving the psychosocial crisis of early school age. Erikson called play the work of childhood. In fact, he warned against thinking of work and play as distinctly different activities.

For the ritualizing power of play is the infantile form of the human ability to deal with experience by creating model situations and to master reality by experiment and planning. It is in the crucial phases of his work that the adult, too, "plays" with past experience and anticipated tasks, beginning with that activity in the autosphere called thinking. But beyond this, in constructing model situations not only in open dramatizations (as in "plays" and in fiction) but also in the laboratory and on the drawing board, we inventively anticipate the future from the vantage point of a corrected and shared past as we redeem our failures and strengthen our hopes. (1982, 51)

Once children start school, play may remain as the primary preferred activity, but the time devoted to it declines. And, in fact, many of the activities that schools treat as play, especially physical fitness and competitive games, may not fulfill a young child's criteria for pleasurable play. As Lois Murphy (1972) described it, "play is most fun and most playful, when it is spontaneous, evolving from an integration of impulse and ideas and providing expression, release, sometimes climax, often mastery, and with a degree of exhilaration, and refreshment. Good play leaves one feeling good, happy, alive" (120–121).

Inhibition

Inhibition can be thought of as the restraint or suppression of behavior. In a psychological context, one might define inhibition as a conscious or unconscious blocking of unacceptable wishes and behaviors. Often, inhibition results when a child experiences guilt associated with certain wishes, or fear due to having been punished for expressing those wishes in the past. Inhibition is assumed to emerge when parents or caregivers use high levels of love withdrawal and guilt-inducing interactions with their children. These kinds of interactions suggest to the child that the parent's love, affection, and approval are conditional upon the child matching certain specific parental standards. In order to adapt in this kind of environment and avoid risking loss of love, the child becomes self-conscious and restrained in his or her actions. In contrast to the sense of confidence and agency implied in the concept of purpose, a child who is inhibited does not want to take the risks associated with imposing a plan or suggesting a direction for fear of parental disapproval.

Lois Murphy (1972) proposed that inhibition has even earlier origins in the mother–infant relationship. She suggested that in "healthy" mother–infant interactions, mothers take care to provide meaningful feedback and consequences for their babies' actions. When mothers are very depressed or psychologically unavailable, they may be unable to engage in the kinds of consistent, rhythmic behaviors that produce early experiences of cause-effect. Children who have never internalized the schemes for these kinds of behaviors cannot impose them on external circumstances. As a result of the lack of early, structured, cause–effect interactions in the mothering relationship, some early-school-age children have a very passive orientation toward play and social interactions. According to Murphy, their inhibition is not so much a product of guilt but a lack of basic early structures or schemes for the positive process of initiation. These children do not impose organization on toys or integrate sensory and motor play into a more complex scenario. They remain focused on the sensory activity itself, like digging in the sand, or on the imitation of very basic behaviors, like feeding the baby.

These children are not at the same level of deficit as are the autistic or seriously withdrawn children described in Chapter 8. However, because these children have difficulty imposing plans and direction on play, they miss the accumulation of positive feedback that builds a sense of purpose during the

[handwritten margin note: An inhibited child misses the positive feedback wmch leads to a sense of purpose]

early-school-age period. Raised in families where caregivers are psychologically unavailable or neglectful, these children are likely to emerge during the subsequent period of middle school as shy, withdrawn, and lonely. Without some form of social intervention, they become increasingly withdrawn and inhibited, not knowing how to impose their ideas into the ongoing activities of the group and not experiencing the confidence-building effects of having their suggestions accepted. Consequently, by the end of the early-school-age period, their inhibition produces new deficits in social skill development.

Thus, inhibition as a core pathology may result from historically more severe deprivation in the mothering relationship that prevents the formation of cognitive structures necessary for imposing a plan and goals on a situation, as well as from later experiences of parental rejection or guilt induction which cause a child to feel that his or her ideas, plans, and strategies for reaching goals are naughty or unworthy.

The Role of Parents and Other Family Members in Fostering Development

As the themes of initiative and purpose suggest, curiosity, experimentation, and exploration are signposts of expanding mental activity during the early-school-age years. Young children are attuned to information that will help them become more skillful, extend their mastery, and resolve their many questions about the order and organization of their social and physical worlds. As a result of this surge in inquisitiveness, children turn to their parents, older siblings, grandparents, and other adults for answers. Mothers, fathers, brothers, sisters, aunts, uncles, cousins, teachers, and baby-sitters become the sources of information about such topics as "how to build a road" and "how a television works," as well as more private concerns about "how long will you be alive" and "what happens when you die," questions that can be asked of some experts but not of others.

Parents who have more than one child recognize how much the younger child learns from older children. Siblings become primary targets for imitation and identification. Much of a child's information and savvy about the world are taught by siblings. Grandparents can represent a substantial teaching presence when they are involved in the life of the family, as can friends, teachers, and others. But at no age is the role of parent as teacher as important as it is during the early-school-age period. The following two sections address the roles of parent as educator and parent as advocate. These roles, which are central to the child's full participation in the complex organizations of the community, also promote new learning for many parents. As adults take on the roles of educator and advocate, they must become increasingly skillful at identifying the resources of the community that are a good match for their family's needs.

Parents as Educators

The central process for the resolution of the psychosocial crisis—identification—often involves the child's intense observation of and interest in one or both parents. Emulating parents in thought and action guides the child's learning during this stage. Through the process of identification, children attempt to incorporate their parents' values, beliefs, emotional responses, verbal expressions, and problem-solving strategies. The developmental tasks of moral development, gender-role development, learning group skills, and constructing a theory of self orient children toward any and all information that will help them understand what others expect of them and how best to conform to these expectations.

Children, who are in need of so much information and encountering so many questions, push their parents into the role of teacher. At the same time, many parents also identify with their children, remembering fragments of their own lives when they were four to six, proudly recalling some of their early experiences of mastery and perhaps regretting the loss of their childhood enthusiasm and curiosity. Thus, parents may teach, encourage, and coach their children, not only because their children invite it but because the parents are invested in re-creating, extending, or fixing their own past through their children's new achievements (Radin, 1976).

At this age, parental nurturance and comfort are a critical foundation permitting the child's natural curiosity and innovativeness to flourish. Positive, responsive, and frequent interactions are essential contributions to a child's cognitive and emotional development. Beyond nurturance, however, children need their parents to "explain things" to them, "show them how" things work, and help them "figure things out." Parents enact the teacher role in many different ways across both the socioemotional and the cognitive domains.

As socioemotional teachers, parents provide models of honesty, kindness, thoughtfulness, and caring, as well as dishonesty, thoughtlessness, cruelty, and insensitivity. They talk about how they feel when positive and negative events occur, and they encourage their children to express their feelings as well. Through their actions, as well as their spoken teachings, parents give children ideas about how to handle strong feelings. Parents introduce children to stories, songs, poems, and fables that help encode basic moral teachings, and then talk together about these messages. Why was Cinderella's stepmother so mean? Why did Simba's father, the Lion King, die? What went wrong for the three little pigs? What are these stories about? Conversations constitute a primary mechanism for much teaching and learning about feelings, moral values, and concerns about the consequences of one's actions for others.

Parents are also important teachers in the cognitive domain. Most parents, regardless of their educational background, have a vast storehouse of knowledge, skills, and problem-solving strategies that are of use and interest to children ages four to six (Hall & Skinner, 1980). Parents answer their children's questions and ask new questions that encourage children to extend their thinking. Parents read with their children, helping their children become comfortable with printed language, the organization of books, and the nature of stories. As they go about their day, parents point out signs and symbols on products, in store windows, and around the home that help children recognize the value of printed words and visual images. Parents give children opportunities to help perform tasks in the kitchen, the yard, in cleaning or repairing, in shopping for groceries, writing letters and stamping envelopes, or doing laundry. In these and other situations, parents point out important features of daily tasks and explain how they are done. They encourage children to help, and they provide constructive feedback to improve their level of performance. Parents and children play games together that may involve counting the dots on dice, reading simple words, or recognizing colors and shapes. As children become more skilled players, parents introduce more complicated games or impose stricter rules on the old games. In Vygotsky's terms, parents urge their children to higher levels of functioning by interacting with them in their zone of proximal development.

Parents differ in their beliefs about how children learn, and, as a result, they differ in their ideas about how to foster this learning. Often, these beliefs are related to the kinds of discipline techniques that parents use—authoritarian, authoritative, permissive, and neglectful parenting styles (Schaefer, 1991). However, parental beliefs about the child as a learner encompass more than how to achieve compliance and the internalization of parental standards. They include ideas about the parent's and the child's role in teaching and learning, how to identify the appropriate goals for learning, and what to expect from teachers and schools in the learning process.

In an intensive study of African-American teenage mothers' beliefs about their preschool children's schooling and learning, three different belief systems were identified: transmissive, maturational, and transactional (Neuman et al., 1995). The *transmissive* view suggests that children are like empty vessels ready to be filled up with appropriate knowledge. Information and skills are transmitted from older, more experienced people to children who do not yet have this information. The transmissive view might be considered adult-centered in that adults determine what children need. The *maturational* view suggests that children have a strong developmental capacity for learning. Mothers who held this view thought that, if children were in a safe, supportive environment where they were exposed to information, they would discover ways of learning it. A lot of emphasis is placed on a child's interests and abilities in guiding the direction of new learning.

The *transactional* view emphasizes the child's meaningful interactions with people and objects in the environment in order to gain knowledge. Children are seen as creative agents; adults are seen as guiding and enriching the learning by their responses. Table 12.1 summarizes the salient beliefs about the parent's role, the child's role, the process of learning, and the role of schooling for each of these three views. More research is needed to help clarify how widely held these three perspectives are, whether these beliefs are systematically linked to particular discipline strategies, and what relationship might exist between these belief systems and a child's approach to schooling and academic tasks.

In David Elkind's book, *The Hurried Child* (1981), he warned about the many pressures on young children to give up their childhood and enter the world of competition and self-reliance too soon. In some families, parents take the role of teacher too far too fast. They impose their own frustrated dreams and goals on their young children, forcing them toward unrealistic levels of achievement and competition. They place their children in accelerated academic programs, introducing expectations for mastery of reading, mathematical, and factual skills at the expense of exploration, experimentation, and fantasy play. They introduce their children to lessons of all sorts, including athletic training and musical instruction in which the

TABLE 12.1

Three Belief Systems about Learning

Beliefs about	Transmissive	Maturational	Transactional
The parent's role	Emphasis on direct teaching; knowledge defined as a set of skills transmitted by adult	Emphasis is on child's abilities to learn through his/her own experiences; parent's role is to provide nurturance and opportunity	Emphasis is on encouraging children to actively construct knowledge through their own initiative with adult facilitation
The child's role	Child learners expected to master what is taught through observation and/or recitation	Learners expected to initiate on the basis of interest and personal/social needs	Child encouraged to ask questions, to reason, and to learn from child-oriented activity (i.e., play)
Learning and literacy	Emphasis on the early acquisition of alphabet, numbers, colors—discrete skills	No particular emphasis; child will learn when "ready"	Emphasis on child developing at his/her own pace; encouragement through engaging in storybook reading, conversations, and responses to questions
Schooling	Teachers should manage instruction; learning should be paced; priority of group over individual interests; product-orientation	Teachers should provide a safe environment; should be positive role model for children; schools should be physically well maintained	Teachers should focus on individual needs of children; provide a learning environment for child-initiated activity and skill learning

Source: Neuman et al., (1995). Toward a collaborative approach to parent involvement in early education: A study of teenage mothers in an African-American community. *American Educational Research Journal, 32,* 811.

children are isolated from peers, have limited contact with the parents, and are expected to reach higher and higher levels of achievement at very young ages.

The movie *Searching for Bobby Fisher* illustrates the danger of adults creating an overly intense, competitive context in their efforts to develop a child's talents. In that movie, parents discovered that their child had a precocious ability to play chess. At first, playing was exciting and novel for the child. But as the parents' ambitions for the child's success grew, they hired a coach, entered the child into higher levels of competition, and placed more and more pressure on his winning. Finally, the child rebelled by deliberately losing a match and refusing to play chess. He needed to find out if anyone cared about him as a person or if they were only interested in him when he won chess matches.

Parents can accomplish a lot with their children when they see themselves as teachers, but they must stay focused on identifying the children's own interests and goals rather than their own. Parents need to recognize and value their children's achievements and provide accurate feedback to help their children progress. At the same time, they should encourage the child's own investigation and remain flexible about the ultimate outcome.

Parents as Advocates

The parents' extension into the teacher role seems to be natural as children and adults interact during the early-school-age years. However, changing historical and cultural conditions have introduced another, more formal role for parents as advocates for their children. *Advocacy* for children means speaking on behalf of children and making their needs known. It may involve participation in the public sector to change policies or inform elected officials of children's needs. It may involve forming partnerships with service agencies, schools, businesses, and other organizations to change practices or improve services in a community. Or it may involve forming support groups within a school or neighborhood to help parents articulate and cope with specific challenges that they and their children face (Goffin & Lombardi, 1988).

Educational reforms in the United States have been characterized by trends toward greater sensitivity to the needs of families and greater accountability for educating a more diverse student population. Public schools are mandated by state and federal laws to provide appropriate accommodations for the special needs of children, including accommodations for physical challenges, health-care needs, and special emotional, behavioral, and cognitive disabilities. Three major areas of legislation have had a significant impact on the expectations for schools' adaptations to students' needs. Public Law 94142, the Special Education Act, covers the responsibilities of schools to provide appropriate, least restrictive environments for children with learning disabilities or multiple handicapping conditions. Section 504 of the Civil Rights Act has been interpreted to mean that accommodations must be made for any handicapping conditions that limit learning. The Americans with Disabilities Act requires that all components of the school environment be accessible to all children, teachers, and staff who might have physical challenges. Although these laws require adaptations on the part of schools, they also place new responsibilities on parents to identify their children's special needs as learners, as well as the resources that are available within their school system to meet those needs, and to influence the school system to adopt appropriate policies, programs, and procedures.

Advocacy usually begins at an individual level as a parent recognizes a child's unique talents or challenges as a learner. For example, Ron and Susan noticed that their child, Matt, who was born small for gestational age and four weeks premature, had many motor difficulties. At age four, Matt still had difficulty with bowel control; he could not use a pair of scissors; and he did not like to stay with any one activity very long. When Ron and Susan observed Matt at his preschool, they noticed that he ran around the other children but rarely played with any of them. Matt's teachers told Ron and Susan that he was a cheerful, energetic child who had trouble focusing his attention. They reassured them that Matt would outgrow his difficulties. However, Ron and Susan wondered if Matt would be ready for kindergarten in the fall. They planned to have a psychologist evaluate Matt to identify any specific learning disabilities. They inquired about special prekindergarten programs and talked with their local school principal about what sorts of adjustments the school could make if Matt were to attend kindergarten there in the fall. At present, they are very worried. They doubt that Matt will be able to handle the demands of a regular kindergarten program, but they have not diagnosed Matt's difficulties well enough to know what specific adaptations to request or which kind of school experience would best meet Matt's needs.

Once parents recognize the nature of their children's special needs, they are likely to learn of other families who are facing similar challenges. When the local school is unable to provide the resources or programs for their children, such as programming for the gifted or bilingual teachers or transportation for physically challenged children, parents may begin to work together to try to bring about change. They may introduce their concerns through a parent–teacher organization or form an advocacy group to raise awareness about the legitimate special needs of their children. They may introduce these concerns to school administrators; identify experts who can address them; try to influence legislators to introduce programs or policies regarding their needs; or raise money to provide resources for their children. Often, advocacy groups also provide a source of emotional and social support for parents whose children share common issues.

Advocacy involves representing a child's needs beyond the supportive boundaries of family and friends. It requires parents to admit and accept their child's special challenges and to engage in a process of social change. Through this work, parents not only foster the optimal development of their own children but also fulfill their own needs for generativity, improving the quality of life for many other children in the future.

Cultural and Ethnic Patterns That Create Distinctive Child-Rearing Environments

Much of the discussion in this and the previous chapter centers on issues that are deeply embedded in the cultural context. In fact, one might say that a primary focus of the early-school-age period is on learning to function as an appropriate member of one's social group: to behave in a moral way, according to expectations of parents, family, and other authority figures, and in conformance with patterns associated with one's gender. The implication is that parents and teachers are in the business of shaping, guiding, and constraining behaviors, and children are in the business of paying attention to important messages that will help them follow the culturally approved path. Often, the process is so seamless and trouble-free that children do not even realize that they have been socialized. Sometimes the messages conflict, the practices are very harsh, or the child temperamentally does not fit the culture's expectations. Under these circumstances, children may experience strong feelings of guilt or be identified as "problem children" by parents and teachers, and a pattern of conflict and confusion is set into motion. The two cultural themes that are taken up in this section are the influence of religion on the moral atmosphere of the home, and cultural definitions of gender.

Religion and the Moral Atmosphere of the Home

It is surprising how little scientific information is available on the role of religion in the socialization and moral education of young children. In 1991, 89% of the U.S. population 18 years and older claimed to have a religious affiliation, and 68% were members of a church or synagogue (U.S. Bureau of the Census, 1994). Religious beliefs typically play a key role in clarifying moral values and views about ethical behavior. Most organized religions support concepts of intimacy, childbearing, and parental responsibility within the context of marriage. In providing moral education for their children, parents are likely to rely heavily on their own religious beliefs and the teachings of their religious leaders to guide their instruction. Many families join a church or synagogue when their children reach the age of four or five so that the children can benefit from formal religious instruction (Stolzenberg et al., 1995).

In this section, we explore some of the possible influences of religion on young children. We do not mean to imply that formal religion is the only or the ideal vehicle for creating a meaningful moral climate for young children, but it is an important force. Religion of one type or another is practiced in almost every culture. Yet religion itself is a very complex concept, incorporating many different patterns of beliefs and practices. In thinking about the influence of religion on young children, we must understand how religious beliefs guide a parent's approach to child-rearing, moral education, and social relationships and how a parent's religiosity may enhance or detract from a child's optimal development.

Religious practices, beliefs, and rituals structure many family activities. Attending religious services, learning to recite prayers, singing religious songs, lighting candles, participating in religious holidays, partaking in a first communion or baptism, or having religious images and symbols in the home all provide children with concrete evidence of the significance and pervasiveness of a religious force in their lives. These factors link a child to a concrete set of actions and images that are integrated into the child's self-concept. They also link a child to a community, a group of people beyond the immediate family who share an understanding of the meaning of these symbols and practices and have common expectations about behavior.

Beyond concrete rituals and symbols, religiosity conveys moral messages about the value of human life, an orientation toward human relationships, especially family, and attitudes about behavior toward others (Brody et al., 1994). There is a consistent, if modest, relationship between religiosity and higher levels of marital stability with less marital conflict (Booth et al., 1995). Religious orientation, particularly when it is conceived of as a central, organizing, and integrating framework through which the person strives to achieve a full, moral life, is also typically associated with high levels of well-being (Ventis, 1995). These by-products of religion, in turn, may be expected to provide a context for more supportive, optimistic, caring parent–child relationships.

Religions offer guidance to parents about marital and parent–child relationships. For example, in the Jewish religion parents are expected to oversee the religious, secular, and practical education of their children. Jewish parents are expected to: "1) instill the moral and ethical values of the Jewish heritage; 2) encourage active observance of the Torah's commandments; 3) transmit knowledge of the Torah, the Talmud, and the major Jewish sources; 4) create a strong sense of identification with and concern for all Jewish people" (Donin, 1972, 130). Jewish tradition also requires parents to teach their children the skills necessary to earn a livelihood.

Children in the early-school-age years are at an ideal age to absorb certain religious concepts. Unlike many adults, they do not have to suspend their rational, critical thinking in order to accept religious ideas since those critical reasoning skills are not yet very fully developed. For example, the idea of one omniscient, omnipotent, and omnipresent god is as plausible in the mind of a five-year-old as are the ideas of Santa Claus, angels, and miracles. Belief in

Early religious teaching typically introduces children to the idea of prayer.

God can be embraced readily by a mind that still accepts the possibility of magic, does not yet understand the scientific principles of the physical world, and is not yet sensitive to the logical inconsistencies that many religious beliefs introduce. Armed with a belief in a God who is watching over them, young children raised in a religious home have additional motivation to behave in a morally acceptable way. In Christian faiths, the life of Jesus is a specific model for living a moral life. This provides each child with a very concrete connection with a loving Father who created him or her. Children learn to fear the possibility of God's displeasure and also to be comforted by the belief that God watches over and cares about them.

The impact of religion on young children depends on a parent's orientation. For example, adults who hold very rigid, dogmatic religious views are likely to have other prejudiced views that they pass on to their children. Adults who believe that their religious views hold the inherent and exclusive truth about morality tend to perceive other views as expressions of evil that must be opposed (Altemeyer & Hunsberger, 1992). Other adults have a more questioning, open approach to religion. They seek answers but acknowledge the complexity of the issues that they are trying to resolve. Adults with this approach are likely to score low on measures of bigotry and prejudice (Hunsberger, 1995).

Some religious practices are physically as well as psychologically harmful to young children. These practices range from the relatively common practices of inculcating feelings of self-doubt and sinfulness to significant acts of actual physical abuse. In a survey of clinical psychologists, psychiatrists, and clinical social workers, roughly one-third of the respondents reported that they had encountered at least one case of ritualistic or religious abuse (Bottoms et al., 1995). Respondents gave detailed information about 1,652 cases that they had encountered over a ten-year period. Three major categories of abuse were identified: abuse related to withholding medical care for religious reasons; abuse related to trying to purge a child of evil or of the devil; and abuse by a person of religious authority, typically sexual abuse. In 75% of the cases of medical neglect and 85% of the cases of purging a child from evil, the primary perpetrator was identified as the parent.

The role of religious education is especially relevant to the psychosocial development of young children since they are so actively attuned to discovering moral principles to guide their behavior. As this discussion suggests, religion has the potential to enrich or detract from a young child's development. A religious home environment characterized by love, caring, and concern for others affects a child directly and shapes the child's interactions with others. However, religion can also create an environment in which intimidation and harsh treatment make a child feel guilty and worthless (see Notebook Page 12.3 on page 524).

Culture and Gender

You may have heard people argue about whether the differences we observe between girls and boys are a product of culture or genetically based biological differences. Do girls play with dolls and boys play with trucks because that is what our culture expects them to do, or because girls are biologically more nurturant and boys more physically active? The concept of sex-role standards that was presented in Chapter 11 assumes that cultures send specific messages about the kinds of behaviors that are desirable and appropriate for males and females. Once internalized, these messages guide children's beliefs about how they should behave and what others expect of them as girls and boys, men and women. Cultures differ in the content of their sex-role standards, how strictly these standards are applied, and the degree of overlap in what is expected of boys and girls, or men and women. In this section, we will discuss two approaches to conceptualizing how cultures define gender roles: the distinction between collectivist and individualist cultures and the distinction between masculine and feminine cultures. We also describe the gender-role expectations of two traditional societies, the Yanomamö and the Maasai.

Individualism and Collectivism

One useful strategy for distinguishing social behavior across cultures is to clarify the relative focus on individualism and collectivism (Kashima et al., 1995; Triandis, 1990). In cultures that place a strong value on *individualism*, personal goals are placed at a higher level of priority than is responsibility to the group, whether it is the family, friendship group, work group, or some other type of group identity. There is wide variability in how people are expected to behave, and demographic characteristics such as age, gender, or family role are not as powerful predictors in guiding individual behavior as are individual talents, goals, and preferences.

In cultures that place a strong value on *collectivism,* an individual's behavior is guided largely by group goals. When conflicts arise between personal and communal needs, individuals are expected to place the group's needs ahead of their own. Within these societies, the integrity of the family group is typically a central value. Relationships are based on friendship and mutual support. Individuals are expected to judge their behavior with an eye toward how others might evaluate their actions rather than whether the actions brought them personal pleasure or advantage.

The more collectivist a culture, the more likely roles are to be defined by gender as well as other group characteristics. Family roles are especially important, and there is a lot of social pressure to ensure that children learn appropriate gender roles that will prepare them to create and preserve stable family and community systems. The more individualist a culture, the more likely that children will be socialized to exercise independent judgment and pursue their particular talents and abilities. Within individualist societies, choices about family life are more likely to be based on personal pleasure and romantic love rather than on the basis of duty or family obligation.

Masculinity and Femininity

Another way of characterizing cultures has been along the dimension of masculinity and femininity (Draguns, 1990; Hofstede, 1986). *Masculine* cultures are characterized as making the greatest distinction between what men and women are expected to do. Masculine cultures emphasize instrumentality and place great value on achievement. *Feminine* societies are more flexible, allowing more overlap in male and female roles. One might think of feminine societies as more androgynous with an expectation that men and women will exhibit many traits in common. In feminine cultures, we would expect to see less distinction in the play behaviors of male and female children and fewer restrictive child-rearing practices intended to socialize male and female children along distinct paths. These cultures also emphasize the value of relationships and expressive behavior.

These different ways of thinking about cultures have implications for how stereotyped or constrained gender roles are likely to be. They do not address the content of these gender roles which will be more closely tied to the economic, historical, and geographic contexts to which the culture must adapt.

The Yanomamö: The Fierce People

The Yanomamö Indians live in South America, in jungle areas of southern Venezuela and northern Brazil. They are an aggressive people, organized into small villages that are continuously at war with one another. The Yanomamö society is characterized as strongly masculine (Chagnon, 1977). Men are valued as warriors and are given a wide range of advantages and preferences in the culture. Male children are preferred to female children, resulting in frequent female infanticide. Young girls may play house and enjoy some moments of fun with their mothers, but at an early age they are expected to help their mothers and to serve their fathers and brothers. They are a major asset to their mothers who have difficult and strenuous tasks to do (including gathering firewood and water).

As soon as girls begin to menstruate, they are hidden from others in their home. After this first confinement, they are ready to become wives and move to their husbands' homes. Girls are promised in marriage without any choice, and must begin married life in the husband's residence serving him and his family. Women are expected to be entirely subservient to their husbands, who frequently beat them to show their displeasure. Women are thought to admire

The Impact of Religion During Early Childhood

The religious environment of the home provides a structure for organizing and orienting a young child's early moral education. Think back to when you were four to six and try to recall the moral climate of your family.

1. To what extent did religion contribute to your moral education as a young child? What religious beliefs, if any, were instilled in you? If no religion was practiced by your family, what early moral concepts do you remember learning?

_____

_____

_____

2. What religious rituals and celebrations, if any, were practiced in your family? If your family did not practice any religious rituals, what reaction did you have to those practiced by your friends?

_____

_____

_____

3. What do you remember about your early ideas of God?

_____

_____

_____

4. What religious stories, songs, poems, prayers, or other teachings do you remember learning during your early childhood years?

_____

_____

_____

5. Who were the people most responsible for your early moral education?

_____

_____

_____

6. Which religious beliefs from childhood are still part of your belief system today?

_____

_____

_____

7. Which religious beliefs from childhood did you revise? What experiences led to the revision of those beliefs?

_____

_____

_____

this aggressiveness in their husbands and to brag to other women by showing off the scars from their husbands' attacks. At the same time, women are mistrustful of men and develop a very cynical, bitter outlook on life. When warfare breaks out between villages, women are often abducted and brutalized, so they are very concerned about the bravery and forcefulness of the men in their village. Most of their power comes from goading their men into action to protect them from possible attack from their enemies by accusing them of cowardice.

Little boys have a much more playful childhood than do girls. They are rarely punished and are encouraged to exercise their aggressiveness toward their parents and especially toward their sisters. They are free to play among themselves, creating pretend huts and imitating their fathers' activities. There is no formal closure to childhood for males, but over time they must assert themselves through their fierceness, their success as hunters and warriors, and their general ability to dominate and direct others.

The Maasai

The Maasai live in Kenya and Tanzania, in the Great Rift Valley of East Africa. They are cattle herders, moving each season to follow the herds in search of grass and water. They have a reputation as fierce warriors, but their lives revolve largely around their cattle, which provide food, wealth, and power. The two things that the Maasai pray for are children and cattle, which go hand in hand. If one has children, one needs cattle to provide for them; if one has cattle, one needs children to help with the herd (Saitoti, 1989).

The Maasai adore their children and are very affectionate toward them. In toddlerhood, the boys and girls mingle freely with everyone in the village. Fathers as well as mothers are tender with their infants. All the men and women of the settlement keep an eye out for the safety of the children, even if they are not related. At about age four, boys are encouraged to associate more with the men and girls to associate more with the women, but women remain the primary caregivers. Boys and girls love to sing, play games, and pretend. Boys build make-believe corrals out of mud and stones and put berries or pebbles inside to represent cattle. Girls make dolls out of mud and grass. At about age five to seven, children learn to take on some responsibilities: Boys help with the calves and may help herd cattle; girls help with household tasks. Children are socialized to understand what is good and bad behavior, especially the importance of behaving well in the presence of their elders and showing respect for them. But punishments are usually mild, and good deeds are rewarded.

By the age of 9 to 12, girls begin to associate more with the warriors and less with the boys their own age. They may begin to adorn themselves with beaded necklaces and patterned hides, making themselves attractive to potential boyfriends and lovers. They also take on more difficult chores, including drawing water, collecting firewood, and even tending the sheep and cattle if their fathers have no sons. Boys begin to engage in more difficult and strenuous tasks; by adolescence, they spend most of their time looking after the cattle. But at night, boys and girls still gather together to sing and listen to stories.

For boys, a major transition occurs at about the age of 16 when they try to convince the elders that they are ready for *circumcision*. Circumcision periods last for three or four years, and then no circumcisions are performed for another 15 years or so. This process leads to the formation of a generational group that emerges from childhood to warrior and elderhood as a collective with its own unique name, an identified leader, and a council that makes decisions and establishes norms for their behavior. For boys, circumcision leads to a new life of greater freedom, respect, and admiration.

There is no waiting period for girls, who are circumcised soon after they reach puberty. It is very important to be circumcised before becoming pregnant, which would be a great embarrassment to the family. Once she has healed from the circumcision, a girl is prepared for married life. The freedom and flirtations that were allowed her during the last years of childhood are now severely restricted as she prepares for marriage. Marriages are arranged by parents, often early in childhood. Typically, Maasai men bring many gifts to the girl's family when the couple is betrothed. Thus, a girl is treated with great value and her family with respect as plans are made for the marriage. Although a girl is advised to respect and obey her husband, she also knows that if life with her husband is very unpleasant, she can return to her family or her clan. A young man is advised to treat his new wife fairly or she is likely to return home and it will be difficult to get her back again.

One finds similarities as well as contrasts in the gender-role socialization of these two traditional societies. Both are characterized by socialization of men toward a warrior role. However, in the Yanomamö, the warrior status is achieved individually through acts of aggressiveness and brutality, whereas the Maasai confer warrior status on a group of young men who have proven themselves worthy. This group moves into young adulthood and eventually into elder status as a cohort, providing cohesiveness and leadership to the community. The socialization of gender roles begins early in both cultures, with sex-role expectations being manifest during the period of four to six. However, Maasai boys and girls continue to have many opportunities to play together and to enjoy each other's company through song, games, and storytelling, whereas the Yanomamö children begin to show evidence of male dominance, with boys bullying girls and girls expected to serve and care for their fathers and younger siblings. Puberty brings a marked transition for girls in both the Yanomamö and the Maasai cultures, serving as the time of entry into the restrictions and responsibilities of married life. For boys, puberty is marked by an important set of ceremonial events among the Maasai but a gradual passage into adulthood among the Yanomamö. In general, men and women in the Maasai share more tasks and show more open affection, whereas the gender roles are much more differentiated among the Yanomamö. Even though the two cultures award great status to the warrior role, the Maasai place a more balanced, even value on males and females, and more freedom is given to women, especially during the periods of childhood and early adolescence. In contrast, the Yanomamö culture creates an intense male–female antagonism, which is established in childhood and expressed in adulthood by men brutally beating their wives and women inciting their husbands to new levels of ferocity.

Societal Issues That Provide Resources or Barriers to Development

Development takes place in a dynamic, changing context of historical, economic, and technological factors. Our expectations for young children, the kinds of resources available to them, and the stressors that they encounter vary from one period to the next. Societal factors become increasingly relevant as we think about the developmental tasks of early-school-age children. During the years from four to six, children are building a foundation of competence on gender roles, morality, social relationships, and self-worth. These competencies influence children's adaptation and success in the critical arenas of family, school, and peer relations. In the sections that follow, we discuss two major societal issues that have an impact on adaptation during early school age: school readiness and television.

School Readiness
In 1989, President Bush and the state governors created an educational agenda for the United States. The first goal was that, by the year 2000, all children in America would start school ready to learn. This goal identified the first years

of schooling as critical in setting the long-term course for school achievement and preparation for adult roles and responsibilities. The goal, which seems positive and appropriate on the face of it, has resulted in important dialogue about what is meant by readiness, how to measure it, what obstacles stand in the way of school readiness, and who should be responsible for achieving it (Lewit & Baker, 1995).

Readiness

The concept of *readiness* is a familiar idea in the study of development. Typically, the term is used to refer to a time when the child's physical, cognitive, social, and emotional maturation is at a level that permits new learning or engaging in a more complex, demanding type of activity or relationship. Sometimes, it is called a sensitive period or a teachable moment. We discussed the idea of readiness in relation to attachment relationships and walking in Chapter 7, language use in Chapter 9, toilet training in Chapter 10, and gender-role identification in Chapter 11. Vygotsky's concept of a zone of proximal development is another way of conceptualizing readiness; it is the next higher level of performance that one can achieve with the help of competent teachers. When thinking about the goal stated above, however, the concept of readiness becomes somewhat more complicated. Does it refer to readiness to learn or readiness to start school? One might argue that all children, except perhaps those with very severe neurological damage, are ready to learn. However, not all children have the combination of physical, cognitive, emotional, and social skills that will allow them to adapt to the demands of the kindergarten classroom environment or to succeed at the academic challenges of the kindergarten curriculum (Kagan, 1990).

How to Measure Kindergarten Readiness?

In the past, kindergarten readiness was established largely by chronological age. School districts typically established a birthday cut-off. For example, if a child was five by December 1 of a given year, he or she could start kindergarten in September of that year. Those who missed the December 1 date had to wait until the following September. In the 1980s, concern about the quality of education in the United States led to an upgrading of the elementary school curriculum. As part of this school reform, academic demands for school performance were raised, and children were exposed to a more challenging curriculum in earlier grades. Many skills that had, in the past, been introduced in first grade are now part of the kindergarten curriculum, and more children are having trouble meeting the expectations for school performance. In efforts to prevent early school failure, some states began to administer school readiness tests. However, there is no agreement or universal acceptance of a measure of kindergarten readiness, and some educators dispute whether any test given to five-year-olds can accurately predict a child's ability to learn in the school environment (American Academy of Pediatrics, 1995).

In the midst of these changes in the school environment, parents began to make their own decisions about whether or not their children were ready for kindergarten. In a 1993 National Household Education Survey, slightly over 8% of children who were eligible by age to attend kindergarten were being held back (National Center for Education Statistics, 1994). An increasingly large group of parents has begun to think that it is better to wait a year and give their children a developmental advantage rather than to have them compete with older children who will outperform them. Although there may be some advantage for the older children in kindergarten, especially in the area of language skills, no special advantage is seen for delayed kinder-gartners over on-time kindergartners by the third grade (Shepard & Smith, 1986).

Given the lack of an objective, accepted measure or screening test, what do parents and teachers think are essential markers of school readiness? How can a parent judge if a child is ready or should wait a year to begin kindergarten? In two separate national surveys, parents and teachers were asked what characteristics should be demonstrated by a child who is ready to start school. Figure 12.1 shows the responses. Some items from the teacher survey were not on the parent survey. Teachers emphasized that children need to be physically healthy, well-rested, and well-nourished as the most important aspect of readiness. Beyond that, teachers emphasized the abilities to communicate effectively, to demonstrate enthusiasm and curiosity, to follow directions, to avoid being disruptive, and to show sensitivity to the feelings of other children as important indicators. Parents tended to empha-size the importance of specific skills, such as using a pencil or scissors, knowing the alphabet or counting to 20 more than did teachers (Lewit & Baker, 1995). Typically, these "expert" opinions about kindergarten readiness place a somewhat greater emphasis on social and emotional competence than on skills and knowledge. Children need to be ready to separate com-fortably from their parents, to interact in a positive way with other children, and to engage in the "appropriate" behaviors associated with the student role: following directions, being quiet when asked, and asking and answer-ing questions.

What Obstacles Stand in the Way of School Readiness?

Success in kindergarten is based on a combination of intellectual and social skills and the motivation to succeed. Most children are excited about going to kindergarten and do well. However, certain demographic character-istics are associated with the likelihood of poor school adjustment, even in kindergarten. These include poverty, limited English-language proficiency, and having a physical, cognitive, or emotional disability (National Commis-sion on Children, 1993). Poverty is perhaps the most serious factor, since 24% of all children under the age of six live in poverty, and 59% of all children liv-ing in mother-headed, single-parent families live in poverty (U.S. Bureau of the Census, 1994). These children are likely to suffer from malnutrition, and many have not been immunized against infectious diseases. Often, they have been exposed to parental distress, which affects their overall sense of confi-dence and self-worth. Many of these children have no access to health or den-tal services. Children growing up in poor, urban neighborhoods are exposed to violence in their streets and even in their schoolyards, and their parents do not have the resources to supplement or complement school activities in order to meet their special needs (Stallings, 1995). The effects of poverty can be seen in the lower reading scores of fourth-grade children from disadvantaged urban communities, as compared with children from other kinds of commu-nities (U.S. Department of Education, 1992).

Parent and Teacher Views of Readiness

Percentage of preschoolers' parents and kindergarten teachers who rate specific characteristics as either "essential" or "very important" to being ready to start kindergarten, 1993

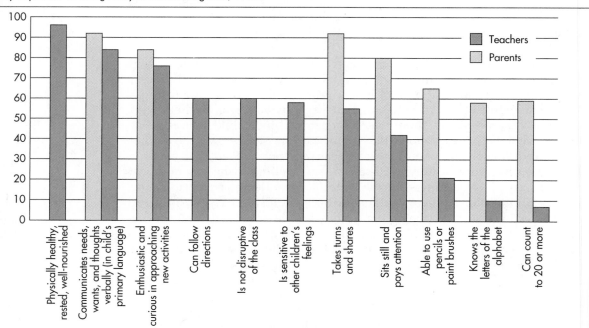

Parents and teachers are arguably the most important forces in a child's early school experiences. This graph, which uses parent responses from the 1993 National Household Education Survey (NHES) and teacher responses from the 1993 kindergarten Teacher Survey on Student Readiness (KTSSR), presents the characteristics that parents and teachers believe are important for being ready to begin kindergarten. For some characteristics, such as physical health and following directions, data are available only for teacher responses from the KTSSR because no parallel question was asked of parents in the NHES.

• Teachers were more likely to rate good health as essential or very important than any other characteristic.
• Parents and teachers agree that both the ability to communicate needs, wants, and thoughts verbally in a child's primary language and the qualities of being enthusiastic and curious in approaching new activities are very important aspects of school readiness.
• Substantially more parents than teachers believe that the more academic items, such as counting to 20 or knowing the letters of the alphabet, are important for school readiness.

FIGURE 12.1

Parents' and teachers' responses to important indicators of school readiness
Source: U.S. Department of Education. Readiness for kindergarten: Parent and teacher beliefs. NCES 93–257. Washington, D.C.: National Center for Education Statistics, Office of Educational Research and Improvement, 1993; National Center for Education Statistics. *Public school kindergarten teachers: Views on children's readiness for school.* Statistical analysis report. Washington, D.C.: U.S. Department of Education, 1993.

Who Is Responsible for Meeting the Goal of School Readiness?

One of the questions raised by establishing a national goal for children to start school ready to learn is "Whose responsibility is it to meet this goal?" Do we need to place more responsibility on families to provide the early experiences that will foster health, confidence, motivation, and cognitive and social development during the first four years of life? Do we need to place more responsibility on schools to provide the environment, services, curriculum, and methods of instruction that will facilitate learning for an increasingly diverse group of students? Do we need to place more responsibility on local, state, and federal governments to sustain and expand programs such as Head Start so that more children can participate in early educational experiences that help offset the negative effects of poverty?

What does Lucy understand from the images she sees on T.V.?

A psychosocial perspective calls for action on all three fronts. The child's chances of success in school will be improved if all interacting systems support one another in achieving the goal of academic success for the widest range of students. Schools, businesses, and families must work together to identify the children who are at greatest risk for school failure in their community and make plans for integrated, long-range multiservice programs (Madden et al., 1993; Stallings, 1995).

The Impact of Television

If you were to visit the homes of American families in the early 1940s, you would find that only a few of the most wealthy families had televisions. Today, over 90% of American families have at least one TV set, and many families have more than one. College students have television sets in their dormitory rooms, hospitals provide television in patients' rooms, and motels and hotels have televisions with additional pay channels for viewing movies. There are televisions that can be plugged into automobile cigarette lighters for "on-the-road viewing," and there are hand-held televisions that people can carry with them just like small radios and tape players. The centrality of television as a force in daily life was vividly portrayed in the movie *Rain Man*, in which the main character becomes intensely anxious if he thinks he is going to miss his regular, daytime television programs.

Televisions are being watched an average of about seven hours per day in American homes (Sternberg, 1985). Studies of the viewing time for different ages suggest that even infants are exposed to about half an hour of television daily. On average, children in the age range four to six watch about two and a half hours of television daily (Liebert & Sprafkin, 1988). This average, of course, gives no indication of the wide variation in practices observed among children in this age range. Some children watch as much as six or eight hours of television a day on weekends. A study of first-graders found that about one-third watched four or more hours of television daily and about 10% watched none (Lyle & Hoffman, 1972).

Since television is so pervasive in our lives, it makes sense to examine its impact on development. How do the amount of time spent watching television and the content of the programs that are watched influence the cognitive and socioemotional development of young children? To what extent can television be a stimulus for optimal development? Can we draw any implications that might be useful to parents and teachers who have responsibility for guiding young children's television viewing?

Cognitive Consequences

Many parents and educators worry that television is turning children into a generation of couch potatoes who are lulled into a life of mental and physical passivity. A review of over 200 studies of the impact of television on children's cognitive development found a mixed picture of television's impact (Landers, 1989a). On the one hand, there is no simple relationship between hours of television viewing and academic performance. On the other hand, children who spend a lot of time watching television do have less time for other stimulating activities and for peer interaction.

Television viewing tends to replace other activities that children might be involved in, such as going to the movies, playing, reading, listening to the radio, and participating in organized sports. In a natural experiment, Williams and Handford (1986) compared the daily activities of adults and children in three Canadian towns: one that had no television (NOTEL), one that had only one television channel (UNITEL), and one that had four channels (MULTITEL). Data were collected before television came to NOTEL and then again four years later. Before television, the children and youths in NOTEL were significantly more involved in community and sports activities than youths in the other two towns. Once NOTEL had television reception, participation in these activities dropped dramatically.

Research on cognitive development suggests that social interaction is an important stimulus for cognitive growth. Children benefit by interacting with others who express ideas and opinions that differ from their own. Day-to-day exchanges with adults and peers force children to examine their own point of view and to "decenter" as they seek solutions to problems or make plans as members of a group. Because television reduces social interaction, it can have a negative effect on cognitive development. The presence of television in a community reduces participation in community activities. Even within the family, when the television is on, conversation dwindles. An observational study of family television viewing periods found that children interacted less with each other and with their fathers during viewing periods than during nonviewing periods (Brody, Stoneman & Sanders, 1980).

The need for peer-group interaction is certainly not met during the hours when a child watches television (Gadberry, 1974). For many young children, watching television is a solitary activity. This is a time when they are interacting neither with peers nor with adults. The noninteractive aspect of television does not serve to reduce the young child's egocentrism, as interaction with other people does.

Television does not appear to replace time spent doing homework. To the distress of many adults, children often have the television on when they do their homework (Sheehan, 1983). Even when the television is on, however, children are not really "glued to the tube." Preschool-age children are observed to tune out frequently while they watch television. They often ignore long portions of the audio component of programs (Hayes & Birnbaum, 1980). They are especially distracted by the presence of toys, by the boring quality of programs, and by the mere fact of having already watched television for a while (Anderson, 1977). A study of five-year-old children in their own homes found that the children were looking at the television only 67% of the time they were in the room while it was on (Anderson et al., 1985). Visual attention to the television appears to peak at about age nine and declines slightly to an adult rate of about 60% of the time (Huston et al., 1992). In any attempt to assess the impact of television, it is important to determine whether heavy viewers are actually focusing their attention on the television or treating it as background for other activities.

Many studies have focused on the potential relationship between television viewing and specific cognitive processes. The results of these studies have shown limited effects (Huston et al., 1992). Television viewing in and of itself is not related to reduced attention span, reduced academic achievement, reduced reading time, or reduced creativity and imagination. Similarly, claims that television viewing enhances cognitive functioning have had little support (Anderson & Collins, 1988). The effects of television are mediated by a child's intelligence, other activities and stimuli in the environment, and the kind and amount of viewing (see Box 12.2). In a synthesis of 23 studies, researchers found an inverted U-shaped relationship between television viewing and academic achievement. Achievement was highest among children who viewed about 10 to 15 hours of television per week (as compared with children who watched fewer than 10 hours), and then declined sharply as viewing hours increased from 20 to 40 hours (Williams et al., 1982).

The lack of clear evidence about negative or positive consequences of television viewing is somewhat counterintuitive. If one compared children who spend time watching television with children who spend time playing video games and computer games, one wonders whether the two forms of leisure activity would be associated with different patterns of mental activity and levels of cognitive functioning.

Socioemotional Consequences

The dominant focus of research on the socioemotional impact of television viewing is the role of televised violence in the beliefs and behaviors of young children. Concern with television violence is particularly relevant to the context of the child's growing moral consciousness. More than 20 years of laboratory experiments, field experiments, and analyses of naturally occurring behaviors have led to the conclusion that televised violence has definite negative consequences for young children's behaviors and beliefs.

Studies of children in the United States and in other countries support the belief that at least three processes may increase the level of aggressiveness in children who watch televised violence (see Table 12.2) (Comstock & Paik, 1991; Huesmann & Eron, 1986; Huesmann & Malamuth, 1986; Huston et al., 1992; Josephson, 1987; Liebert & Sprafkin, 1988). First, children observe

BOX 12.2

What Do Children Understand about Television Advertising?

One aspect of watching television that has received attention is the impact of televised advertising on the attitudes and buying preferences of children (Comstock & Paik, 1991; Liebert & Sprafkin, 1988). Children as young as three and four can usually tell the difference between programs and commercials. Under the age of eight, however, children are not clearly aware of the marketing intention of the advertisement. Young children tend to trust a commercial's message to be accurate and true. They do not understand disclaimers ("some assembly required") or the company's motivation for presenting the commercial. From age 8 up to age 12, there is a marked increase in children's understanding of the profit motive associated with advertising and an accompanying decline in trust in commercial messages.

Advertisements aimed at young viewers have at least two negative consequences. First, children are likely to have conflicts with their parents when they want to buy products that they have seen advertised on television. Since young children are more gullible than adults, they find it hard to accept their parents'

judgment about the actual worth of an advertised product. Parents and children are very likely to differ as to whether the product will really be as much fun as the children have been led to believe. The only way some children can learn to be more discerning is to buy an advertised product and be disappointed.

The second negative consequence applies specifically to highly sugared food products—candies, sweet fruit-flavored drinks, and sugared cereals. Advertisements for these products make up about 80% of children's television advertising (Liebert & Sprafkin, 1988). Exposure to these advertisements is likely to influence young children's beliefs about nutrition as well as their selection of foods and snacks. Young children do not understand that eating these heavily sugared foods causes them to gain excess weight and produces cavities. When children are exposed to commercials for these sugary snacks, they are likely to select them when they have a choice, even when they know that fruits and vegetables are healthier snacks (Gorn & Goldberg, 1982).

televised role models who perform aggressive actions. Children are especially likely to imitate the aggressive actions of a hero who is provoked and retaliates with aggression. Thus, viewing televised violence adds new violent behaviors to the child's repertoire. In addition, when a hero is rewarded or viewed as successful as a result of violent actions, children's tendencies to express aggression are increased (Bandura, 1973).

The second process linked to the impact of televised violence is a heightening of arousal. The fast action that usually accompanies televised violence captures the viewer's attention. The violent incident raises the child's level of emotionality, bringing to the fore other aggressive feelings, thoughts, memories, and action tendencies. The more frequently this network of elements is activated, the stronger their association. Thus, children who have seen a lot of televised violence and are temperamentally aggressive are likely to engage in overt acts of aggression because of the strong arousal prompted by the televised stimulus (Berkowitz, 1984, 1986).

Finally, exposure to televised violence affects a young child's beliefs and values. Children who are exposed to frequent episodes of televised violence are more likely to believe that aggressive behavior is an acceptable way to resolve conflicts, and they become hardened to the use of aggression in peer interactions. They are also more accepting of the use of aggression as a response to frustration. In addition, children (and adults) who are exposed to televised violence are more likely to expect that others will be

TABLE 12.2

Three Processes That May Increase the Level of Aggression in Children Who Watch Televised Violence

Process	Possible Consequence
Observing role models who engage in aggressive actions.	Imitation of violent action likely when: 1. Hero is provoked and retaliates with aggression. 2. Hero is rewarded for violent actions. New violent behaviors added to repertoire.
Viewing aggressive actions leads to heightened level of arousal.	Brings network of aggressive thoughts, feelings, memories, and action tendencies into consciousness. Repeated stimulation strengthens this network. Stimulation interacts with aggressive temperament to increase the likelihood of aggressive action.
Viewing aggression affects beliefs and values.	Aggressive behavior is seen as an acceptable way to resolve conflicts. Viewers are hardened to use of aggression in peer interactions. Aggression is used as a response to frustration. Viewers expect others to be aggressive toward them. Viewers worry about being victims of aggression. Viewers see the world as a dangerous place.

aggressive toward them; they are more likely to worry about being victims of aggression; and they are more likely to see the world as a dangerous place (Bryant et al., 1981; Gerbner et al., 1980; Thomas & Drabman, 1977).

Television as a Stimulus for Optimal Development

Researchers have barely scratched the surface of television's uses for promoting optimal development. There is clear evidence that children who are exposed to prosocial programming can be influenced toward more positive social behavior (Hearold, 1986). Some programs developed for children and others intended for a broader viewing audience convey positive ethical messages about the value of family life and friendship, the need to work hard and sacrifice in order to achieve important goals, the importance of loyalty and commitment in relationships, and many other cultural values. A number of contemporary programs include characters of many races and ethnic backgrounds. Many feature women in positions of authority or performing acts of heroism. A variety of family groupings are represented, including children in single-parent families, stepfamilies, gay and lesbian families, and multigenerational families. Through exposure to these programs, children can learn to challenge racial and gender stereotypes and develop positive images of people of other racial and cultural groups (Liebert & Sprafkin, 1988).

Public television has been successful in developing programs that directly address the educational needs of young children. *Sesame Street* is the best-known and most well-documented of these efforts. It is clear that young children who consistently watch *Sesame Street* benefit in a variety of intellectual tasks, such as recognizing letters, numbers, and shapes; sorting objects into groups; and recognizing relationships among objects. Children who watched *Sesame Street* regularly between the ages of three and five showed measurable improvement in vocabulary. These gains have been documented for boys and girls from a variety of socioeconomic backgrounds (Rice et al., 1990).

After the success of *Sesame Street*, other programs directed at development of literacy, science education, and mathematical skill appeared. Professionals are confident that television can introduce ideas and information to supplement instruction and improve literacy for a broad range of children. However, relatively few resources are directed toward this activity in the United States. Japan, Great Britain, and Australia all invest significantly more toward the development of public television programming for children than the United States does. "In 1985, the British Broadcasting Corp. carried 590 hours of newly produced TV programs for children compared to 87.5 hours in the United States" (Landers, 1989b).

Advice to Parents, Teachers, and Caregivers about Guiding Children's Television Viewing

Many families find that they end up arguing about the amount or kind of television programs that their children watch. (See Notebook Page 12.4.) Withdrawal from television becomes a punishment for a wide range of misbehaviors, from telling a lie to getting in trouble in school. Parents and children may argue about which programs to watch or about turning off the television at bedtime. Conversely, children may find that their parents are so involved in television that they cannot get their attention; and parents may depend on television as a substitute for companionship for their children when they are not home.

Since television is a given in contemporary life, it makes sense to help children get the most out of it. Making it the focus of conflicts over control does not seem very productive. Parents, teachers, and other caregivers need to take a proactive stance with respect to children's experiences with television (Huston et al., 1992; Tangney, 1987). They should emphasize more dos than don'ts.

1. Watch television with young children and talk about the stories and information presented. Talk about how situations that are presented on television may or may not be similar to real life.

The Impact of Television Viewing on Young Children

The literature on the impact of television has focused on cognitive consequences, especially academic achievement, and socioemotional consequences, especially the impact of televised violence. But there are many other themes in the programs that children watch. Spend two hours watching Saturday-morning cartoons and two hours watching educational programming designed for children ages four to six. Keep a record of the following issues.

1. Moral messages: What is right and wrong, good and bad behavior? How should people be treated?

_____

_____

2. Messages about gender: How should boys and girls, men and women behave? (You may detect this from the kinds of actions that males and females perform, as well as from what is said.)

_____

_____

3. Messages about race, culture, and ethnicity: What racial/ethnic groups are depicted? How do they behave toward one another? What characteristics or attributes do the people or characters of various racial groups display?

_____

_____

4. Messages about violence: How is violence portrayed? What happens to people or characters who behave in an aggressive manner?

_____

_____

5. From what you have observed, what would you say are the potential contributions of television (both positive and negative) to a young child's psychosocial development?

_____

_____

537

2. As appropriate, follow up ideas and suggestions presented in educational programming with activities at home or in the classroom. Such activities give children ideas about how to use the information being presented on television more actively.

3. Encourage children to sample a wide variety of television programs. Introduce them to news specials, science programs, opera, concerts, classic movies, and coverage of special events, as well as children's programming.

4. Talk with children about the purpose of commercials, how they are made, how they are intended to influence children's behaviors, and how children should evaluate them.

5. Limit young children's exposure to television violence. It will probably not be possible to eliminate it entirely, but deliberate efforts should be made to reduce the early-school-age child's exposure to violent programming before bedtime, and to talk with children about how and why violence is used on TV. With the newly developed V-chip, it may become possible to prevent many violent programs from being carried in homes where young viewers are present.

6. Talk with children about other activities that they can participate in instead of watching television. Help children choose among many uses of their time.

7. Tape programs that are developmentally appropriate for times when children are sick at home or when regular evening programming is judged to be unsuitable for a child of a certain temperament or developmental level.

The goal is to take advantage of the cognitive and socioemotional resources that television offers without allowing it to dominate a child's time or thoughts with violent, exploitive, and sexist or racist messages.

Optimizing Development for Early-School-Age Children

Early-school-age children push the boundaries of their world through experimentation and inquiry. They are eager for new information, asking questions about anything and everything. Sometimes it may even seem that they are trying to irritate you, constantly poking their "But why?" in your face. Yet, this very spirit of insistent questioning is at the heart of the enthusiasm for learning that will result eventually in a cognitively complex, rational adult who can frame problems and seek information to solve them. For this reason, it is important for adults to be open to young children's inquiries. Adults must learn to listen to the questions and concerns a child raises and provide information that helps resolve these questions. This means taking the child's point of view, responding in ways that legitimize the child's curiosity, without overwhelming the child with too much information. A child who asks where babies come from may want to know that they are formed in the mother's uterus but he or she may not be ready for an entire lecture on sexual reproduction. If an initial answer does not suffice, the child will probably ask more questions.

Most of a young child's inquiry is in areas where adults have quite a lot of expertise. However, it is important that adults let children know that they do not have information about every topic. A child's questioning is a wonderful opportunity to introduce young children to other sources of information—trips to the library, books and magazines at home, information available from television, computer programs, the Internet, friends, family members, and other experts. And as children's information and ideas expand, they may become experts themselves. One four-year-old we know developed a keen interest in geography by playing with his father on big, floor-sized puzzles of the United States and the world. He could spout off quite a lot of facts about cities and countries of the world and entered into conversations about travel with great enthusiasm.

Some of a child's exploration takes place through direct manipulation with objects and materials. Children of this age like to take things apart to see how they operate. They like to mix solutions of various products to create "magic formulas" or new drinks or perfumes. They may enjoy dressing up in odd costumes, creating new looks by "trimming" their hair or "altering" their clothes. Encouraging this kind of "scientific" experimentation requires making material available and giving children a certain leeway in what they can modify or mutilate without negative consequences.

Sometimes, in a spurt of energy, young children try out pranks they have heard about or seen on television. These are years of playful mischief as children begin to comprehend what might create surprise or distress in another person. Annoyed at being locked out of her parents' bedroom, one young girl unscrewed the latch on the door so it couldn't be locked. Another child snuck his parents' car keys into his pocket, opened the car, started the engine, and began playing the car radio.

These efforts at initiative may stretch an adult's patience. A parent may worry that the child will get into trouble in the outside world if he or she doesn't know how to restrain this playful inquisitiveness. It may be funny to hide mother's car keys, but it may not be funny to hide the teacher's purse. A parent may encourage independent judgment at home, but a teacher may feel that a child who insists on his or her own approach to solving a problem is being disrespectful or disruptive. Thus, parents try to socialize their children to community norms in an effort to protect the child and perhaps the family from embarrassment. In this effort, parents may convey the idea that inquiry and experimentation are dangerous or undesirable. This message is full of pitfalls. While too little restraint on the child's initiative may leave the child open to ridicule at school or among other children, too much restraint takes away the creative energy that fuels further growth. Parents and other adults responsible for a young child's education and socialization must find the right balance between fostering a child's enthusiasm for creative inquiry and a respect for the feelings and needs of others, especially when the inquiry threatens to undermine privacy, safety, or moral and ethical taboos of the culture.

Ideas about fostering optimal development during the early-school-age period are listed in Table 12.3. These ideas are taken from the material covered in Chapters 11 and 12 of the text.

TABLE 12.3

Optimizing Development for Early-School-Age Children

Be willing to explore questions about gender and expose children to a variety of male and female images and role models.

Recognize the child's needs to categorize and differentiate activities on the basis of gender.

Remember that this is a time when children will be very receptive to your own values about many issues, including your views on gender roles.

Provide evidence of flexibility in your own behavior and in the behavior of others within the home or school environment to encourage flexible attitudes about gender.

Foster a sense of worth for the child's gender without belittling the opposite gender.

Engage in conversations about moral dilemmas as they arise in play, within the family, on television, or in stories.

In addition to telling a child about your views of right or wrong, encourage him or her to explain to you why something is right or wrong.

Encourage empathy for another person's feelings and life conditions.

Help children think about how situations look from another person's point of view.

Teach children about your moral values through stories, games, songs, poems, and, most important, through your own moral behavior.

When children do things that you disapprove of or think are naughty, use discipline techniques that help them understand the moral implications of their behavior.

Decide which actions are important to restrict or correct; don't try to correct too many behaviors, especially behaviors that may arise out of sincere curiosity or playful experimentation.

Remember that children who identify with their parents are typically very sensitive to even mild messages of disapproval. Too much criticism may make a child feel ashamed and worthless. Too much adult power assertion may lead a child to identify with the assertive method of resolving conflict and become bullying and aggressive with others.

Validate and enjoy the child's enthusiasm for play.

Continue to participate as a play companion.

Recognize the value of a child's friendships, and provide opportunities for your child to spend time with friends.

Help support a child's self-esteem through messages of love and approval.

Provide opportunities for a child to explore many areas of talent and ability.

Give children many situations in which they experience success.

Be reassuring and give helpful, constructive criticism when a child fails. Avoid sarcastic or belittling reactions to a child's failure.

Try to foster a child's sense of optimism about the ability to meet challenges and succeed.

Encourage curiosity.

(continued)

TABLE 12.3 (continued)

Be ready to answer children's questions and to identify additional sources of information.

Encourage the child to experiment with materials and ideas.

Show enthusiasm for a child's suggestions and plans. Try to help a child enact his or her plans when possible.

Encourage parental identification through warmth, through many opportunities for interaction, and by recognizing the similarities between you and your child.

Conceptualize your role as teacher. Help children develop new skills, extend their language abilities, and understand the behaviors of others.

Present some problem-solving opportunities that are a little beyond the child's current level of functioning.

Encourage the child to learn and participate in the rituals and celebrations of the family, including those that are derived from your religious and ethnic heritage. This is an important time for developing a sense of family.

Serve as an advocate for your child by trying to make the best match possible between the child's needs and the resources of the school and community.

Try to gather as much information as you can about what your child is experiencing at school, and try to create a sense of continuity between home and school.

Talk with your child about what he or she is viewing on television.

Use television as a resource for information and entertainment, not as a substitute for other forms of meaningful activity and social interaction.

Chapter Summary

1. The psychosocial crisis of the early-school-age period is initiative versus guilt. Initiative is the active, conceptual investigation of the world. A sense of initiative has direct implications for such essential personality characteristics as self-esteem, creativity, curiosity, and risk taking.

2. Guilt is an emotion that accompanies a sense of responsibility for an unacceptable thought, fantasy, or action. It plays an important role in orienting children toward the implications of their actions for others. In moderation, it appears to be an essential ingredient in preserving social bonds. In the extreme, however, excessive guilt restricts creative thought and action.

3. The central process for resolving the psychosocial crisis is identification. Through identification, children incorporate their parents' beliefs and values and build an ego ideal.

4. The prime adaptive ego quality, purpose, allows children to bring goal-directed planfulness to their action. Much of a young child's purposefulness is expressed through play.

5. The core pathology, inhibition, is associated with self-conscious restraints on behavior, usually linked to fear of loss of love.

6. The developmental direction of the early-school-age period typically evokes new roles for parents, especially the roles of educator and

advocate. As educators, parents play a key role in teaching, coaching, encouraging, and extending their children's academic and socioemotional skills.

7. As advocates, parents try to understand their children's unique talents and needs. They work to create the best match possible between these needs and the resources of the school and community. This role may require parents to join formal or informal support groups that will have an impact on larger organizations.

8. The family's religious beliefs and practices contribute to the moral environment of the home and influence the child's early belief system. Often, these practices and rituals provide a memorable, concrete structure for the child's inquiry about good and evil, family relationships, and the idea of God. Sometimes, religious practices are associated with harsh punishments and engender intense feelings of guilt that detract from optimal development.

9. Cultural practices shape the content of sex-role expectations and guide the development of male and female children along distinct paths toward adolescent and adult roles.

10. Parents and teachers are concerned about how to define school readiness for entry into kindergarten. The goal of having all American children ready to learn when they start school has led to controversies about how to define school readiness and how to overcome the obstacles that place certain children at risk for early school failure.

11. The impact of television on the early-school-age child highlights the interconnectedness of emotional and cognitive development. As an activity, television viewing reduces social interaction. Moderate amounts of television viewing do not appear to disrupt academic achievement.

12. Many studies demonstrate a strong relationship between viewing television violence and increased aggressiveness among young children. The potential for television to contribute to the optimal development of young children has only begun to be realized.

References

Altemeyer, B. & Hunsberger, B. (1992). Authoritarianism, religious fundamentalism, quest, and prejudice. *The International Journal for the Psychology of Religion, 2*, 113–133.

American Academy of Pediatrics. (1995). The inappropriate use of school "readiness" tests. *Pediatrics, 95*, 437–438.

Anderson, D. R. (1977). *Children's attention to television.* New Orleans: Paper presented at the biennial meeting of the Society for Research in Child Development.

Anderson, D. R. & Collins, P. A. (1988). *The impact on children's education: Television's impact on cognitive development.* Washington, D.C.: U.S. Department of Education.

Anderson, D. R., Field, D. E., Collins, E. P. L. & Nathan, J. G. (1985). Estimates of young children's time with television: A methodological comparison of parent reports with time-lapse video home observation. *Child Development, 56*, 1345–1357.

Bandura, A. (1973). *Aggression: A social learning analysis.* Englewood Cliffs, N.J.: Prentice-Hall.

Berkowitz, L. (1984). Some effects of thoughts on anti- and prosocial influences of media events: A cognitive-neoassociation analysis. *Psychological Bulletin, 95*, 419–427.

Berkowitz, L. (1986). Situational influences on reactions to observed violence. *Journal of Social Issues, 42*, 93–103.

Booth, A., Johnson, D. R., Branaman, A. & Sica, A. (1995). Belief and behavior: Does religion matter in today's marriage? *Journal of Marriage and the Family, 57,* 661–671.

Bottoms, B. L., Shaver, P. R., Goodman, G. S. & Qin, J. (1995). In the name of God: A profile of religion-related child abuse. *Journal of Social Issues, 51,* 85–112.

Brody, G. H., Stoneman, Z., Flor, D. & McCray, C. (1994). Religion's role in rural, two-parent African-American families. *Journal of Marriage and the Family, 56,* 878–888.

Brody, G. H., Stoneman, Z. & Sanders, A. K. (1980). Effects of television viewing on family interactions: An observational study. *Family Relations, 29,* 216–220.

Bryant, J., Carveth, R. A. & Brown, D. (1981). Television viewing and anxiety: An experimental examination. *Journal of Communication, 31,* 106–119.

Chagnon, N. A. (1977). *Yanomamö: The fierce people* (2nd ed.). New York: Holt, Rinehart & Winston.

Comstock, G. A. (with Haejung Paik). (1991). *Television and the American child.* San Diego, Calif.: Academic Press.

Coolidge, J. C. (1979). School phobia. In J. D. Noshpitz (Ed.), *Basic handbook of child psychiatry.* New York: Basic Books, 453–463.

Damon, W. & Hart, D. (1988). *Self-understanding in childhood and adolescence.* New York: Cambridge University Press.

Davison, G. C. & Neale, J. M. (1990). *Abnormal psychology: An experimental clinical approach* (5th ed.). New York: Wiley.

Dodge, K. A., Pettit, G. S., McClaskey, C. L. & Brown, M. M. (1986). Social competence in children. *Monographs of the Society for Research in Child Development, 51* (2, Serial No. 213).

Donin, H. H. (1972). *To be a Jew.* New York: Basic Books.

Draguns, J. G. (1990). Normal and abnormal behavior in cross-cultural perspective: Specifying the nature of their relationship. In J. J. Berman (Ed.), *Nebraska symposium on motivation, 1989.* Lincoln: University of Nebraska Press, 235–278.

Elkind, D. (1981). *The hurried child: Growing up too fast too soon.* Reading, Mass.: Addison-Wesley.

Erikson, E. H. (1963). *Childhood and society* (2nd ed.). New York: W. W. Norton.

Erikson, E. H. (1977). *Toys and reasons.* New York: W. W. Norton.

Erikson, E. H. (1978). Reflections on Dr. Borg's life cycle. In E. H. Erikson (Ed.) *Adulthood.* New York: W. W. Norton, 1–31.

Erikson, E. H. (1982). *The life cycle completed: A review.* New York: W. W. Norton.

Freud, S. (1929/1955). Three essays on the theory of sexuality. In J. Strachey (Ed.), *The standard edition of the complete psychological works of Sigmund Freud* (vol. 7). London: Hogarth Press.

Gadberry, S. (1974). Television as baby-sitter: A field comparison of preschoolers' behavior during playtime and during television viewing. *Child Development, 45,* 1132–1136.

Gerbner, G., Gross, L., Morgan, M. & Signorelli, N. (1980). The "mainstreaming" of America: Violence profile no. 11. *Journal of Communication, 30,* 10–29.

Goffin, S. G. & Lombardi, J. (1988). *Speaking out: Early childhood advocacy.* Washington, D.C.: National Association for the Education of Young Children.

Gorn, G. J. & Goldberg, M. E. (1982). Behavioral evidence of the effects of televised food messages on children. *Journal of Consumer Research, 9,* 200–205.

Hall, E. G. & Skinner, N. (1980). *Somewhere to turn: Strategies for parents of the gifted and talented.* New York: Teachers College Press.

Hayes, D. S. & Birnbaum, D. W. (1980). Preschoolers' retention of televised events: Is a picture worth a thousand words? *Developmental Psychology, 16,* 410–416.

Hearold, S. (1986). A synthesis of 1043 effects of television on social behavior. In G. Comstock (Ed.), *Public communications and behavior* (vol. 1). New York: Academic Press, 65–133.

Hoffman, M. L. (1982). Development of prosocial motivation: Empathy and guilt. In N. Eisenberg (Ed.), *The development of prosocial behavior.* New York: Academic Press, 281–313.

Hoffman, M. L. (1990). Empathy and justice motivation. *Motivation and Emotion, 14,* 151–172.

Hofstede, G. (1986). Cultural differences in teaching and learning. *International Journal of Intercultural Relations, 10,* 301–320.

Huesmann, L. R. & Eron, L. D. (1986). *Television and the aggressive child: A cross-national comparison.* Hillsdale, N.J.: Erlbaum.

Huesmann, L. R. & Malamuth, N. M. (1986). Media violence and antisocial behavior: An overview. *Journal of Social Issues, 42,* 1–6.

Hunsberger, B. (1995). Religion and prejudice: The role of religious fundamentalism, quest, and right-wing authoritarianism. *Journal of Social Issues, 51,* 113–129.

Huston, A. C., Donnerstein, E., Fairchild, H., Feshbach, N. D., Katz, P. A., Murray, J. P., Rubinstein, E. A., Wilcox, B. L. & Zuckerman, D. (1992). *Big world, small screen: The role of television in American society.* Lincoln: University of Nebraska Press.

Izard, C. E. (1977). *Human emotion.* New York: Plenum.

Jacobson, E. (1964). *The self and the object world.* New York: International Universities Press.

Josephson, W. L. (1987). Television violence and children's aggression: Testing the priming, social script, and disinhibition predictions. *Journal of Personality and Social Psychology, 53,* 882–890.

Kagan, S. L. (1990). Readiness 2000: Rethinking rhetoric and responsibility. *Phi Delta Kappan, 1,* 21–23.

Kashima, Y., Yamaguchi, S., Kim, U., Choi, S., Gelfand, M. J. & Yuki, M. (1995). Culture, gender, and self: A perspective from individualism-collectivism research. *Journal of Personality and Social Psychology, 69,* 925–937.

Landers, S. (1989a). Watching TV, children *do* learn. *APA Monitor, 20(3),* 25.

Landers, S. (1989b). Big Bird, experts sing praises of kids' shows. *APA Monitor, 20(7),* 32.

Lewit, E. M. & Baker, L. S. (1995). School readiness. *The Future of Children, 5,* 128–139.

Liebert, R. M. & Sprafkin, J. (1988). *The early window: Effects of television on children and youth* (3rd ed.). New York: Pergamon.

Lyle, J. & Hoffman, H. R. (1972). Children's use of television and other media. In E. A. Rubinstein, G. A. Comstock & J. P. Murray (Eds.), *Television in day-to-day life: Patterns of use.* Washington, D.C.: U.S. Government Printing Office, 129–256.

Maccoby, E. E. (1990). Gender and relationships: A developmental account. *American Psychologist, 45,* 513–520.

Madden, N. A., Slavin, R. E., Karweit, N. L., Doaln, L. J. & Wasik, B. A. (1993). Success for all: Longitudinal effects of a restructuring program for inner-city elementary schools. *American Educational Research Journal, 30,* 123–148.

Murphy, L. B. (1972). Infant's play and cognitive development. In M. W. Piers (Ed.), *Play and development.* New York: Norton, 99–126.

National Center for Education Statistics. (1994). *National household education survey of 1993: School readiness data file user's manual.* NCES 94-193. Washington, D.C.: U.S. Department of Education.

National Commission on Children. (1993). *Just the facts: A summary of recent information on America's children and their families.* Washington, D.C.: National Commission on Children.

Neuman, S. B., Hagedorn, T., Celano, D. & Daly, P. (1995). Toward a collaborative approach to parent involvement in early education: A study of teenage mothers in an African-American community. *American Educational Research Journal, 32,* 801–827.

Phelps, L., Cox, D. & Bajorek, E. (1992). School phobia and separation anxiety: Diagnostic and treatment comparisons. *Psychology in the Schools, 29,* 384–394.

Radin, N. (1976). The role of the father in cognitive, academic, and intellectual development. In M. E. Lamb (Ed.), *The role of the father in child development.* New York: John Wiley & Sons, 237–276.

Rice, M. L., Huston, A. C., Truglio, R. & Wright, J. C. (1990). Words from *Sesame Street:* Learning vocabulary while viewing. *Developmental Psychology, 26,* 421–428.

Saitoti, T. O. (1989). With Photographs by Carol Beckwith. *Maasai* (7th printing). New York: Harry N. Abrams, Inc.

Sandler, J., Holder, A. & Meers, P. M. (1963). The ego ideal and the ideal self. *Psychoanalytic Study of the Child, 18,* 139–158.

Schaefer, E. (1991). Goals for parent and future-parent education: Research on parental beliefs and behavior. *Elementary School Journal, 91,* 239–248.

Sheehan, P. W. (1983). Age trends and the correlates of children's television viewing. *Australian Journal of Psychology, 35,* 417–431.

Shepard, L. A. & Smith, M. L. (1986). Synthesis of research on school readiness and kindergarten retention. *Educational Leadership, 44,* 78–86.

Stallings, J. A. (1995). Ensuring teaching and learning in the 21st century. *Educational Researcher, 24,* 4–8.

Sternberg, C. (1985). *TV facts.* New York: Facts on File.

Stolzenberg, R. M., Blair-Loy, M. & Waite, L. J. (1995). Age and family life cycle effects on church membership. *American Sociological Review, 60,* 84–103.

Tangney, J. P. (1987). TV in the family. *Bryn Mawr Now, 14(1),* 14.

Tangney, J. P. (1991). Moral affect: The good, the bad, and the ugly. *Journal of Personality and Social Psychology, 61,* 598–607.

Thomas, M. H. & Drabman, R. S. (1977). Effects of television violence on expectations of others' aggression. San Francisco: Paper presented at the annual convention of the American Psychological Association.

Triandis, H. C. (1990). Cross-cultural studies of individualism and collectivism. In J. J. Berman (Ed.), *Nebraska symposium on motivation, 1989.* Lincoln: University of Nebraska Press, 41–134.

Turner, J. S. & Rubinson, L. (1993). *Contemporary human sexuality.* Englewood Cliffs, N.J.: Prentice-Hall.

U.S. Bureau of the Census. (1994). *Statistical abstract of the United States: 1994* (114th ed.). Washington, D.C.: U.S. Government Printing Office.

U.S. Department of Education. (1992). *Digest of education statistics, 1992.* Washington, D.C.: U.S. Government Printing Office.

Ventis, W. L. (1995). The relationships between religion and mental health. *Journal of Social Issues, 51,* 33–48.

Williams, C. & Bybee, J. (1994). What do children feel guilty about? Developmental and gender differences. *Developmental Psychology, 30,* 617–623.

Williams, P. A., Haertel, E. H., Walberg, H. J. & Haertel, G. D. (1982). The impact of leisure-time television on school learning: A research synthesis. *American Educational Research Journal, 19,* 19–50.

Williams, T. H. & Handford, A. G. (1986). Television and other leisure activities. In T. H. Williams (Ed.), *The impact of television: A natural experiment in three communities.* Orlando, Fla.: Academic Press, 143–213.

Zahn-Waxler, C. & Kochanska, G. (1990). The origins of guilt. In R. A. Thompson (Ed.), *Nebraska symposium on motivation, 1988* (vol. 36). Lincoln: University of Nebraska Press, 183–258.

Zahn-Waxler, C., Kochanska, G., Krupnick, J. & McKnew, D. (1990). Patterns of guilt in children of depressed and well mothers. *Developmental Psychology, 26,* 51–59.

Developmental Tasks of Middle Childhood (Ages 6 to 12)

Chapter 13

Concrete Operations

Conservation

Extensions of Piaget's Ideas about Conservation

Classification Skills

Combinatorial Skills

Skilled Learning

Features of Skilled Learning

Reading

A Model of the Developing Mind

The Social and Cultural Contexts of Skill Development

Self-Evaluation

Self-Efficacy

Social Expectations

Teachers' Expectations: The Self-Fulfilling Prophecy

Parents' Expectations

Friendship

Family Influences on Children's Readiness for Friendships

Three Contributions of Friendship to Social Development

Perspective Taking and Cognitive Flexibility

Social Norms and Peer Group Pressures

Close Friends

Team Play

Interdependence

Division of Labor

Competition

In-Group and Out-Group Attitudes

Chapter Summary

References

Middle childhood is a relatively long period of development during which a tremendous amount of change occurs. The photos of our daughter Rachel at ages 6 and 12 (below) help illustrate some of the changes. You can observe Rachel's physical development, but these changes reflect only one dimension along which maturation takes place. Over these years, she became interested and then disinterested in being an astronaut. She took up tennis, the drums, the saxophone, soccer, softball, basketball, skiing, and rollerblading. She began to write poetry, started worrying about not being popular, and got interested in money. She changed from telling us how stupid teenagers were to admiring them. By age 12, Rachel had developed a point of view; she was able to evaluate her teachers, her friends, her parents, and herself. She could comment on how she did or did not fit in, what made sense to her and what was troubling, what was fun and what was gross.

New tasks for development are highlighted as children become focused on concrete mental operations, skill learning, self-evaluation, friendship formation, and team play. Mastery of these tasks, coupled with new capacities for complex social, emotional, and intellectual activity, produces a remarkable synergy. While play dominates the behavior of early-school-age children, children in middle childhood are characterized by more purposeful, industrious behavior. This is not to say that play is lost. New thrills and excitement are generated by the capacity to engage in more complex forms of play and the desire to take new risks—riding one's bike further from home, jumping and then diving from the high board, going on big, fast amusement park rides without a parent.

Historically, middle childhood was not considered important for an understanding of development. Freud's psychoanalytic theory treated the years following the resolution of the Oedipal conflict as a time when sexual and aggressive impulses are repressed and active only in the unconscious. He

In many war-torn regions of the world, the developmental tasks of middle childhood take a back seat to survival.

called this period the *latency stage,* suggesting that no significant contributions to personality formation could be traced to it. For a long time, psychologists tended not to study psychological development during the middle-school-age years.

More recent interest in the theories of Erik Erikson, Jean Piaget, and Lev Vygotsky stimulated developmental research focusing on children who are between the ages of 6 and 12. Their theories emphasize intellectual growth, competence, and a growing investment in work. During this time of life, children are learning the fundamental skills valued by their society, whether they are reading, writing, and arithmetic or hunting, fishing, and weaving. As children gain confidence in their skills, they begin to have more realistic images of their potential contributions to the larger community. At the same time, learning is taking place in a cultural context that provides the symbol system, values, and specific sources of expertise through which knowledge is passed from one generation to the next.

The competence that develops during middle childhood applies to social as well as to work-related skills. This is a time when parent–child relationships, peer friendships, and participation in meaningful interpersonal communication can give children the social skills they will need if they are to cope with the upcoming challenges of adolescence. Children's cognitive accomplishments appear to develop alongside achievements in the social and emotional domains.

For many children, this is a joyful, vigorous time. The fears and vulnerabilities of their early school days are behind them. Energized by ego qualities of hope, will, and purpose, most children enjoy the resources and opportunities of their communities. Even as the presence of family members continues to comfort them, they begin to explore more complex social relationships with peers and other significant adults.

In some parts of the world, however, and in some communities in the United States, the lives of children ages 6 to 12 are marked by extreme disorganization, terror, and exploitation. For example, during the fighting in Sarajevo, Bosnia-Herzegovina, hundreds of children, many without their mothers or fathers, escaped the war on buses to be relocated in Russia and other parts of Europe (*Columbus Dispatch,* 1992). Firsthand accounts of children growing up in the midst of war illustrate the psychological and physiological consequences of daily exposure to violence, suffering, and destruction that are out of their control (Garbarino et al., 1991).

In some parts of the world, adults travel through impoverished areas kidnaping, buying, or luring children into forms of slavelike labor where they are often beaten, sexually abused, and degraded. Children as young as six are sold or given away by poor families as slaves or bonded laborers. "In Haiti, more than 100,000 children, sold or given away by poor families, toil as domestic servants. . . . In Pakistan as many as 20 million people, 7.5 million of them children, are working as bonded laborers in factories, on farms and on construction projects, unable to pay off employer advances" (*Time,* 1993).

In New Orleans, at the corner of Congress and Law streets, buildings are riddled with bullet holes. In 1994, there were three or more killings per month in the streets surrounding the St. Philip Social Service Center located there. Preschoolers attending school in the center have "shooting drills" in which they are instructed to drop to the floor until an all-clear siren is sounded. In a study of African-American mothers and children ages 9 to 12 living in a similarly violent section of New Orleans, 51% of the children reported being victims of violence, and 91% of the children reported having witnessed some type of street violence (Lacayo, 1996; Osofsky, 1995).

Considering these frightening examples, it can be deemed a societal luxury for young children to have the opportunity to work on developmental tasks such as concrete operational reasoning, skill learning, self-evaluation, friendship formation, and team play. Having the time, resources, and security to promote child development may only be possible within the context of communities that are economically and politically stable and ideologically committed to the future of their children.

Concrete Operations

Intelligence during infancy consists of sensory and motor patterns that children use to explore their environment and gain specific ends. During toddlerhood, children develop a variety of representational skills that free them from complete reliance on their immediate physical environment. They create novel situations and solve problems by using thought, fantasy, and language. Piaget (Piaget & Inhelder, 1969) suggested that at about age six or seven a qualitatively new form of thinking develops, which he called *concrete operational thought.*

Concrete operational thought is based on the Piagetian notion of mental operations. An *operation* is an action that is performed on an object or set of objects. A *mental operation* is a transformation that is carried out in thought rather than in action. Piaget argued that such transformations are built on some physical relationship that the younger child can perform but cannot articulate. For example, a toddler can arrange a graduated set of plastic rings on a stick so that the largest ring is at the bottom of the stick and the smallest ring is at the top. The child does not have words to describe the ordering operation but can perform the action. By middle childhood, however, children can explain the task to a younger child using phrases like "You put them in order from biggest to smallest," or, "You just stack them up like a tower from the big one to the little one." A mental operation is an internal representation of an alteration in the relationship among objects. During the stage of concrete operational thought, children begin to represent many physical actions symbolically and perform them in their mind.

begin to see physical operations symbolically & perform them in their mind.

During the stage of concrete operations, a number of conceptual skills are gradually achieved. The ones that have received the most attention are (1) conservation skills, (2) classification skills, and (3) combinatorial skills. Each one comprises a group of interrelated operations. These skills bring children in touch with the logic and order of the physical world. They allow children to experience the predictability of physical events. As children use logical principles associated with concrete operational thought to solve problems, they generalize these principles to their thinking about friendships, team play and other games with rules, and their own self-evaluation. As the order of the physical world becomes more apparent, children begin to seek logic and order in social and personal domains. Sometimes this search for order is frustrated by the unpredictability of the social world. At other times, children find that they can use their enhanced capacities for reasoning to solve interpersonal problems and to arrange their daily life so that it better meets their interests and needs.

skills – bring logic & order to the physical world.

Conservation

The basic meaning of the *conservation* scheme is that physical matter does not magically appear or disappear despite changes in form or shape, arrangement, or container. The concept of conservation can be applied to a variety of dimensions, including mass, weight, number, length, area, and volume. The child who conserves is able to resist perceptual cues that alter the form of an object, insisting that the quantity remains the same despite the change in form. One of the most common problems of this type that Piaget investigated involves conservation of mass. The child is presented with two clay balls and asked whether they are equal. Once the child is satisfied that the balls are equal, one of the balls is flattened out into a pancake. The child is then asked, "Does one have more or are they the same amount?" Sometimes the child is also asked whether the clay pieces are still the same. The child who does not conserve says that the pancake has more clay because it is a lot wider than the ball. This child is still in the preoperational stage of thought. He or she is using personal perceptions to make judgments. The child who conserves knows that the two pieces of clay are still identical in amount and can explain why.

Three concepts allow the child to ascertain that equality along any physical dimension has not been altered (see Figure 13.1). First, the child may explain that the pancake has the same amount of clay as the ball; no clay has been added or taken away. This is an example of the concept of *identity:* The pancake is still the *same* clay; nothing has been changed except its shape. Second, the child may point out that the experimenter can turn the pancake back into a ball. This is an example of the concept of *reversibility:* The child becomes aware that operations can be reversed, so that their effects cancel each other out. Furthermore, the child can reverse the operation mentally, tracing the

explanation as to why
— IDENTITY
— REVERSIBILITY
— RECIPROCITY

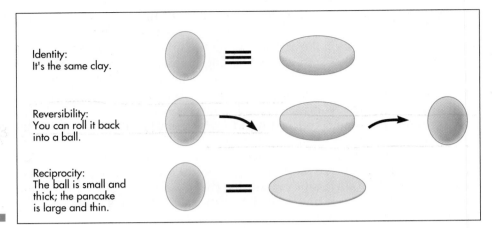

FIGURE 13.1

Three concepts that contribute to conservation

steps to transform the pancake back into the ball. Third, the child may notice that, although the pancake has a larger circumference, the ball is much thicker. When children can mentally manipulate and compare two dimensions such as circumference and thickness, they give evidence of understanding the concept of *reciprocity*. In the clay ball example, change in one dimension is compensated for by change in another; the total mass remains the same. With consolidation of the concepts of identity, reversibility, and reciprocity, the child is able to conserve along any physical dimension (Siegler, 1991).

Children appear to develop the capacity to conserve in a predictable sequence, first conservation of mass and number, then weight, area, and volume. Piaget also noted that the development of conservation does not proceed evenly across all of the physical modes. Research has shown that children who are unable to conserve quantity with an unfamiliar object such as poker chips can do so with a more familiar substance such as M&Ms (Goodnow, 1969; Gulko et al., 1988; Lovell, 1961; Uzgiris, 1964). Differences are seen not only when contrasting familiar and unfamiliar materials. For example, in one set of experiments, girls from low socioeconomic backgrounds were successfully able to perform conservation of liquid when the task was presented in the standard manner comparing the experimenter's glass and their own. However, when the task was posed in a story where juice had to be divided between two dolls, their performance declined. One interpretation of this difference in performance is that the girls identified the correct principles when the task was framed as a scientific exploration and where the experimenter served as an authority figure who expected a certain type of response. But in a story context, the principles of conservation were not obvious to these girls. Evidence of a lack of generalizability of knowledge from in-school to out-of-school contexts is found for other areas of reasoning, especially mathematical codes and scientific principles (Perret-Clermont et al., 1991).

Extensions of Piaget's Ideas about Conservation

Research has raised questions about the meaning of conservation tasks, the timing for the emergence of conservation, and the possibility of teaching children to conserve. The way the task is presented and the kinds of questions that are asked can influence a child's responses. For example, the task can emphasize identity or equivalence. In an identity task, the child is asked to judge whether a clay ball (V) has the same amount of clay after it has been rolled into a sausage (V_1). In an equivalence task, there are two balls of clay. The child is asked to judge whether the ball that is rolled into a sausage has the same amount of clay as the standard, comparison ball. Some studies have found that children can perform the identity task earlier than the equivalence task; some have found just the opposite; and some have argued that identity and equivalence are achieved at the same time (Brainerd & Hooper, 1978; Miller, 1978; Silverstein et al., 1982). In a study of five- to-seven-year-olds, children were asked to say how the materials looked, and then to say how they really were. Alerting the child to this distinction between appearance and reality resulted in more correct answers than the standard procedure, in which this distinction is not made (Bijstra et al., 1989).

Some studies have demonstrated that it is possible to train young children of preschool age to conserve (Brainerd, 1977). These training studies have both theoretical and practical implications. Theoretically, Piaget's view of development suggests that there is a period of maturational readiness for the application of logical operations to physical objects. Thus, explanations of rules and relationships ought not be relevant to a child who is not cognitively ready to understand them. The training studies suggest that it is possible to introduce such concepts as identity and reversibility so that children as young as four can achieve conservation. Further, conservation will be transferred from the tasks involved in training to other materials and dimensions (Field, 1981; May & Norton, 1981). Apparently, the most important element in modifying children's approach to conservation is confronting them with someone else's reasoning that contradicts their own. For this contradiction to be effective, however, the child must be approaching a level of readiness to reorganize his or her thinking, and the gap between the current level of reasoning and the new ideas must not be too great. The implication here is that entry into a new stage of thought may emerge earlier and be more readily influenced by the social environment than Piaget's cognitive developmental theory had predicted.

In fact, contemporary work on cognition emphasizes the idea of the "social construction of meaning." This notion, extended from Vygotsky's theory, emphasizes that in most learning situations the child is not only trying to understand the logical or symbolic features of the problem but is also trying to understand the social meaning of the situation. For example, in one study of six- to ten-year-olds, the children were given a task with incomplete instructions. The focus of the study was on how children would handle the task and the extent to which they would ask for information from the experimenter to fill in the gaps that were omitted from the instructions. Most of the children tried to complete the task on their own, without asking any questions to clarify the instructions. Even older children who were clearly aware that the instructions were inadequate did not ask for clarification. Most of the questions that were asked seemed to be directed to confirming that they were doing the right thing; that is, questions were directed toward gaining social approval from the experimenter rather than toward revealing more about the logic of the task. The study illustrated that learning is influenced by the social norms for interactions between adult authority figures and children. Transactions such as asking questions, which adults may construe as a means of gaining information, are often construed by children as a means of reassuring themselves that they are behaving appropriately and meeting the adult's expectations (Perret-Clermont, Perret & Bell, 1991).

Practically speaking, the implication is that preschool- and kindergarten-age children are capable of integrating and applying more abstract concepts than educators once believed they could. For example, studies of children as young as three and four have shown that they understand the idea that materials are made of tiny particles that retain their properties even when they are invisible. They can use this notion of particles to explain how a substance such as sugar can continue to exist in solution and retain its sweetness even when it is invisible (Au et al., 1993; Rosen & Rozin, 1993). Early-childhood educators have found that, through a planned program of exploring, experimenting, and describing the transformation of materials, young children can be guided to conceptualize the physical world in a more systematic, logical manner.

Classification Skills

The ability to use categories to classify objects was first discussed in Chapter 7 when we described the basic accomplishments of sensorimotor intelligence. One of the adaptive benefits of *categorization* is that one can assume that whatever holds true for one member of a category is likely to hold true for other members of a category. If water and juice are both liquids, then if you can pour water, you can pour juice. Other substances classified as liquids should also have this property, even substances that one has never seen. In middle childhood, children's knowledge of categories and the information that is associated with various categories expand dramatically. Furthermore, children acquire a broad range of categories with which to incorporate a novel observation. The value of *classification skills* is not purely to organize objects or experiences into classes, but to take advantage of what is known about these categories to make inferences about the characteristics and dynamics of members of the same categories, members of hierarchically related categories, and objects that are not members of a specific category (Farrar et al., 1992; Kalish & Gelman, 1992; Lopez et al., 1992).

One component of *classification skills* is the ability to group objects according to some dimension that they share. The other component is the ability to order subgroups hierarchically, so that each new grouping will include all previous subgroups. Vygotsky (1932/1962) suggested a method for studying classification skills in young children. Children are presented with a variety of wooden blocks that differ in shape, size, and color. Under each block is a nonsense syllable. The purpose of the task is to figure out which combination of qualities is linked to which nonsense syllables. Children are instructed to select one block at a time and to try to select all the blocks that have the same syllable. The youngest children, who would be characterized as preoperational in Piaget's stage theory, tend to select the first few blocks by their color. Their technique for grouping is highly associative (Nelson, 1974). When they discover that they have blocks that do not have matching syllables, they choose each new block to match some characteristic of the previous selection. They do not hold in mind a single concept that guides their choices.

Children who have entered the stage of concrete operations tend to focus on one dimension at first, perhaps shape, and continue to select blocks until they discover that they have made an incorrect choice. They use this discovery to change their hypothesis about which characteristics of the blocks are associated with the nonsense syllable. This classification task demonstrates the concrete operational child's ability to hold a concept in mind and to make a series of decisions on the basis of that concept. It also demonstrates that, during the stage of concrete operations, children can use mistakes to reorient a problem-solving strategy.

Piaget studied reasoning about class hierarchies or *class inclusion* by asking questions about whether a group of objects included more members of one subtype than of the group as a whole (Chapman & McBride, 1992; Piaget, 1941/1952). Thus, when a set of pictures shows three ducks, six sparrows, and two robins, one might ask: "Are there more sparrows or more birds in these pictures?" This is an unusual kind of question, one that children are probably rarely asked. By the age of eight or nine, however, many children can respond correctly because they recognize the distinction between classes and subclasses. In order to handle such problems, children have to inhibit their tendency to reinterpret the question in line with a more common comparison, such as "Are there more sparrows than ducks?"

In one study of class inclusion reasoning, an intriguing pattern was found. Children ages three and four, who could not repeat the question and who clearly had not learned any rules about classes, were more likely to answer correctly than children of five and six. Children ages seven and eight performed better than children of all the younger ages. The five- and six-year-olds, who answered quickly and confidently, were consistently incorrect. They seemed unable to inhibit the more obvious comparison in order to consider the actual question (McCabe et al., 1982).

The capacity for classifying and categorizing has been explored in relation to specific domains such as health and illness concepts or concepts of the family. For example, children were told about 21 different human groupings and asked to say whether these groupings were a family. "Here are Mr. Mead and his son Tom. They live together, just the two of them. Are they a family?" The youngest subjects (four- to six-year-olds) had trouble accepting examples involving single parents or biologically related people who did not live in the same home as instances of family. Principles of biological relatedness and shared physical residence were both important to these youngest children's view of family. By middle childhood, children were able to accept a wider variety of groups as meeting certain essential features of family, usually biological relatedness and emotional closeness. Emotional closeness was endorsed by 80% of the subjects as a defining feature of family and was used repeatedly as a basis for judging whether a specific instance of a grouping could be considered a family or not (Newman et al., 1993).

Combinatorial Skills

A third characteristic of concrete operational thought is the development of *combinatorial skills*. Once they have acquired the scheme for conservation of number, children understand that certain physical transformations will not alter the number of units in a set. If ten poker chips are lined up in a row, there will still be ten chips whether they are spread out, squeezed tightly together, or stacked one on top of another. Between the ages of three and four, children begin counting and can use counting to answer a "how many" kind of question. For example, they can assign one number to each item in a set of four poker chips and tell you that there are four chips in all. However, young children have more difficulty selecting a set of six chips from a larger pile of chips or establishing that two sets of chips are equal in number. They also have trouble solving verbal story problems when no concrete objects are present (Jordan et al., 1992; Sophian, 1988). Conservation of number is achieved around age six or seven (Halford & Boyle, 1985). Addition, subtraction, multiplication, and division are all learned during this stage. Children learn to apply the same operations no matter what specific objects or quantities are involved. Piaget claimed that it is no coincidence that schools begin to instruct children in the basic skills of arithmetic at age six. It is probably a strength of our schools that they meet an important aspect of intellectual readiness at the appropriate time.

The period that we have identified as early school age marks the beginnings of concrete operational thought. During this time, children's performances on tests of cognitive maturity are likely to be inconsistent. For example, children may be able to conserve quantity but will make errors in conservation of weight, volume, or space. They may be able to perform a classification task correctly when they sort by one dimension, such as color, but make errors when asked to sort objects that have more than one dimension in common. The conceptual awareness of the process of classifying objects or the logic of conservation is not fully integrated until sometime during middle childhood and may not reach peak performance until later adolescence or adulthood (Flavell, 1982).

As concrete operational intelligence develops, the child gains insight into the regularities of the physical world and the principles that govern relationships among objects. Table 13.1 summarizes the components of concrete operational thought. Perceptions of reality become less convincing than logical understanding of how the world is organized. For example, even though it looks as if the sun sinks into the water at the horizon, we know that what we see is a result of the earth's rotation on its axis. However, exposure in the gro-

---

TABLE 13.1

Components of Concrete Operational Thought

Component	New Abilities
Conservation	Ability to perceive identity
	Ability to perceive reversibility
	Ability to manipulate two dimensions simultaneously in reciprocity
Classification	Ability to group objects according to some common dimension
	Ability to order subgroups in a hierarchy
Combinatorial skills	Ability to manipulate numbers in addition, subtraction, multiplication, and division

BOX 13.1

Metacognition

Piaget's method for understanding the development of concrete operational thought led the way to the study of metacognition. Rather than focusing on the exact answers that children gave to the questions he asked, he was concerned with how they explained their answers. How do children know what they know? What reasons can they give to justify or support their answers? *Metacognition* refers to a whole range of processes and strategies that we use to assess and monitor our knowledge. It includes the "feeling of knowing" that accompanies problem solving, the ability to distinguish those answers about which we are confident from those answers about which we have doubts (Butterfield et al., 1988).

One part of this "feeling of knowing" is understanding the source of one's beliefs. For example, we can be told about something, we can see it for ourselves, or we can feel and touch something. All three of these sources of information might coincide to create a single belief, or we may discover that there are inconsistencies between what someone says is true and what we perceive through sight or touch. By the age of four or five, children are able to understand how all three sources of information contribute to their understanding of an experience (O'Neill & Gopnik, 1991).

Metacognition includes the ability to review various strategies for approaching a problem in order to choose the one that is most likely to result in a solution (Carr et al., 1989). It includes the ability to monitor one's comprehension of the material that one has just read and to select strategies for increasing comprehension (Cross & Paris, 1988).

Metacognition develops in parallel with other cognitive capacities. As children develop in their ability to attend to more variables in solving problems, they simultaneously increase their capacity to take an "executive" posture in relation to cognitive tasks. They can detect uncertainty and introduce strategies to reduce it. They can learn study techniques that will enhance their ability to organize and recall information. These capacities continue to develop as the child becomes a more sophisticated learner. Metacognitive skills are also quite amenable to training, both at home and at school. Metacognition appears to be a natural component of cognitive development. However, just like first-level cognitive capacities, it is constructed in a social context. Interactions between children and adults or other peers can nurture and stimulate metacognition by helping children identify sources of information, talk about and recognize the differences between feelings of certainty and uncertainty in their knowledge, and devise effective strategies for increasing feelings of knowing.

cery store to large, partially filled cereal boxes and attractively shaped bottles of shampoo attest to the occasional failure of the cognitive system to dominate visual perception. We allow the size or shape of the container to override the assessment of the quantity or volume contained within.

As children's understanding of concrete operational reasoning develops, they are able to use conceptual principles as well as direct sensation, perception, and motor skills to solve problems. The fields of science, history, and mathematics are accessible to children who can master the principles of classification and combinatorial skills. As a result of the maturation of concrete operational thought, children are able to manipulate techniques for measurement. They have a growing appreciation of time as a nonsubjective unit. Time, like height and weight, can be measured, and these measurements can be compared. Children are able to entertain an explanatory hypothesis and evaluate evidence that supports or disproves it. All of these cognitive skills allow children to move rapidly beyond the limits of their own experience into consideration of events that happened long ago, might happen in the future, or are hypothesized to be happening all the time (see Box 13.1).

Complex problem solving, such as assembling this circuit board, requires the coordination of many skill areas, including reading, interpreting mechanical drawings, manual dexterity, and scientific reasoning.

In Notebook Page 13.1, you are asked to consider how to facilitate or extend a child's concrete operational reasoning as part of a hypothetical class field trip to a zoo.

Skilled Learning

One area of impressive growth during middle childhood is the acquisition of skills. Skills are the basis of intellectual competence. They combine knowledge (knowing about) and practice (knowing how) directed toward identifying and solving significant, meaningful problems (Gardner, 1983; Kuhn et al., 1995). Typically, a person moves through a developmental progression within a skill area, starting off as a novice, achieving more proficiency, and then, depending on a combination of aptitude, training, and practice, becoming an expert. Cultures differ on the value placed on various skills; in some societies like ours, symbolic skills such as reading, mathematics, and abstract reasoning are highly valued. In other cultures, reading and mathematics are of less use and value than agricultural skills, hunting, or food preparation. In the United States, one observes the emergence of a wide range of valued skills during middle childhood, including:

mathematics	science	theater	art
writing	computer operation	cooking	sewing
sports	mechanics	crafts	reading
music	dance		

Concrete Operational Thought

A class of fourth-graders is planning a visit to the zoo. Think up activities or assignments that might help extend the mental operations associated with concrete operational thinking that could be linked to this trip.

1. What are some activities that could foster the operations underlying conservation (e.g., identity, reversibility, and reciprocity)?

_____

_____

_____

_____

2. What are some activities that could foster the scheme for classification?

_____

_____

_____

_____

3. What are some activities that could foster combinatorial operations?

_____

_____

_____

_____

BOX 13.2

Characteristics of Skilled Reading

Four basic assumptions about the characteristics of skilled reading have been described and appear to have received research support (Hall, 1989; Spiro et al., 1980):

1. Skilled reading depends on perceptual, cognitive, and linguistic processes.
2. Skilled readers obtain information from many levels simultaneously by synthesizing information derived from graphophonemes (the shapes of letters associated with sounds), morphemes (basic units that make up words), semantics (meanings), syntax (rules of grammar that dictate word order), pragmatics (cues provided by the context and past experience), schematics (construction and use of conceptual schema to account for the way information is arranged; prior knowledge about story structure), and interpretation. Reading is a process of simultaneous interactions that do not proceed in strict sequence from basic perceptual units to general interpretation of text.
3. The capacity of the human information-processing system limits the amount that a person can perceive in a single fixation on a text. The speed of eye movement, the number of chunks of information that can be held in short-term memory, and the speed with which information can be retrieved from long-term memory are all factors that influence how much written material a person can process at one time. In the skilled reader, lower-level processes such as decoding function automatically, allowing the reader to attend to higher-order comprehension processes.
4. Reading involves the use of strategies. The skilled reader reads with a purpose and continuously monitors comprehension. Skilled readers perceive breakdowns in understanding, are selective in focusing attention on various aspects of what they are reading, and refine their interpretation of the text as they read.

Much research remains to be done before we can explain how these processes work and identify other processes that are essential for skilled reading. Still, the characteristics that have been identified give us a sense of just how complex the reading process is.

Based on research on how skilled reading develops (for details, see Box 13.2) we can construct a general model for understanding how complex behavioral skills are achieved.

Features of Skilled Learning

First, the development of skill depends on a combination of sensory, motor, perceptual, cognitive, linguistic, emotional, and social processes. In sports, for example, a child must learn to coordinate specific sensory information and motor activities, understand the rules of the game, be able to communicate with the coach and the other players, gain control over emotions such as fear or anger that might interfere with performance, and sustain motivation to keep trying despite errors or defeat.

Second, skills are attained through the simultaneous integration of many levels of the component behaviors. Skills are not acquired in strict sequence, from simple to complex. Children work on the simple and more complex components of the skill at the same time. For example, in art, children may experiment with mixing paints to achieve new colors at the same time as they are experimenting with line drawing, perspective, and shading.

Third, limits of the human system place constraints on an individual's capacity to perform skilled behavior. With practice, lower-level processes begin to function automatically, so a person can attend to higher-order processes. In writing, for example, young children struggle with the physical act of printing and writing, concentrating largely on the motor skills necessary to make each letter, word, and sentence. A skilled writer can manage the mechanics of writing with little effort, focusing attention on the meaning of the writing, the plot, or the character development rather than on the physical aspects of the task.

Fourth, skilled behavior requires the use of strategies. Skillful people operate with purpose and continuously monitor their performance. They perceive breakdowns in performance, are selective in focusing attention on various aspects of what they are working on, and refine higher-order processes as they perform the skill. This model of skill development focuses on the elements that are necessary in order to move from what might be considered a novice level to a more advanced level in skill performance.

One must keep in mind that children vary widely in their rate of intellectual development and in their capacities to perform skills. For example, by the first or second grade, children have been identified as mathematically gifted, normal, or slow to learn (Geary et al., 1991; Geary & Brown, 1991). These designations relate to children's abilities to perform relatively simple mathematical operations such as addition. Differences in early mathematical ability relate to children's capacity for using a variety of counting strategies as well as their ability to retain and recall math facts from memory. In each distinct area of skill development, a combination of maturational factors, aptitude or talent, opportunities for exposure and training, and the value placed on the skill by the family, school, and larger society all play a role in how rapidly and how well a skill will be developed.

In the sections that follow, we look at reading as a specific case of skill development, then more broadly at a model of the developing mind, and finally at the social and cultural contexts within which skilled learning occurs.

Reading

In some ways, reading is the most significant intellectual skill that develops during middle childhood because it opens the door to so many others. Reading provides access to new information, new uses of language, and new forms of thinking. Children are limited in their ability to learn mathematics, social studies, and science if they cannot read. Once a child can read fluently, the possibility for all manner of independent inquiry expands significantly.

Children probably begin to read in a variety of ways. As David and his mother drove from home to preschool everyday, they used a game with street signs along the road to build the bridge from language to literacy. At first, David would ask his mother to tell him what every sign said. After a while, David began to "read" the signs by memorizing words and phrases that were linked to certain shapes and patterns in the signs. Other children begin to read by learning letters and the sounds that are linked to them and by experimenting with sounding out the letters when they are strung together. At first, most children are bewildered and confused by these experiences. This is a time when they require a good deal of support and encouragement for their efforts. Gradually, through a process of trial, feedback, and repetition, children learn to read simple words and simple sentences (Knight & Fischer, 1992).

Early in the process of learning to read, children can understand and communicate orally a great deal more than they can read by themselves. They must learn how to use these oral communication skills in the comprehension of written language (Carroll, 1986). At some point, a child begins to articulate the concept "I can read" or "I am a reader." Once this idea is part of the self-concept, efforts to read increase and are motivated by a confidence in one's potential for success.

Reading is a complex skill involving the acquisition of many interrelated abilities. Box 13.2 helps us to understand the complexity of skilled reading. Children do not have to score extremely high in intelligence tests to make substantial progress in learning to read (Share et al., 1989). The most important factors in learning to read are practice, usually in the presence of a skilled reader, and time spent reading. Unfortunately, most children spend little or no time reading books outside of school. Over time, those who do some reading outside of school show the greatest gains in reading achievement between second and fifth grades (Anderson et al., 1988).

Parents' direct influence on children's reading achievement has been consistently documented. Parents affect their children's reading in at least five ways (Hess & Holloway, 1984; Schickedanz, 1986):

1. In the value they place on literacy,
2. In the emphasis they place on academic achievement,
3. In the reading materials they make available at home,
4. In the time they spend reading with their children, and
5. In the opportunities that they provide for verbal interaction in the home.

Parents who value the ability to read, who urge their children to do well in school, who provide resources for reading, who read with them, and who talk with them produce children who are more skilled readers than parents who don't (Bus et al., 1995).

Parents also have an indirect effect on how well a child learns to read by influencing the child's placement in a school reading group (Goldenberg, 1989). Ability grouping for reading instruction is practically universal in elementary schools (Slavin, 1987). Teachers depend on their perceptions of a child's ability, work habits, and behavior when they assign students to reading groups (Haller & Waterman, 1985). The higher the level of a child's reading group, the better he or she learns how to read. Parents may help a child understand the school's reading curriculum (schools differ in their approaches to teaching reading) and encourage good work habits and appropriate classroom behavior. Parents who do these things may influence a teacher's perception of their child and, as a result, the child's assignment to a particular reading-group level.

A Model of the Developing Mind

Think about the skill development that takes place across so many domains from about age 6 to about age 12. We observe children reaching high levels of functioning in such diverse areas as sports, reading, writing and story telling, mathematical problem solving, art, and science. The expansion of complex thought processes that must be involved to support such advanced functioning is marvelous (see Box 13.3). Demetriou and colleagues (1993) presented a general model of the developing mind that demonstrates some of this complexity (see Figure 13.2). In their model, intellectual development is

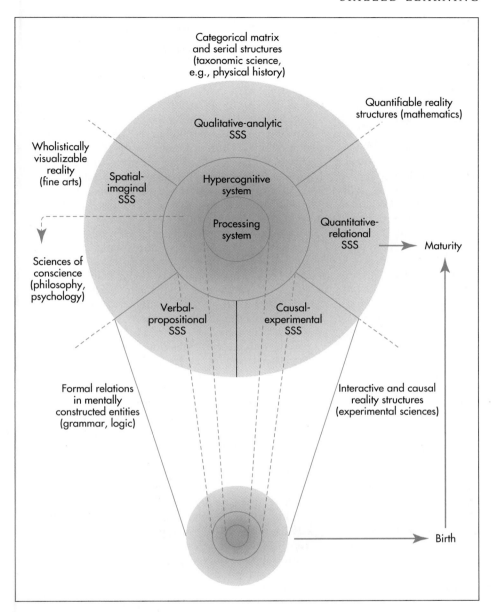

Categorical matrix
and serial structures
(taxonomic science,
e.g., physical history)

Quantifiable reality
structures (mathematics)

Qualitative-analytic
SSS

Wholistically
visualizable
reality
(fine arts)

Spatial-
imaginal
SSS

Hypercognitive
system

Processing
system

Quantitative-
relational
SSS

Sciences of
conscience
(philosophy,
psychology)

Verbal-
propositional
SSS

Causal-
experimental
SSS

Maturity

Formal relations
in mentally
constructed entities
(grammar, logic)

Interactive and causal
reality structures
(experimental sciences)

Birth

FIGURE 13.2

The general model of the developing mind
Source: Demetriou, A., Efklides, A. & Platsidou, M. (1993). The architecture and dynamics of developing mind. *Monographs of the Society for Research in Child Development, 58,* Fig. 13, p. 124. Copyright © 1993 The Society for Research in Child Development, Inc. Reprinted with permission.

a product of the ongoing interactions among three structural systems: the processing system, the hypercognitive system, and the specialized structural systems (SSS).

The *processing system* (the inner circle in Figure 13.2) is composed of the elements of thinking that enter into every form of intellectual endeavor. These elements include the speed of processing information, the control of processing information, and the storage and retrieval of information. According to the model, these processing systems operate in relation to whatever task activates them, whether the stimulus is musical notes, verbal symbols, or mathematical symbols.

BOX 13.3

What Is Intelligence?

The model of the mind developed by Demetriou and colleagues (1993) is not the only approach to conceptualizing intelligence. The term *intelligence* is used in many contexts and has a variety of meanings. At a conceptual level, it may refer to the ability to solve important problems or to adapt to environmental conditions. At a psychometric level, it may refer to the score on a standardized test comprised of one type of item (such as Peabody's Picture Vocabulary Test) or many kinds of items (such as the Stanford-Binet). Some theorists emphasize a general underlying factor, *g*, that reflects what many different types of items have in common (Spearman, 1927). Other models of intelligence offer different ideas about the number and content of distinct areas of specialization.

One might think of intelligence from a developmental perspective. For example, Piaget (1972) described four basic types of intelligence, each emerging at a different period of childhood: sensorimotor intelligence (the ability to know through direct observation and manipulation of objects); representational intelligence (the ability to distinguish between the real and the pretend; to think about and represent objects and events that are not present); concrete operational intelligence (the ability to detect the logical relationships among objects; to place objects in sequences; and to comprehend and manipulate numbers); and formal operational intelligence (the ability to use experimental techniques and hypothetical reasoning to solve problems, to generalize observations from one situation to another, and to relate cause and effect in complex, multidimensional problems). These kinds of intelligence reflect different processes or approaches to solving problems.

Howard Gardner (1983) developed a theory of multiple intelligences that suggests that there are at least seven distinct intelligences, each with its own content, and each contributing in unique ways to solving important, meaningful problems. These include linguistic intelligence, musical intelligence, logical-mathematical intelligence, spatial intelligence, bodily-kinesthetic intelligence, and two forms of personal intelligence, one directed toward understanding one's own internal feelings (intrapersonal intelligence), the other directed toward identifying and differentiating among the characteristics of others (interpersonal intelligence). This theory recognizes domains of human functioning that show evidence of high levels of achievement which are not necessarily related to the scientific reasoning of specific concern to Piaget or to the broader areas of intellectual and scientific thinking discussed by Demetriou and colleagues.

Still another view is represented by Robert Sternberg's (1985) idea of three kinds of intelligence—analytic, creative, and practical. According to Sternberg, only the first is systematically measured by tests of intelligence, but the latter is often required in job performance or adaptation to the demands of daily life. Cultures differ in what kinds of abilities are valued as evidence of intelligence. In many instances, parents value social skills (knowing how to behave appropriately with peers and teachers), practical skills necessary for adjustment to school (completing homework), and motivation (working hard to understand a problem) as more important indications of intelligence than cognitive accomplishments (Okagaki & Sternberg, 1993). Differences in exposure to situations, familiarity with materials, and group values all influence which abilities are valued or viewed as evidence of intelligence (Neisser et al., 1996).

Table 13.2 summarizes some current controversies that are being debated about intelligence by presenting myths, countermyths, and a brief statement of what recent research suggests might be true (Sternberg, 1996). The debate about intelligence is especially relevant for our discussion of the period of middle childhood since this is a time when intelligence tests are administered in school and school placement decisions are made. Furthermore, children begin to hear about the results of these tests and make personal attributions about their ability or potential. Thus, IQ tests may have a direct impact on the kind of educational experiences that children encounter and on their sense of self-efficacy.

The *hypercognitive system* (the circle surrounding the processing system in Figure 13.2) is composed of all the functions that make meaning of something. In this model, the hypercognitive system tries to interpret a particular task or problem, evaluating what is required to solve it, and then assigning the problem to one or more specialized systems that are best equipped to solve

TABLE 13.2

Myths, Mythical Countermyths, and Truths about Intelligence

Myth	Mythical Countermyth	Truth
1. Intelligence is one thing, g (or IQ).	Intelligence is so many things you can hardly count them.	Intelligence is multidimensional but scientifically tractable.
2. The social order is a natural outcome of the IQ pecking order.	Tests wholly create a social order.	The social order is partially but not exclusively created by tests.
3. Intelligence cannot be taught to any meaningful degree.	We can perform incredible feats in teaching individuals to be more intelligent.	We can teach intelligence to at least some degree, but cannot effect radical changes at this point.
4. IQ tests measure virtually all that's important for school and job success.	IQ tests measure virtually nothing that's important for school and job success.	IQ tests measure skills that are of moderate importance in school success and of modest importance in job success.
5. We are using tests too little, losing valuable information.	We're overusing tests and should abolish them.	Tests, when properly interpreted, can serve a useful but limited function, but often they are not properly interpreted.
6. Intelligence is essentially all inherited except for trivial and unexplainable variance.	Intelligence is essentially all environmental except for trivial and unexplainable variance.	Intelligence involves substantial heritable and environmental components in interaction.

Source: Sternberg, R. J. (1996). Myths, countermyths, and truths about intelligence. *Educational Researcher, 25,* Table 1, p. 12. Copyright 1996 by the American Educational Research Association. Reprinted by permission of the publisher.

it. As new skill areas are established, the person will have more alternative strategies to bring to bear on the solution of particular tasks or problems.

The *specialized structural systems* (areas labeled SSS in the outer circle of Figure 13.2) relate to specific types of intellectual domains that require distinct problem-solving skills. In their model, Demetriou and colleagues have identified five SSSs, each one best suited to a particular family of problems and associated with a unique profile of mental abilities. They include: qualitative-analytic (skills related to categorizing and systematically organizing information such as are required in fields like geology or botany); quantitative-relational (skills related to counting, measuring, and comparing information such as are required in fields like mathematics, statistics, or accounting); causal-experimental (skills related to hypothesis raising and hypothesis testing such as are required in any experimental science like psychology, physics, or chemistry); verbal-propositional (skills related to the organization and meaning of language and other symbol systems such as are required in the study of grammar, logic, and law); and spatial-imaginal (skills related to mental imagery and visual and spatial reasoning such as are required in the visual arts, weaving and pottery, or architecture).

In this model, each of the five SSSs can be applied, with its own unique set of concepts or schemes, operations, or strategies, to the task at hand. The more familiar the task and the more fully developed the SSS, the less likely any other SSS will be recruited to aid in the problem-solving process. For example, in the early years of developing the quantitative-relational skills necessary for mathematical problem-solving skills, teachers often rely on spatial and visual examples as well as verbal examples to help clarify mathematical symbols and relations. Once the mathematical symbols and processes such as addition, subtraction, division, and multiplication are understood, children may not need to rely on other SSSs to solve problems in the mathematical domain. However, once students are faced with advanced problems in geometry and calculus, principles from logic and visual/spatial reasoning may again come into play.

According to this model, development occurs in all three components. The processing system can become more efficient; attention can be improved to control the input of information; and storage and retrieval can become more effective. The hypercognitive system can develop as metacognitive capacities mature, allowing the person to make finer and more accurate assessments of the nature of problems and the kinds of skills most appropriate to their solution. Within each SSS, new subcapacities can be acquired. For example, in the causal-experimental domain, the achievement of schemes for conservation are elaborated into more formal scientific hypothesis-raising and hypothesis-testing strategies required for scientific research. Developmental changes may result from maturation of the central nervous system and the perceptual/motor capacities. They may arise from individually guided motivation to increase one's skill level in a particular SSS, or they may arise from external sources. Interactions with peers can result in new approaches to problem solving. Direct instruction or intervention adds to a child's skill level both at the hypercognitive level (teaching new approaches to recognizing and analyzing problems) and at the SSS level (teaching new techniques for representing and solving specific kinds of problems). Over time, and especially from about the ages of 10 to 12, we see a fantastic synergy of maturation, motivation, and external stimulation. The growth process accelerates in such a way that 11- and 12-year-olds appear qualitatively different in their approach to solving problems and enormously more skillful in their day-to-day functioning than younger children.

The Social and Cultural Contexts of Skill Development

Recent attention has been given to the social and cultural contexts in which many skills, especially school-related abilities, emerge (Eccles, 1993). Progress in skill development is influenced by parental and school expectations regarding levels of performance. It is also influenced by a child's motivation to achieve new levels of ability and to direct attention and energy to practice, problem solving, and the formulation of new strategies within a particular domain. Skill development can be enriched by interactions with skillful peers as well as by the appropriate intervention of teachers, coaches, and guides. As discussed in Box 13.3, cultures and subgroups within cultures differ in what skills they value, what behaviors are considered intelligent in a particular situation, and what qualities are viewed as essential for supporting intelligent behavior.

Consider the ongoing concern regarding mathematics ability among U.S. students, especially in comparison with their Japanese and Chinese counterparts. In 1980, comparative studies showed that first- and fifth-grade U.S. students in Minneapolis were substantially behind their age-mates in Sendai, Japan and Taipei, Taiwan in tests of mathematics achievement. In a ten-year follow-up, U.S. children still lagged behind, and by the 11th grade the gap in achievement had widened (Stevenson et al., 1993). Even among the top 10%

A sixth-grade classroom in Tokyo, Japan.

of students tested, the top Minneapolis students scored about at the average of the Taipei and Sendai students. It is difficult to account for these cross-national comparisons on the basis of ability. All three countries have practically universal enrollment of school-age children. Furthermore, when children were compared for general information of the type not included in the school curriculum, U.S. children at first and fifth grades scored higher than the Japanese and Chinese children.

At least four sociocultural factors interact to contribute to the advantage that Japanese and Chinese children show in mathematical skill development. First, there is a difference in parents' expectations for their children. Parents in the United States appear to be satisfied with their children's level of mathematics performance and do not expect their children to do better than they are doing. In contrast, the Japanese and Chinese parents have higher expectations for their children's performance.

Second, there is a difference in parents' evaluations of their children's schools. Parents in the United States are generally satisfied with the school curriculum and think that the schools are doing a good job. Far fewer Japanese and Chinese parents view the schools as good or excellent. The public pressure in these cultures is for increasing improvement in the quality of education. Even though Japanese and Chinese children spend more time on homework than do U.S. children, Japanese and Chinese parents are more likely to encourage even more time devoted to homework.

Third, there are cultural differences in reasons given for success in mathematics. American parents and teachers highlight the importance of natural ability as a major factor in accounting for individual differences in mathematical ability. Japanese and Chinese parents and teachers are more likely to see outstanding performance as a result of studying hard (Holloway, 1988). If a child believes that skill depends on natural ability, then he or she might conclude that there is not much that can be done to improve performance. If the child believes that skill depends on effort, then he or she may be more inclined to devote additional time and focused application to reach a new level of performance.

Finally, in contrast to what might be expected, by 11th grade, U.S. students are more stressed by school than are Chinese or Japanese youths. Students in the 11th grade in the United States reported frequent experiences of stress, anxiety about school, and aggression. They are less clear about the central role of school achievement in their lives. They had more competing demands on their time from after-school jobs, sports, and dating than did the Japanese or Chinese adolescents. One interpretation of this difference is that U.S. families and children set a greater value on freedom of choice and individuality than Japanese or Chinese families. As a result, there is less consistency in the priority that U.S. schoolchildren, their parents, and their teachers place on academic achievement in relation to the many other activities that claim time and attention.

The emphasis on skill building and the energy that children bring to the acquisition of new skills during middle childhood suggest a strong parallel to toddlerhood. At both stages, children's motives for competence and mastery are directed outward to the environment. At both stages, children appear to be delighted by the potential for learning that almost every new encounter offers. However, as a result of their cognitive capacities and their awareness of social expectations, skill learning at middle childhood is part of a much more complex framework of continuous monitoring and self-assessment. In addition, beliefs and attitudes about which skills are important, what you expect of yourself, others' expectations of you, and the influence of competing demands all contribute to the levels of performance that are likely to be achieved (see Notebook Page 13.2).

Self-Evaluation

During middle childhood, the emphasis on skill building is accompanied by a new focus on self-evaluation. Children strive to match their achievements to internalized goals and external standards. Simultaneously, they receive feedback from others about the quality of their performance. During early school age, children begin to receive messages about how well they are accomplishing tasks set before them. They may be designated as "Red Group" readers, or they may see a long line of stars after their names on the bulletin board. They may be asked to sit in the left-hand row in order to receive "special" help or be told to go down the hall for tutoring. These and many other signs of social judgment may be incorporated into children's self-evaluations.

In middle childhood, the process of self-evaluation is further complicated because the peer group becomes an additional source for social comparison, criticism, and approval. Toddlers and early-school-age children are likely to observe and imitate their peers in order to learn new strategies for approaching a task or out of curiosity. But in middle childhood, pressures toward conformity, competition, and the need for approval contribute to the self-evaluation process. Children begin to pay attention to the work of others in order to assess their own abilities (Butler & Ruzany, 1993). The child's athletic skills, intellectual abilities, and artistic talents are no longer matters to

Skilled Learning

Trace the path of skill learning in one important area during your own childhood. Select one area of skilled functioning, such as reading, math, hobby, or athletics.

1. When did you begin showing an interest?

_____

_____

_____

_____

2. What experiences were important (teaching, practice, peer modeling)?

_____

_____

_____

_____

3. What can you recall about the pattern of growth in this skill? Was it steady? Did it occur in spurts? Did you abandon it for awhile and later return?

_____

_____

_____

_____

4. How important is this skill area for you now? What did it lead to?

_____

_____

_____

_____

which only teachers and parents respond. Peers also identify others' skills and begin to generate profiles of one another: "Oh, Rafael is good in math, but he runs like a girl"; "Jane is kind of fat, but she writes great stories"; "I like Rashidah best because she's good at everything." Depending on how successfully the crises of toddlerhood and early school age are resolved, children approach the process of self-evaluation from a framework of either self-confidence or self-doubt. They may expect to accomplish tasks in a competent manner and consequently approach them as a welcome challenge, or they may anticipate failure and approach tasks with trepidation.

In a program of research involving children in the age range 8 to 13, Susan Harter (1985, 1993) devised a method for assessing children's perceptions of competence in five specific domains: scholastic competence, athletic competence, likability by peers, physical appearance, and behavioral conduct. In addition, she measured general or global self-esteem. Her research was based on the idea that, by the age of eight, children would not only be able to differentiate specific areas of competence but would view certain areas as more important to them than others. She found that self-esteem was highest for those children who viewed themselves as competent in domains that they judged to be important. Competence in relatively unimportant domains was not especially strongly related to overall self-esteem. In the sections that follow, we focus on two different paths toward self-evaluation, one that reflects a child's personal judgment of ability (self-efficacy) and one that reflects the impact of others' expectations on a child's performance.

Self-Efficacy

How do children reach an assessment of their competence in a specific ability area? How do they decide whether they are going to be able to perform well at a particular task? Albert Bandura (1982) has theorized that judgments of self-efficacy are crucial to understanding this process. *Self-efficacy* is defined as a person's sense of confidence about performing behaviors demanded in a specific situation. Expectations of efficacy vary with the specific ability required. In other words, a child may view efficacy negatively in a situation requiring mathematical ability but have a positive sense of efficacy where physical strength is required.

Bandura has suggested that four sources of information contribute to judgments of self-efficacy: enactive attainments, vicarious experiences, verbal persuasion, and physical state (see Figure 13.3). *Enactive attainments* are prior experiences of mastery in the kinds of tasks that are being confronted. A child's general assessment of ability in any area (mathematics, writing, gymnastics) is based on accomplishments in that area (Skaalvik & Hagtvet, 1990). Successful experiences increase self-efficacy, whereas repeated failures diminish it. Failure experiences are especially detrimental when they occur early in the process of trying to master a task. Many boys and girls are diverted from mastering such sports as tennis or baseball because they have had negative experiences early in their participation. They develop doubts about their abilities that prevent them from persisting at the task.

The second source is *vicarious experience*. Seeing a person similar to oneself perform a task successfully can raise one's sense of self-efficacy; seeing a person similar to oneself fail at a task can lower it (Brown & Inouye, 1978).

Verbal persuasion is the third source. Children can be encouraged to believe in themselves and to try a new task. Persuasion is likely to be most

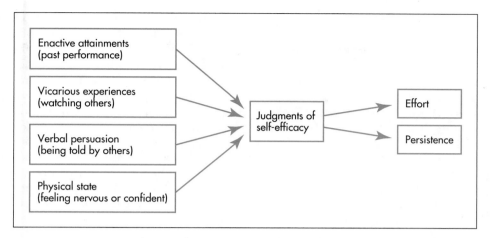

FIGURE 13.3

Four components of self-efficacy

effective in boosting the performance level of children who already have confidence in their abilities.

The fourth source is *physiological state*. People monitor their body states in making judgments about whether or not they can do well. When children feel very anxious or frightened, they are likely to anticipate failure. Children who are excited and interested but not overly tense are more likely to perceive themselves as capable of succeeding.

Self-efficacy judgments are related to children's perceptions of the likelihood of success. They also determine the factors to which children attribute their success or failure (McAuley, Duncan & McElroy, 1989). In the face of difficulty or failure, children who have confidence in their abilities and high self-efficacy will work harder to master challenges. They will attribute their difficulties to failure to try hard enough, and they will redouble their efforts. Children who have a low sense of self-efficacy tend to give up in the face of difficulty because they attribute their failure to a basic lack of ability (Bandura & Schunck, 1981). The level of self-efficacy also affects how children prepare to handle new challenges. Children with high levels of self-efficacy related to academic achievement are likely to set challenging goals for themselves. They are also likely to regulate their learning behaviors by deliberately enlisting a number of strategies, including concentrating, organizing their work, finding a good place to study, taking notes in class, and completing their homework assignments so that they have the best chance of reaching their goals (Zimmerman et al., 1992).

Social Expectations

In modern, postindustrial societies, it is difficult for children to develop independent, internal criteria by which to judge their abilities. If the skills of the culture were more direct and manual, perhaps it would be easier for children to make such judgments. In learning to plow a field, for example, one can look back over the land and see whether the furrows are deep enough and the rows straight. Many important areas of accomplishment, however, have no such clear, objective standards against which a child can readily compare his or her performance. In learning to write an English composition, assume leadership in a group, or prepare a science project, how can a child judge whether he or she has done an adequate job?

Research on self-concept suggests that the appraisals and expectations of others become incorporated into one's own self-evaluation. Self-esteem has been found to be based on the general positive regard and approval of others and on the specific expectations they have for one's ability and achievement in certain areas of performance, as well as on one's own feelings of competence (Harter, 1993; Jussim, 1990a). In attempting to assess their own abilities, children may rely on many external sources of evaluation, including grades, teachers' comments, parental approval, and peer approval (Crooks, 1988). If feedback from important adults suggests to children that they are cooperative, intelligent, and creative, these attributes are likely to be incorporated into their self-evaluations. Children who see themselves as cooperative and intelligent are likely to approach social and intellectual tasks with optimistic expectations about their performance. Conversely, feedback suggesting lack of cooperation, intelligence, and creativity can produce a pessimistic or antagonistic approach to the challenges of skill development. (See Box 13.4.)

The impact of social expectations on self-concept appears to crystallize during the second and third grades. Early-school-age children (four- and five-year-olds) do not typically make systematic use of success or failure feedback in predicting their next success (Parsons & Ruble, 1977). At the start of first grade, children's expectations about the grades they will receive on their first report cards are not clearly related to their IQs or to parents' or teachers' expectations, nor are they closely related to their later estimates of their grades. By the end of the first grade, however, children begin to be more accurate predictors of their performance (Alexander & Entwisle, 1988; Entwisle et al., 1987). By fifth grade, children are very aware of their teachers' expectations for their performance, and they are likely to mirror those expectations in their academic achievement (Weinstein et al., 1987).

Teachers' Expectations: The Self-Fulfilling Prophecy

The feedback that students receive from their teachers is not wholly objective. Teachers' expectations about their students' abilities can be based on objective assessments, but they can also be derived from stereotypes about certain types of children or biases based on prior experiences, such as having a child's older siblings in class in prior years or hearing unfavorable comments from other teachers. Merton (1948) suggested that problems can arise through a process that he called the *self-fulfilling prophecy.* This concept refers to false or inaccurate beliefs that can produce a reality that mirrors these beliefs. For example, if a teacher expects a child to perform poorly even though the child is above average in ability and the child actually does perform poorly, one can infer that the child fulfilled the teacher's low expectations.

In the original study on the effect of teacher expectations on student performance, teachers were led to believe that certain students were "late bloomers" who would show major gains in IQ later on in the school year (Rosenthal & Jacobson, 1968). These children, chosen at random from among first- and second-graders, actually did show significant increases in IQ (10 to 15 points) in comparison with the control group. The effect did not continue into third and fourth grades, and overall the correlation between teachers' expectations and students' measured IQ was modest.

Subsequent naturalistic studies of the self-fulfilling prophecy in classroom settings find that it has a consistent but comparatively small effect on

BOX 13.4

The Illusion of Incompetence

Have you ever noticed that some children who you think are quite capable have a poor opinion of their abilities? These children have a low estimation of their abilities even though the objective evidence suggests that they are capable. This phenomenon, described as the "illusion of incompetence," pertains to children who perform well on tests of academic achievement (at the 90th percentile or above) but perceive themselves as below average in academic ability. These children expect lower levels of success, are less confident, attempt less challenging tasks, and say that their schoolwork is more demanding than peers of similar high ability who have more positive self-evaluations.

It appears that parents play a central role in establishing these children's low assessments of themselves. Children who have an illusion of incompetence think that their parents have a low opinion of their abilities and expect little of them. They see their fathers, in particular, as holding to very rigorous standards that they are not expected to meet (Phillips, 1987, 1984). The parent–child dynamics that are likely to underlie this negative assessment were observed in a study involving children with high academic ability and varying levels of perceived academic competence. Children worked with their mothers and fathers on solvable and unsolvable tasks. The fathers of children who had low perceptions of their academic competence were found to interact with their children in more critical or unsupportive ways than did fathers of children who had high perceptions of their academic competence. Further, the children who held illusions of incompetence were more emotionally upset and dependent when they approached the unsolvable tasks (Wagner & Phillips, 1992).

student performance. One way of expressing the size of the effect is that, if you could control for actual ability and prior achievement, the teachers' erroneous expectations might lead to increases in performance among about 10% of children who were targets of high expectations and decreases in performance among about 10% of children who were targets of low expectations (Jussim, 1990a). The impact of these erroneous perceptions is likely to be increased when the person making the judgments is especially rigid or highly motivated to maintain and confirm negative views about a certain group. Thus, one might expect a stronger impact of biased perceptions and the self-fulfilling prophecy among teachers who endorse prejudiced views, whether the target of prejudice is race, gender, social class, religion, or some other classification.

Teachers' expectations for student performance are influenced by their assessments of both the student's ability and effort. In a study of elementary-school teachers, a relationship was found between the teachers' explanations for students' success and failure and the emotions the teachers felt toward the students under various conditions (see Figure 13.4). It was presumed that these emotional reactions were among the major cues that teachers sent to students about their performances. The teachers were likely to feel angry toward the students if they believed that the students were capable of very good work and their poor performance was due to a lack of effort. When children of low ability suddenly began putting forth a great deal of effort, teachers were likely to experience pride in their own accomplishments with these students. If low-ability students who were trying very hard failed, teachers felt a sense of guilt. Teachers were more willing to accept personal responsibility for certain patterns of student success and failure than for others. The students who made

FIGURE 13.4
Students' ability and
effort—teacher's reaction

teachers angriest were the bright ones who did not try hard. The research on teacher expectations illustrates how social expectations influence both perceptions of other people and the quality of interpersonal communication (Prawat et al., 1983).

Certain conditions can make children more or less vulnerable to internalizing false expectations. Children who are unsure about their abilities or who are learning something for the first time may be more likely to rely on the information that they receive from others to assess their abilities. Being in a new situation, like moving to a new school or changing from elementary to middle school, might increase a child's dependence on social expectations for performance. During middle childhood, many new domains of skill development are just being introduced. Children at this period of life may be more vulnerable to the effects of biased perceptions and erroneous expectations than are older children (Jussim, 1990b).

In addition, some children appear to monitor their social environment more self-consciously than others (Musser & Browne, 1991). High-self-monitoring children are more aware of the emotional and nonverbal behavior of others and make more use of social information in order to evaluate and regulate their own behaviors. These children are more responsive to subtle forms of feedback about their performance. They take in more information about social expectations for their performance than do children who are comparatively oblivious to the intricacies of their social environment.

Parents' Expectations

Parents' as well as teachers' expectations influence their children's perceptions of their abilities. This process is demonstrated in a study of parents' and children's attitudes about math aptitude (Parsons et al., 1982). Children in grades 5 through 11 and their parents were asked about their attitudes toward the children's mathematics achievement. Parents had lower expectations for their daughters' math achievement than for their sons'. They believed that mathematics is more difficult for girls than for boys and requires more effort. Their expectations about their children's aptitude were better predictors of the children's self-assessments than were the children's own past performances in mathematics.

Focusing on the relationship between gender-role bias and the socialization of children's competencies and interests, Eccles (1993) proposed the following model (see Table 13.3):

> The evidence suggests that general (parental) gender-role-beliefs influence perceptions of individual children's competencies and interests, which in turn affect the kinds of experiences parents provide.... Essentially, we believe that parents' gender-role stereotypes, in interaction with their children's sex, affect the following mediators: 1) parents' causal attributions for the children's performance; 2) parents' emotional reaction to their children's performance in various activities; 3) the importance parents attach to their children's acquiring various skills; 4) the advice parents provide their children regarding involvement in various skills; and 5) the activities and toys parents provide. In turn, we predict that these subtle and explicit mediators influence the development of the following child outcomes across the various gender-role-stereotyped activity domains: 1) children's confidence in their ability; 2) children's interest in mastering various skills; 3) children's affective reaction to participating in various activities; and as a

TABLE 13.3

The Relationship Between Parents' Gender-Role-Stereotype Beliefs and Perceptions to Parental Actions and Behaviors and Child Outcomes

Parents' Specific Beliefs and Perceptions	Parents' Specific Actions and Behaviors	Child Outcomes
Parents' casual attributions for child	Parents' advice	Child's motivational and psychological characteristics
Parents' affective reactions to child's performance and activity choices	Provision of equipment and toys	Child's confidence in his/her ability
Parents' perceptions of child's competence and interests	Provision of specific experiences	Child's interests and subjective task value
Parents' expectations for child's success		Child's affective associations and memories ↓
Parents' perceptions of importance of various activities and skills		Child's activity choice
		Child's affective reactions
		Child's persistence and performance

Source: Adapted from Eccles, J. S. (1993). School and family effects on the ontogeny of children's interests, self-perceptions, and activity choices. In J. E. Jacobs (Ed.), Nebraska Symposium on Motivation, 1992. Lincoln: University of Nebraska Press, Figure 6, p. 171. Copyright © 1993 by University of Nebraska Press. Reprinted by permission of University of Nebraska Press.

consequence of these self and task perceptions; 4) the amount of time and type of effort the children end up devoting to mastering and demonstrating various skills. (Eccles, 1993, 170)*

A number of studies support the underlying dynamics of this model. Independent of actual gender differences in specific domains, including math, sports, and English, parents' stereotypes about which gender is more talented in a particular area influence their perceptions of their own children's competence in that area. Parents' perceptions of competence are directly related to their children's perception of competence (Eccles et al., 1990).

The discussion of self-evaluation highlights children's sensitivity to their social environment. Direct experiences with success and failure are important, but they are embedded in a context of social expectations. Children become aware of existing roles, norms, and sanctions for norm violation. Messages of reassurance and encouragement from parents and teachers can play a key role in establishing a sense of competence and motivation for persisting in the face of difficult challenges. The negative effects of erroneous teacher expectations can be counteracted by giving children many opportunities for successful experiences in a particular domain. As children establish a history of success, they will come to trust their own judgments about their abilities. In addition, parents can advise children that some teachers have prejudiced attitudes and help them identify the signs of such attitudes operating in the classroom. By the end of middle childhood, children have had enough school experience that they can detect favoritism, bias, and unfair treatment and can devise strategies to protect themselves from the impact of such negative assessments. The stronger and more supportive children's social relationships are, the more confidence they will have about their worth and the more accurately they will assess their abilities. In addition to family, one of the most salient sources of reassurance and support is likely to come from friends.

Friendship

Can you remember some things about a friend you had when you were ten years old? While friendships of the middle childhood years are not likely to be as enduring as the attachment relationships of infancy, they can be quite memorable for their levels of closeness and affection. At this age, children describe *close friends* as people who like the same activities, share common interests, enjoy each other's company, and can count on each other for help (Ainsworth, 1989; Youniss, 1980).

Friendships may not be as essential to survival as attachment relations, but they clearly provide social and developmental advantages (Ainsworth, 1989; Hartup, 1989). You will recall from Chapter 4 that ethology is the study of behaviors that are associated with the long-term adaptation and survival of groups. According to ethological theory, friendship relations have adaptive advantages. Group cooperation gives a selective advantage to many social

Source: Eccles, J. S. (1993). School and family effects on the ontogeny of children's interests, self-perceptions, and activity choices. In J. E. Jacobs (Ed.), Nebraska Symposium on Motivation, 1992. Lincoln: University of Nebraska Press, p. 170. Copyright © 1993 by University of Nebraska Press. Reprinted by permission of University of Nebraska Press.

species, especially in tracking and hunting for food. From an evolutionary standpoint, individuals who were able to coordinate their activities with others were probably more successful in gathering more food, hunting larger game, and protecting a larger territory. Therefore, the skills of cooperation and sociability are thought to have contributed to fitness for the species as a whole. On an individual level, children who participate in positive peer friendships are likely to experience social support and intellectual and social stimulation that foster their personal development.

Friendships → social support intellectual and social stimulation

In the following discussion of the developmental task of friendship, we begin by considering the role of the family in preparing children to engage in satisfying peer relationships. Then, the role of friendship is considered in promoting flexible perspective taking, exposure to peer norms, and experiences of closeness with peers.

Family Influences on Children's Readiness for Friendships

Not all children enter middle childhood with the same capacity to make friends. Early family experiences contribute to a child's sociability and social competence. The process of learning to be friends may begin in infancy. Children who have secure attachments in infancy are more popular in preschool and engage more freely in social interactions. They are perceived as more helpful and better able to consider the needs of others (Park & Waters, 1989; Sroufe & Fleeson, 1986).

A mother's discipline techniques, the way she speaks to her child, and her parenting values are all linked to a child's social competence and popularity. Mothers who interact in positive, agreeable ways and openly express their feelings are more likely to produce children who have positive friendship relations. These patterns are observable as early as preschool and continue to be found in the elementary grades (Youngblade & Belsky, 1992). Mothers who use power-assertive discipline techniques and believe that aggression is an acceptable way of resolving conflicts have children who expect to get their way by asserting power in peer conflicts (Dishion et al., 1991; Haskett & Kistner, 1991). Researchers carried out observations of the social relationships of 8- to 12-year-old children who had been physically abused. These abused children had low social status among their peers and were described by peers as aggressive and uncooperative. Their teachers described them as showing noticeable behavior problems (Salzinger et al., 1993).

The family environment influences a child's social competence in at least three ways. First, children may directly imitate their parents' positive or negative behaviors. For example, if parents ask many questions and invite their child's opinions, the child may be more likely to show interest in the ideas and opinions of others, which encourages friendships. Second, a parent's discipline technique may influence what a child expects in a social interaction. Children who have been exposed to aggressive parenting techniques believe that these same strategies will work with their peers. However, evidence suggests that children avoid or reject peers who are overly aggressive and bullying in their social behavior. As a result, these children are more likely to experience social rejection. Third, parents who are highly restrictive and try to control their children's behavior are less likely to permit their young children much exposure to peer social interaction. These children arrive at middle childhood with less experience in peer play and, as a result, are less competent at forming and sustaining peer friendships (Hart et al., 1990; Pettit et al., 1988; Putallaz, 1987).

Three Contributions of Friendship to Social Development

[handwritten margin notes:]
— increased appreciation for varying points of view.
— sensitive to social norms & peer group pressures
— close, caring relationship devt.

Children learn at least three lessons from daily interactions with peers. First, friendship teaches an increasing appreciation of the many points of view represented in the peer group. As children play together, they discover that there may be several versions of the same song, divergent sets of rules for the same game, varying interpretations of the same event or conversation, and different customs for the same holiday. Second, friendship teaches children to be increasingly sensitive to social norms and peer group pressures. Third, friendship teaches how to have experiences of closeness and caring with an age-mate as best-friend relationships develop.

Perspective Taking and Cognitive Flexibility

As children interact with peers who see the world differently than they do, they begin to understand the limits of their own points of view. According to Piaget (1932/1948), peers have an important influence in diminishing one another's self-centered outlooks precisely because they interact as equals. Children do not feel forced to accept one another's ideas in the same way as they feel pressure to accept the ideas of adults. They argue, bargain, and eventually compromise in order to maintain friendships. The opportunity to function in social peer groups for problem solving and play leads children away from the egocentrism of early childhood and closer to the eventual flexibility of adult thought. The greatest benefit comes from resolving conflicts due to differences in perspective in the peer group. Growth is especially positive for children who interact with slightly more competent peers whose problem-solving skills are more advanced or flexible than their own (Tudge, 1992).

A substantial body of evidence demonstrates that the behavior of well-adjusted, competent children is maintained in part by a number of social-cognitive abilities, including social perspective taking, interpersonal problem solving, and information processing (Carlo et al., 1991; Dodge et al., 1986; Downey & Walker, 1989; Elias et al., 1989). These cognitive abilities appear to foster a child's entry into successful peer interactions. At the same time, active participation with peers tends to promote the development of these social-cognitive abilities.

Perspective-taking ability relates to other social skills that can contribute to the quality of a child's social relationships. Such skills include analyzing social problems, empathizing with the emotional state of another person, understanding that others may see a situation differently because of their own information or beliefs, and a willingness to accept individual differences in personality or abilities (Chalmers & Townsend, 1990; Montgomery, 1993; Pillow, 1991; Wellman, 1990) (see Box 13.5). Children who are sensitive to the variety of perspectives that coexist in a social situation are also likely to be more positively evaluated by their peers (Pellegrini, 1985). Rejected and withdrawn children often lack the social skills that would win them acceptance by their age-mates (French, 1988; Patterson, 1982).

An interactive process is set in motion. Children who have opportunities to participate in peer friendships make progress in achieving new levels of interpersonal understanding. As interpersonal understanding grows, children acquire the necessary skills and sensitivity to be more effective with—and usually more valued by—their peers. On the flip side, rejected children come to expect negative behaviors from others. A vicious cycle develops between the rejected child and peers, each having negative expectations of the

BOX 13.5

When Friends Disagree

We have suggested that peer interaction fosters cognitive growth because peers are free both to share and to disagree with others' points of view. But does this really happen? Are children more open to and honest with their friends than they are with children who are not their friends? Do children change their views when friends disagree with them?

A study of boys and girls ages eight through ten approached the question of how friends and nonfriends handle conflict (Nelson & Aboud, 1985). Pairs of children who were friends and pairs who were not friends were asked to resolve their differences about a social/ethical problem. Two examples of the problems they had to discuss were: What should you do if you get home and find that you accidentally picked up something at a store and forgot to pay for it? and What should you do if a boy (girl) much smaller than you starts a fight with you? In describing the interactions among the pairs, three differences were observed:

1. Friends offered each other more explanations than did nonfriends.
2. Friends criticized each other more than did nonfriends.
3. Friends who disagreed changed their opinions more readily following discussions than did nonfriends. Further, such changes were likely to be in the direction of a higher level of social responsibility.

Other research supports the finding that good friends do not avoid conflict, but seem to resolve conflicts relatively easily. Their disagreements do not last a long time, and they remain positive in their assessment of their relationship even when they disagree (Parker & Asher, 1993). Although children may not seek out conflict and criticism in their friendship, its presence appears to play a valuable role in promoting moral reasoning and social cognition.

---

other. As this cycle continues, the rejected child acquires an increasingly negative reputation and has little opportunity to develop positive relationship skills (Waas, 1988).

Social Norms and Peer Group Pressures

The peer group evolves norms for acceptance and rejection. As children become aware of these *social norms*, they begin to experience pressures to conform. Adults, particularly teachers, lose some of their power to influence children's behavior. In the classroom, the early-school-age child focuses primarily on the teacher as a source of approval and acceptance, whereas during middle childhood the child perceives the peer group as an equally significant audience. Children often play to the class instead of responding to the teacher. The roles of class joker and class leader emerge during middle childhood as ways of gaining approval from the peer group.

The need for peer approval becomes a powerful force toward conformity (Pepitone et al., 1977). Children learn to dress, talk, and joke in ways that are acceptable to peers. From grades 3 through 9, they become increasingly willing to conform to peer behaviors that might be considered antisocial. For example, it has been reported that ninth-graders are more willing than third-graders to go along with peer cheating, stealing, and trespassing (Berndt, 1979). Antagonism between boys and girls, which is very common during this stage, is perpetuated by pressures toward conformity. If all the fifth-grade boys hate girls, Johnny is not very likely to admit openly that he likes to play with Mary. There are indications that perceived pressures to conform are

Inside jokes, a shared set of signs and symbols, and enjoyment in shared activities bind friends together.

stronger in the fifth and sixth grades than at later times, although the importance of being identified as a member of a specific peer group has not yet peaked (Gavin & Furman, 1989).

Loneliness.   With the increased emphasis on peer acceptance and conformity comes the risk of peer rejection and feelings of loneliness. In a study of over 500 children between the ages of 8 and 11, more than 10% expressed feelings of loneliness and social dissatisfaction (Asher, Hymel & Renshaw, 1984). A significant proportion of the children had trouble making friends (17%) or felt left out (18%) or alone (14%). Not surprisingly, children who were infrequently mentioned as a best friend by others were more lonely than those who were mentioned as a best friend by three or more other children.

Four social characteristics may combine to increase a child's experiences of loneliness. First, children who are withdrawn or prefer to be involved in isolated activities even when peers are present tend to view themselves as socially incompetent. Second, children who have trouble forming any kind of close friendship that provides emotional closeness and support are more likely to feel lonely. Third, peer rejection is especially powerful in producing feelings of loneliness. Children who experience a general positive level of peer acceptance feel less alone than those who are rejected by peers (Crick & Ladd, 1993). Finally, children who tend to blame themselves for their lack of social acceptance feel more lonely and are possibly less likely to believe that they can do anything to improve their situation (Cassidy & Asher, 1992; Renshaw & Brown, 1993; Rubin et al., 1990).

Peer Rejection.   Research has identified three main types of rejected children: Some children who are rejected tend to be disruptive and aggressive with peers; others tend to be socially withdrawn but do not exhibit aggressive tendencies; a third group has been described as both aggressive and withdrawn (French, 1988, 1990; Hymel et al., 1993). All three groups tend to have multiple problems. Children in the *aggressive-rejected* group are more likely than nonaggressive children to attribute hostile intentions to others. They tend to see peer interactions as threatening, and they also say that they would be likely to use aggressive strategies in response to negative peer behaviors (Quiggle et al., 1992; Sancilio et al., 1989). The aggressive children also tend to have a somewhat exaggerated idea about their competence.

Children in the *withdrawn-rejected* group tend to be inhibited, anxious, and interpersonally reserved. They have negative self-concepts and tend to interpret negative peer reactions as a result of their own personal failings (Hymel et al., 1993). They experience difficulty dealing with stress. These children also exhibit inappropriate affect and various unusual behavioral mannerisms that are likely to be ridiculed by peers (French, 1988). Some withdrawn children report close relationships with a favorite sibling. However, having this kind of sibling support does not appear to protect these children entirely from the negative consequences of peer rejection (East & Rook, 1992). The withdrawn-rejected children are more likely to experience higher levels of loneliness and to worry about the quality of their relationships with peers (Parkhurst & Asher, 1992).

Children in the *aggressive-withdrawn-rejected* group tend to be the least well-liked of all three types of rejected children. They exhibit anxiety, poor self-control, and social withdrawal in addition to aggressive behavior. They are rated by other children as being incompetent in school ability, unattractive, poor at leadership, cooperation, or humor, and the most likely to behave inappropriately in school. Despite high levels of peer rejection, however, they do not have the same low self-concept and negative view of their abilities as do the withdrawn-rejected children.

Rejected children tend to retain this status throughout elementary school. They are likely to have future adjustment problems and often require psychiatric treatment in adolescence or adulthood (Coie & Krehbiel, 1984; Hymel et al., 1990) (see Notebook Page 13.3).

Close Friends

The opportunity for peer-group interaction usually leads to the formation of close friends or best-friend relationships that can become quite intimate (Berndt, 1981). Typically, but not always, close friends are of the same sex. In the context of these friendships, children share private jokes, develop secret codes, tell intimate family information, set out on "dangerous" adventures, and help each other in times of trouble. They also fight, threaten, break up, and reunite. Sullivan (1949) pointed out the significance of these early, same-sex friendships as building blocks for adult relationships. With a best friend, a child experiences love and closeness for a peer rather than for an adult, a relationship that is more likely to allow for mutuality of power, status, and access to resources (French, 1984). Conflicts in the relationship can be worked out in terms that the children can control rather than escalating into dimensions requiring adult intervention. One child cannot take away another child's allowance or send the other child out of the room when a conflict

Rejected Children

Consider the issue of peer rejection during middle childhood. Try to recall a rejected or withdrawn child from that time in your life (ages 6 to 12).

1. Describe the child (physical features, notable behaviors, interests, etc).

_____

_____

_____

_____

2. How was the child treated by peers? What evidence are you using to identify this child as rejected or withdrawn?

_____

_____

_____

_____

3. Based on what you have read in the text and your memories, what might have accounted for this child's rejection or withdrawal?

_____

_____

_____

_____

4. If you were this child's teacher, what might you have done to help reduce his or her experiences of rejection or withdrawal?

_____

_____

_____

_____

arises. The children must resolve their differences within the framework of commitment to each other.

In a study of over 800 children in grades 3 through 5, 78% had at least one reciprocated best friend (one child named another as one of his or her three best friends, and that other child named the first child on his or her list as well); and 55% had a *very* best friend. More girls than boys had best friends, and the quality of best friends was somewhat different for girls and boys. Girls and boys described their best-friend relationships quite similarly with respect to having low levels of conflict or betrayal and high levels of companionship and shared recreational activities. However, girls described their best-friend relationships as having higher levels of caring and personal validation ("makes me feel good about my ideas"), intimacy ("we always tell each other our problems"), help and guidance ("help each other with schoolwork a lot"), and conflict resolution ("we make up easily when we have a fight") (Parker & Asher, 1993).

In addition to differences in the characteristics of best-friend relationships, the structures of boys' friendships differ somewhat from those of girls. Boys' friendship networks appear somewhat larger and looser (Karweit & Hansell, 1983). The number of reciprocated female friendships increases with age (Epstein, 1983). During middle childhood, girls spend more time each day talking on the phone to their best friends than do boys, and their time spent talking to friends increases from sixth to eighth grade (Crockett et al., 1984). Girls have more in-school contact with their friends through participation in service clubs and student government, while boys have their greatest contact with close friends through athletics (Karweit, 1983). Boys come into more contact with their best friends at nonschool functions and make more out-of-school friends than girls. Boys are more concerned than girls with status in selecting friends, and they make more unreciprocated friendship choices as a result (Clark & Ayers, 1988; Karweit & Hansell, 1983).

Children's need for the friendship of peers brings them into an increasingly complex social system. They learn that other children do not necessarily share their point of view, that approval is conditional upon conformity to certain norms, and that there are opportunities for unique emotional experiences with friends that cannot be duplicated with the family. Often, it is the desire to spend more time with friends or to become connected to a new group of friends that motivates children to become actively involved in team sports or other types of organized group activities.

Team Play

During middle childhood, a new dimension is added to the quality of a child's play. Children begin to participate in team sports, and, as a result, they gain a sense of team success as well as personal success. Team sports are generally more complicated than the kinds of games described as group play in Chapter 11. The rules are so complex that they may require a referee or an umpire if they are to be followed accurately. In sports, children join together into teams that remain together for the duration of the game. Some children join teams that play together for an entire season, such as Little League. Through participation in team play, one can see a "preworking" of skills and orientations that will apply to the world of work and to the functioning of the family group. Four significant characteristics of team membership are relevant to development during this stage: (1) interdependence, (2) the principle of the division of labor, (3) competition, and (4) the formation of in-group/out-group attitudes.

Interdependence

Team membership carries with it the awareness that one's acts may affect the success or failure of the entire group. There is a definite emphasis on winning and losing. Children may be ostracized or ridiculed if they contribute to a team loss. Although team sports do provide opportunities for individual recognition, it is quite clear that team success casts a halo over even the poorest players and team failure a shadow over even the best. In this sense, participation in team sports is an early lesson about *interdependence*. All of the team members rely on one another, and ideally it is to everyone's advantage to assist the weaker members in improving the quality of their play. The best coaches are noted for inspiring this sense of interdependence and mutual support among team members, urging them to work together to improve their skills. What often happens, however, is that the poorest players are scorned and scapegoated, particularly if the team loses.

Division of Labor

The notion of the *division of labor* as an effective strategy for attaining a goal is experienced through participation with peers on teams. Children learn that each position on a team has a unique function and that the team has the best chance of winning if each player performs a specific function rather than trying to do the work of all the other players. The team concept encompasses the variety of activities in which each of the team members actually engages. A complementary concept is cooperation. Team members learn that if the team as a whole is to do its best, the members must help one another to play their particular roles as well as possible. Cooperation can take many forms: Members share resources, take time to help other team members improve their skills, plan strategies together, work cooperatively on the field, cheer each other up, transport equipment, or clean up after the game. In many sports, there is a dynamic tension between competition and cooperation. Team members may compete with each other for a more desirable position or recognition as the top player. At the same time, the team members know that they have to support each other, especially when they play against another team.

The team may well become an experiential model for approaching other complex organizations (Shears & Bower, 1974). Once children learn that certain goals can best be attained when tasks are divided among a group of people, they begin to conceptualize the principles behind the organization of social communities. They recognize that some children are better suited to handle one aspect of the task and others do better at another aspect. Some children enjoy the skill development associated with team play, others enjoy learning the rules and devising strategies, others especially value the chance for peer companionship, and still others have a strong inner motive to compete and to try to win (Klint & Weiss, 1987). The distribution of roles to fit children's individual skills and preferences is a subtle element of the learning that is acquired through team play.

For many children, team competition increases motivation and performance. For some, it arouses intense anxiety about failure.

Competition

Team play teaches children about the nature of *competition* and the importance of winning. In team sports, both sides cannot win; success for one side must result in failure for the other. If the team experience is a laboratory for learning lessons about the larger social community, this particular aspect promotes a competitive view of social situations. Some children come to think of business, politics, popularity, and even interpersonal conflicts as win–lose situations in which the primary goal is to beat one's opponents. The idea of a win–win strategy to conflict resolution is very foreign in this context.

Winning is a great "high." Many young adults look back fondly on the memories associated with winning an important game and bring that energetic approach to adult tasks. The metaphor of playing on a winning team is deeply interwoven into the world of work, giving a competitive goal orientation to day-to-day work-related obligations and tasks. In one study of women in traditional and nontraditional professions, for example, more professional businesswomen and other women in nontraditional fields remembered experiences playing in competitive sports and being on teams with both males and females during their childhood (Coats & Overman, 1992).

In contrast to those who are energized by the challenges of competition, some children are especially sensitive to the pain of failure and will go to remarkable extremes in order to avoid failing. The public embarrassment and private shame that accompany failure are powerful emotions. Children who have a low sense of self-esteem are more likely to experience intense anxiety about losing in a competitive situation (Brustad, 1988). Losing can be an important lesson for children, but, as Vince Lombardi has been known to say, "Show me a good loser, and I'll show you a loser." The bitterness of losing and the intense drive to win associated with team sports discourage some children from participating.

Team play has implications for both intellectual and social development. Children who play team sports learn to conceptualize the game and their role in it in more relational terms. They see themselves as contributors to a larger effort and learn to anticipate the consequences of their behavior for the group. Games that involve teams are generally so complex that children are called on to learn many rules, make judgments, plan strategies, and assess the strengths and weaknesses of the other players. All of these characteristics of participation in team sports can stimulate cognitive growth (Smith, 1986). In one study, for example, children were divided into soccer "experts" versus soccer "novices" (Schneider & Bjorklund, 1992). The experts had an impressive depth of knowledge about the game of soccer, and when given a memory task involving soccer-related items, they were able to use their expertise to perform the task at a high level.

Interest in sports and competitive team play has been used as a motivational "hook" to interest children in other areas of school ability. For example, in Columbus, Ohio, a former Ohio State University football player who also played professional football organized a summer camp for 5th- through 12th-graders. The focus of the camp was to combine sports with math and science education. The curriculum was developed to teach math and science for 2½ hours each day and to spend the remainder of the day in practical applications in the area of sports. For example, students might learn the principles of physics that account for why a baseball travels faster than a football and then experiment with these principles on the ballfield (Beaulieu, 1992).

In-Group and Out-Group Attitudes

All human societies observe distinctions between in-group and out-group attitudes and behaviors. The *in-group* is a group in which the members share common norms, goals, and values. Within the in-group, the members share a common fate. In the case of sports teams, for example, the team wins or loses as a team. Feelings of cohesiveness and similarity with members of an in-group prompt behaviors that support the group's survival. The *out-group* is any group whose goals are either in opposition or inconsistent with the goals of the in-group. Any group can be perceived as an out-group, even though that group does not actually pose any physical threat to members of the in-group. For sports teams, the out-group's goal of winning is directly in competition with the in-group's similar goal (Triandis, 1990). We learn that moral principles that apply to members of the in-group do not necessarily apply to members of the out-group. In the extreme, adults can justify killing a member of an out-group under conditions of declared war.

The social consequences of team play can be divided into in-group and out-group attitudes. A child in the in-group learns to value and contribute to team goals. Identification with team goals may even require a child to relinquish a personal goal, such as being first at bat, for the good of the team. The child receives feedback on skills from team members that may help him or her to improve. Children learn to value their roles as part of a larger system and to see the interdependence between themselves and the other players. They learn that team victories can give them great personal satisfaction and team defeats can be a source of frustration and depression.

The child learns to see the outcome of competition as a win-or-lose situation, with the other team being the "enemy." Antagonism toward the out-group is valued in team sports.

Many older adolescents recall that both in-group and out-group attitudes were formed within their team, although this may appear contradictory to the concepts of interdependence and group cooperation. Certain children are "earmarked" as the true athletes of the team, and the others may feel like outsiders. Sometimes, parents use their influence to make sure that their children are given special treatment. Sometimes, conflict arises as a result of school or neighborhood rivalries among the children. In these instances, the out-group children may feel that they are not only competing with members of the opposing team, but that they have to protect themselves from insults, pranks, and other ostracizing behavior from their own team members.

In-group and out-group boundaries were observed in a study of sharing (Dickstein, 1979). Children shared more with a friend than they did with a disliked peer. With friends, children always preferred a norm of equal treatment. With nonfriends, children always preferred a norm of rivalry. Even those children who were quite skillful at perspective taking were not likely to apply these abilities to disliked peers.

Children can belong to more than one in-group, and the people who are categorized as members of an out-group can change according to the situation. For example, Ryan and his friend Tom were on the school soccer team together, but they belonged to different summer baseball leagues. During the summer they had to compete against each other, so they usually spent more time together and were closer friends during the school year than they were during the summers. Table 13.4 shows the in-group and out-group attitudes that result from experiences in team play.

Teams that create in-group and out-group attitudes provide a socialization experience that has both positive and negative consequences. For most children, the experiences of belonging to a team, making friends, learning new skills, and enjoying the sense of success that are associated with collaborative effort are very positive (see Notebook Page 13.4). However, we all know of

TABLE 13.4

Development of Attitudes as a Result of Team Play Experiences

In-Group Attitudes	Out-Group Attitudes
The child learns:	The child learns:
1. To value and contribute to team goals.	1. That the outcome of competition is win or lose.
2. To relinquish personal goals for team goals.	2. That the other team is the "enemy."
3. To receive and use feedback and help from team members.	3. That one must try one's hardest to defeat the other team.
4. To value her or his role as an element in a larger system and to perceive interdependence.	4. That there is and should be antagonism between teams.
5. That team victories give personal satisfaction and team defeats bring frustration and depression.	5. That assisting the other team is unethical.

Team Play

Think about a team experience that you had during middle childhood. It might be sports or some other kind of organized team effort such as cheerleading, academic competition, or drama.

1. What positive and negative memories do you have of this team experience?

_____

_____

_____

_____

2. Give examples of the following four constructs from your own experience: interdependence, division of labor, competition, and in-group/out-group attitudes.

_____

_____

_____

_____

3. Give examples of how the developmental tasks of friendship, concrete operations, skill learning, and self-evaluation were elaborated in the context of team play.

_____

_____

_____

_____

instances where rivalries become elaborated into peer hatreds, where children from neighboring schools turn against each other, and where coaches humiliate and degrade children in order to instill a commitment to the team and a determination to win. Perhaps the question is whether the focal point of team sports is to enhance children's natural impulses for competence and skill elaboration or a way for adults to vent their own frustrated needs for domination and power.

Chapter Summary

1. According to Piaget's theory, a qualitatively new stage of cognitive development occurs during middle childhood—the stage of concrete operational thinking. During this period, children begin to solve problems using mental operations to achieve basic transformations. They apply logical principles of cause and effect to physical and social domains.

2. Three major cognitive accomplishments of this period are: (a) the principle of conservation which is gradually applied to many dimensions of the physical world, including mass, weight, number, area, and volume; (b) classification skills, including the capacity to form a logical hierarchy of categories; and (c) combinatorial skills, especially the skills of addition, subtraction, multiplication, and division.

3. Skilled learning advances along a number of dimensions, with most children reaching new levels of expertise in a few skill areas and some children becoming quite advanced in certain special areas such as math, music, and reading. Reading is an example of the complex mental, physical, motivational, and emotional components linked to the development of new skills.

4. A model of the mind helps to clarify the dynamics of complex skill learning, linking activities at three levels: the central processing system capacities that control the speed and storage of information; the hypercognitive system that interprets problems and assesses the skills required to solve them; and the specialized structural systems that accumulate knowledge, as well as techniques appropriate to certain problem-solving domains.

5. Problem solving and skill development must also be understood within a cultural context that provides certain supports and barriers to skill development. The sociocultural context of differences in math achievement is an example of this principle.

6. During middle childhood, there is new awareness of the comparative basis of personal judgments and a heightened capacity for self-evaluation. Two processes contribute to self-evaluation: self-efficacy and its role in promoting confidence and persistence in the learning situation, and social expectations, the evaluative feedback from others about how well or poorly one is expected to perform. Teachers and parents both play key roles in conveying expectations about a child's ability and potential in various skill development areas.

7. During middle childhood, friends provide important sources of companionship, support, encouragement, and feedback. Family experiences play a key role in setting the stage for how children approach friendship in middle childhood. Children learn social skills by observing and imitating their parents' discipline and guidance techniques. As a result, some children are better prepared than others to engage in positive, satisfying social relationships with peers.

8. Three contributions of peer relationships during middle childhood include: new levels of perspective taking and cognitive flexibility; understanding the peer norms for acceptance and rejection; and achieving new levels of intimacy and affection with a close friend.

9. Research on peer rejection finds that roughly 10% of children in middle childhood experience loneliness and dissatisfaction with peer relations. Rejected children are likely to exhibit one of three patterns: aggressiveness, withdrawn but not aggressive, and a combination of aggressive and withdrawn.

10. In addition to the social learning gained in friendships, many children participate in new levels of competitive team sports. These experiences provide insight into the process of interdependence among team members; the principles of division of labor; competition and the meaning of winning and losing; and the formation of in-group and out-group attitudes.

References

Ainsworth, M. D. S. (1989). Attachments beyond infancy. *American Psychologist, 44,* 709–716.

Alexander, K. L. & Entwisle, D. R. (1988). *Achievement in the first two years of school: Patterns and processes.* Monographs of the Society for Research in Child Development, 53 (2, serial no. 218).

Anderson, R. C., Wilson, P. T. & Fielding, L. G. (1988). Growth in reading and how children spend their time outside of school. *Reading Research Quarterly, 23,* 285–303.

Asher, S. R., Hymel, S. & Renshaw, P. D. (1984). Loneliness in children. *Child Development, 55,* 1456–1464.

Au, T. K., Sidle, A. L. & Rollins, K. B. (1993). Developing an intuitive understanding of conservation: Invisible particles as a plausible mechanism. *Developmental Psychology, 29,* 286–299.

Bandura, A. (1982). Self-efficacy mechanism in human agency. *American Psychologist, 37,* 122–147.

Bandura, A. & Schunck, D. H. (1981). Cultivating competence, self-efficacy, and intrinsic interest through proximal self-motivation. *Journal of Personality and Social Psychology, 41,* 586–598.

Beaulieu, L. (1992). Teaching more than just sports. *Columbus Dispatch* (June 28, 1992), 6D.

Berndt, T. J. (1979). Developmental changes in confor-

mity to peers and parents. *Developmental Psychology, 15,* 608–616.

Berndt, T. J. (1981). Relations between social cognition, nonsocial cognition, and social behavior: The case of friendship. In J. H. Flavell and L. D. Ross (Eds.), *Social cognitive development: Frontiers and possible futures.* Cambridge: Cambridge University Press.

Bijstra, J., Van Geert, P. & Jackson, S. (1989). Conservation and the appearance-reality distinction: What do children really know and what do they answer? *British Journal of Developmental Psychology, 7,* 43–53.

Brainerd, C. J. (1977). Cognitive development and concept learning: An interpretive review. *Psychological Bulletin, 84,* 919–939.

Brainerd, C. J. & Hooper, F. H. (1978). More on the identity equivalence sequence: An update and some replies to Miller. *Psychological Bulletin, 85,* 70–75.

Brown, I., Jr. & Inouye, D. K. (1978). Learned helplessness through modeling: The role of perceived similarity in competence. *Journal of Personality and Social Psychology, 36,* 900–908.

Brustad, R. J. (1988). Affective outcomes in competitive youth sport: The influence of intrapersonal and socialization factors. *Journal of Sport and Exercise Psychology, 10,* 307–321.

Bus, A. G., vanIJzendoorn, M. H., Pellegrini, A. D. (1995). Joint book reading makes for success in learning to read: A meta-analysis on intergenerational transmission of literacy. *Review of Educational Research, 65,* 1–21.

Butler, R. & Ruzany, N. (1993). Age and socialization effects on the development of social comparison motives and normative ability assessment in kibbutz and urban children. *Child Development, 64,* 532–543.

Butterfield, E. C., Nelson, T. O. & Peck, V. (1988). Developmental aspects of the feeling of knowing. *Developmental Psychology, 24,* 654–663.

Carlo, G., Knight, G. P., Eisenberg, N. & Rotenberg, K. J. (1991). Cognitive processes and prosocial behaviors among children: The role of affective attributions and reconciliations. *Developmental Psychology, 27,* 456–461.

Carr, M., Kurtz, B. E., Schneider, W., Turner, L. A. & Borkowski, J. G. (1989). Strategy acquisition and transfer among American and German children: Environmental influences on metacognitive development. *Developmental Psychology, 25,* 765–771.

Carroll, D. W. (1986). *Psychology of language.* Pacific Grove, Calif.: Brooks/Cole.

Cassidy, J. & Asher, S. R. (1992). Loneliness and peer relations in young children. *Child Development, 63,* 350–365.

Chalmers, J. B. & Townsend, M. A. R. (1990). The effects of training in social perspective taking on socially maladjusted girls. *Child Development, 61,* 178–190.

Chapman, M. & McBride, M. L. (1992). Beyond competence and performance: Children's class inclusion strategies, superordinate class cues, and verbal justifications. *Developmental Psychology, 28,* 319–327.

Clark, M. L. & Ayers, M. (1988). The role of reciprocity and proximity in junior high school friendships. *Journal of Youth and Adolescence, 17,* 403–411.

Coats, P. B. & Overman, S. J. (1992). Childhood play experiences of women in traditional and nontraditional professions. *Sex Roles, 26,* 261–271.

Coie, J. D. & Krehbiel, G. (1984). Effects of academic tutoring on the social status of low-achieving, socially rejected children. *Child Development, 55,* 1465–1478.

Columbus Dispatch. (1992, May 11). War chases children out of Sarajevo. (Associated Press), 3A.

Crick, N. R. & Ladd, G. W. (1993). Children's perceptions of their peer experiences: Attributions, loneliness, social anxiety, and social avoidance. *Developmental Psychology, 29,* 244–254.

Crockett, L., Losoff, M. & Petersen, A. (1984). Perceptions of the peer group and friendship in early adolescence. *Journal of Early Adolescence, 4,* 155–181.

Crooks, T. J. (1988). The impact of classroom evaluation practices on students. *Review of Educational Research, 58,* 438–481.

Cross, D. R. & Paris, S. G. (1988). Developmental and instructional analyses of children's metacognition and reading comprehension. *Journal of Educational Psychology, 80,* 131–142.

Demetriou, A., Efklides, A. & Platsidou, M. (1993). The architecture and dynamics of the developing mind: Experiential structuralism as a frame for unifying cognitive developmental theories. *Monographs of the Society for Research in Child Development, 58* (5–6, Serial No. 234).

Dickstein, E. B. (1979). Biological and cognitive bases of moral functioning. *Human Development, 22,* 37–59.

Dishion, T. J., Patterson, G. R., Stoolmiller, M. & Skinner, M. L. (1991). Family, school, and behavioral antecedents to early adolescent involvement with antisocial peers. *Developmental Psychology, 27,* 172–180.

Dodge, K. A., Petit, G. S., McClaskey, C. L. & Brown, M. M. (1986). *Social competence in children.* Monographs of the Society for Research in Child Development, *51* (2, serial no. 213).

Downey, G. & Walker, E. (1989). Social cognition and adjustment in children at risk for psychopathology. *Developmental Psychology, 25,* 835–845.

East, P. L. & Rook, K. S. (1992). Compensatory patterns of support among children's peer relationships: A test using school friends, nonschool friends, and siblings. *Developmental Psychology, 28,* 163–172.

Eccles, J. S. (1993). School and family effects on the ontogeny of children's interests, self-perceptions, and activity choices. In J. E. Jacobs (Ed.), *Nebraska Symposium on Motivation: 1992* (vol. 40). Lincoln: University of Nebraska Press, 145–208.

Eccles, J. S., Jacobs, J. E. & Harold, R. D. (1990). Gender-role stereotypes, expectancy effects, and parents' role in the socialization of gender differences in self-perceptions and skill acquisition. *Journal of Social Issues, 46,* 182–201.

Elias, M. J., Beier, J. J. & Gara, M. A. (1989). Children's responses to interpersonal obstacles as a predictor of social competence. *Journal of Youth and Adolescence, 18,* 451–465.

Entwisle, D. R., Alexander, K. L., Pallas, A. M. & Cadigan, D. (1987). The emergent academic self-image of first-graders: Its response to social structure. *Child Development, 58,* 1190–1206.

Epstein, J. (1983). Examining theories of adolescent friendships. In J. Epstein & N. Karweit (Eds.), *Friends in school: Patterns of selection and influence in secondary schools.* New York: Academic Press.

Farrar, M. J., Raney, G. E. & Boyer, M. E. (1992). Knowledge, concepts, and inferences in childhood. *Child Development, 63,* 673–691.

Field, D. (1981). Can preschool children really learn to conserve? *Child Development, 52,* 326–334.

Flavell, J. H. (1982). On cognitive development. *Child Development, 53,* 1–10.

French, D. C. (1984). Children's knowledge of the social functions of younger, older and same-age peers. *Child Development, 55,* 1429–1433.

French, D. C. (1988). Heterogeneity of peer-rejected boys: Aggressive and nonaggressive subtypes. *Child Development, 59,* 976–985.

French, D. C. (1990). Heterogeneity of peer rejected girls. *Child Development, 61,* 2028–2031.

Garbarino, J., Kostelny, K. & Dubrow, N. (1991). *No place to be a child: Growing up in a war zone.* Lexington, Mass.: Lexington Books.

Gardner, H. (1983). *Frames of mind: The theory of multiple intelligences.* New York: Basic Books.

Gavin, L. A. & Furman, W. (1989). Age differences in adolescents' perceptions of their peer groups. *Developmental Psychology, 25,* 827–834.

Geary, D. C. & Brown, S. C. (1991). Cognitive addition: Strategy choice and speed of processing differences in gifted, normal, and mathematically disabled children. *Developmental Psychology, 27,* 398–406.

Geary, D. C., Brown, S. C. & Samaranayake, V. A. (1991). Cognitive addition: A short longitudinal study of strategy choice and speed-of-processing differences in normal and mathematically disabled children. *Developmental Psychology, 27,* 787–797.

Goldenberg, C. N. (1989). Parents' effects on academic grouping for reading: Three case studies. *American Educational Research Journal, 26,* 329–352.

Goodnow, J. J. (1969). Problems in research on culture and thought. In D. Elkind & J. H. Flavell (Eds.), *Studies in cognitive development: Essays in honor of Jean Piaget.* New York: Oxford University Press.

Gulko, J., Doyle, A., Serbin, L. A. & White, D. R. (1988). Conservation skills: A replicated study of order of acquisition across tasks. *Journal of Genetic Psychology, 149,* 425–439.

Halford, G. S. & Boyle, F. M. (1985). Do young children understand conservation of number? *Child Development, 56,* 165–176.

Hall, W. S. (1989). Reading comprehension. *American Psychologist, 44,* 157–161.

Haller, E. & Waterman, M. (1985). The criteria of reading group assignments. *Reading Teacher, 38,* 772–782.

Hart, C. H., Ladd, G. W. & Burleson, B. R. (1990). Children's expectations of the outcomes of social strategies: Relations with sociometric status and maternal disciplinary styles. *Child Development, 61,* 127–137.

Harter, S. (1985). *The self-perception profile for children.* (Manual). University of Denver.

Harter, S. (1993). Visions of self: Beyond the me in the mirror. In J. E. Jacobs (Ed.), *Nebraska symposium on motivation: 1992* (vol. 40). Lincoln: University of Nebraska Press, 99–144.

Hartup, W. W. (1989). Social relationships and their developmental significance. *American Psychologist, 44,* 120–126.

Haskett, M. E. & Kistner, J. A. (1991). Social interactions and peer perceptions of young physically abused children. *Child Development, 62,* 979–990.

Hess, R. & Holloway, S. (1984). Family and school as educational institutions. *Review of child development research: The family* (vol. 7). Chicago: University of Chicago Press, 179–222.

Holloway, S. D. (1988). Concepts of ability and effort in Japan and the United States. *Review of Educational Research, 58,* 327–345.

Hymel, S., Bowker, A. & Woody, E. (1993). Aggressive versus withdrawn unpopular children: Variations in peer and self-perceptions of multiple domains. *Child Development, 64,* 879–896.

Hymel, S., Rubin, K. H., Rowden, L. & LeMare, L. (1990). Children's peer relationships: Longitudinal predictions of internalizing and externalizing problems from middle to late childhood. *Child Development, 61,* 2004–2021.

Jordan, N. C., Huttenlocher, J. & Levine, S. C. (1992). Differential calculation abilities in young children from middle- and low-income families. *Developmental Psychology, 28,* 644–653.

Jussim, L. (1990a). Expectancies and social issues: Introduction. *Journal of Social Issues, 46,* 1–8.

Jussim, L. (1990b). Social realities and social problems: The role of expectancies. *Journal of Social Issues, 46,* 9–34.

Kalish, C. W. & Gelman, S. A. (1992). On wooden pillows: Multiple classification and children's category-based inductions. *Child Development, 63,* 1536–1557.

Karweit, N. (1983). Extracurricular activities and friendship selection. In J. Epstein & N. Karweit (Eds.), *Friends in school: Patterns of selection and influence in secondary schools.* New York: Academic Press.

Karweit, N. & Hansell, S. (1983). Sex differences in adolescent relationships: Friendships and status.

In J. Epstein & N. Karweit (Eds.), *Friends in school: Patterns of selection and influence in secondary schools.* New York: Academic Press.

Klint, K. A. & Weiss, M. R. (1987). Perceived competence and motives for participating in youth sports: A test of Harter's competence motivation theory. *Journal of Sport Psychology, 9,* 55–65.

Knight, C. C. & Fischer, K. W. (1992). Learning to read words: Individual differences in developmental sequences. *Journal of Applied Developmental Psychology, 13,* 377–404.

Kuhn, D., Garcia-Mila, M., Zohar, A. & Andersen, C. (1995). *Strategies of knowledge acquisition.* Monographs of the Society for Research in Child Development, 60 (4, Serial 245).

Lacayo, R. (1996). Law and order. *Time, 147,* 48–56.

Lopez, A., Gelman, S. A., Gutheil, G. & Smith, E. (1992). The development of category-based inductions. *Child Development, 63,* 1070–1090.

Lovell, K. (1961). *The growth of basic mathematical and scientific concepts in children.* New York: Philosophical Library.

May, R. B. & Norton, J. M. (1981). Training-task orders and transfer in conservation. *Child Development, 52,* 904–913.

McAuley, E., Duncan, T. E. & McElroy, M. (1989). Self-efficacy cognitions and causal attributions for children's motor performance: An exploratory investigation. *Journal of Genetic Psychology, 150,* 65–73.

McCabe, A. E., Siegel, L. S., Spence, I. & Wilkinson, A. (1982). Class-inclusion reasoning: Patterns of performance from three to eight years. *Child Development, 53,* 780–785.

Merton, R. K. (1948). The self-fulfilling prophecy. *Antioch Review, 8,* 193–210.

Miller, S. A. (1978). Identity conservation and equivalence conservation: A critique of Brainerd and Hooper's analysis. *Psychological Bulletin, 85,* 58–69.

Montgomery, D. E. (1993). Young children's understanding of interpretive diversity between different-age listeners. *Developmental Psychology, 29,* 337–345.

Musser, L. M. & Browne, B. A. (1991). Self-monitoring in middle childhood: Personality and social correlates. *Developmental Psychology, 27,* 994–999.

Neisser, U., Boodoo, G., Bouchard, T. J., Jr., Bodkin, A. W., Brody, N., Ceci, S. J., Halpern, D. F., Loehlin, J. C., Perloff, R., Sternberg, R. J. & Urbana, S. (1996). Intelligence: Knowns and unknowns. *American Psychologist, 51,* 77–101.

Nelson, J. & Aboud, F. E. (1985). The resolution of social conflict between friends. *Child Development, 56,* 1009–1017.

Nelson, K. (1974). Variations in children's concepts by age and category. *Child Development, 45,* 577–584.

Newman, J. L., Roberts, L. R. & Syre, C. R. (1993). Concepts of family among children and adolescents: Effect of cognitive level, gender, and family structure. *Developmental Psychology, 29,* 951–962.

Okagaki, L. & Sternberg, R. J. (1993). Parental beliefs and children's school performance. *Child Development, 64,* 36–56.

O'Neill, D. K. & Gopnik, A. (1991). Young children's ability to identify the sources of their beliefs. *Developmental Psychology, 27,* 390–397.

Osofsky, J. D. (1995). Children who witness domestic violence: The invisible victims. *Social Policy Report, 9,* 1–16.

Park, K. A. & Waters, E. (1989). Security of attachment and preschool friendships. *Child Development, 60,* 1076–1081.

Parker, J. G. & Asher, S. R. (1993). Friendship and friendship quality in middle childhood: Links with peer group acceptance and feelings of loneliness and social dissatisfaction. *Developmental Psychology, 29,* 611–621.

Parkhurst, J. T. & Asher, S. R. (1992). Peer rejection in middle school: Subgroup differences in behavior, loneliness, and interpersonal concerns. *Developmental Psychology, 28,* 231–241.

Parsons, J. E., Adler, T. F. & Kaczala, C. M. (1982). Socialization of achievement attitudes and beliefs: Parental influences. *Child Development, 53,* 310–321.

Parsons, J. E. & Ruble, D. N. (1977). The development of achievement-related expectancies. *Child Development, 48,* 1075–1079.

Patterson, G. R. (1982). *Coercive family processes.* Eugene, Oreg.: Castalia.

Pellegrini, D. S. (1985). Social cognition and competence in middle childhood. *Child Development, 56,* 253–264.

Pepitone, E. A., Loeb, H. W. & Murdock, E. M. (1977). Social comparison and similarity of children's performance in competitive situations. San Francisco: Paper presented at the annual convention of the American Psychological Association.

Perret-Clermont, A., Perret, J. & Bell, N. (1991). The social construction of meaning and cognitive activity in elementary school children. In L. B. Resnick, J. M. Levine & S. D. Teasley (Eds.), *Perspectives on socially shared cognition.* Washington, D.C.: American Psychological Association, 41–62.

Pettit, G. S., Dodge, K. A. & Brown, M. M. (1988). Early family experience, social problem-solving patterns, and children's social competence. *Child Development, 59,* 107–120.

Phillips, D. A. (1984). The illusion of incompetence among academically competent children. *Child Development, 55,* 2000–2016.

Phillips, D. A. (1987). Socialization of perceived academic competence among highly competent children. *Child Development, 58,* 1308–1320.

Piaget, J. (1932/1948). *The moral judgment of the child.* Glencoe, Ill.: Free Press.

Piaget, J. (1941/1952). *The child's conception of number.* London: Kegan Paul, Trench & Trubner.

Piaget, J. (1972). *The psychology of intelligence.* Totowa, N.J.: Littlefield Adams.

Piaget, J. & Inhelder, B. (1969). *The psychology of the child.* New York: Basic Books.

Pillow, B. H. (1991). Children's understanding of biased social cognition. *Developmental Psychology, 27,* 539–551.

Prawat, R. S., Byers, J. L. & Anderson, A. H. (1983). An attributional analysis of teachers' affective reactions to student success and failure. *American Educational Research Journal, 20,* 137–152.

Putallaz, M. (1987). Maternal behavior and children's sociometric status. *Child Development, 58,* 324–340.

Quiggle, N. L., Garber, J., Panak, W. F. & Dodge, K. A. (1992). Social information processing in aggressive and depressed children. *Child Development, 63,* 1305–1320.

Renshaw, P. D. & Brown, P. J. (1993). Loneliness in middle childhood: Concurrent and longitudinal predictors. *Child Development, 64,* 1271–1284.

Rosen, A. B. & Rozin, P. (1993). Now you see it, now you don't: The preschool child's conception of invisible particles in the context of dissolving. *Developmental Psychology, 29,* 300–311.

Rosenthal, R. & Jacobson, L. (1968). *Pygmalion in the classroom: Teacher expectations and student intellectual development.* New York: Holt, Rinehart & Winston.

Rubin, K. H., LeMare, L. J. & Lollis, S. (1990). Social withdrawal in children: Developmental pathways to peer rejection. In S. R. Asher & J. D. Coie (Eds.), *Peer rejection in childhood.* Cambridge: Cambridge University Press, 217–252.

Salzinger, S., Feldman, R. S., Hammer, M. & Rosario, M. (1993). The effects of physical abuse on children's social relationships. *Child Development, 64,* 168–187.

Sancilio, M. F. M., Plumert, J. M. & Hartup, W. W. (1989). Friendship and aggressiveness as determinants of conflict outcomes in middle childhood. *Developmental Psychology, 25,* 812–819.

Schickedanz, J. A. (1986). *More than the ABCs: The early stages of reading and writing.* Washington, D.C.:

National Association for the Advancement of Young Children.

Schneider, W. & Bjorklund, D. F. (1992). Expertise, aptitude, and strategic remembering. *Child Development, 63,* 461–473.

Share, D. L., McGee, R. & Silva, P. A. (1989). IQ and reading progress: A test of the capacity notion of IQ. *Journal of the American Academy of Child and Adolescent Psychiatry, 28,* 97–100.

Shears, L. M. & Bower, E. M. (1974). *Games in education and development.* Springfield, Ill.: Charles C. Thomas.

Siegler, R. S. (1991). *Children's thinking* (2nd ed.). Englewood Cliffs, N.J.: Prentice-Hall.

Silverstein, A. B., Pearson, L. B., Aguinaldo, N. E., Friedman, S. L., Tokayama, D. L. & Weiss, Z. T. (1982). Identity conservation and equivalence conservation: A question of developmental priority. *Child Development, 53,* 819–821.

Skaalvik, E. M. & Hagtvet, K. A. (1990). Academic achievement and self-concept: An analysis of causal predominance in a developmental perspective. *Journal of Personality and Social Psychology, 58,* 292–307.

Slavin, R. E. (1987). Grouping for instruction in the elementary school. *Educational Psychologist, 22,* 109–127.

Smith, T. L. (1986). Self-concepts of youth sport participants and nonparticipants in grades 3 and 6. *Perceptual and Motor Skills, 62,* 863–866.

Sophian, C. (1988). Limitations on preschool children's knowledge about counting: Using counting to compare two sets. *Developmental Psychology, 24,* 634–640.

Spearman, C. (1927). *The abilities of man.* New York: Macmillan.

Spiro, R. J., Bruce, B. C. & Brewer, W. F. (Eds.). (1980). *Theoretical issues in reading comprehension.* Hillsdale, N.J.: Erlbaum.

Sroufe, L. A. & Fleeson, J. (1986). Attachment and the construction of relationships. In W. W. Hartup and Z. Rubin (Eds.), *Relationships and development.* Hillsdale, N.J.: Erlbaum, 51–72.

Sternberg, R. J. (1985). *Beyond IQ: A triarchic theory of human intelligence.* New York: Cambridge University Press.

Sternberg, R. J. (1996). Myths, counter myths, and truths about intelligence. *Educational Researcher, 25,* 11–16.

Stevenson, H. W., Chen, C. & Lee, S. (1993). Mathematics achievement of Chinese, Japanese, and American children: Ten years later. *Science, 259,* 53–58.

Sullivan, H. S. (1949). *The collected works of Harry Stack Sullivan* (vols. 1 and 2). New York: Norton.

Time. (1993, March 22). Alas, slavery lives: A new report details a world still plagued by human bondage. *141,* 12, 26.

Triandis, H. C. (1990). Cross-cultural studies of individualism and collectivism. In J. J. Berman (Ed.), *Nebraska symposium on motivation: 1989* (vol. 37). Lincoln: University of Nebraska Press, 41–134.

Tudge, J. R. H. (1992). Processes and consequences of peer collaboration: A Vygotskian analysis. *Child Development, 63,* 1364–1379.

Uzgiris, I. C. (1964). Situational generality of conservation. *Child Development, 35,* 831–841.

Vygotsky, L. S. (1932/1962). *Thought and language.* Cambridge, Mass.: MIT Press; New York: Wiley.

Waas, G. A. (1988). Social attributional biases of peer-rejected and aggressive children. *Child Development, 59,* 969–975.

Wagner, B. M. & Phillips, D. A. (1992). Beyond beliefs: Parent and child behaviors and children's perceived academic competence. *Child Development, 63,* 1380–1391.

Weinstein, R. S., Marshall, H. H., Sharp, L. & Botkin, M. (1987). Pygmalion and the student: Age and classroom differences in children's awareness of teacher expectations. *Child Development, 58,* 1079–1093.

Wellman, H. M. (1990). *The child's theory of mind.* Cambridge, Mass.: MIT Press.

Youngblade, L. M. & Belsky, J. (1992). Parent–child antecedents of 5-year-olds' close friendships: A longitudinal analysis. *Developmental Psychology, 28,* 700–713.

Youniss, J. (1980). *Parents and peers in social development: A Sullivan-Piaget perspective.* Chicago: University of Chicago Press.

Zimmerman, B. J., Bandura, A. & Martinez-Pons, M. (1992). Self-motivation for academic attainment: The role of self-efficacy beliefs and personal goal setting. *American Educational Research Journal, 29,* 663–676.

Expanding the Psychosocial Analysis of Middle Childhood

Chapter 14

The Psychosocial Crisis: Industry Versus Inferiority
   Industry
   Inferiority

The Central Process: Education

The Prime Adaptive Ego Quality and the Core Pathology
   Competence
   Inertia

The Interactive Relationship Between the Development of Children and Parents
   Forming the Parent–School Partnership
   The Child as a Stimulus to Adult Learning

Cultural and Ethnic Patterns That Create Distinctive Child-Rearing Environments
   Achievement Strivings and Culture
   Multicultural Education and School Adjustment

Social Issues That Create Barriers to Development
   Parental Divorce and Its Impact on Children
         Phases of Family Restructuring and Reorganization
         Children's Adjustment to and Coping with Parental Divorce
         Loss of Economic and Social Resources
   Violence in the Schools
   Homelessness and Its Impact on Children

Optimizing Development in Middle Childhood

Chapter Summary

References

Psychosocial analysis of development during middle childhood reveals the significant interaction between the child's enormous capacity for skill development and mastery and the various social institutions that can either foster or restrict this direction of growth. This chapter introduces the psychosocial crisis, industry versus inferiority, and the central process, education, through which this crisis is played out and resolved. The prime adaptive ego quality of competence and the core pathology of inertia are described with special attention to the significance and many meanings of competence. Dynamics of family, school, culture, and contemporary society that can influence the direction of development during middle childhood highlight the dramatic complexity and potential instability of demands that many children face today.

The Psychosocial Crisis: Industry Versus Inferiority

According to psychosocial theory (Erikson, 1963), a person's fundamental attitude toward work is established during middle childhood. As children develop skills and acquire personal standards for evaluation, they make an initial assessment of their ability to contribute to the social community. Some children are committed to competing against a standard of excellence and achieving success. Others develop low expectations about the possibility of success and are not motivated by opportunities to achieve. The strength of a child's motivation to achieve success is well established by the end of this stage (Atkinson & Birch, 1978). Children go forward from middle childhood to early adolescence with basic feelings of industry or inferiority to guide them. A basic sense of competence or feelings of inertia will now be associated with a person's approach to the new challenges of this and each succeeding stage (see Notebook Page 14.1).

Industry

The concept of *industry* in this psychosocial stage refers to an eagerness to acquire skills and perform meaningful work. During middle childhood, many aspects of work are intrinsically motivating. Acquiring skills presents new challenges and new opportunities to become more like adults. Mastering new skills allows children some degree of independence and may bring additional responsibilities that heighten their sense of worth. In addition to these self-motivating factors, external sources of reward promote skill development. Parents and teachers encourage children through grades, material rewards, additional privileges, and praise. Peers are also sources of encouragement for skill development, although they may also have some negative input. Certain youth organizations, such as Scouts and 4-H, make skill acquisition a specific route to success and higher status.

Kowaz and Marcia (1991) described three components of personal industry: cognitive, behavioral, and affective. The *cognitive* component of industry was defined as the acquisition of the basic skills and knowledge valued by the culture. The *behavioral* component of industry was defined as the ability to apply skills and knowledge effectively through characteristics such as concentration, perseverance, work habits, and goal directedness. The *affective* component was defined as the positive emotional orientation toward the acquisition and application of skills and knowledge. These include such feel-

Concentration, perseverance, and goal directedness are all evident in Joseph's approach to his school assignments.

ings as a general curiosity and desire to know, a pride in one's efforts, and an ability to handle the distresses of failure as well as the joys of success.

When applied to a society, industry is the aggregate of manufacturing or technically productive enterprises. When applied to a person, industry occurs in an aggregate of skill-development activities. An industrious person is energetic and devoted to activity in any task, diligent, systematic, and organized in work or labor. Just as societal industry relies on social relations as well as manufacturing in order to be productive, personal industry includes skills at managing and relating to others in order to accomplish the task at hand.

Inferiority

Given the thrust toward skill building that is motivated by a sense of competence and external rewards, it might appear that there should be no real conflict at this stage. One might assume that everyone would be united in a commitment to the joy and fulfillment accruing from experiences of competence. However, feelings of worthlessness and inadequacy come from two sources: the self and the social environment. Alfred Adler (1935) directed attention to the central role that organ inferiority can play in shaping a person's perceptions of his or her abilities. *Organ inferiority* is any physical or mental limitation that prevents the acquisition of certain skills. Children who are not capable of mastering particular skills experience some feelings of inferiority.

No one can do everything well. Children discover that they are incapable of mastering every skill that they attempt. Individual differences in aptitude, physical development, and prior experience result in feelings of inadequacy in some domain. Even a child who feels quite positive toward work and finds new challenges invigorating experiences some feelings of inferiority when faced with specific tasks that are difficult to master. We can all recall times when we have exclaimed in frustration: "I just can't do this."

Components of Personality Development in Middle Childhood

According to psychosocial theory, at the beginning of middle childhood a child is armed with certain prime adaptive ego qualities such as hope, will, and purpose, or dominated by certain maladaptive core pathologies such as withdrawal, compulsion, and inhibition. These dynamic components of perspective on selfhood and social relationships have many implications for a child's orientation toward the challenges and opportunities posed by schooling. For example, Christy is seven years old. She approaches school with a strong sense of purpose and tells her mom that she is going to work very hard to get good grades so that she can become a physicist and discover time travel. For each of the following children, create a scenario about the child's outlook on school.

1. Jody: Hope, will, and purpose

_____

_____

_____

_____

_____

2. Jean: Hope, will, and inhibition

_____

_____

_____

_____

3. Kelly: Withdrawal, compulsion, and inhibition

_____

_____

_____

_____

If success in one area compensated for failure in another, we could minimize the effect of individual areas of inadequacy on the overall resolution of the psychosocial conflict. However, the social environment does not reinforce success in all areas equally. During middle childhood, for example, success in reading is much more highly rewarded in U.S. schools than success in fixing broken automobile engines. Success in team sports is more highly valued than success in operating a ham radio. In a study of children ages 8 to 11, various domains of competence were assessed as predictors of global self-worth. At both ages, perceptions of physical appearance were the most powerful predictors of self-worth. However, the second most important predictor shifted from social acceptance and popularity at age 8 to scholastic competence at age 11 (Granleese & Joseph, 1994). Failure in school and consequent public ridicule have been shown to play a central role in establishing a negative self-image. This is especially true when a child's initial self-concept is negative (Calhoun & Morse, 1977). School represents the voice of the larger society. Children who continually fail to meet the standards set by school authorities are likely to incorporate a view of themselves as failures. Sometimes, children defend against this threat by blaming others for their failures or by bragging that they can succeed in other ways. Much as it may appear that these children scorn school goals, school remains a symbol of cultural authority. Failure in school can easily lead a child to feel rejected by the larger social community.

The social environment also generates feelings of inferiority through the process of social comparison. Particularly in the school setting, but even in the home, children are confronted by suggestions that they are not as "good" as some peer, sibling, or cultural subgroup. The intrinsic pleasure of engaging in a task for the challenge it presents conflicts with messages that stimulate feelings of self-consciousness, competitiveness, and doubt: "I like playing ball, but I'm not as good as Ted, so I don't think I'll play." During middle childhood, children may refuse to try a new activity because they fear being bettered by their peers (Crooks, 1988).

Finally, the social environment stimulates feelings of inferiority through the negative value that it places on any kind of failure. Two types of failure messages that may contribute to feelings of inferiority have been described. One type consists of criticisms of the child's *motivation*. Such criticisms imply that failure could have been avoided by really trying. The other type refers more specifically to a *lack of ability*. Here, the implication is that the child does not have the necessary competence to succeed. This type of failure message can lead to a sense of learned helplessness.

Learned helplessness is a belief that one's efforts have little to do with success or failure and that the outcome of most situations is largely outside one's control (Nelson, 1987; Seligman, 1975). Fourth-, fifth-, and sixth-graders were asked to verbalize their thoughts as they worked on various tasks. Mastery-oriented children were able to keep a positive attitude, to increase their problem-solving efforts, and to use past mistakes to correct their approach ("I can get this. It's a lot like the problem we did in class"). Helpless children began to blame themselves ("I never did have a good memory"). They emphasized negative aspects of the task or criticized their abilities and tried to find ways to escape from the situation (Diener & Dweck, 1980). Helpless children tend to discount their successes and respond to even a few remarks about their lack of ability with a pessimistic view about chances for future success (Holloway, 1988; Phillips, 1984).

Normal Experiences of Inferiority

Every child encounters some feelings of inferiority. Children take different lessons away from the situation that may guide their approach to difficult challenges in the future and may shape their sense of self-efficacy.

1. Recall and describe an influential failure experience from your childhood during the years from about 6 through 11.

2. What were your reactions to this failure?

3. What accounted for the failure?

4. How public or private was it? Who knew about it? To what extent did people who were important to you know of it? What were their reactions?

5. What were the consequences for you? How did you cope with this failure? How did it influence your subsequent efforts?

6. Looking back, what might have helped you cope more effectively with this event?

In middle childhood, children are often shamed for failure just as toddlers are shamed when they fail at toilet training. Earlier themes of doubt and guilt are intimately associated with feelings of inferiority. Messages about failure usually suggest that there is an external standard of perfection, an ideal, that the child did not meet. A few failure experiences can generate such strong negative feelings that the child will avoid engaging in new tasks in order to preclude failure.

In extreme cases, we see reluctance, self-doubt, and withdrawal in children who feel very inferior. Such resolutions of the crisis in the direction of inferiority suggest that these children cannot conceive of their potential to contribute to the welfare of the larger community. This is a very serious consequence. It makes the gradual incorporation of the individual into a meaningful social group very difficult. Ironically, the social group, which depends on each individual's motives toward mastery for its survival, also negates those motives by communicating messages of inferiority (see Notebook Page 14.2).

The Central Process: Education

Every culture must devise ways of passing on the wisdom and skills of past generations to its young. This is the purpose of education in its broadest sense. The practice of separating formal educational experiences from practical, hands-on learning at home and in the community is only about 100 years old. Before the Industrial Revolution, most children were educated by participating with their parents in the tasks of home life, farming, commerce with neighbors, and participation in religious life (Coleman, 1987). In the case of the European nobility, children often had tutors who supervised their education at home. By the turn of the twentieth century, funding of public schools and compulsory school attendance laws in the United States resulted in children of all social classes attending school. The Industrial Revolution brought with it the realization that families could not educate their children for the broad range of complex skills and wide variety of occupational roles that were emerging in modern society (Gutek, 1992).

Today, schools bear the primary responsibility for formal education. Teaching, which began as an extension of the parent role, has become a distinct profession. Unlike more traditional cultures, education in our culture is not a continuous interplay between the skilled and the unskilled. Formal learning takes place in a special building during certain hours of the day. To be sure, the impact of schooling on building a child's skills and a sense of the self as a learner depends heavily on the ongoing involvement and commitment of family members (Coleman, 1987; Stevenson & Baker, 1987). For today's children, however, school experiences play a key role in forming a personal sense of industry.

During the elementary-school years, the goal of education is to help children develop the basic tools of learning. Central to this process is an introduction to the language of concepts, theories, and relationships that will allow children to organize experience (Cole & D'Andrade, 1982). Schools strive to develop verbal/analytic problem solving. Throughout the educational process, children are exposed to a range of disciplines and to methods of inquiry to help them analyze and solve complex problems of increasing difficulty

(Tharp, 1989). School provides children with many opportunities to practice their newly developing skills and offers them continuous feedback about their level of competence.

In addition to the acquisition of skills and knowledge, schools emphasize an approach to behavior that can be described as a combination of "citizenship" and "study habits." Schools impart a code of conduct that is intended to enable students to pay attention and to organize and focus on the tasks at hand, while maintaining a respectful, cooperative attitude toward adults and peers. Much of the literature that addresses problems of teacher bias or the self-fulfilling prophecy, which were discussed in Chapter 13, implicates the lack of fit between the students' cultural resources regarding study skills, work habits, demeanor (for example, disruptive behavior, manner of speech, or style of dress) and teachers' expectations.

Ideally, a school environment provides exposure to adult role models who instill a commitment to learning (Rutter, 1983). These adults generally have skills that demonstrate to children some sense of how much more there is to learn (see Notebook Page 14.3). Participation in school, therefore, may provide opportunities not only for mastery but also for setting goals and standards for more advanced skills and knowledge and for observing models engaged in inquiry.

In middle childhood, children are at a stage of cognitive development that permits them to grasp the fundamental principles of the problems posed by school. The art of teaching lies in presenting problems at a level of complexity that will be meaningful to children but just a step beyond their present ability level. This approach, consistent with Vygotsky's notion of the zone of proximal development, creates a context in which learning becomes a tantalizing process of being lured by the problem itself to find its solution. This process is captured in an adult's reminiscences about his music teacher from high school.

> Beyond anything else, Griff wanted you to love and be as deeply affected by music as he was. His daughter, Ann, recently reminded me that when he was sometimes criticized for the problems students experienced with the difficult music he assigned, Griff would respond: "I don't care what a kid does to music. I care what the music does to the kid." Ever since he first convinced me to take voice lessons and seriously consider a career in music, Griff's visions have been a daily realization, as my life's work has, happily, been devoted to the arts. (Mosel, 1992, 12)

Not all children approach schooling with the same expectations for success or the same trust in adults or the formal education process. Some groups view education as the means to economic security, intellectual development, and political empowerment. Others are skeptical of teachers, schools, and education. They expect to be alienated from the learning process because they anticipate that it will devalue their basic language, heritage, and beliefs (Cochran-Smith, 1995). They believe that the only way to improve their condition is through major political and economic change. In their view, education per se will not empower them or their children. Children in these groups may conclude that the only way to retain their basic sense of self-confidence is to withdraw from school and try to establish their competence among their peers (Ogbu, 1987; Spencer, 1985).

Recalling a Favorite Teacher

One of the most significant ways that schooling influences children is through contact with teachers who reach out to them and influence their outlook on learning.

1. Recall and describe a favorite teacher from the years from about 6 through 11. How did you encounter this teacher? Why was this teacher so meaningful for you?

_____

_____

_____

_____

_____

_____

_____

_____

2. What were some of the lasting contributions that this teacher made to your development? In what ways did he or she contribute to your sense of industry and competence?

_____

_____

_____

_____

_____

_____

_____

_____

The Prime Adaptive Ego Quality and the Core Pathology

Competence

The term *competence* has been used broadly and with diverse meanings in the human development literature. Ford (1985) offered a summary of five distinct uses of this concept:

1. *Competence as an outcome measure reflecting one's effectiveness in a specific situation.* For example, one might say that a child was competent at solving a specific problem or finding the necessary resources to meet his or her needs.

2. *Competence as a personality type.* This use of the concept is similar to "resilience," a term used to describe children who successfully overcome stressful life circumstances and continue to perform well in school (Garmezy & Masten, 1991).

3. *Competence as a motivational system.* Robert White (1959) described his belief in a universal tendency to strive toward higher and higher levels of mastery. According to White, once children become competent at a certain level of functioning, they experience the desire to move to a new, more challenging level. This is demonstrated by children's fascination with computer games that are designed to lead players to increasingly difficult levels, introducing new dangers, faster speed of play, or more complex movements.

4. *Competence as a composite of knowledge, skills, and abilities that permit successful adaptation.* For example, language competence encompasses many different kinds of abilities that involve understanding the language of others, expressing one's own thoughts verbally, and adapting to the language demands of specific situations. Each of the developmental tasks might be considered a domain for the development of age-related competence as defined by specific cultural expectations (Masten et al., 1995).

5. *Competence as a belief in one's effectiveness.* This definition refers to a general belief in one's ability to "get the job done." It is closely related to Bandura's concept of self-efficacy which was discussed in Chapter 13.

This last definition is closest to Erikson's (1982) notion of competence as the prime adaptive ego quality, a belief in one's ability to make sense of and master the demands of a situation. "Competence, in turn, is the free exercise of dexterity and intelligence in the completion of tasks, unimpaired by infantile inferiority. It is the basis for cooperative participation in technologies, and it relies, in turn, on the logic of tools and skills" (Erikson, 1978, 30).

Competence provides children with a deep confidence in their ability to engage in new situations and succeed. This idea is illustrated in a study that monitored children's perceptions of competence during school transitions from fifth to sixth grade and from sixth to seventh grade. Those children who had the highest levels of perceived competence also had the strongest positive feelings about how they were doing in school and showed the highest scores on a measure of intrinsic motivation. These children wanted to be challenged by their schoolwork, and they liked to be able to work independently and figure things out for themselves. They expressed curiosity about the tasks, saying they would work hard because of their own interest rather than to please the teacher or to get good grades (Harter, Whitesell & Kowalski, 1992).

Children who have internalized a sense of competence love to learn and work. They are excited about developing new skills and optimistic about being able to achieve success. These children sign up for new activities or start neighborhood clubs, try out for two or three sports teams, look forward to field trips and school projects, and eagerly engage in difficult tasks like planting trees along the highway, building a new playground, or raising money for earthquake victims. In contrast, some children leave this stage with an overwhelming sense of apathy or disinterest, which Erikson referred to as inertia.

Inertia

Inertia is the core pathology of middle childhood. "The antipathic counterpart of industry, the sense of competent mastery to be experienced in the school age, is that inertia that constantly threatens to paralyze an individual's productive life and is, of course, fatefully related to the inhibition of the preceding age, that of play" (Erikson, 1982, 76–77).

Children who leave middle childhood with a sense of inertia are likely to continue to be withdrawn and passive, never engaging psychologically with the demands of their schools or their communities. They have trouble initiating actions or changing the course of events in their lives. They are not likely to address challenges or problems by formulating plans of action, evaluating these plans, and executing them. They do not believe that they can master the challenges they face, and, thus, they are likely to be swept along by the tide of events.

We all experience periods of inertia, times when we cannot muster the energy, enthusiasm, or confidence to take action. We may become besieged by doubts about our competence and worth, doubts that can produce indecision, paralysis, fatigue, listlessness, procrastination, or aimlessness. Typically, one can drift for a few days, even weeks, on "automatic pilot," just doing the bare minimum to survive. And children may be able to get by for quite a while without exercising much energy or direction, especially if they are being sustained by parents and teachers. However, eventually, life demands change, and expectations emerge to meet new challenges that have never been faced before. At those times, children who are burdened with a pervasive sense of inertia are unable to cope.

The Interactive Relationship Between the Development of Children and Parents

The lives of parents and children are continuously intertwined during middle childhood, with children relying on parents for material resources, emotional support, intellectual stimulation, and advocacy in transactions with school, neighborhood, and extended family relationships. Children draw their parents into new domains where they direct energy to new interests and abilities. Parents take on new roles in relation to school and community and develop new areas of expertise in order to support or keep abreast of their child's curiosity and skill development. In this section, we focus on two topics that illustrate the interactive relationship between the development of children during middle childhood and the development of parents: forming parent–school partnerships and the child as a stimulus to adult learning.

Forming the Parent–School Partnership

For most parents in U.S. society, their child's middle childhood is the time for learning to deal with school systems in the communities where they reside. The roles of *parent as advocate* and *parent as educator* (discussed in Chapter 12) are expanded as soon as children enter school. Parents must learn to deal with a complex social institution that dictates much of the day's structure for some members of families. Bus schedules, school holidays, vacation schedules, early-dismissal days, teacher's conferences, money for books and supplies, field trips, rules about absences and truancy, and many other institutional rules and regulations make demands on family life and require family adaptation. Schools may also exert influence on evening and weekend activities, sometimes introducing competing demands on the family's time or value conflicts between home and school.

Many parents cope with the interaction between home and school by forming some type of *parent–school partnership* (Connors & Epstein, 1995). This kind of partnership requires family participation in school activities and knowledge of school issues to help foster their child's academic achievement. It also requires schools to communicate with families regarding their organization, policies, and programs. The results of the partnership may often be invisible to the school, but they occur when parents review a child's homework, keep track of deadlines and due-dates, and advise the child about important school-related decisions.

Often, however, parents take a more visible role in contacting the school and getting to know their children's teachers, the school principal, or the guidance counselor. For example, in interviewing low-income African-American parents and their children who were doing well in school, Cannon-Watkins (1994) found that parents were very specific about getting to know their child's teachers. These parents let the teachers know how to get in touch with them. They were informed about expectations for homework. They used a variety of strategies in order to know about their children's school experiences and to maintain contact with teachers so that any problems that might arise could be handled quickly. Their children knew that any problems at school would soon be dealt with at home and, conversely, that successes at school would be valued and recognized at home.

Many schools offer opportunities for parents to be involved through activities such as volunteering in a classroom or operating a school store during lunch and after school. Sometimes, parents plan and/or help operate a complex venture such as a school show or a field trip. The parent–teacher organization offers parents many other opportunities to be involved and improve the quality of school life. Teachers can actively reach out to families by assigning homework that requires students to discuss a topic with a parent or by creating group problem-solving tasks that children are expected to carry out with other family members (Epstein et al., 1992).

Balancing a full work schedule with school involvement is a major challenge for many parents. This becomes even more difficult when the children in a family attend more than one school. Despite these challenges, most parents do become involved. According to a national survey, about 90% of parents talked to teachers about their children's school progress in the past year; 70% of parents of children ages 6 to 9 and 55% of parents of children ages 10 to 13 helped with a class trip or special school project in the prior year (National Commission on Children, 1991). Most parents place a high priority on being involved in a constructive way with their children's education. This involvement allows parents to be more effective advocates for their children. Furthermore, as parents gain direct knowledge of the school, the teachers, and the curriculum, they can do a better job of helping their children make educational choices.

We hypothesize that through efforts to further their own children's progress in school, parents begin to evolve an attitude toward—even a philosophy of—education (see Notebook Page 14.4). As parents praise, defend, or reprimand their own children about events that take place in school, they clarify their stance toward that institution and its functions. For some parents, their child's school seems like an extension of home, a place where the child is valued and the teachers foster the child's competence and sense of mastery. These parents are likely to encourage a positive outlook toward school for their children and to find many ways to build connections between school and home. Such parents tend to believe that the skills, attitudes, and values that are being fostered in school are essential for their child's success.

For other parents, school appears to be a hostile place. They may have done poorly in school themselves and remember it as a place of rejection or humiliation. Or they may feel that their children and their family are not valued by the school or that the school introduces new conflicts between them and their children. They may express anger or resentment toward the educational system in general or toward school personnel in particular, introducing conflict for their children and creating a barrier to school success.

The Child as a Stimulus to Adult Learning

In other writings, we have suggested that parenting is a process that has the potential for stimulating new directions of growth during adulthood (Newman & Newman, 1988). The period of middle childhood is especially relevant in this regard as the child's desires for increasing competence and the society's expectations for industry lead the child to invest in a new and ever-widening range of interests. Parents respond to this surge of enthusiasm for skill development in a variety of ways, including serving as role models for learning, revisiting prior learning, and developing new interests.

First, parents become increasingly aware of the ways that they serve as role models for their children. For example, in a study of children's feelings of school competence, there was a correlation between children's perceptions of their parents' positive feelings about their employment and their own academic competence (Moorehouse & Sanders, 1992). This relationship was true for both working-class and middle-class families, and for English-speaking as well as Spanish-speaking Mexican immigrant families. The only exception to this pattern was among children of laboring-class Spanish-speaking families in relation to their mothers. For these children, the more negative the mother was about her job, the more positive the children were about their school competence.

This research indicated that when parents express positive feelings about their work, they serve as role models for their children. Parents' expressions of competence, satisfaction in work-related achievements, and enthusiasm about work help bolster their children's confidence about being able to achieve in school-related challenges. However, in the case of the laboring, Spanish-speaking mothers, one might hypothesize that the mothers speak negatively

Parents' Involvement in a Child's Education

Even with their very busy lives, most parents say that they take time to be involved in their children's education. The kinds of involvement may vary with the age of the child, the particular subjects that are being studied, the efforts that the teacher and/or school make to involve parents, and the parent's own motivation for taking an active role in his or her child's education.

1. Describe several ways that your parents (guardians) were involved in your schoolwork or school activities during grades 1 through 6. Try to generate a list of parent involvements, indicating the approximate grade when this involvement took place.

2. As you review this list, what patterns do you observe? Were your mother and father involved in different ways? Did the type of involvement change with your age?

3. Looking back over the list, in what ways did this involvement help support your success in school? Were there ways that your parent(s)' involvement was counterproductive? (For example, did they help so much with your projects that they looked very good but you did not experience any sense of personal accomplishment?)

4. If you were in the parent role (or if you are a parent), what might you do differently with respect to your child's schooling as compared with the ways your parent(s) were involved with your schooling?

about their work in order to encourage their children to strive for something higher; and, conversely, the children in these families who perceive that they are doing well academically realize how difficult and perhaps demeaning their mothers' work may be. In general, the research emphasizes that parents' sentiments about their jobs convey information to children about the hardships as well as the satisfactions of work and influence children's orientation about the value of academic success.

Parents also serve as role models with respect to their specific talents and abilities. Whether parents excel in carpentry, auto repair, fishing, tennis, painting, or scientific experimentation, they begin to pay greater attention to their own areas of expertise as they try to introduce these skills to their children. Explaining what you do to someone else and showing them the "ins-and-outs" of your trade tend to sharpen your own abilities and help you identify aspects of your skills that you may not have recognized or examined in the past.

Second, as children move through grades 1 to 6, they study a variety of topics that open up old files in a parent's educational memory. About 90% of parents of children ages 6 through 9 say they help their child with homework or a school project at least once a week; 76% of parents of children ages 10 through 13 provide this kind of help (National Commission on Children, 1991). Parents may recall studying American history, world geography, astronomy, and English grammar. As they work on school projects with their children, review homework assignments, or help them prepare for a test, parents are reminded of a wealth of information that they have probably forgotten. In some instances, parents become acquainted with new information that had not yet made its way into the elementary school curriculum when they were in school.

Third, children's interests, talents, and abilities draw their parents into new areas of interest. Mothers who never played football become interested in it in order to help their children learn new plays or practice certain drills. Fathers become interested in theater as their children show talent and try out for local acting companies. Children's enthusiasm for camping, sports, hobbies, computer games, music or the arts acts as a stimulus to parents who begin to explore these fields. They may talk to other adults or read books about the topic, attend conferences, offer to volunteer as a coach or assistant, and, as a consequence, expand their own knowledge. It is not uncommon to find parents who say that their own interest and abilities in some significant area were first aroused by their attempt to support their daughter's or son's desire to explore that area.

As the case of Colleen suggests, parents may continue to be involved in a field of interest even after their child's interest wanes. Colleen offered to be a leader for a Cub Scout troop when her son, Eric, was 6. She gathered as much information as she could about being a troop leader, talked to people who had done this before, and became active as a scouting volunteer. She enjoyed planning activities for her son and his friends as they continued in scouting, and she valued the philosophy, goals, and objectives that scouting developed. She continued in this volunteer activity when her second child was old enough to begin scouting. As her sons moved on into more advanced levels of scouting, Colleen began attending workshops to develop her own leadership skills. She began to be invited to do additional training of other volunteers and eventually became one of the most prominent leaders of the Boy Scout program in her state. What started out as an effort to support her children's development became a significant field of expertise for Colleen and a new aspect of her personal identity in her community.

Cultural and Ethnic Patterns That Create Distinctive Child-Rearing Environments

The process of education results from the interaction between schools and children and their families. Culture plays a variety of roles in the educational process by providing the tools, defining the aims, and establishing a shared belief system about the requirements for academic success. In this section, we consider two related but distinct aspects of the impact of culture on education: (1) the significance of culture in defining the role of a good student and beliefs about academic achievement; and (2) the ways that schools attempt to meet the needs of a culturally diverse student population.

Achievement Strivings and Culture

What does it mean to be a good student? Children's approaches to learning and, more specifically, schooling are influenced in part by individual temperament, talents, and abilities and in part by the broader cultural definition of the student role for young children. Cultures vary in their beliefs about being a good student and what accounts for success or failure. In the early socialization process, parents teach children about their culture's valued characteristics. These cultural values contribute to children's beliefs about how they should respond to authority figures, how they should behave in public settings, what constitutes good and naughty behavior, and what is expected of them as they enter the student role. For example, a comparison of the cultural support for schooling in Japan and the United States offers the following contrast in parental values: "In Japan a child is thought to be good if he or she is 'obedient in good grace,' 'mild and gentle,' and 'self-controlled.' In the United States, the 'good child' is more likely to be assertive, independent, courteous, and socially competent with peers" (Hess & Azuma, 1991, 3).

Hess and Azuma argued that these differences in values about being a good child result in children coming to school with different predispositions about the school environment. Japanese children see their failures as due to lack of effort; U.S. children are more likely to explain their failures as due to lack of ability or problems with the school itself. At the same time, Japanese and U.S. schools have distinct approaches to the learning process. Japanese teachers place a strong emphasis on repetition, group response, and slow, deliberate focus on one small aspect of a problem at a time. Children are expected to stay with a problem, examining all sides of it, until they understand it. "Students perceive the situation, realize what is expected of them, and concentrate on living up to the teacher's expectations" (Hess & Azuma, 1991, 7). In the United States, teachers try to identify materials or problems that will appeal to the student. They question students and use feedback to recognize individual contributions. Teachers rely on the quality of the material to evoke curiosity and attention. Discussions often reward different points of view, ideas, and explanations without requiring closure on one correct answer. Rather than expecting students to address and solve problems in a mature, persistent, thoughtful manner, U.S. teachers assume that it is their

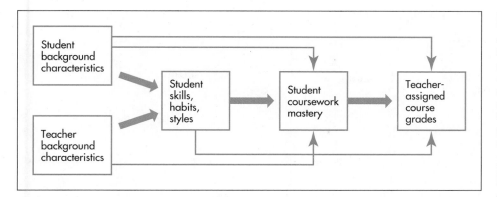

FIGURE 14.1
A model of teacher and student cultural resources and school achievement
Source: Adapted from Farkas et al. (1990). Cultural resources and school success: Gender, ethnicity, and poverty groups within an urban school district. *American Sociological Review, 55,* Figure 1, p. 129. Reprinted by permission.

responsibility to provide curricular materials and use a teaching style that will engage students.

Academic success depends on the interaction between the teacher's background and ability to relate to a diverse student body and the students' cognitive and noncognitive resources, especially their attitudes toward the student role, including "citizenship" and "study habit" behaviors (Alexander et al., 1987). In a test of this notion, children and teachers from 22 middle schools in a center-city school district in the Southwest participated in a study on the relationship between cultural resources and school success. Data were gathered on the teachers' and the students' background characteristics such as gender, race, and family income. In addition, students' basic attendance, skills, study habits, and appearance were assessed by teacher reports, as were their coursework mastery and grades (Farkas et al., 1990). In this particular study, the school district was racially diverse, and many children were from poor families. A model of the analysis of the study is shown in Figure 14.1.

The model suggests that students as well as teachers come to the school situation with cultural and personal background characteristics. The students' characteristics have a direct influence on how they approach schooling, especially such factors as coming to school regularly, trying hard, participating in class, and doing homework. These skills and study habits can have a direct, beneficial impact on the mastery of coursework and on school grades.

In addition to these direct relationships, teachers' perceptions of students' work habits influence the grades they give, even after mastery of the subject matter is taken into account. The study found that Asian-American students benefited most from teachers' perceptions of their high levels of class participation, effort, organization, and good-quality homework. In comparison with Anglos, Hispanics, and African-American students, Asian-American students had lower absenteeism and were judged by teachers to have better study habits, be less disruptive, and arrive at school with a better appearance than their peers. Asian-American children had higher coursework mastery which could account directly for their higher grades, but, in addition, teachers' perceptions of their work habits significantly influenced the way they were evaluated.

Cultural values that support education do not always lead to school success. For example, in a study of Khmer refugees, researchers conducted extensive interviews to try to understand why such a large number of Khmer girls

Consider the challenges faced by this Indo-Chinese family as they leave their rural home and try to adapt to life in the United States.

and young women dropped out of school in the United States (Smith-Hefner, 1993). The Khmer are the predominant population of Cambodia, a culture with a history going back to the fifth century and reaching its prominence in Indochina during the tenth through the twelfth centuries. Khmer parents, although of limited educational background themselves, understood that education was very critical for their children's future life, especially for their future employment. However, the Khmer culture also opposed the idea of women developing a strong sense of personal identity and behavioral autonomy. Thus, Khmer female children were in conflict between preserving continuity with their family's cultural values and successfully adapting to a new country by performing well in school.

A similar finding was attained in a study of Indo-Chinese refugee families (Caplan et al., 1992). In general, this research illustrated the remarkably successful adaptation of Indo-Chinese children to U.S. schools. However, within this ethnic group, some children performed much better than others, depending on the nature of each child's family's values. Egalitarian values and role sharing within the families were strong predictors of school grades. Children whose parents endorsed a wife's submission to her husband's wishes and the importance of a college education for boys but not for girls did significantly less well in school than children whose parents had more egalitarian views. School success did not necessarily mean abandoning all cultural values, however. The Indo-Chinese children who were most likely to perform well continued to have a strong family orientation and saw individual achievement as a path toward improving conditions for the family as a whole.

Cross-cultural research illustrates three different paths through which culture influences school achievement. First, culture influences a child's definition of how to function as a student and what it means to be a good student. Second, it influences teachers' expectations for areas and levels of mastery and evaluations of student behavior. Third, it influences the meaning and value families place on school achievement for their children.

Multicultural Education and School Adjustment

Consider the following example. A group of fourth-grade Hispanic children attended a bilingual school. Their skills in reading Spanish were progressing at an appropriate level, and they were reading and writing book reports in Spanish. However, their English skills lagged far behind. The English class was taught by an English-speaking teacher, and the materials they worked with were at about first-grade level. Frustrated by seeing children work so competently in Spanish and so poorly in English, the school hired a bilingual reading teacher who had high-level reading skills in both English and Spanish. The students were given fourth-grade-level English reading materials for their English class, and the teacher used both English and Spanish to answer their questions. After the children had read the material, they discussed the ideas of the text in a combination of English and Spanish. Over time, the class used more and more English to discuss the English texts, and the children's English reading abilities and comprehension progressed markedly (Moll & Diaz, 1985).

This example raises many questions about the cultural context of the learning environment. How can children be assisted in traversing cultural boundaries in the educational process? How can schooling enhance competence in core skills and knowledge without devaluing the diverse cultural backgrounds of the students?

During the process of schooling, children are exposed to a combined agenda focusing both on the elaboration of skills and on the mastery of behaviors that are associated with success within the culture of school. Within the United States, we have come to believe that contextualizing the learning process is integral to providing a successful educational environment for all children. *Contextualizing* instruction involves teaching in ways that first draw upon a child's existing experiences, knowledge, and concepts, and then expanding that understanding in new directions. Contextualizing may require organizing the classroom in a variety of ways such as encouraging children to work individually and/or in small groups as well as following the traditional model of the large group that listens and responds to the teacher. The teacher uses contextualization to draw upon the heroes and heroines, symbols, stories, songs, customs, beliefs, and myths of a cultural group in order to help children feel comfortable with more abstract concepts. Different modes of expression, patterns of social conversation, and language may be acknowledged. Finally, contextualizing may require the involvement of parents and other important community figures in the learning process so that children are not isolated from their significant social community (Tharp, 1989; Tharp & Gallimore, 1988). Box 14.1 illustrates the approach of eight teachers who were identified as especially effective with low-income, African-American elementary-school children.

All these efforts may be particularly beneficial to groups who have been alienated from or are mistrustful of schooling. When the educational process is contextualized, children's cultural identity is strengthened. When their efforts toward personal and cultural achievement are validated, there is little conflict between school professionals and members of minority cultures. Teachers and school administrators gain more confidence in children's school

BOX 14.1

Culturally Relevant Teaching

How do effective teachers actually bring the idea of contextualized instruction to life? Eight such teachers were identified through a process of parent and principal nominations (Ladson-Billings, 1995). All of these teachers all worked in a low-income, predominantly African-American elementary-school district in northern California. Parents described these teachers as being respectful to them, engendering children's enthusiasm about school and academic goals, and helping their children build positive attitudes toward themselves and others. Principals described these teachers as having excellent classroom management skills and reported high standardized test score results among their students.

Basic characteristics of successful, culturally relevant teaching strategies were derived from in-depth interviews with the teachers, classroom observations, videotaped observations, and the teachers' analysis and interpretation of their own videotapes. These characteristics were divided into three broad areas: the conceptions that teachers had of their students and themselves; the kinds of social relations that teachers developed in the classroom; and the teachers' conceptions of knowledge and the learning process. Some of the major principles that were considered fundamental to their effectiveness as culturally relevant teachers are listed here.

Conception of Self and Others

- Teachers believed that the students were capable of academic success. "Students were not permitted to choose failure. . . . [Teachers] cajoled, nagged, pestered, and bribed the students to work at high intellectual levels." Teachers talked freely about their own difficulties in learning and how they had achieved success.

- Teachers were actively involved in and contributed to the community. Several teachers lived in the community. Others made deliberate efforts to shop, attend events, and spend leisure time in the community.

     One teacher made the community a focus of a class assignment to review an historical document and interview members of the city council and longtime residents.

Social Relations

- Teachers gave students opportunities to function as teachers. Students were asked to explain ideas to others. One teacher identified classroom experts and asked other students to consult with them in carrying out their assignments.

- Teachers established a sense of a community of learners. One teacher shared what she was learning in her own graduate-school class with students once a week. Students were encouraged to teach one another, collaborate on projects, and help each other do better. One class was organized in a buddy system so that each student had a partner to review homework, quiz them in advance of tests, and take notes if he or she was absent from class.

Conceptions of Knowledge

- Teachers believed that knowledge is an active process of construction and revision. Students were encouraged to ask *why* about everything, including why a problem was worth solving or why they should be interested in knowing something. Students were encouraged to use many sources of information, including one another and adults and friends in the community, as well as traditional sources, to complete projects.

- Teachers maintained that knowledge must be critically evaluated. Students were asked to consider whether they were satisfied with an answer that was given by the teacher, other students, or in written materials. They were asked to participate in the evaluation of textbooks and approved reading materials.

- Teachers made multidimensional assessments, covering many areas of performance. Students were asked to contribute to their own evaluations. Students could select sources of evidence in addition to standardized tests to be used in judging their mastery.

abilities, and children are more willing to persist in school-related tasks, thereby achieving new levels of competence (Comer, 1985).

Social Issues That Create Barriers to Development

Societies change, exposing each cohort of children to new challenges as well as new resources. Three of the more troubling issues facing children of the 1990s are increasing parental divorce, violence, and family homelessness.

Parental Divorce and Its Impact on Children

An estimated one million U.S. children experience parental divorce each year, and a similar number are expected to face parental divorce through the end of this century (Glick, 1988; U.S. National Center for Health Statistics, 1991). Divorce involves a number of experiences and changes for both parents and children over an extended period of time. In analyzing the impact of divorce on children, especially during middle childhood, it is important to consider events from the child's point of view.

Phases of Family Restructuring and Reorganization

At least four possible phases can be identified in a family's restructuring and reorganization during the divorce process:

1. The predivorce period when there may be high levels of conflict and distress.
2. The decision to divorce, usually accompanied by the parents' separation, and the establishment of custody arrangements.
3. Living in a single-parent family.
4. The possible remarriage of one or both parents, creating a new, blended family.

This last phase may not occur if both parents remain single.

Children's Adjustment to and Coping with Parental Divorce

Numerous studies have found that many children suffer at least short-term adjustment problems associated with parental divorce. These problems may include increased aggression, depression, anxiety, health problems, declines in academic performance, school behavior problems, and conflicts with or withdrawal from peers (Fogas et al., 1992; Hetherington, 1985; Wallerstein & Kelly, 1980). In contrast, some children seem to cope effectively with the disruptions associated with parental divorce.

Evidence suggests that exposure to parental conflict, whether in the context of intact or divorcing families, is emotionally upsetting to children, leading to increased aggression, behavioral problems, disruption in social skills, anxiety, and depression (Cummings, 1994). Some children worry about how to reduce the level of conflict or assume that they are to blame. Others externalize the stress of the conflict by becoming more aggressive with peers or more disruptive in the classroom. In addition, when parents are in conflict with one another, they are likely to be less emotionally or psychologically available to their children, leaving the children with feelings of rejection or

Exposure to parental conflict is a significant stressor for children.

loss of approval, which may be linked to feelings of inferiority and inertia. Exposure to parental conflict has negative consequences for children, so it may be better for children to escape the conditions of conflict through divorce than to remain in an embattled family (Mechanic & Hansell, 1989).

Exposure to predivorce conflict is not the only source of stress for children in the divorce process. Parents' and children's interpretations of the events related to divorce, the single-parent family, or remarriage may differ. In general, the more negative events that a child associates with the divorce process, the more likely the child is to exhibit problems in psychological adjustment (Sandler et al., 1991). Negative events include a variety of possible losses or denigrations such as separation from a loved parent, moving to a new house or neighborhood, exposure to stigmatizing comments from teachers or peers, and loss of contact with other extended family members such as grandparents, aunts, uncles, and cousins. On the other hand, some children describe positive changes after divorce, such as being spared frequent conflicts between parents, having a more stable living arrangement within the single-parent family, observing the custodial parent's relief or optimism, and receiving support from friends, other family members, or school adults.

Experiencing a series of uncontrollable events during the divorce process may erode a child's sense of competence and locus of control. Children may begin to feel that they are simply helpless to protect themselves from being buffeted by their parents' whims, unable to protect themselves from substantial changes in their family life. In a study of children ages 8 to 15 (mean age 11.2), it was found that the more negative events that the children experienced, the more they were likely to show evidence of an *external locus of control*. This means that they tended to believe that the things that happened in their lives were due to luck, fate, or the nature of the situation rather than to their own efforts and abilities. External locus of control was associated with higher levels of anxiety and depression. Those children who were able to retain a high level of *internal locus of control,* a belief that events in their lives resulted primarily from their own efforts and abilities, were able to protect themselves from these negative emotions. They were better able to separate the things that they could control or improve in their situation and the things over which they really had no control. They were able to continue to use active coping strategies such as seeking help, solving the problems within their sphere of control, and using their social support system to provide encouragement and a sense of value. Those children with an external locus of control were more likely to use passive coping strategies such as wishful thinking, blaming themselves or others, or trying to ignore their problems. Over time, these children are likely to form a view of themselves as being incompetent and unable to guide the course of events in their lives, sentiments that are frequently linked to depression (Fogas et al., 1992) (see Notebook Page 14.5).

Loss of Economic and Social Resources

The loss of control is only one loss associated with the divorce process for children. The majority of divorces involving children award custody to the biological mother. However, mothers typically have fewer economic resources to meet the needs of their children than do fathers. Children of divorce are likely to face new levels of economic hardship, often involving a move to less expensive housing, a poorer neighborhood, a new school, and loss of possessions that must be sold. Economic loss affects children directly through the loss of material resources and indirectly due to the loss of family status and increased stress for the single parent striving to meet daily demands with reduced income.

Children also experience loss when the sense of family stability and the kinship system is disrupted by divorce. Typically, a child's parents decide to marry and to separate as adult life choices. However, children are involuntarily born or adopted into a family that defines their sense of self. The sense of family, like the scheme for the permanent object, attachment to the caregiver, understanding the permanence of gender, and conservation of matter, is a core organizing cognition around which children make meaning of daily experiences. Suddenly experiencing a disruption in this family system is likely to bring into question many foundational issues of self: To whom do I belong? Who cares about me? What is the meaning of family? We hypothesize that a child functioning at the level of concrete operational thought whose family is permanently disrupted by divorce is likely to raise many related questions about the predictability and regularity of other social and physical constructs.

Divorce may also cause loss of contact with the noncustodial parent. In a national survey of children and families, children under the age of 17 reported the amount of contact they have with fathers who live apart from them (National Commission on Children, 1991) (see Figure 14.2). For these children, about 34% see their father daily or weekly. The remaining 64% see their fathers once per month or less, with 18% responding that they have not actually seen their fathers in the past year but have received a phone call or letter and another 18% saying that they have not seen their fathers in the past five years.

Many factors help explain the lack of contact between noncustodial fathers and their children. Some of these include continued conflict between the child's father and mother, court-designated visitation privileges, fathers' discomfort about interacting with children, and geographical separation between fathers and children (MacArthur, 1994). However, this lack of contact is likely to be linked with children's loss of identification and sense of

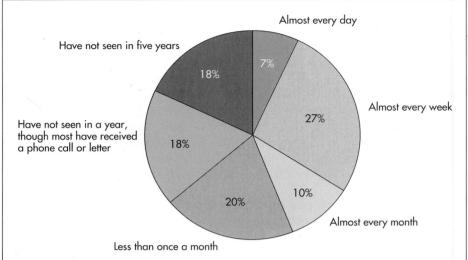

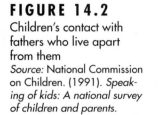

FIGURE 14.2
Children's contact with fathers who live apart from them
Source: National Commission on Children. (1991). *Speaking of kids: A national survey of children and parents.* Washington, D.C.: National Commission on Children, Figure 16, p. 22.

closeness with their fathers. In the same national study cited above, for example, only 55% of children in single-parent families believed that their fathers really cared about them, as compared with 96% in intact families with both biological parents. Only 20% of children in single-parent families said that they looked up to and admired their fathers, as compared with 52% of children in intact families with both biological parents.

Whereas divorce points out how events in the marital relationship can lead to disruption for the child, the next two topics illustrate how factors beyond the family, violence in the schools and homelessness, may have an impact on a child's developing social and intellectual abilities.

Violence in the Schools

In recent years, the problem of violence in the schools threatens to undermine the quality of the educational experience for many American children (see Box 14.2). Despite all the concerns that have been expressed about the high rate of illiteracy in the United States and the poor performance of American children in math and science compared with that of children in other nations, two of the first bills that the current Secretary of Education has sent to Congress address efforts to prevent or reduce violence in schools. The first provides funding for increasing school security, and the other provides resources for violence-prevention programming, including dealing with anger, resolving conflict, reducing racial stereotypes, and training students in peer mediation (Toch, 1993). We are dealing with the very bottom layer in Maslow's famous hierarchy of needs—safety and security. When children are threatened, very little higher-order thinking can be accomplished. The quality of life within the school, the emotional climate, the patterns of interaction between children and adults, as well as among the children themselves, all contribute to children's openness to learning. Children who are relaxed and having a good time and who feel acknowledged and involved in the teaching–learning process are likely to be more attentive, to try harder, and to take pleasure and pride in their achievements (Stevenson, 1992).

Divorce

We know that many children experience the process of parental divorce as a difficult challenge in their lives. At the same time, some children appear to cope more easily with this crisis and recover more readily from its effects.

1. From what you have read in the chapter and your own knowledge of the divorce process, what factors appear to help children cope with divorce?

_____

_____

_____

_____

_____

2. How might you intervene in a family to help prevent long-lasting disruptive effects of parental divorce on the children? In particular, what would you do to help sustain a child's continuing sense of industry, competence, and academic achievement?

_____

_____

_____

_____

_____

3. What could you do to help sustain a child's continuing sense of trust and hope, autonomy and will, initiative and purpose during the divorce process?

_____

_____

_____

_____

BOX 14.2

Violence in American Schools

Times have really changed for America's schools. Consider the comparison presented in the accompanying table that shows the kinds of problems that public school teachers worried about in the 1940s and the kinds of problems they worry about now. The statistics cited in this narrative were taken from an article in the November 8, 1993 *U.S. News and World Report.* In 1993, an estimated 3 million crimes were committed in or near public school buildings around the United States. In a national survey, 16% of eighth-graders said they fear for their safety when they are at school. These fears may be stimulated in part by exposure to violence in the media, but they are also associated with increased levels of actual violence among children in schools. The New York City schools reported 5,761 violent incidents in 1992, and the mayor of New York announced a plan to station police officers in all of the city's public schools. Of the nation's eighth-graders, 9% have carried some type of weapon to school in the past month, and one estimate is that about 270,000 guns are in the schools each day.

Many people focus on children's and youths' access to guns as one source of the problem. Children are lured into a cycle of fear. In order to prevent becoming a victim, children decide that they need to arm themselves in order to be protected. However, the presence of arms increases the likelihood of violence. Most children, whether inner city or suburban, say they would have little difficulty obtaining a gun; stolen guns are available for about $50. The government is struggling to restrict minors' access to guns. For example, Congress passed a Gun-Free School Zones Act in 1990, but the law was declared unconstitutional. In the meantime, school systems are spending scarce educational resources on security systems. In at least 45 urban school districts, children are screened with metal detectors. Some schools are installing bulletproof window glass. Like New York, many districts are increasing police presence in and around their schools. In one elementary school in Connecticut where children saw two fellow students gunned down outside the school, the school principal explained, "Kids didn't want to go to class, they couldn't eat or sleep, they burst out crying. . . . We couldn't think about teaching reading, writing and arithmetic until we dealt with these problems" (Toch, 1993).

Public School Teachers' Perceptions of Top Disciplinary Problems

1940	1990
Talking out of turn	Drug abuse
Chewing gum	Alcohol abuse
Making noise	Pregnancy
Running in the halls	Suicide
Cutting in line	Rape
Dress-code violations	Robbery
Littering	Assault

Source: Toch, T. (1993). Violence in schools: When killers come to class. *U.S. News & World Report, 115,* 34. Reprinted by permission.

Homelessness and Its Impact on Children

In all cultures, the household provides a basic life structure for most people. The household is not only a physical setting but also a shared psychological context for a group of people. In nomadic tribal groups, for example, the continuity of the household is preserved by the group of people and their shared belongings even though the location of the household changes.

The homeless are people who live on the streets or in public shelters. These people have no permanent resting place, no private space (Landers, 1989). In 1990, the Census Bureau identified roughly 50,000 people who appeared to live on the streets and 180,000 who lived in emergency shelters for the homeless (U.S. Bureau of the Census, 1994). The Census Bureau did not claim that this was a complete and accurate count of the homeless, but merely an effort to include the homeless in the decade census tally. Many who fall into this category are mentally ill persons who have been released from mental institutions. Some are drug and alcohol abusers. Some are runaway youths. The fastest-growing segment of the homeless are families, usually single-parent mothers and their children (Bassuk, 1991).

A combination of the reduction in the buying power of social welfare benefits and shortages in low-income housing have contributed to the increase in the number of families with children living in the streets or in emergency shelters. The paths toward homelessness are diverse. Some of the most common precursors are job loss, domestic violence, substance abuse, mental illness, and divorce (Koblinsky & Anderson, 1993). Although some homeless individuals are in a sudden crisis, many have spent years stumbling from one temporary living situation to the next, and others have never really been able to establish a permanent home. Some of these people are overwhelmingly alone, unable to develop even minimal social relationships.

Many homeless mothers have no friends or family to help them. They lack a family social support system or sense of social connection, often as a result of some form of victimization earlier in their lives. They are commonly suffering from emotional dysfunction which may be due to an earlier crisis and is often exacerbated by the use of alcohol and drugs (Grigsby et al., 1990; Wright & Devine, 1993). As a result of drug or alcohol abuse, these women are unable to sustain employment or even avail themselves of community resources (Robertson, 1991). Other women are forced into homelessness when they flee from a violent partner (Browne, 1993).

Homeless children are exposed to a broad range of stressors that compromise their development. In addition to experiencing the loss of a permanent home, they are often in the care of a dysfunctional parent (Hausman & Hammen, 1993). In some instances, a homeless child may actually be functioning at a more competent level than his or her parent. In a comparison between homeless children and very-low-income children who lived in homes, the homeless children fared far less well on many dimensions (Bassuk, 1991; Bassuk & Gallagher, 1990). They experienced many more health problems, with high rates of diarrhea, malnourishment, asthma, and high blood levels of lead. These children were more likely than housed, poor children to have missed immunizations. They were more likely to be victims of abuse. School-age children exhibited high levels of depression, anxiety, and regressive behaviors that appear to be due to the uncertainty and lack of control that they experience in their lives.

School achievement is often severely disrupted for homeless children. The case of Robert, a 12-year-old boy living in a shelter in Boston, illustrates the dilemma.

> Robert said he hated school. He stated that he had no friends and was bored and that he worried his classmates would discover he had no real home. Robert said he was teased by his peers and criticized by adults. He disliked the shelter and the other children there and spoke wistfully of the family's last home in a trailer. Robert was failing in school and had repeated a grade. (Bassuk, 1991, 71)

An estimated 30% of homeless children do not go to school. They are more likely to score below grade level in reading and math, repeat a grade, and do failing work in school. Frequent moves from school to school, numerous absences, and ridicule by peers for their appearance, their hygiene, and even for living in a shelter are likely to turn school into a negative experience rather than a force for stability in their already chaotic lives.

Optimizing Development in Middle Childhood

The ideas about optimizing development in middle childhood are based on the concepts discussed in Chapters 13 and 14. Table 14.1 summarizes these ideas. Middle childhood brings exceptional new growth in a wide range of ego capacities, including skill development, problem solving, social competence, and the ability to conceptualize the self as an object of appraisal by others. Much of this growth is stimulated by active involvement with peers who can challenge one another's point of view and challenge one another to higher levels of skill attainment, while accepting one another as valued friends. Thus, adults can help optimize development by validating a child's interest in peer relationships and helping him or her to develop the kinds of social competence that will permit effective functioning in the peer group.

The child's interests and abilities in a wide range of skills are nurtured by expanding access to new experiences. Children may be taught directly how to perform tasks. Parents, teachers, and other caring adults can also introduce children to new skills by taking them to museums, enrolling them in clubs such as Scouting or 4-H, or arranging for special classes or tutoring in particular interests such as music, dance, or art. They can encourage children to read books and magazines and to seek out other sources of new ideas and information. As children engage a new skill area, adults can identify opportunities where children can succeed and build a sense of confidence and optimism about mastering more challenging levels of ability.

Encourage children to take on new challenges with enthusiasm and optimism.

In addition to exposing children to new skill areas and ideas, it is important to provide experiences where they can experiment with materials, ideas, and information. Adults should talk with children about their observations and inferences and encourage them to consider alternative explanations for their conclusions and to think logically as they make decisions and solve problems.

Parents should be actively engaged in their children's schooling, maintain an open channel of communication with school personnel, and become familiar with the school environment. Children may need help understanding the norms and rules of school behavior; they may encounter nonacademic problems in school that interfere with learning; and they may become restless or disruptive if the level of work is either too difficult or too easy. Parents and other adults can play a critical role in helping a child adapt to the demands and expectations of the school environment. They can also help the school respond sensitively to the child's unique disposition and abilities.

Children will experience their fair share of failures and disappointments as they try new activities and meet new people. It is important for children to know that their parents and teachers have confidence in their ability to succeed. Without setting unrealistic standards for performance, it is important to help a child believe in the possibility of success, strive for goals, and stay with tasks until they are adequately mastered. Eventually, the encouragement and approval that the child senses from others will become internalized as a personal sense of competence and an authentic enthusiasm for taking on new challenges.

TABLE 14.1

Optimizing Development in Middle Childhood

- Provide opportunities for children to carry out systematic investigation of materials.
- Encourage children to make observations and ask questions about the physical properties of objects in their environment.
- Give children opportunities to classify and categorize the characteristics of things that are meaningful to them, such as baseball cards or CDs.
- Provide experiences in understanding the concept of quantity across many different kinds of objects and materials.
- Introduce the four basic combinatorial operations (addition, subtraction, multiplication, and division) and practice solving problems using these operations.
- Foster metacognition by helping children identify the sources of their knowledge.
- Encourage children to talk about their feelings of certainty or uncertainty.
- Introduce children to skill development by providing opportunities for mastery at a beginning level and encourage them to take on increasingly difficult tasks.
- Assist children in becoming fluent readers.
- Encourage the value of reading beyond school assignments.
- Reassure children that you believe in their ability to develop new skills.
- Encourage children to stick with challenges that are difficult for them.
- As a child begins a new skill area, try to structure the situation so that there are frequent experiences of success.
- Make sure that the child knows that you have confidence in her/his ability.
- Avoid expressing gender-role stereotypes that plant doubts in a child's mind about whether she or he has the ability to be competent in certain areas.

(continued)

TABLE 14.1 (continued)

- Avoid setting overly high expectations or being too critical of a child's mistakes.
- Recognize and value the child's need for friendship.
- Model positive, accepting patterns of interaction.
- Provide opportunities for children to spend unstructured time with peers.
- Help children develop perspective-taking skills.
- Encourage children to analyze social situations from varying points of view.
- Recognize the seriousness of peer rejection for children; assist withdrawn and rejected children to participate in programs focusing on social cognition and social skill development.
- Recognize the value of a close-friend or best-friend relationship.
- Recognize the challenges and benefits of team experiences for children.
- Use team experiences to teach about interdependence, cooperation, and division of labor as well as about competition.
- Encourage children to talk about in-group and out-group attitudes that they form as members of teams, and point out the potential risks of forming attitudes that are too intense.
- Avoid humiliating or degrading children in the context of team competition.
- Provide a positive role model for the sense of industry by approaching your own work with high standards, persistence, and a positive attitude.
- Be an active partner in a child's education by being involved at school, with homework, and in learning new things yourself.
- Be enthusiastic about a child's new learning, and support his or her expanding range of interests.
- Help children correctly interpret the valued behaviors associated with the student role in their school and with their teacher.
- Teach children to be proud of their family's ethnic heritage.
- Find ways for the child's school to recognize and validate the child's cultural group(s).

Chapter Summary

1. Industry, as we have discussed it, focuses primarily on building skills and knowledge that are valued by the society, having the ability to apply those skills, and taking pride and pleasure in achieving work-related goals.

2. Personal and physical limitations, as well as social feedback, can cause a child to feel inferior. Multiple experiences of failure and criticisms of one's ability are likely to produce a sense of inferiority.

3. In U.S. society, continuous attention is given to the child's success or failure in basic skill areas at school. The child's emerging sense of industry is closely associated with the quality of the school environment and access to experiences that both foster enthusiasm toward new learning and provide objective feedback about levels of mastery.

4. In addition to teaching skills and knowledge, schools provide a socialization environment for behaviors associated with citizenship and good work and study habits.

5. A critical factor in education is the opportunity to identify with and model effective teachers.

6. The prime adaptive ego quality of middle childhood is competence, a belief in one's ability to make sense of and master the demands of each new situation.

7. An internalized sense of competence equips a child to meet new and increasingly difficult demands for skill development with enthusiasm and optimism.

8. Inertia, the core pathology, is associated with difficulties in taking action to alter the direction of events.

9. The lives of parents and other involved adults are altered by the demands of their children during middle childhood. In particular, parents and other family members may need to be more active in forming a partnership with the school in order to learn more about school expectations and to help resolve conflicts that may arise between their children and the school.

10. Parents are likely to be stimulated by their children's new areas of interest and learning during middle childhood.

11. A child's school success is influenced in part by the family's definition and expectations of the student role. This definition differs from one cultural group to another.

12. In some instances, children encounter conflict between their family's cultural values and the school's expectations for performance.

13. Multicultural education emphasizes contextualizing learning so that it legitimizes and expands a child's existing knowledge, experiences, and concepts.

14. Parental divorce, like other disruptions in the parental relationship, can have a negative impact on a child's sense of competence and school success. Children's feelings of helplessness or inertia are linked to exposure to high levels of parental conflict and frequent, negative family changes during the divorce process.

15. In addition to potentially causing children to lose their sense of control, divorce may expose children to the losses of financial resources, contact with a biological parent (usually the father), and a sense of family stability.

16. Increases in the level of violence in schools threaten the capacity for learning in contemporary U.S. society.

17. An increase in the number of homeless families in U.S. society is another social issue that disrupts children's school attendance and academic achievement. In addition to losing their homes and privacy, homeless children may suffer because their parents are too stressed to provide emotional support or academic guidance. Homeless children are more likely to be absent from school, suffer from a variety of health problems, and experience emotional conflicts that disrupt their concentration on school-related tasks.

References

Adler, A. (1935). The fundamental views of individual psychology. *International Journal of Individual Psychology, 1*, 5–8.

Alexander, K. L., Entwistle, D. R. & Thompson, M. S. (1987). School performance, status relations, and the structure of sentiment: Bringing the teacher back in. *American Sociological Review, 52*, 655–682.

Atkinson, J. W. & Birch, D. (1978). *Introduction to motivation* (2nd ed.). New York: Van Nostrand.

Bassuk, E. L. (1991). Homeless families. *Scientific American, 265,* 66–74.

Bassuk, E. L. & Gallagher, E. M. (1990). The impact of homelessness on children. *Child and Youth Services, 14,* 19–33.

Browne, A. (1993). Family violence and homelessness: The relevance of trauma histories in the lives of homeless women. *American Journal of Orthopsychiatry, 63,* 370–384.

Calhoun, G., Jr. & Morse, W. C. (1977). Self-concept and self-esteem: Another perspective. *Psychology in the Schools, 14,* 318–322.

Cannon-Watkins, G. (1994). A case study of ways that African-American families support academic achievement in middle childhood. Project submitted in partial fulfillment of the Master's degree. The Ohio State University.

Caplan, N., Choy, M. H. & Whitmore (1992). Indochinese refugee families and academic achievement. *Scientific American, 266,* 36–42.

Cochran-Smith, M. (1995). Color blindness and basket making are not the answers: Confronting the dilemmas of race, culture, and language. *American Educational Research Journal, 32,* 493–522.

Cole, M. & D'Andrade, R. (1982). The influence of schooling on concept formation: Some preliminary conclusions. *Quarterly Newsletter of the Laboratory of Comparative Cognition, 4,* 19–26.

Coleman, J. S. (1987). Families and schools. *Educational Researcher, 16,* 32–38.

Coles, R. & Stokes, G. (1985). *Sex and the American teenager.* New York: Harper & Row.

Comer, J. P. (1985). Empowering black children's educational environments. In H. P. McAdoo & J. L. McAdoo (Eds.), *Black children: Social, educational, and parental environments.* Newbury Park, Calif.: Sage, 123–138.

Connors, L. J. & Epstein, J. L. (1995). Parent and school partnerships. In M. Bornstein (Ed.), *Handbook of parenting: Applied and practical parenting* (vol. 4). Mahwah, N.J.: Erlbaum, 437–458.

Crooks, T. J. (1988). The impact of classroom evaluation practices on students. *Review of Educational Research, 58,* 438–481.

Cummings, E. M. (1994). Marital conflict and children's functioning. *Social Development, 3,* 16–36.

Diener, C. I. & Dweck, C. S. (1980). An analysis of learned helplessness: II. The processing of success. *Journal of Personality and Social Psychology, 39,* 940–952.

Epstein, J. L., Jackson, V. E. & Salinas, K. C. (1992). *Manual for teachers: Teachers involve parents in schoolwork.* Baltimore: Johns Hopkins University, Center on Families, Communities, Schools and Children's Learning.

Erikson, E. H. (1963). *Childhood and society* (2nd ed.). New York: W. N. Norton.

Erikson, E. H. (1978). Reflections on Dr. Borg's life cycle. In E. H. Erikson (Ed.), *Adulthood.* New York: Norton, 1–31.

Erikson, E. H. (1982). *The life cycle completed: A review.* New York: W. W. Norton.

Farkas, G., Grobe, R. P., Sheehan, D. & Shuan, Y. (1990). Cultural resources and school success: Gender, ethnicity, and poverty groups within an urban school district. *American Sociological Review, 55,* 127–142.

Fogas, B. S., Wolchik, S. A., Braver, S. L., Freedom, D. S. & Bay, R. C. (1992). Locus of control as a mediator of negative divorce-related events and adjustment problems in children. *American Journal of Orthopsychiatry, 62,* 589–598.

Ford, M. E. (1985). The concept of competence. Themes and variations. In H. A. Marlowe & R. A. Weinberg (Eds.), *Competence development. Theory and practice in special populations.* Springfield, Ill.: Charles C. Thomas.

Garmezy, N. & Masten, A. S. (1991). The protective role of competence indicators in children at risk. In E. M. Cummings, A. L. Greene, & K. H. Karraker (Eds.), *Life-span developmental psychology: Perspectives on stress and coping.* Hillsdale, N.J.: Erlbaum, 151–174.

Glick, P. C. (1988). The role of divorce in the changing family structure: Trends and variations. In S. A. Wolchik & P. Karoly (Eds.), *Children of divorce: Empirical perspectives on adjustment.* New York: Gardner Press, 3–34.

Granleese, J. & Joseph, S. (1994). Reliability of the Harter self-perception profile for children and predictors of global self-worth. *Journal of Geriatric Psychology, 155,* 487–492.

Grigsby, C., Baumann, D., Gregorich, S. E. & Roberts-Gray, C. (1990). Disaffiliation to entrenchment: A model for understanding homelessness. *Journal of Social Issues, 46,* 141–156.

Gutek, G. L. (1992). *Education and schooling in America.* Boston: Allyn & Bacon.

Harter, S., Whitesell, N. R. & Kowalski, P. (1992). Individual differences in the effects of educational transitions on young adolescents' perceptions of competence and motivational orientation. *American Educational Research Journal, 29,* 777–807.

Hausman, B. & Hammen, C. (1993). Parenting in homeless families: The double crisis. *American Journal of Orthopsychiatry, 63,* 358–369.

Hess, R. D. & Azuma, H. (1991). Cultural support for schooling: Contrast between Japan and the United States. *Educational Researcher, 20,* 2–8.

Hetherington, E. M. (1985). Long-term effect of divorce and remarriage on the adjustment of children. *Journal of the American Academy of Child Psychiatry, 24,* 518–530.

Holloway, S. D. (1988). Concepts of ability and effort in Japan and the United States. *Review of Educational Research, 58,* 327–345.

Koblinsky, S. A. & Anderson, E. A. (1993). Studying homeless children and their families: Issues and challenges. *Division 7 Newsletter,* Spring–Summer, 1–3.

Kowaz, A. M. & Marcia, J. E. (1991). Development and validation of a measure of Eriksonian industry. *Journal of Personality and Social Psychology, 60,* 390–397.

Ladson-Billings, G. (1995). Toward a theory of culturally relevant pedagogy. *American Educational Research Journal, 32,* 465–491.

Landers, S. (1989). Homelessness hinders academic performance. *APA Monitor, 20,* 39.

MacArthur, A. (1994). Psychosocial factors related to father involvement with noncustodial children after remarriage. Doctoral dissertation, The Ohio State University, 1994.

Masten, A. S., Coatsworth, J. D., Neemann, J., Gest, S. D., Tellegen, A. & Garmezy, N. (1995). The structure and coherence of competence from childhood through adolescence. *Child Development, 66,* 1635–1659.

Mechanic, D. & Hansell, S. (1989). Divorce, family conflict, and adolescents' well-being. *Journal of Health and Social Behavior, 30,* 105–116.

Moll, L. C. & Diaz, S. (1985). Ethnographic pedagogy: Promoting effective bilingual instruction. In E. Garcia & R. Padilla (Eds.), *Advances in bilingual education research.* Tucson: University of Arizona Press, 127–149.

Moorehouse, M. J. & Sanders, P. E. (1992). Children's feelings of school competence and perceptions of parents' work. *Social Development, 1,* 185–200.

Mosel, S. (Fall 1992). Remembering great teachers at Parker: Chauncey Griffith. *Parker Magazine,* 12.

National Commission on Children. (1991). *Speaking of kids: A national survey of children and parents.* Washington, D.C.: National Commission on Children.

Nelson, E. (1987). Learned helplessness and children's achievement. In S. Moore & K. Kolb (Eds.), *Reviews of research for practitioners and parents* (no. 3). Minneapolis: Center for Early Education and Development, 11–22.

Newman, P. & Newman, B. (1988). Parenthood and adult development. *Marriage and Family Review, 12,* Special Issue on Transition to Parenthood, 313–338.

Ogbu, J. U. (1987). Variability in minority school performance: A problem in search of an explanation. *Anthropology and Education Quarterly, 18,* 312–334.

Phillips, D. A. (1984). The illusion of incompetence among academically competent children. *Child Development, 55,* 2000–2016.

Robertson, M. J. (1991). Homeless women with children: The role of alcohol and other drug abuse. *American Psychologist, 46,* 1198–1204.

Rutter, M. (1983). School effects on pupil progress: Research findings and policy implications. *Child Development, 54,* 1–29.

Sandler, I. N., Wolchik, S. A., Braver, S. L. & Fogas, B. S. (1991). Stability and quality of life events and psychological symptomatology in children of divorce. *American Journal of Community Psychology, 19,* 501–521.

Seligman, M. E. P. (1975). *Helplessness.* San Francisco: W. H. Freeman.

Smith-Hefner, N. J. (1993). Education, gender, and generational conflict among Khmer refugees. *Anthropology and Education Quarterly, 24,* 135–158.

Spencer, M. B. (1985). Racial variations in achievement prediction: The school as a conduit for macrostructural cultural tension. In H. P. McAdoo & J. L. McAdoo (Eds.), *Black children: Social, educational, and parental environments.* Newbury Park, Calif.: Sage, 85–111.

Stevenson, D. L. & Baker, D. P. (1987). The family–school relation and the child's school performance. *Child Development, 58,* 1348–1357.

Stevenson, H. W. (December, 1992). Learning from Asian schools. *Scientific American, 267,* 6, 70–77.

Tharp, R. G. (1989). Psychocultural variables and constants: Effects on teaching and learning in schools. *American Psychologist, 44,* 349–359.

Tharp, R. G. & Gallimore, R. (1988). *Rousing minds to life: Teaching, learning, and schooling in social context.* Cambridge, England: Cambridge University Press.

Toch, T. (with T. Gest & M. Guttman) (October 8, 1993). Violence in schools: When killers come to class. *U.S. News & World Report, 115,* 18, 30–37.

U.S. Bureau of the Census. (1994). *Statistical abstract of the United States, 1994* (114th ed.). Washington, D.C.: U.S. Government Printing Office.

U.S. National Center for Health Statistics. (1991). Monthly vital statistics report, 39. Advance report of final divorce statistics, 1988. Washington, D.C.: U.S. Government Printing Office.

Wallerstein, J. S. & Kelly, J. B. (1980). *Surviving the breakup: How children and parents cope with divorce.* New York: Basic Books.

White, R. W. (1959). Motivation reconsidered. The concept of competence. *Psychological Review, 66,* 297–333.

Wright, J. D. & Devine, J. A. (1993). Family backgrounds and the substance abusive homeless: The New Orleans experience. *The Community Psychologist, 26,* 35–37.

Developmental Tasks of Early Adolescence (Ages 12 to 18)

Chapter 15

Physical Maturation
    Physical Changes in Girls
    Physical Changes in Boys
    The Secular Trend
    Psychosocial Consequences of Differences in Maturation Rate
    Review of Major Trends in Physical Development

Formal Operations
    Piaget's Theory of Formal Operational Thought
    Six Characteristics of Formal Operational Reasoning
    Egocentrism
    Factors That Promote Formal Operational Thought
    Criticisms of the Concept of Formal Operations

Emotional Development
    Developmental Trends over the Course of Early Adolescence
    Eating Disorders
    Delinquency
    Depression
        Factors Associated with Depression in Adolescence
        Gender Differences in Vulnerability to Depression

Membership in the Peer Group
    Cliques and Crowds
    New Learning Linked to Peer-Group Membership

Sexual Relationships
    The Transition to Coitus
    Orientation Toward Sexuality
    Problems and Conflicts Associated with Sexuality

Chapter Summary

References

*E*arly adolescence begins with the onset of puberty and ends around 18 years of age, often with graduation from high school. This stage is characterized by rapid physical changes, transforming a child into a full-sized adult with significant new cognitive abilities, emotional maturation, sexual awakening, and a heightened sensitivity to peer relations. We call the psychosocial crisis of this stage *group identity versus alienation* (Newman & Newman, 1976). Just as toddlers are both driven to and conflicted over autonomous behavior, early adolescents are driven to and conflicted over group behavior. A strong sense of belonging to groups emerges, resulting in the ego quality of loyalty to groups of family members, friends, and others.

In addition, early adolescents rework and synthesize earlier psychosocial orientations as they engage with a more complex and demanding sociocultural environment. At the onset of early adolescence, it is hypothesized that healthy children have 18 complex behavioral systems (see Table 15.1) derived from successfully accomplishing the developmental tasks of the preceding stages, which help them achieve mastery over the environment. During this new stage, rather intense growth and new learning occur in five areas: physical maturation, formal operations, emotional development, membership in peer groups, and sexual relationships. By the end of this stage, young people undergo a metamorphosis from competent hard-working, hard-playing children to almost-mature-looking adults with skills that allow them to function as full members of society (see Notebook Page 15.1).

Table 15.1 recaps the coping systems that are available at the onset of early adolescence, as well as the new tasks of this stage. Each of the behavior systems activated earlier continues to play an important role in enabling a person to cope with the challenges of life and solve emergent life problems. The attachment behavior system, for example, continues to operate through toddlerhood, early school age, middle childhood, and early adolescence. In early adolescence, attachments begin to include peers outside the family. Teenagers derive a sense of security from being near one another. The parent–child attachment is in transition and will undergo continued change through this and succeeding stages. Parents are often disappointed when their children become uncomfortable walking too close to them in public. At the same time, new attachments and new elements of attachment behavior begin to play a role in subsequent adaptation. Examining Table 15.1, it is clear that, while attachment to parents continues independently of other developmental tasks, it is also involved in new tasks, including sexualized attachments, attachments to peers, and the emotional maturation underlying basic feelings related to a sense of connectedness to others. Similar lines of continuity can be drawn in relation to capacities for reasoning and problem solving, emotional expression, complex social relationships, and self-understanding.

Physical Maturation

The onset of early adolescence is marked by rapid physical change. Of course, childhood is marked by continuous physical growth and changes in physical competencies. However, physical maturation at puberty—including a height spurt, increases in weight and muscle strength, the maturation of the reproductive system, the appearance of secondary sex characteristics, and

Understanding the Continued Importance of Previously Activated Coping Skill Areas

By the time a young person enters early adolescence, he or she has addressed 18 developmental tasks of prior stages. Each of these tasks contributes to the young person's coping resources. Using Table 15.1, describe a possible contribution of each of these 18 tasks to meeting one or more of the challenges of the developmental tasks of early adolescence. For example, how might the developmental tasks of self-control, self-theory, and self-evaluation contribute to the ability of early adolescents to cope with their rapid physical changes?

TABLE 15.1

Coping Systems Potentially Available for Increased Mastery over the Environment

Life Stage	Developmental Tasks	New Tasks of Early Adolescence
From infancy:	Social attachment Maturation of sensory, perceptual, and motor functions Sensorimotor intelligence and primitive causality Understanding the nature of objects and the creation of categories Emotional development	Physical maturation Formal operational thinking Emotional development Membership in peer groups Sexual relationships
From toddlerhood:	Elaboration of locomotion Fantasy play Language development Self-control	
From early school age:	Gender-role identification Early moral development Self-theory Group play	
From middle childhood:	Concrete operational thought Skill learning Self-evaluation Friendship Team play	

changes in body shape—result in a total revision of a young person's physical appearance. These changes generally begin at around age 11 for females and 13 for males. Variability in the rate of development is well documented (Brooks-Gunn & Reiter, 1990; Faust, 1977; Tanner, 1978/1990). The time from the appearance of breast buds to full maturity may range from 1½ to 6 years for girls; the male genitalia may take from two to five years to reach adult size. These individual differences in maturation suggest that the chronological peer group is biologically far more diverse during early adolescence than it was during early-school-age and middle childhood. If you have ever attended a middle-school dance, you will have observed this physical diversity firsthand.

Pubertal development can influence psychological and social development in at least three ways (Clausen, 1975). First, physical growth alters a person's actual ability to perform tasks. Early adolescents are taller and stronger than younger children and have greater coordination and endurance. Second, physical growth alters the ways in which one is perceived by others. For example, early adolescents may be viewed by adults as less cuddly or more threatening than younger children. Third, physical growth influences the ways in which adolescents perceive themselves. They may feel more like adults, or, if their growth is disappointing, adulthood may be harder to accept. Of course, the influence of physical maturation will depend largely on how it is viewed and marked by the society.

Girls have their height spurt about two years earlier than boys.

The degree to which one's body matches the culturally desired or socially valued body build influences social acceptance by peers and adults. This match between body shape and cultural values influences the future course of psychosocial development. For example, our culture gives special self-esteem advantages to muscular, well-developed males and petite, shapely females. In contrast, it devalues and detracts from the self-esteem of thin, gangly boys and overweight girls. In other cultures, patterns are different, and some cultures value a greater variety of body builds.

Physical Changes in Girls

For girls, the onset of puberty occurs at approximately 11 years of age—almost two years sooner than the parallel experience for boys. A height spurt is one of the earliest pubertal changes. Initially, a girl may be embarrassed to find herself towering above her male classmates. Girls often slouch in an attempt to disguise their increased height.

The greatest concern that adolescent girls express about their bodies is their perception that they are too fat. In a national survey of adolescents' health concerns, 85% of adolescents said they thought that girls cared a lot about controlling their weight. In contrast, only 30% thought that boys cared a lot about controlling their weight. Despite the strong interest expressed in controlling weight, less than 10% of adolescents thought that their peers cared a lot about eating healthy foods. Among girls, strong concern about controlling weight was more likely to be linked to cigarette use and drug use than to healthy eating patterns (Evans et al., 1995). At the onset of the growth spurt, most girls notice their features getting plumper. In an attempt to ward off what they perceive as a tendency toward obesity, many early adolescent girls begin a regimen of strict and often faddish dieting. This strategy is ill timed since their bodies require well-balanced diets and increased calorie intake during the period of rapid growth.

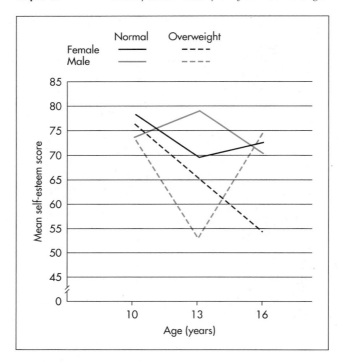

FIGURE 15.1
Self-esteem and body weight for boys and girls ages 10–16
Source: Mendelson, B. K. & White, D. R. (1985). Development of self-body-esteem in overweight youngsters. *Developmental Psychology, 21,* 92. Copyright © 1985 by the American Psychological Association. Reprinted with permission.

During the early adolescent years, obesity is associated with negative feelings about one's appearance and body. This is closely tied to our cultural preference for the slender female body shape, which results in most adult women perceiving that they are overweight, leading almost half of them to some type of weight-loss diet (Thornberry et al., 1986). Research suggests that being overweight has little relation to self-esteem in middle childhood but does begin to have a negative association with self-esteem during early adolescence (see Figure 15.1). At age 10, self-esteem did not differ significantly for normal and overweight boys and girls. Overweight boys had lower self-esteem than boys of normal weight at age 13, but not at younger or older ages. Overweight girls had lower self-esteem than girls of normal weight at 16 (Martin et al., 1988; Mendelson & White, 1985). The impact of obesity on self-esteem illustrates the effect of physical development and body shape on self-evaluation and acceptance during this stage.

Obesity is related to activity level. One of the compounding factors in obesity among many adolescent girls is that they tend to reduce their activity level with age. In an ethnically diverse sample of over 550 girls in grades 5 through 12, only 36% met the national goal for strenuous activity (15 minutes of strenuous activity at least three times per week) (Wolf et al., 1993). The amount of overall activity and strenuous activity decreased with age, and obesity was negatively correlated with activity. The study also revealed differences in total exercise patterns across ethnic groups. Hispanic and Asian-American girls had significantly lower scores on activity level than did African-American and Anglo girls. Two cultural hypotheses were raised to explain this pattern, but neither one was tested. First, it is possible that strenuous physical activity is viewed as especially unfeminine in Asian-American and Hispanic ethnic groups. Second, it is possible that the slender body type is not as desirable in these ethnic groups, so there is less motivation for strenuous exercise. We do not know much about ethnic differences in adolescence, especially as they relate to preferences for body type and standards of physical attractiveness.

For girls, the development of primary sex characteristics includes the maturation of the reproductive organs and the onset of the menstrual cycle. Most girls are prepared by their mothers for the specific events associated with menstruation. However, menstruation is often handled as a matter of hygiene rather than as a sexual transition (Logan, 1980). Many girls do not understand the relation of menstruation to the total process of reproduction (see Chapter 5). They simply accept the fact of monthly periods as another sign of their femininity.

At the age when most girls begin to menstruate (approximately 12 years of age), their male peers may still be ignorant of this phenomenon. Girls are often put in the position of having to explain or hide the facts of menstruation from boys. Girls rarely tell their male peers or their fathers about the onset of menarche, but they do discuss it with their female friends and their mothers. The discrepancy in the onset of puberty in boys and girls and the uneven dissemination of information about it may make it difficult for girls to fully accept the changes that they are experiencing. The memoirs of Simone de Beauvoir (1959) reflect this ambivalence:

> We were staying with friends. . . . I awake horror-stricken one morning: I had soiled my nightdress. I washed it and got dressed: again I soiled my underclothes. I had forgotten Madeleine's vague prophecies, and I wondered what shameful malady I was suffering from. Worried and feeling somehow guilty, I had to take my mother into my confidence: she explained to me that I had now become "a big girl," and bundled me up in a very inconvenient manner. I felt a strong sense of relief when I learned that it had happened through no fault of my own; and as always when something important happened to me, I even felt my heart swell with a sort of pride.

Most girls seem to react to menstruation with a mix of positive and negative feelings. The positive feelings reflect a pride in maturing and in the confirmation of their womanliness. The negative feelings reflect the inconvenience, some unpleasant symptoms, and the possible embarrassment of menstruation (Brooks-Gunn & Reiter, 1990).

The appearance of secondary sex characteristics includes the development of breasts, changes in body shape, and the increased growth of body hair. Typically, girls look upon the development of breast buds as a welcome sign of growing maturity and femininity (Brooks-Gunn & Warren, 1988). Some girls begin to wear bras in anticipation of breast development. However, girls may greet the appearance of dark or thick leg and underarm hair less enthusiastically than do boys. The cultural preference in the United States for smooth-skinned females requires regular shaving of underarms and legs. This shaving ritual, however, is not filled with the same positive sex-role validation as is face shaving for adolescent boys. Adolescent girls thus learn that they must make certain adaptations and alterations to natural pubertal growth in order to meet cultural standards for femininity.

Generally, girls are more dissatisfied than boys with their physical appearance and their overall body image. This pattern has been found among Finns as well as Americans (Petersen et al., 1984; Rauste-von Wright, 1989). For girls, self-consciousness and dissatisfaction with appearance reach their peak between the ages of 13 and 15. By age 18, the more satisfied a young

TABLE 15.2

The Development of Primary and Secondary Sex Characteristics

Females	Average Age of Occurrence	Males
Onset of growth spurt	10–11	
Increased activity of oil and sweat glands (acne can result from clogged glands)	11	Increased activity of oil and sweat glands (acne can result from clogged glands)
Initial breast development	10–11	Onset of growth spurt
Development of pubic hair	11–12	
Onset of menarche (age range is 9–17)	12–13	**Growth of testes** Development of pubic hair
Development of underarm hair		**Growth of penis**
Earliest normal pregnancy	14	Deepening of the voice
Completion of breast development (age range is 13–18)	15–16	**Production of mature spermatozoa** **Nocturnal emissions** Development of underarm and facial hair
Maturation of skeletal system	17–18	Maturation of skeletal system Development of chest hair

Note: Primary sex characteristics are in boldface type.
Source: Adapted from Turner, J. S. & Rubinson, L. (1993). *Contemporary human sexuality.* Englewood Cliffs, N.J.: Prentice-Hall, 421.

woman is with her body image, the more likely she is to have positive social relationships with her family, her peers, and people in general. It is not clear whether it is the positive social support that helps a young woman reach a level of satisfaction with her appearance, or if those young women who feel positive about their appearance are more likely to be confident and outgoing in their social relationships.

Physical Changes in Boys

Physical maturation poses different challenges for males and females (see Table 15.2). Although both sexes must adjust to a changing body image, cultures place distinct values and taboos on the kinds of changes experienced by each. For boys, increased height and muscle mass are welcome changes that bring them one step closer to adult maturity. On the one hand, a mature physique usually brings well-developed physical skills that are highly valued by peers and adults alike. On the other hand, the period of rapid growth may leave a boy feeling awkward and uncoordinated for a time. This awkwardness results because growth does not take place at the same rate in all parts of the body. One particular discrepancy is the time lag between the height spurt and an increase in muscle strength. For boys, the peak increase in muscle strength usually occurs about 12 to 14 months after the peak height spurt (Carron & Bailey, 1974). During this temporary period, a boy simply cannot accomplish what he might expect, given his physical size. Psychologically, this awkward period poses some strong challenges to a boy's self-esteem. He simply looks funny and awkward. He may be easily embarrassed by this condition. He cannot fully accept his new body image at first, and he doubts whether others can.

The growth of the testes and penis also poses important problems for early-adolescent males. Testicular growth is one of the first signs of puberty for boys, and they are generally not well prepared by their parents for the maturation of the reproductive organs (Bolton & MacEachron, 1988). Specifically, they are not taught about spontaneous ejaculation and may be surprised, scared, or embarrassed by it. In a study of first ejaculation, Nigerian boys experienced many of the same patterns that were found for Americans. The main difference was that the Nigerian boys were about two years older at the time of their first ejaculation. Most of the boys were not prepared for this experience; however, those who were prepared received their information largely from male sources, especially older brothers. The experience itself was associated with mild to strong feelings of pride and pleasure, and it made the boys feel grown up. Many boys expressed some mild feelings of upset, embarrassment, and shame. There was no difference in reactions between boys who had been well prepared for their experience and those who had not been prepared (Adejoke, 1993).

The sexual connotation of ejaculation may make it difficult for boys to seek an explanation from their parents. They are left to gain information from friends and reading material or to worry in private about its meaning. For many boys, spontaneous ejaculation provides an important clue to the way in which physical adult sexuality and reproduction are accomplished (Gaddis & Brooks-Gunn, 1985; Marsiglio, 1988).

A third area of physical development that has psychological and social meaning for boys is the development of secondary sex characteristics, particularly the growth of facial and body hair. The equipment and the ritual behaviors associated with shaving are closely linked to the masculine sex role. Most boys are eager to express their identification with this role through the act of shaving, and they use the slightest evidence of hairy outgrowth as an excuse to take razor in hand. The ritual of shaving not only provides some affirmation of a boy's masculinity but also allows him an acceptable outlet for his narcissism. As he shaves, it is legitimate for him to admire his changing image. In some subcultures, facial hair is an important symbol of manliness. Thus, some young men cultivate and admire their mustaches or beards as evidence of their enhanced male status.

The Secular Trend

Given a genetic potential for growth and sexual maturation, the environment can play an important role in an individual's eventual attainment of this potential. A *secular growth trend* is an increase or decrease in a population's average adult height or a change in the average age at which physical maturation takes place for a particular cohort (Van Wieringen, 1978). Changes in hygiene, nutrition, and health care have contributed to an earlier growth spurt over the past century. Children ages 10 to 14 increased in height by an average of 2 to 3 centimeters every decade from 1900 to 1960. Adult height is not necessarily greater; it is simply attained earlier.

Other evidence of a secular trend is provided by the shift in age at menarche. There is some controversy about the extent of this shift. Data reported by Tanner (1978/1990) showed a decrease in average age at menarche (from age 13.5–14 in 1950 to age 12.5–13 in 1970). At present, the mean age at menarche in the United States is 12.3, but the range is from 9 to 17. Age at menarche varies among countries and even among socioeconomic groups within a country. Roman, Islamic, and medieval writings suggest that females have matured in the age range of 12 to 14 for many centuries (Bullough, 1981). Lack of precise records and the confounding of health and social class with age at menarche make it difficult to confirm long-term historical trends. Lower age at the onset of menarche is associated with improved standard of living, including health, diet, and social class (Tanner, 1981). The secular trend has been documented across ethnic groups, provided that samples have comparable access to adequate nutrition (Brooks-Gunn & Reiter, 1990).

What is the relevance of the secular trend for understanding the challenges that face contemporary adolescents in postindustrialized societies? Reproductive capacity and physical adult stature occur at a younger age than at the turn of the century, but full engagement in the adult society requires more training, education, and complex preparation than in the past. Thus, adolescence is prolonged, with more time to experience the risks of unwanted pregnancy, the sense of being in a marginal social status, and disruptions in the transition from childhood to adulthood.

Psychosocial Consequences of Differences in Maturation Rate

The consequences of early and late maturation differ for girls and boys (Dwyer & Mayer, 1971). Both early- and late-maturing girls experience some tension with regard to physical development. Early-maturing girls stand out among all female and later-maturing male age-mates. Their stature and breast development violate the cultural equation of femininity with petiteness. Early onset of menstruation is especially stressful, resulting in heightened self-consciousness and anxiety (Hill, 1988). Early maturers are less likely to have been prepared for the onset of menstruation or to have close friends with whom they can discuss it. For a time, at least, early-maturing girls may be embarrassed by their femininity. Not only do they look very different from their peers, but they are experiencing significant physical changes that they cannot discuss readily with their age-mates.

Several studies suggest that early pubertal onset is a source of stress for girls (Caspi & Moffitt, 1991; Kornfield, 1990). They experience higher levels of conflict with parents and are more likely to report depression and anxiety (Wierson et al., 1993). There is some evidence that early-maturing girls earn lower grades and score lower on academic achievement tests. They are also more likely to be identified as displaying behavior problems in school (Blyth et al., 1981). Early-maturing girls start dating earlier and perceive themselves as more popular with boys than do late-maturing girls. Some studies report that early-maturing girls are more likely to engage in high-risk, promiscuous sexual behavior. In general, however, the timing of the transition to puberty in and of itself is not a strong predictor of a girl's emotional well-being. Rather, timing of puberty interacts with other events such as school transition, family conflict, or peer acceptance to influence a girl's response to this physical transition (Brooks-Gunn & Reiter, 1990; Richards & Larson, 1993).

The timing of pubertal maturation varies for boys just as it does for girls. It has been noted that boys who mature later than their age-mates experience considerable psychological stress and develop a negative self-image (Clausen, 1975; Mussen & Jones, 1957). Late-maturing boys are treated as if they were younger than their age. As a result, they may become isolated from their peers and behave in a silly, childish manner in an attempt to gain attention.

Boys who mature earlier than their age-mates tend to have an advantage. They develop a positive self-image, in part because they are likely to be given increased responsibility by parents and teachers. They are generally more satisfied with their bodies and feel more positive about being boys, and they are likely to be more involved in school activities by the 10th grade than are late-maturing boys (Blyth et al., 1981). Fifth- and sixth- grade boys who are quite physically mature for their age report more positive daily emotions, better attention, more feelings of being strong, and some greater awareness of states of tension (Richards & Larson, 1993). In general, early-maturing boys experience the kind of positive mood and sense of centeredness that are reflected in the social qualities of leadership and personal confidence.

These psychological consequences of the timing of physical maturation highlight the interactions among the biological, psychological, and social systems. Early-maturing girls and late-maturing boys may become isolated from their peers. Individuals who deviate from the normal physical growth pattern may be rejected by the group because they look different and are experiencing different psychological events. Similarly, the advantages of early maturation for boys are primarily a product of the admiration and leadership role accorded to them by their parents and peers. Differences in timing of physical maturation can result in perceptions of body image and dissatisfaction with one's physical appearance that persist well beyond adolescence (Rauste-von Wright, 1989).

Review of Major Trends in Physical Development

Both boys and girls experience parallel phases of physical maturation during early adolescence. Although girls experience these changes somewhat earlier, both sexes must adapt to increases in height and weight and to the maturation of primary and secondary sex characteristics. As a result of earlier maturation of the reproductive system, girls often introduce issues of dating, going together, and romance into the peer culture. Girls' biological changes energize the social system to incorporate and evolve rituals to deal with reproductive and sexual topics. This is an example of how changes in the biological system may modify the social system.

Four points have been made with respect to the psychological meaning of these body changes for males and females:

1. Physical development enables adolescents to think of themselves as approaching adulthood.
2. Physical development influences a young person's identification with the role of man or woman.
3. The developing adolescent becomes more egocentric and self-involved.
4. These physical changes produce ambivalence. If the family and peer group are not supportive, negative feelings and conflicts are likely to result.

BOX 15.1

Safety and Risk Behaviors in Adolescence

One stereotype of adolescence is that it is a time of risk taking. Of course, not all youths expose themselves to risks, and youths are not alone in taking risks. However, some disturbing data suggest that contemporary youths do indeed expose themselves to high rates of preventable injuries. The leading cause of death among U.S. adolescents is accidents, especially motor vehicle accidents, and the second most common cause of death for this group is homicides (U.S. Bureau of the Census, 1994). The death rate from homicides is higher for adolescents than for any other age range.

In addition to risk behaviors that are associated with mortality, adolescents are known for their rejection of safety precautions. The age range 16 to 18 is the peak period for initiation of smoking, drinking, and using illicit drugs. Data from 1994 show that roughly 19% of eighth-graders and 25% of tenth-graders smoke cigarettes and that the rate of cigarette smoking is increasing for this generation of adolescents even while the rate of smoking among adults is declining (Johnston, 1995). About 26% of eighth-graders and 38% of tenth-graders report riding in a car with a driver who was intoxicated or using drugs.

Another area of risk behavior is unprotected sexual activity. One estimate found that one in seven adolescents in the United States has a sexually transmitted disease, and AIDS is the sixth leading cause of death in adolescents and young adults between the ages of 15 and 24 (Sells & Blum, 1996). Among American youth who are sexually active, 47% say that neither they nor their partners systematically use a condom (Benson, 1992; Quadrel et al., 1993).

Weapon carrying has increased dramatically since the mid-1980s. A study of weapon carrying in two junior high schools in Washington, D.C., found that among males, 47% had carried knives and 25% had carried guns during the prior two weeks. Among females, 37% had carried knives and 4% had carried guns (Webster et al., 1993). This problem has such deadly consequences that reducing weapon carrying among adolescents has been formally included as one of the national health objectives for the year 2000.

Adolescents appear to expose themselves to a wider range of high-risk behaviors over the course of the years from 12 through 17, and, during that same time, they use fewer safety precautions. In a study of over 2,000 junior high and high school students in rural and urban areas of Iowa, safety behaviors were assessed. The percentage of adolescents who used a car safety belt while riding in the front or back seat of a car or used any type of helmet while riding a bicycle, moped, skateboard, or snowmobile decreased with age. Similarly, safety strategies associated with swimming, such as checking the depth of the water before diving or always swimming with a partner, decreased with age. At the same time, the percentage who drove a car while drunk or high on drugs increased with age even when opportunities to drive, which normally increase with age, were taken into account (Schootman et al., 1993). In the sections on cognitive and emotional development, we will consider various explanations that have been offered to try to understand the high-risk behavior of youth.

The timing of physical growth can have an impact on whether puberty is experienced as positive or negative (see Notebook Page 15.2). Acceptance of these physical changes requires adequate information, a positive identification with one's gender role, and an atmosphere of family and peer support. The secular trend alerts us to the importance of the psychosocial context of physical development. The fact that reproductive capacity starts earlier than it did 50 years ago poses special challenges to young people who must cope with the expression and regulation of sexual impulses. One consequence of the earlier onset of puberty is that adolescents come into contact with potentially high-risk situations at a relatively young age. Given the kinds of risks present in a technological society, it is not surprising that adolescent exposure to risk behaviors is a major contemporary health concern (see Box 15.1)

Exploring the Psychosocial Consequences of Physical Maturation at Puberty

Use this notebook page to reflect on the relevance of physical maturation at puberty for your own psychosocial development.

1. Did you enter puberty earlier, later, or at the same time as most of your peers?

_____

_____

2. What do you recall as memorable issues related to your physical maturation in adolescence? For example, what worried you about your physical development or body shape? What changes pleased you? Were there any new physical problems that you encountered in adolescence?

_____

_____

3. How did physical maturation influence your perception of yourself as approaching adulthood? For example, were you able to perform new tasks or reach new levels of skill in physical activities?

_____

_____

4. How did physical maturation influence your perceptions of yourself as becoming a woman or man? For example, did you begin to think of yourself as sexually attractive?

_____

_____

5. What issues about physical appearance or physical development that began in adolescence continue to influence your assessment of your body or your physical appearance today?

_____

_____

Formal Operations

As the body undergoes significant changes during puberty, so too does mental activity. Early adolescents begin to think about the world in new ways. Thought processes become more abstract. Young people are able to think in several dimensions at once rather than focusing on just one domain or issue at a time. Thinking becomes more reflective, and adolescents are increasingly aware of their own thoughts as well as the accuracy or inaccuracy of their knowledge. Adolescents are able to generate hypotheses about events that they have never experienced (Keating, 1990). These complex cognitive capacities have been described by Jean Piaget as *formal operations* (Chapman, 1988; Inhelder & Piaget, 1958; Piaget, 1970, 1972).

Studies of the physical maturation of the brain suggest that two distinct phases of new development occur, one linked with the visuoauditory, visuospatial, and somatic systems from about age 13 to 17 and one linked with the frontal executive functions from about age 17 to 21. Figure 15.2 highlights the "spurts" in cortical development during childhood and adolescence as well as the new mental abilities associated with each new phase of development.

Piaget's Theory of Formal Operational Thought

Piaget hypothesized that a qualitative shift in thinking occurs during adolescence from concrete to formal operational thought, which is governed more by logical principles than by perceptions and experiences. In the period of concrete operational thought, children use mental operations to explain changes in tangible objects and events. In the period of formal operational thought, young people use operations to manipulate and modify thoughts and other mental operations (Piaget, 1972). A central feature of formal operational reasoning is being able to consider all the possible combinations of propositions and their interrelations. For example, in thinking about trying to get a part-time job, adolescents may consider the number of hours they want to work, their access to transportation, the kind of work they want to do, and their qualifications before filling out applications. They are able to create different scenarios about working, based partly on what they want and partly on what they know, and then to modify their plan based on new information they get about the jobs that are available.

An important feature of formal operational thought is the ability to raise hypotheses to explain an event, and then to follow the logic that a particular hypothesis implies. One of the classic experiments that Piaget and Inhelder designed to demonstrate the development of hypothetical-deductive reasoning involves the explanation of the swing of a pendulum. The task is to find out what variable or combination of variables controls the speed of the swing. Four factors can be varied: the mass of the object, the height from which the pendulum is pushed, the force with which it is pushed, and the length of the string. To investigate this problem, it is necessary to begin by isolating the separate factors and then varying only one factor at a time, while keeping the others constant. As it happens, only the length of the string influences the speed of the pendulum. The challenge is to demonstrate that the length of the string accounts for the speed and that the other factors do not. Children in the stage of concrete operational thought have difficulty coordinating the interaction among four separate variables and may lose track of what is being

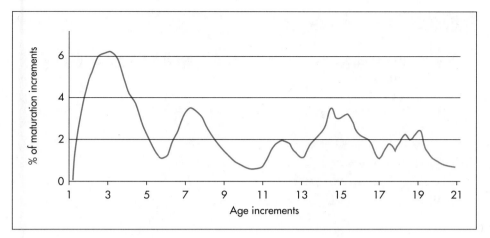

FIGURE 15.2
Peak periods of cerebral maturation. The mean rate of growth for the four regions of the brain reveals the landmarks of cerebral maturation, marked by five distinct peak periods between the ages of 1 and 21. *Peak 1: Ages 1–6.* Rapid brain growth across several areas. Associated with ability to form images, use words, place things in serial order, and solve problems. *Peak 2: Ages 6–10.* Peak growth in the sensory-motor regions. Associated with operational functions such as determining weight and reasoning of mathematical problems. *Peak 3: Ages 10½–13.* New growth in the visual and auditory regions. New abilities to perform calculations and to perceive new meanings and functions for familiar objects. *Peak 4: Ages 13–17.* New growth in the visuo-auditory, visuospatial, and somatic systems. New ability to review mental operations, find flaws in reasoning, and use information to revise problem-solving strategies. *Peak 5: Ages 17–21.* New growth in the frontal executive region. New capacities to question and evaluate information, form new and original hypotheses integrating personal experiences with information from other sources. *Source:* Allison, M. (1992). The effects of neurologic injury on the maturing brain. *Headlines,* October/November, 2–4. Reprinted with permission.

varied and what is held constant. After trying one or two strategies, the child may simply give up. Using formal operational thought, a child can create a matrix of variables and test each factor separately to evaluate its contribution (Flavell, 1963; Inhelder & Piaget, 1958).

Several skills are involved in problem solving of this kind. First, one must be able to identify the separate factors and the possible effect of each factor. Second, one must be able to consider possible interactions among the factors. Third, one must be able to develop a systematic method for testing each factor in combination with each other factor. The conceptual system of the interrelations among possible solutions guides problem solving (Neimark, 1975; Siegler et al., 1973).

Six Characteristics of Formal Operational Reasoning

Six new conceptual skills emerge during the stage of formal operations (Demetriou & Efklides, 1985; Neimark, 1982) (see Table 15.3). Each of these skills has implications for how adolescents approach interpersonal relationships, personal plans, and goals, and for how well they analyze scientific and mathematical information. First, adolescents are able to manipulate mentally more than two categories of variables simultaneously; for example, they can consider the relationship of speed, distance, and time in planning a trip (Acredolo et al., 1984). They can draw on many variables to explain their behavior as well as the behavior of others. Second, they are able to think about things changing in the future; they realize, for instance, that their current friendships may not remain the same in the years ahead. Third, they are able to hypothesize about a logical sequence of possible events; for example, they are able to predict college and occupational options that may be open to them, depending on how well they do in certain academic course work in high school. Fourth, they are able to anticipate consequences of their actions. For instance, they realize that if they drop out of school, certain career possibilities will be closed to them.

Fifth, they have the capacity to detect the logical consistency or inconsistency in a set of statements. They can test the truth of a statement by finding evidence that supports or disproves the statement. They are troubled, for example, by the apparent contradictions between statements such as "All

TABLE 15.3

New Conceptual Skills That Emerge During the Stage of Formal Operational Thought

1. Ability to manipulate mentally more than two categories of variables simultaneously.
2. Ability to think about the changes that come with time.
3. Ability to hypothesize logical sequences of events.
4. Ability to foresee consequences of actions.
5. Ability to detect logical consistency or inconsistency in a set of statements.
6. Ability to think in relativistic ways about self, others, and the world.

people are equal before the law" and the reality that people who have more money can afford better legal representation and are likely to have different experiences with the legal system than those who are poor.

Sixth, they are able to think in a relativistic way about themselves, other individuals, and their world. They know that they are expected to act in a particular way because of the norms of their community and culture. They also know that, in other families, communities, and cultures, different norms may govern the same behavior. As a result, the decision to behave in a culturally accepted manner becomes a more conscious commitment to their society. At the same time, it is easier for them to accept members of other cultures because they realize that these people are the products of societies with different sets of rules and norms (O'Mahoney, 1989).

These qualities of thought reflect what is possible for adolescents rather than what is typical. Most adolescents and older adults approach problem solving in a practical, concrete way in their common, daily functioning. However, under the most supportive conditions, adolescents' more abstract, systematic, and self-reflective qualities of thought can bring a new perspective to their analysis of information and acquisition of knowledge (Eckstein & Shemesh, 1992; Fischer, 1980; Fischer et al., 1993).

In general, the changes in conceptual development that occur during early adolescence result in a more flexible, critical, and abstract view of the world. The abilities to hypothesize logical sequences of action, to conceptualize change, and to anticipate consequences of actions all contribute to a more realistic sense of the future (Klineberg, 1967; Lessing, 1972). The view of the future includes both hopes, such as career goals, educational attainment, and beginning a family, and fears, such as concerns about unemployment or the possibility of war (Gillies, 1989; Nurmi, 1987). Formal operational reasoning also alters a young person's interpersonal behavior and social outlook. It permits an adolescent to speculate about another's point of view and to analyze the consequences of having different opinions or beliefs. It also leads to speculation about how life might be improved if social conditions were altered.

Egocentrism

The term *egocentrism* refers to the child's limited perspective at the beginning of each new phase of cognitive development (Inhelder & Piaget, 1958; Piaget, 1926). In the sensorimotor phase, egocentrism appears as an inability to separate one's actions from their effects on specific objects or people. As the scheme for causality is developed, the first process of *decentering* occurs. Infants recognize that certain actions have predictable consequences and that novel situations call for new, relevant behaviors; for example, one cannot turn the light on by turning the knob on the radio. At each developmental stage, decentering is a process that allows a person to approach situations from a more objective, analytic point of view.

In the phase of preoperational thought, egocentrism is manifested in an ability to separate one's own perspective from that of the listener. When a four-year-old girl tells you about something that happened to her at the zoo, she may explain events as if you had seen them too. When a three-year-old boy is explaining something to his grandmother over the phone, he may point to objects in the room, unaware that his grandmother cannot see over the phone lines.

The third phase of heightened egocentrism occurs in the transition from concrete to formal operational thought. As children develop the capacity to formulate hypothetical systems, they begin to generate assumptions about their own and others' behavior that will fit into these abstract formulations. For example, an early-adolescent boy may insist that cooperation is a more desirable mode of interaction than competition. He argues that cooperation ought to benefit each participant and provide more resources for the group as a whole. This boy may become angry or disillusioned to discover that teachers, parents, and even peers seek competitive experiences and appear to enjoy them. He may think, "If the cooperative system is so superior, why do people persist in their illogical joy in triumphing over an opponent?" This kind of egocentrism reflects an inability to recognize that others may not share one's own hypothetical system.

In early adolescence, decentering requires an ability to realize that one's ideals are not shared by everyone. We live in a pluralistic society in which each person is likely to have distinct goals and aspirations. Early adolescents gradually discover that their neat, logical life plans must be constantly adapted to the expectations and needs of relevant others. As they develop the flexibility of thought that accompanies formal operational perspective taking, their egocentrism should decline.

An early adolescent's egocentrism has two characteristics that may affect social interaction as well as problem solving: preoccupation with his or her own thoughts and a belief that others' thoughts are also preoccupied with him or her. Early adolescents may become somewhat withdrawn and isolated as the domain of their consciousness expands. Thoughts about the possible and the probable, the near and the distant future, and the logical extension of contemporary events to future consequences all flood their minds. David Elkind (1967) described one aspect of this process as the formation of a *personal fable,* an intense investment in one's own thoughts and feelings and a belief that these thoughts are unique. Adolescents may conclude that they alone are having certain insights or certain difficulties and that no one else can understand or sympathize with their thoughts. This tendency to withdraw into their own speculations may cut off adolescents' access to new information or ideas and inhibit social interaction.

Second, early adolescents may assume that they are the center of interest of others' thoughts and attentions. Elkind (1967) referred to this as an *imaginary audience.* Instead of realizing that everyone is equally wrapped up in his or her own concerns and plans, early adolescents envision their own thoughts as being the focus of other people's attention. This subjectivity generates an uncomfortable self-consciousness that makes interaction awkward. There is some controversy about the cognitive processes involved in this heightened self-consciousness. On the one hand, a preoccupation with the idea that others are watching your every move may be an important element in decentering that directs attention to others and their perceptions of you. The concern with others' perceptions thus stimulates cognitive maturation. On the other hand, self-consciousness may be an outcome of an increased ability to consider others' point of view and expectations for your behavior.

Needless to say, egocentrism is not limited to the adolescent years. At each new phase of expanding awareness, people tend to rely heavily on their own experiences and perceptions in order to minimize the anxiety associated with uncertainty. Part of the progress of formal thought implies a reliance on reason over experience. We have more confidence in what we know than in what we can see or hear. Thus, we can find ourselves trapped in an egocentric perspective. We may interpret new experiences as examples of familiar concepts rather than as novel events. We may reject evidence for an argument because it does not support an already carefully developed explanation. The task of searching for new evidence and new explanations is a lifelong challenge. It is much easier to rely on earlier assumptions than to continually call one's perspective into question.

Factors That Promote Formal Operational Thought

Several environmental conditions facilitate the development of formal operational thought and reduce egocentrism. First, early adolescents begin to function in a variety of role relationships that place both compatible and conflicting demands on them. Among these role relationships are son or daughter, worker, student, friend, girlfriend or boyfriend, religious believer, and citizen. Early adolescents experience firsthand the pressures of multiple expectations for behavior. At times, for example, expectations for the student role may be at odds with those for the child or the friend role. Ongoing interactions with parents provide a powerful stimulus for cognitive development, especially when parents encourage children to examine their assumptions, find evidence to support their arguments, and evaluate the sources of information as they approach problems in daily life (Dunham et al., 1988). Participating in a variety of roles also facilitates relativistic thinking by demonstrating that what is acceptable and valued in one situation may not be acceptable or valued in another (Chandler & Boyes, 1982).

The second environmental condition that facilitates the development of adolescent cognitive skills is participation in a more heterogeneous peer group (Looft, 1971). When children move from their community elementary school to more centralized middle and high schools, they are likely to become acquainted with other students whose family backgrounds and social class are different from their own. In working and playing with these friends, they recognize the extent to which their present values and expectations for the future are shaped by the families and neighborhood from which they come.

The use of formal operational skills can be observed in adolescent discussions of peer-related issues and in the formation of intimate/romantic relationships, a new domain that requires a wide range of hypothesis raising and testing. We have observed our own children as they talk with friends in person, over the phone, and through notes, helping each other to generate mul-

The exchange of different points of view among peers promotes formal operational reasoning.

tiple explanations of a given situation. They may use these explanations to put themselves in a more favorable or desirable position, gain a person's confidence, comfort a distressed friend, or escape uncomfortable circumstances. Here is an example of a conversation between a 15-year-old girl and her best friend:

Cindy: I'm so frustrated I can't stand it. Before Stan and I started to date, he was nice to me. I enjoyed being with him. He said hello to me in the halls; we'd walk along together. We talked about all kinds of things. Now that we're going out, he seems rude and uncaring. When we're with other people, he jumps in when I start to talk and his eyes say "be quiet." He breezes by me in the halls sometimes, and when we talk about things (if we talk), he acts as if he is always right. I don't think he cares about me anymore. What's going on?

Donna: I know he likes you because he tells me. Maybe you should talk to him and tell him what he does and how it makes you feel.

Cindy: No, if I do that he'll get mad and he won't like me anymore. Why don't you talk to him?

Donna: No, that wouldn't do any good because then he would know you talked to me about this and he would not like it, or he would just say what he thinks would make him look good.

This conversation goes on and on. Many possible scenarios are offered to explain this behavior, and many possible solutions are proposed. The girls project likely outcomes of each set of possible actions and attempt to evaluate the results of each. Finally, a tentative conclusion is reached: Boys treat girls differently when they are involved in a boyfriend-girlfriend relationship than when they are not. In the "just friends" situation, there is a tendency to treat the girl as an equal; in the boyfriend-girlfriend situation, there is a tendency for the boy to expect that he should dominate the girl. A solution is derived: Cindy must shape Stan up. Because she still likes him very much and wants to go out with him, she must try to tell him how she feels and hope that he will change his behavior so that it is supportive and comfortable for her. She must be the one to do this. Because Stan really does like her and because he may not realize how his behavior is affecting her, chances are good that he will respond positively to Cindy's complaint rather than lose her as a girlfriend.

The context of friendship allows Cindy to trust Donna in discussing her problem so that they can examine it fully. It also allows Donna to disagree with Cindy without terminating the conversation. Thus, Cindy can get a somewhat different point of view on her situation, and the two friends can explore a very personal problem on a more objective, rational basis than Cindy probably could have done on her own.

The third condition that fosters the development of early-adolescent cognitive skills is the content of the high school curriculum. Courses in science, mathematics, and language formally expose students to inherent logical relationships and introduce them to the hypothetical-deductive style of reasoning. The fine arts and the humanities foster conceptions of the past and future. They expand the repertoire of representational thought. According to Gardner's model of multiple intelligences discussed in Chapter 13, the visual arts provide a means of integrating spatial intelligence with interpersonal intelligence. Students who are actively engaged in the more complex and differentiated academic environment of high school can achieve substantial gains in conceptual skills (Kuhn et al., 1988; Linn et al., 1989; Rabinowitz, 1988).

Although schooling may be a vehicle for formal operational reasoning, not all school experiences are equally effective in promoting abstract, hypothetical reasoning. Keating (1990) describes important characteristics for creating a cognitively stimulating school experience:

> Students need to be engaged with meaningful material; training of thinking skills must be embedded in a knowledge of subject matter, for acquisition of isolated content knowledge is likely to be unproductive; serious engagement with real problems has to occur in depth and over time; students need experiences that lead to placing a high value on critical thinking, to acquiring it as a disposition, not just as a skill; and many of these factors occur most readily, and perhaps exclusively, when students have the opportunity for real, ongoing discourse with teachers who have reasonably expert command of the material to be taught. (p. 77)

These key factors for stimulating abstract reasoning and critical thinking may not be present in many high school classrooms.

We do not expect an early adolescent to be a mature scientist or a profound philosopher. A young person's formal operational reasoning awaits encounters with a specific discipline and its full range of significant problems. However, the opportunity for cognitive growth during this period is extensive. Adolescents are capable of generating novel solutions and applying them to current life challenges. They are also able to be increasingly objective about the problem-solving process and to have insight into their own mental activity (see Notebook Page 15.3).

Formal Operational Reasoning

Imagine that you are developing programs for adolescents in schools or other out-of-school settings. Consider what kinds of activities or strategies you might use to promote formal operational reasoning. In particular, describe what you might do to foster the following skills:

Formal Operational Quality	Activities to Promote This Quality
1. Manipulate more than two variables at once:	
2. Think of things changing in the future:	
3. Hypothesize about the logical sequence of events:	
4. Anticipate the possible consequences of actions:	
5. Detect logical inconsistencies:	
6. Think about themselves and their groups in a more relativistic way:	

Criticisms of the Concept of Formal Operations

In Piaget's theory of cognitive development, formal operational reasoning is viewed as the final stage in the development of logical thought. A number of scholars have pointed to limitations in this construction. First, questions have been raised about the extent to which there is a qualitative, stagelike consolidation in the use of formal reasoning. Many studies show that most adolescents and adults do not function at the formal operational level and that their use of formal reasoning is inconsistent across problem areas. For example, Neimark (1975) followed changes in the problem-solving strategies of adolescents over a 3½-year period. Even the oldest subjects in her study, who were 15, did not apply formal operational strategies across all problems. Although performance across problems was not consistent, there did appear to be a progression through levels of problem-solving approaches during the years from 11 to 15. Neimark (1982) described these levels as (1) no rule, (2) limited rules, (3) collection of rules or unelaborated principles, and (4) general principles. In general, research has not been able to confirm Piaget's claims that thinking becomes consistently more propositional across problem areas or that formal operational reasoning is a universal characteristic of adolescent reasoning (Keating, 1980).

A second criticism of formal reasoning as a construct is that it is not broad enough to encompass the many dimensions along which cognitive functioning matures. In the model of the developing mind presented in Chapter 13, there are at least two other domains in which growth takes place: the information processing system and the hypercognitive system. Increases in speed, efficiency, and capacity of information storage have been documented during the period from 11 to 14 (Thatcher et al., 1987). It is quite likely that improvements in logical reasoning are in part a result of being able to process greater quantities of information more quickly and efficiently. In addition to development in basic processing, there are gains in knowledge about a number of topics, both as a result of schooling and increased mastery in specific areas of expertise. One consequence of the combination of greater information-processing capacity and a broader knowledge base is that the hypercognitive processing improves. Adolescents can hold a problem in mind and approach it from several different angles, assessing which domain offers the most promising avenue for a solution (Keating, 1990).

Emotional Development

Descriptions of adolescence often refer to increased emotional variability, moodiness, and emotional outbursts. Adolescents clearly are more aware than younger children of gradations in their emotional states and are able to attribute emotions to a wider range of causes. However, some researchers have questioned whether adolescence really brings the peaks and valleys of emotional intensity that are stereotypically linked to this time of life.

Developmental Trends over the Course of Early Adolescence

In an attempt to assess the question about emotional peaks and valleys, researchers gave an electronic paging device to children and adolescents ages 9 to 15 and asked them to describe their emotional state each time they were paged (Larson & Lampman-Petraitis, 1989). Over one week, each participant responded about 37 times. The variability of emotions was not found to increase with age. However, both boys and girls in the older group expressed fewer extremely positive emotions and more mildly negative emotions than did children in the younger group. In a subsequent study using similar methods, daily emotions were monitored in relation to children's pubertal status (Richards & Larson, 1993). For both boys and girls, those with a more mature body shape at each age reported more frequent thoughts and feelings about love. Pubertal development was slightly related to increased feelings of anger for girls, but, in general, physical maturation was not closely linked to patterns of specific emotions for girls. For boys, the relationships between pubertal development and emotions were much stronger. Those boys who were more physically mature reported more frequent experiences of frustration, tension, and feeling "hyper." They also reported a generally more positive mood, greater ability to focus their attention, and greater feelings of strength in comparison with less physically mature boys. Thus, for boys, pubertal changes were associated with both positive moods and a restless irritability, a pattern that might be characterized as "peaks and valleys."

Adolescents are aware of a more differentiated palette of emotions. Among the more negative of these emotions are anxiety, shame, embarrassment, guilt, shyness, depression, and anger (Adelson & Doehrman, 1980). Adolescent girls are likely to have a heightened awareness of increased negative emotions that focus inward, such as shame, guilt, and depression; boys are likely to have a heightened awareness of increased negative emotions that focus on others, such as contempt and aggression (Ostro et al., 1989; Stapley & Haviland, 1989).

Given the likelihood of a more differentiated range of emotions during adolescence, a major task is accepting one's feelings and not interpreting them as a sign of "going crazy" or being "strange." In a study of the coping styles of adolescents, Moriarty and Toussieng (1976) described adolescents as either *sensers* or *censors*. The sensers were willing to be influenced by new experiences. They preferred to seek out new activities, engage people, and question inconsistencies. They accepted their emotions and sought out experiences that would modify their values. The censors preferred to limit their sensory experiences and to restrict themselves to situations that would not elicit intense emotional reactions. They tried to clarify their parents' values by discovering what was acceptable in society. They had limited peer interaction and were uninvolved with school. They rejected experiences or ideas that did not confirm their traditional views. Both sensers and censors are normal, healthy adolescents whose coping styles work in our society. However, the two orientations reflect distinctly different solutions to the challenge of integrating emotional experiences into the self-concept.

Many of the problems of early adolescence are linked to the expression, control, and overcontrol of emotions. Three topics considered here are eating disorders, delinquency, and depression.

Eating Disorders

One disorder that may be a consequence of anxiety and overcontrol of emotions is *anorexia nervosa* (Yates, 1989). Anorexia is found primarily among girls, and symptoms usually begin shortly after the weight spurt that accompanies puberty. Adolescents with this condition focus their behavior on weight loss. They take an obsessive, determined position in rejecting most foods. They may

Over 80 percent of American youth are involved in some form of delinquent behavior during the teen years. Which of these young people will be drawn into more serious criminal activity is difficult to predict.

experience intense eating binges, followed by prolonged avoidance of food. During the latter phase, they are continuously nauseous and have trouble holding down food. In addition, they tend to have a distorted perception of their body image, seeing themselves as much fatter than they really are. The outcome of this condition is a potentially life-threatening loss of weight.

Another, more common eating disorder in adolescence is *bulimia*, which involves binges of overeating followed by different strategies to prevent the absorption of food such as induced vomiting, the use of laxatives, or strenuous exercise. Bulimia has an incidence of between 5% and 18% of the adolescent population, and is experienced somewhat more evenly by males and females. Although both bulimia and anorexia are associated with serious health risks, anorexia fatalities are more likely to be from the complications of starvation (Millstein & Litt, 1990).

The origins of anorexia nervosa are not fully understood. Many authors implicate the cultural infatuation with thinness as a stimulus for this condition. In addition, the preoccupation with body appearance may be provoked by the relatively rapid physical changes associated with puberty. However, in addition to these factors, which are common to all adolescents, those who suffer from anorexia tend to have difficulty accepting and expressing their emotions. As compared with adolescents who have other types of emotional disorders, anorexics show less emotional expressivity, greater timidity, and more submissiveness. Anorexics have been described as "duty bound, rigidly disciplined, and moralistic with underlying doubts and anxious hesitancy" (Strober, 1981, 289–290).

Delinquency

In contrast to adolescents whose overcontrol of emotions can be problematic, others are impulsive and highly reactive to any emotionally arousing environmental stimulus. They seem to be unable to modify the intensity of their reactions. A consequence of this impulsiveness for a large proportion of normal adolescents is involvement in delinquent acts. "Over 80 percent of American adolescents admit to committing one or more delinquent acts, most of these minor, in the course of a few years of adolescence" (Gold & Petronio, 1980, 523). The inability to exert intellectual control over their impulses is a passing experience for most young people, since the fear and guilt that follow a delinquent act are usually sufficient punishment to prevent further violations.

For some adolescents, however, committing several delinquent acts weakens their ability to impose social constraints on such behavior, and the delinquency intensifies. One national survey categorized about 30% of males and 10% of females as serious violent offenders. These adolescents had committed three or more violent crimes in a one-year period sometime before their 18th birthday. Boys commit more crimes than girls, and their crimes tend to be more serious (Blumenstein et al., 1986; Elliott et al., 1989; McCord, 1990). In 1992, roughly 16% of the total arrests in the United States involved people ages 15 to 18, but this age group accounted for 29% of the serious crimes such as motor vehicle thefts, arson, burglary, and murder (U.S. Bureau of the Census, 1994).

Since so many young people now carry some type of weapon, especially knives and guns, one wonders about the emotional correlates of this type of behavior. Are children who carry weapons primarily motivated by self-defense, or are the weapons an extension of their aggressive motives? In one study, teens who carried guns were found to differ from those who carried knives (Webster et al., 1993). For females, the more victims of violence that the female knew, the more likely she was to carry a knife. Too few females carried guns to identify predictors for that group. For males, two strong predictors for carrying a knife were having been threatened with a knife and frequently being involved in fights that they did not initiate. Correlates of carrying a gun included having been arrested before, being involved in and being an instigator of many fights, and believing that shooting people is justifiable under certain circumstances. In this research, gun-carrying was linked with a much more violent, aggressive orientation that could not really be construed as a strategy for self-protection.

Depression

Depression has received considerable attention in the recent literature (Garrison et al., 1989; Robertson & Simons, 1989). The word *depression* is used in at least three different contexts: depressed mood, depressive syndrome, and a clinical diagnosis of major depressive disorder (Petersen et al., 1993). *Depressed mood* refers to feelings of sadness, a loss of hope, a sense of being overwhelmed by the demands of the world, and general unhappiness. Almost everyone experiences this kind of depression at one time or another. People may refer to it as the "blues," feeling "down in the dumps," or feeling "low." People who are experiencing a depressed mood may have other symptoms including worrying, moodiness, crying, loss of appetite, difficulty sleeping, tiredness, loss of interest or enjoyment in activities, and difficulty concentrating. Depressed mood can range from mild, short-lived periods of feeling sad and discouraged to severe feelings of guilt and worthlessness. Depressed mood can be predictive of more serious emotional disorders, but it is not in itself a clinical diagnosis. One estimate is that about 35% of adolescents (a higher percentage of girls) had experienced a depressed mood in the previous six months.

A *depressive syndrome* refers to a constellation of behaviors and emotions that occur together, including depression and anxiety. It usually includes complaints about feeling depressed, anxious, fearful, worried, guilty, and worthless. Roughly 5% of the normal population experiences this syndrome.

The third use of the concept of depression is its central role in clinical diagnosis. An adolescent diagnosed with *major depressive disorder* will have experienced five or more of the following symptoms for at least two weeks:

> depressed mood or irritable mood most of the day; decreased interest in plea-
> surable activities; changes in weight or perhaps failure to make necessary weight
> gains in adolescence; sleep problems; psychomotor agitation or retardation;
> fatigue or loss of energy; feelings of worthlessness or abnormal amounts of guilt;
> reduced concentration and decision-making ability; and repeated suicidal idea-
> tion, attempts, or plans of suicide. (Petersen et al., 1993, 156)

Depression is of special concern during early adolescence for several rea-
sons (Brooks-Gunn & Petersen, 1991; Maag et al., 1988). First, it is associated with adolescent suicide. Although depression is not always a precursor to suicide, there is some link between depression and suicidal thoughts. Second, depression is linked to alcohol and drug abuse. Adolescents who are strug-
gling with strong feelings of depression may turn to alcohol or other drugs as a way of trying to alleviate or escape from these feelings. Third, depressed adolescents may be unable to participate effectively in the classroom, so their academic performance deteriorates. Finally, depression during adolescence may be a forerunner of severe depression later in adulthood.

Factors Associated with Depression in Adolescence

A number of challenges that adolescents face make them vulnerable to depression. At present, no single theory is accepted as the explanation for depression. Certain factors appear to increase the likelihood of depression, while others seem to buffer adolescents from these feelings. Some research points to genetic factors associated with the clinical diagnosis of depression. However, thinking back to the research on the interaction between depressed mothers and their infants that was discussed in Chapter 7, it is hard to separate genetic and environmental factors in the etiology of clinical depression.

Experiences of parental loss or parental rejection have been found to increase an adolescent's vulnerability to depression (Robertson & Simons, 1989). In one longitudinal study of the consequences of economic pressures on families, a relationship was found between the family's economic stresses and increased parental depression, which in turn produced heightened marital conflict, increased hostility, and less nurturance toward children. Subse-
quent adjustment problems were observed in adolescent daughters, especially hostility and depression (Conger et al., 1993).

In addition, adolescence is a time of life when one is likely to encounter loss, failure, and rejection, as well as accumulated negative events and hassles. Even though we no longer view adolescence as a unique period of emo-
tional turmoil, it is clear that adolescents are exposed to more negative events than are younger children. This may be due in part to the fact that they are more aware of what other people are experiencing. In part, more is expected of adolescents, and so they have more to worry about. And, of course, adolescents have a wider circle of relationships through which they are exposed to more problems, expectations, and disappointments. Adolescents report experiencing problems in the following domains: social alienation (disagree-

ments with teachers, disliking other students); excessive demands (not enough time to meet responsibilities or to sleep); romantic concerns (dissatisfaction about a romantic relationship); decisions about the future (important decisions about a future career); loneliness and unpopularity (being excluded); assorted annoyances and concerns (money problems, disagreement with a boy/girlfriend); social mistreatment (being taken advantage of or betrayed); and academic challenge (struggling to meet other people's standards of performance at school) (Kohn & Milrose, 1993). Adolescents who begin to identify themselves as having a homosexual orientation may be vulnerable to depression, especially if they perceive this orientation to be highly stigmatized in their community. Peer rejection and social isolation place adolescents at risk for depression (Petersen et al., 1991).

Adolescents are relatively inexperienced at coping with these kinds of stressors. They may not have developed strategies for controlling or reducing the feelings of grief or discouragement that are likely to accompany stressful life events. The combination of pressures on parents, especially marital conflicts and economic pressures, plus the adolescent's exposure to failures, disappointments, and loss of relationships with peers and in school, are clearly linked to negative mood, especially sadness and depression (Larson & Ham, 1993). Feelings of depression may also be intensified by accompanying hormonal changes (Susman et al., 1991). Young people may become convinced of their worthlessness, and this distortion of thought may lead them toward social withdrawal or self-destructive actions.

Gender Differences in Vulnerability to Depression

Experiences of depression appear to be more common for adolescent girls than boys. This gender difference has been found when comparing Anglo, African-American, Mexican, and other Hispanic adolescents (Roberts & Sobhan, 1992). In addition, Mexican-American adolescents appear to have a higher incidence of depression than Anglos, African-Americans, or other Hispanic ethnic groups. Evidence of greater risk for depression among females continues to be found in studies of adults (Jones-Webb & Snowden, 1993).

Although prepubescent boys are somewhat more likely to show signs of depression than prepubescent girls, this pattern reverses during adolescence (Nolen-Hoeksema et al., 1991; Petersen et al., 1991). Several theories have been offered to explain this reversal:

- At puberty, girls become especially critical of their bodies, with a particular concern about being overweight and unattractive. This may lead to prolonged feelings of dissatisfaction with the self and subsequent depression.

- Girls tend to look for internal explanations for their failures, blaming problems on their own lack of ability, whereas boys tend to focus on factors outside the self, blaming other people or unfair conditions for their failures.

- Although girls tend to receive strong social support from parents and friends, they are also somewhat more sensitive to the problems that people in their support network are having. Girls who have higher levels of caring and who are likely to get involved in the problems of their close friends are more vulnerable to depression (Gore et al., 1993). The negative experiences that a girl's best friend or members of her friendship group are going through tend to add to her own negative mood.

- Girls tend to persist in trying to account for negative events or to explain them, allowing these events to continue to disturb them. Boys tend to distract themselves with other thoughts or just "put problems out of their mind" (Nolen-Hoeksema, 1987).

- In adolescence, girls begin to experience numerous microaggressions spawned by sexist views of teachers, male peers, and even parents. These negative messages create a worldview in which the adolescent girl is less important, less competent, and less entitled to her own independent ideas than her male peers. The result is increased feelings of insecurity, lack of confidence, and feelings of worthlessness.

Membership in the Peer Group

In discussing the developmental tasks of earlier stages in Chapters 9, 11, and 13, we pointed out the importance of peer interaction for psychological development. Clearly, the capacity to interact effectively with age-mates and to find satisfaction in companionship and closeness with friends provide support for psychosocial development and adaptation throughout life. During early adolescence, peer relations take on a new importance, energized by heightened emotional intensity, a new sensitivity to peer approval, and a new level of structure and social organization within the peer group itself (Newman, 1982). The implications of the individual's relation to the peer group become more clearly defined. Before the adolescent period, it is important to have friends but not so important to be a member of a definable group. A child's friends are often found in the neighborhood, local clubs and sports teams, community centers, or classrooms. Friendship groups are homogeneous. They are the product of informal associations, residential area, and convenience. In early adolescence, young people spend more time away from home; thus, friendships become an increasingly important source of social support, and the quality of these friendships changes (Levitt et al., 1993).

Adolescent friendships provide opportunities for emotional intimacy, support, and understanding, as well as companionship and fun. Talking with friends, either in person or on the telephone, becomes a dominant daily activity, especially for girls (Raffaelli & Duckett, 1989). Early adolescents have the cognitive skills to consider the needs and feelings of others. The qualities of self-disclosure and intimate knowledge of the other become more central to the formation and maintenance of adolescent friendships (Berndt, 1982; Tedesco & Gaier, 1988). Friendships become more intimate and more selective than they were during middle childhood. One adolescent boy described the end of a friendship as follows: "[My friend] is trying to single out his friends now. At the beginning of the year, he was friends with almost everybody because he wanted to be friends over the school year with a lot of kids. Now he's singling out best friends" (Berndt & Hoyle, 1985, 1013).

Cliques and Crowds

In addition to changes in friendships and in the quality and functions associated with close friends, new layers of peer relationships, sometimes known as the clique and the crowd, begin to take shape. *Cliques* are small friendship groups of five to ten friends. Usually these groups provide the framework for frequent interactions both within school and in neighborhoods. Adolescents usually do not refer to their group of friends as a clique, but the term is used to connote a certain "tightness" among the members. These kids hang out together, know about each others' families, plan activities together, and stay in touch with each other from day to day. In the transition from middle school to the larger, more heterogeneous environment of high school, there is a reordering of students according to a variety of abilities and a corresponding reordering of friendship groups. It may take some time for adolescents to find their clique, and the members of this group may change from time to time over the first year or two of high school.

The concept of a *crowd* refers to a large group that is usually recognized by a few predominant characteristics, such as their orientation toward academics, involvement in athletics, use of drugs, or involvement in deviant behavior. When the "leading crowd" of a particular neighborhood elementary or middle school enters a more centralized high school, the members of that group find that they are, to some degree, competing with the leading crowds of the other neighborhood schools from which the high school draws its students. After some contact at the high school, the several "leading crowds" are reordered into a single "leading crowd." Some students find that their social positions have been maintained or enhanced, whereas others find that they have been demoted as a result of a reevaluation of their abilities, skills, or traits.

Popularity and acceptance into a peer group in high school may be based on one or more of the following characteristics: good looks, athletic ability, social class, academic performance, future goals, affiliation with a religious, racial, or ethnic group, sexual orientation, special talents, involvement with drugs or deviant behavior, or general alienation from school. Although the criteria for membership may not be publicly articulated, groups tend to include or exclude members according to consistent standards. Physical attractiveness continues to be a powerful force in determining popularity. Especially for very attractive and unattractive adolescents, physical appearance may be a primary determinant of social acceptance or rejection (Cavior & Dokecki, 1973; Musa & Roach, 1973).

Some of the well-known crowds present in American high schools today are commonly referred to as populars, gangsters or hoods, punkers, jocks, druggies, and nerds. A new group, called the mods or the progressives, expressly rejects this traditional social stratification. The progressives emphasize individuality and the value of forming a personal identity. In setting themselves apart from other groups, however, they form a distinct group themselves (Stevenson et al., 1987). In racially diverse schools, it is not uncommon for students to identify peer groups based specifically on ethnic categories, such as the Asian group, the Mexicans, and the African-Americans. Each of the crowds can be identified within a school setting by their dress, their language, the activities in which they participate, and the school settings in which they are most likely to congregate.

In one analysis of over 3,000 students in grades 9 through 12, drawn from nine high schools in two different states, nine crowd types were identified with a high degree of regularity across the schools. These crowds were labeled by the students as jocks, populars, popular-nice, average-normal, brains, partyers, druggies, loners, and nerds (Durbin et al., 1993). Although many adolescents resist being labeled as part of one crowd or another, they

BOX 15.2

Interracial Friendships Among High School Students

One of the anticipated outcomes of the movement to desegregate America's schools was that children would form interracial friendships through opportunities for daily cross-race interactions and thereby reduce the level of racism in society. To what extent are interracial friendships being formed during the high school years?

Drawing on a national sample of over 58,000 sophomores and seniors at more than 1,000 public and private high schools in the United States, researchers attempted to address this question (Hallinan & Williams, 1989). They considered the possible dyadic (two-person) groups that could be formed among students and then asked whether a friendship existed in these dyads. In other words, of all the two-person groups in a school, how many are friendships in which person A says that person B is a friend? The results showed that cross-race friendships were quite rare. When all factors are taken into account, such as

school size and the proportion of African-American students in a school, same-race friendships were six times more likely than cross-race friendships. However, cross-race friendships were more likely to be reciprocated than same-race friendships. If student A named someone of another race as a friend, that person was very likely to name student A as a friend as well.

The results of this analysis are disappointing. Of more than 18,000 friendships identified by students, only about 350 involved friends of different races. There was no relationship between the proportion of African-American students in a school and the likelihood of identifying interracial friendships. The data suggest that merely bringing adolescents of different races together in the same school does not lead to high levels of interracial friendship. This kind of outcome probably requires additional structural or curricular intervention.

usually recognize that these categories of students exist in their school (Brown, 1990). These crowds appear to reflect prototypical identities, each with its distinct profile with respect to school grades, use of alcohol and drugs, performing delinquent acts, involvement in fights and carrying weapons to school, and perceptions about involvement in the social life at school. Thus, the youth culture, as it is sometimes called, is actually composed of a number of subcultures, each endorsing somewhat different attitudes about adults and other authority figures, school and academic goals, drugs and deviant behavior, partying, and social life (Brown et al., 1993).

Individual adolescents are faced with a variety of choices for peer-group membership. Upon entering high school, adolescents establish a reputation based on how they act, what they seem interested in, and what their friends and acquaintances say about them. They come in contact with a number of people who may offer their friendship. This is the informal route to membership in a peer group. The adolescent learns to look beyond the initial offer of friendship and to assess the group from which the potential friend comes. The person may decide to accept the friendship or reject it on the basis of the potential friend's peer-group reputation (see Box 15.2). While some adolescents accept one of the crowd categories as their appropriate group, others claim that they are friends with people from several different crowds, and still others do not believe that they are a part of any crowd. These adolescents may have a small group of friends with whom they interact, but they reject identifying with any of the stereotypical groups that exist in their school.

Peer groups have boundaries. Membership in cliques is relatively stable but is always vulnerable to change. One description suggests that these groups have some very central members who serve a leadership role, others who are regularly included in the activities of the clique, and others at the periphery. At the same time, there are "wannabe's" who would like to be part of the clique but for one reason or another are never fully included (Hansell, 1985). Some students try to push their way into a certain group; others may fall out of a group. Dating someone who is a member of the clique or getting involved in a school activity (such as athletics or choir) may be a way of moving into a new peer group. What is more likely is that, through gossip, refusal to adhere to group norms, or failure of a romantic relationship, individuals slip outside the boundaries of their cliques. Changing one's crowd identity may be even more difficult than changing from one clique to another. When the school population is relatively stable, it is very difficult to lose a reputational identity that has already been established (Jones, 1976) (see Notebook Page 15.4).

New Learning Linked to Peer-Group Membership

We hypothesize that adolescents learn through becoming a member of a peer group to assess group structure and norms and select the particular group or groups with which they would like to affiliate. For adolescents, the structure may include patterns of dominance, dating, and relationships with others outside the group. Associated with these patterns are norms or expectations for the behavior of the peer-group members. As adolescents discover their positions in the social hierarchy of the group, they learn how they may advance within it and what behaviors are expected of members at various levels. On the basis of all this information, they must decide whether their personal growth is compatible with the peer-group affiliation they have made. There is some evidence that being a member of a supportive peer group is linked to well-being. The peer group serves as a source of social support and helps to buffer members from stress. As time goes on, however, many 11th- and 12th-graders are likely to perceive the close connections with a single clique as less important or central to their social life. Close dyadic friendships and love relationships begin to play a greater role, and, especially for girls, the time and energy that used to be focused toward preserving the friendship group is redirected to these more intimate relationships (Smith, 1987).

Sexual Relationships

During adolescence, peer relationships are modified by new sexual interests and behavior. The impetus for this increased interest in sexual relationships stems from social expectations as well as sexual maturation and related desires for romance and physical intimacy. In many cultures, the act of first intercourse is a significant marker of the transition from adolescence to adulthood. In our own society, the norms for engaging in sexual activity differ by ethnic group and gender. In general, sexual activity has been disengaged from marriage and childbearing. Most adolescents and adults do not believe that sex ought to be reserved for married couples, but in some subcultures this is still held as the ideal. And although males and females are becoming more alike in their patterns of sexual activity, most subcultures continue to endorse a pattern that promotes earlier entry into sexual activity for males and more constraints on sexual activity for females.

Peer-Group Membership

Characterize your clique or small friendship group from your high school years.

1. What activities, interests, and out-of-school behaviors did you and your friends share?

_____

_____

_____

_____

2. What were the crowds in your high school? How could these crowds be identified (for example, by dress, activities, academic track, race)? Which crowd best characterized your clique or friendship group?

_____

_____

_____

_____

3. What memories stand out about peer-group membership from your high school years? Why are these memories so significant to you?

_____

_____

_____

_____

4. What lasting lessons of life do you think you may have learned from your peer-group experiences during high school?

_____

_____

_____

Sexuality adds a new dimension, both pleasurable and troubling, to adolescent peer relationships.

The sexual transition can take place in very different contexts for adolescents. It can be a planned event, or an unplanned impulse, often combined with alcohol or drug use. It can be viewed as a marker of independence or as an act of rebellion and defiance against the family. It can take place in the context of an ongoing close relationship or as part of a casual encounter.

Usually, the earlier the entry into sexual activity and intercourse, the more likely the act is to be part of a profile of high-risk behaviors, including alcohol use, drug use, and delinquent activity. The later the entry, the more likely it is to be seen as a marker of the transition into adulthood or as a planned aspect of deepening commitment in an ongoing relationship (Flannery et al., 1993; Ketterlinus et al., 1992). Michael Storms (1981) has suggested that children who experience sexual maturation at a young age (around 11 or 12) are more likely to have erotic feelings toward children of the same sex, since peer groups are more sex-segregated during middle childhood. Retrospective studies find that gay men and lesbians recall an earlier age of sexual awareness than do heterosexuals. The results of this kind of research are subject to the same criticisms as other types of retrospective studies, in that the recollections may be inaccurate or subject to revision based on subsequent events (Turner & Rubinson, 1993).

The Transition to Coitus

Dating relationships during early adolescence provide the typical context for sexual activity. Pubertal changes may increase a young person's interest in sexual ideation, but the timing of dating per se depends heavily on the norms of the peer group and the community (Garguilo et al., 1987). One of the strongest predictors of early sexual activity is early age of dating. Adolescents who "go steady" with one partner are much more likely to be sexually active than are those who do not (Hanson et al., 1987).

In the United States, the historical trend has been toward earlier involvement in sexual intercourse for both boys and girls and greater sexual activity among girls, with racial and social-class differences in earlier age at first intercourse narrowing from the 1970s to the 1990s (Voydanoff & Donnelly, 1990). Current estimates suggest that about 80% of Anglo and African-American females and 85% of Anglo and 96% of African-American males have had sexual relations at least once by age 19 (Katchadourian, 1990; Moore & Peterson, 1989; Sonenstein et al., 1989). Research has found that the transition to sexual intercourse is strongly predicted by hormonal levels and physical maturation for boys but is more strongly linked to psychosocial factors for girls (see Box 5.1 in Chapter 5).

One of the clearest cultural influences on adolescent sexual behavior is religious participation. Adolescents who attend religious services frequently and who value religion as an important aspect of their lives have less permissive attitudes toward premarital sex. This finding applies equally to Catholic, Protestant, and Jewish young people. The relationship is accentuated for adolescents who describe themselves as fundamentalist Protestant or Baptist. However, an adolescent's attitudes toward premarital sex are shaped by many factors in addition to their religious socialization. By the time young people are making independent decisions about religious participation, they also have opinions about whether or not they believe in premarital sex. Thus, those young people who have more permissive views about sex may also be less likely to attend religious services and find less satisfaction in religious participation (Thornton & Camburn, 1989).

Any data regarding entry into sexual activity and age at first intercourse must be interpreted with caution. First, data reported by race/ethnicity are often compounded by social class. Second, the differences between rural and urban communities are often ignored in the analyses. Third, the reporting is retrospective (asking adolescents to think back to when they first engaged in sexual activities) and is consequently vulnerable to inconsistencies and memory errors (Alexander et al., 1993). Especially at early ages, it is possible that some children overestimate their sexual activity in order to appear "cool" and that others underestimate their sexual activity in order to disguise what might be considered unacceptable behavior.

Of course, sexual relationships do not necessarily involve intercourse. Many levels of sexual activity—from autoerotic sexual fantasies, masturbation, and erotic responses to sexual stimuli, to dyadic behaviors that may include handholding, kissing and hugging, and heavy petting—are involved in becoming a sexually active adult. Furthermore, initial experiences with sexual intercourse do not necessarily result in a pattern of frequent sexual activity. For example, boys who experience an early-pubertal sexual initiation may not have another sexual experience for a year or more (Brooks-Gunn & Furstenberg, 1989).

Orientation Toward Sexuality

Most young people experience sexual arousal and are involved in some form of romantic relationships during adolescence (Levesque, 1993). Some early adolescents are sexually permissive and are regularly active in sex play—from petting to intercourse. Other early adolescents are much less active sexually. Some may remain relatively uninterested in sexual relationships; others think about sexual relationships a good deal. The way that one thinks about sexual relationships can vary. Some early adolescents become preoccupied with thoughts of very romantic relationships. Some are infatuated with rock stars, athletes, movie stars, or other sex symbols. Others manifest rather perverse obsessions with sexual material. Whatever the resulting adult sexual orientation, it can be assumed that the early-adolescent awakenings are representative of a system that is just being started up and tested out. As a result of sexual experiences, adolescents begin to think of themselves as sexual, develop a scheme for sexual behavior, and formulate ideas about features that they find sexually attractive.

Dating patterns that have been characterized as "monogamous" (dating one person at a time, going from one serious relationship to another even if it only lasts a week or two) or as "sexual adventuring" (having multiple, sexual relationships at the same time, none at any great level of intensity) are formulated during this period of life, as are components of both gender identity and sexual orientation.

Sexual orientation refers to one's preference for partners in sexual and affectional relationships. Some people are attracted to partners of the opposite sex (heterosexuals), some to partners of the same sex (homosexuals), and some to members of both sexes (bisexuals). Although one might assume that one's sexual orientation as heterosexual, homosexual, or bisexual begins to take shape in early adolescence, the research literature on this point is sparse. Many adolescents report some kind of homosexual experience such as arousal at the sight of a member of the same sex or a transient infatuation with a same-sex peer. Adult homosexuals often recall the beginnings of their sexual orientation as taking shape in adolescence, but exactly how early-adolescent sexual encounters contribute to the formation of a homosexual orientation is not well understood.

The paths to a gay sexual identity vary widely. In one study of a volunteer sample of 77 gay males, most recalled having an awareness of gay feelings as early as middle school or early adolescence, but they did not label themselves as gay until later adolescence (D'Augelli, 1991). The majority (75%) knew they were gay *before* their first sexual experience. And once they had labeled themselves as gay, they waited an average of eight years to disclose this to someone else. According to Richard Troiden (1988), as children move into adolescence, the sense of being different from their peers is combined with a realization that they are sexually attracted to members of the same sex. They may not know for sure whether this sexual orientation is permanent, and they may not be ready to openly claim a homosexual orientation, but they know that they are not going to embrace heterosexuality as the natural, unconflicted direction of development that they observe in most of their peers.

Reports of adolescents who are openly gay suggest that this is an extremely stressful realization, one that is commonly accompanied by negative reactions from parents and friends and open acts of hostility from school peers (Remafedi, 1987). Anticipating the strong social censure attached to an unconventional sexual orientation, adolescents are likely to deny it or try to function as a heterosexual during this period of life.

Problems and Conflicts Associated with Sexuality

The sexual system is one of the most problematic components of psychosocial development for young people in the United States. Most parents feel uncomfortable discussing sexuality with their children. In addition to private thoughts, impulses, and fantasies which may result in feelings of guilt or confusion, young people confront conflicting messages about sexual behavior from peers, the mass media, and the religious community. Risks of sexually transmitted diseases, especially AIDS, introduce anxiety about expressing sexual impulses. In a sample of over 1,000 students from 13 urban and rural California high schools, only 20% of the students thought that they had some chance of getting AIDS. However, among those who claimed to be sexually active, 60% had actively tried to avoid exposure to AIDS, most commonly using a condom or having their boyfriend use a condom and having fewer sexual partners (Leland & Barth, 1993). The threat of exposure to AIDS is clearly having an impact on how young people think about sexual activity and its associated risks.

Young people see numerous examples of sexual intimacy on television and in films, suggesting that sexual gratification ought to be more immediate and more satisfying than it is likely to be in real life. The emotional closeness and understanding that they may seek in a sexually intimate relationship are often elusive. Furthermore, many adolescents, especially females, are exposed to unwanted sexual activity. In a sample of 7th-, 9th-, and 11th-grade girls, 21% reported unwanted sexual contact, ranging from unwanted touching and fondling to unwanted or forced intercourse (Small & Kerns, 1993). In many instances, unwanted sexual intercourse occurred on the first date or in a dating relationship. This pattern illustrates the problematic nature of sexual contact in early adolescence. The boundaries around acceptable sexual contact are unclear, the sexual agenda for males and females is likely to be very different, and other risk-taking behaviors such as alcohol and drug use can foster an unwanted sexual encounter.

In an effort to learn more about adolescents' reactions following their involvement in sexual intercourse, Australian researchers surveyed students in secondary schools in seven of the eight Australian states and territories (Donald et al., 1995). Students were asked about the context of their most recent sexual experience and how they felt about it. The majority of males and females said they felt good about their most recent sexual experience, with older students (16 and 17) more likely to be positive about it than younger students (15 and under). For girls, five factors were significantly associated with feeling good about their most recent sexual experience: believing that there was a low risk for contracting a sexually transmitted disease; having a "steady" relationship with the partner; having talked with their partner about avoiding pregnancy; having talked with their partner about ways of having sexual pleasure without having intercourse; and not being drunk or high. For boys, two factors were significantly associated with feeling good about their most recent sexual experience: having sex with a "steady" partner and not being drunk or high. Larger percentages of girls than boys were likely to say they felt used or bad after their most recent sexual experience, and younger girls were more likely than older girls to say they felt bad or used. About equal percentages of girls and boys said they felt guilty after their most recent sexual experience. Generally, girls in this sample were more vulnerable to negative emotional reactions to their recent sexual experience, and these negative reactions were associated with having sex with someone who was not a steady partner and with being drunk or high when they had sex.

The lack of both supervision and frank conversation about sexuality with caring adults can place adolescents at risk for early sexual experiences that are negative or abusive. The sex-linked problems that many people encounter—unintended pregnancy, marital infidelity, rape and other forms of unwanted sexual contact, child sexual abuse, pornography, sexually transmitted diseases—are evidence that socialization by parents, teachers, and religious leaders is failing to promote mature sexuality in significant numbers of adolescents and adults in the United States.

Chapter Summary

1. Early adolescence is marked by the rapid physical changes of puberty, including a height spurt, increases in weight and muscle strength, maturation of the reproductive system, appearance of secondary sex characteristics, and changes in body shape.

2. The timing and pattern of physical changes vary widely and are different for males and females. Both boys and girls experience some awkwardness and self-consciousness associated with physical maturation.

3. As a result of modern improvements in hygiene, nutrition, and health care, children enter puberty earlier today than they did in the first half of the century.

4. Psychosocial consequences are associated with early and late maturing. For boys, early maturing is generally linked to increased responsibility, leadership, and self-esteem. For girls, early maturing is more stressful and may be linked with more conflict with parents, poorer school performance, and early entry into dating.

5. The impact of physical development depends in part on the associated social meaning and the reactions of parents, peers, and other community adults.

6. Piaget suggested that a qualitatively new approach to reasoning emerges in early adolescence, which he referred to as formal operational reasoning. This kind of thinking is more abstract, hypothetical, and flexible. It permits one to use thought to manipulate, modify, and reason about one's thoughts.

7. In adolescence, egocentrism reflects a young person's certainty that his or her reasoning is universally correct. Adolescents also tend to be preoccupied by a sense that their thoughts are unique and that everyone is monitoring and judging them.

8. Factors that promote formal operational reasoning include involvement in multiple roles, membership in a heterogeneous peer group, and participation in an academic curriculum that encourages discourse and critical thinking.

9. The notion of a stage of formal operational thought has been criticized on several counts. First, most adolescents and adults do not use formal operational reasoning consistently across problem areas. Second, it does not encompass the many dimensions along which cognitive functioning is expanding during adolescence.

10. Emotional development in adolescence appears to be characterized by an increase in negative moods and a decrease in extremely positive emotions. Physical maturation is also linked to a preoccupation with

love. For boys, physical development tends to be linked with heightened feelings of frustration, tension, and restlessness on the one hand, and a new sense of focus and strength on the other.

11. Three areas of adolescent emotional distress suggest difficulties in managing or expressing emotions: eating disorders, delinquency, and depression. Girls appear to experience more difficulties with eating disorders and depression, whereas boys participate in more serious delinquent acts.

12. Peer relations take on new importance in early adolescence, and the peer group achieves greater structure and social organization.

13. The peer structure has been described in terms of cliques (small groups of five to ten friends) and crowds (prototypes of large groups of adolescents in a high school). Cliques serve functions of intimacy, shared activity, and emotional support. Crowds are more relevant to social reputation and a sense of social identity within the high school.

14. Sexual relationships in adolescence emerge as a result of both physical maturation and social expectations. Early sexual intercourse tends to be associated with other high-risk behaviors.

15. The transition to sexual intercourse is associated with biological factors, new desires for independence, socialization factors including norms and practices of family and friends, religious beliefs, personal aspirations and life goals, and physical attractiveness. Typically, biological factors are a strong predictor of entry into sexual activity for boys, whereas socialization and personal factors are stronger predictors of entry into sexual activity for girls.

16. Patterns show earlier entry into sexual activity in recent years for girls and boys, although methodological problems in reporting sexual activity raise questions about the validity of these data.

17. The formation of a sexual orientation probably begins in early adolescence as children experience arousal and attraction toward members of the same and the opposite sex. Most adults who have a homosexual orientation recall experiences in middle childhood and early adolescence that made them aware that they might not be heterosexual.

18. Adolescents are likely to experience conflict about sexual behavior. About one-fifth of teenage girls report unwanted sexual contact from peers, older men, or family members.

References

Acredolo, C., Adams, A. & Schmid, J. (1984). On the understanding of the relationships between speed, duration, and distance. *Child Development, 55,* 2151–2159.

Adejoke, A. A. (1993). The experience of spermarche (the age of onset of sperm emission) among selected boys in Nigeria. *Journal of Youth and Adolescence, 22,* 201–209.

Adelson, J. & Doehrman, M. J. (1980). The psychodynamic approach to adolescence. In J. Adelson (Ed.), *The handbook of adolescent psychology.* New York: John Wiley & Sons, 99–116.

Alexander, C. S., Somerfield, M. R., Ensminger, M. E., Johnson, K. E. & Kim, Y. J. (1993). Consistency of adolescents' self-report of sexual behavior in a longitudinal study. *Journal of Youth and Adolescence, 22,* 455–473.

Allison, M. (1992). The effects of neurologic injury on the maturing brain. *Headlines, October/November,* 2–6, 9–10.

Beauvoir, S. de (1959). *Memoirs of a dutiful daughter.* New York: World.

Benson, P. L. (1992). *The troubled journey: A profile of American youth.* Minneapolis: RespecTeen/ Lutheran Brotherhood.

Berndt, T. J. (1982). The features and effects of friendship in early adolescence. *Child Development, 53,* 1447–1460.

Berndt, T. J. & Hoyle, S. G. (1985). Stability and change in childhood and adolescent friendships. *Developmental Psychology, 21,* 1007–1015.

Blumstein, A., Cohen, J., Roth, J. A. & Visher, C. A. (1986). *Criminal careers and career criminals* (vol. 1). Washington, D.C.: National Academy Press.

Blyth, D. A., Bulcroft, R. & Simmons, R. G. (1981). The impact of puberty on adolescents: A longitudinal study. Los Angeles: Paper presented at the annual convention of the American Psychological Association.

Bolton, F. G., Jr. & MacEachron, A. E. (1988). Adolescent male sexuality: A developmental perspective. *Journal of Adolescent Research, 3,* 259–273.

Brooks-Gunn, J. & Furstenberg, F. F., Jr. (1989). Adolescent sexual behavior. *American Psychologist, 44,* 249–257.

Brooks-Gunn, J. & Petersen, A. C. (1991). Studying the emergence of depression and depressive symptoms during adolescence. *Journal of Youth and Adolescence, 20,* 115–120.

Brooks-Gunn, J. & Reiter, E. O. (1990). The role of pubertal processes. In S. S. Feldman & G. R. Elliott (Eds.), *At the threshold: The developing adolescent.* Cambridge, Mass.: Harvard University Press, 16–53.

Brooks-Gunn, J. & Warren, M. P. (1988). The psychological significance of secondary sexual characteristics in 9- to 11-year-old girls. *Child Development, 59,* 161–169.

Brown, B. B. (1990). Peer groups and peer cultures. In S. S. Feldman & G. R. Elliott (Eds.), *At the threshold: The developing adolescent.* Cambridge, Mass.: Harvard University Press, 171–196.

Brown, B. B., Mounts, N., Lamborn, S. D. & Steinberg, L. (1993). Parenting practices and peer group affiliation in adolescence. *Child Development, 64,* 467–482.

Bullough, V. L. (1981). Age at menarche: A misunderstanding. *Science, 213,* 365–366.

Carron, A. V. & Bailey, O. A. (1974). *Strength development in boys from 10 through 16 years.* Monographs of the society for Research in Child Development, 39 (4).

Caspi, A. & Moffitt, T. E. (1991). Individual differences are accentuated during periods of social change: The sample case of girls at puberty. *Journal of Personality and Social Psychology, 61,* 157–168.

Cavior, N. & Dokecki, P. R. (1973). Physical attractiveness, perceived attitude similarity, and academic achievement as contributors to interpersonal attractions among adolescents. *Developmental Psychology, 9,* 44–54.

Chandler, M. & Boyes, M. (1982). Social cognitive development. In B. B. Wolman (Ed.), *Handbook of developmental psychology.* Englewood Cliffs, N.J.: Prentice-Hall, 387–402.

Chapman, M. (1988). *Constructive evolution: Origin and development of Piaget's thought.* New York: Cambridge University Press.

Clausen, J. A. (1975). The social meaning of differential physical and sexual maturation. In S. E. Dragostin & G. H. Elder (Eds.), *Adolescence in the life cycle: Psychological change and social context.* Washington, D.C.: Hemisphere.

Conger, R. D., Conger, K. J., Elder, G. H., Lorenz, F. O., Simons, R. L. & Whitbeck, L. B. (1993). Family economic stress and adjustment of early adolescent girls. *Developmental Psychology, 29,* 206–219.

D'Augelli, A. R. (1991). Gay men in college: Identity processes and adaptation. *Journal of College Student Development, 32,* 140–146.

Demetriou, A. & Efklides, A. (1985). Structure and sequence of formal and postformal thought: General patterns and individual differences. *Child Development, 56,* 1062–1091.

Donald, M., Lucke, J., Dunne, M. & Raphael, B. (1995). Gender differences associated with young people's emotional reactions to sexual intercourse. *Journal of Youth and Adolescence, 24,* 453–464.

Dunham, R. M., Kidwell, J. S. & Portes, P. R. (1988). Effects of parent–adolescent interaction on the continuity of cognitive development from early childhood to early adolescence. *Journal of Early Adolescence, 8,* 297–310.

Dunphy, D. C. (1963). The social structure of urban adolescent peer groups. *Sociometry, 26,* 230–246.

Durbin, D. L., Darling, N., Steinberg, L. & Brown, B. B. (1993). Parenting style and peer group membership among European-American adolescents. *Journal of Research on Adolescence, 3,* 87–100.

Dwyer, J. & Mayer, J. (1971). Psychological effects of variations in physical appearance during adolescence. In R. E. Muuss (Ed.), *Adolescent behavior and society: A book of readings.* New York: Random House.

Eckstein, S. & Shemesh, M. (1992). The rate of acquisition of formal operational schemata in adolescence: A secondary analysis. *Journal of Research in Science Teaching, 29,* 441–451.

Elkind, D. (1967). Egocentrism in adolescence. *Child Development, 38,* 1025–1034.

Elliott, D. S., Huizinga, D. & Menard, S. (1989). *Multiple problem youth: Delinquency, substance use, and mental health problems.* New York: Springer-Verlag.

Evans, N., Gilpin, E., Farkas, A. J., Shenassa, E. & Pierce, J. P. (1995). Adolescents' perceptions of their peers' health norms. *American Journal of Public Health, 85,* 1064–1069.

Faust, M. S. (1977). *Somatic development of adolescent girls.* Monographs of the Society for Research in Child Development, 42 (1, serial no. 169).

Fischer, K. W. (1980). A theory of cognitive development: The control and construction of hierarchies of skills. *Psychological Review, 87,* 477–531.

Fischer, K. W., Bullock, D., Rotenberg, E. J. & Raya, P. (1993). The dynamics of competence: How context contributes directly to skill. In R. Wozniak & K. Fischer (Eds.), *Development in context: Acting and thinking in specific environments. JPS Series on Knowledge and Development* (vol. 1). Hillsdale, N.J.: Erlbaum, 93–117.

Flannery, D. J., Rowe, D. C. & Gulley, B. L. (1993). Impact of pubertal status, timing, and age on adolescent sexual experience and delinquency. *Journal of Adolescent Research, 8,* 21–40.

Flavell, J. H. (1963). *The developmental psychology of Jean Piaget.* Princeton, N.J.: Van Nostrand.

Gaddis, A. & Brooks-Gunn, J. (1985). The male experience of pubertal change. *Journal of Youth and Adolescence, 14,* 61–69.

Garguilo, J., Attie, I., Brooks-Gunn, J. & Warren, M. P. (1987). Dating in middle school girls: Effects of social context, maturation, and grade. *Developmental Psychology, 23,* 730–737.

Garrison, C. Z., Schluchter, M. D., Schoenbach, V. J. & Kaplan, B. K. (1989). Epidemiology of depressive symptoms in young adolescents. *Journal of the American Academy of Child and Adolescent Psychiatry, 28,* 343–351.

Gillies, P. (1989). A longitudinal study of the hopes and worries of adolescents. *Journal of Adolescence, 12,* 69–81.

Gold, M. & Petronio, R. J. (1980). Delinquent behavior in adolescence. In J. Adelson (Ed.), *Handbook of adolescent psychology.* New York: Wiley, 495–535.

Gore, S., Aseltine, R. H. & Colten, M. E. (1993). Gender, social-relational involvement, and depression. *Journal of Research on Adolescence, 3,* 101–126.

Hallinan, M. T. & Williams, R. A. (1989). Interracial friendship choices in secondary schools. *American Sociological Review, 54,* 67–78.

Hansell, S. (1985). Adolescent friendship networks and distress in school. *Social Forces, 63,* 698–715.

Hanson, S. L., Myers, D. R. & Ginsburg, A. L. (1987). The role of responsibility and knowledge in reducing teenage out-of-wedlock childbearing. *Journal of Marriage and the Family, 49,* 241–256.

Hill, J. P. (1988). Adapting to menarche: Familial control and conflict. In M. R. Gunnar & W. A. Collins (Eds.), *Development during the transition to adolescence.* Minnesota Symposium on Child Psychology (vol. 21). Hillsdale, N.J.: Erlbaum, 43–77.

Inhelder, B. & Piaget, J. (1958). *The growth of logical thinking from childhood to adolescence.* New York: Basic Books.

Johnston, L. D. (1995). Smoking rates climb among American teenagers, who find smoking increasingly acceptable and seriously underestimate the risks. *The University of Michigan: News and Information Services.* Ann Arbor, Mich., July 17.

Jones, S. S. (1976). High school status as a historical process. *Adolescence, 11,* 327–333.

Jones-Webb, R. J. & Snowden, L. R. (1993). Symptoms of depression among blacks and whites. *American Journal of Public Health, 83,* 240–244.

Katchadourian, H. (1990). Sexuality. In S. S. Feldman & G. R. Elliott (Eds.), *At the threshold: The developing adolescent.* Cambridge, Mass.: Harvard University Press, 330–351.

Keating, D. P. (1980). Thinking processes in adolescence. In J. Adelson (Ed.), *Handbook of adolescent psychology.* New York: John Wiley & Sons, 211–246.

Keating, D. P. (1990). Adolescent thinking. In S. S. Feldman & G. R. Elliott (Eds.), *At the threshold: The developing adolescent.* Cambridge, Mass.: Harvard University Press, 54–90.

Ketterlinus, R. D., Lamb, M. E., Nitz, K. & Elster, A. B. (1992). Adolescent nonsexual and sex-related problem behaviors. *Journal of Adolescent Research, 7,* 431–456.

Klineberg, S. L. (1967). Changes in outlook on the future between childhood and adolescence. *Journal of Personality and Social Psychology, 7,* 185–193.

Kohn, P. M. & Milrose, J. A. (1993). The inventory of high-school students' recent life experiences: A decontaminated measure of adolescents' life hassles. *Journal of Youth and Adolescence, 22,* 43–55.

Kornfield, S. (1990). Impact of parental marital status, gender, and pubertal development on adolescent. University of Georgia: unpublished manuscript.

Kuhn, D., Amsel, E. & O'Loughlin, M. (1988). *The development of scientific thinking skills.* New York: Academic Press.

Larson, R. & Ham, M. (1993). Stress and "storm and stress" in early adolescence: The relationship of negative events with dysphoric affect. *Developmental Psychology, 29,* 130–140.

Larson, R. & Lampman-Petraitis, C. (1989). Daily emotional states as reported by children and adolescents. *Child Development, 60,* 1250–1260.

Leland, N. L. & Barth, R. P. (1993). Characteristics of adolescents who have attempted to avoid HIV and who have communicated with parents about sex. *Journal of Adolescent Research, 8,* 58–77.

Lessing, E. E. (1972). Extension of personal future time perspective, age, and life satisfaction of children and adolescents. *Developmental Psychology, 6,* 457–468.

Levesque, R. P. (1993). The romantic experience of adolescents in satisfying love relationships. *Journal of Youth and Adolescence, 22,* 219–252.

Levitt, M. J., Guacci-Franco, N. & Levitt, J. L. (1993). Convoys of social support in childhood and early adolescence: Structure and function. *Developmental Psychology, 29,* 811–818.

Linn, M. C., Clement, C., Pulos, S. & Sullivan, P. (1989). Scientific reasoning during adolescence: The influence of instruction in science knowledge and reasoning strategies. *Journal of Research in Science Teaching, 26,* 171–187.

Logan, D. D. (1980). The menarche experience in 23 foreign countries. *Adolescence, 15,* 247–256.

Looft, W. R. (1971). Egocentrism and social interaction in adolescence. *Adolescence, 12,* 485–495.

Maag, J. W., Rutherford, R. B., Jr. & Parks, B. T. (1988). Secondary school professionals' ability to identify depression in adolescents. *Adolescence, 23,* 73–82.

Marsiglio, W. (1988). Adolescent male sexuality and heterosexual masculinity: A conceptual model and review. *Journal of Adolescent Research, 3,* 285–303.

Martin, S., Houseley, K., McCoy, H., Greenhouse, P., Stigger, F., Kenney, M. A., Shoffner, S., Fu, V., Korslund, M., Ercanli-Huffman, F. G., Carter, E., Chopin, L., Hegsted, M., Clark, A. J., Disney, G., Moak, S., Wakefield, T. & Stallings, S. (1988). Self-esteem of adolescent girls as related to weight. *Perceptual and Motor Skills, 67,* 879–884.

McCord, J. (1990). Problem behaviors. In S. S. Feldman & G. R. Elliott (Eds.), *At the threshold: The developing adolescent.* Cambridge, Mass.: Harvard University Press, 414–430.

Mendelson, B. K. & White, D. R. (1985). Development of self-body-esteem in overweight youngsters. *Developmental Psychology, 21,* 90–96.

Millstein, S. G. & Litt, I. F. (1990). Adolescent health. In S. S. Feldman & G. R. Elliott (Eds.), *At the threshold: The developing adolescent.* Cambridge, Mass.: Harvard University Press, 431–456.

Moore, K. & Peterson, J. (1989). *The consequences of teenage pregnancy: Final report.* Washington, D.C.: Child Trends.

Moriarty, A. E. & Toussieng, P. W. (1976). *Adolescent coping.* New York: Grune & Stratton.

Musa, K. E. & Roach, M. E. (1973). Adolescent appearance and self-concept. *Adolescence, 8,* 385–395.

Mussen, P. H. & Jones, M. C. (1957). Self-conceptions, motivations, and interpersonal attitudes of late and early maturing boys. *Child Development, 28,* 243–256.

Neimark, E. D. (1975). Longitudinal development of formal operations thought. *Genetic Psychology Monographs, 91,* 171–225.

Neimark, E. D. (1982). Adolescent thought: Transition to formal operations. In B. B. Wolman (Ed.), *Handbook of developmental psychology.* Englewood Cliffs, N.J.: Prentice-Hall, 486–499.

Newman, P. R. (1982). The peer group. In B. B. Wolman (Ed.), *Handbook of developmental psychology.* Englewood Cliffs, N.J.: Prentice-Hall, 526–535.

Newman, P. R. & Newman, B. M. (1976). Early adolescence and its conflict: Group identity versus alienation. *Adolescence, 11,* 261–274.

Nolen-Hoeksema, S. (1987). Sex differences in unipolar depression: Evidence and theory. *Psychological Bulletin, 101,* 259–282.

Nolen-Hoeksema, S., Girgus, J. S. & Seligman, M. E. P. (1991). Sex differences in depression and explanatory style in children. *Journal of Youth and Adolescence, 20,* 233–246.

Nurmi, J. (1987). Age, sex, social class, and quality of family interaction as determinants of adolescents' future orientation: A developmental task interpretation. *Adolescence, 22,* 977–991.

O'Mahoney, J. F. (1989). Development of thinking about things and people: Social and nonsocial cognition during adolescence. *Journal of Genetic Psychology, 150,* 217–224.

Ostrov, E., Offer, D. & Howard, K. I. (1989). Gender differences in adolescent symptomatology: A normative study. *Journal of the American Academy of Child and Adolescent Psychiatry, 28,* 394–398.

Petersen, A. C., Compas, B. E., Brooks-Gunn, J., Stemmler, M., Ey, S. & Grant, K. E. (1993). Depression in adolescence. *American Psychologist, 48,* 155–168.

Petersen, A. C., Sarigiani, P. A. & Kennedy, R. E. (1991). Adolescent depression: Why more girls? *Journal of Youth and Adolescence, 20,* 247–272.

Petersen, A. C., Schulenberg, J. E., Abramowitz, R. H., Offer, D. & Jarcho, H. D. (1984). A self-image questionnaire for young adolescents (SIQYA): Reliability and validity studies. *Journal of Youth and Adolescence, 13,* 93–111.

Piaget, J. (1926). *The language and thought of the child.* New York: Harcourt, Brace.

Piaget, J. (1970). Piaget's theory. In P. H. Mussen (Ed.), *Carmichael's manual of child psychology* (3rd ed., vol. 1). New York: Wiley.

Piaget, J. (1972). Intellectual evolution from adolescence to adulthood. *Human Development, 15,* 1–12.

Quadrel, M. J., Fischhoff, B. & Davis, W. (1993). Adolescent (in)vulnerability. *American Psychologist, 48,* 102–116.

Rabinowitz, M. (1988). On teaching cognitive strategies: The influence of accessibility of conceptual knowledge. *Contemporary Educational Psychology, 13,* 229–235.

Raffaelli, M. & Duckett, E. (1989). "We were just talking . . .": Conversations in early adolescence. *Journal of Youth and Adolescence, 18,* 567–582.

Rauste-von Wright, M. (1989). Body image satisfaction in adolescent girls and boys: A longitudinal study. *Journal of Youth and Adolescence, 18,* 71–83.

Remafedi, G. (1987). Adolescent sexuality: Psychosocial and medical implications. *Pediatrics, 79,* 326–330.

Richards, M. H. & Larson, R. (1993). Pubertal development and the daily subjective states of young adolescents. *Journal of Research on Adolescence, 3,* 145–169.

Roberts, R. E. & Sobhan, M. (1992). Symptoms of depression in adolescents: A comparison of Anglo, African, and Hispanic Americans. *Journal of Youth and Adolescence, 21,* 639–652.

Robertson, J. F. & Simons, R. L. (1989). Family factors, self-esteem, and adolescent depression. *Journal of Marriage and the Family, 51,* 125–138.

Schootman, M., Fuortes, L. J., Zwerling, C., Albanese, M. A. & Watson, C. A. (1993). Safety behavior among Iowa junior high and high school students. *American Journal of Public Health, 83,* 1628–1629.

Sells, C. W. & Blum, R. W. (1996). Morbidity and mortality among U.S. adolescents: An overview of data and trends. *American Journal of Public Health, 86,* 513–519.

Siegler, R. S., Liebert, D. E. & Liebert, R. M. (1973). Inhelder and Piaget's pendulum problem: Teaching preadolescents to act as scientists. *Developmental Psychology, 9,* 97–101.

Small, S. A. & Kerns, D. (1993). Unwanted sexual activity among peers during early and middle adolescence: Incidence and risk factors. *Journal of Marriage and the Family, 55,* 941–952.

Smith, D. M. (1987). Peers, subcultures, and schools. In D. Marsland (Ed.), *Education and youth.* London: Falmer Press, 41–64.

Sonenstein, F. L., Pleck, J. H. & Ku, L. C. (1989). Sexual activity, condom use, and AIDS awareness in a national sample of adolescent males. *Family Planning Perspectives, 21,* 152–158.

Stapley, J. C. & Haviland, J. M. (1989). Beyond depression: Gender differences in normal adolescents' emotional experiences. *Sex Roles, 20,* 295–308.

Stevenson, B. W., Roscoe, B., Brooks, R. H., II & Kelsey, T. (1987). Profiles of mod revivalists: A case study of a reemerging adolescent group. *Adolescence, 22,* 393–404.

Storms, M. D. (1981). A theory of erotic orientation development. *Psychological Review, 88,* 340–355.

Strober, M. (1981). A comparative analysis of personality organization in juvenile anorexia nervosa. *Journal of Youth and Adolescence, 10,* 285–295.

Susman, E. J., Dorn, L. D. & Chrousos, G. P. (1991). Negative hormones and affect levels in young adolescents: Concurrent and predictive perspectives. *Journal of Youth and Adolescence, 20,* 167–190.

Tanner, J. M. (1978/1990). *Fetus into man: Physical growth from conception to maturity.* Cambridge, Mass.: Harvard University Press.

Tanner, J. M. (1981). *A history of the study of human growth.* Cambridge, England: Cambridge University Press.

Tedesco, L. A. & Gaier, E. L. (1988). Friendship bonds in adolescence. *Adolescence, 23,* 127–136.

Thatcher, R. W., Walker, R. A. & Giudice, S. (1987). Human cerebral hemispheres develop at different rates and ages. *Science, 236,* 1110–1113.

Thornberry, O. T., Wilson, R. W. & Golden, P. (1986). Health promotion and disease prevention provisional data from the National Health Interview Survey: United States, January–June 1985. *Vital and Health Statistics of the National Center for Health Statistics, 119,* 1–16.

Thornton, A. & Camburn, D. (1989). Religious participation and adolescent sexual behavior. *Journal of Marriage and the Family, 51,* 641–654.

Troiden, R. R. (1988). *Gay and lesbian identity: A sociological analysis.* Dix Hills, N.Y.: General Hall.

Turner, J. S. & Rubinson, L. (1993). *Contemporary human sexuality.* Englewood Cliffs, N.J.: Prentice-Hall.

U.S. Bureau of the Census. (1994). *Statistical abstract of the United States, 1994* (114th ed.). Washington, D.C.: U.S. Government Printing Office.

Van Wieringen, J. C. (1978). Secular growth changes. In F. Falkner & J. M. Tanner (Eds.), *Human growth* (vol. 2). New York: Plenum, 445–473.

Voydanoff, P. & Donnelly, B. W. (1990). *Adolescent sexuality and pregnancy.* Newbury Park, Calif.: Sage.

Webster, D. W., Gainer, P. S. & Champion, H. R. (1993). Weapon carrying among inner-city junior high school students: Defensive behavior vs. aggressive delinquency. *American Journal of Public Health, 83,* 1604–1608.

Wierson, M., Long, P. J. & Forehand, R. L. (1993). Toward a new understanding of early menarche: The role of environmental stress in pubertal timing. *Adolescence, 28,* 912–924.

Wolf, A. M., Gortmaker, S. L., Cheung, L., Gray, H. M., Herzog, D. B. & Colditz, G. A. (1993). Activity, inactivity, and obesity: Racial, ethnic, and age differences among schoolgirls. *American Journal of Public Health, 83,* 1625–1627.

Yates, A. (1989). Current perspectives on the eating disorders: 1. History, psychological, and biological aspects. *Journal of the American Academy of Child and Adolescent Psychiatry, 28,* 813–828.

Expanding the Psychosocial Analysis of Early Adolescence

The Psychosocial Crisis of Early Adolescence
  Group Identity
  Alienation
The Central Process: Peer Pressure
  The Role of School Adults in Peer-Group Structuring
  Affiliating with a Peer Group
  Peer Pressure in Specific Areas
  Conformity and a Sense of Belonging
  Conflict, Tension, and Alienation
The Prime Adaptive Ego Quality and the Core Pathology
  Fidelity to Others
  Isolation
Significant Factors in the Development of Parents and Other Family Members
  Parents and Their Adolescent Children
    Interactions with Parents and Their Influences on an Adolescent's Well-Being
    Conflicts Between Parents and Adolescents
    Parents and Adolescents Learn One Another's Views
    The Impact of Parenting Practices on Adolescent Development
  Parents Caring for Their Aging Parents
Cultural and Ethnic Patterns That Create Distinctive Child-Rearing Environments
  Cultural Patterns of Rites of Passage
    The Functions of Puberty Rites
    Marking the Transition to Adulthood in the United States
  Ethnic-Group Identity
    The Salience of Ethnic Identity in Adolescence

Chapter 16

    The Development of Ethnic Identity from Early to Later Adolescence
Societal Issues That Provide Resources or Barriers to Development
  Parenthood in Early Adolescence
    Contraception
    Consequences of Teenage Pregnancy
    Adolescent Fathers
  Adolescent Alcohol and Drug Use and Abuse
    Effects of Alcohol on the Body
    Factors Associated with Alcohol Use
    Factors Linked with Early Entry into Alcohol and Drug Use
  Work Experiences in Early Adolescence
    Youth Unemployment
Personal Identity: The Psychosocial Transition to Adulthood
  Two Components of Identity: Content and Evaluation
  Identity Status
    Crisis and Commitment
    Negative Identity
    Identity Confusion
  Gender Variation in the Process of Identity Formation
Optimizing Development in Adolescence
Chapter Summary
References

Adolescence brings rapid change on many fronts, accompanied by entry into a broader sphere of social life. Increased responsibilities and higher expectations for performance, coupled with new opportunities for independent decision making, produce new stressors. Adolescent males, with their larger, stronger bodies, deeper voices, and restless energy are likely to experience more conflicts with parents, teachers, and members of the community. They may encounter suspicion, authoritarian control, and even open hostility in their communities. Adolescent females, with their changing body shape, inexperienced flirtatiousness, and concern about social approval are likely to encounter unwanted sexual advances, exploitation, and open or latent messages of devaluation. In the midst of these private and public transformations, adolescents typically seek support, validation, and protection with peers, a process that has potential for tremendous benefits as well as enormous risk.

This chapter takes a wide-ranging approach to the extension of the psychosocial analysis, focusing first on the psychosocial crisis of early adolescence, group identity versus alienation, with its central process of peer pressure, and the resulting adaptive ego quality of fidelity to others and the core pathology of isolation.

As we pointed out in Chapter 3, these ideas are a departure from Erikson's original theory. He described the psychosocial crisis of adolescence as a conflict between personal identity and identity confusion, a theme that will be addressed at the end of this chapter. However, much of the developmental literature suggests that in early adolescence psychological energy is focused primarily on clarifying one's social identity or connection with others, followed in later adolescence by the clarification of one's personal identity.

The relationship with parents is discussed in some detail since family continues to provide an intimate support system for most adolescents. We also consider some of the competing demands on parents as they try to meet the needs of both their adolescent children and their own aging parents. The discussion of culture and ethnicity focuses on two critical dynamics: rites of passage and ethnic identity. We consider three major societal trends that influence adolescent development today: adolescent parenthood, drug and alcohol use and abuse, and adolescents in the workplace. The chapter ends with a discussion of the psychosocial construct of personal identity and the challenges that face a young person in trying to fashion a sense of self to serve as an orienting guide during the complex transition into adulthood.

The Psychosocial Crisis of Early Adolescence

Throughout life, tensions arise between desires for individuality and desires for connection. Certain cultures emphasize connection over individuality, while others put individuality ahead of connection. However, all societies must deal with both aspects of the ego: the *I* as agent, originator, and executive of one's individual thoughts and actions and the *we* as agent, originator, and executive of collective, cooperative enterprises that preserve and further the survival of the group (Triandis, 1990). During the early years of adolescence, one confronts a new psychosocial conflict in which pressures to ally oneself with specific groups and to learn to be comfortable functioning as a member of a group are major preoccupations (see Notebook Page 16.1). We call this conflict *group identity versus alienation* (Newman & Newman, 1976).

The Orienting Components of Personality Development in Early Adolescence

In Chapter 14, you responded to a notebook page on the orienting effect of the prime adaptive ego qualities or core pathologies. For the early adolescent, we add competence or inertia to the guiding framework for behavior. Return to Chapter 14, Notebook Page 14.1, and look up Jody, Jean, and Kelly. Now try to extend these analyses. For each of these children, create a scenario about the child's outlook toward peers.

1. Jody: Hope, will, purpose, and competence

2. Jean: Hope, will, inhibition, and inertia

3. Kelly: Withdrawal, compulsion, inhibition, and inertia

Group Identity

Group identity refers to the aspect of an individual's self-theory that focuses on membership and connection with social groups. It is an extension of the ego system's sense of *we* which originates in the first attachment relationship of infancy. It is an elaboration of the very early sense of trust, in which an infant establishes a foundation of social connection through which both self and other are defined. The *we* includes the deep desire for and belief in connection with others. The *we* can be compared with the *I* which includes the deep desire to be an independent individual with a sense of personal significance and value. The *we* and the *I* are thus complementary aspects of the ego system, although at times they may be in conflict.

Early adolescents experience a search for membership, an internal questioning about the groups of which they are most naturally a part. They ask themselves, "Who am I, and with whom do I belong?" Although membership in a peer group may be their most pressing concern, questions about other group identifications also arise. Adolescents may seek commitments to religious organizations; they may evaluate the nature of their ties to immediate or extended family members; and they may begin to understand the unique characteristics of their racial, ethnic, or cultural identity. Research confirms that, in the most positive pattern, peer-group membership does not replace attachment to parents or closeness with family. Rather, the adolescent's network of supportive relations is anchored by the family and expands into the domain of meaningful peer relationships. Typically, those adolescents who show strong signs of mental health and adaptive coping strategies can be described as having positive communication and trusting relationships with parents or other close family members, as well as strong feelings of trust and security among friends (Levitt et al., 1993; Raja et al., 1992).

In the process of seeking group affiliation, adolescents are sometimes confronted by clashes between personal and group needs and values. The process of self-evaluation takes place within the context of the meaningful groups with which adolescents identify. Individual needs for social approval, affiliation, leadership, power, and status are expressed by the group identifications that are made and rejected during early adolescence.

A positive resolution of the conflict of group identity versus alienation is one in which adolescents associate with an existing group that meets their social needs and provides them with a sense of belonging. In one attempt to measure this concept, Luhtanen and Crocker (1992) devised a measure of *collective self-esteem*, defined as the relatively stable evaluation of one's group membership. They included several dimensions of group belonging: the enactment of roles prescribed by the group; one's feelings of comfort and belonging with other group members; one's appraisal of the group's status in the eyes of others; and the salience of the group in one's life. All four dimensions contribute to the formation of a positive group identification. In order to experience group identification, a person must be engaged in activities associated with the group. In addition, the group must be positively evaluated by the person for the central role it plays in providing personal meaning and structure.

Alienation

Alienation refers to a sense of social estrangement, an absence of social support or meaningful social connection (Mau, 1992). An alienated adolescent does not experience a sense of belonging to a group; rather, he or she is continually uneasy in the presence of peers. A negative resolution of the conflict, which leaves an adolescent with a pervasive sense of alienation from peers, may result from at least three different circumstances. First, adolescents whose parents pressure them to join a particular peer group that does not accept them will probably experience alienation. Second, adolescents become alienated when they cannot find a group that really meets their personal needs. These adolescents may never become members of a peer group. A third basis for a negative outcome occurs when adolescents are rejected by all peer groups. For example, some young people ascribe too avidly to adult values and norms, causing their peers to see them as goody-goodies or nerds and to exclude them from the peer culture (Allen, Weissberg & Hawkins, 1989). Other adolescents have poor social skills; they are either overly aggressive and domineering or overly withdrawn and socially inept. It is not unusual for adolescents to identify such students in their high school as loners or outcasts (Brown et al., 1993).

During early adolescence, it is common for young people to become preoccupied with their own feelings and thoughts. They may withdraw from social interactions because they are unwilling to risk the vulnerability and confusion that accompany physical, intellectual, and social growth. In this sense, most adolescents feel some of the loneliness and isolation that are implied by the term *alienation*. Even with peers, they feel they must exercise caution in sharing their most private concerns for fear of rejection or ridicule. The maintenance of an interpersonal "cool"—a persona of bravado designed to give the perception of competence and security rather than vulnerability—may stand in the way of building strong, secure bonds of commitment to social groups.

The tension between expectations for group affiliation and barriers to group commitment is a product of the self-consciousness and egocentrism typical of this life stage, as well as the possibility of group rejection. The lack of peer social support that may result from a negative resolution of this crisis can have significant implications for adjustment in school, self-esteem, and subsequent psychosocial development (see Box 16.1). Chronic conflict about integration into a meaningful reference group can lead to lifelong difficulties in personal health, work, and the formation of intimate family bonds (East et al., 1987; Spencer, 1982, 1988).

The Central Process: Peer Pressure

Adolescents' family backgrounds, interests, and styles of dress quickly link them to subgroups of peers who lend continuity and meaning to life within the context of their neighborhoods or schools. The peer-group social structure is usually well established in most high schools, and members exert pressure on newcomers to join one peer group or another. These groups demand conformity to their norms and a demonstration of commitment and loyalty from their members. At the same time, young people outside the groups form expectations that reinforce adolescents' connections to specific peer groups and prohibit their movement to others. An individual who becomes a member of any group is more acceptable to the social system than is someone who tries to remain unaffiliated and aloof.

BOX 16.1

Suicide in Adolescence

Suicide at any age is deeply troubling, but adolescent suicide is cause for special anguish and soul-searching. Why would a young person, with all the endless possibilities and opportunities of life ahead, choose death? Is the prospect of becoming an adult so threatening and terrifying that some young people would rather die than grow up?

Public concern over adolescent suicide has intensified in response to the rising suicide rate among adolescents over the past 30 years. Suicide, which is the third leading cause of death among adolescents ages 15 to 19, rose from 3.6 per 100,000 in 1960 to 11.0 per 100,000 in 1991 (Garland & Zigler, 1993; U.S. Bureau of the Census, 1994). Over this same period, the suicide rate for the total population stayed relatively constant. In a comparison of racial and ethnic groups, Native Americans have the highest suicide rate, especially among Apaches (Berlin, 1987). White males are more likely to commit suicide than are African-Americans. The rate of 11.0 per 100,000 may be an underestimate since social stigma and life-insurance policies may prevent a death from being reported as a suicide. It is suspected that a significant number of adolescent deaths from single-automobile accidents are actually suicides.

The number of actual suicides among adolescents is still relatively small, but many more adolescents have attempted suicide. One estimate suggests that there are 50 suicide attempts for every suicide-related death (Sells & Blum, 1996). Males are four times as likely as females to commit suicide, but females are three times as likely as males to attempt suicide. National surveys find that from 6% to 13% of adolescents say they have attempted suicide at least once; however, very few have actually received any medical treatment or mental health care following the attempt (Garland & Zigler, 1993). Furthermore, a national Gallup survey found that 15% of adolescents had considered suicide (Ackerman, 1993). Widely publicized suicides that lead to the formation of a self-destructive cult, copycat suicides, and clusters of friends who commit suicide as part of a pact suggest that suicidal ideation is not always triggered by internal depression or loss.

Primary risk factors for suicide have been identified by studying the lives of adolescents who have committed suicide (Garland & Zigler, 1993). They may not be very useful in predicting whether a particular individual will commit or attempt suicide, however. These risk factors include:

- Drug and alcohol abuse
- History of psychiatric illness
- Family history of suicidal behavior
- Prior suicide attempt
- History of antisocial, aggressive behavior
- Availability of a firearm

In addition to these factors, there is usually some precipitating event such as a shameful or humiliating experience, a notable failure, rejection by a parent or a romantic partner, or guilt or confusion about one's sexual orientation. Use of drugs that alter cognitive functioning and decrease inhibitions coupled with easy access to a gun, form one likely path from suicidal ideation to suicidal action.

The Role of School Adults in Peer-Group Structuring

School adults appear to accept the peer-group structure as it exists. They make almost no effort to alter this structure of peer organization, which they may remember from their own high school days. In fact, school adults rely on members of specific peer groups to perform certain functions and to act along particular lines. Teachers, as well as students, appear to expect that individuals who dress in a certain way are members of one peer group and that students who have a particular intellectual ability belong to another. School adults often rely on the leaders of various peer groups to convey and enforce school norms for acceptable behavior. The peer-group structure becomes an important vehicle for maintaining a predictable order in school. Far from challenging this arrangement, school adults count on it to facilitate their efforts.

Affiliating with a Peer Group

The process of affiliating with a peer group requires an adolescent to open up to the pressure and social influence imposed by the group. This process provides the context within which the crisis of group identity versus alienation is resolved. Adolescents are at the point in their intellectual development when they are able to conceptualize themselves as objects of expectations. They may perceive these expectations as forces urging them to be more than they think they are—braver, more outgoing, more confident, and so forth. Thus, these expectations help define the zone of proximal development for group skills and social competencies. Peer pressure may have a positive effect on the adolescent's self-image and self-esteem, serving as a motive for group identification. Those dimensions of the self that are valued by the peer group become especially salient in adolescents' self-assessments (Hoge & McCarthy, 1984).

As members of peer groups, adolescents have more influence than they would have as individuals. They begin to understand the value of collective enterprise. In offering membership, peer groups expand adolescents' feelings of connection and protect them from loneliness. When family conflicts develop, adolescents seek comfort and intimacy among peers. In order for adolescents to benefit in these ways from affiliation with a peer group, they must be willing to suppress some of their individuality and focus on attributes that they share with peers.

Peer Pressure in Specific Areas

Peer pressure may be exercised in a variety of areas, including involvement with peers, school, and family; drug use; engaging in misconduct; sexual activity; and conformity to preferences in dress, music, or entertainment. Within a particular group, pressures may be strong in one or two areas but not in others. For example, in a comparison of three peer groups—the "jock-populars," the "druggie-toughs," and the "loners"—the druggie-toughs perceived the strongest peer pressure toward misconduct. Jock-populars perceived greater pressure toward school involvement than did druggie-toughs. However, pressure toward peer involvement (spending free time with peers) was equally high in all three groups (Clasen & Brown, 1985).

Norms for cigarette smoking have been studied as another example of a voluntary behavior that may be influenced by peer pressure. For example, in one study of sources of peer influence on cigarette smoking, the crowd identified as the "burnouts" (combination of "druggies," "radicals," and "punks") smoked four times as many cigarettes per week as the average students and ten times as many cigarettes as the "jock/preps" (Urberg, 1992). One might expect that pressure to conform to this behavior would be exceedingly strong within the "burnouts" crowd, whereas there might be much more variability around norms related to smoking in other groups.

Conformity and a Sense of Belonging

Peer groups do not command total conformity. In fact, most peer groups depend on the unique characteristics of their members to lend definition and vigor to emerging group roles. However, the peer group places considerable

In adolescent peer groups, pressures toward conformity are usually balanced by a degree of freedom for individual personalities and roles.

importance on some level of conformity in order to bolster its structure and strengthen its effectiveness in satisfying members' needs; indeed, most adolescents find some security in peer-group demands to conform. The few well-defined characteristics of the group lend stability and substance to adolescents' identities. In complying with group pressure, an adolescent can state unambiguously that he or she is someone and belongs somewhere (see Notebook Page 16.2).

Conflict, Tension, and Alienation

Adolescents may also find that some peer expectations conflict with their personal values or needs. For example, they may feel that their valued intellectual skills are demeaned by the peer group, that they are expected to participate in social functions they do not enjoy, or that they are pressured to be more independent from their families than they prefer to be. In most cases, peer-group pressure alters adolescents' personal values to make them more similar to those of other group members. If, however, the peer group's expectations are too distant from an adolescent's personal values, establishing a satisfying group identification is much more difficult. Adolescents experience tension and conflict as they try to balance the allure of peer-group membership with the cost of abandoning personal beliefs.

Susceptibility to peer pressure seems to peak at about age 13 or 14 when adolescents are most sensitive to peer approval while making the initial transition toward behavioral autonomy and emotional independence from parents (Lamborn & Steinberg, 1993; Urberg, et al., 1990). During the years from 14 to

Peer Pressure

We have hypothesized that peer pressure is the central process through which peer-group identification is established. Try to recall examples of peer pressure during your adolescence.

1. Describe two examples of positive peer pressure that led you to become involved in stimulating activities, broaden your experiences, or act more responsibly.

   a. _____

   b. _____

2. Describe two examples of negative peer pressure that led you to take dangerous risks, act in a cruel or violent manner, or take a narrow, bigoted stand.

   a. _____

   b. _____

3. How strong were the positive and negative peer pressures on you as an adolescent?

   _____

   _____

   _____

   _____

4. Based on your own experiences as well as your reading, what factors determine how vulnerable an adolescent will be to peer pressure?

   _____

   _____

   _____

   _____

683

16, adolescents become more adept at resisting peer pressure. Through encounters with peer pressure and opportunities to conform or resist, older adolescents develop a growing appreciation for their personal values against the backdrop of peer expectations. If the emotional costs of peer-group pressure become too great, adolescents may not be willing to submit, thus relinquishing the opportunity for group identity that is so central to psychosocial growth. An inability to reduce the tension and conflict between group pressure and personal values produces a state of alienation in which the individual is unable either to identify with social groups or to develop personal friendships.

Peer-group membership may not be as salient for minority youth as it has been described as being for white adolescents. In one study of family and peer relations, after controlling for social class, African-American adolescents reported both higher levels of parental control and higher levels of family intimacy than did white subjects (Giordano et al., 1993). In addition, African-American adolescents reported that they perceived less peer pressure, less need for peer approval, and somewhat lower levels of intimacy in their friendships. One ought not interpret this pattern as an indication that friendship relationships are unimportant for African-American adolescents, but rather that friendships may be less intense for African-American than for white adolescents. African-American adolescents may be socialized to function more independently, to be more flexible in accepting their friends, but less dependent on friends than on family for feelings of self-worth and emotional security. We do not really know much about intragroup differences in sources and quality of social support among minority youth and how these patterns are associated with well-being.

The Prime Adaptive Ego Quality and the Core Pathology

Fidelity to Others

A positive resolution of the psychosocial crisis of group identity versus alienation results in the achievement of the prime adaptive ego quality referred to as *fidelity to others*—a capacity to pledge loyalty to a group and to be faithful to one's promises and commitments. Fidelity to others fosters the necessary motivations to preserve small groups and larger communities through dedication to family, civic pride, and patriotism.

Looking ahead to subsequent life stages, one can anticipate the significant role that this ego quality plays in ensuring long-term faithfulness to friends, marital partners, children, aging parents, and other groups. Research on factors that buffer stress often cites social support as crucial in coping with change and adapting positively to challenges. Social support implies a capacity for fidelity. People who function as sources of support have the ability to remain compassionately connected to others during periods of hardship and loss as well as during periods of success and prosperity. We think of a true friend as someone who stands by us in times of adversity as well as in times of joy.

Fidelity to others fosters family solidarity, for example, when adults are called on to meet the needs of their own aging parents, a topic we will cover later in this chapter. Such a role is largely voluntary, based on one's definition of *filial obligation,* a sense of duty and responsibility to one's family. Surely, the way that adults enact this role reflects their capacity for fidelity to others.

Isolation

Isolation refers to a lack of companions, withdrawal from others, and an inability to experience the bond of mutual commitment. By isolation, we do not mean a preference for being alone, but rather a tendency toward social distancing and a reluctance to make the required commitments for establishing and maintaining enduring friendships. Sometimes this occurs as a result of rejection. Adolescents who experience isolation are likely to mistrust their peers and may even develop an attitude of hostile resentment toward the companionship they observe between others. At a very basic level, any sense of "*we*ness" requires shared understanding between at least two people and a recognition of some common bond, such as a mutual enemy, a shared crisis, or a common goal. The core pathology of isolation occurs when an adolescent is unable to experience the level of mutual understanding or symbolic connection that creates such bonds of "*we*ness."

Significant Factors in the Development of Parents and Other Family Members

Parents and Their Adolescent Children

As we consider the increasingly important role of peer relationships in early adolescence, we must keep in mind that under optimal conditions this process takes place against a background of continuing close, supportive relationships with family members. Adolescents evidence a variety of overt signs of independence from family. They may make decisions about their clothes, dating, and leisure time; they may have cars, stay out late, and earn their own money. However, they typically maintain an emotional attachment to their families and to their family's value orientations.

In the transition from childhood to adolescence, the child's radius of significant relationships changes. One study that looked at the structure and function of social support involved African-American, Anglo, and Hispanic children in three age groups: 7, 10, and 14 (Levitt et al., 1993). In the transition from age 7 to 10, extended-family members become increasingly important to children as a source of support. This pattern was true for all three ethnic groups, but African-American and Hispanic children were more likely to identify extended-family members as a source of support than were Anglo children. From ages 10 to 14, friends become an increasingly important source of support. In addition, the number of people mentioned as friends increases notably from age 7 to age 14. However, at all three ages and for all three ethnic groups, family members continue to be mentioned as the most central support in these children's lives, "the people who are the most close and important to you—people you love the most and who love you the most."

Furthermore, at each age, support from the close, inner circle comprised largely of family members was an important correlate of well-being and sociability.

Interactions with Parents and Their Influences on an Adolescent's Well-Being

How does the quality of parent–adolescent interactions influence an adolescent's well-being? Time spent at home in positive interactions with parents appears to have positive consequences for adolescents. In a study of eighth-graders, spending time in a supportive home was positively related to perceiving the family environment as intellectually and culturally stimulating. There was a strong relationship between time spent at home in leisure and recreational activity and a sense of well-being (McMillan & Hiltonsmith, 1982). At the opposite end of the continuum, experiences of parental rejection or neglect are closely linked to low self-esteem and depression (Robertson & Simons, 1989; Rosenberg et al., 1989).

Time spent in public with adults appeared to be more conflictual. Adolescents who reported a high level of parental companionship in public settings also reported feeling self-conscious about and preoccupied by the evaluations of others (Adams & Jones, 1982). Although adolescents may feel good about being affectionate and close with their parents, they are also sensitive to peer-group expectations that adolescents and parents should not be too chummy. Although frequent open communication between adolescents and their parents contributes to a positive relationship, it is misleading to assume that these interactions are always positive. It is hard work for parents and adolescents to keep channels of communication open.

Conflicts Between Parents and Adolescents

As adolescents go through puberty, conflicts with their parents increase. One way of understanding this phenomenon is to consider the dominant direction of psychosocial development for adolescents and their parents. Adolescents are preoccupied with expressing their own point of view and asserting behavioral and emotional autonomy from parents. They tend to be especially sensitive to parental control, and even mild expressions of parental disapproval or efforts by parents to redirect their behavior are perceived as intrusive. Parents are concerned about generativity; they look on their adolescent children as one expression of their impact on the future. Thus, their efforts to monitor, guide, and control their adolescents' behavior can be interpreted as a way of protecting their stake in their children's future. These two opposing motivations are likely to produce new tensions.

> Developmental success for midlife parents and their adolescent children seems to require cooperation: in order for children to successfully individuate, parents must be willing to yield some control; in order for parents to achieve a sense of generativity and successfully resolve midlife concerns, children must allow themselves to be guided. (MacDermid & Crouter, 1995, p. 32)

Conversations are marked by increased assertiveness on both sides (Papini et al., 1988; Papini & Sebby, 1988). These conflicts tend to be about rather mundane issues such as performing household chores, spending money, doing schoolwork, or abiding by curfews, rather than on basic value issues like political ideology or religious beliefs (Montemayor, 1983; Steinberg, 1990). Resolutions of these family conflicts usually lead to a new balance of power or control within the family (Feldman & Gehring, 1988), which appears to be negotiated differently by male and female adolescents.

Steinberg (1981) described parent–child interactions among boys ages 11 to 14 and their parents. As boys proceed through puberty, parents increasingly interrupt their adolescent sons, and boys increasingly interrupt their mothers during conversations. Parents offer fewer explanations, and family interactions become more rigid. After the period of rapid pubertal growth, adolescent–parent conflicts subside somewhat. Mothers interrupt their sons less, and sons become increasingly deferential to their fathers.

The pattern for girls is a bit different (Hill, 1988). In the months following menarche, parents interrupt their daughters more during conversations. Girls are more likely to yield to their mothers' interruptions, but they do not tend to yield to their fathers' interruptions. Daughters assert themselves with their mothers through a high frequency of interruptions and with their fathers by an unwillingness to yield the conversation when their fathers interrupt them. Over time, parents notably increase their explanations when their opinions differ from their daughters', suggesting a new respect for their daughters' independent views and a redefinition of her power in the family.

Parents and Adolescents Learn One Another's Views

When families have frequent, reasonable interactions and allow for the expression of conflict, parents can communicate more effectively their expectations and children have opportunities to explain their points of view. As a result, parents and adolescents learn one another's opinions on most issues. In one study, parents and adolescents completed the Offer Self-Image Questionnaire (OSIQ) (Offer et al., 1982). Out of 38 items, there were only 12 in which the parents' and the adolescents' endorsements differed by more than 10%. Parents tended to underestimate the importance of their children's having girlfriends or boyfriends. They also underestimated the extent to which their children found dirty jokes amusing. Parents thought that peers found their children more attractive than the children believed they did. Parents thought that their sons' feelings were more easily hurt than the sons thought they were. Parents thought that their daughters were more confident and more prepared to compete in adult life than the daughters thought they were. Parents thought that both their sons and their daughters were less able to take criticism and learn from others than the children thought they were. This discrepancy may result from the fact that children are more willing to take criticism and learn from others than they are from their parents.

This picture of parent–adolescent views is confirmed in a study describing adolescents' discussions with their parents and peers (Hunter, 1985). Over the age ranges 12 to 13 and 14 to 15, adolescents discussed academic/vocational, social/ethical, and family relations topics more often with their parents than with their friends. However, they discussed peer relations more with their friends. Parents may not have as much information about their children's peer relations as about other important topics, and adolescents are likely to perceive their parents as having little understanding about their social life.

The Impact of Parenting Practices on Adolescent Development

It is important to consider that early adolescence comes close on the heels of middle childhood. It does not make sense to assume that, shortly after a period of intense socialization and dependence, a child would be eager to reject most of what has been learned at home. Young adolescents are typically very attached to their parents and need their emotional support and approval. Thus, one might view parent–child conflict as one means for adolescents to achieve autonomy while preserving the bonds of affection and goodwill that have been formed earlier with parents.

The quality of the home environment, especially characteristics of parenting practices, has implications for the adolescent's peer relationships as well as for the quality of parent–child interactions. You will recall from the discussion in Chapter 13 that high levels of power assertion as a parenting practice are associated with a greater likelihood of peer rejection during the middle-school years. Studies of the relationship between parenting practices and adolescent peer-group membership extend this analysis. A model has been proposed that links parenting practices to adolescent behaviors and ultimately to crowd affiliation (Brown et al., 1993; Durbin et al., 1993) (see Figure 16.1). Parenting practices, listed in the left-hand column, were evaluated on three dimensions: the extent to which parents emphasized academic achievement; parental monitoring of adolescent behaviors; and the degree to which parents involved adolescents in decision making. Adolescent behaviors, listed in the center column, were evaluated by examining the students' grade-point averages, drug use, and self-reliance. Finally, students were characterized by one of six crowd affiliations, listed in the right-hand column.

Parenting practices were significantly linked to the child's behavior, which in turn was a strong predictor of crowd affiliation. A positive (+) path indicates a positive correlation between a parenting practice and an adolescent behavior or a particular crowd membership. A negative (−) path indicates an inverse relationship between a parenting practice and an adolescent behavior or crowd membership. The pattern was especially clear for the positive link from parental emphasis on academic achievement, a child's high grades, and association with the "brain" crowd; and for low parental monitoring, little joint decision making, little emphasis on academic achievement, and the high likelihood of an adolescent's use of drugs and identification with the "druggie" crowd. One implication of this study is that, even though adolescents may perceive their involvement with peers as a separate and distinct domain from their family life, the threads of parent socialization practices and their consequences for adolescent behavior continue to exert an influence on peer relations.

Parents tend to view their children's adolescence as extremely trying. Adolescents are likely to strive for a great deal of behavioral independence. They spend most of the day away from home and parental supervision. As adolescents gain in physical stature and cognitive skills, they are likely to challenge parental authority. During this time, the principles that parents have emphasized as important for responsible, moral behavior are frequently tested. Children are exposed to many influences, including the media, popular heroes and heroines, peers, and school adults, that suggest many different ideals and definitions of success. Parents must maintain a degree of authority about standards or limits while permitting their children to exercise their judgment. Parents must also be ready to give support when children fail to meet

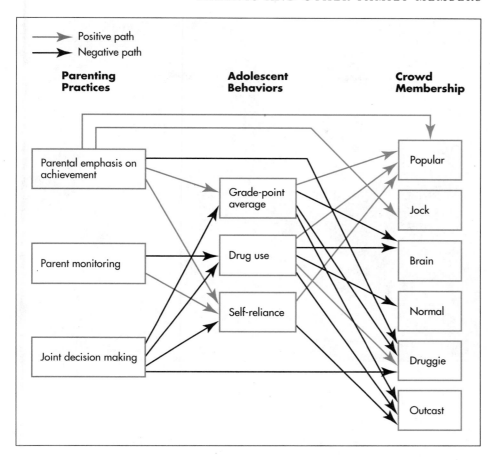

FIGURE 16.1
Parenting practices, adolescent behaviors, and crowd membership
Source: Brown et al. (1993). Parenting practices and peer group affiliation in adolescence. *Child Development, 64,* Figure 3, p. 476. Copyright © 1993 The Society for Research in Child Development Inc. Reprinted with permission.

adult expectations or when they show poor judgment. A balance of freedom, support, and limit setting allows children to become increasingly independent while still being able to rely on an atmosphere of family security (Baumrind, 1991; Newman, 1989; Ryan & Lynch, 1989).

Adolescent children are the front line of each new generation. The questions they raise and the choices they make reflect not only what they have learned in the past but also what they are experiencing in the present and what they anticipate about their future. Parents of adolescents are likely to feel persistent pressure to reevaluate their own socialization as well as their effectiveness as parents. They question their preparation for their own futures as well as their children's. The sense of fulfillment parents get from being perceived by their young children as wise and resourceful is likely to be replaced by doubts as both parents and adolescents face an uncertain future. Parents who can respond to their adolescents in an open, supportive way benefit from the opportunity to clarify their own values. They can begin building a new parent–child relationship that will carry over to their children's adulthood.

Parents Caring for Their Aging Parents

Typically, parents of adolescent children are also children of aging parents. As one ages from 40 to 60, one's parents may age from 65 to 85. Increasing numbers of U.S. families have a living grandparent and even a living great-grand-

Adolescents can gain a new appreciation for their family's history by reminiscing with their grandparents.

parent generation. Older adults who have typically experienced a vigorous and independent later adulthood eventually become frail and need support services. Parents of adolescents are likely to be involved in meeting the needs of aging parents or grandparents at the same time that they are trying to foster the continued development of their children (Aneshensel et al., 1995). In addition, financial resources may be strained as the medical needs of the grandparent generation compete with the costs of education and career training for the adolescents.

The evidence suggests that daughters assume much more of the responsibility for their aging parents than do sons (Finley, 1989). This involvement is one element of the basic "kin-keeping" tasks that have traditionally been incorporated in women's socialization. Daughters are more likely than sons to provide direct care, such as bathing or dressing parents, as well as emotional support, such as listening to parents' concerns or helping them feel important and loved. Sons and daughters are about equally likely to assist in some of the tasks involving relations with health and human service organizations, scheduling medical checkups, and reviewing insurance and other financial matters (Spitze & Logan, 1990).

If this pattern of caregiving is widespread, then we would expect adolescent children to identify the enactment of filial obligation as gender linked. Adolescents are likely to recognize their mothers as the family members who look after the daily well-being of their aging grandparents. Adolescents may be less aware of their fathers' efforts on behalf of their aging grandparents to handle finances, insurance, or other bureaucratic problems unless the parents talk about these matters. Thus, the pattern of gender-linked filial obligation is transmitted from generation to generation through the indirect socialization children receive by observing their parents caring for their grandparents.

Maintaining a relationship with one's parents during adulthood is a matter of choice. Many adult children feel a moral obligation to reciprocate the care and devotion that their parents extended to them when they were young. In addition, a moral obligation to "honor thy father and thy mother" may have been incorporated into the children's religious training. However, the goal of child-rearing in this society generally encompasses promoting the offspring's independence: Children are encouraged to leave home, establish residences of their own, and be economically self-sufficient. After children leave home, many adult parents experience a positive role transition. They enjoy refocusing their time and attention on each other or on new activities and relationships. Reestablishing a parent–child relationship in the parents' old age may involve sharing a household or maintaining frequent contact and interdependence, which do not always come easily to either the adult children or the aging parents. As parents of adolescent children struggle with their responsibilities for their own parents' care, they must weigh them against their commitments to their parental, marital, and work roles. They may begin to feel that they are caught between both ends, imposing unwanted restrictions and limitations on their aging parents as well as on their adolescent children and pleasing neither. Success in this relationship is closely related to the affection that children continue to hold for their parents during the years in which they have lived relatively independent adult lives (Bengston & Roberts, 1991) (see Notebook Page 16.3).

Aging parents are very likely to request help from their adult children during widowhood (Lopata, 1979; O'Bryant, 1987). The loss of a grandparent is likely to be one of a child's first encounters with death of someone close. Often, this first loss occurs in adolescence, when the child is struggling to express his or her own independence and individuality and resolve infantile attachments to parents in favor of a more mutual affection and regard. A grandparent's mortality sheds a new light on the importance of family relationships and may help to refocus the adolescent's commitment to the family. The death of a grandparent also gives an adolescent new insight into his or her parent's role as a child who has lost a parent. This insight, coupled with the child's own sense of loss at the grandparent's death, may create a new bond of identification between parent and child and foster mutual consolation.

Cultural and Ethnic Patterns That Create Distinctive Child-Rearing Environments

Culture imposes special meaning on the period of adolescence. In this section, we consider two complementary processes. First, we describe the idea of rites of passage as mechanisms for orienting young people toward the new status and new roles that accompany the transition from childhood to adolescence and adulthood. Second, we discuss ethnic identity, a process through which adolescents internalize the unique values, beliefs, and shared history of their family's ethnic ancestry.

Adults and Their Aging Parents

What can you recall or what do you know about the relationship between your parents or guardians and their parents?

1. In what ways were your parents or guardians sources of support for their parents? How did they enact their filial obligations?

_____

_____

_____

_____

_____

_____

2. How would you describe the direction of caregiving between the two generations? Were your parents a greater source of support to your grandparents, or were your grandparents a greater source of support to your parents?

_____

_____

_____

_____

_____

_____

3. What do you expect will be your relationship with your aging parents? For example, how close or far away will you live from them? How often will you interact in person or over the phone? What kinds of support do you think that you will be able to provide? What do you think might be areas of conflict?

_____

_____

_____

_____

_____

_____

4. In what ways are the issues that arise between parents and their adolescent children similar to issues that might arise between adults and their aging parents?

_____

_____

_____

_____

_____

_____

Cultural Patterns of Rites of Passage

In all human societies, people have devised rituals and ceremonies to observe significant life transitions such as birth, puberty, marriage, pregnancy, and death. Arnold van Gennep (1909/1960) was the first anthropologist to use the phrase *rites of passage* to describe the ritual celebrations of new life roles. He argued that rites of passage are designed to smooth the transition from one status or role to another. Although the rites are frequently tied to biological events, van Gennep viewed their function as primarily social and psychological. Ritualization helps a person make potentially overwhelming or painful transitions within the enduring context of society.

Puberty rituals or initiation ceremonies are the rites of passage most closely associated with "coming of age" or with a culture's definition of maturity. The content and timing of initiation rites vary widely from one culture to another (Muuss, 1970). Typically, patterns of initiation differ for males and females, and both the severity and educational aspects of the rituals vary across cultures. Among the Aranda (or Arunta) of Central Australia, for example, girls are initiated by rubbing their breasts with fat and ocher when they reach puberty. In contrast, Aranda boys must go through a series of difficult ceremonies designed to test their manhood, teach obedience, and impart tribal secrets. The first of these rites includes separating the boy from all women at about age 10 to 12, tossing him into the air several times, and beating him with a club as he falls to the ground. Later, he is circumcised and taken to the bush to recover. While he is in the bush, men come and bite his scalp to help his hair grow. Finally, there is a period of several months of celebration which ends when the boy goes through tests of fire, including kneeling down on hot coals. Some time later, he is deemed capable of receiving the fetish object from the totem chief and is considered to be a man (Murdock, 1934; Spencer & Gillen, 1966). The pattern described here, where males are subject to more severe rites than females, is not consistent from one culture to the next. In some societies, females also endure painful surgical procedures and periods of social isolation; and in other societies, puberty is not marked with dramatic rites and rituals.

The Functions of Puberty Rites

Several explanations have been offered for the cultural functions of puberty rites or initiation ceremonies. These rites may be closely associated with the biological events of puberty. Margaret Mead (1949/1955) argued that women's lives are marked by clear, well-defined physical events, including menarche, first intercourse, childbirth, and menopause. To enable males to achieve some comparable developmental sequence, some societies introduce rituals and social distinctions that help to clarify a male's social status.

A second explanation is that initiation ceremonies serve to emphasize society's adult gender-role expectations (Brown, 1975; Munroe & Munroe, 1975). In an analysis of cultures whose male initiation ceremony involves circumcision, Burton and Whiting (1961) argued that the purpose of this ceremony is to clarify a boy's identification with the male gender role. They point out that, in some societies that give children exclusive privileges of sleeping with their mother during the first few years of life, a strong mother–son bond develops, as well as a father–son rivalry. Especially when fathers do not participate in the socialization of infants and young children, there are few opportunities for a strong male identification to develop. Society intervenes at puberty to enforce the boy's commitment to the male group. In societies where children sleep with both parents or in the unusual case in which the infant sleeps alone (as in the United States), the initiation rites generally do not involve severe tests of manhood. The transition to the adult male gender role is more gradual.

A third view is that initiation ceremonies reflect a culture's emphasis on continuity or discontinuity in life events from childhood to adulthood (Muuss, 1970). In cultures characterized by continuity, the information and experiences necessary to participate in adult life are gradually integrated into the child's daily life. In Samoa, for example, young children are given increasing responsibility for the care of siblings, household chores, and running errands. Cultural taboos are explained and enforced. Children have the opportunity to observe sexual behavior and gradually participate in sexual exploration. In all these ways, children accumulate skills and knowledge to prepare them for their adult status (Mead, 1928, 1949/1955).

In contrast, some societies make very dramatic distinctions between childhood and adult roles. Children may be prevented from participating in specific activities or from obtaining certain information. Among the Aranda described above, boys are taken away from their mothers at puberty and are eventually "reborn" as males at the end of the initiation ceremonies (Benedict, 1938; Muuss, 1970). Because of the Arandas' secrecy in all aspects of adult religious practices and the intense cultural hostility between males and females, male children have relatively few opportunities to learn the appropriate behaviors that are associated with the adult male role.

Marking the Transition to Adulthood in the United States

In the United States, the change in status from child to adult occurs gradually during the years from about 10 to 21. Specific subcultures retain their own initiation ceremonies, especially around the theme of religious commitment. Religious groups conduct ceremonies of baptism, bar mitzvah, communion, and confirmation to signal the stages in achieving adult status in their community. In addition, a variety of public events by the family, community, and the state recognize a person's increasing competence and the gradual removal of protections and restrictions that accompanies diminishing childhood status (Muuss, 1970). The transitions from elementary school to junior high school to high school and to college are marked by ceremonies and festivities that celebrate increased intellectual competence. Adult privileges such as eligibility for a driver's license and the ability to work without legal restrictions at age 16, the rights to vote and to marry without parental consent at age 18, and the full legal status associated with running for public office and participating in legal contracts at age 21 all acknowledge the passage from one status to another.

Adolescents also create their own "rites of passage," including smoking their first cigarettes, initiating sexual activities, getting drunk, or taking a dare to steal a car or dive into a water-filled quarry. Often, these rites are linked with peer-group membership and emphasize the willingness to put personal safety or well-being at risk in order to show commitment to the group. These kinds of acts of defiance or bravery symbolize a definition of adult status that is quite distinct from adults' perspectives of mature behavior. However, these acts fulfill adolescents' needs to differentiate themselves from the protected status of childhood and to stake a claim for self-determination.

The transition to adulthood is more ambiguous for U.S. adolescents than it is in more traditional societies, possibly because of our lack of clarity about the status of adolescents (Gavazzi, 1995). Some argue that young people are protected too long, perhaps as a way of delaying their entry into the labor market. Others suggest that the requirements of independent living have become so complex that it takes longer to achieve the necessary intellectual competencies and skills to function as an adult in our society than it does in more traditional cultures, and therefore adolescence is prolonged. Still others argue that U.S. society is unclear about its definition of maturity, and adolescent behavior merely reflects this uncertainty.

Ethnic-Group Identity

One of the most challenging aspects of establishing group identity during adolescence is the formation of an ethnic-group identity (Spencer & Markstrom-Adams, 1990). Ethnic identity is not merely knowledge of membership in a certain racial or ethnic group, but a recognition that some aspects of one's thoughts, feelings, and actions are influenced by ethnic identity. As adolescents begin to make important life choices, their ethnic group becomes a significant reference group whose values, outlook, and goals are taken into account.

Native American adolescents strengthen their ethnic identity by joining a dance troupe and performing traditional dances at powwows and festivals.

In the United States, African-Americans, Native Americans, Asian-Americans, and Hispanics have had a history of negative imagery, violence, discrimination, and invisibility. Young people in each of these groups encounter conflicting values between their own ethnic identity and the larger society. They must struggle with the negative or ambivalent feelings that are linked with their own ethnic group as a result of the cultural stereotypes derived from the media and the schools, as well as the scarcity of positive group role models for leadership and authority.

The Salience of Ethnic Identity in Adolescence

Issues of ethnic-group identity may not become salient until early adolescence. As children grow up, they tend to incorporate many of the ideals and values of the Anglo culture; suddenly, in adolescence, they may find themselves excluded from it. At that time, peer groups become more structured. Sanctions against cross-race friendships and dating relationships become more intense, both within the ethnic group and from members of other groups. Adolescents may encounter more overt rejection and failure in areas of academic achievement, employment, and school leadership. Certain adolescents may find that their family and ethnic-group values conflict with the values of the majority culture within their community. They may feel that they have to deny their ethnic-group identity in order to be accepted by the majority group in their high school or community. They may flounder without a clear ethnic identity and struggle through a period of bitter rejection. In other instances, adolescents may create ethnic peer groups in order to affirm the value of their heritage.

The Development of Ethnic Identity from Early to Later Adolescence

Adolescents' efforts to understand their ethnic identities and to clarify their commitment to a particular ethnic subculture lead to self-definition that facilitates a personal identity as well. Forming a clear sense of personal identity requires understanding one's ancestry, especially the cultural and ethnic heritage and the values, beliefs, and traditions that may have shaped one's child-rearing environment and vision of the future. Ethnic-group identity typically involves awareness of ethnic identity; incorporation of ethnic ideals, values, and beliefs; an understanding of how this ethnic group is regarded by outsiders; and self-orientation with respect to the group, that is, association with other members of the group, pride in group membership, and positive attitudes about the group (Cross, 1991).

As you might imagine, young people make the transition from early to later adolescence with different orientations toward their ethnic-group identity. One theory of ethnic identity development offers a five-stage model (Atkinson et al., 1983):

1. *Conformity.* Identification with the values, beliefs, and practices of the dominant culture.
2. *Dissonance.* Recognition and confusion about areas of conflict between the values, beliefs, and practices of the dominant culture and those of one's own ethnic group.
3. *Resistance and immersion.* Rejection of many elements of the dominant culture; education about and involvement with one's own ethnic group and its beliefs, values, and practices.
4. *Introspection.* Critical examination of the values, beliefs, and practices of both the dominant culture and one's own ethnic group.
5. *Articulation and awareness.* Synthesis of values, beliefs, and practices from the dominant culture and one's own ethnic group, which forms a personal, cultural identity.

In this model, ethnic identity and personal identity interact. Of course, not all young people experience all of these stages. Some children are immersed in the values and ritual practices of their ethnic group in infancy and toddlerhood, thus never experiencing conformity. For others, the stage of articulation and awareness may not occur until sometime later in adulthood. But for many later adolescents, the transition from stage 1, conformity, to stages 2 and 3 is commonly stimulated by attending college, where the student body is usually much more diverse than in high school. Young people of many racial, ethnic, social class, regional, and religious backgrounds are expected to live together in college residence halls, learn together in the classrooms, and collaborate in organizations, social activities, sports, and cultural events. This diversity often exposes students to racial and ethnic prejudice, cultural ethnocentrism, and intergroup conflict. At the same time, exposure to the college curriculum offers an intellectual framework for understanding the historical, psychological, and sociological foundations of racism, prejudice, and cultural conflict.

Often, college students seek opportunities to learn more about their ethnic-group identity. They may take courses that address the history, culture, and accomplishments of their group. They may be resentful about the lack of recognition given to their group in the general operations of the university or in the curriculum. They may challenge the university, urging greater efforts to acknowledge and incorporate their group's traditions, customs, and contributions. At the same time, these students experience many pressures to function in accord with the values, beliefs and practices of the dominant culture. As a result, they enter an active process of experimentation with multiple roles.

Eventually, these multiple views of the self must be reconciled somehow. This resolution can be aided by the support of people who have arrived at a similar perspective, who understand and confirm one's beliefs and practices, enjoy celebrating one's ethnicity, and enable one to experience a basic sense of self-acceptance. Students who do not have this support group and continue to experience dissonance may become alienated from the college environment and are likely to leave.

Societal Issues That Provide Resources or Barriers to Development

The societal themes that follow—adolescent parenthood, alcohol and drug use and abuse, and early work experiences—each illustrate the interactions of the biological, psychological, and societal systems in producing developmental outcomes. In adolescence, one can readily appreciate how individuals' choices influence the course of their development. At the same time, the organization of society at a particular historical period determines many of the possible consequences of those choices.

Parenthood in Early Adolescence

In 1992, 532,000 live infants were born to women age 19 or younger, and 326,000 legal abortions were performed on women in this age group. Roughly 900,000 adolescent girls experienced pregnancy in that year, and about 40% terminated their pregnancies through abortion, a reasonable indicator that the pregnancies were unwanted. After several years of a steady birth rate for adolescents, the past few years have seen a new increase. The birth rate for mothers ages 10 to 14 (the number of births per 100,000 women in that age group) increased from 1.1 in 1980 to 1.4 in 1991; and for mothers ages 15 to 19, the rate increased from 53 in 1980 to 62.1 in 1991 (U.S. Bureau of the Census, 1995).

Social policies advocating the prevention of early pregnancy and the role of public programs in family planning and abortion tend to emphasize the negative consequences of pregnancy for adolescent girls and their babies. However, studies of pregnant adolescents generally find that these girls do not differ much in attitudes, mental health, or cognitive abilities from those who are sexually active but have not gotten pregnant. We must be careful not to label a group of adolescents as deviant simply because they have gotten pregnant.

Contraception

A critical factor in explaining the high rate of adolescent pregnancy is the ambivalence of American parents, teachers, and teens toward contraception. In comparison with adolescents in many European countries, the majority of American adolescents do not integrate contraception into their approach to natural sexual activity. American adolescents are largely uninformed about the variety of methods of contraception and their relation to the biological factors that prevent pregnancy (Morrison, 1985). One study of sexually active adolescent girls reported that only 35% consistently used contraceptives, 27% never used them, and 39% were inconsistent in their use (Zelnik & Kantner, 1980).

Use or nonuse of contraceptives is associated with religious beliefs, family attitudes and behavior patterns, and peer norms. For example, low-income African-American female adolescents have more negative attitudes toward birth control than do white adolescents, and they value fertility more. Thus, African-American females who are sexually active are less likely to use contraceptives (Edelman & Pittman, 1986; Pete & DeSantis, 1990; Zabin et al., 1993). However, African-American adolescent males tend to use condoms more consistently than other groups (Pleck et al., 1991).

About 40% of adolescent girls believe that contraception is the responsibility of the male, but most males are ineffective or inconsistent in their use of contraceptives (Franklin, 1988). In one national survey of adolescent males ages 15 to 19, 30% reported regularly using condoms, including with the recent partners and with the last partner, and 57% reported using a condom at their last intercourse. These rates are higher than those observed in the early 1980s (Pleck et al., 1991). However, this still leaves 70% of adolescent males who are inconsistent in their use of condoms or who do not use condoms at all. Males who believe they have a responsibility to prevent pregnancy, are concerned about their partner, and want to avoid contracting AIDS are more likely to be consistent in their use of condoms. Concerns about reduced sexual pleasure and embarrassment about using a condom, coupled with the pattern of having multiple sexual partners, were factors associated with inconsistent condom use.

Consequences of Teenage Pregnancy

Teenage parenthood is a complex phenomenon that touches the lives of the adolescent mother and father, the children born to them, the adolescents' parents, and the schools, counseling services, and family planning services that have been established to help them cope (Caldas, 1993; Franklin, 1988). The consequences for a teenage mother and her infant depend on the psychosocial context within which the pregnancy occurs. There is a big difference between becoming a mother at age 14 or at age 18. Research suggests a strong relationship between a mother's age at first birth and her family income at age 27 (Moore et al., 1993). This effect is mediated by a number of other personal and family factors that appear to follow the first birth, such as continuing on in school, chances of getting married, the mother's work and personal earnings, and the earning capacity of other family members. Among African-American teen mothers, the poverty level is high regardless of age at first birth. However, the earlier that African-American females begin childbearing, the more children they are likely to have, a factor that increases the level of poverty. For Hispanic females, delaying childbearing results in higher educational attainment, which is linked to both higher personal income and higher income among other family members when the mothers reach age 27. For white females, delaying the age of childbearing is associated with older age at first marriage, fewer children, and higher personal earnings. For all

It takes quite a lot of re-sourcefulness for adolescents to continue their education and be nurturing parents.

three ethnic groups, each year of delayed childbearing substantially reduces the chances of living in poverty by age 27.

One of the great paradoxes of adolescent parenthood is the contrast between young girls' aspirations about mothering and the actual experience of child-rearing. Here are the comments of one 14-year-old mother:

> When I got pregnant, my parents wanted me to have an abortion, but I'm an only child, and it's a lonely feeling when you're an only child. I just said, "Well, I'm going to keep the baby because now I'll have somebody I'll feel close to, instead of being lonely all the time." (Fosburgh, 1977, 34)

Many adolescents do not possess the adequate emotional, social, or financial resources to sustain the kind of caring relationship they envision having with their children. They may not anticipate the degree to which their own needs must often be sacrificed to their babies' needs. This discrepancy between aspirations and reality may result in a young mother's hostility toward her baby. The risk of child abuse is great in families with teen parents, especially when aggravated by the factors of poverty and single parenthood (Gelles, 1989; Zuravin, 1988).

Is a pregnant adolescent who marries better off than one who does not? Adolescent pregnancy and adolescent marriage have separate consequences for future educational attainment, occupational achievement, and marital stability. Having a baby in adolescence is associated with lower educational and occupational levels, whether or not the mother marries. Getting married in adolescence is associated with a greater chance of divorce or separation than getting married at age 20 or older. Somewhat surprisingly, however, adolescent marriage without children is somewhat more likely to be associated with later marital instability than is adolescent marriage accompanied by adoles-

BOX 16.2

A Case Study of Five African-American Teen Mothers

In an attempt to understand the factors that lead to certain sexual decisions, including the decision to have a child, Pete and DeSantis (1990) conducted a case study of five African-American girls who were pregnant or had recently delivered a child. One must be cautious about generalizing these observations to all African-American adolescent mothers or to adolescent mothers in general. All five were 14 years old and in the eighth grade. They were from low-income families in Miami, Florida. Despite the very small sample size, the focus of this study is especially relevant because it considers the viewpoint of a critical group. Roughly 23% of all African-American births are to teen mothers (U.S. Bureau of the Census, 1994).

Interviews with these very young mothers both confirm and challenge some of our beliefs about adolescent pregnancy. First, the girls all rejected earlier opportunities to become sexually active. They said that they waited to become sexually active until they had established a relationship that they believed was based on trust and love. They did not delay sexual activity in order to avoid pregnancy. They assumed that the person with whom they had sex would not abandon them if they became pregnant.

Second, they did not use contraceptives for a variety of reasons. Some believed that they were too young to get pregnant. Some relied on their boyfriends to use contraception, but the methods used were inconsistent or nonexistent. Most of the girls were confused about the use of contraceptives or lacked the means to obtain them.

Third, the girls all described a daily life that had a large amount of unsupervised free time. They all lived with adults who did not or could not supervise their behaviors effectively. One girl had moved out of the house when her mother became hooked on crack cocaine. Another girl lived with her grandmother, who never talked with her about sex or her social life. Although the girls all said they felt close to their parents or guardians, these adults did not monitor the girls' social lives or discuss sexual decisions.

Fourth, the girls denied to themselves that they were pregnant as long as they could. "However, even though Deb had missed several periods, was sick every morning, and had fainted several times, she vehemently denied she was pregnant for seven months. . . . As Deb so clearly put it, 'as long as I did not tell anyone I was pregnant, as far as I was concerned, I wasn't pregnant'" (Pete & DeSantis, 1990, 151).

Finally, the girls all believed that once a girl becomes pregnant, it is her responsibility to have and keep the baby. Since they waited so long to admit the pregnancy, abortion was out of the question. Adoption was never considered. The parents or guardians thought that the girls should not get married because they were too young. All the partners continued to maintain contact with their girlfriends and babies, were involved in child care, and provided some financial support. Three of these adolescent fathers took their babies to their homes every other weekend. Even though the girls' parents or guardians were disappointed in the pregnancy, they did not reject the young mothers. The pregnancy and childbirth did not result in a deterioration of the girls' support system.

---

cent childbirth (Teti & Lamb, 1989). Not surprisingly, adolescents who are married when they have their first child have a higher household income than are those who are single when their first child is born (Astone, 1993) (see Box 16.2).

Adolescent Fathers

Although concern over adolescent pregnancy has focused on girls, there is growing attention to adolescent fathers. It is difficult to determine the number of teenage fathers. Many young mothers will not reveal the name of their baby's father. Many of these fathers are not adolescents but older men. National data from 1984 reported that, of 479,647 infants born to teenage mothers, only 19% also had teenage fathers (Hardy & Duggan, 1988). According to census data, only 130,000 males under the age of 20 were named as the fathers in live births for the year 1991 (U.S. Bureau of the Census, 1994). This is a decline from 189,000 in 1970, but an increase from 105,000 in 1986.

Contrary to the stereotype, studies of adolescent pregnancy find that many of the fathers maintain contact with the mother and child. Some adolescent fathers marry the mother; others live with her for awhile. Often, the couple continues to date. In some instances, the couple actually marries several years after the child is born. In many cases, the father contributes financial support to the mother and child, even when the couple does not marry. Many fathers, however, have little education and are minimally employed, so the material support they can provide is very limited (Hardy & Duggan, 1988; Robinson, 1988).

William Marsiglio (1989) compared African-American and white male adolescents' preferences about pregnancy resolution and family formation. These data were gathered from responses to a hypothetical situation: "Please imagine that you have been dating the same girl who is about your age for the past year and that she told you last week that she was two months pregnant with your child. For the purpose of this survey, assume that your girlfriend wants you to live with her and your child." Beginning with this premise, the boys in the survey were asked about how likely they would be to live with the child, their attitudes about doing this, their evaluation of possible positive and negative consequences of this decision, and their overall preference for resolving the pregnancy if it were entirely their decision.

African-American adolescents were significantly less likely to endorse abortion as the solution to this situation. This was true even when the factor of the adolescent's parents' education was controlled. For example, none of the African-American males whose parents were college graduates selected abortion as a solution, while 40% of the white males whose parents were college graduates preferred abortion. African-American and white males were about equally likely to endorse the idea of living with the child and its mother (45% of both groups selected this option). African-American males were more likely than white males to see living with the baby as an opportunity to care for his or her daily physical needs and to assume greater financial responsibility for the situation. In other respects, African-American and white males viewed the positive consequences of the situation quite similarly. White males were more likely to see the situation as reducing their chances of further education or spending time with friends. In other respects, African-American and white males evaluated the negative consequences of the situation quite similarly. African-American males were more likely to assume that living with the child and mother would require having a steady job.

Fathering a child is bound to stimulate conflicting feelings of pride, guilt, and anxiety in an adolescent boy. He must struggle with the fact that his sexual behavior has resulted in a pregnancy that may cause difficulty for someone for whom he cares. He must confront and give consideration to the choices that he and his girlfriend have for coping with an unplanned pregnancy. He may feel isolated from the childbirth process. He may drop out of school and enter the labor market to provide financial support for his girlfriend and child even though he will probably be only minimally employed (Hendricks & Fullilove, 1983).

Not much systematic research has been conducted on the attitudes, knowledge, or behaviors of adolescent fathers or the impact of fatherhood on a teenage boy's subsequent development (Robinson, 1988). Few programs consider the needs of adolescent fathers. Limited evidence suggests, however, that many adolescent fathers experience stress related to the pregnancy and could benefit from some kind of counseling (Lamb & Elster, 1985). Those who have studied the problem of unwed fathers argue that much stronger emphasis ought to be placed on the father's responsibility, not only for financial support but also for continued interaction with the child.

There is no question that early entry into parenthood is problematic for both girls and boys. When adolescent pregnancy is followed by disruption of education, loss of family and peer support, and poverty, opportunities for the young mother and her child are severely curtailed. However, these consequences are not automatic. Much depends on the response of family members, schools, community agencies, and peers. Further, some young parents have greater personal resources to bring to their new parental role than do others. Differences in the way adolescent pregnancy is construed in various racial/ethnic and social class communities must be taken into account when designing prevention and intervention programs.

For both girls and boys, a key factor in preventing early pregnancy is building greater confidence in and commitment to the consistent use of contraception as part of any sexual relationship. For girls, fostering a sense of academic self-efficacy and investment in academic goals leading to postsecondary education and/or professional training is especially crucial (Ohannessian & Crockett, 1993; Plotnick, 1992). For boys, building greater social expectations of and commitment to assuming the financial and social responsibilities associated with fatherhood and devising specific opportunities to enact these responsibilities seem promising directions for intervention (National Urban League, 1987; Olds et al., 1988) (see Notebook Page 16.4).

Adolescent Alcohol and Drug Use and Abuse

American high-school-age youths have a higher level of illicit drug use than those of any other industrialized nation. Roughly 46% of American high-school students have tried an illegal drug, including marijuana, inhalants, amphetamines, heroin and other opiates, cocaine, or barbiturates, by their senior year. While the use of these drugs declined from 1980 to 1992, recent trends show an increase in use at the 8th-grade, 10th-grade, and 12th-grade levels, with large increases in the use of marijuana and small but significant increases in the use of hallucinogens, crack, cocaine, and heroin at the 8th grade. Figure 16.2 shows the lifetime use of illicit drugs by U.S. 12th-graders.

Alcohol use has remained at a stable and relatively high level since 1975. An ongoing national study of high school seniors' drug use and related attitudes shows widespread use of alcohol from 1975 to 1994 (Johnston et al., 1994). Nearly all high-school seniors (87%) had tried alcohol at least once; 67% of 8th-graders had already tried alcohol. Recent trends in alcohol use provide a mixed picture. Among high-school seniors, those who drink monthly declined from 72% in 1980 to 50% in 1994, and daily drinking dropped from 7% in 1979 to 3.4% in 1994. However, initiation into alcohol use appears to be starting at an earlier age today. Among 8th-graders surveyed in 1993 and 1994, 26% reported having been drunk at least once, and 9% said they had been drunk in the past 30 days. In a rural sample of 7th-graders, about 60% had used alcohol in the past year, and about 8% drank four or five times a month (Sarvela & McClendon, 1988). Because of the widespread use of alcohol across many teen subcultures, much of the discussion

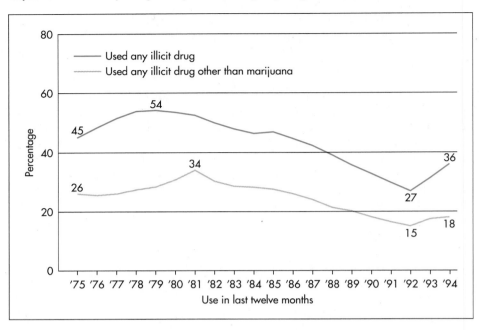

FIGURE 16.2
Annual use of illicit drugs by 12th graders.
Source: Johnston, L. D., O'Malley, P. M., & Bachman, J. G. (1995). *National survey results on drug use from the Monitoring the Future study, 1975–1994. Vol. I: Secondary school students.* (NIH Publication No. 95-4026.) Washington, D.C.: National Institute on Drug Abuse.

in this chapter focuses on understanding factors associated with its use and abuse.

Effects of Alcohol on the Body

Alcohol depresses the central nervous system. Although many people think that alcohol provides a "high," at its greatest levels of concentration in the body it can cause death by suppressing breathing. Although this outcome is extremely rare, it may occur after "chugging" large quantities of alcohol, a practice that is sometimes included in certain adolescent initiation rites and competitions over manliness. There are two other situations in which alcohol use has potentially lethal consequences. One is the use of alcohol in combination with other drugs, especially barbiturates. The other is its use in combination with driving. One study of 10th-, 11th-, and 12th-graders found that 57% had driven while intoxicated, and 78% had ridden in a car while the driver was drinking (DiBlasio, 1986).

Factors Associated with Alcohol Use

Let us consider some factors associated with the use of alcohol and the part that alcohol use plays in adolescents' lives. We are especially concerned with understanding the relationship between alcohol use and the major themes of early adolescence: physical and cognitive development, peer relations, and parent–child relationships.

Physical Effects. The physical development of puberty is accompanied by a heightened awareness of body sensations. In small quantities, alcohol has a relaxing effect that may accentuate pleasurable bodily sensations. Adolescents may use alcohol to increase physical arousal, reduce sexual inhibitions, and minimize the self-consciousness that is a barrier to social interactions. In larger quantities, alcohol may alter perceptions of reality so that

Parenthood in Early Adolescence

One area of social welfare reform that is currently being debated is policy related to adolescent mothers and their children. In answering these questions, consider the adolescent mother, her baby, the baby's father, and the adolescent mother's parents as a family system.

1. What changes might a family system undergo when an adolescent girl has a baby?

_____

_____

_____

2. How might the birth of a child to an adolescent alter her developmental trajectory? How might it alter the development of the baby's father? How might it alter the development of the adolescent mother's parent(s)?

_____

_____

_____

3. What do you consider to be the most important needs that should be met by programs designed to serve adolescent mothers and fathers?

_____

_____

_____

4. If you had an opportunity to develop a program to *prevent* teen pregnancy, what strategies would you use and why?

_____

_____

_____

705

adolescents are willing to take risks or ignore certain physical limitations. While adolescents are intoxicated, the disadvantages of physical appearance, height, weight, or sexual immaturity are minimized. Dissatisfaction with body image may contribute to an inclination to drink heavily in social situations.

Assessment of Risk. Cognitive development during adolescence suggests that young people are increasingly able to anticipate the consequences of their actions. They can hypothesize about events that have not yet occurred and reason about their possible outcomes. Adolescents should be able to manipulate several variables at one time in order to solve a problem or make a decision. These skills imply that adolescents should be able to use information about the influence of alcohol to guide their drinking behavior. However, many adolescents do not view alcohol consumption as terribly risky. In a national survey, 27% of high-school seniors saw daily drinking as involving great risk, and 46.5% of high-school seniors saw binge drinking (five or more drinks once or twice over a weekend) as involving great risk (Johnston et al., 1993). Students who drink alcohol frequently are less likely to see a great deal of risk in drinking, while those who drink little or not at all are more likely to see a great deal of risk (Small, Silverberg & Kerns, 1993). This pattern suggests cognitive consistency; in other words, adolescents who view a certain level of drinking behavior as highly risky are less likely to engage in that behavior. But what factors influence whether one views drinking as risky?

Adults as a Reference Group. The two reference groups that influence the acceptability of drinking and the manner in which alcohol is consumed are the family and the peer group (Brook, Whiteman & Gordon, 1983). There appear to be many similarities between the ways in which students and adults in a community think about and use alcohol. Barnes (1981) surveyed students and adults in the same community to assess their respective patterns of use. Adults and students showed similar patterns of using beer, wine, and other liquors. They described similar patterns of alcohol use in the home on special occasions or at mealtimes. Three basic justifications for drinking were described by the two groups: conforming functions ("so I won't be different from my friends"); social, festive functions ("it's a good way to celebrate"); and personal effects ("it helps relieve pressure"). The first reason was somewhat more important to adolescents than to adults. The second was most important to both groups. The third was somewhat more important to adolescents than to adults. Neither the first nor the third reason helps to predict whether a student or an adult will be a heavy drinker. Barnes concluded that the drinking patterns of students and adults were extremely similar. The adult members of a community set the attitudinal and behavioral tone with regard to alcohol use, and adolescents are socialized to internalize that position.

A somewhat different perspective emerges if adolescents are asked about parental approval of drinking patterns. Adolescents perceive their parents as disapproving of almost any drug use. With respect to alcohol use, over 90% perceive their parents to be disapproving of having one or two drinks a day, and almost all high-school seniors see their parents as disapproving of binge drinking (Johnston et al., 1993).

The impact of parental sanctions against alcohol use depends heavily on the quality of the parent–child relationship:

Compared to users, nonusers feel closer to both parents, consider it important to get along well with them, and want to be like them when they grow up. Nonusers' parents more typically provide praise and encouragement, develop feelings of interpersonal trust, and help with personal problems. Perceived as stricter, nonusers' parents more typically have rules about homework, television, curfew, and drugs and alcohol. Yet, they are not more punitive. Instead, parental control is enhanced by praise and encouragement and by an emotionally close relationship that encourages youngsters to seek parental advice and guidance. Young people who feel loved and trusted by parents want to emulate them, not bring embarrassment by inappropriate behavior. (Coombs & Landsverk, 1988, 480)

Peers as a Reference Group. The peer group also contributes to the patterns of alcohol use in adolescence. Here we see some explanation for the potential inconsistencies in alcohol use. The majority (53%) of high-school seniors say that they spend time with peers who use alcohol to get high, and close to 30% say they spend time with friends who get drunk at least once a week (Johnston et al., 1993). Even for 8th-graders, about 75% say their friends drink.

Most adolescents do not drink every day. However, many do engage in binge drinking, which they perceive as risky but somehow acceptable within the peer context. Binge drinking is more frequent among boys than girls and more frequent among the non-college-bound than among the college-bound. Even though adolescents say they perceive greater risk with binge drinking than with taking one or two drinks every day, they are more likely to disapprove of daily drinking than of binge drinking. Further, adolescents perceive their peers' attitudes as being much more similar to their own and much less disapproving of binge drinking than the attitudes of their parents (Johnston et al., 1987). From our knowledge of the central role of the peer group during this stage of life, we must assume that alcohol use is influenced in part by peer pressure to conform to a group norm.

Alcohol is a part of the life experience of almost every adolescent. Drinking is something an adolescent can do that symbolizes celebration, adult status, and some degree of behavioral independence from parents. Since most adults also drink, adolescents may perceive adult disapproval of adolescent drinking as hypocritical. Thus, drinking can become an avenue for testing the limits of adult authority or expressing behavioral autonomy from parental control.

Factors Linked with Early Entry into Alcohol and Drug Use

Recently, concern has turned to trying to understand why children in middle childhood (4th-, 5th-, 6th-, and 7th-graders) become involved in heavy drug and alcohol use (Farrell et al., 1992; Iannotti & Bush, 1992; Newcomb & Bentler, 1989). Significant predictors of early alcohol use included several peer factors (friends' approval of alcohol and drugs; peer pressure to use alcohol and drugs; having friends with an alcohol or drug problem) and several family factors (being home alone 20 or more times in the past 30 days after school and reporting that half or more of the adults they knew had an alcohol or drug problem).

Risk factors associated with early alcohol use are linked to social class and cultural factors. Control over the sale of alcohol to minors, the cost of alcohol, and the efforts of parents and other adults, including school officials and police, to monitor adolescent alcohol use are all community factors that can have significant influence. In addition, alcohol plays a somewhat different role among various ethnic, cultural, and religious groups. For example, a comparative analysis of African-American, Cuban, other Hispanic, and Anglo sixth- and seventh-grade males in Dade County, Florida, found different rates of alcohol use and patterns of risk factors that predicted early use for the four groups (Vega et al., 1993). In this particular study, Anglos had the highest percentage of early alcohol users (48%), Cubans next highest (41%), other Hispanics next highest (31%), and African-Americans the lowest (25%). For all groups, low family pride and willingness of the adolescent to participate in delinquent behavior or to break the law were significant predictors of early alcohol use.

Alcohol, in particular, may become a part of life for normal adolescents during the high-school years. Experimentation with alcohol is relatively easy to understand in the context of the adolescent's psychosocial needs and the modeling of alcohol use in the family, the peer group, and the community. Although illegal alcohol use might be considered a normative "rite of passage" for most adolescents, it appears that children who begin to drink early in the adolescent years, that is before ninth grade, are especially vulnerable to more serious involvement with alcohol and drug use. These children experience some combination of family, peer, and psychosocial pressures that increase their willingness to engage in deviant behavior and to ignore or minimize the risks associated with drinking.

Work Experiences in Early Adolescence

Many adolescents hold part-time jobs while they attend high school. In 1994, over 50% of 16- to 19-year-olds were in the labor force (U.S. Bureau of the Census, 1995). Only about 7% of graduating high-school seniors say they have never worked for pay (Bachman et al., 1987). There is some controversy about the benefits of working during high school and the extent to which these work experiences actually contribute in a positive way to the occupational component of identity development. Some find that adolescents who work long hours in stressful jobs are more likely to show evidence of increased cigarette smoking, marijuana and alcohol use, truancy and poor academic performance in school (Bachman et al., 1986; Manning, 1990; Steinberg & Dornbusch, 1992). Students who work long hours have less time for school activities, friends, or developing other areas of interest. The kinds of work opportunities that are available to adolescents are usually minimally skilled jobs with high turnover, low pay, and little decision-making responsibility or stimulation for skill development. These kinds of jobs are likely to produce depression and low self-esteem, as well as contributing to alienation from the school environment. For some adolescents, time spent in these kinds of work settings is associated with the development of cynical attitudes toward work and greater acceptance of unethical work practices.

Other researchers emphasize the diversity of work experiences and the potential benefits of certain kinds of work. Students who are able to find and keep a good job may feel more confident about themselves and their promise for future employment (Bachman et al., 1986). When the work does not involve too many hours and fosters skill development that young people see as related to their future career direction, the experience is likely to be associated with higher levels of well-being and less involvement in problem behaviors. For girls, the perception of continuity between school and work and the belief that work improves school performance had an especially positive relationship with mental health and well-being (Mortimer et al., 1992).

Youth Unemployment

Related to the debate about the costs and benefits of working during adolescence, there is growing concern about the problem of youth unemployment. In 1993, when the overall unemployment rate was 6.8%, adolescents in the age range 16 to 19 experienced rates of 20.4% for males and 17.4% for females. Among African-American adolescents in this age range, the unemployment rate was 40.2% for males and 37.5% for females (U.S. Bureau of the Census, 1994). A major segment of U.S. youth are having great difficulty entering the labor market.

The problem appears to be due, in part, to the low level of educational preparation that many high-school students demonstrate as they attempt to enter the work force, coupled with the slow growth of entry-level positions in certain urban centers. From the point of view of business and industry, entry-level workers need to have basic literacy and computational skills, the ability to think logically about a problem and to communicate what they are thinking verbally and in writing, and the capacity to adapt to change and learn new ways of functioning rather quickly (William T. Grant Foundation, 1988).

Results of a national assessment of public education suggest that many contemporary high-school graduates fall short of these expectations. High-school students' reading skills are stronger than their writing skills, which are evaluated as poor or minimal. Many high-school graduates cannot follow written instructions in order to complete a task. The intended meaning of the average written work cannot be understood for certain. Mathematics performance has been improving since the late 1970s, but most of the improvement is in the area of basic skills rather than the higher-order mathematical reasoning that is expected in areas such as algebra and statistics. Computer competence is expanding rapidly, but students in low-income urban centers lag significantly behind students in more affluent school districts, thereby further restricting the competitiveness of these students for higher-paying jobs (U.S. Department of Education, 1992).

A school–business–government partnership is typically advised for improving the transition from school to work for those students who are at risk for long-term unemployment (William T. Grant Foundation, 1988). Each community must evaluate the opportunities for entry-level positions. Local, state, and federal governments may need to intervene in communities where the job market is deteriorating. Businesses and schools need to work together to sponsor apprenticeships and on-the-job training. Schools must ensure that high-school graduates have the basic skills, attitudes, and social competencies to function effectively in the work environment. City, state, and federal government agencies should identify incentives for hiring low-income youth and offer some type of subsidy for personnel to mentor and train these youths. Businesses need to give hiring priority to students who have graduated from high school in their community and who meet the school's instructional and behavioral standards. This ecological-systems approach takes advantage of many different kinds of resources to facilitate the successful transition of youth into the world of work.

Personal Identity: The Psychosocial Transition to Adulthood

We close the psychosocial analysis of adolescence with a discussion of the process of *identity formation*. According to psychosocial theory, this creative construction of a sense of meaning, purpose, and continuity provides the critical foundation for performing the roles and meeting the challenges of adulthood. It serves as a personal blueprint to guide choices and commitments in encountering the great variety of opportunities and demands of adult life.

Later adolescents are preoccupied with questions about their essential character in much the same way that early adolescents are preoccupied with questions about their sense of belonging. In their efforts to define themselves, later adolescents must take into account the bonds that have been built between them and others in the past, as well as the direction that they hope to take in the future. Identity serves as an anchor point of the *I*, providing the adolescent with an essential experience of continuity in social relationships.

> The young individual must learn to be most himself where he means the most to others—those others, to be sure, who have come to mean most to him. The term *identity* expresses such a mutual relation in that it connotes both a persistent sameness within oneself (self-sameness) and a persistent sharing of some kind of essential character with others. (Erikson, 1959, 102)

Two Components of Identity: Content and Evaluation

The structure of identity has two components: content and evaluation (Breakwell, 1986; Whitbourne, 1986). The *content*, what one thinks about, values, believes in, and the traits or characteristics by which one is recognized and known by others, can be further divided into the inner or private self and the public self. The *private self*, often described as a "sense of self," refers to one's inner uniqueness and unity, a subjective experience of being the originator of one's thoughts and actions and of being self-reflective. The private self recognizes the range of values and beliefs to which one is committed and can assess the extent to which certain thoughts and actions are consistent with those beliefs (Blasi, 1991; Glodis & Blasi, 1993).

The elements of the *public self* include the many roles one plays as well as the expectations of others. It develops with greatest intensity during early adolescence. As young people move through the stage of later adolescence (roughly ages 18 to 22), they find that social reference groups including family members, neighbors, teachers, friends, religious groups, ethnic groups, and even national leaders continue to have expectations in regard to their behavior. A young person may be expected to work, attend college, marry, serve the country in the military, attend religious services, vote, have children, and provide economic support for family members. Persistent demands by meaningful others cause certain decisions that might have been made differently or not made at all under a different configuration of social reference groups. In the process of achieving personal identity, the private sense of self must be synthesized with the public self derived from a person's many different roles and relationships.

The second structural component of identity, *evaluation*, refers to the significance placed on various aspects of the identity content. Even though most people play many of the same roles, their identities differ in part because they

By taking on the role of big brother in a volunteer program, Scott explores his own values and begins to formulate the kind of person he hopes to become.

place different values on some of these roles. Some people are quite single-minded, setting great value on success in one domain, such as academic and vocational goals, and placing little stock in others. Other people strive to maintain a balance of roles; they consider themselves successful if they can find enjoyment in a variety of relationships and activities (Reischl & Hirsch, 1989).

Both the content and the evaluation component of identity change over the life course. In later adolescence, the focus is on integrating the various sources of content and determining which elements have the greatest salience. This is a major accomplishment that requires self-awareness, introspection, and active exploration of a variety of roles and relationships. However, the individual identity that is formulated by later adolescents is often very abstract because these youth have not yet encountered many of the responsibilities, pressures, and conflicts of adult life. The ideological framework of identity has not yet been forged in the flames of reality.

The basic conflict of the psychosocial crisis of later adolescence is individual identity formation versus identity confusion. This conflict results from the enormous difficulty of pulling together the many components of the self, including changing perspectives on one's beliefs and values as well as new and changing social demands, into a unified image that can guide a person toward positive, meaningful action. The process of identity formation is confounded by many distractions. Many young people find it very hard to sort out what they want to be from what their parents have urged them to become. Some have received little encouragement to become a separate person with independent feelings and views; others are so beleaguered by feelings of inferiority and alienation that they do not have the necessary optimism for envisioning a positive future. Still others find many paths appealing and have difficulty making a commitment to one.

Identity Status

Identity formation is a dynamic process that unfolds as young people assess their competencies and aspirations within a changing social context of expectations, demands, and resources. Many potential resolutions of the psychosocial crisis of individual identity versus identity confusion have been described. At the positive pole is *identity achievement;* at the negative pole is *identity confusion.* Also discussed are premature resolution, *identity foreclosure;* postponement of resolution, *psychosocial moratorium;* and *negative identity.*

Crisis and Commitment

One of the most widely used conceptual frameworks for assessing identity status was devised by James Marcia (Marcia, 1980; Waterman, 1982). Using Erikson's concepts, Marcia assessed identity status on the basis of two criteria: crisis and commitment. *Crisis* consists of a period of role experimentation and active decision making among alternative choices. Usually, the experience of crisis is accompanied by feelings of confusion and uncertainty about values and goals. *Commitment* consists of a demonstration of personal involvement in the areas of occupational choice, religion, and political ideology. The status of subjects' identity development is assessed on the basis of Marcia's interview (see Table 16.1). People who are classified as identity achieved have already experienced a crisis and made occupational and ideological commitments. People who are classified as identity foreclosed have not experienced a crisis but demonstrate strong occupational and ideological commitments. Their occupational and ideological beliefs appear to be very close to those of their parents. The foreclosed identity is deceptive. A young person of 18 or 19 who can say exactly what he or she wants in life and who has selected an occupational goal may appear to be very mature. This clarity of vision may impress peers and adults as evidence of a high level of self-insight. However, if this solution has been formulated through the wholesale adoption of the young person's family expectations, it may not actually reflect much depth of self-understanding.

People who are classified as being in a state of psychosocial moratorium are involved in ongoing crisis. Their commitments are diffuse. People who are classified as identity confused may or may not have experienced a crisis and demonstrate a complete lack of commitment. Marcia mentions that the identity-confused group has a rather cavalier, playboy quality that allows them to

TABLE 16.1

Relationship of Identity Status, Crisis, and Commitment

	Crisis	Commitment
Identity achievement	+	+
Foreclosure	−	+
Moratorium	+	−
Identity confusion	+/−	−

cope with the college environment. He suggests that more seriously confused persons (such as those described by Erikson, 1959) may not appear in his sample because they are unable to cope with college.

Negative Identity

Sometimes, cultural expectations and demands provide a young person with a clearly defined self-image that is completely contrary to the cultural values of the community. This is called a negative identity (Erikson, 1959). Such expressions as "failure," "good-for-nothing," "juvenile delinquent," "hood," "gangster," and "loser" are negative labels that adult society commonly applies to certain adolescents. In the absence of any indication of possible success or contribution to society, a young person may accept such negative labels as a self-definition and proceed to validate this identity by behaving in ways that confirm it. Some young people grow up admiring adults who have become very successful by following antisocial or criminal paths. Drug lords, gang leaders, leaders of hate groups, and people who use elected political positions for personal gain are all examples of possible role models around which a negative identity may be formed.

A negative identity can also result from a strong identification with someone who is devalued by the family or the community. A loving uncle who is an alcoholic or a clever, creative parent who commits suicide can inspire association with or emulation of shared undesirable characteristics.

Linda, for example, established the negative identity of a person going crazy.

> Her father was an alcoholic, physically abusive man, who terrified her when she was a child. . . . Linda, herself a bright child, became by turns the standard bearer for her father's proud aspirations and the target of his jealousy. Midway through grade school she began flunking all her courses and retreating to a private world of daydreams. . . . "I always expected hallucinations, being locked up, down the road coming toward me. . . . I always resisted seeing myself as an adult. I was afraid that at the point I stopped the tape [the years of wild experimentation] I'd become my parents. . . . My father was the closest person I knew to crazy." (Ochberg, 1986, 296–297)

Identity Confusion

The foreclosed identity and the negative identity both resolve the identity crisis in ways that fall short of the goal of a positive personal identity. Yet both provide a person with a concrete identity. The most psychologically problematic resolution of the crisis is identity confusion. These young people are unable to make a commitment to any single view of themselves. They may be unable to integrate the various roles they play. They may be confronted by opposing value systems or by a lack of confidence in their ability to make meaningful decisions. Within the private, subjective self, some young people may reach later adolescence having difficulty accepting or establishing clear ego boundaries or experiencing feelings of agency. At an unconscious level, they may have incorporated two or more conflicting ideas about the self—for example, an abusive, harsh, rejecting, powerful father and a wise, loving, nurturant, powerful grandmother, who stand in opposition to one another. Under any of these conditions, the demands for integration and synthesis of a personal identity arouse anxiety, apathy, and hostility toward the existing roles, none of which they can successfully adopt.

In comparison with the moratorium group, young people with a confused status are less conscientious, more likely to experience negative emotions, and more disagreeable (Clancy & Dollinger, 1993). They are generally not outgoing, but rather describe themselves as self-conscious and likely to feel depressed. Several studies have found that young people who are characterized as identity confused have had a history of early and frequent involvement with drug use and abuse (Jones, 1992). One might speculate that difficulties resolving earlier psychosocial crises, especially conflicts related to trust versus mistrust, autonomy versus shame and doubt, and initiative versus guilt, leave some young people with deficits in ego formation that interfere with the kind of energy and playful self-assertiveness that are necessary for achieving identity.

In the process of evolving an individual identity, everyone experiences temporary periods of confusion and depression. The task of bringing together the many elements of one's experience into a coordinated, clear self-definition is difficult and time consuming. Adolescents are likely to experience moments of self-preoccupation, isolation, and discouragement as the diverse pieces of the puzzle are shifted and reordered into the total picture. Thus, even the eventual positive identity is the result of some degree of identity confusion. The negative outcome of identity confusion, however, suggests that a person is never able to formulate a satisfying identity that will integrate multiple identifications, aspirations, and roles. Such individuals have the persistent fear that they are losing their hold on themselves and their future (see Box 16.3 and Notebook Page 16.5).

Gender Variation in the Process of Identity Formation

Questions have been raised about the process of identity formation and its outcome for young men and women in our society. For both women and men, identity achievement is associated with positive ego qualities. "Identity achieved youths generally exhibit higher levels of self-esteem, greater cognitive and ego complexity, postconventional levels of moral reasoning, and a strong capacity for inner-directed behavior" (Craig-Bray, Adams & Dobson, 1988, 175). In one analysis of the way older adolescents think about commitments, subjects were asked to define the concept of commitment (Galotti & Kozberg, 1987). Few gender differences were found in these definitions, except that women were more likely than men to cite the importance of keeping a promise or their word of honor. Other themes—mutual trust, expression of one's values, a social contract, ordering of priorities, perseverance, obligation, devotion of the self—were referred to equally often by men and women.

There is evidence that men and women handle the process of role experimentation and identity achievement somewhat differently. The uncertainty of the identity crisis is often accompanied by greater anxiety for women than for men. This anxiety may be linked to concerns over achievement strivings. Many women experience conflict between their image of femininity and their desire to set ambitious personal goals (Ginsburg & Orlofsky, 1981). Anxiety may also be a product of the general distress that women feel when they focus on their own agendas rather than on facilitating the agendas of others, as society appears to expect them to do. In this

BOX 16.3

Parental Attachment and Identity Formation

We tend to think of identity formation as a process that requires young people to distance themselves from the strong expectations and definitions imposed by parents and other family members. To achieve an individual identity, a person must create a vision of the self that is authentic and take hold of his or her destiny in an effort to reach goals that are personally meaningful. Yet recent research has demonstrated that the quality of family relationships contributes significantly to a young person's ability to achieve a personal identity (Kamptner, 1988; Kroger & Haslett, 1988; Papini et al., 1989).

The relationship can be compared with the contribution of secure attachments in infancy to subsequent willingness to explore the environment. Later adolescents who have a secure relationship with parents and are comfortable about loosening those ties can begin to explore the ideological, occupational, and interpersonal alternatives that will become their own identities. In particular, both male and female college students, who have a positive attachment to their mothers are more likely to have an achieved identity, and less likely to be in the moratorium or identity diffused statuses than are students who have insecure, mistrustful relationships with

their mothers. Later adolescents who are still emotionally dependent on parents and who require constant reassurance about their parents' affection experience greater identity confusion (Benson, Harris & Rogers, 1992).

By the time individuals reach later adolescence, those who are securely attached to their parents are confident about their parents' affection and support. At the same time, they trust in their own worth and ability to make decisions (Blain, Thompson & Whiffen, 1993). A sense of family security fosters identity formation in the following ways:

- It fosters confidence in the exploration of social relationships, ideologies, and settings.

- It establishes positive expectations in regard to interpersonal experiences outside the family.

- It fosters the formation of group identities apart from the family, thus providing a transitional context for work on individual identity.

- It provides a basic layer of self-acceptance, permitting the young person to approach the process of identity formation with optimism.

---

context, the moratorium status, which is considered a positive interlude on the path toward achievement, has been found to be linked to higher levels of self-doubt in women than in men.

Other evidence for gender differences lies in the content of the identity. Erikson's (1968, 1982) work emphasized ideological and vocational commitments as central to identity formation. Gilligan (1982) criticized this orientation, arguing that the interpersonal content may be more central for women and that the clarification of interpersonal commitments enables more advanced exploration in vocational and ideological contents. Research findings lend support to this concept (Bilsker et al., 1988; Mellor, 1989; Schiedel & Marcia, 1985). The quality of interpersonal relations and the establishment of satisfying social commitments are more relevant to the development of a woman's identity than to that of a man. Measures of identity status that distinguish between interpersonal and ideological aspects of identity find that women score higher on interpersonal identity achievement than men and are less likely to show evidence of interpersonal identity diffusion (Benson et al., 1992).

For both men and women, differentiation or the capacity to function autonomously without being overly burdened by feelings of responsibility for others is positively associated with psychosocial maturity and identity

The Identity Formation Process

Personal identity provides a guide for the major decisions of early adulthood. How far along are you in formulating your personal identity? In each area listed below, try to identify your values and goals. Then explain the extent to which you have experienced any experimentation, uncertainty, or anxiety about your values and goals concerning this aspect of identity.

1. *Career direction*
   a. Values and goals:

   _____

   _____

   _____

   b. Experiences of experimentation or uncertainty:

   _____

   _____

   _____

2. *Family roles and relationships*
   a. Values and goals:

   _____

   _____

   _____

   b. Experiences of experimentation or uncertainty:

   _____

   _____

   _____

3. *Interpersonal relations*
   a. Values and goals:

   _____

b. Experiences of experimentation or uncertainty:

4. *Religious ideology*
   a. Values and goals:

b. Experiences of experimentation or uncertainty:

5. *Political ideology*
   a. Values and goals:

b. Experiences of experimentation or uncertainty:

achievement. However, some studies suggest that women tend to have less conflict over sustaining high levels of intimacy and identity. Women are more able to find support for their identity in positive relationships with others. On the other hand, the very highest levels of identity are likely to be associated with lower levels of intimacy for men, suggesting that those who are highly individuated tend to experience a loss of connection and closeness with others (Garbarino et al., 1995).

Optimizing Development in Adolescence

Ideas about optimizing development in adolescence are drawn from the topics covered in Chapters 15 and 16 and are summarized in Table 16.2. By the time children reach adolescence, their situations are enormously varied depending upon the life circumstances they have encountered: the degree of love and encouragement they have received from parents and others; their personal and family resources; the quality of their education; their cognitive abilities and talents; and the resources and opportunities available in their communities. Some adolescents compete in science fairs, perform in concerts, have their poems and short stories published, provide leadership to community service activities, excel in highly competitive athletic events, or start their own businesses. Other adolescents are addicted to drugs, serve time in youth detention centers, drop out of school, or commit vandalism, robbery, or murder. Some are already dead as a result of homicide or suicide. Still other adolescents are walking the middle path, taking classes that are mostly boring but not terrible, working 10 to 20 hours a week, spending time with friends, drinking and smoking cigarettes, driving around in their cars, planning what to do on weekends, partying, and dreaming about the future.

It is difficult to generalize about how to optimize development for young people in this age group because the group itself is so varied. Perhaps the first point is to stop considering adolescents as one homogeneous group with a common "youth culture." Recognizing individual differences and responding appropriately to the variety of developmental levels that exist in this chronological age group are important beginnings.

In our opinion, our contemporary society is not providing an optimal developmental environment for many adolescents. Adolescents have great potential for reaching high levels of competence in each of the major domains of functioning: physical, social, intellectual, emotional, and self-understanding. Yet, many young people attend schools that typically do not engage or challenge their problem-solving skills. Many parents are confused about their role as socialization agents during adolescence. Businesses and nonprofit agencies offer relatively few apprenticeships or on-the-job training experiences that help build a sense of competence. Many adolescents are bored or restless; they are not included in the important decisions of family or community, and they do not feel valued or respected by adults. Despite the tremendous need for services in most communities, we have only begun to harness the volunteer potential in the adolescent population. Many adolescents do not have a single meaningful relationship with an adult: Their parents are psychologically unavailable or simply not present when adolescents are at home; many

TABLE 16.2

Optimizing Development in Adolescence

- Teach adolescents about the variations in sequence and timing of physical changes during puberty and help them incorporate the physical changes into a positive body image.
- Foster good nutrition, appropriate physical activity and rest, and personal hygiene.
- Help adolescents understand the risks associated with early entry into sexual activity and use of alcohol and other illegal drugs. Teach them a variety of strategies for resisting these activities when they occur in family or peer settings.
- Encourage adolescents to engage in a variety of roles and relationships to foster flexible problem solving.
- Participate with adolescents in ongoing interactions in which they are encouraged to examine their assumptions, find evidence to support their views, and evaluate the sources of their information.
- Acknowledge the value of participating in a more heterogeneous peer group for the part it plays in fostering formal operational reasoning.
- Encourage adolescents to take challenging high-school courses that introduce the principles of hypothetical-deductive reasoning, the use of symbols and symbol systems, and relativistic thinking.
- Place high expectations on the high school to provide the range of courses and academic experiences that will foster abstract, logical thinking and flexible problem solving.
- Help adolescents to find ways of acknowledging and accepting a variety of emotional experiences as well as devising strategies for expressing and controlling their emotions.
- Teach adolescents new ways of overcoming feelings of worthlessness and depression.
- Help adolescents to identify appropriate community resources for coping with anxiety, depression, and uncontrollable impulses.
- Take any discussion of suicide or evidence of self-destructive behavior seriously, and assist the adolescent in finding professional counseling.
- Acknowledge the significance of peer relations for adolescents, and provide opportunities for adolescents to discuss openly their concerns about their peers.
- Give adolescents support in finding a group of friends that best matches their needs, interests, and abilities.
- Provide opportunities for adolescents to talk about conflicts they experience between going along with their peers and doing what they think is personally right for them. Encourage adolescents to use their judgment in these conflicts, rather than always telling them what to do.
- As adolescents struggle with concerns about peer group affiliation, be sure to tell them that they are valued and respected in their family.
- Let adolescents know that they have a right to resist unwanted sexual contact from any person and that you will help them deal with this problem should it occur.
- Help adolescents to accept their sexual needs as normal and healthy. At the same time, talk with them about finding appropriate, caring, nonexploitive ways of expressing and satisfying these needs.
- Provide evidence in your own behavior for the value of fidelity. Let adolescents know that they can count on your loyalty and support.
- Try to prevent a sense of isolation by empathizing with the adolescent and giving him or her reassurance of being understood and valued.

(continued)

TABLE 16.2 (continued)

- As a parent, continue to find times for meaningful interactions with an adolescent child. Listen while your child tells you what is on his or her mind, and give your child opportunities to hear about the concerns and challenges you face in your life as well.
- Recognize the constructive role of conflict. Try to accept some level of expressing differences of opinion as an important aspect of an adolescent's emerging independence.
- In parenting an adolescent, try to find the right balance of affection and support, appropriately high expectations, reasonable limits, and adequate freedom for the child to make independent decisions.
- Let your adolescent children know about some of the issues you face in caring for your aging parents. Involve them in helping you solve some of these challenges.
- Give adolescents opportunities to know what is expected of them as adults, and encourage them to develop the skills and knowledge that will help them function independently.
- Provide information that will help build a strong ethnic identity, and expose adolescents to information and experiences that will build a positive evaluation of their ethnic heritage.

teachers are regarded with suspicion; and other community agencies are not able to find the key that unlocks their protective facade of cool indifference.

We need to find meaningful roles for adolescents in their communities that bring these young people together with others who have different points of view and different skills so that they can appreciate the value of working together toward common goals. We need to identify roles that allow adolescents to glimpse their possible futures as leaders who give substance to their communities.

Chapter Summary

1. A positive resolution of the psychosocial crisis of group identity versus alienation occurs when adolescents find acceptance and membership in a group that meets their social needs and provides them with a sense of belonging.
2. A negative resolution of the psychosocial crisis of group identity versus alienation leaves adolescents with a pervasive sense of social estrangement and lack of social support.
3. The central process for the resolution of the psychosocial crisis, peer pressure, can have both positive and negative influences on an adolescent's behavior. The concept of peer pressure implies that adolescents are willing to suppress some aspects of their individuality in order to experience acceptance by and affiliation with the group.
4. Peer pressure can result in clarifying individual values and beliefs, especially when group norms conflict with personal values.
5. As a result of resolving the psychosocial crisis of group identity versus alienation in a positive direction, the prime adaptive ego quality of

fidelity to others is established. A negative resolution of the crisis results in the core pathology of isolation.

6. Adolescence brings important changes to the parent–child relationship. Parents and other family members remain an important source of support even while involvements in the peer group are intensifying.

7. Time spent in interaction with parents at home has positive consequences for adolescents.

8. Even though parent–child conflicts increase, they can provide a valuable context in which adolescents express their own independent views and learn about their parents' ideas.

9. Parenting practices, especially the extent to which parents emphasize academic achievement, monitor their adolescents' activities, and involve adolescents in decision making are associated with school performance, peer group affiliation, and drug use.

10. At the same time as parents are involved in meeting the demands of their adolescent children, many are also caring for aging parents. Adolescents have the opportunity to observe the exercise of fidelity to others as they watch their parents try to fulfill the needs of their grandparents.

11. Death of a grandparent is one of the first experiences of death that most children are likely to encounter. This loss helps adolescents to see their parents in a new role as children and stimulates thoughts about the relationship they will have with their parents as both they and their parents grow older.

12. Cultural puberty rites or initiation ceremonies help mark the transition from youth to adulthood. These ceremonies serve a variety of functions and are characterized by wide differences in severity, timing, and content.

13. The transition from youth to adulthood is more gradual in the United States than in many traditional societies, which have a number of shifts in rights, responsibilities, and community recognitions. Lack of clarity about the status of adolescents results in rules and laws about adolescents varying from one state to the next.

14. One of the most challenging aspects of establishing group identity is the formation of an ethnic-group identity. Ethnic identity intensifies as young people move into a more diverse social environment and encounter more ethnic diversity and discrimination.

15. Early parenthood poses a significant challenge to adolescent development. A strong relationship exists between a mother's age at first birth and her family income by age 27. Early parenthood is also associated with lower educational attainment and occupational levels.

16. An emerging literature focuses on adolescent fathers. Most fathers try to stay in contact with the mother and the baby. Many try to contribute financially to the baby's support. There is little research on the psychological consequences of early fatherhood.

17. Many adolescents seek or hold part-time jobs. There is a substantial difference between the benefits of having a good job that is less than 20 hours per week and one that involves minimal skills and requires long hours. Whereas the former appears to be associated with increased well-being, the latter is associated with poor grades and increased cigarette, alcohol, and drug use.

18. Adolescents experience a high rate of unemployment, especially among African-Americans. Problems of entering into the labor market are explained by a combination of factors, including poor academic preparation for work, limited opportunities, and lack of necessary social and motivational attributes.

19. Adolescent drug and alcohol use is higher in the United States than in any other industrialized nation. Recent trends show an increase in cigarette smoking and the use of marijuana and inhalants, as well as small increases in the use of heroin, crack, and cocaine at early (8th-grade) ages. Adolescents appear to be less concerned about the risks associated with the use of alcohol and drugs than they were in the past.

20. Both adults and peers serve as significant reference groups that influence the use of alcohol. The quality of the parent–child relationship appears to be a significant predictor of the age at which a child begins drinking or using drugs and how much a child drinks.

21. Experimentation with alcohol is relatively easy to understand in the context of the adolescent's psychosocial needs and the modeling of alcohol use in the family, the peer group, and the community. Illegal alcohol use appears to serve as a rite of passage for most adolescents.

22. In the transition from adolescence into adulthood, establishing a personal identity is a major psychosocial achievement. Personal identity provides a creative sense of meaning, purpose, and continuity from the past into the future.

23. Identity is comprised of content (what one thinks about, one's values, beliefs, and traits) as well as evaluation (the significance one places on each component of the identity). Identity is usually formed around basic domains such as career, family, personal relationships, political and religious ideologies, and ethnicity.

24. Identity status refers to one's experiences of crisis and commitment. Various identity statuses have been identified: identity achievement, moratorium, foreclosure, identity confusion, and negative identity.

25. For both men and women, identity achievement is associated with positive ego strengths. However, women tend to evaluate interpersonal and family domains more highly, whereas men tend to evaluate career and ideological domains more highly. Women typically experience more anxiety over moratorium than do men. Men experience more conflict between identity and intimacy than do women.

References

Ackerman, G. L. (1993). A Congressional view of youth suicide. *American Psychologist, 48*, 183–184.

Adams, G. R. & Jones, R. M. (1982). Adolescent egocentrism: Exploration into possible contributions of parent–child relations. *Journal of Youth and Adolescence, 11*, 25–31.

Allen, J. P., Weissberg, R. P. & Hawkins, J. A. (1989). The relation between values and social competence in early adolescence. *Developmental Psychology, 25*, 458–464.

Aneshensel, C. S., Pearlin, L. I., Mullan, J. T., Zarit, S. H. & Whitlach, C. J. (1995). *Profiles in caregiving: The unexpected career.* San Diego: Academic Press.

Astone, N. M. (1993). Are adolescent mothers just single mothers? *Journal of Research on Adolescence, 3*, 353–372.

Atkinson, D. R., Morten, G. & Sue, D. W. (1983). *Counseling American minorities: A cross-cultural perspective* (2nd ed.) Dubuque, Iowa.: William C. Brown.

Bachman, J. G., Bare, D. E. & Frankie, E. I. (1986). *Correlates of employment among high school seniors.* (Monitoring the Future Occasional Paper, 20). Ann Arbor, Mich.: Institute for Social Research.

Bachman, J. G., Johnston, L. D. & O'Malley, P. M. (1987). *Monitoring the future: Questionnaire responses from the nation's high school seniors, 1986.* Ann Arbor, Mich.: Survey Research Center, Institute for Social Research.

Baumrind, D. (1991). The influence of parenting style on adolescent competence and substance use. *Journal of Early Adolescence, 11*, 56–95.

Benedict, R. (1938). Continuities and discontinuities in cultural conditioning. *Psychiatry, 1*, 161–167.

Bengston, V. L. & Roberts, R. E. (1991). Intergenerational solidarity in aging families: An example of formal theory construction. *Journal of Marriage and the Family, 53*, 856–870.

Benson, M. J., Harris, P. B. & Rogers, C. S. (1992). Identity consequences of attachment to mothers and fathers among late adolescents. *Journal of Research on Adolescence, 2*, 187–204.

Berlin, I. N. (1987). Suicide among American Indian adolescents: An overview. *Suicide and Life-Threatening Behavior, 17*, 218–232.

Bilsker, D., Schiedel, D. & Marcia, J. (1988). Sex differences in identity status. *Sex Roles, 18*, 231–236.

Blain, M. D., Thompson, J. M. & Whiffen, V. E. (1993). Attachment and perceived social support in late adolescence: The interactions between working models of self and others. *Journal of Adolescent Research, 8*, 226–241.

Blasi, A. (1991). The self as subject in the study of personality. In D. Ozer, J. Healy & A. Stewart (Eds.). *Perspectives in personality* (vol. 3, part A, 19–37). London: Kingsley.

Breakwell, G. M. (1986). *Coping with threatened identities.* London: Methuen.

Brook, J. S., Whiteman, M. & Gordon, A. S. (1983). Stages of drug use in adolescence: Personality, peer, and family correlates. *Developmental Psychology, 19*, 269–277.

Brown, B. B., Mounts, N., Lamborn, S. D. & Steinberg, L. (1993). Parenting practices and peer group affiliation in adolescence. *Child Development, 64*, 467–482.

Brown, J. K. (1975). Adolescent initiation rites: Recent interpretations. In R. E. Grinder (Ed.), *Studies in adolescence* (3rd ed.). New York: Macmillan, 40–51.

Burton, R. B. & Whiting, J. W. M. (1961). The absent father and cross-sex identity. *Merrill-Palmer Quarterly, 7*, 85–95.

Caldas, S. J. (1993). Current theoretical perspectives on adolescent pregnancy and childbearing in the United States. *Journal of Adolescent Research, 8*, 4–20.

Clancy, S. M. & Dollinger, S. J. (1993). Identity, self, and personality: I, identity status and the five-factor model of personality. *Journal of Research on Adolescence, 3*, 227–246.

Clasen, D. R. & Brown, B. B. (1985). The multidimensionality of peer pressure in adolescence. *Journal of Youth and Adolescence, 14*, 451–468.

Coombs, R. H. & Landsverk, J. (1988). Parenting styles and substance use in childhood and adolescence. *Journal of Marriage and the Family, 50*, 473–482.

Craig-Bray, L., Adams, G. R. & Dobson, W. R. (1988). Identity formation and social relations during late adolescence. *Journal of Youth and Adolescence, 17*, 173–188.

Cross, W. E. (1991). *Shades of black: Diversity in African-American identity.* Philadelphia: Temple University Press.

DiBlasio, F. A. (1986). Drinking adolescents on the roads. *Journal of Youth and Adolescence, 15*, 173–188.

Durbin, D. L., Darling, N., Steinberg, L. & Brown, B. B. (1993). Parenting style and peer group membership among European-American adolescents. *Journal of Research on Adolescence, 3*, 87–100.

East, P. L., Hess, L. E. & Lerner, R. M. (1987). Peer social support and adjustment of early adolescent peer groups. *Journal of Early Adolescence, 7*, 153–163.

Edelman, M. W. & Pittman, K. J. (1986). Adolescent pregnancy: Black and white. *Journal of Community Health, 11,* 63–69.

Erikson, E. H. (1959). The problem of ego identity. *Psychological Issues, 1,* 101–164.

Erikson, E. H. (1968). *Identity: Youth and crisis.* New York: W. W. Norton.

Erikson, E. H. (1982). *The life cycle completed: A review.* New York: W. W. Norton.

Farrell, A. D., Danish, S. J. & Howard, C. W. (1992). Risk factors for drug use in urban adolescents: Identification and cross-validation. *American Journal of Community Psychology, 20,* 263–286.

Feldman, S. S. & Gehring, T. M. (1988). Changing perceptions of family cohesion and power across adolescence. *Child Development, 59,* 1034–1045.

Finley, N. J. (1989). Gender differences in caregiving for elderly parents. *Journal of Marriage and the Family, 51,* 79–86.

Fosburgh, L. (1977). The make-believe world of teenage maturity. *New York Times Magazine* (August 7), 29–34.

Franklin, D. L. (1988). Race, class, and adolescent pregnancy: An ecological analysis. *American Journal of Orthopsychiatry, 58,* 339–355.

Galotti, K. M. & Kozberg, S. F. (1987). Older adolescents' thinking about academic/vocational and interpersonal commitments. *Journal of Youth and Adolescence, 15,* 147–163.

Garbarino, J., Gaa, J. P., Swank, P., McPherson, R. & Gratch, L. V. (1995). The relation of individuation and psychosocial development. *Journal of Family Psychology, 9,* 311–318.

Garland, A. F. & Zigler, E. (1993). Adolescent suicide prevention: Current research and social policy implications. *American Psychologist, 48,* 169–182.

Gavazzi, S. M. (1995). The Growing up FAST: Families and adolescents surviving and thriving™ program. *Journal of Adolescence, 18,* 31–47.

Gelles, R. J. (1989). Child abuse and violence in single-parent families: Parent absence and economic deprivation. *American Journal of Orthopsychiatry, 59,* 492–501.

Gennep, A. van (1909/1960). *Rites of passage* (M. B. Vizedon & G. Caffee, trans.). Chicago: University of Chicago Press.

Gilligan, C. (1982). *In a different voice: Psychological theory and women's development.* Cambridge, Mass.: Harvard University Press.

Ginsburg, S. D. & Orlofsky, J. L. (1981). Ego identity status, ego development, and locus of control in college women. *Journal of Youth and Adolescence, 10,* 297–307.

Giordano, P. C., Cernkovich, S. A. & DeMaris, A. (1993). The family and peer relations of black adolescents. *Journal of Marriage and the Family, 55,* 277–287.

Glodis, K. A. & Blasi, A. (1993). The sense of self and identity among adolescents and adults. *Journal of Adolescent Research, 8,* 365–380.

William T. Grant Foundation. (1988). *The forgotten half: Pathways to success for America's youth and young families.* Washington, D.C.: The William T. Grant Commission on Work, Family, and Citizenship.

Hardy, J. B. & Duggan, A. K. (1988). Teenage fathers and the fathers of infants of urban teenage mothers. *American Journal of Public Health, 78,* 919–922.

Hendricks, L. E. & Fullilove, R. E. (1983). Locus of control and use of contraception among unmarried black adolescent fathers and their controls: A preliminary report. *Journal of Youth and Adolescence, 12,* 225–233.

Hill, J. P. (1988). Adapting to menarche: Familial control and conflict. In M. R. Gunnar & W. A. Collins (Eds.), *Development during the transition to adolescence.* Minnesota Symposium on Child Psychology (vol. 21). Hillsdale, N.J.: Erlbaum, 43–77.

Hoge, D. R. & McCarthy, J. D. (1984). Influence of individual and group identity salience in the global self-esteem of youth. *Journal of Personality and Social Psychology, 47,* 403–414.

Hunter, F. T. (1985). Adolescents' perception of discussions with parents and friends. *Developmental Psychology, 21,* 433–440.

Iannotti, R. J. & Bush, P. J. (1992). Perceived versus actual friends' use of alcohol, cigarettes, marijuana, and cocaine: Which has the most influence? *Journal of Youth and Adolescence, 21,* 375–389.

Johnston, L. D., Bachman, J. G. & O'Malley, P. M. (1994). Drug use continues to climb among American teenagers. Ann Arbor, Mich.: *The University of Michigan News and Information Service.* December 8.

Johnston, L. D., O'Malley, P. M. & Bachman, J. G. (1987). *National trends in drug use and related factors among American high school students and young adults, 1975–1986.* Rockville, Md.: National Institute on Drug Abuse.

Johnston, L. D., O'Malley, P. M. & Bachman, J. D. G. (1993). *National survey results on drug use from Monitoring the Future Study, 1975–1992, Volume 1: Secondary school students.* Rockville, Md.: National Institute on Drug Abuse.

Jones, R. M. (1992). Ego identity and adolescent problem behavior. In G. R. Adams, T. P. Gullota & R.

Montemayor (Eds.), *Adolescent identity formation.* Newbury Park, Calif.: Sage, 216–233.

Kamptner, N. L. (1988). Identity development in late adolescence: Causal modeling of social and familial influences. *Journal of Youth and Adolescence, 17,* 493–514.

Kroger, J. & Haslett, S. J. (1988). Separation-individuation and ego identity status in late adolescence:0 A two-year longitudinal study. *Journal of Youth and Adolescence, 17,* 59–80.

Lamb, M. E. & Elster, A. B. (1985). Adolescent mother–infant–father relationships. *Developmental Psychology, 21,* 768–773.

Lamborn, S. D. & Steinberg, L. D. (1993). Emotional autonomy redux: Revisiting Ryan and Lynch. *Child Development, 64,* 483–499.

Levitt, M. J., Guacci-Franco, N. & Levitt, J. L. (1993). Convoys of social support in childhood and early adolescence: Structure and function. *Developmental Psychology, 29,* 811–818.

Lopata, H. Z. (1979). *Women as widows: Support systems.* New York: Elsevier.

Luhtanen, R. & Crocker, J. (1992). A collective self-esteem scale: Self-evaluation of one's social identity. *Personality and Social Psychology Bulletin, 18,* 302–318.

MacDermid, S. & Crouter, A. C. (1995). Midlife, adolescence, and parental employment in family systems. *Journal of Youth and Adolescence, 24,* 29–54.

Manning, W. D. (1990). Parenting employed teenagers. *Youth and Society, 22,* 184–200.

Marcia, J. E. (1980). Identity in adolescence. In J. Adelson (Ed.), *Handbook of adolescent psychology.* New York: Wiley, 159–187.

Marsiglio, W. (1987). Adolescent fathers in the United States: Their initial living arrangements, marital experience, and educational outcomes. *Family Planning Perspectives, 19,* 240–251.

Marsiglio, W. (1989). Adolescent males' pregnancy resolution preferences and family formation intentions: Does family background make a difference for blacks and whites? *Journal of Adolescent Research, 4,* 214–237.

Mau, R. Y. (1992). The validity and devolution of a concept: Student alienation. *Adolescence, 27,* 731–741.

McMillan, D. W. & Hiltonsmith, R. W. (1982). Adolescents at home: An exploratory study of the relationship between perception of family social climate, general well-being, and actual behavior in the home setting. *Journal of Youth and Adolescence, 11,* 301–315.

Mead, M. (1928). *Coming of age in Samoa.* New York: William Morrow.

Mead, M. (1949/1955). *Male and female: A study of the sexes in a changing world.* New York: William Morrow; Mentor Books.

Mellor, S. (1989). Gender differences in identity formation as a function of self-other relationships. *Journal of Youth and Adolescence, 18,* 361–375.

Montemayor, R. (1983). Parents and adolescents in conflict: All families some of the time and some families most of the time. *Journal of Early Adolescence, 3,* 83–103.

Moore, K. A., Myers, D. E., Morrison, D. R., Nord, C. W., Brown, B. & Edmonston, B. (1993). Age at first childbirth and later poverty. *Journal of Research on Adolescence, 3,* 393–422.

Morrison, D. M. (1985). Adolescent contraceptive behavior: A review. *Psychological Bulletin, 98,* 538–568.

Mortimer, J. T., Finch, M., Shanahan, M. & Ryu, S. (1992). Work experience, mental health, and behavioral adjustment in adolescence. *Journal of Research on Adolescence, 2,* 25–57.

Munroe, R. L. & Munroe, R. H. (1975). *Cross-cultural human development.* Monterey, Calif.: Brooks/ Cole.

Murdock, G. P. (1934). *Our primitive contemporaries.* New York: Macmillan.

Muuss, R. E. (1970). Puberty rites in primitive and modern societies. *Adolescence, 5,* 109–128.

National Urban League. (1987). *Adolescent male responsibility pregnancy prevention and parenting program: A program development guide.* New York: National Urban League.

Newcomb, M. D. & Bentler, P. M. (1989). Substance use and abuse among children and teenagers. *American Psychologist, 44,* 242–248.

Newman, B. M. (1989). The changing nature of the parent–adolescent relationship from early to later adolescence. *Adolescence, 24,* 916–924.

Newman, P. R. & Newman, B. M. (1976). Early adolescence and its conflict: Group identity versus alientation. *Adolescence, 11,* 261–274.

O'Bryant, S. L. (1987). Attachment to home and support systems of older widows in Columbus Ohio. In H. Z. Lopata (Ed.), *Widows* (vol. 2). Durham, N.C.: Duke University Press.

Ochberg, R. L. (1986). College dropouts: The developmental logic of psychosocial moratoria. *Journal of Youth and Adolescence, 15,* 287–302.

Offer, D., Ostrov, E. & Howard, K. I. (1982). Family perceptions of adolescent self-image. *Journal of Youth and Adolescence, 11,* 281–291.

Ohannessian, C. M. & Crockett, L. J. (1993). A longitudinal investigation of the relationship between educational investment and adolescent sexual activity. *Journal of Adolescent Research, 8,* 167–182.

Olds, D. L., Henderson, C. R., Jr., Tatelbaum, R. & Chamberlin, R. (1988). Improving the life-course development of socially disadvantaged mothers: A randomized trial of nurse home visitation. *American Journal of Public Health, 78,* 1436–1445.

Papini, D. R., Datan, N. & McCluskey-Fawcett, K. A. (1988). An observational study of affective and assertive family interactions during adolescence. *Journal of Youth and Adolescence, 17,* 477–492.

Papini, D. R. & Sebby, R. A. (1988). Variations in conflictual family issues by adolescent pubertal status, gender, and family member. *Journal of Early Adolescence, 8,* 1–15.

Papini, D. R., Sebby, R. A. & Clark, S. (1989). Affective quality of family relations and adolescent identity exploration. *Adolescence, 24,* 457–466.

Pete, J. M. & DeSantis, L. (1990). Sexual decision making in young black adolescent females. *Adolescence, 25,* 145–154.

Pleck, J. H., Sonenstein, F. L. & Ku, L. C. (1991). Adolescent males' condom use: Relationships between perceived cost-benefits and consistency. *Journal of Marriage and the Family, 53,* 733–746.

Plotnick, R. D. (1992). The effects of attitudes on teenage premarital pregnancy and its resolution. *American Sociological Review, 57,* 800–811.

Raja, S. N., McGee, R. & Stanton, W. R. (1992). Perceived attachment to parents and peers and psychological well-being in adolescence. *Journal of Youth and Adolescence, 21,* 471–486.

Reischl, T. M. & Hirsch, B. J. (1989). Identity commitments and coping with a difficult developmental transition. *Journal of Youth and Adolescence, 18,* 55–70.

Robertson, J. F. & Simons, R. L. (1989). Family factors, self-esteem, and adolescent depression. *Journal of Marriage and the Family, 51,* 125–138.

Robinson, B. E. (1988). Teenage pregnancy from the father's perspective. *American Journal of Orthopsychiatry, 58,* 46–51.

Rosenberg, M., Schooler, C. & Schoenbach, C. (1989). Self-esteem and adolescent problems: Modeling reciprocal effects. *American Sociological Review, 54,* 1004–1018.

Ryan, R. M. & Lynch, J. H. (1989). Emotional autonomy versus detachment: Revisiting the vicissitudes of adolescence and young adulthood. *Child Development, 60,* 340–356.

Sarvela, P. D. & McClendon, E. J. (1988). Indicators of rural youth drug use. *Journal of Youth and Adolescence, 17,* 335–348.

Schiedel, D. G. & Marcia, J. E. (1985). Ego identity, intimacy, sex-role orientation, and gender. *Developmental Psychology, 21,* 149–160.

Sells, C. W. & Blum, R. W. (1996). Morbidity and morality among U.S. adolescents: An overview of data and trends. *American Journal of Public Health, 86,* 513–519.

Small, S. A., Silverberg, S. B. & Kerns, D. (1993). Adolescents' perceptions of the costs and benefits of engaging in health-compromising behaviors. *Journal of Youth and Adolescence, 22,* 73–88.

Spencer, B. & Gillen, F. J. (1966). *The Arunta: A study of a Stone Age people.* Atlantic Highlands, N.J.: Humanities Press.

Spencer, M. B. (1982). Personal and group identity of black children: An alternative synthesis. *Genetic Psychology Monographs, 103,* 59–84.

Spencer, M. B. (1988). Self-concept development. In D. T. Slaughter (Ed.), *Black children in poverty: Developmental perspectives.* San Francisco: Jossey-Bass, 59–72.

Spencer, M. B. & Markstrom-Adams, C. (1990). Identity processes among racial and ethnic minority children in America. *Child Development, 61,* 290–310.

Spitze, G. & Logan, J. (1990). Sons, daughters, and intergenerational social support. *Journal of Marriage and the Family, 52,* 420–430.

Steinberg, L. D. (1981). Transformations in family relations at puberty. *Developmental Psychology, 17,* 833–840.

Steinberg, L. D. (1990). Autonomy, conflict, and harmony in the family relationship. In S. S. Feldman & G. R. Elliott (Eds.), *At the threshold: The developing adolescent.* Cambridge, Mass.: Harvard University Press, 255–277.

Steinberg, L. D. & Dornbusch, S. M. (1991). Negative correlates of part-time employment during adolescence: Replication and elaboration. *Developmental Psychology, 27,* 304–313.

Teti, D. M. & Lamb, M. E. (1989). Outcomes of adolescent marriage and adolescent childbirth. *Journal of Marriage and the Family, 51,* 203–212.

Triandis, H. C. (1990). Cross-cultural studies of individualism and collectivism. In J. J. Berman (Ed.), *Nebraska Symposium on Motivation: 1989* (vol. 37). Lincoln: University of Nebraska Press, 41–134.

Urberg, K. A. (1992). Locus of peer influence: Social crowd and best friend. *Journal of Youth and Adolescence, 21,* 439–450.

Urberg, K. A., Shyu, S. J. & Liang, J. (1990). Peer influence in adolescent cigarette smoking. *Addictive Behavior, 115,* 247–255.

U.S. Bureau of the Census. (1992). *Statistical abstract of the United States, 1992* (112th ed.). Washington, D.C.: U.S. Government Printing Office.

U.S. Bureau of the Census. (1994). *Statistical abstract of the United States, 1994* (114th ed.). Washington, D.C.: U.S. Government Printing Office.

U.S. Bureau of the Census. (1995). *Statistical abstract of the United States, 1995* (115th ed.). Washington, D.C.: U.S. Government Printing Office.

U.S. Department of Education. (1992). *The condition of education, 1992.* Washington, D.C.: National Center for Education Statistics.

Vega, W. A., Zimmerman, R. S., Warheit, G. J., Apospori, E. & Gil, A. G. (1993). Risk factors for adolescent drug use in four ethnic and racial groups. *American Journal of Public Health, 83,* 185–189.

Waterman, A. S. (1982). Identity development from adolescence to adulthood: An extension of theory and a review of research. *Developmental Psychology, 18,* 341–358.

Whitbourne, S. K. (1986). *The me I know: A study of adult identity.* New York: Springer-Verlag.

Zabin, L. C., Astone, N. M. & Emerson, M. R. (1993). Do adolescents want babies? The relationship between attitudes and behavior. *Journal of Research on Adolescence, 3.*

Zelnik, M. & Kantner, J. F. (1980). Sexual activity, contraceptive use, and pregnancy among metropolitan area teenagers: 1971–1979. *Family Planning Perspectives, 12,* 230–237.

Zuravin, S. J. (1988). Child maltreatment and teenage first births: A relationship mediated by chronic sociodemographic stress? *American Journal of Orthopsychiatry, 58,* 91–103.

Glossary

abortion   Termination of a pregnancy before the fetus is capable of surviving outside the uterus.

accommodation   (a) In Piaget's theory of cognitive development, the process of changing existing schema in order to account for novel elements in the object or the event. (b) In vision, change in the curvature of the lens in response to the distance of the stimulus.

achievement motivation   Internal state of arousal that leads to vigorous, persistent, goal-directed behavior when an individual is asked to perform a task in relation to some standard of excellence and when performance will be evaluated in terms of success and failure.

acoustic   Pertaining to the quality of sounds.

acquired immunodeficiency syndrome (AIDS)   A deficiency of the immune system due to infection with the human immunodeficiency virus.

adaptation   The total process of change in response to environmental conditions.

adaptive self-organization   The process by which an open system retains its essential identity when confronted with new and constant environmental conditions. It creates new substructures, revises the relationships among components, and establishes new, higher levels of organization that coordinate existing substructures.

adaptive self-regulation   Adjustment made by an operating system in which feedback mechanisms identify and respond to environmental changes in order to maintain and enhance the functioning of the system.

adequacy   One of the dimensions of attitudes toward pregnancy and childbirth.

advocate   A person who pleads another's cause.

affect   Emotion, feeling, or mood.

affiliative behavior   Actions intended to form positive, affectionate bonds with others.

age-graded expectation   An assumption that someone should do something because of how old he or she is.

agency   Viewing the self as the originator of action.

aggression   Hostile, injurious, or destructive behavior.

aggressive-rejected   A classification referring to children who are disruptive and aggressive with peers.

aggressive-withdrawn-rejected   A classification referring to children who are anxious, aggressive, socially withdrawn, and have poor self-control.

alcoholism   An addiction to alcohol; excessive and compulsive use of alcohol.

alienation   Withdrawal or separation of people or their affections from an object or position of former attachment.

allele   The alternate state of a gene at a given locus.

amino acids   Organic acids that are the basic building blocks of proteins.

amniocentesis   The surgical insertion of a hollow needle through the abdominal wall and into the uterus of a pregnant woman to obtain fluid for the determination of sex or chromosomal abnormality of the fetus.

amniotic sac   A thin membrane forming a closed sac around the embryo and containing a fluid in which the embryo is immersed.

anaclitic depression   More recently referred to as reactive attachment disorder of infancy, a condition involving passivity, limited motor exploration, withdrawal from social interaction, and, over time, physical deterioration.

anal stage   In Freud's psychosexual theory, the second life stage, during which the anus is a primary source of sexual satisfaction. Issues of willfulness and order are central to this stage.

androgyny   The capacity to express both masculine and feminine characteristics as the situation demands.

anesthetic   A substance that produces loss of sensation with or without loss of consciousness.

animosity   Ill will or resentment.

anomaly   Irregularity, something that is inconsistent with the normal condition.

anorexia nervosa   An emotional disorder in which the person loses the ability to regulate eating behavior; the person is obsessed with a fear of being overweight and avoids food or becomes nauseous after eating.

anoxia   A medical term that means complete absence of oxygen within a tissue, such as the brain or a muscle, causing disruption in cell metabolism and cell death unless it is corrected within a few minutes.

anxiety   A painful or apprehensive uneasiness of mind, usually over an impending or anticipated problem.

anxious-avoidant attachment   An attachment pattern in which infants avoid contact with their caregivers after separation and appear to resist the caregiver's attempts to comfort them.

anxious-resistant attachment An attachment pattern in which the infant appears to want to be close to the caregiver after separation, but at the same time is angry and difficult to soothe.

Apgar rating Assessment of the newborn based on heart rate, respiration, muscle tone, response to stimulation, and skin color.

aptitude Potential for learning and future performance of a skill.

arbitrary Selected at random and without logical reason.

articulation and awareness The fifth stage in ethnic identity development referring to a personal synthesis of values, beliefs, and practices from one's ethnic group as well as the dominant culture.

artificial insemination Injection of donor sperm into a woman's vagina to promote conception.

aspiration A strong desire to achieve something.

assimilation In Piaget's theory of cognitive development, the process of incorporating objects or events into existing schema.

assortive mating The process of choosing a partner who has a particular trait.

assumption A fact, statement, or premise that is considered true and that guides the underlying logic of a theory.

attachment The tendency to remain close to a familiar individual who is ready and willing to give care, comfort, and aid in time of need.

attachment behavioral system A complex set of reflexes and signaling behaviors that inspire caregiving and protective responses in adults; these responses shape a baby's expectations and help create an image of the parent in the child's mind.

attachment patterns Distinct behavioral patterns of attachment that are characteristic of infants and seem to lead to different patterns of attachment formation in later relationships: 1. *secure attachment,* 2. *anxious-avoidant attachment,* 3. *anxious-resistant attachment,* and 4. *disorganized attachment.*

attribution The act of ascribing a quality or characteristic to someone else or to oneself.

authoritarian A style of decision making in which the leader assumes total responsibility for making decisions and assigning responsibility. The authoritarian leader or parent expects obedience from everyone in a lower status position.

authority A person who has power and influence and who is seen by others as the legitimate decision maker.

autonomous morality A more mature moral perspective in which rules are viewed as a product of cooperative agreements.

autonomy The ability to behave independently, to do things on one's own.

autosomal A chromosome other than a sex chromosome.

avoidance conditioning A kind of learning in which specific stimuli are identified as painful or unpleasant and are therefore avoided.

Babinski reflex A response in which toes extend and fan out when the sole of the foot is gently stroked. This reflex is a sign of an immature nervous system. Eventually, a stroke on the sole of the foot makes one's toes curl down.

bar mitzvah In the Jewish religion, a ceremony celebrated at age 13 to mark a boy's entry into adult status (bas mitzvah for girls).

bilingualism The ability to speak two languages fluently.

biological adaptation A process whereby species evolve that have characteristics most suitable to the conditions of the environment.

birth order The order in which children in a family were born.

boundaries The criteria that determine who is considered to be a family member and who is an outsider.

bulimia An eating disorder characterized by binging and overeating followed by strategies to prevent the absorption of food.

case study A research method consisting of an in-depth description and analysis of a single person, family, or group.

categorical identification A way of understanding and describing the self with the use of statements describing basic or general characteristics.

categorization The process of arranging, classifying, or describing by labeling or naming.

causal agent A person or object that makes something happen.

causality The relation between a cause and an effect.

cell differentiation A process whereby cells take on specialized structures related to their function.

censor A coping strategy in which one limits exposure to novel experiences and adheres closely to parental values.

central process The dominant context or mechanism through which the psychosocial crisis is resolved.

cephalocaudal The direction of development that follows from the head to the feet.

cerebellum   A part of the brain in the back of the head; the area that coordinates muscle activity and equilibrium.

cerebral cortex   The layer of gray matter in the brain that serves to coordinate central nervous system functions.

cerebrum   The upper part of the brain; the seat of conscious mental processes.

cervix   The narrow lower end of the uterus, which forms the beginning of the birth canal.

cesarean delivery   Delivering a newborn by lifting it out through an incision in the uterine wall.

change   To make the form, nature, content, future course, etc. of something different from what it is, or from what it would be if left alone.

child abuse   The physical, sexual, or emotional intimidation, domination, and exploitation of children.

chromosome   One of the rodlike bodies of a cell nucleus that contain genetic material and that divide when the cell divides. In humans there are 23 pairs of chromosomes.

circular reaction   In cognitive development, the infant's use of familiar actions to achieve familiar results.

circumcision   Removing the foreskin that covers the glans of the penis.

classical conditioning   A form of learning in which a formerly neutral stimulus is repeatedly presented with a stimulus that evokes a specific reflexive response. After repeated pairings, the neutral stimulus elicits a response similar to the reflexive response.

classification   The action of grouping objects according to some specific characteristics they have in common, including all objects which show the characteristic and none which do not.

class inclusion   A component of classification skills referring to the understanding of class hierarchies and subgroups.

clinical studies   Research conducted on populations who are or have been treated for a problem, or who are waiting to be treated.

clique   A small, exclusive group of people.

coconstructed   Built or created together; involving two or more people.

codominance   Both genes at a specific allele contribute to the characteristic that is expressed, as in AB blood type.

cognition   The capacity for knowing, organizing perceptions, and problem solving.

cognitive behaviorism   The study of those cognitive dimensions related to understanding a person's ability to learn and perform tasks.

cognitive competencies   Knowledge, skills, and abilities.

cognitive differentiation   The act of adding additional units of information, which increases the complexity of a concept.

cognitive map   An internal mental representation of the environment.

cognitive smile   A smile in response to recognizing something or someone as familiar, or pleasure in understanding something.

cognitive theory   An analysis of the quality of thought and changes in thought at various stages of development.

cognitive unconscious   The range of mental structures and processes that operate outside awareness but play a significant role in conscious thought and action.

cohort   In research design, a group of subjects who are studied during the same time period.

cohort sequential study   A research design that combines cross-sectional and longitudinal methods. Cohorts consist of participants in a certain age group. Different cohorts are studied at different times. New cohorts of younger groups are added in successive data collections to replace those who have grown older. This design allows the analysis of age differences, changes over time, and the effects of social and historical factors.

collective self-esteem   The relatively stable evaluation of the value of one's group membership.

collectivism   A cultural perspective in which an individual's behavior is guided largely by group values and goals.

commitment   Personal investment and involvement in areas such as occupational choice, religion, political ideology, and social relationships.

communication repairs   In infant–caregiver interaction, when communication is mismatched and the sense of connection is broken, the caregiver takes steps to reestablish connection; for example, by trying to do a better job of matching the infant's state, or by withdrawing and allowing the infant to give a new signal.

communicative competence   The ability to use all the aspects of language that permit effective participation in the language environment of one's culture.

competition   A contest between rivals.

compulsions   Repetitive ritualized actions which serve as mechanisms for controlling anxiety.

concrete operational thought   In Piaget's theory, a stage of cognitive development in which rules of logic can be applied to observable or manipulatable physical relations.

conditioned response   A response that is evoked by a stimulus as a result of repeated, systematic association.

conditioned stimulus   A stimulus that evokes a response as a result of repeated, systematic association.

conformity   The first stage in ethnic development in which one identifies with the values, beliefs, and practices of the dominant culture.

congenital   Existing from the time of birth.

congruence model   A model of sex-role identity which suggests that it is most adaptive for males to adopt a strong masculine sex role and for females to adopt a strong feminine sex role.

conscience   Internalized moral standards and values.

conservation   The concept that physical changes do not alter the mass, weight, number, or volume of matter. This concept is acquired during the concrete operational stage of cognitive development.

constructivist perspective   The theory that gender differences are a product of socially agreed-upon meanings for how males and females are expected to behave in certain situations rather than persistent attributes of men and women.

contextual dissonance   Discrepancy between a characteristic of the individual and norms related to that characteristic within the community; for example, being one of few poor children in a middle-class school.

contextualist   A person who argues that behavior takes its meaning from the situation or circumstances in which it occurs.

contextualization of learning   Offering instruction in ways that first draw upon a child's existing experiences, knowledge, and concepts, and then expand them in new directions.

continual feeders   A pattern of infant nursing among mammals in which infants cling to their mothers or follow their mothers and nurse frequently.

continuity   The state or quality of being continuous.

continuous reinforcement   Giving reinforcement on every learning trial.

contraceptive   A method of preventing conception or impregnation.

contraction   Tightening of the uterine muscles during childbirth.

control   Referring to the experimental method, it ensures that differences among subjects do in fact occur as a result of the experimental manipulation.

control group   The subjects in an experiment who do not experience manipulation or treatment and whose responses or reactions are compared with those of subjects who are treated actively to determine the effects of the manipulation.

conventional morality   A stage of moral reasoning described by Kohlberg in which right and wrong are closely associated with the rules created by legitimate authorities, including parents, teachers, or political leaders.

coordination   In infant–caregiver interaction, it refers to a combination of matching and synchrony. Matching means that the infant and caregiver are involved in similar behaviors or states at the same time. Synchrony means that movement from one state to the next is fluid.

coordination of means and ends   The fourth phase in the development of causal schemes, when infants use familiar actions to achieve new outcomes.

coping   Active efforts to respond to stress. Coping includes gathering new information, maintaining control over one's emotions, and preserving freedom of movement.

coping behavior   Consists of active efforts to resolve stress and create new solutions to the challenges of each developmental stage.

core pathologies   Destructive forces that result from severe, negative resolutions of the psychosocial crises.

corpus luteum (yellow body)   Body of cells or group of cells that appear yellow in color, and produce the hormone progesterone.

correlation   A measure of the strength and direction of the relationship among variables.

correlation coefficient   A statistical value which reflects the strength of relationship among variables.

couvade   A practice in which the expectant father takes to his bed and observes very specific taboos during the period shortly before birth.

creativity   The willingness to abandon old forms or patterns of doing things and to think of new ways.

crisis   In the process of identity development, experiences of uncertainty, questioning, and experimentation about values and goals.

critical period   A time of maximum sensitivity to or readiness for the development of a particular skill or behavior pattern.

criticism   Finding fault or passing judgment.

crossing-over   Interchange of genes or chromosome segments.

cross-sectional study   A research design in which the behavior of subjects of different ages, social backgrounds, or environmental settings is measured once to acquire information about the effects of these differences.

crowd   A large group that is usually recognized by a few predominant characteristics, such as the preppies, the jocks, or the druggies.

cultural continuity   A smooth transition from the role expectations of childhood through adolescence and adulthood.

cultural determinism   The theoretical concept that culture shapes individual experience.

cultural discontinuity   Discrete expectations associated with each stage or period of life.

cultural norms   Shared expectations held by members of society for one another's behavior.

cultural relativism   A premise of cultural anthropology that the meaning of a specific ritual or norm must be interpreted in light of the values and goals of the culture.

cultural theory   The learned systems of meanings and patterns of behaviors that are shaped by a group of people and transmitted from one generation to the next.

culture   The concepts, habits, skills, arts, technology, religion, and government of a group of people during a specific period.

cumulative relation   In heredity, when the allelic states in a single pair of genes combine to influence a trait.

curriculum   The courses offered by an educational institution.

day care   A variety of programs and settings designed to care for infants and young children on a daily basis.

decentering   Gaining some objectivity over one's own point of view; reducing the dominance of one's subjective perspective in the interpretation of events.

defense mechanism   A technique, usually unconscious, that attempts to alleviate the anxiety caused by the conflicting desires of the id and the superego in relation to impulses (e.g., repression, denial, projection).

democratic   A style of decision making in which the leader involves all group members in reaching a decision. The democratic leader expects all members to share responsibility for decisions that are made.

dependent variable   A factor that is defined by a subject's responses or reactions, and that may or may not be affected by the experimenter's manipulation of the independent variable.

depressed mood   Feelings of sadness, loss of hope, or being overwhelmed by the demands of the world.

depression   A state of feeling sad, often accompanied by feelings of low personal worth and withdrawal from relations with others.

depressive syndrome   A constellation of behaviors and emotions including depression and anxiety.

deprivation   The state of being without something one needs.

developmental stage   A period of life dominated by a particular quality of thinking or a particular mode of

social relationships. The notion of stages suggests qualitative changes in competence at each phase of development.

developmental tasks   Skills and competence that are acquired at each stage of development.

dialect   A form of language that differs from the standard in pronunciation, grammar, and word meaning.

dilatation   Condition of being stretched open beyond normal limits.

discipline   A strategy for punishing or changing behavior.

discourse   Conversation, exchange of ideas.

disorganized attachment   Infants appear to have no coherent strategy for managing the stresses of the strange situation. Their behavior is contradictory and unpredictable, suggesting high levels of fear or confusion.

dissonance   The second stage in the development of ethnic identity in which one recognizes conflicts between values, beliefs, and practices of one's ethnic group and those of the dominant culture.

division of labor   Splitting the activities needed to accomplish a task between participants.

dizygotic twins   Two-egg twins that can be of different sexes.

DNA (deoxyribonucleic acid)   DNA molecules are the chemical building blocks of chromosomes found in the cell nucleus.

domains of development   Principally includes the major areas of physical, intellectual, emotional, social, and self development.

dominance   (a) The personal characteristic of asserting oneself in relation to others and of trying to control others. (b) A genetic situation where one allele is present and always observed, whether or not the other allele is the same.

dominant gene   A form of a gene that is always expressed in the phenotype when the gene is present, as in the example of Rr for tongue rolling.

doubt   A sense of uncertainty about one's abilities and one's worth.

Down syndrome   A chromosomal irregularity in which the child has an extra chromosome. The condition results in mental retardation.

dramatic role playing   Taking on a role in fantasy play.

dual-career marriage   A marriage in which both partners have professional, technical, or administrative careers.

dual-earner marriage   A marriage in which both partners work to earn money.

dyadic relationship   A two-person relationship.

early adolescence   The period of psychosocial development that begins with the onset of puberty and ends around 18 years of age, usually with graduation from high school.

early school age   The period of psychosocial development following toddlerhood, from approximately ages 4 to 6.

effacement   The shortening of the cervical canal.

egalitarian   Marked by the treatment of others as peers and equals out of a belief in human equality.

egg cell   The gamete cell produced by a female, containing half of the genetic material present in other body cells.

ego   In psychoanalytic theory, the mental structure that experiences and interprets reality. The ego includes most cognitive capacities, including perception, memory, reasoning, and problem solving.

egocentric speech   Speech directed toward oneself; this kind of speech may not be meaningful to others and is not intended for social communication.

egocentrism   The perception of oneself at the center of the world; the view that others and events base their behavior on or occur as a result of one's own perceptions.

ego ideal   A set of positive standards, ideals, and ambitions that represent the way a person would like to be.

ego strength   The soundness of the individual's personality.

Electra conflict   In Freud's psychosexual theory, the central conflict of the phallic stage for a girl, when she desires intimacy with her father and expresses hostility toward her mother.

electronic fetal heart rate monitoring   Continuous monitoring of fetal heart rate using an electronic amplification device.

embryo   The developing human individual from the time of implantation to the end of the eighth week after conception.

empathy   The capacity to recognize and experience the emotional state of another person.

enactive attainment   Personal experiences of mastery.

enzyme   Complex protein produced by living cells that acts as catalyst for biochemical reactions.

epididymis   A sperm-collecting duct, located near the testis, capable of holding billions of sperm.

epigenetic principle   A biological plan for growth such that each function emerges in a systematic sequence until the fully functioning organism has developed.

equilibration   Effort to reconcile new ideas and information with existing schemes and concepts.

estrogen   The major female sex hormone.

ethics   Principles of conduct founded upon a society's moral code.

ethnic group   People who share socially standardized ways of thinking, feeling, and acting, with other members of their subgroup.

ethnic group identity   Knowing that one is a member of a certain ethnic group; recognizing that aspects of one's thoughts, feelings, and actions are influenced by ethnic membership; and taking the ethnic group values, outlook, and goals into account when making life choices.

ethnicity   Traits, background, allegiance, or associations that are associated with an ethnic group.

ethnic subculture   The cultural values and behavioral patterns characteristic of a particular group in a society that shares a common ancestry; memories of a shared historical past; and a cultural focus on symbolic elements that distinguish the group from others.

ethology   The comparative investigation of the biological bases of behavior from an evolutionary perspective, to determine the proximal causes of behavioral acts, the relative contribution of inheritance and learning to these acts, and the adaptive significance and evolutionary history of different patterns of behavior within and across species.

evolution   A theory that accounts for the changes from one species to another as well as modifications within species over time.

exosystem   Pertains to one or more settings that do not involve the developing person as an active participant, but in which events occur that affect, or are affected by, what happens in the setting containing the developing person.

expansion   Elaborating on a child's expression by adding more words.

expectations   Views held by oneself or by others about what would be appropriate behavior in a given situation or at a given stage of development.

experimental group   The subjects who experience the manipulation or treatment in an experiment.

experimentation   A method of research that is conducted under repeatable and highly controlled conditions, in which some variable or group of variables are systematically manipulated while others are held constant; used to assess cause-and-effect relationships.

experimentation with new means   The fifth phase in the development of causal schemes, when infants modify familiar actions in order to achieve new goals.

extended family   The family group that includes family members other than the nucleus of parents and children.

external ear canal   The visible part of the ear, which collects and transmits sound.

extinction   (a) In classical conditioning, the reduction of an association when the unconditioned stimulus is not presented. (b) The negative pole of the psychosocial crisis of very old age in which it is feared that the end of life is the end of all continuity.

faceness   A property of a visual stimulus that gives it the general appearance of a face.

facilitate   To make easier.

fallopian tube   The tube, extending from the uterus to the ovary, in which fertilization takes place.

family   Any group of persons closely related by blood, such as parents, children, uncles, aunts, and cousins.

family day care   A child-care arrangement in which a person cares for several children in his or her own home, often along with the person's own children.

family of origin   The family to which one is born.

family of procreation   The family one begins as an adult.

family risk factors   Characteristics of the parent, the relationship between the parents, and the social and economic conditions of the family that make it difficult for an adult to respond appropriately or to be psychologically available to a child.

family system   The relationships among all those who comprise the child's significant and intimate family.

fantasy   A form of symbolic thought that is not restrained by the limits of reality.

fast mapping   Forming a rapid, initial, partial understanding of the meaning of a word by relating it to the known vocabulary and restructuring the known-word storage space and its related conceptual categories.

fear of loss of love   A motive for parental identification in which the child tries to be like the parent in order to preserve a sense of closeness with the loved parent.

feedback   Information about how a particular activity is being carried out that returns to a central control mechanism. Feedback may be automatic information from muscles about a physical activity or evaluative information from a teacher about academic performance.

feminine culture   A culture that allows flexible overlap between male and female roles.

fertility   The capacity to reproduce.

fertilization   The penetration of an egg by a sperm.

fertilization in vitro   A process where an egg is removed from an ovary and placed in a petri dish inside an icubator, and a few drops of sperm are added to the dish to create a fertilized egg.

fetal alcohol syndrome   A condition of the fetus involving central nervous system disorders, low birth weight, and malformations of the face; the condition is associated with alcohol consumption during pregnancy.

fetoscopy   Examination of the fetus through the use of a fiberoptic lens.

fetus   The unborn infant. Usually the term *fetus* refers to infants between 12 weeks of gestational age and birth.

fidelity (I)   The ability to freely pledge and sustain loyalties to others.

fidelity (II)   The ability to freely pledge and sustain loyalties to values and ideologies.

filial obligation   The responsibility of adult children for their aging parents.

first experiences   Principally include the concepts of coding at basic levels of concept formation; establishing a foundation for expectations; organizing ideas for self conceptualization; and establishing basic attitudes, standards, and values.

first habits   The second phase in the development of causal schemes, when reflexes are used to explore a wider range of stimuli.

fixation   In psychoanalysis, a preoccupation with the issues and tasks of a particular stage of development; an inability to progress to more mature stages.

fixed action pattern   A genetically guided sequence of complex highly patterned behavior, such as nest building or mating, that is characteristic of a particular species and is prompted or triggered by a specific stimulus pattern that signals or releases the innate behavior pattern.

follicle   A small sac of cells on the surface of an ovary. It reacts to hormones from the brain and produces the hormone estrogen during the ten days before an egg cell is released.

formal operations   In Piaget's theory, the final stage of cognitive development characterized by reasoning, hypothesis generating, and hypothesis testing.

foundational category   A primitive or early basis for grouping and distinguishing one type of stimulus from another, such as living and inanimate, or familiar and novel.

frail elderly   Older people who may have delicate health, one or more inactivating chronic conditions, and possibly some form of dementia.

frame of reference   The events or point of view that influence one's judgments.

fraternal twins   Children born at the same time who developed from two different ova.

full-term baby   A baby who has developed in utero for the complete gestational period of nine months or approximately 36 weeks.

gamete   A mature germ cell involved in reproduction.

gamete interfallopian transfer (GIFT)   A process involving the transfer of eggs and sperm into a woman's fallopian tubes.

gender   The sex of a person.

gender identity   A set of beliefs, attitudes, and values about oneself as a man or woman in many areas of social life including intimate relations, family, work, community, and religion.

gender label   Words that identify one's gender, as boy, girl, man, or woman.

gender role preference   A preference for the behaviors and attitudes associated with being a male or female.

gender schema   A personal theory about cultural expectations and stereotypes related to gender.

gene   The fundamental physical unit of heredity. A gene is a linear sequence of nucleotides along a segment of DNA that carries the coded instructions for synthesis of RNA, which, when translated into protein, leads to hereditary character.

gene pool   Information contained in the genes of the population or culture which provides the genetic ancestry for an individual.

generativity   The capacity to contribute to the quality of life for future generations. A sense of generativity is attained toward the end of middle adulthood.

genetic anomalies   Neurological or physical abnormalities that have a genetic cause.

genetic code   The complete genetic information for human beings.

genetics   The study of heredity.

gene transfer   The insertion of copies of a gene into living cells in order to induce synthesis of the gene's product; the desired gene may be microinjected into the cell directly, or it may be inserted into the core of a virus by gene splicing and the virus allowed to infect the cell and replicate the gene in the cell's DNA.

genitalia   The reproductive organs, especially the external ones.

genital stage   In Freud's psychosexual theory, the final life stage, during which the genitals are the primary source of sexual satisfaction and in which sexual impulses are directed toward members of the opposite sex.

genome   A full set of chromosomes that carries all the inheritable traits of an organism.

genotype   The hereditary information contained in the cells. Genotype may or may not be observable in the phenotype (see **phenotype**).

gestation   The period of carrying a fetus from conception to birth.

gestational age   The age of the fetus from the time of conception.

goals   Personal standards of performance.

grammar   Rules for the arrangement of words and phrases in a sentence and for the inflections that convey gender, tense, and number.

grasp reflex   An automatic involuntary movement present at birth that disappears as the nervous system matures. Any object placed in the infant's palm will be firmly grasped.

group identity   The positive pole of the psychosocial crisis of early adolescence in which the person finds membership in and value convergence with a peer group.

group game   A form of play, such as "Ring Around the Rosie" or "London Bridge," in which an element of fantasy is combined with rules for winning or losing.

growth rate   The amount of growth that occurs during a given period of time.

guilt   An emotion associated with doing something wrong or anticipating doing something wrong.

habituation   A form of adaptation in which the child no longer responds to a stimulus that has been repeatedly presented.

haploid   The number of chromosomes contained by gametes.

hemophilia   A sex-linked hereditary disease in which blood clots very slowly.

heredity   The qualities and potential that are transmitted genetically from one generation to the next.

heterogeneous   Having different qualities.

heteronomous morality   A child's moral perspective in which rules are viewed as fixed and unchangeable.

heterosexual relationships   Associations and friendships with members of the opposite sex.

heterozygous   Characterized by the presence of different alleles of a particular gene at the same locus.

holophrase   A word functioning as a phrase or sentence.

homeostasis   A relatively stable state of equilibrium.

homozygous   Characterized by the presence of matched alleles of a particular gene at the same locus.

hope   An enduring belief that one can attain one's essential wishes.

hormones   A group of chemicals, each of which is released into the bloodstream by a particular gland or tissue and has a specific effect on tissues elsewhere in the body.

household   All persons who occupy a housing unit, including related family members and all unrelated persons.

human immunodeficiency virus (HIV)   The cause of AIDS, it gains access to the body through the bloodstream and attacks the brain, sometimes causing damage and dementia.

hypercognitive system   A component of the model of the mind referring to all the functions that permit the person to make meaning of a stimulus or an event.

hypothesis   A tentative proposition that can provide a basis for further inquiry.

hypothetico-deductive reasoning   A method of reasoning in which a hypothetical model based on observations is first proposed and then tested by deducing consequences from the model.

id   In psychoanalytic theory, the mental structure that expresses impulses and wishes. Much of the content of the id is unconscious.

identical twins   Children born at the same time who developed from the same ovum.

identification   A psychological mechanism in which the people attempt to enhance their own self-concept by incorporating some of the valued characteristics of important others, such as parents, into their own behavior.

identification with the aggressor   A motive for parental identification in which the child tries to be like the parent in order to prevent injury or rejection from the parent.

identity   In cognitive theory, the concept that an object is still the same object even though its shape or location has been changed.

identity achievement   Individual identity status in which, after crisis, a sense of commitment to family, work, political, and religious values is established.

identity confusion   The negative pole of psychosocial crisis of later adolescence in which a person is unable to integrate various roles or make commitments.

identity foreclosure   Individual identity status in which a commitment to family, work, political, and religious values is established prematurely, without crisis.

illusion of incompetence   Expressed by children who perform well in academic achievement tests, yet perceive themselves as below average in academic ability and behave in accordance with this perception.

imaginary audience   The preoccupation with what one believes other people are thinking about him or her.

imaginary companion   A fantasized character created by a child's symbolic capacities.

imitation   Repetition of another person's words, gestures, or behaviors.

imprinting   A process whereby an animal comes to follow a large object, usually its mother, at some point after birth.

impulse   Internal psychological drive for certain types of behavior, such as aggressive or sexual impulses.

incest   Sexual relations between people so closely related that they are forbidden by law to marry.

independent variable   A factor that is manipulated in an experiment, and the effects of the manipulation measured.

individual identity   The commitment to a personal integration of values, goals, and abilities that occurs as personal choices are made in response to anticipated or actual environmental demands at the end of adolescence.

individualism   A cultural perspective that gives personal goals a higher priority than responsibility to the group.

individuation   The process of becoming a unique and distinct person.

induction   A form of discipline that points out the consequences a child's actions have on others.

industry   A sense of pride and pleasure in acquiring culturally valued competence. The sense of industry is usually acquired by the end of the middle childhood years.

inertia   A paralysis of thought and action that prevents productive work.

infancy   The period of psychosocial development that begins when the child is born and ends when the child is approximately two years old.

infantile autism   A rare condition in which infants have extremely impaired social competence, restricted and repetitive behavior patterns, and little or no language development.

infant mortality rate   The number of babies who die during the first year of life per one thousand live births.

inferiority   A sense of incompetence and failure which is built on negative evaluation and lack of skill.

infertility   Inability to conceive or carry a fetus through the gestational period.

in-group   A group of which one is a member; contrasted with **out-group.**

inhibition   A psychological restraint that prevents freedom of thought, expression, and activity.

initiative   The ability to offer new solutions, to begin new projects, or to seek new social encounters; active investigation of the environment.

innate behavior   Existing from birth; inborn; hereditary.

insight   In Piaget's theory of cognitive development, the last phase of sensorimotor intelligence in which children solve problems by thinking over the possible solutions and selecting the correct one to try.

instinct   An inherited and largely unalterable tendency of an organism to make a complex specific response to environmental stimuli.

instrumental conditioning   A form of associational learning in which the behaving organism emits responses that are shaped into the desired response by reinforcement. Once the desired response occurs it is strengthened by continued reinforcement.

interdependence   (a) Marked by all the elements in a system relying on one another for their continued growth. (b) Systems that depend on each other.

intermittent reinforcement   Giving reinforcement every once in a while.

internal conflict   Psychological tension between opposing needs, goals, or values.

internalization   A process in which the values, beliefs, and norms of the culture become the values, beliefs, and norms of the individual.

inter-observer reliability   When observers' codings of the same situation are compared in order to determine whether different observers of the situation are reliable.

intersubjectivity   A shared repertoire of emotions which enable infants and their caregivers to understand each other and create shared meanings; they can engage in reciprocal, rhythmic interactions, appreciate state changes in one another, and modify their actions in response to emotional information about one another.

interview   A research method in which subjects are questioned about various aspects of their lives, including their feelings and thoughts.

introspection   The fourth stage in ethnic identity development referring to critical examination of the values, beiefs, and practices of both the dominant culture and one's own ethnic group.

in utero   In the uterus.

in vitro   In an artificial environment.

in vivo   Biological processes occurring or caused to occur within the living body of a plant or animal.

irregular verbs   Verbs that do not conform to the usual pattern of inflection; for example, sell/sold, see/saw.

irritability   The ease with which stimuli cause disruption or pain.

isolation   A crisis resolution in which situational factors or a fragile sense of self leads a person to remain psychologically distant from others.

kibbutz   An Israeli community in which members share the ownership of all property and the profits from production, and children are reared communally.

kinship   Family relation; kin are all the people to whom one is related by blood, marriage, or a sense of family.

labor   The period of involuntary contractions of the uterine muscles that occurs prior to giving birth.

lactation   Presence and secretion of milk that automatically occurs in the breasts of the mother of a newborn infant.

language perception   The ability to recognize sounds and differentiate among sound combinations before the meanings of these sounds are understood.

language production   The ability to produce sounds, words, and meaningful sentences.

latency   The time that elapses between a signal to act and the act itself.

latency stage   In Freud's psychosexual theory, the fourth life stage, during which no significant conflicts or impulses are assumed to rise. Superego development proceeds during this period.

later adolescence   The period of psychosocial development that begins around the time of graduation from high school and ends in the early twenties.

leading crowd   A group of students identified in James Coleman's research as leaders in high school who tend to associate with one another and who make up the top group in the social hierarchy of the student culture.

learned helplessness   A belief that one's efforts have little to do with success or failure; that the outcome of most situations is largely outside one's control.

learning   Any relatively permanent change in thought and/or behavior that is the consequence of experience.

learning set   A general strategy for problem solving.

learning theory   A set of principles that accounts for changes in behavior at every stage of life, usually focusing on ways in which controlled changes in the environment produce predictable changes in behavior.

life course   Individual life patterns as they are expressed in a social and historical time period.

lightening   The stage of pregnancy in which the movements of the fetus are first felt by the pregnant woman.

linguistic system   Combination of vocabulary, grammar, phonetics, and language customs.

literacy   Being able to read and write.

loneliness   A feeling of sadness related to being alone; failing to meet one's needs for companionship.

longitudinal study   A research design in which repeated observations of the same subjects are made at different times, in order to examine change over time.

love withdrawal   A form of discipline in which parents express disappointment or disapproval and become emotionally cold or distant.

low birth weight   The weight of newborns who weigh less than 2500 grams (about 5 pounds, 8 ounces).

macrosystem   The consistencies in the form and content of lower-order systems (micro-, meso-, and exo-) that exist, or could exist, at the level of the subculture or the culture as a whole, along with any belief systems or ideology underlying such consistencies.

major depressive disorder   A clinical diagnosis reflecting the presence of five or more related symptoms which persist for at least two weeks.

malnutrition   A condition of ill health that results from faulty or inadequate food intake.

masculine culture   Culture that makes very clear distinctions between male and female roles, with a strong emphasis on instrumentality and achievement.

masculinity model   A model of sex-role identity which suggests that a masculine sex-role orientation is most adaptive for females as well as for males.

mastery   Competence or skill.

matched groups sampling   Sampling in which two or more groups of subjects who are similar on many dimensions are selected as the sample for an experiment. The effects of different treatments or manipulations are determined by comparing the behavior of these groups.

maternal deprivation   Lack of opportunities for interaction with a mother or primary caregiver.

maturational view of learning   An outlook that suggests that children have a strong developmental capacity and desire for learning.

maturation rate   The rate at which certain personal, biological, and behavioral characteristics emerge and develop in an individual through the process of growth.

means-end relationship   A sensorimotor scheme for the causal connection between certain actions and certain consequences.

meiosis   An aspect of cell division resulting in the reduction of the number of chromosomes in gamete-producing cells by one half.

menarche   The beginning of regular menstrual periods.

menopause   The ending of regular menstrual periods.

menstruation   The loss of tissue and blood from the uterus, usually lasting four or five days each month.

mental age   One's age as measured by an intelligence test. Usually, mental age is determined by the level of difficulty of the questions the child can answer correctly.

mental image   A form of representational thought which involves the ability to hold the picture of a person, object, or event in one's mind even in the absence of the stimulus itself.

mental operation   A transformation, carried out in thought rather than action, which modifies an object, event, or idea.

mesosystem   It comprises the interrelations among two or more settings in which the developing person actively participates (such as, for a child, the relations among the home, school, and neighborhood peer group; for an adult, among family, work, and social life).

metabolization   The process by which energy is provided for vital processes and activities and new material is assimilated to repair the waste, through the chemical changes in living cells.

metacognition   Thinking about one's own thinking, including what individuals understand about their reasoning capacities and about how information is organized, how knowledge develops, how reality is distinguished from belief or opinion, how to achieve a sense of certainty about what is known, and how to improve understanding.

methodology   Particular techniques used to conduct a research investigation.

microsystem   A pattern of activities, roles, and interpersonal relations experienced by the developing person in a given setting with particular physical and material characteristics.

middle school   A school containing grades 5 through 8.

mistrust   A sense of unpredictability in the environment and suspicion about one's own worth. Experiences with mistrust are most critical during infancy.

mitochondria   A portion of the sperm cell that generates energy.

mitochondrial DNA   DNA from mitochondria, rich in proteins, fats, and enzymes, which are found outside the nucleus of a cell and produce energy for the cell through cellular respiration. The DNA is passed on solely through the mother and can be used to trace genetic lineage.

mitosis   A process, involving five steps, which results in the formation of two new nuclei, each having the same number of chromosomes as the nucleus.

mobility   Ability to engage in movement.

model   In social learning theory, the one who is imitated.

modeling   Demonstrating behaviors that can be imitated by others.

monozygotic twins   Twins who develop from a single fertilized egg. These twins have identical genetic characteristics.

moral development   The process of learning the moral code of one's family and culture, experiencing guilt or remorse when moral standards have been violated, and taking appropriate actions to inhibit harmful behavior or to initiate helpful behavior as the situation requires.

moral judgments   Cognitive decisions about right or wrong behavior which involve an underlying rationale.

moral prescriptions   Positive rules for valued behavior.

moral prohibitions   Rules to suppress negatively valued behavior.

mortality (infant)   The number of deaths per 100,000 of liveborn infants.

motherese   The simplified, redundant style of speaking used by adults and older children so that they are more likely to be understood by a child who is learning language.

motive   Something that causes a person to act.

motor functions   Bodily movements of both voluntary and reflexive types.

multicultural education   An educational approach in which the values and practices of many cultural groups are explained and incorporated into the learning process.

mutations   Any changes in the nucleotide sequence from the original DNA molecule.

mutuality   Ability of two people to meet each other's needs and share each other's concerns and feelings.

myelination   The formation of a soft, white, fatty material called myelin around certain nerve axons, to serve as an electrical insulator that speeds nerve impulses to muscles and other effectors.

naturalistic observation   A research method in which subjects' behavior is observed and described as it occurs in its natural setting without experimental intervention.

natural selection   A process whereby those individuals best suited to the characteristics of the immediate environment are most likely to survive and reproduce.

negative feedback loops   Patterns of communication that operate to diminish certain types of interactions.

negative identity   A clearly defined self-image that is completely contrary to the cultural values of the community.

negative reinforcers   Stimuli, such as electric shock, that increase the rate of response when removed.

negativism   Refusal to comply with others' requests.

neonatal   Affecting the newborn, especially during the first month of life.

nerve conduction velocity   The speed of neural firing.

nerve pathways   Bundles of axons from many neurons in the brain that send information away from the billions of neural cells.

neutral stimulus   One of the four basic elements in a classical conditioning experiment.

neural tube   The hollow longitudinal tube formed by infolding and subsequent fusion of the opposite ectodermal folds in the vertebrate embryo.

neurological development   Growth of the nervous system.

neuron   A nerve cell with specialized processes that is the fundamental functional unit of nervous tissue.

nondisjunction   An event occurring during cell division, in which both chromosomes of a pair go to the same new cell. Nondisjunction results in chromosomal irregularities, including Down syndrome.

norms   Collective expectations, or rules for behavior, held by members of a group or society.

nuclear family   A household grouping that includes the mother, father, and their children.

nurturance   The tendency to attempt to care for and further the growth and development of another.

obesity   A condition characterized by being excessively fat.

objective   When observations accurately reflect the events that are taking place and are not unduly influenced by what the observer hopes to see.

object permanence   A scheme acquired during the sensorimotor stage of development in which children become aware that an object continues to exist even when it is hidden or moved from place to place.

observation   A research method in which behavior is watched and recorded.

observational learning   Changes in thought or behavior that result from watching others.

obsessions   Persistent repetitive thoughts which serve as mechanisms for controlling anxiety.

Oedipal conflict   In Freud's psychosexual theory, the central conflict of the phallic stage, in which the boy has strong desires for the mother, strong aggressive feelings toward his father, and strong fears of castration by the father.

oocytes   The large number of immature egg cells that human females have at birth.

open systems   Structures that maintain their organization even though their parts constantly change.

operant conditioning   A form of learning in which new responses are strengthened by the presentation of reinforcements.

operational definition   In research, the way an abstract concept is defined in terms of how it will be measured.

optimal ability   The level of performance of which one is capable at the highest levels of motivation and preparation.

oral stage   In Freud's psychosexual theory, the first life stage, during which the mouth is the primary source of sexual satisfaction. Issues of self-concept and personal worth are important at this stage.

organ inferiority   In Adler's theory, a strong sense that some organ of one's body is weak and inferior. The person becomes preoccupied with thoughts of this weakness.

out-group   A group that competes with one's own group; contrasted with **in-group.**

oviducts   Short tubes situated near the ovaries, commonly referred to as the fallopian tubes.

ovulation   The process of an egg cell being released from the ovary.

ovum   An egg; the female germ cell.

palate   The roof of the mouth, separating the mouth from the nasal cavity.

paradox   A statement that may appear to be opposed to common sense, yet is true.

peer   A person belonging to the same group, often on the basis of age or grade.

peer pressure   Expectations and demands to conform to the norms of one's peer group.

penis   A male organ used for reproduction and for the excretion of urine.

perception   The recognition and organization of sensory experiences.

perineum   The area between the anus and the back of the vagina.

peristalsis   Successive waves of involuntary contractions passing along the walls of the intestine or other hollow muscular structure, forcing the contents onward.

permissive   Marked by a relatively easygoing and tolerant discipline technique that allows the child's desires to be asserted.

personal fable   An intense investment in one's own thoughts and feelings and a belief that these thoughts are unique.

personal identity   A creative construction of a sense of meaning, purpose, and continuity.

person-environment fit   The fit between the person's needs, skills, and interpersonal style and the characteristics of the environments in which the person participates.

perspective taking   The ability to consider a situation from the point of view of another person or angle.

phallic stage   In Freud's psychosexual theory, the third stage of development, during which the Oedipal and Electra conflicts occur.

phenotype   Observable characteristics that result from a particular genotype and a particular environment.

phenylketonuria (PKU)   A genetic disease that restricts intellectual development if it is not treated.

phobia   An intense, irrational fear.

phonetics   The sound system of a language.

physical culture   The objects, technologies, structures, tools, and other artifacts of a culture.

physiological feedback   One component in building a sense of self-efficacy which refers to monitoring one's physical state as one approaches a challenge; reading physical cues such as nervousness, excitement, or fear.

placenta   The vascular organ that connects the fetus to the maternal uterus and mediates metabolic exchanges.

plans   The strategies one develops for achieving goals.

plasticity   The capability of being molded and modified by experience.

polygamy   A family organization in which a spouse may have more than one mate.

population   All units for potential observation.

positive feedback loops   Patterns of communication that operate to stabilize or increase certain types of behavior.

positive reinforcers   Stimuli, such as food and smiles, that increase the rate of response when present.

postconventional morality   In Kohlberg's stages of moral reasoning, the most mature form of moral judgments. Moral decisions are based on an appreciation of the social contract which binds members of a social system and on personal values.

postpartum depression   A period of sadness that may be experienced by the mother after giving birth and that appears to be related to hormonal activity.

power assertion   A discipline technique involving physical force, harsh language, or control of resources.

precarious   Characterized by a lack of stability or security.

preconscious   Absent from consciousness, but capable of being readily brought into consciousness.

preconventional morality   In Kohlberg's stages of moral reasoning, the most immature form of moral judgments. Moral decisions are based on whether the act has positive or negative consequences, or whether it is rewarded or punished.

preoperational thought   In Piaget's theory of cognitive development, the stage in which representational skills are acquired.

pretense   Symbolic or fantasy play.

pretend identity   Allowing an object or person to stand for something else; i.e., a bucket is a crown; a block is gold.

pre-term baby   A baby who is born before the full gestational period.

primal wishes   Very early needs and desires.

primary process   The seemingly unorganized mental activity, characteristic of the id and the unconscious, that occurs in dreams, fantasies, and related processes. Characterized by an absence of negatives, a here-and-now focus, and symbolic flexibility.

primate   Any of various omnivorous mammals of the order Primates, including the three suborders Tarsioidea (tarsiers), Prosimii (lemurs, loris, and their allies), and Anthropoidea (humans, great apes, gibbons, Old World monkeys, and New World monkeys). Distinguished by varied locomotion, use of hands, and flexible, complex behavior involving a high level of cultural adaptability and social interaction.

prime adaptive ego qualities   Mental states that form a basic orientation toward the interpretation of life experiences; new ego qualities emerge in the positive resolution of each psychosocial crisis.

primiparas   A woman who has borne one child or who is pregnant for the first time.

primitive causality   An understanding of cause and effect acquired by infants which is based solely on sensory and motor experience, not symbolic logic.

private self   A subjective sense of uniqueness and unity.

processing system   A component of the model of the mind referring to basic neurological processes that are required in all intellectual functioning.

progesterone   A hormone related to pregnancy.

prompting   Urging a child to say more about an incomplete expression.

prosocial behavior   Positive social behavior such as helping another person.

proximodistal   Development in the direction from the center of the body to the extremes.

psychosexual theory   Freud's theory of psychological development, which proposed that cognitive, emotional, and social growth were associated with predictable changes in sexual sensitivity during childhood. This theory is sometimes called psychoanalytic theory.

psychosocial crisis   A predictable life tension that arises as people experience some conflict between their own competence and the expectations of their society.

psychosocial evolution   The contribution of each generation to the knowledge and norms of the society.

psychosocial moratorium   A period of free experimentation before a final identity is achieved.

psychosocial orientation   The assumption that development is a product of the continuous interplay between individuals and their social environments.

psychosocial theory   A theory of psychological development that proposed that cognitive, emotional, and social growth were the result of the interaction between social expectations at each life stage and the competence that people bring to each life challenge.

puberty   The period of physical development at the onset of adolescence when the reproductive system matures.

public self   The many roles one plays and the expectations of others.

purpose   The ability to imagine and pursue valued goals.

quasi-experimental   A type of research design that allows researchers to observe the impact of naturally occurring life events. The differences in outcome can be observed but not controlled.

quickening   Sensation of fetal movement, usually during the second trimester of fetal growth.

radius of significant relationships   The groups of important people in one's life; the breadth and complexity of these groups change over the life span.

random   Characteristic of a situation in which each event of a set of events is equally likely to occur.

random sampling   A method for choosing the sample for a study in which each member of the population under investigation has an equal chance of being included.

rapport   Harmony and understanding in a relationship.

reaction range   The range of possible responses to environmental conditions that is established through genetic influences.

reaction time   The time that lapses between the signal to make a response and the response itself.

reality principle   The motivating force or mechanism by which the ego protects the person by preventing id impulses from being gratified until a socially acceptable form of expression can be found.

receptive language   The ability to understand words.

recessive gene   A form of a gene that is expressed in the phenotype only when a similar allele is present. In combination with a dominant gene the characteristics associated with the recessive gene are masked.

reciprocal   Interactions in which the behavior of each participant influences the responses of the other.

reciprocal roles   Each role is partly defined by the other roles that support it.

reciprocity   A scheme describing the interdependence of related dimensions, such as height and width or time and speed.

reference group   A group with which an individual identifies and whose values the individual accepts as guiding principles.

reflex   An involuntary response to a simple stimulus.

reflexive self-concept   Bernstein's concept of the influence of language on shaping a self-concept that is sensitive to social relationships and roles.

reinforcement   In operant conditioning, the positive consequence that follows a given behavior.

reinforcement patterns   The frequency and timing with which reinforcements are presented.

releasing stimulus   An odor, color, movement, sound, shape, pattern of events, or relationship among any of these that elicits the performance of a fixed action pattern in a particular species.

reliability   The consistency of a test in measuring something.

repeatable   When someone else can approach the research task and observe the same things as the original investigator.

representational skills   Skills learned in the preoperational stage, including mental imagery, symbolic play, symbolic drawing, imitation, and language, that permit the child to represent experiences or feelings in a symbolic form.

repression   A defense mechanism that involves pushing unacceptable anxiety-provoking impulses, memories, thoughts, or feelings into the unconscious.

resilience   The capacity to recover from stress.

resistance and immersion   The third stage in the development of ethnic identity in which one rejects many aspects of the dominant culture and becomes immersed in the values, beliefs, and practices of one's ethnic group.

retrospective study   A research design in which subjects are asked to report on experiences they had earlier in their lives.

reversibility   A scheme describing the ability to undo an action and return to the original state.

reward   A positive consequence that follows desired behavior.

rite of passage   A ritual associated with a crisis or a change of status (for example, marriage for an individual).

RNA (ribonucleic acid)   A compound that conveys the information in the DNA strands to the cytoplasm in order to stimulate the production of specific amino acids.

role   A set of behaviors that have some socially agreed-upon functions and for which there exists an accepted code of norms, such as the role of teacher, child, or minister.

role compatibility   Partners in a relationship approach situations in a manner that works well; their behaviors and responses complement one another.

role diffusion   The negative role of the psychosocial crisis of later adolescence in which the person cannot make a commitment to any unified vision of the self.

role enactment   Patterned characteristics of social behavior that one performs as a result of being in a specific role.

role expectations   Shared expectations for behavior that are linked to a social role.

role experimentation   The central process for the resolution of the psychosocial crisis of later adolescence, which involves participation in a variety of roles before any final commitments are made.

role prescription   The specific behaviors and norms associated with a particular role.

role strain   The conflict and competing demands made by several roles that the person holds simultaneously.

role-taking abilities   Skills related to understanding and enacting the roles of others.

rooting   An infant reflex in which the baby's head turns toward the direction of the cheek that is stimulated.

saline solution   A solution containing salt.

sample   The group of people who have been selected to participate as subjects in a research project.

sampling   A method of choosing subjects in a study.

sanction   A negative consequence that occurs when a standard or rule has been violated.

scaffolding   A process through which a child and an adult attempt to arrive at a shared understanding about a communication, at which point the adult interacts so as to expand or enrich the child's communicative competence.

schedules of reinforcement   The frequency and regularity with which reinforcements are given.

scheme   In Piaget's theory, the organization of actions into a unified whole; a mental construct.

school phobia   A strong, irrational fear of some aspect of the school situation, interpreted in psychoanalytic theory as an expression of a child's reluctance to leave the mother.

school readiness   A broad term suggesting that a child has reached a level of development which would permit him or her to function effectively in and take advantage of educational experiences in a formal school environment.

scientific observation   Characterized by three essential qualities: it must be objective, repeatable, and systematic.

scientific process   A process for building a body of knowledge involving observation, theory construction, operationalizing the theory, testing the theory, evaluating and revising the theory.

scrotum   The pouch that houses the testes, located just below the penis.

secondary process   The conscious mental activity and logical thinking controlled by the ego and influenced by environmental demands.

secular trend   A tendency observed since approximately 1900 for more rapid physical maturation from one generation to the next, probably as a result of favorable nutrition, increased mobility, and greater protection from childhood diseases.

secure attachment   A pattern of infant attachment in which infants can explore their environment freely, the caregiver is effective in reassuring and comforting the infant, and the infant can recover readily from distress and continue to explore.

self-concept   The characteristics and attributes one applies to oneself.

self-control   The ability to control impulses and the ability to control events.

self-control strategies   Techniques an individual develops for regulating his or her own behavior.

self-efficacy   A sense of confidence that one can perform the behaviors that are demanded in a specific situation.

self-encodings   Evaluations and concepts related to information about oneself.

self-esteem   The evaluative dimension of the self that includes feelings of worthiness, pride, and discouragement.

self-fulfilling prophecy   False or innacurate beliefs that can produce a reality that mirrors those beliefs.

self-presentation bias   When subjects present themselves in the way they want the interviewer to see them.

self-theory   An organized set of ideas about the self that is accumulated through daily interactions.

semantic contingency   The immediate matching of an adult's utterance to the content or topic of a child's verbalization.

semen   Whitish fluid produced by the male reproductive system, and emitted during ejaculation.

semiotic thinking   The understanding that one thing can stand for another.

sensitive period   A span of time during which a particular skill or behavior is most likely to develop.

sensitivity (of caregiver)   Attentiveness to an infant's state, accurate interpretation of the infant's signals, and well-timed responses that promote mutually rewarding interactions.

sensorimotor intelligence   In Piaget's theory of development, the first stage of cognitive growth during which schema are built on sensory and motor experiences.

sensorimotor play   Sensory exploration and motoric manipulation that produce pleasure.

sensors   A coping strategy in which people seek out new activities and experiences that will challenge their preconceptions and values.

sensory functions   The responses of the body and nervous system to a variety of stimuli; vision, hearing, taste, smell, and touch.

sensory receptors   Millions of microscopic structures throughout the body that collect information about the external environment or the body's internal state. Receptors are attuned to particular stimuli, and they fire when excited.

separation anxiety   Feelings of fear or sadness associated with the departure of the object of attachment.

sex education   An organized curriculum focusing on the biological, psychological, cultural, and interpersonal aspects of love, sexuality, and reproduction.

sex hormones   Hormones that are produced as a result of stimulation by hormones produced in the brain and mainly including estrogen, testosterone, and progesterone.

sex-linked characteristics   Characteristics for which the allele is found on the sex chromosomes.

sex-role identification   The integration of knowledge about one's gender, awareness of cultural expectations associated with each sex, identification with the like-sex parent, and preference for one's sex role.

sex-role preference   A positive value for the expectations and norms held for a specific gender group.

sex-role standards   Attributes held by the culture for males and females. These attributes can include both precepts and sanctions.

sexual orientation   One's preference for partners of the same or the opposite sex in sexually intimate relationships.

shame   An intense emotional reaction to being ridiculed or to a negative self-assessment.

shaping   In operant conditioning, altering behavior by reinforcing progressively closer approximations of the desired behavior.

sibling   Brother or sister.

sibling rivalry   Jealousy or competiton among siblings.

sign   Something that represents something else, usually in an abstract, arbitrary way; for example, a word for an object.

social attachment   A strong, affectionate bond that develops between infants and their caregivers.

social cognition   Concept related to understanding interpersonal behavior and the point of view of others.

social competence   The skills involved in making friends, maintaining friendships, and enjoying the benefits of close peer relations.

social convention   Socially accepted norms and regulations that guide behavior.

social culture   The norms, roles, beliefs, values, and customs of a culture.

social desirability   The quality of a person's responding or behaving in ways that are viewed as acceptable or proper by others.

socialization   The process of teaching and enforcing group norms and values to the new group members.

social learning theory   A theory of learning that emphasizes the ability to learn new responses through observation and imitation of others.

social pretend play   Fantasy or symbolic play involving two or more play companions.

social referencing   The process by which infants use facial features and verbal expressions as clues to the emotional responses of another person, often the mother, and as information about how to approach an unfamiliar, ambiguous situation.

social ridicule   Making fun of someone through embarrassing remarks or derisive comments.

social roles The parts or identities a person assumes.

social role theory   The theory that emphasizes participation in varied and more complex roles as a major factor in human development.

social smile   Smile in response to humans, other living creatures, or stimuli that have the appearance of a face, usually a signal of recognition, interest, and an invitation for continued communication.

social support   Information leading people to believe that they are cared for and loved, that they are esteemed and valued, and that they belong to a network of communication and mutual obligation.

socioeconomic status   One's ranking on a number of social and financial indicators, including years of education, kind of work, and salary.

solicitude   Attentive care and protectiveness.

solitary pretense   Fantasy or symbolic play carried on alone or with an imaginary companion.

somatic processes   All those processes necessary for the functioning of the biological organism; for example, the sensory capacities.

soothability   The ability to regain a calm state following irritation or pain.

spaced feeders   A pattern of infant nursing among mammals in which mothers leave their infants in a nest and return to nurse periodically.

specialized structural systems   A component of the model of the mind referring to types of intellectual domains that require unique problem-solving skills.

sperm   The male germ cell.

stage of development   A period of life that is characterized by a specific underlying organization.

stages   Periods where there are qualitative differences in how one's life is experienced.

stimulus   Any change in the energy of the environment that has the potential to influence a perceiver.

stimulus generalization   The capacity for similar stimuli to evoke the same response.

stranger anxiety   Feelings of fear or apprehension in the presence of unfamiliar people, especially during infancy.

strange situation   A standard laboratory procedure designed to describe patterns of attachment behavior. A child is exposed during a 20-minute period to a series of events that are likely to stimulate the attachment system. Child and caregiver enter an unfamiliar laboratory setting; a stranger enters; the caregiver leaves briefly; and the caregiver and infant have opportunities for reunion while researchers observe child, caregiver, and their interactions.

stratification   The process of dividing the larger population into subgroups that are unlikely to intermarry.

stratified sampling   A method for choosing the sample for a research study in which subjects are selected from a variety of levels or types of people in the population.

subcultural norms   Views shared by members of an ethnic group or subculture on such issues as the definition of appropriate child behavior and successful maturity, the nature of gender roles, and the proper balance between individual achievement and responsibility to family and community.

subordinate   One who is of a lower, submissive rank.

substantive complexity   The degree to which one's work requires thought, independent judgment, and frequent decision making.

sudden infant death syndrome   The sudden, unexpected death of an apparently healthy baby who seems well when put to sleep, but later is found dead.

superego   In psychoanalytic theory, the mental function that embodies moral precepts and moral sanctions. The superego includes the ego ideal, or the goals toward which one strives, as well as the punishing conscience.

surrogate mother   A woman who conceives and bears a child for an infertile couple.

survey   A research method in which carefully worded questions are asked of a large number of respondents, either orally or in writing.

swaddling   The practice of wrapping an infant snugly in strips of cloth.

symbol   An object, image, or word that represents something. A symbol can be a word that represents an object, such as *chair*, or an object that represents a concept, such as a dove.

symbolic drawing   Drawing that represents a specific thought.

symbolic play   Imaginative or pretend activities that express emotions, problems, or roles.

synchronize   To coincide or agree in time.

synchrony   Caregiver–infant interactions that are rhythmic, well-timed, and mutually satisfying.

syntax   The rules for ordering words in a specific language.

system   A combination of things or parts, forming a complex or unitary whole and functioning as a unit.

systematic approach   Conducting research in a careful and orderly way.

systems theory   A perspective that the whole is greater than the sum of its parts.

taboo   Proscribed by society as improper or unacceptable.

tactile stimulation   Any stimuli that evoke a response from the sensory receptors in the skin. Touching, tickling, pinching, and rubbing are examples.

talent   Areas of skill or competence.

teachable moments   The times when a person is maturationally most ready to learn a new skill.

technology   A technical method of achieving a practical purpose.

telegraphic speech   Two-word sentences, used by children, that omit many parts of speech but convey meaning.

temperament   Innate characteristics that determine the person's sensitivity to various sense experiences and his or her responsiveness to patterns of social interaction.

teratogens   Agents that might produce malformations during the formation of organs and tissues.

test   Groups of questions or problems that usually indicate and measure abilities, potentials, or psychological characteristics.

testosterone   A hormone that fosters the development of male sex characteristics and growth.

theory   A logically interrelated system of concepts and statements that provides a framework for organizing, interpreting, and understanding observations, with the goal of explaining and predicting behavior.

toddlerhood   The period of psychosocial development including the ages two and three.

toxemia   The presence of toxins produced by bacteria in the bloodstream.

transactional view of learning   A view of learning which suggests that children gain knowledge through meaningful interactions with people and objects in the environment.

transmissive view of learning   A view of learning which suggests that children are like empty vessels ready to be filled with information.

trauma   In psychoanalytic theory, an emotional shock that has long-lasting psychological consequences.

trial-and-error learning   A mode of learning in which the solution is discovered by observing the consequences of each response.

trimester   A period of three months during the nine months of pregnancy.

trust   An emotional sense that both the environment and oneself are reliable and capable of satisfying basic needs.

ultrasound   A technique for producing visual images of the fetus in utero through a pattern of deflected sound waves.

unconditioned response   A response that is evoked by a stimulus prior to opportunities for learning; sometimes described as a reflexive response.

unconditioned stimulus   A stimulus that evokes a response prior to opportunities for learning.

unconscious   In Freud's psychosexual theory, a reservoir of wishes, needs, and fantasies that influence behavior but of which we are not normally aware.

uterus   In the female reproductive system, the hollow muscular organ in which the fertilized ovum normally becomes embedded and in which the developing embryo and fetus is nourished and grows.

vagina   A muscular passageway that connects to the uterus and to the outside of the body.

validity   The extent to which a test measures what it is supposed to measure.

value   A principle or quality that is intrinsically desirable.

variables   Dimensions that can have a number of different values.

verbal persuasion   Encouragement from others.

verbatim   Word for word; using the exact words.

vernix caseosa   A coating of dead cells and oil that covers the skin during fetal development.

vicarious   An experience achieved through the imagined participation in events that happen to another person.

vicarious reinforcement   When negative behaviors go unpunished, they are likely to be imitated by others.

vigilant interest   Intense, focused attention; characteristic of toddlers as they watch their mothers caring for a new sibling.

visual acuity   The ability to detect visual stimuli under various levels of illumination.

visual tracking   Following an object's movement with one's eyes.

vocabulary   A list of the words a child uses and understands.

volunteer sampling   A method of sampling in which subjects for a study are selected from volunteers.

vulnerability   One of the dimensions of attitudes toward pregnancy and childbirth.

weaning   Shifting an infant from nursing or bottle feeding to other food sources.

will   The determination to exercise free choice and self-control.

withdrawal   Becoming socially and emotionally detached.

withdrawn-rejected   A classification referring to children who are inhibited, anxious, and interpersonally reserved.

world view   A way of making meaning out of the relationships, situations, and objects encountered in daily life.

zone of proximal development   The emergent developmental capacity that is just ahead of the level at which the person is currently functioning.

zygote   The developing individual formed from two gametes.

Photo Credits

Name Index

Abel, E. L., 196
Aber, J. A., 294
Aboud, F. E., 579
Ackerman, G. L., 680
Acredolo, C., 44, 645
Action for Children, 324
Adams, B. N., 162
Adams, G. R., 686, 714
Adamson, L. B., 332
Adejoke, A. A., 639
Adelson, J., 653
Adler, A., 414, 599
Adler, N. E., 223, 225
Ainsworth, M. D. S., 18, 251,
    252, 253, 255, 257, 258,
    259, 295, 316, 331, 576
Albert, S., 399
Aleksandrowicz, D. R., 200
Aleksandrowicz, M. K., 200
Alessandri, S. M., 297
Alexander, C. S., 664
Alexander, K. L., 210, 433,
    572, 612
Allen, J. P., 294, 328, 679
Allen, L., 467
Als, H., 200
Altemeyer, B., 521
Alter, R. C., 226
Ambrose, J. A., 275
American Academy of
    Pediatrics, 315, 528
American Psychiatric Asso-
    ciation, 301, 400
American Psychological
    Association, 47, 48
Anderson, D. R., 533
Anderson, E. A., 623
Anderson, R. C., 562
Anderson, W. F., 171
Andersoon, B., 327
Andrews, L. B., 150
Aneshensel, C. S., 690
Anglin, J. M., 354
Anthony, J. E., 17
Aoki, C., 240
Apgar, V., 236, 237
Archer, J., 92
Armstrong, B. G., 197, 198
Aronfreed, J., 466
Asher, S. R., 579, 580, 581,
    583
Aslin, R. N., 241, 242
Astone, N. M., 701
Atkinson, D. R., 697

Atkinson, J. W., 598
Au, T. K., 554
Avis, J., 478
Ayers, M., 583
Azuma, H., 612

Bachman, J. G., 708
Badzinski, D. M., 476
Bahr, S. J., 130
Bailey, J. M., 456, 462, 463
Bailey, O. A., 638
Baillargeon, R., 268, 269
Bakeman, R., 331
Baker, D. P., 603
Baker, L. S., 528, 529
Baker, S. P., 320
Bales, R. F., 127
Balogh, R. D., 243
Ban, B., 317
Bandura, A., 114, 115, 131,
    382, 397, 461, 467, 534,
    570, 571, 606
Banks, M. S., 241
Barbee, A. H., 46
Barinaga, M., 166
Barnes, G. M., 706
Barrett, K. C., 276
Barrett, M., 47–48
Barth, R. P., 666
Bartsch, K., 478
Basic Behavioral Science
    Task Force, 44
Bassuk, E. L., 623
Bates, E., 347, 348, 397
Bates, J. E., 168, 250, 251
Bathurst, K., 322
Bauer, P. J., 459
Baulieu, E., 220
Baumgardner, A. H., 490
Baumrind, D., 420, 463, 689
Baur, K., 187
Beaulieu, L., 586
Beauvoir, S. de, 637
Becker, T. M., 317
Beere, C. A., 458
Beit-Hallahmi, B., 473
Bell, D. M., 327
Bell, N., 554
Bell, S. M., 295
Belsky, J., 12, 251, 275, 295,
    303, 306, 323, 416, 577
Bem, S. L., 457, 459, 465
Benedict, R., 123, 127, 695
Benedict, S., 123

Benenson, J. F., 484
Bengston, V. L., 691
Benn, R., 310
Benson, J. B., 268
Benson, M. J., 715
Benson, P. L., 642
Bentler, P. M., 707
Berger, J., 19
Berkowitz, L., 382, 534
Berlin, I. N., 680
Berndt, T. J., 579, 581, 658
Bernstein, P., 275
Berrueta-Clement, J. R., 431
Bertenthal, B. I., 267
Betancourt, H., 122
Bettelheim, B., 66
Biddle, B. J., 127, 128, 130
Bidell, T. R., 269
Biernat, M., 412
Bigler, R. S., 459
Bijstra, J., 553
Billy, J. O. G., 146
Bilsker, D., 715
Binet, A., 103
Birch, D., 598
Birch, H., 249
Biringen, Z., 363
Birnbaum, D. W., 533
Bitman, J., 315
Bjorklund, D. F., 586
Blain, M. D., 715
Blasi, A., 710
Blass, E. M., 243, 244
Bleuler, E., 103
Block, J., 17
Block, J. H., 17
Bloom, L., 349
Blos, P., 60, 66, 344
Blos, R., 59
Blum, R. W., 642, 680
Blumenstein, A., 655
Blyth, D. A., 640, 641
Boas, F., 123
Bohan, J. S., 453
Bolton, F. G., Jr., 639
Booth, A., 520
Borke, H., 475
Bornstein, J. H., 242
Bornstein, M. H., 241, 242,
    306, 331, 373
Borton, R. W., 246
Boss, P., 13
Bottoms, B. L., 521
Bouchard, T. J., 175

Bowen, M., 133
Bower, E. M., 584
Bower, T. G. R., 246
Bowlby, J., 251, 253, 293, 331
Boyce, W. T., 297
Boyes, M., 476, 648
Boyle, F. M., 556
Brackbill, Y., 200
Bradley, R. H., 331, 427
Bradley, R. M., 242
Braine, M. D. S., 350
Brainerd, C. J., 553
Brasel, J., 194
Braungart, J. M., 249
Brazelton, R. B., 295
Brazelton, T. B., 196, 200,
    248
Breakwell, G. M., 710
Bretherton, I., 255
Breuer, J., 98
Bridges, L. J., 255
Brim, O. G., Jr., 127
Brockner, J., 489
Brody, G. H., 415, 416, 520,
    532
Bronfenbrenner, U., 131
Bronson, G. W., 200, 252
Brook, M. S., 706
Brooks-Gunn, J., 146, 239,
    634, 637, 639, 640, 656,
    664
Brown, B. B., 660, 679, 681,
    688
Brown, I., Jr., 570
Brown, J. D., 489, 490
Brown, J. K., 694
Brown, J. L., 427
Brown, J. R., 360, 379, 414
Brown, P. J., 580
Brown, R., 127, 351
Brown, S. C., 561
Browne, A., 623
Browne, B. A., 574
Brustad, R. J., 585
Bryant, J., 535
Buchsbaum, H. K., 486
Buehler, 317
Buescher, P. A., 195
Buie, J., 432
Bukowski, W. M., 484
Bullock, M., 382, 383
Burchinal, M., 430
Burke, B., 373
Burke, C., 239

Burr, W. R., 490
Burt, R. D., 210
Burton, R. B., 694
Bus, A. G., 562
Bush, G., 527
Bush, P. J., 707
Buss, A. H., 16, 168, 249
Bussell, D., 223
Butler, R., 491, 568
Butterfield, E. C., 557
Bybee, J., 504, 506
Byrne, G., 149, 150

Caldas, S. J., 699
Caldera, Y. M., 462
Caldwell, B. M., 331
Calhoun, G., Jr., 601
Calkins, S. D., 250
Camburn, D., 664
Campbell, J., 490
Campos, J. J., 249, 267, 268, 276
Campos, R. G., 294
Camras, L. A., 273
Canfield, R. L., 242
Cannon-Watkins, G., 608
Caplan, M., 380
Caplan, N., 614
Carey, S., 349
Carlo, G., 578
Carlson, V., 257
Caron, A. J., 242
Caron, R. F., 277
Carr, M., 557
Carroll, D. W., 562
Carroll, J. L., 467, 470
Carron, A. V., 638
Carter, D. B., 459
Caspi, A., 9, 17, 640
Cassady, G., 194, 195, 237
Cassidy, J., 293, 580
Castro, K. G., 317
Caughy, M. O., 430
Cavior, N., 659
Cernoch, J. M., 243
Chagnon, N. A., 418, 422, 523
Chalmers, J. B., 578
Chamberlain, P., 409
Chandler, M., 476, 648
Chandler, M. J., 203
Chapman, M., 379, 555, 644
Chappell, C. K., 130
Charlesworth, W. R., 93, 94
Chase-Lansdale, P. L., 260, 423
Chasnoff, I. J., 196
Chazen, S. E., 269
Chen, Y., 314
Cherlin, A. J., 309, 310
Chess, S., 16, 168, 249, 250

Children's Defense Fund, 324, 326, 327
Chilmonczyk, B. A., 318
Christensen, C., 490
Ciaramitaro, V., 243, 244
Cicchetti, D., 275, 436
Cicirelli, V. G., 491
Clancy, S. M., 714
Clark, J. E., 364, 365
Clark, M. C., 332
Clark, M. L., 583
Clark, R. D., III, 475
Clark, R. M., 17
Clarke-Stewart, K. A., 323, 326, 431
Clarren, S. K., 196
Clasen, D. R., 681
Clausen, J. A., 634, 641
Clayman, C. B., 149, 168, 171, 211
Clifton, R., 241
Coats, P. B., 585
Cochran-Smith, M., 604
Cohler, B. J., 17
Cohn, J. F., 295
Coie, J. D., 581
Cole, D., 371
Cole, M., 603
Cole, R., 60
Coleman, J. S., 603
Collins, P. A., 533
Colombo, J., 241
Columbo, J., 39
Comer, J. P., 617
Comstock, G. A., 533, 534
Conger, R. D., 656
Connolly, K., 262
Connors, K., 297
Connors, L. J., 608
Constantinople, A., 84
Coolidge, J. C., 504
Coombs, R. H., 707
Copans, S. A., 203
Corcker, J., 678
Corine, D. P., 347
Corter, C. M., 315
Coster, W. J., 360
Cote, T. R., 317
Coulton, C. J., 433
Cowan, C. P., 130, 302, 303, 306
Cowan, E. L., 17
Cowan, P. A., 130, 302, 303, 306
Cowley, G., 317
Cox, M. J., 251, 303, 332
Craig-Bray, L., 714
Crain, W. C., 84
Crain-Thoreson, C., 358
Creswell, J. W., 28
Crick, N. R., 580

Crittenden, P., 302
Crockett, L., 583
Crockett, L. J., 703
Cronin-Golomb, A., 347
Crooks, R., 187
Crooks, T. J., 572, 601
Cross, D. R., 557
Cross, W. E., 697
Crouter, A. C., 686
Crystal, R. G., 169, 171
Culbertson, S. A., 113
Cullen, C., 112
Cummings, E. M., 75, 382, 617
Cummings, J. S., 382
Cunningham, F. G., 168, 192, 208, 220

Dale, P. S., 358
Dalgeish, M., 262
Daling, J. R., 210
Damon, W., 468, 481, 485, 486, 502
D'Andrade, R., 603
Dann, S., 36
Dannemiller, J. L., 241
Darney, P. D., 199
Darwin, C., 92, 93, 131
Darwin, D., 93
D'Augelli, A. R., 665
Davey, G., 112
Davis, A., 40
Davis, M. M., 198
Davis-Floyd, R. E., 214
Davison, G. C., 504
Davison, M. L., 61
Dawson, G., 299
de Alteriis, M., 223
DeCasper, A. J., 241
DeLoache, J. S., 345
DeMeis, D. K., 324
Demetriou, A., 562, 564, 565, 645
Demo, D. H., 423
DeMulder, E. K., 302
Denham, S. A., 403
DeSantis, L., 699, 701
de St. Aubin, E., 307
Devine, J. A., 623
DeVos, J., 268, 269
Diaz, R. M., 361
Diaz, S., 615
DiBlasio, F. A., 703
Dickstein, E. B., 587
Dickstein, S., 332
Didow, S. M., 373, 374, 398
Diener, C. I., 601
Dinges, D. F., 198
DiPietro, J. A., 239
Dishion, T. J., 577

DiVitto, B., 238
Dobson, W. R., 714
Dodge, K. A., 274, 503, 578
Doehrman, M. J., 653
Dokecki, P. R., 659
Dolgin, K., 242
Dollinger, S. J., 714
Donald, M., 666
Donin, H. H., 520
Donnelly, B. W., 664
Donovan, W. L., 260
Dornbusch, S. M., 708
Downey, G., 578
Drabman, R. S., 535
Draguns, J. G., 523
Dubow, E. F., 12
Duck, S., 78
Duckett, E., 658
Duggan, A. K., 701, 702
Duncan, G. J., 424, 426
Duncan, T. E., 571
Dunham, R. M., 648
Dunn, J., 360, 368, 373, 379, 409, 414, 415
Durbin, D. L., 659, 688
Dweck, C. S., 300, 601
Dwyer, J., 640

East, P. L., 581, 679
Easterbrooks, M. A., 238, 330
Eccles, J. S., 566, 575
Eckerman, C. O., 373, 374, 398
Eckstein, S., 646
Edelbrock, C., 458
Edelman, M. W., 699
Eder, R. A., 488
Edwards, C. P., 378, 483
Efklides, A., 645
Egeland, B., 293, 332
Eiger, M. S., 314, 315
Einstein, A., 98
Eisenberg, N., 474
Elder, G. H., Jr., 13
Elias, M. J., 578
Elkind, D., 516, 647
Elliott, D. S., 655
Ellsworth, C. P., 270
Elmer-Dewitt, P., 149, 150
Elson, J., 151
Elster, A. B., 703
Emde, R. N., 379, 381, 474, 486
Emerson, P. E., 252
Emery, A. E. H., 171
Emery, R. E., 435
Entwisle, D. R., 210, 433, 572
Epstein, J., 583
Epstein, J. L., 608
Epstein, S., 484

Erikson, E. H., 36, 59, 60–65, 66, 70, 77–78, 80, 81, 82, 84, 96, 99, 100, 107–108, 126, 294, 300, 308, 311, 314, 372, 395, 400, 418, 421, 480, 499, 502, 509, 512, 549, 598, 606, 607, 710, 715
Erikson, J. M., 294, 308
Eron, L. D., 533
Evans, N., 635

Fabes, R. A., 476
Fagot, B. I., 457
Farkas, G., 612
Farrar, M. J., 554
Farrell, A. D., 707
Faust, M. S., 634
Fawcett, J. T., 206
Fechter, L. D., 197
Fein, G. G., 323, 431
Feinman, C. F., 199
Feinman, S., 253
Feldman, D. H., 470
Feldman, H., 128
Feldman, M., 128
Feldman, S. S., 687
Fenson, L., 346, 348, 350
Fenster, L., 198
Fentress, J. C., 246
Fernald, A., 347
Ferster, C. B., 113
Field, D., 553
Field, T., 294, 297, 327
Field, T. M., 188, 242, 254, 274
Fifer, W., 241
Fincham, F. D., 423, 483
Finley, N. J., 690
Fischer, K. W., 61, 246, 263, 267, 269, 561, 646
Flaks, D. K., 463
Flannery, D. J., 663
Flavell, J. H., 61, 367, 476, 556, 645
Fleeson, J., 577
Fleming, A. S., 203, 315
Fogas, B. S., 617, 619
Folkman, S., 80
Fonagy, P., 259
Ford, C. S., 215, 216
Ford, M. E., 606
Forehand, R., 416
Fosburgh, L., 699
Fowler, F. L., Jr., 39
Fox, N. A., 250, 255, 323
Francis, P. L., 237
Franklin, D. L., 699
Franz, C. E., 307
French, D. C., 578, 581
Freud, A., 36, 59, 60, 62, 99, 414, 461

Freud, S., 57, 59, 96–100, 251, 316, 383, 396, 472, 473, 474, 508, 548
Frey, K. S., 491
Fried, P. A., 197
Froming, W. J., 467
Frye, K. F., 260
Fu, V., 420
Fuller, B., 430
Furman, W., 580
Furstenberg, F. F., 309, 310
Furstenberg, F. F., Jr., 146, 664

Gadberry, S., 532
Gaddis, A., 639
Gaier, E. L., 658
Gaines, J. A., 297
Gallagher, E. M., 623
Gallagher, F. M., 489
Galligan, R., 130
Gallimore, R., 615
Galotti, K. M., 714
Gandhi, M., 36, 61, 469
Ganong, L. H., 423
Gant, N. F., 192, 208, 220
Garbarino, J., 433, 550, 718
Garcia, E. E., 361
Gardner, H., 558, 564
Garguilo, J., 663
Garland, A. F., 680
Garmezy, N., 12, 17, 426, 606
Garner, P. W., 416
Garrison, C. Z., 655
Garton, A. F., 348
Garvey, C., 480
Gavazzi, S. M., 695
Gavin, L. A., 580
Geary, D. C., 561
Gehring, T. M., 687
Gelles, R. J., 699
Gelman, S. A., 554
Gerbner, G., 535
Gervai, J., 458
Getchell, N., 364, 366
Giacola, G. P., 201
Gibbs, J. C., 468
Gibson, E. J., 246
Gibson, J. J., 244
Gilbert, M. S., 188
Gildea, P. M., 350
Giles-Sims, J., 132
Gillen, F. J., 694
Gillies, P., 646
Gilligan, C., 84, 715
Ginsburg, A. L., 146
Ginsburg, S. D., 714
Giordano, P. C., 684
Glass, P., 198
Glenn, N. D., 303

Glick, P. C., 617
Glick, W., 317
Glodis, K. A., 710
Godwin, A., 326
Goedert, J. J., 317
Goffin, S. G., 518
Goffman, E., 19
Gold, M., 655
Goldberg, M. E., 534
Goldberg, S., 238, 318
Goldberg, W., 420
Goldenberg, C. N., 562
Goldfield, E. C., 248
Goldsmith, H. H., 249
Golinkoff, R. M., 350
Golombok, S., 151
Goodnow, J. J., 552
Gopnik, A., 268, 270, 557
Gordon, A. S., 706
Gore, S., 657
Gorer, G., 217
Gorman, C., 157
Gorn, G. J., 534
Gotleib, I. H., 303
Gottfried, A. E., 322
Gottfried, A. W., 322
Gottman, J. M., 13
Gould, R., 84
Gralinski, J. H., 407, 408, 419
Grandquist, H., 216
Granleese, 601
Gratch, G., 264
Green, R., 462
Greenberger, E., 411, 420
Greene, A.-L., 75
Greenfield, P. M., 348
Greenhouse, 223
Grigsby, C., 623
Grossman, F. K., 203
Grusec, J. E., 78, 115
Grych, J. H., 423
Gubrium, J. F., 37
Gulko, J., 457, 552
Gunnar, M. R., 16, 253, 254, 277
Gutek, G. L., 603
Guthrie, D., 297

Habenstein, R. W., 418, 420, 421
Habicht, J. P., 195
Hagtvet, K. A., 570
Hahn, R. A., 206, 212, 216, 218
Haith, M. M., 242, 264
Hakuta, K., 361
Hala, S., 368
Halford, G. S., 556
Hall, E. G., 515
Hall, W. S., 560
Haller, E., 562

Hallinan, M. T., 660
Halpin, G. J., 212
Halton, A., 186, 200
Halverson, C. F., 459
Ham, M., 75, 657
Hamilton, C. E., 326
Hammen, C., 623
Handford, A. G., 532
Hans, S. L., 198
Hansell, M. J., 195
Hansell, S., 583, 618, 661
Hanson, S. L., 146, 663
Hardy, J. B., 701, 702
Harmon, 330
Harris, M., 345, 348
Harris, P., 267
Harris, P. B., 715
Harris, P. L., 367, 371, 478
Hart, B., 357
Hart, C. H., 473, 577
Hart, D., 485, 486, 502
Harter, S., 488, 570, 572, 607
Hartup, W. W., 576
Harwood, R. L., 276, 419
Haskett, M. E., 577
Haskins, R., 430, 431
Haslett, S. J., 715
Haswell, K., 405
Hausman, B., 623
Havighurst, R. J., 59, 65–67
Haviland, J. M., 653
Hawkins, J. A., 679
Hay, D. F., 254
Hayes, D. S., 533
Haynes, O. M., 292
Hearold, S., 535
Heath, S. B., 356
Hebel, 197
Heckhausen, I., 331
Heinicke, C. M., 189, 297, 303
Heitlinger, A., 206
Helman, C. G., 207, 213
Henderson, V. K., 431
Herkovits, M., 122
Hernandez, D. J., 422
Hess, R., 562
Hess, R. D., 612
Hetherington, E. M., 80, 310, 617
Hickey, T. L., 241
Higgins, E. T., 78
Hill, J. P., 640, 687
Hill, R., 13
Hiltonsmith, R. W., 686
Hirsch, B. J., 711
Hock, E., 324
Hodges, J., 293
Hoffman, 405
Hoffman, H. R., 532
Hoffman, L. W., 322, 324

Hoffman, M. L., 473, 474, 475, 504
Hoffman, S. J., 359
Hoffmeyer, L. B., 243
Hoffner, C., 476
Hofstede, G., 523
Hoge, D. R., 681
Hohmann, M., 439
Holden, C., 166, 167
Holden, G. W., 332
Holloway, S. D., 430, 562, 567, 601
Holmes, J. G., 290
Holmes, T. H., 206
Holstein, J. A., 37
Homans, G. C., 19
Hooper, F. H., 553
Hopkins, B., 246
Hopkins, J. R., 60
Horn, J. D., 224
Hornik, R., 277
Horobin, K., 44
Horowitz, F. D., 237
Horowitz, L. M., 294
Howe, N., 416
Howes, C., 326, 327, 369, 373, 431, 484
Howes, P, 260
Hoyle, S. G., 658
Hubert, J., 314
Hubert, N. C., 168, 249
Huesmann, L. R., 533
Hunsberger, B., 521
Hunt, J. M. V., 268
Hunter, F. T., 687
Huston, A. C., 423, 533, 536
Huston, T. L., 303, 304
Hutt, S. J., 372
Huxley, J., 59, 96
Hyman, 434
Hymel, S., 580, 581

Iannotti, R. J., 382, 707
Inhelder, B., 263, 550, 644, 645, 646
Inouye, D. K., 570
Isabella, R. A., 251, 259, 295, 303
Izard, C. E., 254, 260, 274, 276, 503

Jacklin, C. N., 453, 483
Jacobs, J. E., 575
Jacobson, E., 461, 508
Jacobson, L., 572
Jacobson, S. W., 241, 260
Jacobvitz, D., 332
Jaeger, E., 322
James, W., 484, 485
Jarboe, P. J. D., 206

Jaroff, L., 156
Jaspars, J., 483
Jayakody, R., 426
Jeliffe, D., 315
Jeliffe, E. F. P., 315
Jensen, R., 467
Johnston, L. D., 642, 703, 706, 707
Jones, K. L., 196
Jones, M. C., 641
Jones, R. M., 686, 714
Jones, S. S., 350, 661
Jones-Webb, R. J., 657
Jordan, B., 212, 214, 215
Jordan, N. C., 556
Joseph, 601
Josephson, W. L., 533
Josselson, R., 84
Jouriles, E. N., 413
Judson, F. N., 199
Jussim, L., 572, 573, 574

Kagan, J., 9, 275, 461
Kagan, S. L., 528
Kagitcibasi, C., 122
Kahn, R. L., 129
Kalish, C. W., 554
Kalleberg, A. L., 412
Kalverboer, A. F., 364
Kamptner, N. L., 715
Kantner, J. F., 699
Kantor, D., 132
Kantor, N., 300
Kantrowitz, B., 238
Kaplan, N., 293
Karow, W. G., 200
Karraker, K. H., 75
Karweit, N., 583
Kashima, Y., 522
Katchadourian, H., 664
Katz, D., 129
Kaufmann, G., 397
Kavanaugh, R. D., 367, 371
Keating, D. P., 644, 650, 652
Kegan, R., 491
Keil, P. F., 262
Kelly, J. B., 617
Kelly, M. L., 426
Keltenbach, K., 253
Kennell, J. H., 203
Kermoian, R., 268
Kerns, D., 666, 706
Kessen, W., 34, 242
Ketterlinus, R. D., 663
Kilbourne, B. W., 317
Kimura, D., 186, 187
King, M. L., 469
King, R. A., 331
Kistner, J. A., 577
Kivnick, H. Q., 294, 308

Klackenberg-Larsson, I., 464
Kliman, D. G., 203
Klineberg, S. L., 646
Klinnert, M. D., 277
Klint, K. A., 584
Knight, C. C., 561
Koblinsky, S. A., 623
Kochanska, G., 34, 381, 405, 408, 473, 477, 504
Kohl, R., 203
Kohlberg, L., 456, 468, 470
Kohn, M. L., 411
Kohn, P. M., 657
Kohut, H., 473
Kolb, B., 190
Konner, M., 314, 315, 417
Koop, C. E., 223
Kopp, C. B., 274, 378, 407, 408, 419
Kornfield, S., 640
Koslowski, B., 248, 295
Kostelny, K., 433
Kowalski, P., 607
Kowaz, A. M., 598
Kozberg, S. F., 714
Krannich, R. S., 218
Krehbiel, G., 581
Kroger, J., 715
Kroonenberg, P. M., 259, 293
Kropp, J. P., 292
Kuczynski, L., 34, 398, 409
Kuhl, P. K., 241, 347
Kuhn, D., 558, 650

Labouvie-Vief, G., 80
Lacayo, R., 151, 550
Ladd, G. W., 373, 580
Ladson-Billings, G., 616
Lamb, G. S., 207
Lamb, M. E., 255, 701, 703
Lamborn, S. D., 682
Lampman, Petraitis, C., 652
Landau, G. M., 372
Landers, S., 532, 536, 622
Landsverk, J., 707
Lang, M., 303
Lang, M. E., 323, 328
Larson, M. C., 253
Larson, R., 75, 640, 641, 652, 653, 657
Laszlo, E., 131
La Voie, J. C., 371
Lazarus, A., 226
Lazenby, A., 317
Leavitt, L. A., 260
Lee, L. C., 480
Lehr, W., 132
Leigh, G. K., 130
Leinbach, M. D., 457

Leland, N. L., 666
Lemkau, J. R., 225, 226
Lenneberg, E. H., 353
Lerner, J. V., 249
Lerner, R. M., 168, 249
Lessing, E. E., 646
Lester, B. M., 198, 200
Levan, A., 153
Levesque, R. P., 664
Levin, H., 307
Levin, I., 61
LeVine, R. A., 318
Levinson, D., 84
Levitt, M. J., 332, 658, 678, 685
Levy, G. D., 459
Levy-Schiff, R., 238
Lewis, H. B., 397
Lewis, M., 41, 253, 317, 368
Lewit, E. M., 528, 529, 530
Lewit, L. S., 530
Liben, L. S., 459
Lieberman, A. F., 298
Liebert, R. M., 531, 533, 534, 536
Lin, C. Y. C., 420
Lindblad, B. S., 194
Lindbohm, M., 200
Linn, M. C., 650
Lipkin, M., 207
Lipps, T., 103
Litt, I. F., 654
Lobel, T. E., 459
Loftus, E. F., 44
Logan, D. D., 637
Logan, J., 690
Lombardi, J., 518
Lombardi, V., 585
Long, B. H., 491
Longeway, K. P., 254
Looft, W. R., 648
Lopata, H. Z., 691
Lopez, A., 554
Lopez, S. R., 122
Lorenz, K. F., 292
Lovell, K., 552
Lowenthal, M., 84
Lozoff, B., 214, 215
Lucariello, J., 368
Ludemann, P. M., 242, 277
Luhtanen, R., 678
Luther, M., 61
Lutkenhaus, P., 382, 383
Lyle, J., 532
Lynch, J. H., 689
Lyons-Ruth, K., 293
Lytton, H., 78

Maag, J. W., 656
MacArthur, A., 619

Maccoby, E. E., 307, 406, 420, 453, 462, 473, 483, 506
MacDermid, S. M., 304, 686
MacDonald, P. C., 192, 208, 220
MacEachron, A. E., 639
MacFarlane, J. A., 243
MacLean, D. J., 267
MacTurk, R. H., 265
Mactutus, C. F., 197
Madden, N. A., 531
Mahler, M., 344
Mahler, M. S., 473
Main, N., 293, 295
Makin, J. W., 243
Malamuth, N. M., 533
Malatesta, C. A., 276
Malle, B. F., 294
Malone, S., 214, 215
Mandel, D. R., 347
Mankowski, T. A., 489
Manning, W. D., 708
Marcia, J., 84
Marcia, J. E., 598, 712, 715
Markman, H. J., 260
Markstrom-Adams, C., 695
Marsiglio, W., 639, 702
Martin, C. L., 458, 459, 465
Martin, G. B., 475
Martin, N. G., 161
Martin, S., 636
Marx, J., 166
Maslow, A., 620
Masten, A. S., 606
Matheny, A. P., Jr., 249
Mau, R. Y., 678
May, R. B., 553
Mayer, J., 640
McAdams, D. P., 307
McAdoo, H. P., 490
McAuley, E., 571
McBride, M. L., 555
McBride, S. L., 324
McCabe, A. F., 555
McCarthy, J. D., 681
McCarthy, K., 434
McClearn, G. E., 248
McClelland, D. C., 307
McClelland, J. L., 109
McClendon, E. J., 703
McCloskey, L. A., 344
McCord, J., 655
McCoy, J. K., 416
McCubbin, H., 13
McDonald, A. D., 197, 198
McElroy, M., 571
McGrath, S., 203
McGue, M., 175
McHale, S. M., 304

McInnes, R. R., 158, 161
McKey, R. H., 430
McLanahan, S., 303
McLeod, J. D., 424
McLeod, P. J., 246
McLouth, G., 226
McLoyd, V. C., 424, 425, 426
McMillan, D. W., 686
McNeely, E., 66
Mead, M., 124, 126, 212, 216, 694
Mechanic, D., 618
Melhuish, E. C., 327
Mellor, S., 715
Meltzoff, A., 246, 268, 270
Menaghan, E. G., 411
Menashri, J., 459
Mendel, G., 157, 162
Mendelson, B. K., 636
Merton, R. K., 572
Mertz, K. J., 212
Messer, D. J., 383
Messick, S., 39
Metropolitan Human Services Commission, 324
Millar, W. S., 239
Miller, D., 311
Miller, D. C., 32
Miller, G. A., 350
Miller, N. B., 306, 344
Miller, P. H., 56, 61, 84
Miller, S., 397
Miller, S. A., 553
Miller, W. B., 226
Mills, R. S. H., 408
Millstein, S. G., 654
Milrose, J. A., 657
Mirowsky, J., 81
Mischel, W., 120, 380, 382, 383, 461, 467, 473
Mistretta, C. M., 242
Mitchell, J. M., 157
Miyake, K., 276
Mofese, D. L., 346
Moffitt, T. E., 640
Moll, L. C., 615
Mollnow, E., 196, 197, 201
Money, J., 144
Montemayor, R., 687
Montgomery, D. E., 578
Moore, K., 664
Moore, K. A., 699
Moore, K. L., 185, 187, 201
Moorehouse, M. J., 609
Morelli, C., 354
Moriarty, A. E., 653
Morris, R. A., 201
Morrison, A. P., 395
Morrison, D. M., 699

Morse, W. C., 601
Mortimer, J. T., 709
Mosel, S., 604
Moskowitz, B. A., 354, 356
Moss, P., 327
Mother Theresa, 469
Muecke, M. A., 206, 212, 216, 218
Mueller, R. F., 171
Muir, D. W., 242
Munn, P., 409
Munroe, R. H., 694
Munroe, R. L., 694
Murdock, G. P., 215, 218, 694
Murphy, L. B., 513
Musa, K. E., 659
Mussen, P. H., 641
Musser, L. M., 574
Muuss, R. E., 693, 694, 695
Myers, B. J., 310
Myers, D. R., 146

National Center for Education Statistics, 528
National Commission on Children, 330, 424, 425, 429, 431, 433, 434, 529, 609, 611, 619, 620
National Commission to Prevent Infant Mortality, 212
National Research Council, 435
National Urban League, 703
Naulty, J. S., 200
Neale, J. M., 504
Neimark, E. D., 645, 652
Neisser, U., 39, 40
Nelson, C. A., 242, 277
Nelson, E., 601
Nelson, J., 579
Nelson, K., 351, 358, 554
Neugarten, B., 309
Neuman, S. B., 516, 517
Newcomb, M. D., 707
Newcomber, S., 146
Newman, B. M., 306, 609, 632, 676, 689
Newman, J. L., 555
Newman, P. R., 84, 306, 609, 632, 658, 676
Newman, R. M., 84
Newton, N., 212, 216
Niedenthal, P. M., 490
Nolen-Hoeksema, S., 657, 658
Norem, J. K., 300
Norton, J. M., 553
Notarius, C. I., 382

Nsamenang, A. B., 124, 126
Nurmi, J., 646

O'Bryant, S. L., 691
O'Campo, D., 188
Ochberg, R. L., 713
Oden, M. M., 46
Offer, D., 687
Ogakaki, L., 564
Ogan, T. A., 277
Ogbu, J. U., 604
Ohannessian, C. M., 703
Olds, D. L., 703
Olds, S. W., 314, 315
O'Leary, S., 406
Olsen, L., 361
Olson, M. V., 156, 158
O'Mahoney, J. F., 646
O'Neill, D. K., 557
Oosterwegel, A., 488
Oppenheim, D., 255
Oppenheimer, L., 488
O'Reilly, A. W., 373
Orlofsky, J. L., 714
Osofsky, J. D., 297, 550
Oster, H., 277
Ostrov, E., 653
Overman, S. J., 585
Owen, M. T., 260
Oyserman, D., 310

Padawer, J. A., 210
Paik, H., 533, 534
Palkovitz, R., 203
Palm, G. F., 203
Palmer, C. F., 267
Papini, D. R., 686, 715
Papousek, H., 275
Pappaioanou, M., 317
Parcel, T. L., 411
Paris, S. G., 557
Park, K. A., 481, 577
Parke, R. D., 306, 310, 322, 332
Parker, A. L., 212
Parker, J. D., 214
Parker, J. G., 579, 583
Parkhurst, J. T., 581
Parsons, J. E., 572, 574
Parsons, T., 127
Passman, R. H., 254, 310
Patterson, C. J., 463
Patterson, D., 173
Patterson, G. R., 409, 578
Pavlov, I. P., 108
Pawl, J. H., 298
Peck, R., 84
Pedersen, F. A., 244
Peduzzi, J. D., 241
Pelham, B. W., 491

Pellegrini, D. S., 382, 578
Pensky, E., 303
Pepitone, E. A., 579
Perret, J., 554
Perret-Clermont, A., 552, 554
Peskin, J., 368
Pete, J. M., 699, 701
Petersen, A. C., 637, 655, 656, 657
Peterson, J., 664
Petronio, R. J., 655
Pettit, G., 168
Pettit, G. S., 473, 577
Phelps, L., 504
Phillips, D. A., 326, 327, 431, 573, 601
Phillipsen, L., 484
Piaget, J., 34, 37, 38, 44, 59, 101–105, 107–108, 131, 262, 263, 264, 267, 268, 269, 372, 468, 469, 476, 549, 550, 551, 552, 554, 555, 557, 564, 578, 644, 645, 646, 652
Pick, H. L., 364
Piers, M. W., 372
Pillow, B. H., 578
Pipp, 330
Pittman, K. J., 699
Pleck, J. H., 699
Plomin, R., 16, 161, 167, 168, 176, 248, 249, 250, 414
Plotnick, R. D., 703
Pokalo, 434
Polednak, A. P., 211
Pollitt, E., 427
Popkin, B. M., 315
Porter, R. H., 243
Posada, G., 293
Powlishta, K. K., 457
Prawat, R. S., 574
Presser, H. B., 311
Putallaz, M., 577
Pye, C., 356

Quadrel, M. J., 642
Queen, S. A., 418, 420, 421
Quiggle, N. L., 581
Quilligan, E. J., 201
Quinn, J. B., 432

Rabinowitz, M., 650
Radin, N., 310, 515
Radke-Yarrow, M., 34, 257, 302, 331, 379, 381, 398
Radman, M., 159, 161
Raffaelli, M., 658
Rahe, R. H., 206
Raja, S.N., 678

Ramsay, D. S., 267
Rauste-von Wright, M., 637, 641
Raymond, C., 347
Reagan, R., 223
Redl, F., 66
Reinisch, J. M., 200
Reischl, T. M., 711
Reiter, E. O., 637, 640
Reiter, M. P., 634
Remafedi, G., 665
Remple, J. K., 290
Renshaw, P. D., 580
Repetti, R. L., 411
Rest, J. R., 467, 470
Rheingold, H. L., 18
Rice, M. L., 349, 356, 536
Richards, M. H., 640, 641, 653
Ricks, M. H., 259
Ridenour, M. V., 366
Rieder, 436
Rindfuss, R. R., 464
Risley, T. R., 357
Roach, M. E., 659
Roberton, M. A., 364
Roberts, L., 169
Roberts, R. E., 657, 691
Robertson, J., 253
Robertson, J. F., 655, 686
Robertson, M. J., 623
Robinson, B. E., 702
Robinson, J. L., 379, 381
Rochat, P., 265
Rock, S. L., 331
Rogers, C. S., 368, 403, 715
Rogers, M. F., 317
Rogoff, B., 354
Rogosch, F. A., 434
Rohner, R. P., 122
Rollins, B. C., 130
Rook, K. S., 581
Rooparine, J., 324
Rosch, E., 270
Rose, S. A., 239, 244
Rose, S. P., 246
Rosen, A. B., 554
Rosenberg, M., 490, 686
Rosenblatt, R. A., 220
Rosenfeld, R. A., 412
Rosenthal, R., 572
Ross, C. E., 81
Ross, S. A., 254
Roth, W. E., 216
Rothbart, M. K., 16
Rovee, C. K., 262
Rovee, D. T., 262
Rovee-Collier, C., 240, 265
Rovine, M., 303
Rozin, P., 554

Rubenstein, J., 244
Rubin, K. H., 373, 408, 580
Rubinson, L., 146, 153, 504, 663
Ruble, D. N., 491, 572
Ruff, H. A., 244, 265
Ruffman, T., 368
Rumelhart, D. E., 109
Runyan, W. M., 36
Russo, N. R., 224
Rutter, M., 17, 80, 293, 297, 301, 604
Ruzany, N., 568
Ryan, R. M., 689
Ryff, C. D., 83

Sagi, A., 255, 475
Saitoti, T. O., 526
Saltz, E., 373
Saltz, R., 373
Salzinger, S., 577
Sameroff, A. J., 129, 131, 203
Sancilio, M. F. M., 581
Sanders, A. K., 532
Sanders, P. E., 609
Sanders, S. A., 200
Sandler, I. N., 618
Sandler, J., 508
Sanson, A., 16
Sargent, J. D., 318
Sarvela, P. D., 703
Sawyers, J. K., 368, 403
Schaefer, E., 516
Schaffer, H. R., 252
Schaie, K. W., 46
Schatz, J. A., 264
Schatz, M., 351
Schickedanz, J. A., 359, 562
Schiedel, D. G., 715
Schneider, W., 586
Schneider-Rosen, K., 275
Schootman, M., 642
Schrag, L., 326
Schroeder, S. R., 201
Schuler, M., 267
Schunck, D. H., 571
Schuster, C. S., 201
Schwartz, R., 224
Schweinhart, L. J., 430
Sciarillo, W. G., 318
Scott, J. P., 292
Seabrook, C., 199
Sears, R. R., 46, 307
Sebby, R. A., 686
Segal, L. B., 242
Self, P. A., 237
Seligman, M. E. P., 601
Selik, R. M., 317

Sells, C. W., 642, 680
Selman, R. L., 476
Sera, M. D., 267
Serbin, L. A., 457, 458, 459
Serson, J., 60–61
Setterlund, M. B., 490
Sexton, M., 197
Shakespeare, W., 128
Shannon, M. J., 424
Share, D. L., 562
Shatz, C. J., 190
Shears, L. M., 584
Sheehan, P. W., 533
Shelov, S. P., 318
Shemesh, M., 646
Shepard, L. A., 529
Shostak, A., 226
Shuster, C., 324
Siegler, R. S., 552, 645
Siekevitz, P., 240
Signorella, M. L., 459
Silverberg, S. B., 706
Silvern, L., 61, 263
Silverstein, A. B., 553
Simon, R. W., 412
Simons, R. L., 655, 686
Singer, D. J., 374, 381
Singer, J. L., 374, 381
Singer, W., 240
Singh, G. K., 211
Siskind, V., 314
Skaalvik, E. M., 570
Skinner, B. F., 111, 114, 131
Skinner, N., 515
Skjoerven, R., 211
Slade, A., 373
Slavin, R. E., 562
Sloan, M., 197, 198
Slobin, D. I., 350
Small, S. A., 666, 706
Smart, S. A., 490
Smetana, J. G., 459, 472
Smith, D. M., 661
Smith, D. W., 196
Smith, J. H., 348
Smith, L. B., 350
Smith, M. L., 529
Smith, P. K., 308, 483
Smith, R. S., 17
Smith, T. L., 586
Smith-Hefner, N. J., 614
Snow, C. E., 356, 361
Snowden, L. R., 657
Snyder, C. R., 83, 300
Snyder, S. S., 470
Sobhan, M., 657
Sonenstein, F. L., 330, 664
Sophian, C., 267, 556
Sosa, R., 203
Soule, B., 203

Spearman, C., 564
Spelke, E. S., 267
Spence, M. J., 241
Spencer, B., 694
Spencer, M. B., 604, 679, 695
Sperling, D., 149
Spiro, R. J., 560
Spitz, R. A., 301
Spitze, G., 690
Sprafkin, J., 531, 533, 534, 536
Sprunger, L. W., 297
Sroufe, L. A., 260, 262, 275, 293, 332, 577
Stack, D. M., 242
Stallings, J. A., 529, 531
Standley, K., 203
Stanger, C., 41
Stannard, D. E., 50
Stapley, J. C., 653
Stattin, H., 464
Stechler, G., 186, 200
Steinberg, L., 420
Steinberg, L. D., 682, 687, 708
Stephens, S., 417
Stern, E., 150–151
Stern, W., 150–151
Sternberg, C., 531
Sternberg, R. J., 564
Stevens, J. H., Jr., 331, 332
Stevenson, B. W., 659
Stevenson, D. L., 603
Stevenson, H. W., 566, 620
Stevenson, M. F., 328
Stewart, P., 431
Stipek, D., 486, 491
Stocker, C., 415
Stolzenberg, R. M., 520
Stoneman, Z., 415, 416, 532
Storms, M. D., 663
Strange, M., 194, 195, 237
Strayer, J., 474
Streissguth, A. P., 197
Strober, M., 654
Sugawara, A. I., 458
Sullivan, H. S., 581
Sullivan, M. W., 41, 274
Super, C. M., 240
Susman, E. J., 657
Sutton-Smith, B. A., 480
Swann, W. B., Jr., 489
Swyer, P. R., 195
Szocka, A., 320

Tangney, J. P., 396, 504, 536
Tanner, J. M., 196, 634, 640
Taylor, C. E., 319

Taylor, J. H., 12, 470, 479
Taylor, M., 374
Tedesco, L. A., 658
Tellegen, A., 161
Teller, D. Y., 242
Terman, L. M., 46
Teti, D. M., 381, 701
Tharp, R. G., 604, 615
Thatcher, R. W., 652
Thelen, E., 247
Thomas, A., 16, 168, 249, 250
Thomas, E. J., 127
Thomas, M. H., 535
Thompson, J. M., 715
Thompson, L., 453
Thompson, M. W., 158, 161, 171
Thompson, R., 310
Thompson, R. A., 260
Thompson, S. K., 457
Thornberry, O. T., 636
Thornton, A., 664
Tichauer, R., 217
Tiedje, L. B., 412
Tijo, J. H., 153
Tinsley, B. J., 310
Tinsley, V. S., 352
Tizard, B., 293
Toch, T., 620, 622
Tolman, E. C., 120
Tolson, T. F. M., 311
Tomlin, A. M., 310
Toosa, M. W., 201
Toufexis, A., 198
Toussieng, P. W., 653
Townsend, M. A. R., 578
Tracy, R. L., 255, 258
Trefil, J., 161
Trethowan, W., 207
Triandis, H. C., 122, 522, 586, 676
Trickett, P. K., 435, 436
Troiden, R. R., 665
Tronick, E. Z., 248, 271, 274, 276, 295
Tudge, J. R. H., 105, 578
Tureil, E., 470
Turner, J. S., 146, 153, 504, 663
Turner, P. J., 458

Udry, J. R., 146
Umbe., V. M., 361
United States Bureau of Census, 32, 192, 208–209, 211, 320, 322, 429, 434, 519, 529, 622, 642, 655, 698, 701, 708, 709

United States Department of Education, 529, 709
United States National Center for Health Statistics, 617
Urberg, K. A., 681, 682
Uzgiris, I. C., 268, 552

Vaillant, G. E., 307
Valdez-Menchaca, M. S., 358
Vandell, D. L., 431
van Gennep, A., 693
van Ijzendoorn, M. H., 257, 258, 259, 293
Van Wieringen, J. C., 639
Vasek, M. E., 368
Vaughan, T. L., 210
Vaughn, B. E., 203, 260, 379, 380
Vega, W. A., 708
Ventis, W. L., 520
Vizziello, G. F., 207
Volling, B. L., 306, 416
von Bertalanffy, L., 129
Vorhees, C. V., 196, 197, 201
Voydanoff, P., 412, 664
Vygotsky, L. S., 101, 105–108, 108, 367, 371, 372, 385, 386, 516, 528, 549, 553, 554, 604

Waas, G. A., 579
Wagner, B. M., 573
Wagner, E., 379
Wagner, R., 159, 161
Walaskay, M., 84
Walden, T. A., 277
Walker, A. S., 246
Walker, E., 578
Walker, L. J., 12, 470, 479
Walker-Andrews, A. S., 277
Wallace, A. R., 93
Wallace, P. M., 303
Waller, A. E., 320
Wallerstein, J. S., 617
Walters, R. H., 114, 115
Warren, M. P., 637
Waterman, A., 84
Waterman, A. S., 712
Waterman, M., 562
Waters, E., 577
Waters, H. S., 352
Watson, J. S., 275
Weber, R. A., 332
Webster, D. W., 642, 655
Weikart, D. P., 430, 439
Weinberg, R. A., 40

Weinberger, J., 307
Weinraub, M., 322
Weinstein, R., 309
Weinstein, R. S., 572
Weiskopf, S., 242
Weiss, B., 406, 436
Weiss, M., 41
Weiss, W. R., 584
Weissberg, R. P., 679
Wellman, H. M., 267, 478, 578
Wenar, C., 382, 405
Wentworth, N., 264
Werker, J. F., 241
Werner, E. E., 17, 81, 310, 311
West, J. R., 196
Westoff, C. F., 464
Weston, D. R., 298
Westra, E., 246
Whiffen, V. E., 715
Whitall, J., 366
Whitbourne, S. K., 84, 710
White, B. L., 355
White, D. R., 215, 636
White, R. W., 59, 78, 396, 606
Whitebrook, M., 326, 327
Whitehead, M. B., 150–151
Whitehurst, G. J., 358
Whiteman, M., 706
Whitesell, N. R., 607
Whiting, B. B., 483
Whiting, J. W. M., 316, 694
Wierson, M., 640
Wilcox, A. J., 211
Willard, H. F., 158, 161
Williams, C., 504, 506
Williams, P. A., 533
Williams, R. A., 660
Williams, T. H., 532
William T. Grant Foundation, 709
Willwerth, J., 199
Wilmoth, G.H., 223
Wilson, B. J., 13
Wilson, K. S., 431
Wilson, M. N., 311
Wilson, R. S., 249
Wilson, S., 42
Winterhoff, P. A., 105
Wittenberg, J., 317
Wolf, A. M., 636
Wolf, D. A., 330
Wolff, P. H., 271, 275
Work, W. C., 17
Wortman, C. B., 412
Wright, J. D., 623

Yaffe, S. J., 201
Yang, R. K., 200, 203

Yarrow, L. J., 244, 265, 292
Yavuz, T., 319
Yengo, L., 267
Yin, R. K., 36
Young, K. T., 326
Youngblade, L. M., 373, 577
Younger, B., 270

Youniss, J., 576
Yu, S. M., 211
Yurdakok, K., 319

Zabin, L. C., 699
Zahniser, S. C., 208
Zahn-Waxler, C., 331, 379,

381, 382, 398, 504,
506
Zanna, M. P., 290
Zelnik, M., 699
Zeskind, P. S., 272
Zigler, E., 323, 326, 328, 680
Zimmerman, B. J., 571

Zimmerman, M. A., 83
Zucker, K. J., 242, 456, 462,
463
Zuckerman, B., 198
Zuravin, S. J., 699
Zussman, J. V., 408

Subject Index

Abortion, 218–227
 legal, characteristics of
  women undergoing,
  225t
 legal context of, 220–223
Abortion research
 difficulties in evaluating,
  223–224
 results of, 224–227
Academic achievement, day
 care and, 430–431
Accommodation, 102
Achondroplasia, 170t
Acquired immunodefi-
 ciency syndrome
 (AIDS). See AIDS
Actions, early moral development and, 466
Adaptation, 102
 sensorimotor, 262
Adaptive self-organization,
 131
Adaptive self-regulation,
 131
Addictive drugs, prenatal
 development and,
 198–199
Adenine, 158, 159
Adequacy, pregnancy and
 childbirth and,
 217–218
Adolescence
 alcohol and drug
  use/abuse in, 703–708
 early. See Early adoles-
  cence
 optimizing development
  in, 718–720, 719–720t
 suicide in, 680
 transition to adulthood,
  710–718
Adolescent fathers, 701–703
Adulthood, psychosocial
 transition to, 710–718
Adult-infant communica-
 tion, emotions as chan-
 nel for, 276–277
Advertising, television,
 children's understand-
 ing of, 534
Advocacy, parents and,
 518–519
African-Americans
 belief systems among, 516

genetic disease in, 171
infant mortality rates for,
 211
peer pressure and, 684
role of grandmothers in
 child-rearing among,
 311
teenage mothers among,
 701
Age, maternal
 live birthrates by, 202t
 prenatal development
  and, 201–202
Age-graded expectations,
 66
Aggression, in children,
 television violence and,
 535t
AIDS
 adolescents and, 642, 666
 congenital, 317–318
 intravenous drug use
  and, 199
Aid to Families with De-
 pendent Children
 (AFDC), 423
Albinism, 170t
Alcohol, prenatal development and, 196–197
Alcohol use/abuse, in
 adolescence, 703–708
Alienation, in early adoles-
 cence, 678–679
Alleles, 162
Allied Chemical, 200
Americans with Disabilities
 Act, 518
Amniocentesis, 192
Amniotic sac, 183
Anaclitic depression, 301
Analytic Institute, 99
Anesthetics, obstetric, new-
 born and, 200
Anger, control in children,
 382
Anomalies, 168
Anorexia nervosa, 653–654
Anxious-avoidant attach-
 ment, 258
Anxious-resistant attach-
 ment, 258
Apgar scoring chart, 237t
Apgar scoring method,
 236–237

Aranda, rites of passage of,
 693–694
Arousal states, in newborns,
 271t
Articulation, ethnic-identity
 development and, 697
Artificial insemination, 149
Ashkenazi Jews, genetic
 disease in, 171
Assimilation, 102
Assumptions, 57
As You Like It, 128
Attitudes, team play and,
 586–589, 587t
Attractiveness, first sexual
 intercourse and, 146
Autism, infantile, 301
Autonomy
 promoting, cultural dif-
  ferences in, 418–420
 in toddlerhood, 395
Autosomal, 153
Avoidance conditioning,
 internalization and, 467
Awareness, ethnic-identity
 development and, 697

Babbling, 347–348
Babinski reflex, 187
Baby and Me, 440
Baganda, child-rearing
 among, 419–420
Baka, reasoning of children
 of, 478
Bali, fantasy play among,
 418
Bases, 157–158
Behavior, impact of heredity
 on, 173–176
Behavioral genetics,
 174–176
Behaviorism, cognitive,
 120–121, 121t
The Behavior of Organisms,
 111
Beliefs, reasoning about, 478
Beyond Freedom and Dignity,
 111
Bias, self-representation, 37
Bilingualism, 361
Biological clock, 157
Birth culture, 212–213
 in Sweden and Nether-
  lands, 215

in traditional societies,
 215–218
in United States, 213–214
Birth process, 207–212
Body weight, self-esteem
 and, 636f
Bottle feeding, cultural and
 ethnic factors in,
 314–315
Boundaries, 132
Boy Scouts, 611
Brain
 development of, 190–191
 language processing and,
  347
Breast-feeding, cultural and
 ethnic factors in,
 314–315
British Broadcasting Corp.,
 536
Bulimia, 654

Caffeine, prenatal development and, 198
Caregiver, mutuality with,
 294–295
Case study, 36
Case study method, 36–37
Categorization, 270
Causality, 262
 sensorimotor, develop-
  ment of, 263–265, 264t
Causal schemes, develop-
 ment in infants,
 263–265, 264t
Cayapo Indians, playful-
 ness among, 419
Cell division, 153–156
Censors, 653
Central process, 76
 in early school age,
  506–509
 in middle childhood,
  603–604
 in toddlerhood, 397–399
Cerebral maturation, peak
 periods of, 645f
Cesarean delivery, 208–210
Chamber of Commerce,
 440
Chemical pollutants
 children's health and, 318
 fetuses and newborns
  and, 201

Child abuse, 433–438
  effects of, 435–438
  prevention and treatment of, barriers to, 434
Childbirth
  adequacy vs. vulnerability and, 217–218
  attitudes toward, 216–218, 217f
  cultural complexity and, 218
  impact of culture and, 212–218
Child care, directions for future of, 431–433
Child development
  classical conditioning and, 109
  cognitive behaviorism and, 121
  cognitive development theory and, 104–105
  content of, 5–9
  contexts of, 11–14
  continuity in, 9
  cultural determinism and, 124–126
  designs for studying, 43–46
  domains of, 6, 6f
  evolutionary theory and, 93–94
  heredity and environment and, 16–17
  ongoing study of, 50–52
  operant conditioning and, 113–114
  optimizing, vital families and, 12–13
  poverty and, 424–425
  psychosexual theory and, 97–99
  scientific observation in, 28–31
  social learning theory and, 118
  social role theory and, 128
  stages of, 6–8
  systems theory and, 132–135
  Vygotsky's theory and, 107
Childhood
  early school age. See Early school age
  first experiences in, 17–18
  middle. See Middle childhood
  skill development and learning in, 19–20
  universal characteristics of, 17–20, 21t

Childhood and Society, 61
Childhood phobias, 504
Child-rearing environments
  in early adolescence, cultural and ethnic patterns in, 691–698
  in early school age, cultural and ethnic patterns in, 519–527
  in infancy, cultural and ethnic patterns in, 311–320
  in middle childhood, cultural and ethnic patterns in, 612–617
  in toddlerhood, cultural and ethnic patterns in, 416–422
Children
  in families, 18–19
  reared by gay or lesbian parents, 463
Chinese, individual achievement and, 420
Chromatids, 155
Chromosomal disorders, examples of, 170t
Chromosomes, 153, 154–155, 157–158
  male, 158f
  sex, 164–166
The Chrysanthemum and the Sword, 123
Cigarette smoking
  peer pressure and, 681
  prenatal development and, 197
Circular reactions, 264
Circumcision, in Maasai society, 526
Civil Rights Act, 518
Classical conditioning, 108–109, 110f, 121t
Classification skills, in middle childhood, 554–555
Class inclusion, 555
Cliques, 658–661
Close friends, in middle childhood, 581–583
Cocaine, prenatal development and, 198–199
Codominance, 163
Cognition, 101
Cognitive behaviorism, 120–121, 121t
Cognitive competencies, 120
Cognitive development
  television viewing and, 532–533

Vygotsky's concepts of, 105–108
Cognitive development theory, 101–108
  child development and, 104–105
  early moral development and, 468–472
  psychosocial theory and, 107–108
Cognitive flexibility, friendship and, 578–579
Cognitive map, 120
Cognitive smile, 275
Cohorts, 46
Cohort sequential design, 46
  elements of, 47f
Collective self-esteem, 678
Collectivism, cultural differences and, 522–523
Color blindness, 170t
Combinatorial skills, in middle childhood, 555–558
Commitment, identity status and, 712–713
Communication, adult-infant, emotions as channel for, 276–277
Communication development
  in infancy, 346–349
  milestones in, 346–354
Communicative competence, 345
  in toddlerhood, 349–352
Community, optimizing development in toddlerhood and, 440–441
Companionate grandparents, 309
Competence, in middle childhood, 606–607
Competition, team play and, 585–586
Compulsion, in toddlerhood, 399–400
Concrete operational thought, 104
  components of, 556t
  in middle childhood, 550–558
Conditioned response (CR), 109
Conditioned stimulus (CS), 109
Conditioning
  avoidance, internalization and, 467

classical, 108–109, 110f, 121t
  operant, 111–114, 121t
Conflict
  family environment and, 412–413
  among friends, 481–483
Conformity
  ethnic-identity development and, 697
  peer pressure and, 681–682
  social norms and peer group pressures and, 579–581
Congenital disorders, 168–169
  causes of, 169f
Conscience, development of, research on, 473
Conscious, 96
Conservation, in middle childhood, 551–554
Content, identity and, 710
Contextual dissonance, self-esteem and, 490
Contextualism, 105
Contextualizing, education and, 615
Continual feeders, 313–314
Continuity, 124
Continuous reinforcement, 113
  vs. intermittent reinforcement, 114f
Contraception, 698–699
Control, experimentation and, 42
Control group, 41
Conventional morality, 469
Cooperative Extension Service, 440
Coordination, 295
Coordination of means and ends, 264–265
Coping behavior, 78–82
Core pathology, 82
  at each life stage, 82t
  in early adolescence, 685
  in early school age, 513–514
  in infancy, 300–302
  in middle childhood, 607
  in toddlerhood, 399–400
Corpus luteum, 144
Correlation, 34–35
  patterns reflecting, 35f
Correlation coefficient, 35
Coughing reflex, 246
Couvade, 207

Crack cocaine, prenatal development and, 198–199
Crisis, identity status and, 712–713
Criticism, shame and, 395
Crossing over, 155
Cross-sectional method, 44–46
Crowds, 658–661
Crying, 271–272
Cub Scouts, 611
Cultural complexity, pregnancy and childbirth and, 218
Cultural determinism, 123
   psychosocial theory and, 126–127
Cultural theory, 122–127
Culture
   achievement strivings and, 612–615
   development and, 11
   discipline practices and, 420–422
   gender differences and, 522–527
   impact on pregnancy and childbirth, 212–218
   physical, 122
   skill learning and, 566–568
   social, 122
Cumulative relation, 163
Cystic fibrosis, 170t, 171
Cytoplasm, 151
Cytosine, 158, 161

Day care, 427–433
   affordable, quality, 431–432
   availability of, 324–326
   costs of, 327
   impact of, 429–431
   quality of, 326–327
Deception, in toddlerhood, 368
Declaration of Independence, 418
Delinquency, in early adolescence, 654–655
Dependent variable, 40
Depression
   anaclitic, 301
   in early adolescence, 655–658
Depressive syndrome, 656
Desires, reasoning about, 478
Development
   abnormal, genetic determinants of, 168–169

child. See Child development
   prenatal. See Prenatal development
   rate of, genetic determinants of, 166–167
Developmental research
   ethics and, 47–48
   evaluating, 47–48
   methods of, 33–43
Developmental stages, 60–65
Developmental tasks, 8–9, 65–70
   associated with life stages, 71t
   psychosocial crises and, 75
Developmental viability, abortion and, 221
Digyzotic twins, 149
Diploid, 153
Disagreement, friendship and, 579
Disciplinarians, 405
Discipline, 404
   co-constructed, 406
   moral development and, 477–480
   parental beliefs and, 407
   religion and, 421
Discipline practices, 405–406
   culture and, 420–422
Discontinuity, 124
Disease, protecting children from, cultural and ethnic factors in, 317
Disequilibrium, 101
Disorganized attachment, 258
Dissonance, ethnic-identity development and, 697
Division of labor, in team play, 584
Divorce
   impact on children, 617–620
   poverty and, 423
DNA, 154, 156–158
   mutations in, 161
   replication of, 159–161, 160f
Dominance relation, 164
Dominant gene, 164
Doubt, in toddlerhood, 395–397
Down syndrome, 170t, 201–202
   mental retardation and, 174
   reaction range and, 173–174

Dramatic role playing, 371
Drugs
   addictive, prenatal development and, 198–199
   prescription, prenatal development and, 199–200
Drug use, maternal, prenatal development and, 196–200
Drug use/abuse, in adolescence, 703–708
Duchenne muscular dystrophy, 170t
Dwarfism, 170t
Dyads, 484

Early adolescence
   alcohol and drug use/abuse in, 703–708
   alienation in, 678–679
   central process in, 679–684
   child-rearing environments in, cultural and ethnic patterns in, 691–698
   core pathology in, 685
   delinquency in, 654–655
   depression in, 655–658
   development in, societal issues and, 698–709
   eating disorders in, 653–654
   egocentrism in, 646–648
   emotional development in, 652–658
   ethnic-group identity in, 695–698
   fidelity to others in, 684–685
   formal operational thought in, 644–652
   group identity in, 678
   interracial friendships in, 660
   isolation in, 685
   optimizing development in, 718–720, 719–720t
   parenthood in, 698–703
   parents and, 685–689
   peer group membership in, 658–661
   peer pressure in, 679–684
   physical maturation in, 632–642
   prime adaptive ego quality in, 684–685
   psychosocial crisis of, 676–679
   safety and risk behaviors in, 642

self-esteem and body weight in, 636f
   sexual relationships in, 661–667
   work experiences in, 708–709
Early school age
   central process in, 506–509
   changes in gross motor skills during, 365t
   child-rearing environments in, cultural and ethnic patterns in, 519–527
   core pathology in, 513–514
   development in, societal issues and, 527–538
   fostering development in, role of parents and family members in, 514–519
   gender-role identification in, 452–465
   group play in, 480–484
   guilt in, 503–506
   identification in, 506–509
   inhibition in, 513–514
   initiative in, 502–503
   moral development in, 465–480
   optimizing development for, 538–539, 540–541t
   prime adaptive ego quality in, 509–513
   psychosocial crisis of, 502–506
   purpose in, 509–513
   school readiness and, 527–531
   self-esteem and, 491–492
   self-theory and, 484–492
   television viewing and, 531–538
Eating disorders, in early adolescence, 653–654
Education
   culturally relevant, 616
   in middle childhood, 603–604
   multicultural, 361
   school adjustment and, 615–617
Egg, fertilization of
   through reproductive technology, 149–151
   through sexual intercourse, 145–149
Egg cells, 142, 144, 151–153
   meiosis in, 155–156

Ego, 97, 472
Egocentric empathy, 474–475
Egocentric speech, 385
Egocentrism, in early adolescence, 646–648
Ego ideal, 396, 509
Electronic fetal heart rate monitoring, 192
Embryo, 183
Embryonic period, 183–186
Emotional development
   in early adolescence, 652–658
   ethnic groups and, 15
   in infants, 270–277
Emotional state, maternal, prenatal development and, 202–203
Emotions
   as channel for adult-infant communication, 276–277
   early moral development and, 466
Empathy
   development of, 474–476
   guilt and, 504
   in toddlerhood, 379–380
Enactive attainments, judgments of self-efficacy and, 570
Environment, child development and, 16–17
Environmental toxins, prenatal development and, 200–201
Epididymis, 142
Epigenetic principle, 63
Equilibrium, 101–102
Estrogen, 143–144
Ethical Principles in the Conduct of Research with Human Participants, 48
Ethics, developmental research and, 47–48
Ethnic-group identity, in early adolescence, 695–698
Ethnic groups, development and, 11–13, 15
Ethnicity and, genetic disease and, 171
Ethology, 93
Evaluation, identity and, 710–711
Evolutionary theory, 92–96
   child development and, 93–94
   psychosocial theory and, 96

Exosystem, 131
Expectancies, 120
Experimental group, 41
Experimental method, 40–43
Experimentation, 40–42
Experimentation with new means, 265
External locus of control, 618

Fables, 421
Faceness, 242
Fallopian tube, 143, 145–146
Familial Mediterranean fever, 171
Family
   children in, 18–19
   children's readiness for friendship and, 577
   development and, 11, 12–13
   development during toddlerhood, 403–416
   establishing functional rhythm in, 297
   impact of conflict on, 412–413
Family life
   managing work and, 409–413
   siblings and work and, 417
Family relationships, influence of genetics on intelligence and, 175–176
Fantasy play
   cultural differences in, 417–418
   during toddlerhood, 366–375
Fear of loss of love, parental identification and, 461
Feedback loops, 133
Feedback mechanisms, 131
Feeding, ethnic and cultural factors in, 313–314
Female reproductive system, 143, 144f
Femininity, cultural differences and, 523
Fertilization
   in vitro, 149–150
   in vivo, 150
   merger of genetic information during, 153
   through reproductive technology, 149–151
   through sexual intercourse, 145–149

Fetal alcohol syndrome, 196–197
Fetal development. *See* Prenatal development
Fetal heart rate monitoring, electronic, 192
Fetal period, 186–187
Fetoscopy, 192
Fetus, 186
   impact on pregnant woman, 203–207
   monitoring, 192–193
Fidelity to others, in early adolescence, 684–685
Filial obligation, 685
First habits, 264
Fitness, 92
Fluorocarbon 22, fetal damage and, 200
Follicle, 144
Food additives, newborns and, 201
Formal operational thought, 104
   characteristics of, 645–646
   conceptual skills emerging during stage of, 646t
   in early adolescence, 644–652
   factors promoting, 648–650
Formal operations, 644
Foundational category, 270
Fragile X syndrome, 165, 170t
France, parental leave policies in, 328t
Fraternal twins, 149
Friendship
   disagreements and, 579
   interracial, 660
   in middle childhood, 576–583
   social development and, 578–583
Friendship groups, 481–484
   sex-segregated, 483–484

Gamete intrafallopian transfer (GIFT), 150
Gametes, 142, 151–153
Ganda, weaning practices among, 316
Gandhi's Truth, 36
Gay parents, children reared by, 463
Gender, 456
   identity formation and, 714–718
   understanding, 456–457

vulnerability to depression and, 657–658
Gender differences
   culture and, 522–527
   individual differences vs. constructivist perspectives on, 453–456
Gender identity, androgynous, reaction to abortion and, 225–226
Gender role, 456
Gender-role bias, parental, children's competencies and interests and, 575t
Gender-role identification, 452–465
   dimensions of, 465t
Gender-role preference, formation of, 462–465
Gender schemes, 458–459
Generativity, 84
Genes, 153, 157–158
   abnormal development and, 168–169
   dominant, 164
   individual traits and, 167–168
   rate of development and, 166–167
   recessive, 164
Gene therapy, 169–171
Genetic code, 156
Genetic counseling, 171–173
Genetic disorders
   examples of, 170t
   race and ethnicity and, 171
Genetic information, transmission of, 156–166
Genetic markers, 169
Genetic technology
   ethical issues in, 173
   psychosocial evolution and, 169–173
Genotype, 163–164
Germany, parental leave policies in, 328t
Germinal period, 183
Gestational age. *See* Small for gestational age
Gesturing, in infants, 348
Global empathy, 474
Glucose-6PD deficiency, 171
Goal attainment, in toddlerhood, self-regulated, 383–386
Goals and plans, 121
Gonads, 154
Goodness of fit model, 168
Grammar, development in toddlerhood, 351–352

Grammatical inflections, basic sequence in adding, 352*t*

Grandparenthood, transition to, 308–311

Grandparents
companionate, 309
impact on grandchildren, 310–311
involved, 309–310
remote, 309

Grasping reflex, 246

Grasp reflex, 187

Gratification, children delaying, process of, 382–383

Group games, 480–481

Group identity, in early adolescence, 678

Groups, friendship, 481–484
sex-segregated, 483–484

Guanine, 158, 159

Guilt, in early school age, 503–506

Gymboree, 440

Habituation, 240

Habituation event, object permanence and, 269*f*

Haploid, 153

Head Start, 32, 440, 530

Healthy People 2000, 209

Hearing, development in infants, 241

Hemophilia, 170*t*
sex-linked inheritance of, 165–166, 165*f*

Herbicides, prenatal development and, 201

Heredity
child development and, 16–17
impact on behavior, 173–176
laws of, 161–166

Heroin, prenatal development and, 198–199

Heteronomous morality, 468

Heterozygosity, 162

High/Scope Preschool, 439

HIV, intravenous drug use and, 199

HIV infection, in infants, 317–318

Holophrases, 348

Home
dangers in, infant and child safety and, 318–320

moral atmosphere of, early school age moral development and, 519–522

Homelessness, in middle childhood, 622–623

Homosexual orientation, 665
adolescent depression and, 657

Homozygosity, 162

Hope, in infants, 300

Hopi Indians
albinism among, 171
family discipline among, 421
fantasy play among, 418

Hormones
reproductive system and, 143–145
sex, 143–144

Human Development and Education, 66

Human genome, 156

Human immunodeficiency virus (HIV). *See* HIV

Huntington's chorea, 170*t*

The Hurried Child, 516

H-Y antigen, 186

Hypercognitive system, 564

Hysteria, 98

Id, 97, 472

Identical twins, 147–149

Identification, parental, 459–462
in early school age, 506–509
motives for, 461*t*

Identification with aggressor, parental identification and, 461

Identity, 551
components of, 710–711

Identity achievement, 712

Identity confusion, 712, 713–714

Identity crisis, 70

Identity foreclosure, 712

Identity formation, 710
gender variation in, 714–718
parental attachment and, 715

Identity status, 712–714

Imaginary audience, 647

Imaginary companions, in toddlerhood, 374
toddlers' descriptions of, 375–376*t*

Imitation, 76, 114
in toddlerhood, 397–399

Immersion, ethnic-identity development and, 697

Imprinting, 292

Impulse control, in toddlerhood, 379–383
factors associated with, 381*f*

Incest, 504

Incompetence, illusion of, 573

Independent variable, 40

Individualism, cultural differences and, 522–523

Individuality, genetic sources of, 166–173

Individual traits, genetic determinants of, 167–168

Indo-Chinese refugees, cultural values supporting education among, school success and, 614

Inductions, discipline and, 405

Industrial Revolution, 603

Industry, in middle childhood, 598–599

Inertia, in middle childhood, 607

Infancy. *See also* Infants
child-rearing environments during, cultural and ethnic patterns in, 311–320
communication accomplishments in, 346–349
core pathology in, 300–302
prime adaptive ego quality in, 300
psychosocial crisis in, 290–294
self-theory and, 486

Infant-adult communication, emotions as channel for, 276–277

Infant attachment, 251–262
anxious-avoidant, 258
anxious-resistant, 258
critical period for, 292–293
development of, 252–255
disorganized, 258
formation with mother, father, and others, 255
maternal employment and, 322–323
object permanence and, 269
patterns of, 255–259

quality of, parental sensitivity and, 259–262, 260*f*
secure, 258
trust and, 290–291

Infant care
alternative
parental employment and, 320–330
social policies and, 327–330

Infantile autism, 301

Infant mortality, 211–212

Infant mortality rate, in United States, 192

Infants. *See also* Newborns
attachment in. *See* Infant attachment
categorization of objects and, 269–270
cognitive development in, promoting, 330–331
communicating with gestures, 348
development of causal schemes in, 263–265, 264*t*
emotional development in, 270–277
emotional differentiation in, 271–273
emotional regulation in, 274–276
experience organization in, 262–263
first words, 348–349
hope in, 300
meaning of smiles of, 275
monitoring brain activity of, 299
motor development in, 244–249, 247*f*
mutuality with caregiver, 294–295
nature of objects and, 265–269
parents with psychological problems and, 297–299
precursors of self-control in, 378
rules and prohibitions for, 407*t*
sensory/perceptual development in, 240–244
social referencing and, 277
temperament in, 249–251
trust vs. mistrust in, 290–294
vocabulary development in, 349

Inferiority, in middle child-hood, 599–603
Infertility, reproductive technology and, 149
In-group attitudes, team play and, 586–589, 587t
Inhibition, in early school age, 513–514
Initiative, 65, 84
  in early school age, 502–503
Insecticides, children's health and, 318
Insight, 265
Institute of Genetics, 153
Intellectual development, ethnic groups and, 15
Intelligence
  day care and, 430–431
  hereditary influences on, 174–176
  myths, mythical coun-termyths, and truths about, 565t
  perspectives on, 564
  reaction ranges for, 174f
  sensorimotor, 103–104
Interdependence, in team play, 584
Interdependent elements, 129
Intermittent reinforcement, 113
  vs. continuous reinforce-ment, 114f
Internal conflict, shame and, 396
Internalization, 465–466
Internal locus of control, 618
International Congress on Psychoanalysis, 98
Interobserver reliability, 35
Interracial friendship, 660
Interview method, 37–38
Intimacy, marital satisfac-tion, parental effective-ness, and psychosocial development and, 308f
Introspection, ethnic-iden-tity development and, 697
Inventory of Psychosocial Development, 84
In vitro fertilization, 149–150
In vivo fertilization, 150
Involved grandparents, 309–310

Japan, cultural support for schooling in, 612

Job loss, poverty and, 423
Just the Facts, 424

Kachinas, 421
Kanjar, gender roles among, 452–453
Khmer refugees, cultural values supporting education among, school success and, 613–614
Kindergarten readiness, measuring, 528–529
Klinefelter's syndrome, 170t
Knowledge, early moral development and, 466
!Kung San, nursing patterns among, 314

Labor, 207–208
  psychological stages of, significant events of, 210t
  stages of, 208, 209f
Lack of ability, feelings of inferiority and, 601
Language
  brain processing, 347
  at home and at school, 361
  receptive, 348
Language development, 345–361
  beyond toddlerhood, 352–354
  interaction and, 355–358
  milestones in, 346–354, 353t
  parenting style during, 357t
  strategies for enhancing, 358–360
Language environment, 354–361
Language games, enhanc-ing language develop-ment and, 358–360
Language perception, 347
Language production, 348
Latency, 100
Law, abortion controversy and, 220–223
Law of natural selection, 92
Lead poisoning, infants and young children and, 201, 318
Learned helplessness, feel-ings of inferiority and, 601
Learning
  belief systems about, 517t
  in childhood, 19–20
Learning processes, 121t

Learning theory, 108–122
  classical conditioning, 108–109, 110f, 121t
  cognitive behaviorism, 120–121, 121t
  moral development and, 466–467
  operant conditioning, 111–114, 121t
  psychosocial theory and, 122
  social learning theory, 114–118, 121t
Leeway of mastery, 372
Lesbian parents, children reared by, 463
Life span, eleven stages of, 64f
Life stages
  core pathologies at, 82t
  developmental tasks associated with, 71t
  organization of, 86–87t
  psychosocial crises of, 72–75, 72t
Little League, 583
Locomotion, elaboration in toddlerhood, 361–366
Loneliness, in middle child-hood, 580
Longitudinal study, 46
Love withdrawal, discipline and, 405

Maasai, gender roles among, 526–527
Macrosystem, 131
Major depressive disorder, 656
Male reproductive system, 142, 143f
Malnutrition, prenatal development and, 194–196
Marfan's syndrome, 170t
Marital satisfaction, transi-tion to parenthood and, 303
Masculinity, cultural differ-ences and, 523
Matched groups, 33
Matching, 295
Maternal age
  live birthrates by, 202t
  prenatal development and, 201–202
Maternal drug use, prenatal development and, 196–200
Maternal emotional state, prenatal development and, 202–203

Maternal employment
  infant attachment and, 322–323
  parental values about, 323–324
  role of grandparents in child-rearing and, 311
Maternal nutrition, prenatal development and, 194–196
Mate selection, social chem-istry of, 162–163
Maturation, genetic deter-minants of, 166
Maturational view, 516
Medicaid, 212
Medical and Family Leave Act, 328
Meiosis, 153–156
  phases of, 155f
  timing for males and females, 156
Menstrual cycle, 144
  onset of, 637
Menstruation, 144
Mental operation, 550–551
Mental retardation, genetic irregularities and, 174–175
Mercury, prenatal develop-ment and, 200–201
Mesosystem, 131
Metacognition, 557
Metapelets, 255
Methadone, prenatal devel-opment and, 198–199
Methyl mercury, prenatal development and, 200–201
Microsystem, 131
Middle childhood
  central process in, 603–604
  child-rearing environ-ments in, cultural and ethnic patterns in, 612–617
  classification skills in, 554–555
  combinatorial skills in, 555–558
  competence in, 606–607
  concrete operations in, 550–558
  conservation skills in, 551–554
  core pathology in, 607
  development in, social issues and, 617–623
  education in, 603–604
  friendship in, 576–583
  homelessness and, 622–623

interactive parental relationships in, 607–612
optimizing development in, 624–625, 626–627t
parental divorce and, 617–620
prime adaptive ego quality in, 606–607
psychosocial crisis in, 598–603
reading in, 561–562
school violence and, 620, 622
self-efficacy in, 570–571
self-evaluation in, 568–576
skilled learning in, 558–568
social expectations in, 571–576
team play in, 583–589
Midwifery, 215
Mind, developing, model of, 562–566, 563f
Mistrust, in infants, 291–294
Mitochondrion, 151
Mitosis, 153–155
phases of, 154f
Model for imitation, 414
Models, 114–115
Monozygotic twins, 147
Moral development
contributions to study of, 479t
early, 465–480
Morality
conventional, 469
heteronomous, 468
postconventional, 469
preconventional, 469
Moral judgment, stages of, 469t
Mother-infant relationship, disruption in, 292–293
Motivation
criticism of, feelings of inferiority and, 601
first sexual intercourse and, 146
Motor development, in infants, 244–249, 247f
nature and nurture and, 248–249
Motor skills, changes during toddlerhood and early school age, 365t
Multicultural education, 361
school adjustment and, 615–617
Mutations, 161

Mutuality, with caregiver, 294–295
Myths, 421

National Household Education Survey, 528
Native Americans
infectious disease among, 317
role of grandparents among, 311
suicide among, 680
Naturalistic observation, 34
Natural selection, 92
Need for status and power, parental identification and, 461
Negative feedback loops, 133
Negative identity, 712, 713
Negative reinforcer, 112
Negativism, in toddlerhood, 404–405
Nerve pathways, 190
Netherlands, birth culture in, 215
Neuron, 190
Neutral response (NR), 109
Neutral stimulus (NS), 109
Newborns, 236–238. See also Infants
states of arousal in, 270t
very small, 238–239
New Jersey Supreme Court, 150
Nicotine, prenatal development and, 197
Nucleotides, 158
Nutrition, maternal, prenatal development and, 194–196

Obesity, in adolescent girls, 636
Object permanence, 267–268
attachment and, 269
habituation and test events and, 269f
precursors of, 268–269
Observation, naturalistic, 34
Observational method, 34–36
Obsessions, in toddlerhood, 400
Obstetric anesthetics, newborn and, 200
Offer Self-Image Questionnaire (OSIQ), 687
Office of Technology Assessment, 149
Oocytes, 153

Open discourse, 404
Open systems, 129
Operant conditioning, 111–114, 121t
Operation, 550
Organ inferiority, 599
The Origin of Species, 93
Out-group attitudes, team play and, 586–589, 587t
Ovaries, 143
Ovulation, 156

Parental attachment, identity formation and, 715
Parental beliefs, socialization process and, 406–408
Parental discipline, moral development and, 477–480
Parental employment, infant child care and, 320–330
Parental expectations, in middle childhood, 574–576
Parental identification, 459–462
in early school age, 506–509
motives for, 461t
Parental leave, 328, 328t
Parental sensitivity, quality of attachment and, 259–262, 260f
Parent-child interaction, language competence and, 355–356
Parenthood
adolescent, 698–703
role strain and, 130
transition to, 302–308
Parenting
adolescent development and, 688–689
contextual factors supporting, 331–332
language development and, 357t
poverty and, 424–425
as stimulus for adult development, 306–308
work and, 411
Parents
adolescent children and, 685–689
as advocates, 331, 518–519
caring for aging parents and, 689–691
as educators, 514–517
gay or lesbian, children reared by, 463
nonparents compared, 304

as play companions, 402–404
as socialization agents, 404–409
Parent-school partnership, 608–609
Passive behavior, gender differences in, 453
Patterns of Culture, 123
Peer groups
adolescent alcohol use and, 707
early adolescence and, 658–661
formal operational thought and, 648
Peer-group structuring, role of school adults in, 680–681
Peer pressure
conformity and, 579–581
in early adolescence, 679–684
Peer rejection, in middle childhood, 580–581
Penis, 142
Perceived similarity, parental identification and, 461–462
Perceptual development, in infants, 240–244
Peristalsis, 192
Perry Preschool Project, 431
Personal identity, 84, 710–718
Perspective taking
friendship and, 578–579
moral development and, 476–477
Pesticides, prenatal development and, 201
Phenotype, 163–164
Phenylketonuria (PKU), mental retardation and, 174–175
Phenylthiocarbamide, 167
Phobias, childhood, 504
Physical culture, 122
Physical development, ethnic groups and, 15
Physical environment, optimizing development in toddlerhood and, 439–440
Physical maturation, in early adolescence, 632–642
boys and, 638–639
girls and, 635–638
psychosocial consequen[...]
640–641

Physical punishment, discipline and, 421–422
Physiological state, judgments of self-efficacy and, 571
Placenta, 183–185
functions of, 186f
Play. *See also* Fantasy play; Team play
purpose and, 512–513
social, 369
social pretend, 369
Play companions
parents as, 402–404
role of, 373–374
Polar bodies, 155
Population, 32
Positive feedback loops, 133
Positive reinforcer, 112
Positron emission tomography (PET), 347
Postconventional morality, 469
Poverty, 422–427
child development and, 424–425
conditions leading to, 422–424
factors mediating impact of, 426
prenatal development and, 195
toddlerhood and, 426–427
Power assertion, discipline and, 405, 421–422
Preconscious, 96
Preconventional morality, 469
Prednisone, birth weight and, 199–200
Pregnancy
adequacy vs. vulnerability and, 217–218
attitudes toward, 216–218, 217f
cultural complexity and, 218
first trimester of, fetal development in,
3–187
t of culture and,
218
reactions to,

notions and,
roll
205 ontext of,

nd,

second trimester of, fetal development in, 187–191
solicitude vs. shame and, 216–217
teenage, consequences of, 699–701
third trimester of, fetal development in, 192–194
toxemia of, 205
Pregnant woman, impact of fetus on, 203–207
Prenatal development
critical periods in, 187f
in first trimester, 183–187
major developments during, 183t
maternal age and, 201–202
maternal drug use and, 196–200
maternal emotional state and, 202–203
maternal nutrition and, 194–196
optimizing, 227, 227t
phases of, 182–194
in second trimester, 187–191
in third trimester, 192–194
Preoperational thought, 104
Prescription drugs, prenatal development and, 199–200
Pretense, distinguishing, 367–368
Primary sex characteristics
development in boys, 638t, 639
development in girls, 637, 638t
Prime adaptive ego quality, 80–81
at each psychosocial stage, 81t
in early adolescence, 684–685
in early school age, 509–513
in infancy, 300
in middle childhood, 606–607
in toddlerhood, 399
Private self, 710
Processing system, 563
Psychoanalytic theory, early moral development and, 472–474
Psychosexual theory, 96–101

child development and, 97–99
psychosocial theory and, 99–101
Psychosocial crisis, 70–77
developmental tasks and, 75
of early adolescence, 676–679
of early school age, 502–506
of infancy, 290–299
of life stages, 72–75, 72t
of middle childhood, 598–603
process for resolving, 75–77, 76t
of toddlerhood, 394–397
Psychosocial development, positive and negative, mechanism for, 86f
Psychosocial evolution, 59, 96
genetic technology and, 169–173
Psychosocial moratorium, 712
Psychosocial orientation, 5
Psychosocial stages
Erikson's, 63f
prime adaptive ego quality at, 81t
Psychosocial theory, 57–59
basic concepts of, 59–82, 62f
cognitive development theory and, 107–108
coping behavior in, 78–82
cultural determinism and, 126–127
developmental tasks in, 65–70
evaluation of, 82–88, 83t
evolutionary theory and, 96
learning theories and, 122
psychosexual theory and, 99–101
psychosocial crisis in, 70–77
radius of significant relationships in, 77–78, 77f
social role theory and, 128–129
stages of development in, 60–65
systems theory and, 135
Puberty, psychological and social development and, 634

Puberty rites, functions of, 694–695
Public self, 710
Purpose
in early school age, 509–513
play and, 512–513

Quasi-experimental, 42
Quickening, 188–189

Race
genetic disease and, 171
United States population by, 14t
The Races of Mankind, 123
Radius of significant relationships, 77–78, 77f
Random sample, 32
Range of applicability, 57
Rapport, 37
Reaction range, 173–174
for intelligence, 174f
Reactive attachment disorder of infancy, 301
Reading
in middle childhood, 561–562
skilled, characteristics of, 560
Reading games, enhancing language development and, 358–360
Receptive language, 348
Recessive gene, 164
Reciprocal roles, 128
Reciprocity, 552
Reflexes, infant, 263–264
Reinforcement, 112–113
continuous, 113
continuous vs. intermittent, 114f
intermittent, 113
vicarious, 115
Religion
adolescent sexual behavior and, 664
discipline and, 421
socialization and moral education of young children and, 519–522
Remote grandparents, 309
Reproduction. *See* Sexual reproduction
Reproductive system
female, 143, 144f
hormones and, 143–145
male, 142, 143f
Reproductive technology, fertilization through, 149–151
Research design, 31–48

Research methods, 33–43
 advantages and disadvantages of, 43t
 case study, 36–37
 experimental, 40–43
 interview, 37–38
 observational, 34–36
 surveys and tests, 38–40
Resilience, 426
Resistance, ethnic-identity development and, 697
Retrospective study, 44
Reversibility, 551
Risk behaviors, in early adolescence, 642
Rites of passage, cultural patterns of, 693–694
Rituals, in toddlerhood, 399–400
Roe v. *Wade*, 221, 224
Role enactment, 128
Role expectations, 128
Roles, 127–128
 pregnancy and, 205–206
Role strain, parenthood and, 130
Rooting reflex, 246
RU 486, abortion and, 220
Rules, 132

Safety, infant, cultural and ethnic factors in, 316–320
Samoa, puberty rites in, 694
Samples
 random, 32
 stratified, 33
 volunteer, 33
Sampling, 32–33
Scaffolding, enhancing language development and, 358
Schedule of reinforcement, 113
School adjustment, multicultural education and, 615–617
School readiness, 527–531
Schools, violence in, 620, 622
Scientific observation, in child development, 28–31
Scientific theory, 56–57
Searching for Bobby Fisher, 517
Secondary sex characteristics
 development in boys, 638t, 639
 development in girls, 637, 638t

Secure attachment, 258
Self-control
 components of, 378f
 precursors in infancy, 378
 in toddlerhood, 376–386
Self-control strategies, 121
Self-development, ethnic groups and, 15
Self-efficacy
 components of, 571f
 in middle childhood, 570–571
Self-encoding, 120
Self-esteem, 488–491, 678
 body weight and, 636f
 contextual dissonance and, 490
 early school age and, 491–492
Self-evaluation, in middle childhood, 568–576
Self-fulfilling prophecy, 572–574
Self-representation bias, 37
Self-theory, 484–492
 developmental changes in, 486–488
Self-understanding, developmental model of, 485f
Semen, 142, 145
Seminal fluid, 142
Seminal vesicles, 142
Semiotic thought, 345
Sensers, 653
Sensitive periods, 66
Sensorimotor adaptation, 262
Sensorimotor causality, development of, 263–265, 264t
Sensorimotor intelligence, 103–104
Sensorimotor play, 367
Sensory development, in infants, 240–244
Separation anxiety, 253–255
Sephardic Jews, genetic disease in, 171
Sesame Street, 536
Sex characteristics, secondary, development of, 144, 638t
Sex chromosomes, 164–166
 abnormalities of, 170t
Sex hormones, 143–144
Sex-linked characteristics, 164–166
Sex-Role Learning Index, 458
Sex-role standards, learning, 457–459

Sexual intercourse
 fertilization through, 145–149
 first, social context of, 146
Sexually transmitted disease (STD), adolescents and, 642, 666
Sexual orientation, 665
 parental sexual orientation and, 463
Sexual relationships, in early adolescence, 661–667
Sexual reproduction
 cellular basis of, 151–156
 process of, 142–151
Shame
 pregnancy and childbirth and, 216–217
 in toddlerhood, 395–397
Shaping, 112
Sibling relationships, similarity in intelligence for levels of, 176f
Sibling rivalry, 414–416
Siblings, work and family life and, 417
Sickle-cell anemia, 170t, 171
Signs, 106
Sioux Indians, fantasy play among, 418
Skill development, in childhood, 19–20
Skilled learning
 features of, 560–561
 in middle childhood, 558–568
Skilled reading
 characteristics of, 560
 social and cultural contexts of, 566–568
Skinner box, 111
Small for gestational age (SGA), 194, 237
Smell, development in infants, 242–243
Smoking, prenatal development and, 197
Social conditions, development and, 13–14
Social controls, first sexual intercourse and, 146
Social convention transgressions, 470–472
Social culture, 122
Social development
 ethnic groups and, 15
 friendship and, 578–583
Social expectations, in middle childhood, 571–576

Socialization, 404–409
 co-constructed, 406
 parental beliefs and, 406–408
Social learning theory, 114–118, 121t
Social norms, conformity and, 579
Social play, 369
Social pretend play, 369
Social Readjustment Rating Scale, 206
Social referencing, 277
Social ridicule, shame and, 395–396
Social roles, 128
Social role theory, 127–129
 child development and, 128
 psychosocial theory and, 128–129
Social smiles, 275
Socioeconomic status, child abuse and, 435
Socioemotional competencies, day care and, 431
Solicitude, pregnancy and childbirth and, 216–217
Solitary pretense, 369
Spaced feeders, 313–314
Special Education Act, 518
Specialized structural system, 565–566
Speech attainment, in toddlerhood, 383–386
Sperm, fertilization of egg by, 145–147
Sperm banks, 150
Sperm cells, 142, 151
 meiosis in, 155–156
Spherocytosis, 171
Status, pregnancy and, 205–206
Stepping reflex, 246
Stories, 421
Stranger anxiety, 253
Strange situation procedure, 255–256, 257t
 validity in different cultures, 259
Stratified sample, 33
Sucking reflex, 244–246
Sudden infant death syndrome (SIDS), cocaine-exposed infants and, 198
Suicide, adolescent, 680
Superego, 97, 472
Surrogate mother, 150
Survey research, 38–40

Swaddling, 243, 248
  prolonged, dangers of,
    318–319
Sweden
  birth culture in, 215
  infant mortality rate in,
    211
  parental leave policies in,
    328*t*
Symbolic play, emergence
  of, 367–368
Synchrony, 295
Systems, relationships
  among, 132*f*
Systems theory, 129–135
  child development and,
    132–135
  psychosocial theory and,
    135

Taboos, 504
Taste, development in
  infants, 242–243
Tay-Sachs disease, 170*t*,
  171
Teachable moments, 66
Teachers, 405
Teachers' expectations, in
  middle childhood,
  572–574
Team play
  competition and, 585–586
  division of labor in, 584
  in-group and out-group
    attitudes and, 586–589,
    587*t*
  interdependence in, 584
  in middle childhood,
    583–589
Teenage pregnancy, conse-
  quences of, 699–701
Telegraphic speech, 350
Television advertising,
  children's understand-
  ing of, 534
Television viewing
  early school age and,
    531–538
  as stimulus for optimal
    development, 535–536
Television violence
  aggression in children
    and, 535*t*
  socioemotional conse-
    quences of, 533–535
Telophase I, 155
Temperament
  genetic determinants of,
    167–168
  in infants, 249–251
Teratogens, 185

Test events, object perma-
  nence and, 269*f*
Testis-determining factor
  (TDF), 165
Testosterone, 143–144
  prenatal development
    and, 200
Test research, 38–40
Thalassemia, 171
Thalidomide, 199
Theory, 56–57
Thymine, 158, 159
Time urgency, 411
Tobacco, prenatal development and, 197
Tobacco smoke, exposure
  to, respiratory illness
  among infants and,
  318
Toddlerhood, 344–345. *See
  also* Toddlers
  autonomy in, 395
  becoming a sibling in,
    413–416
  central process in,
    397–399
  changes in gross motor
    skills during, 365*t*
  child-rearing environ-
    ments during, cultural
    and ethnic patterns in,
    416–422
  communicative compe-
    tence in, 349–352
  compulsion in, 399–400
  core pathology in,
    399–400
  deception in, 368
  elaboration of locomotion
    in, 361–366
  family development
    during, 403–416
  fantasy play in, 366–375
  goal attainment in, self-
    regulated, 383–386
  imaginary companions
    in, 374
  imitation in, 397–399
  impulse control in,
    379–383
  language and communi-
    cation in, 345–361
  language development
    beyond, 352–354
  optimizing development
    in, 438–442, 442–443*t*
  poverty and, 426–427
  prime adaptive ego qual-
    ity in, 300
  psychosocial crisis of,
    394–397

psychosocial develop-
  ment in, societal issues
  and, 422–438
role of play companions
  in, 373–374
self-control in, 376–386
self-theory and, 486
shame and doubt in,
  395–397
speech attainment in,
  383–386
will in, 399
Toddlers
  day care and, 427–433
  play companions for,
    402–404, 404*t*
  rules and prohibitions for,
    407*t*
Toilet training, 396
Tools, 106
Touch, development in
  infants, 243–244
Toxemia of pregnancy,
  205
Toxins, environmental,
  prenatal development
  and, 200–201
Toys and Reason, 512
Trainers, 405
Traits, individual, genetic
  determinants of,
  167–168
Transactional view, 516
Transference, 19
Transmissive view, 516
Trimesters, 183
Trust, in infants, 290–291
Turner's syndrome, 170*t*
Twins, 147–149
  dizygotic, 149
  fraternal, 149
  identical, 147–149
  monozygotic, 147
Two-word sentences,
  350–351

Ultrasound, fetal imaging
  and, 192
Unconditioned response
  (UR), 109
Unconditioned stimulus
  (US), 109
Unconscious, 96
Undue burden, 223
United States
  children in poverty in,
    424
  cultural support for
    schooling in, 612
  infant mortality in,
    211–212

infant mortality rate in,
  192
medical birth culture in,
  213–214
parental leave policies in,
  328*t*
school violence in, 620,
  622
transition to adulthood
  in, 695
United States Congress, 328,
  620
United States population,
  by race and Hispanic
  origin, 14*t*
United States Public Health
  Service, 209
United States Supreme
  Court, 221, 226
Uterus, 143

Vagina, 143
Validity, test, 39
Values, 121
Vas deferens, 142
Verbal persuasion, judg-
  ments of self-efficacy
  and, 570–571
Vernix caseosa, 189
Vicarious experience, judg-
  ments of self-efficacy
  and, 570
Vicarious reinforcement,
  115
Vienna Psychoanalytic
  Society, 60
Vigilant interest, 414
Violence
  in schools, 620, 622
  television, 533–535, 535*t*
Vision, development in
  infants, 241–242
Visual cortex, 190
Vital Involvement in Old Age,
  61
Vocabulary, development
  in toddlerhood,
  349–350
Volunteer samples, 33
Vulnerability, pregnancy
  and childbirth and,
  217–218

Walden Two, 111
Walkers, injuries from,
  319–320
Weaning
  cultural and ethnic fac-
    tors in, 315–316
  ethnic and cultural fac-
    tors in, 313–314

Will, in toddlerhood, 399
Withdrawal, in infants, 300–302
Women, Infants, and Children (WIC) food program, 195
Work
    parenting and, 411
    siblings and family life and, 417

Work experiences, in early adolescence, 708–709

X chromosome, 153, 164–165

Yanomamo
    family discipline among, 422
    fantasy play among, 418

gender roles among, 523–525
Y chromosome, 153, 164–165, 186
Youth unemployment, 709
Yurok, self-restraint among, 421

Zambia, infant behavior in, 248–249

Zinacantecos, child-rearing practices among, 248
Zone of proximal development, 106, 372
Zygote, 147

To The Owner Of This Book

We hope that you have enjoyed *Childhood and Adolescence* as much as we enjoyed writing it. We would like to know as much about your experience as you would care to offer. Only through your comments and those of others can we learn how to make this a better text for future readers.

School: _____ Your instructor's name: _____

1. What did you like most about the book? _____

_____

_____

_____

2. Do you have any recommendations for ways to improve the next edition of this text?

_____

_____

_____

3. In the space below or in a separate letter, please write any other comments you have about the book. (For example, were any chapters or concepts particularly difficult?) We'd be delighted to hear from you!

_____

_____

_____

_____

_____

_____

_____

_____

_____

_____

_____ Date: _____

...uote you, either in promotion for *Childhood and Adolescence* or in
...g ventures?

_____ No: _____

Sincerely,

Philip and Barbara Newman

FOLD HERE

- -

||।....||.।.।....।.।.।।....।.।.।....।.।।.।.।....।.।।

- -

FOLD HERE